TABLE B MEASURES OF U.S. INCOME, PRICES, AND FEDERAL DEBT

Year	GNP	Net National Product	National Income	Personal Income	Disposable Income	GNP Deflator (1982 = 100)		CPI (1982–1984 = 100)		Federal Budget Deficit	Federal Debt
						Index Number	Percent Change	Index Number	Percent Change		
		Billions of Dollars								*Billions of Dollars*	
1929	103.9	94.0	84.7	84.3	81.7	14.6				0.7	16.9
1933	56.0	48.4	39.4	46.3	44.9				–5.1%	–2.6	22.5
1939	91.3	82.3	71.2	72.1	69.7	12.	–0.8%	13.9	–1.4%	–2.8	48.2
1940	100.4	91.1	79.6	77.6	75.0	13.0	2.0%	14.0	0.7%	–2.9	50.7
1941	125.5	115.3	102.8	95.2	91.9	13.8	6.2%	14.7	5.0%	–4.9	57.5
1942	159.0	147.7	136.2	122.4	116.4	14.7	6.6%	16.3	10.9%	–20.5	79.2
1943	192.7	181.1	169.7	150.7	132.9	15.1	2.6%	17.3	6.1%	–54.6	142.6
1944	211.4	199.4	182.6	164.5	145.6	15.3	1.4%	17.6	1.7%	–47.6	204.1
1945	213.4	201.0	181.6	170.0	149.2	15.7	2.9%	18.0	2.3%	–47.6	260.1
1946	212.4	198.2	180.7	177.6	158.9	19.4	22.9%	19.5	8.3%	–15.9	271.0
1947	235.2	217.6	196.6	190.2	168.8	22.1	13.9%	22.3	14.4%	4.0	257.1
1948	261.6	241.2	221.5	209.2	188.1	23.6	7.0%	24.1	8.1%	11.8	252.0
1949	260.4	238.4	215.2	206.4	187.9	23.5	–0.5%	23.8	–1.2%	0.6	252.6
1950	288.3	264.6	239.8	228.1	207.5	23.9	2.0%	24.1	1.3%	–3.1	256.9
1951	333.4	306.2	277.3	256.5	227.6	25.1	4.8%	26.0	7.9%	6.1	255.3
1952	351.6	322.5	291.6	273.8	239.8	25.5	1.5%	26.5	1.9%	–1.5	259.1
1953	371.6	340.7	306.6	290.5	255.1	25.9	1.6%	26.7	0.8%	–6.5	266.0
1954	372.5	340.0	306.3	293.0	260.5	26.3	1.6%	26.9	0.7%	–1.2	270.8
1955	405.9	371.5	336.3	314.2	278.8	27.2	3.2%	26.8	–0.4%	–3.0	274.4
1956	428.2	390.1	356.3	337.2	297.5	28.1	3.4%	27.2	1.5%	3.9	272.7
1957	451.0	409.9	372.8	356.3	313.9	29.1	3.6%	28.1	3.3%	3.4	272.3
1958	456.8	414.0	375.0	367.1	324.9	29.7	2.1%	28.9	2.8%	–2.8	279.7
1959	495.8	451.2	409.2	390.7	344.6	30.4	2.4%	29.1	0.7%	–12.8	287.5
1960	515.3	468.9	424.9	409.4	358.9	30.9	1.6%	29.6	1.7%	0.3	290.5
1961	533.8	486.1	439.0	426.0	373.8	31.2	1.0%	29.9	1.0%	–3.3	292.6
1962	574.6	525.2	473.3	453.2	396.2	31.9	2.2%	30.2	1.0%	–7.1	302.9
1963	606.9	555.5	500.3	476.3	415.8	32.4	1.6%	30.6	1.3%	–4.8	310.3
1964	649.8	595.9	537.6	510.2	451.4	32.9	1.5%	31.0	1.3%	–5.9	316.1
1965	705.1	647.7	585.2	552.0	486.8	33.8	2.7%	31.5	1.6%	–1.4	322.3
1966	772.0	709.9	642.0	600.8	525.9	35.0	3.6%	32.4	2.9%	–3.7	328.5
1967	816.4	749.0	677.7	644.5	562.1	35.9	2.6%	33.4	3.1%	–8.6	340.4
1968	892.7	818.7	739.1	707.2	609.6	37.7	5.0%	34.8	4.2%	–25.2	368.7
1969	963.9	882.5	798.1	772.9	656.7	39.8	5.6%	36.7	5.5%	3.2	365.8
1970	1015.5	926.6	832.6	831.8	715.6	42.0	5.5%	38.8	5.7%	–2.8	380.9
1971	1102.7	1005.1	898.1	894.0	776.8	44.4	5.7%	40.5	4.4%	–23.0	408.2
1972	1212.8	1104.8	994.1	981.6	839.6	46.5	4.7%	41.8	3.2%	–23.4	435.9
1973	1359.3	1241.2	1122.7	1101.7	949.8	49.5	6.5%	44.4	6.2%	–14.9	466.3
1974	1472.8	1335.4	1203.5	1210.1	1038.4	54.0	9.1%	49.3	11.0%	–6.1	483.9
1975	1598.4	1436.6	1289.1	1313.4	1142.8	59.3	9.8%	53.8	9.1%	–53.2	541.9
1976	1782.8	1603.6	1441.4	1451.4	1252.6	63.1	6.4%	56.9	5.8%	–73.7	629.0
1977	1990.5	1789.0	1617.8	1607.5	1379.3	67.3	6.7%	60.6	6.5%	–53.6	706.4
1978	2249.7	2019.8	1838.2	1812.4	1551.2	72.2	7.3%	65.2	7.6%	–59.2	776.6
1979	2508.2	2242.4	2047.3	2034.0	1729.3	78.6	8.9%	72.6	11.3%	–40.2	828.9
1980	2732.0	2428.1	2203.5	2258.5	1918.0	85.7	9.0%	82.4	13.5%	–73.8	908.5
1981	3052.6	2704.8	2443.5	2520.9	2127.6	94.0	9.7%	90.9	10.3%	–78.9	994.3
1982	3166.0	2782.8	2518.4	2670.8	2261.4	100.0	6.4%	96.5	6.2%	–127.9	1136.8
1983	3405.7	3009.1	2719.5	2838.6	2428.1	103.9	3.9%	99.6	3.2%	–207.8	1371.2
1984	3772.2	3356.8	3028.6	3108.7	2668.6	107.7	3.7%	103.9	4.3%	–185.3	1564.1
1985	4014.9	3577.6	3234.0	3325.3	2838.7	110.9	3.0%	107.6	3.6%	–212.3	1817.0
1986	4231.6	3771.5	3412.6	3526.2	3013.3	113.8	2.6%	109.6	1.9%	–221.2	2120.1
1987	4515.6	4028.6	3660.3	3766.4	3194.7	117.4	3.2%	113.6	3.6%	–149.7	2345.6
1988	4873.7	4359.4	3984.9	4070.8	3479.2	121.3	3.3%	118.3	4.1%	–155.1	2600.8
1989	5200.8	4646.4	4223.3	4384.3	3725.5	126.3	4.1%	124.0	4.8%	–152.0	2866.2
1990	5463.0	4887.4	4417.5	4645.6	3945.8	131.5	4.1%	130.7	5.4%	–220.4	3206.3

SOURCE: *Economic Report of the President*, February 1991.

ECONOMICS
A Contemporary Introduction
Second Edition

William A. McEachern
Professor of Economics
University of Connecticut

COLLEGE DIVISION South-Western Publishing Co.

CINCINNATI

HB83BA

Sponsoring Editor: James M. Keefe
Developmental Editor: Brigid M. Harmon
Production Editor: Judith O'Neill
Production House: Lifland et al., Bookmakers
Cover and Interior Designer: Craig LaGesse Ramsdell
Photo Researcher: Diana Fears
Marketing Manager: Scott D. Person

Copyright © 1991

by SOUTH-WESTERN PUBLISHING CO.
Cincinnati, Ohio

Library of Congress Cataloging-in-Publication Data

McEachern, William A.
    Economics : a contemporary introduction / William A. McEachern. —
2nd ed.
        p.   cm.
    Includes bibliographical references and index.
    ISBN 0-538-80832-2
    1. Economics   I. Title.
HB171.5.M475   1991
330 — dc20   90-35835
                                                                         CIP

COVER PHOTO: Philadelphia Museum of Art: A. E. Gallatin Collection

Printed in the United States of America

2   3   4   5   6   RN   5   4   3   2   1

Preface

Economics has a short history but a long past. As a distinct discipline, economics has been studied for only a few hundred years, but civilizations have confronted the economic problem of scarce resources and unlimited wants for thousands of years. Economics may be centuries old, but it is new every day. Each day offers fresh evidence that can be used to support or reshape evolving economic theory. In this book I try to convey the vitality and timeliness of the discipline — and I believe that I am new enough to the task to keep the discussion fresh but experienced enough to get it right.

Remember the last time you were in an unfamiliar neighborhood and had to ask for directions? Along with the directions came the standard comment "You can't miss it!" So how come you missed it? Because the landmark that was obvious to the neighborhood resident who gave you directions might as well have been invisible to you, a stranger. Writing a principles text is much like giving directions. The author's familiarity with the material can be both a strength and a weakness. Knowing the material is obviously essential to the task. But familiarity can dull one's perceptions: those who have worked for years with economic concepts may have trouble seeing them with fresh eyes. As a result, principles authors sometimes have difficulty describing an economic point to someone unfamiliar with it. Some authors try to compensate by telling all they know about a subject, in the process overwhelming the student with so much detail that the central point gets lost. Other authors take a minimalist approach, offering little discussion of institutional detail or of what students may already know intuitively, and instead talking abstractly about good x and good y, units of labor and units of capital, or the proverbial widget. Otherwise sensible textbook authors

put their economist caps on and go into a sort of trance, lapsing into a style of presentation that turns economics into a foreign language. This approach may work with advanced undergraduates and with other economists, but it doesn't work with principles students.

Students typically arrive the first day of class with eighteen or more years of experience with economic institutions and economic choices. Each student grew up in a household — the central economic institution. As consumers, students are familiar with fast food restaurants, movie theaters, car dealers, and dozens of stores at the mall. Most students have also been resource suppliers: as high school students, more than half were employed outside of school. Students have experience with government: they know about sales taxes, drivers licenses, speed limits, public schools, and colleges. And they have a growing awareness of the rest of the world: they buy imported goods, and the nightly news tells them about trade deficits, famines in Africa, and the market revolution in Eastern Europe.

Thus from the rise of the shopping mall to the fall of the Berlin Wall, students have abundant experience with economic events, economic choices, and economic institutions. But many principles authors miss the boat by not tapping into this rich lode of student experience, believing instead that they must create for the student a new world based on economics as a foreign language. These authors miss the chance to make the connection between economics and "the ordinary business of life." And when principles books use examples that are not familiar to students, instructors must take up precious time explaining the examples. I believe that examples should be self-explanatory; they should convey the point quickly and directly. Having to explain an example is like having to explain a joke — the impact is lost.

Good directions rely on landmarks familiar to us all: a gas station, a fork in the road, a white picket fence. Likewise, a good textbook builds bridges from the familiar to the unknown. In this book I draw on common experience to convey economic points. I try to create graphic pictures in students' minds by using examples that need little explanation. I try to elicit from the reader that light of recognition, that "aha!" Clear and palpable examples allow me to jump-start the analysis, pushing it further and faster than is possible in books that rely on less obvious or more abstract examples. Throughout, I provide just enough intuitive information and institutional detail to get the point across without overwhelming the student. My approach is to start where students are, not where we would like them to be. For example, to explain the division of labor, rather than refer to Adam Smith's pin factory, I call attention to the division of labor at McDonald's. Similarly, I explain resource substitution by talking about specific examples of alternative labor-capital mixes — for example, a drive-through car wash versus a Saturday morning send-the-band-to-Disney-World charity car wash — rather than by referring to abstract units of labor and capital.

Since instructors can cover only a fraction of the material in class, principles texts should, to the extent possible, be self-explanatory, thereby providing instructors with greater flexibility. This book provides much "running room" — by not requiring instructors to cover everything in the chapter, it leaves them free to explore in greater detail topics of special interest. And because the examples are so contemporary, instructors can draw on more traditional examples to provide students with additional insight. I believe the use of familiar experiences and the clarity of exposition are what make this book effective and even enjoyable.

Growing Significance of the World Economy

This edition reflects the growing impact of the world economy on U.S. economic welfare. International issues are introduced early and are discussed often. The book stresses the interdependence of the U.S. economy and the rest of the world. For example, the rest of the world is introduced as an economic actor in Chapter 1 and comparative advantage and the production possibilities frontier are each discussed from a global perspective in Chapter 2. The international coverage is not simply added on; it enhances the entire presentation. For example, students gain greater perspective about unemployment and inflation when U.S. rates are compared to those in other key countries around the world. Likewise, students can better understand how free markets allocate resources when the effects of trade barriers are considered. And recent trends in the competitive structure of the U.S. economy cannot be understood without examining the role of imports and foreign investment. To heighten student awareness of international coverage, international passages are denoted by a small globe that appears in the margin.

Introductory Chapters

Topics common to both macroeconomics and microeconomics are covered in the first four chapters. Limiting the introductory material to four chapters saves precious class time, particularly at institutions where students can take macro and micro courses in either order (and hence are likely to end up repeating the introductory chapters).

Macroeconomics

At no time since World War II has the field of macroeconomics been in such disarray. This lack of consensus poses a real problem for the principles author. Some texts present a smorgasbord of alternative macroeconomic approaches, leaving it to the student to choose among them. The problem with this approach is that students lack sufficient background to evaluate the alternatives, so competing theories often seem unrelated and confusing.

Rather than dwell on the differences among competing schools of thought, I use the aggregate demand and aggregate supply model to focus on the fundamental distinction between those economists who believe that the economy is essentially stable and self-correcting and those who believe that the economy is unstable and in need of government intervention. This approach allows for a discussion of the policy prescriptions that flow from these differences between activists and nonactivists.

Wherever possible, I rely on the students' experiences and intuition to explain the theory behind macroeconomic abstractions such as aggregate demand and aggregate supply. To this end, Chapter 10 has been revised to provide a more intuitively appealing explanation for the shapes of the short-run and long-run aggregate supply curves. For example, to explain how output can temporarily exceed its potential rate, I note how students, as the term draws to a close, can temporarily shift into high gear to study for final exams and finish term papers.

Some emerging issues of macroeconomics receive special scrutiny. There is a chapter on the declining growth in U.S. productivity and a chapter on the federal deficits and debt. This edition also discusses the savings and loan crisis, the market revolution in Eastern Europe, monetary targeting, policy credibility, rules versus discretion, and the natural rate hypothesis.

Microeconomics

My approach to microeconomics underscores the role of time and information in production and consumption. The presentation also reflects the growing interest in economic institutions, particularly the internal organization of firms and governments. More generally, I try to convey the idea that most microeconomic principles operate like gravity: market forces work whether or not particular economic actors understand them.

In light of the growing concern about the environment, a new chapter entitled "Externalities and the Environment" discusses the economic implications of current, though controversial, issues such as global warming and the destruction of the tropical rain forests. A major section on corporate finance has been added to explain recent developments in financial markets, such as the market for corporate control and leveraged buyouts. Other emerging issues of microeconomics that receive greater attention in this second edition are contestable markets, vertical integration, economies of scope, principal-agent problems, signaling, screening, comparable worth, rent seeking, and public choice.

Organization

In many principles texts chapters are interrupted by boxed case studies, parenthetical explanations, qualifying footnotes, and other distractions that disrupt the flow of the presentation. Segregating case studies from the mainstream of a chapter leaves students uncertain about when or if they should read the case studies.

In contrast, this book has a natural flow. Each chapter opens with a motivating paragraph and a list of key concepts, then tells a compelling story using logical sections and subsections. Qualifying footnotes are used sparingly, and parenthetical explanations are used hardly at all. Moreover, although they are self-contained, case studies appear in the natural sequence of the chapter. Students can thus read each chapter smoothly from beginning to end. Each chapter includes the following features.

Captioned Exhibits A caption beneath each exhibit explains the lessons to be drawn from the analysis.

Marginal Definitions Important economic terms appear in boldface in the body of the text and are also defined in the margins.

Case Studies As already noted, case studies are identified as such but are integrated into the body of the text. The student therefore has no doubt about when to read them. Each case study draws out the economic implications of a contemporary event. These self-contained features show the link between economic theory and everyday life.

Profiles of Famous Economists The profiles of famous economists discuss their contributions to economic thought rather than focusing primarily on biographical information. These profiles are placed so as to complement other analysis presented in a chapter.

End-of-Chapter Material The conclusion of each chapter draws the discussion to a close; a summary reviews the key points. The number of end-of-chapter questions has been increased by half in this edition. Most of the new questions are analytical, requiring the student to do calculations or to draw graphs. Suggested answers to these questions and problems are provided in the *Instructor's Manual*.

Appendixes Several end-of-chapter appendixes provide more detailed treatment of various topics. The appendix to Chapter 1 is recommended for all students unfamiliar with variables, graphs, slopes, and the like. Other appendixes are optional in the sense that subsequent material does not rely on them. Including the more difficult material in this way offers the instructor greater flexibility of coverage with no loss of continuity.

Glossary Key terms are listed alphabetically in the glossary, which appears just before the index.

Supplementary Items for Students

Study Guide The chapters of the student *Study Guide* correspond to the chapters in the text. Each chapter includes (1) an introduction; (2) a chapter outline, with definitions of all terms; (3) a discussion of the chapter's main points; (4) a "lagniappe," which supplements the material in the chapter and is accompanied by a "Question to Think About"; (5) a list of key terms; (6) a variety of questions, including completion, true/false, multiple choice, and discussion questions; and (7) answers to all these questions.

MacroGraph and MicroGraph Microcomputer tutorials convey difficult material from the text in a dynamic way — students can actually see curves shift from one equilibrium to another. *MacroGraph's* four modules illustrate key ideas in macroeconomics; *MicroGraph's* four modules illustrate key ideas in microeconomics. These tutorials are available free of charge from your South-Western representative. They can be copied and given to students, or they can be placed in a microcomputer lab.

Supplementary Items for Instructors

Instructor's Manual The *Instructor's Manual* includes (1) an outline and brief overview of each chapter; (2) a summary of each chapter's main points; (3) pedagogical tips that expand on points raised in the chapter; (4) a list of additional readings; and (5) suggested answers to the end-of-chapter questions and problems. Three suggested outlines for one-term courses are provided at the beginning of the manual.

Teaching Assistance Manual The *Teaching Assistance Manual* provides additional support beyond the *Instructor's Manual* and may be especially useful to new instructors, graduate assistants, and teachers who would like to generate more class discussion. This manual offers (1) an overview and detailed outline of each chapter; (2) chapter objectives and quiz material; (3) material for class discussion; (4) a discussion of chapter topics that warrant special attention; (5) supplementary examples; and (6) lists of "What if?" discussion questions. Four appendixes provide guidance on presenting material; generating and sustaining class discussions; preparing, administering, and grading quizzes; and coping with the special problems confronting foreign graduate assistants.

Hypercard Tutorial The *Hypercard Tutorial* is a computer program developed especially for *Economics: A Contemporary Introduction* to animate the exhibits in the book by showing movements from one equilibrium to another, providing alternative views of graphs, and illustrating the results of what-if propositions — all accompanied by rolling text explanations. The tutorial includes nearly six hundred visual displays that provide ideal teaching support in the classroom. It also comes with a search capability to display the definition of any key term in the book. The images and text can be projected with a Macintosh computer, a standard overhead projector, and a projection pad hookup. The tutorial may also be used during student labs or may be copied and distributed to students for their personal use. The computer disc containing this program is offered free to adopters of *Economics: A Contemporary Introduction.*

Innovative Teaching Transparencies Accompanying this new edition is an expanded and improved set of transparencies. The transparencies number 150 rather than 100 and many are in three or four colors. One-third of the transparencies have hinged overlays, allowing step-by-step exposition of complicated diagrams.

Test Bank The *Test Bank* has been thoroughly revised since the first edition, and the number of multiple choice questions has nearly doubled, to about five thousand. The *Test Bank* also contains 360 true/false questions. All questions have been scrutinized by a panel of reviewers. None of the questions duplicates those in the *Study Guide.* The *Test Bank* is available in two volumes — macro and micro — and on a computer disk that can be used with either IBM- or Macintosh-compatible microcomputers. The software allows instructors to edit questions and to print graphs in the body of the test.

Videotapes Videotapes are available to qualified adopters. These videos are designed to supplement the text and to promote class discussion. The videotape series is the latest version of the *Economics U$A Telecourse,* which consists of twenty-eight half-hour programs showing economic principles in action through films of key historical events, news broadcasts, and interviews with well-known economists, business leaders, and public officials.

The Teaching Economist South-Western publishes a semiannual newsletter, *The Teaching Economist,* aimed at making classes more interesting and more fun for both students and instructors. In this newsletter, I will discuss new and imaginative ways to present topics — for example, how to integrate more international topics into the course material or how to generate and sustain class discussion.

Acknowledgments

Many people contributed to this book's development. I would like to thank my colleagues at the University of Connecticut who provided helpful feedback for the second edition, especially Francis Ahking, Peter Barth, Dimitris Hatzinikolaou, Dennis Heffley, William Lott, Steve Miller, Steve Sacks, and Imanuel Wexler.

I also gratefully acknowledge the helpful comments of those who reviewed material for the second edition:

David W. Brasfield	*Murray State University*
Jeffrey A. Buser	*Murray State University*
Charles Callahan III	*SUNY, College at Brockport*
Larry A. Chenault	*Miami University*
Curtis R. Clarke	*Eastfield College*
Steven A. Cobb	*Xavier University*
Jim M. Cox	*DeKalb College*
Jerry L. Crawford	*Arkansas State University*
Joseph P. Daniels	*Marquette University*
David Dean	*University of Richmond*
Justino de la Cruz	*Wharton Econometrics*
Donald S. Elliot	*Southern Illinois University, Edwardsville*
G. Rod Erfani	*Transylvania University*
T. Windsor Fields	*James Madison University*
Gary M. Galles	*Pepperdine University*
James R. Hill	*Central Michigan University*
Janice Holtkamp	*Iowa State University*
Joseph M. Lammert	*Raymond Walters General and Technical College*
Thomas M. Maloy	*Muskegon Community College*
Wolfgang Mayer	*University of Cincinnati*
Floyd McFarland	*Oregon State University*
Martin I. Milkman	*Murray State University*
Kathryn A. Nantz	*Fairfield University*
Mitch Redlo	*Monroe Community College*
Rexford E. Santerre	*Bentley College*
Robert J. Stonebreaker	*Indiana University of Pennsylvania*
Tom TenHoeve	*Iowa State University*
David R. Weinberg	*Xavier University*
Richard D. Winkelman	*Arizona State University*
Mesghena Yasin	*Morehead State University*

I also thank those who, as reviewers, contributed to the success of the first edition:

Polly Reynolds Allen	*University of Connecticut*
Jacquelene Browning	late of *Texas A&M University*
Art Goldsmith	*Washington and Lee University*
Rich Hart	*Miami University*
Andrew J. Policano	*SUNY at Stony Brook*
Steven M. Sheffrin	*University of California, Davis*
Roger Sherman	*University of Virginia*
Houston Stokes	*University of Illinois at Chicago*
Gregory H. Wassall	*Northeastern University*
William C. Wood	*James Madison University*
Leland B. Yeager	*Auburn University*

I relied on comparative advantage and the division of labor to prepare the most complete teaching package on the market today. My colleague at the University of Connecticut, Richard Langlois, wrote the profiles of famous economists featured throughout the book. John Lunn of Louisiana State University authored the *Study Guide*, and Steven Cobb of Xavier University authored the *Instructor's Manual*. My coauthors on the *Test*

Bank were Nancy Fox of St. Joseph's University, John Golden of Allegheny College, Sharon Linard of Indiana University-Purdue University at Fort Wayne, Alannah Orrison of Saddleback College, and William Witter of the University of North Texas. John Pisciotta of Baylor University developed the *Hyper-Card Tutorial*. I am grateful to all of them for their contributions to the project.

The talented staff at South-Western Publishing offered invaluable editorial, administrative, and sales support. I would like to thank Jim Keefe, Sponsoring Editor, who coordinated resources for the many parts of the package, and Judy O'Neill, Production Editor, who was responsible for the editorial production schedule and who provided helpful comments along the way. I especially would like to thank Brigid M. Harmon, Developmental Editor, who worked with me, sometimes daily, to ensure the excellence of the second edition. I also gratefully acknowledge the support of South-Western's service and sales force, for in a significant way they contributed to the gratifying success of the first edition that made the second edition possible.

Finally, I owe a special debt to my wife, Pat, who has now had to suffer through two editions. For her patience and good humor, I dedicate this book to her.

William A. McEachern

Contents in Brief

Contents

PART TWO   *Fundamentals of Macroeconomics*   **99**

PART FOUR *Introduction to the Market System*   *435*

PART FIVE   Market Structure, Pricing, and Government Regulation   523

William A. McEachern

William A. McEachern is professor of economics at the University of Connecticut, where he has taught principles of economics since 1973 and has developed a series of annual workshops for teaching assistants. He earned an undergraduate degree *cum laude* in the honors program from Holy Cross College and an M.A. and a Ph.D. from the University of Virginia. He has published several books and monographs on public finance, public policy, and industrial organizations. His research has appeared in a variety of journals, including *Economic Inquiry*, *National Tax Journal*, *Journal of Industrial Economics*, *Kyklos*, *The Quarterly Review of Economics and Business*, *Challenge*, and *Public Choice*. Professor McEachern has advised federal, state, and local governments on policy matters and directed a bipartisan commission charged with examining Connecticut's finances. He has addressed well over one hundred groups and has received the University of Connecticut's Faculty Award for Distinguished Public Service.

P A R T   O N E

Introduction to Economics

The Art and Science of Economic Analysis

You have been reading and hearing about economic issues for years—the unemployment rate, the inflation rate, the price of oil, the federal deficit, higher tuition, the price of rock concert tickets. When the explanations of these issues go into any depth, your eyes probably glaze over, and you tune out the same way you do when the weather forecaster tries to provide an in-depth analysis of high-pressure fronts colliding with moisture carried in from the coast. Because of a negative experience with economics, some of you may have been dreading this course. Some of you may have had to work up your courage just to open this book.

What many people fail to realize is that economics is much more alive than the dry accounts provided by the news media. Economics is about making choices, and you make economic choices every day—choices about whether to live in the dorm or off-campus, take a course in accounting or one in music appreciation, pack a lunch or buy a Big Mac. Because you, as an economic decision maker, are the subject of this book, you already know much more about economics than you may think you do. You bring to the subject a rich personal experience, an experience that will be tapped throughout the book to reinforce your understanding of the basic concepts. This chapter will introduce you to the art and science of economic analysis. Topics discussed in this chapter include

- Scarce resources
- Unlimited wants
- Rational self-interest
- Marginal analysis

- Scientific method
- Normative versus positive analysis
- Pitfalls of economic thinking

THE ECONOMIC PROBLEM:
SCARCE RESOURCES BUT UNLIMITED WANTS

Would you like a new car, a bigger dorm room, better meals, more free time, a more interesting social life, more spending money, more sleep? Yes, you say? Even if you are able to satisfy some of these desires, others will keep popping up. *The problem is that although your wants, or desires, are virtually unlimited, your resources are scarce.* A resource is **scarce** when there is not enough of it to satisfy people's wants. Because of scarce resources, you must choose from among your many wants and, whenever you choose, you must forgo satisfying some wants.

*A resource is **scarce** when there is not enough of it to satisfy all of the people's wants, or desires, for it.*

This problem of scarce resources but unlimited wants is faced to a greater or lesser extent by each of the five billion people around the world. It is faced by taxicab drivers, by farmers, by politicians, by shepherds, by everybody. The taxicab driver uses the cab and other scarce resources—knowledge of the city, driving skills, time—to earn income, which can be exchanged for housing, groceries, clothing, trips to Atlantic City, and other goods and services aimed at satisfying the driver's unlimited wants.

Economics is the study of how people choose to use their scarce resources in an attempt to satisfy unlimited wants.

Economics is the study of how people choose to allocate their scarce resources to produce, exchange, and consume goods and services in an attempt to satisfy their unlimited wants. We shall first consider what we mean by resources, next examine goods and services, and finally focus on the heart of the matter—the necessity of making economic choice, which arises from scarcity.

Resources

*Land is all plots of ground and other natural resources used in the production of goods and services. Resource owners receive **rent** for the use of their land.*

Resources are divided into four broad categories: land, labor, capital, and entrepreneurial ability. These resources are combined in various ways to produce goods and services. **Land** represents not only land in the conventional sense of plots of ground but all other natural resources, including rivers, trees, minerals, and even animals. **Labor** comprises the broad category of human effort, both physical and mental. The efforts in this category can range from those of the cab driver to those of the brain surgeon. Note that labor itself is derived from a more fundamental scarce resource: *time*. Time is really the ultimate raw material of life. Without it we can accomplish nothing; with it, much is possible. Our time can be put to alternative uses: we can *sell* our time as labor, or we can *spend* our time doing other things.

*Labor is the physical and mental effort of humans, who receive **wages** for their labor.*

*Capital includes all buildings, equipment, and human skills used to produce goods and services. Resource owners receive **interest** for the use of their capital.*

Capital represents human creations that are used in the production of goods and services. We often distinguish between human capital and physical capital. *Human capital* consists of the knowledge and skills people develop (through education and formal or on-the-job training) that enhance their ability to produce, such as the taxi driver's knowledge of the city's streets or the surgeon's knowledge of the human body. *Physical capital* consists of buildings, machinery, tools, and other manufactured items that are used to produce goods and services. Physical capital includes the driver's cab, the surgeon's scalpel, the ten-ton press used to print *Newsweek*, and the building where your economics class meets.

A special kind of human skill is called **entrepreneurial ability** — the rare talent required to build a better mousetrap. The entrepreneur identifies the need for a new product or finds a better way to produce an existing product. After figuring out how best to produce the product, an entrepreneur brings together the land, labor, and capital required for production and assumes the risk of success or failure. The entrepreneur tries to discover and act on profitable opportunities. The largest firms in the world today began as ideas in the minds of individual entrepreneurs.

Resource owners are paid for the *time* their resources are employed by entrepreneurs, so resource payment has a time dimension, as in a wage of $10 per hour or rent of $600 per month. Resource owners are paid **rent** for their land, **wages** for their labor, and **interest** for their capital. **Profit** is the difference between the price the entrepreneur is paid for a product and the wages, rent, and interest the entrepreneur must pay for the resources employed. Thus, we say that the entrepreneur is the *residual claimant*, who earns whatever income is left after all other resources are paid for. Sometimes the entrepreneur ends up in the hole.

Entrepreneurial ability includes managerial and organization skills together with the willingness to take risks. Resource owners receive profit for their entrepreneurial ability.

Goods and Services

Land, labor, and capital can be combined by the entrepreneur in a variety of ways to produce goods and services to satisfy our wants. A farmer, a tractor, fifty acres of land, plus seeds and fertilizer produce a good: corn. One hundred musicians, musical instruments, some chairs, a conductor, a musical score, and a music hall combine to produce a service: Ravel's *Bolero*. Corn is a **good** because it is something you can see, feel, and touch that requires scarce resources to produce and is used to satisfy wants. The book you now hold, your last meal, and the clothes you have on are all goods. The rendition of *Bolero* is a **service** because it is not something tangible, yet it uses scarce resources and is used to satisfy wants. Lectures, movies, and haircuts are all services.

A good is a tangible item, such as a doughnut or a sweater, that is used to satisfy wants.

A service is an intangible activity, such as a bus ride or a movie, that is used to satisfy wants.

Because goods and services require scarce resources, they are themselves scarce. Goods and services are *scarce* if the amounts people desire exceed the amounts that are freely available. Since we cannot have all the goods and services we would like, we must continually choose among them. We must choose among better living quarters, better meals, nicer clothes, higher-quality entertainment, more late-night pizza, and so on. Making choices in a world of scarcity means that some goods and services must be passed up.

A few goods and services are considered *free* because the amount freely available exceeds the amount people desire. For example, air and seawater are often considered free because we can breathe all the air we want and have all the seawater we can haul away. Yet, despite the old saying that "The best things in life are free," most goods and services are scarce, not free, and even free goods come with strings attached. For example, *clean* air and *clean* seawater have become increasingly scarce because the atmosphere is used as a gas dump and the ocean as a sewer.

Sometimes we mistakenly think of certain goods as free because they involve no apparent cost to us. Those subscription cards that keep falling out of magazines appear to be free. At least it seems we would have little difficulty rounding up about three thousand if necessary! Their production, however, uses up scarce economic resources, resources drawn away from competing uses, such as producing higher-quality magazines perhaps. You may have heard the expression "There is no such thing as a free lunch." The lunch may be free to us, but it draws scarce resources away from the production of other economic goods. Without scarcity, there would be no economic problem. Goods and services that are truly free are not the subject matter of the economist.

Economic Actors

There are four types of actors in the U.S. economy: households, firms, governments, and the rest of the world. Households play the leading role. As consumers, households demand the goods and services produced, and as resource owners, households supply the land, labor, capital, and entrepreneurial ability to firms and to governments. Firms and governments are supporting actors because they supply the goods and services demanded by households. The rest of the world includes foreign households, firms, and governments, which supply products to U.S. markets and demand U.S. products.

Markets are the means by which buyers and sellers carry out exchange. Markets are often physical places, such as the supermarket, a department store, or a shopping mall. Markets also include the arrangements by which buyers and sellers communicate their intentions, such as letters, phone calls, classified ads, and radio and television ads. These market mechanisms provide information about the quantity, quality, and price of products offered for sale. Goods and services are bought and sold in **product markets**; resources are bought and sold in **resource markets**. The most important resource market is the labor market, or job market. Think of your experience looking for a job, and you get some idea of this market.

Microeconomics and Macroeconomics

Although you have made thousands of economic choices, if you are like most people, you have seldom reflected on your own economic behavior. For example, why did you choose to spend your scarce resource—time—reading this book right now rather than doing something else? **Microeconomics** is the study of your economic behavior and the economic behavior of other economic actors making choices about such matters as what to buy and what to sell, how much to work and how much to play, how much to borrow and how much to save. Microeconomics examines the

*A **market** is a set of arrangements through which buyers and sellers carry out exchange at mutually agreeable terms.*

*A **product market** is one in which goods and services are exchanged; domestic and foreign households are demanders in such markets, whereas domestic and foreign firms and governments are suppliers.*

*A **resource market** is one in which resources are exchanged; domestic and foreign households are suppliers in such markets, and firms and governments are demanders.*

***Microeconomics** is the study of the economic behavior of decision makers.*

factors that affect individual economic choices, how changes in these factors alter such choices, and how the choices of various decision makers are coordinated.

You have perhaps given little thought to the factors influencing your own economic behavior. You have probably given even less thought to the way your choices link up with the billions of choices made by hundreds of millions of other individuals to cause changes in economy-wide aggregate variables such as inflation, unemployment, and the extent of poverty. **Macroeconomics** studies the performance of the economy as a whole. Whereas microeconomics is a study of the individual pieces of the economic puzzle, macroeconomics tries to put all the pieces together to focus on the big picture. Macroeconomics considers the combined effects of individual choices on the overall performance of the economy as reflected by such measures as the nation's average price level, total production, and level of employment. Microeconomics, in contrast, focuses on the determination of prices, output levels, and employment in individual markets, such as the market for textbooks.

Macroeconomics is the study of the behavior of entire economies.

Just as the whole consists of the sum of its parts, the economy is ultimately driven by the individual choices made by people like you in responding to changes in their economic environment. Thus, a study of the big picture — of economic aggregates such as unemployment and inflation — must be based on an understanding of the individual choices behind those aggregates.

THE ART OF ECONOMIC ANALYSIS

Our economic system results from millions of individuals making billions of choices while attempting to satisfy their unlimited wants. Because these choices lie at the very heart of the economic problem — the problem of allocating scarce resources — they deserve closer scrutiny. Developing an understanding of the factors that shape economic choices is the first step toward mastering the art of economic analysis.

Rational Self-Interest

A key economic assumption is that individuals rationally select choices they perceive to be in their best interest. By *rational* we mean simply that people do not consciously make themselves less happy or less satisfied. The economist does not claim that each individual knows with certainty which alternatives are best. The economist merely maintains that individuals make choices they believe will achieve the desired results and that these choices are influenced in predictable ways by changes in each individual's economic situation, such as changes in income or in prices.

This reliance on *rational self-interest* should not be viewed as blind materialism, pure selfishness, or greed. Your self-interest often includes the welfare of your family, your friends, and perhaps the poor of the world. But your concern for others is tempered by economic considerations. You are more likely to donate your old clothes than your new ones to organizations such as Goodwill Industries. You may volunteer to drive a friend to the airport on Saturday afternoon, but you are less likely to offer a ride if your friend's plane leaves at 6:00 A.M. People are more inclined to give to their favorite charities if their contributions are tax deductible. The point is that the notion of self-interest does not rule out concern for others; it simply means that concern for others is to some extent influenced by the same economic factors that influence other economic choices. The lower the personal cost of helping others, the more help will be offered.

Economic Analysis Is Marginal Analysis

Economic choice usually involves some adjustment to the existing situation or to the status quo. The president of a computer software company must decide whether to develop a new word processing program. The town manager must decide whether to buy another garbage truck. Your favorite jeans are on sale, and you must decide whether to buy another pair. You are wondering whether you should carry an extra course next semester. You have just finished dinner and must decide whether to have dessert.

Economic choices may involve working a little more or a little less, studying a little more or a little less, buying a little more or a little less, selling a little more or a little less. The decisions are based on a comparison of the expected marginal costs and the expected marginal benefits of the change under consideration. **Marginal** means "incremental" or "decremental"; it refers to a change in an economic variable. For example, the marginal cost of production when a firm alters its level of output is the change in production cost. *You, as a rational decision maker, will change the status quo as long as your expected marginal benefit from the change exceeds your expected marginal cost.* Thus, you compare the marginal benefit you expect from the dessert—your additional enjoyment from consuming it—with its marginal cost—the extra money, extra time, and extra calories.

Marginal means "incremental" or "decremental"; it refers to a change in an economic variable.

Typically the change under consideration is small, but marginal choices can involve major economic adjustments, as in the decision to quit school and join the Marines. For a firm, a marginal choice might mean producing a new product, building a plant in Taiwan, or even filing for bankruptcy. By focusing on the effects of marginal adjustments to the status quo, the economist is able to cut the analysis of economic choice down to manageable size. Rather than confront head-on a bewildering economic reality, the economist can begin with marginal choices, then see how these marginal choices affect particular markets and help shape the economic system as a whole.

Choice Requires Time and Information

Rational choice takes time and requires information; both time and information are scarce and valuable. Thus, we seldom know all we would like to know prior to making choices. If you have any doubts about the time and information required to make choices, talk to someone who recently purchased a house, a car, or a personal computer. Talk to a corporate official who is trying to decide whether to introduce a new product or whether to buy a new machine. Consider your own experience in selecting a college. You probably talked to friends, relatives, teachers, and guidance counselors; very likely you looked at school catalogs and the various college guides; you may have visited a few campuses to meet with the admissions staff and with anyone else who was willing to talk. The decision took time and money, not to mention creating aggravation and anxiety.

Because information is costly to acquire, we are often willing to pay others to gather and digest it for us. The market for stock analysts, travel agents, real estate brokers, career counselors, restaurant guidebooks, and *Consumer Reports* magazine indicates our willingness to pay for information that will facilitate our economic choices.

To review: The art of economic analysis focuses on how individuals use their scarce resources in an attempt to satisfy their unlimited wants. Rational self-interest guides individual choice. Choice involves a comparison of the marginal costs and marginal benefits of alternative actions, a comparison that requires time and information. To understand when and why marginal changes are made, we must examine the impact of economic events on individual choices. The economist studies such impacts in a systematic manner called the scientific method. The science of economic analysis will be examined next.

THE SCIENCE OF ECONOMIC ANALYSIS

*A **theory**, or **model**, is a simplification of economic reality designed to capture the important elements of the relation under consideration.*

Economists use the science of economic analysis to develop theories, or models, to explain how some aspect of the economy works. A **theory**, or **model**, is a simplification of economic reality that captures only the important elements of the relation under consideration. Theories, or models, *are used to make predictions about the real world.* Economic theories need not contain every detail and interrelation. In fact, the more details they contain, the more unwieldy they become and the less useful they are. The world we confront is so complex that we have to abstract from the billions of relations to make any sense of things. Theories can be presented verbally, graphically, or mathematically.

The Role of Theory

The role of theory is usually not well understood. Perhaps you have heard someone say "Oh, that's fine in theory, but in practice it's another matter." The implication is that the theory provides no aid in practical matters. Individuals who say this fail to realize that what they are actually doing is substituting their own theory for a theory they either do not believe or do not understand. In effect, they are saying "I have my own theory, which works better."

All of us use theories, however poorly defined or understood, to operate. A person who pounds on the Pepsi machine that just ate his quarter has a crude theory about how that machine works and what just went wrong. One version of that theory might go: "The quarter drops through a series of whatchamacallits, but sometimes the quarter gets stuck. *If* I pound on the machine, *then* I can free up the quarter and send it on its way." Evidently this theory works well enough that many individuals continue to pound on machines that fail to produce (a real problem for the vending machine industry). Yet if you asked these mad pounders if they had a "theory" about how the machine operates, they would look at you as if you were crazy.

The Scientific Process

The process of theoretical investigation can be understood most easily by breaking down the scientific methodology into four steps.

*A **variable** is any quantity that can take on different values.*

Step One The first step is to identify and define the key variables that are relevant to the economic problem under consideration. A **variable** is a quantity, such as the unemployment rate or the price of zucchini, that can take on different possible values. The variables of concern become the basic elements of the theory, so they must be selected with care.

*The **other-things-constant assumption** allows economists to focus on key economic variables by assuming that other variables are constant.*

Step Two The second step is to state the assumptions that specify the conditions under which the theory is to apply. One major category of assumptions is the **other-things-constant assumption**—in Latin, the *ceteris paribus* assumption. The idea is to identify those variables of interest, then to assume that nothing else of importance will change. For example, suppose that we are interested in how the quantity of Pepsi purchased per week is influenced by changes in its price. Since we wish to isolate the relation between the price of Pepsi and the quantity purchased, we assume that there will be no changes in other important variables such as consumer income, the price of Coke, and the average temperature.

*Behavioral assumptions** describe the objectives of economic actors and how these decision makers are expected to behave.*

We also make assumptions about individual behavior; these are called **behavioral assumptions**. Perhaps the most fundamental behavioral assumption is that of rational self-interest. As noted earlier, we assume that individual decision makers rationally pursue their self-interest and make choices accordingly. For consumers, rationality implies allocating their resources in a way that maximizes their expected levels of satisfaction. For producers, rationality implies making choices about inputs, prices, and outputs that maximize expected profits. These kinds of assumptions are known as behavioral assumptions because they specify how individuals are expected to behave—what makes them tick, so to speak.

*A **hypothesis** is a statement about relations among variables.*

Step Three The third step of the scientific method is to formulate a **hypothesis**, which is a theory about how key variables relate. For example, one hypothesis holds that *if* the price of a six-pack of Pepsi goes up, other things constant, *then* the quantity purchased per week will go down. Thus, the hypothesis becomes a prediction of what will happen to the quantity purchased if the price goes up. The purpose of this theory, like that of any theory, is to make predictions about the real world.

Step Four The validity of the theory must be tested by confronting its predictions with evidence. Testing hypotheses, the fourth step, is perhaps the most difficult step because data must be collected in a way that focuses attention on the variables in question, while other effects are carefully controlled for. The test will lead us either to reject the theory as inconsistent with the evidence or to continue using the theory until another one comes along that predicts even better. It may be that a theory is not a good predictor at all times, yet still does a better job of predicting than competing theories.

Predictions Versus Forecasts

The predictions of a theory are not the same as an economic forecast. Economic theory might predict that *if* consumer spending increases, *then* unemployment will decrease, other things constant. A theory is usually offered as a *conditional* statement. In contrast, an *economic forecast* might simply state that unemployment will go down next year. The forecaster might be guessing that consumer spending will increase next year and that unemployment will therefore go down. If the forecast about unemployment turns out to be wrong, this does not necessarily mean that the underlying economic theory is faulty. The forecaster may simply have guessed wrong about an increase in consumer spending.

Remember this distinction between the predictions of economic theory and the forecasts of economists. Predictions are conditional statements of the *if-then* variety, whereas forecasts are more like guesses about what will actually occur. It is the forecaster you hear from most often in the media. *Although the economist may be the most informed forecaster, keep in mind that forecasts are nothing more than educated guesses.*

Predicting Average Behavior

The task of economic theories, then, is to try to predict the effects of economic changes on economic choices and, in turn, the effects of these choices on particular markets and on the economy as a whole. Does this mean that economists try to predict the behavior of particular individuals? No, because any particular individual may behave in an unpredictable way. But the unpredictable actions of numerous individuals tend to cancel one another out, so the average behavior of groups can be predicted with greater accuracy. For example, the professor cannot predict very well which particular students will be absent on a given day, but can predict fairly accurately what percentage of the class will be absent. Likewise, the manager of

Burger King does not know who in particular will order a Whopper, but can predict with great accuracy the number of Whoppers that will be sold on a particular day. And if the price of a Whopper increases by 20 percent, the manager can better predict how total sales will change than how a particular customer will respond. The random actions of individuals tend to offset one another so that *the average behavior of a large group can be predicted more accurately than can the behavior of a particular individual.* Consequently economists focus on the average behavior of people in groups rather than on the specific behavior of particular economic actors.

Normative Versus Positive Analysis

Economists, through their simplifying models, attempt to explain how the world works. But sometimes economists concern themselves not with how the world works but with how it *should* work. Compare these two statements: "The U.S. unemployment rate is 6 percent" and "The U.S. unemployment rate should be lower." The first is called a **positive economic statement** because it is an assertion about economic reality that can be supported or rejected by reference to the facts. The second statement is called a **normative economic statement** because it reflects an opinion, and an opinion cannot be shown to be true or false by reference to the facts. Positive statements concern what *is*; normative statements concern what, in someone's opinion, *should be*. Positive statements do not have to be true, but they must be subject to possible verification by reference to the facts.

Theories are expressed as positive statements, such as "If the price increases, the quantity demanded will decrease." Most of the disagreement among economists involves matters of normative policy questions rather than positive analysis. To be sure, many theoretical issues still are unresolved, but there is broad consensus in the economics profession about most fundamental theoretical principles—that is, there is much agreement about positive economic analysis. For example, in a survey of two hundred U.S. economists,[1] 90 percent agreed with the statement "A minimum wage increases unemployment among young and unskilled workers"; 98 percent agreed with the statement "A ceiling on rents reduces the quantity and quality of housing available." Both of these are positive statements because they can be shown to be consistent or inconsistent with the evidence. In contrast, there was much less agreement on normative statements, such as "The government should be an employer of last resort and initiate a guaranteed job program." Only 53 percent of the economists surveyed agreed with that statement.

Economists Tell Stories

Despite economists' reliance on the scientific method for developing and evaluating theories, economic analysis is perhaps as much art as science.

*A **positive economic statement** is one that can be tested by reference to facts.*

*A **normative economic statement** is one that represents an opinion, which cannot be proved or disproved.*

---

[1] J. Kearl et al., "A Confusion of Economists," *American Economic Review* 69 (May 1979): Table 1.

Observing some phenomenon in the real world, isolating the key variables, formulating a theory to predict how these variables relate, and devising an unambiguous way to test the predictions all involve more than simply an understanding of economics and scientific methodology. These steps depend on intuition for identifying, relating, measuring, and testing theories.

Economic analysis also calls for the imagination of a storyteller. Economists tell stories about how they think the world works. Although these are technically called theories or models, they are stories nonetheless. To tell a compelling story, the economist relies on case studies, anecdotes, parables, and the personal experience of the listener. The story about the Pepsi machine was an example. Throughout this book you will hear stories that bring you closer to the concepts under consideration. These stories help to breathe life into economic theory and allow you to personalize abstract ideas.

Some Pitfalls of Faulty Economic Analysis

Economic investigation, like other forms of scientific inquiry, is subject to common mistakes in reasoning that can cause the unwary to draw faulty conclusions. We will discuss three sources of confusion.

The Fallacy That Association Is Causation   Does this sound familiar: "The stock market was higher today as traders reacted favorably to diminished tensions in the Middle East"? Although it is comforting to think that a movement in stock prices resulting from millions of individual trades can be traced to a single event, such simplifications are often misleading and even wrong. To assume that event B was caused by event A simply because B and A are associated in time is to fall into the **fallacy that association is causation**, a common error. The simple fact that one event follows another or that one event occurs with another does not necessarily imply that one causes the other. Remember: Association is not necessarily causation.

*The **association-causation fallacy** is the mistaken idea that if two variables are associated in time, one must necessarily cause the other.*

The Fallacy of Composition   Suppose a farmer with an abundant harvest anticipates a financially successful year, only to discover that the other farmers have also had abundant harvests and the increase in supply has depressed farm prices enough to *reduce* farm revenues. The farmer has committed the **fallacy of composition**, which is an erroneous belief that what is true for the individual or for the part is also true for the group or the whole.

*The **fallacy of composition** is the erroneous belief that what is true for the individual or part must necessarily be true for the group or whole.*

The Mistake of Ignoring the Secondary Effects   Many city officials, because of concern about escalating rents, have imposed rent controls on housing. The *primary effect* of this policy, the effect on which policy makers focus, is to keep rents from rising. Over time, however, fewer new units are built because the rental business becomes less profitable. Moreover, existing rental units deteriorate because owners cannot recover rising maintenance costs through higher rents. Thus, the quantity and quality of housing may well decline as a

Secondary effects of economic actions are unintended consequences that develop slowly over time as people react to events.

result of what appeared to be a reasonable public policy of keeping rents from going up. The policy makers' mistake was to ignore the **secondary effects** of their policy. Economic actions have secondary effects that often turn out to be more important than the primary effects. Secondary effects may develop more slowly and may not always be obvious, but good economic analysis takes them into account.

Minimum-wage legislation represents another policy with important secondary effects. The initial effect of a minimum-wage law is to raise the wages of workers at the bottom of the wage scale. The secondary effect, however, may be to put some of these same people out of work, particularly those with the least experience, such as teenagers. Employers do not find their labor worth the higher wage.

IF ECONOMISTS ARE SO SMART, WHY AREN'T THEY RICH?

Why aren't economists rich? Well, some of them are. Some economists earn as much as $20,000 per appearance on the lecture circuit. Others earn thousands of dollars a day as consultants. Economists have been appointed to many high-level government positions, including not only positions for which they have clear expertise, such as Chairman of the Federal Reserve Bank, Director of the Office of Management and Budget, Chairman of the President's Council of Economic Advisers, Secretary of Commerce, Secretary of the Treasury, and Secretary of Labor, but also other positions for which the connection is less obvious, such as Secretary of State and Secretary of Defense. Both presidents Reagan and Bush majored in economics. Economics is the only social science and the only business discipline for which the prestigious Nobel Prize is awarded, and pronouncements by economists are reported in the media daily.

Leonard Silk, an economic columnist for the *New York Times*, writes: "Businessmen employ economists in large numbers or consult them at high fees, believing that their cracked crystal balls are better than none at all. The press pursues the best-known seers. While many laymen may be annoyed by economists, other social scientists *hate* them—for their fame, Nobel Prizes, and ready access to political power."[2] Despite its critics, the economics profession thrives because its models usually do a better job of making economic sense out of a confusing world than do alternative approaches. In the land of the blind, the one-eyed person is king.

But not all economists are rich, nor is wealth the objective of the discipline. In a similar vein, not all doctors are healthy (some of them even smoke); not all carpenters live in perfectly built homes; not all marriage

---

[2] Leonard Silk, *Economics in Plain English* (New York: Simon and Schuster, 1978), 17 (emphasis in original).

counselors are happily married; and not all child psychologists have well-adjusted children.

CONCLUSION

This textbook describes how economic factors affect individual choices and how all these choices come together to shape the economic system. Economics is not the whole story, and economic factors are not always the most important. But economic factors have important and predictable effects on individual choices and these choices help shape the way we live. Economics is a challenging discipline, but it is also an exciting and rewarding one. The good news is that you already know a great deal about economics. But to use your knowledge of economics, you must cultivate the art and science of economic analysis. You must be able to simplify the real world to isolate the key variables and then tell a persuasive story about how these variables relate.

An economic relation can be stated in words, represented as a schedule of quantities, described by a mathematical equation, or illustrated as a graph. The appendix to this chapter provides an introduction to the use of graphs. Some of you may find the appendix unnecessary. If you are already familiar with relations among variables, slopes, tangents, and the like, you can probably just browse. Those of you with little recent experience with graphs, however, will benefit from a more careful reading. In the next chapter we will introduce some key ideas of economic analysis. Subsequent chapters will use these ideas to explore economic problems and to explain economic behavior that may otherwise appear puzzling. You must walk before you can run, however, and in the next chapter you will take those first wobbly steps.

Summary

1. Economics is the study of how people choose to use their scarce and limited resources to produce, exchange, and consume goods and services in an attempt to satisfy their unlimited wants. The economic problem arises from the conflict between scarce resources and unlimited wants. If wants were limited or if resources were not scarce, there would be less need to study economics.

2. Economic resources are combined in a variety of ways to produce goods and services. Major categories of resources include (1) land, representing all natural resources, (2) labor, (3) capital, and (4) entrepreneurial ability. Because economic resources are scarce, only a limited amount of goods and services can be produced with them; hence, choices must be made.

3. Microeconomics focuses on choices in households, in firms, and in governments. These choices are assumed to be guided by rational self-interest and are based on the marginal cost and the marginal benefit associated with each

action. Choice requires time and information, both of which are scarce and valuable. Whereas microeconomics examines the individual pieces of the puzzle, macroeconomics steps back to consider the big picture — the performance of the economy as a whole.

4. Economists use theories, or models, to help predict the effects that changes in economic factors will have on choices and, in turn, the effects these choices will have on particular markets and on the economy as a whole. Economists employ the scientific method to (1) identify the key variables, (2) state the assumptions under which the theory operates, (3) derive predictions about how, according to the theory, the variables relate, and (4) test the theory by comparing these predictions with the evidence. Some theories may not work perfectly, but they will continue to be used as long as they predict better than competing theories.

5. Positive economic analysis is aimed at discovering how the world works. Normative economic analysis is more concerned with how, in someone's opinion, the world should work. Economic analysis, if not pursued carefully, can result in inaccurate conclusions based on the fallacy that association is causation, the fallacy of composition, or ignorance of secondary effects.

Questions and Problems

1. (Definition of Economics) Recently some economists have conducted controlled experiments on animals. They claim that some animals act according to basic economic theory. That is, the animals act as though they are seeking to satisfy goals subject to the imposition of external constraints. If the researcher changes the constraints, the animals exhibit predictable behavioral changes. How does such constrained goal seeking conform to the definition of economics given in the text? Are animals different from humans when it comes to economic behavior?

2. (Resources) Determine which category of resources each of the following belongs in:
   a. A taxicab
   b. Computer software
   c. One hour of legal counsel
   d. A parking lot
   e. A forest
   f. The Mississippi River
   g. A prison

3. (Goods and Services) Explain why each of the following should *not* be considered a "free lunch" for the economy as a whole:
   a. Food stamps

   b. U.S. aid to developing countries
   c. Corporate charitable contributions
   d. Noncable television programs
   e. High school education

4. (Resources) California, New York, and Michigan have high per-capita incomes; some other states have low per-capita incomes. Can these differences be explained by scarcity of resources?

5. (Resources and Scarcity) "The only real resource that the human race has is the human mind." This line is often used to counter arguments that society is running out of its scarce resources. Is there truth in the statement? Are the resources of land, labor, and capital being depleted faster than they can be replaced?

6. (Micro Versus Macro) Some economists believe that in order to really understand macroeconomics, one must fully understand microeconomics. How does microeconomics relate to macroeconomics?

7. (Rational Self-Interest) Classical economists maintained that society would be optimally arranged if individual members of society

pursued their own self-interest. Is such a sweeping generalization possible? What about such problems as traffic jams, litter, and runs on banks? Doesn't self-interest need to be considered in the context of the aggregation of individual goals and their feasibility?

8. (Marginal Analysis) A small pizza store must decide whether to increase the radius of its delivery area by a mile. What considerations must be taken into account if such a decision is to contribute to profitability?

9. (The Value of Time) Economists often attempt to measure the value of time by using wage rates or average salary levels. According to these measures, the value of time in growing economies is always rising. How does the growing value of time affect the types of products and services being introduced into the economy? How might this increase in the value of time be related to the widespread use of microwave ovens, video cassette recorders, McDonald's, and automatic tellers at banks?

10. (Pitfalls of Economic Thinking) Using the discussion of pitfalls in economic thinking, identify the fallacy or mistake in thinking in each of the following statements:

a. Raising taxes will always increase government revenues.

b. Whenever there is a recession, imports tend to decrease. Thus, to stop a recession, we should increase imports.

c. Thriftiness is a sound virtue for the family and for the nation as a whole.

d. Capitalist economies do well in wartime because war promotes full employment and growing incomes. Hence, an economic boom can lead to conditions favorable to war.

e. Air bags in automobiles can reduce accidental death from collision. Therefore, air bags in cars make good economic sense.

f. Gold sells for about $400 per ounce. Therefore, the U.S. government could sell all of the gold in Fort Knox at $400 per ounce and eliminate the national debt.

11. (Role of Theory) What good is economic theory if it can't predict anybody's behavior?

12. (Rational Self-Interest) If behavior is governed by rational self-interest, why do people give to charitable institutions?

APPENDIX
Understanding Graphs

Take out a pencil and a blank piece of paper. Go ahead, do it. Put a point in the middle. That will be the point of departure, called the **origin**. With your pencil at the origin, draw a straight line off to the right; this line is called the **horizontal axis**. Returning to the origin, draw another line up, or north; this line is called the **vertical axis**. The value of the variable x measured along the horizontal axis increases as you move to the right of the origin. Similarly, the value of the variable y measured along the vertical axis increases as you move upward. The basic elements of a graph are presented in Exhibit 1. Within the space framed by the axes, we can plot combinations of the variables under consideration. For example, point a represents the combination where x equals 10 and y equals 5. Point b represents 5 units of x and 15 units of y.

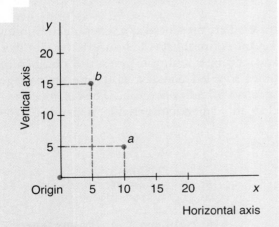

EXHIBIT 1   BASICS OF A GRAPH

Any point on a graph represents a combination of particular values of two variables. Here point a represents the combination of 10 units of variable x (measured on the horizontal axis) and 5 units of variable y (measured on the vertical axis). Point b represents 5 units of x and 15 units of y.

It has been said that a picture is worth a thousand words. **Graphs** are pictures showing how variables relate. Consider Exhibit 2, which shows the U.S. unemployment rate for each year since 1900. As you can see, the year is measured along the horizontal axis, and the unemployment rate along the vertical axis. Exhibit 2 is a **time-series graph** because it conveys how a variable, in this case the unemployment rate, changes over time. If you had to describe the information presented in Exhibit 2 in words, it would take pages. The picture shows not only how one year compares to the next but also how one decade compares to another and what the trend is over time. The eye can wander over the hills and valleys to observe patterns that would be hard to express in words. The dramatically higher unemployment rate during the Great Depression of the 1930s is unmistakable. The graph also reveals that the average unemployment rate has drifted upward since the 1940s. Thus, graphs convey information in a compact and efficient way.

This appendix shows how graphs are used to express a variety of relations among variables. Most of the graphs of interest in this book reflect the relation between two economic variables, such as the year and the unemployment rate, the price of a commodity and the quantity demanded, or the cost of production and the quantity produced. Because we focus on just two variables, we must abstract from other details in the economy.

We often observe that one thing appears to depend on another. The time it takes you to drive home depends on your average speed. Your weight depends on how much you eat. The amount of Pepsi purchased depends on its price. A **functional relation** exists between two variables when the value of one variable *depends* on the value of another variable. The value of the **dependent variable** is determined by the value of the **independent variable**. Your weight, the dependent variable, is determined by how much you eat, the independent variable. This is not to say that

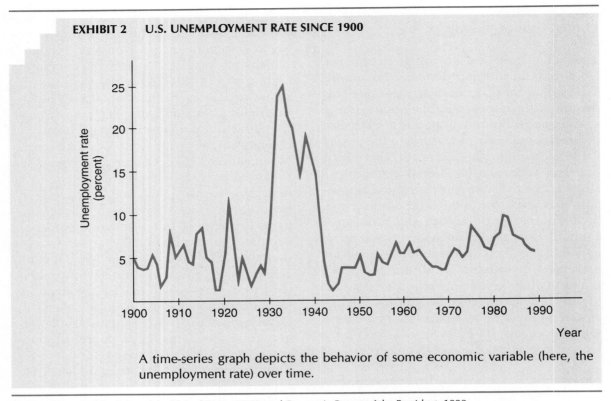

EXHIBIT 2   U.S. UNEMPLOYMENT RATE SINCE 1900

A time-series graph depicts the behavior of some economic variable (here, the unemployment rate) over time.

Sources: *Historical Statistics of the United States*, 1970, and *Economic Report of the President*, 1990.

other factors, such as exercise and age, do not affect your weight, but we typically focus on the relation between the two key variables, assuming other factors constant. The task of the economist is to isolate economic relations and determine the direction of causality. Recall that one of the pitfalls of economic thinking is the erroneous belief that association is causation. We cannot conclude that, simply because two events are related in time, one causes the other.

Drawing Graphs

Consider a very simple relation. Suppose you are planning a trip across the country and want to determine how far you will travel each day. You estimate that your average driving speed will be 50 miles per hour. Possible combinations of driving time and distance

traveled are presented as a schedule in Exhibit 3. One column lists the hours driven per day, and the next column gives the number of miles traveled per day, assuming an average speed of 50 miles per hour. The distance traveled, the dependent variable, depends on the

EXHIBIT 3
SCHEDULE RELATING DISTANCE TRAVELED TO HOURS DRIVEN

	Hours Driven per Day	Distance Traveled per Day
a	1	50
b	2	100
c	3	150
d	4	200
e	5	250

number of hours driven, the independent variable. We identify combinations of hours driven and distance traveled as *a*, *b*, *c*, and so on.

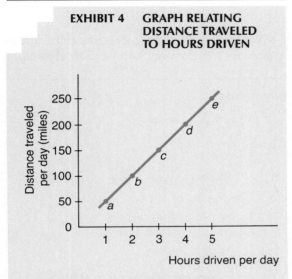

EXHIBIT 4   GRAPH RELATING DISTANCE TRAVELED TO HOURS DRIVEN

Points *a* through *e* depict different combinations of hours driven per day and the corresponding distances traveled. Connecting these points creates a graph.

We can plot the combinations from Exhibit 3 on a graph (Exhibit 4), with hours driven per day measured along the horizontal axis and total distance traveled along the vertical axis. Each combination of hours driven and distance traveled is represented by a point in Exhibit 4. For example, point *a* shows that when you drive for only 1 hour, you travel only 50 miles. Point *b* indicates that when you drive for 2 hours, you travel 100 miles. By connecting the points, we create a line running upward and to the right.

Three types of relations between variables can be expressed: (1) as one variable increases, the other increases as well, in which case there is a **positive**, or **direct**, **relation** between the variables; (2) as one variable increases, the other decreases, in which case there is a **nega-**tive, or **inverse**, **relation**; and (3) as one variable increases, the other remains the same, in which case the two variables are said to be *independent*, or *unrelated*. The relation between hours driven and distance traveled is positive, or direct.

In later chapters we will consider demand, a key economic concept. The *demand curve* shows the relation between the quantity of a product demanded and the price of that product. Exhibit 5 depicts the relation between the price of Pepsi and the quantity of Pepsi demanded per week. This demand curve is identified simply as *D*. As you can see, more Pepsi is demanded at lower prices than at higher prices: there is an inverse, or negative, relation between price and quantity demanded. Inverse relations are expressed by downward-sloping curves. One of the advantages of graphs is that they easily convey the relation between variables. We need not examine the particular combinations of numbers; we need only focus on the shape of the curve.

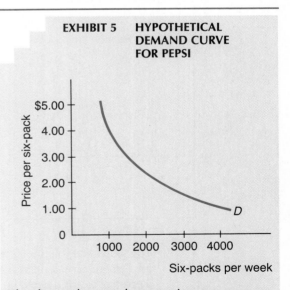

EXHIBIT 5   HYPOTHETICAL DEMAND CURVE FOR PEPSI

The demand curve shows an inverse, or negative, relation between price and quantity demanded. The curve slopes downward from left to right, indicating that the quantity demanded increases as the price falls.

Economists usually measure price, the independent variable, along the vertical axis, and quantity demanded, the dependent variable, along the horizontal axis. This arrangement appears odd to mathematicians, who usually put the independent variable on the horizontal axis and the dependent variable on the vertical axis. In another context, however, the cost of production might be the dependent variable and quantity produced the independent variable, so for consistency economists measure dollar amounts on the vertical axis and quantity on the horizontal axis.

The Slopes of Straight Lines

A more precise way to describe the shape of a curve is to measure its slope. The **slope** of a

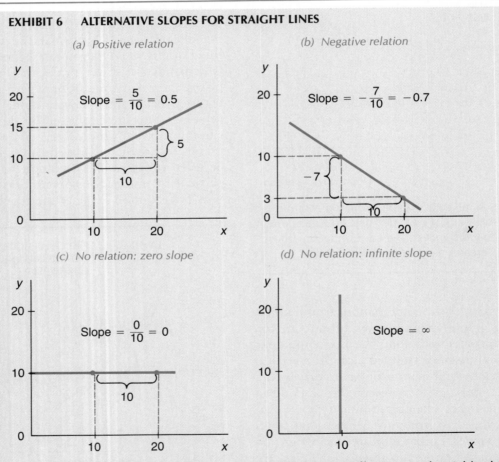

EXHIBIT 6   ALTERNATIVE SLOPES FOR STRAIGHT LINES

(a) Positive relation

Slope $= \dfrac{5}{10} = 0.5$

(b) Negative relation

Slope $= -\dfrac{7}{10} = -0.7$

(c) No relation: zero slope

Slope $= \dfrac{0}{10} = 0$

(d) No relation: infinite slope

Slope $= \infty$

The slope of a line indicates how much the vertically measured variable changes for a given increase in the variable measured on the horizontal axis. Panel (a) shows a positive relation between two variables; the slope is 0.5, a positive number. Panel (b) depicts a negative, or inverse, relation. When the x variable increases, the y variable decreases; the slope is −0.7, a negative number. Panels (c) and (d) represent situations in which two variables are unrelated. In panel (c), the y variable always takes on the same value; the slope is 0. In panel (d), the x variable always takes on the same value; the slope is infinite.

line indicates how much the vertical variable changes for a given increase in the horizontal variable. Specifically, the slope between two points along any straight line is the vertical change between those two points divided by the horizontal change, or

$$\text{Slope} = \frac{\textbf{Change in the vertical distance}}{\textbf{Change in the horizontal distance}}$$

For short, we refer to the slope as the *rise over the run*, where the *rise* is the vertical change and the *run* is the horizontal change.

The four panels in Exhibit 6 each indicate the vertical change given a 10-unit increase in the horizontal variable. In panel (a), the vertical distance increases by 5 units when the horizontal distance increases by 10 units. The slope of the line in panel (a) is therefore 5/10, or 0.5. Notice that the slope in this case is a positive number because the relation between the two variables is positive, or direct. This slope indicates that for every 1-unit increase in the horizontal variable, the vertical variable increases by 0.5 unit. The slope, incidentally, does not imply causality — the increase in the horizontal variable does not necessarily cause the increase in the vertical variable. The slope simply indicates in a uniform way how much the vertical variable changes with every 1-unit increase in the horizontal variable.

In panel (b), the vertical distance declines by 7 units when the horizontal distance increases by 10 units, so the slope equals − 7/10, or − 0.7. The slope in this case is a negative number because the two variables have a negative, or inverse, relation. In panel (c), the vertical variable remains unchanged as the horizontal variable increases by 10, so the slope equals 0/10, or 0. These two variables are unrelated. Finally, in panel (d), the vertical variable can take on any value, though the horizontal variable remains constant. In this case any change in the vertical measure is divided by 0, since the horizontal value remains fixed. Any number divided by 0 is

infinitely large, so we say that the slope of a vertical line is infinite. Again, the two variables are unrelated.

Slope Depends on How Units Are Measured

The mathematical value of the slope depends on the units of measurement on the graph. For example, suppose copper tubing costs $1 per foot to produce. Graphs depicting the relation between output and total cost are shown in Exhibit 7. In panel (a), total cost increases by $1 for each 1-foot increase in the amount of tubing produced. Thus, the slope in panel (a) equals 1/1, or 1. If the cost per foot remains the same but the unit of measurement is not *feet* but *yards*, the relation between output and total cost is as depicted in panel (b). Now total cost increases by $3 for each 1-yard increase in output, so the slope equals 3/1, or 3. Because of differences in the units used to measure copper tubing, the two panels reflect different slopes, even though the cost of tubing is $1 per foot in each panel. So keep in mind that the slope will depend in part on the way units are measured.

Marginal Analysis and the Slope

As noted earlier, economic analysis usually involves *marginal analysis*. Thus, economic analysis might relate to the marginal cost of producing one more unit of output. The slope is a convenient device for measuring marginal effects because it reflects the change in total cost along the vertical axis for each 1-unit change along the horizontal axis. For example, in panel (a) of Exhibit 7, the marginal cost of another *foot* of copper tubing is $1, which also equals the slope of the line. In panel (b), the marginal cost of another *yard* of tubing is $3, which, again, is the slope of that line. Because of its applicability to marginal analysis, the slope has significance in economics.

EXHIBIT 7   SLOPE DEPENDS ON THE UNIT OF MEASURE

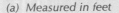

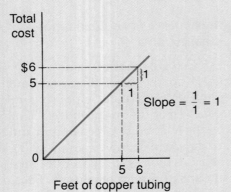

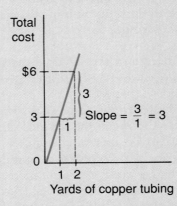

(a) Measured in feet   *(b) Measured in yards*

The value of the slope depends on the units of measure. In panel (a), output is measured in *feet* of copper tubing; in panel (b), output is measured in *yards*. Although the cost of production is $1 per foot in each panel, the slope is different in the two panels because copper tubing is measured using different units.

The Slopes of Curved Lines

The slope of a straight line is the same everywhere along the line, but the slope of a curved line usually varies at every point along the curve. Consider the curve in Exhibit 8. To find the slope of that curved line at a particular point, draw a straight line that just touches the curve at that point but does not cut or cross the curve. Such a line is called a **tangent** to the curve at that point. The slope of the tangent is the slope of the curve at that point. Consider the line *AA*, which is tangent to the curve at point *a*. As the horizontal value increases from 0 to 10 along *AA*, the vertical value drops from 40 to 0. Thus, the vertical change divided by the horizontal change equals − 40/10, or − 4.0, which is the slope of the curve at point *a*.

Alternatively, consider *BB*, a line drawn tangent to the curve at point *b*. The slope of *BB* is the change in the vertical divided by the change in the horizontal, or − 10/30, which equals − 0.33. This slope is negative because the curve slopes downward, reflecting a negative, or inverse, relation between the two variables (as one declines, the other increases). As you can see, the curve gets flatter as the hori-

EXHIBIT 8   SLOPES AT DIFFERENT POINTS ON A CURVED LINE

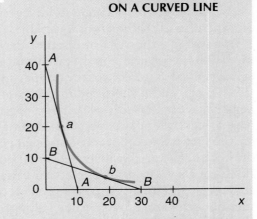

The slope of a curved line varies from point to point. At a given point, such as *a* or *b*, the slope of the curve is equal to the slope of the straight line that is tangent to the curve at that point.

zontal variable increases, so the value of the slope approaches 0.

Other curves, of course, will reflect different slopes as well as different changes in the slope along the curve. Downward-sloping curves have a negative slope, and upward-sloping curves, a positive slope. Sometimes curves are more complex, having both positive and negative ranges. For example, consider the hill-shaped curve in Exhibit 9. For relatively low values of x, there is a positive relation between x and y. As the value of x increases, however, its positive relation with y diminishes, eventually becoming negative. We can divide the curve into two segments: (1) the segment between the origin and point a, where the slope is positive, and (2) the segment of the curve to the right of point a, where the slope is negative. The slope of the curve at point a is 0. This type of curve could be used to show the relation between the temperature of a swimming pool and your enjoyment of a swim. The horizontal axis could represent the water temperature, and the vertical axis could represent some measure of your enjoyment. At very low temperatures, swimming is not much fun because the water is too cold. As the temperature increases, your enjoyment level increases. At some point, say at 85 degrees, your level of enjoyment reaches a maximum. Thus the value of x at point a equals 85 degrees. At still higher temperatures, the water becomes uncomfortably hot, so your level of enjoyment falls. The U-shaped curve represents the opposite relation: x and y are negatively related until point b is reached; thereafter they are positively related. The slope equals 0 at point b.

Curve Shifts

Now that you have some feel for curves, you should know that economic analysis often involves shifts in the curves under consideration. Exhibit 10 depicts a hypothetical demand curve, D, for Pepsi, first presented as Exhibit 5. The curve reflects the inverse rela-

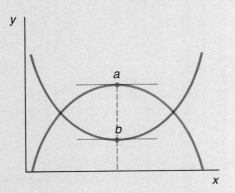

EXHIBIT 9   CURVES WITH BOTH POSITIVE AND NEGATIVE RANGES

Some curves have both positive and negative slopes. The red curve has a positive slope to the left of point a, a slope of 0 at point a, and a negative slope to the right of that point. The blue curve starts off with a negative slope, has a slope of 0 at point b, and has a positive slope to the right of that point.

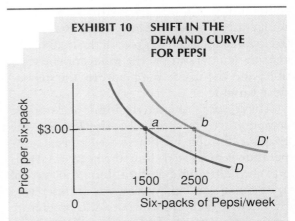

EXHIBIT 10   SHIFT IN THE DEMAND CURVE FOR PEPSI

The demand curve D shifts to the right to D' because higher consumer income increases the demand for Pepsi. After the shift in the demand curve, more Pepsi is demanded at each price. For example, at a price of $3 per six-pack, the quantity demanded per week increases from 1500 to 2500.

tion between the price of Pepsi and the quantity demanded. Suppose an increase in consumer income makes consumers demand more Pepsi at each price level. As a result, the demand for Pepsi shifts to the right from D to D'. After the shift in the demand curve, more Pepsi is demanded at each price. For example, the original demand curve indicates at point a that 1500 six-packs of Pepsi were demanded per week when the price was $3 per six-pack. After the increase in demand, the quantity demanded at that price is 2500 six-packs per week, as reflected by point b. Conversely, we could trace the effects of a decrease in consumer income on the demand for Pepsi. A decrease in income would shift the demand for Pepsi to the left, so less Pepsi would be demanded at each price level.

Of Mice and Fleas: The 45-Degree Line from the Origin

As we said earlier, economists tell stories to convey concepts. Picture a family of mice living in the belfry of a country church. Because the belfry is unheated and drafty, the temperature inside is always the same as the temperature outside. Thus, when it is 0 degrees outside, it is 0 degrees in the belfry. The outside temperature is the independent variable, and the inside temperature, the dependent variable.

The relation between the inside and outside temperatures is shown by the line on the graph in Exhibit 11, where the external temperature is measured along the horizontal axis and the belfry temperature along the vertical axis. Since the belfry temperature increases by 1 degree each time the outside temperature increases by 1 degree, the slope of the line is equal to 1. The line bisects, or cuts in half, the angle formed by the two axes so that every point on the line is an equal distance from both axes. We say that the line is a **ray** drawn from the origin, forming a 45-degree angle with the horizontal axis. (By the way, the degrees measuring an angle have nothing to

do with the temperature degrees in our example.) Many rays can be drawn from the origin, but only a 45-degree line exactly bisects the 90-degree angle formed by the two axes. Expressing this line as an equation, we have $B = E$, where B is the belfry temperature and E the external temperature.

Although the church belfry is unheated, the main hall of the church is heated in winter and cooled in summer. The parishioners might prefer to maintain the temperature of the hall at 72 degrees all year round, but keeping this drafty building at such a constant temperature would cost more than the parish can afford. Consequently, the temperature in the church hall varies, depending on the external temperature, as shown by the upward-sloping line in Exhibit 12(a). As you can see, even when it is 0 degrees outside, it is still 54 degrees in the church hall. As the outside temperature gets warmer, the inside tem-

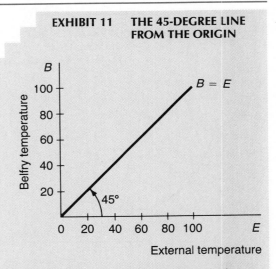

EXHIBIT 11   THE 45-DEGREE LINE FROM THE ORIGIN

The 45-degree line extending from the origin has a slope equal to 1. At each point along the line, the value of what is measured on the horizontal axis (here, the external temperature) is equal to the value of what is measured on the vertical axis (the internal temperature of the belfry).

perature increases too, but not by as much. Specifically, each 4–degree increase in the external temperature raises the inside temperature by 1 degree. Thus, the slope of this temperature function equals 1 divided by 4, or 0.25. This line can be expressed algebraically as $H = 54 + 0.25E$, where H represents the temperature in the church hall and E the external temperature. Notice again that when E is 0, H equals 54 degrees. This point, where the line cuts the vertical axis, is called the vertical **intercept**. When E equals 100, H equals 54 plus 25, or 79.

In Exhibit 12(b) we again present the temperature function for the church hall, but to add perspective we also include the 45-degree line indicating all points at which the external temperature equals the temperature in the church hall. Notice that the temperature function for the church hall intersects the 45-degree line at 72 degrees. Thus, at the point of intersection, the external temperature equals the temperature in the church hall. When the outside temperature is less than 72 degrees, the heat is on in the church hall. When the outside temperature is above 72 degrees, air conditioning keeps the hall from heating up as much as the outside temperature. When it is exactly 72 degrees outside, neither heating nor cooling is required.

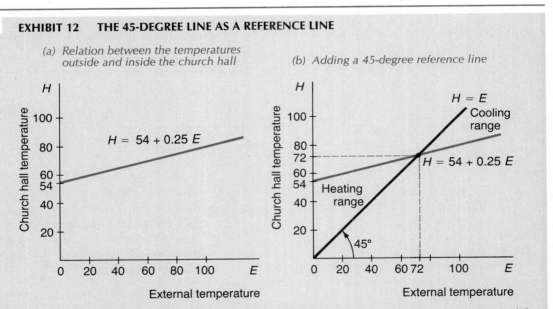

EXHIBIT 12   THE 45-DEGREE LINE AS A REFERENCE LINE

Panel (a) is a graph showing the relation between the external temperature and the church hall temperature. When the external temperature, E, is 0, the hall temperature is 54 degrees. For each 4-degree increase in external temperature, the hall temperature increases by 1 degree. The slope of the line is 0.25.

Panel (b) introduces a 45-degree line showing all points at which external temperature and hall temperature are equal. The two lines intersect at an external temperature of 72 degrees. At external temperatures below 72 degrees, the hall temperature exceeds the external temperature because the heating system is operating. At external temperatures above 72 degrees, the external temperature exceeds the hall temperature because the air conditioning is on.

To finish the story, why haven't the mice migrated south to the balmy church hall? Because of the cat—a restless cat that patrols the hall, ever vigilant to the stirrings of creatures, especially mice. Why is the cat so restless? Because of the fleas—fleas that live in the cat's thick fur. The fleas' environment is maintained by the cat's body heat at a constant 101.8 degrees, regardless of the temperature outside. The fleas never eat out. The relation between the temperature on the cat's back and the external temperature is a horizontal line drawn at 101.8 degrees, as shown in Exhibit 13. We can express the relation as simply $C = 101.8$, where C is the temperature in the cat's fur. Thus, the temperature in the snug little world of the fleas is independent of the outside temperature.

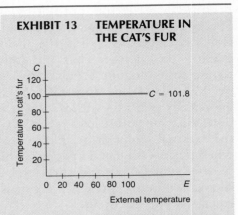

EXHIBIT 13   TEMPERATURE IN THE CAT'S FUR

The temperature in the cat's fur is independent of the external temperature. This is illustrated by a horizontal line with a height equal to 101.8 degrees, the temperature in the cat's fur. The line has a slope of 0, indicating that the value of the variable measured on the vertical axis is independent of the value of the variable measured on the horizontal axis.

Appendix Questions

1. (Use of Graphs) Graph the relationship $TC = 10 + 12Q$, where TC = total cost (in dollars) and Q = dozens of eggs.
   a. What is the intercept?
   b. What is the slope?
   c. How would the slope change if you graphed total cost against single eggs rather than dozens of eggs?
   d. What is the marginal cost of an egg?

2. (Use of Graphs) Suppose you have collected the following data on automobiles:

Observation	Mileage	Weight	Transmission
1	40 mpg	1500 lb	manual
2	30 mpg	2500 lb	manual
3	20 mpg	1500 lb	automatic
4	10 mpg	2500 lb	automatic

   a. An engineer looking at the second and third observations might conclude that mileage improves when auto weight increases. What

is wrong with this analysis?
   b. Draw a graph relating auto weight (on the horizontal axis) to mileage (on the vertical axis) for cars with manual transmissions.
   c. How would changing the transmission influence your graph?

3. (Use of Graphs) A demand curve shows a relation between the price of an item and the quantity demanded.
   a. Construct a demand curve based on the following data:

Quantity Demanded	Price	Income of Demander
0	$50	$100
10	$40	$150
15	$20	$100
20	$10	$100

   b. What is the intercept?
   c. What is the slope?

C H A P T E R   2

Some Tools of Economic Analysis

In the first chapter you learned that because of scarcity, choices must be made. These choices are guided by rational self-interest and require both time and information. But the first chapter said little about how to analyze economic choices. In this chapter we develop the framework with which to explore economic choices—choices about what goods and services are produced, how they are produced, and for whom they are produced. First we consider the costs involved in selecting one alternative over others. We then develop tools to explore the production choices available to the economy. In particular, we examine how resources are employed efficiently. Finally, we consider how different economies address the economic choices they confront. Topics discussed in this chapter include

- Opportunity cost
- Production possibilities frontier
- Specialization
- Comparative advantage

- Division of labor
- Three economic questions
- Economic systems

CHOICE AND OPPORTUNITY COST

In Chapter 1 we noted that human wants are unlimited but resources are scarce. Because resources are scarce, not all wants can be satisfied. Therefore, we must choose from among our many wants. But in choosing, we must forgo satisfying other wants.

Your Opportunity Cost

Suppose you spend $300 on a compact disc player. Let's say your best alternative to spending that money on a CD was spending it on a trip south during spring break. So in buying the CD, you had to forgo the vacation. Or consider an actual decision you just made: the decision to read this book now rather than use the time to sleep, study for another course, watch TV, or do something else. Suppose your best alternative to reading now is getting some sleep. The cost of spending your time reading economics, therefore, is passing up some sleep. Because of scarcity, you incur an opportunity cost whenever you make a choice. The **opportunity cost** of the chosen item or the chosen activity is the benefit expected from the *best alternative* that is forgone. You might think of opportunity cost as the *opportunity lost* when choices are made. Often, though not always, opportunity cost can be measured in monetary terms.

How many times have you heard people say they did something because they "had nothing better to do"? They actually mean they had few alternatives, so they were sacrificing very little to undertake the chosen activity. According to the concept of opportunity cost, people always do what they do because they have nothing better to do. The choice selected seems, at the time, preferable to all other possible choices. You are reading this book right now because you have nothing better to do. In fact, you are attending college for the same reason: college appears more attractive than your best alternative. Consider the opportunity cost of attending college in the following case study.

*The **opportunity cost** of a chosen item or chosen activity is the benefit expected from the best alternative forgone.*

CASE STUDY

The Opportunity Cost of College

In the movie classic *Animal House*, Bluto, after hearing the news that he just flunked out of college, wails, "Seven years of college down the drain!" What does it cost you per year to attend college full-time—that is, what is your opportunity cost? What was the best alternative you gave up by coming to college? It was probably a full-time job. Based on the experiences of others who took jobs right out of high school, you likely had some notion of what your prospects for employment were. Suppose you expected to land a job paying $15,000 a year. As a college student, you are still able to work in the summer and earn, say, $4,000. Thus, each year you are giving up net earnings of $11,000 ($15,000 − $4,000) to attend college.

There is also the direct cost of college itself. Suppose you pay $10,000 per year for tuition, fees, and books. This income is therefore unavailable to you (or your family) to spend on other things. Hence, the opportunity cost of paying for tuition, fees, and books is the forgone benefit you expected from the alternative goods and services that money could have purchased. The cost of room and board must be considered more carefully, because even if you had not gone to college, you would still have to live somewhere and eat something. In fact, whether or not you attended college, you would still face outlays for items such as entertainment, clothes, and laundry. Such expenses do not represent an opportunity cost of attending college. They are the upkeep costs that arise regardless of what you are doing. For simplicity, let's assume that these outlays are the same whether or not you attend college, so we can forget them. Thus, the net forgone earnings of $11,000 per year plus the $10,000 per year direct costs yield an opportunity cost of attending college of $21,000 per year.

The preceding analysis assumes that other things are constant. If, in your view, attending college is "more of a pain" than you expected the best alternative to be, the opportunity cost of attending college is even higher. That is, if you are one of those people who find college difficult, often boring, and in most ways more unpleasant than a full-time job right out of high school would have been, then the cost in money terms understates your full opportunity cost. Not only are you incurring the added expense of college, you are also forgoing a more pleasant quality of life. If, on the contrary, you think the wild and crazy life of a college student is more enjoyable on balance than a job, then $21,000 per year overstates your true opportunity cost because the best alternative involves a less satisfying quality of life.

Note that this analysis of opportunity cost focuses primarily on the forgone value of your best alternative; the analysis ignores the benefits you expect to derive from a college education. Thus, the focus is on the cost of your choice, not its benefit. Evidently, you view college as a good investment in your future even though it is costly and perhaps even painful. For you, the net benefits expected from college exceed those expected from the best alternative, and that is why you as a rational decision maker chose the college option.

Opportunity Cost Is Subjective

Opportunity cost is a subjective notion. Only the individual chooser can estimate the expected value of the best alternative. In fact, we seldom know the actual value of the forgone alternative, because by definition that opportunity lost is "the road not taken"—the alternative passed up in favor of the preferred option. Thus, if you gave up an evening of pizza and conversation with friends to work on an English paper, you will never know the exact value of what you gave up. You know only what you *expected*. Evidently, you considered the marginal benefit of working on your paper to be greater than your best alternative. Incidentally, focusing on the *best* alternative forgone makes all other alternatives irrelevant.

Calculating Opportunity Cost Requires Time and Information People, in employing their scarce resources, rationally choose the use that promises the highest expected net benefit. This does not mean that people exhaustively calculate costs and benefits for all possible alternatives. Since acquiring information about alternatives is often costly and time-consuming, people usually make choices based on limited or even wrong information about their opportunity costs. Indeed, some choices may turn out to be poor ones (for example, you went on a picnic and it rained; the movie you selected was a bore). At the time you made the choice, however, you thought you were making the best use of all your scarce resources, including the time required to gather information about your alternatives. Consider the opportunity cost of time in the next case study.

CASE STUDY

Opportunity Cost in a Land of Plenty

If uninvited guests arrive for dinner, the Sultan of Brunei should be able to find an extra place at the table—his home seats forty-three hundred for dinner. If some guests need to spend the night, the sultan should be able to put them up—the place has 1788 rooms. For a friendly polo match the sultan has two hundred ponies from which to choose, and for a drive in the country he can select from among his forty cars—perhaps the Aston-Martin or the Maserati will do.

Several thousand members of his personal staff attend to the sultan's every need. Brunei, you see, is a small, oil-rich country in the South China Sea, and the sultan's home is, in fact, a palace built at a cost of half a billion dollars and said to be the most lavish in the world. The billions of dollars in oil revenues that flow into this tiny country each year provide the sultan with a grand standard of living. Surrounded by such opulence, the sultan would appear to have resolved the economic problem caused by scarce resources but unlimited wants.

Even if the sultan can buy whatever he wants, however, he has limited *time* in which to enjoy these goods and services. If he pursues one activity, he cannot at the same time do anything else. Each activity he undertakes has an opportunity cost. If the sultan chooses to play polo over his best alternative, a drive through the country in his Maserati, the opportunity cost of playing polo is the forgone benefit expected from a drive through the country. Consequently, the sultan must make choices among the competing uses of his scarcest resource, time.

Opportunity Cost May Vary with Circumstance Since opportunity cost depends on the alternatives, the opportunity cost of consuming a particular good or undertaking a certain activity will vary with circumstance. This is why you are less likely to study on a Saturday night than on a Wednesday night. On a Saturday night the opportunity cost of studying is greater because you have more alternative activities, and usually the expected benefit of at least one of these alternatives exceeds the expected benefit from studying. Suppose you decide on a movie for Saturday night. The opportunity cost of the movie may not be forgoing your studies, because the best alternative might be attending a basketball game. For some of you, studying on Saturday night may be well down the list of alternatives—perhaps ahead of reorganizing your closet but behind watching trucks being unloaded at the supermarket.

Although opportunity cost is a subjective notion, in some circumstances money paid for goods and services becomes a reasonably good approximation of the opportunity cost of their consumption. But the monetary cost definition may leave out some important elements, particularly the time involved. In addition to the ticket price, a trip to the movies costs travel time, gas, and the two hours it takes to watch the show.

Sunk Costs and Choice

Suppose you have just finished shopping for groceries and are wheeling your basket up to the check-out counters. How do you decide which line to join? You pick the line you think will require the least time. Suppose that after waiting in line for 10 minutes, you realize that another line has moved more quickly and is now much shorter than yours. Do you switch lines? Or do you think, "I've already spent 10 minutes in this line, so I'm going to stay in this line." The 10 minutes spent in the original line represents a **sunk cost**, which is a cost that cannot be recovered regardless of what you do. Such costs should be ignored in making economic choices. Economic decision makers should weigh only those costs that are affected by the choice. Sunk costs are not affected by your choice and are therefore irrelevant.

*A **sunk cost** is a cost that cannot be recovered and is therefore irrelevant in making economic choices.*

Opportunity cost underscores what you must give up each time choices are made under conditions of scarcity. Just as resources are scarce for the individual, they are scarce for the economy as a whole. In the next section we develop a tool to explore opportunity cost for the economy.

THE ECONOMY'S PRODUCTION POSSIBILITIES

An economy has millions of different resources, which can be combined in all kinds of ways to produce millions of possible goods and services. In this section we consider a model for examining the economy's production possibilities. Here are the model's assumptions. To reduce the analysis to manageable proportions, we limit the output of the hypothetical economy to just two products—in our example they are food and education. The focus is on a particular time period—in this case, a year. We assume that the amount of resources available in the economy is fixed during the time period—there is only so much labor, so much land, so much capital, and so much entrepreneurial ability. These resources can be combined in a variety of ways to produce food and education. We also assume that society's knowledge about how these resources can be combined to produce output—that is, society's available technology—remains fixed during the year.

*The **production possibilities frontier**, or **PPF**, is a curve showing all combinations of goods that can be produced when available resources are used fully and efficiently.*

Efficiency and the Production Possibilities Frontier

Given the resources and the technology available in the economy, the **production possibilities frontier**, or **PPF**, reveals the various possible

combinations of the two goods that can be produced when the resources are
being used fully and efficiently. Resources are used with **efficiency** when no
change in the way the resources are combined could increase the production
of one good without decreasing the production of the other good. *Efficiency
involves getting the maximum possible output from available resources.*

The economy's PPF for food and education is shown by the curve *FE* in
Exhibit 1, where *F* represents the amount of food produced per year if *all* the
economy's resources are used efficiently to produce food and *E* represents
the amount of education produced per year if all the economy's resources are
used efficiently to produce education. Points along the curve between *F* and
E represent the possible combinations of food and education that can be
produced when all the economy's resources are used efficiently to produce
both goods. Points inside the PPF, such as *J*, represent combinations of food
and education that do not employ resources fully or employ them ineffi-
ciently; points outside the PPF, such as *K*, represent unattainable combina-

EXHIBIT 1   THE ECONOMY'S PRODUCTION POSSIBILITIES FRONTIER

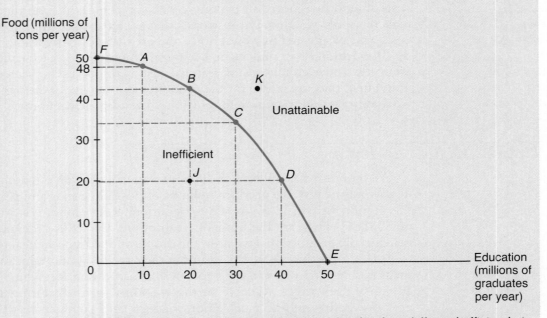

If the economy uses its available resources and technology fully and efficiently in
producing food and education, it will be on its production possibilities frontier,
curve *FE*. The PPF is bowed out to illustrate the law of increasing opportunity cost:
additional units of education require the economy to sacrifice more and more units
of food. Note that more food must be given up in moving from *D* to *E* than in
moving from *F* to *A*, though in each case the gain in education is 10 million
graduates. Points inside the PPF, such as *J*, represent inefficient use of resources.
Points outside the PPF, such as *K*, represent unattainable combinations.

tions of food and education given the resources and the technology available.

Notice that if you start from any point inside the PPF, such as *J*, it is always possible to increase the production of one good without reducing the production of the other good. For example, from point *J* it is possible, by combining resources more efficiently or by employing previously idle resources, to move to point *B* and produce more food without reducing the amount of education. Thus, the economy can increase the production of food by 22 million tons without reducing the amount of education produced. Alternatively, it is possible, by using resources more efficiently or by employing previously idle resources, to move from point *J* to point *D* and thereby increase the amount of education produced without reducing the production of food. Indeed, as you can see, it is possible to move from point *J* to any point between *B* and *D* along the PPF, such as point *C*, and thereby increase the production of both food and education.

The Shape of the Production Possibilities Frontier

Any movement along the PPF involves giving up some units of one good to get units of the other. Movements down the curve indicate that the opportunity cost of more education is less food. *The PPF in Exhibit 1 is curved out like a bow because the resources in the economy are not all perfectly adaptable to the production of both food and education.*

Although all resources are used efficiently at point *F*, certain resources contribute little to the production of food, as some economics professors make terrible farmers and school buildings are not easily adapted to the production of food. Moving from point *F* to point *A* increases the number of graduates per year from none to 10 million and reduces food production by only 2 million tons, from 50 million to 48 million tons. Increasing the number of graduates per year to 10 million causes food production to fall very little because it draws upon those resources, such as classrooms and teachers, that add very little to food output but are quite productive in education.

The opportunity cost of more education is the forgone food. As shown by the dashed lines in Exhibit 1, each additional 10 million graduates reduces food production by more and more. Larger and larger amounts of food must be sacrificed because, as more education is produced, the resources drawn away from food are those that are more important in food production. In other words, the opportunity cost of education increases as more education is produced.

The **law of increasing opportunity cost** *states that as more of a particular good is produced, the opportunity cost of its production rises.*

This relation reflects the law of increasing opportunity cost. If the economy's resources are already used fully and efficiently, the **law of increasing opportunity cost** states that as more of a particular commodity is produced, larger and larger quantities of the alternative good must be sacrificed. The PPF derives its bowed shape from the law of increasing opportunity cost. For example, whereas the first 10 million college graduates have an opportunity cost of only 2 million tons of food, the final 10 million—that is, those produced between point D and point E—have an opportunity cost of 20 million tons of food. Notice that the *slope* of the PPF indicates the opportunity cost of an additional unit of education. As you move down the curve, the slope gets steeper, reflecting the higher opportunity cost of education in terms of food.

The law of increasing opportunity cost also applies in moving from the production of education to the production of food. When all resources in society are concentrated on education, as at point E, certain resources, such as tractors and cows, make little contribution. (In fact, the cows foul the sidewalks and block the hallways if they are allowed to hang around the schools.) Thus, in shifting resources into the production of food, little education must be surrendered initially. As more food is produced, however, resources that are of greater value in the production of education must be used, invoking the law of increasing opportunity cost. *If resources were perfectly adaptable to alternative uses, the PPF would be a straight line, reflecting a constant opportunity cost as we moved along the PPF.*

Shifts in the Production Possibilities Frontier

When we construct the production possibilities frontier, we assume that the quantity of resources available in the economy and the level of technology are constant. Over time, however, the PPF may shift as a result of a change in resource availability or a technological breakthrough.

Changes in Resource Availability For example, if individuals in the economy decided to work longer hours, this decision would shift the PPF out so that more of both goods could be produced, as depicted in Exhibit 2(a). An increase in the size of the labor force, an increase in the skills of the labor force, or an increase in the availability of other resources would also shift the PPF outward. In contrast, a decrease in the availability or the quality of resources would shift the PPF inward, as depicted in panel (b). The shifts in panels (a) and (b) appear to be parallel, indicating that the resource whose availability is altered is perfectly adaptable to the production of both goods. If that resource is better suited to the production of one good—say, education—then the shift on the education axis will be greater than the shift on the food axis, so the shift in the PPF will be skewed.

Increases in the Capital Stock An economy's production possibilities frontier depends on its stock of human and physical capital. The more capital an economy produces in one period, the more output that capital can produce in the next period. Thus, increased production of capital this period will increase the economy's PPF next period. To produce more capital this period, an economy must reduce current consumption. In fact, the choice is typically between producing goods for current consumption and producing

EXHIBIT 2   SHIFTS IN THE ECONOMY'S PRODUCTION POSSIBILITIES FRONTIER

(a) *Increase in available resources*   (b) *Decrease in available resources*

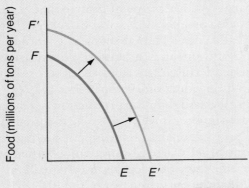

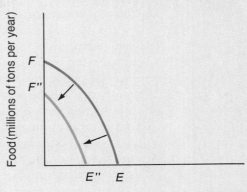

(c) *Technological advance in food production*

(d) *Technological advance in education production*

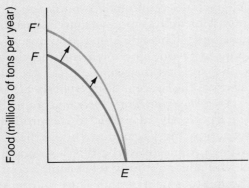

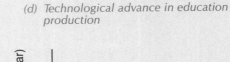

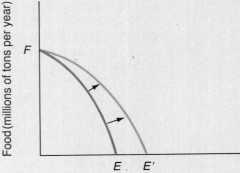

When the resources available to an economy change, the PPF shifts. If more resources become available, the PPF shifts outward, as in panel (a), indicating that more output can be produced. A decrease in available resources causes the PPF to shift inward, as in panel (b). Technological changes also shift the PPF. Panel (c) shows the effect of a technological improvement in food production. More food can now be produced for any given level of education. Panel (d) shows the effect of a technological advance in the production of education.

goods for future production and consumption. In Exhibit 2(a), the more education produced this period, the greater the economy's stock of human capital next period, so the farther out the PPF will shift.

Effects of Technological Change Another type of change that could cause the economy's PPF to shift out is some technological discovery that combines available resources more efficiently. The effect of a technological break-through in the production of food, such as a more bug-resistant strain of some crop, is demonstrated in Exhibit 2(c). As you can see, such a development primarily increases the production of food. Exhibit 2(d) shows the result of a technological breakthrough in the production of education, such as the development of a computer program for self-instruction. Some discoveries could enhance production of both products, such as a managerial innovation designed to control the use of resources more efficiently. Break-throughs that improve the efficiency of resources used equally in producing both products are reflected by the outward shift of the PPF in Exhibit 2(a).

What We Can Learn from the PPF

The production possibilities frontier demonstrates several concepts introduced thus far. The first is *scarcity*: the economy can produce only so much. The second is *efficiency*: the PPF describes the efficient combinations of output that are possible, given the economy's resources and technology. Some combinations are impossible unless more resources become available or better technology is developed. The PPF slopes downward, indicating that the more that is produced of one good when using the economy's resources fully and efficiently, the less that can be produced of the other good. This tradeoff demonstrates the concept of *opportunity cost*. The bowed-out shape of the PPF reflects the *law of increasing opportunity cost*, which arises because not all resources are perfectly adaptable to the production of all goods. Individuals in the economy must somehow choose the combination of goods along the PPF to be produced, so the PPF also underscores the need for *choice*. The choice will affect not only what can be consumed this period but the size of the capital stock next period. The resulting shifts in the PPF reflect *economic growth*. The way individuals select the combination will depend on the decision-making rules operating in the economy. Later in this chapter we will consider some alternative decision-making rules that have evolved in different economic systems, but first you must learn more about production and efficiency.

SPECIALIZATION, COMPARATIVE ADVANTAGE, AND EXCHANGE

Suppose you live in the dormitory, where your meals and chores are taken care of. You and your roommate have such busy social and academic schedules that you each can spare only about an hour per week for such mundane tasks as typing and ironing. Each of you must turn in a three-page typewritten paper every week, and you each prefer to have your shirts ironed if you have the time. Let's say you take 10 minutes to type one page, or half an hour to type a three-page paper. Your roommate is from the hunt-and-peck school and takes about 20 minutes per page, or an hour for the three pages. But your roommate is talented at ironing and can iron a shirt in 5 minutes flat (or should that be iron it flat in 5 minutes?). You need about twice as long, or 10 minutes, to iron a shirt.

The typing takes priority during the hour available for typing and ironing. If you and your roommate each do your own typing and ironing every week, it takes you half an hour to type the paper; in the remaining half hour you iron three shirts. Your roommate needs the entire hour to type the paper and so has no time left for ironing. Thus, with each of you performing your own tasks, the combined output is two papers and three shirts.

The Law of Comparative Advantage

Before long, you realize that combined output would increase if you did all the typing and your roommate did all the ironing. In the hour available for these tasks, you type both papers and your roommate irons twelve shirts. Total output has increased by nine shirts as a result of specialization. A deal is struck to exchange your typing for your roommate's ironing, so that each of you ends up with a typed paper and six ironed shirts. Thus, each of you is better off as a result of specialization.

By specializing in the tasks that you each do best, you and your roommate are applying the **law of comparative advantage**, which states that the individual with the lowest opportunity cost for producing a particular output should specialize in producing that output. In this example it is clear that you are the better typist and your roommate the better ironer, and we need no economic law to figure out that there are gains from specialization. In a more complicated situation the law of comparative advantage is not quite so obvious, yet there are still gains from specialization, as we shall now see.

*The **law of comparative advantage** states that the individual with the lowest opportunity cost of producing a particular good should specialize in producing that good.*

Absolute and Comparative Advantage

The gains from specialization and exchange in the example above are intuitively obvious. A more interesting case arises if we change the example so that you are not only a faster typist than your roommate but also a faster ironer. Suppose your roommate needs 12 minutes to iron a shirt, compared to your 10 minutes. You now have an absolute advantage in performing both tasks because you can do each task in less time than can your roommate. More generally, having an **absolute advantage** means having the ability to produce the output with fewer resources than other producers use.

***Absolute advantage** is the ability to produce something with fewer resources than other producers use.*

Does your absolute advantage in both activities mean specialization is no longer a good idea? Recall that the law of comparative advantage states that the individual with the lower opportunity cost of producing a particular good should specialize in producing that good. You still need 10 minutes to type a page and 10 minutes to iron a shirt, so in the time it takes you to type one page you could iron one shirt. Therefore, your opportunity cost per page of typing is not ironing one shirt. Your roommate takes 20 minutes to type a page and 12 minutes to iron a shirt, so your roommate could iron 1 ⅔ shirts in the time taken to type one page. Therefore, your roommate's opportunity cost per page of typing is not ironing 1 ⅔ shirts. Because your opportunity cost of typing is lower than your roommate's, you have a comparative advantage in typing; your roommate has a comparative advantage in ironing. Thus, you should do all the typing, and your roommate, all the ironing.

Comparative advantage is the ability to produce something at a lower opportunity cost than other producers face.

Although you have an absolute advantage in both tasks, your **comparative advantage** calls for specializing in the task for which you have the lower opportunity cost—in this case, typing. If you did not specialize, you could type one paper and iron three shirts in an hour; your roommate could still just type one paper. So the combined output would remain at two papers and three shirts. But if you each specialized according to the law of comparative advantage, you could type the two papers in an hour and your roommate could iron five shirts. Thus, specialization increases total output by two ironed shirts. Exhibit 3 summarizes the example. Even though you are better at both tasks than your roommate, you are comparatively better at typing. Put another way, your roommate, although worse at both tasks, is not quite as poor at ironing as at typing.

Don't think this is simply common sense. Common sense would lead you to do your own ironing and typing, since you are more skilled at both tasks than your roommate. Spend a little time reviewing Exhibit 3. Try approaching the problem in terms of the opportunity cost of ironing, working it through until you are satisfied that the outcome is the same—that is, that specialization increases output.

The law of comparative advantage applies not only to individuals but to firms, to regions of a country, and to countries. Those individuals, firms, regions, or countries with the lowest opportunity cost of producing a particular good should specialize in producing that good. Because of such factors as climate, availability of natural resources or capital, and the education level of the work force, certain parts of the country or certain parts of the world have a comparative advantage in producing particular goods. Regardless of what is being produced—from Apple computers in California's "Silicon Valley" to oranges in Florida, from VCRs in Korea to bananas in Honduras—*resources are allocated most efficiently across the country and around the world when production and trade conform to the law of comparative advantage.* You might imagine a production possibilities frontier for the entire world economy. We would be on that frontier only when production around the globe conformed to the law of comparative advantage.

Specialization and Exchange

Barter is the exchange of one good for another without the use of money.

In the previous example you specialized in typing and your roommate specialized in ironing, and you exchanged your products. No money changed hands. In other words, you engaged in barter. **Barter** is a system of

EXHIBIT 3
COMPARATIVE ADVANTAGE: MAXIMIZING OUTPUT

CASE 1: You are a faster typist and your roommate is a faster ironer.

Output per Hour

	Each Does Own		Each Specializes	
	Typed Pages	**Ironed Shirts**	**Typed Pages**	**Ironed Shirts**
You	3	3	6	0
Roommate	3	0	0	12
Total	6	3	6	12

CASE 2: You are a faster typist and a faster ironer,
but you are a comparatively faster typist.

Output Per Hour

	Each Does Own		Each Specializes	
	Type	**Iron**	**Type**	**Iron**
You	3	3	6	0
Roommate	3	0	0	5
Total	6	3	6	5

Cases 1 and 2 both show gains from specialization and exchange for you and your roommate. In both cases it takes you half an hour to type the paper and 10 minutes to iron one shirt. In both cases your roommate takes 1 hour to type the paper. But, whereas in Case 1 it takes your roommate only 5 minutes to iron a shirt, in Case 2 it takes 12 minutes to iron a shirt. In Case 1 you have an absolute advantage and a comparative advantage in typing, so total output is greater if you do all the typing and your roommate does all the ironing. In Case 2 you have an absolute advantage in both typing and ironing. But you have a comparative advantage only in typing because you have a lower opportunity cost of typing than does your roommate. So in Case 2 output is maximized if you do all the typing and your roommate does all the ironing.

exchange in which products are traded directly for other products. Barter works satisfactorily in very simple economies where there is little specialization and few different goods to trade, but for economies with greater specialization, money plays an important role in facilitating exchange. Money serves as a *medium of exchange* because it is the one thing that everyone is willing to accept in return for all goods and services.

Because of specialization and comparative advantage, most people consume little of what they produce and produce little of what they consume. People specialize in particular activities and exchange their products for money, which, in turn, is exchanged for goods produced by others. Thus, people sell their specialized products in one market and buy the products of others in another market. Did you make a single article of clothing you are now wearing? Probably not. Consider the degree of specialization that went into your cotton shirt or blouse. Some farmer in a warm climate grew the cotton and sold it to someone who spun it into thread, who sold it to someone who wove it into fabric, who sold it to someone who made the shirt, who sold it to a wholesaler, who sold it to a retailer, who sold it to you. Your shirt or blouse was produced by many specialists.

Division of Labor and Gains from Specialization

Think about your last trip to McDonald's: "Let's see, I'll have a Big Mac, an order of fries, and a chocolate shake." About 30 seconds later your order was ready. In contrast, consider how long it would take you to prepare the same meal yourself. It would take at least 15 minutes to make a homemade version of the Big Mac with all its special ingredients. Peeling, slicing, and frying the potatoes would take another 15 minutes. With the ice cream on hand, you should be able to make the shake in 5 minutes. If you add in the time it takes to buy the ingredients and to clean up afterward, meal preparations would take you at least an hour.

*The **division of labor** is the organization of production into tasks in which people specialize.*

Why is the McDonald's meal faster, cheaper, and (for some people) better than one you could make yourself? Why is fast food so fast? The manager of McDonald's is taking advantage of the gains resulting from the **division of labor**. Rather than have each worker prepare an entire individual meal, McDonald's separates the meal preparation process into various tasks and assigns individuals to specialize in these separate tasks. This division of labor allows the group to produce much more than it could if each person tried to do it all. Instead of making twenty complete meals in an hour by each doing it all, the twenty employees specialize and produce more than two hundred meals per hour.

__Specialization__ occurs when individuals confine their work to a particular product or to a single task.

How is this tenfold increase in productivity possible? First, the manager can assign tasks according to individual preferences and abilities. The employee with the toothy smile and pleasant personality can handle the customers up front; the employee with the strong back but few social graces can handle the 50-pound sacks of potatoes out back. Second, as each individual performs the same task again and again, he or she gets better at it. Experience is a good teacher. The employee operating the cash register, for example, becomes better at handling the special problems that arise in dealing with customers. Third, there is no time lost in moving from one task to another. Finally, and perhaps most importantly, the **specialization** of labor allows for the introduction of more sophisticated production techniques, which would not make economic sense on a smaller scale. For example, McDonald's does not prepare each milkshake separately but mixes ingredients in a machine that shakes gallons at a time. Such machines would be impractical in the home. The specialization of labor allows for the introduction of specialized machines, and these machines make each worker more productive.

When workers fail to specialize according to the law of comparative advantage, output is not being produced efficiently. Only when labor and other resources are employed according to the law of comparative advantage is the economy operating on its production possibilities frontier.

The specialization of labor takes advantage of individual preferences and natural abilities, allows workers to develop more experience at a particular task, reduces the time required to shift between different tasks, and permits the introduction of labor-saving machinery. Specialization and the division of labor occur not only among individuals, but also within firms, states, and indeed entire countries. For example, clothing production often involves growing cotton in one country, turning the cotton into cloth in another, making the clothing in a third country, and marketing that clothing in a fourth country. When countries around the globe specialize according to the law of comparative advantage, the world economy is operating on its production possibilities frontier.

In closing, we should note that specialization can create problems, since doing the same thing eight hours a day often becomes tedious. Consider, for example, the assembly line worker whose task is to tighten a particular bolt on each product. Such a job could drive that worker crazy. Thus, the gains from breaking production down into individual tasks must be weighed against the problems caused by assigning workers to repetitive and tedious jobs.

THREE ECONOMIC QUESTIONS: WHAT, HOW, AND FOR WHOM

The focus to this point has been on how individuals choose to use their scarce resources to satisfy their unlimited wants—more specifically, how they specialize based on comparative advantage. This emphasis on the individual has been appropriate because the world of economics is driven by the choices of individual decision makers, whether they are consumers, producers, or public officials. These individual choices tie into the entire economy and allow all economies, regardless of their structure, to answer the three fundamental questions that each must resolve.

What Will Be Produced?

As you observe the economy around you, you take for granted the incredible number of choices that go into deciding what gets produced. For example, of the thousands of potential rock stars, which ones will make albums, and how many albums will be produced? Which fruits will be grown? Which new kitchen appliances will be introduced? Which new roads will be built? An economic system must resolve millions of such questions to determine what gets produced. Although different economies resolve these questions using different decision-making rules and mechanisms, all economies must make these decisions in the face of scarce resources.

Adam Smith
(1723–1790)

Britain in the eighteenth century was at the forefront of industrialization, but by modern standards it was still very much a developing country. It is not surprising, then, that economic thought of the time was concerned centrally with economic growth. What constitutes national wealth? Where does it come from? What can we do to get more of it? In 1776 a bookish professor of moral philosophy from Scotland answered these questions in a way that was to have a lasting effect on the way we think about economics.

Adam Smith was born in the village of Kirkcaldy, near Edinburgh. After studying at Oxford University—largely without the assistance of professors—he returned to Scotland to begin a teaching career. In person Smith was awkward and absentminded, a kind of eighteenth-century nerd. But no one doubted his brilliance, and he quickly rose to prominence within the important intellectual movement now known as the Scottish Enlightenment. After publishing a well-received book on moral philosophy in 1759, Smith turned his attention to political economy. The result was a rich and scholarly treatise called *The Wealth of Nations*.

National wealth, said Smith, is not gained by amassing money at the expense of other countries. True wealth lies in the country's productive capacity, especially in the skill and ability of its workers. To increase wealth, a country must increase productive capacity, or efficiency. And, for Smith, the most potent source of increased efficiency was specialization, what he called the division of labor. The subdivision of tasks saves time, increases the level of skill, and leads to innovation. The result is "that universal opulence which extends itself to the lowest ranks of the people"—new and cheaper products and a higher standard of living for all.

How can a country secure this kind of productivity growth? Smith's answer was truly a radical one. Rather than attempting to control resources and guide investment, a country should instead rely on a set of institutions Smith called "the system of natural liberty"—what is now sometimes called *laissez faire*. By this he meant a system of rights and laws that would harness individual self-interest and allow people to take the best advantage of their localized skills and knowledge. Smith's famous metaphor leaves a vivid image: the decentralized market system allocates resources as if by an invisible hand.

Richard Langlois

How Will Goods Be Produced?

The economic system — or, more specifically, individual decision makers in the economic system — must determine how output is to be produced. Which resources should be used, and how should they be combined to produce each product? How much labor should be used and at what skill level? What kinds of machines should be used? How much fertilizer should be used to grow the best sweet peas? Should the factory be built in the city or closer to the interstate highway? Again, billions of individual decisions must be made to determine which resources are to be employed and how these resources are to be combined.

For Whom Will Goods Be Produced?

Finally, the economic system must decide how to divide the fruits of production among the population. Who will actually consume the goods and services produced? Should equal amounts of the good be provided to everyone in the economy? Should the weak and the sick receive more? Should goods be allocated according to height? Weight? The value of resources supplied? Political connections? The question "For whom will goods be produced?" is often referred to as the distribution question. Consider your own situation. What determines your share of the goods and services produced? Money from your parents, earnings from summer and part-time jobs, and possibly loans and student aid are the primary determinants. In short, your income from various sources determines how much you are able to purchase. In our economic system, your income depends on who your parents are, your labor skills, how hard you work, your ownership of other resources, and the relative scarcity of your resources.

Although the three questions have been discussed separately, they are closely interwoven. The answer to one depends very much on the answers to the others. For example, the answer to what is to be produced will depend on who will receive the good. An economy that distributes goods and services in uniform amounts to all will, no doubt, answer the what-is-to-be-produced question differently from an economy that somehow allows each individual to choose a unique bundle of goods and services.

ALTERNATIVE WAYS OF ANSWERING THE THREE ECONOMIC QUESTIONS

Each economy resolves the three questions — what, how, and for whom — differently. The laws about resource ownership and the extent to which the government attempts to coordinate economic activity determine the "rules of the game" — the set of conditions that shape individual incentives and constraints. Along a spectrum ranging from the most free to the most regimented type of economic system, pure capitalism would be at one end and the command economy would be at the opposite end.

Pure Capitalism

Pure capitalism is an economic system characterized by private ownership of resources and the use of prices to coordinate economic activity in free, competitive markets.

Under **pure capitalism**, the rules of the game include the private ownership of resources and the coordination of economic activity by the price signals generated in free, competitive markets. Any income derived from the use of land, labor, capital, or entrepreneurial ability goes to the individual owners of those resources. Owners have *property rights* to the use of their resources and are therefore free to sell their resources to the highest bidder. Producers are free to make and sell whatever output they think will be profitable. Consumers are free to buy whatever goods they can afford. All this voluntary buying and selling is coordinated by competitive markets, where buyers and sellers make their wishes known. Market prices guide resources to their highest-valued use.

Under pure capitalism, markets direct the what, how, and for whom of production. Markets transmit information about relative scarcity, provide individual incentives, and distribute income among resource suppliers. No single individual or small group coordinates these activities. Rather, it is the voluntary choices of many buyers and sellers responding only to their individual incentives and constraints that direct resources and products to the highest bidder. According to Adam Smith, one of the first to explain the allocative role of markets, the market forces coordinate as if by an "invisible hand": an unseen force that harnesses the pursuit of self-interest to direct resources where they earn the greatest return, in the process promoting the general interest. Thus, although each individual pursues his or her self-interest, the invisible hand promotes the general welfare. Pure capitalism is sometimes called *laissez-faire* capitalism; translated from the French, this phrase means "to let do," or to let people do as they choose without government intervention. Thus, *under pure capitalism, voluntary choices based on rational self-interest are made in competitive markets to answer the questions what, how, and for whom.*

Command Economy

A command economy is characterized by public ownership of resources and the coordination of economic activity through centralized planning.

In a **command economy**, there is public, or communal, ownership of property. Resources are directed and production coordinated through some form of *central planning*. The collective will of the people is, in theory, reflected by the decisions of the central planners. These planners, as representatives of all the people, determine how much steel, how many cars, how many tubes of toothpaste, and how many personal computers to produce. The central planners also determine how these goods are to be produced and who will receive the goods. In theory, the command economy incorporates individual choice into collective choice which, in turn, is reflected in central planning decisions.

Mixed Economies

No country on earth exemplifies either type of economic system in its pure form. The United States represents a *mixed capitalist economy*, with governments directly accounting for a little more than one-third of all economic activity. But even the economic activity carried out by the private sector is often regulated by government in a variety of ways.

About 25 percent of the world's population lives in the People's Republic of China, perhaps the most centrally planned of economies. Even in China, however, workers are entitled to their wages, and marketlike mechanisms are being introduced with increasing frequency, allowing some private businesses to operate. The Soviet Union is another example of a command economy that has recently introduced more market incentives through an economic restructuring called *perestroika*. For example, the Soviet Union now permits limited forms of private enterprise. For the first time since the 1920s, families are allowed to operate small businesses, such as restaurants and laundries.

Although public ownership of the resources usually goes hand in hand with centrally planned coordination, hybrid systems are developing. Yugoslavia, for example, has a system called *market socialism*, in which public ownership of some resources, particularly capital, is combined with relatively free markets to direct economic activity. Hungary and Poland are also experimenting with a profusion of small, consumer-oriented businesses. Indeed, most countries in Eastern Europe are now trying to introduce market forces into their economies.

Finally, some economic systems are directed largely by custom or religion. Laws of the Muslim religion set limits on the rate of interest that can be earned on certain investments. The caste system in India and elsewhere often restricts the occupations available to individuals. Hence, religion, custom, and family relations play important roles in the organization and coordination of economic activity. Your own pattern of consumption and choice of occupation may be influenced by some of these factors.

CONCLUSION

This chapter introduced some of the key concepts of economics: opportunity cost, production possibilities, efficiency, specialization, comparative advantage, and the questions of what, how, and for whom. Although economies can answer the three economic questions in a variety of ways, this text will focus primarily on the mixed form of capitalism found in the United States. This type of economy blends private choice, guided by the price system in competitive markets, with public choice, guided by representative democracy in political markets. The study of mixed capitalism is becoming more relevant as capitalist economies and command economies grow more alike.

If you quit right now, you would already know more about economic analysis than most people. But you learned about these analytical tools so that you could use them to make sense out of the world, as we will attempt to do in the next chapter on resource allocation through competitive markets.

Summary

1. Scarcity arises because resources are limited but wants are unlimited. Since we cannot satisfy all wants, we must make choices, and choice involves opportunity cost. The opportunity cost of the preferred option is the forgone benefit from the best alternative.

2. The production possibilities frontier is a curve that shows the productive capabilities of the economy during a particular time period, assuming all resources are used fully and efficiently. Points inside the frontier represent inefficient use of resources; points outside the frontier are unattainable given the economy's resources and technology. This frontier's bow shape reflects the law of increasing opportunity cost, which exists because resources are not perfectly adaptable to the production of all goods.

3. Over time, the production possibilities frontier can shift in or out as a result of changes in the availability of resources or in technology. The frontier demonstrates several economic concepts, including scarcity, efficiency, the law of increasing opportunity cost, choice, and economic growth.

4. The law of comparative advantage states that the individual, firm, region, or country with the lowest opportunity cost of producing a particular good should specialize in the production of that good. Specialization according to the law of comparative advantage promotes the most efficient use of resources.

5. All economic systems, regardless of their decision-making process, must answer three fundamental questions: What is to be produced? How is it to be produced? For whom is it to be produced? Nations answer the questions differently, depending on who owns their resources and how their economic activities are conducted and directed. Two extremes of ownership and coordination are represented by pure capitalism and a pure command economy. All countries exemplify a mix of both elements, with some leaning more toward capitalism and others leaning more toward a command economy. Economic systems have been growing more alike over time.

Questions and Problems

1. (Opportunity Costs) Discuss the ways in which the following conditions might affect the opportunity cost of going to a movie.
   a. You have a final exam the next day.
   b. School will be out for one month starting today.
   c. The same movie will be shown on TV tomorrow night.
   d. The school dance or concert is the same night as the movie.

2. (Opportunity Costs) "You should never buy precooked frozen foods because you are paying for the labor costs of preparing the food." Is this statement always true, or can it be invalidated by the principle of comparative advantage?

3. (Production Possibilities) During the late 1960s and early 1970s Mao Zedong and the leaders of the Great Proletarian Cultural Revolution forced highly educated professionals in China to move to farms and work as peasants. The action was justified by arguing that

such professionals, by becoming acquainted with honest labor, would learn to respect the common laborer. This policy created a massive reduction in productivity, incentives, and economic growth, and it was later abandoned. How does such a policy relate to the production possibilities frontier?

4. (Production Possibilities) In response to what seemed to be a flood of illegal aliens, Congress made it a federal offense to hire illegal aliens. How will the measure affect the U.S. production possibilities frontier? Will all industries be affected equally? Which individuals in society will be helped, and which will be hurt?

5. (Production Possibilities) "If society decides, by way of the marketplace, to use its resources fully (that is, to keep the economy on the production possibilities frontier), then future generations will be worse off because they will not be able to use these resources." If this assertion is true, full employment of resources may not be a good thing. Comment on the validity of the assertion.

6. (Production Possibilities) People are often confused about what will shift the production possibilities frontier. For example, someone might think that a reduction in the unemployment rate would shift the PPF outward. Explain why this is *not* the case.

7. (Specialization) Discuss the strengths and weaknesses of the practice at universities of having each subject taught by a different professor. Why not have one professor teach history, economics, physics, mathematics, and so on?

8. (Comparative and Absolute Advantage) In the United States some states specialize in the production of certain products. For example, over 50 percent of the apples consumed in the United States come from the Pacific Northwest. Identify states that have absolute advantages in the production of their goods and states that have comparative advantages in the production of their goods.

9. (Comparative Advantage) Corporate executives often use limousines, even though the executives are perfectly good drivers. Suppose that a certain executive is a better driver than her chauffeur. Use the principle of comparative advantage to show that the executive should still employ the driver rather than drive the car herself.

10. (Opportunity Cost) Frick can pick twelve bushels of corn in one hour; Frack can pick twenty bushels. If Frick spends his hour fishing, he can catch three fish; Frack can catch four fish in the same amount of time.
    a. What is the (opportunity) cost of a fish for Frick? For Frack?
    b. What is the (opportunity) cost of a bushel of corn for Frick? For Frack?
    c. What is the greatest number of fish the two can catch together if they also pick twenty bushels of corn? Explain.

11. (Production Possibilities) Suppose a production possibilities frontier includes the following data points:

Cars	Washing Machines
0	1000
100	600
200	0

    a. Graph the production possibilities frontier, assuming that it has no curved segments.
    b. What is the cost of a car when 50 cars are produced?
    c. What is the cost of a car when 150 cars are produced?
    d. What is the cost of a washing machine when 50 cars are produced? 150 cars?
    e. What do your answers tell you about opportunity costs?

12. (Sunk Cost) You go to a restaurant and buy an expensive meal. Halfway through, in spite of feeling stuffed, you decide to clean your plate. After all, you think, you paid for the meal, so you are going to eat all of it. What's wrong with this thinking?

13. (Opportunity Cost) You win a full scholarship to go to graduate school. You aren't sure that you will benefit much from going, but you decide to go because it is free. What's wrong with this thinking?

C H A P T E R   3

The Market System

Why are tomatoes cheaper in August than in January? Supply and demand. Why are hotel rooms in Phoenix, Arizona, cheaper in the summer, when the temperature is 110 degrees, than in the winter, when the temperature is 70 degrees? Supply and demand. Why is the designer-original dress from Paris more expensive than a similar dress off the rack from K-Mart? You guessed it: supply and demand.

It seems that many economic questions boil down to the workings of supply and demand. Indeed, some people believe that if you programmed a computer to respond "supply and demand" to economic questions, you could put many economists out of work. The concepts of supply and demand are the most fundamental and the most powerful of all economic tools. An understanding of the two will take you far in developing your skills in the art and science of economic analysis. This chapter will introduce the underpinnings of supply and demand and show how the two interact in competitive markets. As you will see, the correct analysis of supply and demand takes skill and care. The chapter uses graphs extensively, so you may want to refer back to the appendix of Chapter 1 for a refresher. Topics discussed in this chapter include

- Demand
- Substitution and income effects
- Changes in demand
- Supply
- Changes in supply

- Markets
- Transaction costs
- Equilibrium price and quantity
- Disequilibrium

DEMAND

If the price of Pepsi is $1 a six-pack, how many six-packs will be demanded each week? How many will be demanded if the price is $2? If the price is $3? The answers to these questions provide a schedule conveying the relation between the price of Pepsi and the quantity demanded. This schedule is called the demand for Pepsi. More generally, **demand** is a relation indicating the quantity of a well-defined commodity that consumers are both *willing* and *able* to buy at each possible price during a given period of time, other things constant. Because demand is calculated for a specific period of time, such as a day, a week, or a month, demand is best thought of as the desired *rate* of purchase at each possible price. Note that demand reflects the quantity that consumers are both *willing* and *able* to buy at each alternative price. For example, you may be *able* to buy a motorcycle at a price of $2000 because you have enough money to pay for it, but you may not be *willing* to buy one if motorcycles do not interest you.

Demand is a relation indicating the quantity of a well-defined good that consumers are willing and able to buy at each possible price during a given period of time, other things constant.

The Law of Demand

In a remote region of western Pennsylvania is a poorly lit, run-down yellow building known as Pechin's Mart. The aisles are unmarked and strewn with half-empty boxes arranged in no apparent design. The sagging roof leaks when it rains. Why do shoppers come from as far away as Maryland and put up with the chaos and the grubbiness to buy as many groceries as they can haul away? The store has violated nearly all the rules of retailing, yet it thrives, with annual sales more than four times the average for supermarkets around the country. The store thrives because it follows a rule merchants have known for thousands of years—its prices are the lowest around.

You as a consumer have little trouble grasping the notion that people will buy more of a particular good at a lower price than at a higher price. Sell the product for less, and the world will beat a path to your door. In fact, the relation between the price of a good and the quantity demanded has been elevated to the status of an economic law. The **law of demand** states that in a given time period the quantity demanded of a product is inversely related to its price, other things constant. Thus, the higher the price, the smaller the quantity demanded; the lower the price, the greater the quantity demanded.

The *law of demand* states that the quantity of a good demanded during a given time period is inversely related to its price, other things constant.

Demand, Wants, and Need Consumer *demand* and consumer *wants* are not the same thing. As we have seen, wants are unlimited. You may *want* a Mercedes, but at a price of $60,000, it is likely to be beyond your budget (that is, the quantity you demand at that price is zero). Nor is *demand* the same as *need*. You may *need* a new muffler for your car, but when the price is $100, you may decide "I am not going to pay a lot for this muffler." Evidently, you believe you have better ways to spend your money. If, however, the price of mufflers falls far enough, say to $40, then you will be both willing and able to buy one.

Other Prices Held Constant Notice that the definition of demand includes the other-things-constant assumption. Since demand is influenced by factors other than the price, the law of demand is applicable only as long as these other factors do not change. For example, Pepsi and Coke represent alternative ways of quenching a thirst. Therefore, the quantity of Pepsi demanded will depend not only on the price of Pepsi but also on the price of Coke, as well as on the prices of other alternatives. In order to isolate the relation between the price of Pepsi and the quantity of Pepsi demanded, we must assume that the prices of Coke and other alternatives remain constant. By assuming other prices remain constant, we are able to consider the effect of a change in the price of one good, Pepsi, *relative to the prices of other goods*. Thus we focus on the effects of a change in what is called the *relative price* of Pepsi. If the price of Pepsi increases while the price of other goods remains constant, the relative price of Pepsi has increased.

The Substitution Effect of a Price Change What explains the law of demand? Why, for example, is less demanded when the price is higher? The explanation begins with scarce resources meeting unlimited wants. Many goods and services are capable of satisfying particular wants. For example, your hunger can be satisfied by pizza, tacos, cheese sandwiches, sirloin steak, or fried chicken. Similarly, your desire for warmth in the winter can be met by warm clothing, home insulation, heating oil, or a trip to Hawaii. Clearly, some ways of satisfying your wants will be more appealing to you than others. Most of us would prefer dining on filet mignon at a posh French restaurant to eating a peanut butter sandwich at home. In a world without scarcity, there would be no prices, so you would always choose the most attractive alternative. Scarcity, however, is an overriding reality, and the degree of scarcity of one good relative to another determines their relative prices.

When the price of one good goes up and prices of other goods do not change, this good becomes relatively more costly. Consumers therefore tend to substitute other goods for the higher-priced good. If the price of pizza goes up, you tend to eat less pizza and more of other foods. This phenomenon is called the **substitution effect** of a price change: an increase in the price of one good encourages consumers to substitute other goods, which are now relatively cheaper. On the other hand, a decrease in the price of one good causes consumers to substitute that good for other goods, which are now relatively more expensive. Consumers are more *willing* to purchase the good when its relative price falls. Remember that it is the change in the *relative* price — the price of one good relative to the prices of other goods — that causes the substitution effect. If all prices rise by the same percentage, there is no change in relative prices, so there is no substitution effect.

*The **substitution effect** is a change in the pattern of consumption caused by a price change. When the price of a good falls, consumers are more willing to substitute this good for other goods, so the quantity demanded increases.*

The Income Effect of a Price Change A rise in price often causes a decline in quantity demanded for another reason. Suppose you have $30 a week to spend on midnight snacks and you are a pizza fanatic who buys six pizzas a

Real income *is mea-sured in terms of the goods and services it can buy.*

*A change in price of a good has an **in-come effect** by alter-ing consumers' purchasing power. A fall in the price of a good increases con-sumers' purchasing power, making them more able to pur-chase all normal goods, so the quan-tity demanded increases.*

week at $5 per pizza. What will happen to the quantity you demand if the price doubles to $10? At that price you can buy at most three pizzas a week. The increase in the price of pizza has reduced your **real income**—that is, your income measured in terms of the goods and services it can buy. The quantity of pizza you demand is reduced because of this **income effect** of a price increase.

More generally, as the price of a particular good goes up, other things constant, your real income declines. Because of this decline in real income, your *ability* to purchase this good (and all other goods) declines. Therefore, you typically reduce the quantity of this good demanded. Conversely, as the price of a particular good declines, other things constant, your real income increases, so you typically increase the quantity of that good demanded.

The income effect of a price change is greater for products on which you spend a large portion of your budget, such as housing and cars, than for smaller items, such as soap and doughnuts. The higher the percentage of your budget devoted to expenditures on a particular good, the more your budget is affected by changes in the price of that good. For example, suppose housing accounts for $300 of your $600 monthly budget. If the price of housing drops by 33 percent, other things constant, you can purchase the same amount of housing for $200, thus freeing up $100 in your budget to be spent on more housing and more of other goods.

Now consider a change in the price of a much less important item. Suppose you eat, on average, a dozen doughnuts a month at a total cost of $3. This expenditure constitutes 0.5 percent of your $600 monthly budget. A 33 percent drop in the price of doughnuts reduces the cost of purchasing a dozen doughnuts by $1 per month, thereby freeing up just $1 per month, which you can spend on more doughnuts and more of other goods. As you can see, the income effect of a change in the price of housing is likely to be greater than the income effect of a change in the price of doughnuts. You may buy more doughnuts when the price falls, but this is due primarily to the *substitution* effect, not the *income* effect.

The Demand Schedule and Demand Curve

Demand can be expressed as a *demand schedule* or as a *demand curve*. Panel (a) of Exhibit 1 shows a hypothetical demand schedule for milk. When we describe demand, we must be specific about the units being measured and the time period under consideration. In our example, the price is for a quart of milk, and the period is a month. The schedule lists alternative prices, along with the quantity demanded at each price. At a price of $1.25 per quart, for example, consumers will demand 8 million quarts per month.

As you can see, the lower the price, the greater the quantity demanded: if the price drops as low as $0.25, 32 million quarts will be demanded per month. As the price of milk falls, consumers substitute milk for other goods since milk becomes relatively cheaper. The income effect also increases the quantity of milk demanded. Because milk expenditures typically represent a

EXHIBIT 1   THE DEMAND SCHEDULE AND DEMAND CURVE FOR MILK

(a) *Demand schedule*   (b) *Demand curve*

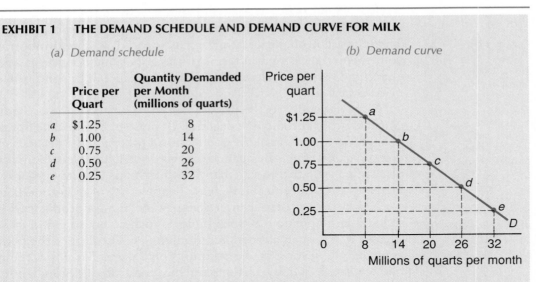

	Price per Quart	Quantity Demanded per Month (millions of quarts)
a	$1.25	8
b	1.00	14
c	0.75	20
d	0.50	26
e	0.25	32

The market demand curve, *D*, shows the quantity of milk demanded, at various prices, by all consumers.

small fraction of each consumer's budget, however, the income effect is probably small.

*A **demand curve** is a downward-sloping curve showing the quantity of a specific commodity demanded at various possible prices.*

The demand schedule in panel (a) is presented as a **demand curve** in panel (b). Price is measured on the vertical axis and the quantity demanded is measured on the horizontal axis. Each combination of price and quantity demanded listed in the demand schedule in panel (a) is represented by a point in panel (b). Point *a*, for example, indicates that at a price of $1.25, 8 million quarts will be demanded per month. These points are connected to form the demand curve for milk, which is labeled *D*. Note that the demand curve slopes downward, reflecting the *law of demand*: price and quantity demanded are inversely related, other things constant.

Take care to distinguish between the *demand* for milk and the *quantity demanded*. The demand for milk is not a specific quantity but the entire relation indicating the quantity demanded at each price. *Demand* is represented by the complete demand schedule or demand curve. Individual points along the demand curve show the *quantity demanded* at each price. For example, at a price of $0.75 per quart, the quantity demanded is 20 million quarts. When the price of milk changes, this change is expressed by a movement along the demand curve. Movements along the curve, say from point *a* to point *b*, reflect *changes in quantity demanded*, not changes in demand.

At times it is useful to distinguish between *individual demand*, which is the demand of an individual consumer, and *market demand*, which is the sum of the individual demands of all consumers in the market. Market demand conveys the relation between the price of a good and the quantity that all consumers in the market are willing and able to buy. In most markets there are many consumers, sometimes millions. Unless otherwise noted, when we talk about demand, we will be referring to market demand, as in the first two exhibits.

CHANGES IN DEMAND

To isolate the relation between the price of a good and the quantity demanded, we have assumed that other factors that could affect demand remained unchanged. Consider how changes in these other factors will affect the demand curve. Variables that can affect market demand are (1) consumer incomes, (2) the prices of related goods, (3) consumer expectations, (4) the number of consumers in the market, and (5) consumer tastes.

Changes in Income

In Exhibit 2 we have reproduced the market demand curve, *D*, for milk. This demand curve assumes a given level of consumer income. Suppose consumer incomes increase. Consumers will then be willing and able to purchase more milk at each price level, so the demand curve for milk will shift to the right, as reflected by the movement from *D* to *D'*. For example, at a price of $1, the quantity demanded increases from 14 million to 20 million quarts per month, as indicated by the movement from point *b* on *D* to point *g* on *D'*.

But an increase in the demand for milk also means that consumers are willing and able to pay a higher price for each *quantity* of milk. For example, consumers were initially willing and able to pay $1 per quart for 14 million quarts, as reflected by point *b*. After the increase in demand, consumers are willing and able to pay $1.25 per quart for 14 million quarts, as reflected by point *f* on the new demand curve, which is directly above point *b* on the original demand curve. In short, an increase in demand—that is, a shift to the right in the demand curve—means that consumers will buy more units at each price level, or will pay more per unit at each quantity level.

*The demand for **normal goods** increases as income rises. The demand for **inferior goods** decreases as income rises.*

We classify goods into two broad groupings depending on how demand for the good responds to changes in income. The demand for **normal goods** increases as income increases. Because the demand for milk increases when consumer income increases, milk is considered to be a normal good. Most goods are normal goods. In contrast, the demand for **inferior goods** actually declines as income increases. Examples of inferior goods include ground beef, trips to the laundromat, and bus rides. As income increases, consumers tend to switch from consuming these inferior goods to consuming normal goods (steak, their own washer and dryer, automobile or plane rides), so the demand curve for inferior goods shifts to the left.

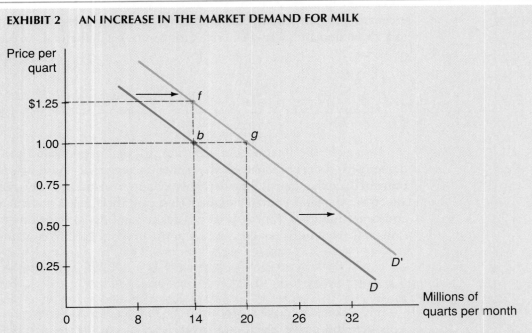

EXHIBIT 2   AN INCREASE IN THE MARKET DEMAND FOR MILK

An increase in the demand for milk is reflected by an outward shift in the demand curve. After the increase in demand, the quantity of milk demanded at a price of $1 per quart increases from 14 million quarts (point *b*) to 20 million quarts (point *g*). Another way to interpret the shift is to say that the maximum price consumers are willing to pay for 14 million quarts has increased from $1 per unit (at point *b*) to $1.25 per unit (at point *f*).

Changes in the Prices of Complements and Substitutes

As noted earlier, there are alternative ways of trying to satisfy any particular want. For example, thirst can be quenched not only by drinking milk but also by drinking a soft drink, fruit juice, or water. These goods are, to a certain extent, substitutes in satisfying the particular want, thirst. Consumers choose among substitutes partly on the basis of their relative prices. Consider two substitutes, milk and juice. Obviously, they are not perfect substitutes (you wouldn't pour juice on cereal), but an increase in the price of juice, other things constant, will encourage some consumers to buy less juice and more milk. Two goods are **substitutes** if an increase in the price of one leads to an increase in the demand for the other, and conversely, if a decrease in the price of one leads to a decrease in the demand for the other.

Goods are complements if they are used in combination to satisfy some particular want. For example, milk and chocolate chip cookies, computer hardware and software, and popcorn and movies are considered complements because they are often used in combination. A decrease in the price of

*Two goods are **substitutes** if an increase in the price of one leads to an increase in demand for the other.*

chocolate chip cookies will increase the quantity of those cookies demanded, which will increase the demand for milk. Two goods are **complements** if a decrease in the price of one leads to an increase in the demand for the other, and conversely, if an increase in the price of one leads to a decrease in the demand for the other. Most pairs of goods selected at random are *unrelated*. For example, the demand for milk has no relation to the price of string beans or to the price of an airline ticket from Denver to Chicago.

Changes in Consumer Expectations

Another factor that can shift the demand curve is a change in consumer expectations about factors that influence demand, such as future income and the future price of a good. A consumer who is expecting a pay increase may increase current demand in anticipation of that pay increase. For example, a college senior who lands that first job may buy a car even before graduation in anticipation of a steady paycheck. Demand in this case is based not on current income but on expected income. Changes in price expectations can also affect demand. For example, if consumers expect the price of new housing to go up next year, they will probably increase their demand for new housing this year. On the other hand, expectations of a lower price in the future will encourage consumers to postpone purchases. Changes in expectations will have less effect if the good in question is perishable. If you expect the price of milk to go up next month, you will not buy twenty extra quarts today. Even in this case, though, expectations will still matter to some degree: if you expect the price of milk to go up tomorrow, you will likely buy a little extra today.

Changes in the Number of Consumers

We mentioned earlier that market demand is the sum of the individual demands of all consumers in the market. If the number of consumers in the market changes, demand will change. For example, if the population grows, the demand for food will increase. Even if the total population remains the same, demand could change as a result of a change in the composition of the population. For example, if the number of retired couples increases, the demand for recreational vehicles will probably increase. If the baby population declines, the demand for baby food will decrease.

Changes in Tastes

Do you like anchovies on your pizza? How about sauerkraut on your hot dog? Do you wear designer jeans? Choices in food, clothing, movies, music, reading—indeed, all consumption choices—usually are influenced by consumer tastes. *Tastes* are nothing more than your likes and dislikes as a consumer. What determines tastes? Who knows? Economists certainly don't, nor do they spend much time worrying about it. Economists do recognize, however, that tastes are very important in shaping demand, and that a change in tastes can change demand.

Because tastes are so difficult to observe, we should be reluctant to attribute a change in demand to a change in tastes. In our analysis of consumer demand, we will assume that tastes are given and are relatively stable over time. Otherwise, there is a temptation to explain any shift in demand by a change in tastes. For example, the question "Why did the demand for milk change?" could be answered by saying "Obviously, the preferences for milk changed." But since there is no way to test such an assertion, we will use the change-in-tastes explanation sparingly and only after other possible changes have been ruled out. At times a change in tastes may be identified by tracing the change to specific events. For example, if health officials warn that milk consumption is linked to heart disease, the demand for milk is likely to fall. Similarly, the demand for milk could fall if the public developed the perception that only wimps drink milk.

It is important to understand that only a **change in the quantity demanded** of a good results from a change in the good's price. A **change in demand** results from a change in one of the determinants of demand that causes a shift in the entire demand curve. The crucial distinction between a change in demand and a change in the quantity demanded may be confusing at first, so be careful.

> A **change in quantity demanded** is a movement along a given demand curve in response to a change in the price of the good.

> A **change in demand** is a change in the entire relation between price and quantity demanded in response to a change in one of the variables that influence demand. A change in demand is reflected by a shift in the demand curve.

SUPPLY

> **Supply** is a relation indicating the quantity of a well-defined good that producers are willing and able to sell at various prices during a given time period, other things constant.

Just as demand is the relation between price and quantity demanded, supply is the relation between price and quantity supplied. Specifically, **supply** indicates how much of the good producers are both *willing* and *able* to offer for sale in a given time period at each possible price, other things constant. The relation between price and quantity supplied is normally, though not always, a direct one; that is, more is supplied at a higher price than at a lower price, other things constant.

The Supply Schedule and Supply Curve

> A **supply curve** shows the quantity of a well-defined good supplied at various possible prices.

Exhibit 3 presents the market supply schedule and market **supply curve**, *S*, for milk, showing the quantity of milk supplied at various possible prices by thousands of dairy farmers. As you can see, price and quantity supplied are directly, or positively, related. More is offered for sale at a higher price than at a lower price, so the supply curve slopes upward. There are two reasons producers tend to offer more goods for sale when prices are higher. The first has to do with a *willingness* to offer more for sale at a higher price than at a lower price. An increase in the price of milk provides farmers with an incentive to shift some resources out of the production of other goods, such as corn, for which the price is now relatively lower, and into milk, for which the price is now relatively higher. Prices act as signals to existing and

EXHIBIT 3   THE SUPPLY SCHEDULE AND SUPPLY CURVE FOR MILK

(a) Supply schedule

Price per Quart	Quantity Supplied per Month (millions of quarts)
$1.25	28
1.00	24
0.75	20
0.50	16
0.25	12

(b) Supply curve

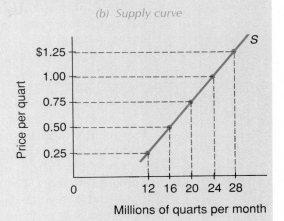

The market supply curve, *S*, shows the quantity of milk supplied, at various prices, by all farmers.

potential suppliers about the relative rewards for producing various goods. *A higher milk price attracts resources from less-valued uses to the higher-valued use.* As the price of a good increases, other things constant, a producer is more *willing* to supply the good.

A second reason the supply curve tends to slope upward is that higher prices increase the *ability* to supply the good. The law of increasing opportunity cost states that as more of a particular good is produced, the opportunity cost of additional output becomes greater—that is, the *marginal cost* increases. Since producers face a higher marginal cost for additional output, they must receive a higher price for that output to be *able* to increase the quantity supplied. For example, when milk production is low, farmers are able to employ resources that are well suited to the task. As output increases, however, producing the additional increments of milk requires resources that may be better suited to the production of other goods. To feed additional cows, for example, a farmer may have to convert a productive wheat field into grazing land. Therefore, additional output has a higher opportunity cost. *Higher milk prices make farmers more able to draw resources away from alternative uses.*

Thus, a higher price makes producers more *willing* and more *able* to increase the quantity of goods offered for sale. Producers are more *willing* because production of the higher-priced good is now relatively more attractive than the alternative uses of the resources involved. Producers are more *able* because the higher price allows them to cover the higher marginal costs typically involved with higher rates of production.

As with demand, we distinguish between *individual* supply and *market* supply. Market supply is the sum of the amount supplied at each price by all the individual suppliers. Unless otherwise noted, when we talk about supply, we will be referring to market supply. We also distinguish between *supply* and *quantity supplied*. Supply is the relation between the price and quantity supplied, as expressed by the entire supply schedule or supply curve. Quantity supplied refers to a particular amount on a given supply curve.

CHANGES IN SUPPLY

The supply curve expresses the relation between the price of a good and the quantity supplied, other things constant. Thus, the supply curve is drawn under the assumption that no changes occur in other factors that determine supply. Such factors include (1) the state of technology, (2) the cost of relevant resources, (3) the prices of alternative goods, (4) producer expectations, and (5) the number of producers in the market. We will consider how a change in each of these determinants of supply will affect the supply curve.

Changes in Technology

Recall from Chapter 2 that the state of technology represents the economy's stock of knowledge about how resources can be combined most efficiently. Technology is assumed to be constant for a given supply curve. If some new method is devised to produce the good more efficiently, production costs will fall, so suppliers will be more willing and more able to supply the good at each price. Supply will increase, as reflected by a shift to the right in the supply curve. For example, suppose a new milking machine called The Invisible Hand has a very soothing effect on cows; cows find the new machine so "udderly" delightful that they produce more milk. Such a technological advance is reflected by a shift to the right in the market supply curve for milk, as shown by the shift from S to S' in Exhibit 4.

Notice that just as a change in demand can be interpreted in two different ways, so can a change in supply. First, an increase in supply means dairy farmers supply more milk at each possible price. For example, when the price rises to $1 per quart, the quantity of milk supplied increases from 24 million to 28 million quarts per month, as shown by the movement from point h to point i in Exhibit 4. Second, an increase in supply means that farmers are willing and able to supply the same quantity at a lower price. For example, farmers originally supplied 24 million quarts when the price was $1.00 per quart; on the new supply curve, that same quantity is supplied for only $0.75 per quart, as shown by the movement from point h to point j.

Changes in the Cost of Relevant Resources

Suppose the price of milking machines falls. This lower price for a resource reduces the cost of milk production. Dairy farmers are therefore more willing and able to supply milk, and the supply curve for milk shifts to the right, as was shown in Exhibit 4. On the other hand, an increase in the

EXHIBIT 4   AN INCREASE IN THE SUPPLY OF MILK

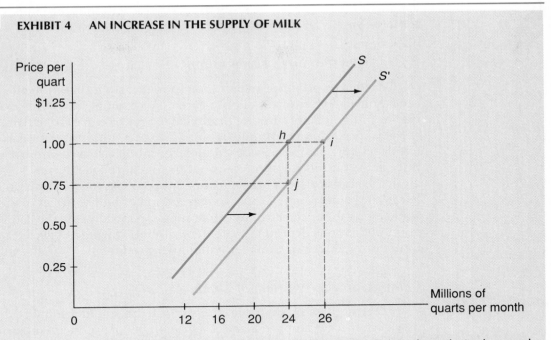

An increase in the supply of milk is reflected by a shift to the right in the supply curve, from *S* to *S'*. After the increase in supply, the quantity of milk supplied at a price of $1 per quart increases from 24 million quarts (point *h*) to 28 million quarts (point *i*). Another way to interpret the shift is to say that it shows a reduction in the minimum price suppliers require in order to produce 24 million quarts. Previously, a price of $1 per quart was required (point *h*); after the increase in supply, suppliers require a price of only $0.75 per quart (point *j*).

price of a relevant resource will reduce supply. For example, higher electricity rates would increase the cost of lighting the barn and operating the milking machines. These higher production costs would be reflected by a shift to the left in the supply curve.

Changes in the Prices of Alternative Goods

Nearly all resources have alternative uses. The farmer's field, tractor, barn, and labor could be used to produce a variety of goods. *Alternative goods* are goods that use some of the same resources as are used to produce the good under consideration. For example, suppose the production of corn uses some of the same resources as the production of milk. An increase in the price of corn will raise the opportunity cost of producing milk. Because the production of corn is now relatively more rewarding, resources will shift from milk production to corn production. With fewer resources supplied to the production of milk, the supply of milk will decrease, or shift to the left. On the other hand, a fall in the price of an alternative good will make milk production relatively more attractive. As resources shift into milk production, the supply of milk will increase, or shift to the right.

Changes in Producer Expectations

Changes in producer expectations about factors that influence supply can result in a shift of the supply curve. For example, a farmer expecting higher prices for milk in the future may begin to expand the dairy today, thereby increasing the supply of milk. When a good can be easily stored (crude oil, for example, can be left in the ground), an expectation of a higher price in the future will prompt producers to reduce their current supply and await the higher price. Their reduction in supply is reflected by a shift to the left in the supply curve. Thus, an expectation of higher prices in the future could increase or decrease the current supply, depending on the nature of the good under consideration. More generally, any change expected to affect future profitability in a market will influence supply.

Changes in the Number of Producers

Since the market supply is the sum of the amount supplied by each producer, market supply depends on the number of producers in the market. If the number of producers increases, supply will shift to the right; if the number decreases, supply will shift to the left. For example, during the 1980s the number of stores renting movie videos mushroomed, so the supply of videos available for rent increased sharply, shifting the supply curve to the right.

*A **change in quantity supplied** is a movement along a given supply curve in response to a change in the price of the good.*

Before leaving this section on supply, notice that supply and demand have some similar determinants. Both depend on the prices of related goods, price expectations, and the number of participants in the market. Note also that we distinguish between a **change in the quantity supplied**, which is represented by a movement between points along a given supply curve in response to a change in the price of the good, and a **change in supply**, which is a shift in the entire supply curve in response to a change in one of the determinants of supply. We are now ready to bring supply and demand together.

*A **change in supply** is a change in the entire relation between price and quantity supplied in response to a change in one of the variables that influence supply. A change in supply is reflected by a shift in the supply curve.*

PUTTING IT ALL TOGETHER: SUPPLY, DEMAND, AND EQUILIBRIUM

Suppliers and demanders have different views of price because demanders *pay* the price and suppliers *receive* the price. Thus, higher prices tend to be bad news for consumers but good news for producers. As the price rises, consumers reduce the quantity demanded and producers increase the quantity supplied. How is this ongoing conflict between producers and consumers resolved?

Markets

The differing views of price held by suppliers and demanders are sorted out by the market for the product. A *market*, a term first introduced in Chapter 1, is an impersonal mechanism that coordinates the independent decisions of buyers and sellers. A market represents all the arrangements used to buy and sell a particular commodity. Markets reduce the cost of bringing buyers and sellers together and allow them to find out what's for sale, at what price and of what quality. Thus, we say that markets reduce the **transaction costs** of exchange — the cost of time and information required for exchange. For example, suppose you are looking for a summer job. One approach would be to go from employer to employer inquiring about job openings. But this would be time-consuming and could involve extensive travel. Alternatively, you could pick up a copy of the local newspaper and let your fingers do the walking through the help-wanted ads. These ads, which are one element of the job market, reduce the cost of time and information required to bring workers and employers together. Different markets provide different amounts of information about the item being exchanged, and this information is diffused, or communicated, at different speeds. For example, the stock market provides up-to-the-minute information about the price and quantity of thousands of stocks.

The **transaction costs** of an exchange are the costs of the time and information required to carry it out.

The coordination that occurs through markets takes place not because of some central plan but because of Adam Smith's "invisible hand." For example, most of the auto dealers in your community tend to be located together, usually on the outskirts of town. The car dealers locate on the outskirts of town because that type of business uses much land, and land is cheaper farther from the center of town. The dealers congregate not because they like one another's company but because each dealer wants to be where customers shop for cars — that is, near other dealers. This common location makes it easier for buyers to go from dealer to dealer to make comparisons. For the same reason, stores group together downtown and in shopping malls.

Specialized Markets

Markets can encompass the entire world, such as the market for wheat, or they can be as narrow as the competing gas stations at an intersection. Some markets are very specialized; others are more general. In Quincy Market, a shopping center in Boston, a store called The Bear Facts sells nothing but toy bears. In a rural community outside of Boston, there is a general store where you can buy anything from a lug wrench to a pound of lamb chops. Why do some stores sell many different products while others specialize?

Again, Adam Smith gave us the answer more than two hundred years ago when he noted that *the degree of specialization is limited by the extent of the market.* The larger the market — that is, the greater the potential number of customers — the greater the degree of specialization. The shopping complex in

Boston attracts millions of shoppers each year. Even if just a tiny fraction of them buy toy bears, the store can thrive. The general store, however, relies on a much smaller market—the several dozen homes scattered across the surrounding countryside—so it must offer a wider range of choice to sell enough goods to stay afloat. Thus, specialty stores are more likely to locate in major population areas than in rural communities.

Similarly, some magazines, such as *Time* and *People*, are aimed at a general readership, so their subject matter and advertisements reflect this general interest. Other periodicals, such as the *American Economic Review* and the *Teddy Bear Review*, contain subject matter and advertising reflecting the narrow interests of their readers.

Market Equilibrium

We will examine how a market works by bringing together market supply and market demand. Exhibit 5 shows the supply and demand for milk, using schedules in panel (a) and curves in panel (b). To see how market forces operate, suppose the price initially is $1 per quart. At that price producers supply 24 million quarts, but consumers demand only 14 million quarts. Thus, when the price is $1 per quart, the quantity supplied exceeds the quantity demanded, resulting in an *excess quantity supplied,* or a **surplus**, of 10 million quarts. The 10 million quarts of unsold milk signals producers that the price is too high. Unless the price falls, the surplus will continue and milk will sour on store shelves. How can the surplus be eliminated? By lowering the price. Thus, the suppliers' desire to eliminate the surplus creates downward pressure on the price, as reflected by the arrow pointing downward in panel (b). As the price falls, producers reduce the quantity supplied and consumers increase the quantity demanded. As long as quantity supplied exceeds quantity demanded, the resulting surplus will create pressure for a lower price.

Alternatively, suppose the price is initially $0.50 per quart. You can see from Exhibit 5 that the quantity supplied at that price is 16 million quarts but the quantity demanded is 26 million quarts. Thus, when the price is $0.50 per quart, the quantity demanded exceeds the quantity supplied, resulting in an *excess quantity demanded*, or a **shortage,** of 10 million quarts. Producers notice that the quantity supplied has quickly sold out and customers are grumbling because milk is no longer available. Empty store shelves and frustrated consumers create market pressure for a higher price, as reflected by the arrow pointing upward in panel (b). As the price rises, producers increase the quantity supplied and consumers reduce the quantity demanded. The price will continue to rise as long as quantity demanded exceeds quantity supplied.

Thus, a surplus creates downward pressure on the price, and a shortage creates upward pressure on the price. As long as quantity demanded and quantity supplied differ, market forces will create pressure for a price change, which in turn will affect quantity demanded and quantity supplied. When the quantity consumers are willing and able to buy equals the quantity pro-

*A **surplus** is an excess of quantity supplied over quantity demanded at a given price.*

*A **shortage** is an excess of quantity demanded over quantity supplied at a given price.*

EXHIBIT 5   EQUILIBRIUM IN THE MILK MARKET

(a) Market schedules

Millions of Quarts per Month

Price per Quart	Quantity Demanded	Quantity Supplied	Surplus or Shortage	Price Will
$1.25	8	28	Surplus of 20	Fall
1.00	14	24	Surplus of 10	Fall
0.75	20	20	Equilibrium	Remain the same
0.50	26	16	Shortage of 10	Rise
0.25	32	12	Shortage of 20	Rise

(b) Market curves

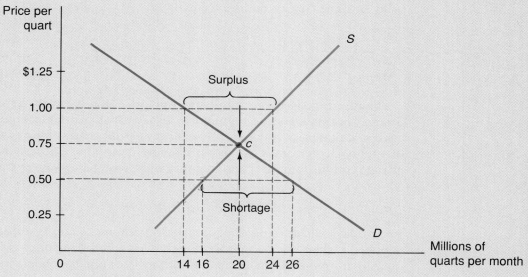

Market equilibrium occurs at a price at which the quantity demanded by consumers is equal to the quantity supplied by producers. This is shown at point c. At prices above the equilibrium price, the quantity supplied exceeds the quantity demanded; at these prices there is a surplus, and there is downward pressure on the price. At prices below equilibrium, quantity demanded exceeds quantity supplied; the resulting shortage puts upward pressure on the price.

Equilibrium is a situation in which the plans of buyers match the plans of sellers; no market forces are present that would cause price or quantity to change.

ducers are willing and able to sell, the market is said to be in equilibrium. In **equilibrium**, the independent wishes of both buyers and sellers exactly match, so market forces will exert no pressure for a change in price or quantity.

In panel (b) of Exhibit 5, the eye is drawn to the intersection of the demand and supply curves, identified as point *c*. At this *equilibrium point*, the *equilibrium price* is $0.75 per quart and the *equilibrium quantity* is 20 million quarts per month. At the equilibrium price and quantity, the market *clears*;

there is no shortage or surplus. Once equilibrium is achieved, there will be no tendency for price or quantity to change as long as demand and supply remain unchanged.

Note that an equilibrium is achieved through the independent actions of thousands, or even millions, of buyers and sellers in the market. Prices are signals of relative scarcity. The equilibrium price rations the product to those consumers most willing and able to pay that price. In one sense the market is very personal because each consumer and producer makes a personal decision regarding how much to buy or sell at a given price. In another sense the market is very impersonal because it typically involves no conscious coordination among consumers or producers. *Impersonal market forces synchronize the personal and independent decisions of many individual buyers and many individual sellers to determine equilibrium price and quantity.* At the equilibrium price, all consumers buy the amount they want, all producers sell the amount they want, and the two amounts are equal.

CHANGES IN EQUILIBRIUM PRICE AND QUANTITY

Equilibrium is that combination of price and quantity at which the desires of demanders and suppliers are exactly matched. Once equilibrium is achieved, that price and quantity will prevail unless one of the determinants of supply or demand changes. A change in any one of these factors will change equilibrium price and quantity in a predictable way, as we shall see.

Impact of Demand Shifts on Equilibrium Price and Quantity

In Exhibit 6 the initial equilibrium price and quantity of milk are as depicted earlier: the price is $0.75 per quart and the quantity is 20 million quarts per month. Suppose that one of the determinants of demand changes in a way that shifts the demand curve to the right from D to D'. Any of the following changes could result in such a shift: (1) an increase in consumer income (as long as milk is a normal good); (2) an increase in the price of a substitute, such as juice, or a decrease in the price of a complement, such as cereal; (3) a change in consumers' expectations that encourages them to buy more milk now; (4) an increase in the number of consumers; or (5) a change in consumer tastes—based, for example, on a growing awareness that the calcium in milk builds stronger bones.

After the increase in demand, as reflected in Exhibit 6, the quantity demanded at the original price of $0.75 is 30 million quarts, which obviously exceeds the quantity supplied of 20 million quarts. Thus the quantity demanded exceeds the quantity supplied by 10 million quarts. This shortage puts upward pressure on the price. As the price increases, the quantity demanded decreases along the new demand curve and the quantity supplied increases until the two are in equilibrium once again. The new equilibrium price is $1 per quart, and the new equilibrium quantity is 24

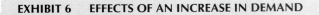

EXHIBIT 6   EFFECTS OF AN INCREASE IN DEMAND

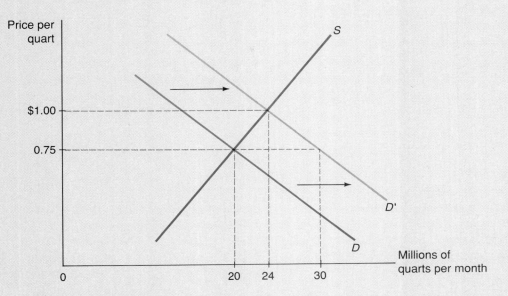

After an increase in demand shifts the demand curve from *D* to *D′*, quantity demanded exceeds quantity supplied at the old price of $0.75 per quart. As the price rises, quantity supplied increases along supply curve *S*, and quantity demanded falls along demand curve *D′*. When the new equilibrium price of $1 per quart is reached, the quantity demanded will once again equal the quantity supplied. Both price and quantity are higher following the increase in demand.

million quarts per month. Thus, given an upward–sloping supply curve, an increase in demand increases both the equilibrium price and the equilibrium quantity. In contrast, a decrease in the demand curve would result in a lower equilibrium price and quantity. We can summarize these results as follows: *as long as the supply curve slopes upward and is unchanging, any increase or decrease in demand will change equilibrium price and quantity in the **same** direction as the change in demand.*

Impact of Supply Shifts on Equilibrium Price and Quantity

In Exhibit 7 the initial equilibrium price is $0.75 per quart and the initial equilibrium quantity is 20 million quarts. Suppose one of the determinants of supply changes, resulting in a supply increase from *S* to *S′*. Consider the kinds of changes that could shift the supply curve to the right: (1) improved technology in milk production, such as a more efficient milking machine; (2) a reduction in the price of a resource, such as electricity; (3) a reduction in the price of an alternative good, such as corn; (4) a change in expectations that encourages farmers to produce more milk now; or (5) an increase in the number of dairy farmers.

EXHIBIT 7   EFFECTS OF AN INCREASE IN SUPPLY

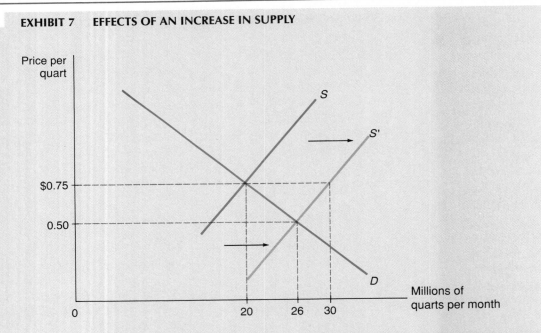

An increase in supply is depicted as a shift to the right in the supply curve, from *S* to *S'*. At the new equilibrium, quantity is higher and price is lower than before the increase in supply.

After the shift in supply in Exhibit 7, the quantity supplied at the initial equilibrium price of $0.75 increases to 30 million quarts, yielding a 10-million-quart surplus at the initial price. This surplus forces the price down. As the price falls, the quantity supplied falls along the new supply curve and the quantity demanded increases until a new equilibrium point is established. The new equilibrium price is $0.50 per quart, and the new equilibrium quantity is 26 million quarts. As a result of the increase in supply, the equilibrium price falls and the equilibrium quantity rises.

Alternatively, a reduction in supply—that is, a shift to the left in the supply curve—will cause the equilibrium quantity to fall but the equilibrium price to rise. Thus, *a shift in the supply curve, with the demand curve held constant, will cause the equilibrium quantity to change in the same direction as the change in supply but will cause the equilibrium price to change in the opposite direction.* An easy way to remember this is to picture the supply curve moving along a given downward-sloping demand curve. As the supply curve shifts to the left, price increases but quantity decreases; as the supply curve shifts to the right, price decreases but quantity increases.

Simultaneous Shifts in Supply and Demand

As long as only one curve shifts at a time, we can say what will happen to the equilibrium price and quantity. But if both curves shift simultaneously, the outcome is less obvious. For example, suppose a decline in the price of chocolate chip cookies increases the demand for milk. At the same time, a technological development increases the supply of milk. As we shall see, such shifts increase the equilibrium quantity, but the effect on the equilibrium price depends on which shifts more, supply or demand. In panel (a) of Exhibit 8, demand shifts more than supply. In panel (b), supply shifts more than demand. In both panels, the equilibrium quantity increases; the equilibrium price, however, rises in panel (a) and falls in panel (b). The effect on the equilibrium price depends on the shift in demand *relative* to the shift in supply. If the shift in demand is greater, as in panel (a), the equilibrium price increases. If the shift in supply is greater, as in panel (b), the equilibrium price falls.

Conversely, if both curves decrease, the equilibrium quantity decreases, but again we cannot say what will happen to the equilibrium price unless we examine the relative shifts. (You can picture reductions in supply and demand in Exhibit 8 by imagining that D' and S' are the initial curves.) If the reduction in demand exceeds the reduction in supply, the price will fall. If the reduction in supply exceeds the reduction in demand, the price will rise. What will happen to equilibrium price when both curves shift in the same direction can be summarized as follows: *if the shift in demand is greater, the equilibrium price will increase when both curves shift to the right and will decrease when both curves shift to the left.*

If supply and demand move in opposite directions, without reference to

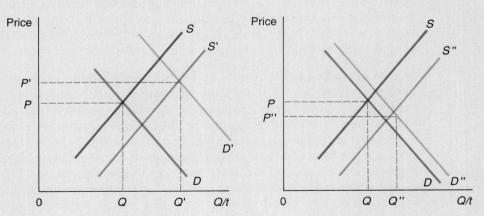

**EXHIBIT 8   INDETERMINATE EFFECT OF AN INCREASE IN BOTH SUPPLY
AND DEMAND**

(a) Shift in demand dominates   *(b) Shift in supply dominates*

When both supply and demand increase, the quantity exchanged—the equilibrium quantity—also increases. The effect on price depends on which curve shifts farther. In panel (a), the shift in demand is greater than the shift in supply; as a result, the price rises. In panel (b), the shift in supply is greater, so the price falls.

EXHIBIT 9   EFFECTS OF CHANGES IN BOTH SUPPLY AND DEMAND

	Change in Demand	
	Demand Increases	**Demand decreases**
Supply increases	Equilibrium price change is indeterminate. Equilibrium quantity increases.	Equilibrium price falls. Equilibrium quantity change is indeterminate.
Supply decreases	Equilibrium price rises. Equilibrium quantity change is indeterminate.	Equilibrium price change is indeterminate. Equilibrium quantity decreases.

Change in Supply

When the supply and demand curves shift in the same direction, equilibrium quantity also shifts in that direction; the effect on equilibrium price depends on which curve shifts more. If the curves shift in opposite directions, equilibrium price will move in the same direction as demand; the effect on equilibrium quantity depends on which curve shifts more.

---

particular shifts we cannot say what will happen to the equilibrium quantity, but we can say what will happen to the equilibrium price: the equilibrium price will increase if demand increases and supply decreases, and the equilibrium price will decrease if demand decreases and supply increases. These results are probably somewhat confusing to you, but Exhibit 9 summarizes the possibilities. Take time now to think about some hypothetical shifts in supply and demand to develop an understanding of the process.

Markets are efficient devices for allocating scarce resources to their highest-valued use. The measure of value is consumers' willingness and ability to pay. In a market economy, those who are unable to pay go without. Many people view this feature of the market system as a flaw. Some observers are troubled, for example, that more than $20 billion is spent each year on pet food at a time when thousands of homeless people are sleeping on the nation's streets. On your next trip to the supermarket, notice how much shelf space is devoted to pet products—often an entire aisle. In the next section we consider some ways in which government intervenes in markets to redirect production and consumption.

DISEQUILIBRIUM PRICES

A surplus triggers market forces that exert downward pressure on the price; a shortage exerts upward pressure on the price. Markets, however, do not always attain equilibrium instantaneously. During the time it takes to adjust, the market is said to be in disequilibrium. *Disequilibrium* is usually a temporary phase while the market gropes for equilibrium. But at times, as a result of government intervention, disequilibrium can last a long time. We will consider some of the ways in which market forces can be subverted.

Price Floors

Prices are sometimes fixed at a level above the equilibrium value. For example, the federal government often regulates the prices of agricultural commodities in an attempt to ensure farmers a higher and more stable income than they would otherwise have. To achieve higher prices, the government sets a *minimum*, or a *floor*, on the price at which certain farm products can be sold. The effect of this floor on the milk market is shown in panel (a) of Exhibit 10, where we assume that a minimum price of $1 per quart has been established. At that price farmers supply 24 million quarts per month, but consumers demand only 14 million quarts. Thus the price floor results in a surplus of 10 million quarts.

Unless this surplus is somehow eliminated, it will create downward

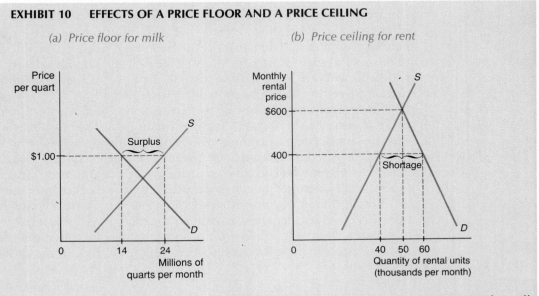

EXHIBIT 10   EFFECTS OF A PRICE FLOOR AND A PRICE CEILING

(a) *Price floor for milk*   (b) *Price ceiling for rent*

If a price floor is established above the equilibrium price, a permanent surplus will result. A price floor established at or below the equilibrium price will have no effect. If a price ceiling is established below the equilibrium price, a permanent shortage will result. A price ceiling established at or above the equilibrium price will have no effect.

pressure on the price of milk. So, as part of the price support program, the government agrees to buy the surplus milk to take it off the market. The federal government, in fact, spends billions of dollars each year on surplus agricultural goods. The government tries on occasion to distribute this surplus to the poor here and abroad, but the government's distribution must not displace market demand since a drop in demand would increase the surplus even more. Thus the government simply stores much of the surplus.

Price Ceilings

Sometimes public officials try to keep prices below their equilibrium values by establishing a *maximum*, or a *ceiling*, on the price that can be charged. For example, concern about the rising cost of rental housing in some cities prompted legislation that imposed rent ceilings. Panel (b) depicts the supply and demand for rental housing in a hypothetical city; the number of rental units is measured on the horizontal axis, and the monthly rent on the vertical axis. The equilibrium, or market-clearing, price is $600 per month, and the equilibrium quantity is 50 thousand housing units.

Assume that the ceiling on rents has been set at $400 per month. At that price 60 thousand rental units are demanded, but only 40 thousand are supplied, resulting in a shortage of 20 thousand units. With so much excess demand, price no longer serves as a sufficient mechanism to fully ration housing units to those who value the housing most highly. Consequently, other rationing devices emerge, such as waiting lists, political connections, and the willingness to pay under-the-table charges, such as "key fees," "finder's fees," excessive deposits, and the like. Advocates of rent control often ignore the secondary effects that such ceilings have on the quantity of housing supplied and demanded. And the rentals that are available do not go to those who are most needy. Many of the rich and famous who live at fancy addresses in New York City reportedly pay only about 20 percent of the market price for their rent-controlled apartments.

Government restrictions distort the market's ability to ration goods to those consumers who value them most highly. The problem is that artificially high prices encourage too much production, whereas artificially low prices discourage sufficient production and encourage consumption. These restrictions will give rise to various nonprice allocation devices to deal with the surpluses or shortages produced by the market interference.

Not all disequilibrium situations are caused by government. Although our market-adjustment model assumes the market will adjust rather quickly to equate quantity supplied with quantity demanded, often the adjustment process can take months or even years, as you will see in the case study.

CASE STUDY

Supply and Demand in the Cabbage Patch

The toy business is not much fun. Each year thousands of new toys are introduced and thousands are dropped. A few toys have staying power, such as G.I. Joe, who, with over twenty-five years in the service, could collect military retirement benefits, and Barbie, who has been all dolled up for over thirty years. But those are rare exceptions. Most toys don't survive from one season to the next.

Store buyers must order in February for Christmas delivery. Can you imagine the uncertainty of this market? Who, for example, could have anticipated the phenomenal success of the Cabbage Patch Kids, Nintendo, or Teenage Mutant Ninja Turtles? Although more than twenty million Cabbage Patch dolls were sold for $30 each between mid-1983 and the end of 1984, there was still excess demand. When the established price is below the equilibrium level, price does not serve as a full rationing mechanism, so other rationing schemes take over. The most dramatic forms of rationing were the near riots that broke out each time a store sprouted a new patch of dolls. Stores established waiting lists to allocate their monthly allotments, and the waits lasted up to eight months.

The inability of the manufacturer to keep up with the quantity demanded attracted others into the market. For example, boatloads of counterfeit dolls were reportedly pouring into the country from overseas. Some of these illegal aliens were detained at the border, but many more made it through. Classified ads also appeared, offering dolls for as much as $250. Another rationing scheme was practiced by some car dealers and furniture stores that promised to throw in a free doll to anyone making a major purchase. These different responses could have been predicted in a situation where the market price did not rise enough to eliminate excess demand.

Why didn't Coleco, the manufacturer, simply allow the price to seek its market level? Suppose, for example, that the market-clearing price had been $60, twice the established price. Consumers might have resented paying such a high price for a doll, and Coleco, a producer of a variety of toys, may not have wanted to risk criticism for being an opportunist, or a "price gouger." After all, a firm's reputation is important. Suppliers who hope to retain customers for a long time often avoid appearing greedy. That's why the local hardware store doesn't raise the price of snow shovels after the first winter storm, and why K-Mart doesn't jack up the price of air conditioners during the dog days of summer.

But perhaps the doll manufacturer should have charged higher prices. Coleco's sales peaked at $600 million in 1985. Once the Cabbage Patch craze quieted down, the company lost its fizz; it filed for bankruptcy in 1988.

CONCLUSION

Although markets usually involve the interaction of many buyers and sellers, markets are seldom consciously designed by any individual or group. Just as the laws of gravity work whether or not we understand Newton's principles, market forces operate whether or not market participants grasp the logic of supply and demand. These forces arise naturally, much like the car dealers that congregate on the outskirts of town.

Supply and demand are the foundation of market economies. To build on that foundation, we must take a closer look at key economic decision makers and how they interact. In the next chapter we focus on four economic actors: households, firms, governments, and the rest of the world.

Summary

1. Demand is a relation between the price of a good and the quantity consumers are willing and able to buy per period, other things constant. According to the law of demand, the price of a good is inversely related to the quantity demanded during a given time period, other things constant. This inverse relation between price and quantity is expressed graphically by a downward-sloping demand curve.

2. Demand curves slope downward because of both the substitution and the income effect of a price change. The substitution effect arises because a decrease in the price of one good makes consumers more willing to substitute the now relatively cheaper good for other goods. The income effect arises because the real value of each consumer's income increases as the price of the good declines, making consumers more able to buy the good as the price declines.

3. The factors that can affect the demand for a product are (1) consumer income, (2) the prices of substitutes and complements, (3) consumer expectations, (4) the number of consumers in the market, and (5) consumer tastes.

4. Price and quantity supplied are usually directly, or positively, related, so the supply curve typically slopes upward. Price and quantity sup-plied are usually positively related because higher prices offer suppliers more incentive to produce and allow them to cover the higher marginal cost associated with greater output rates.

5. The factors that can affect the supply of a product are (1) the state of technology, (2) the cost of resources, (3) the prices of alternative goods, (4) producer expectations, and (5) the number of producers.

6. Demand and supply come together in a market. A major function of markets is to provide information about the price, quantity, and quality of the item for sale. Markets reduce the transaction costs of exchange — the cost of time and information required to undertake exchange. The interaction of supply and demand guides resources and products to their highest-valued use.

7. The equilibrium price and quantity exactly match the independent wishes of both buyers and sellers. Equilibrium will continue unless there is a change in one of the determinants of supply or demand. Although disequilibrium is usually a temporary phase while markets seek equilibrium, government policies sometimes create chronic shortages or surpluses.

Questions and Problems

1 (Demand and Quantity Demanded) According to the text, what variables increase the demand for normal goods? Explain why a reduction in the price of a normal good does *not* increase the demand for the good.

2. (Income Effects) Often economists use the size of the income effect to classify a good or service as a luxury or necessity. What do people commonly mean by *luxuries*, and how ple commonly mean by *luxuries*, and how would income effects be related to this meaning of *luxuries*?

3. (Shifting Demand) Using supply and demand curves, show the effect of each of the following events on the market for cigarettes:
   a. A cure for lung cancer is found.
   b. There is an increase in the price of cigars and pipes.
   c. There is a substantial increase in wages in states that grow tobacco.

d. A fertilizer that increases the yield per acre of tobacco is discovered.

e. There is a substantial rise in the price of matches and cigarette lighters.

f. An embargo is placed on foreign tobacco products.

4. (Substitutes) During 1973 and 1974, there was a sharp rise in the price of oil. How might this event be related to the subsequent rise in Cadillac sales in Eastern Kentucky and West Virginia?

5. (Equilibrium) Determine whether each of the following is true or false. Then provide a short explanation for your answer.

a. At equilibrium, all sellers can find buyers.

b. At equilibrium, no buyer is willing and able to buy more than that buyer is being sold.

c. At equilibrium, there is no pressure on the market to produce or to consume more than is being sold.

d. At prices *above* equilibrium, the quantity exchanged is larger than the quantity demanded.

e. At prices *below* equilibrium, the quantity exchanged is equal to the quantity supplied.

6. (Demand) Water is essential for life, whereas diamonds are not essential for life. Yet a bucket of diamonds is worth far more (in dollars) than a bucket of water. Explain why.

7. (Supply and Demand) How did each of the following affect the world price of oil? (Use basic supply and demand analysis.)

a. Tax credits for home insulation

b. Completion of the Alaskan oil pipeline

c. Decontrol of oil price ceilings

d. Discovery of oil in Mexico and the North Sea

e. Mass production of smaller and lighter automobiles

f. Increased use of nuclear power

g. Increased fighting among OPEC members

8. (Price Floor) There is considerable interest in whether the minimum wage rate contributes to teenage unemployment. Draw a supply and demand diagram for the unskilled labor market and discuss the effects of a minimum wage. Who is helped, and who is hurt? Does the minimum wage make society worse off?

9. (Price Ceiling) Often a sick person will have to wait a considerable amount of time to see a doctor. How is the value of the time spent in the office, along with the price of the doctor's service, related to the market-clearing price of the office visit?

10. (Supply and Demand) Tuition at many U.S. universities is rising each year. At some places the cost of attending school is approaching $20,000 per year. Using supply and demand analysis, explain why this is happening. Do you think this trend will continue?

11. (Equilibrium) If a price is not an equilibrium price, there will be a tendency for it to move to its equilibrium value. Regardless of whether the price was too high or too low to begin with, the adjustment process will increase the quantity of the good purchased. Explain, using a supply-demand diagram.

12. (Income Effects) When you move along the demand curve, you must hold income constant. Yet one reason the quantity demanded changes is an "income effect." Explain.

13. (Equilibrium) We have all observed that in December there is an increase in both the price of evergreen trees and the quantity purchased. In January, price and quantity both fall. In the case of apples, the price is lower in the fall than in the spring, and the quantity purchased is higher. How can we explain these apparently contradictory phenomena with the same theory of supply and demand?

14. (Price Ceiling) Suppose the supply and demand curves for rental housing units have the typical slopes, and that rent control establishes a rent level below the equilibrium level.

a. What happens to the quantity of housing consumed?

b. Who gains from rent control?

c. Who loses from rent control?

The Economic Actors: Households, Firms, Governments, and the Rest of the World

To develop a deeper understanding of the power of economic analysis, we must become more familiar with key actors in the economy. In this chapter we examine the four main actors: households, firms, governments, and the rest of the world. We begin with a simple model to show the interplay between households and firms, and then consider the structure, organization, and objectives of the four economic actors. You already know more than you realize about these actors; this chapter will remind you of the abundant personal experience you bring to the class. Topics discussed in this chapter include

- The circular flow
- Evolution of the household
- Household production
- Evolution of the firm

- Kinds of firms
- Rationale for government
- Tax principles
- Role of the rest of the world

THE CIRCULAR FLOW OF RESOURCES, PRODUCTS, AND INCOME

Consider the relations among the four economic actors. Households supply land, labor, capital, and entrepreneurial ability to resource markets and, in turn, demand goods and services, such as notebooks, medical care, and bananas. Household demand ultimately determines what goods and services are produced. Thus, the starring role is played by households because they supply the resources for production and demand the goods and services produced.

An idea of how economic actors operate in the economy can be conveyed by the circular flow model. The **circular flow model** describes the flow of resources, products, and income among economic actors. For simplicity, we will focus initially on just two actors: households and firms. Exhibit 1 depicts their interaction in a circular pattern, with households on the left and firms on the right. Households demand goods and services in the *product market* and supply land, labor, capital, and entrepreneurial ability to the *resource market*. Households ultimately own all resources. Firms supply goods and services to the product market and demand land, labor, capital, and entrepreneurial ability in the resource market. Supply and demand in the product market determine equilibrium prices for goods and services. Supply and demand in the resource market determine equilibrium prices for resources.

Let's make one loop around the circular flow using a particular good. Suppose households buy a million microwave ovens, paying $300 each, the equilibrium price established in the product market. Thus household expenditures and firm revenue both amount to $300 million, as reflected by the flow of spending in the upper half of Exhibit 1. Firms use this revenue to pay resource owners for land, labor, capital, and entrepreneurial ability in the resource market (the bottom half of Exhibit 1). These resource payments flow as income to the households that supplied the resources. Note that resources and products flow in a counterclockwise direction, and the corresponding payments for these products and resources flow in the opposite direction.

*The **circular flow model** describes the flow of resources, products, and income among economic actors.*

STARRING: THE HOUSEHOLD

Households are *the* key actors in the economy. Although households usually consist of several individuals, each household is viewed as acting as a single decision-making unit. As suppliers of resources and demanders of goods and services, households make all kinds of choices, such as where to live, where to work, what to buy, and how much to save. These decisions of households are crucial factors in determining what is produced.

Households Maximize Utility

What exactly do households attempt to accomplish in making decisions? Economists assume that households attempt to maximize their level of satisfaction, sense of well-being, or overall welfare. For short, we say that households attempt to maximize **utility**. Households, like other economic actors, are viewed as rational decision makers, meaning that they act in their own best interests and would not deliberately select an option expected to make them worse off. Utility maximization is based on each household's

***Utility** is the satisfaction received from consuming a good or service.*

EXHIBIT 1   THE CIRCULAR FLOW OF RESOURCES, PRODUCTS, AND INCOME

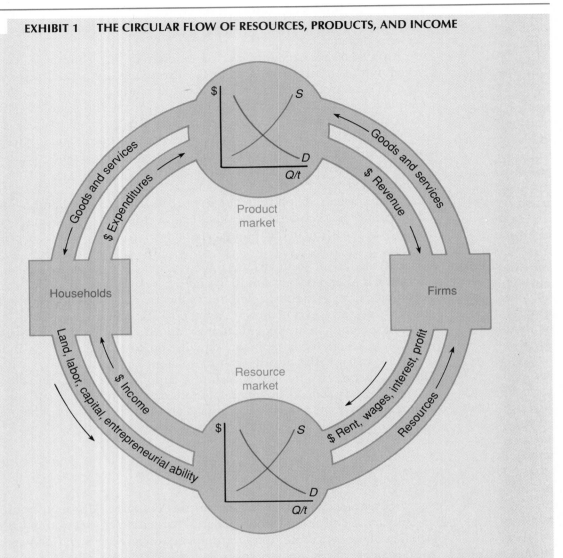

Households demand goods and services in the product market (the upper half of the circle) and supply resources to the resource market (the lower half of the circle). Firms supply goods and services to the product market and demand resources in the resource market. Products and resources flow in a counterclockwise direction; payments for these items flow in the opposite direction.

subjective goals, not on some objective standard. The subjectivity of utility allows for a wide range of household behavior, all consistent with utility maximization. Some households live in the city; others settle down in the country. Some households are large; others are small. Some households maintain a manicured front lawn; others allow junk cars to accumulate.

A House Is Not Necessarily a Home

There are more than ninety million households in the United States. All those who live under one roof are considered part of the same household. When we think of the household, we usually think of Mom, Dad, the kids, and Rover. However, the two-parent household, though still in the majority, is less common now than it once was. In 1950 married couples made up 78 percent of households, but in 1988 they numbered less than 57 percent. The major shifts have been in the percentage of households with women as family heads, which increased from 8 percent to 12 percent, and in the percentage of households consisting of people living alone or with unrelated individuals, which has climbed from 11 to 28 percent of all households. Because of these shifts, the size of the average household has decreased by over 20 percent since 1950.

Households as Resource Suppliers

Households use their limited resources in an attempt to satisfy their unlimited wants. They can use these resources to produce goods and services in their homes—they can prepare their own meals or fix that leaky roof, for example. Or they can sell these resources in the resource market and use the income to buy goods and services in the product market.

Labor is the most valuable resource owned by most households. Unfortunately, members of some households, because of poor education, disability, or bad luck, have few resources that are valued in the resource market. Also, many single parents must remain at home to care for small children. Society has made the political decision that individuals in such circumstances are entitled to some form of public assistance. Thus, some households receive **transfer payments** from the government. *Cash transfers* are monetary payments, such as Aid to Families with Dependent Children or Social Security benefits. *In-kind transfers*, such as food stamps and free medical care, support specific goods and services.

Transfer payments are cash or in-kind benefits received by individuals as outright grants from government.

Exhibit 2 shows the various sources of personal income received by U.S. households in a typical year. As you can see, about two-thirds of personal income comes from wages and salaries. A distant second on the list is interest earnings, followed by cash transfer payments and proprietors' income. *Proprietors* are people who work for themselves rather than for employers—farmers, plumbers, and doctors are examples. Less than 3 percent of personal income is received in the form of rents and dividends. Thus, *the majority of personal income in the United States is derived from labor earnings rather than from the ownership of other resources such as capital and land.*

Households as Demanders of Goods and Services

What happens to personal income once it comes into the household? Households can allocate their income in three ways. They can spend it on

EXHIBIT 2
SOURCES OF PERSONAL INCOME IN 1989

Source	Billions of Dollars	Percent of Total
Wages and salaries	2880.4	65
Personal interest	657.8	15
Transfer payments	417.9	9
Proprietors' income	352.2	8
Dividends	112.4	2
Rental income	8.0	1
Total	4428.7	100

Source: *Economic Report of the President*, February 1990.

privately provided goods and services such as food and housing; such household spending is called *personal consumption*. About 80 percent of U.S. personal income went to such expenditures in 1989. They can save it; about 5 percent is usually saved. Or they can pay it to the government as taxes to support publicly provided goods and services and transfer payments. About 15 percent of U.S. personal income goes to taxes. Because decisions about government are made by all voters collectively through some sort of public process, each individual household has little say about the percentage of income allocated to taxes.

Personal consumption is divided into three broad categories: (1) consumption of *durable goods*, such as refrigerators and cars, (2) consumption of *nondurable goods*, such as potato chips and soap, and (3) consumption of *services*, such as medical care and bus rides. Of the amount spent on personal consumption in 1989 in the United States, 14 percent was on durable goods, 32 percent was on nondurable goods, and 54 percent was on services, up from 47 percent a decade earlier. The services sector is the fastest-growing area of personal consumption because many activities, such as entertainment and meal preparation, that formerly were carried out in the household are now more often purchased in the market. The changes that have occurred in the household deserve closer attention.

The Evolution of the Household

In earlier times, when the economy was primarily agricultural, roles for individual family members reflected the division of labor and specialization of tasks on the farm. Parents were assisted in these tasks by their many children, who often specialized in specific chores. The household as an economic unit was much more self-sufficient than is the modern household. Food, clothing, and shelter were produced primarily within the household. Farm products not required for domestic consumption were sold in the market, and the money was used to purchase tools and any other special items that could not be produced by the household.

With the introduction of new seed varieties, fertilizers, and labor-saving machinery, farm productivity increased sharply. The invention of the reaper, for example, allowed one farmer to accomplish what previously had taken many to do. Therefore, not as many farm hands were needed to grow enough food to feed a nation. Simultaneously, the growth of factories in the cities created an increased demand for labor in urban areas. As a result, more people moved from farms to the cities, where they were far less self-sufficient.

Since World War II, the household has continued to change in important ways. Perhaps most significant has been the dramatic increase in the number of married women in the U.S. labor force. In 1950 only about 15 percent of married women with children under eighteen years of age were in the labor force, compared with more than 50 percent today. Economists who have studied the matter argue that the greater demand for labor was the primary reason for the rising tide of married women in the work force. Rising wages and expanded job possibilities have increased the opportunity cost of working in the home. Many women found opportunities in the labor market more attractive than those available at home.

The rise of the two-earner household has affected the family as an economic unit. Less production takes place in the home, and more goods and services are demanded in the market. For example, child-care services, fast food, and frozen dinners have displaced some household production. Since less is produced in the home, there is less need for a division of labor in household production. The rise of the two-worker family therefore reduced the advantages of specialization within the household—a central feature of the farm family. Nonetheless, some production still occurs in the home. The decisions about what is produced in the home and what is purchased in the market will be explored in the next section.

SUPPORTING ACTOR: THE FIRM

As noted earlier, the household once built its own home, made its own clothes and furniture, grew its own food, and provided its own entertainment. Over time, however, the efficiency gains from comparative advantage resulted in a greater specialization among resource suppliers. What we explore in this section is why *firms* evolved to promote this greater specialization.

Transaction Costs and Evolution of the Firm

Specialization and comparative advantage explain why households gradually became less self-sufficient, but why couldn't households specialize? Why was the firm necessary to capture the gains arising from specialization? Suppose a consumer wanted to buy a sweater. Couldn't that consumer take advantage of specialization by relying on some household that raised sheep for the wool, another that spun the wool into yarn, a third that dyed the yarn, and finally a household that knit the yarn into a sweater?

Production could occur through such household specialization, but the consumer would have to reach separate agreements with each specialist about quantity, quality, and price. How much wool would be needed? How much time would be required to spin the wool into yarn? How much yarn of each color would be necessary? Thus, transacting each contract would involve much information and much time. These *transaction costs* could easily erase the efficiency gains arising from the greater specialization of labor.

Instead of negotiating with each specialist, the consumer could simply purchase the sweater from someone who would do all that bargaining. The consumer could buy the sweater from an *entrepreneur* who contracted for all the resources necessary to knit a sweater. The entrepreneur, by arranging for the production of many sweaters rather than just one, specializes in resource contracting and is thereby able to reduce the transaction costs per sweater.

The Cottage Industry Era For hundreds of years, profit-seeking entrepreneurs relied on "putting out" raw material such as wool and cotton to rural households that turned this raw material into finished goods. The system developed on the British Isles, where workers' simple thatched cottages served as tiny factories, each specializing in one stage of production. This approach to production, which came to be known as the *cottage industry* system, imposed much of the production costs on workers, who used their own homes and their own equipment. All the entrepreneur needed was the ability to transport and store the raw material and the finished goods. The cottage industry system still exists in some parts of the world today.

The Industrial Revolution As the economy began to expand in the eighteenth century, entrepreneurs began organizing the various stages of production under one roof. Technological developments increased the productivity of each worker and contributed to the shift of employment from the farm to the factory. *Work thus became organized in large, centrally powered factories, which promoted a more efficient division of labor, the direct supervision of production, reduced transport costs, and the use of machines far bigger than anything that had been used in the home.* The development of large-scale factory production came to be known as the *Industrial Revolution*, which began in Great Britain and subsequently spread to other parts of the world.

The Firm Thus, production has evolved from self-sufficient, rural households through the cottage industry system to the current system of handling much production under one roof. Today, entrepreneurs combine resources in firms such as factories, mills, offices, stores, and restaurants. **Firms** are therefore economic units formed by profit-seeking entrepreneurs, who combine the other resources—land, labor, and capital—to produce goods and services. *Firms are convenient devices for reducing the transaction costs involved in hiring and directing a variety of resources to produce a particular good or service.* Just

Firms are economic units, formed by profit-seeking entrepreneurs, that employ resources to produce goods and services.

as we assume that households attempt to maximize utility, we assume that firms attempt to *maximize profit*.

Why Does Household Production Still Exist?

If firms are such convenient units for reducing the transaction costs of bringing together specialized resources, why doesn't all production occur within firms? Why are activities such as house cleaning, meal preparation, and child care still undertaken primarily by households and not by firms? Indeed, some people repair their own cars, paint their own homes, and perform many other tasks that are also performed by firms. Why hasn't all productive activity shifted to the market? In general, if a household's opportunity cost of performing a task is less than the market price, the task will usually be performed by the household. The households with the lowest opportunity cost of time will do more for themselves. For example, whereas janitors typically would mow their own lawns, physicians might hire someone to do the job. Consider some of the factors that could make household production relatively more attractive than firm production.

Some Household Production Requires Few Specialized Resources As efficient as firms are at reducing the transaction costs of bringing specialized resources together, some activities require so few specialized resources that households may find it cheaper to do these jobs themselves. Sweeping the floor requires only a broom and some time and is usually performed by household members. Shampooing the rug, however, can involve expensive machinery and specialized skills, and thus this service is often purchased in the market. Similarly, although you would not hire someone to brush your teeth, filling a cavity is another matter. Household tasks that demand neither particular skills nor specialized machinery are usually performed by household members.

Technological Advances Have Simplified Household Production Technological breakthroughs have not been confined to firms. Some machines have made time spent in household production more efficient. Vacuum cleaners, dishwashers, and microwave ovens reduce the time and often the skill required to perform household tasks. The demand for professional laundry service has declined as a result of the invention of automatic washers and dryers and wrinkle-resistant, easy-care clothing. Therefore, some technological breakthroughs have increased the household production of some services.

Household Production Avoids Taxes Income taxes, sales taxes, and other taxes are usually collected on the basis of market transactions. Suppose you are trying to decide whether to hire a painter or to paint your own house. If the income tax rate averages one-third, a painter who charges you $3000 for the job will net only $2000 after paying $1000 in taxes. In order to have the $3000 in after-tax income to pay the painter, you must earn $4500 before taxes. Because taxes take one-third of your income and one-third of the painter's income, you must earn $4500 so that the painter can net $2000 after taxes. If you paint the house, however, no taxes need be paid. The tax-free nature of do-it-yourself activity often creates a bias in favor of household production rather than market purchases.

Households Have More Control over Products Finally, some households prefer home production because it affords more personal control over the output than is available in the market. For example, many people prefer home-cooked meals to restaurant food, in part because home-cooked meals can be prepared according to individual tastes.

Why Do Some Firms Specialize?

If the firm is such an efficient device for combining resources under one roof, why aren't all phases of production combined within a single firm? For example, why do sweater companies purchase wool from other firms rather than raise their own sheep? Or why do sweater producers sell their finished products to retailers rather than directly to households? For that matter, why isn't there a single large firm that produces everything? To answer these questions, we must consider the costs and benefits of coordinating activity within the firm versus coordinating through markets.

Although firms are convenient devices for assembling and coordinating specialized factors of production under one roof, the gains from this coordination are limited. Like other people, entrepreneurs have *bounded rationality*, which means that they face limits on their ability to monitor all the specialists, exercise quality control at each stage, and keep track of the entire process. As firms draw together more and more specialized resources, the cost of all this internal coordination grows. At some point these costs exceed the benefits, so things start to go wrong. The firm tries to become a jack-of-all-trades, but ends up a master of none. Thus, firms become more efficient by purchasing certain specialized inputs from other firms. The market, relying only on the profit-maximizing motives of each entrepreneur, guides resources through the intermediate steps "as if by an invisible hand," coordinating the task of linking one firm's output with another firm's input to produce the final good.

Consequently, firms often find that they are more efficient if they specialize in a single product or in a limited range of products. For instance, many seasoned travelers are wary of eating at hotel restaurants, despite their convenience, because of the difficulty of operating both a nice hotel and a fine restaurant. Different entrepreneurs have different opinions about their abilities to coordinate production in the firm, so some hotels have restaurants and some do not.

Kinds of Firms

There are about seventeen million businesses in the United States. Two-thirds of these are small farms, small retail businesses, or small services. Each year many new firms are started, and many fail. In fact, three of five new businesses go "belly up" before their third year of operation. A firm can be organized in one of three ways: as a sole proprietorship, as a partnership, or as a corporation. The advantages and disadvantages of each structure will be examined next.

Sole Proprietorships The simplest form of organization is the **sole proprietorship**, a single-owner firm: Pop's corner store, the local realtor, the family physician. A sole proprietorship is easy to organize, and the owner is in complete control. No special legal requirements are involved; the firm simply opens for business. But the owner has unlimited liability for any debts the business incurs, so the owner's personal possessions could be sacrificed to cover such debts. Also, since the sole proprietor has no partners or other financial backers, raising start-up money can be difficult. One final disadvantage is that sole proprietorships usually go out of business upon the death of the proprietor. Sole proprietorships are the most common form of business organization, accounting for 71 percent of all businesses. Because this type of firm is typically small, however, proprietorships generate a small portion of all business sales — only 6 percent.

> *A **sole proprietorship** is a firm with a single owner who has the right to all profits and who bears unlimited liability for the firm's debts.*

Partnerships A more complicated form of business organization is the **partnership**, which involves two or more individuals who agree to contribute some of their own resources to the business in return for a share of the profit or loss. Law, accounting, and medical partnerships typify this business form. To organize, the partners simply must reach some accord about the division of responsibilities and rewards. Partners have strength in numbers and often find it easier than the sole proprietor to raise the start-up funds. But partnerships also have disadvantages. Decision making can be more difficult with partners than with a single owner. Also, usually each partner faces unlimited liability for all the debts and claims against the partnership, so one partner could lose everything because of another's mistake. Finally, the death or departure of one partner may disrupt the firm's continuity and could require a complete reorganization. The partnership is the least common form of business organization, making up only 10 percent of all firms and accounting for only 4 percent of all firm sales.

> *A **partnership** is a firm with multiple owners who share the firm's profits and who each bear unlimited liability for the firm's debts.*

Corporations By far the most complicated form of business organization is the corporation. The **corporation** is a legal entity recognized by the state through articles of incorporation. The owners of the corporation are issued shares of stock, entitling them to corporate profits in proportion to their stock ownership. The corporation has a life separate and apart from those of the owners; it can be taxed and sued as if it were a person. A major advantage of the corporate form is that many individuals — hundreds or even thousands — can pool their money to finance the firm. Incorporating therefore represents the easiest way to amass large sums of financing. Also, stockholders have *limited liability*, meaning their liability for the firm's losses is limited to the value of their stock. A final advantage of this form is that the

> *A **corporation** is a legal entity owned by stockholders, whose liability is limited to the value of their stock.*

corporation has a life of its own, even if ownership of the firm changes hands.

The corporate form has some disadvantages as well. A stockholder's ability to influence corporate policies is limited to helping elect a board of directors, who oversee the operation of the firm. Each share of stock usually carries with it one vote; the typical stockholder of a large corporation owns only a tiny fraction of the shares. Only stockholders who own a significant share of the firm exercise any real control. Whereas the income from sole proprietorships and partnerships is taxed only once, corporate income is taxed twice: first corporate profit is taxed, and then stockholder income is taxed, either as corporate dividends or as realized capital gains. A *realized capital gain* is any increase in the market value of a share that occurs between the time the share is bought and the time it is sold.

Corporations make up only 19 percent of all businesses, but because they tend to be much larger than the other two forms of business, corporate sales represent 90 percent of all business sales. Exhibit 3 summarizes the importance of each kind of business in terms of total numbers and total sales. As we have said, the sole proprietorship is the most important in terms of numbers, but the corporation is the most important in terms of sales.

EXHIBIT 3   NUMBER AND SALES OF EACH TYPE OF FIRM, 1985

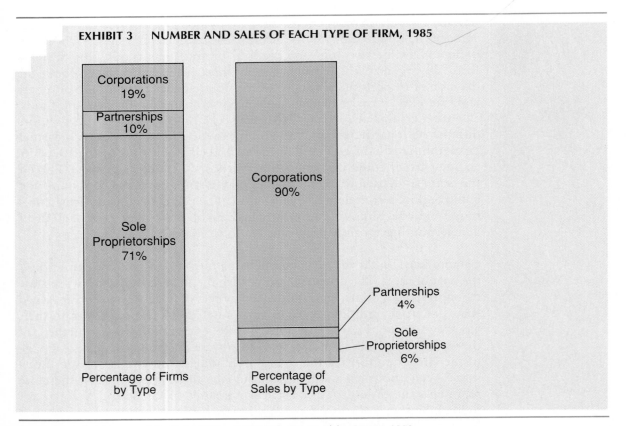

Source: *Statistical Abstract of the United States: 1989*, U.S. Bureau of the Census, 1989.

Nonprofit Institutions

To this point we have considered firms that maximize profit. But some institutions, such as nonprofit hospitals, the Red Cross, the Salvation Army, churches and synagogues, and perhaps the college you are attending, do not have profit as an explicit objective. Even these nonprofit institutions, however, must cover the cost of the resources they employ, and they raise money to do this through some combination of contributions and charges for the services they provide. When we talk about firms in this book, however, we will be referring to for-profit firms.

SUPPORTING ACTOR: THE GOVERNMENT

Why does the economy need producers other than firms? Since firms maximize profit by attempting to satisfy consumer demands, why not end the story here? Why is it necessary for yet another economic unit to get into the act? For reasons that will be examined next, voluntary exchange through private markets does not guarantee a socially desirable outcome.

The Role of Government

The unrestrained operation of markets may at times result in an allocation of resources that society finds undesirable. Too much of some goods may be produced and too little of other goods. In this section we consider the sources of **market failure** and the ways in which society's welfare may be improved by government intervention.

Market failure occurs when the unrestrained operation of markets yields results that are viewed as socially undesirable.

Establishing and Enforcing the Rules of the Game Private markets are based on people like you voluntarily employing their resources to maximize their utility. What if you were robbed of your paycheck on the way home from work each week, or what if your employer told you after a week's work that you would not be paid? The system of private markets would break down if you could not safeguard your private property or if you could not enforce contracts. Governments play a role in *protecting private property* through police protection and in *enforcing contracts* through a judicial and penal system. More generally, governments attempt to see that participants in markets abide by the "rules of the game."

Promoting Competition Although the "invisible hand" of competition generally promotes an efficient allocation of resources, some firms try to avoid market discipline through *collusion*, which is an agreement among firms on prices or market shares. Or individual firms may pursue *anticompetitive* behavior: unfair trade practices aimed at driving competitors out of business. For example, to eliminate local competitors, a large firm may temporarily sell at a price below its cost. Government *antitrust laws* are designed to *promote competition* by prohibiting collusion and other anticompetitive practices.

Regulating Natural Monopolies Typically, when a number of firms compete, resources are employed more efficiently than when only one firm, a **monopoly**, is the sole producer in a market. Certain goods and services, however, are provided more efficiently by one firm than by several firms. For example, electricity is provided more efficiently by a single firm that is responsible for all the electrical lines running through the community than by several firms that each run lines. When it is cheaper for one firm to serve the market than for two or more firms to do so, that firm is called a **natural monopoly**. Since a natural monopoly faces no price competition, the government usually regulates the prices charged by natural monopolies.

Providing Public Goods Once produced, **public goods**, such as national defense and a system of justice, are available to all. These goods will not likely be produced by private, for-profit firms, since firms cannot prevent people who fail to pay from receiving the good. Consequently, one way the demand for public goods is supported is through public financing. The government has the police power to enforce payment of the taxes or user charges that finance public goods.

Dealing with Externalities Another problem with private, competitive markets is that not all the costs and benefits of consumption or production are reflected in market prices. Market exchange reflects only the *private*, or personal, costs and benefits of buyers and sellers. But some consumption or production may impose *external* costs or *external* benefits on the rest of society. **Externalities** are unpriced by-products of production or consumption that impose external costs or external benefits on some people who are not directly involved in the transaction. *Negative externalities* impose external costs, such as the harm caused by factory pollution. *Positive externalities* convey external benefits, such as the benefits neighbors enjoy when a homeowner maintains a beautiful home and lawn. Because unrestrained market prices do not reflect these externalities, governments often employ taxes, subsidies, and regulations to promote positive externalities and to discourage negative externalities.

Providing for More Equality in the Distribution of Income As noted earlier in the discussion of household income, some households may be unable to earn enough to support themselves because of a lack of education, mental or physical disabilities, or perhaps the need to care for small children at home. Since the resource markets do not guarantee households even a minimum level of income, the government often provides transfer payments to ensure some basic standard of living to all households. Nearly all people agree that, through government, society should alter some of the results of the competitive market by redistributing the fruits of the economy to the poor. (Notice the normative aspect of this economic statement.) Where the differ-

---

*A **monopoly** is the single producer of a product for which there are no good substitutes.*

*A **natural monopoly** occurs when one firm can serve a market more cheaply than two or more firms can.*

*Once produced, **public goods** are available for all residents to consume, regardless of who pays and who does not, since there is no practical way to exclude non-payers.*

*An **externality** is an unpriced by-product of consumption or production that harms or benefits individuals who are not involved in the transaction.*

ences of opinion arise is in deciding just how much redistribution is appropriate and what form that redistribution should take.

Promoting Full Employment, Price Stability, and Adequate Growth The government, through its ability to tax, to spend, and to regulate the money supply, attempts to promote full employment, price stability, and an adequate rate of growth in the economy. The government's pursuit of these objectives through its taxing and spending powers is called **fiscal policy**. The government's pursuit of these objectives through the regulation of the money supply is called **monetary policy**. The implementation of these policies is often controversial; each type of policy receives extensive scrutiny in the study of macroeconomics.

Government's Structure and Objectives

The United States has a *federal system* of government, meaning that responsibilities are shared across levels of government. The state government grants some powers to local government and surrenders some powers to the national, or federal, government. As the system has evolved, the federal government has primary responsibility for the security of the nation and stability of the economy. State governments support higher education and roads and, with aid from the federal government, assist those unable to care for themselves. Local governments' responsibilities include primary and secondary education, plus police and fire protection.

Perhaps the best way to understand government is by comparing it to something we have already discussed: households and firms. We will examine how government differs from these other economic actors.

Difficulty in Defining Government Objectives We assume that households maximize utility and firms maximize profits, but what assumptions can we make about government behavior? What do governments—or, more specifically, government decision makers—attempt to maximize? One problem with focusing on the government's objectives is that our federal system consists of not one government but many governments—more than eighty thousand separate jurisdictions in all. Also, the federal government was developed under a system of offsetting, or countervailing, powers among the *executive*, *legislative*, and *judicial* branches, so government does not act as a single, consistent decision maker. Even within the federal executive branch there are so many agencies and bureaus that at times they appear to be working at cross purposes. For example, at the same time the U.S. Surgeon General tries to discourage cigarette smoking, the U.S. Department of Agriculture subsidizes tobacco farmers. Given this tangle of jurisdictions, branches, and bureaus of government, one theory of government behavior is that elected officials make decisions with the objective of maximizing the number of votes they will receive in the next election. Thus, we can assume that elected officials are *vote maximizers*.

Fiscal policy is the use of government spending, taxes, and borrowing to influence aggregate economic activity.

Monetary policy is the regulation of the economy's money supply to influence aggregate economic activity.

Voluntary Exchange Versus Coercion Market exchange is based on the voluntary behavior of all firms and households associated with the transaction; no coercion is involved. If you don't like tofu, no problem—just don't buy any. In political markets, any voting rule that requires less than unanimous consent implies some government coercion. Public choices are enforced by the police power of the state. Those who fail to pay their taxes could go to jail even if they object to the programs funded by the taxes.

Absence of Market Prices Another distinguishing feature of governments is that the selling price of the output is usually either zero or some amount below the cost of that output. If you are now attending a state college or university, your tuition probably covers only about one-fourth of the total cost of providing your education. (Why are taxpayers willing to subsidize your education?) Since the revenue side of the government budget is usually separate from the expenditure side, there is no necessary link between the cost of the program and its benefits. In the market system, on the other hand, if the price of a good fails to cover its cost, the good will no longer be produced.

Size and Growth of Government

One way to consider the relative size of government participation in the economy is by measuring government spending as a share of the gross national product. The *gross national product*, or *GNP*, is the total value of all final goods and services produced in the economy each year. In 1929, the year the Great Depression began, government spending, mostly state and local, accounted for 10 percent of GNP. The federal government at that time played a minor role in the economy. In fact, during the country's first one hundred and fifty years, federal spending, except during times of war, never amounted to more than 3 percent of GNP.

The Great Depression, World War II, and a change in mainstream macroeconomic theory increased the role of the federal government in the economy. Exhibit 4 shows the big jump in federal spending during World War II and the steady growth in government spending as a percentage of the gross national product since 1950. In 1989 spending by all levels of government in the United States was 34 percent of GNP. In comparison, government spending as a percent of GNP was 46 percent in West Germany, Canada, and the United Kingdom; 50 percent in Italy; and 53 percent in France. Among countries with developed economies, only Japan, with 33 percent, had a level of government spending below the U.S. level.

The federal government accounts for about two-thirds of all government spending. Exhibit 5 gives a detailed view of the composition of federal outlays since 1940. As you can see, the percentage of federal spending allocated to defense was high during World War II, went down and up after the war, declined between the early 1950s and the mid-1970s, and has been relatively flat since then. Since the early 1950s, the fastest-growing spending area has been payments to individuals, which now make up half of the

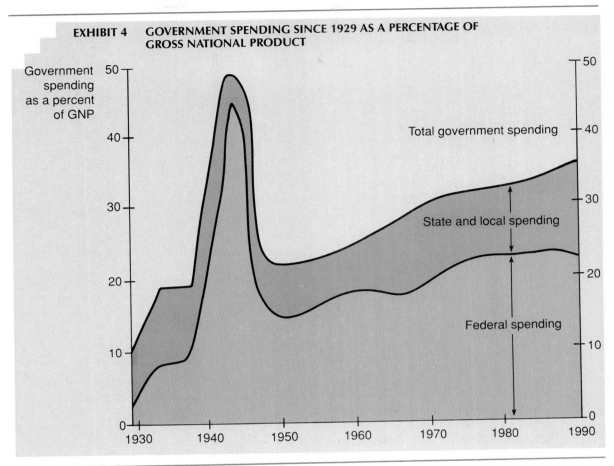

EXHIBIT 4   GOVERNMENT SPENDING SINCE 1929 AS A PERCENTAGE OF GROSS NATIONAL PRODUCT

Government spending as a percent of GNP

Total government spending

State and local spending

Federal spending

Source: *Economic Report of the President*, February 1990.

federal budget. Most important among payments to individuals are benefits for Social Security, unemployment compensation, medical care, and welfare.

Sources of Revenue

Taxes provide the bulk of revenue at all levels of government. The federal government relies primarily on the individual income tax, the state government on the sales tax, and the local government on the property tax. In addition to taxes, other revenue sources include borrowing, particularly at the federal level, and user charges, such as highway tolls and fishing licenses. Many states run lotteries designed solely to raise money. Some states also monopolize the sale of liquor—again, to raise money.

Exhibit 6 illustrates the share of each major revenue source as a percentage of all federal receipts since 1940. The individual income tax has accounted for a little over 40 percent of federal revenues since about 1945. In

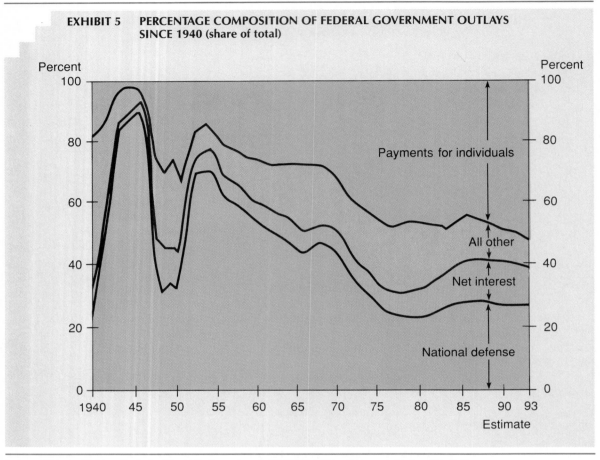

EXHIBIT 5   PERCENTAGE COMPOSITION OF FEDERAL GOVERNMENT OUTLAYS SINCE 1940 (share of total)

Source: Historical tables, *Budget of the U.S. Government, FY 1989*, Office of Management and Budget.

the early 1950s, payroll taxes accounted for only about 10 percent of federal receipts, compared to 37 percent by 1990. *Payroll taxes* are deducted from paychecks to support Social Security, unemployment benefits, and medical care for the elderly. Corporate income taxes and *excise*, or sales, taxes have generally declined as a share of the total since the 1940s, though the share of corporate income tax has increased slightly since the mid–1980s.

Tax Principles

A tax is often justified on the basis of one of two general principles. The first is that a tax should be related to the individual's *ability to pay* so that those with a greater ability pay more taxes. Income or property taxes are often based on this principle. The second tax principle is that of *benefits received*, which argues that taxes should be in proportion to the benefits the individual receives from the government activity funded by the tax. For example, the tax on gasoline, which is earmarked to fund highway construction

EXHIBIT 6   PERCENTAGE COMPOSITION OF FEDERAL GOVERNMENT RECEIPTS SINCE 1940 (share of total)

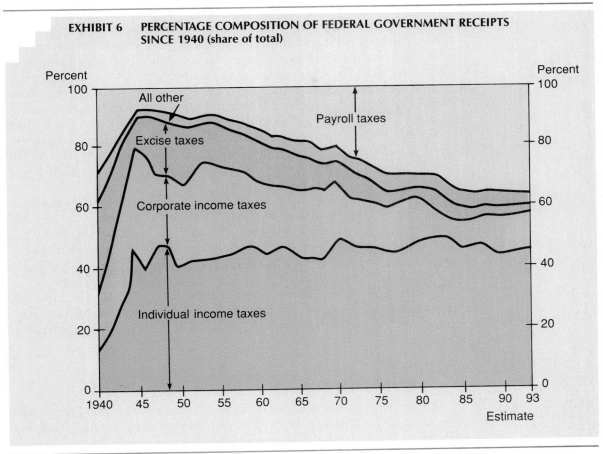

Source: Historical tables, *Budget of the U.S. Government, FY 1989*, Office of Management and Budget.

and maintenance, links the amount paid to road use. Thus, the benefits-received principle links the revenue side of the budget with the spending side of the budget. The trouble with the benefits-received principle is that benefits of government programs often cannot be traced to particular individuals, and even when the beneficiaries can be identified, these people may be too poor to pay for the benefits received.

Tax Incidence

Tax incidence indicates who actually bears the burden of a tax.

Tax incidence indicates who actually bears the burden of the tax. One way of evaluating tax incidence is by measuring the tax as a percentage of income. Under *proportional taxation*, taxpayers at all income levels pay the same percentage of their income in taxes. For example, if the proportional tax rate were 10 percent, an individual with an income of $10,000 would pay $1000 in taxes and an individual with an income of $100,000 would pay $10,000. A proportional tax is often called a *flat-rate tax* because the tax as a percentage of income remains constant as income changes.

Under *progressive taxation*, the percentage of income paid in taxes increases as income increases; that is, the marginal tax rate increases with income. The *marginal tax rate* indicates how much of each additional dollar of income must be paid in taxes. A marginal tax rate of 10 percent means a person must pay $0.10 in taxes for each additional $1 in income. High marginal rates can reduce people's incentives to work and to invest. Until 1986, the federal individual income tax had fourteen marginal tax rates, or tax brackets, starting at 11 percent and rising to 50 percent. The Tax Reform Act of 1986 reduced the number to three: 15 percent, 28 percent, and, over a limited income range, 33 percent. Thus, the individual income tax is still generally progressive, but it now has fewer rates and the difference between the bottom and top rates is less dramatic.

Under *regressive taxation*, the percentage of income paid in taxes decreases as income increases: the marginal tax rate declines as income increases. The Social Security tax is a regressive tax: in 1990 it was 7.65 percent of the first $50,400 of earnings; above $50,400 the marginal tax rate was zero. Therefore, for someone earning $100,800 the percentage of income devoted to taxes would be only half what it was for someone earning $50,400.

This discussion of revenue sources brings to a close, for now, our examination of the role of government in the economy. Government has a pervasive influence on the economy, and its role will continue to surface in our discussions.

SUPPORTING ACTOR: THE REST OF THE WORLD

Thus far we have focused on institutions within the United States — that is, on *domestic* households, firms, and governments. This initial focus was appropriate because our primary objective has been to understand the workings of the U.S. economy. But the success of the U.S. economy depends in part on the rest of the world. For example, political unrest in the Persian Gulf can interrupt the flow of oil, raising the price Americans pay for energy. Asian economies such as those of Japan and South Korea supply U.S. markets with autos, electronic equipment, and other manufactured goods, affecting U.S. prices, wages, and profits. Banks in the United States have loaned billions of dollars to developing countries, and the stability of our banks is affected by whether these loans are repaid. Thus, foreign actors have a profound effect on the U.S. economy — on the resources U.S. households supply and on the goods and services U.S. firms produce.

The *rest of the world* consists of the households, firms, and governments in more than 150 foreign countries; some of these countries have formed economic alliances, such as the European Economic Community. Because the rest of the world consists of so many economic actors, we should not view the rest of the world as maximizing any one particular objective.

International Trade

In Chapter 2 you learned about the principle of comparative advantage and the gains from specialization. These gains explain why households stopped trying to do everything for themselves and began to specialize. International trade arises for the same reasons. Simply put, if VCRs can be produced for less in South Korea than in the United States, U.S. households, if given the opportunity, will purchase VCRs imported from South Korea. Production and exchange among countries follow the law of comparative advantage. *International trade occurs because the opportunity cost of producing specific goods differs across countries.*

A country tends to export goods that require relatively large amounts of the resources it has in abundance. For example, Taiwan, with much semi-skilled labor, produces goods such as textiles that employ large amounts of this type of labor. A country tends to import goods that require relatively large amounts of its most scarce resource. For example, Taiwan imports sophisticated machinery and computers.

Trade Restrictions

Tariffs are taxes on imports or exports.

Quotas are legal limits on the quantity of a particular commodity that can be imported or exported.

Although there are clear gains from international specialization and exchange, nearly all countries impose some restrictions on trade. These restrictions can take the form of (1) **tariffs**, which are taxes on imports or exports; (2) **quotas**, which are legal limits on the quantity of a particular commodity that can be imported or exported; and (3) other restrictions, such as the agreement by Japanese car manufacturers to voluntarily limit their exports to the United States from 1981 to 1985.

If specialization according to comparative advantage is so beneficial, why do most countries restrict trade? Restrictions are introduced primarily to benefit some domestic producers, although such protection occurs at the expense of domestic consumers. For example, U.S. textile manufacturers, facing stiff competition from foreign producers, have sought and received protective legislation to restrict textile imports. As a result, the price of textiles in the United States is higher than it would be without the restrictions. Such restrictions interfere with the free flow of products across borders and tend to harm the overall economy.

Exchange Rates

Foreign exchange is the currency of another country needed to carry out international transactions.

The exchange rate measures the price of one currency in terms of another.

Trade across international borders is complicated by the lack of a common currency. How many U.S. dollars are required to purchase a Mercedes selling for 100,000 marks in West Germany? An American customer who purchases the auto cares only about the dollar cost; the West German manufacturer cares only about the marks received.

To facilitate trade between nations, a market for foreign exchange has developed. **Foreign exchange** is the currency of another country needed to carry out international transactions. The supply and demand for foreign exchange come together in *foreign exchange markets* to yield an equilibrium exchange rate around the world. The **exchange rate** measures the price of one currency in terms of another. For example, the exchange rate between U.S. dollars and German marks might indicate that one mark can be exchanged for 52 cents. The greater the demand for a particular foreign currency or the smaller the supply, the higher its exchange rate will be — that is, the more dollars it will cost. The exchange rate affects the prices of imports and exports and thus influences the flow of foreign trade.

U.S. Trade Experience

Americans import raw materials such as crude oil and sugar and finished goods such as cameras, VCRs, and jeans. The United States exports sophisticated equipment such as computers and airplanes, as well as agricultural products such as wheat and corn. International trade between the United States and the rest of the world has been rising sharply in recent decades. In 1970 U.S. imports amounted to only about 6 percent of the gross national product. By 1989 that figure had doubled to about 12 percent of GNP. American exports have also grown, from about 7 percent of GNP in 1970 to about 10 percent in 1989. The United States' chief trading partners are Canada, Japan, Mexico, West Germany, Great Britain, France, and South Korea.

*A nation's **merchandise trade balance** during a particular time period equals the value of commodities exported minus the value of commodities imported.*

The **merchandise trade balance** equals the value of commodities exported minus the value of commodities imported. In recent years the United States has experienced a *deficit* in its merchandise trade balance, meaning that the value of U.S. imports has exceeded the value of U.S. exports. In 1989 this deficit amounted to $113 billion. Just as a household must cover its spending, so too must a nation. A nation's **balance of payments** is the record of transactions between its residents and residents of the rest of the world. The balance of payments is made up of several accounts, such as the merchandise trade balance. Without detailing those accounts here, we can say that a deficit in the merchandise trade balance must be offset by surpluses in one or more of the other balance-of-payments accounts. During most of the 1980s, Americans were consuming more than they were producing and were borrowing from abroad to finance the difference. Americans now owe more to the rest of the world than does any other nation.

*A nation's **balance of payments** is the record of transactions between its residents and residents of the rest of the world.*

CONCLUSION

In this chapter we examined the four most important economic actors in the economy: households, firms, governments, and the rest of the world. Domestic households are by far the most important actors, for they, along with foreign households, supply all the resources and demand the goods and services produced. In recent years the U.S. economy has come to depend more on the rest of the world both for products and as a source of investment funds.

This chapter completes our introduction to economics. From now on discussion will focus primarily on either macroeconomics or microeconomics.

Summary

1. There are four kinds of actors in the economy: households, firms, governments, and the rest of the world. Households are the key actors because they supply the resources employed and demand the goods and services produced.

2. Most household income arises from the sale of labor, and most household income is spent on personal consumption. Personal consumption consists of expenditures on durable goods, nondurable goods, and services—the fastest-growing portion of personal consumption. Income not spent on personal consumption is either saved or paid as taxes.

3. Firms are convenient devices for bringing together specialized resources. But when the net benefits of organizing production within the firm are exhausted, market exchange becomes a more efficient way to coordinate production. The market, relying only on the profit motives of each firm, guides resources through the intermediate stages required to produce the final good.

4. Firms can be organized in three different ways: as sole proprietorships, partnerships, or corporations. The sole proprietorship is the most common form of business organization, and the partnership the least common form. Because the corporation is typically large, corporations account for the bulk of all firms' sales.

5. When private markets give rise to socially undesirable results, voters seek government inter-

vention to correct these market failures. Government programs are designed to (1) protect private property and enforce contracts; (2) promote competition; (3) regulate natural monopolies; (4) provide public goods and services; (5) discourage negative externalities and promote positive externalities; (6) provide for greater equality in the distribution of income; and (7) promote full employment, price stability, and growth.

6. Taxes are the primary source of revenue to fund public programs. Other revenue sources include user charges and borrowing. The federal government in the United States relies primarily on the personal income tax, states on the sales tax, and localities on the property tax. A tax is usually based either on the individual's ability to pay the tax or on the benefits the individual receives from those activities financed by the tax.

7. The rest of the world is also populated by households, firms, and governments. Despite the gains from comparative advantage that arise from international trade, nearly all countries introduce trade restrictions to protect specific industries. Since trade involves two different currencies, a rate of exchange between these currencies is established in foreign exchange markets. The transactions between the residents of one country and the residents of the rest of the world are summarized in the balance of payments.

Questions and Problems

1. (Consumption) It is now well known that the service sector of the U.S. economy has been growing very fast. Many economists claim that this sector will provide most new jobs in the future. What services will be important in the future, and what skills, if any, will be

needed by the workers in those industries?

2. (Consumption) What factors come into play when a consumer considers buying a durable good such as an automobile or a refrigerator?

3. (Household Production) Technological breakthroughs have made household production possible in some cases. What are some technological advances that have made household production of entertainment possible? How has the entertainment industry reacted to such devices?

4. (Household Production) Many households supplement their food budget by cultivating small vegetable gardens. Explain how each of the following might affect this kind of household production:
   a. Both husband and wife are professionals earning high salaries.
   b. The household is located in the city rather than in the country.
   c. The household is located in the South rather than in the North.
   d. The household is located in a region where there is a high sales tax on food.
   e. The household is located in a region that has a high property tax rate.

5. (Specialization) Why did the institution of the firm appear after the advent of the Industrial Revolution in the nineteenth century? What type of business organization existed before this?

6. (Corporations) Why do most large businesses organize as corporations rather than as partnerships or sole proprietorships? Must corporations always be large in terms of sales and production?

7. (Government) Economists sometimes argue over whether the government should provide a particular service. However, even when everyone agrees that the government should provide the service, it must still be decided whether the government service is best provided by the local, state, or federal government. What factors are important in determining which level of government should provide the service?

8. (Government) One of the most important government services is provided by the National Weather Service. Why isn't it possible for a private weather service to provide information and predictions about the weather? Why is it necessary to have a National Weather Service?

9. (Government) Often it is said that government is necessary when private markets fail to work effectively and fairly. Based on your reading of the text, discuss how private markets might break down.

10. (Government) How is each of the following related to the various services that government is responsible for providing?
    a. The Food and Drug Administration
    b. The Pentagon
    c. The Supreme Court of the United States
    d. The progressive income tax system
    e. State-supported universities
    f. State utility rate commissions

11. (Tax Rates) Suppose taxes are related to income level as follows:

Income	Taxes
1000	200
2000	350
3000	450

    a. What percentage of income is paid in taxes at each level?
    b. Is the tax progressive, proportional, or regressive?
    c. What is the marginal tax rate on the first $1000 of income? The second $1000? The third $1000?

12. (Externality) Suppose a good has an external cost associated with its production. What's wrong with letting the market decide how much should be produced?

13. (Circular Flow) Using the circular flow diagram in Exhibit 1, show what might happen in the product and resource markets if households decided to save more of their income.

14. (International Trade) Suppose a VCR costs 10,000 yen in Japan. If the exchange rate is $1 = Y200, how much will a Japanese VCR cost here? What would the cost be if the dollar strengthened to $1 = Y250? If a bushel of wheat costs $10 in the United States, how much will it cost in Japan under each of these two exchange rates?

Fundamentals of Macroeconomics

C H A P T E R 5

Introduction to Macroeconomics

In macroeconomics we think big—not about the supply and demand for chewing gum but about the supply and demand for everything produced in the economy; not about the price of floppy disks but about the average price of all products sold in the economy; not about consumption by the Jackson household but about consumption by all households combined; not about the investment by General Motors but about the investment by all firms combined.

We are concerned not only with determining such aggregates as the level of the economy's prices, employment, and output but also with understanding the movements in these aggregates over time. What determines the ability of the economy to use available resources productively, to adapt, to grow? As we shall see, the economy has a certain rhythm of its own. We want to feel the beat. *The ultimate objective of macroeconomics is to develop and test theories about how the economy works—theories that can be used to predict the consequences of economic events.*

Economists agree less on macroeconomics than on microeconomics. Disagreement centers first on how stable the economy is and second on what should be done when the economy fails to perform as we would like. The first disagreement is over economic theory, the second over economic policy. Theory and policy intertwine more closely in macroeconomics than in microeconomics. Topics discussed in this chapter include

- The national economy
- An analogy between the human body and the economy
- The business cycle
- Aggregate demand and aggregate supply
- A short history of the U.S. economy
- Demand-side policies and supply-side economics

THE NATIONAL ECONOMY

Macroeconomics concerns the overall performance of the economy. The term *economy* can be defined as the structure of economic life or economic activity in a community, a region, a country, a group of countries, or the world. We could talk about the St. Louis economy, the Missouri economy, the Midwest economy, the U.S. economy, the North American economy, or the world economy. The performance of an economy can be measured in different ways, such as the number of individuals employed, the size and number of producers, or the average earnings of labor. One measure, however, appears to capture the most economic information and is most effective for considering the same economy over time or for comparing different economies at the same time: the gross product.

The *gross product* is the market value of final goods and services produced in a particular geographical region during a given time period, usually one year. If the focus is the Missouri economy, we consider the gross *state* product. If the U.S. economy is the object of interest, we consider the gross *national* product, an expression introduced in Chapter 4 and to be examined more carefully in Chapter 6.

What Is Special About the National Economy?

Consider the reasons for treating the national economy as a special entity. If you were to drive west on Interstate 10 in Texas, you would hardly notice crossing the state line into New Mexico. If you took the Juarez exit off I-10 south to Mexico, however, you would become quite aware that you were crossing an international border. You would have to present personal identification, provide reasons for your trip, and prepare to be searched. Like other countries of the world, the United States and Mexico typically allow freer movement of people and goods *within* their borders than *across* their borders.

The differences between the United States and Mexico are far greater than the differences between Texas and New Mexico. For example, each country has its own culture and language, its own communication and transportation systems, its own unique mix of economic resources, its own system of government, its own currency, and its own "rules of the game" — that is, its own regulations for conducting economic activity both within and across its borders. More fundamentally, each country answers the three economic questions — what is to be produced, how is it to be produced, and for whom is it to be produced — in different ways.

The focus of macroeconomics is the performance of the national and world economies. To gain some notion of the complicated nature of the U.S. economy, consider a profile of households, firms, and governments. There are more than ninety million households "getting and spending," more than seventeen million firms producing goods and services, and more than eighty thousand separate governments ensuring that dogs are properly licensed and nuclear missiles properly maintained. And there are more than one hundred and fifty sovereign countries throughout the world, ranging from Djibouti, a tiny country in East Africa with a population smaller than that of any state in the United States, to the People's Republic of China, with a population of over one billion. Such snapshots convey an idea of the economic actors, but our interest in the economy is not like a coroner's interest in a lifeless body. The economy is dynamic—living, breathing, constantly changing.

The economy is too complex to be confronted head on, which is why we use theoretical models to simplify and crystallize the key relations. Perhaps the easiest way to introduce macroeconomics is to compare the national economy to something more familiar. Let's consider the similarities and differences between the human body and the economy.

Similarities Between the Human Body and the Economy

The body is made up of millions of individual cells, each carrying out particular functions yet each linked to the operation of the entire body. Similarly, the economy is composed of millions of individual economic units, each acting with some independence yet each interconnected with the economy as a whole. The economy, like the body, is continually renewing itself, with new households, new firms, new foreign competitors, and an ever-changing cast of public officials.

Blood is a medium that circulates throughout the body, facilitating the exchange of vital nutrients among cells. Similarly, money is a medium that circulates throughout the economy, facilitating the exchange of resources and products among individual economic units. In fact, money is called a *medium of exchange*. As noted in the last chapter, the pattern traced by the movement of money, products, and resources throughout the economy is a *circular flow*, as is the pattern traced by the movement of blood and nutrients throughout the body.

Stocks and Flows Just as the same blood is recirculated again and again in the body, the same money recirculates several times during the year to finance many transactions. The same dollars you use to pay for croissants may then be used by the baker to buy butter and then by the dairy farmer to buy radial tires. We often distinguish between stocks and flows. A **stock** variable represents an amount of something at a particular time, such as the amount of blood in your body or the number of dollars in your wallet right now. A **flow** variable represents an amount per unit of time, such as heartbeats per minute or the spending in the economy per year. If a time dimension is required to convey meaning (i.e., per hour, per day, per year, etc.), the variable is a flow variable.

*A **stock** is a variable that measures the amount of something at a particular time. A **flow** is a variable that measures the amount of something over an interval of time.*

Role of Expectations In both medicine and economics, *expectations* play an important role in the performance of the system. If the patient expects a certain medicine to provide a cure, the body often promotes a cure, even if the medicine is only a sugar pill, or placebo. A similar mechanism operates in the economy. If firms expect greater demand for their products, they will invest more capital and hire more labor to produce more output. As more resources are demanded, households, as suppliers of those resources, earn greater incomes and therefore increase their demand for goods and services. Thus, when producers expect greater demand for their products, their behavior often fosters the very prosperity they expect. Negative expectations can also be self-fulfilling. If firms expect the demand for their products to fall, they will reduce their investment and cut back on employment. As the demand for resources falls, household incomes decline, thereby reducing the demand for goods and services.

Differences of Opinion Both in medicine and in macroeconomics, problems are often seen from varying viewpoints. First, diagnoses of what ails the patient or the economy may differ. Second, even when doctors or economists agree about the nature of the malady, they may disagree about the best remedy. Medicine and the other natural sciences, however, have one major advantage in the development and evaluation of new theories: the ability to test these theories in a laboratory setting.

Testing New Theories

Physicians and other natural scientists can conduct experiments under controlled conditions to test their theories, but macroeconomists have no laboratory and little ability to run experiments of any kind. Granted, economists can study the workings of many economies throughout the world. Each economy displays such a unique blend of economic conditions, however, that comparisons across countries are tricky. Testing a drug or medical procedure in a variety of circumstances offers medical researchers something that is typically unavailable to macroeconomists: an opportunity to make the chance, or serendipitous, discovery. With only one patient, the macroeconomist cannot introduce particular policies in a variety of ways. Therefore, the unexpected discovery (such as penicillin) that often characterizes breakthroughs in the natural sciences is unlikely in economics. Cries of "Eureka!" are seldom heard among macroeconomists.

Knowledge and Performance

Throughout history we had little knowledge of how the body works, yet many people enjoyed good health. Not until 1638, for example, did we discover that the blood actually circulates through the body; it took another one hundred and fifty years to determine why. Similarly, over the millenia various complex economies have developed and flourished, though at the time there was little understanding or even concern about how these economies worked.

The economy is much like the body: as long as it functions smoothly, we need not understand its operation. But if a problem develops—high inflation, severe unemployment, or stagnant growth, for example—we need to know how a healthy economy works before we can consider if and how the problem can be corrected. We need not know every detail of the economy, just as we need not know every detail of the body. But we must understand the essential relations among key elements of the economy. For example, we would like to know to what extent the economy is self-organizing and self-adjusting. Does the economy work well enough on its own, or does it generally perform so poorly as to require constant government intervention? If it does perform poorly, are there reliable public policies to ensure that the desired objectives are attained, or do corrective efforts ultimately do more harm than good?

When doctors did not understand how the body worked, the cure was often worse than the disease. Much of the history of medicine describes misguided attempts to deal with disease. As recently as the nineteenth century, medical "remedies" included "bleeding, cupping, violent purging, the raising of blisters by vesicant ointments, the immersion of the body in either ice water or intolerably hot water, endless lists of botanical extracts evoked up and mixed together under nothing more than pure whim."[1]

Likewise, national policy makers have often implemented the wrong economic prescriptions because of a flawed theory about how the economy works. At one time, for example, a nation's economic vitality was thought to spring from the stock of precious metals the nation could accumulate in its treasury. This theory spawned a policy called *mercantilism*, which restricted international trade and consequently suppressed the gains from specialization and exchange that arise from trade. As another example, when the nation was in the grip of the Great Depression, unemployment was extremely high, yet President Herbert Hoover recommended a major tax *increase* to cure the economy's ills. Policy makers have since learned that such a policy does more harm than good.

We all have some acquaintance with cycles in nature—the changing seasons, the ebb and flow of the tides, the regular movements of celestial bodies, the rhythms of the body. As we shall see, the economy also has a rhythm of its own.

THE BUSINESS CYCLE

*The **business cycle** is the rise and fall of economic activity relative to the long-term growth trend of the economy.*

Economic activity, like cycles in nature, fluctuates in a fairly regular way. The U.S. economy and other industrial market economies experience alternating periods of expansion and contraction in the level of economic activity. These fluctuations give rise to a roller coaster–like effect called the business cycle. The **business cycle** reflects the rise and fall of economic

---

[1] As described by Lewis Thomas in *The Youngest Science: Notes of a Medicine Watcher* (New York: Viking Press, 1983), 19.

activity relative to the long-term growth trend of the economy. These fluctuations in the level of economic activity vary a great deal in length and intensity, yet some features appear common to all cycles. First, these ups and downs involve the entire nation and often the world, and they affect nearly all dimensions of economic activity, not simply the employment and output levels. Second, these cycles have staying power, usually spanning several years.

Business Cycle Analysis

Perhaps the easiest way to understand the business cycle is to break it down into its components. During the 1920s and 1930s, Wesley C. Mitchell (1874–1948), Director of the National Bureau of Economic Research (NBER), became famous for his analysis of business cycles. In simplest terms, the economy, according to Mitchell, has two phases: periods of expansion and periods of contraction. Before World War II, some periods of contraction were so severe and so prolonged that they were called depressions. Although there is no official definition, a **depression** can be viewed as a severe reduction in the nation's total production accompanied by high unemployment that lasts several years. Since World War II, periods of contraction have taken a milder form called a **recession**. According to the NBER definition, a recession is a decline in the nation's total production that lasts six months or more.

Over the long run, enhanced technology and increases in the amount and quality of resources tend to expand an economy's output. Exhibit 1 shows this long-term growth trend as an upward-sloping straight line. The business cycle reflects movements around this growth trend. The exhibit depicts a full cycle. A recession begins after the previous expansion has reached its peak and continues until the economy reaches a trough. Thus, the period between the peak and the trough is called a recession, and the period between the trough and the subsequent peak is called an *expansion*.

The actual experience of the U.S. economy is pictured in Exhibit 2, which shows the growth in GNP around its trend line during the last hundred years. As you can see, the phases of the cycle vary widely in duration and in rate of change. The big declines during the Great Depression of the 1930s and the sharp gains during World War II stand in sharp contrast. Analysts at NBER have been able to track the U.S. economy back to 1854. Since then the country has gone through more than thirty expansions and contractions. No two business cycles have been exactly alike. The shortest expansion lasted only 10 months, during 1919 and 1920, and the longest was 106 months, from 1961 to 1969. The shortest contraction lasted only 6 months, in 1980; the longest lasted 65 months, from 1873 to 1879. The U.S. economy entered a period of expansion in November, 1982, that was still going as of mid-1990, making this the longest *peacetime* expansion since the 1920s.

Since 1933 the U.S. economy has completed about ten cycles. During this period peacetime expansions averaged about three years, and peacetime

*A **depression** is a severe reduction in the economy's total production, accompanied by high unemployment, that lasts several years.*

*A **recession** is a decline in the economy's total production that lasts six months or longer.*

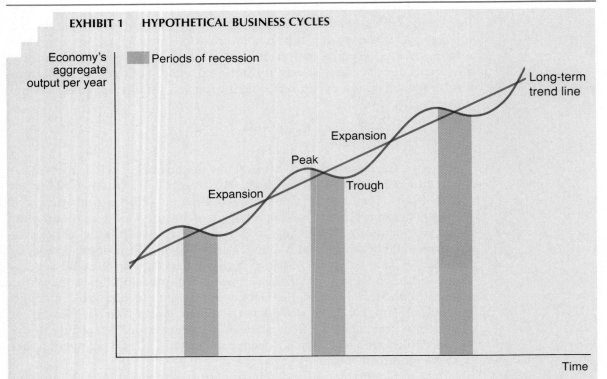

EXHIBIT 1   HYPOTHETICAL BUSINESS CYCLES

Economy's aggregate output per year

Periods of recession

Long-term trend line

Expansion

Peak

Trough

Expansion

Expansion

Time

The business cycle reflects movements of economic activity around a trend. A recession (shown in red) begins after a previous expansion has reached its peak and continues until the economy reaches a trough. An expansion begins when economic activity starts to increase and continues until the economy reaches a peak.

contractions about one year; wartime expansions were longer. In contrast, during the ten cycles preceding 1933, expansions lasted about two years, and contractions a little less than two years.[2] Not only have the recessions become shorter since 1933; they have also become less severe. Depressions were a common feature of earlier business cycles, but none has occurred since World War II. There has been a clear shift toward longer expansions and shorter contractions. The entire cycle, however, still lasts about four years on average.

Because of seasonal fluctuations, the economy does not move smoothly through the business cycle. We cannot always distinguish between short-run blips in economic activity and actual turning points in the cycle. The drop in production in a particular period may be the result of a snowstorm or a poor harvest rather than the onset of a recession. Turning points in the business cycles—peaks and troughs—are thus identified by the NBER only

[2] These data are found in Victor Zarnowitz, "Recent Work on Business Cycles in Historical Perspective," *Journal of Economic Literature 23* (June 1985): 525.

**EXHIBIT 2   HISTORICAL BUSINESS CYCLES
IN THE UNITED STATES**

Business scale (percent)

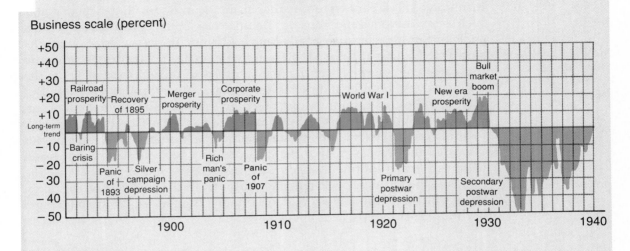

Business scale (percent)

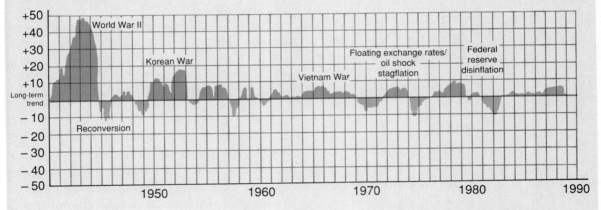

This historical chart shows the phases of the U.S. business cycle since 1890. The vertical scale indicates the percentage by which the level of business activity exceeded or fell short of the long-term trend.

Source: "American Business Activity from 1790 to Today," Ameritrust Corporation, January 1988.

after the fact. Since a recession involves declining output for two consecutive quarters, a recession is not officially so designated until at least six months after it starts.

Leading Economic Indicators

Certain events foreshadow a turning point in the business cycle. Months before a recession is fully under way, changes in the leading economic indicators portend the coming storm. In the early stages of a recession, fewer new firms are started, orders for machinery and equipment begin to fall, and the stock market, perhaps in anticipation of lower profits, begins to turn down. Households, too, reduce their spending on "big-ticket" items, such as automobiles and housing. Because residential construction permits and housing starts have especially long lead times, they slow down when the storm clouds first appear. All these activities are called **leading economic indicators** because they are the first variables to predict movements in the business cycle. Leading indicators also signal recovery from a recession. But leading indicators cannot predict precisely *when* turning points will occur.

*The **leading economic indicators** are economic statistics that foreshadow future business activity.*

Our introduction to the business cycle has been largely mechanical, focusing on the history and measurement of the business cycle. We have not discussed the reasons behind the cycle, in part because such a discussion requires a firmer footing in macroeconomic theory and in part because the causes of the business cycle remain in dispute. In the next section we begin laying the foundations for a macroeconomic framework by introducing a key model of analysis.

AGGREGATE DEMAND AND AGGREGATE SUPPLY

The economy is so complex that we need to simplify or to abstract from the millions of relations in order to capture the important elements under consideration. We must step back from all the individual economic decisions to survey the resulting mosaic. Perhaps the clearest way to characterize the operation of the entire economy is with familiar tools: demand and supply.

Aggregate Demand

The demand for food shows the relation between the average price of food and the quantity of food demanded. When we consider the demand for food, we implicitly view the average price of the diverse array of foods—from freshly picked corn to live lobsters. Moving from a specific product, fresh corn, to a general product, food, requires a higher level of abstraction, but such an aggregation process is not conceptually difficult.

Aggregate output is *the total quantity of final goods and services produced in the economy during a given time period.*

To consider aggregate demand, we must move from the demand for food or housing or clothing or entertainment to the demand for all goods and services produced in the economy—the demand for what we refer to as aggregate output. **Aggregate output** is the total quantity of final goods and services produced in the economy during a given time period. A unit of aggregate output is a composite measure of all output in the same sense that a unit of food is a composite measure of all food.

*The **aggregate demand curve** shows the relation between the general price level and the amount of aggregate output demanded per period of time.*

The **aggregate demand curve** shows the relation between the general price level—an average of all prices in the economy—and the aggregate output demanded per period of time, other things constant. Exhibit 3 presents a hypothetical aggregate demand curve, *AD*. Aggregate output per period of time is measured along the horizontal axis, and the general price

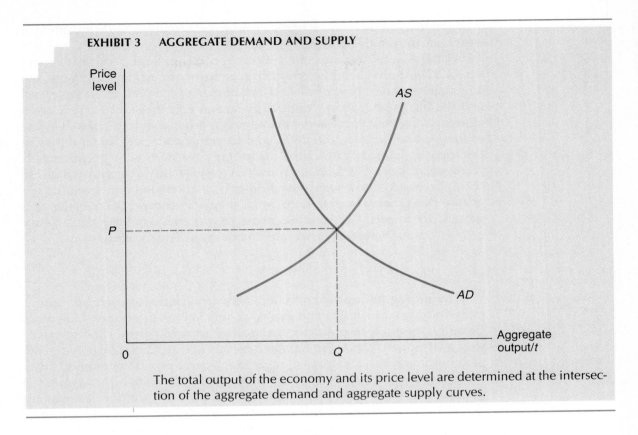

EXHIBIT 3   AGGREGATE DEMAND AND SUPPLY

The total output of the economy and its price level are determined at the intersection of the aggregate demand and aggregate supply curves.

level along the vertical axis. You are perhaps more familiar than you think with aggregate output and the price level. Reports in the media about the gross national product are referring to the most common measure of aggregate output. And the general price level is nothing more than the "cost of living" so often mentioned in the media.

The aggregate demand curve in Exhibit 3 reflects an inverse relation between the price level and the quantity of output demanded in the economy. As average prices in the United States fall, households demand more washers and Wheaties, firms demand more trucks and typewriters, governments demand more computer software and military hardware, and the rest of the world demands more U.S. grain and U.S. aircraft.

Consider why the quantity of aggregate output and the price level are inversely related. The quantity of aggregate output demanded depends in part on household *wealth*. Some wealth is held in dollar amounts, such as money in a savings account. A reduction in the price level increases the amount of goods and services that can be purchased with a given amount of savings. Therefore, households feel richer with a decrease in average prices, so they increase the quantity of aggregate output demanded. Conversely, an increase in the price level decreases the amount of goods and services that can be purchased with a given amount of savings. Households feel poorer when there is an increase in average prices, so they decrease the quantity of aggregate output demanded.

The aggregate demand curve reflects both domestic and foreign demand for U.S. output. Therefore, another reason for the negative slope of the aggregate demand curve involves the relation between the *domestic* price level and the *foreign* price level. Among the factors held constant along a given aggregate demand curve is the price level in other countries, as well as the exchange rate between the dollar and foreign currencies. When the price level in the United States falls, the average price of U.S. products falls relative to the price of foreign products. Consequently, Americans increase their purchases of now relatively cheaper U.S. goods and buy fewer foreign goods. Foreigners also find U.S. goods relatively cheaper, so they demand more U.S. exports. Conversely, a rise in the price level reduces the quantity of U.S. output demanded by both Americans and foreigners.

Aggregate Supply

*The **aggregate supply curve** shows the relation between the general price level and the amount of aggregate output supplied per period of time.*

The **aggregate supply curve** indicates the quantity of aggregate output that producers are willing and able to supply at each price level. How does quantity supplied respond to changes in average prices? The upward-sloping supply curve, *AS*, in Exhibit 3 depicts a positive relation between the price level and the quantity of aggregate output producers supply, other factors that affect supply held constant. Recall that when the economy's production possibilities frontier was developed, the supply of resources available in the economy and the state of technology were held constant. Those same factors are held constant along a given aggregate supply curve. *As long as the average price producers receive for their output rises more than the cost of producing that output, producers find it profitable to expand output as the price level increases.*

Also held constant along a given aggregate supply curve is the price level prevailing in other countries, as well as the exchange rate between the dollar and foreign currencies. As average prices in the United States rise relative to average prices in other countries, U.S. producers find domestic markets more attractive than export markets, so the quantity of aggregate output supplied increases. Thus, the quantity of aggregate output supplied and the price level are positively related. We should caution, however, that the shape and explanation of the aggregate supply curve are much debated among macroeconomists.

Equilibrium

The intersection of the aggregate demand and aggregate supply curves determines the equilibrium levels of average prices and aggregate output in the economy. Only at the equilibrium level will the desires of buyers and sellers match. If for some reason the price level is initially higher than the market-clearing, or equilibrium, level, the resulting excess supply will force the price level down until quantity demanded and quantity supplied are equal. If the price level is initially below the equilibrium level, the resulting shortage of goods and services will put upward pressure on the price level until the shortage is eliminated.

Although employment is not measured directly along the horizontal axis, firms must hire additional workers to produce more goods and services. Thus, higher levels of aggregate output reflect higher levels of employment. In terms of economic policy, greater aggregate output seems desirable for two reasons. First, greater output means that more goods and services are available in the economy. Second, greater output means that more people in the economy are employed and fewer are unemployed. According to the supply curve in Exhibit 3, more aggregate output will usually be supplied only if the price level increases. As we shall see later, however, a rising price level may create another set of problems, so greater output is not always the only goal of the economy.

Perhaps the best way to convey an understanding of aggregate demand and supply is to apply these new tools to the U.S. economy. In the next section we greatly simplify U.S. economic history to show how the price level and level of aggregate output have related over time.

A SHORT HISTORY OF THE U.S. ECONOMY

The history of the U.S. economy can be crudely divided into three economic eras: (1) before World War II, (2) between World War II and the early 1970s, and (3) since the early 1970s. The first era was marked by a series of economic depressions, culminating in the Great Depression of the 1930s. These depressions were often accompanied by a falling price level. The second era was one of generally strong economic growth, with only moderate increases in the average level of prices. The third era was characterized by problems with both inflation and unemployment.

Before World War II

"It is a gloomy moment in history. . . . In our own country there is . . . panic and thousands of our poorest fellow-citizens are turned against the approaching winter without employment, and without the prospect of employment." The quotation, taken from the October 10, 1857, issue of *Harper's Weekly*, describes the Panic of 1857. As we have mentioned, U.S. economic history records alternating periods of prosperity and depression before World War II. There was the depression of the 1820s, followed a decade later by the Panic of 1837. The economy gradually recovered, but the Panic of 1857 brought on the depression described in the quote. Depression hit again between 1873 and 1879, when eighty railroads went bankrupt and most of the steel industry was shut down. Another depression in the 1890s lasted four years, but this was followed by more than thirty years of relative prosperity, interrupted only by two brief crises. The prosperity of the

Roaring Twenties hit a dead end with the stock market crash of October, 1929. This crash set off what was to become the most severe economic contraction in our nation's history, the Great Depression of the 1930s.

In terms of aggregate demand and aggregate supply, the Great Depression can be viewed as a shift to the left in the aggregate demand curve, as shown in Exhibit 4. *AD* is the aggregate demand curve before the onset of the depression, and *AD'* the demand curve after the depression set in.[3] With this fall in aggregate demand, both the equilibrium price level and the equilibrium quantity of aggregate output declined. Between 1929 and 1933, the price level decreased by 23 percent and aggregate output fell by 30 percent. As aggregate output declined, the unemployment rate increased, climbing from about 3 percent in 1929 to 25 percent in 1933. Why did aggregate demand fall so dramatically? Though the causes are still subject to debate, most economists agree that grim expectations and the subsequent collapse of the banking system contributed to the decline in aggregate demand.

EXHIBIT 4   THE DECREASE IN AGGREGATE DEMAND BETWEEN 1929 AND 1933

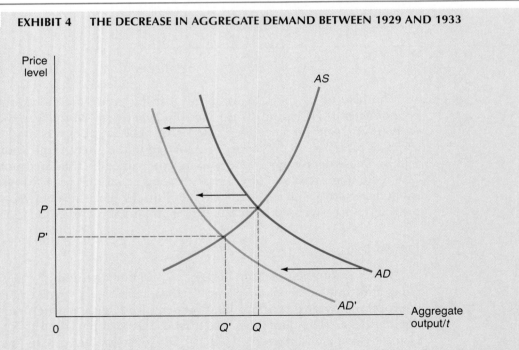

The Great Depression of the 1930s can be represented by a shift to the left of the aggregate demand curve, from *AD* to *AD'*. As a result of the depression, aggregate output fell from *Q* to *Q'*, and the price level dropped from *P* to *P'*.

---

[3] The aggregate supply curve probably also shifted somewhat during the period, but for simplicity we assume it was unchanged. Most economists agree that the shift in the aggregate demand curve was the dominant factor.

How did the government respond to these economic calamities? Before the Great Depression, public policy was based on the laissez-faire philosophy of Adam Smith. Recall that Smith argued in *The Wealth of Nations* that if people were allowed to pursue their self-interest in a free market, resources would be guided as if by an "invisible hand" to produce the greatest, most efficient level of aggregate output. The policy pursued by governments before the Great Depression was based on the theory that the economy would perform better if left alone than if government intervened. Though the U.S. economy had suffered through at least six major depressions since the beginning of the nineteenth century, the common view each time was that these contractions were unfortunate but essentially *self-correcting*. Each economic crisis and subsequent depression was viewed as a natural phase of the economy, which would improve without government intervention. President Herbert Hoover said at the onset of the Great Depression that prosperity was "just around the corner."

The Age of Keynes

It took the Great Depression to prompt at least one economist to argue that depressions were not necessarily self-correcting. John Maynard Keynes (1883–1946) argued that aggregate demand was inherently unstable, in part because investment decisions were often guided by the unpredictable "animal spirits" of business expectations. He saw no natural forces operating to ensure that the economy, even if allowed abundant time, would return to a higher level of aggregate output and employment.

Keynes proposed that the federal government shock the economy out of its depression by increasing aggregate demand. This could be done directly, by increasing government spending, or indirectly, by cutting taxes to stimulate the primary components of private-sector demand, consumption and investment. Either way, government spending would likely exceed government revenues, resulting in a **federal budget deficit**. Thus, Keynes recommended an *expansionary fiscal policy* and called for a federal budget deficit. If this policy worked as Keynes expected, aggregate demand would increase, as represented in Exhibit 5 by a shift to the right in the aggregate demand curve, from *AD'* back to its original position, *AD*. Most importantly, such a shift would raise the equilibrium level of aggregate output and employment. This change also would raise the price level, but changes in the price level were of less concern to Keynes.

According to the Keynesian prescription, the miracle drug of government fiscal policy — changes in government spending and taxes — was needed to compensate for what Keynes viewed as the inherent instability of private spending, especially investment. If demand in the private sector declined, it became the government's responsibility to pick up the slack. We can think of the Keynesian approach as **demand-side economics** because it focused on how increases in aggregate demand could promote full employment. Government spending, if injected into the circular flow at the

The **federal budget deficit** is the excess of the federal government's annual expenditures over its annual revenues.

Demand-side economics uses government policies in an effort to regulate aggregate demand to promote full employment and price stability.

EXHIBIT 5   KEYNESIAN POLICY TO INCREASE AGGREGATE DEMAND

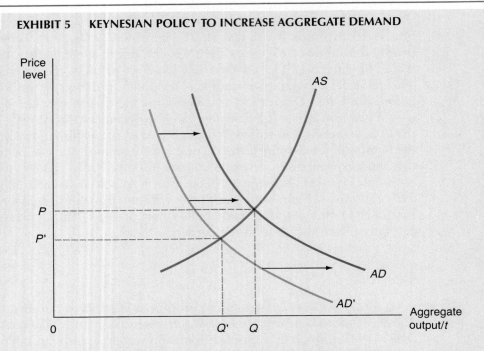

Keynes proposed that the government stimulate aggregate demand to help the economy recover from the Great Depression. A tax cut or an increase in government spending would shift the aggregate demand curve from *AD'* to *AD*. Aggregate output would then increase from *Q* to *Q'*, and the price level would rise from *P'* to *P*.

right time and in the proper dose, could be just the tonic to shock the economy out of its depression and back to health.

The additional demand created by World War II brought the economy out of the depression and seemed to provide confirmation of the powerful role that government spending could play in boosting output and employment. After the war, memories of the depression were still vivid, and everyone wanted to avoid a recurrence. Congress, therefore, approved the *Employment Act of 1946*, which imposed a clear responsibility on the federal government to foster, in the language of the act, "maximum employment, production, and purchasing power." One provision of the act set up the Council of Economic Advisers and required the President to report annually on the state of the economy. In the introduction to his first *Economic Report*, President Harry Truman wrote: "The job at hand is to see to it that America is not ravaged by recurring depressions and long periods of unemployment, but that instead we build an economy so fruitful, so dynamic, so progressive that each citizen can count upon opportunity and security for himself and his family."[4]

Implemention of Keynesian policies was cautious at first. The economy seemed to prosper during the 1950s largely without the help of expansionary fiscal policies. The decade of the 1960s, however, proved to be the *Golden Age of Keynesian economics*, a period when policy makers believed that by manipulating government taxation and spending, they could "fine-tune" the economy to avoid the recessionary phase of the business cycle. During the 1960s nearly all developed economies of the world enjoyed low unemployment and healthy growth in output with only modest inflation. The value of U.S. exports exceeded that of U.S. imports, and income flowed into the country from extensive U.S. investments in foreign countries.

Toward the end of the 1960s, some economists were beginning to speak of the obsolescence of the business cycle. As a sign of the times, the federal government changed the name of a publication called *Business Cycle Developments* to *Business Conditions Digest*. As it turned out, reports of the death of the business cycle were premature. In the early 1970s, the cycle returned with a fury. Prior to 1970 the problem of inflation occurred primarily during expansions, but after 1970 inflation plagued the economy during two recessions. The confidence economists had in Keynesian policies began to crumble, and the expression "fine-tuning" passed from economists' vocabularies. What happened in the short span of a few years to end the Golden Age of Keynesian economics?

The Great Stagflation

During the late 1960s, the federal government stepped up the war in Vietnam and increased spending on social programs at home. These simultaneous efforts increased aggregate demand enough that in 1968 the **inflation rate**, the annual percentage change in the price level, moved above 4.0 percent for the first time since 1951. Inflation drifted to 5.2 percent in 1969, and to 5.8 percent in 1970. These rates, which appear normal by today's standards, were so alarming that in August of 1971 President Richard Nixon introduced measures to freeze prices and wages. The initial three-month freeze was followed by several "phases" of controls that imposed varying wage and price restrictions during 1972 and 1973.

*The **inflation rate** is the annual percentage increase in the general price level.*

These freezes were lifted about the time grain prices were driven up by crop failures in several key locations, such as the Soviet Union. Moreover, giant increases in oil prices were pushed through by the suddenly powerful Organization of Petroleum Exporting Countries (OPEC). All of these shocks hit the economy hard. The favorable balance of trade the United States had experienced with the rest of the world reversed during the 1970s. In part because of the higher price of imported oil, Americans for the first time in decades were spending more on imports than they received for their

---

[4] *Economic Report of the President* (Washington, D.C.: U.S. Government Printing Office, 1947), 7.

exports, which resulted in a deficit in our merchandise trade balance. This trend, which was to worsen during the 1980s, showed how vulnerable the U.S. economy had become to economic forces around the world.

Whereas macroeconomic fluctuations during the 1960s seemed to be dominated by movements in the aggregate demand curve along a given aggregate supply curve, the shocks of the early 1970s reduced aggregate supply. A reduction in aggregate supply—a shift to the left in the aggregate supply curve—touched off the so-called *Great Stagflation* of the 1970s. This reduction in aggregate supply, shown in Exhibit 6 by the shift to the left in the aggregate supply curve, from *AS* to *AS'*, resulted in the twin problems of higher average prices and a lower level of aggregate output and employment. Aggregate output declined from *Q* to *Q'*, and the price level increased from *P* to *P'*. **Stagflation** means **stag**nation, or contraction, in the economy's aggregate output and an in**flation**, or increase, in the price level. In 1973 inflation was 5.5 percent, and the unemployment rate was 4.9 percent. By 1975 inflation had climbed to 8.9 percent, and unemployment had jumped to 8.5 percent.

Since the problem was on the supply side, not on the demand side, the demand-management prescriptions of Keynes were less effective in the 1970s. A government-induced increase in aggregate demand would merely

Stagflation is a contraction of the nation's output accompanied by inflation.

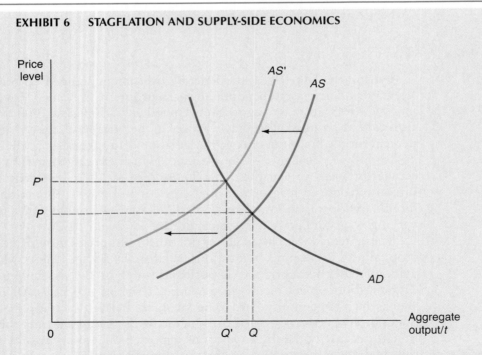

EXHIBIT 6   STAGFLATION AND SUPPLY-SIDE ECONOMICS

The stagflation of the 1970s can be represented as a reduction in aggregate supply from *AS* to *AS'*. Aggregate output fell from *Q* to *Q'* (stagnation), and the price level rose from *P* to *P'* (inflation).

aggravate the inflation. Stagflation appeared again in 1979 and 1980, partly as a result of another boost in oil prices; the inflation rate climbed to over 10 percent at a time when the unemployment rate was also rising. Macroeconomics has not been the same since.

Supply-Side Economics

Supply-side economics uses tax reductions in an effort to increase aggregate supply by stimulating production.

Increasing aggregate supply seemed an appropriate way to combat stagflation, for such a move would both lower inflation and increase output and employment. Attention therefore turned from aggregate demand to aggregate supply. A key idea behind so-called **supply-side economics** was that the federal government, by lowering taxes, would provide resource owners with greater incentives to supply their land, labor, capital, and entrepreneurial ability. This greater supply of resources for productive activity would increase aggregate supply. One hoped-for outcome is represented in Exhibit 6: a shift in the aggregate supply curve from *AS'* back to *AS*. Theoretically, an increase in aggregate supply would have the happy result of increasing the aggregate output while reducing the price level. But this was easier said than done.

To provide economic incentives and thereby increase aggregate supply, President Ronald Reagan and Congress cut income tax rates by 23 percent between 1981 and 1983. Their hope was that aggregate output would increase enough that the lower tax rate would actually result in more tax revenue. Put another way, the tax cuts would stimulate enough of an expansion of the economic pie that the government's smaller share of the bigger pie would be greater than its larger share of the smaller pie.

The expected tax revenue did not materialize, however, in part because in 1981 the economy entered a major recession that drove the unemployment rate in 1982 to nearly 10 percent. The federal deficit climbed each year, topping $220 billion in 1986. The economic stimulus offered by these giant federal deficits helped lower unemployment to 5.2 percent by 1989. After reaching a low of 1.9 percent in 1986, the inflation rate has remained relatively modest: 3.6 percent in 1987, 4.1 percent in 1988, and 4.8 percent in 1989. In Chapter 16 we will examine more closely the effects of these giant deficits on the equilibrium levels of price and output.

On the international scene, the U.S. trade balance deteriorated during the 1980s, with the trade deficit exceeding $150 billion in 1987. These trade deficits meant that foreigners were accumulating dollars from their net sales to the United States. Foreigners used these dollars to invest in U.S. firms, to buy U.S. stocks and bonds, and to buy other U.S. assets such as real estate. Thus there were twin deficits during the 1980s — the federal budget deficits and the balance-of-trade deficits — and the two were related. The rest of the world took the dollars accumulated because of our trade deficits and lent them back to the United States, thereby helping us finance the federal budget deficits. As noted in the previous chapter, the United States has now borrowed more from the rest of the world than has any other nation.

CONCLUSION

We have attempted to relate in a simple fashion the course of economic activity over the years. During the 1960s the Keynesian demand-side view prevailed. When stagflation appeared to limit the relevance of demand-side policies, interest shifted to other approaches, including supply-side economics. But there are more than two sides to this story. As we shall see, some economists have focused on the role of monetary policy, others on the role of expectations. Different economists may have different interpretations of the events discussed in this chapter. At this point there is no dominant macroeconomic theory about how the economy works. There are still many mysteries and much controversy.

These differing views present a real challenge to the beginning student. You might well ask, "If the experts can't agree on how the economy works, how can those who have much less training in the subject be expected to understand macroeconomics?" That is a reasonable question. Some books lay out the competing theories, leaving it to the reader to select an alternative. Rather than describe each theory of the economy in great detail, we will attempt to integrate the theories whenever possible to find the common ground among them.

Because macroeconomists have no test subjects and cannot rely on luck, they hone their craft by developing models of the economy and closely observing the economy's performance for evidence to support or refute these models. In this sense macroeconomics is largely retrospective, always looking at recent history for hints about which model works best. The macroeconomist is like a traveler who has a view of only the road behind, not the road ahead, and must find the way using a collection of poorly drawn maps. The traveler is not sure which map is correct or, indeed, whether any map is better than nothing. Consequently, the traveler must continually check each map (or model) against the landmarks passed, to see if one map appears more consistent with the terrain than the others. Hence, each new batch of information about the economy's performance causes macroeconomists to shuffle through their "maps" of the economy to re-evaluate their models.

The next chapter will help you "get the lay of the land" by providing an overview of how to measure economic activity. Then Chapter 7 will take a closer look at the two central problems of our economy, unemployment and inflation. In macroeconomics there seems to be an emphasis on what can go wrong with the economy. Problems associated with unemployment, inflation, and faltering economic growth capture much of the attention in macroeconomic theory and policy. We should not forget, however, that we must understand how a healthy economy operates before we can consider remedial policies when the economy fails in some important way.

Summary

1. Because each country has a unique economic setting, the focus of macroeconomics is on the national economy. A standard way of gauging an economy's performance is by measuring its gross national product, the value of final goods and services produced during a year.

2. The business cycle reflects the rise and fall of economic activity relative to the long-term growth trend of the economy. The economy has two phases: periods of expansion and periods of contraction. Although business cycles differ, contractions last about a year on average, and expansions average about three years.

3. The aggregate demand curve slopes downward, reflecting a negative, or inverse, relation between the price level and the quantity of aggregate output demanded. The aggregate supply curve slopes upward, reflecting a direct relation between the quantity of aggregate output supplied and the price level. The intersection of the two curves determines the economy's equilibrium price and output levels.

4. The Great Depression prompted Keynes to argue that the economy was inherently unstable, largely because the components of private spending, particularly business investment, were erratic. Keynes did not believe that depressions were self-correcting. He believed that whenever aggregate demand declined, the federal government should spend more or tax less. Keynes's demand-side policies dominated macroeconomics between World War II and the late 1960s.

5. During the 1970s supply shocks caused by higher energy prices and global crop failures reduced aggregate supply. The result was stagflation, the troublesome combination of slumping production and a higher rate of inflation. Demand-side policies appeared less effective in an economy suffering from a reduction in aggregate supply.

6. Supply-side tax cuts in the early 1980s were supposed to increase aggregate supply, thereby increasing output while dampening inflation. One effect of the tax cuts, however, was to increase the federal deficit. Giant deficits continued through the 1980s.

Questions and Problems

1. (Stocks and Flows) Wages and profits are considered flows; the money supply and the federal debt are considered stocks. Explain why this is the case. What is the relationship between the federal budget deficit and the federal debt and between the level of investment and the value of the capital stock?

2. (Business Cycles) Some businesses do well during a recession and tend to experience a drop in sales when the economy is recovering. Give some examples of such counter-cyclical businesses.

3. (Business Cycles) Explain why each of the

following is used by the Commerce Department as a component in the index of leading economic indicators:

a. Average work week
b. Number of unemployment claims
c. Orders for consumer goods
d. New building permits
e. Inventories
f. Stock prices
g. The money supply

4. (U.S. Economic History) During the Vietnam War there was a considerable increase in government spending without much additional taxation. How can the government spend without taking in sufficient tax revenues?

5. (Aggregate Demand and Supply) Explain why a decrease in the aggregate demand curve results in a lower level of employment, given a fixed aggregate supply.

6. (Stagflation) Discuss some causes of the stagflations of 1973 and 1979. What differences are there between these episodes of stagflation and the Great Depression of the 1930s?

7. (Aggregate Demand and Supply) Is it possible for prices to be falling while production and employment are rising? How might this happen?

8. (The Macroeconomy) When someone gets sick, doctors often claim that the body will cure itself. Is it reasonable to believe that the economy also will return to normal business conditions after experiencing a recession, assuming that government takes no action? Why or why not?

9. (Aggregate Demand and Supply) Use an aggregate demand-supply diagram to predict the change in aggregate output and price under the following conditions:

a. A decrease in wealth
b. An increase in the resource base
c. An increase in the price of OPEC oil
d. An increase in foreign price levels
e. An increase in the value of the dollar against foreign currencies

10. (Business Cycles) Using the constant (1982) dollar GNP figures from Table A on the inside front cover, identify peak years, trough years, and recession years for the U.S. economy.

11. (Supply-Side Economics) One supply-side measure pushed by the Reagan administration was a cut in income tax rates. Use an aggregate demand-supply diagram to show what the intended effect was to be. Show what might happen if such tax cuts also generated an increase in aggregate spending.

12. (Trade Deficit) Explain how a desire by foreigners to invest in this country (e.g., buy real estate, Treasury bills, factories) could foster a trade deficit.

Measuring Economic Aggregates and the Circular Flow of Income

Where in the newspaper do you find the scores? You probably think of the sports section, but in fact more scores are reported in the business section: the prices of thousands of stocks, bonds, and commodities ranging from platinum to pork bellies. You may not be able to find the price of tea in China, but you can find the price of hogs in Iowa or the current price for coffee to be grown next year.

In this chapter you will learn how to keep score of billions of economic transactions. The scorecard is the national income accounting system, which reflects the performance of the economy as a whole by reducing a huge network of economic activity to a few aggregate measures. This chapter focuses on one of the most important scores: the gross national product. As we shall see, the gross national product can be calculated either from the total spending on output or from the total income generated by producing that output. We examine each approach, show how the two approaches are equivalent, and discuss how to adjust the gross national product for the effects of inflation. To clarify the equalities of the national income accounts, we use a more sophisticated version of the circular flow model first introduced in Chapter 4.

The major components and important equalities built into the national income accounts are presented as another way of understanding how the economy works—not as a foreign language to be mastered before the next exam. The emphasis is more on economic intuition than on accounting precision. This chapter includes sufficient detail about the national income accounts to provide the background you need for later chapters, but it only scratches the surface. Additional detail plus some complications are presented in the appendix to the chapter. Topics discussed in this chapter include

- Gross national product
- Expenditure and income approaches
- Disposable income
- Circular flow of income and spending

- Limitations of national income accounting
- Implicit price deflator
- Consumer price index

GROSS NATIONAL PRODUCT

How do we measure the economy's performance? During much of the seventeenth and eighteenth centuries, when the dominant economic policy was mercantilism, many thought that economic prosperity was best measured by the *stock* of precious metals a nation accumulated. François Quesnay (1694–1774) was the first to measure economic activity as a *flow*. In 1758 he published his *Tableau Économique*, a book that described the circular flow of goods and income among different sectors of the economy. His insight was probably inspired by his knowledge of the circular flow of blood in the body—Quesnay was the court physician to Louis XV of France.

Rough measures of national income were developed in England more than two hundred years ago, but detailed calculations built up from microeconomic data were first developed by Simon Kuznets during the Great Depression. The resulting *national income accounting system* organizes the tremendous quantities of data that are collected from a variety of sources around the country. These data are summarized, assembled into a coherent framework, and reported periodically by the federal government. Our national income accounts describe the largest and most complex economy in history. They are the most widely reported and the most highly regarded in the world and have earned their developers Nobel Prizes.

Market Value of Final Goods and Services

How do the national income accounts keep track of the incredible variety of goods and services produced, from phone service to chain saws? As mentioned earlier, the *gross national product*, or *GNP*, measures the market value of all final goods and services produced in the United States during a particular time period, usually a year. The national income accounts are based on a double-entry bookkeeping system in which sales of aggregate output are recorded on one side and payments for resources producing that output are recorded on the other side. Therefore, GNP can be measured by looking at total spending or by looking at total income received. The **expenditure approach** involves adding up the aggregate expenditure on all final goods and services produced during the year. But the production of

*The **expenditure approach** to calculating GNP involves adding up expenditures on all final goods and services produced during the year.*

final goods and services results in income to those who produce that output. Hence, the **income approach** to calculating GNP involves computing the aggregate income earned by resource suppliers: the returns on land, labor, capital, and entrepreneurial ability.

The *income approach* to calculating GNP involves adding up all payments to owners of resources used to produce output during the year.

The gross national product includes only **final goods and services**, which are goods and services sold to the final, or ultimate, user. A toothbrush, a pair of contact lenses, and a bus ride are examples of final goods and services. Whether a sale is to the final user often depends on who buys the product. Your purchase of a chicken from the grocer is reflected in GNP. When a Kentucky Fried Chicken franchise purchases chicken, this transaction is not directly recorded in GNP because the franchise is not the final consumer; only when the chicken is fried and sold to consumers is a sale recorded as part of GNP.

Final goods and services are those that are sold to ultimate users.

Intermediate goods and services are those purchased for additional processing and resale, such as the chicken purchased by a franchise. This additional processing may be imperceptible, as when the corner grocer buys goods to stock the shelves. Or the intermediate goods can be dramatically altered, as when paint and canvas are turned into a work of art. Sales of intermediate goods and services are excluded from GNP to avoid the problem of *double counting*, which is counting an item's value more than once. For example, suppose the grocer buys a can of tuna for $0.60 and sells it for $1. If GNP included both the intermediate transaction of $0.60 and the final transaction of $1, that same can of tuna would be counted twice in GNP, and the recorded value would be $0.60 more than the final value of the good.

Intermediate goods and services are those that are purchased for further reprocessing and resale.

The gross national product reflects production in a particular year, so purchases of goods produced in prior years, such as used cars, previously owned homes, and used textbooks are also excluded from current GNP. These goods were added to GNP the year they were produced.

GNP Based on the Expenditure Approach

As we have said, one way to measure the value of GNP is by keeping track of the aggregate expenditure on final goods and services produced in the economy during the year. Perhaps the easiest way to grasp the notion of aggregate expenditure is to divide it into its four components: consumption, investment, government purchases, and net exports. We will discuss each in turn.

Consumption includes all household purchases of final goods and services.

Consumption consists of purchases of final goods and services by households during the year. Consumption is the largest spending category but also the easiest to understand. Along with services, it includes purchases of nondurable goods, such as soap and soup, and durable goods, such as stereos and station wagons. Durable goods are those expected to last for more than a year.

Investment is all output produced during a year but not used for present consumption.

Investment consists of all output produced during the year but not used for present consumption. The most important category of investment is **physical capital**, such as buildings, machinery, tools, and other manufactured items purchased by firms and used to produce goods and services.

Physical capital is manufactured items used to produce goods and services.

Investment also includes new residential construction. Physical capital can range from the smallest screwdriver to the largest steam shovel, from a toolshed to the Sears Tower in Chicago. Purchases of stocks and bonds are not considered investment for purposes of national income accounting because such transactions simply reflect the transfer of financial assets among buyers and sellers, not the production of physical capital.

Inventories are stocks of finished goods and goods in process held by producers.

Firm inventories are another category of investment. Firm **inventories** are stocks of final goods and goods in process that help insulate the firm against unanticipated changes in the supply of its resources or in the demand for its product. For example, an auto manufacturer maintains stocks of both auto components and finished autos. A *net* increase in inventories during the year is counted as investment, since this production is not used for current consumption. For example, suppose General Motors sells one hundred thousand fewer cars than expected, so dealer inventories grow by that amount during the year. The gross national product will increase by the value of net inventory increases. Using the expenditure approach, you can think of the car dealers as buying this inventory from General Motors. Conversely, a net inventory reduction during the year is counted as negative investment, or *disinvestment*, since inventory reductions represent the sale of output already credited to a prior year's GNP.

Government purchases include spending for goods and services by all levels of government.

Government purchases include spending by all levels of government for goods and services from clearing snow to clearing court dockets. According to the national income accounts, governments are viewed as the final users of the goods and services they purchase, even though governments presumably function on behalf of the public. Government purchases, and therefore GNP, do not include transfer payments, such as Social Security and welfare benefits. Such payments merely reflect an outright grant from government to recipients and are therefore not part of GNP. Since transfer payments are excluded, the government budget is actually much larger than government purchases indicate.

The final component of aggregate expenditure results from the interaction of the U.S. economy with the rest of the world. The U.S. GNP includes only goods and services produced in the United States, so the expenditure approach measures spending on U.S. products only. Exports from the United States reflect the sale of domestic production, so the market value of exports must be added to GNP. But imported goods and services are not produced in this country, so spending on imports must be subtracted from total spending in order to arrive at total spending on U.S. products. **Net exports** equal the value of U.S. exported goods and services minus the value of U.S. imported goods and services. The net export accounts include not only merchandise trade — that is, commodities — but also so-called *invisibles*, such as earnings from foreign investments and tourism. Prior to 1983 the United States was a net exporter, meaning net exports were positive. Since then, net exports have been negative, meaning imports have exceeded exports.

Net exports are the value of domestic products purchased by foreigners minus the value of foreign products purchased by domestic residents.

Aggregate expenditure is the total spending on final goods and services at a given price level.

With the expenditure approach, the nation's aggregate expenditure is set equal to GNP. **Aggregate expenditure** is equal to the sum of consumption,

C; investment, *I*; government purchases, *G*; and net exports, (*X* − *M*), which is exports, *X*, minus imports, *M*. Summing these components gives aggregate expenditure:

$$C + I + G + (X - M) = \textbf{GNP}$$

GNP Based on the Income Approach

Whereas the expenditure approach to GNP involves totaling the aggregate spending on production, the income approach involves adding up the aggregate income arising from that production. The practice of double-entry bookkeeping ensures that the value of aggregate output must equal claims on its value by the individuals who owned the resources used to produce that output: the wages, rent, interest, and profit arising from production. The price of a Hershey Bar represents income to all the resources employed to bring that bar to the grocer's shelf. **Aggregate income** equals the sum of all the income earned by resource suppliers in the economy. Thus we can say that

Aggregate income is the sum of all the income earned by resource suppliers in the economy.

Aggregate expenditure = GNP = aggregate income

Most final goods and services are processed by several firms on their way to the consumer. Furniture starts as raw timber, which is cut by one firm, milled by another, made into furniture by a third, and retailed by a fourth. Double counting can be avoided either by including only the market value of final goods or services produced or by carefully *calculating the value added at each stage of production*. The **value added** by each firm equals that firm's selling price minus the amount paid to other firms for materials. The value added at each stage represents income to resource suppliers at that stage. The sum of the value added at each stage equals the market value of the final good, and the sum of the value added for all final goods and services equals the GNP based on the income approach.

Value added is the difference, at each stage of production, between the value of products a firm sells and the cost of the materials purchased to make those products.

To understand the concept of value added, consider the following example. Suppose you spend $10 for a 16-ounce steak at the Raging Bull Steak House. Because you are the ultimate consumer of this steak, your $10 payment represents the market value of the final good and is added directly into GNP. Consider the history of that steak. The steer that gave its life for your lunch was born and raised on the range until the rancher sold it to a meat packer for $1.50 per pound. The meat packer processed the beef and sold it for $2.50 per pound to a wholesaler, who delivered it to the restaurateur for $4 per pound. The restaurant broiled it medium rare over a flaming pit and served it to you with a smile for $10 per pound.

Column (1) of Exhibit 1 lists the selling price of the steak at each stage of production. If each of these transactions were added to GNP, the steak would add a total of $18 to GNP. To avoid double counting, we include as part of GNP only the value added at each stage of production, listed in column (3) as the difference between the purchase price and the selling price

EXHIBIT 1
COMPUTATION OF VALUE ADDED
PER POUND OF BEEF

Stage of Production	Sale Value (1)	Cost of Intermediate Goods (2)	Value Added (3)
Rancher	$ 1.50	—	$ 1.50
Meat packer	2.50	1.50	1.00
Wholesaler	4.00	2.50	1.50
Restaurateur	10.00	4.00	6.00
			$10.00

of the beef. Suppose the rancher started from scratch and added $1.50 per pound to the value of the beef. The meat packer paid $1.50 per pound for the beef and sold it for $2.50, in the process adding $1 to the value. The wholesaler added $1.50, and the restaurateur added a whopping $6 to the value. The value added at each stage equals the income to all who supplied resources at that stage. For example, the $6 in value added by the restaurant represents income to all who contributed resources at that final stage, from the linen supplier to the newspaper that carried the restaurant's advertising. The sum of this value added at all stages equals $10, the final market value of the steak and the total income earned by all resource suppliers along the way.

Disposable Income

Because of taxes, not all aggregate income earned in the economy is available to households, the resource suppliers. Governments impose taxes that claim a portion of aggregate income. With this tax revenue, governments purchase goods and services and make transfer payments, which flow to certain households. Therefore, the **disposable income** available to households consists of aggregate income minus taxes plus transfer payments.[1] Disposable income is the take-home pay that households have available to spend or save.

Disposable income is the income available for households to spend or to save after personal taxes have been paid and transfers received.

We are most interested in how disposable income is actually allocated, or *disposed* of, during the year. Households have only two choices in allocating disposable income; they can spend it or save it. More precisely, we say that disposable income, DI, goes either to personal consumption, C, or to personal saving, S, which consists of all uses other than personal consumption. Thus

$$DI = C + S$$

---

[1] This is a rough definition of disposable income. A more precise definition, based on a fuller examination of the national income accounts, is provided in the appendix.

THE CIRCULAR FLOW
OF INCOME AND SPENDING

The equalities among GNP, aggregate expenditure, and aggregate income can be clarified by examining the circular flow diagram in Exhibit 2, which portrays the flows discussed so far. Whereas only households and firms were reflected in the circular flow model presented in Chapter 4, Exhibit 2 includes governments and the rest of the world. And whereas the circular flow presented earlier included the flow of products and resources, Exhibit 2 concentrates on the flow of income and spending.

The leading actors in the circular flow are domestic *households,* which make the key decisions about how much to spend on consumption and how much to save. The supporting actors are *governments*, which make decisions about government purchases, transfers, and taxes; domestic *firms*, which make production and investment decisions; and *the rest of the world*, where decisions are made regarding purchases of U.S. exports and production of U.S. imports.

Income flows through the bottom half of the diagram, and spending flows through the top half. The money mainstream flows clockwise around the circle, first as income from firms to households, then as spending from households back to firms. At various points around the loop, the flow of money is diverted from the mainstream. Any diversion of aggregate income from the domestic spending stream is called a **leakage** from the circular flow. In the lower portion of the loop, taxes paid to governments represent a leakage from the income stream. In the upper portion of the loop, saving going to financial markets and spending on imports represent leakages from the domestic spending stream.

Any diversion of aggregate income from the domestic spending stream is called a **leakage**. *Leakages include saving, taxes, and imports.*

Any payment of income other than by firms or any spending other than by domestic households is called an **injection**. *Injections include investment, government purchases, transfer payments, and exports.*

Leakages from the circular flow are offset by injections of income and spending into the mainstream. Any payment made into the income stream other than by firms or any expenditure made into the spending stream other than by domestic households is called an **injection**. In the bottom half of the circular flow, transfer payments are injections into the income stream. In the upper half of the diagram, investment, government purchases, and money received for exports are injections into the expenditure stream. As we shall see, the sum of the leakages must equal the sum of the injections.

The Income Half of the Circular Flow

Although we could pick up the flow at any point around the circle, the logic of the model is clearest if we begin at juncture (1), where U.S. firms make their production and investment decisions. The circular flow is a continuous process, but production usually must occur before output can be purchased. For example, General Motors must build autos before autos can be sold. Therefore, firms must decide how much to produce before spending actually occurs, so they must estimate the amount of output that will be sold and then produce accordingly.

Aggregate output, or GNP, gives rise to an equal amount of aggregate

EXHIBIT 2   THE CIRCULAR FLOW OF INCOME AND EXPENDITURE

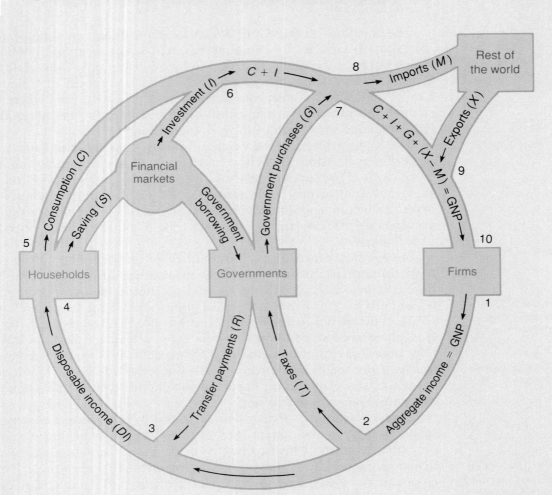

The circular flow diagram captures important relationships in the economy. The bottom half of the diagram depicts the income flow arising from production. At juncture (1) GNP equals aggregate income. Taxes leak out of the flow at point (2), but transfer payments augment the flow at point (3). Aggregate income minus taxes plus transfer payments equals disposable income, which flows to households at juncture (4).

The top half of the diagram shows the flow of expenditures on GNP. At juncture (5) households split their disposable income between consumption and saving. The saving stream flows into financial markets, where it is channeled to government borrowing and to business investment. At point (6) the injection of investment spending augments household consumption spending. At juncture (7) government spending represents another injection into the circular flow. At point (8) imports are a leakage of spending, and at point (9) exports are an injection of spending into the circular flow. Consumption plus investment plus government purchases plus exports minus imports equals the aggregate expenditure on GNP faced by firms at point (10).

income. Households supply their land, labor, capital, and entrepreneurial ability to firms and receive rent, wages, interest, and profit. We can therefore say that at juncture (1) GNP equals aggregate income. Not all that income becomes available to households. At juncture (2) governments impose taxes, T, to support government programs. Some of these tax dollars, however, are returned to the flow of income as transfer payments, R, at point (3). Consequently, aggregate income has been reduced by taxes but increased by transfer payments. By subtracting taxes and adding transfers, we transform aggregate income into disposable income, DI, which flows to households at juncture (4).

The bottom half of this circular flow can be viewed as the *income half* because it focuses on the income stemming from production. Two measures of income are identified: (1) aggregate income, which is the total income arising from producing GNP, and (2) disposable income, DI, the income that remains after taxes have been paid and transfers received. To streamline the discussion, we will define *net taxes* as taxes, T, minus transfer payments, R, or $(T - R)$. Thus, we can say more simply that aggregate income equals disposable income plus net taxes:

$$\textbf{GNP = Aggregate income = DI} + (\textbf{\textit{T}} - \textbf{\textit{R}})$$

To review: At juncture (4) firms have produced output and have paid resource suppliers; governments have collected taxes and distributed transfers; households have received their disposable income and must now decide how much to spend and how much to save. Firms in particular are eager to see how much consumers and other demanders are willing to spend, since firms have already produced the output and have paid resource suppliers. Should any output go unsold, it must become part of firms' inventories.

The Expenditure Half of the Circular Flow

Thus households, with disposable income in hand, make the critical decisions of how much to spend and how much to save. The stream of disposable income splits in two at juncture (5): part flows to consumption, C, and the remainder to saving, S. Dollars spent on consumption remain in the circular flow and represent the most important component of aggregate expenditure. Personal saving flows to financial markets, identified by the small circle. **Financial markets** consist of banks and other institutions that provide a link between savers and borrowers. For simplicity, we assume that households are the only savers, although governments, firms, and the rest of the world could be savers, too. The primary borrowers are firms and governments.

Financial markets consist of banks and other institutions that facilitate the flow of funds from savers to borrowers.

Since firms in our simplified model pay resource suppliers an amount equal to the entire value of output, firms have no money left for investment. Thus, if firms want to invest, they must go through financial markets to borrow money from households that save. Firms must borrow to finance purchases of physical capital plus any increases in their inventories. Households also may borrow from financial markets to purchase new homes. Therefore, investment, I, consists of capital investment by firms, changes in business inventories, and residential construction. Investment represents the second injection of spending into the circular flow, shown at juncture (6), and brings aggregate spending at that point to $C + I$.

Governments must borrow whenever their total outlays—transfer payments plus purchases of goods and services—exceed their revenues. Simply put, governments must borrow whenever they incur deficits. Government *budget deficit* is a flow variable that measures for a particular period the amount by which one flow, total government outlays, exceeds another flow, taxes. In contrast, government *debt* is a stock variable that measures the net accumulation of all prior deficits. For example, in 1989 federal outlays exceeded federal revenues by about \$150 billion, a deficit that raised the federal debt to well over \$2 trillion. Government outlays are made up of transfer payments and purchases of goods and services. Transfer payments were already mentioned in the discussion of the lower half of the circular flow. Government purchases of goods and services, represented by G at juncture (7), are an injection of spending into the circular flow.

Some spending on consumption, investment, and government purchases actually goes for imports. Since spending on imports does not flow to U.S. producers, imports are a leakage from the circular flow, reflected by M at juncture (8). But the rest of the world also buys U.S. products, and exports are an injection into the circular flow, reflected by X at juncture (9). The net impact of *the rest of the world* on aggregate expenditure equals exports minus imports, or $(X - M)$.

The upper half of the circular flow can be viewed as the expenditure half because it focuses on the components that make up aggregate expenditure: consumption, C; investment, I; government purchases, G; and net exports, $(X - M)$. Aggregate expenditure flows into firms at juncture (10). The amount spent in the economy equals the market value of aggregate output in the economy, or GNP. In other words,

$$\text{GNP} = \textbf{aggregate expenditure} = C + I + G + (X - M)$$

Leakages and Injections

Let's step back now and consider the big picture. In the lower half of the circular flow, aggregate income equals disposable income plus net taxes. In the upper half, aggregate expenditure equals the sum of the spending by each sector. As noted earlier, the aggregate expenditure on output equals the aggregate income arising from that output. Thus, aggregate income (disposable income plus net taxes) equals aggregate expenditure (spending by each sector), or

$$\underbrace{DI + (T - R)}_{\substack{\textbf{Aggregate} \\ \textbf{income}}} = \underbrace{C + I + G + (X - M)}_{\substack{\textbf{Aggregate} \\ \textbf{expenditure}}}$$

We know, however, that disposable income equals consumption plus saving. If we substitute $C + S$ for DI in the above equation and then subtract C from both sides and add M to both sides, we get

$$S + (T - R) + M = I + G + X$$

On the left-hand side, saving plus net taxes plus imports represents the leakages from the circular flow. On the right-hand side, investment plus government purchases plus exports represents the injections into the circular flow. This leakages-injections equation demonstrates a second accounting identity: according to the principles of double-entry bookkeeping, *the leakages from the circular flow must equal the injections into that flow.*

Planned Investment Versus Actual Investment

As we have said, at juncture (1) in the circular flow, firms make production decisions plus decisions about how much they plan to invest. Their investment plans may go awry, however, if aggregate expenditure does not match firms' expectations. Suppose, for example, that firms produce $5 trillion in output, but aggregate consumption plus planned investment plus government purchases plus net exports adds up to only $4.8 trillion. Firms must add $200 billion in unsold products to their inventories. Since increases in inventories are counted as investment, actual investment is $200 billion greater than firms had planned. Note the distinction between **planned investment**, the amount firms plan to invest before they know how much each sector will spend, and **actual investment**, which includes both planned investment and unplanned changes in inventories.

Planned investment is the amount of investment firms plan to undertake during a year. Actual investment is the amount actually invested during the year; it is equal to planned investment plus unplanned changes in inventories.

The relationship between actual and planned investment will be examined more closely in Chapter 9; for now, you need only understand that the national income accounting system reflects *actual* investment, not *planned* investment. *The national income accounts always look at economic activity after transactions have occurred—after the dust has settled.*

In summary, the practice of double-entry bookkeeping provides the underpinnings for national income accounting. Economic activity can be measured in two fundamental ways: by determining the market value of spending on all final goods and services produced in the economy during the year or by totaling the income arising from that production. The national income accounting system was developed over the years to trace economic activity consisting of billions of individual transactions. Such an all-purpose system, however, is bound to have limitations, as we shall see next.

LIMITATIONS OF NATIONAL INCOME ACCOUNTING

Imagine the difficulty of developing an accounting system that must capture the subtleties of such a complex and dynamic economy. In the interest of clarity and simplicity, some features of the economy are neglected; others receive perhaps inordinate weight. In this section we examine some limitations of the national income accounting system, beginning with productive activity that is not captured by GNP.

Some Production Is Not Included in GNP

With some minor exceptions, GNP includes only those products that are sold in formal markets. It thus misses all household production. Child care, meal preparation, laundry, house cleaning, leaf raking — all household services not purchased in the market — are excluded from GNP. Thus an economy in which households are largely self-sufficient will have a much lower GNP than will an economy in which households specialize and sell goods and service to one another.

This irregularity of the national income accounts has been a factor in the growth of GNP in recent years. During the 1950s more than 80 percent of mothers with small children stayed at home caring for the family, but all this care counted not one whit toward GNP. Today more than half the mothers with small children are in the work force, where their labor services are reflected in GNP. Moreover, with more mothers working, households are more likely to purchase goods and services that formerly tended to be produced by the household, such as meals and child-care services. Consequently, the measured GNP has increased, both because more mothers are in the work force and because activities that had been carried out within the household are now more frequently recorded as market transactions. Typically, the more developed the economy, the less economic activity is of the "do-it-yourself" variety. Because official GNP figures ignore most home production, these figures tend to understate the quantity of goods and services actually available to households in less developed countries.

*The **underground economy** is a term that describes all economic activity not reported to the government.*

Estimates of GNP also fail to capture transactions of which no official records are kept. The **underground economy** is an expression used to describe all market exchange that goes unreported either because it is illegal or because those involved want to evade taxes. Although there are no official estimates on the extent of the underground economy, most economists agree that it is substantial. One Census Bureau study suggests that the nation's underground economy amounts to about 7.5 percent of GNP, which in 1989 would have been nearly $400 billion. Other estimates range as high as 20 percent of GNP.

Even though some kinds of production are not reflected in GNP, the *imputed income* from certain activities that do not pass across recorded markets *is* included. Income must be imputed, or estimated, because market exchange does not occur. For example, homeowners are assumed to receive an imputed rental income from owning their home, even though no rent is actually paid or received, and this value is included in GNP. (This implicit rent is discussed in the appendix to this chapter.) Dollar values are also imputed for wages paid *in kind*, such as employers' payments for employees' medical insurance. A farm family's income includes an imputed value for food produced on the farm for that family's own consumption. The national income accounts consequently reflect some economic production that does not involve market exchange.

GNP Ignores Quality and Variety

The average work week is much shorter now than it was years ago, so people work less to produce today's output. The increase over the years in the amount of leisure time available has resulted in a higher quality of life. But leisure time is not reflected in GNP because leisure is not explicitly bought and sold in the market. The quality and variety of products available have also improved over the years, as a result of technological advances and competition. Today's cars, for example, are quieter, more fuel-efficient, and more comfortable than the hulking steel carriers produced twenty years ago. Similar improvements can also be noted in televisions, stereo systems, computers, running shoes, and so on. Also, many new products are introduced each year, such as video cassette recorders and compact-disc players. *The gross national product ignores changes in the availability of leisure time, changes in the quality of products, and changes in the availability of new products.*

Gross National Product Is Really Gross

Depreciation *measures the value of capital stock used up during a year in producing GNP.*

Net national product *equals GNP minus depreciation.*

As GNP is produced, some capital stock wears out or becomes obsolete. **Depreciation** measures the value of the capital stock used up in the production process. The gross national product is called "gross" because it fails to reflect this depreciation. Depreciation is subtracted from GNP to yield a measure called the **net national product**. The net national product and several other key measures of economic activity are discussed in the appendix to this chapter.

GNP Values All Output Equally

In GNP, the market price of output is used as the measure of its value. Therefore, each dollar spent on nuclear missiles is counted in GNP the same as each dollar spent on health care. Positive economic analysis is designed to avoid value judgments about how people choose to spend their money. Because the level of GNP provides no information about its composition, some economists question whether GNP is a good measure of the country's economic welfare. For example, at a time when many people in the nation are hungry and homeless, Americans spend billions of dollars on tobacco products—a leading cause of death in the United States.

GNP Does Not Reflect All Costs

The production and consumption of goods degrades the quality of our environment: passenger cars pump carbon monoxide into the atmosphere, housing developments displace forests, paper mills foul the lungs and burn the eyes, and chemical firms generate toxic waste and increase the possibility of poisonous gas leaks. These negative externalities—the unpriced by-products of production—are largely ignored in GNP accounting, even though they affect the quality of life. To the extent that growth in GNP also involves growth in such negative externalities, a rising GNP may not be as attractive as it would first appear.

GNP Comparisons Across Countries Are Tricky

Observers are tempted to make much of international differences in various economic measures, particularly when GNP per capita is measured, but such comparisons are fraught with complications. The United States has perhaps the most thorough and systematic national income accounting system in the world. Some less developed countries, however, are simply too poor to support the sophisticated surveys required to monitor economic activity. Thus, the national income statistics generated in poor countries tend to be unreliable. In centrally planned countries, such as the Soviet Union and the countries of Eastern Europe, the definition of final output often excludes "nonproductive" services, such as personal transportation and communications, as well as government and most professional services. Final output in centrally planned economies also excludes a return on capital or land. Moreover, governments in centrally planned economies establish many prices, so such prices reflect bureaucrats' decisions rather than market forces. Therefore, international comparisons of GNP data should be viewed with caution.

Despite the limitations and inaccuracies associated with official GNP estimates, the trend of GNP over time provides a fairly accurate picture of the overall movement of the U.S. economy. As a vehicle for observing what happens to the economy from year to year, GNP remains a useful measure of economic activity. Inflation, however, distorts the direct comparability of dollar amounts from one year to the next. In the next section we examine ways of adjusting GNP for changes in the general price level.

ACCOUNTING FOR PRICE CHANGES

As noted earlier, the national income accounts are based on the market values of the goods and services produced in the particular year. The gross national product is therefore computed in *current dollars*—that is, in the dollars actually paid or received at the time of the transaction. If GNP is based on current dollars, then the national income accounts measure the **nominal value** of national output. Hence, the current-dollar GNP and nominal GNP are identical; both are based on the prices prevailing at the time of the transaction.

*A **nominal value** is measured in current-year dollars.*

The system of national income accounting based on current dollars, or nominal values, allows us to make comparisons among income or expenditure components in a particular year. But the economy's price level tends to change over time, making current-dollar comparisons across years less meaningful. For example, between 1979 and 1980, nominal GNP increased by about 9 percent. That sounds like an impressive growth in production, but the economy's price level grew at about the same rate. Thus, the growth in nominal GNP between 1979 and 1980 was the result of inflation. The **real value** of GNP — that is, GNP measured in terms of actual production — was unchanged.

*A **real value** is measured in dollars of fixed purchasing power.*

To make meaningful comparisons of GNP across years, we must adjust GNP for changes in the price level, so that only actual, or real, changes in production are measured. To do this, we must first compute the average of all prices in the economy and then devise a way to compare the price level in one year with the level in another year. Such a comparison requires that we establish a reference point that can be used to measure the year-to-year changes in the price level.

The Price Index

To compare the price level over time, we must first select a reference point that can be used to construct index numbers. To see how index numbers are used, consider the simplest case imaginable. Suppose bread is the only good produced in the economy. As a reference point against which to measure price changes, we choose the price of bread in some specified period. The year selected is called the *base year*, and prices in other years are expressed in terms of the base-year price.

Suppose the base year chosen is 1988, a year during which a loaf of bread in our simple economy sold for $1.25. Suppose the price of bread increased to $1.30 in 1989, and to $1.40 in 1990. We construct a price index by dividing each year's price by the price in the base year, as in Exhibit 3. For 1988, the base year, we divide the base price of bread by itself, $1.25/$1.25, so the price index in the base year equals 1. The index in 1989 is $1.30/$1.25 = 1.04, which is 4 percent higher than in the base year. In 1990 the index is $1.40/$1.25 = 1.12, which is 12 percent higher than in the base year. In

EXHIBIT 3
HYPOTHETICAL EXAMPLE OF A PRICE INDEX
(base year = 1988)

Year	Price of Bread in Current Year (1)	Price of Bread in Base Year (2)	Price Index (3) = (1)/(2) × 100
1988	$1.25	$1.25	100
1989	1.30	1.25	104
1990	1.40	1.25	112

reporting the price index, it is customary to multiply the index by 100. Thus, *in the base period the index is always 100*; the index is 104 in 1989 and 112 in 1990.

The price index not only permits comparisons between the base year and any other year but also makes comparisons between any two years easy. For example, what if you were presented with the indexes for 1989 and 1990 and asked to determine what happened to the price level between the two years? By dividing the 1990 price index by the 1989 price index, 112/104, you would find that the price level increased by about 8 percent.

This section has shown how the price index is computed if we know average prices. A more difficult task is to compute the price level in the economy. Two approaches are to construct the implicit price deflator and to calculate the consumer price index.

Implicit Price Deflator

Exhibit 4 illustrates how to compute an implicit price deflator. For simplicity, we assume that the economy produces only three outputs: Twinkies, fuel oil, and cable TV service. The production of each in the current year is listed in column (1); current prices are listed in column (2), and current expenditures in column (3).

Current expenditures on each item equal the output in the current year multiplied by the price in the current year. The current-year GNP is simply the sum of expenditures on all items, which equals $51,750 for this hypothetical economy. What would the value of this same output be if, instead of using current-year prices, we used the prices prevailing in the base year? All we need do is substitute the base-year prices for the current-year prices and recompute total expenditures. Column (4) lists the base-year prices. Multiplying these prices by the quantities listed in column (1) yields the base-year equivalent expenditures in column (5).

Whereas GNP in current prices, or nominal GNP, is $51,750, GNP computed in base-year prices, or real GNP, is $41,350. The price index is

EXHIBIT 4
HYPOTHETICAL DATA USED TO DEVELOP
THE IMPLICIT PRICE DEFLATOR

Good or Service	Output in Current Year (1)	Prices in Current Year (2)	Expenditures in Current Year (3) = (1) × (2)	Base-Year Prices (4)	Base-Year Equivalent Expenditure (5) = (1) × (4)
Twinkies	15,000 packages	$ 0.45/package	$ 6,750	$ 0.49	7,350
Fuel oil	10,000 gallons	1.50/gallon	15,000	1.00	10,000
Cable TV	1,200 months	25.00/month	30,000	20.00	24,000
			$51,750		$41,350

The ***implicit price deflator*** *is a price index for the economy's aggregate output; it is the ratio of nominal GNP to real GNP, multiplied by 100.*

found by dividing expenditures in current-year prices by expenditures on that same output in base-year prices, then multiplying by 100. This price index is called the **implicit price deflator**; it is also referred to as the *implicit GNP deflator*. In our example the implicit price deflator equals 125.2 ($51,750/$41,350 × 100). This deflator says that, on average, prices in the current year are 25.2 percent higher than prices in the base year. *We can compute the implicit price deflator for any year by dividing nominal GNP in that year by real GNP in that year.* Thus

Implicit price deflator = (nominal GNP/real GNP) × 100

Suppose nominal GNP increases in a given year. Part of this increase may simply be the result of inflation — pure hot air. To *deflate* GNP — take out the hot air — we hold prices constant, thereby eliminating increases due solely to increases in the price level. The calculations required to develop real GNP for the U.S. economy involve thousands of prices, but the principle is the same as in our simple example. The federal government has deflated GNP over time by applying 1982 prices to the output produced each year. The record of the U.S. economy since 1960 is presented in Exhibit 5. The blue line indicates nominal GNP, or GNP measured in the prices that prevailed each year. The red line indicates real GNP, or GNP measured in 1982 prices.

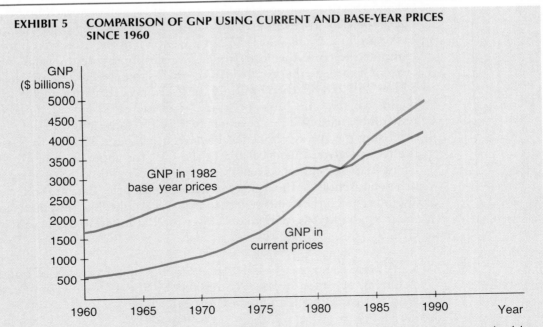

EXHIBIT 5   COMPARISON OF GNP USING CURRENT AND BASE-YEAR PRICES SINCE 1960

Since 1960 GNP measured in current prices has increased every year. Much of that increase, however, has been due to price changes. Real GNP, measured in 1982 prices, has increased more slowly and has fallen during some years.

Notice that for years prior to 1982, real GNP exceeds nominal GNP because the 1982 prices used to compute real GNP on average exceed the prices that prevailed prior to 1982. After 1982, however, real GNP is below nominal GNP because 1982 prices on average are below the prices since 1982. Real GNP and nominal GNP are identical in the base year, 1982, since for that year 1982 prices are used to compute both measures of GNP.

Consumer Price Index

*The **consumer price index** (CPI) measures changes in the cost of a fixed "market basket" of consumer goods and services over time.*

Perhaps the price index most familiar to you is the **consumer price index**, or **CPI**, which measures changes over time in the cost of buying the "market basket" of goods and services purchased by a typical family. The cost of buying this same basket each year is computed based on the current prices each year. Changes in the cost of this basket are often referred to as changes in the "cost of living." To show how the CPI is calculated for a simple case, we will develop a hypothetical market basket for the base year. For simplicity, suppose a typical family's market basket for the year includes 365 packages of Twinkies, 500 gallons of fuel oil, and 12 months of cable TV service. Prices in the base year are listed in column (2) of Exhibit 6. The annual cost of each product in the base year is found by multiplying price times quantity, as shown in column (3). The total cost of such a market basket in the base year is shown at the bottom of column (3) to be $918.85.

Current-year prices are listed in column (4). Notice that not all prices changed by the same amount. The price of fuel oil increased by 50 percent, but the price of Twinkies actually declined. The cost of purchasing that same basket in the current year is $1214.25, shown as the total of column (5). To compute the consumer price index, we simply divide the total cost in the current year by the total cost of that same basket in the base year, $1214.25/$918.85, then multiply by 100. This calculation yields 132.1. We could say that the "cost of living" has increased by 32.1 percent, but remember that not all prices increased by the same amount.

Using the average price level between 1982 and 1984 as the base value, the federal government calculates the CPI for about four hundred items. These items are chosen as representative of the bundle purchased by a typical urban household in the base year. Each month price data are collected from about eighteen thousand sellers in fifty-six localities across the country. In the next chapter we will take a closer look at inflation as measured by the CPI.

A price index can be calculated for any market basket of goods. Two examples of other indexes computed by the U.S. government are the producer price index and the export price index.

Differences Between the Implicit Price Deflator and the CPI

Price indexes are weighted averages of various prices. Whereas the implicit price deflator includes the prices of *all* final domestic production in a

EXHIBIT 6
HYPOTHETICAL MARKET BASKET USED TO DEVELOP THE CONSUMER PRICE INDEX

Good or Service	Quantity in Market Basket (1)	Prices in Base Year (2)	Cost of Basket in Base Year (3) = (1) × (2)	Prices in Current Year (4)	Cost of Basket in Current Year (5) = (1) × (4)
Twinkies	365 packages	$ 0.49	$178.85	$ 0.45	$ 164.25
Fuel oil	500 gallons	1.00	500.00	1.50	750.00
Cable TV	12 months	20.00	240.00	25.00	300.00
			$918.85		$1214.25

year, the CPI focuses on the prices of a market basket of specific items consumed by a typical household—just a sample of current production. Since consumers buy imported goods as well as domestically produced goods, a sample of imported goods is included in the CPI market basket.

Both the implicit price deflator and the CPI compare current prices to prices in a base period. The primary difference between the two is in the weight that each price receives when the index is computed. By maintaining the same market basket over time, the CPI holds the weights of each price constant over time. The implicit price deflator, however, weights prices according to each product's importance in GNP each year, so these weights can change from year to year. Since the two price indexes measure inflation in different ways, we should not be surprised that they yield different measures of inflation.

Problems with Inflation Measures

There is no perfect way to measure the cost of living. All price indexes involve certain distortions or biases.

Quality Improvements As already noted, the quality and variety of products are on the average improving all the time, so some price increases may be as much a reflection of quality improvements as of inflation. There have been some attempts to account for quality differences over time in computing changes in the price level, but these efforts fail to reflect all quality changes. Thus we say there is a *quality bias*, since each price index assumes that quality remains relatively constant over time even though quality has generally improved. As a result, *the true extent of inflation tends to be overstated*.

Buyer-Response Bias Recall that the CPI, in order to focus on the pure effect of price changes, holds constant the kind and amount of goods and services in the typical market basket. But not all prices change by the same percentage. And a family would probably respond to changes in relative prices by consuming more of the relatively cheaper goods and less of the relatively more expensive goods. Because the CPI calculations hold constant the bundle of commodities consumed over time, this approach does not recognize that consumers adjust to changes in relative prices. The CPI calculations thus imply uneconomical consumer behavior, thereby *overstating the true extent of inflation experienced by the typical family*.

Whereas the CPI assumes the same consumption bundle over time, even in the face of sharp changes in relative prices, the implicit price deflator calculates the effects of inflation based on the quantities of goods actually produced each year. Hence, if the quantity of fuel oil demanded falls because of its higher relative price, oil will receive less weight in the implicit price deflator. The implicit price deflator in this sense offers a truer measure of inflation than does the CPI for products actually produced and consumed. Because the CPI holds the commodity bundle constant over time, it tends to yield a higher measure of inflation than does the implicit price deflator. Between 1970 and 1989, for example, the average annual increase in the CPI was 6.3 percent, compared to an average increase in the implicit price deflator of 6.0 percent.

CONCLUSION

Necessity was the mother of invention in the development of the national income accounts. The Great Depression created the demand for more information about the economy. The national income accounts are not perfect, but they do offer a reasonably accurate measure of year-to-year movements in the economy. The national income accounts are published in much greater detail than the preceding discussion suggests. The appendix to this chapter discusses the national income accounts in greater depth.

This chapter explained how to adjust GNP for changes in the economy's price level. In the following chapters we will often refer to distinctions between real and nominal values. As we do this, keep in mind that no adjustment for the effects of inflation is perfect. Though no price index is perfect, the price indexes now in use provide reasonably good measures of the trend in price levels over time.

Summary

1. The gross national product measures the total market value of all final goods and services produced in the economy during a particular year. There are two ways of measuring GNP: the expenditure approach and the income approach. The expenditure approach involves adding up the market value of all final goods

and services produced in the economy during the year. The income approach involves adding up all the income generated as a result of production during the year.

2. The circular flow of income summarizes the flow of income and spending through the

economy. Disposable income is either spent or saved. Saving, net taxes, and imports represent leakages from the circular flow. These leakages must equal the injections into the circular flow: investment, government purchases, and exports.

3. GNP reflects mostly recorded market exchanges; household production and the underground economy are not included. Improvements in the quality and variety of goods are generally not reflected in GNP either. In other ways GNP may overstate the true amount of production that occurs. GNP fails to account for depreciation of the capital stock or for any externalities arising from production.

4. GNP values output based on its market value. Changes in GNP over time may reflect changes in the amount produced or changes in the prices at which goods are sold. Nominal GNP must therefore be adjusted to filter out the effects of changes in the price level. The implicit price deflator accounts for changes in the prices of all final goods and services produced in the nation during each year. The consumer price index focuses on a base-year sample of goods and services consumed by a typical family. Although no adjustment for changes in the price level is perfect, an examination of real GNP over time provides a useful picture of the trend in economic activity.

Questions and Problems

1. (National Income Accounting) Identify the component of aggregate expenditure to which each of the following belongs:
   a. purchase of a new Japanese automobile
   b. purchase of one hour of legal counsel by a household
   c. construction of a new house
   d. an increase in semiconductor inventories over last year's level
   e. acquisition of ten new police cars for a city

2. (Circular Flow) Suppose that consumers decide to cut spending by 20 percent. This will cause a rise in firms' inventories. How will such inventories, which have accumulated unexpectedly, be financed by the firms?

3. (Injections and Leakages) Explain why injections must equal leakages if aggregate expenditure is equal to aggregate income.

4. (Leakages and Injections) Japan has one of the highest saving rates in the world. Some economists say it is because Japan has a policy of forced early retirement; others say it is because the country lacks a social security system such as the one in the United States; and still others say it is because of the extraordinary cost of buying living space. Expand the equation of leakages and injections found in this chapter to include net exports, and discuss the Japanese situation.

5. (Investment) In the national income accounts, one part of measured investment is net changes in inventories. Last year's inventories are subtracted from this year's inventories to obtain a net change. Explain why this variable is considered part of the national income. Also, discuss why it is not sufficient to measure inventories only for the current year. (Remember the difference between stocks and flows.)

6. (Underground Economy) Many underdeveloped countries do not use checking accounts. If such countries placed high income taxes on the working population, what do you expect would happen to their underground economies? Why is the use of currency so essential to the underground economy?

7. (Price Index) Home computers and video cassette recorders have not been part of the U.S. economy for very long, and both goods have been decreasing in price and improving in quality. What problems does this situation

pose for people who are responsible for computing a price index?

8. (Price Index) Compute a new price index for the data in Exhibit 4 in this chapter, given that the current price of fuel oil is $0.46 per gallon. Is the current price level higher or lower than that of the base year?

9. (Price Index) The health expenditure component of the price index has been steadily rising. How might this index be biased by quality and substitution effects? Are there any substitutes for health care?

10. (Inflation) Inflation is a continuous and prolonged rise in the level of prices. Hyperinflation is unusually high rates of inflation — for example, 40 percent per month. Who would be hurt by hyperinflation? How would a government cope with the increased demand for currency?

11. (National Income Accounting) Suppose a company produces something nobody wants. Since production of the good generates income to the resources used, it is included in GNP on the income side. How would it be counted on the expenditure side?

12. (Circular Flow) Using the national income identity in which aggregate income equals aggregate expenditure, show how government budget deficits must be financed from a combination of imbalances between (a) exports and imports and (b) saving and investment.

13. (Price Index) Consider the following data.

Good	Current Output Level (units)	Typical Household Consumption Level (units)	Base Price (per unit)	Current Price (per unit)
Clothing	100,000	2	$10	$12
Food	120,000	3	$ 2	$ 4
Durables	6,000	1	$50	$40

a. Calculate the rate of price increase from the base period to the current period, using both the implicit GNP deflator and the Consumer Price Index methods.
b. Explain why the two measures are different.
c. Which is better?

14. (Gross National Product) Explain why each of the following should be taken into account when GNP data are used to compare the "level of well-being" in different countries.
a. Population levels
b. Distribution of income
c. The amount of production that takes place *outside* of markets (e.g., housekeeping by a family member)
d. The length of the average work week
e. The degree of pollution in the environment

APPENDIX
A Closer Look at the National Income Accounts

This chapter has focused on two key definitions of output and income: gross national product and disposable income. Although these two measures will be of most interest in subsequent chapters, other economic aggregates also convey useful information and receive media attention. In this appendix we examine these other aggregate measures.

Net National Product

In the course of producing GNP, some capital stock becomes worn out, grows obsolete, or becomes damaged during the year. For example, a new truck that logs a hundred thousand miles its first year has been subject to wear and tear and therefore has a diminished value as a resource. A truer picture of the *net* production that actually occurs during the year is found by subtracting this *depreciation* from GNP. The *net national product*, or **NNP**, equals GNP minus depreciation—the value of the capital stock used up in the production process.

We can now distinguish between two definitions of investment. **Gross investment** measures the value of all investment during the period, including investment required to replace capital used up during the production process. Gross investment is used in computing GNP. **Net investment** equals gross investment minus depreciation. The economy's productive abilities depend on what happens to net investment. If net investment is negative—that is, if depreciation exceeds gross investment—the capital stock declines, so its contribution to output declines as well.[2] If net

investment is zero, the capital stock remains constant, as does its contribution to output. And if net investment is positive, the capital stock grows, as does its contribution to the economy's ability to produce.

As the names imply, the *gross* national product includes *gross* investment and the *net* national product includes *net* investment. If we let D represent the value of depreciation and I' net investment, then $I - D = I'$ and

$$GNP - D = NNP = C + I' + G + (X - M)$$

Developing a figure for depreciation involves much guesswork. For example, what is the appropriate measure of depreciation for the parking lots at Disney World, the metal display shelves at Sears, or the 5000-gallon casks used to age wine in the Napa Valley? Exhibit 7 uses data for 1989 to show that NNP is derived by subtracting depreciation from GNP.

EXHIBIT 7
DERIVING NET NATIONAL PRODUCT AND NATIONAL INCOME USING 1989 DATA
(in billions of dollars)

Gross national product (GNP)	$5233.2
Minus depreciation	− 552.2
Net national product	4681.0
Minus indirect business taxes (net of subsidies)	− 416.0
National income (NI)	4265.0

Source: *Economic Report of the President,* February 1990.

National Income

The value of final goods and services is computed at market prices, but some products sell for less, and others for more, than resource suppliers receive. Because of **government subsidies**, such as payments to

---

[2] This discussion assumes there is no major change in inventories during the period. As we have said, changes in inventories are reflected in investment. A major reduction in inventories could result in a negative net investment even when the capital stock has not declined.

suppliers of low-income housing, some products sell for less than resource suppliers receive. Because of **indirect business taxes**, such as sales, excise, and property taxes, some products sell for more than resource suppliers receive. For example, a gallon of gasoline may sell for $1.25, but about $0.25 in taxes must be paid to the government before any resource supplier receives a penny.

Since subsidies are received as income, they should be included in national income, even though they are not part of the selling price. And since indirect business taxes are not received as income by any individual, they should not be included in national income, even though they are part of the selling price. **National income**, or **NI**, therefore equals net national product plus government subsidies minus indirect business taxes. Since indirect business taxes are about twenty times greater than government subsidies, we simplify the reporting by computing indirect business taxes net of subsidies. Exhibit 7 shows how to go from net national product (NNP) to national income (NI).

We have now moved from gross national product to net national product to national income. Next we peel back yet another layer to arrive at personal income, the income people actually receive.

Personal Income

Some of the income received this year was not earned this year, and some of the income earned this year is not actually received this year by those who earned it. By adding to national income the income received but not earned and subtracting from it the income earned but not received, we convert national income into all income *received* by individuals, which is termed **personal income**, or **PI**. Personal income, a widely reported measure of economic welfare, is computed by the government monthly.

The adjustment from national income to personal income is shown in Exhibit 8. In-come earned but not received includes (1) Social Security taxes paid by employers, (2) corporate income taxes, and (3) undistributed corporate profits, which are profits the firm retains rather than pays as dividends. Income received but not earned in the current period includes (1) government transfer payments, (2) receipts from private pension plans, and (3) interest paid by government and by consumers.

Disposable Income

Although several taxes have been considered so far, we have not yet discussed personal taxes. Personal taxes consist primarily of the federal and state personal income tax and the employee's share of the Social Security tax. Subtracting personal taxes and other government charges from personal income yields disposable income, or DI, which is the amount available for spending or saving—the amount that can be "disposed of" by the household. Think of disposable income as

EXHIBIT 8 DERIVING PERSONAL INCOME AND DISPOSABLE INCOME USING 1989 DATA (in billions of dollars)	
National income (NI)	$4265.0
Minus income earned but not received (Social Security taxes, corporate income taxes, undistributed corporate profits)	− 665.1
Plus income received but not earned (government and business transfers, net personal interest income)	828.8
Personal income (PI)	4428.7
Minus personal tax and nontax charges	− 648.7
Disposable income (DI)	3780.0

Source: *Economic Report of the President,* February 1990.

take-home pay. Exhibit 8 shows that personal income (PI) minus personal taxes and other government charges yields disposable income (DI).

Summary of National Income Accounts

The income side of national income accounts can be summarized as follows. We begin with GNP, the market value of final goods and services produced during the year. We subtract depreciation from GNP to yield the net national product (NNP). From NNP we subtract indirect business taxes (net of subsidies) to yield national income (NI). We obtain personal income (PI) by subtracting from NI all income earned but not received (e.g., undistributed corporate profits) and adding to NI all income received but not earned (e.g., transfer payments). By subtracting personal taxes and other government charges from PI, we arrive at the bottom line: disposable income (DI), the amount people are actually free either to save or to spend. The components of the national income accounts are summarized below.

GNP = market value of output *produced* during the year

NNP = market value of output *available for use* by households, firms, governments, and foreign purchasers

NI = amount of income *earned* by suppliers of resources employed to produce GNP

PI = amount of income *received* by households before personal taxes have been paid

DI = amount of *spendable* income for saving and consumption after personal taxes have been paid

We now have a more detailed picture of the income side of the national income accounts. As we have said, GNP can be computed either by considering aggregate expenditures on production or by allocating the income arising from that production. The relationship

between these two approaches to national income accounting resembles on a large scale the relationship between the two sides of a balance sheet in business accounting. Next we will discuss how these two sides of the ledger fit together.

Summary Income Statement of the Economy

Exhibit 9 presents an income statement for the entire economy. The upper portion lists aggregate expenditure, which consists of consumption, gross investment, government purchases, and net exports. As you can see, during 1989 imports exceeded exports, so net exports were negative. You might think of aggregate expenditure as the revenue of a giant firm. The income from this expenditure is broken down in the lower portion of Exhibit 9. After depreciation and indirect busi-

---

EXHIBIT 9
EXPENDITURE AND INCOME STATEMENT FOR THE U.S. ECONOMY USING 1989 DATA
(in billions)

Aggregate Expenditure

Consumption (C)	$3470.3
Gross investment (I)	777.1
Government purchases (G)	1036.7
Net exports (X − M)	− 50.9
GNP	5233.2

Allocation of Income

Depreciation	$ 552.2
Net indirect business taxes	416.0
Compensation of employees	3145.4
Proprietors' income	352.2
Corporate profits	298.2
Net interest	461.2
Rental income of persons	8.0
GNP	5233.2

Source: *Economic Report of the President*, February 1990.

ness taxes, the remaining allocations equal national income. National income, which represents the sum of all earnings from producing national product, can be divided into its five components: employee compensation, proprietors' income, corporate profits, net interest, and rental income of persons.

Employee compensation, which is by far the largest source of income, includes both money wages and payments made to cover Social Security taxes, medical insurance, and other fringe benefits. **Proprietors' income** includes the earnings of farmers and other owners of unincorporated business. **Corporate profits** are the net revenues received by incorporated businesses before subtraction of corporate income taxes. **Net interest** is the interest received by individuals, excluding interest paid by consumers to businesses and interest paid by government.

Each family that owns its own home is viewed as a tiny firm that rents its home to itself. Since homeowners do not, in fact, rent homes to themselves, an *imputed* rental value must be developed based on what the market rent would be. **Rental income of persons** consists primarily of the imputed rental value of owner-occupied housing minus the costs of owning that property (such as property taxes, insurance, depreciation, and interest paid on the mortgage). From the totals in Exhibit 9, you can see that aggregate spending in the economy equals the income generated by that spending.

Appendix Question

1. (National Income Accounts) Use the following data to answer the questions below.

Net investment	$100
Depreciation	40
Exports	50
Imports	30
Government spending	150
Consumption	400
Indirect business taxes (net of subsidies)	35
Income earned but not received	60
Income received but not earned	70

Personal income taxes	50
Employee compensation	460
Corporate profits	60
Rental income	20
Net interest	40
Proprietor's income	55

a. Calculate GNP using the income-based and expenditure methods.
b. Calculate gross investment.
c. Calculate NNP, NI, PI, and DI.
d. What percent of personal income is employee compensation?
e. What percent of personal income goes to personal income taxes?

C H A P T E R 7

Unemployment and Inflation

In this chapter we explore the two macroeconomic phenomena that usually pose the greatest problems for the economy: unemployment and inflation. Although unemployment and inflation are often related, we will initially describe each separately. Our focus will be more on the extent and consequences of these problems than on their causes. The causes of each and the relationship between the two will become clearer as you learn more about the economy.

As this chapter will show, not all unemployment or inflation harms the economy. Even in a healthy economy, there are certain kinds of unemployment that reflect the voluntary choices of workers seeking their best job opportunities. And inflation that is fully anticipated creates fewer distortions in the economy than does unexpected inflation. Topics discussed in this chapter include

- Measuring unemployment
- Frictional, structural, seasonal, and cyclical unemployment
- Meaning of full employment
- Sources and consequences of inflation
- Relative price changes
- Nominal and real interest rates

UNEMPLOYMENT

"They scampered about looking for work.... They swarmed on the highways. The movement changed them; the highways, the camps along the road, the fear of hunger and the hunger itself, changed them. The children without dinner changed them, the endless moving changed them."[1]

There is no question that a long stretch of unemployment can have a profound effect on an individual or a family. The most obvious loss is that of a steady paycheck, but the unemployed often also suffer a loss of self-esteem. Moreover, researchers have found that unemployment appears to be linked to a greater incidence of crime and to a variety of afflictions including heart disease, suicide, and mental illness. However much they complain about their jobs, workers tend to rely on these jobs not only for income but also for part of their personal identity. So the loss of a job involves some loss of that identity.

In addition to these personal costs, unemployment imposes a cost on the economy as a whole because fewer goods and services are produced. When the economy does not generate enough jobs to employ all those who are willing and able to work, that unemployed labor service is lost forever. *This lost potential output coupled with the economic and psychological damage to unemployed workers represents the real cost of unemployment.* As we begin our analysis of unemployment, keep in mind that unemployment statistics reflect millions of individuals with their own stories. For some, unemployment is inconvenient but brief. For others, unemployment is a major problem that has profound effects on their own and their families' stability and economic welfare.

Measuring Unemployment

"The unemployment rate was up slightly in September, but administration officials noted that there is no cause for alarm." So reads a typical news story on the unemployment rate, perhaps the most widely reported measure of the nation's economic condition. What does the unemployment rate measure, what are the sources of unemployment, and how does unemployment change over time? These are some of the questions explored in this section. To start, we will consider how unemployment is measured.

The **labor force** includes all individuals 16 years of age and older who are either working or actively looking for work.

The **unemployment rate** expresses the number of unemployed workers as a percentage of the labor force.

We will begin with the U.S. noninstitutional adult population, which consists of all persons 16 years of age and older, except those in prisons and in mental facilities. In this chapter when we refer to the *adult population*, we will mean the noninstitutional adult population. The **labor force** consists of those in the adult population who are either working or looking for work. Those looking for work are considered unemployed. More specifically, the Bureau of Labor Statistics counts people as unemployed if they have looked for work at least once in the preceding four weeks. The unemployment rate measures the percentage of those in the labor force who are unemployed. Thus, the **unemployment rate** equals the number unemployed—that is, the number looking for work—divided by the number in the labor force.

---

[1] John Steinbeck, *The Grapes of Wrath* (New York: Viking Press, 1939), 392.

Only a fraction of those adults not working are actually counted as unemployed. The others may be retired, may choose to remain at home to care for children or perform household tasks, or may be full-time students. The "idle rich" may pursue a life of leisure. Some people may be unable to work because of long-term illness or disability. Finally, some people may have given up their job searches in frustration. Since these so-called **discouraged workers** have, in effect, dropped out of the labor force, they are not counted as unemployed. *Because the official unemployment rate does not include discouraged workers, the true extent of unemployment in the economy tends to be understated.*

The above definitions are illustrated in Exhibit 1, where circles represent the various groups and subgroups. The circle on the left depicts the entire U.S. labor force, including both those employed and those unemployed. The circle on the right represents those in the adult population who are not working, for whatever reason. The two circles, representing those *not working* and those in the *labor force*, together reflect the entire adult population. The intersection of the two circles identifies those who are *unemployed*—that is, those who are in the labor force but not working.

Unemployment Rate You can see from the circles that all those who are unemployed are counted as not working, but not all those who are not working are counted as unemployed. The number of individuals in each category and subcategory is listed in parentheses (in millions). Of the 126.3 million in the labor force in November of 1989, 6.7 million were unemployed. The unemployment rate is found by dividing the number of unem-

*A **discouraged worker** is a person who has dropped out of the labor force because of failure to find a job.*

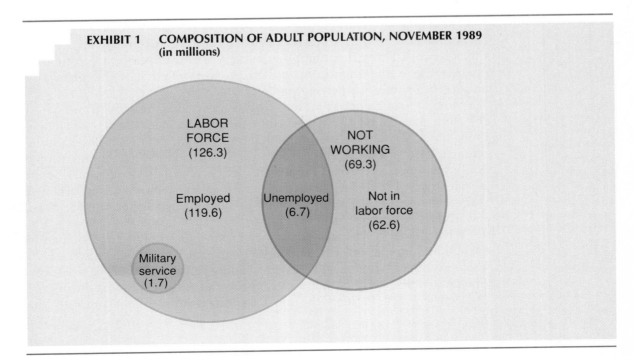

EXHIBIT 1   COMPOSITION OF ADULT POPULATION, NOVEMBER 1989
(in millions)

LABOR FORCE (126.3)

NOT WORKING (69.3)

Employed (119.6)

Unemployed (6.7)

Not in labor force (62.6)

Military service (1.7)

Source: *Economic Report of the President*, February 1990.

ployed workers by the number in the labor force; in November, 1989, the unemployment rate averaged 5.3 percent.

Labor Force Participation Rate Another measure of interest when we study employment is the labor force participation rate, which indicates the proportion of the adult population that is in the labor force. In Exhibit 1 the adult population equals those in the labor force (126.3 million) plus those not in the labor force (62.6 million): a total of 188.9 million.[2] The **labor force participation rate** therefore equals the number in the labor force divided by the adult population, or 66.9 percent (126.3/188.9), which is the highest labor participation rate since World War II.

*The **labor force participation rate** is the ratio of the labor force to the population of working age.*

Civilian Unemployment Rate Those in military service are depicted by the small circle identifying that subset of the labor force. Since all those in the military are considered employed (even those who "only stand and wait"), this small circle does not intersect the "not working" circle. Official unemployment statistics often distinguish between the overall unemployment rate, which was just discussed, and the civilian unemployment rate, which is found by dividing the number unemployed by the civilian labor force. Until the reporting method was changed by the Reagan administration, the military figures were not included in the labor force. Including them lowers the official unemployment rate below the civilian unemployment rate.

Changes over Time in Unemployment Statistics

The adult population changes slowly over time. The only way to join that group is to become 16 years of age or to immigrate to the United States; the only way to leave the adult population is to die or to emigrate to another country. Since 1950 the adult population in the United States has grown by an average of only 1.6 percent per year.

Moving in and out of the labor force is easier than moving in and out of the adult population. Thus, the labor force participation rate can change more quickly than the adult population. Since the 1950s, for example, women have increased their labor force participation rate dramatically. Among women, the participation rate climbed from 36 percent in 1955 to 57 percent in 1989. The participation rate among men, however, declined from 85 percent in 1955 to 76 percent in 1989, primarily because of a trend toward earlier retirement.

What changes even more quickly over time than labor force participation or the adult population is the unemployment rate. Exhibit 2 depicts the U.S. unemployment rate since 1900, with shading to indicate years of recession. The rates were clearly higher during recessions and were lowest during the two world wars. Perhaps the most striking feature of the graph is the

---

[2] Prior to the 1940 census, "workers" could include anyone 10 years of age or older. In 1940 age 14 became the lower limit, and in 1966 the lower limit was raised to 16, where it remains.

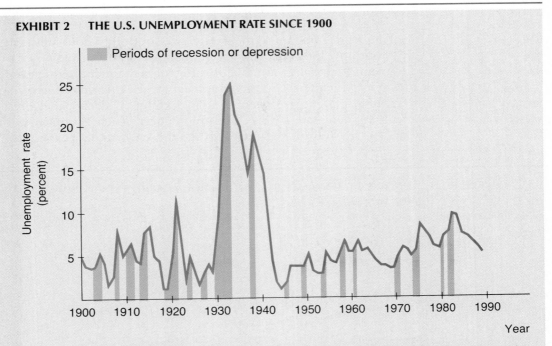

EXHIBIT 2   THE U.S. UNEMPLOYMENT RATE SINCE 1900

Since 1900 the unemployment rate has fluctuated widely, rising during recessions and falling during expansions. During the Great Depression of the 1930s, the rate rose as high as 25.2 percent. Since 1950 there has been an upward trend in the unemployment rate.

Source: *Historical Statistics of the United States,* 1970, and *Economic Report of the President,* 1990.

dramatic jump that occurred during the Great Depression, when the unemployment rate climbed above 25 percent.

Note that since 1950 there has been an upward trend in the unemployment rate. Between 1950 and 1970, for example, the rate averaged 4.6 percent, never reaching 7.0 percent any year during that stretch. Since 1970, however, the unemployment rate has averaged 7.0 percent, never falling as low as 4.6 percent. These numbers imply that the number of people who have been unable to find work at any given time has been about 2.5 million people higher since 1970 than it was between 1950 and 1970. We should also note, however, that the labor force grew sharply between these two periods because of a growing population and a rising labor force participation rate. Thus although the number of unemployed increased, the number employed increased as well, growing by more than 40 million since 1970. In fact, the United States has been called an "astounding job machine," and this feature of our economy is the envy of the world. At the same time the U.S. economy was creating forty million jobs, the industrialized countries of Western Europe saw little employment growth. In 1989 the civilian unemployment rate averaged 5.3 percent in the United States, compared to about 7.5 percent in European Common Market countries.

Unemployment in Various Groups

The overall unemployment rate says nothing about who are unemployed or how long they have been unemployed. Even a low rate of unemployment often belies some wide differences in unemployment rate across ages, races, genders, and geographical areas. Unemployment rates since 1972 for different groups appear in Exhibit 3. Each panel presents the unemployment rate by race and by gender; panel (a) considers those 20 years of age and older, and panel (b) those 16 to 19 years old. Years of

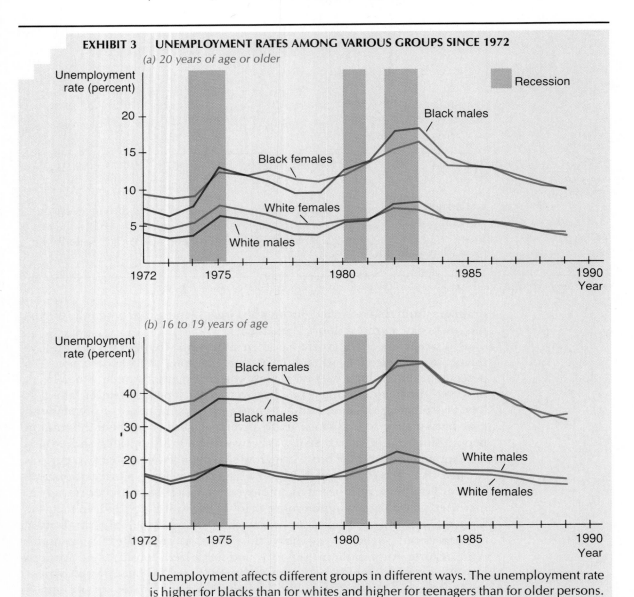

EXHIBIT 3   UNEMPLOYMENT RATES AMONG VARIOUS GROUPS SINCE 1972

(a) 20 years of age or older

(b) 16 to 19 years of age

Unemployment affects different groups in different ways. The unemployment rate is higher for blacks than for whites and higher for teenagers than for older persons.

recession are shaded. As you can see, rates are higher among blacks than among whites, and rates are higher among teenagers than among those age 20 and older. The rates of all groups climbed during recessions. Unemployment also varies by occupational group. Historically, professional and technical workers have experienced lower unemployment rates than blue-collar workers, especially those in construction.

Duration of Unemployment

Any given unemployment rate says little about how long people have been unemployed — that is, the *average duration of unemployment*. The average duration of unemployment in 1989 was 11.9 weeks. Some people were unemployed longer than others: 49 percent were unemployed fewer than 5 weeks; 30 percent from 5 to 14 weeks; 11 percent from 15 to 26 weeks; and 10 percent 27 weeks or longer. Typically, a rise in the unemployment rate is due to both a larger number of people unemployed and a greater average duration of unemployment.

Unemployment Differences Across the Country

The national unemployment rate masks much variance in rates across the country. For example, during 1988, when the U.S. unemployment rate averaged 5.5 percent, more than one hundred counties had unemployment rates exceeding 15 percent and thirty counties had rates exceeding 25 percent. To look behind the numbers, we examine one county's experience with high unemployment in the following case study.

CASE STUDY

Poor King Coal

For decades McDowell County, West Virginia, prospered by supplying the coal that fired the nation's steel mills. Mining jobs were abundant and wages attractive; many miners earned over $40,000 a year in 1980. Most young people became miners rather than finishing their educations. The mining companies dominated the county. They owned most of the property and discouraged other types of economic development.

Then, during the first half of the 1980s, the value of the dollar rose relative to foreign currencies, so American steel became more expensive overseas and foreign steel became cheaper in the United States. As the demand for U.S. steel fell, so did the demand for the coal needed to produce that steel. Coal mines in McDowell County shut down, and by 1988 the official unemployment rate for the county had reached a whopping 32 percent. Local officials claimed the actual rate was higher.

The county tried to attract new industry — even bidding for the controversial federal nuclear-waste dump — but met with little success. The county's poor roads and bridges and a labor force trained only for mining are not attractive features for potential employers. In short, the county had all its eggs in one basket, and the basket fell.

Source: Alan Murray, "Unemployment Tops 25% in Some Regions Mired in Deep Poverty," *Wall Street Journal*, 21 April 1988.

Sources of Unemployment

Consider all the ways in which people can become unemployed. They may quit or be fired from their jobs. They may be looking for a first job because they just turned 16 or graduated. Or they may be trying to reenter the labor force after an absence. An examination of the reasons behind unemployment during 1989 indicates that 46 percent of those unemployed lost their previous jobs, 16 percent quit their previous jobs, 10 percent were entering the labor market for the first time, and 28 percent were reentering the market. *Thus most were unemployed because they either quit their jobs or were just joining or rejoining the labor force.*

Pick up any metropolitan newspaper and thumb through the classified pages. The "Help Wanted" section may run more than forty pages and include more than ten thousand jobs, listed alphabetically from accountants to x-ray technicians. Why, when millions are unemployed, are so many jobs unfilled? To understand this paradox, we must take a closer look at the reasons behind unemployment statistics. Based on the source of unemployment, we distinguish among four basic types: frictional, structural, seasonal, and cyclical unemployment.

Frictional Unemployment Just as employers do not often hire the first applicant who comes through the door, workers do not always accept their first job offer. Both employers and job applicants need time to explore the job market. Employers need time to find out about the talent available, and job seekers need time to find out about openings. During the time required to accumulate and act on all this information, job vacancies remain unfilled. The time required to bring together labor suppliers and labor demanders results in **frictional unemployment**. Although unemployment often creates economic and psychological hardships, not all unemployment is necessarily bad. Frictional unemployment does not last long and results in a better match-up between workers and jobs, so the entire economy becomes more efficient.

Frictional unemployment is unemployment that arises because of the time required to match job seekers with job openings.

Structural Unemployment A second reason job vacancies and unemployment can occur simultaneously is that unemployed workers often do not have the skills demanded by employers or do not live in the area where their skills are in demand. Unemployment arising from a mismatch of skills or geographic location is called **structural unemployment**. Structural unemployment occurs because changing demand and changing technology reduce the demand for certain skills and increase the demand for other skills. In our dynamic economy, some job seekers—such as coal miners in McDowell County, West Virginia, oil rig operators in Texas, or bank tellers displaced

Structural unemployment is unemployment that arises because those who are unemployed do not possess the skills demanded by employers or do not live in regions where the jobs are.

by automatic teller machines—are stuck with skills that are no longer demanded in the job market. Whereas most frictional unemployment is short term and voluntary, structural unemployment poses more of a problem because workers must seek work elsewhere or must develop other skills. For example, miners, oil riggers, or auto workers who are unemployed must look for work in other industries or in other regions. Displaced bank tellers may have to learn other skills such as computer programming.

Moving to where the jobs are is easier said than done. Obviously people prefer to remain near friends and relatives. Those laid off from high-wage jobs may be reluctant to leave the area because they hope to be rehired. Families in which the spouse is employed may be unwilling to give up one partner's job to find work for the other. Finally, the available jobs may be in areas where the cost of living is much higher. For example, the average price of a three-bedroom home in the depressed oil-based economy of Houston was about $86,000 in 1989. In that year jobs were abundant around Boston, but the average price of a three-bedroom home in the Boston suburbs was over $200,000. Workers are understandably wary of moving where housing costs so much more.

Seasonal unemployment is unemployment caused by seasonal shifts in labor supply and demand.

Seasonal Unemployment Unemployment caused by seasonal shifts in labor supply and demand during the year is called **seasonal unemployment**. It occurs in industries such as construction, agriculture, and tourism, where the weather affects the demand for labor. Little farming or building occurs during winter months in regions where the ground freezes. Likewise, the tourist trade in places such as Miami and Phoenix wilts in the summer heat. The Christmas holidays increase the demand for those who can serve as sales clerks, postal carriers, or Santa Clauses. Those employed in seasonal occupations know they will probably be unemployed during particular months. Some may even have purposely chosen a seasonal occupation. To eliminate seasonal unemployment, we might have to outlaw winter and abolish Christmas. Official employment statistics spread out seasonal unemployment over the year and thus mask the bulges that occur in particular months because of seasonal factors.

Cyclical unemployment is unemployment that occurs because of the decline in the economy's aggregate output during recessions.

Cyclical Unemployment Recall that Exhibits 2 and 3 indicated an increase in the unemployment rate during recessions. Because of the general decline in output during a recession, most firms reduce their demand for inputs, including labor. **Cyclical unemployment** reflects the decline in aggregate output that occurs during the recessionary phase of the business cycle. Between 1932 and 1934, when unemployment averaged about 24 percent, there was clearly much cyclical unemployment. Between 1942 and 1945, when the unemployment rate averaged only 1.6 percent, there was no cyclical unemployment. Government policies that stimulate aggregate demand during recessions have more impact on cyclical unemployment than on the other types of unemployment.

The Meaning of Full Employment

When economists talk about "full employment," they do not mean zero unemployment. In an ever-changing economy such as ours, where entrepreneurs are continually introducing new products, shifts in demand and technology alter the supply and demand for existing products. Consequently, even when the economy is at *full employment*, there will be some frictional, structural, and seasonal unemployment. After all, often more than half those unemployed have quit their last job or are new entrants or reentrants into the labor force. A large proportion of this group could be counted among the frictionally unemployed.

Most economists believe that unemployment of the frictional-structural-seasonal variety has risen since the late 1950s, perhaps from 4 percent to 5 or 6 percent; that low an unemployment rate would now constitute full employment. Why did this increase occur? The full employment level may have changed over time primarily because of changes in the composition of the labor force and changes in the institutional structure of the economy. When many new workers flood into the labor market for the first time, unemployment increases, because even a healthy economy needs time to absorb these new workers. Teenagers, for example, tend to have higher unemployment rates because they are new entrants who arrive with no particular skills and no job experience.

Since the 1950s the composition of the labor force has shifted. Today, groups that have historically experienced lower unemployment rates comprise a smaller proportion of the labor force. For example, the group that experiences the lowest average unemployment in the labor force—white males 20 years of age and older—made up about two-thirds of all workers in 1955. By 1989 they made up only about half of the labor force.

Unemployment Insurance

As noted earlier, unemployment often imposes an economic and psychological hardship on those who are affected. For a variety of reasons, however, the burden on those who are unemployed may not be as severe today as it was during the Great Depression. Today, with so many more women in the labor force, households with an unemployed worker are now somewhat more likely to have someone else in the household who has a job. When a household has more than one breadwinner, the economic distress of unemployment is to some extent cushioned. Moreover, workers who lose their jobs usually receive unemployment benefits.

In response to the massive unemployment of the Great Depression, Congress passed the Social Security Act of 1935, which provided for an unemployment insurance system financed by a tax on employers. Unemployed workers who meet certain qualifications can receive *unemployment benefits* for up to six months, provided they actively seek employment. The insurance is aimed primarily at those who have lost jobs. Not covered are those just entering or reentering the labor force, those who quit their last job, or those fired for just cause such as excessive absenteeism or stealing. Because of these restrictions, slightly fewer than half of all unemployed workers receive unemployment benefits.

Unemployment benefits usually replace more than half of a person's take-home pay. In 1989, for example, an average of $150 per week was paid to the unemployed who received benefits. But high insurance benefits may create work incentive problems, because these benefits reduce the opportunity cost of remaining unemployed. Thus an individual who receives benefits may be less interested in finding a job, at least right away. For example, if you faced the choice of washing dishes for a take-home pay of $200 per week or collecting $150 per week in unemployment benefits, which would you choose? Evidence suggests that unemployed workers who receive insurance benefits tend to search less actively than those without such benefits. Thus, although unemployment insurance provides a safety net for the unemployed, it may also reduce the urgency of finding work, thereby contributing to an increase in frictional unemployment. On the plus side, unemployment insurance may allow for a higher-quality search, since the individual has "walking-around" money and need not take the first job available.

International Comparisons

In 1989 the U.S. unemployment rate of 5.3 percent was below the rates in West Germany (5.7 percent), France (10.1 percent), Britain (6.4 percent), and Italy (7.8 percent), but above the 2.5 percent rate in Japan. We should view international comparisons with caution, however, because the definitions of unemployment may differ across countries with respect to age limits, the criteria used to determine whether a person is looking for work, the way layoffs are treated, how the military are counted, and in other subtle ways, and these differences can affect estimates of unemployment. For example, most countries in North and South America and some European countries base their unemployment estimates on periodic surveys of the labor force. Experts believe that such sample surveys yield the most accurate results. But most other countries, including West Germany, Great Britain, and a majority of less developed countries, base official estimates on registrations with government employment offices. Reliance on such self-reporting tends to underestimate the actual level of unemployment, particularly in less developed countries, where there are few jobs, no unemployment benefits, and hence no real reason to bother registering as unemployed with the government. Centrally planned economies do not usually report unemployment rates at all.

Underemployment *occurs when workers are overqualified for their jobs, such as the artist who can find work only as a house painter.*

Official unemployment statistics are not without their problems. As we said earlier, dropping discouraged workers from the official labor force understates unemployment. Official employment data also ignore the problem of **underemployment**, which arises because people are counted as employed even if they work only part time and even if they are vastly overqualified for the job, as when someone with a Ph.D. in literature can find employment only as a bookstore clerk. For social or cultural reasons, the amount of underemployment may differ from country to country. In Japan, for example, many firms offer an implicit promise to provide employment security for life. As a result, employees in Japan may be underemployed or no longer working, yet still be carried on the company's payroll. Thus, the true extent of unemployment in Japan is higher than official figures indicate.

Not counting discouraged workers as unemployed and counting part-time workers and the underemployed as employed tend to understate the actual amount of unemployment. On the other hand, because some welfare programs require recipients to seek employment, some people may act as if they are looking for work just to qualify for such programs. If these people do not in fact want to find a job, their inclusion among the unemployed will tend to overstate the official unemployment figures. *On net, however, most experts believe that official unemployment figures tend to underestimate the true extent of unemployment because of the exclusion of discouraged workers.* Despite several qualifications and limitations, the unemployment rate is a useful measure of unemployment trends over time. We turn next to the second major concern in today's economy: inflation.

INFLATION

We begin our discussion of inflation with a case study that highlights the cost of inflation by focusing on the recent experience of Bolivia.

CASE STUDY

Wild Inflation in Bolivia

In the spring of 1985, the inflation rate in Bolivia was running at 25,000 percent a year, one of the highest in history. That high rate, coupled with high rates for the two previous years, meant that in 1985 it took more than five thousand pesos to equal the purchasing power of one 1982 peso. To put this in perspective, if that rate prevailed in the United States, the price of a gallon of gasoline would have climbed from $1.25 in 1982 to $6250 in 1985. A pair of jeans that sold for $35 in 1982 would have cost $175,000 in 1985!

Cash registers in Bolivia did not contain enough zeros to ring up even a hamburger. Prices were no longer printed on menus. With the value of the Bolivian peso cheapening by the hour, people understandably did not want to hold pesos. As soon as workers were paid, they tried to get rid of pesos, either by buying goods and services before prices increased further or by exchanging pesos for a more stable currency, such as the U.S. dollar. With such wild inflation, everyone, including merchants, had difficulty keeping track of prices. Price differences among sellers of the same product became greater, prompting shoppers to incur the "shoe-leather cost" of walking around in search of the lowest price.

With the peso worth so little, carrying money for spending was a real burden. Bolivians became accustomed to lugging incredible wads of pesos in sacks or in blankets slung over their shoulders—whatever would do the job. Money was folded in individual packets of one million pesos, and the packets were tied into foot-long bundles. Few people bothered to count the money in each packet—they simply counted the packets.

To focus on the sheer physical effort required to carry money, think again in terms of dollars. Suppose the dollar became so inflated that it took $5000 in today's dollars to purchase what one dollar had purchased three years ago. To carry the equivalent of $5 in the spending power of three years ago, you would need $25,000 in today's dollars ($5 × 5000). Can you imagine toting around $25,000 just to pay for lunch or a movie? To carry the equivalent of $200 in preinflated spending power for a shopping trip, you would have to load yourself down with a million dollars. If you carried this amount in dollar bills, it would weigh a ton—literally. Even with $100 bills, your wallet would still weigh more than 20 pounds.

Lugging money around, shopping for the lowest price, and continually attending to money matters all involve a great deal of time and effort—time and effort not devoted to production. Thus, the high and unpredictable inflation in Bolivia and more recently in Brazil results in much activity that is rational for each individual but unproductive for the economy as a whole. When people pay constant attention to wages, prices, and the value of the currency, the economy's productivity suffers.

Source: "Bolivia Struggles to Curb World's Highest Inflation," *Hartford Courant* (July 21, 1985): A12.

Inflation is a sustained and continuous increase in the price level.

A very high rate of inflation is called **hyperinflation***.*

Deflation is a sustained and continuous decrease in the price level.

We have already discussed inflation in different contexts. **Inflation** is a sustained and continuous increase in the average level of prices. If the price level bounces around—moving up one month, falling back another — any particular increase in the price level will not necessarily be called inflation. A sustained and continuous price increase implies that prices rise month after month. We typically describe inflation on an *annual* basis. Very high inflation, as in Bolivia, is often called **hyperinflation**. **Deflation** is a sustained and continuous decrease in the average level of prices. In this section we first briefly consider two sources of inflation. We then examine in more detail the extent and consequences of inflation in the United States.

Two Sources of Inflation

Inflation can be depicted as an increase in average prices resulting from an increase in aggregate demand or a decrease in aggregate supply. Panel (a) of Exhibit 4 shows that an increase in aggregate demand raises the price level from P to P'. Inflation that arises from an increase in aggregate demand is often called **demand–pull inflation**. In such cases a rising aggregate demand curve *pulls up* the price level. To generate repeated and continuous price increases, the aggregate demand curve would have to keep shifting out.

Alternatively, inflation can arise from a reduction in aggregate supply, as

Demand-pull inflation is a sustained and continuous rise in the price level caused by increases in aggregate demand.

**EXHIBIT 4   INFLATION CAUSED BY SHIFTS IN THE AGGREGATE DEMAND AND
SUPPLY CURVES**

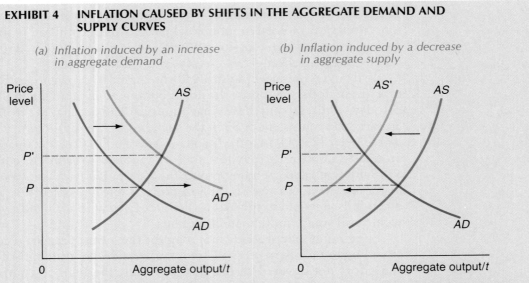

*(a) Inflation induced by an increase
in aggregate demand*

*(b) Inflation induced by a decrease
in aggregate supply*

Panel (a) illustrates demand-pull inflation. An outward shift of the aggregate
demand to *AD'* "pulls" the price level up from *P* to *P'*. Panel (b) shows cost-push
inflation, in which a decrease in aggregate supply to *AS'* "pushes" the price level up
from *P* to *P'*.

shown in panel (b) of Exhibit 4, where a shift to the left in the aggregate
supply curve raises the price level. For example, crop failures and reductions
in the supply of oil during the 1970s reduced aggregate supply, thereby
raising the price level. Inflation stemming from a decrease in aggregate
supply is often called **cost–push inflation**, suggesting that an increase in the
cost of production has *pushed up* the price level. Again, to generate sustained
and continuous price increases, the aggregate supply curve would have to
keep shifting to the left.

*Cost-push inflation is
a sustained and con-
tinuous increase in
the price level caused
by decreases in ag-
gregate supply.*

A Historical Look at Inflation and the Price Level

In the last chapter we considered the two most widely used measures of
inflation: changes in the consumer price index and changes in the implicit
price deflator. The consumer price index is the measure you are likely to
encounter most frequently, so it will receive the greatest attention here.
Exhibit 5 indicates the movement of the price level in the United States since
1900, as measured by the consumer price index. Panel (a) shows the *level* of
prices in each year, which is measured by an index relative to the base period
of 1982–1984. As you can see, the price level was not much higher in 1940
than in 1900. Since 1940, however, it has risen steadily, especially during the
1970s. Of most concern is not the level of prices but the change in the price
level. Panel (b) shows the annual *rate of change* in the price level, or the annual
inflation rate, since 1900.

EXHIBIT 5   CONSUMER PRICE INDEX SINCE 1900

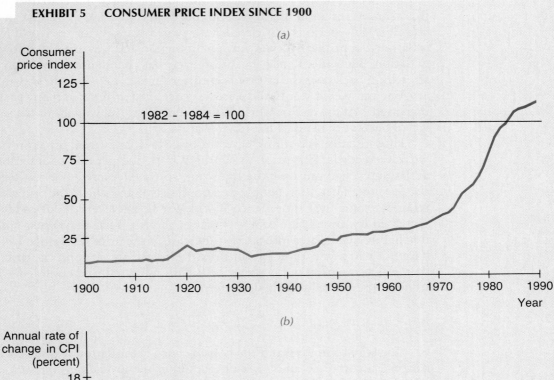

(a)

Consumer price index

1982 - 1984 = 100

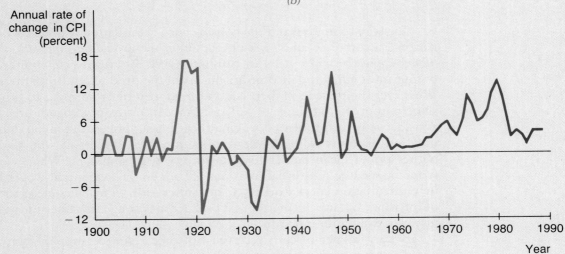

(b)

Annual rate of change in CPI (percent)

Panel (a) shows that, despite some fluctuations, the price level was not much higher in 1940 than it had been in 1900. Since 1940 the price level has risen almost every year.

Panel (b) shows the annual rate of change in the price level. Between 1900 and 1946, the average annual inflation rate was 1.3 percent. Since 1946 the inflation rate has averaged 4.4 percent annually.

The decade of the 1970s was not the only period of high inflation during this century. Inflation was also in double digits from 1917 to 1920, in 1942, and in 1947—periods associated with world wars. Prior to World War II, inflation was primarily a wartime phenomenon and was usually followed by deflation. Such an inflation-deflation cycle has characterized war and peace stretching back over the last two centuries. In fact, between the Revolutionary War and World War II, the price level declined in about as many years as it increased.[3] At the end of World War II, the price level was about the same as it had been at the end of the Civil War.

Thus inflation is nothing new; the price level has varied for as far back as we have records. But prior to World War II, the periods of inflation and deflation evened out over the long run, so the *purchasing power of the dollar changed little*. Therefore, people had good reason to believe the dollar would retain its value over time. Since World War II, however, the price level has increased by an average of 4.4 percent per year. That may not sound like much, but it translates into a *sixfold* increase in the price level since 1946. We have not had a year of deflation since 1955, and the drop in the price level that year was a mere 0.4 percent. So inflation has reduced confidence in the value of the dollar over the long term.

Why Is Inflation So Unpopular?

One way to understand the consequences of inflation is in terms of the national income accounts. Recall that either the *expenditure approach* or the *income approach* can be used to compute GNP. Aggregate expenditure on output must equal the income arising from the production of that output. Whenever the price level increases, more money must be spent to buy the same output. If you think of inflation only in terms of expenditures, you consider only the problem of paying those higher prices. But if you think of inflation in terms of the higher money incomes that result, you see that higher prices mean higher receipts for resource suppliers. When viewed from the income side, inflation is not so bad. To the extent that wages keep up with inflation, most workers do not suffer a loss of real income as a result of inflation. In fact, during the last two decades, wage increases on average just kept even with inflation.

If every higher price is received by some resource supplier, why are people so troubled by inflation? Why do public opinion polls consistently indicate that inflation is at or near the top of public concerns? Presidents Ford and Carter could not control inflation and were turned out of office. Inflation fell significantly during the Reagan administration, and President Reagan was reelected in a landslide, even though the level of unemployment was higher during his first term than during President Carter's tenure. During the 1988 election, George Bush kept reminding voters what the rate

---

[3] Arthur F. Burns, "Our Inflation in Historical Perspective," *Atlantic Community Quarterly* 19 (Spring 1981): 70–77.

of inflation was the last time a Democrat was president. Inflation, or the fear of inflation, continues to be a key campaign issue.

One major difference between inflation and unemployment is that at any particular time unemployment affects only a fraction of the labor force, usually less than 10 percent. In contrast, inflation affects everyone, whether in or out of the labor force, employed or unemployed, buying or selling goods, borrowing or lending money. *People are more concerned with inflation than with unemployment because more people are affected by inflation.* Also, whereas people view their higher incomes as the just rewards for their labor, they see inflation as a penalty that unjustly robs them of purchasing power. Most people do not stop to realize that, without an increase in real output per worker, producers cannot pay higher wages unless they charge higher prices. Prices and incomes are two sides of the same coin.

Anticipated Versus Unanticipated Inflation

What is the effect of inflation on the economy's performance? *Unanticipated inflation* creates more problems for the economy than does *anticipated inflation*. To the extent that inflation is higher or lower than anticipated, it arbitrarily creates winners and losers. If inflation is higher than expected, the winners are all those who had contracted to buy for a price that did not reflect the higher inflation. For example, someone who borrows money at a rate that turns out to be below the rate of inflation is a winner. The losers are all those who contracted to sell at that price. For example, someone who lends money at a rate below the rate of inflation is a loser. If inflation is lower than expected, the situation is reversed: the winners are all those who contracted to sell at a price that anticipated higher inflation, and the losers are all those who contracted to buy at that price.

Suppose inflation next year is expected to be 5 percent, and you agree to sell your labor for a *nominal*, or money, wage that is 5 percent higher than your wage this year. In this case you expect your *real* wage — that is, your wage measured in terms of the quantity of goods and services it will buy — to remain the same. If inflation turns out to be 5 percent, you and your employer will both be satisfied with your wage increase of 5 percent. If inflation turns out to be 10 percent, your real wage will fall and you will be a loser. If inflation turns out to be 2 percent, your real wage will increase and you will be a winner. The arbitrary gains and losses arising from unanticipated inflation are additional reasons why inflation is so unpopular.

The Transaction Costs of Variable Inflation

During long periods of price stability, people correctly believe that they can predict future prices and can therefore plan accordingly. As Keynes once said, money is an important "link between the present and the future."[4]

---

[4] J. M. Keynes, *The General Theory of Employment, Interest, and Money* (London: Macmillan, 1936), 293.

Uncertainty about inflation undermines the ability of money to serve as such a link. When inflation grows unexpectedly, the purchasing power of the dollar declines unexpectedly and the future value of the dollar becomes more uncertain. Since the future is more cloudy, planning for that future becomes more difficult. A sound economy is built on a sound dollar.

Some economists suspect that the high and variable inflation rate in the United States during the 1970s contributed to the slower growth rate of the economy during the decade. Firms that deal with the rest of the world face more complications, for they must not only attempt to plan for U.S. inflation, but also anticipate how the the value of the dollar might change relative to foreign currencies. Inflation uncertainty and the resulting exchange-rate uncertainty increase the difficulty of making business decisions. In this more uncertain environment, managers must shift their attention from worrying about productivity to anticipating the effects of inflation and exchange-rate variations on the firm's finances.

Inflation forces individuals and firms to try to hedge against unexpected changes in the dollar's value. This hedging has taken such forms as including cost-of-living escalators in wage settlements, making adjustments in accounting procedures, and basing investment decisions on expected inflation. During the 1970s, for example, the variable-rate home mortgage began replacing the fixed-rate mortgage typically offered by banks. The interest rate on a variable-rate mortgage varies from year to year, depending on the market rate of interest. There was also a trend toward mortgages shorter than the standard thirty-year variety, and the length of corporate bonds was shortened. Lenders became more apprehensive about inflation over the long term, so they wanted to get their money back sooner. The transaction costs of drawing up contracts, particularly long-term contracts, increased.

Adapting to Relative Price Changes

Inflation has been defined as a sustained and continuous rise in the price level. This definition, however, misses an important problem with inflation: not all prices change at the same rate. Consider the changes in relative prices discussed in the following case study.

CASE STUDY

Changes in Relative Prices

As we have seen, inflation does not mean that all prices rise by the same amount or by the same proportion. During the last twenty years, for example, the price level in the United States roughly tripled, yet the prices of color televisions, VCRs, pocket calculators, and many other items declined steadily. Because the prices of various goods change by different amounts, *relative prices* change. Whereas the price level describes the terms by which some representative bundle of goods is exchanged for *money*, relative prices describe the terms by which individual goods are exchanged for *one another*.

Let's examine more closely the composition of inflation and the change

EXHIBIT 6
CASE STUDY OF DISINFLATION
BETWEEN 1978–1980 AND 1982–1984

Item	Weight in CPI	Annual Percentage Change in CPI		Contribution of Item to Disinflation (percentage points)
		1978–1980	1982–1984	
All items	100.0	12.4	3.7	− 8.7
Housing	42.7	13.9	3.4	− 4.5
Food	19.0	9.6	3.0	− 1.3
Clothing	4.5	5.7	2.2	− 0.2
Motor fuel	6.1	37.1	− 2.4	− 2.4
Electricity and gas	4.0	13.9	6.3	− 0.3
New cars	3.1	8.0	2.7	− 0.2
Used cars	4.5	5.5	12.6	+ 0.3
Medical care	4.7	10.1	7.5	− 0.1
Entertainment	3.4	7.8	4.0	− 0.1
Other goods and services	4.3	7.9	8.8	+ 0.1

Source: Bureau of Labor Statistics; *Economic Report of the President,* January 1987.

in inflation between two periods. Exhibit 6 compares the composition of inflation during 1978–1980 with that during 1982–1984. Each major consumer item is listed, along with the weight that item receives in the consumer price index. Keep in mind that the prices of about four hundred individual products are included in the market basket, so we are considering here only summary statistics for the major groupings. For example, the food category is a summary of price movements for more than a hundred items, from soup to nuts. Of the major components listed, housing plays the most important role, accounting for 42.7 percent of the budget.

The highest single stretch of inflation since 1947 occurred between 1978 and 1980, when annual inflation averaged 12.4 percent. Notice, however, the difference in price changes across major components. The annual rate of price increase for clothing was less than half the average increase. On the other hand, because of OPEC-related price hikes, the price of motor fuel increased by almost three times the average increase. The first lesson we learn from the exhibit is that *the rates of price increases can differ sharply among items.*

During the 1982–1984 period, inflation declined to an annual rate of 3.7 percent, less than one-third the rate during 1978–1980. A reduction in the rate of inflation is called **disinflation**. Make no mistake: the price *level* was still rising during this disinflation, but the *rate* of increase in the price level was falling. During the 1982–1984 period, some prices increased faster than the average and some increased slower than the average. The price of used cars went up by more than three times the average rate; the price of motor fuel actually dropped. Hence, not only was the price level changing, but

Disinflation *is a reduction in the rate of inflation.*

relative prices were changing as well. Motor fuel became relatively cheaper compared to other goods, and used cars became relatively more costly.

Based on the data provided in the first three columns of Exhibit 6, we can calculate the contribution each major component made to the disinflation that occurred. For example, the average increase in housing costs dropped from 13.9 percent to 3.4 percent between the two periods, for a difference of 10.5 percent. If we multiply this difference by housing's share of the total budget, we get 4.5 percent (10.5 × 0.427). Thus, of the 8.7 percent average reduction in inflation between the periods 1978–1980 and 1982–1984, 4.5 percent, or about half of the total, can be traced to the lower inflation rate in housing costs. The second leading contributor to disinflation was the drop in the price of motor fuel, which accounted for 2.4 percent of the 8.7 percent drop in the inflation rate.

Source: This way of examining inflation was developed by Otto Eckstein in "Disinflation," in *Issues in Contemporary Macroeconomics and Distribution*, ed. G. W. Feiwel (Albany, N.Y.: State University of New York Press, 1985), 297–323.

During periods of volatile inflation, there is greater uncertainty about the price of one good relative to another—that is, about relative prices. Milton Friedman, in his Nobel Prize address, noted, "The more volatile the rate of general inflation, the harder it becomes to extract the signal about relative prices from the absolute prices; the broadcast about relative prices is, as it were, being jammed by the noise coming from the inflation broadcast."[5] But relative price changes are important for allocating the economy's resources efficiently.

If all price changes moved together, producers could simply link the selling price of their goods to the overall inflation rate. Since not all prices move in unison, however, tying a particular product's price to the overall inflation rate may result in a price that is too high or too low for market conditions. The same is true of agreements by employers to raise wages in accord with inflation. If the price of an employer's product lags behind the inflation rate, the employer will be hard-pressed to increase wages by the rate of inflation. Consider the problem confronting oil producers who had signed labor contracts agreeing to pay their workers cost-of-living wage increases. In 1986 those employers had to provide pay increases at a time when the price of oil was falling like a rock.

International Comparisons of Inflation Statistics

In 1989 the U.S. inflation rate of 4.8 percent was below those of Great Britain (7.8 percent) and Italy (6.6 percent), but above the rates in France (2.6 percent), West Germany (2.7 percent), and Japan (1.3 percent). Several factors should be kept in mind, however, in comparing inflation rates across

---

[5] Milton Friedman, "Nobel Lecture: Inflation and Unemployment," *Journal of Political Economy* 85 (June 1977): 467.

countries. As with unemployment statistics, the quantity and quality of data collected to track movements in the price level vary across countries. The data are less comprehensive in less developed countries, where fewer products are sampled and the geographical region covered is often limited to the capital city. Whereas some four hundred items are sampled in the United States, as few as thirty might be sampled in some less developed countries.

In centrally planned economies, reported inflation must be viewed with caution, since most prices in such countries are established and controlled by the government. Because of shortages of many consumer items, the official prices are not market-clearing prices. The fact that inflation is low in centrally planned economies may offer little comfort to consumers who find store shelves bare because of artificially low prices.

Even with market-clearing prices and the most sophisticated sampling techniques, however, there is still debate over which measure best captures inflation. For example, in the previous chapter we examined how the CPI, by fixing the bundle of goods and services in the consumer basket, does not reflect rational consumption behavior in the face of changes in relative prices. Therefore, the CPI tends to overstate the extent of inflation.

Inflation and Interest Rates

The **interest rate** *is the amount of money paid for the use of a dollar for one year.*

No discussion of inflation would be complete without a consideration of the role of interest. Interest is the reward offered savers, or lenders, to forgo present consumption. Specifically, the **interest rate** can be viewed as the amount of money earned for supplying the use of one dollar for one year. For example, if the interest rate is 5 percent, the lender earns $0.05 per $1 lent per year. The greater the interest rate, other things constant, the greater the reward for lending money. Thus the quantity of money people are willing to lend increases as the interest rate rises, other things constant. The supply of loanable funds therefore slopes upward, as indicated by line *S* in Exhibit 7.

These funds are demanded by firms and individuals who want to finance purchases, such as buildings, machinery, and homes. The lower the interest rate, other things constant, the lower the opportunity cost of borrowing funds. Hence, the quantity of loanable funds demanded increases as the interest rate falls, other things constant. The demand for loans therefore slopes downward, as indicated by line *D* in Exhibit 7. The downward-sloping demand for loanable funds and the upward-sloping supply of loanable funds intersect at the equilibrium point to yield the equilibrium rate of interest, *i*.

The **nominal rate of interest** *measures interest in terms of the actual dollars paid even if inflation has eroded the value of those dollars.*

The **nominal rate of interest** measures interest in terms of the actual dollars paid even if inflation has eroded the value of those dollars. The nominal rate of interest is the rate that appears on the borrowing agreement; it is the rate discussed in the news media and is often of political significance. The **real rate of interest** is the nominal rate of interest minus the inflation rate:

The **real rate of interest** *is the nominal rate of interest minus the inflation rate.*

Real rate = nominal rate – inflation rate

EXHIBIT 7   THE MARKET FOR LOANS

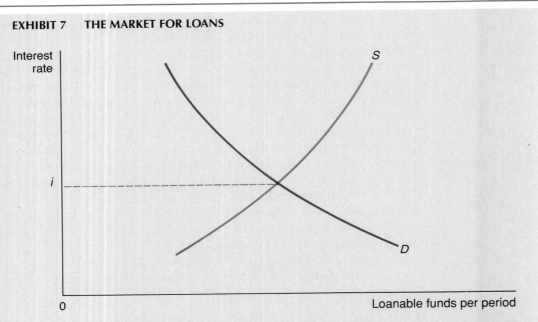

The upward-sloping supply curve, *S*, shows that more savings are supplied to financial markets at higher interest rates. The downward-sloping demand curve, *D*, shows that the quantity of loanable funds demanded is greater at lower interest rates. The two curves intersect to determine the equilibrium interest rate, *i*.

For example, if the nominal rate of interest is 10 percent and the annual rate of inflation is 6 percent, the real rate of interest equals 4 percent. With no inflation, the nominal rate of interest and the real rate of interest will be identical. But inflation erodes the real value of interest, so with inflation the real rate of interest will be less than the nominal rate of interest. Therefore, the higher the *expected* rate of inflation, the higher the nominal rate of interest. The real rate of interest, however, is known only after the fact—that is, only after inflation actually occurs. Because the future is uncertain, lenders and borrowers base their decisions on the *expected* real interest rate, which equals the nominal rate minus expected inflation. In an inflationary world, therefore, lenders and borrowers look beyond the nominal interest rate to base their decisions on the expected real interest rate.[6]

CONCLUSION

To the extent that the level and composition of inflation are fully anticipated by all market participants, inflation is of little concern in macro-

---

[6] Although the discussion has implied that there is only one rate of interest, a variety of rates can exist simultaneously, depending on differences in such factors as the risk and maturity of different loans.

economic analysis. But unanticipated inflation arbitrarily creates winners and losers and reduces the ability to make long-term plans. Unanticipated inflation redistributes income and wealth from one group to another. The more variable and unpredictable inflation is, the greater the difficulty of negotiating long-term contracts. The overall productivity of the economy falls, because people must spend more time coping with the uncertainty created by inflation and less time producing goods and services.

This chapter has focused on two problems with the economy: unemployment and inflation. In the next chapter we begin building a model of the economy by examining some components of aggregate demand. Once we have a better idea of how a healthy economy works, we can consider the policy choices that must be made in the face of high unemployment or high inflation.

Summary

1. The unemployment rate equals the number of people looking for work divided by the number in the labor force. Since the 1950s women have increased their labor force participation rate, but many older workers have retired earlier. The overall unemployment rate hides the variety of rates among particular groups. The lowest rate is among adult white males; the highest rate is among black teenagers.

2. There are four basic types of unemployment. Frictional unemployment arises because job seekers and employers need time to find one another. Structural unemployment arises because some unemployed workers do not have the skills demanded by employers or are not located where the jobs are. Seasonal unemployment stems from the effects of the weather and the calendar on certain industries, such as construction and agriculture. Cyclical unemployment results from the decline in production during recessions.

3. Unemployment imposes both an economic and a psychological burden on those who are unemployed. For some people this burden is reduced by unemployment insurance, which typically replaces more than 50 percent of take-home pay. Unemployment insurance provides a safety net for people who are unemployed, but it also may reduce their incentive to find work.

4. Inflation is a sustained and continuous rise in the average level of prices. Demand-pull inflation results from an increase in aggregate demand. Cost-push inflation results from a decrease in aggregate supply. Until World War II, both increases and decreases in the price level were common, but since then the price level has steadily increased.

5. Anticipated inflation causes fewer distortions in the economy than does unanticipated inflation. Unanticipated inflation arbitrarily creates winners and losers and forces people to spend more time and energy coping with inflation. The negative effects of high and variable inflation on an economy's productivity can be observed in those countries that have experienced hyperinflation.

6. Because not all prices change by the same amount during inflationary periods, people have difficulty keeping track of relative prices. Uncertainty about relative prices makes economic activity more costly and more risky.

7. The intersection of the supply and demand curves for loanable funds indicates the equilibrium interest rate. The nominal rate of interest equals the real rate of interest plus the rate of inflation. The higher the expected inflation, the higher the nominal rate of interest.

Questions and Problems

1. (Labor Force) Refer to Exhibit 1 in this chapter to determine whether the following are true or false.
   a. Some people who are unemployed are not in the labor force.
   b. Some people in the labor force are not working.
   c. All people who are not unemployed are in the labor force.
   d. Some people who are not working are not unemployed.

2. (Frictional Unemployment) Why might there be less frictional unemployment in a small, developed country than in a large, less developed country? Does the geographic size of a country have anything to do with the amount of frictional unemployment it has?

3. (Unemployment Across Industries) The rate of unemployment in such industries as financial services, transportation, and public utilities is consistently below that in manufacturing, which in turn is below that in construction. Are there any fundamental economic or social reasons why this is so? Explain.

4. (Structural Unemployment) Which industries in the U.S. economy are most likely to develop large-scale structural unemployment? Are colleges preparing students for such structural changes? Are unskilled workers more or less likely to become structurally unemployed than educated and skilled workers are?

5. (Unemployment Insurance) It is commonplace to hear that the average duration of unemployment in the United States is greatly influenced by the fact that this country has unemployment insurance. In Japan companies offer bonuses to workers who accept reduced hours or different jobs rather than stay on unemployment insurance. Some countries in Europe scale down the unemployment benefits the longer an individual stays on unemployment insurance. How would such programs work in the United States? What problems are associated with such programs?

6. (Inflation) (See Exhibit 5 in this chapter.) Using the concepts of aggregate supply and demand, explain why inflation usually rises during wartime.

7. (Inflation) If actual inflation is higher than anticipated inflation, who will lose purchasing power and who will gain?

8. (Anticipated Inflation) What are the benefits associated with correctly anticipating inflation? Is such anticipation free, or does it require some of the economy's scarce resources? Why would greater uncertainty about inflation inhibit the undertaking of long-term capital spending by business?

9. (Real Interest Rates) During much of the 1970s, real interest rates in the United States were negative. How can bankers and other lenders carry out their business when they are lending at negative interest rates? What caused lenders to lend consistently at rates that were too low?

10. (Nominal Versus Real Interest Rates) Why does a 10 percent tax imposed on nominal interest earned result in more than a 10 percent tax on real interest earned when there is inflation?

11. (Unemployment Rate) Suppose that the U.S. noninstitutional adult population is 180 million and the labor force participation rate is 65 percent.
    a. What is the size of the U.S. labor force?
    b. If 70 million of the adult population are not working, what is the unemployment rate?
    c. If the number of adults in the military is 2 million, what is the civilian unemployment rate?

12. (Unemployment Rate) Suppose that the unemployment rates for population subgroups remain constant as follows:

Teenagers	18%
Young adults (20–39)	9%
Older adults (40–65)	3%

a. Explain how changes in the composition of the population across these subgroups lead to changes in the overall unemployment rate.

b. Calculate the overall unemployment rate given the composition of the labor force in the two years shown below.

	1960	1985
Teenagers	40%	20%
Young adults	30%	50%
Older adults	30%	30%

13. (Inflation) Explain why steady inflation is likely to be less harmful to an economy than a situation in which inflation rates fluctuate a lot.

14. (Relative Prices) Suppose the elderly poor spend all of their incomes on just three items in the following proportions:

Food	35%
Housing	50%
Medical care	15%

Using the data in Exhibit 6, calculate the inflation rate for this group for 1978–1980 and 1982–1984, and compare your answer to the CPI figures for all items.

15. (Nominal Versus Real Interest Rates) Using a supply-demand diagram for loanable funds (like Exhibit 7), show what happens to nominal interest rates, real interest rates, and the equilibrium quantity of loans when both borrowers and lenders increase their estimates of the expected inflation rate from 5 percent to 10 percent (assume an initial equilibrium nominal interest rate of 8 percent).

C　H　A　P　T　E　R　　8

Aggregate Demand: Consumption, Investment, and Net Exports

Chapter 5 introduced the aggregate demand and aggregate supply curves. The intersection of these two curves determines the economy's equilibrium price level and the equilibrium quantity of aggregate output. Using these concepts, we developed a rough idea of how the economy works and considered the problems arising from unemployment and inflation.

In this chapter and the next, we focus on aggregate demand, especially the main private-sector components of aggregate demand—consumption and investment. The chapter's appendix examines the rest of the world.

In Chapter 10 we will discuss aggregate supply and show how it acts together with aggregate demand arising from the private sector to create the economy's equilibrium level of price and output. When the private-sector equilibrium occurs where there is much unemployment, the question is whether self-correcting forces operate in the economy to promote full employment or whether government intervention is necessary.

We will begin by considering some early views of the macroeconomy and discussing the reexamination of these views caused by the Great Depression. Topics discussed in this chapter include

- Say's Law
- Consumption function
- Shifts in the consumption function

- Investment demand
- Investment function
- Shifts in the investment function

EARLY VIEWS OF
THE MACROECONOMY

In Chapter 6 we mentioned Quesnay's contribution to our understanding of the circular flow of income. He had other insights into the economy's performance that contributed to subsequent developments in macroeconomics. Quesnay argued that even though people were motivated by self-interest, the economy was ruled by natural laws, laws that government intervention would only distort. The phrase "laissez-faire et laissez-passer" — roughly, let it alone and let it flow — came to be associated with the view that unfettered markets best promote national economic prosperity.

The Classical View

Quesnay's notions of a natural economic order and his philosophy of laissez-faire influenced Adam Smith (1723–1790), whose *The Wealth of Nations* is the most famous book in economics. Published in 1776, Smith's study argues for a "system of natural liberty." Smith, like Quesnay, had no misconception about individual motives; he too assumed that people pursued their own self-interest. Fortunately for humankind, according to Smith, the "great Director of Nature" led individuals as if "by an invisible hand" to promote the general good.

To understand the revolutionary nature of Smith's declaration of economic independence, you must keep in mind that during the previous two hundred years European countries had followed a mercantilist policy, which carefully regulated international trade in order to accumulate gold and silver in the public treasury. Smith established a school of thought that came to be called classical economics. *Classical economists* criticized mercantilism and advocated laissez-faire. These economists did not deny the existence of depressions and unemployment, but they argued that the sources of such crises lay outside the economic system, in the effects of wars, tax increases, and changing tastes. Such external "shocks" could reduce aggregate demand. The resulting disequilibrium, however, was viewed as a short-run phenomenon that would be essentially corrected by natural market forces, particularly the flexibility of prices and wages. Simply put, classical economists argued that if the price level was too high to sell all that was produced, prices would fall until the quantity supplied equaled the quantity demanded; if wages were too high to employ all workers, wages would fall until the quantity of labor supplied equaled the quantity demanded.

Consumption, Saving, and Investment

Classical economists addressed common fears that the sharp depressions of the period implied that the quantity of goods supplied could exceed the quantity demanded, resulting in a "general glut" of goods. Thus, the important question for the classical economist was "Will the aggregate quantity demanded be sufficient to purchase the aggregate quantity supplied, or will goods be left unsold?" *As long as all output was purchased, firms would continue to employ the labor necessary to supply that output. As long as resource owners spent all their earnings, total spending would equal total income. If, however, resource owners spent less than they earned, some output might remain unsold. If the excess supply persisted, unemployment would result, since firms would not continue to produce goods they could not sell.*

The income that arises from supplying aggregate output in the economy provides sufficient power to purchase that level of output. Smith divided this purchasing power into two flows, consumption and saving; saving represented a potential diversion from the circular flow. For example, if only 80 percent of income was spent on consumption and if consumption represented the only source of demand in the economy, then not all output would be purchased, so output and employment would fall.

Smith, however, believed that people saved only because they wanted to invest. Thus saving was not a leakage of purchasing power from the circular flow because it was directly converted into investment demand. To Smith, saving was "the immediate cause of the increase in capital."[1] Moreover, even if not every saver was also an investor, the interest rate would adjust in the market for loanable funds until planned saving equaled planned investment. So saving was actually a virtue because the resulting increase in investment expanded the economy's capital stock, thereby enhancing the economy's ability to produce. According to Smith, *the combination of consumption demand and investment demand would always be sufficient to clear the market of total output, so aggregate demand would always equal aggregate supply.*

Say's Law: Quantity Supplied Creates Its Own Quantity Demanded

Say's Law *holds that production of a given amount of output creates sufficient demand for that output.*

The classical view of the economy's natural ability to sell all that was produced is perhaps best reflected by **Say's Law**, which holds that the quantity supplied creates its own quantity demanded. According to this law, people supply their resources to the market only because they want to buy something in return. Consequently, every supplier is also a demander. Although Say's Law is credited to the French economist Jean Baptiste Say (1767–1832), it is actually a collection of related propositions embellished by a number of economists of the period. Some of the most important propositions are as follows:

1. The total income received by resource suppliers must equal the total value of goods on the market. Thus, total resource payments received for aggregate output must necessarily be sufficient to purchase that output.

---

[1] Adam Smith, *The Wealth of Nations*, bks. I–III, with an introduction by Andrew Skinner (Great Britain: Penguin Books, 1970), 437.

2. There is no loss of purchasing power throughout the economy. People save only to the extent that they want to invest. Thus, desired saving always equals desired investment. Even if savers and investors are not the same people, interest rates in the market for loanable funds adjust to ensure that the quantity saved equals the quantity invested.

3. Individuals produce only because of their demand for products. Hence, the quantity supplied creates its own quantity demanded.

In summary, since the quantity supplied would create an equal quantity demanded, the quantity demanded would always be sufficient to clear the market of production, regardless of how fast or how large the economy grew. Although widespread unemployment could arise temporarily because of external shocks to the economy, natural market forces in the form of price and wage adjustments would correct this imbalance and reduce unemployment. Therefore, *classical economists believed that in the long run a high level of output and employment could be sustained naturally with no assistance from government. Production generated the purchasing power required to demand that output. Markets would always clear.*

The history of economic thought reflects the interplay of theory and events. The classical belief in laissez-faire and the self-correcting nature of markets dominated economic thinking through much of the nineteenth and early twentieth centuries. New theories of macroeconomics evolve as existing theories are shaken by economic events, however, and the Great Depression was such a theory-shaking event.

Keynes and the Great Depression

Although classical economists had admitted that capitalistic, market-oriented economies could experience temporary unemployment, the prolonged depression of the 1930s strained belief in the economy's self-correcting ability. As discussed earlier, the Great Depression was marked by severe unemployment and much unused plant capacity. With abundant unemployed resources, output and income fell far short of the economy's potential.

The stark contrast between the full-employment predictions of the classical theory and the years of high unemployment during the Great Depression represented a collision of theory and fact. In 1936 John Maynard Keynes, of Cambridge University in England, published *The General Theory of Employment, Interest, and Money*, a book that disputed the classical view of the economy and touched off what has come to be called the Keynesian revolution. Keynesian theory and policy were developed to address the problem of unemployment arising from the Great Depression.

The main quarrel Keynes had with the classical economists was that prices and wages did not appear sufficiently flexible to ensure the full employment of resources. Keynes also argued that saving and investment were carried out by different groups of people for different reasons, and there was no reason to expect these two groups to have identical intentions. In the classical view, the interest rate continually adjusted to ensure a match between saving and investment, but Keynes believed that business expectations might at times be so grim that even very low interest rates would not be sufficient to induce firms to invest all that consumers might save. Thus, in Keynes's view, the interest rate, which operates through the market for loanable funds, would not ensure that desired saving equaled desired investment.

Once the link between the amount households plan to save and the amount firms plan to invest is broken, it becomes possible for saving to exceed investment. Thus the leakage of planned saving from the circular flow may exceed the injection of planned investment into the circular flow. *If saving exceeds the amount firms plan to invest, then the quantity of aggregate output demanded will fall short of the quantity of aggregate output supplied. Some goods will remain unsold, causing firms to reduce production, so the levels of aggregate income and employment will fall.* In the classical model, flexible wages, prices, and interest rates would adjust to increase income and employment, returning the economy to its full employment level. According to Keynes, however, prices and wages were relatively inflexible — they were "sticky" — so natural market forces would not return the economy to full employment.

Though Keynes and the classical economists had differing views of how the economy works, there was still much agreement. Both Smith and Keynes focused on the combined effect of consumption and investment in the context of the circular flow. Indeed, Keynes once said that his intent was "to use what we have learned from modern experience and modern analysis, not to defeat but to implement the wisdom of Adam Smith."[2]

In the balance of this chapter we shift gears to discuss the main private-sector components of aggregate demand: consumption and investment. In Chapter 9 we will combine these components and show how to derive the aggregate demand curve. Chapter 10 will introduce aggregate supply.

CONSUMPTION

Suppose a new friend at college invited you home for the weekend. One of the things you would learn from your visit is how well off the family is — you would get an impression of their standard of living. Is their home something you might see on "Lifestyles of the Rich and Famous," or is it more modest? Do they drive a new Mercedes, or do they take the bus? What do they eat? What do they wear? The simple fact is that consumption tends to reflect income. You can usually tell much about a family's economic status

---

[2] Speech in the House of Lords, December 18, 1945, as quoted in Eric Roll, *A History of Economic Thought*, 3d ed. (Englewood Cliffs, N.J.: Prentice-Hall, 1964), 525.

by observing their consumption pattern. Although you sometimes come across people who live well beyond their means or people who still have the first nickel they ever earned, by and large consumption and income tend to be highly correlated. *The positive and stable relation between consumption and income, both for the household and for the economy as a whole, is the central idea of this chapter.*

An Initial Look at Consumption and Income

Keynes observed that the most important determinant of how much people spend is how much they have available to spend. Although his observation seems obvious, it is fundamental to an understanding of how the economy works. Exhibit 1 depicts real disposable income in the United States since 1929 as a red line, and real consumer spending as a blue line. *Disposable income*, remember, is the income actually available for spending or saving. (The use of the term "real" here and later indicates that the data have been corrected to eliminate the effects of inflation.)

Note in Exhibit 1 that consumer spending and disposable income tend to move together over time. Consumer saving is the difference between disposable income and consumer spending; it is indicated in Exhibit 1 by the

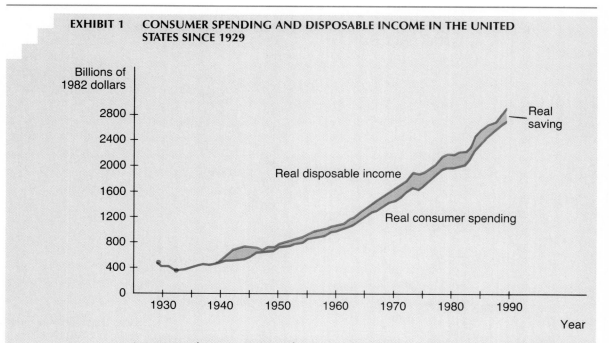

EXHIBIT 1   CONSUMER SPENDING AND DISPOSABLE INCOME IN THE UNITED STATES SINCE 1929

Income and consumer spending move together over time. Consumer saving is the difference between disposable income and consumer spending and is shown by the blue shaded area on the graph. Saving was close to zero during the Great Depression of the 1930s.

Source: *Economic Report of the President,* January 1990.

vertical distance between the red and blue lines. During the Great Depression, the two lines were close together, indicating that households spent all their income. Because of military demands during World War II, however, fewer consumer goods were available; many items were rationed. With little to buy, people saved more during the war. Since World War II, the relation between income and consumption has been relatively stable. Both have increased nearly every year.

Another way to graph the relation between income and consumption over time is shown in Exhibit 2, where disposable income is measured along the horizontal axis and personal consumption along the vertical axis. Notice that each axis measures the same units: dollars. The exhibit focuses on the relation between income and consumption in the United States since 1950. Each year is depicted by a point that reflects two values: disposable income and consumption. For example, in 1964 disposable income (read from the horizontal axis) was $1291 billion, and consumption (read from the vertical axis) was $1171 billion.

As you can see, there is a clear and direct relation between consumption and disposable income, a relation that should come as no surprise after Exhibit 1. You need little imagination to see that by connecting the points on

EXHIBIT 2   CONSUMER SPENDING AND DISPOSABLE INCOME IN THE UNITED STATES SINCE 1950

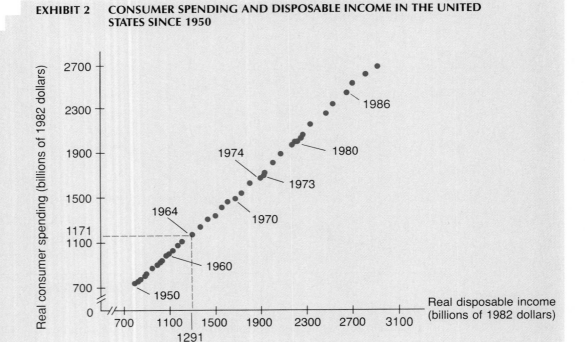

The clear, direct relation between consumption and disposable income is apparent when the two variables are plotted against each other on the same graph.

the graph in Exhibit 2, you could trace a line relating consumption to income. Such a relation has special significance in macroeconomics.

The Consumption Function

We have examined the link between consumption and disposable income and have found it to be quite stable, particularly since World War II. The table in Exhibit 3 illustrates such a relation with a hypothetical schedule. The first column lists various possible levels of disposable income in the economy. Given the level of disposable income, consumers decide how much to consume and how much to save. So consumption depends on disposable income. Disposable income is the independent variable, and consumption the dependent variable.

Notice that at very low levels of disposable income, consumption actually exceeds income. For example, if disposable income equals $1200 billion, consumption equals $1300. How is this possible? Households can borrow or can draw from their stock of savings, as they did during the Great Depression. Hence, when consumption exceeds income, saving is negative; households are *dissaving*. As disposable income increases, both consumption and saving also increase. At a given income level, the decision as to how much to spend also determines how much to save. Individuals save both for unforeseen emergencies and for fully anticipated expenses, such as college tuition or a down payment on a house.

Because consumption depends on income, we say that consumption is a

EXHIBIT 3
HYPOTHETICAL DATA SHOWING THE CONSUMPTION AND SAVING FOR VARIOUS LEVELS OF DISPOSABLE INCOME
(billions of dollars)

Disposable Income	=	Personal Consumption	+	Personal Saving
$1200		$1300		− 100
1400		1450		− 50
1600		1600		0
1800		1750		50
2000		1900		100
2200		2050		150
2400		2200		200
2600		2350		250
2800		2500		300
3000		2650		350
3200		2800		400
3400		2950		450
3600		3100		500

function of income. In fact, from the hypothetical data in Exhibit 3, we can construct the consumption function, *C*, shown in Exhibit 4. The **consumption function** shows the relation between the amount spent on consumption and the level of income in the economy, other determinants of consumption held constant. One of the determinants we hold constant is the price level prevailing in the economy; another is the market rate of interest. The consumption function answers the following question: How does consumption relate to the level of disposable income, other things constant? Notice that our hypothetical consumption function in Exhibit 4 looks similar to the actual historical relation between consumption and disposable income, shown in Exhibit 2.

To gain perspective on the relation between consumption and income, we use a handy analytical device: the 45-degree line first discussed in the appendix to Chapter 1. Recall that the special feature of this line is that any

EXHIBIT 4   THE CONSUMPTION FUNCTION

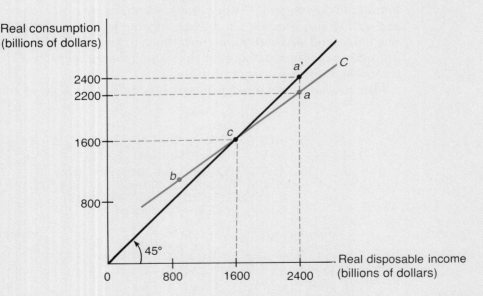

The consumption function, *C*, shows the relation between consumption expenditure and disposable income. Where the consumption function intersects the 45-degree line at point *c*, consumption and income are both equal to $1600 billion; nothing is saved.

When disposable income is less than $1600 billion (as at point *b*), the consumption function lies above the 45-degree line. Consumption exceeds disposable income, and saving is negative. When income is greater than $1600 billion, the consumption function lies below the 45-degree line. At an income of $2400 billion, for example, consumption is $2200 billion (point *a*). The vertical distance between consumption (point *a*) and income (point *a'*) shows the amount of saving.

point along it is exactly the same distance from each axis. Since the line identifies all points where income and consumption are equal, it offers an easy way of examining income, consumption, and saving. In Exhibit 4 the consumption function intersects the 45-degree reference line at point *c*, where the levels of both consumption and income equal $1600 billion. Consumers at this point spend all of their disposable income on consumption; nothing is saved. When disposable income is less than $1600 billion, as, for example, at point *b*, the consumption function lies above the 45-degree line, indicating that consumption actually exceeds disposable income. Households in this case are dissaving. When disposable income exceeds $1600 billion, the consumption function lies below the reference line, indicating that consumption is less than disposable income, so saving is positive.

At any particular level of income, the vertical distance between the consumption function and the 45-degree line indicates the amount of saving or dissaving that occurs at that level of disposable income. For example, suppose disposable income equals $2400 billion. First find that amount along the horizontal axis. Now move vertically from that level of income up to point *a* on the consumption function. The vertical distance between the horizontal axis and point *a* equals $2200 billion, the level of consumption when income equals $2400 billion. The vertical distance between point *a* and point *a'* on the 45-degree reference line equals $200 billion, the amount saved. Consumption plus saving equals $2400 billion, the disposable income. Adding consumption and saving at any particular level of disposable income will always give the amount of disposable income.

Nonincome Determinants of Consumption

Along a given consumption function, consumer spending depends on the level of disposable income in the economy, other things constant. Now let's see what factors could cause the entire consumption function to shift.

Net wealth is the value of assets minus liabilities.

Net Wealth and Consumption Given the level of income in the economy, an important factor influencing the desired level of consumption is each household's **net wealth**—that is, the value of all the assets that each household owns minus any liabilities, or debts owed. Consider your own family. Your assets may include a home, cars, furniture, money in the bank, and the value of stocks, bonds, and pension funds. Your liabilities, or debt, may include a mortgage, car loans, credit card balances, and the like. To increase net wealth, your family can save or can pay off debts.

The greater the level of net wealth, the more willing households are to consume instead of save their income. To see why, suppose you discover that those dusty paintings in the attic are Rembrandts and are worth a bundle. This increase in wealth reduces the primary motive for saving—namely, the desire to increase net wealth. Hence, an increase in net wealth, other things constant, encourages households to save less and spend more at each level of income. The original consumption function is depicted as line *C* in Exhibit

Franco Modigliani
(b. 1918)

Do rich people save a larger fraction of their income than poor people do? Both theory and evidence seem to suggest that they do. The easier it is to make ends meet, the more likely it is that money will be left over for saving. Does it follow from this that richer *societies* save more than poorer ones—that societies save a larger fraction of total disposable income as they grow? In his famous book *The General Theory*, published in 1936, John Maynard Keynes drew exactly this conclusion. But as economists studied the data—such as that presented in Exhibit 2—it soon became clear that Keynes was wrong. For *societies*, the fraction of total disposable income saved seems to stay constant as income grows.

Economists don't like paradoxes, and this was a particularly troubling one. By the early 1950s, several solutions had been proposed. One of the most important of these—the life cycle model of consumption—was largely the work of an Italian immigrant named Franco Modigliani.

Why do people save? One of the main motives, said Modigliani, is to provide for themselves in their old age. As a matter of fact, he reasoned, people who don't bequeath money to their children *don't save at all*, at least not over the whole cycle of their lives. They save when they're young but then *dissave* the same amount to support themselves when they're old. So for societies, saving doesn't depend on current income alone; it also depends on the relative number of young savers and old dissavers in the population. This way of thinking has implications not only for theories of the consumption function but also for the analysis of social security programs.

Franco Modigliani was born and educated in Rome. At the outbreak of World War II, he fled to the United States, and by 1944 he had earned a Ph.D. from the New School for Social Research in New York City. Modigliani taught at a number of universities before settling in at the Massachusetts Institute of Technology in 1962. He became known for work in several areas of economics, including the theory of corporate finance. In 1985 Modigliani received the Nobel Prize in Economics.

Richard Langlois

EXHIBIT 5   SHIFTS IN THE CONSUMPTION FUNCTION

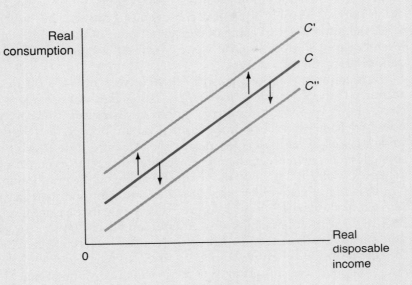

An upward shift in the consumption function, such as from C to C', can be caused by an increase in wealth, a decrease in the price level, a favorable change in consumer expectations, or a decrease in the interest rate. A downward shift, such as that from C to C'', can be caused by a decrease in wealth, an increase in the price level, an unfavorable change in expectations, or an increase in the interest rate.

5. As a result of an increase in net wealth, the consumption function shifts from *C* up to *C'*, as households spend more at every level of income.

Conversely, the lower the level of net wealth, the less willing households are to consume instead of save their income. For example, during the stock market crash of October, 1987, stock prices fell sharply. Stockholders on average experienced a decrease in their net wealth, so we would expect them to reduce their consumption. They reportedly did just that; the demand for real estate, expensive cars, and jewelry declined. The effect of a decrease in net wealth is reflected in Exhibit 5 by a drop in the consumption function from *C* down to *C''*.

Again, *it is a change in net wealth, not a change in income, that shifts the consumption function. Changes in income simply result in a movement along a given consumption function, not a shift in the function.* Be mindful of the difference between a *movement along* the consumption function, which results from a change in income, and a *shift in* the consumption function, which results from a change in one of the nonincome determinants of consumption, such as net wealth.

The Price Level Another variable that can affect the consumption function is the price level prevailing in the economy. As we have said, household wealth is an important determinant of consumption. The greater the household wealth, other things constant, the greater consumption will be at each level of income. Much household wealth is held in assets whose values are fixed in dollar terms. The most obvious of these is money itself. The higher the price level, the lower the real value of a given amount of money. When the price level changes, so does the real value of savings accounts and other dollar-denominated financial assets.

For example, suppose your wealth consists of $10,000 in a savings account. If the price level increases by 10 percent, these savings will purchase about 10 percent fewer real goods and services. Since your savings now buy less, you feel poorer because you are poorer. To rebuild the real value of your wealth to some desired level, you decide to save more and spend less. An increase in the price level therefore reduces consumption and increases saving at each level of income by reducing the purchasing power of wealth held in fixed-dollar assets. So the consumption function shifts from C to C'', as shown in Exhibit 5. Conversely, a drop in the price level increases the real value of dollar-denominated assets and thereby increases consumption at every level of income. A drop in the price level is reflected by a shift in the consumption function from C up to C'. In effect, a change in the price level influences consumption by affecting the real value of net wealth.

Expectations As noted early in this book, expectations influence economic behavior in a variety of ways. For example, suppose you are a senior in college and you land a high-paying job to start upon graduation. Your consumption will probably jump long before the job actually begins because you anticipate a higher income. You will likely make credit card purchases, borrow for a new car, and draw down whatever savings you had. You will probably spend more than friends who have not yet secured a job or those who plan to pursue graduate study. More generally, your college years are a period in which your consumption usually far outstrips your income, all in anticipation of higher income after graduation. Any change that leads you to expect higher income in the future will shift your consumption function up. Conversely, the worker who receives a "pink slip" announcing a layoff that is to take effect at the end of the year will probably reduce consumption immediately, well before the actual date of the layoff.

Expectations about inflation also affect consumption. An expectation of a higher price level in the future encourages people to consume more now. On the other hand, an expectation of a lower price level in the future makes people defer major purchases until after the price level falls. Thus, expectations affect spending at each level of income, and a change in expectations shifts the consumption function.

The Interest Rate As mentioned in Chapter 7, interest is the reward paid to savers to defer consumption and the amount charged borrowers to secure current spending power. When graphing the consumption function, we assume a given interest rate. If the rate of interest increases, other things constant, savers, or lenders, are rewarded more, and borrowers are charged more. The higher the interest rate, the less will be spent on those items typically purchased on credit. Thus, at a higher rate of interest, households will save more, borrow less, and spend less. Greater saving at each level of income means less consumption. Simply put, a rise in the interest rate, other things constant, will shift the consumption function down. Conversely, a drop in the interest rate will shift the consumption function up.

This concludes our introduction to consumption. Again, keep in mind the distinction between movements along a given consumption function as a result of a change in income and shifts in the consumption function. We now consider the other major component of aggregate expenditure: investment. Our objective is to work up to an aggregate expenditure function and from there to aggregate demand.

INVESTMENT

The second major component of aggregate expenditure is investment. Investment consists of spending on (1) the construction of factory plants and equipment, (2) the construction of housing, and (3) net increases in inventories. Investment adds to the economy's stock of physical capital and is measured by spending on currently produced capital goods and by inventory changes.

The Demand for Investment

Just as we assumed that consumption decisions are based on utility-maximization by households, we assume that investment decisions are based on profit-maximization by firms. Thus, investment is undertaken because those who run the firm believe that such spending will increase the firm's profit. But simply knowing that profit is the rationale for investment is not enough. We need to know what factors affect the profitability of particular investments.

An investment represents a commitment of current resources in expectation of a future stream of profit. Some machines, for example, are expected to last five years, others thirty years. Since the payoff occurs in the future, a potential investor must estimate how much profit a particular investment will yield this year, next year, the year after, and in all future years covered by the productive life of the investment. *Firms buy capital goods only if they expect the investment to be more profitable than other possible uses of funds.*

To understand the investment decision, consider a simple example. The operators of the Hacker Haven Golf Club are contemplating buying additional solar-powered golf carts to rent to golfers. The model under consideration, called the Weekend Warrior, sells for $2000, requires no maintenance or operating expenses, and is expected to last indefinitely. In this simplified example, the *expected rate of return* equals the annual dollar earnings expected from the investment divided by its dollar cost. The first cart purchased is expected to earn a rental income of $400 per year. Dividing this income by the cost of the cart, we find that the first cart purchased can be expected to yield a rate of return of $400/$2000, or 20 percent per year. Additional carts will be used less. A second cart is expected to generate $300 per year in rental income, yielding a rate of return of $300/$2000, or 15 percent; a third cart, $200 per year, or 10 percent; and a fourth cart, $100 per year, or 5 percent. A fifth cart would not be used at all, so it has an expected rate of return of 0 percent.

Should the operators of Hacker Haven purchase any carts, and if so, how many? Suppose they plan to borrow the money to buy the carts. The number of Weekend Warriors they should purchase will depend on the rate of interest they must pay to borrow money. If the rate of interest exceeded 20 percent, their cost of borrowing would exceed the expected rate of return on even the first cart, so no carts would be purchased. What if the course operators already have the money to buy the carts? The market rate of interest also reflects what the club owners could earn by lending money. If the interest rate exceeded 20 percent, they would earn a higher rate of return by lending any funds on hand than by investing these funds in golf carts. Thus, if the market rate of interest exceeded 20 percent, no carts would be purchased even if the course operators had the money on hand. *The market rate of interest represents the opportunity cost of investing in capital.*

Suppose the market rate of interest is 8 percent per year. At that rate of interest, the first three carts, with expected rates of return above 8 percent, would more than pay for themselves. A fourth cart would lose money, since its expected rate of return is below 8 percent. This reasoning is easier to understand if you refer to Exhibit 6, where the expected rate of return and market rate of interest are measured along the vertical axis, and the amount invested in golf carts is measured along the horizontal axis. The steplike relation shows the expected rate of return earned on additional dollars invested in golf carts. This relation also indicates the amount invested in golf carts by course operators at each interest rate, so you can view this steplike relation as the operators' demand for this type of investment.

The horizontal line at 8 percent indicates the market rate of interest, which represents the opportunity cost of investment funds to the firm. This line can be viewed as the supply of investment funds available to the course operators. Recall that the course operators' objective is to choose an investment strategy that maximizes profit. Profit is maximized when $6000 is invested in the carts—that is, when three carts are purchased. The expected return from a fourth cart is below the opportunity cost of funds. Therefore, investing in four or more carts would lower total profit.

From Micro to Macro

So far we have examined the investment decision for a single golf course, but there are over thirteen thousand golf courses in the United States. The industry demand for investment in golf carts shows the relation between the amount all course operators invest and the rate of return on that type of

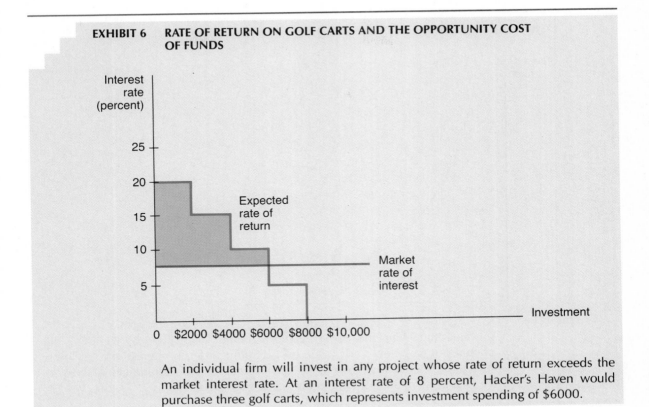

EXHIBIT 6   RATE OF RETURN ON GOLF CARTS AND THE OPPORTUNITY COST OF FUNDS

An individual firm will invest in any project whose rate of return exceeds the market interest rate. At an interest rate of 8 percent, Hacker's Haven would purchase three golf carts, which represents investment spending of $6000.

investment. Like the relation in Exhibit 6, the investment demand curve for the golf industry would slope downward.

Now let's move beyond golf carts and consider the investment decisions in all industries: plumbing, publishing, pig farming, and thousands more. Individual industries generally have a downward-sloping demand for investment. More is invested when the cost of borrowing is lower. An investment demand curve for the entire economy could be derived, with some qualifications, from a horizontal summation of each industry's investment demand curve. The economy's demand curve for investment is represented as *D* in Exhibit 7. Given business expectations, the lower the market rate of interest, the greater the quantity of investment demanded.

Investment and Disposable Income

To integrate the discussion of investment with our earlier analysis of consumption, we need to know if and how planned investment varies with the level of disposable income in the economy. Whereas we were able to present empirical evidence relating consumption to the level of income over time, there is less of a link between investment and income. *Investment varies*

EXHIBIT 7   INVESTMENT DEMAND FOR THE ECONOMY

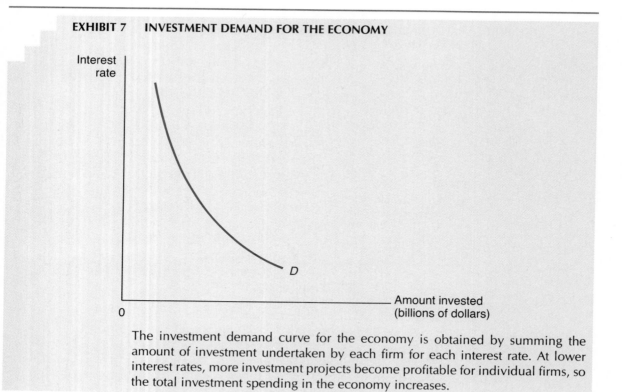

The investment demand curve for the economy is obtained by summing the amount of investment undertaken by each firm for each interest rate. At lower interest rates, more investment projects become profitable for individual firms, so the total investment spending in the economy increases.

greatly from year to year, depending more on interest rates and on business expectations than on the prevailing level of income in the economy. The investment decision is said to be "forward looking," based more on expected profit than on current income levels.

So how does the amount invested relate to the economy's level of income? The simplest investment model assumes that planned investment is unrelated to the current level of disposable income; investment is said to be **autonomous**. For example, suppose that, given the market rate of interest and business expectations, firms plan to invest $300 billion per year; they will do so regardless of the level of income prevailing in the economy. Exhibit 8 measures disposable income on the horizontal axis and planned investment on the vertical axis. Investment of $300 billion is shown by the flat autonomous investment function, *I*.

Autonomous means "independent"; autonomous investment is unrelated to the level of income.

Changes in Investment

The autonomous investment function isolates the relation between income and planned investment, other things constant. We have already mentioned two important components that are held constant: the market rate of interest and the expected rate of return at each level of investment.

EXHIBIT 8   AUTONOMOUS INVESTMENT FUNCTION

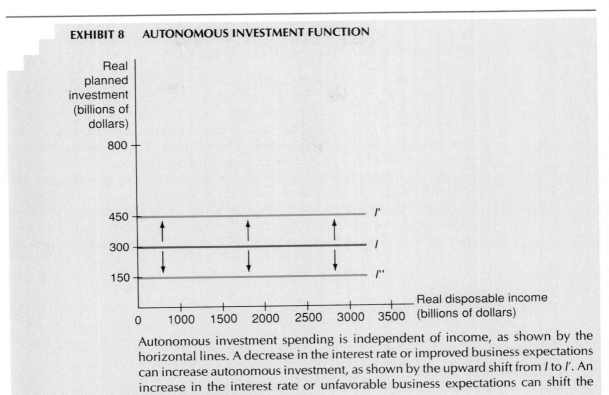

Autonomous investment spending is independent of income, as shown by the horizontal lines. A decrease in the interest rate or improved business expectations can increase autonomous investment, as shown by the upward shift from *I* to *I'*. An increase in the interest rate or unfavorable business expectations can shift the investment function down to *I''*.

Now let's consider the effect of changes in these factors on autonomous investment.

Market Interest Rate Autonomous investment, I, is based on a given interest rate. If the interest rate falls, say because of some change in the nation's monetary policy, the cost of borrowing will be reduced, so firms will be willing to invest in capital projects with lower expected rates of return. Households will also be more willing to invest in housing. The resulting increase in planned investment is reflected in Exhibit 8 by a shift in the autonomous investment function from I up to I'. Conversely, an increase in the rate of interest will raise the cost of borrowing and will lower the autonomous investment function from I down to I''.

Business Expectations As noted in Chapter 5, investment depends primarily on business expectations, or on what Keynes called the "animal spirits" of business. If firms in general become more optimistic about profit prospects, perhaps expecting an economic expansion next year, their planned investment will increase at every level of income, as reflected in Exhibit 8 by an increase in the autonomous investment function from I up to I'. On the contrary, if profit expectations sour, firms will be less willing to invest, thereby reducing the autonomous investment function from I down to I''. Factors that could affect business expectations are political events, changes in business taxes, and the cost of capital equipment.

CONCLUSION

We have now considered the main private-sector components of aggregate expenditure: consumption and investment. Consumption relates positively to the level of income in the economy. The level of investment, however, is related more to such factors as the interest rate prevailing in the economy and profit expectations than to the level of income. In the appendix to this chapter we bring in the rest of the world and discuss the third private-sector component of aggregate expenditure: net exports. In the next chapter we will again focus on consumption and investment, to derive the equilibrium quantity of aggregate output demanded.

Summary

1. Classical economists believed that planned saving would equal planned investment, so the aggregate quantity demanded would usually be sufficient to purchase the aggregate quantity supplied. Although unemployment could arise temporarily because of external shocks to the economy, natural market forces, including adjustments in prices, wages, and interest rates, would restore the economy to full employment.

2. The Great Depression was so deep and so prolonged that belief in the natural recuperative powers of the economy faded. Keynes argued that planned saving could exceed planned investment, so some goods would remain unsold. This would cause firms to cut production, creating unemployment. According to Keynes, wages and prices were relatively sticky, so they would not adjust to ensure full employment.

3. One of the most predictable and useful relations in macroeconomics is that between consumption and income. The more disposable income people have, the more they spend on consumption, other things constant. At low levels of disposable income, consumption exceeds income, so saving is negative. At high levels of disposable income, income exceeds consumption, so saving is positive.

4. Certain factors can cause the consumption function to shift. An increase in net wealth will reduce the need to save and hence increase consumption at every level of income. A lower price level will increase the value of dollar-denominated assets and thereby increase consumption. Expectations about future income and price levels will also influence consumption. Finally, a reduction in the interest rate will make saving less rewarding and borrowing less costly and hence will increase consumption.

5. Planned investment depends on the market rate of interest and the expected rate of return on investment. For simplicity, we assume that planned investment is unrelated to the economy's level of income; we say that investment is autonomous, or independent of income. Autonomous investment will change in response to changes in expected profits or in the interest rate.

1. (Classical Economic Theory) It is sometimes said that the classical economic system assumed flexible prices in all markets. Discuss how flexible prices and wages would eliminate excess production of goods, excess supply of labor, and excess supply of savings — all of which occur during a recession.

2. (Classical Versus Keynesian Economics) Why was the flexibility of wages, prices, and interest rates such an important issue between Keynesian and classical economists?

3. (Consumption) For each of the following cases, discuss which way the consumption function will shift; that is, will it shift up or down — or are you unable to tell?
   a. Wealth increases, and interest rates fall.
   b. Wealth increases, and the price level increases.
   c. Interest rates rise, and people expect a recession.
   d. The price level increases, and people expect prices to rise more in the future.

4. (Consumption Function) How does an *increase* in each of the following variables affect the consumption function? The savings function?
   a. lump-sum taxes
   b. interest rates
   c. consumer optimism, or confidence
   d. price level
   e. real wealth
   f. disposable income

5. (Wealth and Consumption) Two people have the same annual income, but one has a higher level of real wealth. Economists would expect the person with greater wealth to spend a greater fraction of total disposable income. Why?

6. (Investment Spending) One of the most unstable components of investment spending is construction, both residential and commercial. One of the most unstable prices in the economy is the level of interest rates. Is there a relationship between the two? What are some possible reasons for the volatility of interest rates?

7. (Autonomous Investment) Some investment projects are relatively insensitive to the *current* level of income in the economy. Give some examples of such investment projects. Why are they so insensitive?

8. (Investment) Consider Exhibit 6 in this chapter. If the owners of the golf course revised their estimates of the revenue from the golf carts so that each cart earned $100 less, how many carts would they buy when the interest rate was 8 percent? How many would they buy when the interest rate was 3 percent?

9. (Investment) Why would the following investment expenditures rise as interest rates fell?
   a. purchase of a new plant and equipment
   b. construction of new housing
   c. accumulation of planned inventories

10. (Keynes) According to the national income accounting rules discussed in Chapter 6, leakages equal injections into the circular flow. In a model containing only households and firms, therefore, $S = I$. Why doesn't this disprove the Keynesian criticism of the classical model — namely, that interest rates need not cause savings and investment to balance?

11. (Consumption) Use the following data to answer the questions below.

Disposable Income	Consumption
100	150
200	200
300	250
400	300

   a. Graph the consumption function with consumption on the vertical axis and disposable income on the horizontal axis.
   b. If the consumption function is a straight line, what are its intercept and slope?
   c. If investment is equal to $100, what level of disposable income causes savings to equal investment?

APPENDIX
The Rest of the World

Thus far this chapter has focused on two important components of spending: consumption and investment. But in recent years, the rest of the world has had a growing influence on the U.S. economy. In this appendix we examine the relation between the rest of the world and the U.S. level of income.

Net Exports and Disposable Income

The rest of the world affects U.S. aggregate expenditure through imports and exports. How do imports and exports relate to the level of income in the economy? When their disposable income rises, U.S. households spend more on all normal goods, including imports. Higher incomes lead to more spending on German automobiles, French wines, Japanese VCRs, and thousands of other imports. Thus, the relation between imports and disposable income is positive, as expressed by the upward–sloping import function, *M*, in panel (a) of Exhibit 9.

How does the value of exports relate to the economy's level of disposable income? The amount of U.S. exports purchased by the rest of the world depends on the income of foreigners, not on the U.S. level of income. An increase in U.S. income has little to do with the desire of the French to purchase U.S. computers or the desire of the government of Saudi Arabia to purchase U.S. military hardware. We therefore assume that foreign purchases of U.S. exports are autonomous, or independent of the level of income in the United States. Suppose the rest of the world spends $200 billion per year on U.S. exports; the export function, *X*, would be as shown in panel (b) of Exhibit 9.

So far we have considered imports and exports as separate functions of U.S. disposable

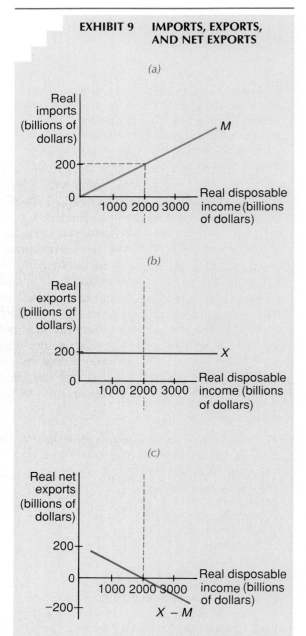

EXHIBIT 9   IMPORTS, EXPORTS, AND NET EXPORTS

Imports are positively related to disposable income, as shown in panel (a). Exports are independent of the level of disposable income, as shown in panel (b). Net exports equal exports minus imports; net exports are negatively related to disposable income, as shown in panel (c).

income. What matters in terms of total spending on U.S. products is net exports: exports, X, minus imports, M. By subtracting the import function depicted in panel (a) from the export function in panel (b), we derive the net export function, depicted by $X - M$ in panel (c). Note that when disposable income is $2000 billion, *imports* in panel (a) equal $200 billion. Since *exports* equal $200 billion at all levels of income, net exports equal zero when U.S. income equals $2000 billion. At levels of income below $2000 billion, net exports are positive because exports exceed imports. At levels of disposable income greater than $2000 billion, net exports are negative because imports exceed exports. Recall that the United States has experienced negative net exports since the mid–1980s. Our trade deficit can be traced in part to the healthy level of economic expansion in the United States during that period.

The net export function presented in panel (c) shows the relation between net exports and disposable income, other things constant. Factors held constant include the U.S. price level, the price levels in other countries, interest rates here and abroad, foreign income levels, and the exchange rate between the dollar and foreign currencies. Consider the effects of a change in one of these factors. Suppose the value of the dollar falls relative to foreign currencies. With the dollar worth less on world markets, U.S. products become cheaper for foreigners and foreign products become more expensive for Americans, leading to an increase in exports but a decrease in imports at each level of income. This increase in exports and decrease in imports increases the net export function, as shown in Exhibit 10 by the shift from $X - M$ up to $X' - M'$. A rise in the dollar's value will have the opposite effect, decreasing exports and increasing imports, as reflected in Exhibit 10 by a shift down in the net export function from $X - M$ to $X'' - M''$. Countries often attempt to de-

value their currency as a way of increasing their net exports.

In summary, *imports are positively related to the level of disposable income, whereas exports are independent of the domestic level of income. Net exports, which equal exports minus imports, therefore vary inversely with the level of disposable income.* The net export function shifts up if the value of the dollar falls and shifts down if the value of the dollar rises. During the 1980s the value of U.S. exports increased very little, but the value of imports nearly doubled. This means that Americans are depending more on the output supplied by the rest of the world, but the rest of the world has not increased its reliance on U.S. goods and services.

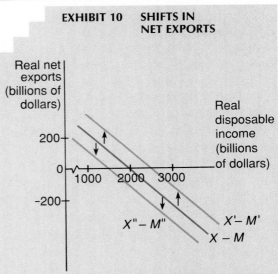

EXHIBIT 10 SHIFTS IN NET EXPORTS

A decline in the value of the dollar, other things constant, will increase exports and reduce imports, thereby contributing to an increase in net exports, as shown by the shift from $X - M$ to $X' - M'$. A rise in the value of the dollar will reduce exports and increase imports, causing net exports to fall, as shown by the shift from $X - M$ to $X'' - M''$.

Appendix Question

1. (Rest of the World) Using a graph of net exports $(X - M)$ against disposable income, show the effects of the following:
   a. an increase in the foreign income level
   b. an increase in the U.S. income level
   c. an increase in U.S. interest rates
   d. an increase in the value of the dollar against foreign currencies

   Explain each of your answers.

C H A P T E R   9

Aggregate Expenditure and Demand-Side Equilibrium

Thus far we have considered in detail two components of aggregate spending: consumption and investment. We showed that whereas consumption appears to be closely related to the level of income in the economy, investment depends more on other factors, such as business expectations and the interest rate. In this chapter we continue to focus on these two private sector components of spending. Our objective is to explore in a simple model the underpinnings of the aggregate expenditure framework.

We will spend most of the chapter deriving a single point on the aggregate demand curve by determining what quantity of aggregate output is demanded at a particular price level. We will then show how changes in the price level affect the quantity of aggregate output demanded. Ultimately we will derive the economy's aggregate demand curve and examine shifts in that curve. The rest of the world is discussed in Appendix A, and an algebraic approach to the material is developed in Appendix B. Aggregate supply will be developed in the next chapter; government will be introduced in Chapter 11. Topics discussed in this chapter include

- Aggregate expenditure function
- Equilibrium aggregate expenditure
- Marginal propensities to consume and save
- The multiplier
- Effect of changes in the price level
- Aggregate demand curve

EQUILIBRIUM AGGREGATE EXPENDITURE

We begin developing the aggregate demand curve by asking how much will be demanded at a given price level. With the quantity demanded at a particular price level, we will establish a single point on the aggregate demand curve. Because the focus is on aggregate demand, we will largely ignore aggregate supply. We will assume that firms are willing to produce however much is demanded at the given price level. Firms at this point aim to please.

The Components of Aggregate Expenditure

Suppose the price level is P, and we want to see how much will be spent by households and firms at various levels of real income. We continue to ignore the rest of the world, so there are no exports or imports. We also continue to ignore government, so there are no taxes or transfers. Finally, we ignore depreciation and business saving, so GNP equals aggregate income and also equals disposable income. Thus the focus will be on the relation between aggregate spending and the real GNP in the economy. By *real GNP* we mean GNP measured in terms of real goods and services produced.

Exhibit 1 presents hypothetical data that will serve as building blocks for constructing the aggregate expenditure curve. The first column lists the level of real income and output, as measured by real GNP and denoted by

EXHIBIT 1
HYPOTHETICAL SCHEDULES FOR REAL GNP, CONSUMPTION, SAVING, INVESTMENT, AND AGGREGATE EXPENDITURE
(billions of dollars)

Real GNP Income = Output (Y) (1)	Consumption (C) (2)	Saving (S) (3)	Planned Investment (I) (4)	Planned Aggregate Expenditure ($C + I$) (5)	Unintended Inventory Adjustment (6)	Actual Investment (7)
1600	1600	0	300	1900	− 300	0
1800	1750	50	300	2050	− 250	50
2000	1900	100	300	2200	− 200	100
2200	2050	150	300	2350	− 150	150
2400	2200	200	300	2500	− 100	200
2600	2350	250	300	2650	− 50	250
2800	**2500**	**300**	**300**	**2800**	**0**	**300**
3000	2650	350	300	2950	50	350
3200	2800	400	300	3100	100	400
3400	2950	450	300	3250	150	450
3600	3100	500	300	3400	200	500

the symbol Y. Households have only two possible uses for income: consumption and saving. The levels of consumption, C, and saving, S, associated with each level of income are listed in columns (2) and (3) of Exhibit 1. You can see that both consumption and saving increase as income increases. Besides consumption, the other component of spending is investment. Column (4) lists planned investment, I, the amount of investment firms want to make at each level of income. Planned investment equals $300 billion regardless of the level of income; thus, investment is autonomous. The planned aggregate expenditure at each level of income is simply the total of consumption plus planned investment, or $C + I$, and is shown in column (5).

Graphical Analysis

Some people find it easier to observe relations in graphs. The consumption and investment schedules in Exhibit 1 are graphed in Exhibit 2(a), which also shows the 45-degree line. Real GNP, measured along the horizontal axis, can be interpreted both as the value of aggregate output and as the aggregate income generated by that level of output. Aggregate expenditure is measured on the vertical axis. Because income is measured on the horizontal axis and expenditure is measured on the vertical axis, this diagram is frequently called the *income-expenditure model*.

The consumption function, C, is drawn to reflect the hypothetical data presented in Exhibit 1. Notice again that the consumption function intersects the 45-degree line at point c, indicating that when real GNP equals $1600 billion, consumption also equals $1600 billion. Because the consumption function is above the 45-degree line for income levels less than $1600 billion, we can conclude that consumption exceeds income at these low levels of income, so saving is negative. Because the consumption function is below the 45-degree line for income levels greater than $1600 billion, consumption at these higher levels of real GNP is less than income, so saving is positive.

Panel (b) has been placed under panel (a) so that the various levels of real GNP, measured along the horizontal axis in each panel, align. Autonomous investment is reflected in the lower panel by a horizontal line, I, drawn at the $300 billion level. The **saving function**, S, relates saving to the level of income. Notice that in the upper panel, households spend all their income when real GNP equals $1600 billion, so saving in the lower panel equals 0 at that level of income.

Panel (a) includes a line that represents the sum of the autonomous investment function, I, and the consumption function, C; adding these two functions vertically yields the aggregate expenditure function, $C + I$. The **aggregate expenditure function** shows, for a given price level, the total planned spending at each income level. The consumption function and the aggregate expenditure function are parallel; the vertical difference between the two equals the $300 billion in planned investment.

*The **saving function** relates saving to the level of income.*

*The **aggregate expenditure function** shows, for a given price level, the total amount of planned spending for each level of income.*

EXHIBIT 2   CONSUMPTION, INVESTMENT, AGGREGATE EXPENDITURE, AND EQUILIBRIUM OUTPUT DEMANDED FOR A GIVEN PRICE LEVEL

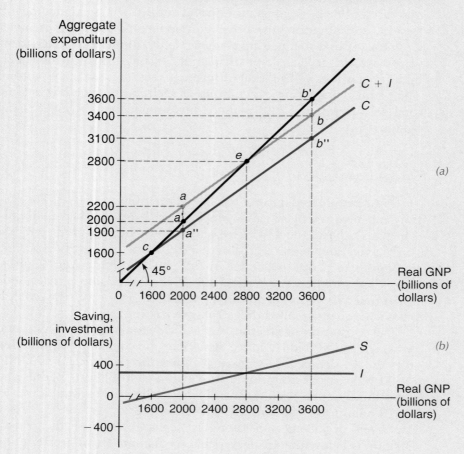

At real GNP of $2800 billion, the economy is in equilibrium, as shown by the intersection of the aggregate expenditure line with the 45-degree line in panel (a). Total spending (*C* + *I*) just equals GNP of $2800 billion at point e. In panel (b), saving equals planned investment at the same level of real GNP.

At any other level of GNP, the economy will be out of equilibrium. For example, at GNP of $2000 billion, consumption spending is $1900 billion (point *a*″). That, combined with investment spending of $300 billion, gives aggregate expenditure of $2200 billion (point *a*), which exceeds GNP by $200 billion (the distance between *a* and *a*′). Since spending exceeds GNP, the economy cannot be in equilibrium there.

Equilibrium Quantity of Real GNP Demanded

Equilibrium will be reached when the amount households and firms plan to spend equals real GNP. Real GNP, recall, is the amount produced and also the amount of income generated by that output. Thus, *equilibrium will be reached when aggregate expenditure equals aggregate output*. To understand the underlying forces that result in the equilibrium quantity of real GNP demanded, suppose real GNP initially equals $2000 billion. Point a'' on the consumption function indicates that consumption is $1900 billion when real GNP equals $2000 billion. This rate of consumption can also be found in column (2) of Exhibit 1.

The $300 billion in planned investment is reflected by the vertical distance between the consumption function and the aggregate expenditure function. When income is $2000 billion, aggregate expenditure equals $1900 billion in consumption plus $300 billion in planned investment, for a total of $2200 billion, identified by point a on the aggregate expenditure function. Column (5) of Exhibit 1 also lists this level of aggregate expenditure.

Equilibrating Forces

Recall that points along the 45-degree line are exactly the same distance from each axis and consequently measure identical amounts along each axis. This line can therefore be used to show where aggregate output equals aggregate expenditure. An aggregate output of $2000 billion, for example, can be measured vertically to correspond to point a', which lies on the 45-degree line directly above the $2000 billion level of real GNP. As you can see, when aggregate output is $2000 billion, aggregate expenditure, as measured by point a, exceeds the value of output, as measured by point a'. The difference between points a and a' represents the shortfall in output—the amount by which planned aggregate expenditure exceeds aggregate output.

When planned spending and output do not match up, something has to give. What gives in this model is *inventories*. If planned spending exceeds output, firms must reduce their inventories to cover the shortage. For example, when income equals $2000 billion, planned spending, as identified on the aggregate expenditure function, exceeds output by $200 billion, so firms must draw down their inventories by $200 billion to satisfy the additional spending. This unintended inventory reduction is listed in column (6) of Exhibit 1 as a negative $200 billion. Since firms cannot draw down inventories indefinitely, these reductions prompt firms to increase production.

A $200 billion decrease in inventories causes firms to increase their rate of production from $2000 billion per year to $2200 per year. However, as you can see from the first two exhibits, if output and therefore income increase from $2000 billion to $2200 billion, consumption will increase from $1900 billion to $2050 billion. Thus, a $200 billion increase in output and income prompts a $150 billion increase in consumption. Since planned investment remains at $300 billion, aggregate spending increases to $2350 billion, so aggregate spending still exceeds aggregate output. Firms must increase output again or have their inventories reduced indefinitely.

At all levels of real GNP below $2800 billion, planned spending exceeds output. As long as planned spending exceeds output, inventories will fall and firms will increase production to make up the difference. When output equals $2800, planned spending exactly matches output, so no unintended inventory adjustments occur. More importantly, when income equals $2800, the amount households and firms plan to spend just equals the amount produced and just equals the amount of income available for spending. Therefore, $2800 billion is the equilibrium level of aggregate output demanded. Hence, we say that when the price level is *P*, the equilibrium quantity of real GNP demanded is $2800 billion. In terms of the symbols introduced earlier, we say that *the equilibrium quantity of real GNP demanded, denoted as Y, equals aggregate expenditure—the sum of consumption, C, plus planned investment, I,* or

$$Y = C + I$$

Perhaps the logic of the model will be reinforced if we assume that initially $3600 billion in output is produced, thereby generating that amount of income to resource suppliers. When income is $3600 billion, consumption will be $3100 billion and planned investment will be $300 billion, for an aggregate expenditure of $3400 billion. In Exhibit 2(a), point *b* lies on the aggregate expenditure function directly above the level of $3600 billion produced. Output exceeds aggregate expenditure by $200 billion, as reflected by the vertical distance between *b'* and *b*. These unsold goods become unintended increases in inventories. Swelling inventories signal firms to reduce their production. Firms cut output, but as they do, income also falls, so consumption falls, prompting firms to lower production yet again. Firms will cut production until their output just equals aggregate expenditure, at a level of real GNP of $2800 billion.

Investment and Unintended Inventory Adjustments

In the income-expenditure model, firms dip into their inventories when planned spending exceeds output and add to their inventories when output exceeds planned spending. Recall that changes in inventories are viewed as changes in investment. Column (7) in Exhibit 1 lists the actual investment that occurs at each level of income. *Actual investment* equals planned investment plus any unintended change in inventories. If the unintended change in inventories is negative—that is, if inventories are reduced during the period—actual investment is less than planned investment. For example, when income is $2000 billion, planned investment is $300 billion, but a $200 billion unintended reduction in inventories reduces actual investment to only $100 billion, as listed in column (7). If the unintended change in inventories is positive, actual investment exceeds planned investment. For example, when income equals $3600 billion, the planned investment of $300 billion is augmented by an unintended $200 billion increase in inventories, yielding an actual investment of $500 billion.

At any level of real GNP, consumption plus actual investment equals real GNP. *From the viewpoint of the national income accounts, the amount produced will always equal the amount purchased, even if some purchases are attributed to firms' making unintended increases or decreases in inventories—that is, even if the amount purchased is not an equilibrium level, or a level that can be sustained.* As mentioned in Chapter 6, the national income accounts are settled after the fact and do not necessarily reflect planned investment. Also, at any level of real GNP, the amount saved equals the amount firms actually invest.

Production of the equilibrium quantity of aggregate output demanded generates just enough income to purchase that output. At any other level of real GNP, planned aggregate expenditure either exceeds or falls short of aggregate output. Consider the equalities that hold in equilibrium. At the equilibrium point *e* in Exhibit 2(a), aggregate expenditure equals the amount produced and also equals the income arising from that production. Planned investment, the injection into the circular flow, equals saving, the leakage from the circular flow, as shown in panel (b) of Exhibit 2. Finally, in equilibrium planned investment equals actual investment, since there are no unintended inventory changes.

Thus, given the price level, the equilibrium level of aggregate output demanded is achieved only when planned aggregate expenditure equals real GNP, which happens only when the amount households save equals the amount firms plan to invest. *Hence, for a given price level, there is only one quantity of output demanded at which income is equal to planned spending.* We have now established the forces that determine the equilibrium quantity of real GNP demanded for a given price level.

Marginal Propensities to Consume and to Save

In Chapter 1 we noted that economic analysis focuses on activity at the margin. Economists are usually interested in changes from one period to the next. How much did the economy grow this year? What growth rate is expected next year? To focus on such changes, we must apply marginal analysis to our income-expenditure model.

The **marginal propensity to consume** is a change in consumption divided by the change in income that caused it.

The **marginal propensity to save** is a change in saving divided by the change in income that caused it.

The effect of a change in income on consumption is of special interest. Suppose households receive another billion dollars in disposable income. Some of this additional income will be spent and some will be saved. The fraction, or proportion, of that additional income that is consumed is called the marginal propensity to consume. More precisely, the **marginal propensity to consume** equals the change in consumption divided by the change in income. Likewise, the fraction of that additional income that is saved is called the marginal propensity to save. Again, more precisely, the **marginal propensity to save** equals the change in saving divided by the change in income.

These propensities can be understood best by reference to Exhibit 3,

EXHIBIT 3
MARGINAL PROPENSITY TO CONSUME AND MARGINAL PROPENSITY TO SAVE
(billions of dollars)

Income (real GNP) (Y) (1)	Change in Income (ΔY) (2)	Consumption (C) (3)	Change in C (ΔC) (4)	Saving (S) (5)	Change in Saving (ΔS) (6)	$MPC = (4) \div (2)$ (ΔC/ΔY) (7)	$MPS = (6) \div (2)$ (ΔS/ΔY) (8)
2000		1900		100			
	200		150		50	150/200 = 3/4	50/200 = 1/4
2200		2050		150			
	200		150		50	3/4	1/4
2400		2200		200			
	200		150		50	3/4	1/4
2600		2350		250			
	200		150		50	3/4	1/4
2800		2500		300			
	200		150		50	3/4	1/4
3000		2650		350			
	200		150		50	3/4	1/4
3200		2800		400			
	200		150		50	3/4	1/4
3400		2950		450			
	200		150		50	3/4	1/4
3600		3100		500			

which uses the hypothetical data on income, consumption, and saving presented earlier. Column (1) presents alternative levels of income, beginning with $2000 billion and increasing in increments of $200 billion. The marginal increases in income are listed in column (2). The consumption and saving associated with each level of income are given in columns (3) and (5). The marginal increases in consumption and in saving resulting from each $200 billion increase in income are listed in columns (4) and (6).

For example, if income increases by $200 billion, from $2000 billion to $2200 billion, consumption increases by $150 billion, from $1900 billion to $2050 billion. The marginal propensity to consume equals the change in consumption divided by the change in income, which in this case equals $150/$200, or 3/4. The marginal propensity to consume, or MPC, is listed in column (7). The hypothetical data in Exhibit 3 indicate that each time income increases by $200 billion, consumption increases by $150 billion. Therefore, the MPC is 3/4 at all levels of income. Likewise, saving increases by $50 billion with each $200 billion increase in income, so the marginal propensity to save, or MPS, equals $50/$200, or 1/4, at all levels of income. Since disposable income is either spent or saved, the marginal propensity to consume plus the marginal propensity to save must add up to 1. In our example, 3/4 + 1/4 = 1. We can say more generally that

$$MPC + MPS = 1$$

You may recall from the appendix to Chapter 1 that the slope of a straight line is equal to the vertical distance between any two points divided by the horizontal distance between those points. Consider, for example, the slope between points *a* and *b* on the consumption function in Exhibit 4(a). The vertical distance between these points represents the change in consumption (denoted ΔC), in this case $150 billion; the horizontal distance represents the change in income (denoted ΔY), in this case $200 billion. The

EXHIBIT 4   MARGINAL PROPENSITIES TO CONSUME AND TO SAVE

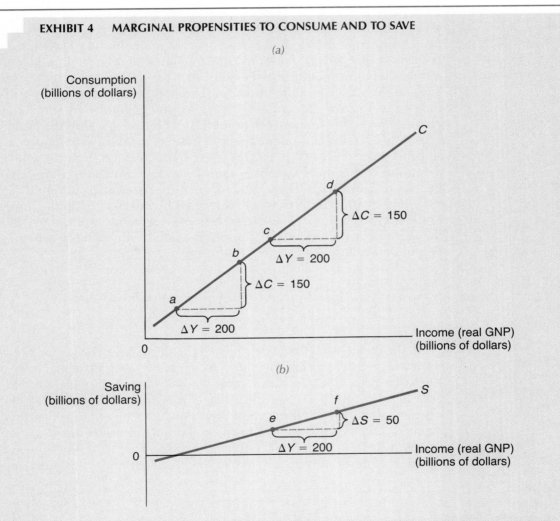

The slope of the consumption function is the marginal propensity to consume. For the straight-line consumption function of panel (a), the slope is the same at all levels of income and is given by the change in consumption divided by the change in income that causes it. Hence, the marginal propensity to consume is $\Delta C/\Delta Y$, or $150/200 = 0.75$. The slope of the saving function is the marginal propensity to save, $\Delta S/\Delta Y$, or $50/200 = 0.25$.

slope is therefore equal to $150/$200, or 3/4, which equals the marginal propensity to consume.

Thus, *the marginal propensity to consume is measured graphically by the slope of the consumption function.* After all, the slope is nothing more than the increase in consumption divided by the increase in income. *Because the slope of any straight line is constant everywhere along the line, the MPC for any linear, or straight-line, consumption function will be constant at all levels of income.* Our hypothetical data yield a consumption function that is linear, with a constant marginal propensity to consume. Note, however, that we make this constant-value assumption for simplicity and ease of exposition. In reality, the marginal propensity to consume will not necessarily be constant. *The consumption function could be curved, so that the MPC was greater at lower levels of income.*

The saving function can be subjected to the same sort of graphical analysis as the consumption function. The slope between any two points on the saving function measures the change in saving divided by the change in income. For example, between points *e* and *f* in Exhibit 4(b), the change in income is $200 billion and the resulting change in saving is $50 billion. The slope between these two points therefore equals $50/$200, or 1/4, which by definition equals the marginal propensity to save. Since the marginal propensity to consume and marginal propensity to save are simply different sides of the same coin, from here on we will focus mainly on the marginal propensity to consume. In the next section we examine the effect of a shift in the aggregate expenditure function on the equilibrium quantity of aggregate output demanded.

SHIFTS IN THE AGGREGATE EXPENDITURE FUNCTION AND THE MULTIPLIER

In the previous section we employed the aggregate expenditure function to determine the equilibrium level of aggregate output demanded for a particular price level. In this section we will continue to assume that the price level is given, as we trace the effects of a shift in the aggregate expenditure function on the equilibrium quantity of aggregate output demanded. Like a stone thrown into a still pond, any shift in the aggregate expenditure function causes ripples through the economy, generating changes in aggregate output that may far exceed any initial shift in spending.

Effects of an Increase in Investment

We begin in equilibrium at point *e* in Exhibit 5. The equilibrium point shows where planned spending of $2800 billion equals output, or real GNP. Suppose firms become more optimistic about the future, so they increase planned investment. Specifically, suppose planned investment increases by $100 billion per year, from $300 billion to $400 billion, as reflected in Exhibit 5 by an increase in the aggregate expenditure function, which shifts up by $100 billion, from $C + I$ to $C + I'$. What interests us is what happens to

EXHIBIT 5   EFFECT OF AN INCREASE IN AUTONOMOUS INVESTMENT

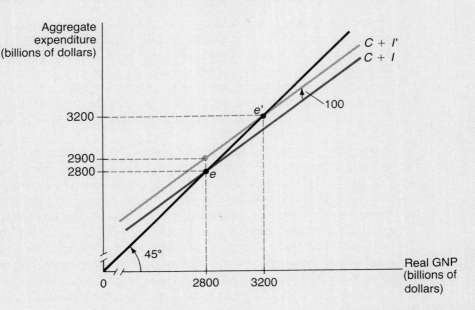

The economy is initially in equilibrium at point e, where spending and real GNP both equal $2800 billion. A $100 billion increase in autonomous investment shifts the aggregate expenditure function vertically from C + I to C + I'. Real GNP rises until it equals spending at point e'. As a result of the $100 billion increase in autonomous investment, real GNP demanded increases by $400 billion, to $3200 billion.

the equilibrium level of income and spending. An instinctive response is to conclude that equilibrium spending will increase by $100 billion, but in this case instinct is a poor guide. In Exhibit 5 you can see that at point *e,* the initial equilibrium, the amount of real GNP demanded equals $2800 billion. As a result of the $100 billion increase in aggregate expenditure, the equilibrium shifts up to point *e',* where the quantity of real GNP demanded equals $3200 billion. The $100 billion increase in investment has somehow increased the equilibrium quantity of real GNP demanded by $400 billion. Thus, each dollar of increased investment has been multiplied fourfold. The **multiplier** equals the ratio of a change in equilibrium output to the initial change in expenditure that caused it. In our example the multiplier equals $400/$100, or 4. Later we will provide a more specific formulation for the multiplier, but first we will explore the source of the multiplier magic.

*The **multiplier** equals the ratio of a change in equilibrium income to the initial change in expenditure that caused it.*

The Multiplier and the Circular Flow

The idea of the circular flow is central to understanding the adjustment process from one equilibrium quantity of output demanded to another.

Recall that production yields income, which generates spending. We can think of each trip around the circular flow as a "round" of income and spending. A shift up in the aggregate expenditure function means that planned spending exceeds output at the initial equilibrium level. Whenever planned spending exceeds output, production must increase. This increase in production increases income, which in turn increases planned spending. This increase in planned spending fuels yet another round of adjustments. *As long as planned spending exceeds output, production will expand, thereby yielding more income, which will generate still more spending.* Now we will describe what happens in each round when planned investment increases by $100 billion.

Round One Suppose firms decide to spend $100 billion per year on additional investment—new buildings, machines, trucks, computers, and the like. Firms that produce these capital goods respond by increasing production by $100 billion. This additional production generates $100 billion in income to all those who supplied their resources to the production of capital goods. Thus, total spending and total income increase by $100 billion in what is the first round of new spending arising from the increase in investment. The income-generating process does not stop there, however, because those who receive this additional income spend some of it and save some of it, laying the basis for round two of spending and income.

Round Two Given a marginal propensity to consume of 3/4, or 0.75, those who receive the $100 billion as income will spend a total of $75 billion on toasters, books, movies, and thousands of other goods and services; the other $25 billion of that $100 billion will be saved. Thus, during the second round, the $100 billion in new income supports a $75 billion increase in consumption and a $25 billion increase in saving. (Keep in mind that we do not necessarily expect the real-world MPC to equal 0.75 or any other constant value.)

Round Three and Beyond Focus now on the $75 billion that went toward consumption during round two. Production increases in the second round by $75 billion to satisfy the increase in spending and generates an equal amount of income to those who produced those additional goods and services purchased. Again, based on the marginal propensity to consume, we know that three-quarters of the additional income will be consumed and one-quarter will be saved. Thus, $56.25 billion will be spent on still more goods and services, and $18.75 billion will be saved. This spending continues to generate income, three-quarters of which is spent, thereby generating still more income.

When does the income-generating machine run out of gas? Saving leaks from the circular flow during every round. *The more income that leaks as saving, the less that remains to fuel still more spending and income.* When the entire $100 billion increase in investment has drained from the circular flow as saving, no new income or spending can be created, so the process stops. Exhibit 6 summarizes in a more systematic way the multiplier process. The table

John Maynard Keynes
(1883–1946)

The economy is a complicated but largely self-balanced system; any shocks to the system set in motion forces that eventually put the system back on track. This notion is Adam Smith's legacy to economists. During the Great Depression of the 1930s, however, this inheritance began to look increasingly threadbare and faded. Economists of the time quickly recognized that the system had somehow fallen seriously off track—and most agreed that, contrary to a popular myth, the system was going to need a push to get back on track. But the classical legacy had not left a well-developed theory of derailed economies.

Into this theoretical void sprang John Maynard Keynes with a book called *The General Theory of Employment, Interest, and Money*. Keynes's intentions were in no way modest. He wanted nothing less than to change the way economists look at the economic system.

In person, Keynes was everything Smith was not. He was worldly, self-confident, articulate, political. A Cambridge don and the son of a famous economist, Keynes moved within the most exalted intellectual circle of his age: the Bloomsbury group, named after the section of London in which they gathered. The members of this group—artists, writers, critics—shared an aristocratic belief in the powers of the mind. Like his compatriots, Keynes liked to take chances with ideas. He also liked to take chances with money, and he made a fortune for himself and his college by playing the market each morning while still in bed.

The contrast with Smith extends to economics as well. Whereas Smith was a system builder, Keynes was an astute intellectual tactician, a brilliant improvisor. *The General Theory* is an attempt to flesh out the intuition that a depressed economy needs a kick. But Keynes does not try to show how a basically self-adjusting system can get back on track; rather, he tries to prove that the system is fundamentally *not self-adjusting*. Here Keynes's fascination with financial markets shows through. Because organized financial markets have become so important, he argues, speculation—not the interest rate—is what largely controls the level of investment. The effect is to cut the classical feedback link between the decision to save and the decision to invest.

In one respect, though, Keynes was very much like Smith. He left a legacy whose implications economists are still debating and trying to understand.

Richard Langlois

EXHIBIT 6
TRACKING THE ROUNDS OF SPENDING
FOLLOWING A $100 BILLION INCREASE
IN AUTONOMOUS SPENDING
(billions of dollars)

Round (1)	New Spending This Round (2)	Cumulative New Spending (3)	New Saving This Round (4)	Cumulative New Saving (5)
1	100	100	—	—
2	75	175	25	25
3	56.25	231.25	18.75	43.75
4	42.19	273.44	14.06	57.81
⋮ ∞	⋮ 0	⋮ 400	⋮ 0	⋮ 100

reflects the new spending and saving generated during each round plus the cumulative effects on spending and saving. The first several rounds are listed, and subsequent rounds are summarized. For example, the cumulative new spending after the third round is $231.25 billion: the sum of the first three rounds of spending. The cumulative new saving after the third round is $43.75 billion. When the increase in spending has run its course, the cumulative effect has been to increase spending by $400 billion and to increase saving by $100 billion. Saving increases just enough to finance the $100 billion increase in autonomous investment. Note that in our example planned investment increased by $100 billion per year. *If this higher level of planned investment is not sustained in the following year, equilibrium spending will fall.* For example, if planned investment returns to $300 billion, other things constant, equilibrium spending will return to $2800 billion.

Tracking Rounds with the Income-Expenditure Model

Yet another way to understand the workings of the multiplier is to follow the rounds of spending by reference to the aggregate expenditure function presented in Exhibit 7. We begin as before at point *e*, where income and spending equal $2800 billion. Recall that changes in spending are measured along the vertical axis and changes in income are measured along the horizontal axis. The first round of spending results from the $100 billion increase in investment, reflected by the shift in the expenditure function from *C + I* up to *C + I'*. This new spending is satisfied initially by an unplanned reduction in inventories. The initial increase in spending is reflected by the movement from point *e* to point *a* on the new aggregate expenditure function.

A reduction in inventories does not translate directly into an increase in income, because these inventories generated income when they were pro-

EXHIBIT 7   THE GEOMETRY OF THE MULTIPLIER

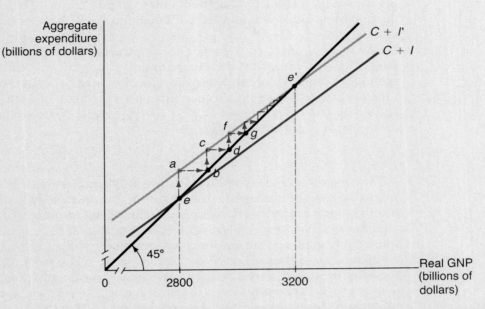

With the economy in equilibrium at point *e*, spending increases by $100 billion. At the initial level of income, this is shown by the movement from point *e* on the old aggregate expenditure function (*C + I*) to point *a* on the new one (*C + I'*). As businesses expand production to satisfy the increased demand, output and income rise by $100 billion, as expressed by the movement from point *a* to point *b*. This is round one.

With income now $100 billion higher, consumption spending rises by $75 billion. This spending causes a reduction in inventories, shown by the movement from point *b* to point *c*. As firms increase output to satisfy the higher level of spending, income also increases by $75 billion, as indicated by the movement from point *c* to point *d*. This process continues until equilibrium is reestablished with aggregate expenditure equal to income at point *e'*.

duced in some previous period. But as firms expand output by $100 billion to replenish their inventories, total income also increases by $100 billion, as expressed by the move from point *a* to point *b*. The movement from point *e* to point *b* represents the first round in the multiplier process.

After the first round, both spending and income have increased by $100 billion. This increase in income results in an increase in spending in the second round of $75 billion, which is initially met by reductions in inventories, as shown by the movement from point *b* to point *c*. But as firms expand output to satisfy the new, higher level of spending, income to those who produced that output also increases by $75 billion, as indicated by the movement from point *c* to point *d*. The process continues in this fashion, with each new round of spending generating an equal amount of income until the new equilibrium quantity of real GNP demanded is reached at point e'. Given a constant price level, the equilibrium quantity of real GNP demanded increases from $2800 billion to $3200 billion. The equilibrium quantity demanded will remain at $3200 billion only if investment remains at its new level.

As we will see later, the equilibrium quantity of real GNP demanded would have increased by the same amount if consumers had decided to spend $100 billion more at each level of income—that is, if the consumption function rather than the investment function had shifted up by $100 billion. *What is important is the effect of a change on the aggregate expenditure function, not which spending component changes.*

Numerical Value of the Multiplier

Tracing the rounds of spending is one way to determine the effects of a particular change in spending, but this process is slow and tedious. What we need is a quick way of translating spending changes into changes in the equilibrium level of real GNP demanded. Recall that the expansion stemming from an increase in autonomous spending was limited by the leakage of income to saving. There is a relation between the multiplier and the marginal propensity to save that proves useful in formulating the multiplier. *The smaller the saved portion of a change in income, the more that is respent each round, so the greater the multiplier. The marginal propensity to save and the multiplier are inversely related; the larger the MPS, the smaller the multiplier.*

$$\text{The simple multiplier} = \frac{1}{\text{MPS}}$$

In our model the simple multiplier is the reciprocal of the MPS. Since the MPS is 1/4, the multiplier equals the reciprocal of 1/4, which is 4. If the MPS were 1/5, the multiplier would be 5. If the MPS were 1/3, the multiplier would be 3.

Recall that the MPC and the MPS add up to 1, so the MPS equals 1 minus the MPC. With this information, we can define the demand multiplier in terms of the MPC as follows:

$$\text{The simple multiplier} = \frac{1}{1 - \text{MPC}}$$

When we state the equation this way, we can see that the larger the MPC, the larger the fraction of each fresh round of income that is spent, so the larger the multiplier will be.[1]

---

[1] A more formal way of deriving the multiplier is to total the additions to spending arising from each new round of income and spending. For example, a $1 increase in investment generates $1 in spending in the first round. In the second round, it generates $1 times the MPC. In the third round, the new spending equals the spending that arose in the second round ($1 × MPC) times the MPC. This goes on round after round, with each new round equal to the spending from the previous round times the MPC. Mathematicians have shown that the sum of this infinite series of rounds, each of which is a constant fraction of the previous round, is 1/(1 − MPC), which in our context is the simple multiplier.

Effects of an Increase in Saving

Thus far we have considered the multiplier effect of an increase in spending, but the multiplier is a two-edged sword that works in reverse for a decrease in investment or consumption. Now we will consider the effect of a decrease in the consumption function. We begin at our initial equilibrium level of $2800 billion, identified by point *e* in panel (a) of Exhibit 8. Suppose that households suddenly see dark clouds on the economic horizon and decide to save more for a rainy day. Specifically, suppose saving increases by $100 billion at every level of income, as reflected in panel (b) of Exhibit 8 by the shift up in the saving function from *S* to *S'*. Since saving and consump-

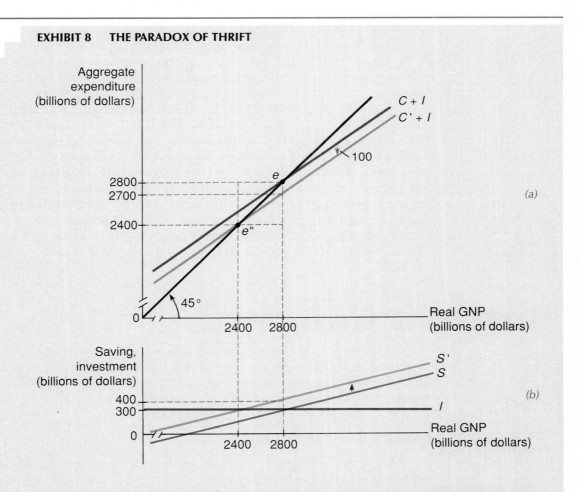

EXHIBIT 8   THE PARADOX OF THRIFT

If households try to increase their saving by $100 billion, as shown in panel (b), the consumption function will shift down by $100 billion at each level of income, as shown in panel (a). The decline in spending sets off a multiplier reaction that causes income to fall by a multiple of $100 billion. With a marginal propensity to consume of 4, income and output will decline by $400 billion.

tion are mirror images, this increase in saving means that consumption will fall by $100 billion at every level of income, as shown in panel (a). A shift in consumption at every level of income is called a change in *autonomous consumption*. As a result of this decline in autonomous consumption, people buy fewer autos and other goods; auto workers therefore receive less income and buy fewer bowling balls and other goods; those who produce bowling balls buy less spaghetti sauce and other goods; and so on. We have the multiplier at full throttle, but in reverse. The downward spiral continues until output and income just equal aggregate expenditure along the now-lower aggregate expenditure function, at point e'' in panel (a) of Exhibit 8. As you can see, the $100 billion decline in spending gets multiplied by a factor of 4, reducing the equilibrium quantity of real GNP demanded from its original level of $2800 billion to $2400 billion.

Notice in panel (b) of Exhibit 8 that the saving function has shifted up by $100 billion, from S to S'. Saving for a rainy day is generally thought of as a responsible endeavor, but if all consumers save for a rainy day, other things constant, increased household saving reduces the equilibrium quantity of aggregate output demanded. At the initial equilibrium level, households increase their saving from $300 billion to $400 billion, but that higher level of saving means that less is spent, and the drop in spending reduces equilibrium income. At the new, lower equilibrium level of aggregate expenditure, saving falls to equal investment of $300 billion. This equality of saving and planned investment helps explain an ironic feature of the income-expenditure model known as the paradox of thrift. The **paradox of thrift** says that if all households try to save more, they may be unable to do so. *The reduced consumption will lower the equilibrium quantity of aggregate output demanded, thereby reducing income and saving until saving once again equals planned investment.*

The **paradox of thrift** says that if all households try to save more, they may be unable to do so.

EFFECT OF CHANGES IN THE PRICE LEVEL

Thus far in this chapter we have used the aggregate expenditure function to derive the equilibrium quantity of real GNP demanded *for a given price level*. For each price level there is a specific aggregate expenditure function, which yields a unique equilibrium quantity of output demanded.

Changes in the Price Level

What is the effect of an increase in the price level on the economy's aggregate expenditure function and, in turn, on the equilibrium quantity of aggregate output demanded? Recall that consumers hold many assets that are fixed in money terms, and an increase in the price level reduces the real value of these dollar-denominated assets. Consumers therefore feel poorer as a result of an increase in the price level, so they are less willing to spend at every level of income. As a result of the higher price level, consumers are more inclined to increase saving in order to restore their assets to some desired level. *An increase in the price level therefore lowers the consumption function and consequently lowers the aggregate expenditure function.* A decline in the aggregate expenditure function reduces the equilibrium quantity of aggregate output demanded.

The opposite holds if the price level decreases. At a lower price level, the value of assets fixed in dollars increases; consumers on average are wealthier and therefore inclined to spend more at every level of income. This greater willingness to spend is reflected by a shift up in the consumption function and, consequently, a shift up in the aggregate expenditure function. The higher aggregate expenditure function leads to a higher equilibrium quantity of aggregate output demanded.

The effects of changes in the price level on the quantity of real GNP demanded can be examined in the two panels in Exhibit 9. Each panel represents a different way of expressing the effects of a change in the price level on the quantity demanded. Panel (a) presents the income–expenditure framework, and panel (b) the aggregate demand framework. Again, the two panels are aligned so that the various levels of real GNP on the horizontal axes correspond. At the initial price level, P, the aggregate expenditure function, $C + I$, intersects the 45-degree line at point e to yield Y, the equilibrium quantity of real GNP demanded. At that level of real GNP, planned spending equals real GNP. Panel (b) shows more directly the link between the quantity of real GNP demanded and the price level. You can see that when the price level is P, the quantity demanded equals Y. This combination of price and quantity is identified by point e on the aggregate demand curve. Thus, the equilibrium quantity of real output demanded at a particular price level in panel (a) yields one combination of price and quantity demanded, point e, on the aggregate demand curve in panel (b).

Consider now the effects of an increase in the price level from P to P'. As explained earlier, an increase in the price level reduces the value of assets fixed in dollars, so consumers spend less at all levels of income. This reduced spending is reflected in panel (a) by a decrease in the aggregate expenditure function from $C + I$ to $C' + I$. (The assumption here is that only consumption is affected by the price change.) A decline in planned spending at each level of income reduces the equilibrium level of real GNP demanded from Y to Y', as indicated by the intersection of the lower aggregate expenditure function with the 45-degree line at point e'. This same price increase can be viewed more directly in panel (b). As you can see, when the price level increases from P to P', the quantity of real GNP demanded declines from Y to Y'.

Return now to the initial price level, P, and consider the effect of a decrease in the price level. Suppose the price level falls from P to P''. The value of all assets fixed in dollars increases, so people are more willing to spend, as reflected by the shift up in the expenditure function from $C + I$ to $C'' + I$ in panel (a) of Exhibit 9. As a result of this greater spending, the equilibrium quantity of real GNP demanded increases from Y to Y''. Panel (b) again conveys the effect of such a price reduction more directly. The reduction in the price level from P to P'' increases the quantity demanded from Y to Y''.

EXHIBIT 9   THE INCOME-EXPENDITURE APPROACH AND THE AGGREGATE DEMAND CURVE

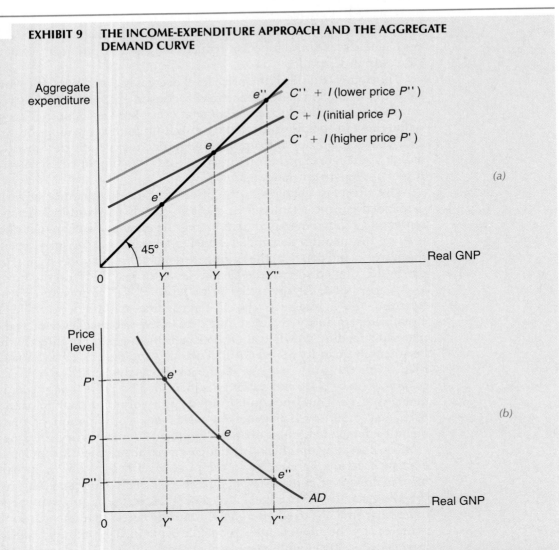

At the initial price level of *P*, aggregate expenditure is *C* + *I*, and equilibrium GNP is *Y*. Hence, price level *P* is associated with the level of output *Y* to determine one point (point *e*) on the aggregate demand curve in panel (b).

At the higher price level *P'*, consumption is lower (*C'*), aggregate expenditure is lower (*C'* + *I*), and equilibrium GNP is lower (*Y'*). This price-output combination is plotted as point *e'* in panel (b). At the lower price level of *P"*, aggregate expenditure is higher (*C"* + *I*), and so is equilibrium GNP (*Y"*). That price-output combination is plotted as point *e"* in panel (b).

Connecting points *e*, *e'*, and *e"* gives us the downward-sloping aggregate demand curve that shows how much real GNP will be demanded at each price level.

The aggregate expenditure function and the aggregate demand curve portray real GNP from different perspectives. The aggregate expenditure function shows, for a given price level, how consumption plus planned investment relates to the level of real GNP in the economy. The aggregate demand curve shows, for various prices, the quantity of real GNP demanded.

The Multiplier and Shifts in Aggregate Demand

Now that we have some idea how the aggregate expenditure function and the aggregate demand curve relate, we can trace the link between a shift in the aggregate expenditure function caused by some factor other than a change in price and the resulting shift in the aggregate demand curve. Exhibit 10 shows how shifts in the aggregate expenditure function and shifts in the aggregate demand curve are related. In panel (a), a $100 billion increase in investment shifts the aggregate expenditure function up by $100 billion, from $C + I$ to $C + I'$. As we have seen, because of the multiplier effect, this increase in spending ultimately raises the equilibrium quantity of real GNP demanded from $2800 billion to $3200 billion. Panel (b) shows the effects of the increase in investment on the aggregate demand curve. The aggregate demand curve has shifted to the right, from AD to AD'. At the prevailing price level, P, the quantity demanded has increased from $2800 billion to $3200 billion as a result of the $100 billion increase in investment.

CONCLUSION

The central idea of this chapter is the relation between the spending multiplier and changes in the equilibrium level of aggregate output demanded. Our discussion of the multiplier exaggerates the actual effect we might expect from a given change in consumption or investment. For one thing, we assume that the price level remains constant in the face of shifts in the aggregate demand curve. The next chapter introduces aggregate supply. Incorporating aggregate supply into the analysis tends to reduce the size of the multiplier because of resulting price changes. Moreover, there are other leakages in the circular flow in addition to saving, such as taxes and imports, and these leakages also tend to reduce the size of the multiplier. Finally, although we have presented the process in a timeless framework, the multiplier takes time to work itself out—perhaps two years.

So our simple multiplier overstates the real-world multiplier. Our approach to calculating the simple multiplier is akin to determining the miles a car travels on a gallon of gasoline by testing cars on a treadmill, where they confront no wind resistance, no hills, no potholes, and no bad drivers. Although the tests are obviously unrealistic, the results are still valuable for comparative purposes. We can say, for example, that a Honda Civic has twice the fuel efficiency of a Lincoln Town Car. Similarly, we can examine the effects of various changes in the aggregate expenditure function to see

**EXHIBIT 10   A SHIFT IN THE AGGREGATE EXPENDITURE FUNCTION AND A
SHIFT IN THE AGGREGATE DEMAND CURVE**

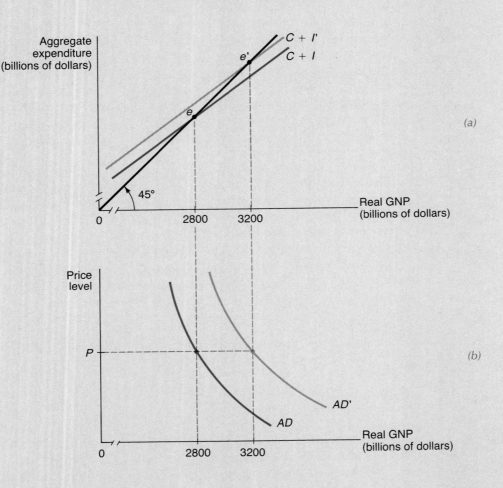

A shift in the aggregate expenditure function that is not due to a change in the price
level will cause a shift in the aggregate demand curve. In panel (a), an increase in
investment spending, with the price level fixed at P, causes aggregate expenditure
to increase from $C + I$ to $C + I'$. As a result, the equilibrium level of real GNP
demanded increases from $2800 billion to $3200 billion. In panel (b), the aggregate demand curve has shifted from AD to AD'. At the prevailing price level P, the
amount of output demanded has increased by $400 billion.

which changes have the greatest impact on the quantity of real GNP
demanded. The simple multiplier provides a first approximation of the
effect of a change in spending on the equilibrium quantity of real GNP

demanded, just as mileage tests on a treadmill provide a first, albeit high, estimate of actual fuel efficiency.

This chapter focused on consumption and investment, ignoring the rest of the world. Appendix A integrates the rest of the world into the framework. Since imports represent a leakage from the circular flow, including the rest of the world in the analysis reduces the size of the multiplier.

Thus far we have determined the equilibrium quantity of aggregate output demanded using several approaches. We told stories, examined tables, and graphed the aggregate expenditure function. With the various approaches we showed that for each price level there is a specific quantity of aggregate output demanded, other things constant. In Appendix B we will use algebra to derive the same equilibrium conditions.

Summary

1. By vertically summing the consumption and planned investment functions, we derive the aggregate expenditure function, which indicates, for a given price level, the amount that households and firms plan to spend at each level of income.

2. At a given price level, the equilibrium quantity of aggregate output demanded is achieved at the level of income where the amount firms and households plan to spend just equals the amount produced. Planned spending equals income. In our simple economy this means that the amount that firms plan to invest equals household saving.

3. The marginal propensity to consume equals the change in consumption divided by the change in income. The slope of the consumption function equals the marginal propensity to consume. The marginal propensity to save equals the change in saving divided by the change in income. The slope of the saving function equals the marginal propensity to save.

4. Any given change in spending will generate a change in income that, in turn, affects spending. The multiplier indicates the multiple by which a given shift in desired spending changes the equilibrium level of aggregate output demanded. The simple multiplier examined in this chapter equals $1/(1 - MPC)$. The greater the MPC, the more of each dollar of income that will be spent, and the greater the multiplier.

5. A change in the price level changes the amount consumers purchase at each level of real income. A higher price level results in a downward shift in the aggregate expenditure function, leading to a lower equilibrium quantity of aggregate output demanded. A lower price level creates an upward shift in the aggregate expenditure function, leading to a greater equilibrium quantity of aggregate output demanded. By tracing the equilibrium output demanded at alternative price levels, we can use the income-expenditure framework to derive the aggregate demand curve.

Questions and Problems

1. (Actual Investment Versus Planned Investment) Recently General Motors experienced inventories equal to about one hundred days' production. Usual inventories are about thirty days' production. How does this situation relate to the concept of unplanned investment as discussed in the chapter? How will GM react to such a problem?

2. (MPC and MPS) Why must it always be true that a rise in the MPC will force a fall in the MPS? Why do economists believe that the MPC is a fraction between zero and one?

3. (MPC and MPS) Why would the MPC be different for different countries? For example, how would Japan's MPC compare with that of the United States? How would the MPC of Chad compare with that of the United States?

4. (Equilibrium) What roles do inventories play in the establishment of equilibrium for aggregate output? To answer this question, suppose that firms are either overproducing or underproducing.

5. (The Multiplier) Suppose that the MPC for the United States is about 0.90 and that a movie studio travels to Montana to make an adventure film. The production of the movie will inject $30 million into the Montana economy initially. One bright economics student claims this $30 million will generate $300 million in additional income for the state. However, some people believe this is an overestimate. What information is needed to decide who is correct?

6. (The Multiplier) What factors would speed up or slow down the multiplier process?

7. (The Multiplier) "A rise in planned investment spending in an economy will lead to a rise in consumer spending." Use the concept of the multiplier to verify this statement.

8. (The Multiplier) Complete a table similar to Exhibit 6 in this chapter, given that the marginal propensity to consume is equal to 0.90. Assuming the same $100 billion increase in autonomous spending, list the values for each of the first four rounds and determine the overall effect of the increase.

9. (Paradox of Thrift) When consumer confidence falls, consumers generally attempt to save a little more money to prepare for bad times ahead. Why does such rational action by consumers make society worse off?

10. (Aggregate Expenditure Function) People who are unfamiliar with economics often have trouble understanding why aggregate expenditure both depends on income and determines income. Use the economic concept of equilibrium to resolve this seeming paradox.

11. (Multiplier) Suppose that the marginal propensity to consume is 0.8 and autonomous investment is $500 billion. Assume that the world consists of only households and firms.
   a. What is the level of saving at equilibrium quantity of aggregate output demanded? Explain.
   b. Suppose that consumption equals $100 billion when aggregate output (income) is 0. Graph the saving function and the investment function, showing equilibrium quantity of output demanded.
   c. What is the value of the multiplier?
   d. Explain why the multiplier is related to the slope of the consumption function.

12. (Multiplier and Aggregate Demand) Suppose that at an average price level of 100, equilibrium output demanded is $1000 billion, and that each point change in the price level causes the aggregate expenditure function to shift by $5 billion. Using a multiplier of 4, do the following:
   a. Construct the aggregate demand curve.
   b. Determine its slope.
   c. Explain how a change in the multiplier would affect the slope of the aggregate demand curve.
   d. How much would an increase in saving of $100 billion affect the aggregate demand curve? Be specific.

APPENDIX A
The Rest of the World

The rest of the world has been ignored in this chapter. But U.S. residents buy foreign products and foreigners buy U.S. products. To focus on purchases of U.S. products, aggregate expenditure should exclude U.S. spending on imports but include foreign spending on U.S. exports. Thus, aggregate spending should reflect net exports, $X - M$, which are exports minus imports.

In the appendix to the last chapter we derived the net export function and showed that net exports and the level of income are inversely related. This function is presented in panel (b) of Exhibit 11. The higher the income level in the economy, the more that is imported, so the lower the net exports. Panel (a) of Exhibit 11 shows the $C + I$ spending function as developed in the chapter. As you can see, when only consumption and investment are included in the aggregate expenditure function, equilibrium output and spending equal $2800 billion.

We add the net export function to the $C + I$ function to derive the $C + I + (X - M)$ spending function. Perhaps the easiest way to see how the addition of net exports affects aggregate expenditures is to begin where real GNP equals $2000 billion. Since net exports equal zero when real GNP equals $2000 billion, the addition of net exports has no effect on the aggregate expenditure at that level of income. Therefore, the $C + I$ function and the $C + I + (X - M)$ function intersect where income equals $2000 billion. At income levels below $2000 billion, net exports are positive, so the $C + I + (X - M)$ function is above the $C + I$ function. At income levels greater than $2000 billion, net exports are negative, so the $C + I + (X - M)$ function is below the $C + I$ function.

With the addition of net exports, spending by the private sector includes consumption, investment, and net exports. *Because net ex-*

ports and income are inversely related, the addition of net exports has the effect of reducing the slope of, or flattening out, the aggregate expenditure function. Notice that because the aggregate expenditure function has flattened out, equilibrium output has fallen. The negative net exports have reduced equilibrium output from $2800 billion to $2571 billion. (This new equilibrium value will be derived algebraically in Appendix B.)

The effect of net exports on equilibrium output depends on the level of income at which net exports equal zero. For example, if net exports were zero when income was $4000 billion, then net exports would be positive when income equaled $2800 billion. If net exports were positive, the inclusion of net exports would boost equilibrium output above $2800 billion, the equilibrium excluding net exports. If, by coincidence, net exports were zero at an income level of $2800 billion, equilibrium output would remain unchanged after the addition of net exports to consumption and investment.

Net Exports and the Spending Multiplier

The inclusion of net exports makes the model more realistic but more complicated, and it requires a reformulation of the multiplier. In the absence of net exports, the marginal propensity to consume determines how much will be spent and how much will be saved when income increases. The inclusion of net exports adds the additional option of spending the money on imports. As income increases, U.S. residents spend more on imports. The **marginal propensity to import**, or **MPI**, indicates the fraction of each additional dollar of income that is spent on imported products. But imports represent a leakage from the circular flow. Thus there are now two leakages from the circular flow: saving and imports. The introduction of this additional leakage changes the value of the multiplier from 1/MPS to

$$\text{Multiplier with net exports} = \frac{1}{\text{MPS} + \text{MPI}}$$

EXHIBIT 11   NET EXPORTS AND THE AGGREGATE EXPENDITURE FUNCTION

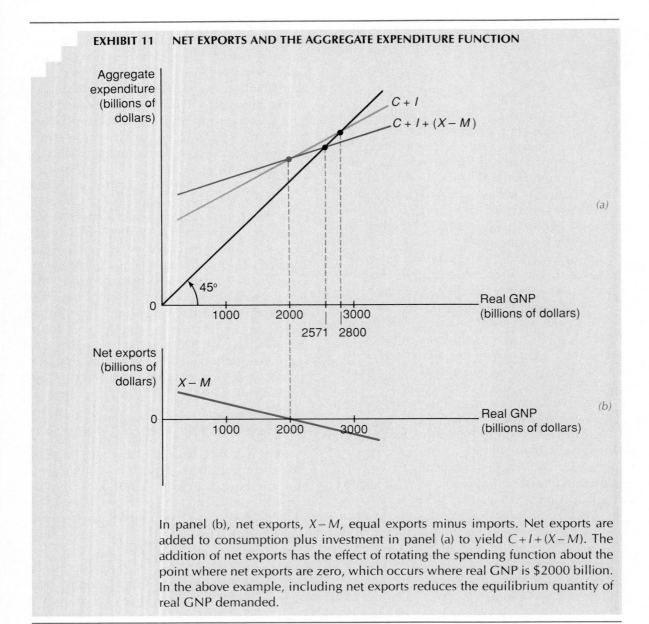

In panel (b), net exports, *X – M*, equal exports minus imports. Net exports are added to consumption plus investment in panel (a) to yield *C + I + (X – M)*. The addition of net exports has the effect of rotating the spending function about the point where net exports are zero, which occurs where real GNP is $2000 billion. In the above example, including net exports reduces the equilibrium quantity of real GNP demanded.

The larger the marginal propensity to import, the greater the leakage during each round of respending and the smaller the resulting spending multiplier. In the United States, about 10 percent of additional income is spent on imports, so the MPI equals about 1/10, or 0.10. If the marginal propensity to save is 0.25 and the marginal propensity to import is 0.10, then only 65 cents of each additional dollar of income is spent on U.S. products. We can compute the new multiplier as follows:

$$\text{Multiplier} = \frac{1}{\text{MPS} + \text{MPI}} = \frac{1}{0.25 + 0.10}$$

$$= \frac{1}{0.35} = 2.86$$

Thus the inclusion of net exports reduces the multiplier in our hypothetical example from 4 to less than 3. Because some of each additional dollar of income is spent on imports, less is spent on U.S. products, so any given shift in the aggregate expenditure function will have less of an impact on equilibrium output.

A Shift in Net Exports

What is the effect of a shift in the net export function on equilibrium GNP? Let's begin in Exhibit 12 with an aggregate expenditure function of $C + I + (X - M)$ and a hypothetical equilibrium output level of $2571 billion. Suppose now that a drop in the value of the dollar relative to foreign currencies makes im-

ports more costly to U.S. residents and exports cheaper to foreigners. As a result, suppose net exports increase by $100 billion at every level of income. This increase in net exports will shift the entire aggregate expenditure function up by $100 billion, from $C + I + (X - M)$ to $C + I + (X' - M')$, as shown in Exhibit 12. As you can see, equilibrium output demanded increases from $2571 billion to $2857 billion, representing an increase of $286 billion, which is $100 billion times the multiplier of 2.86. The derivation of the initial equilibrium level of income and the multiplier will be illustrated in Appendix B. (Incidentally, the effect on equilibrium output demanded would be the same had either the investment function or the consumption function shifted up by $100 billion.)

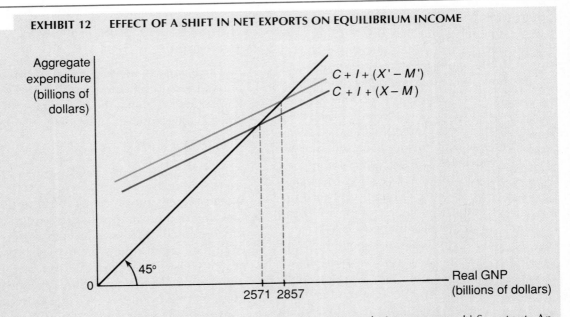

EXHIBIT 12   EFFECT OF A SHIFT IN NET EXPORTS ON EQUILIBRIUM INCOME

An increase in net exports means that more is being spent on U.S. output. An increase in net exports, other things constant, shifts the spending function up from $C + I + (X - M)$ to $C + I + (X' - M')$, yielding a larger equilibrium quantity of real GNP demanded.

APPENDIX B
Algebra of Private Sector Demand

This appendix will explain the algebra behind the material in the chapter deriving the equilibrium value of aggregate output demanded. You should see some similarity between the presentation here and the description of the circular flow explaining the national income accounts.

The Aggregate Expenditure Function

We begin with the heart of the income-expenditure model: the consumption function. The consumption function used throughout this chapter was a straight line; the equation for this line can be written as

$$C = 400 + 0.75Y$$

where Y equals the level of real GNP, or level of real income. This line, or consumption function, has a vertical intercept of $400 billion and a slope of 0.75. Consumption at each level of income therefore equals $400 billion plus 0.75 times the level of income. So $400 billion will be spent on consumption even if income is zero; this amount is called *autonomous consumption*. Consumption will increase by $0.75 for each $1 increase in income; thus, increases in consumption are said to be *induced* by increases in income. Therefore, consumption has an autonomous element, $400 billion, and an induced element, $0.75Y$.

The second component of spending is investment. The equation for autonomous investment used throughout the chapter can be written simply as $I = 300$. Combining these equations for consumption and investment yields

$$C + I = 400 + 0.75Y + 300 = 700 + 0.75Y$$

The right-hand expression describes the aggregate expenditure function used throughout this chapter. This line has an intercept of $700 billion and a slope of 0.75. Thus, autonomous consumption plus autonomous investment equals $700 billion. In equilibrium, real GNP, Y, equals aggregate spending ($C + I$):

$$Y = C + I$$

To find the equilibrium level of Y, we find the value of Y in the following equation:

$$Y = 700 + 0.75Y$$

By rearranging terms, we find

$$0.25Y = 700$$

Dividing both sides of the equation by 0.25 indicates that the equilibrium value of Y is $2800 billion.

A More General Form of Demand-Side Equilibrium

The beauty of algebra is that it allows us to derive the equilibrium quantity of real GNP demanded in a much more general way. Consider a consumption function of the general form

$$C = a + bY$$

where a equals autonomous consumption, the amount of consumption that occurs when income equals 0 ($400 billion in our previous example), and b equals the marginal propensity to consume. We can also say that investment equals I. At equilibrium, therefore, the quantity of GNP demanded equals the sum of consumption and investment, or

Income = Expenditure
$$Y = a + bY + I$$

Again, by rearranging terms and isolating Y on the left-hand side of the equation, we get

$$Y = \frac{1}{1-b}(a + I)$$

The $(a + I)$ term represents autonomous spending—that is, the amount of spending that occurs even if the level of income equals 0. And $(1 - b)$ equals 1 minus the MPC. In the chapter we showed that $1/(1 - \text{MPC})$ equals the multiplier. One way of viewing the forces that underlie the determination of equilibrium is that autonomous spending is *multiplied* through the economy until the equilibrium quantity of aggregate output is demanded.

The formula that yields the equilibrium quantity of aggregate output demanded can be used to focus on the origin of the demand multiplier. We can increase autonomous spending by, say, $1 billion to see what happens to the equilibrium quantity demanded. We begin by adding $1 billion to the equilibrium level of income:

$$Y' = \frac{1}{1-b}(a + I + \$1)$$

The difference between this expression and the initial equilibrium (that is, between Y' and Y) is $\$1/(1 - b)$. Since b equals the MPC, the multiplier equals $1/(1 - b)$. Thus, the change in equilibrium output equals the change in autonomous spending times the multiplier.

Adding the Rest of the World

The effect of adding the rest of the world will depend on net exports. We begin by stating the equilibrium condition when net exports are added to consumption plus investment:

$$Y = C + I + (X - M)$$

Exports are autonomous and have been assumed to equal $200 billion. Imports are induced by increases in income, and the marginal propensity to import has been assumed to equal 0.10. Therefore, net exports will be

$$X - M = 200 - 0.10Y$$

After incorporating the values for C and I as presented earlier, we can express the full equilibrium condition as

$$Y = 400 + 0.75Y + 300 + 200 - 0.10Y$$

which reduces to $0.35Y = 900$, or $Y = 2571$. This is lower than the original equilibrium of $2800 billion, which included only consumption and investment.

Algebra can be used to generalize these results. If m represents the marginal propensity to import, net exports become $X - mY$. The equilibrium output can be found by solving for Y in the expression

$$Y = a + bY + I + X - mY$$

which yields

$$Y = \frac{1}{1 - b + m}(a + I + X)$$

The expression in parentheses represents autonomous consumption plus autonomous investment plus autonomous exports. In the denominator, $1 - b$ is the marginal propensity to save and m is the marginal propensity to import. We learned in Appendix A that $1/(\text{MPS} + \text{MPI})$ equals the multiplier when net exports are included. Thus, equilibrium output equals the spending multiplier times autonomous spending.

Appendix Questions

1. (The Spending Multiplier) Suppose that the marginal propensity to consume (MPC) is 0.8 and the marginal propensity to import (MPI) is 0.05.
   a. What is the value of the multiplier?
   b. What would be the change in equilibrium output if investment increased by $100 billion?
   c. Using your answer to part b, calculate the change in the trade balance (net exports) caused by the change in aggregate output.

2. (Equilibrium) Suppose that when aggregate output equals 0, consumption equals $100 billion, autonomous investment equals $200 billion, and net exports equal $100 billion. Suppose also that MPC = 0.9 and MPI = 0.1.

   a. Construct a table showing the level of aggregate spending, net exports, and saving for aggregate output levels of 0, $500 billion, and $1000 billion.
   b. Use autonomous spending and the multiplier to calculate the equilibrium quantity of aggregate output demanded.
   c. What would the new equilibrium quantity of output demanded be if an *increase* in U.S. interest rates caused net exports to change by $50 billion? Explain.

C H A P T E R   1 0

Aggregate Supply

Up to this point we have focused on the quantity of aggregate output demanded for a given price level. Firms have not figured into our discussion of demand-side equilibrium. We assumed that producers stood ready to supply whatever amount of output was demanded at each price level, reducing their inventories to cover shortfalls and accumulating inventories to absorb any unsold goods. We were not concerned with what producers would be willing and able to supply. Thus, we have not yet introduced a theory of aggregate supply.

Perhaps no area of macroeconomics is subject to more debate among economists than that of aggregate supply. In this chapter, however, we will attempt to develop a single, coherent framework. Although our focus continues to be on economic aggregates, you should not lose sight of the fact that aggregate supply reflects billions of individual production decisions made by millions of individual resource suppliers and firms in the economy. Each firm operates in its own little world, dealing with regular suppliers and customers and keeping a watchful eye on existing and potential competitors. Yet each firm also recognizes that its success in large measure is linked to the performance of the economy as a whole. Thus, the theory of supply we describe here must be consistent with both the microeconomic behavior of individual producers and the macroeconomic behavior of the economy. In the appendix to this chapter we will examine resource markets more closely to strengthen your understanding of the underpinnings of aggregate supply. Topics discussed in this chapter include

- Expected price levels and long-term contracts
- Potential output
- Short-run aggregate supply
- Long-run aggregate supply
- Expansionary and contractionary gaps
- Changes in aggregate supply

225

AGGREGATE SUPPLY IN THE SHORT RUN

As you know, *aggregate supply* is the relation between the price level in the economy and the quantity of aggregate output firms are willing and able to supply, other things constant. The other things held constant along a given aggregate supply curve include the supply of resources in the economy and the state of technology. The greater the supply of resources or the better the technology, the greater the aggregate supply. We begin by looking at the supply of the most important resource: labor.

Labor Supply and Aggregate Supply

The supply of labor in an economy depends on the size and quality of the labor force and household preferences for work versus leisure. Along a given labor supply curve—that is, for a given labor force and given preferences for work versus leisure—the quantity of labor supplied depends on the wage. The higher the wage, other things constant, the greater the quantity of labor supplied.

So far, so good. Things start getting complicated, however, because the purchasing power of any given dollar wage will depend on the price level in the economy. The higher the price level, the less any given dollar wage will purchase. Therefore, we begin our examination of labor supply by distinguishing between the nominal wage and the real wage. The **nominal wage** is the wage measured in current dollars. The **real wage** is the nominal wage adjusted for the effects of changes in the price level. The real wage is thus the wage measured in terms of the quantity of goods and services it will purchase. The real wage is equal to the nominal wage divided by the price level. For example, suppose the nominal wage rate is $10 per hour and the economy's price level averages $2 per unit of output. The real wage is the amount of aggregate output that could be purchased with an hour's wages, which is $10/$2, or 5 units of output. If both the nominal wage and the price level double—to $20 per hour and $4 per unit, respectively—the real wage of $20/$4, or 5 units of output, remains unchanged.

Compensation is usually negotiated in terms of the nominal wage, not the real wage. Both firms and workers are concerned about the real wage, so they would like to agree on the nominal wage only *after* they know what price level will prevail in the economy. However, resource suppliers and firms typically negotiate the nominal wage (as well as the prices of other resources, such as interest on loans and rent on buildings) *before* the start of the period and hence *before* they know exactly what price level will prevail during the period. Moreover, some resource prices, such as wages that are set by long-term contracts, must be agreed upon for extended periods, sometimes a year or more. So workers and firms must reach wage agreements based on *expected* price levels.

Even where there are no explicit labor contracts, there is often an implicit agreement between employer and employee regarding the nominal wage over some time period. For example, in many firms the standard practice is

*The **nominal wage** is the wage measured in terms of current dollars; the **real wage** is measured in terms of the quantity of goods and services it will purchase.*

to revise wages annually. Thus, wage agreements may be either *explicit*, based on a labor contract, or *implicit*, based on the customs or conventions of the market. These explicit and implicit agreements make it difficult to change the nominal wage during the contract period even when the price level turns out to be higher or lower than expected. Some contracts may call for cost-of-living adjustments to be made annually during the life of the contract, but research shows that even these adjustments only partially compensate for unexpected changes in the price level.

Potential Output and the Natural Rate of Unemployment

Firms and resource suppliers each begin the production period expecting a certain price level to prevail in the economy; we will call the expected price P^*. Based on those expectations, they reach agreements on resource prices. If firms' and workers' price-level expectations are realized, the agreed-upon nominal wage yields the expected real wage, so everyone is satisfied with the way things work out. When the actual price level equals the expected price level, we call the resulting level of output the economy's **potential output**. (The concept of potential output will be developed more fully in the appendix to this chapter.) *Thus, the potential output is the amount produced when there are no surprises associated with the price level.*

Potential output is the level of real GNP produced when the actual price level equals the expected price level.

In thinking about potential output, it is useful to return to the idea of the economy's production possibilities frontier, which was introduced in Chapter 2. We can think of the potential output level as the economy's maximum *sustainable* output level, given the supply of resources and the state of technology. Potential output is also referred to by other terms including the *natural rate of output*, the *high-employment level of output*, and the *full-employment level of output*.

If the economy is producing its potential output, does this mean that all resources in the economy—every worker, every machine, every acre of land—are employed? No. Remember from our discussion of unemployment that even in a vibrant, dynamic economy some workers are unemployed. In a healthy economy there are always both job openings and job applicants. Other resources may be periodically unemployed as well. To remain productive, farmland must at times lie fallow. Machines must regularly be shut down for maintenance and repair. Even entire plants may be closed for retooling.

The *natural rate of unemployment* is the rate that occurs when the economy is producing its potential level of GNP.

The unemployment rate that occurs when the economy is producing its potential GNP is called the **natural rate of unemployment**. The natural rate of unemployment reflects a certain amount of frictional, structural, and seasonal unemployment. When the economy is producing its potential output, the number of job openings is equal to the number unemployed for frictional, structural, and seasonal reasons. During the 1960s a widely accepted figure for the natural rate of unemployment was 4 percent of the labor force. Since then the percentage has drifted up for reasons discussed in Chapter 7; today estimates of 5 or 6 percent are most often mentioned.

Potential output depends largely on the supply of labor and the productivity of that labor. The supply of labor, in turn, depends on household choices between labor and leisure. At the turn of the century, the average work week was about 54 hours. Because human and physical capital and technology improved during the century, worker productivity per hour increased. The resulting higher real incomes have prompted many households to increase their consumption of leisure, so the average work week is now about 40 hours. Thus, potential output is lower today than it would be had the labor force not reduced average hours worked.

Potential output provides a reference point for the analysis in this chapter. Any increase in the supply of resources in the economy or any technological breakthroughs in the way resources can be combined will increase the economy's potential output.

Actual Price Level Greater Than Expected

When the actual price level turns out as anticipated, the expectations of both workers and firms are fulfilled. Complications arise, however, when the actual price level that occurs in the economy differs from the expected price level.

Any discussion of aggregate supply should distinguish between the short run and the long run. The *short run* is a period so brief that firms and those who supply resources to firms have insufficient time to adjust to an unexpected price level. In the *long run*, firms and resource suppliers have time to adjust completely to a price level that differs from their expectations.

As we said, each firm's objective is to maximize profit. Profit equals total revenue minus total cost. In the short run, the costs of many resources used to produce output are fixed by contract. Suppose the price level turns out to be greater than expected. What happens to the quantity of aggregate output supplied? Does it exceed the economy's potential, fall short of that potential, or equal that potential? The quantity supplied when the price level increases depends on the profitability of additional production. If firms expect to increase profits by expanding output when the price level rises, the quantity supplied will increase. Put another way, when the price level rises, if the additional revenue of expanded output exceeds the additional cost, then firms have a profit incentive to increase production. Since the prices of many resources have been fixed for the duration of contracts, firms welcome a price level that is higher than expected. After all, in that situation the prices of their products, on average, are higher than expected, while the costs of at least some of the resources they employ remain constant.

If the total revenue the firm receives for the product rises faster than the firm's total cost of production, then profits rise as the price level increases. Because a higher price level results in higher profits in the short run, firms expand aggregate output beyond the economy's potential level. At first it might appear contradictory to talk about producing beyond the economy's potential, but remember that potential output implies not zero unemployment but the *natural rate* of unemployment. Even in an economy producing its potential output, there is some unemployed labor and some unused production capacity. The economy has the resilience to push output beyond its potential, and when it does so the unemployment rate falls below the natural rate. If you think of potential GNP as the economy's normal capacity, you get a better understanding of how the economy can temporarily exceed that capacity. During World War II, the United States pulled out all the stops to win the war. Factories operated around the clock. The unemployment rate fell below 2 percent. Overtime was common. People worked longer and harder than they normally would.

Consider your study habits. During most of the term you display your normal capacity for academic work. As the end of the term draws near, however, you probably shift into high gear, finishing term papers, studying late into the night for final exams, and generally running yourself ragged trying to pull things together. During those final frenzied weeks of the term, you study beyond your normal capacity, beyond the schedule you would prefer to follow on a regular or sustained basis.

We often observe workers exceeding their normal capacity for short bursts: fireworks displayers around the Fourth of July, accountants during tax preparation time, farmers during harvest time, and elected officials during the last days of a campaign or a legislative session. Similarly, firms and their workers are able, for limited periods, to push output beyond its potential.

Why Costs Rise When Output Exceeds Potential

The economy is flexible enough to expand output beyond potential GNP, just as you can extend yourself during final exams. However, neither you nor the economy's resources can be stretched indefinitely without putting pressure on production costs. Even though many workers are bound by contracts, wage agreements may require overtime pay for extra hours or weekend work. Firms may have to spend more on recruiting, particularly to hire workers who had been frictionally unemployed. Some firms must resort to hiring workers who are not properly prepared for the available jobs: those who had been structurally unemployed. Retirees may need an extra bonus to draw them back into the labor force. If few additional workers are available, if available workers are less qualified, or if workers require additional pay for overtime, the marginal cost of labor will increase as output expands in the short run, even though most workers are bound by nominal wage agreements.

The marginal cost of other resources may also increase as output is pushed beyond the economy's potential. As production expands, the demand for resources increases, so the prices of those resources purchased in markets where prices are flexible—such as the spot market for oil—will increase, reflecting their greater scarcity. Thus, the marginal cost per unit of output rises when production is pushed beyond the economy's potential GNP. But *because the costs of some resources are fixed in the short run by contracts, the marginal cost of production rises less than does the marginal revenue resulting from the higher price level, prompting profit-maximizing firms to expand output.* In summary, if the price level is greater than expected, firms have a profit incentive to increase the quantity of aggregate output supplied. As firms increase the quantity supplied, however, the marginal cost of output increases. Thus, when the price level increases, firms will maximize profits by expanding output as long as the marginal revenue of additional production exceeds the marginal cost of that production. Output expansion will cease when marginal revenue equals marginal cost.

The Price Level, Real Wages, and Labor Supply

As the price level rises, the real value of an agreed-upon nominal wage declines. We might ask why workers are willing to increase the quantity of labor they supply when the price level increases. One answer is that since labor agreements require workers to offer their labor at the agreed-upon nominal wage, workers are simply complying with their contracts. Another possible explanation is that the contracted wage is higher than it needs to be to attract enough workers. The **efficiency wage theory** argues that by keeping wages above the level required to attract a sufficient number of workers, some firms ensure an abundant worker pool from which to hire. Since wages are higher than they need to be, workers gladly increase the quantity of labor supplied when firms expand output.

A final possible explanation for increases in the quantity of labor is that nominal wages increase somewhat as firms increase output. Nominal wages increase because of overtime pay and because of the higher pay necessary to attract retirees and the frictionally unemployed back to work. Some workers may mistakenly believe that an increase in the nominal wage is in fact an increase in real wages, so they increase the quantity of labor supplied. Such workers are said to suffer from *money illusion*, which means they respond to increases in the nominal wage, even though real wages may not have increased.

*According to the **efficiency wage theory**, keeping wages above the level required to attract sufficient workers makes workers compete to keep their jobs and results in greater productivity and a larger pool of workers from which to draw.*

Actual Price Level Less Than Expected

We have discovered that when the price level is greater than expected, firms expand output, but as they do, the marginal cost of production increases. Now let's examine the effects of a price level that is lower than expected. Again, suppose that resource suppliers and firms are expecting the price level to be P^*.

If the price level turns out to be lower than expected, production is less attractive to firms. The price firms receive for their output is lower than expected, but many of their production costs do not fall. For example, since the nominal wage has been fixed by labor contracts, a lower price level means that the real wage firms must pay workers actually increases. *Since production is less profitable when the price level is lower than expected, firms reduce their output, and the economy produces less than its potential.* The result is that more workers become unemployed, employed workers may work fewer hours, and unemployment rises above the natural rate. Not only is less labor employed, but machines go unused and delivery trucks sit idle—entire plants may even shut down.

Just as some costs increase in the short run when output is pushed beyond the economy's potential, some costs decline when output falls below the economy's potential. As output falls below potential, resources become unemployed, so the prices of resources purchased in markets where the price is flexible decline. Moreover, with an abundance of unemployed resources, firms can be more selective about which resources to employ, laying off the least productive first.

The Short-Run Aggregate Supply Curve

To review: If the price level turns out to be greater than expected, the quantity supplied increases beyond the economy's potential output. As output expands, however, the marginal cost of production increases. Output expands until the marginal cost of additional production equals the marginal revenue generated. If the price level turns out to be lower than expected, the quantity supplied shrinks below the economy's potential output. As output falls, the marginal cost of production declines. Thus, in the short run, there is a positive relation between the price level and the quantity of aggregate output supplied.

What we have described is the short-run aggregate supply curve, which shows the relation between the price level and the quantity of aggregate output producers in the economy are willing and able to supply. The **short run** in this context is the period during which some resource prices, especially those for labor, are fixed by agreement. For simplicity, we can think of the short run as the duration of labor contracts.

The **short run** is the period during which some resource prices, especially those for labor, are fixed by agreement.

The short-run aggregate supply curve is drawn for a particular contract period based on the given expected price level, P^*. It slopes upward, as $SRAS(P^*)$ does in Exhibit 1. Note that if the price level turns out as expected, producers supply the economy's potential level of output, denoted as Y^*. This combination of price and quantity supplied is indicated by point e^*. If P^* turns out to be the actual price level, all firms and all resource suppliers will be content to supply that amount, because they based their supply and demand decisions on that price level. Nobody is surprised. In Exhibit 1, levels of output that fall short of the economy's potential are shaded in pink and levels of output that exceed the economy's potential are shaded in blue.

The slope of the aggregate supply curve depends on how quickly the marginal production costs rise as aggregate output expands. If the increases in marginal costs are relatively modest, the supply curve will be relatively flat. If marginal costs increase sharply with increased production, the supply curve will climb sharply with output. Notice that the short-run aggregate supply curve gets steeper as output increases. This increasing steepness stems from sharply rising marginal costs as production expands and resources become more scarce.

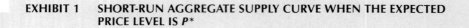

**EXHIBIT 1   SHORT-RUN AGGREGATE SUPPLY CURVE WHEN THE EXPECTED
PRICE LEVEL IS P^***

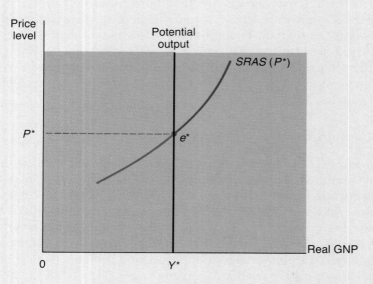

The short-run aggregate supply curve is drawn for a given expected price level, P^*.
Point e^* shows that if the actual price level equals the expected level, producers
supply the potential level of output, Y^*. If the price level exceeds P^*, firms increase
the quantity supplied. As they do, the cost of production per unit of output rises.
With a price level below P^*, firms decrease the quantity supplied. As they do, their
cost per unit of output falls. Levels of output that fall short of the economy's
potential are shaded pink; levels of output that exceed the economy's potential are
shaded blue.

AGGREGATE SUPPLY IN THE LONG RUN

A price level that is higher or lower than the expected price level on
which the prevailing resource agreements were based will, in the long run,
bring about additional adjustments. In the long run, firms and resource
suppliers are able to renegotiate all agreements based on knowledge of the
actual price level. In this section we examine this long-run adjustment.

Actual Price Level Higher Than Expected

Let's begin in Exhibit 2 with an expected price level of P^*. The short-run
aggregate supply curve for that expected price level is $SRAS(P^*)$. If the price
level turned out as expected, firms would be willing to supply the economy's
potential level of output, Y^*. Thus point e^* would reflect the equilibrium
combination of price and output levels. Suppose that aggregate demand
turns out to be greater than expected, so the actual price level is P, a price

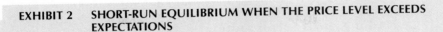

EXHIBIT 2   SHORT-RUN EQUILIBRIUM WHEN THE PRICE LEVEL EXCEEDS EXPECTATIONS

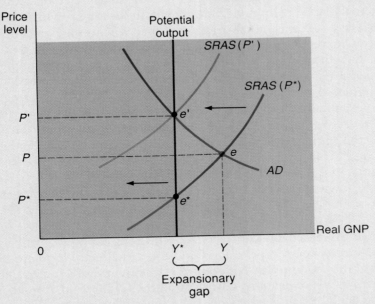

If the expected price level is P^*, the short-run aggregate supply curve is $SRAS(P^*)$. If the actual price level turns out as expected, the quantity supplied is the potential output, Y^*. If the price level is higher than expected, output exceeds potential, as shown by the short-run equilibrium at point e. The amount by which output, Y, exceeds the economy's potential output is referred to as the expansionary gap. In the long run, price expectations will be revised upward. As costs rise, the short-run aggregate supply curve shifts upward to $SRAS(P')$, and the economy moves to long-run equilibrium at point e'.

level higher than expected. When the price level is P, in the short run firms supply Y, a quantity exceeding the economy's potential of Y^*. This price and output combination is represented by point e, the intersection of the aggregate demand curve, AD, with the short-run aggregate supply curve, $SRAS(P^*)$. Note again that levels of output exceeding the economy's potential are shaded in blue, and output levels below the economy's potential are shaded in pink.

The amount by which actual output in the short run exceeds the economy's potential is often referred to as the **expansionary gap**; it is measured in Exhibit 2 as the distance between Y^* and Y. At Y the level of unemployment is below the natural rate. As we will see, output exceeding potential GNP creates inflationary pressure on the economy. Employees are working overtime, machines are being pushed to the limit, and farmers are sandwiching extra crops between usual plantings. The more the actual output exceeds

The amount by which actual output in the short run exceeds the economy's potential is called the **expansionary gap**.

the economy's potential, the larger the expansionary gap and the greater the upward pressure on the price level.

The **long run** is a period during which previous wage settlements and other resource agreements no longer hold and must be renegotiated.

The **long run** is a period during which firms and resource suppliers have the opportunity to renegotiate resource payments based on a knowledge of the actual market conditions. Simply put, in the long run firms and resource suppliers know the actual price level that will result from the aggregate demand curve AD and are able to negotiate settlements based on that price level. As workers and other resource suppliers renegotiate higher resource payments, the short-run aggregate supply curve shifts to the left to reflect the higher cost of resources. In Exhibit 2, the short-run aggregate supply curve eventually shifts back to $SRAS(P')$, which is based on an expected price level of P'. Notice that the short-run aggregate supply curve shifts up along the aggregate demand curve until the economy's potential output is the equilibrium quantity. Thus actual output can exceed the economy's potential in the short run but not in the long run.

As shown in Exhibit 2, the expansionary gap is closed by the shift in the short-run aggregate supply curve from $SRAS(P^*)$ to $SRAS(P')$. Whereas $SRAS(P^*)$ was based on contracts reflecting an expected price level of P^*, $SRAS(P')$ is based on contracts reflecting an expected price level of P'. Because the expected price level and the actual price level are identical at point e', the economy at that point is not only in short-run equilibrium but also in *long-run equilibrium*. Consider all the equalities that hold at point e': (1) the actual price level equals the expected price level; (2) the quantity supplied in the short run equals potential output, which also equals the quantity supplied in the long run; and (3) the quantity supplied equals the quantity demanded. Point e' will continue to be the equilibrium point unless there is some change in aggregate supply or aggregate demand.

Note that in real terms the situation at e' is no different from what had been expected at e^*. At both points, firms are willing and able to supply the economy's potential level of output, Y^*. The same amounts of labor and other resources are employed, and though the price level, the nominal wage rate, and other nominal resource payments are higher at point e', real wages and the real return to other resources are the same as they would have been at point e^*. For example, suppose that the nominal wage rate was $10 per hour when the expected price was P^*. If the expected price level increased by 10 percent, from P^* to P', the nominal wage rate would also increase by 10 percent, to $11 per hour. With no change in the real wage between points e^* and e', firms demand enough labor to produce Y^* and workers supply enough labor to produce Y^*.

If suppliers were continually surprised by higher-than-expected price levels, they would continue trying to expand output in the short run beyond the economy's potential level of output. As the economy adjusted in the long run to the higher-than-expected price levels, the short-run aggregate supply curve would shift up, creating an inflation spiral. Thus, in the short run, a higher-than-expected price level prompts an increase in the quantity of aggregate output supplied; in the long run, these incorrect expectations lead to a shift up in the short-run aggregate supply curve, resulting in a higher price level and a lower level of output.

If a given increase in the price level, or a given amount of inflation, came to be predicted with accuracy year after year, firms and resource suppliers would build these higher expected price levels into their agreements, raising resource prices enough to keep the real return to resources unchanged. Thus, the price level would move up each year by the expected amount, but the economy's output would remain at the potential GNP, thereby skipping the round trip beyond the economy's potential and back.

Actual Price Level Lower Than Expected

Let's begin again with an expected price level of P^* as presented in Exhibit 3, where blue shading indicates output levels exceeding potential and pink shading indicates output levels below potential. If the price level turned out as expected, the resulting equilibrium combination would occur at e^*. Suppose this time that aggregate demand is less than expected so the price level falls below expectations. The intersection of the aggregate demand curve, AD, with $SRAS(P^*)$ establishes the short-run equilibrium point, e. Production at Y is below the economy's potential at Y^*. The amount by which output falls short of potential GNP is called the **contractionary gap**, indicating that the unemployment rate is above the natural rate.

*The amount by which actual output in the short run falls below the economy's potential is called the **contractionary gap**.*

For resource owners working under long-term agreements, the nominal wage remains relatively fixed in the short run at this new short-run equilibrium. Because the price level, P, is lower than the expected level, P^*, this nominal wage translates into a higher real wage. But, in the long run, all labor contracts are subject to renegotiation. Since the price level is lower than expected, employers are no longer willing to offer as high a nominal wage. And with unemployment higher than the natural rate, more workers are competing for jobs. At least in theory, the combination of an increase in the pool of unemployed workers and a decline in the price level should make workers more willing to accept a lower nominal wage.

If firms and workers agree on a lower nominal wage, production costs decline, shifting the short-run aggregate supply curve outward. The short-run supply curve will continue to shift outward until it intersects the aggregate demand curve where the economy produces its potential output. This increase in supply is reflected in Exhibit 3 by a shift to the right in the short-run aggregate supply curve from $SRAS(P^*)$ to $SRAS(P')$. Thus *if the price level and nominal wages are flexible, the short-run aggregate supply curve will move outward until the economy produces its potential output*, Y^*. The new short-run aggregate supply curve is based on an expected price level of P'. Because the expected price level and the actual price level are the same, the economy is now in long-run equilibrium at point e'.

Although the nominal wage is lower at point e' than what was originally agreed upon when the expected price level was P^*, the real wage is the same

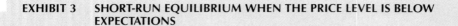

**EXHIBIT 3   SHORT-RUN EQUILIBRIUM WHEN THE PRICE LEVEL IS BELOW
               EXPECTATIONS**

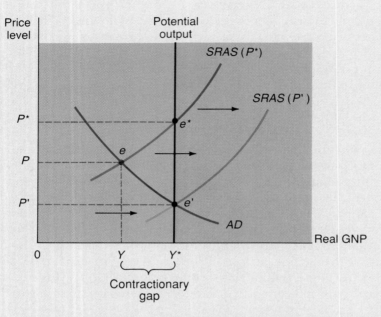

When the price level is below expectations, as indicated by the intersection of the
aggregate demand curve *AD* with the short-run aggregate supply curve *SRAS(P*)*,
short-run equilibrium occurs at point *e*. Production is below the economy's
potential by the amount of the contractionary gap, $Y^* - Y$. In the long run, resource
suppliers will lower their price expectations. As resource costs fall, the short-run
aggregate supply curve shifts out to *SRAS(P')*, and the economy moves to long-run
equilibrium at point *e'*, with output at the potential level, Y^*.

at *e'* as it would have been at *e**. Since the real wage is the same, the amount of
labor that workers supply is the same and real output is the same. Thus, all
that has changed between *e'* and *e** is the price level, the nominal wage, and
other nominal resource payments. In reality, the wage adjustment resulting
from a contractionary gap need not involve a decline in the *nominal* wage. All
that is required is a fall in the *real* wage; the real wage can fall because wage
increases are smaller than, or lag behind, increases in the price level. If prices
increase by 6 percent and the wage increases by only 4 percent, the real wage
falls, increasing the amount of aggregate output supplied. It was classical
economists who first argued that flexible wages and prices promote an
adjustment that can restore the economy to its potential output.

   Thus, when incorrect expectations cause firms and resource suppliers to
overestimate the price level, output in the short run falls below the economy's potential. As long as wages and prices remain flexible, firms and
workers should be able in the long run to adjust their wage agreements as

existing contracts expire; a drop in the nominal wage will shift the short-run aggregate supply curve to the right until the economy once again produces its potential level of output. The necessary fall in real wages may also occur if wage increases lag behind increases in the price level. *If wages and prices do not adjust very quickly to a contractionary gap—that is, if they are, in Keynes's word, "sticky"—then shifts in the short-run aggregate supply curve may be very slow to move the economy to its potential output. The economy can therefore appear stuck at an output and employment level below its potential.*

Tracing Potential Output

If wages and prices are flexible enough, the economy in the long run will produce its potential level of output, as indicated in Exhibit 4 by the vertical line drawn at the economy's potential GNP, Y^*. *The potential level of output depends on the supply of resources in the economy and on the level of technology.* The vertical line drawn at potential GNP is called the economy's *long-run aggregate supply (LRAS) curve.*

Note that as long as wages and prices are flexible, the economy's potential GNP is consistent with any level of prices. *In the long run, the actual price level depends only on the location of the aggregate demand curve.* In Exhibit 4 the initial price level, P^*, is determined by the intersection of AD^* with the

EXHIBIT 4   LONG-RUN AGGREGATE SUPPLY CURVE

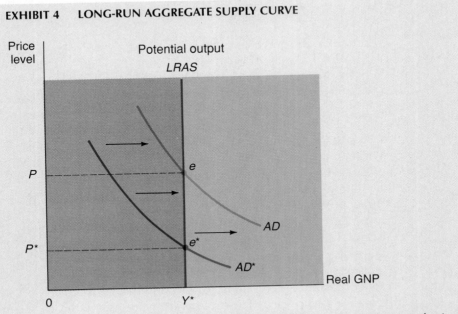

In the long run, when the expected price level equals the actual price level, output will be at the potential level, Y^*. That amount of output will be supplied regardless of the actual price level. The long-run aggregate supply curve, LRAS, is a vertical line at potential GNP.

long-run aggregate supply curve. If the aggregate demand curve shifts out to *AD*, then in the long run the equilibrium price level will increase to *P*, but equilibrium output will remain at the economy's potential GNP. Conversely, a fall in aggregate demand will in the long run lead only to a fall in the price level, with no change in output. We stress that these long-run movements are more like tendencies than smooth adjustments. The time required for resource prices to adjust may be quite long, particularly with a contractionary gap.

Evidence on Aggregate Supply

What evidence is there that when workers and firms have time to adjust to changes in the price level, the long-run aggregate supply curve can be depicted by a vertical line drawn at the economy's potential GNP? Except during the Great Depression, unemployment over the last century varied from year to year but typically returned to what would be viewed as the level that was consistent with potential GNP—about 4 or 5 percent.

As the Great Depression has taught us, however, the adjustment toward potential output can take years. Herein lies the problem: whereas expansion of output beyond the economy's potential creates labor shortages that result in a higher nominal wage and a higher price level, reductions in output below the economy's potential GNP do not appear to generate enough downward pressure to lower the nominal wage. Studies have found that the nominal wage is slow to adjust to high unemployment. Seldom have we observed actual declines in nominal wages, especially since World War II.

When unemployment is extensive, why do employers appear reluctant to cut nominal wages or to replace existing employees with lower-paid workers from the pool of the unemployed? One possible explanation has already been mentioned. Recall that the efficiency wage theory argues that by keeping wages above the level required to attract enough workers, firms make workers compete to keep their jobs. This competition in job performance results in greater productivity. During recessions, firms prefer to lay off workers and reduce the hours of employment for remaining workers rather than cut wages. Wage cuts may save payroll costs, but they can also reduce morale and have negative effects on worker productivity.

Other possible reasons why downward movement of wages might be sticky include workers' psychological resistance to wage cuts, minimum wage laws, long-term wage contracts, union resistance to lower wages, and the fact that recessions since World War II have been shorter and less severe than earlier ones.

Hence, nominal wages do not adjust downward as quickly or as substantially as they do upward. The downward response that does occur tends to be slow and relatively weak. Consequently, we say that nominal wages tend to be sticky in the downward direction. *Since nominal wages fall slowly, if at all, the natural supply-side adjustments needed to return the economy to potential output may take so long as to seem ineffective.* Therefore, unemployment in excess of the natural rate may linger.

There is one final but important point to note. *Even though the nominal wage seldom falls, a contractionary gap can be closed as long as increases in the nominal wage lag behind increases in the price level, thereby decreasing the real wage.* As long as the real wage falls enough, firms will be willing to demand enough additional labor to produce the economy's potential output. Thus, an actual decline in the nominal wage is not necessary to close a contractionary gap.

CHANGES IN AGGREGATE SUPPLY

Supply shocks *are unexpected events that affect aggregate supply, sometimes only temporarily.*

Thus far we have shown that, given the supply of resources in the economy and the state of technology, the short-run aggregate supply curve depends on the expected price level. Also, when the actual price level differs from the price level on which prevailing contracts were based, market forces are set in motion that, in the long run, shift the short-run aggregate supply curve until the economy produces its potential level of output. In this section we will consider factors other than the expected price level that may affect aggregate supply. We distinguish between long-term trends in aggregate supply and **supply shocks**, which are unexpected events that affect aggregate supply, sometimes only temporarily.

Increases in Aggregate Supply

The economy's potential output is based on the willingness and ability of households to supply resources to firms. Any change in the supply of resources or in the way existing resources can be combined to produce goods and services will affect the economy's potential output.[1] For example, labor supply may change because of a change in the size of the labor force or a change in household preferences for labor versus leisure. The U.S. labor force has doubled since 1948 as a result of a growth in population and a rising labor force participation rate, especially among women. Job training, education, and on-the-job experience have increased the quality of labor. Increases in both the quantity and the quality of the labor force have increased the economy's potential GNP, or long-run aggregate supply.

The quantity and quality of other resources also change over time. The capital stock—the amount of machines, buildings, and trucks—increases whenever the economy's gross investment exceeds the depreciation of capital. Even the quantity and quality of land can be increased—for example, by claiming land from the sea, as is done in the Netherlands, or by revitalizing soil that has lost its fertility. These increases in the quantity and quality of resources expand the economy's potential output. *Changes in the labor force and in the supply of other key resources tend to occur gradually over time.*

Exhibit 5 shows the effects of a shift in the economy's potential level of

---

[1] Changes in the economy's potential GNP over time are discussed in greater detail in Chapter 17, which examines U.S. economic growth and productivity.

EXHIBIT 5   EFFECTS OF A GRADUAL CHANGE IN THE SUPPLY OF RESOURCES

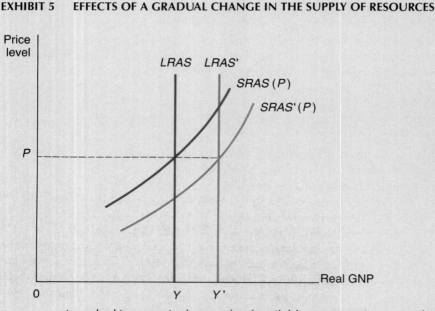

A gradual increase in the supply of available resources increases the potential level of GNP from Y to Y'. Both the long- and short-run aggregate supply curves shift to the right.

output from Y to Y'. Notice that, given contracts based on an expected price level of P, the short-run aggregate supply curve shifts to the right as well, from $SRAS(P)$ to $SRAS'(P)$. Thus, improvements in the economy's ability to produce will shift both the economy's potential output and its short-run aggregate supply curve.

In contrast to the gradual or long-term changes that often occur in the supply of resources, *beneficial supply shocks* are unexpected events that increase aggregate supply. For example, in the mid–1980s, the per-barrel price of oil dropped from over $30 to about $10. Other beneficial shocks include abundant harvests around the world that increase the supply of food, discoveries of natural resources, such as the oil in Alaska and the North Sea, and technological breakthroughs that allow firms to combine resources more efficiently. For example, a new computer chip might monitor resources in a firm, eliminating waste and reducing production time.

Exhibit 6 reflects the effect of a beneficial supply shock on short-run and long-run aggregate supply. Note that, *for a given aggregate demand curve, the happy outcome of a beneficial supply shock is an increase in output and a decrease in the price level.* For example, the 1986 decline in oil prices helped boost output and lower the inflation rate that year to only 1.9 percent, the lowest rate since the early 1960s. A beneficial supply shock might be only temporary. For example, one season's favorable growing conditions do not represent a permanent change in the climate, so the aggregate supply might decrease if

EXHIBIT 6   EFFECTS OF SUPPLY SHOCKS ON AGGREGATE SUPPLY

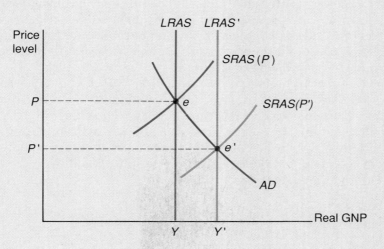

Given the aggregate demand curve, a supply shock shifts both the short-run aggregate supply curve and the long-run aggregate supply curve, or potential output. A beneficial supply shock lowers the price level and increases output, as reflected by the change in equilibrium from point e to point e'. An adverse supply shock can be represented by a move from point e' to point e, where the price level is higher but output is lower.

weather patterns created less favorable growing conditions the following season.

Decreases in Aggregate Supply

Any reduction in the supply of a key resource reduces both potential output and the short-run aggregate supply. We noted earlier that the average work week has become shorter, decreasing from about 54 hours at the turn of the century to about 40 hours today. This decline in the supply of labor has reduced potential output below what it would have been had hours not declined. A change in the composition of the work force in favor of younger, less experienced workers could also reduce aggregate supply. As we said, changes in the supply of labor tend to occur gradually over time. In Exhibit 5, such a drop in supply would be represented by a shift to the left in potential output, from Y' to Y.

Adverse supply shocks are unexpected events that affect aggregate supply, often only temporarily. For example, a national drought could temporarily reduce the supply of a variety of products, including food, building materials, and raw materials such as cotton and flax used in textiles. A lack of rain could also affect water-powered energy sources. A drought clearly reduces the supply of goods and services, and it is reflected by a shift to the left in the short-run aggregate supply curve and a decrease in the level of potential output. Imagine starting at equilibrium point e' in Exhibit 6, where the output level is Y' and the price level is P'. Given the aggregate demand curve, the effect of an adverse supply shock would be represented by a shift up and to the left in the equilibrium point, from point e' to point e, reducing output to Y and increasing the price level to P.

The combination of reduced output and a higher price level is often referred to as stagflation. The United States encountered stagflation during the 1970s, when the economy was rocked by a series of adverse supply shocks, such as crop failures around the globe and the fourfold increase in oil prices achieved by OPEC in 1974. If the condition that reduces aggregate supply is only temporary, as with a drought, aggregate supply should increase when the source of the shock disappears.

CONCLUSION

Perhaps no subject in macroeconomics remains more debatable than that of aggregate supply. No two introductory economics books are likely to discuss the topic the same way. This chapter called attention to the expected price level as a key determinant of the resource prices that shape aggregate supply in the short run. If firms and resource suppliers can, in the long run, fully adjust to unexpected changes in the price level, the economy will produce its potential output.

The appendix to this chapter examines resource markets and potential output. The next chapter will introduce government and show how fiscal policy can be instrumental in moving the economy toward its potential GNP.

Summary

1. Firms and resource suppliers make supply decisions based on the expected price level. The prices of some resources are agreed upon before the actual price level is known. Short-run aggregate supply is based on resource contracts that reflect the expected price level. If the anticipated price level actually occurs, the economy produces its potential level of output. If the actual price level exceeds the expected price level, aggregate output in the short run exceed the economy's potential. If the actual price level is below the expected price level, output in the short run falls short of the economy's potential. Hence the short-run aggregate supply curve slopes upward.

2. Output can exceed the economy's potential in the short run, but in the long run a higher nominal wage will be negotiated at the first opportunity. This higher nominal wage increases the cost of production, shifting the short-run aggregate supply curve back until equilibrium output equals the economy's potential.

3. If output in the short run falls short of the economy's potential, and if wages and prices in the economy are flexible, then a lower nominal wage will be negotiated. This lower nominal wage will reduce production costs, shifting the short-run aggregate supply curve out until equilibrium output equals the economy's potential. Even if the nominal wage does not fall, short-run aggregate supply will increase as long as the nominal wage increases by less than the price level. Thus, as long as real wages fall, a contractionary gap can be closed.

4. Empirical evidence suggests that when output exceeds the economy's potential, wage and price levels will increase and output will fall. But there is less evidence to support a downward movement of wage and price levels when output is below the economy's potential. Wages appear to be somewhat "sticky" in the downward direction. Still, all that is required to correct a contractionary gap is for the nominal wage to grow more slowly than the price level.

5. The long-run aggregate supply curve, or the economy's potential level of output, depends on the amount and quality of resources available in the economy and the state of technology. Increases in resource availability or improvements in technology shift the long-run supply curve to the right. Supply shocks are unexpected and often temporary changes in aggregate supply. Beneficial supply shocks lead to increased output and a lower price level. Adverse supply shocks result in stagflation: reduced output and a higher price level.

Questions and Problems

1. (Short Run) In the short run, prices may go up faster than costs do. The chapter discusses why this might happen. Suppose that labor and management agree to adjust wages for changes in the price level. How would such adjustments affect the slope of the aggregate supply curve?

2. (Real Wages) Suppose that nominal wages in the economy are rising at 10 percent per year and the price level is rising at 8 percent per year. What is happening to the real wage rate under these circumstances? Will workers immediately notice what is happening to their real wages?

3. (Potential Output) What factors might affect the potential level of output of the economy? Would a severe epidemic be likely to alter the level of potential output? Would the effect depend on the length of the epidemic?

4. (Natural Rate of Unemployment) How is it possible for the natural rate of unemployment to remain constant (or even to rise) while the level of potential output rises? Is this happening in the United States today?

5. (Expansionary Gap) Why doesn't a reduction in the supply of resources create an expansionary gap? Is it possible for the price level to rise without creating an expansionary gap?

6. (Contractionary Gaps) After reviewing Exhibit 3 in this chapter, explain why contractionary gaps occur only in the short run and only when the actual price level is below what was expected.

7. (Shifts in Aggregate Supply) How have advances in medicine and pharmaceuticals affected aggregate supply in the United States over the last fifty years? When the population is growing and new jobs must be found, how important is technology for maintaining low unemployment?

8. (Long Run) The long-run aggregate supply curve is vertical at the economy's potential output level. Why would the long-run aggregate supply curve have to be centered at this level of output rather than below or above the potential level?

9. (Long-Run Adjustment) In the long run, why do differences between the actual price level

and the expected price level lead to changes in the level of nominal wages? Why do these changes cause shifts in the short-run aggregate supply curve?

10. (Wages) In Exhibit 2 in this chapter, how does the real wage rate at point e^* compare with the real wage rate at point e'? How do nominal wages compare?

11. (Supply) Describe how each of the following influences the slope of the aggregate supply curve in the short run.

a. The level of the natural rate of unemployment
b. The efficiency wage theory
c. The degree of money illusion among workers

12. (Long-Run Adjustment) The ability of the economy to eliminate any imbalances between actual output and potential output is sometimes called "self-correction." Using an aggregate supply and aggregate demand diagram, show why this self-correction process involves only *temporary* periods of inflation or deflation.

APPENDIX
The Market for Resources

So far we have not discussed in detail the pricing and output decisions of individual firms and resource suppliers. This appendix describes the behavior of resource markets, particularly the labor market. Resource markets play a key role in shaping aggregate supply.

The key actors on the supply side are households and firms. We already know that (1) households supply resources and demand goods and services to maximize utility and (2) firms demand resources and supply goods and services to maximize profit. The willingness and ability of households to supply resources to firms depend on the expected earnings of these resources. The higher the expected earnings, other things constant, the greater the quantity of resources supplied to firms. We initially assume that resource suppliers and demanders, when they formulate their wage agreements, know what price level to expect and are able to adjust their supply and demand based on that expected price level.

Although many resources are required for production, we focus primarily on labor because it is by far the most important cost of production. Moreover, aggregate employment is a key measure of the economy's performance and is thus of special interest to public policy makers.

The Market for Labor

The interaction between the supply of labor by households and the demand for labor by firms determines the equilibrium wage rate and employment level in the economy. The level of employment, in turn, determines the quantity of aggregate output supplied in the economy. Even without a full-scale discussion of the market for labor, we can get some idea of the forces shaping the supply and demand for labor.

Supply of Labor Individuals can use their time in two ways: for labor or for leisure. For simplicity, let's define "leisure" as all noncompensated uses of time, including watching TV, sleeping, and making a sandwich. The wage rate is the reward per unit of time for supplying labor to the market. The higher the wage rate, other things constant, the greater the reward for working—that is, the more goods and services that can be purchased with the earnings from each hour devoted to market work. One of the factors held constant when we compare alternative wage rates is the expected price level. For a given expected price level, any change in the nominal wage—the wage measured in terms of current dollars—also produces a change in the expected real wage—the wage measured in terms of the quantity of goods and services it will purchase. *For a given expected price level, workers believe they can buy more goods and services as the nominal wage increases.*

The higher the nominal wage, given an expected price level, the more goods and services that can be exchanged for an hour of work. Hence, the higher the nominal wage, the higher the opportunity cost of leisure, so the more labor households will supply. *The supply curve for labor by households therefore slopes upward, indicating that the quantity of labor supplied increases as the nominal wage rate increases, other things constant.*

Exhibit 7 presents such an upward-sloping market supply curve for labor, *SL*. The nominal wage rate is measured on the vertical axis, and the quantity of labor on the horizontal axis. This market supply curve for labor is the horizontal sum of all individual workers' supply of labor curves. Because the market supply curve is drawn for a given expected price level *P*, increases in the nominal wage along the supply curve also represent increases in the expected real wage.

Demand for Labor What determines how much of a particular resource a firm will employ? A firm values resources because they

EXHIBIT 7   LABOR SUPPLY

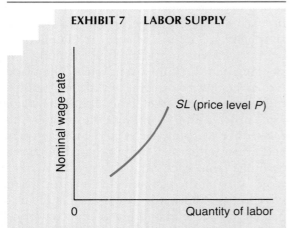

For a given price level *P*, an increase in the nominal wage rate means an increase in the real wage rate. A higher real wage makes individuals more willing to supply labor; thus the labor supply curve, *SL*, slopes upward.

produce goods and services, which can be sold for a profit. A firm will employ additional labor as long as doing so adds more to the firm's revenue than to its cost. A firm will stop hiring more labor when additional units of labor add more to cost than to revenue. So each unit of labor (as well as each unit of other resources) must at least pay for itself. The most a firm is willing to pay for an additional unit of labor is its marginal value: the increase in revenue it produces. The question is, What happens to the marginal value of labor as additional units of labor are employed? Does it go up, go down, or remain the same?

The **law of diminishing returns** says that as additional units of labor are employed while the quantity of other resources is held constant, at some point the quantity of additional output produced begins to decline. This law tells us that the more labor employed, the lower the marginal value added by each additional unit of labor. Remember, the firm will pay no more for additional units of labor than the marginal value of that labor. Since the marginal value of labor declines as

more labor is employed, the amount a firm is willing to pay for each additional unit of labor, which is shown by the firm's demand curve for labor, also declines as more labor is employed.

The demand for labor in the economy is reflected by the downward-sloping market demand curve for labor, *DL*, in Exhibit 8. The market demand curve for labor is the horizontal sum of all firms' demand for labor curves. This downward-sloping demand curve shows that, given the expected price level in the economy *P*, the lower the nominal wage, the greater the quantity of labor firms demand. Because the market demand curve is drawn assuming a given expected price level, decreases in the nominal wage along the demand curve also represent decreases in the expected real wage. The supply and demand curves for labor intersect at the equilibrium point, *n*, to yield the equilibrium wage rate, *W*, and the equilibrium quantity of labor, *N*.

EXHIBIT 8   THE LABOR MARKET

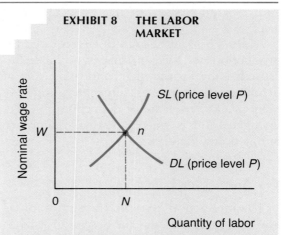

The downward-sloping labor demand curve, *DL*, indicates that firms are willing to hire more labor as the real wage falls. For a given price level *P*, the intersection of the labor supply and demand curves at point *n* determines the nominal wage rate, *W*, and the equilibrium level of employment, *N*.

Changes in the Expected Price Level

What will happen to the wage and employment level if the price level expected to prevail in the economy is higher than *P*? Suppose it is *P'*.

Supply Response With a higher expected price level, workers expect that a given nominal wage will be worth less in real terms because each dollar is expected to purchase less in real goods and services. So under these conditions a higher nominal wage will be required to coax workers to give up the same amount of leisure as they did when the expected price level was lower.

The labor supply curve will therefore shift to the left, from *SL* to *SL'*, as shown in Ex-

EXHIBIT 9   EFFECT OF A HIGHER EXPECTED PRICE LEVEL ON NOMINAL WAGE AND EMPLOYMENT

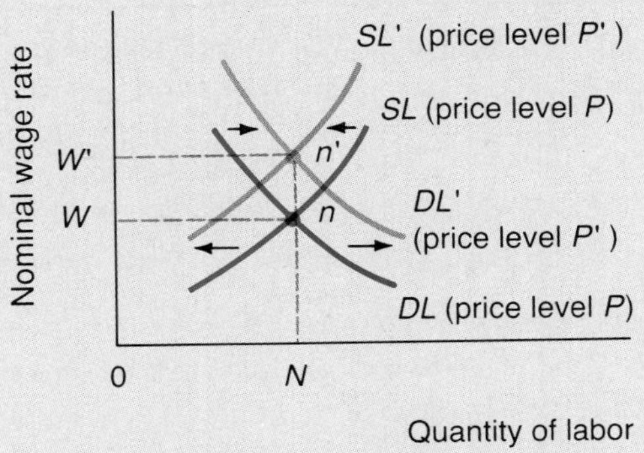

A higher price level reduces the quantity of labor supplied at any given nominal wage rate; the labor supply curve shifts from *SL* to *SL'* as the price level rises from *P* to *P'*. At the same time, the higher price level increases the quantity of labor firms demand at any given nominal wage rate; the labor demand curve shifts from *DL* to *DL'*. These two effects of a given increase in the price level offset each other, so the equilibrium level of employment is unchanged at *N*. The real wage at point *n'* is the same as at point *n*.

hibit 9, indicating that workers have reduced the quantity of labor they supply at each nominal wage, or that they now require a higher nominal wage for each quantity of labor supplied. If the expected price level increases by 10 percent, workers must be paid a nominal wage that is 10 percent higher than before to supply any given quantity of labor. Thus, at any given level of employment, the new supply curve is 10 percent above the initial supply curve.

Demand Response The demand for labor, like the demand for other resources, is based on the value of output produced by each additional unit of that resource. A higher expected price level means that the nominal value of labor's output is expected to be greater because product prices are expected to be higher. Since an increase in the expected price level increases the revenue generated by each additional unit of labor, firms will be willing to pay a higher nominal wage for each additional unit of labor. This increase in labor demand is reflected in Exhibit 9 by a shift of the labor demand curve to the right, from *DL* to *DL'*. This increased demand for labor indicates that firms are willing to hire more workers at each nominal wage, or are willing to pay a higher nominal wage for a given quantity of labor. Specifically, if the expected price level increases by 10 percent, firms' demand for labor increases by 10 percent, indicating that for any given level of employment, firms are willing to pay a nominal wage that is 10 percent higher than before.

New Equilibrium As a result of the higher expected price level, the new supply and demand curves intersect at point *n'*, which corresponds to a higher nominal wage rate, *W'*. Notice that the increased demand for labor just offsets the decreased supply of labor, leaving the equilibrium quantity of labor unchanged at *N*. The nominal wage has increased, but the increase in the expected price level has left the real wage unchanged. As noted earlier, to derive the expected real wage, we can divide the nominal wage by the expected price level. Specifically, the higher wage rate, W', divided by the higher expected price level, P', is equal to the original wage rate, W, divided by the original expected price level, P:

$$\frac{W'}{P'} = \frac{W}{P}$$

Thus, if both expected prices and nominal wages go up by 10 percent, the expected real wage remains unchanged. Because the expected real wage is the same, the equilibrium quantity of labor remains unchanged.

Effects of a Lower Expected Price Level If we traced the effects of a lower expected price level on the market for resources, we would find that the equilibrium nominal wage falls by the same percent as the expected price level. With wages and expected prices falling by the same percentage, the expected real wage remains unchanged, so equilibrium employment also remains unchanged. Let's consider why this would be true. Because of the lower expected price level, firms would offer and workers would accept a lower nominal wage for the same amount of labor as they provided when the expected price level was higher. Although the nominal wage would be lower, the real wage would remain unchanged; hence, the quantity of labor employed would also remain unchanged. After all, firms and workers are interested in the real wage, not the nominal wage. Suppose the expected price level was 10 percent lower than the price level P. After workers and firms fully adjusted to the lower price level, the equilibrium wage rate would fall by 10 percent, so the real wage rate and the level of employment would be the same as they were when the price level was P.

Potential GNP

For a given expected price level, there is a

supply and demand for each type of resource in the economy. The intersection of supply and demand yields for each resource an equilibrium resource price and quantity employed. Imagine all these resource markets as operating simultaneously. How do all these inputs relate to aggregate output? The amount of output a given amount of resources can produce depends on the state of technology that exists in the economy. The more advanced the technology, the more output that can be produced from given amounts of resources. The quantities of the various resources employed, combined with the state of technology prevailing in the economy, determine the level of aggregate output for the given expected price level. Point e in Exhibit 10 indicates that when the expected price level is P, the level of real GNP in the economy is Y^*, as measured along the horizontal axis.

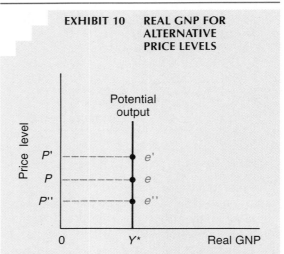

EXHIBIT 10   REAL GNP FOR ALTERNATIVE PRICE LEVELS

In the long run, changes in the price level will be matched by changes in the nominal wage rate. With the real wage unchanged, the level of employment is unchanged. With employment unchanged, potential output does not vary. So regardless of the price level, the long-run quantity of output supplied is Y^*.

As we have seen, if the expected price level is higher or lower than P and if firms and resource suppliers can adjust their supply and demand for resources to reflect the difference, then the same quantities of resources are employed. If the quantities of resources employed remain unchanged, aggregate output also remains unchanged at Y^*. Point e' in Exhibit 10 shows that when the expected price level is P', output is Y^*. Point e'' shows that when the expected price level is lower, say P'', the economy's output is still Y^*.

The vertical line at the level of output Y^* in Exhibit 10 traces the relation between alternative expected price levels and the quantity of output produced. Y^* is the economy's potential GNP, the amount produced when all resource owners and firms have *fully adjusted* to the actual price level in the economy; in other words, the quantity supplied equals the quantity demanded in each resource market, and the expected price level equals the actual price level. For example, the amount of labor that workers are willing and able to supply at the prevailing wage just equals the amount of labor firms are willing and able to demand. Notice that potential GNP is the same regardless of the price level: the amount of output produced in the economy is independent of the expected price level. *Potential output is determined by real factors: the quantity and quality of resources available and the level of technology.*

Appendix Questions

1. (Labor Supply Curve) In Exhibit 7, the supply of labor slopes upward against the nominal wage level. Yet some economists believe that at a high enough nominal wage rate, the supply curve might bend backward. Can you suggest a reason why this might be true?

2. (Equilibrium Level of Employment) Use labor supply and labor demand curves to show the impact on the equilibrium level of employment (and therefore on potential output) of each of the following:
   a. An increase in the price level
   b. A technological improvement
   c. A reduction in the size of the labor force

PART THREE

Fiscal and Monetary Policy

Fiscal Policy, Aggregate Demand, and Equilibrium Output

So far we have examined aggregate demand only in the private sector, focusing primarily on consumption and investment. In this chapter we add government to the picture. In particular, we explore the effects of government purchases, transfer payments, and taxes on the equilibrium quantity of GNP demanded. We then include net exports, which until now have been relegated to appendixes. Next we bring in aggregate supply and consider the impact of government and net exports on the equilibrium level of income and employment in the economy. We examine the role of fiscal policy in moving the economy to its potential level of output. Finally, we examine fiscal policy as it has been practiced since World War II. Throughout the chapter we will use intuition and graphs. Algebraic formulations, particularly the relevant multipliers, are derived in the appendix to the chapter. Topics discussed in this chapter include

- Government purchases of goods and services

- Lump-sum taxes and proportional income taxes

- Transfer payments

- Marginal propensity to import

- Discretionary fiscal policy

- Automatic stabilizers

- Limits of fiscal policy

THEORY OF FISCAL POLICY

Fiscal policy is the deliberate control of government spending, transfer payments, and taxes in order to influence macroeconomic variables such as employment, price level, and level of GNP. Using the aggregate expenditure framework, we will initially focus on the demand side to consider the effect of changes in government purchases, taxes, and transfer payments on the equilibrium level of real GNP demanded.

The Effect of Government Purchases

We begin with the activity that directly and immediately affects aggregate demand: government purchases of goods and services, denoted as G. We assume that government purchases are under the control of policy makers and, consequently, do not depend directly on the level of income in the economy. Thus, for simplicity, we assume government purchases are *autonomous*, or independent of the level of income. We also ignore taxes at the outset.

At any given price level, the equilibrium quantity of real GNP demanded is achieved when planned spending equals output — that is, once we introduce government, where the sum of consumption, C, investment, I, and government purchases, G, equals GNP. In terms of the symbols introduced earlier, we can summarize this statement as follows:

$$\mathbf{GNP} = \boldsymbol{C + I + G}$$

Exhibit 1 shows how the economy converges to the equilibrium level of real GNP demanded, given the price level. Suppose planned investment equals $300 billion and government purchases equal $500 billion per year, regardless of the level of income. The first column lists the levels of output and income in the economy. The income level determines how much households consume, which is listed in column (2), and how much they save, listed in column (3). Each number in column (1) is the sum of the numbers in columns (2) and (3).

Note that each time income increases by $200 billion, consumption increases by $150 billion and saving increases by $50 billion, so the marginal propensity to consume is 0.75. Columns (4) and (5) list planned investment and government purchases. Column (6) lists the aggregate expenditure, which is simply the sum of columns (2), (4), and (5). Recall that equilibrium is achieved when the amount people spend equals the amount produced. As you can see, equilibrium occurs where spending and output equal $4800 billion.

The same situation can be depicted graphically by vertically summing consumption, investment, and government purchases. To the consumption function in Exhibit 2, we add autonomous investment of $300 billion and government purchases of $500 billion to get an aggregate expenditure function of $C + I + G$. The 45-degree reference line provides a ready way of identifying where the amount people want to spend equals the amount firms produce. Again, when output equals $4800 billion, the planned spending of households, firms, and governments just equals output.

The private sector equilibrium of $Y = C + I$, derived in Chapter 9, was

EXHIBIT 1
SCHEDULES FOR REAL GNP, CONSUMPTION,
SAVING, INVESTMENT, GOVERNMENT PURCHASES,
AND AGGREGATE EXPENDITURE
(billions of dollars)

Real GNP Income = Output (1)	Consumption (C) (2)	Saving (S) (3)	Planned Investment (I) (4)	Government Purchases (G) (5)	Aggregate Expenditure (C + I + G) (6)
2800	2500	300	300	500	3300
3000	2650	350	300	500	3450
3200	2800	400	300	500	3600
3400	2950	450	300	500	3750
3600	3100	500	300	500	3900
3800	3250	550	300	500	4050
4000	3400	600	300	500	4200
4200	3550	650	300	500	4350
4400	3700	700	300	500	4500
4600	3850	750	300	500	4650
4800	**4000**	**800**	**300**	**500**	**4800**
5000	4150	850	300	500	4950
5200	4300	900	300	500	5100

$2800 billion. Adding autonomous government purchases to total spending, other things constant, shifts the aggregate expenditure function up by $500 billion, from $C + I$ to $C + I + G$. The process of earning income and spending it multiplies through the economy until the $500 billion has increased the quantity demanded at the given price level from $2800 billion to $4800 billion.

Since equilibrium output increases by $2000 billion as a result of the introduction of $500 billion in government purchases, the government-purchases multiplier in our example is equal to $2000/$500, or 4. *The multiplier for any change in autonomous government purchases, other things constant, equals 1/(1 − MPC), or 1/(1 − 0.75) in our example.* Thus, we can say that for a given price level,

$$\textbf{Change in } Y = \textbf{change in } G \times \frac{1}{1 - \textbf{MPC}}$$

For example, if government purchases increased by $50 billion, other things constant, the equilibrium quantity of aggregate output demanded in our example would increase by $50 billion × 4, or $200 billion. This same multiplier was discussed in Chapter 9, where we focused on changes in autonomous consumption and autonomous investment.

Since we have not yet introduced taxes, how can government purchases

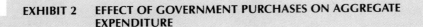

EXHIBIT 2   EFFECT OF GOVERNMENT PURCHASES ON AGGREGATE EXPENDITURE

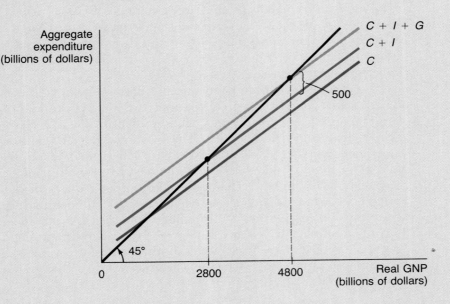

The introduction of government spending increases aggregate expenditure by $500 billion at each level of income. This effect is shown by the shift in the aggregate expenditure line from $C + I$ to $C + I + G$. As a result of this extra spending, the level of real GNP demanded increases from $2800 billion to $4800 billion.

be financed? By government borrowing. As you can see from column (3) in Exhibit 1, when income is $4800 billion, saving equals $800 billion. Saving, the leakage from the circular flow, just equals planned investment plus government purchases, the injections into the circular flow. *In equilibrium, not only does planned spending equal output, but also leakages equal planned injections.*

Taxes and Equilibrium Income

Until now we have ignored taxes; we have assumed that government purchases are financed by borrowing. In reality, of course, taxes play a major role in financing government expenditures. The introduction of taxes, other things constant, reduces disposable income, so households spend less. The simplest kind of tax to consider is a **lump–sum tax**, in which the same amount of revenue is collected regardless of the level of income. Suppose a lump–sum tax of $400 billion is introduced, reducing disposable income by that amount. Households consequently spend less and save less at each level of real GNP. Consumption falls by the amount of the tax times the marginal propensity to consume. In our example, consumption at each level of income falls by $400 billion×0.75, or $300 billion.

With a **lump-sum tax**, a fixed amount of tax revenue is collected regardless of the level of income.

This reduction in consumption is reflected in Exhibit 3 by a downward shift from C, the pre-tax consumption function, to C', the after-tax consumption function. Since a lump-sum tax is the same at all levels of real GNP, consumption falls by the same amount at all levels of income, so the two lines are parallel. The vertical distance between the two in Exhibit 3 is $300 billion. The consumption function does not drop by the full $400 billion because $100 billion of the tax comes out of income that would otherwise have been saved.

The overall effect of introducing this lump-sum tax is shown in Exhibit 4. The initial equilibrium occurs at point e, the level of real GNP where the pre-tax aggregate expenditure function, identified as $C + I + G$, intersects the 45-degree line. At that initial level of output, the $400 billion tax causes aggregate spending to fall by $300 billion. This drop in spending means that output of $4800 billion now exceeds desired spending, so firms reduce output by $300 billion. That decline in output reduces income by $300 billion. Since output and income decline by $300 billion, households reduce consumption by another $225 billion, which equals the decline in their income multiplied by the marginal propensity to consume. This additional decline in consumption results in another drop in income, which causes consumption to decline yet again. The downward spiral continues until the spending multiplier runs out of steam. As a result of the tax, the equilibrium

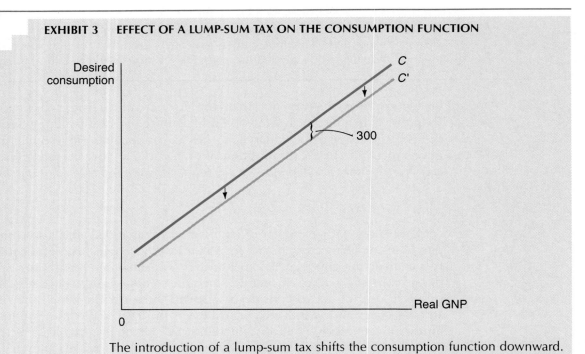

EXHIBIT 3   EFFECT OF A LUMP-SUM TAX ON THE CONSUMPTION FUNCTION

The introduction of a lump-sum tax shifts the consumption function downward. The tax reduces disposable income, so consumption falls by the change in disposable income times the marginal propensity to consume.

EXHIBIT 4   EFFECT OF A LUMP-SUM TAX ON AGGREGATE EXPENDITURE

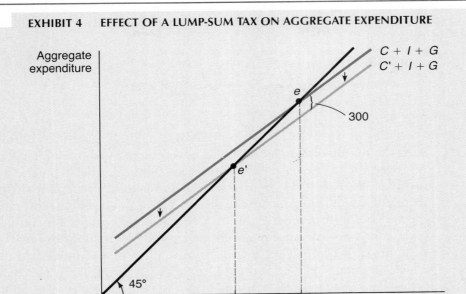

As a result of the introduction of a lump-sum tax, the consumption function shifts downward, as does the aggregate expenditure function. A $300 billion decline in aggregate expenditure reduces the level of GNP demanded by $1200 billion.

level of real GNP demanded declines by $1200 billion, from $4800 billion to $3600 billion per year.

For any given increase in lump-sum taxes, autonomous consumption goes down by the amount of the tax times the marginal propensity to consume. When we introduced lump-sum taxes of $400 billion, we saw autonomous consumption decline by $300 billion, or $400 billion × 0.75. *The change in the equilibrium quantity of aggregate output demanded equals the change in autonomous consumption times the autonomous spending multiplier, which still equals 1/(1 − MPC).* Thus, we can say that for a given price level,

$$\text{Change in } Y = (-\,\text{MPC} \times \text{change in } T) \times \frac{1}{1 - \text{MPC}}$$

This equation can be rewritten as

$$\text{Change in } Y = \text{change in } T \times \frac{-\,\text{MPC}}{1 - \text{MPC}}$$

The second equation shows that the multiplier for a change in lump-sum taxes equals − MPC/(1 − MPC). For example, with an MPC of 0.75, the multiplier equals − 3; an increase in lump-sum taxes of $50 billion would reduce the equilibrium quantity of aggregate output demanded by $150 billion:

$$\textbf{Change in } Y = 50 \times \frac{-0.75}{0.25} = 50 \times -3 = -150$$

It may prove useful at this point to compare the lump-sum tax multiplier with the multiplier for autonomous government purchases. First, changes in government purchases and taxes have opposite effects on the level of income. Whereas a rise in government purchases, other things constant, increases equilibrium income, a rise in taxes, other things constant, decreases equilibrium income. Second, the absolute value of the multiplier is greater for a given change in government purchases than for an equal change in lump-sum taxes. This is true because government purchases directly affect aggregate spending; each $1 increase in government purchases increases spending in the first round by $1. In contrast, taxes work indirectly on consumption and thus on aggregate spending through their effect on disposable income. So a $1 reduction in taxes increases disposable income by $1, which, with an MPC of 0.75, increases consumption in the first round by $0.75.

Transfer Payments

The effect of a change in transfer payments on equilibrium real GNP demanded is equal to but opposite that of a change in lump-sum taxes. Suppose, for example, that transfers increase by $100 billion at all levels of income. With a marginal propensity to consume of 0.75, autonomous consumption will increase by $75 billion, so equilibrium income will increase by $300 billion (75 × 1/0.25). Thus, the multiplier resulting from a change in transfers equals MPC/(1 − MPC). Since the multiplier for changes in transfers is equal to the multiplier for lump-sum taxes but of opposite sign, if taxes and transfers increase by the same amount, equilibrium real GNP demanded remains unchanged.

Taxes and Government Purchases Combined

We are now in a position to consider the combined effects of changes in government purchases and in taxes. The effect of a change in G on Y equals the change in G times 1/(1 − MPC). The effect of a change in T on Y equals the change in T times − MPC/(1 − MPC). The overall effect of changing government purchases and taxes can be determined by combining their individual effects:

$$\text{Change in } Y = \left(\text{change in } G \times \frac{1}{1-\text{MPC}}\right) + \left(\text{change in } T \times \frac{-\text{MPC}}{1-\text{MPC}}\right)$$

For example, suppose government purchases increase by $150 billion and lump-sum taxes increase by $100 billion:

$$\text{Change in } Y = \left(150 \times \frac{1}{0.25}\right) + \left(100 \times \frac{-0.75}{0.25}\right)$$

$$= 600 - 300 = 300$$

The net effect is an increase of $300 billion in the equilibrium quantity of aggregate output demanded at a given price level. As another example, suppose government purchases and lump-sum taxes each increase by $100 billion:

$$\text{Change in } Y = \left(100 \times \frac{1}{0.25}\right) + \left(100 \times \frac{-0.75}{0.25}\right)$$

$$= 400 - 300 = 100$$

The **balanced budget multiplier**, which is equal to 1, shows the effect on GNP of changes of equal size in government purchases and lump-sum taxes.

It is no coincidence that if government purchases and taxes change by the same amount, equilibrium real GNP demanded also changes by that amount. Recall that throughout these examples the multiplier for autonomous government purchases has been 4, but the lump-sum tax multiplier has been − 3. Adding these two multipliers together yields a net multiplier of 1—what is called the balanced budget multiplier. The **balanced budget multiplier** indicates that if lump-sum taxes and government purchases change by the same amount, other things constant, the equilibrium quantity of aggregate output demanded also changes by that amount.

Proportional Income Tax

With a **proportional income tax**, the percentage of income collected is the same at all levels of income.

Our analysis can be made more realistic by considering an income tax rather than a lump-sum tax. With a **proportional income tax**, a constant percentage of income is collected regardless of the income level. For example, suppose a tax rate of 20 percent is imposed on income, meaning that taxes amount to 20 percent of income, regardless of the level of income. Without taxes, real GNP equaled disposable income. After this proportional tax is introduced, disposable income is 20 percent less than real GNP. Since disposable income falls, both consumption and saving fall as well. Specifically, *at each level of real GNP, consumption falls by tax revenues times the marginal propensity to consume*.

To show the effect of this tax on equilibrium GNP demanded, we again begin where equilibrium equals $4800 billion per year before any tax is imposed. The aggregate expenditure function before the tax is shown by $C + I + G$ in Exhibit 5. After the proportional income tax is imposed, the

**EXHIBIT 5   EFFECT OF A PROPORTIONAL INCOME TAX ON AGGREGATE
EXPENDITURE**

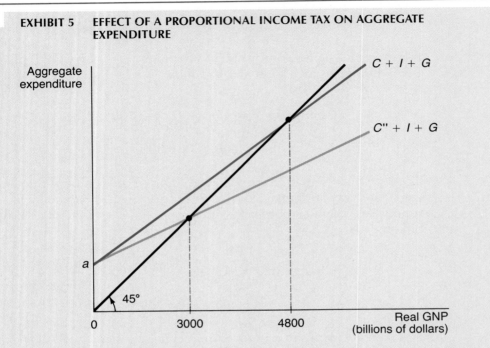

Imposition of a proportional income tax causes both the consumption function and
the aggregate expenditure function to rotate downward. As a result of the tax,
equilibrium income falls from $4800 billion to $3000 billion.

aggregate expenditure function moves down to $C'' + I + G$. When income is
0 the income tax is 0, so the two spending functions intersect at the vertical
axis. As income increases tax revenues grow, so the vertical distance between
the two spending functions increases. The vertical distance between the two
functions equals the fall in consumption caused by the tax; at each level of
real GNP, this fall in consumption equals the taxes collected multiplied by
the marginal propensity to consume.

As you can see, the imposition of a 20 percent income tax causes
equilibrium income to fall from $4800 billion to $3000 billion, a decline of
$1800 billion. Incidentally, at the new equilibrium, income taxes collected
equal the tax rate of 20 percent times $3000 billion, which yields $600
billion. Since government purchases equal $500 billion per year, govern-
ment is operating with a budget surplus of $100 billion per year.

If a lower tax rate were chosen, taxes would be reduced at every level of
real GNP. Picture the spending function rotating up (with point *a* as a pivot)
as the tax rate falls, resulting in a higher equilibrium level of real GNP. If a
higher tax rate were selected, the spending function would rotate down and
equilibrium GNP would fall. *Other things constant, the higher the proportional
tax rate, the less households have to spend and the lower the equilibrium quantity of real
GNP demanded.*

The Income Tax Multiplier

Now consider a proportional income tax rate equal to t, where t is some fraction between 0 and 1. Tax receipts equal the tax rate, t, multiplied by real GNP. What is the effect of an income tax on the expenditure multiplier? An income tax reduces the autonomous spending multiplier because less of each dollar of income is available for spending during each round. Let's focus on what happens during the first round of spending. In the absence of an income tax, a $1 increase in income translates into $1 \times$ MPC in new spending the first round. With an MPC equal to 0.75, a $1 increase in income causes households to spend $0.75 in the first round. Spending each round is 0.75 times the spending during the previous round.

With an income tax, however, the government gets the first bite from each dollar, leaving households with only $1 \times (1 - t)$ in after-tax, or disposable, income. For example, when the tax rate equals 20 percent, disposable income equals $1 \times (1 - 0.2)$, or $0.80. The change in consumption resulting from a $1 increase in before-tax income equals the change in disposable income, $1 \times (1 - t)$, times the MPC. In our example this is 0.80×0.75, which equals $0.60. Thus, with no income tax, consumers spend $0.75 of each dollar increase in GNP, but with an income tax of 20 percent, consumers spend only $0.60 of each dollar increase in GNP. *An income tax, by reducing spending during each round, drains power from the spending multiplier.*

We showed in Chapter 9 that when each successive round of spending was equal to the MPC times spending in the previous round, the sum of all this spending was equal to $1/(1 - \text{MPC})$. Similarly, with a proportional income tax, each round of spending equals the spending in the previous round times MPC$(1 - t)$. The sum of spending from all rounds is

$$\textbf{Spending multiplier with income tax} = \frac{1}{1 - \textbf{MPC}(1 - t)}$$

In our example the MPC equals 0.75, and the tax rate equals 20 percent. If we substitute these values into the multiplier formula, we get

$$\frac{1}{1 - (0.75 \times 0.80)} = \frac{1}{1 - 0.6} = \frac{1}{0.4} = 2.5$$

Thus a 20 percent income tax reduces the autonomous spending multiplier in our example from 4 to 2.5. *The higher the income tax rate, other things constant, the smaller the multiplier.* Incidentally, if income taxes and government purchases were both increased by the same amount, the balanced budget multiplier would equal one, just as with the lump-sum tax.

To summarize, the overall impact of government on aggregate demand will depend on the combined effect of taxes, government purchases, and transfers. Generally, *an increase in government purchases and transfers or a reduction in taxes, other things constant, will increase the equilibrium quantity of aggregate output demanded.* If government purchases plus transfers exceed taxes, there will be a budget deficit; deficits are discussed in greater detail in Chapter 16.

The Inclusion of Net Exports

Thus far discussion of the foreign sector has been limited to the appendixes of Chapters 8 and 9. The impact of the foreign sector on equilibrium income depends on exports minus imports, or net exports. If net exports are positive, then foreigners spend more on domestic goods and services than domestic residents spend on foreign goods and services. Positive net exports represent an injection of spending into the circular flow of income. This injection is subject to the multiplier and thus has a magnified effect on the equilibrium quantity of aggregate output demanded. When domestic residents spend more on foreign products than foreigners spend on domestic products, net exports are negative. *Negative net exports represent a leakage of spending from the circular flow, reducing equilibrium output by some multiple of negative net exports.*

The **marginal propensity to import** equals the fraction of an additional dollar of disposable income that is spent on imports.

Exports tend to be independent of the level of real income in the exporting country. Thus we will assume that exports are constant. But a country's imports increase with an increase in its level of real GNP; that is, the **marginal propensity to import** is positive. *Since exports are constant but imports increase with real income, net exports—exports minus imports—decrease as real income increases.* At low levels of real income, exports exceed imports so net exports are positive. At some higher level of real income, imports increase enough to equal exports so net exports equal zero. And at still higher levels of income, imports exceed exports so net exports are negative. Thus, the higher the real income in the domestic economy, other things constant, the more likely net exports are to be negative.

The effect of adding net exports to the aggregate expenditure function is shown in Exhibit 6, where $C + I + G$ is the aggregate expenditure function without net exports and $C + I + G + (X - M)$ is the expenditure function with net exports. The addition of net exports causes the aggregate expenditure function to rotate clockwise, pivoting on point *a*, which identifies the level of output where net exports are zero. To the left of point *a*, net exports are positive, so the effect of including the foreign sector is to increase desired spending. To the right of point *a*, net exports are negative, so the effect of including the foreign sector is to reduce desired spending.

Thus, *the addition of net exports causes the aggregate expenditure function to flatten out, because net exports decrease as real income increases.* The fraction of each additional dollar of income that is spent on imports is specified by the marginal propensity to import. Dollars spent on imports go to foreigners, not to domestic residents. With less of each dollar of income spent on domestic goods, the force of the multiplier is diminished. In our hypothetical example, the equilibrium level of real income declines from $3600 billion to $3257 billion. (The appendix to this chapter gives a detailed derivation of the equilibrium with net exports.) From now on, when we discuss aggregate demand, we will include net exports.

EXHIBIT 6   THE ADDITION OF NET EXPORTS TO THE AGGREGATE EXPENDITURE FUNCTION

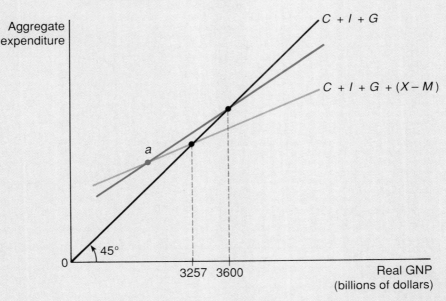

Because net exports fall as real income increases, the addition of net exports to the aggregate expenditure line causes that line to rotate about point a. To the left of point a, net exports are positive, so the inclusion of net exports causes aggregate spending to increase. To the right of point a, net exports are negative, so their inclusion causes aggregate spending to fall. At point a, net exports are zero, so their inclusion has no effect on aggregate spending.

Thus far in this chapter we have ignored the supply side, focusing on the quantity of aggregate output demanded at the given price level. We are now in a position to consider the effects of aggregate supply.

COMBINING AGGREGATE DEMAND WITH AGGREGATE SUPPLY

In the previous chapter we introduced the possibility that natural market forces may take a long time to close a contractionary gap. Let's consider the effect of fiscal policy in such a situation.

Fiscal Policy with a Contractionary Gap

With long-term labor contracts reflecting the expected price level, P^*, firms plan to produce the economy's potential level of output, Y^*, as shown in Exhibit 7. Suppose aggregate demand, which now includes both the

EXHIBIT 7   FISCAL POLICY AND A CONTRACTIONARY GAP

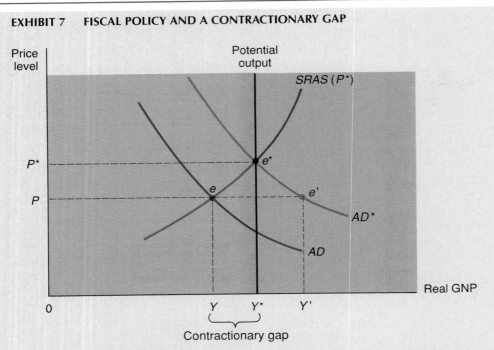

The aggregate demand curve, *AD*, and the short-run aggregate supply curve, *SRAS* (*P**), intersect at point e. Because the price level, *P*, is below the expected price level, *P**, the level of output falls short of the economy's potential. The distance *Y** − *Y* shows the resulting contractionary gap. This gap can be closed by an expansionary fiscal policy. An increase in government spending, a decrease in taxes, or some combination of the two could shift aggregate demand to *AD**, moving the economy to its potential level of output at e*.

government sector and net exports, is not sufficient to clear the market at the expected price level. The short-run aggregate supply curve, $SRAS(P^*)$, and the aggregate demand curve, AD, intersect at point e to yield the short-run equilibrium output, Y, and price level, P. Since the price level turns out to be lower than expected, output falls short of the economy's potential. There is a contractionary gap equal to the difference between Y^* and Y, as Exhibit 7 shows.

If markets adjusted to the resulting increase in unemployed resources, the money price of all resources would in the long run drop enough that the short-run aggregate supply curve would shift out and return the economy to its potential output. However, history suggests that wages and other resource prices may be slow to adjust to a contractionary gap. Suppose policy makers believe that the return to potential output will take too long. Just the right fiscal policy can be used to stimulate aggregate demand enough to return the economy to its potential level of output.

When the economy is at a level of output that is below its potential, what is the effect of an expansionary fiscal policy, such as increasing government purchases, increasing transfer payments, decreasing taxes, or some combination of the above? Suppose an increase in government purchases provides the fiscal stimulus that shifts the aggregate demand curve to the right, as shown in Exhibit 7 by the shift from AD to AD^*. If the price level remained at P, this injection of additional spending would increase the equilibrium quantity demanded from Y to Y'. This increase reflects the multiplier effect, given a constant price level.

Because the aggregate supply curve slopes upward, however, the price level must rise to call forth more quantity supplied, so there is an excess quantity demanded at price level P. This excess quantity demanded causes the price level to rise, in the process increasing the quantity supplied and decreasing the quantity demanded. Let's review why the quantity demanded decreases as the price level increases. As the price level increases, other things constant, the value of fixed-dollar assets declines, so households feel poorer and consequently spend less. A higher domestic price level, other things constant, also makes domestic products more expensive to foreigners and foreign products relatively cheaper to domestic residents. Thus, as the price level rises, exports decrease and imports increase, thereby reducing net exports. This decline in consumption and in net exports reduces the quantity demanded along the new aggregate demand curve AD^*. The price level will rise and the quantity demanded will fall until the quantity demanded equals the quantity supplied. In Exhibit 7, the aggregate supply curve intersects the new aggregate demand curve at e^*, where the price level is the one originally expected and output equals potential GNP, Y^*.

Since P^* was the price level on which producers originally based their production plans, the intersection at point e^* is not only a short-run equilibrium but also a long-run equilibrium. If fiscal policy makers have been accurate enough (or lucky enough), they have provided just enough fiscal stimulus to close the contractionary gap and foster a long-run equilibrium at potential GNP. Note, however, that the increase in output is accompanied by a rise in the price level.

Suppose policy makers overshoot the mark, and aggregate demand turns out to be greater than needed to achieve potential GNP. As we have shown, the economy will in the short run produce beyond its potential level of output. In the long run, however, we expect that firms and resource owners will adjust to the unexpectedly high price level. The short-run supply curve will shift back until it intersects the aggregate demand curve at potential output, increasing the price level but reducing the level of output.

Fiscal Policy with an Expansionary Gap

Suppose the short-run equilibrium price level exceeds the level on which long-term contracts are based, so output exceeds potential GNP. In Exhibit 8, the short-run aggregate supply curve is again based on an expected price level of P^*, but the aggregate demand curve, AD'', is such that the actual price level, P'', exceeds the expected price level. So the short-run level of

EXHIBIT 8   FISCAL POLICY AND AN EXPANSIONARY GAP

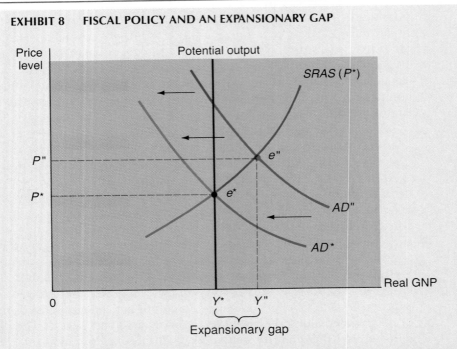

With the price level, P'', above the expected level at point e'', there is an expansionary gap equal to $Y'' - Y^*$. The gap can be eliminated by a contractionary fiscal
policy. An increase in taxes, a decrease in government purchases, or some combination of the two will shift the aggregate demand curve back to AD^* and return
the economy to potential output at point e^*.

equilibrium output is initially at Y''', an amount exceeding the economy's
potential output, Y^*. The economy therefore faces an expansionary gap
measured as the difference between Y''' and Y^*. Ordinarily, this gap would be
closed by an upward shift in the short-run aggregate supply curve, which
would return the economy to the potential level of output but in the process
increase the price level.

The use of fiscal policy, however, opens the door to another possibility.
By increasing taxes, reducing government purchases and transfers, or using
some combination of these approaches, government can use fiscal policy to
reduce aggregate demand, thereby returning the economy to its potential
level of output while avoiding an increase in the price level. If the fiscal
policies are successful, the aggregate demand curve in Exhibit 8 will shift to
the left along the short-run aggregate supply curve, from AD'' to AD^*, and
equilibrium will move from point e'' to point e^*. Again, with just the right
reduction in aggregate demand, the price level will fall to P^*, the level
originally expected, and output will fall to Y^*, the potential GNP. Closing
the expansionary gap in this way results in a lower price level, not a higher
price level. Such a precisely calculated fiscal policy is hard to accomplish,

however, for it assumes that the relevant spending multipliers can be predicted with accuracy, that aggregate demand can be shifted by just the right amount, and that the short-run aggregate supply curve will remain unchanged.

The Multiplier and the Time Horizon

We can now consider the relationship between the multiplier and the time horizon of the aggregate supply curve, generalizing the discussion to include both increases and decreases in aggregate demand. In the short run, the aggregate supply curve slopes upward, so a shift in aggregate demand changes both the price level and the level of output. Because the change in the price level dampens the effect of any shift in aggregate demand on output, the short-run multiplier is smaller than the multiplier assuming a constant price level. The exact value of the short-run multiplier depends on the steepness of the aggregate supply curve. *The steeper the short-run aggregate supply curve, the smaller the value of the multiplier—that is, the less impact a given shift in the aggregate demand curve will have on equilibrium output.*

If the economy is already producing its potential output, in the long run any change in fiscal policy aimed at stimulating demand will increase the price level but will not affect the output level. Therefore, *if the economy is already at the potential level of output, the spending multiplier in the long run is zero.* We now have some idea of how fiscal policy can work in theory. Let's look at how fiscal policy has been applied over the years.

FISCAL POLICY IN PRACTICE

It is said that geologists learn much more about the nature of the earth's crust from one major upheaval, such as an earthquake or a volcanic eruption, than from a dozen more common events. Likewise, economists learned more about the economy from the Great Depression than from many more modest economic fluctuations. Even though it occurred a half a century ago, economists continue to sift and refine the data from that economic calamity, looking for hints about how the economy works.

The Great Depression and World War II

Until the 1930s fiscal policy was not used as a tool to influence the performance of the macroeconomy. Since the classical approach assumed that the economy would tend toward its potential GNP, there appeared to be no need for government intervention in the economy. At the time economists believed that any attempted cure could do more harm than the disease.

Three developments in the years following the Great Depression helped change the role of fiscal policy in the United States. The first was the influence of Keynes's *General Theory*, which argued that the economy would not naturally tend toward potential output. Keynes thought the economy could become stuck at a level of output that was well below its potential, in which case it would be necessary to increase aggregate demand so as to stimulate output and employment. The second development was the persuasive evidence offered by World War II of the positive effects of increased aggregate demand on output and employment. The demands of war greatly increased expenditures and in the process virtually eliminated unemployment, pulling the U.S. economy out of the depression. The third development was the passage of the Employment Act of 1946, which gave the federal government the responsibility for full employment and price stability.

Prior to the Great Depression, the most important fiscal policy was matching revenues and expenditures to balance the budget. Indeed, to offset a modest federal deficit in 1932, a tax increase was approved, an increase that deepened the depression. In the wake of Keynes and World War II, however, economists and policy makers grew more receptive to the view that the fiscal policy could be used to influence aggregate demand and thereby improve economic stability. The objective of fiscal policy was no longer to balance the budget but to promote full employment with price stability.

Automatic Stabilizers

Automatic stabilizers are structural features of the economy that smooth fluctuations in disposable income over the business cycle.

Discretionary fiscal policy is the deliberate manipulation of government spending or taxation in order to promote full employment and price stability.

The tools of fiscal policy can be divided into two major categories: automatic stabilizers and discretionary fiscal policy. **Automatic stabilizers**, such as the federal income tax and the unemployment compensation program, are stabilization policies that, once adopted, require no congressional action to operate year after year. **Discretionary fiscal policy** requires ongoing decisions about government spending and taxation to promote full employment and price stability. So far this chapter has focused on discretionary fiscal policy: conscious decisions to change government spending or taxation. Now let's get a clearer picture of automatic stabilizers.

Automatic stabilizers smooth fluctuations in disposable income over the business cycle, so that consumption varies by less than does GNP. They stimulate aggregate demand during periods of recession and dampen aggregate demand during periods of expansion. Let's consider the federal income tax. As the economy expands and employment increases, more and more taxpayers join the tax rolls. Because the personal income tax is progressive, the fraction paid in taxes increases with income, so tax payments grow faster than income. With a growing share of income going to taxes during expansions, there is proportionately less available for consumption. So the progressive income tax relieves inflationary pressures that could arise during periods of rising incomes. Conversely, when the economy is in recession, taxes fall, so disposable income does not fall as quickly as does GNP. Thus, declines in disposable income, in consumption, and in aggregate demand are cushioned by the progressive income tax. A proportional income tax also serves as an automatic stabilizer, though not as well as a progressive tax.

Another automatic stabilizer is unemployment insurance. During periods of economic expansion, employment grows and the premiums paid into the unemployment fund increase. So during good times the unemployment system automatically increases the flow of funds from the income stream to an unemployment insurance fund, thereby moderating aggregate demand. During a recession unemployment increases and the system reverses itself: unemployment compensation automatically flows from the insurance fund to those unemployed, thereby increasing their disposable income and propping up consumption and aggregate demand. Likewise, welfare benefits automatically increase as more people become eligible during hard times. *As a result of these built-in stabilizers, disposable income varies less over the business cycle than does GNP.*

Most automatic stabilizers, such as unemployment insurance, welfare benefits, and the progressive income tax, were designed not as stabilizers but as income redistribution programs. Their beneficial roles as automatic stabilizers are secondary effects of the legislation. Automatic stabilizers do not eliminate the fluctuations in the economy that are caused by the business cycle, but they do reduce the magnitude of the fluctuations. The stronger and more effective the automatic stabilizers are, the less need there is for discretionary fiscal policy.

The Golden Age of Fiscal Policy

The 1960s were the Golden Age of fiscal policy. John F. Kennedy was the first U.S. president to argue that a federal budget deficit would stimulate an economy experiencing a contractionary gap. He expanded the scope of fiscal policy from simply moderating business fluctuations to promoting long-term economic growth, and he set numerical targets of no more than 4 percent unemployment and no less than a 4.5 percent annual growth rate of output. Fiscal policy was also used on occasion to provide an extra kick to a recovery, as in 1964, when the income tax rate was cut to keep a recovery alive. *This tax cut, introduced to stimulate business investment, consumption, and employment, was perhaps the shining example of the successful use of fiscal policy during the Golden Age.* The tax cut seemed to work wonders, increasing disposable income and consumption. The unemployment rate dropped below 5 percent for the first time in seven years, and the inflation rate was under 2 percent.

Fiscal policy is a type of demand-management policy because the approach is to increase or decrease aggregate demand to smooth business fluctuations. But the problem during much of the 1970s was stagflation, the double trouble of higher inflation and higher unemployment resulting from a decrease in aggregate supply. Demand-management policies were ill-suited to solving the problem of stagflation because an increase in aggregate demand would increase inflation, whereas a decrease in aggregate demand would increase unemployment.

Other concerns spurred economists and policy makers to question the effectiveness of fiscal policy: the time lags involved in implementing fiscal policy, the difficulty of estimating the natural rate of unemployment, the distinction between current and permanent income, and possible feedback effects of fiscal policy on aggregate supply. We will consider each of these concerns in turn.

Lags in Fiscal Policy

The time required to approve and implement fiscal legislation may hamper its effectiveness and weaken fiscal policy as a tool of economic stabilization. Even if the fiscal prescription is appropriate for the economy at the time it is proposed, the months and sometimes years required to marshal enough political support to ensure passage of the required legislation and to implement the change may make the medicine too little too late, taking effect only after the economy has already turned itself around.

Fiscal Policy and the Natural Rate of Unemployment

As we have said, the unemployment rate that occurs when the economy is producing its potential GNP is called the natural rate of unemployment. For policy purposes it is important that public officials correctly estimate this natural rate. Suppose the economy is producing at its potential output, and the natural rate of unemployment is 5 percent. What if government officials believe the natural rate is 4 percent and attempt to increase output and reduce unemployment through fiscal policy? Fiscal policy will appear to succeed in the short run because output will expand. But stimulating aggregate demand will in the long run result only in a higher price level, while the level of output falls back to the economy's potential. Thus, temporary increases in output may persuade policy makers that their plan was a good one, even though attempts to increase production beyond potential GNP in the long run lead only to inflation.

Discretionary Policy and Permanent Income

At one time it was thought that discretionary fiscal policy could be turned on and off like a water faucet, stimulating the economy by just the right amount. Given the marginal propensity to consume, a relationship that Keynes believed was among the most stable in macroeconomics, tax changes could increase or decrease disposable income to bring about the desired change in consumption. A more recent view is that people base their consumption decisions not on their current, or transitory, income, but on their permanent income.

Permanent income is the income that individuals expect to receive on average over the long term.

Permanent income is the income a person expects to receive on average over the long term. If people base consumption decisions on their permanent incomes, consumption will be less responsive to temporary changes than to permanent changes in income. The short-term manipulation of the tax rates to achieve potential output will not yield the desired effects as long as people view the tax changes as only temporary. For example, in 1967, at a time when the U.S. economy was producing its potential level of output, the escalating war in Vietnam stimulated large increases in military spending, pushing the economy beyond its potential. The combination of a booming domestic economy and a widening war had produced an expansionary gap by 1968. In that year Congress approved a temporary tax surcharge, which raised income tax rates for eighteen months. The idea was to reduce disposable income, thereby reducing consumption and aggregate demand as a way of relieving inflationary pressure. But the reduction in aggregate demand turned out to be disappointingly small, and inflation was little affected. Although several factors may have contributed to the failure of this tax increase to reduce consumption, most economists agree that the *temporary* nature of the tax increase meant that consumers faced only a small downward revision in their permanent income. Since permanent income changed little, consumption changed little. Consumers simply saved less. *To the extent that consumers make decisions based on permanent income, attempts to fine tune the economy over the business cycle with temporary tax-rate adjustments will be less effective.*

Feedback Effects of Fiscal Policy on Aggregate Supply

So far we have limited our discussion of fiscal policy to its effect on aggregate demand. Fiscal policy may also affect aggregate supply, though often the effect is unintentional. For example, suppose the government increases transfer payments to the jobless and finances the transfers by an increase in income taxes on those who have jobs. Since the increase in transfers is offset by an increase in taxes, there should be no net effect on disposable income. If the marginal propensity to consume is the same for all groups, the reduction in spending by those whose taxes increase will be just offset by the increase in spending by transfer recipients. Thus, according to a theory of fiscal policy focusing on demand, there should be no change in aggregate demand and hence no change in equilibrium income.

But consider the possible effects of these changes on the supply of labor. The unemployed who benefit from the increase may decide to conduct a more leisurely job search. Conversely, workers who find their take-home wage rate reduced by the higher tax may be less willing to work extra hours or to work a second job. In short, the supply of labor could fall as a result of an increase in transfers to the unemployed. A decrease in the supply of labor will decrease aggregate supply, reducing the economy's potential GNP.

Both automatic stabilizers and discretionary fiscal policy may affect individual incentives to work, to spend, and to save, though these effects are usually unintended. We should keep these secondary effects in mind when we evaluate fiscal policies. It was concern about the effects of taxes on the supply of labor that served as a basis for tax cuts introduced in 1981, as we will see next.

Giant U.S. Budget Deficits of the 1980s

In 1981 President Reagan and Congress agreed on a 23 percent tax reduction over three years and a major buildup in defense spending, with no substantial offsetting reductions in domestic programs. This tax cut reflected a supply-side theory that reductions in taxes would make people willing to work harder because they could keep more of what they earned. Lower taxes would increase the supply of labor and other resources in the economy and thereby increase aggregate supply and the economy's potential GNP. In its strongest form, the supply-side theory held that enough additional real GNP would be generated by the tax cut that total tax revenues would actually increase.

Productivity did increase during the 1980s: output per worker increased at an annual rate of 1.6 percent, compared to only 0.8 percent from 1973 to 1979. Research and development, the fountainhead of technological break-throughs, also increased dramatically. Despite the growth in labor productivity, however, real GNP did not grow enough to generate the required tax revenues, and the resulting budget deficits were huge. Until 1981 deficits had been relatively small, typically less than 1 percent of the economy's potential GNP. But deficits had grown to about $200 billion a year by the middle of the decade—5 percent of GNP. These deficits were the greatest ever experienced during peacetime. The federal debt rose from about 25 percent of GNP in 1980 to well over 40 percent of GNP later that decade.

These deficits were the result of a supply-side experiment that failed to yield the expected revenues. Although they did not make a conscious decision to do so, policy makers in effect implemented an expansionary fiscal policy. (In Chapter 16 we will look at the effects of these deficits in detail. The results of the entire supply-side experiment are examined more closely in Chapter 17.) *The stimulus of huge federal deficits prompted a continued expansion during the 1980s—the longest peacetime expansion in this century.*

Some advocates of supply-side economics argue that the deficits resulted from a failure to cut taxes enough or to reduce government spending enough. Ironically, *the very magnitude of the federal deficits ruled out the active use of discretionary expansionary fiscal policy during the period.* Given a deficit of some $200 billion, the thought of introducing still more fiscal stimulus to reduce unemployment seemed foolish.

CONCLUSION

Because of huge federal deficits, the explicit use of discretionary fiscal policy as a tool for economic stabilization has been in decline, though the fiscal stimulus provided by these deficits looms large. Another important tool for economic stabilization is monetary policy, which is the regulation of the money supply by the Federal Reserve System. In the next two chapters we will introduce money and financial institutions, examine monetary policy, and compare the impact of monetary and fiscal policy on economic stability and growth.

Summary

1. The effect of a change in autonomous government purchases on the equilibrium quantity of aggregate output demanded is the same as that of a change in any other type of autonomous spending. The simple multiplier equals $1/(1 - MPC)$. A change in taxes affects consumption by changing disposable income; thus a given change in taxes does not affect spending as much as an identical change in government purchases would. A change in government transfers also affects consumption by changing disposable income.

2. If both taxes and government purchases change by the same amount, the equilibrium quantity of aggregate output demanded will also change by that amount. A proportional income tax reduces the autonomous spending multiplier because during each round of the multiplier, the income tax reduces the amount of income that can be spent.

3. In order to close a contractionary gap, government purchases or transfer payments can be increased or taxes reduced to increase aggregate demand. Because the aggregate supply curve slopes upward, the increase in aggregate demand will raise both output and the price level. Fiscal policy aimed at reducing aggregate demand in order to close an expansionary gap will result in a reduction in both output and the price level.

4. Fiscal policy focuses primarily on the demand side, not the supply side. The problems of the 1970s, however, appeared to result more from a decline in aggregate supply than from a decline in aggregate demand. Since then, a variety of concerns have tempered the explicit use of fiscal policy to influence aggregate demand. The tax cuts of the early 1980s were introduced as a way of increasing aggregate supply. These tax cuts gave rise to huge deficits, thereby stimulating aggregate demand.

Questions and Problems

1. (Lump-Sum Taxes) Would people who expected their incomes to rise in the future favor a lump-sum tax or a proportional income tax? Would lump-sum taxes be easy to institute in the United States? What groups would favor a lump-sum tax, and what groups would oppose it?

2. (Balanced Budget Multiplier) "Taxes are just the opposite of government spending. Therefore, a rise in taxes must completely offset an equal rise in government spending." Although this argument sounds true, it is actually false. Use the concept of the balanced budget multiplier to explain the error in logic.

3. (Tax Multiplier) Explain why the tax multiplier for lump-sum taxes is equal to the government spending multiplier times the marginal propensity to consume. If the MPC falls, what happens to the tax multiplier?

4. (Automatic Stabilizers) Often during recessions there is a large increase in the

number of young people who volunteer for military service. Would this rise be considered a type of automatic stabilizer? Why or why not?

5. (Automatic Stabilizers) Recent federal legislation requires welfare recipients to work at certain public jobs in order to receive their benefits. Without debating the merits of the program, explain whether you think this plan would strengthen or weaken the automatic stabilizer effect of the welfare system. Why?

6. (Permanent Income) "If the federal government wants to stimulate consumption by means of a tax cut, it should set up tax cuts that last a long time. If the government wants to stimulate savings in the short run, it should create a one-year tax cut." Evaluate these statements.

7. (Fiscal Policy) Will a 10 percent cut in a proportional income tax rate reduce government revenues by 10 percent? Why or why not? What would happen if there were a 10 percent cut in lump-sum taxes?

8. (Fiscal Policy) The chapter shows that increased government spending, with taxes held constant, can eliminate a deflationary gap. How might a tax cut achieve the same results? Must the tax cut be larger than the earlier increase in government spending? Why or why not?

9. (Fiscal Policy) Proponents of the federal highway bill, which passed in 1987 over presidential veto, claimed that such spending would be good for the economy. How would you justify their claims? How would you justify the administration's opposing position?

10. (Effects of Fiscal Policy) Recently some legislators have called for tax increases to reduce the federal budget deficit. Conservatives have countered that such tax increases could plunge the economy into a recession. Using aggregate supply and aggregate demand, explain how increases in taxes would lead to a loss of output and a dampening of prices. What would the expected effect be on interest rates? Are there arguments on both sides?

11. (Fiscal Policy) Suppose that the economy is experiencing a contractionary gap of $500 billion. Answer the following questions, assuming that autonomous spending equals $400 billion, all taxes are lump sum, the MPC equals 0.9, and the price level remains constant.

a. What is the level of potential output?

b. What change in government spending would eliminate this contractionary gap?

c. What change in the lump-sum tax would eliminate this gap?

d. What "balanced budget" change in government spending would eliminate this gap?

e. How would your answers change if the price level changed?

f. How would your answers to part (b) change if taxes were proportional to income?

12. (Fiscal Policy) Explain why effective discretionary fiscal policy requires information about each of the following:

a. The slope of the short-run aggregate supply curve

b. The slope of the aggregate demand curve

c. The natural rate of unemployment

d. The size of the multiplier

e. The speed with which self-correcting forces operate

13. (Consumption) Answer the questions below, using the following data.

Disposable Income	Consumption
$ 0	$ 500
500	900
1000	1300
1500	1700

   a. Assuming that taxes are equal to $200 regardless of the level of income, graph consumption against income (as opposed to disposable income).

   b. How would an increase in taxes to $300 affect your consumption function?

   c. If the level of taxes were related to the level of income (i.e., income tax were proportional), how would this affect your consumption function?

APPENDIX
The Algebra of Fiscal Policy

In this appendix we will continue to focus on aggregate demand, using algebraic analysis. We will first solve for the equilibrium quantities of aggregate demand found in this chapter and derive the relevant multipliers. Then we will incorporate net exports into the framework. Simple multiplier effects assume a given price level, so we will limit the analysis to shifts in the aggregate demand curve.

The equilibrium quantity of aggregate output demanded is where aggregate expenditure equals real GNP (Y). Aggregate expenditure, before the introduction of net exports, is equal to the sum of consumption (C), investment (I), and government purchases (G). Algebraically, we can write the equilibrium condition as

$$Y = C + I + G$$

To determine the equilibrium aggregate expenditure, we begin with the first spending component, consumption. In the absence of tax considerations, the consumption function was

$$C = 400 + 0.75Y$$

where 400 is autonomous consumption measured in billions of dollars, 0.75 is our hypothetical marginal propensity to consume, and Y is income, or real GNP. The two other components of aggregate expenditure are independent of income. We assumed investment spending to be fixed at $300 billion and government purchases to be $500 billion. Now we can write the equilibrium condition as

$$Y = C + I + G$$
$$Y = (400 + 0.75Y) + 300 + 500$$

Notice that there is only one variable in this expression: Y. If we rewrite the expression as

$$Y - 0.75Y = 400 + 300 + 500$$
$$0.25Y = 1200$$

we can solve for the equilibrium level of aggregate output demanded:

$$Y = \frac{1200}{0.25}$$
$$= 4800$$

Now consider the effects of a lump-sum tax, T, on equilibrium income. Recall that households make their consumption decisions based on disposable income, which differs from Y by the lump-sum tax, T. Since disposable income equals Y minus T, the consumption function should be written as

$$C = 400 + 0.75(Y - T)$$

With a lump-sum tax of $400 billion, investment of $300 billion, and government purchases of $500 billion, the aggregate expenditure function is

$$Y = 400 + 0.75(Y - 400) + 300 + 500$$

which reduces to $0.25Y = 900$, or $Y = 3600$.

Government Purchases Multiplier

The benefit of algebra is that we can derive equilibrium in a more general way. With a lump-sum tax, the general form of the consumption function is

$$C = a + b(Y - T)$$

where a equals autonomous spending and b equals the marginal propensity to consume. To consumption, we add the other spending components, G and I, to yield

$$Y = a + b(Y - T) + I + G$$

By rearranging terms and isolating Y on the left-hand side of the equation, we get

$$Y = \frac{a - bT + I + G}{1 - b}$$

which is the equilibrium quantity of GNP demanded, given the prevailing price level. Notice that when b, the marginal propensity to consume, is equal to 0.75, the equilibrium GNP is

$$Y = \frac{1}{0.25} \times (a - 0.75T + I + G)$$

$$= \textbf{multiplier} \times \textbf{autonomous spending}$$

To derive the government purchases multiplier, let's consider the effect of a $1 increase in government purchases:

$$Y' = \frac{a - bT + I + G + \$1}{1 - b}$$

The difference between Y' and Y—that is, the difference in the equilibrium quantity demanded after addition of $1 in government purchases—is

$$Y' - Y = \frac{\$1}{1 - b}$$

Thus, the effect of adding $1 to government purchases is to increase the equilibrium quantity of GNP demanded by $1 divided by $(1 - b)$, or 1 divided by $(1 - MPC)$. Dividing a number by $(1 - MPC)$ is the same as multiplying it by $1/(1 - MPC)$. So the multiplier for a change in autonomous spending is the same as the one derived previously in connection with changes in autonomous consumption and investment.

Lump-Sum Tax Multiplier

Instead of focusing on a $1 increase in government purchases, consider the effects on the equilibrium quantity of GNP demanded of a $1 increase in the lump-sum tax. We begin with Y, the equilibrium derived earlier, add $1 in taxes, then see what happens to the equilibrium level of GNP. Adding $1 to lump-sum taxes yields

$$Y'' = \frac{a - b(T + \$1) + I + G}{1 - b}$$

The difference between this equilibrium and the original equilibrium is

$$Y'' - Y = \frac{\$1 \, (-b)}{1 - b}$$

Since b is the marginal propensity to consume, this difference in equilibrium values can be expressed as $1 times $- MPC/(1 - MPC)$, the lump-sum tax multiplier discussed in this chapter. With the MPC equal to 0.75, the lump-sum tax multiplier equals $- 0.75/0.25$, or $- 3$, so the effect of increasing the lump-sum tax by $1 is to reduce equilibrium income by $3.

The Multiplier When Both G and T Change

In this chapter we discussed the combined effects of government purchases and taxes. Suppose that both increase by $1. We can bring together the two changes in the following equation:

$$Y^* = \frac{a - b(T + \$1) + I + G + \$1}{1 - b}$$

The difference between this equilibrium and Y, the income level before introduction of any changes in T or G, is

$$Y^* - Y = \frac{\$1(-b) + \$1}{1 - b}$$

which can be simplified to

$$Y^* - Y = \frac{1 - b}{1 - b} = 1$$

Equilibrium income increases by $1 as a result of $1 increases in both government purchases and lump-sum taxes.

More generally, we can say that if ΔT is the change in lump-sum taxes and ΔG is the change in government purchases, the resulting change in equilibrium income, ΔY, can be expressed as

$$\Delta Y = \frac{\Delta G - b\Delta T}{1 - b}$$

The Multiplier with an Income Tax

The lump-sum tax is relatively easy to manipulate, but it is not very realistic. Instead of a lump-sum tax, suppose a proportional income tax is employed whereby a fraction t of income is collected. Tax collections equal income, Y, times the tax rate, t. With tax collections of Yt, disposable income equals

$$Y - Yt = Y(1 - t)$$

We plug this value for disposable income into the consumption function to yield

$$C = a + bY(1 - t)$$

To consumption, we add the other components of aggregate expenditure, I and G, to get

$$Y = a + bY(1 - t) + I + G$$

Moving all the Y terms to the left-hand side of

the equation yields

$$Y - bY(1 - t) = a + I + G$$

or

$$Y[1 - b(1 - t)] = a + I + G$$

If we isolate Y on the left-hand side of the equation, we have

$$Y = \frac{a + I + G}{1 - b(1 - t)}$$

The numerator on the right-hand side consists of the autonomous spending components. A $1 change in any of these components would change equilibrium income by

$$\Delta Y = \frac{\$1}{1 - b(1 - t)}$$

Thus, the autonomous spending multiplier when there is a proportional income tax equals $1/[1 - b(1 - t)]$. Note that as the tax rate increases the denominator increases, so the multiplier gets smaller. *The higher the tax rate, other things constant, the smaller the multiplier, because disposable income is reduced during each round of spending in the expansion process.*

The Inclusion of Net Exports

If you have been reading the appendixes along with the chapters, you are familiar with how net exports fit into the picture. With net exports equal to $X - M$, equilibrium income can be derived from the following equation:

$$Y = C + I + G + X - M$$

Suppose government purchases equal $500 billion and lump-sum taxes equal $400 billion. As in the earlier chapters, autonomous exports equal $200 billion and imports equal 0.10 of disposable income. So net exports equal exports of $200 billion minus imports of $0.10(Y - 400)$, where $(Y - 400)$ equals income minus lump-sum taxes, or disposable income. Equilibrium income therefore equals

$$Y = 400 + 0.75(Y - 400) + 300$$
$$+ 500 + 200 - 0.10(Y - 400)$$

which boils down to $0.35Y = 1140$, or $Y = 3257 billion. The inclusion of net exports reduces the equilibrium income from $3600 billion to $3257 billion because net exports are negative over the relevant levels of income. Negative net exports represent a leakage of spending from the circular flow.

When a proportional income tax is employed, equilibrium income can be derived algebraically as

$$Y = a + bY(1 - t) + I + G + X - mY(1 - t)$$

where m is the marginal propensity to import.

This equation reduces to

$$Y = \frac{a + I + G + X}{1 - b + m + t(b - m)}$$

The numerator equals autonomous spending, and 1 over the denominator equals the spending multiplier for a model with proportional income taxes and a foreign sector. The higher the marginal propensity to consume, b, the smaller the denominator and the greater the value of the multiplier. The higher the marginal propensity to import, m, the larger the denominator, so the smaller the spending multiplier. The higher the proportional tax rate, t, the larger the denominator, so the smaller the multiplier. Thus, *the multiplier is reduced by a lower marginal propensity to consume, a higher marginal propensity to import, and a higher proportional tax rate.*

Since we first introduced the simple spending multiplier, we have examined a variety of factors that reduce the multiplier. When we introduce money in the next two chapters, we will consider other constraints on the multiplier.

Appendix Questions

1. (Equilibrium) Suppose that the autonomous levels of consumption, investment, and net exports are $500 billion, $300 billion, and $100 billion, respectively. Suppose further that the MPC is 0.85, the marginal propensity to import (MPI) is 0.05, and income is taxed at a proportional rate of 0.25. If aggregate equilibrium output is $2500 billion,

    a. What is the level of autonomous government spending?

    b. What is the size of the government deficit (or surplus) at this equilibrium output?

    c. What is the size of the trade balance at this output?

    d. What is the level of savings at this output?

    e. What change in autonomous spending is required to change equilibrium output by $500 billion?

2. Using a 45-degree line diagram, show the following:

   a. The size of the multiplier when the slope of the aggregate expenditure function is 1

   b. The size of the multiplier when the slope of the aggregate expenditure function is 0

   c. How increases in MPS, the marginal propensity to import, and the proportional income tax rate affect the slope of the aggregate expenditure function and therefore the size of the multiplier

Money and the Financial System

Money has been a source of fascination since earliest times. It has come to symbolize all personal and business finance. There is *Money* magazine, the "Money" section of *USA TODAY*, and cable TV shows such as "Moneyline" and "Your Money." Money in today's economy represents a sophisticated system of IOUs. With money, you can articulate your preferences clearly — after all, money talks.

Money is the oil that lubricates the wheels of commerce. Just as oil makes for an easier fit among interacting gears, money reduces the friction of voluntary exchange. Too little oil can leave some parts creaking; too much oil can gum up the works. Similarly, too little or too much money in circulation makes exchange more difficult and creates economic problems.

In this chapter we will first discuss the evolution of money, moving from the most primitive economy to our own. Then we will review monetary developments in the United States, focusing primarily on the twentieth century. Topics discussed in this chapter include

- Barter and the double coincidence of wants
- Functions of money
- Commodity, fiduciary, and fiat moneys
- Federal Reserve System
- Depository institutions
- Financial deregulation of the 1980s

THE EVOLUTION OF MONEY

In the beginning there was no money. The earliest families were largely self-sufficient. Each family produced all it consumed and consumed all it produced, so there was little need for exchange. Without exchange, there was no need for money. When specialization first emerged, as some people went hunting and others took up farming, hunters and farmers had to trade. Thus, the specialization of labor resulted in exchange, but the kinds of goods traded were limited enough that people could easily exchange their products directly for other products—a system called *barter*.

Barter and the Double Coincidence of Wants

A ***double coincidence of wants*** *occurs when a trader is willing to exchange his or her product directly for what the other trader is selling.*

Barter depends on a **double coincidence of wants**, which occurs only when traders are willing to exchange their products for what others are selling. The hunter must be willing to exchange hides for the corn offered by the farmer, *and* the farmer must be willing to exchange corn for the hides offered by the hunter.

As long as specialization was limited, mutually beneficial trades were relatively easy to make. As the economy developed, however, greater specialization in the division of labor increased the difficulty of finding goods that each trader wanted to exchange. Rather than just two possible types of producers, there were, say, a hundred types of producers.

In a barter system, not only must traders discover a double coincidence of wants; they also must agree on a rate of exchange after they connect—that is, how many hides should be exchanged for a bushel of corn. When only two goods are produced, only one exchange rate must be determined, but as the number of goods produced in the economy increases, the number of exchange rates grows sharply. For example, for one hundred different goods, $(100 \times 99)/2 = 4950$ exchange rates would have to be determined. Increased specialization made the barter system of exchange more time-consuming and cumbersome.

Negotiating the exchange rates among commodities is complicated in a barter economy because there is no common measure of value. Sometimes differences between the values of products made barter difficult. For example, suppose the hunter wanted to buy a home, which exchanged for 2000 hides. The hunter would be hard-pressed to find a home seller in need of that many hides. These difficulties with barter have led people in even very simple economies to use money.

Earliest Money and Its Functions

Nobody actually recorded the emergence of money. Thus, we can only speculate about how money first came into use. Through repeated exchanges, traders may have found that there were certain goods for which there was always a ready market. If a trader could not find a good he or she desired personally, some good with a ready market could be accepted instead. So traders began to accept certain goods not for immediate consumption but because these goods would be accepted by others and therefore could be retraded later. For example, corn might become accepted because traders knew corn was always in demand. As one good became

Money is anything that is generally acceptable in exchange for goods and services.

generally accepted in return for all other goods, that good began to function as **money**. As we will see, anything that is used as money fulfills three important functions: it serves as a medium of exchange, a standard of value, and a store of wealth.

*Money is a **medium of exchange** because it facilitates trade by being generally acceptable to all parties.*

Commodity money serves as both money and a commodity.

Medium of Exchange   If a community, by luck or by design, can find one commodity that everyone will accept in exchange for whatever is sold, traders can save much time, disappointment, and sheer aggravation. Separating the sale of one good from the purchase of another requires something acceptable to all parties involved in the transaction. Suppose corn plays this role, a role that clearly goes beyond its usual function as food. We then call corn a medium of exchange because it is accepted in exchange by all buyers and sellers, whether or not they want it to use as food. A **medium of exchange** is anything that is generally accepted in payment for goods and services sold. The person who accepts corn in exchange for some product may already have more corn than the entire family could eat in a year, but the corn is not accepted with a view toward consumption. It is accepted because it can be used to purchase whatever is desired whenever it is desired. Because in this example corn both is a commodity and serves as money, we call it a **commodity money**. The earliest money was commodity money.

*Money serves as a **standard of value** by being a yardstick for measuring the value of all goods and services.*

Standard of Value   As one commodity, such as corn, becomes widely accepted, the prices of all other goods come to be quoted in terms of that good. The chosen commodity becomes a common **standard of value**. The price of shoes or pots is expressed in terms of bushels of corn. Thus, not only does corn serve as a medium of exchange; it also becomes a yardstick for measuring the value of all goods and services. Rather than having to quote the rate of exchange for each good in terms of every other good, as was the case in the barter economy, people can measure the price of everything in terms of corn. For example, if a pair of shoes sells for two bushels of corn and a five-gallon pot sells for one bushel of corn, then one pair of shoes has the same value as two five-gallon pots.

*Money serves as a **store of wealth** by retaining its purchasing power over time.*

Store of Wealth   Because people often do not want to make purchases at the time they sell an item, the purchasing power acquired through sales must somehow be preserved. Money serves as a **store of wealth** because it retains purchasing power over time. The cobbler exchanges shoes for corn in the belief that other suppliers will accept corn in exchange for whatever the cobbler demands later. Corn represents a way of conserving purchasing power so that purchases can be deferred until later. The better money is at preserving purchasing power, the better it serves as a store of wealth.

Any commodity that acquires a high degree of acceptability throughout an economy thereby becomes money. Consider some commodities used as money over the centuries. Cattle served as money, first for the Greeks and then for the Romans. In fact, the word "pecuniary" ("of or relating to money") comes from the Latin word *pecus,* meaning "cattle." Other commodity moneys used at various times include tobacco and wampum (polished strings of shells) in colonial America, tea pressed into small cakes in Russia, and dates in North Africa. Whatever serves as a medium of exchange is called money, no matter what it is, no matter how it first comes to serve as a medium of exchange, and no matter why it continues to serve this function.

Problems with Commodity Money

There are problems with most commodity moneys, including corn. First, corn must be properly stored or its quality deteriorates; even then, it will not maintain its quality for long. Second, corn is bulky, so exchanges for major purchases become unwieldy. For example, if a new home cost 50,000 bushels of corn, many truckloads of corn would be involved in its purchase . Third, if all corn is valued equally in exchange, people will tend to keep the best corn and trade away the lowest-quality corn. The quality of corn in circulation will therefore decline, reducing its acceptability. Sir Thomas Gresham, founder of the Royal Exchange of London, pointed out back in the sixteenth century that "bad money drives out good money," and this has come to be known as **Gresham's Law**. When moneys of different quality circulate side by side, people tend to trade away the inferior money and hoard the best.

*According to **Gresham's Law**, people tend to trade away inferior money and hoard the best.*

A final problem with corn, as with other commodity money, is that the value of corn depends on its supply and demand, which may vary unpredictably. If a bumper crop increased the supply of corn, corn would likely become less valuable, so more corn would be exchanged for all other goods. Any change in the demand for corn as food would alter the amount available as a medium of exchange, and this, too, would influence the value of corn. Erratic fluctuations in the value of corn limit its usefulness as money, particularly as a store of wealth. If people cannot rely on the value of corn over time, they will be reluctant to hold it as a store of wealth. More generally, *since the value of money depends on its limited supply, anything that can be easily gathered or produced by anyone does not serve well as a commodity money.* For example, leaves would not serve well as a commodity money.

Metallic Money and Coinage

Throughout history several metals, including iron and copper, have been used as commodity moneys. Most important, however, were the precious metals—silver and gold—which have always been held in high regard. The division of commodity money into units was often quite natural, as in a bushel of corn or a head of cattle. When rock salt was used as money, it was cut into uniform bricks. Since salt was usually of consistent quality, a trader had only to count the bricks to determine the amount of money. With precious metals, however, both the quantity and the quality became open to question. Because precious metals could be debased with cheaper metals, the quantity and the quality of the metal had to be ascertained with each exchange.

This quality-control problem was addressed by coining the metal. *Coinage determined both the amount of metal and the quality of the metal.* The use of coins allowed payment by count rather than by weight. Initially, coins were stamped on only one side, but undetectable amounts of the metal could be shaved from the smooth side of the coin. To prevent shaving, coins were stamped on both sides. But another problem arose. Because the borders of coins remained blank, small amounts of the metal could be clipped from the edges. To prevent clipping, coins were bordered with a well-defined rim and were milled around the edges. If you have a dime or a quarter, notice the tiny serrations on the edge and the words along the border. These features, throwbacks from the time when these coins were silver rather than a cheaper alloy, prevented the recipient from "getting clipped."

The power to coin money was viewed as an act of sovereignty, and counterfeiting as an act of treason. When the face value of the coin exceeds the cost of coinage, the minting of coins becomes a source of revenue to the sovereign. **Seigniorage** refers to the revenue earned from coinage by the sovereign, or seignior. Debasement of the currency represented a potential source of profit for governments. **Token money** is the name given to coins whose face value exceeds their metallic value. Coins now in circulation in the United States are token money. For example, the twenty-five-cent coin costs the U.S. Mint only 2.5 cents to make.

Seigniorage is the revenue earned by a sovereign from coining money; it is the difference between the face value of the money and the cost of coining it.

Coins whose face values exceed their metallic values are called token money.

Money and Banking

Banking, as the term is understood today, dates back to London goldsmiths of the seventeenth century. Because goldsmiths had safes in which to store gold, others in the community came to rely on goldsmiths to hold their money and other valuables for safekeeping. The goldsmiths found that when they held money for many customers, deposits and withdrawals tended to balance out, so the pool of deposits in the safe remained fairly constant. Loans could be made from this pool of idle cash, and the goldsmiths could thus earn interest.

Keeping one's money on deposit with a goldsmith was safer than leaving the money where it could be easily stolen, but it was a bit of a nuisance to have to visit the goldsmith each time money was needed. For example, the farmer would visit the goldsmith to withdraw enough money to buy a horse. The farmer would then pay the horse trader, who would promptly deposit the receipts with the goldsmith. Thus, money took a round trip from goldsmith to farmer to horse trader and back to goldsmith. Because depositors grew tired of going to the goldsmith every time they needed to make a purchase, they instituted a practice whereby a purchaser, such as the farmer, could write the goldsmith instructions to pay someone else, such as the horse trader, a given amount from the purchaser's account. The payment amounted to having the goldsmith move gold from one stack (the farmer's) to another (the horse trader's). *These written instructions to the goldsmith were the first checks.*

By combining the idea of cash loans with checking, the goldsmith soon discovered how to make loans by check. The check was a claim against the goldsmith, but the borrower's promise to repay the loan became the goldsmith's asset. *The goldsmith could extend a loan by creating an account against which the borrower could write checks. In this way goldsmiths, or banks, were able to "create money"—that is, to create claims against themselves that were generally accepted as a means of payment—as a medium of exchange.* This money, though based only on an entry in the goldsmith's ledger, was accepted because of the public's confidence that these claims would be honored.

The total claims against the bank consisted of customer deposits plus deposits created through loans. Because these claims against the bank exceeded the bank's gold and other reserves, this was the beginning of a **fractional reserve banking system**, a system whereby bank reserves amount to only a fraction of deposits. The *reserve ratio* measures reserves as a proportion of total deposits. For example, if the goldsmith had gold valued at $5000 but total accounts valued at $10,000, the reserve ratio would be 50 percent.

*In a **fractional reserve banking** system, bank reserves amount to only a fraction of bank deposits.*

Paper Money

Another way a bank could create claims against itself was to issue bank notes. In London, goldsmith bankers introduced bank notes about the same time they introduced checks. **Bank notes** were pieces of paper promising that the bearer would receive a specific amount in gold upon presenting the notes to the issuing bank for redemption. *Whereas checks could be redeemed only by the individual to whom the deposit was directed, notes could be redeemed by anyone who held them.* Notes redeemable for gold or another valuable commodity are called **fiduciary money**. Fiduciary money was often "as good as gold," since the bearer could, upon request, redeem the note for gold. In some ways fiduciary money was better than gold because it took up less space and was easier to carry.

***Bank notes** were promises to pay a specific amount of money to the bearer in gold.*

***Fiduciary money** is redeemable for gold or another valuable commodity.*

The amount of fiduciary money issued depended on the bank's estimate of the proportion of notes that would be redeemed for gold. The greater the redemption rate, the fewer notes that could be issued based on a given amount of gold reserves. Initially, these promises to pay in gold were issued by private individuals or banks, but over time governments took a larger role in printing and circulating notes.

Once fiduciary money became widely accepted, it was perhaps inevitable that governments would begin issuing **fiat money**, which consists of notes that derive their status as money from the power of the state, or by *fiat*. Fiat money is money because the government says it is money. Fiat money is not redeemable for anything other than more fiat money; it is not backed by a promise to pay something of intrinsic value. You can think of fiat money as mere paper money. It is acceptable not because it is intrinsically useful or valuable—as was corn or gold—but because the government requires that it be accepted as payment. Fiat money is declared **legal tender** by the government, meaning that creditors must accept it as payment for debts. *Gradually, people came to accept fiat money because they believed that others would accept it as*

***Fiat money** is not redeemable for any commodity; its status as money is conferred by the government.*

***Legal tender** is anything that creditors are required by law to accept as payment for debts.*

well. The money issued in the United States today, and indeed paper money throughout most of the world, is largely fiat money. In a way, fiat money is more economical than fiduciary money — fiat money uses only the resources required to produce and police the money supply, whereas fiduciary money requires that some commodity be held in reserve to back up the system.

The Value of Money

Why does money have value? As we have seen, various commodities served as the earliest moneys. Commodities such as corn or tobacco had value in use even if for some reason they became less acceptable in exchange. The commodity feature of early money bolstered confidence in its accept-ability. When paper money came into use, its acceptability was initially fostered by the promise to redeem it for gold or silver. But since most paper money throughout the world is now fiat money, there is no promise of redemption.

So why can a piece of paper bearing the image of Alexander Hamilton and the number 10 in each corner be exchanged for a large pepperoni pizza or anything else selling for $10? People accept these pieces of paper because they believe others will do so. *Fiat money has no value other than its ability to be exchanged for goods and services now and in the future. Its value lies in people's belief in its value.*

The value of money is reflected in its purchasing power: the rate at which money is exchanged for goods and services. The higher the price level, the fewer goods and services that can be purchased with each dollar, so the less each dollar is worth. The purchasing power of each dollar can be compared over time by accounting for changes in the price level. To measure the purchasing power of the dollar in a particular year, first compute the price index for that year, then divide 100 by that price index. For example, relative to the base period 1982–1984, the consumer price index for February 1990 was 128. The value of a dollar in February 1990 was therefore 100/128, or about $0.78, measured in 1982–1984 dollars. Exhibit 1 chronicles the steady decline since 1960 in the value of the dollar, measured in terms of its average value in 1982–1984.

Too Much and Too Little Money

One way to understand the functions of money is to look at situations in which money did not perform these functions well. Money may not func-tion well as a medium of exchange because there is too much money or too little money, or because the price system is not allowed to operate. In Chapter 7 we examined the results of too much money in the hyperinflation of Bolivia. With prices growing by the hour, money no longer represented a stable store of wealth, so people were unwilling to hold money. With rapidly rising prices, some merchants were quicker to raise prices than others, so relative prices also became distorted. Buyers and sellers had difficulty know-ing the appropriate price of each good. Thus, money became less useful as a

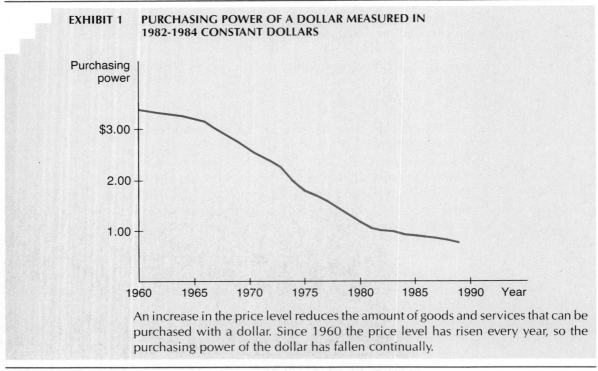

EXHIBIT 1   PURCHASING POWER OF A DOLLAR MEASURED IN
             1982-1984 CONSTANT DOLLARS

An increase in the price level reduces the amount of goods and services that can be purchased with a dollar. Since 1960 the price level has risen every year, so the purchasing power of the dollar has fallen continually.

Source: *Economic Report of the President*, February 1990.

standard of value — that is, as a way of comparing the price of one good to that of another. Money still served as a medium of exchange, but as larger and larger amounts of money were needed to carry out the simplest purchases, exchange demanded more time and energy. In short, *when there is too much money, the economy becomes less productive because more time and energy must be devoted to coping with the effects of inflation.*

At some point, the currency may become so inflated that people will no longer accept it in payment and will resort to barter. Barter is inefficient compared to a smoothly functioning monetary system, but it may be more efficient than trying to use money during hyperinflation. Likewise, if there is too little money in the economy or if the price system is not allowed to function properly, barter may be the only remaining alternative. For example, just after World War II, money in Germany became largely useless because, despite tremendous inflationary pressure in the economy, the occupation forces imposed strict price controls. Since prices were set well below what people thought they should be, sellers stopped accepting money, forcing people to use barter. Experts estimate that because of the lack of a viable medium of exchange, the German economy produced only half the output that it would have produced with a smoothly functioning monetary system. The "economic miracle" that occurred in Germany after 1948 can be credited in large part to that country's adoption of a reliable monetary system.

For a more recent example, consider Panama, a Central American country that relies on the U.S. dollar as a medium of exchange. In 1988 the United States, in response to charges that the leader of Panama was involved in drug dealing, froze Panamanian assets in the United States, precipitating a run on Panama's banks. Those banks were forced to close for nine weeks. The flow of dollars in circulation dried up, so people resorted to barter. Because barter is much less efficient than a smoothly functioning monetary system, Panama's GNP reportedly fell by 30 percent in 1988.

It has been said that no machine increases the economy's productivity as much as a properly functioning money system. Indeed, it seems hard to overstate the value of a reliable monetary system. Consider the following case study, another example of the official currency's failing to serve well as a medium of exchange.

CASE STUDY

The Kent Standard

Until the recent revolutions throughout Eastern Europe, most prices in these Communist bloc countries were set by the government, not by supply and demand. Prices for agricultural products were typically fixed well below their market-clearing level, so the quantity demanded exceeded the quantity supplied.

At the farmers' market in Bucharest, Romania, for example, the frenzied activity would begin at dawn. Long lines of customers would wait with a handful of *lei*, the official Romanian currency. Because prices were set so low, farmers were not anxious to accept lei. Rather than exchange their goods for the official currency at below-market prices, farmers preferred to barter for other goods, thereby bypassing the official price system altogether.

One good in particular was preferred in Romania to all the others: Kent cigarettes. Flash a pack of Kents and go to the head of any line. You could buy anything you wanted: a taxi ride, fine cuts of meat, fresh fruit—you name it. Ironically, few people smoked Kents, in part because they were so valuable in exchange.

Several kinds of money circulated in Romania. First, there was the official currency, the lei; second, the black market currencies, or so-called hard currencies, such as the U.S. dollar; and third, Kent cigarettes, a commodity money. Whereas the black-market money was illegal, Kent cigarettes were not. Public officials chose to look the other way rather than outlaw Kent cigarettes because the prohibition of Kents as a medium of exchange would simply have forced people into black-market currencies.

Source: Roger Thurow, "In Romania, Smoking a Kent Cigarette Is Like Burning Money," *Wall Street Journal*, 3 January 1986.

Because the official currency did not perform well as a medium of exchange, people in Romania adopted Kents as a crude money. The situation is worse in the Soviet Union, where the ruble can barely be called money since there are few goods available for sale. Moreover, the ruble is not convertible into any other medium of exchange.

Now let's consider some cases where there was too little money. Money became extremely scarce during the nineteenth century in Brazil because of a copper shortage. Money-financed transactions were temporarily impossible because copper coins could no longer be minted. In response to this crisis, some merchants and tavern keepers printed vouchers redeemable in goods and services. These vouchers circulated as a crude form of money until copper coins returned to circulation. Similarly, there was often a shortage of money in the early American colonies. One way people dealt with the problem was by keeping careful records of credit, showing who owed what to whom.

Thus, *when there is too little money or when the official money fails to serve as a medium of exchange, some other form of money may arise to facilitate exchange. But this second-best alternative is seldom as efficient as a smoothly functioning money system because more resources must be diverted from production to exchange.*

FINANCIAL INSTITUTIONS IN THE UNITED STATES

Financial intermediaries are institutions that serve as go-betweens linking savers and borrowers.

Depository institutions are commercial banks and other financial institutions that accept deposits from the public.

Commercial banks are depository institutions that make short-term loans primarily to businesses rather than to households.

Demand deposits are accounts on which depositors can write checks to obtain their deposits at any time.

Thrift institutions, or thrifts, are financial institutions that make long-term loans primarily to households.

We discussed the origin of banks in goldsmiths who lent money from deposits held for safekeeping. So you already have some idea of the way banks operate. Recall from the circular flow model discussed earlier that household saving flows into financial markets and is made available for loans. Financial institutions attract the funds of savers and lend these funds to borrowers, serving as intermediaries that link savers to borrowers. Financial institutions, or **financial intermediaries**, earn a profit by "buying low and selling high"—that is, by paying a lower interest rate to savers than they charge borrowers.

A wide variety of financial intermediaries respond to the economy's demand for financial services. **Depository institutions**, such as commercial banks, savings and loan associations, mutual savings banks, and credit unions, obtain funds primarily by accepting *deposits* from the public—hence their name. Other financial intermediaries, such as finance companies, insurance companies, and pension funds, acquire funds not through customer deposits but by collecting premiums or by borrowing. Our emphasis will be on depository institutions because they play an important role in providing the nation's money supply. Depository institutions can be classified broadly into two types: commercial banks and thrift institutions.

Commercial banks are the oldest, largest, and most diversified of depository institutions. They are called **commercial banks** because they make loans primarily to commercial ventures, or businesses, rather than to households. Until recently, commercial banks were the only depository institutions that offered demand deposits, or checking accounts. **Demand deposits** are so named because a depositor with such an account can write a check to *demand* those deposits at any time. **Thrift institutions**, or **thrifts**, include savings and loan associations, mutual savings banks, and credit unions. Historically, savings and loan associations and mutual savings banks specialized in making mortgage loans, which are loans to finance real estate purchases. Credit unions extended loans for purchases of major consumer goods such as cars.

Development of the Dual Banking System

Before 1863 each commercial bank in the United States was chartered by the state in which it operated. These banks, like the English goldsmiths, issued bank notes redeemable in gold. Because state regulations were lax, bank failures were common and many people were stuck with worthless notes. There was growing dissatisfaction with what some people viewed as disarray in note issues by *state banks*—that is, banks with state charters.

The National Banking Act of 1863 and its later amendments created a new system of federally chartered banks called *national banks*. National banks were authorized to issue notes and were regulated by the Office of the Comptroller of the Currency, part of the U.S. Treasury. At this time a tax was introduced on the notes issued by state-chartered banks, the idea being to tax state bank notes out of existence. But state banks survived by substituting checks for notes. Borrowers were issued checking accounts rather than bank notes. State banks thereby held on, and to this day the United States has a *dual banking system* consisting of both state banks and national banks.

Birth of the Federal Reserve System

During the nineteenth century, the economy experienced a number of panic "runs" on banks by depositors. A panic was usually set off by the failure of some prominent financial institution. Following such a failure, banks were besieged by fearful customers. Borrowers wanted additional loans and extensions of credit, and depositors wanted their money back.

The failure of the Knickerbocker Trust Company in New York set off the Panic of 1907. This financial calamity underscored the lack of stability in the existing system and so aroused the public that Congress established the National Monetary Commission to study the banking system and make recommendations. That group's deliberations led to the Federal Reserve Act, passed in 1913 and implemented in 1914, which established the **Federal Reserve System** as the central bank and monetary authority of the United States. *Throughout most of its history, the United States had had what is called a decentralized banking system. The Federal Reserve Act moved the country toward a system that was partly centralized and partly decentralized.*

Although most countries have a single large central bank, the U.S. public's suspicion of such monopoly power led to the establishment of not one central bank but separate semiautonomous central banks in twelve Federal Reserve districts around the country. The new banks were named after the cities in which they were located—the Federal Reserve Bank of New York, Chicago, San Francisco, and so on. All national banks were required to become members of the Federal Reserve System and became

*The **Federal Reserve System** is the central bank and monetary authority of the United States.*

subject to new regulations issued by "the Fed." For state banks, membership was voluntary; most state banks did not join because they did not want to comply with the new regulations.

Powers of the Federal Reserve System

According to the 1913 act, the Federal Reserve System was to be directed by the Federal Reserve Board. This board was authorized "to exercise general supervision" over the twelve Reserve banks. The Federal Reserve's task was to ensure the availability of enough money and credit in the banking system to support a growing economy.

The power to issue bank notes was taken away from national banks and turned over to the Federal Reserve banks. (Take out a dollar bill and notice what it says across the top: FEDERAL RESERVE NOTE. The seal to the left of George Washington's picture identifies which Reserve bank issued the note.) The Federal Reserve was also given other powers: the abilities to buy and sell government securities, to extend loans to member banks, to clear checks, and to require that member banks hold reserves equal to some fraction of their deposits.

Federal Reserve banks typically do not deal with the public directly. Each may be thought of as a bankers' bank. Reserve banks hold deposits of member banks, just as commercial banks hold deposits of households and firms. In fact, the Federal Reserve banks get their name from the fact that they hold member bank *reserves* on deposit, both to promote banking safety and to facilitate interbank transfers of funds. These reserves allow Reserve banks to clear checks written by a depositor in one commercial bank and deposited in another commercial bank. This check clearance is, on a larger scale, much like the goldsmith's moving of reserves from the farmer's account to the horse trader's account. Reserve banks also make loans to member banks, just as commercial banks extend loans to the public. In addition to serving as bankers' banks, Reserve banks serve as bankers to the federal government, holding government deposits and lending money to the government by purchasing federal securities.

Member banks are required to own stock in the Federal Reserve bank in their district, but this ownership conveys no control over Reserve banks. Member banks' input is purely advisory, through the *Federal Advisory Council*, which consists of twelve commercial bankers, one representing each Federal reserve district. Moreover, member banks receive only a modest return on their ownership of the Reserve banks. Any additional profits earned by the Reserve banks are turned over to the U.S. Treasury.

Banking During the Great Depression

From 1913 to 1929, both the Federal Reserve System and the national economy performed relatively well. But the stock market crash of 1929 was followed by the Great Depression, bringing a new set of problems for the Federal Reserve System. The Fed failed to respond to the crisis caused by the depression. It did not act as a lender of last resort—that is, it did not lend banks the money they needed to satisfy deposit withdrawals in cases of runs on otherwise sound banks. Between 1930 and 1933, about 9000 banks failed—roughly half of the banks in existence.

The Federal Reserve System was established precisely to prevent such panics and to add stability to the banking system. What went wrong? In a word, everything. The support offered by the Federal Reserve System seemed to crumble in stages between 1930 and 1933. As businesses failed, they were unable to repay their loans. The bank failures at the outset of the depression were probably the result of these loans' going sour. As the crisis deepened, the public grew more concerned about the safety of deposits, so cash withdrawals increased. To satisfy this increased demand for currency, banks were forced to sell their securities. But with many banks looking to sell and with few buyers, the securities market collapsed, sharply reducing the value of these bank assets. Many banks did not have the resources to survive.

The Fed should have extended loans on a large scale to banks experiencing a short-run shortage of cash, much as it did during the stock market crash of 1987. The Fed failed to act because it did not understand either the gravity of the situation or its own power to assist troubled banks. The Fed viewed bank failure as a regrettable but inevitable consequence of poor bank management or prior speculative excesses, or simply as the effect of a collapsing economy. The Fed did not seem to understand that the banking system's instability was contributing to the deterioration of the economy. For example, securities markets collapsed in part because many banks were trying to sell their securities at the same time. And the collapse came just when banks were badly in need of cash. Fed officials appeared more concerned about the solvency of the Federal Reserve banks. *They did not seem to realize that because Federal Reserve banks had unlimited money-creating power, they could not fail.*

Roosevelt's Reforms

In his first inaugural address, President Franklin D. Roosevelt said, "The only thing we have to fear is fear itself," a view that was especially applicable to a fractional reserve banking system. Most banks were sound as long as people had confidence in the safety of their deposits. *But if many people became frightened and tried to withdraw their money, they could not do so because each bank held reserves amounting to only a fraction of its deposits.*

Upon taking office in March of 1933, President Roosevelt attempted to soothe prevailing fears by declaring a "banking holiday," which closed all banks for a week. A national suspension of banking business for a week was unprecedented, yet it was welcomed as a sign that something would be done. President Roosevelt also proposed the Banking Acts of 1933 and 1935 and other measures to introduce a variety of reforms aimed at shoring up the banking system and centralizing the power of the Federal Reserve in Washington. Let's consider the most important features of this legislation.

Board of Governors The Federal Reserve Board was renamed the Board of Governors, and it became responsible for setting and implementing the nation's monetary policy. Recall that monetary policy is the regulation of the economy's money supply to promote macroeconomic objectives. All twelve Reserve banks came under the authority of the Board of Governors, which consists of seven members appointed by the president and confirmed by the Senate. Each governor serves a fourteen-year term, and the terms are staggered so that one governor is appointed every two years. The president also appoints one of the governors to chair the board for a four-year term. A president bent on changing the direction of monetary policy could be sure of changing only two members in a single presidential term and four members in two terms. Thus, board membership is relatively stable, and in theory any president has only limited control over the board's monetary policy. *The idea was to insulate monetary authorities from short-term political whim.*

Open market operations are purchases and sales of government securities by the Federal Reserve intended to change the economy's supply of money.

Federal Open Market Committee Originally, the power of the Federal Reserve was vested in each of the twelve Reserve banks. The Banking Acts established the Federal Open Market Committee (FOMC) to consolidate decisions about the most important tool of monetary policy — **open market operations**, which are purchases and sales of government securities by the Fed. (Open market operations will be examined in Chapter 13.) The FOMC consists of the seven board governors plus five presidents from the Reserve banks. The president of the New York Fed is always on the FOMC, and the other positions rotate. Each Federal Reserve bank uses its authority over the depository institutions within its region to implement the monetary policy adopted by the FOMC. The organizational structure of the Federal Reserve System as it now stands is presented in Exhibit 2.

Reserve Requirements and the Discount Rate As we noted earlier, because reserves amount to only a fraction of deposits, we have a *fractional reserve* banking system. Specific reserve requirements had been established by the Federal Reserve Act of 1914. Member banks were required to hold reserves equal to a certain percentage of their deposits. The Banking Acts of 1933 and 1935 authorized the Board of Governors to vary reserve requirements within a range, thereby giving the Fed an additional tool of monetary policy. The interest rate at which member banks could borrow from a Federal Reserve bank, called the **discount rate**, was also to be set by the Board of Governors rather than left to the discretion of each Reserve bank.

*The **discount rate** is the interest rate charged by the Federal Reserve to financial institutions that are borrowing reserves.*

Thus, as of 1935, the Federal Reserve System had a variety of tools to regulate the money supply, including *(1) open market operations — buying and selling government securities; (2) setting the legal reserve requirement for member banks; and (3) setting the discount rate — the interest rate charged by the Reserve banks for money lent to member banks.* We will explore these tools in greater detail in Chapter 13.

FDIC and FSLIC The Federal Deposit Insurance Corporation (FDIC) was established in 1933 to insure each deposit account held in member banks for

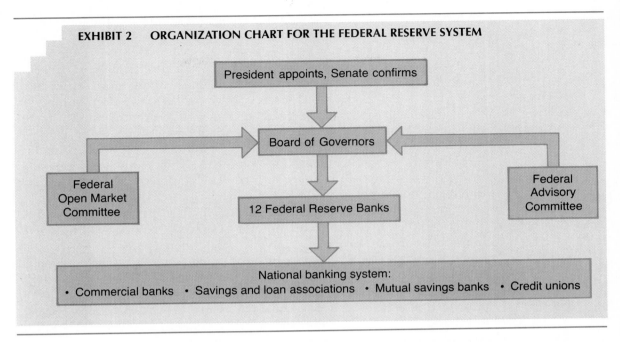

EXHIBIT 2   ORGANIZATION CHART FOR THE FEDERAL RESERVE SYSTEM

President appoints, Senate confirms

Board of Governors

Federal Open Market Committee

Federal Advisory Committee

12 Federal Reserve Banks

National banking system:
• Commercial banks   • Savings and loan associations   • Mutual savings banks   • Credit unions

up to $2500. Today the ceiling is $100,000. Members of the Federal Reserve System are required to purchase FDIC insurance; the program is voluntary for others. Today about 97 percent of the 15,000 commercial banks belong to the FDIC. Similarly, the Federal Savings and Loan Insurance Corporation (FSLIC) was established in 1934 to insure accounts in savings and loan associations. In 1989, about 90 percent of the 2900 savings and loan associations in the nation were insured by the FSLIC. *Federal insurance worked wonders to reduce bank runs by calming fears about the safety of deposits.*

Regulation Q The Great Depression was thought to have resulted in part from interest-rate competition among banks for customer deposits. To reduce such competition, the Fed was empowered under *Regulation Q* to set the maximum interest rates that could be paid on commercial bank deposits. A similar regulation was introduced years later for savings and loan associations. All interest-rate ceilings are somewhat loosely referred to as Regulation Q restrictions.

Restricting Bank Investment Practices As part of the Banking Act of 1933, commercial banks were forbidden to buy and sell corporate stocks and bonds. The belief was that these assets were too risky for commercial banks to hold. When commercial banks hold assets that fluctuate widely in value, the stability of the banking system is endangered. *The act limited bank assets primarily to loans and government securities.*

Branch Banking Restrictions

The United States has more commercial banks than any other country, and the ten largest commercial banks hold less than 30 percent of banking industry assets. In contrast, as few as five banks dominate the industry in other developed countries, such as Canada and the United Kingdom. *So the United States has many banks, and bank assets are distributed more evenly among banks in the United States than in other countries.* The proliferation of banks in this country reflects restrictions on *branches*, which are additional offices that carry out banking operations. Each state controls the type and number of branches that a bank can open. States on the East Coast and West Coast tend to be more lenient about branches than do states in between. Eight states, all in middle America, prohibit branching within the state. Federal legislation prohibits interstate branching. The combination of intrastate and interstate restrictions on branching spawned the many commercial banks that exist today, most of which are relatively small.

*A **bank holding company** is a corporation that owns banks.*

Two developments have allowed banks to skirt branching restrictions. The first is the rise of the bank holding company. A **bank holding company** is a corporation that may own several different banks; this arrangement allows the company to circumvent branching restrictions. Many states now permit holding companies to cross state lines and thereby get around federal prohibitions against interstate banking. Moreover, the holding company can provide other services that banks are not authorized to offer, such as financial advising, leasing, and credit card services. Finally, the holding company has the ability to attract funds from sources that are not available to banks. Holding companies have blossomed in recent years, and today more than three-quarters of the nation's demand deposits are in banks owned by holding companies. The nation's major banks are all owned by holding companies.

The other important development that has allowed banks to extend their presence is the invention of automatic teller machines. In some states banks have bypassed branching restrictions by having several banks share the same machine. Thus, *holding companies and automatic teller machines have allowed banks to avoid branching restrictions and thereby cover more territory.*

The Quiet Life of Depository Institutions

Restrictions imposed on depository institutions during the 1930s made this a heavily regulated industry, something like a public utility. The federal government insured most deposits. Depository institutions, in turn, surrendered much of their freedom to wheel and deal. The assets they could acquire were carefully limited, as were the interest rates they could offer depositors.

Households typically left their money in savings accounts earning 5 percent or less; checking deposits earned no interest. Banks and thrifts quietly accepted these deposits and made loans, earning their profit on the interest differential. The banking business became comfortable and was largely insulated from the rigors of competition. As the expression "banker's hours" suggests, banks closed at 2:00 or 3:00 in the afternoon and remained closed on weekends. Banking was considered stuffy, even boring. In this staid business climate, offering a free toaster as a deposit bonus was considered a bold move.

Thrifts, particularly savings and loan associations and mutual savings banks, were even more sheltered than commercial banks. They might pay 5 percent interest on deposits that were loaned out at 7 percent interest for thirty-year home mortgages. If the loan went into default and the mortgage had to be foreclosed, rising postwar housing values made the house worth more than the unpaid loan. Under the circumstances, it was difficult to make a bad mortgage loan. But the quiet world of banking was shaken by changes in the 1970s that ultimately led to the elimination of many restrictions introduced during the 1930s. Let's look at what happened.

RECENT PROBLEMS WITH DEPOSITORY INSTITUTIONS

*A **money market mutual fund** is a portfolio, or collection, of short-term interest-earning assets.*

The surge of inflation during the 1970s increased the level of interest rates in the economy, and the sleepy world of the banker has not been the same since. In October 1972, Merrill Lynch, a major brokerage house, introduced an account combining a **money market mutual fund** with check-writing privileges. Money market mutual fund shares represent a claim on a portfolio, or collection, of short-term interest-earning assets. By pooling the funds of many shareholders, the managers of a money market mutual fund can acquire a diversified portfolio of assets offering shareholders higher rates of interest than those offered by most depository institutions. Money market mutual funds proved to be stiff competitors for bank deposits.

Depository Institutions Were Losing Deposits

Because Regulation Q set ceilings on the interest rates that depository institutions could offer their depositors, this regulation for the most part eliminated interest-rate competition for deposits among depository institutions when interest rates were at or near the ceiling. Of course, depository institutions still competed for deposits in other ways, such as by offering toasters or providing drive-through windows. As long as the interest-rate ceilings were in accord with prevailing market rates of interest, the banking system as a whole did not have to worry about outside competition for customer deposits. Thus, in a world of relatively low interest rates, Regulation Q had served as an anticompetitive device that banks and thrifts found attractive. *When market interest rates rose above the ceiling banks and thrifts could offer, however, Regulation Q limited the ability of depository institutions to compete with other financial institutions for funds.* Many savers withdrew their deposits from banks and thrifts and put them into higher-yielding alternatives, such as money market funds.

As banks and thrifts lost deposits, they had to support their outstanding loans by borrowing at prevailing interest rates, which were typically higher than those being earned on their loans. Because their loans were typically for short periods, commercial banks encountered less of a problem when interest rates rose. Their problem could be resolved in the short run as outstanding loans were repaid. But thrifts had made loans for long-term mortgages, loans that had to be carried for years. *Because thrifts had to pay more interest to borrow funds than they were earning on these mortgages, they were in big trouble.*

Deregulation of 1980

In response to the problems facing depository institutions, Congress passed the *Depository Institutions Deregulation and Monetary Control Act of 1980,* the most significant banking legislation since the reforms of the 1930s. The "Depository Institutions Deregulation" part of the act gave banks and thrifts greater discretion in their operations. For example, the interest-rate ceilings for deposits were eliminated by 1986. Also, all depository institutions were authorized to offer checking accounts, and thrifts were given wider latitude in making loans.

The "Monetary Control" part of the act imposed uniform reserve re-quirements on all depository institutions, whether or not they were mem-bers of the Federal Reserve System. The act also gave all depository institu-tions equal access to the Fed's services, such as lending and clearing checks. These provisions largely eliminated distinctions between member and non-member commercial banks and also eliminated many important distinctions between commercial banks and thrifts.

All depository institutions were thus put on more equal footing and brought under greater control of the Fed. The Fed had pushed for such provisions, because many commercial banks had dropped their Fed membership when state regulations began to look more attractive than regulations imposed by the Fed. Such dropouts had reduced the Fed's ability to implement monetary policy.

Today, about one-third of all commercial banks are national banks, and two-thirds are state banks. National banks must belong to the Federal Reserve System; state banks may become members if they satisfy certain requirements. Of the 15,000 commercial banks in the United States, about 5800 are members of the Federal Reserve System. Because larger banks tend to belong to the system, member banks account for about 75 percent of the total deposits in commercial banks.

Further Deregulation of 1982

The U.S. banking system experienced more change and upheaval during the 1980s than at any other time since the Great Depression. Hundreds of troubled major banks such as Continental Illinois and First Republic Bank of Dallas were taken over by the FDIC or forced to merge with healthier banks. Other major banks remain in trouble, many with questionable loans still on the books. For example, huge loans extended during the 1970s by the nation's largest banks to developing countries, particularly in Latin America, are now long overdue. The amount of these loans often exceeds the bank's net worth. Also, the oil-industry depression of the mid-1980s and low agricultural prices hit some banks especially hard. Banks in Texas and Oklahoma failed because drilling and agricultural loans went sour. Between 1980 and 1988, 821 banks failed — 200 in 1988 alone, far more than had failed during the latter years of the Great Depression.

The 1980 banking reforms did not relieve the pressure on the ailing thrift industry. In 1980 there were about 4600 S&Ls in the United States; by the end of 1982 there were 780 fewer, a decline of 17 percent. In 1982 Congress passed the *Garn-St.Germain Act*, which expanded the borrowing power of federally chartered savings and loan associations and also improved their flexibility in acquiring assets. Additionally, all depository institutions were allowed to offer money market deposit accounts in order to compete more effectively with those money market funds already offered by other financial institutions. These accounts soon became very popular at depository institutions.

Some states, such as California and Texas, largely deregulated state-chartered savings and loan associations. The combination of deposit insurance, unregulated interest rates, and wide latitude in the kinds of assets that could be purchased gave savings and loan associations a green light to compete for large sums of money in national markets and to acquire assets as they pleased. Once-staid financial institutions moved into the fast lane.

Thus, with deregulation, thrifts could wheel and deal, but with the benefit of deposit insurance. Many troubled thrifts could attract funds only by offering high interest rates. The high rates they had to pay to attract deposits required thrifts to gamble for higher returns on the assets acquired. Some economists argue that deposit insurance encouraged the insured institutions to take unwarranted risks because they knew their depositors would be protected against bankruptcy. For people who managed depository institutions, gambles became "heads, we win; tails, federal insurers rescue our depositors." Many thrifts failed. The number of thrifts in existence had dropped from 3800 in 1982 to 2900 by 1989, including 500 that were expected to fail in the near future.

The number of failed thrifts and commercial banks did not reveal the full extent of the problem, however. Throughout most of the 1980s, regulatory authorities lowered their auditing standards to reduce the numbers of closings and to reduce the cash drain on the FDIC and FSLIC funds. Still, the FSLIC fund reserves fell from $6.4 billion in 1984 to minus $16 billion in 1988. Investigations of failed depository institutions turned up not only poor management but also outright criminal behavior.

Bailing Out the Thrifts

The insolvency and collapse of a growing number of thrifts prompted Congress in August of 1989 to approve the largest financial bailout of any industry in history—a measure estimated to cost at least $400 billion. The money is to be spent over a period of years to shut down failing thrifts and pay off insured depositors. Taxpayers are expected to pay nearly two-thirds of the total cost, with the thrift industry paying the remaining third through higher deposit insurance.

The measure abolished the FSLIC, along with the body that had regulated thrifts. Thrifts were put under the supervision of the U.S. Treasury, and thrift deposits became insured by a new fund established by the FDIC, the insurer of commercial bank deposits. The FDIC was also charged with selling the $400 billion in office buildings, shopping malls, apartment buildings, land, and other assets formerly held by insolvent S&Ls.

The bailout measure imposed new regulations on the composition of thrift portfolios. Thrifts are not allowed to buy junk bonds and must sell their current holdings of junk bonds within five years. Thrifts must now hold at least 70 percent of their assets in mortgages. The measure also made it easier for commercial banks to acquire thrifts. When the dust settles, failures and mergers could reduce the number of thrifts to as few as 1000. Despite the billions that will be spent on the rescue, more funds may yet be needed. Some experts believe that the 1989 bailout measure is just the first step toward ending the S&L crisis.

CONCLUSION

Banking has evolved from one of the most staid industries to one of the most variable. Deregulation and branching innovations have made it easier to enter the industry and have increased the kinds of activities that banks can undertake. Reforms have given the Fed more uniform control over all depository institutions and have given the institutions greater access to the services provided by the Fed. Thus, all depository institutions can compete on more equal footing.

Deregulation provides greater freedom not only to prosper but also to fail. Prior to the deregulation of the airline industry, no major carrier had failed; now they fail all the time. Similarly, in the Darwinian world of deregulated banking, only the fittest will survive. Failures of depository institutions create a special problem, however, because these institutions provide the financial underpinning of the nation's money supply, as we will see in the next chapter. There we will examine more closely how banks operate and how banks help supply the nation's money.

Summary

1. Barter was the first form of exchange. As the degree of specialization grew, it became more difficult to discover the double coincidence of wants required for barter. The time and inconvenience associated with barter led even simple economies to introduce money.

2. Money fulfills three primary functions: it serves as a medium of exchange, a standard of value, and a store of wealth. The first money was commodity money: a good such as corn or gold also served as money. With the second type of money, fiduciary money, what changed hands was a piece of paper that could be redeemed for something of value, such as silver or gold. The third type of money introduced was fiat money, which is paper money that cannot be redeemed for anything other than more paper money. Fiat money is given its status as money by law. Most currencies throughout the world today are fiat money.

3. People accept fiat money because they believe others will do so as well. The value of money depends on how much it will buy. If money fails to serve as a medium of exchange, traders will resort to some second-best means of exchange, such as barter, a careful system of record keeping, or some informal commodity money. When there is too much or too little money, more time must be devoted to ex-

change and less to production, so the economy's efficiency suffers.

4. The Federal Reserve System was established in 1914 to stabilize the banking system. After many banks failed during the depression, the powers of the Fed were increased and centralized. The Fed's control over all depository institutions was extended by legislation passed during the 1980s. The primary powers of the Fed are (1) to conduct open market operations (buying and selling government securities to control the money supply), (2) to establish reserve requirements for depository institutions, and (3) to set the discount rate (the rate at which depository institutions can borrow from the Fed).

5. Regulations introduced during the depression turned banking into a closely regulated and quite predictable industry. But high interest rates during the 1970s disturbed the quiet life of depository institutions. Reforms in the 1980s were designed to give depository institutions greater flexibility in competing with other kinds of financial institutions. Many thrifts used this flexibility to gamble on investments, but these gambles often failed, causing hundreds of thrifts to go bankrupt. In 1989 Congress approved a measure to pay off insured deposits in failed thrifts and to regulate the operations of remaining thrifts.

Questions and Problems

1. (Barter) Most of us have heard stories of the old general store, where many different goods could be exchanged. Why would such a store help reduce transactions costs in economies where there was a considerable amount of barter? Would flea markets that met twice a month have the same effect?

2. (Commodity Money) In medieval Japan rice was used for money. Why do you think this commodity was chosen to serve as money? What would happen to prices in general if there was a particularly good harvest one year?

3. (Store of Wealth) "If an economy had only two goods (both nondurable), there would be no need for money because exchange would always be between those two goods." Does this statement disregard some important function of money?

4. (Gresham's Law) Early in the history of the United States, tobacco was used as money. If you were a tobacco farmer and you had two loads of tobacco that were of different qualities, which would eventually be used for money and which for smoking? Under what conditions would both types of tobacco be used for money?

5. (Fractional Reserve Banking System) What factors or conditions in the economy would lead a bank to increase the fraction of its deposits held as reserves? Would a bank hold greater reserves during certain seasons? Why?

6. (Fiat Money) Most economists believe that fiat money has value only to the extent that people believe it will retain its value. What does this seemingly circular statement mean? How could people lose faith in that money?

7. (Savings and Loans) In the early 1980s, the number of savings and loan institutions in the United States decreased drastically. Why? How did the government deal with the situation?

8. (Federal Reserve System) Why are most Federal Reserve Banks located in the East?

9. (Bank Failures) Why has the steep reduction in the prices of oil and farmland led to the largest number of bank failures in the United States since the Great Depression? Would the United States be better off with higher oil prices and higher food prices? Why or why not?

10. (Regulation Q) Eurodollars are dollar-denominated deposits held in banks outside the United States. Such deposits earn high rates of interest. Did Regulation Q help to foster the development of the Eurodollar market?

11. (Money Versus Barter) "Without money, everything would be more expensive." This statement is both true and false. Explain.

12. (Money) Show that a barter system with n goods has $n(n-1)/2$ exchange rates but this same system with money added has only n exchange rates.

13. (Money) When monetary systems were based on monetary units whose values were determined by their gold content, new discoveries of gold were frequently followed by periods of inflation. Explain.

14. (Banks and Interest Rates) Banks and other financial intermediaries typically borrow short (e.g., accept short-maturity deposits) and lend long (e.g., offer thirty-year mortgages). Because long-term interest rates generally are higher than short-term rates, banks can "live off the spread." Why do you think that rising rates, even without Regulation Q, can create profit problems for banks?

15. (Deregulation) Some economists argue that deregulated deposit rates combined with deposit insurance have led to financial "black holes." Why do you think they make such an argument?

C H A P T E R   1 3

Depository Institutions, the Federal Reserve, and the Money Supply

In this chapter we take a closer look at the role of depository institutions in the economy. Why are we so interested in depository institutions? After all, isn't banking a business like any other—dry cleaning, clam digging, or house painting? Why not devote the chapter to house painting? Banks and other depository institutions are of special interest in macroeconomics because, like the London goldsmith, they can change a borrower's IOU into money. *Depository institutions have the ability to create money, and money is a key ingredient in a healthy economy.*

We will first consider the role of depository institutions in the economy and the types of deposits they hold. Then we will examine how depository institutions work and show how the money supply expands through the creation of deposits. We will also consider the operation of the Federal Reserve System in more detail. As we will see, the Federal Reserve attempts to control the growth of the money supply by controlling bank reserves. Topics discussed in this chapter include

- Checkable deposits
- Near moneys
- Monetary aggregates
- Bank's balance sheet

- Money creation process
- Money multiplier
- Sterilization

DEPOSITORY INSTITUTIONS, THEIR DEPOSITS, AND THE MONEY SUPPLY

Depository institutions attract their funds from savers, who make deposits out of habit or convenience, often for short periods. These funds are lent to borrowers, who are often too small or too poor a risk to secure funds through more formal means, such as issuing stocks or bonds in securities markets. Thus, *savers need a safe place for their money and borrowers need credit, and the depository institution tries to earn a profit by serving both groups.*

Depository institutions attempt to identify borrowers who are willing to pay interest but who also are able to repay the loans. At the same time, these institutions must attract and retain deposits from savers who believe their money will be looked after carefully. Hence, banks and thrifts try to present an image of sober dignity—an image meant to foster assurance. Even their names are selected to inspire depositor confidence. Depository institutions are more apt to be called First Trust, Security National, or Federal Savings than Benny's Bank, Easy Money Bank and Trust, or Last Chance Savings and Loan. In contrast, *finance companies* are financial intermediaries that do not get their funds from depositors, so they can choose names aimed more at borrowers, such as The Money Store and Household Finance.

Role of Depository Institutions

Depository institutions perform three important functions in the economy: (1) they serve as financial intermediaries; (2) they provide expertise in extending, structuring, and monitoring loans; and (3) they make many different loans and thereby reduce each saver's risk in the event that a borrower defaults. Let's consider each of these functions in greater detail.

Intermediation Depository institutions gather various amounts from those who are willing to save and package these funds into the amounts demanded by borrowers. The amount and duration of saving differs among savers. Some savers need their money back next week, some next year, some only after retirement. Likewise, the amount and duration of borrowing varies among borrowers. Depository institutions bring together savers and borrowers, matching amounts and durations to the preferences on each side of the market. They are able to repackage funds because there are so many savers and borrowers. By matching amounts and durations on each side of the market, depository institutions serve as financial intermediaries.

Expertise with Loans Because they specialize in making loans, depository institutions have the experience and expertise to evaluate and compare the credit worthiness of loan applicants. An individual saver who wanted to lend money directly to a corporation would ordinarily lack the background needed to evaluate the terms of the loan. Depository institutions also reduce the cost of contracting. Because they have abundant experience in drawing up and enforcing contracts with borrowers, they can do so more cheaply than could an individual saver. The economy is more efficient because depository institutions develop expertise in selecting loan candidates, structuring loans, and enforcing loan contracts.

Minimization of Risk Through Diversification By creating a diversified portfolio of assets rather than lending funds to a single borrower, depository institutions reduce the risk to each individual saver. All the eggs are not in one basket. A bank or thrift lends a tiny fraction of each saver's deposits to each of the many borrowers it finances. If one of these borrowers defaults, such a failure will hardly make a ripple in the balance sheet of a large, diversified depository institution. Certainly, such a failure does not represent the personal disaster it would if one saver's entire nest egg had been loaned directly to the failed borrower.

Depository institutions play a key role in determining the money supply. Let's take a look at the money supply to see how depository institutions fit into the process of providing money.

Money and Liquidity

*A **liability** is anything that is owed to another individual or institution.*

When a depository institution accepts a deposit, it promises to repay the depositor. The deposit therefore becomes an amount the depository institution owes—it becomes a **liability**. When the depository institution lends these funds to a borrower, the borrower's promise to repay these funds becomes an amount owed to the depository institution—it becomes an **asset**. Although the principle is the same, different kinds of depository institutions have different kinds of liabilities and assets.

*An **asset** is something of value that is owned.*

Suppose you have some cash in your pocket. If you deposit this cash in a checking account, you can then write checks instructing your bank to pay someone else money out of your account. When you think of money, what most likely comes to mind is currency—dollar bills and coins. In reality, however, money consists primarily of a particular class of bank liabilities—**checkable deposits**, or deposits against which checks can be written. Depository institutions hold a variety of checkable deposits. The most important checkable deposits over the years have been demand deposits, which are held by commercial banks and do not earn interest. In recent years financial institutions have developed other kinds of accounts that carry check-writing privileges while also earning interest, such as NOW accounts and credit union share draft accounts. *The number of these interest-bearing accounts expanded rapidly after Congress passed the Depository Institutions Deregulation and Monetary Control Act of 1980*, a bill discussed in the previous chapter.

***Checkable deposits** are deposits against which checks can be written.*

M1 is a measure of the supply of money in the form of currency and coin held by the public, checkable deposits, and traveler's checks.

The money supply is most narrowly defined as **M1**, which consists of currency (including coins) held by the nonbanking public, checkable deposits, and traveler's checks. Currency has been declared legal tender by the federal government; you'll recall that this means creditors must accept currency as payment for debts. Currency held by banks is not counted as part of the money supply. Checkable deposits are the liabilities of the issuing depository institutions, which stand ready to convert these deposits into currency. Checks are not legal tender, so sellers need not accept checks, as signs that say "No Checks!" attest. Yet checks are so widely accepted as a medium of exchange that checkable deposits are considered part of the money supply.

The primary currency is Federal Reserve notes, which are issued by and are the liability of the Federal Reserve banks (although the notes are actually printed by the U.S. Bureau of Engraving in Washington, D.C.). Federal Reserve notes are IOUs from the Fed to the bearer, but unlike other IOUs, they are paid off only with more IOUs. If you present a $20 bill to the Fed for redemption, you will receive your choice of two $10s, four $5s, twenty $1s, or some other combination of currency and coins totaling $20. Since Federal Reserve notes are redeemable for nothing other than more Federal Reserve notes, U.S. currency is fiat money, as noted in the previous chapter. The other component of currency is coins, manufactured and distributed by the U.S. Bureau of the Mint. Our coins are token coins because their metal value is much less than their face value.

Liquidity is the ease with which an asset can be exchanged for money without a significant loss of value.

The ease with which an asset can be converted into the medium of exchange without a significant loss of value determines its **liquidity**. The most liquid asset is money itself—currency held by the nonbanking public and checkable deposits, with currency being the more liquid of the two. In contrast, assets such as autos, real estate, and rare stamps are not very liquid. True, you could sell your car in minutes if you were willing to exchange it for a pittance, but selling your car at its market value would take time and involve some inconvenience.

Other Deposits: Near Moneys

We regard currency and checkable deposits as money because each serves as a medium of exchange, a standard of value, and a store of wealth. Some other kinds of assets appear to perform the standard-of-value and store-of-wealth functions as well and are also readily convertible to currency or to checkable deposits. Because these financial assets are so close to money, we call them **near moneys**. Near moneys are like money in all ways except that they do not serve as a medium of exchange; thus near moneys are less liquid than money. Important forms of near money include time deposits, savings deposits, and money market mutual fund accounts.

Near moneys are financial assets that are like money except that they do not serve as a medium of exchange.

Time deposits earn a fixed rate of interest if they are held for the specified period, which can range anywhere from thirty days to over eight years. Premature withdrawals are penalized. Commercial banks and savings and loan associations offer *nonnegotiable certificates of deposit*, which provide a fixed rate of interest on deposits of specific denominations, such as $5000 or $10,000. These financial assets are called nonnegotiable because depositors must usually hold them to maturity and cannot sell them to a third party.

Savings deposits earn interest but have no specific maturity date. Typically called *passbook savings accounts*, savings deposits are held in commercial banks, mutual savings banks, savings and loan associations, and credit unions. Neither time nor savings deposits serve directly as a medium of exchange, so they are not included in the narrow definition of money. A holder of a time or savings deposit who needs cash must make a trip to the bank, withdraw the money, and, in the case of time deposits, perhaps pay a penalty for early withdrawal.

Money market mutual fund accounts, discussed in the previous chapter, represent another near money. These very popular accounts are not viewed as money because of restrictions on the minimum balance, the number of checks that can be written per month, and the minimum amount of each check.

Because of the similarity between money and near moneys, we often broaden the definition of money to include near moneys. **Monetary aggregates** are various measures of the money supply used by the Federal Reserve. **M2** is a monetary aggregate that includes M1 plus savings deposits, small time deposits, and money market mutual funds. **M3** includes M2 plus *negotiable certificates of deposit*, which are issued by commercial banks to large savers in minimum denominations of $100,000. Negotiable certificates of deposit can be sold to a third party before maturity, hence they are "negotiable." In subsequent discussions when we refer to the "money supply," we will be talking about money as it is narrowly defined by M1.

The size and relative importance of each monetary aggregate are presented in Exhibit 1. As you can see, M2 is about four times larger than M1, and M3 is about five times larger. Thus, *the narrow definition of the money supply describes only a small fraction of the more broadly defined money supply*.

You may be curious about why we have not mentioned credit cards, such as VISA and MasterCard, in our discussion of money. After all, most stores accept credit cards as readily as they do cash or checks. Shouldn't credit cards therefore be included in any definition of money? Credit cards are not really money but simply a means of obtaining a short-term loan from the bank or other company that issued the card. If you purchase plane tickets for a trip to Florida using a credit card, the transaction is not complete until you repay the loan with money weeks or months after the purchase. The credit card has not eliminated the use of money; it has merely postponed the payment of money.

Of the variety of liabilities issued by depository institutions, checkable deposits are of most interest in macroeconomics.

Monetary aggregates are measures of the economy's money supply.

M2 is a monetary aggregate consisting of M1 plus savings deposits, small time deposits, and money market mutual funds.

M3 is a monetary aggregate consisting of M2 plus negotiable certificates of deposit.

HOW DEPOSITORY INSTITUTIONS OPERATE

Banks and thrifts are profit-making institutions in the business of taking people's money on deposit and lending out a large portion of that money, earning a profit on the interest differential. We could consider the operation of any type of depository institution (commercial bank, savings and loan, mutual savings bank, or credit union), but we will focus on commercial banks because they are the most important depository institutions in terms of total assets. The operat-

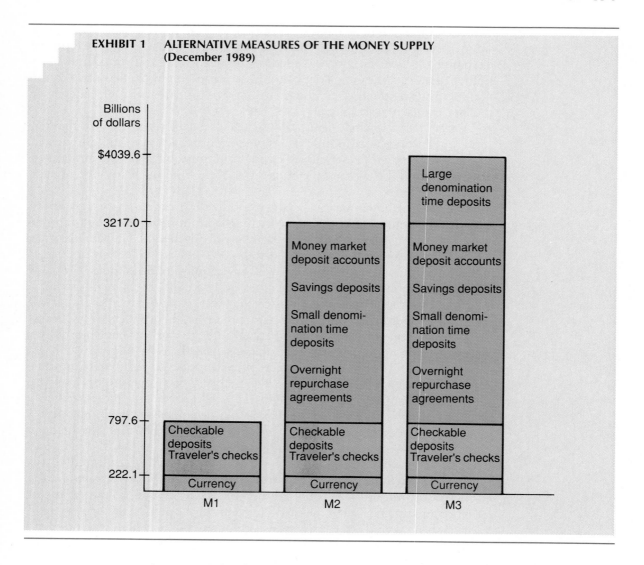

EXHIBIT 1   ALTERNATIVE MEASURES OF THE MONEY SUPPLY (December 1989)

ing principles that apply to credit expansion in commercial banks, however, generally apply to other depository institutions as well.

Starting a Bank

Let's begin with the formation of a bank. Suppose some business leaders in your home town decide to form a commercial bank called Home Bank. To obtain a *charter*, or the right to operate, they must apply to the U.S. Comptroller of the Currency in the case of a national bank or to the state banking authority in the case of a state bank. When the chartering agency reviews the application, it considers the quality of the bank's management, the amount of money the owners plan to invest in the bank, the need for an additional bank in the region, and the probable earnings of the bank.

Suppose the founders plan to invest $100,000 in the bank, and they so indicate on their application for a national charter. When their application is approved, they issue themselves shares of stock — paper certificates indicating ownership. Thus, they exchange $100,000 in cash for shares of stock in the bank. This stock, which provides evidence of ownership, is called the *owners' equity*, or the **net worth**, of the bank. Part of the owners' contribution, say $20,000, they use to buy shares in their district Federal Reserve bank, thereby establishing Home Bank as a member of the Federal Reserve System. (Recall that all national banks must belong to the Fed.) With the remaining $80,000, the owners acquire and furnish the bank building.

Net worth is the difference between an institution's assets and its liabilities.

To focus our discussion, we will examine the bank's **balance sheet**, presented in Exhibit 2. As the name implies, a balance sheet shows a balance between the two sides of the bank's accounts. The left-hand side lists the bank's assets. An asset is any physical property or financial claim owned by the bank. At this early stage, assets include the building and equipment owned by Home Bank plus its stock in the district Federal Reserve bank.

*A **balance sheet** is a financial statement that shows assets, liabilities, and net worth at a given point in time.*

EXHIBIT 2
HOME BANK'S BALANCE SHEET

Assets		Liabilities and Net Worth	
Building and furniture	$ 80,000	Net worth	$100,000
Stock in district Fed	20,000		
Total	$100,000	Total	$100,000

The right-hand side lists the bank's liabilities and net worth. So far the right-hand side includes only the net worth of $100,000, which equals the bank's assets to this point. The two sides of the ledger must always be equal, or in *balance* — hence the name balance sheet. Since the two sides must be in balance, assets must equal liabilities plus net worth:

Assets = liabilities + net worth

The bank is now ready to open. Opening day is the bank's lucky day, because its first customer comes in with a briefcase full of $100 bills and puts $1,000,000 into a checkable deposit account. As a result of this deposit, the bank's assets increase by $1,000,000 in cash, and its liabilities increase by $1,000,000 in checkable deposits. Exhibit 3 shows the effects of this transaction on Home Bank's balance sheet.

The customer has deposited $1,000,000 in the bank, and the bank owes the customer the amount deposited. On the right-hand side there are now two kinds of claims on the bank's assets: claims by the owners, called net worth, and claims by nonowners, called liabilities, which at this point consist of checkable deposits.

EXHIBIT 3 HOME BANK'S BALANCE SHEET AFTER $1,000,000 DEPOSIT			
Assets		**Liabilities and Net Worth**	
Cash	$1,000,000	Checkable deposits	$1,000,000
Building and furniture	80,000	Net worth	100,000
Stock in district Fed	20,000		
Total	$1,100,000	Total	$1,100,000

Reserve Accounts

Where do we go from here? As mentioned in the previous chapter, banks are required by the Federal Reserve System to set aside, or hold in reserve, a certain percentage of their deposits. Reserves can legally be held in two forms: as cash each bank keeps in its vault and as non–interest bearing reserve deposits at the Fed. The **required reserve ratio** dictates the *proportion* of deposits that must be held in reserve. **Required reserves**, the *dollar* amount that must be set aside, equal deposits multiplied by the required reserve ratio.

The ***required reserve ratio*** *is the proportion of deposits that a depository institution must hold in the form of reserves.*

Suppose the required reserve ratio on checkable deposits is 10 percent. Home Bank must hold an amount equal to 10 percent of its checkable deposits, or $100,000 ($0.10 \times \$1,000,000$), as required reserves. Before the banking act of 1980, only member banks were bound by the reserve requirements established by the Fed; nonmember banks were subject to reserve requirements determined by each state. *Now all banks are subject to the reserve requirements established by the Fed.*

Required reserves *are the actual reserves, expressed in terms of a dollar amount, that must be held; they equal the required reserve ratio times the amount of deposits.*

Suppose Home Bank opens a reserve account with the district Federal Reserve bank and deposits $100,000 in cash. Home Bank's balance sheet now looks like Exhibit 4, where reserves are divided between cash in the vault and deposits with the Fed. Home Bank's reserves exceed the required reserves by $900,000. Reserves in excess of required reserves are called **excess reserves**. A bank's total reserves therefore consist of required reserves plus excess reserves.

Excess reserves *are reserves held in excess of required reserves.*

So far Home Bank has not earned a penny. Excess reserves, however, can be used to make loans or to purchase other interest-bearing assets, such as government securities.

EXHIBIT 4

HOME BANK'S BALANCE SHEET AFTER DEPOSITING $100,000 WITH THE FED

Assets		Liabilities and Net Worth	
Deposits with Fed	$ 100,000	Checkable deposits	$1,000,000
Cash	900,000	Net worth	100,000
Building and furniture	80,000		
Stock in district Fed	20,000		
Total	$1,100,000	Total	$1,100,000

Competing Objectives: Liquidity Versus Profitability

Like the early goldsmiths, modern-day banks must be prepared to satisfy depositors' requests for funds. A bank loses reserves whenever a depositor demands cash or whenever a depositor writes a check that gets deposited in another bank. The bank wants to be in a position to satisfy all demands for its reserves, even if many depositors ask for their money at the same time or if many checks are written against its checkable deposits. Banks could fail if they lacked sufficient reserves to meet all depositor requests for funds. Required reserves are not meant to be used to meet depositor requests for funds, so banks often hold excess reserves or hold some assets that can be easily liquidated to satisfy any unexpected demand for funds. Banks may also want to have excess reserves on hand in case a valued customer needs an immediate loan.

The bank manager must therefore structure the portfolio of assets with an eye toward liquidity but must not forget that the bank's survival also depends on profitability. *The two objectives of liquidity and profitability are often at odds.* For example, the bank may find that the assets offering the highest interest rate tend to be less liquid than other assets. The most liquid asset is reserves, either on account with the Fed or in the bank's vault as cash, but reserves yield no interest. At one extreme, consider a bank that is completely liquid, holding all its assets as reserves. Such a bank would clearly have no difficulty meeting depositors' demands for funds. Since it held no interest-earning assets, however, the bank would earn no income and would fail. At the other extreme, imagine a bank that uses all its excess reserves to acquire high-yielding but highly illiquid assets, such as long-term loans. Such a bank would run into liquidity problems any time a withdrawal was made.

The bank portfolio manager's task is to strike just the right balance between liquidity and profitability. The manager's choice of assets is limited by legal restrictions on the kinds of assets a commercial bank can own. Recall that as a result of bank failures during the Great Depression, the kinds of assets banks can acquire were limited primarily to loans and government securities. We should note, however, that in recent years regulatory authorities have allowed banks greater latitude in the way they use their excess reserves.

Suppose Home Bank extends a $400,000 building loan to a local business. The bank also lends $100,000 to households for home improvements, car purchases, and other major consumer purchases. In addition to making loans, Home Bank also purchases $250,000 worth of U.S. government securities and $100,000 worth of other securities, primarily those issued by state and local governments. Finally, to ensure sufficient liquidity, the bank keeps $50,000 in cash as excess reserves. Exhibit 5 reflects Home Bank's revised balance sheet. The bank has exchanged $850,000 of its $900,000 in excess reserves for interest-earning assets. It still has $150,000 in reserves: $100,000 in required reserves on deposit with the Fed and $50,000 in excess reserves as cash in the vault.

EXHIBIT 5
HOME BANK'S BALANCE SHEET AFTER
PURCHASING ASSETS WITH EXCESS RESERVES

Assets		Liabilities and Net Worth	
Deposits with Fed	$ 100,000	Checkable deposits	$1,000,000
Cash	50,000	Net worth	100,000
Business loans	400,000		
Consumer loans	100,000		
U.S. government securities	250,000		
Other securities	100,000		
Building and furniture	80,000		
Stock in district Fed	20,000		
Total	$1,100,000	Total	$1,100,000

Since reserves earn no interest, depository institutions usually try to keep their excess reserves to a minimum. Banks do not let excess reserves remain idle even overnight. They continuously "sweep" their accounts to find excess reserves that can be put to some interest-bearing use.

The **federal funds market** provides for day-to-day lending and borrowing among banks of excess reserves on account at the Fed. For example, suppose that at the end of the business day Home Bank has excess reserves of $50,000 on account at the Fed and is willing to loan that amount to another bank that finished the day with a reserve deficiency of $50,000. These two banks are brought together by a broker who specializes in the market for federal funds—that is, the market for excess reserves at the Fed. The interest rate paid on this loan is called the **federal funds rate**, which is determined by the supply and demand for federal funds. Borrowers in the federal funds market tend to be large commercial banks in New York and Chicago that need reserves because of large, unexpected outflows of deposits.

The **federal funds market** *provides for day-to-day lending and borrowing of reserves among depository institutions.*

The **federal funds rate** *is the interest rate prevailing in the federal funds market.*

To get some feel for banks in the United States, consider the consolidated balance sheet for all commercial banks, shown in Exhibit 6. The consolidated picture bears some resemblance to that of our hypothetical bank, particularly on the assets side. On the liabilities side, bank deposits are sorted into three types: checkable deposits, savings deposits, and time deposits. The reserve requirement on savings and time deposits is lower than the reserve requirement on checkable deposits.

EXHIBIT 6
CONSOLIDATED BALANCE SHEET OF U.S.
COMMERCIAL BANKS AS OF NOVEMBER 1989
(billions of dollars)

Assets		Liabilities and Net Worth	
Deposits with Fed	$ 38.7	Checkable deposits	$ 602.5
Cash	196.1	Savings deposits	537.6
Loans	2187.6	Time deposits	1081.0
U.S. government securities	375.8	Borrowings	542.2
Other securities	173.7	Other liabilities	235.2
Other assets	229.5	Net worth	202.9
Total	$3201.4	Total	$3201.4

Source: *Federal Reserve Bulletin*, February 1990.

Before we discuss how Home Bank can create money, we must bring into the picture another important institution: the Federal Reserve. We will take a closer look at how the Fed operates, beginning with a simplified version of the Fed's balance sheet.

The Fed's Balance Sheet

In its capacity as a bankers' bank, the Fed clears checks for, extends loans to, and holds deposits of depository institutions. In its capacity as banker to the federal government, the Fed lends funds to the federal government by purchasing its securities and also holds deposits of the U.S. Treasury. Although the president appoints members of the Board of Governors, the Fed operates independently of Congress and the president, though both may try to influence the Fed.

The operation of Federal Reserve banks, like that of depository institutions, can be best studied by reviewing their balance sheet. Exhibit 7 presents a consolidated balance sheet for all Federal Reserve banks. *Over three-fourths of the Federal Reserve's assets are U.S. government securities.* These securities are assets of the Fed because they are IOUs from the federal government. Another asset is discount loans extended by the Fed to depository institutions. These loans are assets of the Fed because they are IOUs

EXHIBIT 7
CONSOLIDATED BALANCE SHEET OF FEDERAL RESERVE
BANKS AS OF NOVEMBER 1989
(billions of dollars)

Assets		Liabilities and Net Worth	
U.S. government		Federal Reserve notes	$235.3
securities	$223.1	Deposits of depository	
Discount loans to		institutions	37.3
depository institutions	0.2	U.S. Treasury deposits	5.5
Coin	0.5	Other liabilities	9.1
Other assets	68.7	Net worth	5.3
Total	$292.5	Total	$292.5

Source: *Federal Reserve Bulletin*, February 1990.

from the borrowing institutions. As we will see, an increase in either the Fed's securities holdings or its discount loans increases the reserves of depository institutions, which, in turn, allows the banking system to expand the money supply.

Turning now to the other side of the balance sheet, we can see that *Federal Reserve notes account for over three-fourths of the Fed's liabilities.* Just as the goldsmiths issued notes, the Fed issues financial claims on itself. These notes represent *accounting* liabilities to the Fed because note holders can redeem them with the Fed. As we have said, however, since we have a fiat money system, those who redeem notes are simply given other notes, so these *notes are not true economic liabilities.*

Since depository institutions can ask for their deposits back at any time, these deposits are another liability of the Fed. These deposits are an important part of bank reserves and facilitate the check-clearing process, which will be examined shortly. The deposits of the U.S. Treasury are also a liability of the Fed.

The two primary assets held by the Federal Reserve banks — government securities and discount loans — earn interest for Reserve banks, whereas their two primary liabilities — Federal Reserve notes and the deposits of depository institutions — require no interest payments by Reserve banks. *The Fed is therefore both literally and figuratively a money machine. It is literally a money machine because it provides the economy with Federal Reserve notes, and it is figuratively a money machine because its assets earn interest but its liabilities pay no interest.* The Fed finances its operations with this interest income. Since the Fed does not rely on congressional appropriations, Congress cannot attempt to influence the Fed by withholding funds. The Fed returns any surplus revenue to the Treasury. In 1989, for example, the Fed turned over about $18 billion to the Treasury.

What the balance sheet does not reflect is the Fed's responsibility for the stability of financial markets. The Fed, through its regulation of financial markets, tries to prevent major disruptions and widespread panics. For example, during the stock market crash of 1987, Fed Chairman Alan Greenspan worked behind the scenes to ensure that banks had enough liquidity to provide the essential borrowing needed to calm the panic. In 1989, when a similar crash threatened, the Fed again promised to supply the necessary liquidity.

HOW DEPOSITORY INSTITUTIONS CREATE MONEY

We are now in a position to examine how an individual depository institution and the banking system as a whole can affect the supply of money as defined by M1—currency plus checkable deposits and traveler's checks. Since you already have some acquaintance with balance sheets, we will consider only those entries that change. In the process we will also see how the Federal Reserve System can influence the money supply. *The key to the whole process is that an important liability of depository institutions, checkable deposits, circulates as a medium of exchange. When depository institutions acquire more assets, they can make more loans in the form of checkable deposits, creating more money.* Our discussion will focus on the behavior of commercial banks because these are the largest and most important of depository institutions, but you should keep in mind that thrifts can carry out similar activities.

Creating Money Through Excess Reserves

The Fed can affect the amount of banks' excess reserves by buying and selling government securities, lending reserves to banks through the discount window, and altering the required reserve ratio. The most important of these tools for implementing monetary policy is the buying and selling of government securities. Because the IOUs of the federal government are continually traded in the open market, the Fed's purchases and sales of these securities are called open market operations.

Assume that there are no excess reserves in the banking system initially and that the reserve requirement established by the Federal Reserve is 10 percent. To start the process rolling, suppose the Federal Reserve purchases a $1000 government security from Home Bank, increasing Home Bank's reserve account at the district Federal Reserve bank by $1000. The increase in Home Bank's deposits at the Fed represents an additional liability to the Fed.

Exhibit 8 shows *changes* in the Fed's and Home Bank's balance sheets. On the Fed's asset side, government securities are up by $1000, and on the Fed's liability side, Home Bank's deposits with the Fed are also up by $1000. Home Bank's balance sheet indicates that it has simply exchanged one asset, government securities, for another asset, reserves on deposit with the Fed.

So far the money supply has not changed because neither government securities nor Home Bank's reserves at the Fed are part of the money supply. Nor have Home Bank's total assets changed. But the increase in reserves will bring about an increase in the money supply, as we will observe in the following series of rounds.

EXHIBIT 8
CHANGES IN THE FED'S AND HOME BANK'S BALANCE SHEETS AFTER THE FED BUYS $1000 IN SECURITIES FROM HOME BANK

Fed's Balance Sheet

Assets		Liabilities and Net Worth	
U.S. securities	+ 1000	Depository institution deposits	+ 1000

Home Bank's Balance Sheet

Assets		Liabilities and Net Worth
Deposits with Fed	+ 1000	
U.S. securities	− 1000	

Round One After selling the security, Home Bank has $1000 in excess reserves. Since excess reserves burn the proverbial hole in the bank's pocket, the bank immediately puts these reserves to some interest-earning use. Suppose Home Bank is your regular bank and you apply for a $1000 student loan to help pay tuition. Home Bank approves your loan and consequently increases your checking account by $1000. Home Bank has converted your promise to repay the loan, your IOU, into a $1000 checkable deposit, thereby increasing the money supply by $1000. Home Bank has created money from your promise—it has created money out of thin air. Exhibit 9 shows how Home Bank's balance sheet changes as a result of the loan. On the asset side, loans increase by $1000 because your IOU becomes an asset to the bank. On the liability side, checkable deposits increase by $1000 because Home Bank has increased your account by that amount. Exhibit 9 also illustrates how your balance sheet changes. On the asset side, your checkable deposits are now up by $1000. On the other side, your loan from Home Bank increases your liabilities by $1000.

EXHIBIT 9
CHANGES IN HOME BANK'S BALANCE SHEET
AND YOUR BALANCE SHEET
AFTER HOME BANK LENDS YOU $1000

Home Bank's Balance Sheet

Assets		Liabilities and Net Worth	
Loans	+ 1000	Checkable deposits	+ 1000

Your Balance Sheet

Assets		Liabilities and Net Worth	
Checkable deposits	+ 1000	Loan from Home Bank	+ 1000

Round Two When you write a $1000 check to your college, your college promptly deposits the check in its checking account at College Bank. College Bank then increases the college's account by $1000 and presents the check to the Fed. The Fed reduces Home Bank's reserve deposits by $1000 and increases College Bank's reserve deposits by the same amount. The Fed then sends the check to Home Bank, which reduces your checkable deposits by $1000. The Fed has cleared your check by settling the claim that College Bank had on Home Bank. Consider the balance sheets in Exhibit 10, which reflect the changes after your check clears. Deposits at the Fed and checkable deposits are both down by $1000 at Home Bank and up by $1000 at College Bank. Checkable deposits have simply shifted from one bank to another.

Let's review what has happened to Home Bank's balance sheet. Home

EXHIBIT 10
CHANGES IN HOME BANK'S AND COLLEGE BANK'S
BALANCE SHEETS AFTER YOUR TUITION
CHECK TO COLLEGE BANK CLEARS

Home Bank's Balance Sheet

Assets		Liabilities and Net Worth	
Deposits with Fed	− 1000	Checkable deposits	− 1000

College Bank's Balance Sheet

Assets		Liabilities and Net Worth	
Deposits with Fed	+ 1000	Checkable deposits	+ 1000

Bank initially exchanged securities for excess reserves (Exhibit 8), then extended a loan based on your IOU by increasing your checking account by $1000 (Exhibit 9). When the check you wrote to your college cleared, Home Bank lost its excess reserves to College Bank and reduced your checking account by $1000 (Exhibit 10). Home Bank, by selling securities to the Fed and lending out the excess reserves, has exchanged one asset, government securities, for another asset, loans. But in the process the reserves in the banking system and the money supply have increased, for reserves and checkable deposits at College Bank are now up by $1000 and checkable deposits are money.

So College Bank has $1000 more in reserves on deposit with the Fed. After setting aside $100, or 10 percent of the college's growth in deposits, as required reserves, College Bank has $900 in excess reserves, which can be loaned, used to purchase some other interest-bearing asset, or simply left idle. Suppose these excess reserves are loaned to an enterprising business student who plans to open an all-night bait-and-doughnut shop to lure early morning anglers on their way to a nearby lake. College Bank extends the loan by providing the entrepreneur with a checking account balance of $900. As shown in Exhibit 11, College Bank's assets are up by the $900 loan, and its liabilities are up by the $900 increase in checkable deposits extended as a loan to the business student. *College Bank has converted the student's promise to repay the loan into money.*

EXHIBIT 11
CHANGES IN COLLEGE BANK'S BALANCE SHEET
AFTER MAKING A $900 LOAN

Assets		Liabilities and Net Worth	
Loans	+ 900	Checkable deposits	+ 900

Suppose the student spends the $900 on equipment at Wholesale Hardware, which deposits the check in its bank, Merchants Trust. Merchants Trust increases the hardware store's checkable deposits by $900 and sends the check to the Fed for clearance. The Fed increases Merchants Trust's reserve deposits by $900 and decreases College Bank's reserve deposits by the same amount. The Fed then sends the check to College Bank, which reduces the borrower's checkable deposit account by $900.

Exhibit 12 shows the effects of these transactions on the balance sheets of the two banks. As you can see, deposits at the Fed and checkable deposits are down by $900 at College Bank and up by that amount at Merchants Trust. Checkable deposits in the banking system at this point are $1900 over what they were before we started: your college has $1000 more in checkable deposits at College Bank because you paid tuition, and the hardware store

EXHIBIT 12

**CHANGES IN COLLEGE BANK'S AND MERCHANTS TRUST'S
BALANCE SHEETS AFTER THE BORROWER'S CHECK
FOR $900 TO HARDWARE STORE CLEARS**

College Bank's Balance Sheet

Assets		Liabilities and Net Worth	
Deposits with Fed	− 900	Checkable deposits	− 900

Merchants Trust's Balance Sheet

Assets		Liabilities and Net Worth	
Deposits with Fed	+ 900	Checkable deposits	+ 900

has $900 more in its account at Merchants Trust because of the enterprising student's equipment purchase.

Round Three and Beyond Merchants Trust holds $90 of the $900 deposited as required reserves, which leaves $810 in excess reserves. Suppose this $810 is loaned to an unscrupulous English major who is starting a new venture called "Term Papers 'R' Us." The English major hopes to sell research to students with more money than brains. Exhibit 13 shows that Merchants Trust's assets are up by $810 in loans, and its liabilities are up by the same amount in checkable deposits.

EXHIBIT 13

**CHANGES IN MERCHANTS TRUST'S BALANCE SHEET
AFTER MAKING $810 LOAN TO ENGLISH MAJOR**

Assets		Liabilities and Net Worth	
Loans	+ 810	Checkable deposits	+ 810

The loan is spent at the college bookstore for a complete set of *Cliff's Notes*. The bookstore then deposits the check in its account at Fidelity Bank. Fidelity Bank credits the bookstore's checkable deposits and sends the check to the Fed for clearance. The Fed reduces Merchants Trust's reserves by $810 and increases Fidelity Bank's by the same amount. The Fed then sends the check to Merchants Trust, which reduces the English major's checkable deposits by $810. Exhibit 14 presents the changes in the balance sheets of Merchants Trust and Fidelity Bank after the check clears. Deposits at the Fed

EXHIBIT 14
CHANGES IN MERCHANTS TRUST'S AND FIDELITY BANK'S BALANCE SHEETS AFTER ENGLISH MAJOR'S CHECK TO BOOKSTORE CLEARS

Merchants Trust's Balance Sheet

Assets		Liabilities and Net Worth	
Deposits with Fed	− 810	Checkable deposits	− 810

Fidelity Bank's Balance Sheet

Assets		Liabilities and Net Worth	
Deposits with Fed	+ 810	Checkable deposits	+ 810

and checkable deposits are down by $810 for Merchants Trust but up by the same amount for Fidelity Bank.

Recall that checkable deposits at Merchants Trust initially increased by $900 as a result of the hardware store's deposit. After Merchants Trust extended a loan, its checkable deposits were briefly up by an additional $810 until the borrower's check to the bookstore cleared. After the check cleared, deposits at the Fed and checkable deposits were down by $810 for Merchants Trust but up by the same amount for Fidelity Bank.

At this point checkable deposits in the banking system, and the money supply in the economy, are up by $2710: your college's $1000 deposit at College Bank, plus the hardware store's $900 deposit at Merchants Trust, plus the bookstore's $810 deposit at Fidelity Bank. We could continue the credit expansion process with Fidelity Bank, which sets aside $81 in required reserves and uses the $729 in excess reserves as a basis for additional loans, but by now you get the idea.

Notice the pattern of deposits and loans emerging from the analysis. Each time a bank receives new deposits, 10 percent is set aside to satisfy the reserve requirement. The balance represents excess reserves, which can be lent, used to purchase securities, or left idle. In our example excess reserves were lent and then spent by the borrower. This spending became another bank's checkable deposits, thereby generating excess reserves to fund still more loans. Thus, the excess reserves created initially by the Federal Reserve's securities purchase were passed from one bank to the next in the chain. Each bank set aside 10 percent of new deposits as required reserves and loaned out the remaining 90 percent.

An individual bank in a banking system can lend no more than its excess reserves because borrowers usually spend the amount borrowed. When a check clears, it reduces the reserves for one bank but does not reduce reserves for the banking system as a whole. A check drawn against one account will typically be deposited in another account—if not in the same bank, then in another. Thus, when a bank makes a loan and creates deposits, the excess reserves on which that loan was based find their way back into the banking system. The recipient bank uses the new deposit to extend more loans and create more deposits. The potential expansion of checkable deposits in the banking system therefore equals some multiple of the initial increase in excess reserves.

Summary of Rounds

To review: The initial and most important step in the process described in the preceding section is the injection of $1000 in new reserves into the banking system, which results from the Federal Reserve's purchase of government securities. Home Bank uses this $1000 in excess reserves to offer you a college loan. You pay your college bill, and your college deposits the check in its bank. This deposit precipitates a series of rounds that expand the money supply. These rounds are summarized in Exhibit 15, where the banks are listed along the left-hand margin. Column (1) lists the increase in checkable deposits (and reserves) at each bank, column (2) lists the increase in required reserves resulting from the increase in checkable deposits, and column (3) lists the increase in loans each bank extends as a result of the increase in checkable deposits. As you can see, the change in loans equals the change in checkable deposits minus the change in required reserves. Each bank loans out an amount equal to its excess reserves.

The increase in College Bank's checkable deposits is the change in the money supply arising from the first round. This $1000 deposit translates into $900 in loans plus $100 in required reserves. The $900 lent by College Bank ends up as checkable deposits in Merchants Trust, which sets aside $90 in required reserves and lends the balance of $810. The loan is spent and is deposited in an account at Fidelity Bank, which sets aside 10 percent and

EXHIBIT 15
SUMMARY OF THE CREDIT EXPANSION PROCESS
RESULTING FROM THE FED'S PURCHASE
OF $1000 IN U.S. SECURITIES
FROM HOME BANK

Bank	Increase in Checkable Deposits (1)	Increase in Required Reserves (2)	Increase in Loans (3) = (1) − (2) (3)
1. College Bank	$ 1,000	$ 100	$ 900
2. Merchants Trust	900	90	810
3. Fidelity Bank	810	81	729
All remaining rounds	7,290	729	6,561
Totals	$10,000	$1,000	$9,000

lends the balance of $729. Theoretically, the process will continue until there are no more excess reserves in the system to serve as a basis for additional loans.

The banking system increases the money supply by a multiple of new reserves and thereby appears to perform magic. Can banks simply create credit balances out of thin air? As we have seen, the answer is yes. However, since people borrow money not to hold idle checkable deposits but to spend the borrowed funds, banks must have enough excess reserves to back up their loans. Credit expansion stops when the new reserves introduced into the banking system have been converted into required reserves. In our example, $1000 in new reserves was introduced when the Fed purchased securities from Home Bank. The credit expansion process stopped when the increase in required reserves resulting from credit expansion equaled $1000.

Some Other Possibilities

Suppose that, instead of buying the $1000 worth of securities from Home Bank, the Fed buys them from a securities dealer and pays by issuing $1000 in Federal Reserve notes. Exhibit 16 shows the resulting change in the Fed's and the dealer's balance sheets. The Fed acquires assets of $1000 in securities; liabilities increase by $1000 in the form of new Federal Reserve notes. The securities dealer's balance sheet simply reflects a change in the mix of financial assets, with securities down by $1000 and currency up by the same amount. The Fed has increased the money supply by $1000 by exchanging Federal Reserve notes, which are part of the money supply when in the hands of the public, for government securities, which are not part of the money supply. Once the securities dealer puts this cash into a

EXHIBIT 16
CHANGES IN THE FED'S AND SECURITIES DEALER'S BALANCE SHEETS AFTER THE FED PURCHASES $1000 IN SECURITIES FROM THE DEALER AND PAYS WITH $1000 IN FEDERAL RESERVE NOTES

Fed's Balance Sheet

Assets		Liabilities and Net Worth	
U.S. securities	+ 1000	Federal Reserve notes	+ 1000

Securities Dealer's Balance Sheet

Assets		Liabilities and Net Worth
U.S. securities	− 1000	
Cash	+ 1000	

checkable deposit—or spends the cash, so the money ends up in someone else's checkable deposit—the banking system's credit expansion process will be off and running.

Recall that when the Fed buys government securities from banks, bank reserves are increased; *the excess reserves serve as fuel for the money expansion process.* When the Fed buys securities from the nonbanking public, such as securities dealers, the money supply is increased directly. When deposited in banks, these new deposits generate excess reserves to fuel the money expansion process. Thus, whether the Fed buys securities from banks or from the public, the purchase sooner or later increases bank reserves, thereby promoting the expansion of credit.

The Fed expands the money supply when it purchases government securities, but it also expands the money supply whenever it pays for anything else, from the salaries of the Board of Governors to new carpeting for its Washington, D.C. offices. Conversely, the Fed reduces the money supply when it sells government securities, but it also reduces the money supply whenever it sells anything else, from Fed publications to used furniture. In this chapter we limited discussion of the Fed's buying and selling to government securities because open market operations represent the overwhelming share of the Fed's total buying and selling. Since the Fed is the only bank with the authority to print money, it is the only bank not constrained by reserve requirements. Indeed, the expressions "required reserves" and "excess reserves" do not apply to the Fed. Thus, the Fed has quite a free hand to print whatever money it needs.

Excess Reserves, Reserve Requirements, and Credit Expansion

*The **money multiplier** is the multiple by which the money supply increases as a result of an increase in the banking system's excess reserves.*

*The **simple money multiplier** equals the reciprocal of the required reserve ratio, or 1/r.*

One way the banking system as a whole eliminates excess reserves is by expanding credit. With a 10 percent reserve requirement, an initial injection of $1000 in new reserves by the Fed may support a maximum of $10,000 in checkable deposits in the banking system as a whole, assuming no bank holds excess reserves and nobody withdraws cash. We can think of the $1000 injection as the source of the $1000 in reserves required to support the expansion of $10,000 in new checkable deposits.

The multiple by which the money supply increases as a result of an increase in the banking system's excess reserves is called the **money multiplier**. The **simple money multiplier** equals the reciprocal of the required reserve ratio. The simple money multiplier is therefore $1/r$, where r is the reserve requirement. In our example the reserve requirement was 10 percent, or 0.10, so the reciprocal is $1/0.10$, which equals 10. The formula for the multiple expansion of checkable deposits can be written as

$$\text{Change in checkable deposits} = \text{change in excess reserves} \times 1/r$$

If depository institutions hold no excess reserves, then total reserves must equal checkable deposits times the reserve requirement. Or, total reserves divided by the reserve requirement must equal checkable deposits. Since we assume that banks are "all loaned up," any increase by the Fed in bank reserves is an increase in excess reserves. Thus, if the Fed increases bank reserves, the potential increase in checkable deposits equals the increase in excess reserves divided by the reserve requirement, which is the multiple expansion formula just presented.

Thus, *the simple money multiplier indicates by what multiple checkable deposits can be expanded based on a given amount of excess reserves introduced into the banking system. The simple multiplier assumes that banks hold no excess reserves and the public withdraws no cash.* The higher the reserve requirement, the more of each deposit that must be held as reserves, so the less there is available in excess reserves, and the smaller the money multiplier. If the reserve requirement were 20 percent instead of 10 percent, each bank would have to set aside twice as much for required reserves. The simple money multiplier in this case would be $1/0.20 = 5$, and the potential increase in checkable deposits resulting from an initial $1000 increase in excess reserves would therefore be $1000 \times 5 = \$5000$. Deposits in the banking system could be expanded by only half as much as when the reserve requirement was 10 percent. Excess reserves fuel the deposit expansion process, and a higher reserve requirement drains this fuel from the banking system, thereby reducing the money multiplier.

On the other hand, with a reserve requirement of only 5 percent, banks would set aside less for required reserves and would consequently be able to make more loans because they would have greater excess reserves. The simple money multiplier in that case would be $1/0.05 = 20$. With $1000 in new reserves and a 5 percent reserve requirement, the banking system could increase the money supply by $1000 \times 20 = \$20,000$.

In summary, it all begins with an injection of new reserves into the banking system by the Fed. An individual bank loans only an amount equal to its excess reserves. The proceeds of this loan are redeposited in the banking system and serve as the basis for additional excess reserves. With the help of a cooperative public that redeposits funds, the banking system is able to create money. An increase in bank reserves gives rise to a multiple expansion of checkable deposits, and checkable deposits are money. *The fractional reserve requirement is the key to the multiple expansion of checkable deposits in the banking system.* If each deposit had to be backed by 100 percent reserves, each $1 injected into reserves could create at most a $1 expansion of the money supply; there would be no multiple expansion of the money supply.

Now that we have been through the entire money expansion process, we can return to the beginning and consider what would happen if Home Bank, instead of extending loans, used its excess reserves to purchase securities. If Home Bank purchases securities from the public, those who sell securities will deposit their receipts in checking accounts and these fresh deposits will fuel the money creation process. For the money multiplier to operate, the bank need not use excess reserves in a specific way; the bank could use them to pay all its employees a Christmas bonus, for that matter. *As long as the bank does not allow excess reserves to sit idle and does not simply buy government securities from the Fed, these excess reserves can fund an expansion of the money supply.*

Limitations of Money Expansion

Various leakages from the multiple expansion process tend to reduce the magnitude of the money multiplier, which is why we refer to $1/r$ as the *simple money multiplier*. Here we will consider leakages into cash and into excess reserves. Our example assumed that people never choose to withdraw a portion of their new deposits in cash. *To the extent that people do prefer to hold cash, the actual money multiplier is less than the simple money multiplier because cash withdrawals reduce reserves in the banking system.* With a reduction in reserves, banks have less ability to extend loans or buy securities. Likewise, if banks chose to allow their excess reserves to sit idle, these idle reserves would not fuel expansion of the money supply. However, since banks earn no interest on idle reserves but do earn interest on loans and investments, banks carefully monitor their excess reserves, keeping them as low as possible.

Multiple Contraction of Money and Credit

We have already outlined the mechanics of the banking system, so the story of how the Federal Reserve System can reduce bank reserves, thereby reducing banks' ability to increase loans, can be a brief one. Again, we begin with no excess reserves and a reserve requirement of 10 percent. Suppose that, rather than buying securities, the Fed *sells* Home Bank $1000 worth of government securities. Home Bank pays with a check written against its reserve account at the district Federal Reserve bank. The Fed therefore reduces Home Bank's reserve account by $1000. As Exhibit 17 indicates, the Fed's assets have declined by the $1000 by which the government securities have been reduced. On the liability side is a $1000 reduction in Home Bank's deposits with the Fed. Home Bank's balance sheet indicates the change in the composition of assets: its deposits with the Fed are down by $1000, and securities are up by that amount.

Because Home Bank had no excess reserves at the outset, something has to give. To replenish reserves, Home Bank can recall loans, sell some other asset, or borrow additional reserves. Suppose Home Bank calls in loans amounting to $1000, and those who repay the loans do so with checks written against College Bank. When the checks clear, Home Bank's reserves are up by $1000, just enough to satisfy the reserve requirement, but College Bank's reserves are down by $1000. Since we assumed that there were no excess reserves at the outset, the loss of $1000 in reserves leaves College Bank short of its required reserves. Specifically, in keeping with the legal reserve requirement, College Bank had $100 in required reserves supporting the $1000 checkable deposits, so its reserves are $900 below the required level. College Bank must therefore recall $900 in loans or otherwise try to replenish its depleted reserves.

EXHIBIT 17
**CHANGES IN BALANCE SHEETS AFTER THE FED
SELLS $1000 IN SECURITIES TO HOME BANK**

Fed's Balance Sheet

Assets		Liabilities and Net Worth	
U.S. securities	− 1000	Depository institution deposits	− 1000

Home Bank's Balance Sheet

Assets		Liabilities and Net Worth
U.S. securities	+ 1000	
Deposits with Fed	− 1000	

And so it goes down the line. The Federal Reserve's sale of securities reduces bank reserves, forcing banks to recall loans or to replenish reserves somehow. *The maximum possible effect is to reduce the money supply by the amount of the original reduction in bank reserves times the simple money multiplier, which again equals 1 divided by the reserve requirement, or 1/r.* In our example the Fed's sale of $1000 in government securities to Home Bank leads to a reduction in the money supply of up to $10,000.

The Fed and the Money Supply

Note the control that the Fed has over the money creation process. Through open market operations, the Fed can vary the supply of new reserves by buying or selling government securities. In our example it was the purchase of $1000 worth of government securities that started the ball rolling. The Fed can also increase reserves by lending reserves to banks through the discount window. Finally, the Fed can control the availability of excess reserves by varying reserve requirements. As we have seen, the smaller the reserve requirement, the greater the excess reserves available from a given deposit and the greater the money multiplier.

The Fed is also an active trader in foreign exchange markets. Foreign currency operations are carried out by the FOMC through the New York Fed's foreign trading desk in cooperation with the U.S. Treasury. Some of the "other" Fed assets listed back in Exhibit 7 are securities issued by foreign governments. For example, the Fed can sell West German securities and

Sterilization is the process whereby the Fed uses open market operations to offset the effects of its foreign currency transactions on the domestic money supply.

receive marks in exchange. The marks can then be used to buy dollars from a U.S. bank. These transactions increase the supply of marks and the demand for dollars, thereby affecting the exchange rate. Buying dollars from the U.S. bank, however, also reduces the bank's reserve deposits at the Fed, thus affecting the domestic money supply. If the Fed wants to influence the exchange rate without affecting the domestic money supply, it can engage in offsetting open market operations in a process called **sterilization**. For example, the sale of marks to a U.S. bank may be offset by the purchase of U.S. government securities.

CONCLUSION

Depository institutions play a unique role in the economy because they can transform someone's IOU into a checkable deposit, and a checkable deposit is money. The banking system's ability to expand the money supply depends on the amount of excess reserves in the system. Thus, if the Fed wants to pursue an expansionary monetary policy, it can (1) purchase government securities either from depository institutions or from the public, (2) lower the discount rate to encourage depository institutions to borrow from the Fed through the discount window, or (3) reduce the reserve requirement to create more excess reserves and increase the money multiplier. If it wants to pursue a tight monetary policy, one aimed at slowing the growth of the money supply, the Fed can (1) sell government securities, (2) raise the discount rate, or (3) increase the reserve requirement.

In practice, the Fed rarely changes the reserve requirement because of the disruptive effect of such a change on the banking system. And the Fed uses changes in the discount rate more as a signal of its policy goals than as a means of altering the money supply. *The Fed relies primarily on open market operations to control the money supply.* In the next chapter we will consider the effects of the money supply on the economy.

Summary

1. Depository institutions are unlike other businesses in that they can turn a borrower's IOU into money—they can create money. Depository institutions match the varying desires of savers for particular amounts and durations of saving with the varying desires of borrowers. Depository institutions evaluate loan applications and they develop diversified portfolios of assets to minimize the risk to any one saver.

2. The money supply is most narrowly defined as M1, which consists of currency held by the nonbanking public plus checkable deposits and traveler's checks. Broader monetary aggregates include other kinds of deposits. M2 includes M1 plus savings deposits, small time deposits, and money market mutual funds. M3 includes M2 plus large time deposits, or what are called negotiable certificates of deposit.

3. In acquiring portfolios of assets, depository institutions attempt to maximize profits while simultaneously maintaining liquidity sufficient to satisfy depositors' demands for funds. There is often a tradeoff between profitability and liquidity.

4. Any single bank can expand the money supply by the amount of its excess reserves. The banking system as a whole, however, can expand the money supply by an amount equal to the excess reserves in the banking system times the money multiplier. The simple money multiplier equals the reciprocal of the reserve ratio.

5. The Fed tries to direct monetary policy through its control over excess reserves in the banking system. The key to changes in the money supply is the effect of the Fed's actions on excess reserves in the banking system. To pursue an expansionary monetary policy, the Fed can buy government securities, lower the discount rate, or lower the reserve requirement. To pursue a tight monetary policy, the Fed can sell government securities, increase the discount rate, or increase the reserve requirement. The most important monetary tool for the Fed is open market operations — buying or selling U.S. securities.

Questions and Problems

1. (Demand Deposits) Checks are not used in some countries, such as Japan and Taiwan. What costs are associated with relying only on currency? What benefits might there be? Why do you think such countries elect to avoid demand deposits?

2. (Near Moneys) Coke is a good substitute for Pepsi. Coffee is probably a poor substitute. How can the same principle be applied to the various types of money? Are a hundred pennies a perfect substitute for a dollar bill?

3. (Bank Balance Sheets) Show how each of the following initially affects bank assets and liabilities. Assume a required reserve ratio of 0.05.

   a. The Fed purchases $10 million worth of securities from banks.

   b. The Fed loans the banking system $5 million.

   c. The required reserve ratio is raised to 0.10.

4. (Reserves) Technically bank reserves are defined as vault cash plus bank deposits held at the Federal Reserve. These can be divided between required reserves and excess reserves. Usually banks hold some positive amount of excess reserves. During the Great Depression, excess reserves rose dramatically.

What reasons can you suggest for this increase?

5. (Reserve Requirements) Explain why a reduction in the required reserve ratio cannot increase reserves in the banking system. Is the same true of discount loans from the Fed? What would happen if the Fed bought securities from or sold securities to the banking system?

6. (Money Supply) Why are there different measures of money (for example, M1 and M2)? Could one measure of money rise while another measure fell? How?

7. (Money Supply) Suppose that $1000 is moved from a savings account at a commercial bank to a checking account at the same bank. Which of the following statements will be true and which will be false?

   a. The level of currency will initially fall.

   b. The level of M1 will initially rise.

   c. The level of M2 will initially rise.

   d. The level of bank reserves will increase.

8. (Money Supply) Often it is claimed that banks create money by making loans. How can private banks create money? Isn't the government the only institution that can legally create money?

9. (Credit Cards) Many people have complained recently about the high interest rates consumers are being charged for the use of credit cards. What are the arguments for and against the high rates?

10. (Money Multiplier) Suppose that the Federal Reserve lowers the required reserve ratio from 0.10 to 0.05. How will this affect the money multiplier, assuming that excess reserves are held to zero and there are no currency leakages?

11. (Bank Balance Sheet) Show how each of the following would affect a bank's balance sheet.

    a. Someone makes a $10,000 deposit.

    b. The bank makes a $3000 cash loan.

    c. The bank makes a line-of-credit loan of $1000 by establishing a checking account for $1000.

    d. The line-of-credit loan gets spent.

    e. The bank has to write off a loan because the borrower defaults.

12. (Bank Management) Explain why the bank's manager must strike a balance between liquidity and profitability on the bank's balance sheet.

13. (Money Creation) Suppose Bank A, which faces a reserve requirement of 10 percent, receives a $1000 deposit.

    a. Assuming it wishes to hold no excess reserves, determine how much the bank should lend. Show your answer on Bank A's balance sheet.

    b. Assuming that the loan shown in Bank A's balance sheet is redeposited in Bank B, show the changes in B's balance sheet as it lends out the maximum possible.

    c. Repeat this process for Banks C, D, and E.

    d. Using the simple money multiplier, calculate the total change in the money supply resulting from the $1000 initial deposit.

    e. Calculate the changes in the balance sheets for Banks A, B, C, D, and E if each wished to hold 5 percent excess reserves. How would this level of excess reserves affect the total change in the money supply?

14. (Reserve Requirements) As part of the Monetary Control Act of 1980, the Fed was given the power to set reserve requirements for *all* depository institutions. Because the effect was to increase the reserve ratio for many institutions, the changes were phased in over a seven-year period. Why do you think such a long phase-in period was selected?

Monetary Theory and Policy

Monetary policy is the Fed's role in supplying money to the economy.

Monetary theory is the study of the effect of money on the economy.

Thus far we have focused on how money is created in the banking system. We have established that the Federal Reserve can influence the supply of money in the economy. The Fed's role in supplying money to the economy is called **monetary policy**. The problem of modern monetary policy is *how* the Fed should use this power. More fundamentally, what is the relation between the supply of money and the economic health of the economy?

The study of the effect of money on the economy is called **monetary theory**. A central concern of monetary theory is the effect of the quantity of money on the economy's price level and on the level of output. What have economic theory and the historical record taught us about the relation between the quantity of money in the economy and other macroeconomic variables?

Until now we have not emphasized differences among competing theories of the economy. The role of money in the economy, however, remains subject to debate. In this chapter we will consider two approaches to the way money affects the economy: the Keynesian view and the monetarist view. The Keynesian view will be discussed first because we have already used it to develop the concept of aggregate demand. Then we will consider the monetarist view and show how the two are related. Our discussion will present a simplified version of each theory, ignoring variations among subscribers' interpretations. Note that although these two theories are different, they are not mutually exclusive. Each emphasizes different aspects of the economy, and each contributes to our overall understanding of how the economy works. Many economists subscribe to elements of both theories.

Topics discussed in this chapter include

- Demand for money
- Supply of money
- Keynesian view of monetary policy
- Monetarist view of monetary policy

- Equation of exchange
- Velocity of money
- Monetary targets

THE DEMAND AND SUPPLY OF MONEY

We begin with an important distinction: the distinction between *money* and *income*. Earlier we explained the difference between stocks and flows. You will recall that a stock is an amount measured at a particular point in time, such as the amount of food in your refrigerator or the amount of gasoline in your car's tank. In contrast, a flow is an amount per unit of time, such as the calories you consume per day or the miles you drive per week.

How much money do you have with you right now? That amount is a stock. Likewise, the *stock* of money in the economy is measured at a particular point in time; it equals the amount people have with them (both currency and traveler's checks) and the amount deposited in their checking accounts, plus any money squirreled away in mattresses, coffee cans, or wherever. Income, in contrast, is a *flow*, indicating how many dollars you receive per period of time. Income has little meaning unless the time period is specified. You would not know whether to be impressed that a friend earned $100 unless you knew whether this was earnings per week, per day, or per hour.

The demand for money is a desire to hold a particular amount of money. It may seem odd at first to be talking about the demand for money. You might think that people would demand all the money they could get their hands on. But remember that money, the stock, is not the same as income, the flow. People express their demand for income by selling their labor and other resources. People express their demand for money by holding money even though there is an opportunity cost of doing so. But we are getting ahead of ourselves.

The question we want to ask initially is why people demand money. Why do people maintain cash balances in their checking accounts and have money in their purses or wallets? The most obvious reason people demand money is because it is a convenient medium of exchange. People demand money to carry out transactions.

The Demand for Money

Because barter represents an insignificant portion of exchange in the modern industrial economy, households, firms, governments, and foreigners need money to conduct their daily transactions. Consumers need money to buy products, and firms need money to pay for resources. When credit cards are involved, the payment of money is delayed, but all accounts must eventually be settled with money. Thus, *money allows people to carry out their economic transactions more easily.*

The demand for money to support exchange is called the **transactions demand for money**. The greater the number of transactions to be financed in a given period, the greater the quantity of money demanded for transactions. So the more active the economy—that is, the greater the volume of exchange as measured by real GNP—the greater the transactions demand for money. Also, the higher the average selling price of each unit of output, the greater the transactions demand for money. The more things cost, the more dollars required to purchase them.

Your transactions demand for money supports both expenditures you expect in the course of your normal economic affairs and certain unexpected expenditures. If you plan to buy lunch tomorrow, you will carry enough money to pay for it. But you also want to be able to pay for other possible contingencies. For example, you could have car trouble or you could come across an unexpected sale on a favorite item. You may have a little extra money with you right now for who knows what. Even *you* don't know.

The transactions demand for money is rooted in money's role as a medium of exchange. As we have seen, however, money is more than a medium of exchange; it is also a store of wealth. Because a household's income and expenditures are not perfectly matched each period, purchasing power is often stored to finance future expenditures. People save for a new home, for college, for retirement. The Keynesian view of money focuses on two ways in which people can store their purchasing power: (1) in the form of money (currency, traveler's checks, and checkable deposits—what we have defined as M1) and (2) in the form of other financial assets, such as bonds. When people purchase bonds and other financial assets, they are lending their money and are paid interest for doing so.

The demand for any asset depends on the flow of services it provides. The big advantage of money as a store of wealth is its liquidity: money can be immediately exchanged for whatever is for sale. In contrast, other financial assets must first be *liquidated*, or exchanged for money, which can then be used to buy goods and services. Money, however, has one major disadvantage when compared to other types of financial assets. Until the recent monetary reforms, money earned no interest at all. Even after the reforms, only a fraction of M1 earns interest, and the rate of interest earned is typically below that earned on other financial assets.

So those who hold their wealth in the form of money forgo some interest that could be earned on some other financial asset. For example, suppose a corporation could earn 5 percent more by holding financial assets other than money. The opportunity cost of holding $10 million as money rather than as some other financial asset would amount to over $40,000 per month. The interest forgone represents the opportunity cost of holding money. When interest rates are high, as they were during the early 1980s, people move their money out of checkable deposits and into higher-yielding assets, such as money market mutual funds.

Money Demand and Interest Rates

When the market rate of interest is low, other things constant, the cost of holding money — the cost of liquidity — is low, so people hold a larger fraction of their wealth in the form of money, as narrowly defined. When the market rate of interest is high, the cost of holding money is high, so people hold less of their wealth in money and more of their wealth in other financial assets. Thus, other things constant, the quantity of money demanded varies inversely with the market rate of interest.

The money demand curve, D_m, in Exhibit 1 shows the quantity of money people demand at alternative interest rates, other things constant. *The money demand curve slopes downward because the lower the interest rate, the lower the opportunity cost of holding assets as money.* Movements along the curve reflect the effects of changes in the interest rate on the quantity of money demanded. *Held constant along the curve are the price level and the level of real GNP. If either increases, the transactions demand for money increases, which shifts the money demand curve to the right.*

Supply of Money and the Equilibrium Interest Rate

The supply of money — the stock of money available in the economy at a particular time — is determined primarily by the Fed. We can express the

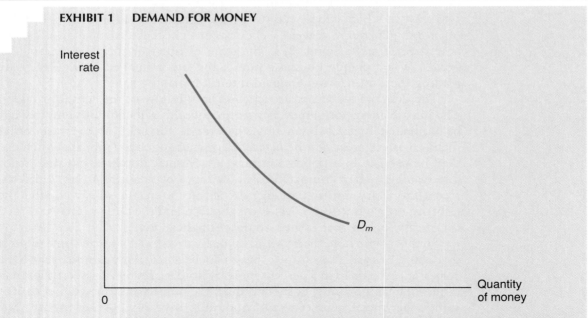

EXHIBIT 1   DEMAND FOR MONEY

The demand for money curve, D_m, slopes downward. As the interest rate falls, so does the opportunity cost of holding money; the quantity of money demanded increases.

supply of money, S_m, as a vertical line, as in Exhibit 2. *By drawing the supply curve as a vertical line, we are making the simplifying assumption that the quantity supplied is independent of the interest rate.* (In reality, financial institutions tend to hold fewer excess reserves as the interest rate rises, so the money supply is directly related to the interest rate; that is, the money supply curve tends to slope upward.)

The intersection of the supply of money, S_m, and the demand for money, D_m, determines the equilibrium rate of interest, i: the interest rate that equates the quantity of money supplied in the economy with the quantity of money demanded. At interest rates above the equilibrium level, the opportunity cost of holding money is higher, so the quantity of money people want to hold is less than the existing supply. At interest rates below the equilibrium level, the opportunity cost of holding money is lower, so the quantity of money people want to hold is greater than the existing supply.

If the Fed increases the money supply, the money supply curve shifts to the right, as shown by the movement from S_m to S'_m in Exhibit 2. The quantity supplied now exceeds the quantity demanded at the original inter-

EXHIBIT 2   EFFECT OF AN INCREASE IN THE MONEY SUPPLY

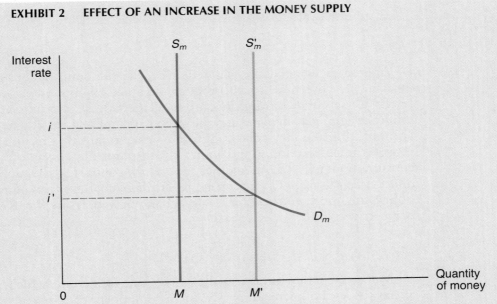

Since the supply of money is determined by the Federal Reserve, it can be represented by a vertical line. The intersection of the supply of money, S_m, and the demand for money, D_m, determines the equilibrium interest rate, i.

Following an increase in the money supply to S'_m, the quantity of money supplied exceeds the quantity demanded at the original interest rate, i. People who are holding more money than they would like attempt to exchange money for bonds or other financial assets. In doing so, they drive the interest rate down to i', where quantity demanded equals the new quantity supplied.

est rate, i. Because of the increased supply of money, there is more money in the hands of the public. People thus are *able* to hold a greater quantity of money, but at interest rate i they are *unwilling* to hold that much. Since people are now holding more of their wealth as money than they would like, they attempt to exchange money for other financial assets, such as bonds.

Because people are more willing to exchange money for other financial assets, the interest rate declines. The interest rate falls until people are both *willing* and *able* to hold the increased supply of money. With the decline in the rate of interest to i' in Exhibit 2, the opportunity cost of holding money falls just enough that the public is willing to demand, or to hold, the greater quantity of money supplied. *For a given demand for money, increases in the supply of money lower the rate of interest, and decreases in the supply of money raise the rate of interest.*

Now that you have some idea how money demand and supply determine the market rate of interest, you are ready to see how money fits into the model of the macroeconomy we have developed thus far. Specifically, we will observe how changes in the supply of money affect aggregate demand and equilibrium output.

MONEY AND AGGREGATE DEMAND

Aggregate demand, as you will recall, is the sum of consumption, investment, government expenditures, and net exports at various price levels. We saw that through fiscal policy, the federal government tries to influence aggregate demand and the level of income and employment in the economy. Fiscal policy affects aggregate demand directly through changes in government spending and indirectly through the effects of taxes on consumption, investment, and net exports. In contrast to the more or less direct effects fiscal policy has on aggregate demand, the effects of monetary policy are more indirect, at least when viewed from the Keynesian perspective.

Interest Rates and Planned Investment

Monetary policy influences the market rate of interest, which, in turn, affects the level of planned investment, a component of aggregate demand. Let's work through the sequence of causality in a specific economic setting. Suppose the Federal Reserve believes that the economy is operating well below its potential level of output and decides to increase the money supply to stimulate output and employment. Recall that the Fed can expand the money supply by (1) conducting open market operations (that is, purchasing government securities), (2) lowering the discount rate (the rate at which banks can borrow from the Fed), or (3) lowering reserve requirements. Open market operations are by far the most important monetary tool.

As we have seen, the opportunity cost of holding money—the interest

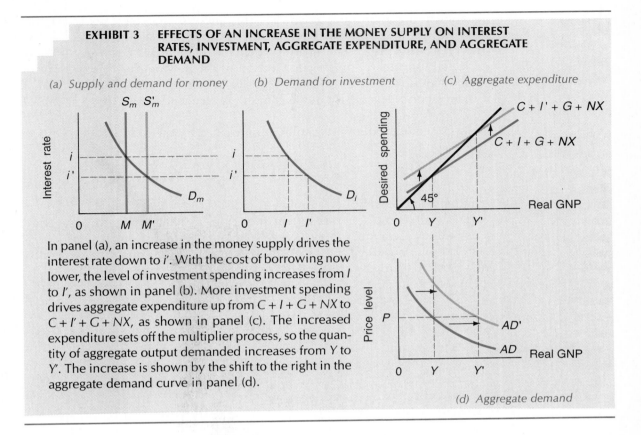

EXHIBIT 3   **EFFECTS OF AN INCREASE IN THE MONEY SUPPLY ON INTEREST RATES, INVESTMENT, AGGREGATE EXPENDITURE, AND AGGREGATE DEMAND**

(a) Supply and demand for money   *(b) Demand for investment*   *(c) Aggregate expenditure*

(d) Aggregate demand

In panel (a), an increase in the money supply drives the interest rate down to i'. With the cost of borrowing now lower, the level of investment spending increases from I to I', as shown in panel (b). More investment spending drives aggregate expenditure up from $C + I + G + NX$ to $C + I' + G + NX$, as shown in panel (c). The increased expenditure sets off the multiplier process, so the quantity of aggregate output demanded increases from Y to Y'. The increase is shown by the shift to the right in the aggregate demand curve in panel (d).

rate—depends on the supply and demand for money. Suppose the Fed purchases government securities and thereby increases the money supply, as shown in panel (a) of Exhibit 3 by the shift to the right in the money supply curve from S_m to S'_m. With the increase in the supply of money, people end up holding more of their wealth in money than they would like at interest rate i, so they try to exchange one form of wealth, money, for other financial assets.

This greater willingness to lend has no direct effect on aggregate demand, but it does reduce the interest rate from i to i'. A decline in the interest rate, other things constant, reduces the opportunity cost of financing purchases of new plant and equipment, thereby making new business investment more profitable. Likewise, a lower interest rate reduces the cost of a mortgage on new housing, so housing investment increases. Thus, the decline in the rate of interest increases the quantity of investment demanded. Panel (b) shows the demand for investment, D_i. As you can see, when the interest rate falls from i to i', the quantity of investment demanded increases from I to I'.

The aggregate expenditure function in panel (c) shifts up by the increase in autonomous investment, from $C + I + G + NX$ (where NX equals the value of exports minus the value of imports) to $C + I' + G + NX$.

The spending multiplier magnifies this increase in investment, leading to a greater increase in the equilibrium quantity of real GNP demanded at the prevailing price. The quantity demanded increases from Y to Y', as reflected in panel (c) by the intersection of the new aggregate expenditure function with the 45-degree line. This same increase is also reflected in panel (d), given price level P, by the shift in the aggregate demand curve from AD to AD'.

The sequence of events can be summarized by the following flowchart:

$$M\uparrow \rightarrow i\downarrow \rightarrow I\uparrow \rightarrow (C + I + G + NX)\uparrow \rightarrow AD\uparrow \rightarrow Y\uparrow$$

An increase in the money supply, M, reduces the interest rate, i. The lower interest rate stimulates investment spending, I, which shifts the aggregate expenditure function, $C + I + G + NX$, up, increasing the quantity of aggregate output demanded from Y to Y'. This increase in the quantity demanded at a particular price level is reflected by a shift to the right in the aggregate demand curve, AD.[1]

We will now trace the same sequence in reverse, although we will dispense with the graphs. (You provide them.) Suppose the Federal Reserve decides to reduce the growth in the money supply to cool down an over-heated economy. Given the money demand curve, a reduction in the supply of money means that people are now holding less money than they would like at the existing interest rate. The excess demand for money at the initial interest rate means that people will attempt to exchange other financial assets for money. These efforts to get more money do not affect the stock of money, but they do raise the interest rate, or the opportunity cost of holding money. The interest rate increases until the quantity of money demanded declines enough to just equal the reduced money supply.

At the higher interest rate, businesses find it more costly to finance plants and equipment and households find it more costly to finance new homes. Hence, a higher rate of interest reduces the quantity of investment de-manded. The resulting decline in investment is magnified by the autono-mous spending multiplier, leading to a greater decline in aggregate demand.

As long as money demand and investment demand are each sensitive to changes in the interest rate — that is, as long as each demand curve slopes downward — changes in the supply of money affect aggregate demand. The extent to which a given change in investment affects aggregate demand depends on the size of the autono-mous spending multiplier.

---

[1] The graphs are actually a bit more complicated than those we have presented. Since the demand for money depends on the level of real GNP, an increase in the quantity of real GNP demanded would shift the money demand curve to the right in panel (a). For simplicity, we have not shown a shift in the money demand curve. If we had shifted the money demand curve, the equilibrium interest rate would still have fallen, but not by as much, so investment and aggregate demand would not have increased by as much.

Money and the Shape of the Aggregate Demand Curve

When we introduced the aggregate demand curve, we offered two reasons for its shape. You may recall that because consumers hold some dollar-denominated assets (assets such as money and bonds), any change in the price level changes the real value of their assets. If the price level increases, the value of the dollar-denominated assets decreases, thereby reducing the wealth of consumers who own such assets. Since consumers are poorer, they now want to save more, so they spend less. This drop in consumption reduces the quantity of aggregate output they demand. Conversely, when the price level decreases, the value of dollar-denominated assets increases. Since consumers are wealthier, they reduce saving and increase consumption, thereby increasing the quantity of aggregate output demanded. Hence, the first reason the aggregate demand curve slopes downward is because changes in the price level affect the real value of money holdings and other dollar-denominated assets.

A second rationale for the shape of the aggregate demand curve stems from the effect of the price level on net exports. As the U.S. price level increases, other things constant, U.S. products become more costly to foreigners and foreign products become relatively cheaper to Americans. So exports decrease and imports increase, causing net exports to fall. Since net exports are a component of aggregate expenditure, a fall in net exports results in a decline in the quantity of aggregate output demanded.

Based on the discussion of money and the interest rate, we are now in a position to explore an additional reason for the shape of the aggregate demand curve. Money is demanded primarily to carry out transactions—to pay for goods and services. The amount of money required to finance transactions depends on the price level, among other things. The higher the price level, the higher the average dollar cost of each transaction, and the more money it takes to pay for a given level of real GNP. So the demand for money increases as the price level increases, other things constant. For a given supply of money, an increase in the demand for money leads to a higher interest rate. An increase in the interest rate raises the opportunity cost of investment, reducing the quantity of planned investment. This decline in investment reduces the quantity of aggregate output demanded.

The two panels of Exhibit 4 represent this relationship graphically. Panel (a) shows the economy's supply and demand for money, and panel (b) shows the aggregate demand curve. We begin with an interest rate of i in panel (a) and a price level of P in panel (b). The equilibrium interest rate is determined by the intersection of the money supply curve, S_m, and the money demand curve, D_m; this intersection occurs at point a in panel (a). Note that D_m is the demand for money when the price level is P. Point a in panel (b) indicates that when the price level is P, the quantity of real GNP demanded is Y.

If the price level increases to P', the amount of money needed to fund a given level of transactions increases, so the demand for money shifts to the

**EXHIBIT 4   EFFECT OF A CHANGE IN THE PRICE LEVEL ON QUANTITY
DEMANDED**

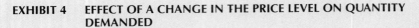

(a) *Supply and demand for money*   (b) *Aggregate demand*

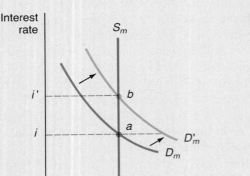
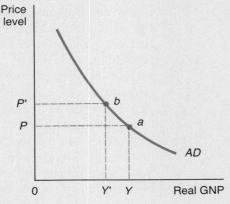

An increase in the price level from P to P' increases the transactions demand for money from D_m to D'_m and drives the interest rate up from i to i'. The rise in the interest rate reduces investment spending and aggregate expenditure. Through the multiplier process, the quantity of aggregate output demanded falls from Y to Y'. Panel (b) shows that higher price levels are associated with lower quantities of real output demanded. Changes in the price level lead to movements along the aggregate demand curve.

right, from D_m to D'_m in panel (a). People demand more money at every interest rate. An increase in the demand for money means that there is now an excess demand for money at the initial interest rate, i.

People try to get more money to support transactions at the higher price level by exchanging some of their other financial assets for money. But S_m is the existing money stock; there is no more. *As they try to get more money, people drive up the interest rate, which is the opportunity cost of holding money and the reward for lending it.* The interest rate rises until the quantity of money demanded just equals the given supply of money, as shown by equilibrium point b in panel (a).

An increase in the interest rate has a now-familiar effect on the quantity of aggregate output demanded. When the interest rate increases, investment becomes more costly, so investment spending declines. Thus, as the price level increases from P to P' in panel (b), the higher demand for money drives up the interest rate and reduces the quantity of investment demanded. This decline in investment results in a reduction in the quantity of aggregate output demanded from Y to Y', reflected by the movement along the aggregate demand curve in panel (b) from point a to point b.

In summary, the aggregate demand curve is drawn assuming a given supply of money in the economy. Changes in the price level alter the amount of money required to carry out transactions, thereby shifting the money demand curve. A higher price level leads to a higher interest rate, which results in less investment and a decrease in the quantity of aggregate output demanded. A lower price level leads to a lower interest rate, resulting in more investment and an increase in the quantity of aggregate output demanded. This relation between the price level and the interest rate provides another important reason why the aggregate demand curve slopes down to the right.

Adding Aggregate Supply

Even after we determine the effect of a change in the money supply on aggregate demand, we still have only half the story. To determine the ultimate effects of monetary policy on the equilibrium level of real GNP in the economy, we must introduce the supply side. We need an aggregate supply curve to tell us how a given shift in aggregate demand affects real GNP and the price level. In the short run, the aggregate supply curve slopes upward, so the quantity supplied will expand only if the price level increases. *For a given shift in the aggregate demand curve, the steeper the short-run aggregate supply curve, the smaller the increase in real GNP and the larger the increase in the price level.*

Assume the economy is producing at point *e* in Exhibit 5, where the aggregate demand curve, *AD*, intersects the short-run aggregate supply curve, *SRAS(P*)*, yielding a short-run equilibrium output of *Y* and a price level of *P*. As you can see, the actual price level is below the expected price level of *P**, so the short-run equilibrium output is below the economy's potential of *Y**. The contractionary gap equals the difference between *Y* and *Y**. (Output levels below the economy's potential are shaded in pink, and those above that potential are shaded in blue.)

The Fed can wait to see whether natural market forces close the gap by shifting the aggregate supply curve to the right. Or the Fed can intervene and attempt to close the gap with an expansionary monetary policy. Suppose the Fed decides to increase the money supply in order to lower interest rates and increase investment. The increased investment, magnified by the autonomous spending multiplier, shifts aggregate demand from *AD* out to *AD**. Recall that the autonomous spending multiplier is computed at a given price level. If the price level were to remain at *P*, equilibrium would shift out from *e* to *e'*, increasing equilibrium output from *Y* to *Y'*.

Once we introduce aggregate supply, it becomes obvious that the price level cannot remain constant. At the original price level, *P*, the quantity demanded, *Y'*, exceeds the quantity supplied, *Y*, so the price level rises. Because the aggregate demand curve has a negative slope, quantity demanded decreases as the price level increases. At the same time, the rising price level increases the quantity supplied. If the Fed increases the money supply by exactly the appropriate amount, the new equilibrium is achieved where the new aggregate demand curve intersects the aggregate supply

EXHIBIT 5   **EXPANSIONARY MONETARY POLICY TO CORRECT
A CONTRACTIONARY GAP**

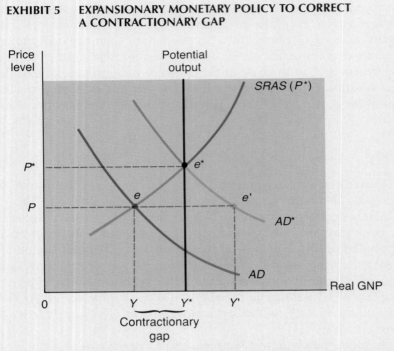

At point e, the economy is producing below potential. There is a contractionary
gap equal to $Y^* - Y$. If the Federal Reserve increases the money supply, the
aggregate demand curve shifts to AD^*. At the old price level, P, the quantity of
output demanded is Y' but the quantity supplied is Y. The excess demand causes
the price level to rise. Equilibrium will be reestablished at point e^*, with price level
P^* and output at the potential level, Y^*.

curve (point e^*), so the economy is producing its potential output. Given all
the connections in the chain of causality between changes in the money
supply and changes in equilibrium output, not to mention the international
effects on the value of the dollar, it would actually be quite difficult for the
Fed to execute such a precise monetary policy—but more on that later.

To review: An initial increase in the money supply reduced the rate of
interest, resulting in an increase in investment and a consequent increase in
aggregate demand. As aggregate demand increased along a given short-run
aggregate supply curve, both equilibrium price and output increased. *As long
as the short-run aggregate supply curve slopes upward, the short-run effect of an
increase in the money supply is an increase in both output and the price level.*

Fiscal Policy with Money

Now that we have introduced the effects that money has on aggregate
demand and equilibrium output, we can take another look at the effects of

fiscal policy, this time incorporating monetary effects. Suppose there is an increase in government spending, other things constant. In Chapter 11 we found that an increase in government spending increases aggregate demand and, in the short run, leads to both a greater output and a higher price level. Once money enters the picture, however, we must recognize that an increase in either real output or the price level increases the demand for money.

Thus, an increase in government spending increases money demand. For a given supply of money, an increase in money demand leads to a higher interest rate. But a higher interest rate *reduces* the quantity of investment demanded. We therefore say that the fiscal stimulus of government spending *crowds out* some investment. (Crowding out will be considered more carefully in a later chapter.) This reduction in investment will, to some extent, dampen the expansionary effects of fiscal policy on real output. Hence, *the inclusion of money in the fiscal framework introduces yet another reason why the simple spending multiplier overstates the increase in real output arising from any given fiscal stimulus.*

Moreover, any fiscal policy designed to reduce aggregate demand will be tempered by monetary effects. Suppose government spending is reduced in an attempt to cool inflation. As aggregate demand declines, equilibrium output and the price level fall in the short run. With a lower level of output and a lower price level, less money is needed to carry out transactions, so the demand for money falls. Again, with the supply of money unchanged, a drop in the demand for money leads to a lower interest rate. This drop in the interest rate stimulates investment spending, to some extent offsetting the effects of the drop in government spending. Thus, *for a given supply of money, the impact of changes in the demand for money on interest rates reduces the effectiveness of fiscal policy.*

Monetarism *is a school of thought that emphasizes the effects of changes in the money supply on economic activity.*

In the Keynesian framework, money influences aggregate demand and equilibrium output through its effect on the interest rate. Another framework, called **monetarism**, focuses more directly on the effects of changes in the money supply on aggregate demand. We now introduce this approach.

MONETARISM AND THE QUANTITY THEORY

The Keynesian approach assumes that the only alternative to holding money as a store of wealth is holding other *financial* assets. In this view, an increased supply of money makes people want to exchange money for other financial assets, which lowers the rate of interest and stimulates investment. Thus, changes in the money supply affect aggregate demand through changes in the interest rate. Another group of economists, called *monetarists*, concurs that money works through interest rates, but they also see a more direct role for money in aggregate spending.

Monetarism

The father of modern monetarism is Milton Friedman, the economist profiled in this chapter. Friedman argues that people hold their wealth in several forms. Money is just one asset among many that can serve as a store of wealth. In addition to other financial assets, people hold *real* assets, such as real estate, cars, and video recorders. An increase in the money supply means that at the initial interest rate the quantity of money supplied exceeds the quantity demanded. People are therefore holding more of their wealth in the form of money than they would like. As they attempt to reduce their money holdings, people increase their demand for all kinds of assets, including homes and other durable goods. So in the monetarist view, an increase in the supply of money increases the demand for a variety of real assets. This increased desire to spend increases aggregate demand directly. Monetarists rely on a framework called the equation of exchange, which we will examine next.

The Equation of Exchange

The **equation of exchange** says that the quantity of money, M, multiplied by its velocity, V, equals nominal income—the product of the price level, P, and real GNP, Y.

Every transaction in the economy involves a two-way swap: the seller surrenders goods and services for money, and the buyer surrenders money equal in value to the asking price. One way of expressing this relation among key variables in the economy is the **equation of exchange**, first developed by the classical economists. Although this equation can be arranged in different ways depending on the variables to be emphasized, the basic version is

$$M \times V = P \times Y$$

The **velocity of money** is the average number of times per year a dollar is used to purchase final goods and services.

where M is the quantity of money in the economy; V is the **velocity of money**, or the average number of times per year each dollar is used to purchase final goods and services; P is the price level; and Y is real national output, or real GNP. The equation of exchange says that the quantity of money in circulation, M, multiplied by the number of times that money turns over (changes hands), V, equals the price level of products sold, P, times the quantity sold, Y. The price level, P, times real output, Y, equals the economy's nominal income and output.

Consider a simple economy in which total sales during the year consist of 1000 bags of popcorn at $1 each and 1000 six–packs of Pepsi at $3 each. The price level of output produced is $2 per unit, and total output equals 2000 units. The nominal value of output, $P \times Y$, equals 2×2000, or $4000, which also equals the income received by resource suppliers.

Suppose the total money supply in this economy is $500. How often is each dollar used on average to pay for purchases during the year? In other words, what is the velocity of money? If $500 is used to pay for $4000 in output, each dollar must be used an average of eight times during the year. We can derive the velocity by rearranging the equation of exchange to yield

$$V = \frac{P \times Y}{M} = \frac{\$4000}{\$500} = 8$$

Milton Friedman
(b. 1912)

The Great Depression was a cataclysmic event not only in society but also in economic thought. It was widely perceived—and continues to be widely perceived—as a failure of the market system. Keynesian economics formalizes this perception, arguing that the market system requires continual deliberate adjustment to stay in balance and achieve full employment.

But this view of the Great Depression is by no means universal—least of all among economists. According to many economists, the depth and severity of the depression resulted not from the failure of the unfettered economy but precisely from mismanaged attempts to regulate that economy. The most influential voice in this corner belongs to Milton Friedman. In Friedman's view, it is the U.S. Federal Reserve System that is largely to blame for turning an ordinary bank panic into the worst economic crisis of the modern world.

Bold opinions of this sort are Friedman's stock-in-trade. And his disagreements with Keynesian economists go well beyond the diagnosis of the causes of the Great Depression. Friedman is the modern-day father of monetarism, a set of related theories linking monetary policy to inflation and other macroeconomic effects. In *A Monetary History of the United States*, Friedman and coauthor Anna Schwartz detailed the close historical relationship between the price level and the quantity of money, a relation captured in the equation $MV = PY$. Friedman's version of monetarism first gained prominence in the 1950s and 1960s, and represents an attack on Keynesianism that is as significant as Keynes's own attack on classical economics.

One implication of Friedman's views is that discretionary control of the economy by government—Keynesian "fine-tuning," as it is sometimes called—may cause more harm than good. For one thing, Friedman would replace discretionary monetary policy at the Fed with a fixed rule for growth in the money supply.

Milton Friedman was born to poor immigrant parents in New York City. He was educated at Rutgers and Columbia universities, and he spent most of his professional life at the University of Chicago, where he was a leader in the postwar Chicago School of Economics. This school is noted not only for monetarism but also for influential views on the nature of economic reasoning, microeconomic theory, and the role of economic freedom in society. Friedman received the Nobel Prize in 1976.

Richard Langlois

Given the value of total output and the money supply, each dollar on average must have turned over eight times. There is no other way purchases could have been made. Velocity is implied by the values of the other variables.

Classical economists developed the equation of exchange as a way of explaining how much money was needed to finance a given amount of spending. The equation says that total spending ($M \times V$) is always equal to total receipts ($P \times Y$), as was the case in our circular flow analysis. As described thus far, however, the equation of exchange is simply an *identity*—a relation expressed in such a way that it is true by definition. Another example of an identity would be a relation equating miles per gallon to the distance driven divided by the gasoline required.

The Quantity Theory of Money

*According to the **quantity theory of money**, velocity is stable or predictable, so changes in the money supply have predictable effects on nominal income.*

How do monetarists use the equation of exchange? They claim that, although velocity may change over time, it changes little in the short run, and any changes that do occur are systematically related to other forces in the economy. Changes in velocity therefore can be predicted. By arguing that velocity is relatively stable and predictable, monetarists transformed the equation of exchange from an identity into a theory: the quantity theory of money. The **quantity theory of money** states that if the velocity of money is stable or at least predictable, then the equation of exchange can be used to predict the effects of changes in the money supply on nominal income, $P \times Y$. For example, if M is increased by 10 percent and if V remains constant, then $P \times Y$, which measures nominal income, must also increase by 10 percent.

Thus, increases in the money supply increase aggregate demand, and the increase in aggregate demand results in a higher nominal income. How is this increase in nominal income ($P \times Y$) divided between changes in the price level and changes in real GNP? The answer does not lie in the quantity theory, for that theory is stated only in terms of nominal income. The answer lies in the shape of the aggregate supply curve. In the short run, the aggregate supply curve slopes upward, so a shift to the right in the aggregate demand curve will increase both real output and the price level. If there is much unemployment and much idle capacity, changes in the price level may be very small. If the economy is already producing its potential output, price level changes will be relatively larger.

So, *in the short run, changes in nominal output are divided between changes in real GNP and changes in the price level*. In the long run, the aggregate supply curve is vertical at the economy's potential level of output. Therefore, a shift to the right in the aggregate demand curve will increase only the price level, leaving output unchanged at potential GNP. Thus, *in the long run, increases in the money supply result only in higher prices*. Note that the economy's potential level of output is not affected by changes in the money supply.

Although monetarists believe that there is a relation between changes in the money supply and changes in nominal income, they caution that there may be long and unpredictable time lags before changes in the money supply affect aggregate demand. Consequently, monetarists consider monetary policy a poor instrument for changing nominal income. In the next chapter we will examine the problem of lags in monetary policy and consider the policy implications of these lags.

To review: *What turns the equation of exchange from an identity into a theory is the monetarist assertion that the velocity of money is relatively stable, at least in the short run.* If velocity is relatively stable, changes in the money supply affect nominal income. Velocity is therefore a key component of the quantity theory of money. Let's consider some factors that influence velocity.

What Determines the Velocity of Money?

Velocity depends on the customs and conventions of commerce. In colonial times money might be tied up in transit for days as a courier on horseback carried a payment from a merchant in Boston to one in Baltimore. Today the electronic transmission of funds takes only seconds, so the same stock of money can move around much more quickly to finance many more transactions. *The velocity of money has also been increased by a variety of commercial innovations that have facilitated exchange.* For example, wider use of charge accounts and credit cards has reduced the need for shoppers to carry cash to support transactions. Likewise, automatic teller machines have made cash more accessible any time, so people have reduced their "walking around" money. Monetarists argue that although such changes can affect velocity, financial innovations do not occur suddenly or frequently. Moreover, their effects are predictable, so the quantity theory remains a useful model.

Another institutional factor that determines velocity is the frequency with which people get paid. If workers are paid $1000 every two weeks and gradually spend the entire paycheck during that period, each worker's average money balance is $500. If workers are paid $500 once a week, however, their average money balance falls to $250. Thus, *the more often workers are paid, other things constant, the lower their average money balances, so the more active the money and the greater its velocity.* Again, payment practices change slowly over time, and the effects of these changes on velocity are predictable.

The better money serves as a store of wealth, the more of it people want to hold, so the lower its velocity. For example, the introduction of interest-bearing checking accounts made money a better store of wealth. On the other hand, when inflation is high, it serves poorly as a store of wealth, so it becomes like the proverbial hot potato. People become more reluctant to hold it and try to exchange it for some asset that retains its value during inflation. This reduction in people's willingness to hold money increases the velocity of money. Thus, *velocity increases with a rise in inflation, other things constant.*

The Keynesian Approach and the Equation of Exchange

How does the Keynesian approach look from the viewpoint of the equation of exchange? Recall that since the equation of exchange is an identity, not a theory, we should be able to explain how the Keynesian theory accords with this identity. Suppose some change in autonomous spending increases aggregate demand. As aggregate demand increases, the price level or the level of real output or both increase, thereby increasing the transactions demand for money. For a given supply of money in the economy, an increase in the money demand curve raises the interest rate. The higher opportunity cost of holding money reduces the quantity of money held as an asset, so the velocity of money increases. Because of this increase in velocity, a given supply of money is able to support the increase in aggregate demand.

Thus, in the Keynesian framework, an increase in aggregate demand increases the velocity of money enough that the existing money supply is sufficient to support the higher level of nominal spending. Dollars that had been relaxing comfortably in checking accounts or coffee cans are put to work. The equation of exchange remains in balance, $M \times V = P \times Y$, even though M has not changed. The increase in V allows the existing supply of money to support a higher level of nominal income. *Money works harder when the interest rate rises*.

Conversely, suppose a reduction in autonomous spending reduces aggregate demand, thereby reducing the transactions demand for money. For a given supply of money in the economy, a drop in the demand for money results in a lower interest rate, which lowers the opportunity cost of holding money. With the opportunity cost lower, people increase the quantity of money demanded, so idle money balances increase and the velocity of money falls. The existing money supply supports a lower level of nominal output.

In the Keynesian approach, the velocity of money varies directly with the interest rate. This link between the interest rate and velocity weakens the force of the quantity theory of money. Here is why. The quantity theory states that because velocity is relatively stable, an increase in the supply of money leads to an increase in nominal income. But since an increase in the supply of money reduces the interest rate, people may be content to hold some of the increased supply of money as cash balances. If a decline in the interest rate reduces velocity, then increases in the money supply are to some extent offset by reductions in velocity. But as long as we can predict the effect of changes in the money supply on velocity, we can still say what will happen to nominal output, so the quantity theory can still be useful for predicting nominal income.

Monetarism, Keynesianism, and the Equation of Exchange

Comparing and contrasting extreme versions of the monetarist and Keynesian views will help illuminate the issues involved. As a reference point, we return to our original example of the equation of exchange, where $M = \$500$, $V = 8$, and $P \times Y = \$4000$. Let's consider what would happen if the money supply doubled to $1000. We will examine three possibilities.

1. *Extreme Monetarist View.* If we assume that velocity is constant, then nominal income must double if the money supply doubles, so

$$\$1000 \times 8 = \$8000$$

Thus, in an extreme monetarist view, there is a direct relation between changes in the money supply and changes in nominal income.

2. *Extreme Keynesian View.* In an extreme Keynesian view, changes in velocity offset any changes in the money stock, so if the money supply doubles, the velocity of money falls by one-half, leaving nominal income unchanged:

$$\$1000 \times 4 = \$4000$$

When the money supply increases, the velocity drops proportionately, so the quantity of money people want to hold increases by the same amount as the money supply. In this extreme view, money is completely powerless to affect nominal income.

3. *Intermediate View.* If the money supply doubles, interest rates fall, reducing velocity. A doubling of the money supply causes velocity to fall by less than one-half. Thus, nominal income rises, but proportionately not by as much as the money stock rises:

$$\$1000 \times 6 = \$6000$$

The empirical question is whether view 1 or view 2 more closely resembles the actual operation of the economy. The usefulness of the modern quantity theory hinges on how stable and predictable the velocity of money is. Even a small unexpected change in velocity could undermine the ability of the equation of exchange to predict nominal income. For example, if velocity turned out to be 5 percent less than expected, then nominal GNP would also be 5 percent less than expected. Let's examine the stability of velocity over the years.

How Stable Is Velocity?

Exhibit 6 graphs velocity since 1915, measured as nominal GNP divided by M1. Based on this exhibit, is it reasonable to conclude that velocity is relatively stable? That depends on the time period considered and what is meant by "relatively stable." As you can see, from 1915 to 1947 velocity fluctuated greatly, but the trend was downward. From 1947 to 1979 there was an overall upward trend in velocity, with less variability than before. In

EXHIBIT 6   HISTORICAL RECORD OF VELOCITY (GNP/M1)

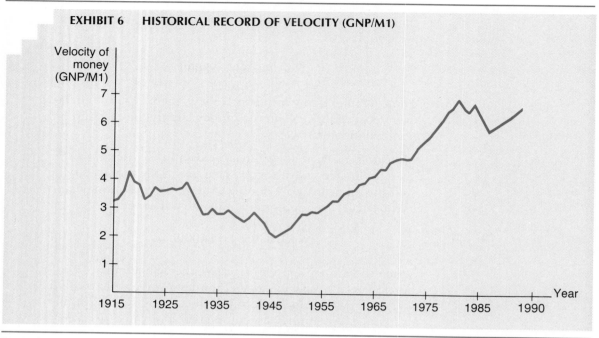

Source: *Long-Term Economic Growth, 1860–1970* (Washington, D.C.: U.S. Government Printing Office, 1973) and *Economic Report of the President*, February 1990.

fact, between 1973 and 1979 velocity grew each year at a rate of between 3.0 and 4.3 percent. *Velocity appeared so relatively stable during this six-year stretch that some economists began to talk about an economic law relating the money supply to nominal GNP.* More attention was thus accorded monetarism during the latter part of the 1970s. Whereas the decade of the 1960s was the high point of Keynesianism, the period of the late 1970s was perhaps the high point of monetarism.

After 1979, however, the velocity of M1 became more erratic. After jumping by 4.9 percent in 1981, it dropped by 4.6 percent during the recession year of 1982, the largest decline since 1947. This swing meant that nominal GNP was 9.1 percent lower in 1982 than it would have been had velocity continued to grow in 1982 as it had in 1981. Velocity dropped by 2.1 percent in 1983, jumped by 4.3 percent in 1984, dropped by 5.3 percent in 1985 and 9.7 percent in 1986, and jumped by 3.2 percent in 1987, 2.8 percent in 1988, and 6.2 percent in 1989.

Thus, between 1979 and 1989 the average growth in the velocity of M1 decreased sharply, whereas year-to-year changes in velocity increased. The equation of exchange consequently became a less reliable predictor of the effects of a change in M1 on nominal GNP. There is less talk now about economic laws relating money supply to nominal GNP. Some economists believe that the link between the money supply and nominal GNP has been disturbed only temporarily. Others aren't so sure.

The deregulation of the interest paid on checkable deposits has been identified as the possible source of the demise of a predictable relation between M1 and nominal income. Recall that prior to 1980, with minor exceptions, interest was not paid on checkable deposits. Since people can now earn interest on their checking accounts, they choose to hold more money, thus reducing the velocity of money.

Some economists argue that the definition of money has really changed as a result of the 1980 act. Therefore, a new definition of money—one that will perhaps be less sensitive to interest rates—should be developed. In fact, the velocity of M2 has been more stable than the velocity of M1. In setting targets for monetary growth, the Fed now relies more on M2 than on M1.

MONETARY TARGETS: MONEY SUPPLY VERSUS INTEREST RATES

According to the Keynesian view, monetary policy affects the economy largely by influencing the market rate of interest. Monetarists think the linkage is more direct—that changes in the growth of the money supply affect how much people want to spend. The Keynesian approach suggests that monetary authorities should worry about interest rates; the monetarist approach suggests that the money supply is of more direct importance. There is much debate over whether monetary authorities should focus on keeping the money stock stable or on keeping the interest rate stable. The Fed does not have enough tools to do both.

Contrasting Policies

To demonstrate the effects of different policies, we will begin with the money market in equilibrium at point e in Exhibit 7. The interest rate is i and the money stock is M, values the monetary authorities find quite appropriate. Suppose there is an increase in the demand for money in the economy, perhaps because the level of income and output in the economy increases. The money demand curve shifts to the right from D_m to D'_m.

When confronted with an increase in the demand for money, monetary authorities can do one of the following two things: they can do nothing, allowing the interest rate to rise, or they can increase the supply of money in an attempt to keep the interest rate constant. If monetary authorities do nothing, the quantity of money in the economy will remain the same, but the interest rate will rise because the greater demand for money will shift the equilibrium up from point e to point e'. Thus, the do-nothing course will leave the money stock unchanged but allow interest rates to rise from i to i'. Alternatively, monetary authorities can keep the interest rate at its initial level by increasing the supply of money from S_m to S'_m. In terms of possible combinations of the money stock and the interest rate, monetary authorities must choose from points lying along the new money demand curve.

A growing economy usually needs a growing money supply. If monetary authorities maintain a steady growth in the money supply, the interest

EXHIBIT 7   TARGETING INTEREST RATES VERSUS THE SUPPLY OF MONEY

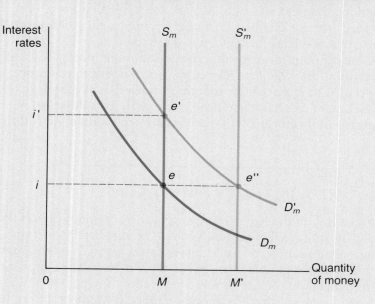

An increase in the price level or in real GNP increases the demand for money from D_m to D'_m. If the Federal Reserve holds the money supply at S_m, interest rates will rise from i (at point e) to i' (at point e'). Alternatively, the Fed could hold the interest rate constant by increasing the supply of money to S'_m. The Fed may choose any point along the new money demand curve, D'_m.

rate will probably fluctuate unless the supply of money grows just enough to match a steady increase in the demand for money. Alternatively, monetary authorities could try to adjust the money supply in each period by the amount needed to keep the interest rate stable. With this approach, variable changes in the money supply would have to offset any variable changes in the demand for money.

Interest-rate fluctuations could be considered undesirable if they created similar fluctuations in investment. For interest rates to remain stable during economic expansions, the growth in the supply of money should just match the growth in the demand for money. Likewise, for interest rates to remain stable during economic contractions, the rate of growth in the money supply should decline by the amount by which demand declines. Hence, if monetary authorities attempted to maintain the interest rate at some predetermined level, the money supply would grow faster during periods of economic expansion and grow more slowly or even shrink during periods of economic contraction. Unfortunately, *such changes in the money supply tend to reinforce fluctuations in economic activity, thereby adding more instability to the economy.*

Targets in Recent Years

Between World War II and October 1979, the Fed attempted to stabilize interest rates. Stable interest rates were viewed as a prerequisite for an attractive investment environment and, thus, for a stable economy. Friedman and other monetarists argued that this exclusive attention to interest rates made monetary policy a major source of instability in the economy because changes in the money supply affected nominal output. Monetarists proposed that the Fed pay less attention to interest rates and instead focus on a steady and predictable growth in the money supply.

The debate raged during the 1970s, and monetarists were making some important converts. Amid growing concern about the rising inflation rate, the Fed, under its new chairman, Paul Volcker, announced in October 1979 that it would deemphasize interest rates and focus more on specified targets for monetary growth. Not surprisingly, the interest rate became much more volatile. What *is* surprising, however, is that the deemphasis on interest rates did *not* result in a more stable growth in the money supply. After October 1979 fluctuations in the rate of money supply growth *increased* rather than decreased.

Many observers believe that a sharp reduction in money growth in the latter half of 1981 was an important factor in the recession of 1982, one of the most severe since the Great Depression. Inflation declined rapidly, but the unemployment rate jumped to over 10 percent. People got worried. As you might expect, the Fed was widely criticized for its monetary policy. Volcker was denounced by farmers, politicians, and businesspeople. Feelings ran high. Volcker was reportedly even given Secret Service protection.

In October 1982, three years after the focus on interest rates was dropped, the Fed backed off. Volcker announced that the Fed would no longer attempt to focus primarily on money growth but would try to pay attention to both interest rates *and* money growth. Monetarists do not acknowledge that the attempt to focus on monetary targets was a failure. Rather, they argue that the Fed never really implemented a policy of steady, predictable growth in the money supply, so the three-year period should not be viewed as a test of the effectiveness of monetarism. Some monetarists even believe that the Fed espoused monetarism simply as a smokescreen for putting the brakes on an overheated economy.

Most observers of monetary policy think that since October 1982 the Fed has abandoned its experiment of controlling the money supply and has returned to trying to prevent wide swings in the interest rate. As we have seen, however, this approach tends to increase the money supply growth during periods of expansion and to reduce the money supply growth during periods of contraction, a monetary policy that could be called procyclical.

Interest Rates and International Finance

Thus far we have confined the discussion of monetary policy to domestic issues. But international transactions complicate the picture, as savers throughout the world have a strong financial incentive to seek out the highest interest rate. For a Japanese saver, for example, the alternatives might be to put funds into Japanese corporate bonds paying, say, 5 percent or to invest in U.S. corporate bonds paying 8 percent. To purchase U.S. bonds, that Japanese saver would have to purchase U.S. dollars with Japanese yen. Therefore, relatively high interest rates in the United States cause foreigners to exchange their own currencies for dollars. This increase in the demand for dollars causes the dollar to appreciate relative to other currencies.

During the first half of the 1980s, real interest rates in the United States were much higher than foreign interest rates, and the U.S. dollar appreciated by about 55 percent. Real interest rates in the United States began a sharp decline in early 1985, a decline that continued until 1987. During that same period, the U.S. dollar fell by nearly 50 percent. When U.S. interest rates exceed those in other countries, foreign savers want to put their funds in U.S. securities so they exchange their currencies for U.S. dollars, driving up the value of the dollar in the process. When U.S. interest rates fall relative to foreign interest rates, the foreign demand for U.S. dollars also falls and the dollar tends to depreciate.

The interest rate, therefore, affects not only domestic investment but the value of the dollar on world currency markets. Higher U.S. interest rates, other things constant, increase the value of the dollar on world markets. An appreciated dollar means that U.S. residents find foreign goods cheaper and foreigners find U.S. goods more expensive, so imports increase and exports decrease. The resulting reduction in aggregate demand reduces the level of output in the economy.

Recent Fed Policy

In the latter part of the 1980s, the economy continued to grow in what became the longest peacetime expansion since World War II. Concern about inflationary pressure prompted the Fed in March of 1988 to allow short-term interest rates to climb. Over the next year, the federal funds rate, the rate charged for overnight borrowing of reserves between banks, climbed from 6.5 percent to nearly 10 percent. Some observers were concerned that the Fed would become too earnest in its efforts to cool the economy and would instead cause a recession.

To reduce the possibility of a recession, the Fed, in June of 1989, began pursuing a policy aimed at lowering interest rates. In the process, the Fed also wanted to halt the appreciation of the dollar that had occurred during the first half of 1989. In response to this easier monetary policy, the federal funds rate dropped from 10 percent in June of 1989 to about 8.5 percent by the end of that year. The value of the dollar on world markets also dropped.

The Fed is always feeling its way along, looking for signs about the direction of the economy and clues to what its monetary policy should be. In its quest for price stability, the Fed has recently developed a new monetary indicator. We close this chapter with a case study discussing this indicator.

The Fed's New Monetary Indicator: The Long-Run Price Level

In their pursuit of price stability, Fed officials have begun considering a new indicator of inflationary pressure in the economy: the *long-run equilibrium price level*, which is the level that prices are expected to reach when the economy produces its potential output. By comparing the long-run price level to the current price level in the economy, Fed officials hope to develop insight into the likely course of inflation.

The long-run price level, as estimated by the Fed, is derived from the equation of exchange, $M \times V^* = P^* \times Y^*$, where M is the money supply (measured as M2), V^* is the average velocity of M2 over the long run, P^* is the long-run equilibrium price level, and Y^* is real potential output. The equation of exchange can be rearranged to yield the long-run equilibrium price level: $P^* = (M \times V^*)/Y^*$. You can think of P^* as the price level that will eventually occur when the economy achieves its potential output, given the current money supply and the average velocity of money.

In deriving P^*, the Fed knows the value of M2, but it must estimate both potential output and the average velocity. Estimates of potential output are based on an analysis of the U.S. economy's long-run trend in real output. The velocity of M2 varies in the short run, but research shows that over sufficiently long periods, velocity returns to an average value; that is, the velocity of M2 seems constant over the long run. As an estimate of long-run velocity, the Fed uses the average value of velocity since 1955.

Once they estimate P^*, Fed analysts compare it to the economy's current price level. The difference between the two price levels provides policy makers with an indication of the likely direction of inflation. Empirical evidence suggests that when the long-run equilibrium price level is below the current price level, inflation tends to decrease. When the long-run equilibrium price level exceeds the current price level, inflation tends to increase. And when the long-run equilibrium price level equals the current price level, inflation remains the same. Therefore, the difference between the current price level and the long-run equilibrium price level provides the Fed with additional information on how to pursue price stability. For example, if the current price level is below the long-run equilibrium price level, it is likely that there is inflationary pressure in the economy, so the Fed may want to pursue a less inflationary monetary policy.

Using the tools of aggregate supply and aggregate demand developed earlier, we can offer a crude explanation for the empirical relation observed between the current price level and the long-run equilibrium price level. Exhibit 8 presents the economy's long-run aggregate supply curve as a vertical line drawn at the economy's potential output, Y^*. The long-run equilibrium price level, P^*, is determined by the intersection of the aggregate demand curve and the long-run aggregate supply curve. Suppose, however, that the short-run equilibrium occurs at point e, where current output is below the economy's potential. At point e, the current price level, P, exceeds the long-run equilibrium price level, P^*, indicating that the price level will tend to fall in the long run. This is the same adjustment we

**EXHIBIT 8   LONG-RUN PRICE LEVEL AS AN INDICATOR OF THE LIKELY COURSE
OF INFLATION**

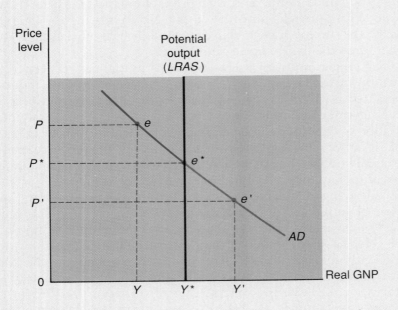

The difference between the current price level and the long-run equilibrium price
level provides Fed officials with an indication of the likely course of inflation. If the
current price level, *P*, exceeds the long-run price level, *P**, inflation will tend to fall
over the long run. If the current price level, *P'*, is below *P**, inflation will tend to
increase. And if the current price level equals *P**, inflation will remain unchanged.

discussed in earlier chapters: the price level falls as natural market forces
close the contractionary gap between *Y* and *Y**.

Conversely, if the short-run equilibrium occurs at point *e'*, current
output, *Y'*, exceeds the economy's potential output and the current price
level, *P'*, is below the long-run equilibrium price level. The Fed's model
predicts that when the current price level is below the long-run equilibrium
price level, the price level will tend to rise. Again, this is the natural market
adjustment to an expansionary gap. If the short-run equilibrium occurs at
point *e**, the current price level equals the long-run price level, so the price
level (or inflation) is expected to remain stable.

Sources: John B. Carlson, "The Indicator P-Star: Just What Does It Indicate?" *Economic Commentary*, Federal Reserve Bank of
Cleveland, September 15, 1989; and Thomas M. Humphrey, "Precursors of the P-Star Model," *Economic Review*, Federal Reserve Bank
of Richmond, July/August 1989.

CONCLUSION

We have described two ways of viewing the effects of money on the economy's performance, but we should not overstate the differences. In the Keynesian model, an increase in the money supply means that people are holding more money than they would like at prevailing interest rates, so they exchange one form of wealth, money, for other financial assets, such as bonds. This increased demand for other financial assets has no direct effect on aggregate demand, but it does reduce the interest rate, thereby increasing planned investment. The increase in planned investment is magnified by the spending multiplier, thereby increasing aggregate demand. The ultimate effect of this increase in demand on real output and the price level will depend on the shape of the aggregate supply curve.

In the monetarist framework, changes in the money supply act more directly on both output and prices. If velocity is relatively stable or at least fairly predictable, then changes in the money supply will have a predictable effect on nominal income and output in the economy. The mechanism through which changes in money translate into changes in nominal income is no more complicated than the equation of exchange. Increase the supply of money, and people try to reduce their money balances to the desired level by exchanging money for other assets, including houses and cars. This greater spending leads to an increase in aggregate demand and to a greater nominal output.

Each model employs a different perspective to examine the way the economy works. The Keynesian approach uses the 45-degree income-expenditure model, with the components of aggregate expenditure as basic building blocks. The monetarist approach uses the equation of exchange, with the elements of that equation as basic building blocks. To understand why these are alternative ways of viewing the same thing, consider the following analogy.

Suppose city officials, concerned about traffic congestion, ask their engineers and planners to estimate the total number of trips made from the suburbs to the city each month. The city engineers check with the state department of motor vehicles and find that 100,000 cars are registered to suburban residents. The engineers then estimate that each car makes an average of 15 trips to the city per month, for a total of 1.5 million trips. In contrast, the city planners consider the number of trips to the city by suburban residents. They estimate that those suburbanites who commute to work make 700,000 trips per month, shoppers make 500,000 trips per month, and joyriders make 300,000 trips per month, for a total of 1.5 million trips.

The engineers focus on the number of cars and the average number of trips taken by each. Likewise, monetarists, to arrive at total spending, focus on the money supply and the average number of "trips" each dollar takes — that is, the average number of times each dollar is spent. Note that the engineers count all registered vehicles, even though some may sit in garages. Similarly, monetarists count all dollars, even though some remain idle in checking accounts or coffee cans. In contrast, the city planners focus not on the number of cars but on the different sources of trips to the city by suburban residents. Likewise, Keynesians focus not on the money stock but on the aggregate demand generated by various sectors in the economy.

Summary

1. The demand for money represents the sum of the transactions demand for money and the demand for money as a store of wealth. The opportunity cost of holding money is the higher interest that could be earned by holding other financial assets. The quantity of money demanded is inversely related to the interest rate. The demand for money increases with an increase in the price level or in real GNP.

2. The supply of money is regulated by the Fed. The intersection of the supply and demand for money determines the equilibrium interest rate. According to the Keynesian view, an increase in the supply of money reduces the rate of interest, which increases investment. This increase in investment increases aggregate demand and the equilibrium level of income and output in the economy.

3. Monetarists focus on the role of money through the equation of exchange, which states that the money stock, M, times the average number of times each dollar is used to pay for output, V, equals the price level, P, times real GNP, Y.

4. Monetarists and Keynesians agree that an increase in the supply of money results in a lower interest rate and greater investment. But monetarists also claim that when the supply of money increases, people exchange money for real assets, such as homes and cars. Monetarists argue that velocity is stable enough that the effect of changes in the money supply on nominal output can be predicted. During most of the 1970s, velocity appeared relatively stable, but since 1979 velocity has been so variable that economists have begun to question the usefulness of the quantity theory, at least in the short run.

5. The Fed's model, based on the long-run equilibrium price level, predicts that inflation (1) will fall when the current price level is above the long-run equilibrium price level, (2) will rise when the current price level is below the long-run equilibrium price level, and (3) will remain unchanged when the current price level equals the long-run equilibrium price level.

Questions and Problems

1. (Transactions Demand for Money) It is sometimes said that not only consumers but also businesses have a transactions demand for money. Explain why businesses would hold both demand deposits and currency. Are the factors that affect the demand for money by consumers the same as those that affect the demand by businesses?

2. (Opportunity Costs) How has lifting the prohibition against paying interest on checkable deposits affected the opportunity cost of holding currency? What has the effect been on the opportunity cost of holding checkable deposits? Will currency leakages and thus the money multiplier also be affected?

3. (Chain of Causation) There are two important links in the chain of causality for monetary policy: the link between an increase in the money supply and a drop in interest rates and the link between a drop in interest rates and a rise in investment spending. What would cause these two links to fail? Might both links fail at the same time?

4. (Demand for Money) If money is so versatile and can buy anything, why don't people demand an *infinite* amount of money? Does it really make sense to talk about a demand for money?

5. (Demand for Money) Would the quantity of money demanded be less sensitive to changes in interest rates if we defined money as M2 instead of M1? Would the same hold true if there was a ceiling on interest paid on savings accounts?

6. (Fiscal Policy and Monetary Policy) Explain why incorporating money into our macroeconomic framework moderates the effects of fiscal policy. That is, how does the existence of the supply and demand for money diminish the effects of increased government spending?

7. (Monetarism) Monetarists claim that a steady, constant growth in the money supply that is compatible with the long-run economic growth of the economy is the best type of monetary policy. What are the strengths and weaknesses of this approach?

8. (Velocity) The existence of automatic tellers for twenty-four-hour withdrawal of cash may have led to a reduction in the average amount of currency held by individuals. What effect would such a reduction have on the velocity of money? Have any other financial innovations affected velocity?

9. (Velocity) Why do some economists believe that higher expected inflation will generally lead to a rise in velocity?

10. (Monetary Targets) One problem with targeting the money supply is that it is not measured continuously as interest rates are. However, there are also some problems associated with using an interest-rate target for monetary policy. What are these problems?

11. (Monetary Policy) Using money supply-demand and aggregate expenditure diagrams, show how the sensitivity of money demand and aggregate expenditure to interest-rate changes influences the effectiveness of monetary policy in shifting the aggregate demand curve.

12. (Money Demand) Suppose the amount of money you hold for transactions purposes equals your average checking account balance (i.e., you never carry cash). Assume that your paycheck of $1000 per month is deposited directly into your account and you spend your money at a uniform (constant) rate such that at the end of each month your checking balance is zero.

   a. What is your transactions demand for money?

   b. How would each of the following affect your money demand level?

      i. You are paid $500 twice a month instead of $1000 once a month.

      ii. You are uncertain about your total spending each month.

      iii. You spend a lot in the beginning of each month (e.g., for rent) and little at the end of each month.

      iv. Your annual income increases.

13. (Interest Rates) In Chapter 7 we noted that interest rates are determined in the loanable funds market. How is this fact consistent with the idea that interest rates are based on money demand and money supply?

14. (Velocity of Money) Using the equation of exchange, show why fiscal policy alone can- not increase nominal GNP if the velocity of money is constant.

15. (Velocity and Money Demand) How would the sensitivity of money demand to interest- rate levels be likely to influence the stability of the velocity of money?

The Policy Debate:
Activism Versus Nonactivism

Now that we have considered the effects of both fiscal policy and monetary policy, we are in a position to examine economic stabilization policy more generally. In this chapter we will compare the merits of active government intervention in the economy with those of passive reliance on natural market forces. We will also consider the crucial role that expectations play in determining the effectiveness of stabilization policy. We will show why unanticipated stabilization policies have more impact on employment and output than do anticipated policies. The chapter closes with a consideration of the tradeoff between unemployment and inflation. As you read, keep in mind that issues of macroeconomic policy remain the most widely debated of economic questions. Topics discussed in this chapter include

- Activist versus nonactivist policy

- Self-correcting mechanisms

- Rational expectations

- Policy rules

- The short-run and long-run Phillips curves

- Normal rate hypothesis

ACTIVISM VERSUS NONACTIVISM

Activists consider the private sector to be relatively unstable and able to absorb shocks only with the aid of discretionary fiscal policy.

Nonactivists consider the private sector to be relatively stable and able to absorb shocks without discretionary government policy.

Although we distinguished between Keynesians and monetarists in the last chapter, in matters of public policy it is more descriptive to speak of activists and nonactivists. **Activists** consider the private sector to be relatively unstable and unable to absorb shocks when they occur; **nonactivists** consider the private sector to be relatively stable and able to absorb shocks when they occur. According to activists, economic fluctuations arise primarily from the private sector, particularly investment. Nonactivists believe that discretionary government policy is a primary source of instability in the economy. Thus, *according to activists, discretionary government policy can reduce the costs imposed by an unstable private sector. According to nonactivists, discretionary policy is part of the problem, not part of the solution.*

Another difference between activists and nonactivists is in their beliefs about how quickly wages and prices adjust to an excess supply or excess demand for labor—that is, how quickly natural market forces operate. Perhaps the best way to describe the views of each group is by examining a particular macroeconomic problem.

Closing a Contractionary Gap

Suppose the economy is in short-run equilibrium at point *e* in Exhibit 1, with output, *Y*, below the economy's potential, *Y**. At output level *Y*, the contractionary gap results in unemployment that exceeds the natural rate (the rate of unemployment when the economy is producing its potential output). What should public officials do when confronted with this situation?

Nonactivists, like their classical predecessors, have more faith in the self-correcting mechanisms of the economy than do activists. In what sense is the economy self-correcting? According to nonactivists, wages and prices are flexible enough to adjust within a reasonable period to labor shortages or surpluses. The high unemployment in Exhibit 1 will cause wages to fall, which will reduce production costs, which will increase the short-run aggregate supply curve. (Money wages need not actually fall; money wage increases may simply lag behind increases in the price level so that real wages fall.) According to the nonactivists, the short-run aggregate supply curve will soon shift out from *SRAS(P*)* to *SRAS(P′)*, moving the economy to its potential level of output at point *e′*. *Nonactivists view the economy as inherently stable, gravitating fairly quickly toward potential GNP. Consequently they see little reason for active government intervention.* The *nonactivist* approach is to make no policy changes.

Activists, on the other hand, argue that prices and wages are not very flexible, particularly in the downward direction. When supply shocks or sagging demand results in unemployment that exceeds the natural rate, the economy does not quickly adjust to eliminate this unemployment. Activists believe that even when there is much unemployment in the economy, the

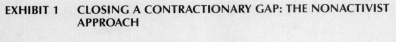

EXHIBIT 1   CLOSING A CONTRACTIONARY GAP: THE NONACTIVIST APPROACH

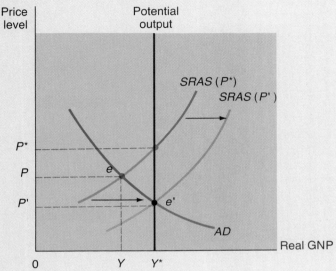

At point e, the economy is in short-run equilibrium, producing output Y. Unemployment is above the natural rate. That high unemployment will eventually cause wages to fall, reducing firms' cost of doing business. The decline in costs will cause the short-run aggregate supply curve to shift out to *SRAS(P')*, moving the economy to its potential level of output at point e'.

renegotiation of long-term wage contracts in line with a lower expected price level may take a long time. Thus the wage reductions (or the slowing in wage growth) required to shift the short-run aggregate supply curve out may also take a long time, even years. The longer natural market forces take to lower unemployment to the natural rate, the greater the forgone output during the adjustment period and the greater the economic and psychic costs to those who are unemployed during that period. Because activists associate a high cost with the nonactivist approach, they believe that the economy needs a fiscal and monetary stabilization policy.

A decision by the government to intervene in the economy to speed the return to potential output — that is, a decision to use discretionary policy — reflects an *activist* approach. By increasing aggregate demand through monetary policy, fiscal policy, or some mix of the two, policy makers can attempt to reduce unemployment and return output to the economy's potential, moving equilibrium from point *e* to *e** in Exhibit 2. If policy makers could quickly stimulate aggregate demand as desired, the activist approach would be relatively attractive. One cost of such a policy, however, is an increase in the price level. To the extent that the stimulus to aggregate demand arises

EXHIBIT 2   CLOSING A CONTRACTIONARY GAP: THE ACTIVIST APPROACH

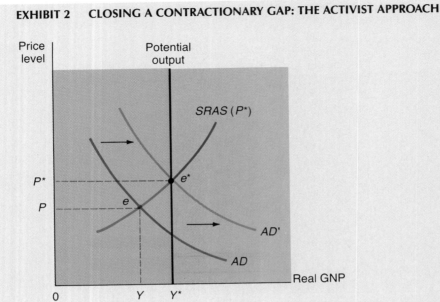

At point e, the economy is in short-run equilibrium, producing output Y. Unemployment is above the natural rate. To reduce the level of unemployment, the government employs an activist policy to shift the aggregate demand curve from AD to AD'. Doing so will cause the economy to move to its potential level of output at point e*.

from a budget deficit, another cost of the policy is an increase in the national debt, a cost that will be examined more closely in the next chapter.

Closing an Expansionary Gap

Let's consider the situation in which the short-run equilibrium output exceeds the economy's potential. Suppose that the actual price level, P', exceeds the expected price level, $P*$, causing an expansionary gap between Y' and $Y*$, as shown in Exhibit 3. In the absence of any discretionary government policy, natural market forces will, according to theory, prompt firms and workers to negotiate higher wage agreements. These higher nominal wages will increase production costs, shifting the short-run supply curve up and to the left, from $SRAS(P*)$ to $SRAS(P'')$, leading to a higher price level and reducing output to the economy's potential. So the natural adjustment process will result in a higher price level, or inflation.

Activists see discretionary policy as a way of returning the economy to its potential without fostering inflation. Activists believe that if aggregate

EXHIBIT 3   POLICY RESPONSES TO AN EXPANSIONARY GAP

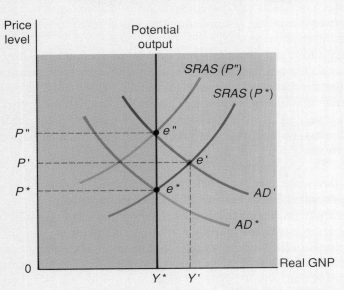

At point e', the economy is in short-run equilibrium, producing output Y'. Unemployment is below the natural rate. If the government makes no change in policy, natural market forces will eventually bring about a higher negotiated wage, shifting the short-run supply curve up to SRAS(P"). The new equilibrium at point e" will result in a higher price level and a lower level of output and employment. An activist policy might be able to reduce aggregate demand, shifting the equilibrium from point e' to point e*, thus closing the expansionary gap without increasing the price level.

demand can be reduced from *AD'* to *AD**, then the equilibrium point will move down along the initial supply curve from *e'* to *e**. *Whereas natural market forces close an expansionary gap by raising the price level, just the right discretionary policy closes the gap by lowering the price level.* Thus, the correct discretionary policy can relieve the inflationary pressure associated with an expansionary gap.

Problems with Activist Policy

The timely adoption and implementation of an appropriate activist policy is not easy. One problem confronting policy makers is the difficulty of identifying the economy's potential level of output and the amount of unemployment associated with that level of output. Suppose the natural rate of unemployment is 5 percent, but policy makers believe it is 4 percent. As they pursue their elusive objective of 4 percent unemployment, the economy will be constantly pushed beyond its potential, creating higher prices in the long run with no permanent reduction in unemployment. Recall that in the short run, if output is pushed beyond the economy's potential, an expansionary gap will be created, which will cause a shift up in the short-run aggregate supply curve until the economy returns to its potential level of output at a higher price level.

Even if policy makers can accurately estimate the economy's potential level of output, formulating an effective policy requires abundant knowledge of the current and future economy. To pursue an effective activist policy, policy makers must first be able to forecast what aggregate demand and aggregate supply would be without government intervention. Simply put, policy makers must be able to predict what would happen with no change in policy. Second, policy makers must have in their discretionary arsenal the tools necessary to achieve the desired result relatively quickly. Third, policy makers must be able to forecast the effects of any new policy on the economy's key performance measures. Fourth, policy makers must work together. Fiscal policy and monetary policy are pursued by separate government bodies that often fail to coordinate their efforts. To the extent that an activist policy requires such coordination, the policy may not work as desired. Fifth, policy makers must be able to implement the appropriate policy, even if that policy involves short-term political costs. For example, during inflationary times the optimal policy may call for a tax increase or slower money growth, changes that may not be popular because of their negative effects on employment. Finally, policy makers must be able to deal with a variety of lags. As we will see next, these lags compound the problems of pursuing an activist policy.

The Problem of Lags

So far we have ignored the need for time in which to implement policy. That is, we have assumed that the desired policy was selected and implemented in no time. Once implemented, the policy worked as advertised—again, in no time. Actually, there are often long, sometimes unpredictable, delays at several stages in the process. These lags prevent stabilization policy from quickly achieving the desired results.

The **recognition lag** *is the time it takes to identify the existence of a macroeconomic problem and its degree of seriousness.*

First, there is a **recognition lag**, which is the time it takes to identify a problem and determine how serious it is. Time is required to accumulate data indicating that the economy is indeed performing well below its potential. Even if initial data provide early warning signals, policy makers often await additional evidence of trouble rather than risk responding to what may turn out to be a temporary aberration. In mid-1989 the Fed pursued lower interest rates largely because May unemployment statistics showed a weakening economy. But May employment figures were later revised sharply upward, suggesting that the economy was not in fact weakening. To reduce such false alarms, a recession does not become official until more than six months after it begins.

When enough evidence has accumulated, policy makers usually take

The **decision-making lag** *is the time it takes to decide what to do about a macroeconomic problem.*

The **implementation lag** *is the time it takes to introduce a change in monetary or fiscal policy.*

The **effectiveness lag** *is the time it takes for a change in monetary or fiscal policy to have an effect on the economy.*

time deciding what to do, so there is a **decision-making lag**. In the case of fiscal policy, Congress and the president must develop and agree upon an appropriate course of action. Fiscal legislation usually takes months; it can take more than a year. Federal Reserve authorities can decide on the appropriate monetary policy much more quickly than can those in charge of fiscal policy, so the decision-making lag is shorter for monetary policy.

Once a decision has been made, the new policy must be introduced, which often involves an **implementation lag**. Again, monetary policy has the advantage: after a policy has been adopted, the Fed can buy or sell bonds, change the discount rate, or alter reserve requirements relatively quickly. The implementation lag is longer for fiscal policy. If tax rates change, new tax forms must be printed and distributed. If government spending changes, the appropriate government agencies must get involved. The implementation of fiscal policy can take more than a year. For example, in February 1983 the nation's unemployment rate reached 10.3 percent, with 11.5 million unemployed. The following month the Emergency Jobs Appropriation Act was passed, providing $9 billion to create what supporters of the measure claimed would be hundreds of thousands of new jobs. Fifteen months later, only $3.1 billion had been spent and only 35,000 new jobs had been created, according to a Government Accounting Office study. By that time, the economy had recovered on its own, reducing the unemployment rate to 7.1 percent and increasing the number of employed workers by 6.2 million. Thus, this public spending program was implemented only after the recession had bottomed out.

Once a policy has been implemented, there is an **effectiveness lag** before the full impact of the policy registers on the economy. One problem with monetary policy is that the lag between a change in the money supply and its effect on aggregate demand and output is long and variable, ranging from several months up to thirty-six months. Once enacted, fiscal policy usually requires three to six months to take effect and between nine and eighteen months to register its full effect.

These various lags make an activist policy difficult to pursue. If natural market forces fail to reduce unemployment, then longer lags increase the total output forgone by the economy and the psychic costs imposed on unemployed workers. The more variable the lags are, the harder it is to predict when a particular policy will take effect and what the state of the economy will be at that time. To nonactivists, these lags are reason enough to avoid discretionary policy, particularly since the average postwar contraction, or recession, has lasted only eleven months. *Nonactivists argue that an active stabilization policy imposes troubling fluctuations in the price level and in the level of output because it often takes hold only after market forces have already returned the economy to its potential level of output.*

Review of Policy Perspectives

Activists and nonactivists have fundamentally different views on the natural stability of the economy and the ability of the government to implement appropriate discretionary policies. Hence they disagree about the role of government in the economy. As we have seen, activists think that the natural adjustments of wages and prices can be excruciatingly slow, particularly when unemployment is high, as during the Great Depression. Prolonged high unemployment means that much output must be sacrificed, and the unemployed must suffer personal hardship during the slow adjustment period. If high unemployment lasts a long time, labor skills may grow rusty, some long-term unemployed workers may drop out of the labor force, and firms may neglect their capital stock, causing it to depreciate faster. Therefore, prolonged unemployment may cause the economy's potential GNP to fall.

Thus activists associate a high cost with the failure to pursue a discretionary policy. And despite the lags involved, activists prefer action to inaction, whether through fiscal policy, monetary policy, or some combination of the two. Nonactivists, on the other hand, believe that uncertain lags and ignorance about how the economy works prevent the government from accurately determining or effectively implementing the appropriate activist policy. Therefore, nonactivists would rather rely on the economy's natural ability to correct itself than pursue a misguided activist policy.

MACROECONOMIC POLICY AND EXPECTATIONS

According to the **rational expectations** school of thought, people form expectations based on all available information, including government policy.

The effectiveness of a particular government policy depends very much on what people expect. As we observed in Chapter 10, the short-run aggregate supply curve is drawn for a given expected price level, which is reflected in long-term wage contracts. If workers and firms expect more inflation, their labor agreements will reflect these inflationary expectations. An influential school of thought in macroeconomics, called the **rational expectations** school, argues that people form expectations on the basis of all available information, including information about the probable future action of policy makers. Thus, aggregate supply depends on what sort of macroeconomic course policy makers are expected to pursue. For example, if people observe that the government tries to stimulate aggregate demand every time real output falls below the economy's potential, they will come to anticipate the effects of this policy on the level of price and output.

Monetary authorities must testify before Congress regularly, indicating the monetary policy they plan to pursue. We will consider the role of expectations in the context of monetary policy by examining the relation between policy pronouncements and equilibrium output. (We could employ a similar approach with fiscal policy, but discretionary fiscal policy over the last decade has been overshadowed by the huge federal deficits.)

Monetary Policy and Expectations

Suppose the economy is humming along at its potential rate of GNP. At the beginning of the year, firms and employees must negotiate wage agreements. While negotiations are under way, the Fed announces that throughout the year its policy will be one of slow growth in the money supply, a policy aimed at keeping the economy producing its potential GNP. This appears to be the appropriate policy, since the level of unemployment is already at the natural rate, but until the year is under way and monetary policy is actually implemented, the public cannot be sure what the Fed will do. Firms and workers understand that the Fed's plans appear optimal under the circumstances, since increasing the money supply sharply would, in the long run, simply lead to a higher price level. Either workers can agree to low wage increases, which would be consistent with the Fed's announced policy and a low expected rate of inflation, or they can shoot for higher wages.

One strategy is for workers and firms to settle on wage increases in accord with expectations of low inflation. If the low wage increase is agreed to and if the Fed follows a slow-money-growth policy, as promised, then inflation will turn out to be modest, output will remain at the economy's potential, and unemployment will remain at the natural rate. Low inflation is the optimal outcome in the long run. The situation is depicted in Exhibit 4. In accordance with the Fed's policy pronouncements, the short-run aggregate supply curve, $SRAS(P^*)$, is based on wage contracts reflecting an expected price level of P^*. If the Fed follows the announced course, aggregate demand will be AD^* and equilibrium will be at point e^*, where the price level is as expected and the economy is producing its potential level of output.

Suppose, however, that after workers and firms have signed low-wage-increase labor pacts — that is, after the short-run aggregate supply curve has been determined — public officials become dissatisfied with the prevailing level of unemployment. Perhaps election-year concerns about unemployment, an underestimation of the natural rate of unemployment, or a false alarm about a rising unemployment rate prompts officials to pressure the Fed into stimulating aggregate demand and lowering unemployment in the short run by increasing the money supply more than was expected.

The unexpected increase in the money supply increases aggregate demand beyond AD^*, the level anticipated by firms and employees, to AD. The expansionary monetary policy stimulates output and employment in the short run because long-term contracts prevent nominal wages from increasing in proportion to price increases. Output increases to Y, and the price level increases to P. This temporary reduction in unemployment lasts perhaps long enough to help public officials get reelected.

In the short run, workers are locked into wage levels that, because of the higher price level, are lower in real terms than they had bargained for. At their next opportunity, they will negotiate higher wages. These higher wage agreements will eventually cause the short-run aggregate supply curve to shift up until equilibrium output once again returns to the economy's potential GNP, identified as point e' in Exhibit 4.

Thus the greater-than-expected increase in the money supply causes a short-run increase in output and employment; in the long run, the increase

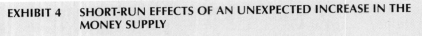

**EXHIBIT 4   SHORT-RUN EFFECTS OF AN UNEXPECTED INCREASE IN THE
MONEY SUPPLY**

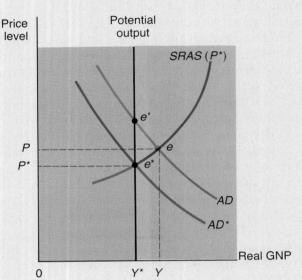

At point e*, firms and workers expect the price level to be P*; supply curve
SRAS(P*) reflects those expectations. If the Federal Reserve unexpectedly increases the money supply, the aggregate demand curve will be AD rather than
AD*. Output will temporarily rise above the potential rate (at point e), but in the
long run it will fall back to the potential rate at point e'. The short-run effect of
monetary policy is a higher level of output, but the long-run effect is just an
increase in the price level.

in the aggregate demand results only in a higher price level, or inflation.
After a short-run surge in output, the short-run aggregate supply curve
shifts to the left, the price level climbs, and output returns once again to the
economy's potential.

Anticipating Monetary Policy

Suppose the resulting inflation becomes a matter of growing concern, so
the next time around the Fed once again announces that it will pursue a
slow-growth monetary policy, one aimed at keeping the economy's output
at its potential. From their previous experience, however, workers and firms
have learned that the Fed is willing to trade higher inflation for a temporary
reduction in unemployment. Consequently, the slow-growth announcements by the Fed are taken with a grain of salt. Workers, in particular, do not
want to get caught again with their real wages down should the Fed
implement a stimulative monetary policy, so a high-wage-increase settlement is reached.

In effect, workers and firms are betting that when the chips are down, monetary authorities will pursue an expansionary monetary policy. The short-run aggregate supply curve reflecting these high-wage-increase agreements is depicted by $SRAS(P')$ in Exhibit 5, where P' is the expected price level. Note that AD'' is the aggregate demand expected if the announced low-money-growth policy is pursued, and AD' is the aggregate demand expected to result from a high-money-growth policy. Firms and workers have agreed to wage settlements that will produce the economy's potential level of output if the Fed behaves as *expected*, not as *announced*.

Monetary authorities must now decide whether to stick with their announcement of a low rate of increase in the money supply or follow a more expansionary monetary policy. If they follow the low-growth-rate policy, aggregate demand will turn out to be AD'' and the price level will be P'', which is lower than the level expected when the wage contracts were negotiated. The quantity of output firms will be willing to supply will decline because prices will be lower than expected and real wages will be

EXHIBIT 5   SHORT-RUN EFFECTS OF AN UNEXPECTED DECREASE IN THE MONEY SUPPLY

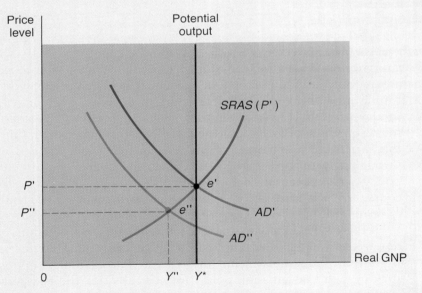

At point e', output is at potential and unemployment is at the natural rate. The Fed announces a slow-growth monetary policy. Firms and workers, however, do not believe the announcement; they think the monetary policy will be expansionary. The short-run aggregate supply curve, $SRAS(P')$, reflects their forecasts of the price level. The Fed must then decide what to do. If it follows the slow-growth policy, aggregate demand will be AD'' and output will fall below potential to point e''. To keep the economy performing at its potential, the Fed must increase the money supply by as much as workers and firms expected.

higher than expected. Thus, if the Fed follows through as announced, output will fall to Y''', which is below the economy's potential, resulting in unemployment above the natural rate.

If the monetary authorities want to keep the economy performing at its potential, they have only one alternative: they *must* increase the money supply by more than they had announced in order to meet workers' and firms' expectations. Such a policy will result in an aggregate demand of AD', and the economy will achieve its potential output and the expected price level, P', reflected in the wage contracts.

Thus firms and workers enter their negotiations with the realization that the Fed has an incentive to pursue a high-growth-rate monetary course. Therefore, workers and firms agree to high wage increases, and the Fed follows with a high-money-growth policy. This pattern of behavior results in more inflation. Once workers and firms come to expect an expansionary monetary policy and the resulting inflation, the growing money supply does not spur even a temporary boost in output beyond the economy's potential. *The rational expectations school believes that an expansionary monetary policy, if fully and correctly anticipated, has no effect on output or employment. Only unanticipated or incorrectly anticipated changes in policy can have an impact on output and employment.*

Policy Credibility

An unexpected increase in the money supply provides some initial short-term gains in the form of lower unemployment. The costs, however, are not only inflation in the long term but also a loss of credibility the next time around. Is there any way out of this cycle? For the Fed to get on a slow-money-growth, slow-inflation course, its announcements of slow growth must somehow be *credible*, or believable. Firms and workers must believe that when the time comes to make a hard decision, the Fed will follow through as promised. Perhaps the Fed could offer some sort of insurance policy to make everyone believe that policy makers who deviate from the set course will pay dearly—for example, the chairman of the Fed could promise to resign if the Fed does not pursue the announced course.

If the monetary policy makers thought of their reputations as valuable resources to be handled with care, they might be more reluctant to seek short-term reductions in unemployment. For example, suppose that by sticking to a low-inflation policy for several years, the Fed persuaded the public that such a policy would continue in future years. As firms and workers came to realize that the Fed was credible, they would be more willing to sign low-wage-increase contracts.

Much depends on the Fed's time horizon. If policy makers take the long view of their duties, they will be reluctant to risk their long-run policy effectiveness for a temporary reduction in unemployment. If Fed officials realize that their credibility is hard to develop but easy to undermine, they will carefully weigh the effects of their actions on their reputations and follow what monetarists believe is the optimal policy: slow, steady growth in the money supply.

Because of the market revolution in Eastern Europe, economic and political events there provide fresh evidence of the often hard choices government policy makers face. Policy issues involving the reunification of East and West Germany are discussed in the following case study.

After losing World War II, Germany was divided into West Germany, which evolved into one of the strongest capitalist countries in the world, and East Germany, which joined the Communist Bloc and lagged far behind. By 1990, because of antiquated factories, outdated production methods, and a different system of incentives, output per worker in East Germany was only about one-third that in West Germany.

Consequently, household income in East Germany was only about one-third that in West Germany. This lower income level translated into a much lower standard of living in East Germany. For example, nearly all West German households owned an automobile; only one in two East German households did. Also, nearly all West German households had phones, compared to only one in fourteen East German households.

Most East German households did not own color televisions, but they did have black-and-white sets, and these sets were often tuned to West German stations. East Germans therefore could see how low their own standard of living was in comparison. Pressure from East Germans for a better life was among the forces that helped to undermine the East German government, contributing to the fall of the Berlin Wall in November of 1989 and eventually ending nearly a half century of Communist rule. After the fall, East Germans streamed into West Germany at a rate that would be comparable to eleven million Americans' leaving the United States each year. The loss of skilled workers brought the already sagging East German economy to the brink of disaster. Something had to be done.

Public officials in both countries agreed that the ultimate solution was to reunify the two countries, allowing East Germany to be nourished by the economic strength of West Germany. That meant that East Germany would have to get rid of central planning and become more market oriented. But unless real incomes in East Germany could be moved closer to those in West Germany, East Germans would continue to seek higher-paying jobs in West Germany. This could spark an economic collapse in East Germany even after reunification. For reunification to work, East German productivity had to improve.

To increase labor productivity, West Germany would have to spend billions of marks to modernize deteriorating East German factories. What's more, East Germany needed billions to repair its roads and rail system, and billions more for environmental cleanup (East Germany was an environmental disaster). These additional spending requirements would necessitate both higher taxes and increased borrowing.

As a first step toward reunification, the two countries had to agree on a common currency. The West German mark was respected around the world and was the natural choice of a currency for a united Germany. But East Germans had 160 billion East German marks in savings accounts plus another 17 billion marks in circulation. The political sticking point in the reunification negotiations was the rate at which East German marks would be converted to West German marks.

Before reunification was contemplated, the exchange rate on the black market was 6 East German marks for 1 West German mark. Based on an accord reached in May 2, 1990, however, an official one-to-one conversion rate was set for wages, pensions, rents, and (with some exceptions) personal savings of up to 4000 marks. The conversion rate was set at 2 East German marks for 1 West German mark for company debt, personal savings above 4000 marks (most East Germans had less than 4000 marks in their savings accounts), and all other monetary exchanges. Thus the agreed-upon exchange rate amounted to a windfall gain to East Germans, who were able to convert their marks at far more favorable terms than was reflected by market forces.

If all East German marks were converted to West German marks and became part of the money supply, the supply of West German marks could double. Such an increase in the money supply would not generate inflation as long as the output of a united Germany increased proportionately. But public officials feared that the large increase in the number of West German marks in circulation would not be matched by an increase in productivity from East Germany's decaying economy. For one thing, the demand for East German goods was expected to fall once West German goods became available in East Germany. East German manufacturers had been able to sell their often inferior products only because most foreign competition was prohibited. For example, prior to the fall of the Berlin Wall, there was a fourteen-year waiting list for the only model of automobile produced in East Germany, the Trabant. The Trabant was a two-cycle, twenty-six horsepower piece of junk that reputedly tended to rust out after only 10,000 miles. The demand for Trabants was expected to fall sharply once East Germans were free to purchase the products of Mercedes-Benz and BMW. East Germans would use their newly converted marks to buy West German goods, creating unemployment in East German factories but raising prices for West German goods as demand outstripped production.

The merger was also expected to hurt West Germany's trade balance, which would move from a surplus to a deficit as goods and services flowed to East Germany rather than to the rest of the world. During the spring of 1990, the West German mark fell in value relative to the dollar as investors anticipated a jump in West German inflation, greater borrowing requirements by both government and private investors, and possible tax increases to finance East Germany's reconstruction.

Thus the monetary union fueled inflationary fears because West Germany was expected to have to pump money into the East German economy. In the spring of 1990, European interest rates soared because of the higher expected borrowing and higher expected rate of inflation. In response, interest rates in the United States rose as well. Because of the globalization of financial markets, news of financial developments flash with electronic speed around the world. Not too long ago, Fed officials focused almost exclusively on the U.S. economy; now, in order to have any effect on U.S. interest rates, they must consider the impact of economic events around the globe.

Sources: Richard Rustin and Michael Sesit, "German Bond Market Reels as Fear Grows Over Reunification's Impact," *Wall Street Journal*, 14 February 1990; Terence Roth, "East German Winners In Election Now Seek Fast Monetary Union," *Wall Street Journal*, 20 March 1990; John Bader, "Dollar Posts Gains Against the Mark Despite German Monetary Agreement," *Wall Street Journal*, 3 May 1990; and Timothy Aeppel, "East, West Germany Reach Accord on Plan for Merging of Economies," *Wall Street Journal*, 3 May 1990.

POLICY RULES

As we have noted, activists believe that the economy is inherently unstable and that a discretionary fiscal and monetary policy is needed to eliminate excessive unemployment when it arises. Nonactivists believe that the economy is inherently stable, so discretionary policy not only is unnecessary but causes destabilizing swings in the economy that ultimately lead to more inflation. In place of discretionary policy, nonactivists advocate predetermined rules to guide the actions of policy makers. In this section we examine the arguments for rules versus discretion, again in the context of monetary policy.

Rationale for Monetary Rules

As noted in the previous chapter, monetarists believe that changes in the quantity of money have a major influence on changes in nominal income. They also believe that stability in the behavior of the money stock is better for the economy in the long run than any discretionary monetary policy. In fact, monetarists attribute most past instability in nominal income to unstable money growth. Perhaps the strongest advocate of a monetary rule is Milton Friedman, who said:

> My own prescription is still that the monetary authority go all the way in avoiding such swings by adopting publicly the policy of achieving a specified rate of growth in a specified monetary total. The precise rate of growth, like the precise monetary total, is less important than the adoption of some stated and known rate.[1]

----

[1] Milton Friedman, "The Role of Monetary Policy," *American Economic Review* 58 (March 1968): 16.

In addition, Friedman contends that in the long run *excessive* increases in the money supply result in inflation. Exhibit 6 illustrates the relation between the average growth rate in the money supply and the average rate of inflation between 1980 and 1987 for ninety-one countries. As you can see, the points fall rather neatly along the trend line, showing a positive relation between money growth and inflation. Most countries are bunched below an inflation rate of 20 percent. The four countries that experienced annual inflation exceeding 100 percent also had an annual growth in the money supply exceeding 100 percent. For example, Bolivia, which had the highest average annual inflation rate, at 602 percent, also had the highest annual rate of growth in the money supply, at 589 percent. Conversely, countries such as Japan, West Germany, the Netherlands, and Austria had very low rates of inflation and very low rates of money growth. Such evidence has led Friedman and others to advocate a steady *and moderate* increase in the money supply year after year.

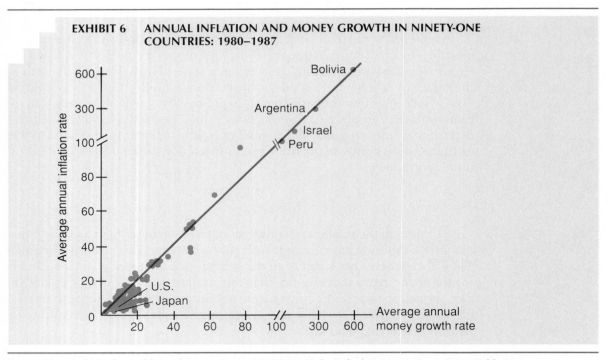

EXHIBIT 6   ANNUAL INFLATION AND MONEY GROWTH IN NINETY-ONE COUNTRIES: 1980–1987

Source: The World Bank, *World Development Report 1989* (New York: Oxford University Press, 1989), Table 13.

Kinds of Rules

A *monetary rule* specifies the relation that ties policy instruments, such as the growth in the money supply, to policy objectives, such as keeping inflation below a certain rate. A rule can specify that there is no policy relation. For example, it might state that the rate of growth in the money supply will be constant regardless of how the economy actually performs. Such a rule represents the most passive form of monetary policy.

A more active approach might be to link money supply growth to some measure of economic performance. For example, a rule might state that the money supply will grow as fast as real GNP, that the money supply will be adjusted to offset the growth in inflation (as inflation heats up, the growth in the money supply will be slowed), that the money supply will be adjusted to maintain a constant interest rate, or that the money supply will be adjusted to maintain a constant rate of inflation. These monetary policies are active in the sense that they respond to events. But because the response has been predetermined—that is, because it has been established by a previously adopted policy — little discretion is required of policy makers. Such a policy, however, does not completely eliminate discretion on the part of policy makers, because they must still determine what growth rate in the money supply will achieve the desired results. Policy makers must decide, for example, how much money should grow next year to match the growth in real GNP or to keep interest rates constant.

If monetary authorities are not penalized for departing from a predetermined rule, then it is not much of a rule. During the mid-1980s the Fed set targets for the growth in M1. When actual money growth exceeded planned growth, the Fed simply increased its targets during the year. Although actual money growth still exceeded the revised target, Fed officials were not penalized for overshooting their targets. Later in the decade, the Fed dropped M1 as a target and began announcing targets for M2 and M3, but only in 1988 did money growth conform to the announced targets.

Rationale for Rules

Some economists argue that binding constraints should be placed on the Fed. The rationale for rules arises from two different models of how the economy works. One group of economists contends that *the economy is so complex and economic aggregates interact in such inscrutable ways and with such varied lags that monetary authorities cannot comprehend what is going on well enough to pursue an appropriate discretionary policy.* Milton Friedman is perhaps the best-known advocate of this position. He argues that although there is a link between money growth and the growth in nominal GNP, the exact relation is hard to specify because of long lags in the response of economic activity to changes in money growth. If the central bank adopts a discretionary policy that is based on an incorrect estimate of the lag, money may expand just when a tighter monetary policy is more appropriate. Many economists believe that even if an appropriate monetary policy would have the desired result, nobody knows enough about how the economy works to implement that policy at the right time.

So on one hand, rules are advocated because of the complexity of the economy. To avoid doing the wrong thing at the wrong time, Friedman recommends that the Fed follow a fixed-growth-rate monetary policy year after year, such as an annual growth rate of 3 percent in the money supply. In order to achieve long-run price stability, the growth in the money supply should be just enough on average to match the underlying real growth of the economy. You might think of the constant-growth rule as being designed to reduce the risk of implementing the wrong policy at the wrong time.

A comparison of economic forecasters and weather forecasters may help you to understand the position of those who advocate the use of monetary rules to offset our ignorance of the workings of the economy. Suppose you are in charge of the heating and cooling system at the local shopping mall. You realize that weather forecasters have a poor record in your area, particularly in the early spring, when days can be either warm or cold. Each day you must guess what the temperature will be and, based on that guess, decide whether to fire up the heater or turn on the air conditioner. Because the ventilation system and the mall are so large, you must start up the system long before you know for sure what the weather will be. Once the system has been turned on, it cannot be turned off until later in the day.

Suppose you guess the day will be cold, so you turn on the heat. If the day turns out to be cold, your policy is correct and the mall temperature will be just right. But if the day turns out to be warm, the heater will make the mall unbearable. You would have been better off with no heat. In contrast, if you turn on the air conditioner expecting a warm day but the day turns out to be cold, the mall will be very cold. The lesson is that if you have little ability to predict the weather, you should use neither heat nor air conditioning. Similarly, if monetary officials cannot predict the course of the economy, they should not try to fine-tune monetary policy. Complicating the prediction problem is the fact that monetary officials are not sure about the lags involved with monetary policy. The situation is comparable to your not knowing for sure when you turn the heat on, how long it will take to come on.

The above analogy applies only if the cost of doing nothing—using neither heat nor air conditioning—is relatively low. In the early spring, you can assume that there is little risk of the temperature's being so extreme that pipes will freeze or the furnace will melt down. This assumption is like the nonactivists' assumption that the economy is inherently stable and periods of prolonged unemployment are unlikely. In such an economy, the costs of *not* intervening are relatively low. In contrast, activists believe that there can be wide and prolonged swings in the economy (analogous to wide and prolonged swings in temperature), so the nonactivist approach of doing nothing involves significant risks.

Rules and Rational Expectations

Another group of economists also advocates economic rules, but not because they believe we know too little about how the economy works. Proponents of the rational-expectations approach claim that people on average have a good idea about how the economy works and what to expect from policy makers. Individuals and firms are aware enough of the monetary and fiscal policies pursued in the past that they can anticipate future policies and the effects of these policies on the economy with reasonable accuracy. Some individuals will forecast too high and some too low, but on average forecasts will turn out to be correct.

Earlier we argued that only when the public was surprised by the Fed did monetary policy have an effect on output. *To the extent that monetary policy is fully anticipated by workers and firms, it has no effect on the level of output; it affects only the level of prices.* Thus, only unexpected changes in policy can bring about short-run changes in output.

Since in the long run changes in the money supply affect only the rate of inflation, not real output, followers of the rational expectations theory believe that the Fed should not try to pursue a discretionary monetary policy. Instead, the Fed should follow a predictable monetary rule, perhaps a rule that allows for adjustments in response to feedback. Because monetary surprises cause the actual price level to diverge from the expected price level, monetary policy should avoid such surprises. A monetary rule would reduce monetary surprises and would therefore reduce departures from the natural rate of output. *Whereas Friedman advocates a rule because of the Fed's ignorance about the lag structure of the economy, those who subscribe to the rational expectations theory want a predictable rule to avoid monetary surprises, which result in departures from the natural rate of output.*

Despite support by some economists for rules rather than discretion, central bankers appear reluctant to follow hard-and-fast rules about the course of future policy. Discretion appears to rule the day. As Paul Volcker, the former Fed chairman, argued:

> The appeal of a simple rule is obvious. It would simplify our job at the Federal Reserve, make monetary policy easy to understand, and facilitate monitoring of our performance. And if the rule worked, it would reduce uncertainty.... But unfortunately, I know of no rule that can be relied on with sufficient consistency in our complex and constantly evolving economy.[2]

THE PHILLIPS CURVE

At one time, policy makers thought they faced a fairly stable long-run tradeoff between inflation and unemployment. This view was suggested by the research of British economist A. W. Phillips, who in 1958 published an article that examined the historical relation between inflation and unemployment, using data from the United Kingdom.[3] Based on about one

---

[2] Statement of Paul Volcker, Chairman of the Board of Governors of the Federal Reserve System, before the Subcommittee on Domestic Monetary Policy of the Committee on Banking, Finance and Urban Affairs, U.S. House of Representatives, August 1983.

[3] A. W. Phillips, "Relation Between Unemployment and the Rate of Change in Money Wage Rates in the United Kingdom, 1861-1957," *Economica* 25 (November 1958): 283-299.

hundred years of evidence, his data suggested an inverse relation between the unemployment rate and changes in money wages (serving as a measure of inflation). This relation implied that the opportunity cost of reducing unemployment was higher inflation, and the opportunity cost of reducing inflation was higher unemployment.

The *Phillips curve* shows possible combinations of the inflation rate and the unemployment rate, given the expected price level.

The possible options with respect to unemployment and inflation are illustrated by the **Phillips curve** in Exhibit 7. The unemployment rate is measured along the horizontal axis, and the inflation rate along the vertical axis. Let's begin at point *a*, which depicts one possible combination of unemployment and inflation. Fiscal or monetary policy could be used to stimulate output and thereby reduce unemployment, moving the economy from point *a* to point *b*. Notice, however, that the reduction in unemployment comes at the cost of higher inflation. A reduction in unemployment with no offsetting change in inflation would be represented by point *c*. But as you can see, that alternative is not an option available on the curve. Thus, policy makers were thought to face a difficult tradeoff: they could choose either lower inflation or lower unemployment, but not both.

Although not everyone accepted the policy implications of the Phillips curve, during the 1960s policy makers increasingly came to believe that they faced a stable, long-run tradeoff between unemployment and inflation. The

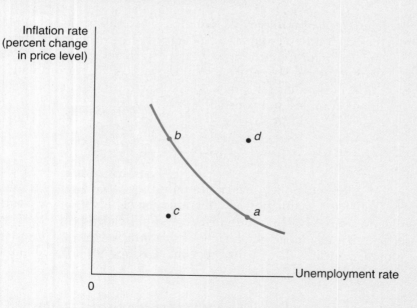

EXHIBIT 7   HYPOTHETICAL PHILLIPS CURVE

Points *a* and *b* lie on the Philllips curve and represent alternative combinations of the inflation rate and the unemployment rate that are attainable as long as the curve itself does not shift. Points *c* and *d* are off the curve; they are not attainable combinations.

Phillips curve was developed during a period when the primary disturbances in the economy were to aggregate demand. Changes in aggregate demand can be viewed as movements along a given short-run aggregate supply curve. If aggregate demand increased, the price level increased, but unemployment decreased. If aggregate demand decreased, the price level decreased, but unemployment increased. Many economists therefore assumed that there was a tradeoff between inflation and unemployment; hence, with appropriate demand-management policies, government policy makers could choose any point along the Phillips curve.

The experience in the 1970s proved this view wrong for two reasons. First, some of the biggest disturbances were supply shocks, such as the shocks created by the oil embargoes; these shocks resulted in leftward shifts in the aggregate supply curve. A reduction in aggregate supply led to both higher inflation and higher unemployment. This stagflation was at odds with the Phillips curve. Second, economists learned that when the short-run equilibrium output exceeds potential output, the economy opens an expansionary gap. As this gap is closed by the upward movement of the short-run aggregate supply curve, the results are greater inflation and higher unemployment — results inconsistent with a given Phillips curve.

The combination of high inflation and high unemployment resulting from stagflation and expansionary gaps is represented by an outcome such as point *d* in Exhibit 7. By the end of the 1970s, increases in inflation and unemployment suggested either that the Phillips curve had shifted out or that it no longer existed. The situation called for a reexamination of the Phillips curve, a reexamination that led economists to distinguish between short-run Phillips curves and the long-run Phillips curve.

Short-Run Phillips Curve

To discuss the underpinnings of the Phillips curve, we must return to the short-run aggregate supply curve. We begin by assuming that the price level *this year* is reflected by a price index of, say, 100. Suppose that people expect prices to be about 4 percent higher next year than this year, so the expected price level next year is 104. Workers will therefore negotiate labor contracts based on an expected price level of 104, which is 4 percent higher than the current price level. As the short-run aggregate supply curve in Exhibit 8(a) indicates, if AD^* is the aggregate demand curve and the price level is 104, as expected, output will equal the economy's potential GNP, Y^*. Recall that when the economy produces its potential GNP, unemployment is equal to the natural rate.

The short-run relation between inflation and unemployment is presented in Exhibit 8(b), where the unemployment rate is measured along the horizontal axis and the inflation rate along the vertical axis. Panel (a) showed that when the inflation rate is 4 percent, the economy produces its potential GNP. When the economy produces its potential GNP, unemployment is at the natural rate, which we assume to be 6 percent in panel (b). The combina-

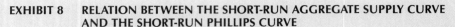

**EXHIBIT 8   RELATION BETWEEN THE SHORT-RUN AGGREGATE SUPPLY CURVE
AND THE SHORT-RUN PHILLIPS CURVE**

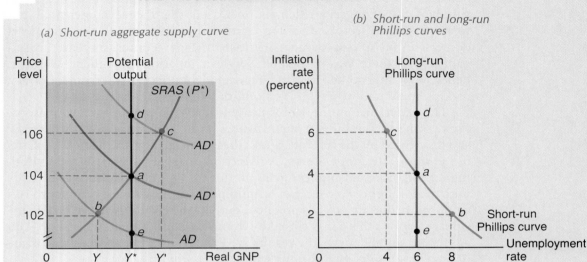

(a) Short-run aggregate supply curve

*(b) Short-run and long-run
Phillips curves*

If people expect a price level of 104, which is 4 percent higher than the current
level, and if AD^* is the aggregate demand curve, then the price level will actually
be 104 and output will be at the potential rate. Point a in both panels represents this
situation. Unemployment will be at the natural rate, 6 percent.

If aggregate demand is less than expected (AD rather than AD^*), short-run
equilibrium will be at point b; the price level, 102, will be lower than expected,
and output, Y, will be below the potential rate. The lower inflation rate and higher
unemployment rate are shown as point b in panel (b). If aggregate demand is
higher than expected (AD'), the economy will be at point c in both panels. In panel
(b), points a, b, and c trace the short-run Phillips curve.

In the long run, the actual price level equals the expected price level and output
is at the potential level, Y^*, in panel (a), and unemployment is at the natural rate, 6
percent, in panel (b). Points a, d, and e represent that situation; they lie on the
vertical long-run Phillips curve.

tion of 4 percent inflation and 6 percent unemployment is reflected by point
a in panel (b), which corresponds to point *a* in panel (a).

What if aggregate demand turns out to be less than expected, as indicated by *AD* in panel (a)? In the short run, the lower demand results in
equilibrium point *b*, where the price level of 102 is lower than the expected
level reflected in labor contracts and output, *Y*, is below potential GNP.
With a lower-than-expected price level, the inflation rate is 2 percent rather
than the expected 4 percent. With output below the economy's potential, the
unemployment rate is 8 percent, which exceeds the natural rate. This

combination of lower-than-expected inflation and higher-than-expected unemployment is reflected by point *b* on the curve in panel (b).

If the aggregate demand curve turns out to be *AD′*, then the short-run equilibrium is identified by point *c* in panel (a), with a price level of 106 and an output level of *Y′*. Since the price level is greater than the expected level reflected in wage contracts, the inflation rate is also greater than expected. Specifically, the inflation rate turns out to be 6 percent, not 4 percent. Output now exceeds the economy's potential, so the unemployment rate falls below the natural rate, to 4 percent. This combination of a higher inflation rate and a lower level of unemployment is depicted by point *c* in panel (b), which corresponds to point *c* in panel (a).

As you can see, the short-run aggregate supply curve in panel (a) can be used to establish the inverse relation between the inflation rate and the level of unemployment illustrated in panel (b). This latter curve is called a *short-run Phillips curve*, and it is generated by the intersection of alternative aggregate demand curves with a given short-run aggregate supply curve. The short-run Phillips curve is therefore based on labor contracts reflecting a given expected price level, which implies a given expected rate of inflation. The short-run Phillips curve in panel (b) is based on an expected inflation rate of 4 percent. If inflation turns out as expected, unemployment will equal the natural rate. If inflation is lower than expected, unemployment in the short run will exceed the natural rate. If inflation is higher than expected, unemployment in the short run will fall below the natural rate.

Long-Run Phillips Curve

If inflation is higher than was expected when long-term labor contracts were negotiated, output can exceed the economy's potential in the short run, but not in the long run. Labor shortages and worker dissatisfaction with shrinking real wages will lead to higher wage agreements during the next round of negotiations. The short-run aggregate supply curve will shift up to the left until it passes through point *d* in Exhibit 8(a), returning the economy to its potential level of output. Point *d* represents a higher price level and hence a higher rate of inflation, but notice that the higher inflation is no longer associated with reduced unemployment. The economy, in closing the expansionary gap, thus experiences both higher unemployment and higher inflation. At point *d* in panel (a), the economy is producing its potential GNP, which means that unemployment equals the natural rate. This combination of higher inflation and the natural rate of unemployment is depicted by point *d* in panel (b). The unexpectedly higher aggregate demand has no lasting effect on output or unemployment. Note that whereas points *a, b,* and *c* are on the same short-run Phillips curve, point *d* is not.

To trace the long-run effects of a lower-than-expected price level, let's return again to point *b* in Exhibit 8(a). At this point the actual price level is below the expected level reflected in long-term contracts, so output is below potential GNP. If, over time, firms and workers negotiate lower money wages (or if the growth in nominal wages trails inflation), the short-run aggregate supply curve will shift to the right until it passes through point *e*, where the economy returns once again to its potential level of output. Both inflation and unemployment will fall, as reflected by point *e* in panel (b).

Note that points *a*, *d*, and *e* in panel (a) depict long-run equilibrium points, so the expected price level equals the actual price level. At those same points in panel (b), the expected inflation equals the actual inflation, so unemployment equals the natural rate. We can connect points *a*, *d*, and *e* in panel (b) to form what is called the *long-run Phillips curve*. *When employers and workers have the time and the ability to adjust fully to any unexpected change in aggregate demand, the long-run Phillips curve is a vertical line drawn at the economy's natural rate of unemployment*, as shown in panel (b). As long as prices and wages are flexible, the rate of unemployment is, in the long run, independent of the rate of inflation. *Thus, in the long run, policy makers cannot choose between unemployment and inflation. They can choose only among alternative levels of inflation.*

Natural Rate Hypothesis

*According to the **natural rate hypothesis**, the natural rate of unemployment is largely independent of the stimulus provided by monetary or fiscal policy.*

As mentioned in Chapter 10, the natural rate of unemployment is the rate of unemployment that is consistent with the economy's potential level of output, which we have discussed extensively already. An important idea to emerge from this reexamination of the Phillips curve is the **natural rate hypothesis**, which holds that in the long run the economy tends toward the natural rate of unemployment. This natural rate is largely independent of the level of the *aggregate demand* stimulus provided by monetary or fiscal policy. Policy makers may be able to push the economy beyond its natural or potential rate of production temporarily, but only if the public does not anticipate the resulting level of aggregate demand and the resulting price level.

The *weak version* of the natural rate hypothesis is that policy makers can influence the tradeoff between unemployment and inflation in the short run but not in the long run. Unemployment could be maintained below the natural rate, but only at the cost of ever-increasing inflation. For example, if the Fed increased the money supply at a faster and faster rate, actual inflation would rise faster and faster, continually exceeding expected inflation. But such a policy is clearly self-limiting. In the long run, monetary or fiscal policy affects only the rate of inflation, not the rate of unemployment; in the long run, there is no tradeoff between inflation and unemployment.

In the *strong version* of the natural rate hypothesis, even this short-run kick becomes smaller and smaller over time. According to the rational expectations theory, market participants gain experience as time goes by, so they adjust more and more rapidly to policy decisions expected to affect the price level. As market participants learn more about the behavior of policy makers, the cycles generated by short-run fluctuations in inflation and unemployment that result from discretionary policy get smaller and smaller. People become more adept not only at predicting the effects of a policy on the economy but also at predicting the policy itself. It becomes more and more difficult for policy makers to surprise the public. Therefore, the short-run gains in employment resulting from monetary or fiscal surprises diminish as the public comes to expect as much. An implication of the natural rate hypothesis is that *regardless of policy makers' concerns about unemployment, the policy that results in low inflation is generally going to be the optimal policy in the long run.*

Inflation and Unemployment Evidence

What has been the actual relation between unemployment and inflation in the United States? In Exhibit 9, the relation for each year since 1960 is represented by a point, with the unemployment rate measured along the horizontal axis and the inflation rate measured along the vertical axis. Superimposed on these points is a series of short-run Phillips curves showing patterns of unemployment and inflation during four distinct periods since 1960. Remember, each short-run Phillips curve is drawn for a given expected rate of inflation. A change in inflationary expectations results in a shift in the short-run Phillips curve.

Notice that the clearest tradeoff between unemployment and inflation seems to have occurred between 1960 and 1969; the points for those years fit neatly along the curve. In the early part of the decade, inflation was low, but unemployment was high; as the 1960s progressed, unemployment declined, but inflation increased. The average inflation rate during the decade was only 2.5 percent, and the average unemployment rate was 4.8 percent.

The short-run Phillips curve appears to have shifted up to the right for

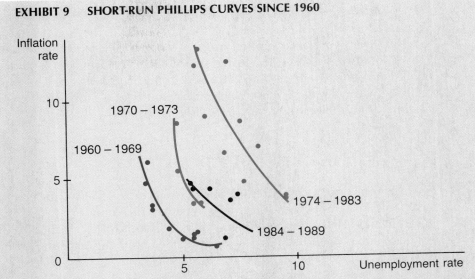

EXHIBIT 9   SHORT-RUN PHILLIPS CURVES SINCE 1960

The figure shows unemployment-inflation rate combinations since 1960. Note that the short-run Phillips curve has shifted as inflation expectations have changed.

the period 1970 to 1973, when inflation and unemployment both climbed to an average of 5.2 percent. In 1974 sharp increases in oil prices and crop failures around the world sparked another shift in the curve. Though points for the decade between 1974 and 1983 do not lie as neatly along the curve as points for earlier periods do, a tradeoff between inflation and unemployment is still evident. During the 1974–1983 period, inflation rose on average to 8.2 percent and unemployment climbed on average to 7.5 percent.

Finally, after recessions in the early 1980s, the short-run Phillips curve seems to have shifted down for the balance of the 1980s; average inflation for 1984–1989 fell to 3.7 percent, and average unemployment fell to 6.4 percent. Changes in the average unemployment rate across periods since 1960 suggest that the underlying natural rate of unemployment may have shifted as well. (You'll recall that earlier we discussed the possibility that the natural rate has drifted higher since the 1960s.)

In Pursuit of Zero Inflation

In 1989 a resolution was proposed in Congress directing the Fed "to adopt and pursue monetary policies leading to, and then maintaining, zero inflation." According to the resolution, inflation would be considered eliminated "when the expected rate of change in the general level of prices ceases to be a factor in individual decisionmaking."[4] Inflation between 1982 and the end of the decade averaged about 4 percent—much lower than the 8.6 percent average that prevailed between 1970 and 1981. Still, many believe that, despite the lower rate, uncertainty about future prices causes business planners to postpone or cancel investment programs that could add to income and employment.

Federal Reserve Chairman Alan Greenspan testified in support of the congressional resolution, stating that he thought the goal was attainable within the five years specified in the resolution. He said that although the zero inflation goal could involve some reduced output in the short run, it need not create a recession. Short-run output losses could be more than offset by the long-run gain that would result from a more stable investment and employment climate.[5]

CONCLUSION

This chapter examined the policy implications of activism versus nonactivism. The important question is whether the economy is (1) essentially stable and self-correcting when it gets off track or (2) essentially unstable and in need of activist policies. Activists believe that the federal government

---

[4] House Joint Resolution 409, 101st Congress, 1st Session, September 25, 1989.

[5] Greenspan's testimony was reported by Lindley H. Clark in "Do We Want or Need Zero Inflation," *Wall Street Journal,* November 6, 1989.

should reduce swings in the business cycle by stimulating a sluggish economy when output falls below its potential level and dampening an overheated economy when output exceeds its potential level. They argue that government attempts to insulate the economy from the ups and downs of the business cycle may be far from perfect, but they are better than nothing. Nonactivists, on the other hand, believe that discretionary policy may contribute to the cyclical swings in the economy, leading to higher inflation in the long run with no permanent effect on either output or employment.

The activist-nonactivist debate in this chapter has focused on monetary policy primarily because the debate over fiscal policy in recent years has been confined to discussions of the impact on the economy of huge federal deficits. In the next chapter we will take a closer look at these deficits.

Summary

1. Activists view the private sector—particularly, fluctuations in investment—as the main source of economic instability in the economy. Because the return to potential output can be slow and painful, activists recommend that the government intervene with monetary or fiscal policy to stimulate aggregate demand when output is below potential output.

2. Nonactivists view the private economy as essentially stable, except when misguided discretionary government policy creates instability. Nonactivists argue that the economy has a natural resiliency which will cause output to return to its potential level within a reasonable amount of time. Nonactivists also point to the variable and uncertain lags associated with monetary and fiscal policy as reason enough to steer clear of active intervention.

3. Nonactivists suggest that the government should follow steady and predictable policies and avoid trying to stimulate or dampen aggregate demand over the business cycle. Rules dictating a predictable and moderate growth in the money supply have been supported by monetarists and rational expectationists.

4. At one time public officials were thought to face a tradeoff between higher unemployment and higher inflation. Recent evidence suggests that if there is a tradeoff, it is only in the short run, not in the long run. Expansionary fiscal or monetary policies, if unexpected, can stimulate output and employment in the short run. But if the economy is already at or near its potential output, these expansionary policies will in the long run result only in higher inflation.

Questions and Problems

1. (Activists Versus Nonactivists) One issue that activists and nonactivists argue about is whether interest rates can be kept low by the actions of the Federal Reserve. Does it seem reasonable that the Fed can keep nominal interest rates permanently low by injecting more and more money into the economy? Why or why not?

2. (Aggregate Supply) What is the variable that naturally adjusts in the labor market, shifting the aggregate supply curve to guarantee full employment at the natural rate? Is it reasonable to assume that the aggregate supply curve shifts up more easily and quickly than it shifts down? Why or why not?

3. (Rational Expectations) Can the government fool the public with erratic monetary and fiscal policy if the public has rational expectations? Suppose that the government uses a monetarist rule. How will rational expectations affect the impact of the rule?

4. (Rational Expectations) Some economists in the late 1970s believed that it might be possible to reduce the very high inflation rate then prevailing without causing higher unemployment. However, they emphasized that the Fed would have to make clear its intention and stick to its policy. In the end, inflation fell dramatically, but not without producing very high unemployment. Is this evidence against the rational expectations hypothesis? Why or why not?

5. (Macroeconomic Policy) Some economists argue that only unanticipated increases in the money supply cause increases in GNP. Explain why this may be the case.

6. (Macroeconomic Policy) An activist economist in the government argues that the current rate of unemployment could be greatly reduced through fiscal and monetary policies. The nonactivist claims that such policies would create price instability. What information must the government have to decide whose advice is better?

7. (Rules) There has been a great deal of talk about a balanced-budget amendment to the Constitution. This would be a rule for fiscal policy. How would you evaluate this rule based on the macroeconomic model discussed in the text?

8. (Phillips Curve) Why does a movement up the short-run Phillips curve imply a declining real wage for workers? Would workers allow this decline to continue unabated? How would the short-run Phillips curve adjust to changes in workers' perceptions about their real wage?

9. (Natural Rate of Unemployment) The natural rate of unemployment was once characterized as "inevitable unemployment" in the *Economic Report of the President*. Why would such words be chosen? What determines the natural rate of employment?

10. (Potential GNP) Why is it hard for policy makers to decide if the economy is operating at its potential output level? Why don't they just look to see if there is full employment?

11. (Activists Versus Nonactivists) Discuss the role each of the following should play in the debate between activists and nonactivists.

a. The speed of adjustments in nominal wages

b. The speed of adjustments in expectations about inflation

c. The existence of lags in policy creation and implementation

d. Variability in the natural rate of unemployment over time

12. (Phillips Curve) Describe the different Phillips curve tradeoffs implied by the activist viewpoint, the weak version of rational expectations, and the strong version of rational expectations.

13. (Phillips Curve) The original Phillips curve research compared the unemployment rate with the rate of nominal wage adjustment (i.e., it was a wage Phillips curve). Show how you would construct a price Phillips curve, like those shown in the text, based on a wage Phillips curve.

Budgets, Deficits, and Public Policy

The word *budget* is derived from the Old French word *bougette*, which means "little bag." The federal budget is now well over $1,000,000,000,000 — over $1 trillion. Big money! If this "little bag" contained $100 bills, it would weigh over 10,000 *tons*! This annual budget is more than enough to cover all the rent and mortgage payments for every family in the country each year.

In this chapter we will first examine the federal budget process, then spend the balance of the chapter on what appear to be the major budget concerns today: the giant budget deficits generated during the 1980s and the national debt, which has grown to more than $3 trillion. We will look at the source of deficits over the years and the immediate effects of deficits on the economy. We will then examine the short-run and long-run effects of the national debt. Topics discussed in this chapter include

- The budget process
- Rationale for deficits
- Impact of deficits

- The burden of the debt
- Measures to reduce deficits

THE BUDGET PROCESS

The **government budget** is a plan for government expenditures and revenues for a specified period, usually a year. The period covered by the federal budget is called the *fiscal year*, which runs from October 1 of one

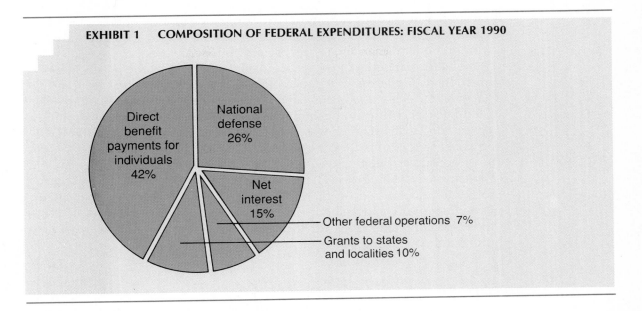

EXHIBIT 1   COMPOSITION OF FEDERAL EXPENDITURES: FISCAL YEAR 1990

*The **government budget** is a plan for government expenditures and revenues for a specified period, usually a year.*

calendar year to September 30 of the following calendar year. About one-third of the federal budget is spent directly on goods and services, mostly for national defense. The rest goes to transfer payments for Social Security, income-support programs, aid to state and local governments, farm subsidies, and interest on the national debt. Exhibit 1 provides a percentage breakdown of federal spending by major category.

The Presidential Role in the Budget Process

Before 1921 the federal government played a minor role in the economy, with federal spending, except during wartime, accounting for less than 3 percent of GNP (versus more than 22 percent today). Federal agencies applied directly to Congress for their appropriations. Congress had no systematic way of reviewing and evaluating these budget requests, and the president was completely bypassed in the budget process.

Procedures changed with the Budget and Accounting Act of 1921, the first of many laws aimed at putting the president into the budget picture. The act created the Office of Management and Budget (OMB) to examine agency budget requests and help the president develop a budget proposal. Later, the Employment Act of 1946 created the Council of Economic Advisers to forecast economic activity and assist the president in formulating an appropriate fiscal policy. (You'll recall that *fiscal policy* involves the use of taxation and government spending to influence aggregate economic variables, such as GNP, employment, and inflation.)

During the 1960s and 1970s, various measures were introduced by the executive branch to improve the evaluation of government programs. By the mid-1970s the president had in place the staff and the procedures to translate policy into a budget proposal to be presented to the Congress. Development of the President's budget begins a year before it is submitted to Congress, with each agency preparing a budget request.

The formal budget process begins in January, with the president's submission to Congress of a fat book called *The Budget of the United States Government*. This document details the president's proposals about what should be spent in the upcoming year and how this spending should be financed. At this stage, however, the president's budget is little more than detailed suggestions for congressional consideration.

Soon after a budget is proposed, the *Economic Report of the President* is also transmitted to Congress. This report, required under the Employment Act of 1946 and written by the Council of Economic Advisers, reflects the administration's views about the state of the economy and includes fiscal policy recommendations for fostering "maximum employment, production, and purchasing power."

The Congressional Role in the Budget Process

Since the Congressional Budget Act was passed in 1974, budget committees in the House and the Senate have been responsible for the overall budget policy. These budget committees agree on the size of the budget, spending by major category, and expected revenues. A comparison of their figures for total spending and total revenue produces an estimated deficit or surplus, which reflects the budget's underlying fiscal policy. *The Budget Act was conceived as a way of allowing Congress to participate in fiscal policy, for only if Congress viewed the budget in broad outline rather than as a collection of many separate programs could the fiscal effect of the budget on the economy be perceived.*

Once an overall budget strategy has been passed by Congress as a *budget resolution*, this resolution is supposed to discipline the many committees and subcommittees that authorize spending by establishing the framework within which spending and revenue decisions should be confined. Specific appropriations and tax measures should conform to the overall plan. The process allows committees some flexibility until a binding budget resolution is passed by both houses.

The Congressional Budget Act also provided a timetable for making budget decisions. The process begins in January, when the presidential budget is delivered to Congress, and ends October 1, when the new fiscal year begins. Thus, the federal budget has a congressional gestation period of about nine months, though, as we have noted, the president's budget begins taking shape a year before the January submission.

The spending side of the budget is usually outlined in more detail than the revenue side. Most taxes are collected on the basis of certain rules and schedules that change infrequently. Of special interest is the bottom line, the relation between *budgeted* expenditures and *projected* revenues. The difference between expenditures and revenues is one measure of the budget's fiscal impact. *When expenditures exceed revenues, the budget is projected to be in deficit; a rising deficit is expected to stimulate aggregate demand.* Recall that if government spending increases, other things constant, then the change in aggregate demand equals the change in government spending times the autonomous spending multiplier. Alternatively, *when revenues exceed expenditures, the budget is projected to be in surplus; a rising surplus is expected to dampen aggregate demand.*

Problems with the Budget Process

Despite reforms introduced by the 1974 Congressional Budget Act, the federal budget process still appears to be out of control. There are several major problems.

Overlapping Committee Authority The new approach retained all the old committees and simply added the budget committees as another layer of authority. Thus, all the existing authorizing, appropriating, and tax-writing committees still have to do their work on the budget. Since the overlap in budget authority across committees was not eliminated, the executive branch must defend the same section of the president's budget before several committees in both the House and the Senate. Hence, *those responsible for running the federal government end up spending much of their time testifying before assorted congressional committees.* Because several committees have jurisdiction over the same area, no committee really has final authority, so matters often remain unresolved even after extensive committee deliberations.

Lengthy Budget Process The executive branch takes about a year to prepare the budget it proposes to Congress. Congress then has nine more months to refashion the president's budget to members' liking. In practice, Congress usually takes longer. You can imagine the difficulty of using the budget as a tool of fiscal policy when the process takes so long. Given that the average recession lasts only about a year and that budget preparations begin more than a year and a half before the budget goes into effect, planning discretionary fiscal measures to deal with recessions through the budget process is nearly impossible.

Continuing Resolutions Instead of Budget Decisions The budget timetable discussed above has been largely ignored by Congress. Because deadlines are often missed, budgets typically run from year to year based on *continuing resolutions*, which are agreements to allow agencies, in the absence of an approved budget, to spend at the rate of the previous year's budget. Poorly conceived programs continue through sheer inertia; successful programs remain in limbo and cannot be expanded. On occasion the president has to shut down the entire government temporarily because not even the continuing resolution can be approved in time.

Overly Detailed Budget The federal budget is divided into thousands of accounts and subaccounts. Congress tends to budget in such minute detail that the big picture often gets lost. To the extent that the budget is a way of making political payoffs, such micromanagement allows Congress to reward friends and punish enemies with great precision. Moreover, the president has little control over the specifics of the budget and must either accept or veto the entire budget as is. Since the president usually receives the budget at the eleventh hour, a veto would shut down the government, so budget vetoes are rare. This *detailed budgeting not only is time-consuming, but also reduces the flexibility of fiscal policy.* When economic conditions change or when there is a shift in the demand for certain kinds of publicly provided goods, the federal government cannot easily reallocate funds from one account to another.

Uncontrollable Budget Items Congress has only limited control over much of the budget. Some budget items, such as interest on the national debt, cannot be changed in the near term. *About three-quarters of the budget falls into expenditure categories that are determined by existing laws.* For example, once Congress establishes eligibility criteria, entitlement programs such as Social Security take on a life of their own, with each annual appropriation simply reflecting the amount required to support the expected number of eligible beneficiaries. Congress has no say in such appropriations unless it chooses to change the eligibility criteria or the level of benefits.

Suggested Budget Reforms

Several reforms have been suggested to improve the budget process. First, the annual budget could be converted into a two-year budget, or *biennial budget.* As it is, Congress spends nearly all of the year working on the budget. The executive branch is always dealing with three budgets: administering an approved budget, defending a proposed budget before congressional committees, and preparing yet another budget for submission to Congress. If decisions were made for two years at a time, Congress would not be continually involved with budget deliberations, and executive branch heads could run their agencies rather than marching from committee hearing to committee hearing. Two-year budgets, however, would require longer-term economic forecasts of the economy and would be even less useful than the one-year budget as a tool of fiscal policy.

Another possible reform would be for Congress to simplify the budget document by concentrating on major groupings and eliminating line items. Each agency head could then be given an overall budget, along with the discretion to allocate funds in a manner consistent with the perceived demands for agency services.

FEDERAL BUDGET DEFICITS

The big budget story in recent years has been the giant federal deficits, deficits nobody appears to want. These deficits add up. It took thirty-nine presidents, six wars, the Great Depression, and more than two hundred years for the federal debt to reach $1 trillion, as it did in 1982. It took only eight more years for that debt to reach $3 trillion. Ironically, this tripling of the national debt occurred primarily under President Reagan, who was initially elected on a promise to balance the budget. To place deficits in perspective, we will first examine the economic rationale for deficit financing.

Rationale for Deficits

Deficit financing has been justified for outlays that increase the economy's productivity — outlays for investments such as highways, waterways, and dams. The cost of these capital goods should be borne in part by future taxpayers, who will also benefit from these investments. This rationale is used to fund capital projects at the state and local level, but a capital budget as such has not been part of the federal budget process.

Until the Great Depression, only wars generated deficits at the federal level. Because wars involved much hardship, public officials were understandably reluctant to increase taxes to finance war-related expenditures. Deficits arising during wars were largely self-correcting, however, because after each war public expenditures dropped faster than did public revenues.

The depression led John Maynard Keynes to develop a new role for deficit spending. As you know, the Keynesian prescription for fighting an economic slump was for the federal government to stimulate aggregate demand through deficit spending. Certain *automatic stabilizers* (first discussed in Chapter 11) were also introduced; these increase government spending during recessions and decrease it during expansions.

The federal deficit increases during recessions because the federal government avoids raising tax rates or imposing deep cuts in government spending during these troubled times. Rather, *as economic activity slows down, unemployment rises, increasing government outlays for unemployment benefits and other transfer payments.* Furthermore, tax revenues decline during recessions. During the 1981–1982 recession, for example, tax revenues from corporations fell by $19 billion (even after accounting for federal tax cuts in 1981), while transfer payments jumped by more than $30 billion. An economic recovery is the other side of the coin. As business activity expands, so do jobs, personal income, and corporate profits, causing federal revenues to swell. With reduced joblessness, transfer payments decline. Thus, the federal deficit falls.

Budget Philosophies and Deficits

Several budget philosophies have emerged over the years. Fiscal policy prior to the Great Depression aimed at maintaining an *annually balanced budget*. Such an approach calls for the government to reduce spending when tax revenues fall during recessions and to increase spending as revenues rise during expansions. A major disadvantage of this approach is that the federal government reinforces business cycle fluctuations.

A second budget philosophy is to have a *cyclically balanced budget*, which requires that the federal government run deficits during recessions and surpluses during expansions, balancing the budget over the course of the business cycle. Fiscal policy is thereby able to dampen swings in the business cycle, but it does not accumulate a growing national debt over the years. Many state governments have established "rainy day" funds in which budget surpluses accumulate during the good times, for use during the periods when revenues lag behind expenditures. The problem with this approach is that the fluctuations in economic activity are not usually symmetrical enough to ensure that the surplus will offset the deficit.

A third budget philosophy is *functional finance*, which says that policy makers should be less concerned with balancing the budget annually or even over the business cycle than with seeing that the economy produces its potential GNP. If the budget needed to keep the economy operating at its potential involves chronic deficits, so be it. According to the functional finance philosophy, one of the federal government's primary responsibilities is to promote economic stability at the potential level of output.

In this country since the Great Depression, budgets have been neither annually nor cyclically balanced. *Although budget deficits have been greater during recessions than during recoveries, the federal budget has been in deficit in all but eight years since 1931.* In fact, the budget has been in deficit every year since 1970. Exhibit 2 shows the deficit since 1979, with periods of recession shaded. As you can see, deficits worsened during the recessions of the early 1980s. But even during expansions there were deficits. The largest deficits in the country's history occurred during the four years of recovery between 1983 and 1986, when the deficit amounted to about 5 percent of GNP.

*The **structural deficit** measures what the federal budget deficit would be if the economy were producing its potential level of output.*

Because GNP fluctuates as the economy moves through the business cycle, actual budgets are not a good measure of fiscal policy. For example, the government could be pursuing a tight fiscal policy, reducing discretionary expenditures and increasing taxes, yet a recession could still create a substantial deficit. The **structural deficit** is an estimate of what the deficit or surplus would be if the economy were producing at its potential; that part of the deficit or surplus arising from the business cycle is filtered out. *The larger the structural deficit, the more stimulative the fiscal policy.* The structural deficit since 1979 is also presented in Exhibit 2. Notice that during the 1980s the structural deficit has been stimulative.

Deficits in the 1980s

In 1981 President Reagan, charged up by his stunning election victory, secured a three-year budget resolution that included a historic tax cut, increases in defense spending, and reductions in some domestic programs. The congressional budget resolution adopted in 1981 was based on the assumption that unspecified spending cuts would bring the two sides of the budget into balance, but the promised cuts were never made. Moreover, overly optimistic revenue projections were built into the budget. Some supply-side proponents argued that tax cuts would stimulate enough economic activity to keep tax revenues from falling.

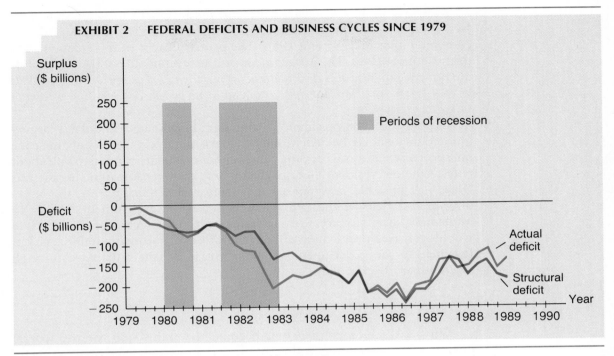

EXHIBIT 2   FEDERAL DEFICITS AND BUSINESS CYCLES SINCE 1979

Source: Federal Reserve Bank of St. Louis, *Monetary Trends*, various issues.

The budget projected that real GNP would grow by 5.2 percent in 1982, but the economy actually fell into a recession and output dropped by 2.1 percent. *The recession caused the automatic stabilizers in the budget to take effect, thereby reducing revenues and increasing spending still more.* Revenues dropped below budget forecasts for two reasons. First, the recession reduced profits and income. Second, an unexpected drop in inflation reduced the windfall revenues the federal government reaped from inflation. During the 1970s the progressive income tax coupled with sharply higher inflation had moved many taxpayers into higher tax brackets, thereby increasing federal revenues. The sharp drop in inflation, from 8.9 percent in 1981 to 3.8 percent in 1982, reduced the federal revenue resulting from such "bracket creep." (Beginning in 1985 personal income tax brackets were indexed for inflation, so personal income taxes no longer increase automatically because of inflation.) Since spending was underestimated and revenue was overestimated, the deficit in 1982 was $146 billion, at the time the largest in history.

The deficit served as a backdrop for budget debates in the early 1980s. President Reagan's budget strategy called for increases in defense spending, but he promised to veto any new taxes or any cuts in Social Security. The deficit worsened to $176 billion in 1983. During the presidential campaign of 1984, candidate Walter Mondale warned that taxes would have to be increased to close the budget deficit. President Reagan, however, blamed the deficits on the recession and predicted that as the economy improved, the deficit would disappear even without tax increases; he claimed the country would grow out of the deficit.

Reagan won the 1984 election but lost the argument about the deficit. In fact, even though the recession was long since over, the annual deficit climbed higher in 1985 and 1986. The primary cause of these deficits was the tax cuts of 1981. The government cut the revenue side of the budget but did not cut expenditures. *Federal spending rose from 22.5 percent of GNP in 1980 to 24.4 percent in 1986. Receipts during the same period fell from 20.3 percent of GNP to 19.5 percent.*

During the 1988 presidential campaign, both major candidates largely ignored the issue of the deficit, since to make much of it would only raise the question of what was to be done, and neither candidate wanted to talk about taxes. One of President George Bush's best known campaign slogans was "Read my lips: No new taxes." As mentioned in Chapter 11, the large, unwanted deficits of the 1980s have reduced the government's ability to implement discretionary fiscal measures during a recession. A recession would increase the deficit because of the effects of automatic stabilizers, but few believe the government should increase deficits still more through discretionary fiscal policy.

Why Deficits? Why Now?

Why has a budget in deficit become the status quo for the federal government? As mentioned already, the deficits of the 1980s were caused by the tax cuts in the early part of the decade and the failure to make comparable cuts in spending. But why has the budget been in deficit for all but eight years since 1931?

As an explanation, let's consider one widely accepted model of public choice. Elected officials attempt to maximize political support, including votes and campaign contributions. Voters enjoy public goods but dislike taxes, so public expenditure programs win support but taxes lose support. Because of this asymmetry in the relative payoffs, *elected officials attempt to maximize their chances of being elected by offering a budget that is long on benefits but short on taxes.* Moreover, the many fragmented congressional committees push their favorite programs with little concern about the overall budget. For example, the 1990 defense authorization bill included eighteen F-14D fighter jets and thirty-six V-22 Osprey aircraft because the planes were produced by firms located in key congressional districts, even though the Pentagon did not want the planes.

This asymmetry in favor of spending may explain why we have deficits, but it does not explain why deficits were not typical before the Great Depression. If politicians have always favored spending programs over taxes, why has it been only since the depression that deficits have predominated? Nobel laureate James Buchanan has argued that the rational self-interest of elected officials has always given them a preference for nontax sources of revenue. Prior to Keynes, however, they were constrained from resorting to deficit financing by the view that such a fiscal policy was *immoral.* According to Buchanan, Victorian fiscal morality dictated adherence to a balanced budget. Keynes revolted against those precepts, replacing the notion of the moral superiority of a balanced budget with an economic argument about why deficits could be good for the country. *After Keynes, it was no longer considered immoral for people, through their government, to spend more than they were willing to tax themselves.*

The Relation Between Deficits and Other Aggregate Variables

There is much talk in the news media about the relations among deficits, interest rates, and inflation. To develop a clearer understanding of these relations, let's consider the following simplification. We begin with the federal budget in balance and the economy producing its potential GNP (point e^* in Exhibit 3). Thus, *the structural deficit—the deficit when the economy produces its potential output—is equal to zero.* The short-run aggregate supply curve is based on long-term labor contracts reflecting an expected price level of P^*.

EXHIBIT 3   DEFICITS AND OTHER MEASURES OF THE ECONOMY'S PERFORMANCE

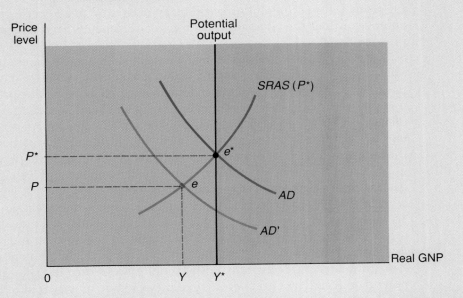

At point e^*, the federal budget is in balance and output is at potential. A decline in aggregate demand to AD' triggers automatic stabilizers. Tax revenues fall, transfer payments increase, and the budget moves to a deficit position. In this case the deficit is associated with falling output and a falling price level.

With the economy now at point e, suppose policy makers stimulate aggregate demand through expansionary fiscal policy. Tax revenues fall, government expenditures increase, and the deficit grows larger. Here the deficit is associated with rising output and a rising price level.

Suppose an unexpected decline in private sector spending reduces aggregate demand. As output and employment decline, the automatic stabilizers kick in, reducing tax revenues and increasing transfer payments. These stabilizers keep aggregate demand from falling as much as it would without them. Still, the aggregate demand curve drops from *AD* to *AD'*, resulting in a short-run equilibrium at output level *Y*. This combination of reduced tax revenues and increased government outlays results in a budget deficit. According to research, every 1 percent increase in the unemployment rate increases the federal deficit by over $30 billion.

Now let's consider the association between this deficit and what happens to real output, the price level, and interest rates. The first two are easy to predict: the deficit resulting from the automatic stabilizers is associated with falling real output and a falling price level. But the interaction of two opposing forces determines the interest rate. First, when output and the price level decline, the transactions demand for money declines as well, so the interest rate will tend to fall. Second, to finance the government deficit, the U.S. Treasury must sell securities, and this additional supply of securities in the market will put upward pressure on interest rates. The net effect on interest rates will depend on which force is stronger, the falling demand for money or the rising supply of government securities. Thus, a deficit resulting from automatic stabilizers will be associated with a lower level of price and output, but the effect on the interest rate depends on opposing market pressures.

At point *e*, the economy is in recession, with a short-run equilibrium output that is below the economy's potential. Either policy makers can do nothing and wait for natural market forces to correct the problem of unemployment or they can intervene in some way. Recall that activists believe that if no government action is taken, the adjustment to potential output could be long and painful, with much unemployment and much forgone output. Nonactivists believe that government intervention involves unpredictable lags and may affect aggregate demand only after the economy has naturally returned to its potential.

Suppose the government increases its spending without changing taxes. To finance this increase in the deficit, the Treasury must sell more securities to the public, a move that tends to put upward pressure on interest rates. According to the activist view, the correct increase in government spending will stimulate aggregate demand just enough to return the economy to its potential GNP. The effects of this policy would be represented in Exhibit 3 by a movement from point *e* back to point *e**. In essence, increased government demand offsets the decline in private sector demand. You might say that this is fiscal policy at its best; the deficit is used to nudge the economy back to its potential output.

What is the relation between the deficit that results from this discretionary fiscal policy and the other macroeconomic aggregates of concern? This deficit is associated with a greater output and a higher price level. The interest rate rises not only because the Treasury sells bonds to finance the deficit but also because the higher price and output levels increase the demand for money. Thus, *the deficit that arises from discretionary fiscal policy is associated with a higher real output, a higher price level, and a higher interest rate.*

Consequently, there is no necessary relation between deficits and various measures of economic performance. In each case the deficit is the result of fiscal policy. In the first instance the deficit results from the operation of automatic stabilizers that cushion the fall in private sector spending; in the second instance the deficit results from a discretionary fiscal policy aimed at increasing aggregate demand.

Crowding Out

Suppose the federal government decides to develop a new defense system that will cost $100 million, but taxes are not increased to finance it. To pay for the new system, the U.S. Treasury sells securities, or IOUs. *The government's increased demand for credit raises interest rates in the market for loans. Higher interest rates in turn discourage, or crowd out, some private investment, reducing the expansionary effect of the deficit.*

Crowding out occurs when increased government spending drives up interest rates and displaces interest-sensitive private spending.

The extent of **crowding out** is a matter of debate. Some argue that although borrowing from the public may displace some private sector borrowing, discretionary fiscal policy will result in a net increase in aggregate demand, leading to greater output and employment. Others believe the crowding out is more extensive, so borrowing from the public in this way could result in little or no increase in aggregate demand and output.

The Twin Deficits

We have already discussed the huge federal deficits that began in the early 1980s. To finance the deficits, the U.S. Treasury had to sell securities, driving up the market rate of interest. With U.S. interest rates relatively higher, foreigners were more willing to save by investing in dollar-denominated assets. To buy such assets, foreigners had to exchange their currencies for dollars. This greater demand for dollars caused the dollar to appreciate relative to foreign currencies. The rising value of the dollar made foreign goods cheaper in the United States and U.S. goods more expensive abroad. Thus, U.S. imports increased and U.S. exports decreased, so the foreign trade deficit increased. *The higher trade deficits meant that foreigners were accumulating dollars. Foreigners invested these dollars in U.S. assets, including U.S. government securities, and thereby helped fund the giant federal deficits.*

The increase in funds from abroad in the 1980s has been both good news and bad news for the U.S. economy. *The good news is that the supply of foreign funds has increased investment in the United States over what it would have been in the absence of these funds.* Higher investment leads to greater worker productivity and more economic growth. In a community where foreigners have just built a plant, ask residents what they think of the new foreign investment; they will likely say it's great.

But the foreign supply of funds means that Americans are spending more than they are producing, and such a pattern could have troubling consequences in the long run. The U.S. saving rate is now about the lowest it has been since the Great Depression, and the United States is now the largest borrower in the world. The United States has surrendered a certain amount of control over its economy to foreign investors. The return on foreign investments in the United States will flow abroad.

THE NATIONAL DEBT

Whereas the federal deficit is a flow variable measuring the amount by which expenditures exceed revenues in a particular year, the *national debt* is a stock variable measuring the net accumulation of past deficits. We distinguish between the total national debt and debt held by the public. The total debt includes U.S. Treasury securities purchased by various federal agencies, such as the Social Security trust fund. Since this is debt the federal government owes to itself, we typically disregard this part of the debt and focus on debt held by the public, which includes debt held by banks (including Federal Reserve banks), firms, individuals, and foreign entities.

The National Debt Since World War II

The top line in Exhibit 4(a) represents the debt held by the public since World War II, as measured in current dollars. At the end of World War II, the federal debt held by the public was $242 billion, about $200 billion of which had resulted from financing the war. Between 1946 and the mid–1970s, the national debt grew slowly. By 1974 the national debt had increased to only $346 billion; by 1990, however, the debt held by the public had jumped to over $2.3 trillion.

Because of inflation, the 1990 dollar purchases far less than did the 1946 dollar. Thus, a dollar's worth of debt in 1990 does not represent as great a liability as a dollar's worth of debt in 1946. To adjust for inflation, we can measure the debt in constant dollars. As the lower line in Exhibit 4(a) shows, *in 1946 constant dollars, the national debt actually declined from $242 billion in 1946 to $124 billion in 1974, but then climbed to $345 billion in 1990*. Hence, when figures are adjusted for inflation, the growth of the national debt is not nearly as dramatic. Measured in *constant dollars*, the federal debt declined at an average annual rate of 2.2 percent between 1946 and 1974 but grew at an average annual rate of 6.6 percent between 1974 and 1990.

Debt Relative to GNP

Another way to measure debt over time is to relate it to the economy's production and income, or GNP (just as a bank might compare the size of a mortgage to a borrower's income). Exhibit 4(b) shows debt held by the public as a percentage of GNP. In 1946 the national debt was 114 percent of GNP. Between 1946 and 1974, debt as a percentage of GNP declined steadily to only 24 percent, but then climbed above 42 percent by 1990.

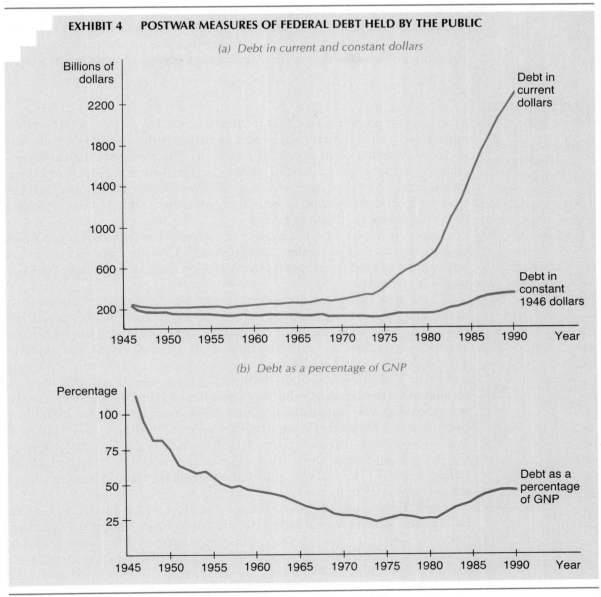

EXHIBIT 4   POSTWAR MEASURES OF FEDERAL DEBT HELD BY THE PUBLIC

(a) Debt in current and constant dollars

(b) Debt as a percentage of GNP

Source: Computed using data from *Economic Report of the President*, January 1990.

Let's consider briefly why debt has changed relative to GNP. For debt as a percentage of GNP to decline, GNP must grow faster than debt. Nominal national debt grew by only 1.3 percent per year between 1946 and 1974, a period during which nominal GNP grew by 7.1 percent per year. National debt as a percentage of GNP therefore fell between 1946 and 1974, as reflected in Exhibit 4(b). Between 1974 and 1990, however, nominal debt grew by a whopping 12.6 percent per year, whereas nominal GNP grew by only 8.6 percent per year, so debt as a percentage of GNP increased.

Thus far we have examined the national debt using the federal government's accounting system, which is unlike the system used by General Motors or Motown Records. The following case study considers what would happen to the deficit if we used conventional accounting practices.

Another View of Federal Debt

Firms in the private sector budget by (1) capital accounts, which reflect spending for such capital resources as plant and equipment, and (2) current accounts, which include expenditures for all other resources, such as wages, energy, and raw materials. The federal budget mixes current and capital expenditures together. Robert Eisner of Northwestern University argues that the federal accounting system, by neglecting a capital budget, yields a distorted measure of national debt.

Eisner develops a capital budget to derive what he believes is a more realistic federal budget picture. Although we will use his figures for 1980 as an example of how to carry out the calculations, his methodology could be used for any year.

Eisner first computes the federal government's "net debt," which is its financial liabilities minus its financial assets. The primary liability is government securities. To derive the 1980 market value of government securities, Eisner had to find the market value of all security issues outstanding. Securities that were initially sold at an interest rate below the 1980 rate would be less attractive than 1980 issues; they would sell at a *discount*, meaning that their market value was lower than their face value. Conversely, securities that were initially sold when interest rates were higher than those prevailing in 1980 would be more attractive than 1980 issues and would sell at a *premium*, with a market value exceeding their face value. According to Eisner's computations, the market value of the federal debt totaled $1154 billion in 1980. (The market value of the federal debt would be nearly three times higher in 1990.)

Next, Eisner adds up federal financial assets: cash on hand, taxes still to be received, and loans extended by the federal government to students, businesses, farmers, home buyers, and other countries. He adjusts the value of these loans as he does the value of liabilities. In 1980 these financial assets had a market value of $707 billion. By subtracting the market value of these assets from the market value of debt, Eisner derived a "net debt" of $447 billion, less than half the reported national debt in 1980 of $930 billion.

But Eisner is not finished yet. He further argues that the federal government, like businesses, owns tangible assets, such as buildings, power plants, military installations, highways, hospitals, public housing, and millions of acres of land. He calculated that the value of these tangible assets in 1980 was $727 billion. These assets minus the government "net debt" of $447 billion yields a government "net worth" of $280 billion. Thus, in Eisner's view, instead of being "in the red" by nearly a trillion dollars in 1980, the federal government was "in the black" by $280 billion. Eisner performed these calculations for several years between 1946 and 1980, and his findings indicate that net worth was climbing during that period.

Note that Eisner's results are very sensitive to prevailing interest rates. High interest rates in 1980 reduced the market value of outstanding debt because much of the debt had been issued at lower rates of interest. Thus, the positive net worth for the U.S. government in 1980 stems from the high interest rate that year.

This broader view of the budget points to the false economy associated with attempting to balance the budget by selling federal assets, such as national park land. Selling tangible assets to finance current expenditures reduces the current deficit but also reduces the federal government's net worth.

Source: Robert Eisner, *How Real Is the Federal Deficit?* (New York: Free Press, 1986).

Interest Payments on the Debt

Holders of the debt range from individuals who purchase $25 savings bonds to institutions that buy $1 million Treasury notes. As bonds mature, the government borrows more money to pay them off. Because most government securities are short term, the national debt "turns over" rapidly. About 45 percent of the debt is refinanced every twelve months. With over $75 billion coming due each month, debt service payments are quite sensitive to movements in interest rates. A 1 percent increase in the interest rate paid by the government increases its annual interest costs by about $10 billion.

Since there are no plans to pay back the national debt, we can focus on the interest outlays. Annual interest payments on the debt grew every year between 1961 and 1990. *Between 1980 and 1990, interest increased from $52.5 billion to over $170 billion, accounting in 1990 for about 15 percent of the federal budget.* In 1961 interest payments were only about 7 percent of the budget.

The Interest Payments and Seigniorage

One factor that influences interest payments is *seigniorage*. You'll recall that this term was originally used to refer to the profit a king derived from issuing coins whose metallic value was less than their face value. In the modern setting, seigniorage refers to the revenue that the U.S. Treasury receives because the Federal Reserve System can create money. As you know, the Fed adds money to the economy by purchasing Treasury securities from the public. Although the Fed earns interest on these securities, it pays no interest on the money it creates.

Some of the interest received by the Fed is used to cover its operating expenses, including a modest return to member banks, which own the Federal Reserve banks. Most of the interest, however, is returned to the U.S. Treasury. Since 1913 the Fed has returned an average of 87 percent of its earnings to the Treasury. For example, in 1989 the Federal Reserve System returned $18 billion to the Treasury. *Seigniorage, a by-product of monetary policy, reduces the net interest payment in any given year and thereby reduces the deficit.*

Who Bears the Burden of the Debt?

Deficit spending is a way to increase current consumption. Some people suggest that the national debt raises moral questions about the right of one generation of taxpayers to bequeath to the next generation the burden of its own borrowing. The director of the Congressional Budget Office has argued before Congress that "by running up large federal deficits, the current generation is lowering the living standard for its children and grandchildren." Similarly, Nobel laureate Franco Modigliani believes that deficit spending amounts to "enjoying it now and paying it later" by pushing the bill on to future generations in the form of the higher taxes that will be required to cover interest and principal. To what extent do budget deficits shift the burden to future generations? Let's consider arguments about the burden of the debt.

Foreign Ownership of Debt It is often argued that the debt is not a burden to future generations because, although future generations must service the debt, those same generations will receive the debt service payments. It's true that if U.S. citizens forgo present consumption to buy bonds, they or their heirs will receive the interest payments, so debt service payments will stay in the country. If foreigners purchase the bonds, however, they forgo the present consumption and receive the future benefits. An influx of foreign capital reduces the amount of consumption that Americans must sacrifice to finance the national debt. This inflow of credit from abroad helps keep interest rates lower than they would otherwise be. A reliance on foreigners, however, increases the burden of the debt on future generations because future debt service payments no longer remain in the country. Foreign holdings of debt have ranged between 10 and 15 percent of the total.

Crowding Out and Capital Formation As we have said, government borrowing drives up interest rates, crowding out private investment by making it more costly. The higher interest rates resulting from government borrowing increase foreign demand for dollars, as foreigners try to invest in dollar-denominated assets. This increased demand for dollars causes the dollar to appreciate on foreign exchange markets, leading to more imports and fewer exports. Thus, higher interest rates could reduce net exports as well as crowd out some domestic investment.

The short-run effect is that deficit spending does not expand equilibrium output as much as the autonomous spending multiplier would suggest. The long-run effect is a reduction in total investment and a reduction in the fraction of investment funded by U.S. residents. The long-run opportunity cost of this crowding out will depend on how the government spends the borrowed dollars. If additional federal outlays are oriented toward investments such as improving interstate highways or educating the work force, the public investment may be as productive as any private investment forgone. Hence, there should be no harmful effects on the economy's long-run productive capability. If, however, the additional borrowed dollars go toward current consumption, such as farm subsidies or retirement benefits, the economy's capital formation will be less than it would otherwise be. With less investment today, there is less of an endowment of capital equipment and technology for future generations.

Between 1987 and 1989, U.S. investment as a percentage of GNP averaged 10 percent, much lower than both the 18 percent rate in Japan during the same period and the 12 percent rate in the United States between 1979 to 1982. Over time, a decline in the rate of investment would reduce the amount and quality of capital available in the economy, which would reduce both productivity and the economy's ability to grow. Thus, the government deficits of one generation can reduce the standard of living of the next. In this sense the deficit of one generation can impose a burden on future generations.

REDUCING THE DEFICIT

Among economists, there is some disagreement over whether the current deficits pose a major problem for the country. Most agree that chronic deficits are undesirable, but few proposals have emerged for reducing the deficits. One way of eliminating the deficit is to raise taxes enough to cover it, but some economists believe that higher taxes could substantially slow the economy and possibly precipitate a recession. Some also believe that the giant deficits have served to check the growth in federal spending (indeed, federal spending as a percentage of GNP fell slightly between 1986 and 1989). According to this view, a tax hike would simply foster higher government spending.

As mentioned earlier, elected officials pay a political price for raising taxes and thus are understandably reluctant to do so. A promise to raise taxes could prove hazardous to a politician's career, as Walter Mondale can attest. Instead, members of Congress pursue reelection by supporting innumerable programs for special-interest constituencies. Individual members of Congress tend to spend for narrow purposes and in so doing to overspend in total.

Line-Item Veto

Some observers argue that an outside force is needed to control spending. One proposal designed to reduce the impact of special interests on the budget and at the same time provide the executive branch with more flexibility is to give the president the line-item veto. The *line-item veto* would allow the president to reject particular portions of the budget rather than simply accept or reject the entire budget, as is now the case. An argument for the line-item veto is that the president is the only elected representative with a broad enough constituency to reject the special-interest programs often embedded in the budget.

Gramm-Rudman-Hollings

Another measure proposed to resolve the deficit problem is the Gramm-Rudman-Hollings law. The Gramm-Rudman-Hollings (GRH) proposal was introduced in 1985 as an attempt to eliminate the deficit over five years. Provisions of the proposal required automatic across-the-board budget reductions if Congress and the president could not approve measures to reduce the projected deficit to certain target levels each fiscal year. But two-thirds of the budget was exempted from such cuts, and the Supreme Court ruled parts of the law unconstitutional.

Congress vowed to maintain the spirit of the law, but the budget-balancing measure seemed to lose its punch the first time it was applied. According to the law, the deficit for fiscal year 1987 was supposed to be reduced to $144 billion, but the actual deficit was $150 billion despite fiscal gimmickry. (For example, certain payments were backdated so that they would fall into the 1986 budget.) The target deficit for 1988 was $108 billion, well below the actual deficit of $155 billion. Fiscal year 1989 was the seventh year in a row with a federal deficit in excess of $150 billion. The failure to meet the projected GRH targets in fiscal year 1990 triggered a $16 billion spending reduction, or *sequester*—the first such cut. Thus, GRH has had a spotty record, but it has at least provided budget benchmarks for Congress to consider in its deliberations.

Balanced Budget Amendment

Another attempt to force the government to control spending is a proposed amendment to the U.S. Constitution requiring a balanced federal budget. James Buchanan argues that a balanced budget amendment could replace the moral force that required balanced budgets before Keynes freed lawmakers of this constraint.

There have been two kinds of criticisms of the balanced budget amendment. The first stems from the belief that the amendment would work too well. Both autonomous and discretionary fiscal policy uses deficits and surpluses as policy tools to stimulate the economy during recessions and to dampen the economy during expansions. A balanced budget requirement would reduce the government's ability to employ fiscal policy to address business fluctuations, particularly recessions. To allow some room for fiscal policy, proposed balanced budget amendments typically allow Congress to override this restriction with a greater-than-majority vote, such as two-thirds or three-fifths. Despite this escape clause, some policy makers remain concerned that fiscal policy would be undermined by a balanced budget amendment. But fiscal policy has been effectively undermined anyway by large chronic deficits.

A second line of criticism of a balanced budget amendment is that any budget restriction would probably be difficult to specify and easy to bypass. Even if such a measure held down spending by the federal government, authority for certain types of spending could simply be pushed down to lower levels of government. Another fear is that the federal government would use greater regulation of the economy to achieve what it failed to bring about directly through the budget. For example, rather than subsidizing an employment training program for unskilled workers, the government might simply require employers to hire and train such workers. Some people think that such government intervention in the market might ultimately prove to be less efficient than using the budget to achieve the desired outcome.

CONCLUSION

Keynes introduced the idea that federal deficit spending is an appropriate fiscal policy when private aggregate demand is lacking. The federal budget has not been the same since. The federal budget has been in deficit every year for the last three decades. During the 1980s giant federal deficits dominated the fiscal policy debate. But thanks to the longest economic peacetime expansion in U.S. history, the federal deficit as a percentage of GNP shrank between the mid and late 1980s. These giant deficits also slowed the growth of the federal budget during the last half of the decade.

The macroeconomic focus thus far has been on the effects of fiscal and monetary policy on full employment and price stability. In the next chapter we will consider another macroeconomic policy objective: economic growth.

Summary

1. The federal budget process suffers from a variety of problems, including overlapping committee jurisdictions, lengthy budget deliberations, extensive use of continuing resolutions, budgeting in too much detail, and a lack of year-to-year control over a large fraction of the budget. Several improvements have been suggested, including instituting a biennial budget and budgeting in less detail.

2. Deficits usually rise during wars and severe recessions, but the largest deficits in U.S. history occurred during the economic expansion of the 1980s, as a result of the 1981 tax cuts. In current dollars, national debt more than tripled during the 1980s.

3. There is no clear, consistent relation between deficits and other measures of macroeconomic performance, such as output, the price level, and interest rates. If a fall in aggregate demand results in recession, deficits increase as automatic stabilizers operate, but output, the price level, and, at times, the interest rate all tend to

decline. If discretionary fiscal policy is used to rekindle aggregate demand, deficits rise, and so do output, the price level, and the interest rate.

4. To the extent that deficits crowd out private capital formation, this decline in investment reduces the economy's ability to grow. To the extent that deficits drive up interest rates, the greater demand for dollars on foreign exchange markets drives up the value of the dollar and reduces net exports. Thus, the deficits of one generation can reduce the standard of living of the next. Foreign holdings of debt also impose a burden on future generations because future payments to service this debt are paid to foreigners and are consequently not available to U.S. citizens.

5. Several proposals have been put forth to reduce the giant deficits of the 1980s. These measures include tax increases, expenditure reductions, the line-item veto, the Gramm-Rudman-Hollings measure, and a balanced budget amendment.

Questions and Problems

1. (Federal Budget Process) Why wouldn't a general freeze on federal government spending stop some government spending from increasing? Why can't the government control expenditures on interest payments on the national debt in the short run?

2. (Government Budget Deficits) Recessions have often led to large budget deficits. However, the years 1983–1987 were years of recovery for the economy. How, then, were the largest deficits in history produced during these years?

3. (Government Budget Deficits) During the 1984 presidential campaign, President Reagan claimed that the country would grow out of the deficit it was experiencing. What was the reasoning behind his statement? Did the economy in fact grow out of the deficit?

4. (Crowding Out) Is it possible for U.S. federal budget deficits to crowd out investment spending in other countries? How could German or British investment be hurt by large U.S. budget deficits?

5. (Government Debt) Consider a capital budget for the government, as described in the chapter. Suppose that interest rates in the United States rose. How would this affect the net worth of the government, as computed by Eisner? If the government attempted to sell off assets to reduce the deficit, what effect would this sale of assets have on the government's net worth?

6. (Seigniorage) Earlier in the text we noted that the Fed pays no interest to commercial banks that hold reserves with the Fed. If the Fed were forced to pay interest, how would this affect the level of seigniorage returned to the U.S. Treasury? How might this complicate attempts to reduce federal budget deficits?

7. (Government Sale of Assets) Some commentators have satirically suggested that the government sell Yellowstone National Park to reduce the deficit. Assuming more appropriate candidates could be found, there are still problems with the sale of assets. Why do such sales reduce the deficit only in the year of sale? Are there other reasons to conduct such sales? How would you decide which assets should be sold and which should not be sold?

8. (Budget Deficits) One alternative to annually or cyclically balancing the budget is to produce a government budget that would be balanced if the economy were at full-employment output. Given the cyclical nature of government tax revenues and spending, how would the budget deficit or surplus vary over the business cycle?

9. (Crowding Out) One kind of crowding out caused by government budget deficits is called *international* crowding out. Explain why a reduction in net exports is likely to occur.

10. (Budget Deficits) If individuals continually spend more than they take in, eventually they must declare bankruptcy. Why is this not the case with the federal government?

11. (Debt Burden) Suppose that government budget deficits are financed to a considerable extent by foreign sources. How does this create a potential burden for the domestic economy in the future?

12. (Balancing the Budget) Explain how a rule *requiring* the federal government to annually balance its budget could be *de*stabilizing to the economy as far as fiscal activity is concerned.

Productivity and Growth

A nation prospers by making more efficient use of its resources. Growing productivity is therefore key to a higher standard of living. During the last century, the real goods and services produced by each hour of labor in the United States increased more than *tenfold*. But in recent years, productivity has not increased as fast as it did during the 1950s and early 1960s. This slowdown could affect continued prosperity. In this chapter we consider the sources of economic growth and examine the recent slowdown in productivity growth. We also analyze government's role in fostering economic growth and productivity.

Economic growth is a complicated process and one we do not yet fully understand. Since before Adam Smith inquired into the *Wealth of Nations*, economists have been trying to discover what makes some economies prosper and others founder. Because the capitalist economy is not the product of conscious design, however, it does not divulge its secrets readily, nor can it be easily manipulated in pursuit of growth objectives. We cannot simply push here and pull there to achieve the desired result. Changing the economy is not like remodeling a home by moving a wall out to expand the kitchen. Since we have no clear copy of the economy's blueprint, we cannot make changes to specifications. So keep in mind as you read this chapter that economics is both an art and a science. Topics discussed in this chapter include

- Labor productivity
- Slowdown in productivity growth
- Technological change

- Research and development
- Policies to change potential GNP
- Supply-side tax cuts

ECONOMIC GROWTH AND PUBLIC POLICY

The population of the United States is continually increasing. Therefore, the economy must grow just to maintain the existing standard of living—that is, just to maintain the same quantity of goods and services available per capita. If the amount of real GNP grows faster than the population, then the standard of living on average should rise. To explore the idea of economic growth, we will consider the production possibilities frontier, introduced in Chapter 2.

Growth and the Production Possibilities Frontier

Production can be thought of as a process that transforms inputs into outputs. Resources coupled with technology yield output. The *production function* describes the relation between inputs and outputs, indicating the maximum output obtainable with given quantities of inputs and a given level of technology.

The production possibilities frontier reflects the underlying production functions involved in producing the output under consideration. Let's briefly review the assumptions employed in developing this frontier. During the period under consideration, resources in the economy and technology are assumed to be fixed. We classify all output into two broad categories—in this case, consumption goods and investment goods. Consumption goods are directly available for current consumption. Investment goods are used to produce other goods. Thus the economy can make cars, or it can make the machines used to make cars. Cars are consumption goods, and machines are investment goods.

The production possibilities frontier, *CI*, in Exhibit 1 shows the possible combinations of consumption goods and investment goods that can be produced by the economy per year when resources are used fully and efficiently. Point *C* depicts the amount of consumption goods that can be produced if all the economy's resources are used efficiently to produce consumer goods. Point *I* depicts the same for investment goods. Points inside the frontier show inefficient combinations, and points outside the frontier are unattainable, given the resources and technology available. The frontier is bowed out because all resources are not perfectly suited to the production of both goods; some resources are specialized.

Economic growth is reflected by an outward shift in the production possibilities frontier, as shown by the movement from *CI* to *C'I'*. What will cause the frontier to shift out? Most important are changes in resource availability and technology. Any increase in the availability of resources such as the labor supply or the capital stock expands the frontier. Labor can increase either because the population increases or because the existing population becomes more willing to supply its labor. The stock of physical capital will expand only if the production of investment goods exceeds depreciation in the capital stock. The more investment goods produced,

EXHIBIT 1   ECONOMIC GROWTH AS A SHIFT IN THE PRODUCTION POSSIBILITIES FRONTIER

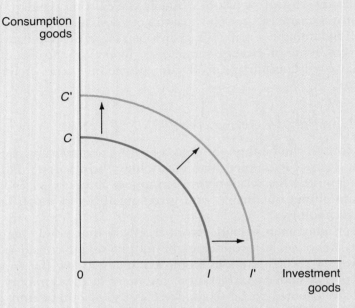

Increased availability of resources or improvements in technology cause the production possibilities frontier to shift outward from *CI* to *C'I'*. As a result, the economy can generate more consumption goods and more investment goods.

the more the economy will grow, as reflected by an outward shift in the production frontier. Any improvement in technology also expands the frontier by making use of existing resources more efficient. *Technological change often improves the quality of capital, but it can enhance the productivity of any resource.*

Postwar Growth Policy

World War II shocked the nation out of the Great Depression, and the U.S. economy surged. The Employment Act of 1946 focused primarily on preventing another depression, which some observers predicted would come as soon as the aggregate demand generated by a wartime economy abated. Once federal policy makers realized that the economy would survive the transition to peace, more lofty national objectives captured their attention. One objective that received more attention was economic growth.

Growth policies implemented in the 1950s and 1960s were of two types. *The first type focused on aggregate supply by stimulating all types of investment and promoting efficiency through greater competition.* Investment occurs in a variety of forms: investment in human capital through education and training; investment in physical capital, such as manufacturing plants and equipment; investment in technological advances through research and development outlays; and investment in the public infrastructure, such as the interstate highway system. Measures to enhance competition included reducing international barriers to free trade, enforcing laws designed to restrict anticompetitive behavior, reducing business regulations, and reducing federal subsidies. Thus, the aggregate-supply approach to growth focused on increasing the economy's productive capacity — to increase long-run aggregate supply — through greater investment and more efficient use of resources.

The second way growth was encouraged was by stimulating aggregate demand to call forth more output, *thereby moving the economy closer to the production possibilities frontier.* Note that stimulating aggregate demand cannot really increase the economy's potential output; it can only close any contractionary gap in output. The tax cut of 1964 is often mentioned as a sterling example of the beneficial effects of public policy on economic growth. The reduction in tax rates on business investment could be viewed either as a demand-side approach aimed at increasing aggregate demand through greater investment spending or as a supply-side approach aimed at expanding the economy's potential output through greater investment.

The Vietnam War eclipsed concerns about national growth during the late 1960s and early 1970s. Moreover, in the early 1970s the country was beset with both inflation and unemployment, so economic growth became a lower national priority. In the latter part of the 1970s, however, concern about growth surfaced again. Policy makers who believed that the federal government should take an active role in directing and nurturing economic growth enacted the Full Employment and Growth Act of 1978. The act set several macroeconomic targets, including an unemployment rate of 3 percent. The act also called for "a balanced federal budget, adequate productivity growth, proper attention to national priorities, achievement of an improved trade balance through increased exports and improvements in the international competitiveness of agriculture, business, and industry, and reasonable price stability." (Whew!) One goal was piled on another to attract the support of legislators, but the broad mandate weakened the act's overall impact. This puffed-up piece of legislation was quickly ignored.

Another progrowth movement that began in the 1970s had a more lasting impact. Policy makers were becoming increasingly concerned that the country was suffering from a shortage of new plants and equipment, a shortage some believed could be overcome if tax rates were reduced enough to stimulate investment. Additional investment incentives were built into the corporate income tax in 1981, and the highest personal income tax rate on capital gains was reduced to 20 percent. (Recall that a capital gain is the difference between an asset's purchase price and its sale price.) But subsequent revisions reduced investment incentives, and the Tax Reform Act of 1986 raised the highest marginal rate on capital gains to 33 percent. In 1989 President Bush tried to reduce the capital gains tax rate, but the measure died in Congress amid controversy about cutting taxes for the rich.

PRODUCTIVITY

Productivity measures how efficiently resources are employed. In simplest terms, the greater the productivity, the more goods and services that can be produced from a given amount of resources. **Productivity** is defined as the ratio of a specific measure of output to a specific measure of input. It usually reflects an average, expressing total output divided by the total input of a specific kind of resource.

We can talk about the productivity of any resource, such as land, labor, or capital. In preindustrial times agricultural products made up the bulk of total output, so land productivity was an important measure of economic welfare. Where soil was rocky and barren, people were less prosperous than where soil was fertile and fruitful. Even today, in many developing countries throughout the world, the productivity of the soil determines the standard of living in the region. Industrialization and trade, however, have liberated many economies from dependence on soil quality. Today some of the world's richest countries are land poor.

Labor Productivity

Labor is the resource most commonly used in measuring productivity. Why labor? First, labor accounts for a relatively large share — about three-fourths — of the cost of production. Second, labor is more easily measured than other inputs, whether we speak of hours per week or full-time workers per year. Statistics about employment and hours worked are more readily available and more reliable than information about the use of other resources.

The ratio of GNP to total employment measures *labor productivity*. In 1989, when the GNP was $5.2 trillion and total employment was about 120 million, U.S. labor productivity was about $43,300 per worker. We should distinguish between the *level* of productivity, which measures the economy's productive capability, and the *growth* in productivity, which measures changes in that productive capability over time. Changes in productivity over time focus on real GNP and indicate what happens to the amount of goods and services produced per worker. If labor productivity grows, more output is produced using a given amount of labor. *As long as the rate of employment growth at least keeps up with the rate of growth in the population, growing labor productivity ensures more real GNP per capita and a higher standard of living.*

Exhibit 2 offers a long-run perspective on growth in the United States, showing annual productivity growth over the last 110 years as measured by real GNP per work hour. Productivity growth is averaged by decade, beginning with the decade that ended in 1880 and ending with the decade that ended in 1980. During the entire period, the labor productivity growth rate averaged 2.3 percent per year. This may not seem like much, but because of the power of compounding, real GNP per work hour grew by about 1100 percent during the 110 years. *Over long periods, tiny differences in productivity growth rates can have significant impact on production.* For example, if productivity had grown by 2.0 percent per year instead of 2.3 percent during the period, output per work hour would have increased by only 780 percent, not

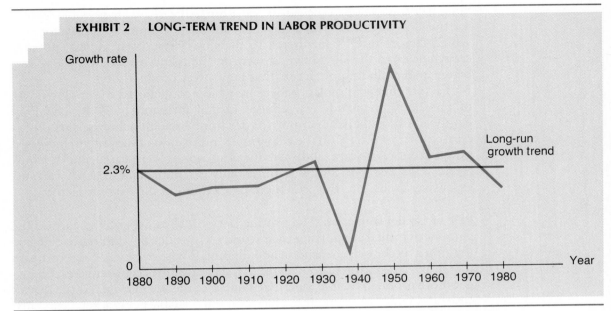

EXHIBIT 2   LONG-TERM TREND IN LABOR PRODUCTIVITY

Source: Angus Maddison, *Phases of Capitalist Development* (New York: Oxford University Press, 1982), 212.

1100 percent. On the other hand, if productivity had increased an average of 2.6 percent per year, output per work hour would have increased by 1580 percent! The wheels of progress grind slowly but they grind very fine, and the cumulative effect is impressive.

The data presented in Exhibit 2 are averages for each decade ending with the 1970s. By focusing on annual data, however, we can compare productivity growth during the 1980s to growth trends during two other major periods since World War II. The growth in output per labor hour declined from 2.8 percent per year between 1948 and 1973 to 0.7 percent per year between 1973 and 1981. Productivity growth then rebounded somewhat to 1.3 percent between 1981 and 1988. *Thus, the rate of growth in labor productivity during the last two decades has been less than half what it was during the quarter century following World War II.*

Such a drop in labor productivity, if it were to be lasting, could spell big trouble for the United States. The United Kingdom once had the richest economy on earth, but half a century of productivity growth that lagged behind that of the United States by less than 1 percentage point has left the United Kingdom one of the poorest industrial countries.

Some Reasons for the Slowdown in Labor Productivity Growth

A thorough explanation of the recent slowdown in productivity growth should not only account for the overall trend from period to period but also explain differences in productivity growth across economic sectors. Nobody has yet developed such an explanation. All we have are possible reasons for the slowdown. As you will see, economists are unable to say for sure which factors really contributed to the slowdown. Nonetheless, possible contributors to the slowdown are worth discussing because they give us a better understanding of factors that may affect productivity.

Factors that economists believe may have contributed to the slowdown of productivity include (1) reduced capital formation, (2) the changing composition of the labor force, (3) declining student achievement, (4) increased energy prices, (5) the changing composition of output, (6) increased government regulation, and (7) reduced spending on research and development. This last possibility is potentially so important that it warrants extensive discussion. But let's begin by examining the first six factors.

Rate of Capital Formation The productivity of labor depends in part on the amount of capital supporting each worker. Consider the difference between digging a ditch with a teaspoon and digging it with a shovel. Now compare that shovel to a backhoe. You can see that the addition of capital makes the digger more productive. A standardized index of the use of capital is the *capital-labor ratio*, which measures the value of capital available per worker. Generally, we expect labor productivity to increase as the capital–labor ratio increases.

Consider again the production possibilities frontier introduced earlier. The amount of capital the economy produces this year will affect the location of the frontier next year. The initial production possibilities frontier in each panel of Exhibit 3 is *CI*. If the economy generates combination *A* along *CI*, the capital produced this year will shift the production possibilities frontier from *CI* out to *C'I'*, as shown in panel (a). However, if more investment goods are produced this year, as reflected by point *B* in panel (b), the production possibilities frontier will shift out even more, to *C"I"*.

A slowdown in the growth of the capital-labor ratio has been suggested as a major reason for the slower productivity growth, but not all researchers agree on the relative contribution of changes in the capital-labor ratio to the slowdown. Edward Denison, who is perhaps the leading authority on U.S. productivity, concludes that the small decline in the growth of the capital-labor ratio contributed only modestly to the fall in productivity growth.[1]

Changing Composition of the Labor Force An important component in the production function is the quality of labor. Some economists argue that changes in the composition of the labor force have contributed to the decline in productivity growth experienced since the mid-1960s. Individuals who are just entering the labor force are typically less productive because they have fewer skills and less experience than those who are already in the labor force. As long as the proportion of new workers remains constant over time, their presence should not affect productivity measures. However, if the share

---

[1] Edward F. Denison, *Trends in American Economic Growth, 1929–1982* (Washington, D.C.: Brookings Institution, 1985).

EXHIBIT 3   THE EFFECT OF INVESTMENT ON ECONOMIC GROWTH

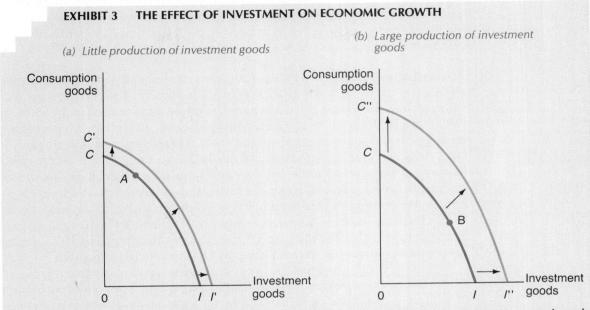

(a) Little production of investment goods

(b) Large production of investment goods

In panel (a), the economy generates the combination of consumption goods and investment goods represented by point *A* on production possibilities curve *CI*. The added investment goods contribute to the available stock of capital, so the production possibilities curve shifts outward to *C'I'*. In panel (b), the economy generates combination *B*. With more investment goods produced, the capital stock grows faster and the curve shifts out farther, to *C"I"*. If consumers forgo consumption today, the economy generates an improved standard of living in the future.

of employment accounted for by new workers increases, as it has since 1966, then productivity growth may suffer. Offsetting to some extent the increase in the number of less experienced workers has been the increase in the education and training of the work force as a whole. *Most researchers agree that the net effect of the change in composition of the work force on the decline in the growth of labor productivity is small.* Furthermore, as the labor force matures and workers develop more experience, labor productivity should increase.

Declining Student Achievement Improvements in the amount and quality of schooling have contributed substantially to productivity growth for much of this century. Beginning in 1967, however, standardized test scores declined nationwide.[2] This fall in test scores, which continued until 1980, suggests that the quality of young entrants into the work force declined. Such a decline has been identified as another source of the decline in

---

[2] See John H. Bishop, "Is the Test Score Decline Responsible for the Productivity Growth Decline?" *American Economic Review* 79 (March 1989): 178–97.

productivity growth. Even though standardized test scores began showing some improvement during the 1980s, student achievement (and thus the quality of the work force) will continue to be below what it would have been without the decline.

Higher Energy Prices in the 1970s The sharp rise in energy prices during the 1970s has been put forth as a cause of the decline in productivity growth during the period. The price of a barrel of crude oil increased from $5.68 in 1973 to $18.06 in 1975 (measured in 1982 constant dollars). With higher energy prices, some existing capital stock became uneconomical, since it was designed during an era of relatively cheap fuel. *Higher energy prices encouraged firms to substitute labor for energy in the production process, which increased labor usage per unit of output.* During the conversion to a more energy-efficient economy — so the argument goes — the growth rate was held down. Real GNP declined by 1.8 percent between 1973 and 1975. Several economists conclude that the increase in energy prices that began in 1973 was an important contributor to the decline in U.S. productivity growth.[3]

Not everyone agrees that higher energy costs were an important factor in the productivity slowdown. *Some economists argue that energy costs represent such a small proportion of total costs that higher energy costs should not greatly affect productivity growth.* Denison says that higher energy costs during the 1970s contributed only 0.1 percent to the decline in productivity growth. During the 1980s the reduction in energy prices caused yet another major conversion in resource usage, a shift that should eventually enhance labor productivity.

Changing Composition of Output Average productivity will decline if workers shift from sectors where substantial capital formation and technological change increase labor productivity to sectors where capital formation and technological change are less important. Labor productivity can be increased more easily in manufacturing, where machines can be readily introduced, than in the service sector, where machines are less important. For example, there are more opportunities for technological change on the assembly line than in the classroom.

Some researchers have argued that *the service sector's growing share of GNP has lowered the growth rate of productivity in the economy as a whole.* Nearly all economists who have explored the issue agree that the shift from high-productivity to low-productivity sectors accounts for some of the slowdown. But economists' estimates of the effect on productivity vary. Some say that the shift had little effect; others hold it responsible for more than half the decline.

Growing Government Regulation Another factor cited as a source of slower productivity growth is the more pervasive role of government in the economy, both in its regulatory functions and more generally in its impact on the

---

[3] See, for example, Dale W. Jorgenson, "Productivity and Postwar U.S. Economic Growth," *Journal of Economic Perspectives* 2 (Fall 1988): 23–41.

direction of economic activity. Government regulation grew sharply between the mid–1960s and the late 1970s. In one three-year period, five major regulatory bodies were established by the federal government, including the Environmental Protection Agency and the Occupational Safety and Health Administration.

As a result of government regulations, resources may be diverted from direct production to areas such as pollution abatement and occupational safety. For example, requirements for greater safety in coal mines have been cited as a source of the decline in productivity in that industry. The control of toxic emissions, the improvement of safety in the workplace, and the like may ultimately increase the quality of life in the nation, but they add little to output as measured by GNP.

Earlier we noted that as long as employment growth keeps pace with population growth, higher labor productivity implies a higher GNP per capita and therefore a higher standard of living. If, however, productivity is inversely related to other measures of welfare, such as safety and health in the workplace or clean air and water, then higher productivity may not be the most appropriate national objective. Since GNP does not reflect qualitative changes in working conditions or in the environment, the apparent slowdown in productivity may not be as troubling as it at first appears, for it may reflect qualitative improvements in working conditions and, more generally, in the quality of life. Thus, *even if government regulations reduce the growth of productivity based on measured GNP, they may improve our standard of living as defined more broadly than simply by GNP per capita.*

One way to view government's role in the economy in a wider context is to look at the relation between economic growth and the share of GNP that goes to the federal government. Herbert Stein notes that in the thirty-seven years between 1892 and 1929, federal expenditures were about 4.5 percent of GNP and federal revenues about 3.5 percent, with most of the difference due to deficits created during World War I.[4] In the thirty-seven years between 1948 and 1985, federal expenditures averaged about 20 percent and revenues about 18.5 percent of GNP. During the earlier period, real GNP rose at an annual rate of 3.4 percent. In the more recent period, the era of big government, real GNP also rose by 3.4 percent annually. In terms of productivity, output per worker-hour rose by 1.5 percent per year during the small-government period and by 2.4 percent per year during the big-government period. These statistics do not necessarily indicate that big government causes economic growth. The point is that *it is simplistic to say that government is the major obstacle to economic growth and productivity.*

Perhaps the single most important contributor to productivity growth is technological change. In the next section we will examine research and development, the source of technological change.

---

[4] Herbert Stein, "Should Growth Be a Priority of National Policy?" *Challenge* (March-April 1986): 11–17.

RESEARCH AND DEVELOPMENT

Simon Kuznets, who won the Nobel Prize in part for his analysis of the sources of growth, claimed that technological changes and the ability to apply these changes to all aspects of production were the driving force behind modern economic growth in developed market economies. Kuznets argued that changes in the *quantities* of labor and capital accounted for only one-tenth of the increase in economic growth. Nine-tenths of the increase was a result of improvements in the *quality* of inputs.

Basic and Applied Research

A major contributor to productivity has been an improvement in the quality of human and physical capital. In terms of the work force, this quality improvement results from more education and more job training. In terms of physical capital, quality improvement results from better technology embodied in this capital. Improvements in technology arise from scientific discovery, which is the result of research.

Basic research *is the search for knowledge without regard to how that knowledge will be used.*

We distinguish between basic research and applied research. **Basic research** is the search for knowledge without regard to how that knowledge will be used. It is a necessary element in technological improvements. In terms of economic growth, however, scientific discoveries are meaningless until they are implemented—which requires applied research. **Applied research** typically seeks to answer particular questions or to apply scientific discoveries to the development of specific products. Since technological breakthroughs may or may not have commercial possibilities, basic research has less of an immediate payoff than applied research.

Applied research *tries to answer specific questions or to apply scientific discoveries to the development of specific products.*

When a technological breakthrough is thought to have economic value in the marketplace, it becomes *embodied* in new capital. Such technological innovation increases the productivity of other resources by permitting them to be combined in more efficient ways, so total output is increased. *From the wheel to assembly-line robots, capital embodies the fruits of scientific inquiry and serves as the primary engine for economic growth.*

Technological Change Can Increase Available Resources

Technological change can sometimes free resources for new uses. For example, now that fiber optics technology has become the best means of communicating, the copper from existing telephone lines is becoming available for other uses. In fact, AT&T controls most of the world's known copper deposits in the form of wires and cables that are already in place.

Throughout history technological change has reduced the number of workers needed to produce the same output. For example, since 1870 there has been a twelvefold increase in U.S. output per worker. As a result, workers often fear that technological change will throw people out of work. Intuition suggests that with continuing technological change the economy might simply employ fewer workers. Won't machines replace workers, and won't unemployment swell?

In some instances technological change may mean that fewer workers will be needed to produce particular goods. We know that structural unemployment can arise from changing technology. But as long as wants are unlimited, there will always be a demand for workers. The displaced workers will typically go on to find other jobs producing the goods and services demanded in a growing economy. Although data for the nineteenth century are sketchy, the evidence suggests that the unemployment rate is no higher today than it was in 1870. Rising productivity has allowed workers to enjoy not only rising real incomes but more leisure: the average work week has fallen by over 25 percent since the turn of the century.

Expenditures for Research and Development

Since technological advances spring from the process of research and development, R&D expenditures represent one measure of the economy's efforts to improve productivity through technological discovery. R&D expenditures reached a peak in the United States around 1968, dropped slightly in the early 1970s, and then recovered somewhat in the late 1970s. Measured as a percentage of sales, R&D expenditures declined from 4.2 percent in 1968 to a low of 2.6 percent in 1979, then increased to 3.7 percent by 1982 and remained at that level through the mid–1980s.

R&D expenditures can be divided into the share financed by business and the share financed by the federal government. Federally supported R&D fell from 2.7 percent of sales in 1967 to 0.7 percent in 1979 but grew somewhat in the early 1980s. Company-financed R&D stayed fairly constant during the period, *so the variation from the late 1960s to the early 1980s can be traced to changes in federal support.* Changes in federal funding reflect the shifting emphasis on military spending. Since much federally supported R&D is for military use, there is some question about its broader applicability.

Some economists believe that the slowdown during the 1970s in the growth of R&D proved very costly to the economy in terms of forgone growth opportunities. As we have seen, the decline in federal R&D was part of the problem. But *research suggests that a dollar of federally supported R&D contributes less to economic growth than a dollar of company-supported R&D,*[5] perhaps because much federally supported R&D has military objectives. Thus, although the decline in federal R&D may have contributed to the slowdown in productivity during the 1970s, the impact would have been greater if the decline in R&D had occurred in the private sector.

Measured as a percentage of GNP, nonmilitary R&D in the United States stood at 1.8 percent during the 1980s, compared to over 2.0 percent in both

---

[5] See, for example, Zvi Griliches,"Productivity, R&D, and Basic Research at the Firm Level in the 1970s," *American Economic Review* 76 (March 1986): 141–54.

Japan and Germany. The federal government has tried to stimulate private R&D by providing special investment tax incentives for this activity. A review of the effects of this program, however, indicates that federal tax incentives introduced in 1981 to stimulate new R&D expenditures were not cost-effective.[6] Because of the special tax benefits accorded R&D outlays, firms became much more liberal in their definitions of R&D. The program cost about $1.5 billion per year in forgone tax revenue, yet it increased R&D by only $0.5 billion.

Thus far we have discussed R&D and the other components of labor productivity in terms of statistics, but behind the numbers are individual cases. The following case study compares the rates of productivity at two auto factories in Ohio.

CASE STUDY

Productivity on the Line

In Marysville, Ohio, the new Honda factory is thriving. One hundred miles away, in Toledo, the antiquated Jeep factory appears to be on its last legs. Each day Honda produces 875 cars; Jeep produces 750. Honda employs 2400 auto workers; Jeep employs *double* that number. Honda turns out its cars in 1.7 million square feet of floor space; Jeep uses more than triple that space.

How does the Honda plant produce more cars with fewer resources? Part of the difference in productivity lies in the many options offered on Jeeps. Honda assembles long runs of nearly identical cars, a far more efficient method but one that offers consumers fewer choices.

Output is a matter not just of quantity but also of quality. Are Hondas perhaps of lower quality than Jeeps? Apparently not; according to the frequency-of-repair data published annually by *Consumer Reports*, Honda is rated "much better than average," and Jeep is rated "much worse than average."

Because the Honda plant is new, it reflects the latest technology. Vehicles at Honda move automatically along the entire assembly line. At the Jeep plant, vehicles must be manually dragged between certain points along the line. At Honda parts are stored by suppliers and delivered to the assembly points just hours before they are needed. At Jeep it takes a day or two simply to move the 12,000 different parts to points along the line. Both plants have huge stamping machines to bend sheet metal into fenders and the like. Honda's machine is designed so that the stamping molds can be changed in ten minutes; the same changes take several hours at Jeep.

Employee attitudes also appear to differ between the plants. Honda is not unionized and has fewer job classifications than does Jeep. For example, at Honda one worker moves parts from the nearby inventory to the assembly line; at Jeep that task calls for three workers, each with a different job

---

[6] Edwin Mansfield, "The R&D Tax Credit and Other Technology Policy Issues," *American Economic Review* 76 (May 1986): 190–94.

classification. As a result, labor costs represent a smaller fraction of total costs at Honda than at Jeep.

Honda employees refer to one another as "associates." All employees, including management, wear white coveralls with their name stitched above the pocket. At Honda there are no executive dining rooms, no reserved parking places, no enclosed offices. At Jeep distinctions between labor and management are clear, resulting in a more adversarial relation of the "us versus them" variety. Absenteeism is also more of a problem at Jeep than at Honda. On one balmy Friday afternoon, 15 percent of Jeep employees failed to show up for work, forcing the plant to shut down. That same afternoon Honda had an absentee rate of only 2 percent.

All these differences are reflected in the outlook and financial vitality of the two companies. Honda spent about 4 percent of its sales on research and development in 1986. American Motors, Jeep's parent company in 1986, spent only about 1 percent. Honda has been very profitable, with a rising stock price and bright prospects. American Motors was losing money regularly and in 1987 was acquired by the Chrysler Corporation.

Sources: John Merwin, "A Tale of Two Worlds," *Forbes* (June 16, 1986): 101–106; "Frequency-of-Repair Records, 1983–1988," *Consumer Reports 1990 Buying Guide Issue*, 192–93.

INTERNATIONAL COMPARISONS

So far we have focused on growth as measured by rising labor productivity—that is, growth achieved by getting more output from each hour worked. The economy may also grow by employing more workers. *Output per capita* captures the combined effects of growing productivity and a growing work force. If the work force grows faster than the population as a whole, output per capita can increase faster than productivity per labor hour.

Exhibit 4 presents the *real GNP growth rate per capita* for three periods between 1948 and 1988 for the United States and six other leading industrial countries. The 2.2 percent U.S. annual growth rate during 1948–1973 was half the 4.7 percent average for the six other developed countries. The United States had the lowest growth rate during that time largely because World War II had not ravaged the United States the way it had all the other countries except Canada. During 1973–1981 the U.S. annual growth rate of 1.1 percent was little more than half the 2.0 percent average growth rate for the six other countries. During the 1980s, however, the U.S. annual growth rate of 2.0 nearly caught up with the 2.2 percent average for the six other countries. In fact, between the periods 1948–1973 and 1981–1988, the U.S. annual growth rate declined from 2.2 percent to 2.0, but growth rates for the other six countries declined on average from 4.7 to 2.2. Japan's growth rate fell by more than half, from 7.8 percent to 3.2 percent, between those two periods. *So during the 1980s the growth rate in GNP per capita in the United States nearly caught up with averages for the six other developed economies and nearly caught up with its own record during 1948–1973.*

EXHIBIT 4
AVERAGE GROWTH RATE PER YEAR
IN GNP PER CAPITA,
1948–1988

Country	1948–1973	1973–1981	1981–1988
United States	2.2%	1.1%	2.0%
Japan	7.8	2.7	3.2
West Germany	5.7	2.0	1.9
United Kingdom	2.6	0.7	2.7
Italy	5.0	2.2	2.0
France	4.3	2.1	1.3
Canada	2.8	2.5	2.2

Source: *Economic Report of the President*, January 1989, Table 1–1.

Perhaps we should not make too much of the recent slowdown in productivity growth, particularly since growth as measured by real GNP per capita seems to have rebounded somewhat during the 1980s. Also, if you flip back to Exhibit 2, you will notice that productivity growth between 1960 and 1980 is in line with the growth rate for the sixty years prior to 1929.

The economy's potential output can be increased either by increasing output per labor hour or by increasing the number employed. One way to increase employment is to reduce the number unemployed. We next consider government policies and employment practices that affect the unemployment rate.

GOVERNMENT POLICIES AND EMPLOYMENT PRACTICES THAT CHANGE POTENTIAL GNP

Unemployed workers cannot be immediately matched with job vacancies because of imperfections in the labor market. Reducing these imperfections can increase the economy's potential GNP. By spelling out these imperfections and exploring policy options for reducing them, we can better understand how the economy works.

Policies to Reduce Skills Mismatch

As we have mentioned, the classified ads may be filled with job openings at the same time that millions of people are unemployed. Many unemployed workers simply do not have the skills required to fill the available jobs. For example, new entrants into the work force, particularly teenagers, have never held a job and have never had an opportunity to develop marketable skills.

For most new entrants, the problem is landing that first job. Government policies that promote education and training of those who are most vulnerable to structural unemployment will reduce this source of unemployment and increase the economy's potential GNP. Primary and secondary schools impart the basic knowledge that is usually demanded by employers, but acquiring the desired skills often requires vocational training or higher education or both.

Wage subsidy programs encourage employers to hire and train those who otherwise lack the necessary skills to get jobs. For years employers have had training programs to teach specific job skills. But a shrinking labor pool has forced employers to do more than simply wait for job applicants to come through the door. Some employers have been forced to recruit potential workers and to teach them more basic skills, such as how to apply for a job, how to dress, and how to get along with other employees.

Policies to Reduce Location Mismatch

This is a big country, and the national unemployment rate often masks wide differences among regions, as noted in Chapter 7. At any given time, the unemployment rate in some states may be less than half the national average, while other states are experiencing rates far exceeding the national average. Some unemployment arises from a locational mismatch: those seeking employment in one region are qualified only for job openings in another region. Employment opportunities may differ even within a metropolitan area. Those unemployed in the central city may qualify for job openings in the suburbs but may be unaware of these opportunities or may be unable to commute to the suburbs.

Programs that help job searchers to identify and secure positions will reduce unemployment that arises from locational mismatches. By establishing government employment agencies and making moving expenses tax deductible (for taxpayers who itemize), the government has tried to encourage mobility to find work. As an example of what can be done to reduce structural unemployment, consider one company's efforts. During the late 1980s, the hotels and casinos in Atlantic City, New Jersey, had hundreds of job openings that could not be filled from the local labor pool. Representatives from one hotel went to a region of Ohio where there was high unemployment to interview job applicants. With the help of local officials in Ohio, the hotel hired and relocated over 100 people.

Because local employment opportunities reflect the ups and downs of local economies, however, interregional differences in unemployment are difficult to eliminate altogether. The demand for labor is derived from the market value of labor's product. When the prices of goods produced in a particular region change, this change can result in drastic changes in employment opportunities. For example, when oil prices were climbing, the Texas economy blossomed and jobs were abundant. Migrants from the energy-poor Northeast poured into Houston and Dallas looking for work. When oil prices tumbled, the Texas economy withered and the unemployment rate increased, leaving many recent migrants stranded without jobs and without family ties.

Legal and Social Practices

Economic and social policies serve a variety of objectives. A side-effect of laws and social conventions that interfere with the free functioning of the labor market may be an increase in unemployment.

The Minimum Wage Law The minimum wage law makes it more difficult for individuals who have few or no skills to find work. Some people, particularly those just entering the labor market, are handicapped by the minimum wage law because they lack the skills necessary to make employers want to hire them at that wage. Imagine trying to climb a ladder when the bottom rung has been removed. Workers who are unable to reach the next highest rung — that is, those who lack the skills to warrant even a minimum wage — may be shut out of the job market entirely. If labor markets were allowed to move to a market-clearing wage, unemployment would be reduced. Moreover, to the extent that the minimum wage law places a floor under wages, wages are less flexible downward and are therefore less likely to fall when unemployment is high.

Restricted Entry and Discrimination Any practice that prohibits qualified workers from entering certain trades or professions reduces employment opportunities and lowers the economy's potential GNP. Labor unions and professional associations often control entry into certain jobs and prevent some people from pursuing those trades. Restrictions based on any criteria other than ability, such as race or gender, increase the unemployment rate within the groups that are discriminated against. This problem can be resolved by ensuring that all qualified applicants are allowed to compete for any job. In an effort to ensure equal access to jobs and promotions, the Equal Employment Opportunity Commission was established by the Civil Rights Act of 1964.

Incentive Problems Finally, some are concerned that the existing social service support system, by providing unemployment benefits that replace most of the after-tax income that could be earned by working, may decrease employment incentives. Public officials are torn between providing adequate support for a family in need and providing incentives to promote self-sufficiency. However, most unemployment assistance goes to the ill, the old, dependent children, and others who cannot work anyway, so decreased incentive is not a problem among the majority of transfer beneficiaries. To address this issue, federal and state governments have introduced welfare reforms aimed at providing recipients with the incentive and the training to enter the work force.

THE SUPPLY-SIDE EXPERIMENT

In 1981 President Reagan said that his proposed tax cut would revive lagging productivity, restore U.S. competitiveness in world markets, and spur the steady growth of jobs, production, and real income. The tax cut was heralded as more than just tax relief for individual taxpayers. It was a way of achieving economic growth, a means of unleashing the animal spirits of enterprise to foster productive activity. According to proponents of the supply-side philosophy that motivated the tax cut, the ensuing economic growth would yield enough new revenue to offset the direct loss of revenue from the lower tax rates. The higher level of economic activity would also generate the additional saving required to finance an increase in investment.

The supply-side tax cut of 1981 therefore hinged on generating enough growth to balance the budget. The economy's potential GNP was supposed to increase dramatically. Otherwise, federal revenues would fall short of federal expenditures, and the resulting budget deficit would soak up the private saving needed to finance investment.

The largest income tax cut in history, the 1981 tax cut emphasized reductions in the marginal tax rates. The measure also accelerated the rate at which businesses could deduct capital costs in computing their corporate income taxes. Thus, there were tax cuts for both individuals and businesses. What has transpired since the tax cut? In earlier chapters we briefly discussed the results of the supply-side experiment. Taking the 1981–1988 period as the time frame for examining the results, we can make some tentative observations.

Results of the Experiment

Although it is difficult to untangle the growth generated by the tax cuts from the cyclical upswing following the recession of 1981–1982, we can say that between 1981 and 1988 employment climbed by 15 million and unemployment fell by 2 million workers. This combination of rising employment and falling unemployment spurred the growth in output per capita. As we already observed in our discussion of Exhibit 4, the growth rate in output per capita increased by 2.0 percent per year between 1981 and 1988. This rate was higher than the 1.1 percent average during 1973–1981 but lower than the 2.2 rate during 1948–1973. *Despite the growth in employment, government revenues did not expand enough to offset tax cuts, and the resulting federal deficits have been huge, as has been well documented already. The federal debt tripled during the 1980s.*

Does the growth in employment and in real GNP per capita mark the supply-side experiment as a success? The growth in employment and output could be explained by the economic stimulus provided by the huge federal deficits during the period. Perhaps the only surprising result of the experiment was that despite the federal deficit, which would tend to crowd out private investment, the proportion of national income that went to business investment during the years following the recession of 1982 was the same as the average during the five expansionary periods between 1954 and 1980. Investment failed to decline because there was an unusually large inflow of saving from abroad. High real interest rates, a strong dollar, and a stable political climate combined to make the United States an attractive place for foreigners to put their savings during the 1980s. In 1984 U.S. private saving was 7.4 percent of GNP. Because of the large federal deficit, dissaving by the government sector (including federal, state, and local governments) amounted to 3.4 percent of GNP. Without foreign capital, private saving could only have supported investment amounting to 4.0 percent (7.4 percent minus 3.4 percent) of GNP. But actual domestic investment amounted to 6.4 percent of GNP, with the difference of 2.4 percent coming from the foreign inflow of saving.

Some economists view the inflow of saving from abroad as one of the few bright spots to emerge from the supply-side experiment. But enthusiasm for this source of funds should be tempered by the realization that foreigners are accumulating U.S. assets. The return on these investments will flow to foreigners, not to Americans.

During the years of large federal deficits, U.S. consumption, investment, and government purchases exceeded U.S. income and output. How could this be? Domestic spending could exceed domestic income because of foreign saving. Domestic spending could exceed domestic output because of foreign production. Thus, during this period U.S. imports exceeded exports, and the resulting trade deficit was financed in part by foreign borrowing.

CONCLUSION

The productivity of an economy depends on the availability and quality of various resources, the level of technology, methods for organizing production, the energy and enterprise of entrepreneurs and workers, and a variety of institutional and social factors that affect the incentives and behavior of various resource suppliers. These factors interact to determine the level and growth of productivity. The factors that contribute to productivity are strongly correlated with one another. A country with low productivity will probably be deficient in the quality of its work force, in the quantity or quality of its capital, and in the level of its technology. Similarly, a country with high productivity is likely to excel in all measures.

Recent productivity growth appears slow compared to the high growth rates immediately following World War II, but not when viewed from the long-term perspective. Many economists believe that the rapid growth between 1940 and 1960 occurred because the economy was catching up after the doldrums of the Great Depression and that such growth should not be used as the benchmark against which to judge current growth rates. Growth over the last two decades was not far below the long-term historical trends. During the 1980s U.S. productivity rebounded somewhat from the 1970s and more closely paralleled growth rates in other industrial economies. If U.S. productivity grew at a rate of 2.3 percent per year — the long-term trend — output per worker would double every thirty years, so in one hundred years each hour of labor would produce nine times more real goods and services than it produces today. Not a bad prospect.

Summary

1. Because the population is continually increasing, economies must produce more goods and services simply to maintain the standard of living. If output grows faster than the population, the standard of living will rise.

2. Over the last century, labor productivity has increased an average of 2.3 percent per year. The wheels of progress appear to turn very slowly, but the cumulative effect is powerful: the output per hour of work was twelve times greater in 1980 than in 1870. Research suggests that the quality of labor and capital is much more important than the quantity of these resources.

3. Productivity growth has slowed somewhat in the last two decades but only in comparison to the robust growth during and immediately following World War II. Recent rates of productivity growth are consistent with those experienced during the sixty years between 1870 and 1929.

4. A variety of factors have been considered to explain the recent decline in productivity growth, including (1) the rate of capital formation, (2) the changing composition of the labor force, (3) the decline in educational achievement, (4) higher energy prices during the 1970s, (5) the changing composition of output, (6) growth in government regulations, and (7) a decline in research and development expenditures.

5. Various government policies are aimed at reducing imperfections in the labor market so as to lower the natural rate of unemployment and thereby expand the economy's potential output. Some programs are aimed at reducing the skills mismatch and the location mismatch. Potential output is diminished when any restriction prevents workers from selling their labor where it is valued the most.

6. Supply-side economic policies of the 1980s included tax cuts to provide incentives to increase aggregate supply. The resulting growth in output fell short of the amount necessary to balance the budget, and the national debt exploded during the 1980s.

Questions and Problems

1. (Education and Growth) Many developing countries pay for students to come to the United States to study. How might those countries benefit from such expenditures? Does the United States also benefit? What groups might be hurt?

2. (Agricultural Productivity) As population

grows, land of lower quality is brought under cultivation to produce more food. This suggests that in predominantly agricultural economies with growing populations, agricultural productivity must fall. Is this a valid conclusion?

3. (Japanese Productivity) Japanese universities graduate more engineers each year than U.S. universities do. However, the United States graduates vastly more attorneys. How would you relate these facts to the slow growth in U.S. productivity compared to that of Japanese productivity? Is the United States burdened by too much regulation and litigation? Can productivity conflict with fairness and justice?

4. (Japanese–U.S. Productivity) The Japanese secondary school year is considerably longer than the U.S. year. However, a smaller percentage of secondary school graduates go to college in Japan. Do differences in educational systems explain the differences in productivity growth between the two countries? Why or why not?

5. (Capital Formation and Productivity) There has been much debate in the United States over the long-run effects of the Social Security system on growth and productivity. The current program transfers taxes directly to older individuals, who spend the transfers. The young see their contributions as savings, but are these contributions really savings? How could such a system reduce the overall rate of saving and capital formation in the economy?

6. (Quality and Productivity) Some economists have argued that it is not simply the quantity of investment in the economy that determines productivity growth but also the quality of investment expenditures. What is meant by the "quality of investment," and how might such quality be improved?

7. (Expanding Potential Output) Explain how the community college system, which offers a wide range of practical courses at night, affects the nation's potential output level. What impact does it have on structural unemployment?

8. (Job Location Mismatch) What factors might contribute to a worker's decision to remain unemployed rather than move to another region where work is available? Consider such issues as marriage, children, and home ownership.

9. (Supply-Side Economics) During the early years of the Reagan administration, there was considerable optimism about supply-side economics. How were tax cuts expected to affect aggregate supply? What other incentives for growth and productivity were advocated? Were such measures successful? Why or why not?

10. (Technology and Productivity) What measures can government take to promote the development of practical technologies? Is the strict enforcement of patent laws important to research and development? Why or why not?

11. (Productivity and Living Standards) A considerable amount of regulatory legislation involves so-called environmental impact considerations. The result has been a reduction in output per unit of labor, which some say has lowered our standard of living. Defend or refute this position.

12. (Investment Policies) Using a supply-demand diagram for loanable funds (see Chapter 7 for review), show the consequences for capital formation, and therefore productivity growth, of each of the following:
    a. Repeal of the deductibility of consumer interest payments
    b. A reduction in the tax rate on corporate income
    c. Elimination of the deductibility of mortgage interest payments

13. (Trade and Productivity) International trade is supposed to enhance efficiency by allowing greater specialization of resources. Yet it may well result in an increase in structural unemployment. Explain.

14. (Supply-Side Economics) Supply-side policies are supposed to increase potential GNP by stimulating resources and productivity. Yet cuts in personal tax rates create higher federal budget deficits and crowding out. Doesn't this contradict the supply-side story?

PRICE ELASTICITY OF DEMAND

Producers find it valuable to know the magnitude of the impact of a price change on quantity demanded. For example, if consumers sharply reduce their taco purchases when the price of tacos goes up, taco producers may find that total revenue falls. Consider the two demand curves in Exhibit 1. In each case the price per unit has increased by 25 percent, from $1 to $1.25, but the effect on the quantity demanded differs in the two panels. In panel (a), the quantity demanded drops from 100 to 90, a 10 percent decline, and in panel (b), it drops from 100 to 70, a 30 percent decline. Consumers are much more responsive to the price increase in panel (b) than in panel (a). The responsiveness of quantity demanded to a change in price is measured by the price elasticity of demand. *Elasticity* is simply another word for *responsiveness*.

Calculating Price Elasticity of Demand

*The **price elasticity of demand** measures the responsiveness of quantity demanded to a price change; it is the percentage change in quantity demanded divided by the percentage change in price.*

In simplest terms, the **price elasticity of demand** is equal to the percentage change in the quantity demanded divided by the percentage change in price. This relationship can be represented by the equation

$$\text{Price elasticity of demand} = \frac{\text{percentage change in quantity demanded}}{\text{percentage change in price}}$$

Recall that the law of demand states that price and quantity demanded are inversely related: the change in price and the change in quantity demanded will always be in opposite directions. Hence, in the preceding elasticity formula the numerator and the denominator will have opposite signs, and the price elasticity of demand will always have a negative value. For simplicity, we use the *absolute value* of the elasticity, which means that we drop the minus sign.

In panel (a) of Exhibit 1, when the price increases from $1.00 to $1.25, an increase of 25 percent [(1.25 − 1.00)/1.00], the quantity demanded decreases from 100 to 90, a drop of only 10 percent [(90 − 100)/100]. In this case the resulting elasticity is − 10%/25%, which has an absolute value of 0.4. In panel (b), the price increase is also 25 percent, but the quantity demanded falls from 100 to 70, or by 30 percent [(70 − 100)/100]. Thus the resulting elasticity is − 30%/25%, which has an absolute value of 1.2.

Note that elasticity expresses the relation between relative amounts — the percentage change in quantity divided by the percentage change in price. Since we are considering only the percentage change, we need not be concerned about how price or output is measured. For example, suppose the good in question is cotton. It makes no difference in the elasticity formulation whether we express the price in terms of dollars per pound, dollars per bale, or dollars per ton. In fact, it doesn't matter whether we use dollars, pesos, francs, or any other currency. All that matters is that the price went up

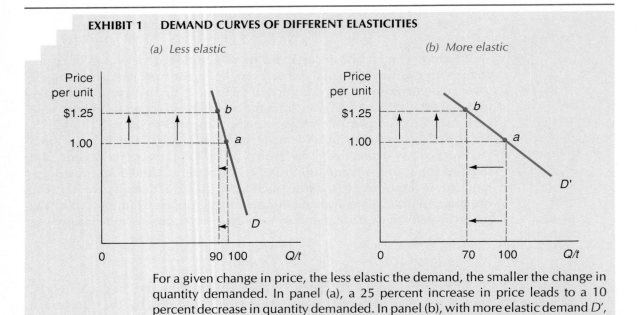

EXHIBIT 1   DEMAND CURVES OF DIFFERENT ELASTICITIES

For a given change in price, the less elastic the demand, the smaller the change in quantity demanded. In panel (a), a 25 percent increase in price leads to a 10 percent decrease in quantity demanded. In panel (b), with more elastic demand D', the same 25 percent price increase leads to a 30 percent decrease in quantity demanded.

25 percent. Similarly, in measuring quantity demanded, all that matters is the percentage change in quantity demanded, not how we measure quantity demanded.

Categories of Price Elasticity of Demand

*Demand is **inelastic** when the price elasticity of demand has a value less than 1.0; it is of **unitary elasticity** when the elasticity value equals 1.0; and it is **elastic** when the elasticity value exceeds 1.0.*

Price elasticity of demand can be divided into three general categories, based on how responsive quantity demanded is to changes in price. If the percentage change in quantity demanded is less than the percentage change in price, the resulting price elasticity has a value less than 1.0, and demand is said to be **inelastic**. For example, in the range of prices depicted in panel (a) of Exhibit 1, demand is inelastic. If the percentage change in quantity demanded just equals the percentage change in price, the resulting price elasticity has a value equal to 1.0, and demand is said to be of **unitary elasticity**. Finally, if the quantity demanded changes by a greater percentage than does the price, the resulting price elasticity has a value greater than 1.0, and demand is said to be **elastic**. For example, in the price range depicted in panel (b) of Exhibit 1, demand is elastic. In summary, *demand is inelastic if price elasticity is less than 1.0, of unitary elasticity if price elasticity is equal to 1.0, and elastic if price elasticity is greater than 1.0.*

Refining the Calculations: The Midpoint Formula

The discussion to this point has glossed over a tricky little problem in calculating elasticity. Using our simple formula, we get a different elasticity value depending on whether we move from point *a* to point *b* or from point *b* to point *a*. Consider the case in panel (a) of Exhibit 1, where the price increases from $1.00 to $1.25, an increase of 25 percent, and the quantity decreases from 100 to 90 units, a decrease of 10 percent. The elasticity was calculated as − 10%/25%, which has an absolute value of 0.4. If, however, we begin with a price of $1.25 and lower it to $1.00, this change represents a price drop of 20 percent [(1.00 − 1.25)/1.25]; quantity demanded then increases from 90 to 100, an increase of 11 percent [(100 − 90)/90]. The resulting elasticity is − 11%/20%, which has an absolute value of 0.55.

The problem is that although the sizes of changes in price and in quantity are the same whether we go from the higher to the lower price or the other way around (that is, the price changes by $0.25, and the quantity demanded changes by 10 units), the *base* for calculating the percentage change depends on the initial price and the initial quantity. Consequently, when we begin with $1.00 and raise the price by $0.25, the base is different from what it is when we begin with $1.25 and lower the price by $0.25. Economists have solved the problem by using the *midpoint* between the initial value and the new value as the base. The midpoint is simply the average of the initial value and the new value. The *midpoint formula* for calculating the price elasticity of demand for any change in price is

$$E_D = \frac{Q'_D - Q_D}{(Q'_D + Q_D)/2} \div \frac{P' - P}{(P' + P)/2}$$

where E_D is the price elasticity of demand, Q_D is the initial quantity, Q'_D is the quantity after the price change, P is the initial price, and P' is the new price. Thus, when the price increases from $1.00 to $1.25, the base used in calculating the percentage change is not $1.00 but ($1.25 + $1.00)/2 = $1.125. The percentage change in price is therefore 0.25/1.125, or 22 percent. And the base will be the same whether we consider a change from $1.00 to $1.25 or from $1.25 to $1.00.

The same holds for changes in quantity demanded. When the quantity demanded falls from 100 to 90, the base is not 100 but (90 + 100)/2 = 95. Thus, the percentage change in quantity demanded calculated by the mid-point method is 10/95, which equals 10.5 percent. The resulting elasticity of demand is the percentage change in quantity, 10.5 percent, divided by the percentage change in price, 22 percent, which is equal to 0.48. Because the midpoint formula uses the same base, the value for the elasticity will be the same for a price drop from $1.25 to $1.00 as for a price increase from $1.00 to $1.25.

Elasticity and Total Revenue

Total revenue equals price multiplied by the quantity sold at that price.

Producers want to know the price elasticity of demand because it tells them what will happen to their total revenue if the price is changed. **Total revenue** is the price of the product multiplied by the quantity sold at that price. In a graph, total revenue at any point along a demand curve can be represented by the area of the rectangle under the demand curve, where the height of the rectangle equals the price and the width equals the quantity demanded.

What happens to total revenue when the price decreases? According to the law of demand, if the price falls, the quantity demanded increases. The lower price means that revenue per unit sold decreases, which tends to decrease total revenue. But the greater quantity demanded means that the number of units sold increases, and this tends to increase total revenue. The overall change in total revenue resulting from a lower price is the net result of these opposite effects. If the positive effect of a greater quantity demanded exceeds the negative effect of a lower price, total revenue will rise. More specifically, when demand is *elastic*, the percentage increase in quantity demanded exceeds the percentage decrease in price, so a price decrease will increase total revenue. When demand is of *unitary elasticity*, the percentage increase in quantity demanded is just equal to the percentage decrease in price, so a price decrease will not change total revenue. Finally, when demand is *inelastic*, the percentage increase in quantity demanded is less than the percentage decrease in price, so a price decrease will decrease total revenue.

Price Elasticity and the Linear Demand Curve

The price elasticity of demand usually varies along a demand curve. An examination of the elasticity of a particular type of demand curve, the linear demand curve, will tie together the concepts examined thus far. A *linear demand curve* is simply a straight-line demand curve. Panel (a) of Exhibit 2 presents a linear demand curve; panel (b) presents a curve reflecting the total revenue generated at each price along the demand curve. Total revenue, you will remember, is price times quantity demanded at that price.

In panel (a) of Exhibit 2, the price elasticity of demand is greater on the higher-price end of the demand curve than on the lower-price end. Since this demand curve is linear, a given decrease in price always causes the same increase in quantity demanded; a $10 price drop always increases quantity demanded by 100 units. At the upper end of the curve, however, a $10 decrease in price is a small percentage change because the price level is high, and the corresponding 100-unit increase in quantity is a large percentage change because the quantity is low. The situation is reversed at the lower end of the demand curve: a $10 price drop when the price is low is a large percentage change in price, and a 100-unit quantity change when the quantity is great is a small percentage change in quantity demanded.

Consider a movement from point *a* to point *b* on the higher end. Using the midpoint formula, we find that a $10 price drop amounts to a percentage change of 10/85, or about 12 percent. The 100-unit increase in quantity demanded is a percentage change of 100/150, or 66 percent. Therefore, the price elasticity between points *a* and *b* is 66%/12%, which equals 5.5. Between points *d* and *e* on the lower end, however, the $10 price change is a

EXHIBIT 2   DEMAND, ELASTICITY, AND TOTAL REVENUE

(a) Demand and elasticity

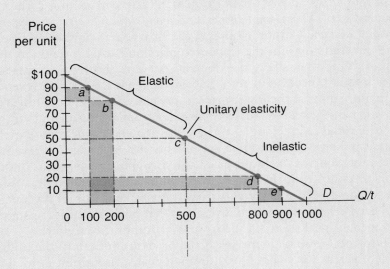

(b) Total revenue

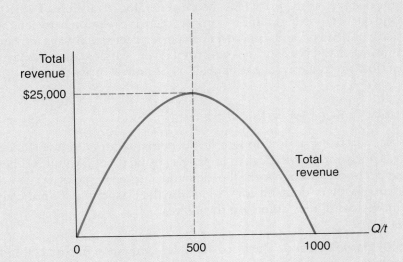

Where demand is elastic in panel (a), total revenue in panel (b) increases following a price decrease. Total revenue attains its maximum value at the level of output where demand is of unitary elasticity. Where demand is inelastic, further decreases in price cause total revenue to fall.

percentage change of 10/15, or 66 percent, and the 100-unit quantity change is a percentage change of 100/850, or only 12 percent. The price elasticity thus falls to 12%/66%, or 0.18. In other words, *if the demand curve is linear, consumers are more responsive to price changes when the price range for a product is relatively high than when the price range is relatively low.*

The price elasticity of demand falls steadily as we move down the curve. At a point halfway down the linear demand curve in Exhibit 2, the elasticity is equal to 1.0. *This midpoint divides the demand curve into an elastic upper half and an inelastic lower half.* You can observe the clear relation between the elasticity of the demand curve in the upper diagram and total revenue in the lower diagram. Note that where the demand curve is elastic, a decrease in price results in a net increase in total revenue because the gain in revenue from selling more units at the lower price (represented by the large blue rectangle in the top panel) exceeds the loss in revenue from selling all units at the lower price (the small red rectangle). Where the demand curve is inelastic, a price decrease reduces total revenue on net because the gain in revenue from selling more units at the lower price (the small blue rectangle) is less than the loss in revenue from the price drop (the large red rectangle). Where the demand curve is of unitary elasticity, the gain and loss of revenue exactly cancel each other out, so total revenue at that point remains constant (hence total revenue "peaks out" in the lower portion of the exhibit).

Thus, total revenue increases as the price declines until the midpoint of the curve is reached, where total revenue peaks. In Exhibit 2, total revenue peaks at $25,000 when total sales equal 500 units. Below the midpoint, total revenue declines as the price falls. More generally, regardless of whether the demand curve is a straight line or a curve, there is a relation between the price elasticity of demand and total revenue: a price decrease always *increases* total revenue if demand is elastic, *decreases* total revenue if demand is inelastic, and *has no effect* on total revenue if demand is of unitary elasticity.

Constant-Elasticity Demand Curves

Price elasticity varies along a linear demand curve unless the demand curve is horizontal or vertical, as in panels (a) and (b) of Exhibit 3. These two demand curves, along with the demand curve in panel (c), are called constant–elasticity demand curves because the elasticity does not change as you move to different points on the curves.

*A **perfectly elastic demand curve** is horizontal. The quantity demanded can increase even with no change in price, but any price increase reduces the quantity demanded to 0. The value of the price elasticity of demand is infinitely large.*

Perfectly Elastic Demand   The horizontal demand curve in panel (a) indicates that consumers will demand all that is offered for sale at price *P*. If the price rises above *P*, however, the quantity demanded will go to zero. This demand curve is said to be **perfectly elastic**, and its numerical elasticity value is infinity, the highest possible value. You may think this is an odd sort of demand curve: consumers, as a result of a small increase in price, go from demanding as much as is available to demanding nothing. As you will see later, this curve describes the demand for the product of any individual producer when many producers are selling identical goods. If, for example, the market price of wheat is $5 per bushel, all that each farmer wants to supply can be sold at that price. But any farmer who charges a higher price

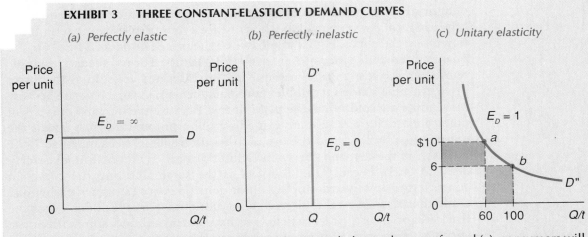

EXHIBIT 3   THREE CONSTANT-ELASTICITY DEMAND CURVES

(a) Perfectly elastic   *(b) Perfectly inelastic*   *(c) Unitary elasticity*

Along the perfectly elastic (horizontal) demand curve of panel (a), consumers will purchase all that is offered for sale at price *P*. Along the perfectly inelastic (vertical) demand curve of panel (b), consumers will purchase quantity *Q* regardless of price. Along the unitary elastic demand curve of panel (c), total revenue is the same for every price-quantity combination.

will find no buyers because consumers can buy wheat from other farmers for the market price of $5 per bushel.

Perfectly Inelastic Demand The vertical demand curve in panel (b) of Exhibit 3 represents the situation in which quantity demanded does not vary when the price changes. This demand curve expresses consumers' sentiment that "price is no object." For example, if you were very rich and needed insulin injections to stay alive, price would be no object. No matter how high the price of the insulin, you would continue to demand the same quantity. If an oil tycoon came across a diamond necklace that she simply had to have, price would be no object. Such demand curves are called **perfectly inelastic** because price changes do not affect quantity demanded, at least not over the range of prices depicted by the demand curve. Since the percentage change in quantity is zero for any given percentage change in price, the numerical value of the elasticity is zero, which is the lowest possible numerical value.

In reality, of course, if the price rises high enough, people will be unable to afford the good regardless of how much they desire it. Recall that demand reflects the quantity people are both *willing* and *able* to demand at alternative prices. For example, the wealthy oil tycoon might buy the necklace even if the price were $1 million, but if the price were $1 billion, she simply could not afford it. Thus, a demand curve may be perfectly inelastic, but only over realistic price ranges. To be accurate, we should say that price is no object over the realistic range of possible prices.

Unitary Elasticity Panel (c) in Exhibit 3 presents a demand curve that is of unitary elasticity everywhere along the curve. This means that a percentage

*A **perfectly inelastic demand curve** is vertical. A price change has no effect on the quantity demanded. The value of the price elasticity of demand is 0.*

change in price will always result in an identical percentage change in quantity. Because percentage changes in price and quantity will be equal and offsetting, total revenue will be the same for every price-quantity combination along the curve. For example, when the price falls from $10 to $6, the quantity demanded increases from 60 to 100 units. The red shaded rectangle represents the loss in total revenue because all units are sold at the lower price; the blue shaded rectangle represents the gain in total revenue because more units are sold when the price drops. Because the demand curve is of unitary elasticity, the revenue gained by selling more units just equals the revenue lost by lowering the price, so total revenue is unchanged at $600.

The price elasticity of demand takes on the same value at every point along a **constant-elasticity** *demand curve.*

Each of the demand curves in Exhibit 3 is called a **constant-elasticity** demand curve because the elasticity is the same all along the curve. In contrast, the downward-sloping linear demand curve examined earlier had a different elasticity value at each point along the curve. Exhibit 4 lists the five categories of price elasticity we have discussed and summarizes the varying effects of a 10 percent increase in the price on quantity demanded and on total revenue. Give this exhibit some thought and see if you can draw a demand curve to reflect each type of elasticity.

EXHIBIT 4
SUMMARY OF PRICE ELASTICITY EFFECTS

		Effects of a 10 Percent Increase in Price	
Absolute Price Elasticity Value	Type of Demand	What Happens to Quantity Demanded	What Happens to Total Revenue
$\|E_D\| = 0$	Perfectly inelastic	No change	Increases by 10 percent
$0 < \|E_D\| < 1$	Inelastic	Drops by less than 10 percent	Increases by less than 10 percent
$\|E_D\| = 1$	Unitary elasticity	Drops by 10 percent	No change
$1 < \|E_D\| < \infty$	Elastic	Drops by more than 10 percent	Decreases
$\|E_D\| = \infty$	Perfectly elastic	Drops to 0	Drops to 0

DETERMINANTS OF THE PRICE ELASTICITY OF DEMAND

Thus far we have explored the technical properties of demand elasticity. We have not yet considered why the price elasticities of demand vary for different goods. Several characteristics influence the price elasticity of demand for a good. We will examine each of these in some detail.

Availability of Substitutes

As noted in Chapter 3, your particular wants can be satisfied in a variety of different ways. If the price of pizza increases, foods that are close substitutes become relatively cheaper. If close substitutes are available, an increase in the price of pizza will cause you to shift to these substitutes and lower the quantity of pizza you demand. But if nothing else comes close to satisfying your desire for pizza, you may reduce your quantity of pizza demanded very little. *The greater the availability of substitutes for a good and the closer these substitutes are to the good demanded, the more elastic the price elasticity of demand.*

The number and similarity of substitutes depend on how we define the good. *The more broadly we define a good, the fewer substitutes there will be and the less elastic the demand will be.* For example, the demand for shoes will be less elastic than the demand for running shoes because there are few substitutes for shoes but several substitutes for running shoes, such as sneakers, tennis shoes, and the like. The demand for running shoes, however, will be less elastic than the demand for Nikes because the consumer has more substitutes for Nikes, including Reeboks, New Balance, and so on. Finally, the demand for Nikes will be less elastic than the demand for a specific model of Nikes, such as Nike Airs.

For some goods there are simply no close substitutes. When a diabetic needs insulin, nothing else will do. The demand for such goods tends to be inelastic. Because producers would like to be able to increase their prices without having you switch to substitutes, they would like you to think there are no substitutes for their products. Much advertising is aimed at establishing in the consumer's mind the uniqueness of a particular product. For example, Nike would like consumers to believe that there is no close substitute for Nike Airs; likewise, Bayer aspirin spends millions of dollars trying to distinguish its product from other brands.

Proportion of the Consumer's Budget Spent on a Good

Recall that a higher price reduces quantity demanded in part because a higher price causes the real spending power of consumer income to decline. A demand curve reflects both the willingness and the ability to purchase a good at alternative prices.

Because expenditures for certain goods represent a large share of the consumer's budget, changes in the prices of these goods have a substantial impact on the quantity that consumers are able to purchase. An increase in the price of housing, for example, greatly affects the ability to buy housing. The income effect of higher housing prices significantly reduces the quantity of housing demanded. Thus, the price elasticity of demand for housing will be large. In contrast, the income effect of an increase in the price of paper towels is trivial because expenditures on paper towels represent such a small proportion of any budget. *The more important the item is as a proportion of the household budget, other things constant, the more elastic its demand will be.* The smaller the item is as a proportion of the budget, the less elastic its demand will be. Hence, the demand for housing, cars, and major appliances tends to be more elastic than the demand for paper towels, pencils, and flashlight batteries.

A Matter of Time

Consumers can substitute lower-priced goods for higher-priced goods, but this substitution often takes time. Suppose your college announces a substantial increase in room and board fees effective immediately. Some students will move off campus as soon as they can. Others will wait until the end of the school year. And, over time, fewer students may apply for admission, and more incoming students will choose off-campus housing. *Thus the longer the adjustment period considered, the greater the ability to substitute away from relatively higher-priced products toward lower-priced substitutes, and the more responsive the change in quantity demanded to a given change in price.*

Exhibit 5 demonstrates how demand becomes more elastic over time. Assuming that the initial price is $1.00, let D_d be the demand curve one day after a price change; D_m, one month after; and D_y, one year after. If the price increases from $1.00 to $1.25, the reduction in quantity demanded will be greater as consumers have longer to identify and adopt substitutes. For example, the demand curve D_d shows that one day after the price change the

EXHIBIT 5   DEMAND BECOMES MORE ELASTIC OVER TIME

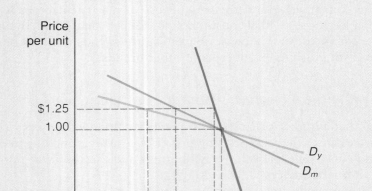

D_d is the demand curve one day after a price increase from $1.00 to $1.25. Along this curve, quantity demanded falls from 100 to 95. One month after the price increase, quantity demanded has fallen to 75 along D_m. One year after the price increase, quantity demanded has fallen to 50 along D_y. D_y is more elastic than D_m, which is more elastic than D_d.

quantity consumed has been reduced very little — in this case from 100 to 95. The demand curve D_m indicates a greater reduction in quantity demanded after one month, and demand curve D_y shows the greatest reduction in quantity demanded after one year. Notice that *among these intersecting demand curves, the flatter the demand curve, the more elastic the demand.*

Luxuries Versus Necessities

Even if the price of food increases, people must eat. They may substitute cheaper cuts of meat for steak and canned tuna for shrimp, but they will probably go without something else in their budget before going without food. Food may be viewed as a *necessity*; people must buy necessities even if the price increases. On the other hand, a higher price for movie tickets may cause people to seek other forms of entertainment; movies may be viewed as *luxuries*. Similarly, higher transportation costs encourage people to reduce their "joy rides" and to vacation closer to home. *The price elasticity of demand is lower for necessities than for luxuries.*

Elasticity Estimates

As a way of breathing some life into the discussion, let's consider some estimates of the price elasticity of demand for particular goods and services. As we have said, the substitution of lower-priced goods for higher-priced goods often takes time. Thus, when estimating price elasticity, we often distinguish between a period during which consumers have little time to adjust — let's call it the short run — and a period during which consumers can fully adjust to a price change — the long run. Neither the short run nor the long run is a uniform length of time; it depends on the good in question. For example, consumers will take longer to adjust fully to a change in the price of housing than to a change in the price of milk.

Exhibit 6 provides short-run and long-run price elasticity estimates for

EXHIBIT 6
SELECTED PRICE ELASTICITIES OF DEMAND

Product	Short Run	Long Run
Air travel	0.1	2.4
Electricity	0.1	1.9
Gasoline	0.2	0.5
Medical care and hospitalization	0.3	0.9
Movies	0.9	3.7
Milk	0.4	—
Automobiles	—	1.5
Chevrolets	—	4.0

Source: H. S. Houthakker and L. D. Taylor, *Consumer Demand in the United States: Analyses and Projections*, 2d ed. (Cambridge, MA: Harvard University Press, 1970).

selected products. Notice that *the price elasticity tends to be greater in the long run because consumers have more time to adjust*. For example, if the price of electricity rose tomorrow, consumers could make some minor adjustments in their use of electricity. Over time, however, they could buy more energy-efficient appliances, replace electric heat with oil or gas heat, and make other major changes to reduce electricity consumption. So the demand is more elastic in the long run than in the short run. Notice also that the long-run price elasticity of demand for Chevrolets exceeds the price elasticity for automobiles in general. There are many more substitutes for Chevrolets than for automobiles.

PRICE ELASTICITY OF SUPPLY

The **price elasticity of supply** measures the responsiveness of quantity supplied to a price change; it is the percentage change in quantity supplied divided by the percentage change in price.

Prices signal both sides of the market about the relative scarcity of products; high prices discourage consumption but encourage production. The price elasticity of demand is a measure of how consumers respond to a price change. Similarly, the **price elasticity of supply** measures how responsive producers are to a price change. This elasticity is calculated in the same way as demand elasticity, but using the percentage change in quantity supplied instead of the percentage change in quantity demanded. We use the midpoint formula to express the price elasticity of supply as follows:

$$E_S = \frac{Q'_S - Q_S}{(Q'_S + Q_S)/2} \div \frac{P' - P}{(P' + P)/2}$$

where E_S is the price elasticity of supply, Q_S is the original quantity supplied, Q'_S is the quantity supplied after the price change, P is the original price, and P' is the price after the price change. Recall that if the price increases, the quantity supplied typically increases, so the percentage change in price and the percentage change in quantity tend to move in the same direction. Since changes in output and in price tend to move in the same direction, supply elasticity is usually positive.

Categories of Supply Elasticity

The terminology for supply elasticity is the same as for demand elasticity: if supply elasticity has a value greater than 1.0, supply is *elastic*; if the value is less than 1.0, supply is *inelastic*; and if the value is equal to 1.0, supply is of *unitary elasticity*. There are some special values of supply elasticity to be considered.

Perfectly Elastic Supply At one extreme is the horizontal supply curve, such as supply curve S in Exhibit 7. In this case producers will supply none of the good at a price below P but will supply any amount at a price of P (the quantity actually supplied at price P will depend on the quantity demanded at that price). Because a tiny increase from a price just below P to a price of P

EXHIBIT 7   TWO EXTREME SUPPLY ELASTICITIES

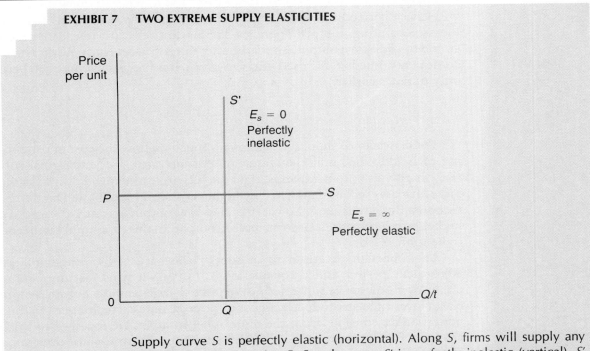

Supply curve *S* is perfectly elastic (horizontal). Along *S*, firms will supply any amount of output at price *P*. Supply curve *S'* is perfectly inelastic (vertical). *S'* represents a situation in which the quantity supplied is independent of the price.

*A **perfectly elastic supply curve** is horizontal. The quantity supplied can increase even with no change in price, but any price decrease reduces the quantity supplied to 0. The value of the price elasticity of supply is infinitely large.*

will result in an unlimited supply, this curve is said to reflect **perfectly elastic supply**, which has a mathematical elasticity value of infinity.

As individual consumers, we typically face perfectly elastic supply curves. When we go to the supermarket, we usually can buy as much as we want at the prevailing price. This is not to say that all consumers together could buy an unlimited amount at the prevailing price. Recall the fallacy of composition: what is true for any individual consumer is not necessarily true for all consumers as a group. Even though an individual consumer faces a horizontal supply curve, it is the market supply curve that determines what price consumers as a group must pay. Typically, though not always, the market supply curve slopes upward.

*A **perfectly inelastic supply curve** is vertical. A change in price results in no change in quantity supplied. The value of the price elasticity of supply is 0.*

Perfectly Inelastic Supply The most unresponsive relation between price and quantity supplied is the one in which there is no change in the quantity supplied when the price changes. Such a case is represented by the vertical supply curve *S'* in Exhibit 7. Because the percentage change in quantity supplied is zero, regardless of the change in price, the value of the supply elasticity equals zero. This curve reflects **perfectly inelastic supply**. This year's crop of strawberries is an example of a product with a perfectly inelastic supply curve. Once the crop is grown, not another strawberry can be produced this season no matter how high the price. Any good that is in fixed supply, such as Picasso paintings or 1978 Dom Perignon champagne, will have a perfectly inelastic supply curve. (Not surprisingly, the price of Picasso's paintings jumped upon news of his death because his death meant an end to additional output. Similarly, after the pop artist Andy Warhol died, art dealers immediately raised prices to as much as triple what they had been only minutes earlier.)

Determinants of Supply Elasticity

The elasticity of supply depends very much on how the cost of producing each additional unit changes as output increases. If the marginal cost rises sharply as output expands, then the incentive to expand output as the price increases will be dampened by higher costs, and supply will tend to be inelastic. But if the marginal cost rises slowly as output expands, the lure of a higher price will cause a large increase in output. In this case supply will tend to be more elastic.

An important determinant of supply elasticity is the length of the adjustment period under consideration. Just as demand becomes more elastic over time as consumers adjust to price changes, supply becomes more elastic over time as producers adjust to price changes. The longer the time period under consideration, the more able producers are to adjust to price changes. Exhibit 8 presents a different supply curve for each of three time periods. S_d is the supply curve when the period of adjustment is a day. As you can see, a higher price will not elicit much of a response in quantity supplied because the firms have little time to adjust. Thus, such a supply curve will tend to slope steeply, reflecting inelastic supply.

S_m is the supply curve when the adjustment period under consideration is a month. In that time firms can more easily adjust the rate at which they employ some resources. As a result, firms have a greater ability to vary output. Thus the supply curve is more elastic when the adjustment period is a month than when it is a day. The supply curve is still more elastic when the adjustment period is a year, as shown by S_y. In a year firms can vary most, if not all, inputs, and new firms may be drawn into the market as a result of a higher price. So a given price increase will elicit a greater response in quantity supplied. *The elasticity of supply is therefore greater the longer the period of adjustment.*

Firms' ability to adjust to a price change differs across industries. Producers of electricity, more fuel-efficient automobiles, and prime timber may take years to make any substantial changes in quantity supplied in response to a change in price. The quantity of services supplied by real estate agents, rock groups, and lunch wagons, however, seems to adjust almost overnight to changes in the price.

Now that you have been introduced to the elasticities of demand and supply, we will reinforce your understanding of elasticity by working through an example using both demand and supply. In the next section we show the effects of a sales tax on price and quantity and link these effects to elasticities.

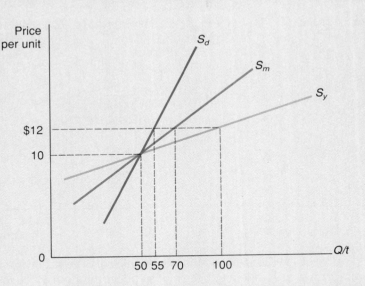

The supply curve one day after a price increase, S_d, is less elastic than the curve one month later, S_m, which is less elastic than the curve one year later, S_y. Given a price increase from $10 to $12, quantity supplied increases to 55 units after one day, to 70 units after one month, and to 100 units after one year.

ELASTICITY AND TAX INCIDENCE: AN APPLICATION

Tax incidence identifies who ultimately pays a tax.

The sales tax is the major source of state government revenue. There is much confusion about who exactly pays the tax. Is it paid by producers or by consumers? As you will see, the **tax incidence** — that is, who ultimately pays the tax — depends on the elasticities of supply and demand.

Demand Elasticity and Tax Incidence

Panel (a) in Exhibit 9 depicts the supply and demand for cigarettes. Before a tax is imposed, the equilibrium price is $1 per pack, and the equilibrium quantity is 10 million packs per day. Now suppose a tax of $0.20 is imposed on each pack of cigarettes produced. Recall that the supply curve represents the amount that producers are willing and able to supply at each price. If producers are now required to pay the government $0.20 for each pack of cigarettes they sell, at each price they will supply fewer packs. Put another way, once the tax is imposed, producers must be paid $0.20 more per pack at each quantity level to supply that quantity. The tax can be viewed as an addition to the supply price at each quantity. Because it adds $0.20 to the supply price at each level of output, the tax causes a $0.20

**EXHIBIT 9   EFFECTS OF DIFFERENT DEMAND ELASTICITIES ON SALES TAX
INCIDENCE**

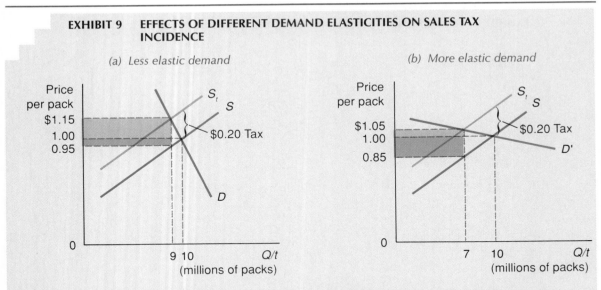

The imposition of a $0.20 sales tax shifts the supply curve vertically from S to S_T. In panel (a), with less elastic demand, the market price rises from $1.00 to $1.15 per pack and the quantity demanded and supplied falls from 10 million packs to 9 million. In panel (b), with more elastic demand, the same sales tax leads to an increase in price from $1.00 to $1.05 per pack; the quantity demanded and supplied falls from 10 million packs to 7 million. The more elastic the demand, the more the tax is paid by producers in the form of a lower price net of taxes.

vertical shift in the supply curve, from S up to S_t. In short, *the effect of the tax is to reduce the supply of cigarettes.* The demand curve remains the same since nothing has happened to shift demand; only the quantity demanded will change.

Since suppliers are the ones who collect the tax for the government, they at first appear to be the ones who pay the tax. But let's take a closer look. The result of the tax in panel (a) is to raise the price to $1.15 and to decrease the equilibrium quantity to 9 million packs. The shaded area represents the amount of tax collected, which equals the tax per pack times the number of packs sold, or $1.8 million ($0.20 × 9 million). Notice that the price does not increase by the full $0.20 because, although producers are willing to supply 10 million packs at a price of $1.20, consumers are not willing to purchase that many. The higher price resulting from the tax reduces the quantity demanded. Therefore, at a price of $1.20, a surplus would develop, causing the price to fall.

As a result of the tax, consumers pay $0.15 more per pack, and producers receive, net of the tax, $0.05 less. Thus, $0.15 of the $0.20 tax is paid by consumers in the form of a higher price, and $0.05 is paid by suppliers in the form of a reduction in the amount they receive per pack. You can see that the original price line of $1 divides the shaded area into two segments, representing the portion of the total tax revenues paid by consumers through a higher price (the lighter shading) and the portion paid by producers now receiving a lower net price (the darker shading).

The same situation is depicted in panel (b) of Exhibit 9, with the single difference being that the demand curve, D', is more elastic than the demand curve in panel (a). In panel (b), the quantity demanded is more responsive to a change in price, so the suppliers cannot pass the tax increase along as easily in the form of a higher price. Hence, the price increases by only $0.05, to $1.05, and the net-of-tax receipts of producers decline by $0.15 per pack, to $0.85. Total tax revenues equal $0.20 per pack times 7 million packs sold, or $1.4 million. Again, the light blue rectangle depicts the portion of the total taxes paid by consumers through a higher price, and the dark blue rectangle depicts the portion of the total taxes paid by producers through a lower price net of taxes. Note that the sum of the price increase and the reduction in producers' net receipts must always equal $0.20, the amount of the tax per unit.

From this example we can conclude that, *other things constant, the more elastic the demand, the less the tax can be passed on to consumers in the form of higher prices, and the more the tax will be absorbed by the producers.* Also note that the amount sold falls more in panel (b) than in panel (a): total tax revenues are lower when demand is more elastic.

Supply Elasticity and Tax Incidence

The effect of the elasticity of supply on the tax incidence is shown in Exhibit 10. The supply curve in panel (a) is more elastic than the one in panel (b). In both panels the demand curve is the same and the supply curve shifts vertically by $0.20 to reflect the $0.20 tax. Notice that in panel (a) the equilibrium price rises to $1.15 — a $0.15 increase over the pretax price. But in panel (b) the price increases by only $0.05. Thus, more of the tax is passed on to consumers in panel (a) than in panel (b). More generally, *other things constant, the more elastic the supply, the more suppliers pass taxes along to consumers in the form of higher prices.*

We conclude that the more elastic the demand and the less elastic the supply, the lower the proportion of the tax paid by consumers. Put another way, the more consumers reduce their quantity demanded in response to an increase in the price they pay and the less suppliers reduce their quantity supplied in response to a decrease in the price they receive, the less the tax is passed on to consumers and the more it is absorbed by producers.

OTHER ELASTICITY MEASURES

The price elasticities of demand and supply are frequently used in economic analysis, but other elasticities also provide useful information. The price elasticity of demand measures the responsiveness of the quantity of a particular product demanded to changes in its price, but we are also

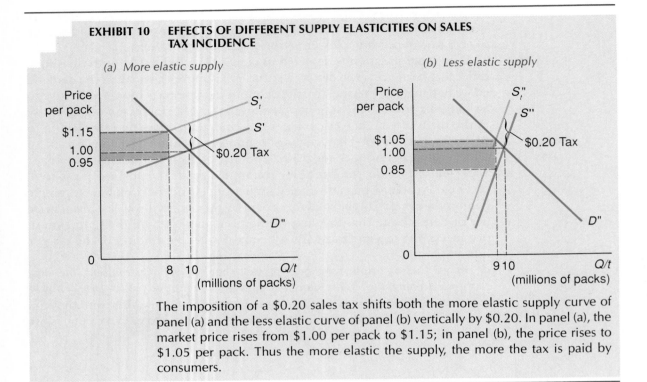

EXHIBIT 10   EFFECTS OF DIFFERENT SUPPLY ELASTICITIES ON SALES TAX INCIDENCE

(a) More elastic supply

(b) Less elastic supply

The imposition of a $0.20 sales tax shifts both the more elastic supply curve of panel (a) and the less elastic curve of panel (b) vertically by $0.20. In panel (a), the market price rises from $1.00 per pack to $1.15; in panel (b), the price rises to $1.05 per pack. Thus the more elastic the supply, the more the tax is paid by consumers.

interested in how demand responds to other events, such as a change in consumer income or a change in the price of a related good.

Income Elasticity of Demand

The income elasticity of demand is the percentage change in quantity demanded at a given price level divided by the percentage change in income.

What happens to the demand for new cars, dental floss, air conditioners, and bicycles if consumer income increases by 20 percent? The answer to this question is of great interest to producers of these goods because it allows them to predict the effect of rising incomes on unit sales and total revenues. The **income elasticity of demand** measures how demand changes in response to a change in income, with prices held constant. Whereas the price elasticity of demand measures changes along the demand curve, the income elasticity of demand measures horizontal shifts in the demand curve in response to a change in income. More specifically, the income elasticity of demand measures the percentage change in quantity demanded divided by the percentage change in income.

As noted in Chapter 3, the demand for some goods, such as hamburger and bus rides, actually declines as income increases. Thus, the value of the income elasticity of demand for such goods will be negative. Goods with a value of income elasticity less than 0 are called *inferior goods*. The demand for most goods increases as income increases. These goods are called *normal goods*, and they have a value of income elasticity greater than 0.

Let's take a closer look at normal goods. Sometimes demand increases with rising income but by a smaller percentage than that by which income increases. In such cases the value of income elasticity is greater than 0 but less than 1. For example, people spend more on food as their income rises, but the percentage increase in spending is less than the percentage increase in income. As a result, the fraction of the family's budget spent on food tends to decline as income increases. Normal goods with a value of income elasticity less than 1 are said to be *income inelastic* and are sometimes called *necessities*. Goods with a value of income elasticity greater than 1 are said to be *income elastic* and are sometimes called *luxuries*. Expensive jewelry, vintage wine, swimming pools, and rare art work are luxury goods.

Exhibit 11 presents income elasticity estimates for various goods and services. Demand for major items such as private education, owner-occupied housing, automobiles, and furniture is income elastic. Products with a value of income elasticity less than 1 tend to be necessities, such as food, physicians' services, gasoline, and rental housing. Thus, whereas restaurant meals are income elastic, more direct food purchases are inelastic. As income increases, spending at the grocery store increases less than spending at restaurants. Similarly, owner-occupied housing is income elas-

EXHIBIT 11
SELECTED INCOME ELASTICITIES OF DEMAND

Product	Income Elasticity
Private education	2.46
Automobiles	2.45
Owner-occupied housing	1.49
Furniture	1.48
Dental services	1.42
Restaurant meals	1.40
Shoes	1.10
Clothing	1.02
Beer	0.93
Physicians' services	0.75
Food	0.51
Cigarettes	0.50
Gasoline and oil	0.48
Rental housing	0.43
Coffee	0.29
Flour	-0.36

Sources: T. F. Hogerty and K. G. Elzinga, "The Demand for Beer," *Review of Economics and Statistics* (May 1972); H. S. Houthakker and L. D. Taylor, *Consumer Demand in the United States: Analyses and Projections*, 2d ed. (Cambridge, MA: Harvard University Press, 1970); J. J. Hughes, "Note on the U.S. Demand for Coffee," *American Journal of Agricultural Economics* (November 1969); S. M. Sackrin, "Factors Affecting the Demand for Cigarettes," *Agricultural Economics Research* (July 1962); H. Wold and C. E. Leser, "Commodity Group Expenditure Functions for the United Kingdom, 1948–57," *Econometrica* (January 1961).

tic but rental housing is inelastic, suggesting that as income rises the demand for rental housing rises less than the demand for owner-occupied housing. Flour appears to be an inferior good because it has negative income elasticity. As income increases, consumers switch from home baking to purchasing baked goods.

Exhibit 11 indicates that the demand for food is income inelastic. The demand for food also tends to be price inelastic. This combination of price and income inelasticities creates special problems in agricultural markets, as described in the following case study.

<table>
<tr><td>

CASE STUDY

The Demand for Food and the Farm Problem

</td><td>

In the late 1980s, net farm income in the United States, adjusted for inflation, was only about half what it had been in the early 1950s. Despite decades of federal support through various farm assistance programs, the number of farms continues to dwindle. By the end of the 1980s, the United States had fewer than 5 million farms, down from 23 million in 1950. The demise of the family farm can be traced to the price and income elasticities of demand for farm products and to technological breakthroughs that made larger farms more efficient.

Most firms can choose the rate of production expected to maximize profits. But many of the forces that determine farm production are beyond the farmer's control. Temperature, rain, insects, and other external forces affect crop size and quality. For example, the summer of 1988 was hot and dry, cutting farm production sharply. These swings in production create special problems for farmers because the demand for most farm crops, such as milk, corn, potatoes, oats, sugar, and beef, is price inelastic. Enough farm products are price inelastic that the demand for food in general can be said to be price inelastic (recall that the more broadly defined the product is, the less price elastic its demand).

The effect of an inelastic demand curve on farm revenue is illustrated in Exhibit 12. Suppose farmers in a normal year supply 10 billion bushels of output at a market price of $5 per bushel. Total revenue, which is price times quantity, comes to $50 billion in our hypothetical example. Suppose that more favorable growing conditions increase crop production to 11 billion bushels, an increase of 10 percent. Because demand is inelastic, the average price in our example must fall by more than 10 percent, say to $4 per bushel, in order to clear the market of the additional billion bushels. Thus, the 10 percent increase in farm production results in a 20 percent decrease in the market price.

Because, in percentage terms, the drop in price exceeds the increase in output, total revenue declines—from $50 billion to $44 billion. So, farm revenue drops by over 10 percent, despite the 10 percent increase in produc-

</td></tr>
</table>

tion. *An inelastic demand curve magnifies the effects of any change in output on farm income.* Of course, the up side of an inelastic demand curve is that lower-than-normal crop production results in a proportionately higher price and a higher total revenue.

EXHIBIT 12   THE DEMAND FOR FARM PRODUCTS

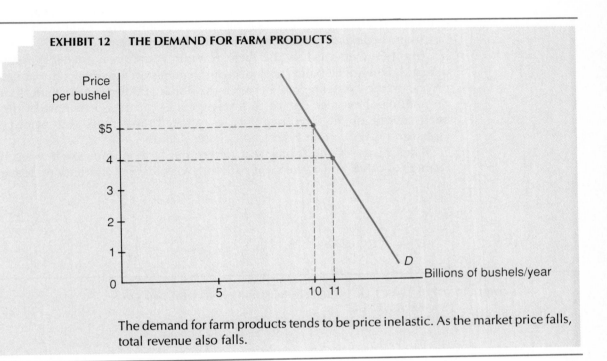

The demand for farm products tends to be price inelastic. As the market price falls, total revenue also falls.

Weather-generated changes in farm production create substantial year-to-year swings in farm revenue. This problem is compounded in the long run by the fact that the demand for food tends to be *income inelastic*. People can eat only so much, and they do not eat much more in response to an increase in income. As their incomes increase, people may spend more to eat because they cook less and buy more prepared foods and more restaurant meals. But the switch from home cooking to packaged foods and restaurant meals has little effect on the demand for farm products. Thus, as the economy grows over time and real incomes rise, the demand for farm products tends to increase by less than real income does, as reflected by the shift in the demand curve from *D* to *D'* in Exhibit 13.

Although the demand for farm products has not kept up with the growth in real income, the supply has increased sharply because of technological improvements in production. Farm output per worker was over six times greater in 1988 than in 1950 because of such factors as more sophisticated machines, better fertilizers, and healthier seed strains. Exhibit 13 shows the supply of farm products increasing from *S* to *S'*. The increase in supply exceeds the increase in demand, so the price level falls. And because the demand for farm products is price inelastic, the percentage drop in price can exceed the percentage increase in output. The combined effect in our hypothetical example is a lower total farm revenue.

Another wild card in the farm revenue equation is unstable foreign demand. Foreign demand for U.S. crops depends on foreign production and prices, on the exchange rate between the dollar and foreign currencies, and on public policy with regard to foreign trade. Farm exports have at times been caught up in foreign policy, as when President Carter placed an embargo on U.S. grain sales to the Soviet Union.

Thus many of the forces that determine farm output are beyond the farmer's control, and at the same time an inelastic price elasticity of demand

EXHIBIT 13   THE EFFECT OF INCREASES IN SUPPLY AND DEMAND ON FARM REVENUE

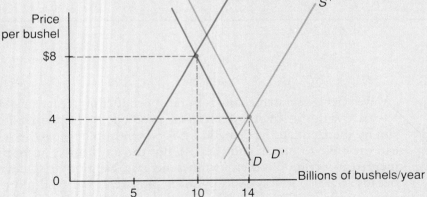

Over time, technological advances in farming have increased the supply of farm products sharply. In addition, increases in household income over time have increased the demand for farm products. But because increases in the supply of farm products have exceeded increases in demand, the combined effect has been a drop in the market prices and a fall in total farm revenue.

and an inelastic income elasticity of demand magnify the effects of changes in output on total revenue. The results for farmers have been widely fluctuating real incomes in the short term and generally declining real incomes in the long term. Federal farm subsidies, which will be examined in a later chapter, represent efforts to stabilize farm income.

Source: *Economic Report of the President*, 1989, Tables B-97 to B-100.

Cross-Price Elasticity of Demand

The **cross-price elasticity of demand** is the percentage change in quantity demanded of one good divided by the percentage change in price of another good.

The responsiveness of demand for one good to changes in the price of another good is called the **cross-price elasticity of demand**. It is defined as the percentage change in quantity demanded of one good divided by the percentage change in price of another good. Its numerical value can be positive, negative, or 0, depending on whether the two goods in question are substitutes, complements, or unrelated.

Substitutes If an increase in the price of one good leads to an increase in the demand for another good, the value of their cross-price elasticity is positive, and the goods are considered *substitutes*. For example, an increase in the price of Coke, other things constant, will increase the demand for Pepsi, reflecting the fact that the two are substitutes.

Complements If an increase in the price of one good leads to a decrease in the demand for another good, the value of their cross-price elasticity is negative, and the goods are considered *complements*. For example, an increase in the price of gasoline, other things constant, will reduce the demand for tires because people will drive less and so will replace their tires less frequently. Gasoline and tires have a negative cross-price elasticity and are complements.

In summary, when the change in demand for one good has the same sign as the change in price of another good, the two goods are substitutes; when the change in demand for one good has the opposite sign from the change in price of another good, the goods are complements. Most pairs of goods selected at random are unrelated, so the value of their cross-price elasticity is 0.

CONCLUSION

Because this chapter has tended to be more quantitative than earlier chapters, you may have been preoccupied with the mechanics of the calculations and thus may have overlooked the intuitive appeal and the neat simplicity of the notion of elasticity. *An elasticity measure represents the willingness and ability of buyers and sellers to alter their behavior in response to a change in their economic circumstances.* For example, if the price of a good falls, consumers may be able but not willing to increase their consumption of the good. In this case the demand would be inelastic.

Elasticities of demand and supply have been calculated for all kinds of goods and services, ranging from eggs to electricity. The objective of this kind of research is to predict the effects of changes in relative prices and in income. The empirical results are generally consistent with the theoretical conclusions presented in this chapter.

Corporations expend a great deal of effort trying to estimate the price elasticity of demand for their products. Since a corporation often produces an entire line of products, it also has a special interest in certain cross-price elasticities. For example, the Coca-Cola Corporation needs to know how changing the price of Cherry Coke will affect sales of Classic Coke. Similarly, Procter and Gamble wants to know how changing the price of Safeguard soap will affect sales of Ivory soap. Governments, too, have an ongoing interest in various elasticities. The members of the Organization of Petroleum Exporting Countries (OPEC), for example, are concerned about the price elasticity of demand for oil. A state government in the United States may want to know the effect of a 1 percent increase in the sales tax on total tax receipts, or how an increase in income will affect the demand for real estate and hence the revenue generated by a property tax. Many questions can be answered by referring to particular elasticities.

Summary

1. The price elasticities of demand and supply indicate how sensitive buyers and sellers are to changes in the price. The greater the response, the greater the elasticity; the less the response, the smaller the elasticity.

2. The price elasticity of demand equals the percentage change in quantity demanded divided by the percentage change in price. If the elasticity has a value of less than 1.0, demand is inelastic; if the value is greater than 1.0, demand is elastic; and if the value is equal to 1.0, demand is of unitary elasticity.

3. If demand is inelastic, a price increase will increase total revenue and a price decrease will reduce total revenue. If demand is elastic, a price increase will reduce total revenue and a price decrease will increase total revenue. And if demand is of unitary elasticity, a price change will leave total revenue unchanged.

4. The midpoint formula uses the average price and average quantity as the base values for computing percentage changes in price and quantity. Computing elasticities based on the midpoint formula ensures that the elasticity calculated between two points on a demand curve will be the same whether the price goes up or down.

5. Usually, demand curves reflect different elasticities for different price changes. Along a linear, or straight-line, demand curve, for example, the elasticity of demand falls steadily as the price falls. Constant-elasticity demand curves have the same elasticity everywhere along the curve.

6. Several factors affect the price elasticity of demand. Demand will be more elastic (1) the greater the availability of substitutes and the more they resemble the good demanded, (2)

the more narrowly the good is defined, (3) the larger the proportion of the consumer's budget spent on the product, (4) the longer the time available to adjust to a change in price, and (5) the more the good tends to be viewed as a luxury rather than a necessity.

7. For the price elasticity of supply, we use the same kind of calculations and the same terminology as for the price elasticity of demand. If costs rise sharply as output expands, supply will be less elastic. Also, the longer the time period under consideration, the more elastic the supply.

8. The income elasticity of demand measures the responsiveness of demand to changes in consumer income. The value of income elasticity of demand is positive for normal goods and negative for inferior goods.

9. The cross-price elasticity of demand measures the responsiveness of demand to changes in the price of another product. Two goods are defined as substitutes, complements, or unrelated, depending on whether the value of their cross-price elasticity of demand is positive, negative, or equal to 0.

Questions and Problems

1. (Demand Elasticity) How is it possible for many elasticities to be associated with a single demand curve?

2. (Demand Elasticity) Suppose that a company is concerned only with maximizing its gross revenues. What pricing policy should it follow?

3. (Midpoint Elasticity) Suppose the initial price and quantity demanded of a good are $1 per unit and 50 units, respectively. A reduction in price to $0.20 results in an increase in quantity demanded to 70 units. Show that these data yield a midpoint elasticity of 0.25. A 10 percent rise in the price can be expected to reduce the quantity demanded by what percentage?

4. (Linear Demand and Elasticity) Must the elastic and inelastic sections of a linear demand curve always be of equal length? Why or why not?

5. (Perfectly Inelastic Demand) Why is it impossible for a demand curve to be perfectly inelastic for *all* prices? Consider very high and very low prices.

6. (Demand Elasticity Determinants) What happens to the elasticity of demand for auto-mobile towing services during a large snowstorm? How might this change be different for low-income people and high-income people?

7. (Perfectly Inelastic Supply) Although Picasso paintings are technically in fixed supply, how might their availability be increased?

8. (Tax Incidence) Often it is claimed that a tax on the sale of a specific good will simply be passed on to consumers. What is necessary for this to happen? In what cases might very little of the tax be passed on to consumers?

9. (Cross-Price Elasticity) Rank the following in order of increasing cross-price elasticity (from negative to positive) with coffee:
   a. Mustard
   b. Tea
   c. Cream
   d. Cola

10. (Price Elasticity) Explain why the price elasticity of demand for Coke is greater than that for soft drinks generally. How would one define the price of soft drinks generally in this case?

11. (Elasticity) Fill in values for each point listed in the following table.

P	Q	Price Elasticity	Total Spending
$10	0	—	
9	1		
8	2		
7	3		
6	4		
5	5		
4	6		
3	7		
2	8		
1	9		
0	10		

12. (Demand and Elasticity) Suppose that crime and drug spending are directly related (i.e., the level of crime increases as drug spending increases) and that the demand for drugs is inelastic. What would happen to the level of crime under each of the following anti-drug policies?
   a. Prosecute pushers only
   b. Prosecute users only
   c. Prosecute both

13. (Tax Incidence) Using supply and demand curves, show why the economic incidence of a sales tax is independent of the statutory incidence (i.e., who legally pays the tax).

14. (Taxes and Elasticity) Suppose a tax is imposed on a good that has a completely inelastic supply curve.
   a. Who pays the tax?
   b. Using supply and demand curves, show how much tax revenue is collected.
   c. How would this tax revenue change if the supply curve became more elastic?

15. (Income Elasticity) Calculate the income elasticity of demand for each of the following goods.

	Income = $10,000	Income = $20,000
Good 1	10	20
Good 2	4	5
Good 3	3	3

16. (Substitutes and Complements) Using supply and demand curves, predict the impact on the price and quantity of Good 1 (above) of an increase in the price of Good 2 if
   a. they are substitutes.
   b. they are complements.
   c. good 2 is price inelastic.

Consumer Choice and Demand

You already know two reasons demand curves slope downward. The first is the substitution effect of a price change. When the price of a good falls, consumers substitute the now-cheaper good for other goods that provide alternative ways of satisfying the same want. The second reason demand curves slope downward is the income effect of a price change. When the price of a good falls, the real incomes of consumers increase, so more of the good will be purchased (if the good is normal).

Because the law of demand is so important, in this chapter we present another way to derive it, a way that focuses on the logic of consumer choice in a world of scarcity. First we will develop utility analysis, which we use to predict which goods and services will be consumed and in what quantities. Then we will show how this analysis relates to the law of demand. The objective of this chapter is not to tell you how to maximize your utility — you already know how to do that — but to examine more closely what you already do and to help you understand more fully the economic implications of your behavior. Topics discussed in this chapter include

- Total and marginal utility
- The law of diminishing marginal utility
- Measuring utility
- Utility-maximizing conditions
- Consumer surplus
- The role of time in demand

UTILITY ANALYSIS

Utility describes the power of goods and services to satisfy wants. It is the sense of pleasure and satisfaction that comes from consumption. Utility is inherently subjective.

Suppose you and a friend dine together. If, after dinner, your friend asks how you enjoyed your meal, you might say, "It was fine" or "I liked it better than my last meal here." You would not say, "It deserves a rating of 85 on the standard utility index." Nor would you say, "I liked it better than you liked your meal." The utility you derived from that meal cannot be measured objectively. You cannot give your meal an 85 utility rating and your friend's meal an 81. Each of us can tell whether one personal experience is more pleasant than another, but we cannot make comparisons across individuals. What we *can* do, even though utility is subjective, is infer from your behavior that you receive more utility from apples than from oranges if, when the two are priced the same, you always buy apples.

Tastes and Preferences

The utility you derive from consuming a particular good depends on your tastes and preferences. Some goods are extremely appealing to you, and others are not. You may not understand, for example, why someone would pay good money for raw oysters, chicken livers, or country music. We will have little to say about why some people like raw oysters and some do not. *We simply assume that tastes are given and are relatively stable.*

Although we know little about the origin of tastes and preferences, some people are obviously influenced by the consumption behavior of others. The typical consumer may look to supposedly more knowledgeable consumers for advice. Young athletes may want to wear the same brand of athletic shoes as Michael Jordan or use the same tennis racket as Steffi Graf. Manufacturers understand this and are willing to pay large sums for product endorsements. Rolex, for example, offers to let trend setters have its $5000 watch free just so that others will notice that famous people wear that brand.

The other side of the coin is that some people apparently derive utility from advertising their own consumption choices, even to the point of wearing the label on the outside. Conspicuous consumption of designer jeans, Gucci handbags, and the ultimate driving machine suggests that the utility of some products is linked to public recognition of one's supposedly superior consumption choices.

The Law of Diminishing Marginal Utility

Imagine that it is a hot day. You have just mowed the lawn and are extremely thirsty. You pour yourself a glass of cold water. That first glass is wonderful, and it puts a serious dent in your thirst; the next one is not quite as wonderful, but it is still good; the third is just fair; and you barely finish the fourth glass.

We distinguish between the **total utility** you derive from your consumption of water and the **marginal utility** you derive from consuming one more glass. Your experience with the water reflects the most basic principle of utility analysis: the **law of diminishing marginal utility**. This law states that the more of a good an individual consumes per time period, other things constant, the smaller the increase in total utility received from each additional unit consumed. The marginal utility you derive from each glass of water declines as your consumption increases. You enjoy the first glass immensely, but each additional glass provides less and less marginal utility. If someone forced you to drink a fifth glass, you probably would not enjoy it; your marginal utility from a fifth glass would likely be negative.

Although diminishing marginal utility is a feature of all consumption, marginal utility does not always decline very quickly. For example, you may eat many potato chips before the marginal utility of additional chips drops sharply. For other goods the drop in marginal utility with additional consumption is more dramatic. A second Big Mac may provide some marginal utility, but the marginal utility of a third one during the same meal would be slight or even negative. A second copy of the same daily newspaper would likely provide you with no marginal utility (in fact, the designs of newspaper vending machines rely on the fact that you will not want more than one paper). After a long winter, that first warm day of spring is something special and is the cause of "spring fever." The fever is cured, however, by many warm days like the first. By the time August arrives, people attach little marginal utility to yet another warm day.

Total utility is the total satisfaction derived from consumption.

Marginal utility is the change in total utility derived from a 1-unit change in the consumption of a good.

According to the *law of diminishing marginal utility*, the more of a good that is consumed per period, the smaller the marginal utility, other things constant.

MEASURING UTILITY

So far our descriptions of utility have used such words as "wonderful," "good," and "fair." We cannot push the analysis of utility very far if we are limited to such subjective language. If we want to predict behavior based on changes in the economic environment, we must develop a consistent way of viewing utility.

Units of Utility

Although there really is no objective way of measuring utility, if pressed you could be more specific about how much you enjoyed each glass of water. For example, you might say the first glass was twice as good as the second, the second was twice as good as the third, the third was twice as good as the fourth, and a fifth glass would have reduced your level of satisfaction. Let's assign arbitrary numbers to the amount of utility from each quantity consumed, such that the pattern of numbers matches the pattern of your satisfaction.

To be more specific, suppose we talk in terms of units of satisfaction, or

Alfred Marshall
(1842–1924)

Natura non facit saltum. This Latin motto adorns the title page of Alfred Marshall's *Principles of Economics*. Literally translated, it means "nature doesn't make leaps"—in other words, change in nature is gradual and evolutionary. It is a well-chosen motto, for it sets the tone both for Marshall's conception of economics and for his own style as an economist.

Alfred Marshall was born in Clapham, England. His domineering father pushed him to enter the ministry, but the young Marshall rebelled and instead studied mathematics at Cambridge University. Soon Marshall was teaching mathematics, studying the works of the classical economists, and quietly developing his own ideas. In 1884 he was called to the Chair of Political Economy at Cambridge, a position he occupied well into the twentieth century and from which he exerted a tremendous influence on British eco-

nomics. In 1890 Marshall published his *Principles*, the most important text of its age.

Marshall's concern with gradual change appears throughout the book. His approach to economic theory was fundamentally incremental. For example, one of Marshall's most important contributions is the method of partial-equilibrium analysis: don't try to examine all the complex interconnections in the economy at once, he advises; instead, look at a single market in isolation while holding all other things constant.

Marshall was something of a gradualist in his professional style as well. In 1871 several European economists (including W. Stanley Jevons of England) had proposed looking at the theory of value in a new way. The classical economists had focused on costs of production as the prime determinant of market price. These "marginalist" economists focused instead on utility—

marginal utility—as the main determinant of market price. In fact, many historians call the work of Jevons and the others the "marginalist revolution." By 1871 Marshall had probably developed the idea of marginal utility on his own. A meticulous thinker and writer, Marshall refused, however, to publish his ideas until he had worked everything out to his satisfaction. Moreover, Marshall was less of a revolutionary than Jevons. He saw himself not as overthrowing the classical economics of Smith but as adding to it. The *Principles* thus combines in many ways the best of the classical and marginalist ideas. John Maynard Keynes, Marshall's most famous pupil, put it this way: "Jevons saw the kettle boil and cried out with the delighted voice of a child; Marshall too had seen the kettle boil and sat down silently to build an engine."

Portrait by Historical Pictures Service, Chicago

Richard Langlois

utils. Let's say the first glass of water provides you with 40 utils of satisfaction, the second glass yields 20, the third yields 10, and the fourth yields 5 utils. A fifth glass would yield a negative utility, or − 2 utils. You might think of utils as imaginary numbers that allow us to be more specific in attaching relative weights to the utility derived from consumption. More generally, **utils** measure pleasure, satisfaction, or utility and can be used to compare the total utility you receive from different goods as well as the marginal utility you derive from additional units of the same good. Thus, we can use utils to evaluate your preferences for various goods. Note, however, that we cannot compare utils across consumers. *Each individual has a uniquely subjective util scale.*

A unit of satisfaction, or utility, is called a ***util****; a util is a subjective measure that is unique to an individual consumer.*

The first column of Exhibit 1 lists possible quantities of water you might consume after mowing the lawn; the second presents the total utility, measured in utils, derived from that consumption; and the third column shows the marginal utility of each additional glass of water consumed. You can see from the second column that total utility increases with each of the first four glasses, but by smaller and smaller amounts. The third column shows that you derive a marginal utility of 40 utils from the first glass, 20 utils from the second glass, and so on. Marginal utility declines after the first glass of water, becoming negative with the fifth glass. The total utility is the sum of the marginal utilities; it is graphed in panel (a) of Exhibit 2. Again, because of diminishing marginal utility, each glass adds less and less to total utility, so total utility increases but at a decreasing rate. Marginal utility is presented in panel (b).

EXHIBIT 1
UTILITY YOU DERIVE FROM WATER
AFTER MOWING THE LAWN

Units of Water Consumed (8-ounce glass)	Total Utility (utils)	Marginal Utility (utils)
0	0	—
1	40	40
2	60	20
3	70	10
4	75	5
5	73	− 2

Utility Maximization in a World Without Scarcity

Your objective in the consumption of water, as in all consumption, is to *maximize total utility.* So how much water do you consume? If the price of water is 0, you drink water as long as each additional glass increases total utility, which means you consume four glasses of water. *So when a good is free, you consume as long as additional units provide positive marginal utility.*

EXHIBIT 2   UTILITY YOU DERIVE FROM WATER AFTER MOWING THE LAWN

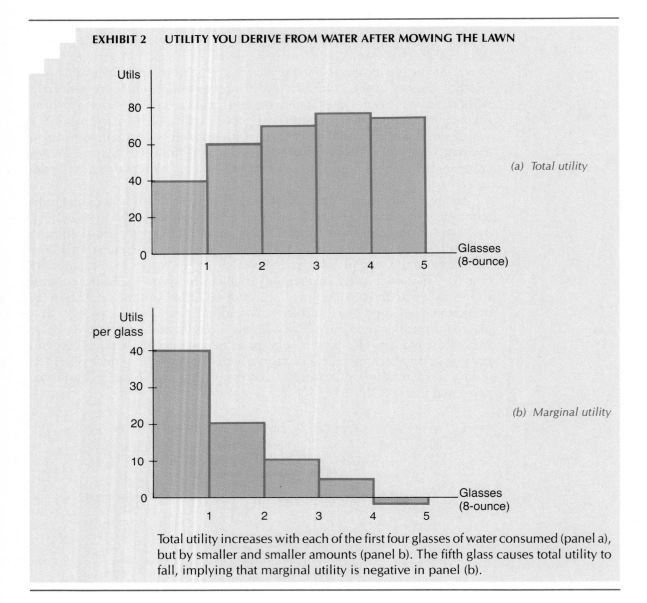

Total utility increases with each of the first four glasses of water consumed (panel a), but by smaller and smaller amounts (panel b). The fifth glass causes total utility to fall, implying that marginal utility is negative in panel (b).

Let's extend the analysis of utility to a world where you have only two goods from which to choose: food and clothing. We will continue to translate the relative satisfaction you receive from consumption into utils. Suppose the total utility and the marginal utility for alternative rates of consumption of these goods, given your tastes and preferences, are as presented in Exhibit 3. You can see from columns (3) and (7) that both goods exhibit diminishing marginal utility.

Given this set of preferences, how much of each good will you consume? That depends on the prices of the goods and your income. Without scarcity, the price of each good would be 0 and you would increase consumption as

EXHIBIT 3

TOTAL AND MARGINAL UTILITY FROM FOOD AND CLOTHING

Units of Food Consumed per Period (1)	Total Utility of Food (utils) (2)	Marginal Utility of Food (utils) (3)	Marginal Utility of Food per Dollar Expended (price = $4) (4)	Units of Clothing per Period (5)	Total Utility of Clothing (utils) (6)	Marginal Utility of Clothing (utils) (7)	Marginal Utility of Clothing per Dollar Expended (price = $2) (8)
0	0	—	—	0	0	—	—
1	25	25	6.25	1	20	20	10.00
2	41	16	4.00	2	34	14	7.00
3	53	12	3.00	3	44	10	5.00
4	62	9	2.25	4	50	6	3.00
5	68	6	1.50	5	54	4	2.00
6	72	4	1.00	6	57	3	1.50

long as you derived positive marginal utility from additional units of each good. Thus, in a world without scarcity you would consume at least the first 6 units of each good because both goods generate positive marginal utility at that level of consumption. Did you ever go to a party where the food and drinks were free to you? How much did you eat and drink? You probably ate and drank until you didn't want any more—that is, until the marginal utility of each good consumed declined to 0.

Utility Maximization in a World of Scarcity

Alas, scarcity is our lot, so we should focus on how a consumer chooses in a world dominated by scarcity. To make our example more realistic, assume the price of food is $4 per unit, the price of clothing is $2 per unit, and your income is $20 per period. Under these conditions, the utility you receive from different goods relative to their prices determines how you allocate your income.

How do you allocate income between the two goods so as to maximize utility? Suppose you start off with some bundle of food and clothing. If you can increase your utility by reallocating expenditures, you will do so, and you will continue to make adjustments as long as you can increase your utility. There may be some trial and error involved in your consumption decision at first, but as you learn from your mistakes you move toward the utility-maximizing position. When no further utility-increasing moves are possible, you have settled on the bundle that maximizes your utility within the limit of your budget; you have arrived at the equilibrium combination. Once you reach this equilibrium, you will maintain this consumption pattern. You have no reason to choose differently unless there is a change in one of the factors that influence your demand, such as your tastes, your income, or prices.

To get the allocation process rolling, suppose you start off spending your entire budget of $20 on food, purchasing 5 units for a total utility of 68 utils per period. But you quickly realize that if you reduce food consumption by 1 unit, you can buy the first 2 units of clothing. You thus give up 6 utils, the marginal utility of the fifth unit of food, but you gain a total of 34 utils from the first 2 units of clothing. Total utility increases from 68 utils to 96 utils per period. Then you notice that if you reduce your food consumption to 3 units, you give up 9 utils from the fourth unit of food but gain 16 utils from the third and fourth units of clothing. This is another utility-increasing move. Further reductions in food consumption, however, would reduce your total utility because you would lose 12 utils from the third unit of food and would gain only 7 utils from the fifth and sixth units of clothing.

Thus, by trial and error, you find that the utility-maximizing equilibrium is to consume 3 units of food and 4 units of clothing, for a total utility of 103 utils. This involves an outlay of $12 on food and $8 on clothing. *You are in equilibrium when consuming this bundle because any change permitted by your budget would only lower your total utility.*

To make sure you understand the utility-maximizing choice, analyze the situation again, but this time begin by assuming that all your income is spent on clothing. You should be able to work through the trial-and-error process of finding the utility-maximizing consumption bundle. You should once again end up with 3 units of food and 4 units of clothing. Try it. It doesn't matter where you start — the effort to maximize utility always leads to the same consumption bundle for a given level of income and prices.

The Utility-Maximizing Conditions When a consumer is in equilibrium, there is no way to increase utility by reallocating the budget. In fact, as you can see from the previous example, once equilibrium has been achieved, any shift in spending from one good to another will decrease utility. The example also illustrates a special property of the utility-maximizing combination: in equilibrium the last dollar spent on each good yields the same utility. More specifically, *utility is maximized when the marginal utility of a good divided by its price is identical for the last unit of each good purchased.* If this were not so, you could always reallocate your budget to increase your total utility. Let's see how this works.

Consumer equilibrium is achieved when the budget is completely exhausted and the last dollar spent on each good yields the same utility.

Columns (4) and (8) in Exhibit 3 indicate the marginal utility of each dollar's worth of food and clothing. Column (4) is derived by dividing the marginal utility of food by the price of a unit of food, which is $4. Column (8) is derived the same way, using the marginal utility of clothing and a price of $2. You can see that the equilibrium choice of 3 units of food and 4 units of clothing yields 3 utils for the last dollar spent on either good. **Consumer equilibrium** is achieved when the budget is completely exhausted and the last dollar spent on each good yields the same utility, or

$$\frac{MU_F}{P_F} = \frac{MU_C}{P_C}$$

where MU_F is the marginal utility of the last unit of food consumed, P_F is the price of food, MU_C is the marginal utility of the last unit of clothing consumed, and P_C is the price of clothing. If food yields a lower marginal utility per dollar than does clothing, total utility can be increased by reducing food purchases and increasing clothing purchases. For example, if you allocated your budget to 4 units of food and 2 units of clothing, then the last dollar spent on food would yield 2.25 utils whereas the last dollar spent on clothing would yield 7 utils. By reducing your food consumption and increasing your clothing consumption, you could increase your total utility. Although we have considered only two goods, the logic of utility maximization applies to any number of goods.

In equilibrium, higher-priced goods must generate greater utility than do lower-priced goods—enough greater utility to compensate for the higher price. In our example, the third unit of food costs twice as much as the fourth unit of clothing, but the marginal utility of the third unit of food is twice that of the fourth unit of clothing. *Thus you, as a consumer, must consider several factors when deciding how much of each good to purchase: your relative preferences for the alternative goods, the prices of the alternative goods, and your income.*

A Caveat The presentation in Exhibit 3 is correct as far as it goes, but this comparative tabular approach cannot be used for examining all goods. An assumption implicit in the analysis is that the goods under consideration are unrelated—they are neither substitutes nor complements. Food and clothing satisfy different wants and can reasonably be considered unrelated. If this assumption does not hold, the marginal utility you receive from consuming one good depends in part on how much of the other good you consume. For example, suppose you have a choice of water or lemonade. If you view the two as close substitutes, the marginal utility you receive from each additional glass of water per day will depend on the amount of lemonade you consume. The marginal utility of the first glass of water will be higher if you are consuming no lemonade than if you are already consuming three glasses of lemonade per day. Thus, you cannot consider the marginal utility of each glass of water without taking into account your consumption of lemonade. By assuming that food and clothing satisfy independent wants, we have avoided the need to hinge the utility of food on the quantity of clothing consumed. The appendix to this chapter develops an alternative approach to utility that permits analysis of both related and unrelated goods.

Deriving the Law of Demand from Marginal Utility

The purpose of utility analysis is to provide information about the demand curve. How does the previous analysis relate to your individual demand for food? It yields a point on your demand curve for food: at a price of $4 per unit, you will demand 3 units per period. This point on the demand curve for food is based on a given income of $20 per period, a given price for clothing of $2 per unit, and given consumer preferences reflected in your utility schedules.

This point alone, however, gives us no idea about the shape of your demand curve. To generate another point, let's change the price of food, other things constant, and see what happens to the quantity demanded. Suppose the price of food drops from $4 to $3 per unit. What will happen to your consumption decision, given the preferences already outlined in the discussion of Exhibit 3? Your original consumption choice was 3 units of food and 4 units of clothing, but you will no longer consume that combination. The marginal utility per dollar of expenditure for the third unit of food is now 4 utils (12/3), which exceeds the 3 utils received from the fourth unit of clothing consumed. The marginal utility of the last dollar spent on each good is no longer equal across goods. Moreover, if you maintained the original mix of food and clothing, you would have $3 left over in your budget because you would be spending only $9 on food. You can increase your utility by consuming a different bundle.

In light of your utility schedules in Exhibit 3, you should increase your consumption of food to 4 units per period. This increase exhausts your budget and equates the marginal utility of the last dollar expended on each good. Your consumption of clothing remains the same, as does the marginal utility for the last dollar spent on clothing. But as your consumption of food increases to 4 units, the marginal utility of the fourth unit, 9 utils, divided by the price of $3 yields 3 utils per dollar of expenditure, which is the same as for clothing. You are in equilibrium once again. Your total utility increases by the 9 utils you receive from the fourth unit of food; hence, you are clearly better off as a result of the price decrease.

Thus when the price of food is $3 per unit, the quantity demanded is 4 units per period. When the price of food falls, other things constant, the quantity demanded increases. We now have a second point on your demand curve for food; the two points are presented as *a* and *b* in Exhibit 4. We could continue to change the price of food and thereby generate additional points on the demand curve, but we get some idea of the demand curve's slope from these two points. Similarly, we could generate the demand curve for clothing. The shape of the demand curve for food conforms to our expectations based on the law of demand: price and quantity demanded are inversely related. (Can you determine the price elasticity of demand between points *a* and *b*?)

We have gone to some length to explain how you (or any consumer) maximize utility. Using utils as a subjective measure, we determined the marginal utility you derived from additional units of the good. This allowed us to construct the table in Exhibit 3 in order to analyze your consumption choices. In reality, you do not need to perform such calculations, at least not explicitly. Your tastes and preferences will naturally guide you to the most preferred bundle, given your income and the prices of goods and services.

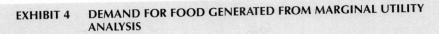

EXHIBIT 4   DEMAND FOR FOOD GENERATED FROM MARGINAL UTILITY ANALYSIS

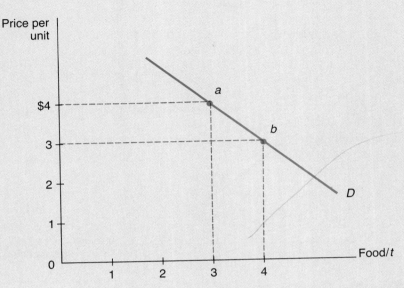

At a price of $4 per unit of food, the consumer is in equilibrium when consuming 3 units of food (point a). Marginal utility per dollar is the same for all goods consumed. If the price falls to $3, the consumer will increase consumption to 4 units of food (point b). Points a and b are two points on this consumer's demand curve for food.

You are probably not conscious of your behavior. The urge to maximize utility is like the force of gravity: both work whether or not you understand them.

Now that you have some idea of utility, let's consider consumer surplus, an application of utility analysis.

CONSUMER SURPLUS

In our example, total utility increased when the price fell from $4 to $3. In this section we take a closer look at how consumers benefit from a lower price. Suppose your demand for pizza is as shown in Exhibit 5, which measures on the horizontal axis the number of medium-size pizzas demanded per month. Recall that in constructing a demand curve, we hold tastes, income, and the prices of related goods constant; only the price of pizza varies.

At a price of $8 or above, you find that the marginal utility of other goods that you could buy for $8 is higher than the marginal utility of a pizza. Consequently, you buy no pizza. At a price of $7, you buy one pizza per

EXHIBIT 5   CONSUMER SURPLUS

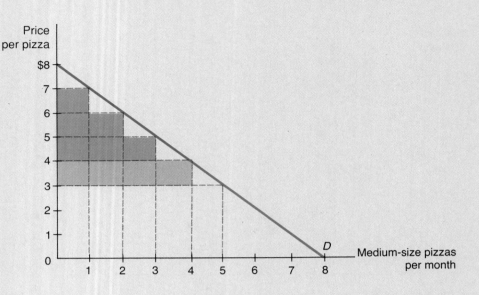

At a given quantity of pizza, the height of the demand curve shows the value of the last unit purchased. The area under the demand curve up to a specific quantity shows the total value the consumer places on that quantity. At a price of $4, the consumer purchases four pizzas. The first pizza is valued at $7, the second at $6, the third at $5, and the fourth at $4; the consumer values four pizzas at $22. Since the consumer pays $4 per pizza, all four can be obtained for $16. The difference between what the consumer would have been willing to pay ($22) and what the consumer actually pays ($16) is called consumer surplus. When the price is $4, the consumer surplus is represented by the dark blue area under the demand curve above $4.

month, so the marginal utility of the first pizza evidently exceeds what you could have received by spending that money on your best alternative — say, a movie, some popcorn, and a Coke. A price of $6 prompts you to buy two pizzas a month. Apparently, your marginal valuation of the second pizza is at least $6. At a price of $5, you buy three pizzas a month, and at $4, you buy four pizzas a month.

In each case the value to you of the last unit purchased must at least equal the price; otherwise, you would not have purchased that unit. Along the demand curve, therefore, the price reflects your **marginal valuation** of the good, or the dollar value of the marginal utility derived from consuming each additional unit.

Notice that when the price is $4, you purchase each of the four pizzas for that price even though you would have been willing to pay more than $4 apiece for the first three pizzas. The first pizza provides marginal utility you

*The **marginal valuation** of a good is the dollar value of the marginal utility derived from consuming each additional unit.*

value at $7; the second, marginal utility valued at $6; and the third, marginal utility valued at $5. In fact, you would have been willing to pay $7 for the first, $6 for the second, and $5 for the third. The value of the total utility of the first four pizzas is $7 + $6 + $5 + $4 = $22. Note, however, that when the price is $4, you get all four pizzas for $16. Thus, a price of $4 confers a **consumer surplus**, or bonus, equal to the difference between the maximum amount you would have been willing to pay ($22) and what you actually paid ($16). When the price is $4 per pizza, your consumer surplus is $6, as shown by the six dark blue blocks in Exhibit 5. The consumer surplus is equal to the difference between the value of the total utility you receive from consuming the pizza and your total expenditure.

Consumer surplus is the difference between the maximum amount a consumer is willing to pay for a given quantity of a good and what is actually paid.

If the price falls to $3, you purchase five pizzas a month. Evidently you feel that the marginal benefit you receive from the fifth unit is worth at least $3. The lower price means that you get to buy all the pizzas for $3 even though most are worth more than $3 to you. Your consumer surplus when the price is $3 is the value of the total utility conferred by the first five pizzas, which is $7 + $6 + $5 + $4 + $3 = $25, minus the cost, which is $3 × 5 = $15. Thus the consumer surplus is $25 − $15 = $10, as indicated by the dark and light blue blocks in Exhibit 5. When the price declines to $3, you are able to purchase all units for less, so your consumer surplus increases by $4, as indicated by the four light blue blocks in Exhibit 5. You can see why consumers benefit from lower prices.

MARKET DEMAND AND CONSUMER SURPLUS

The market demand curve is simply the horizontal sum of the individual demand curves for all consumers in the market. Exhibit 6 shows how the demand curves for three consumers in the market are summed horizontally to yield the market demand curve. At a price of $5 per unit, for example, consumer A demands 30 units, consumer B demands 20 units, and consumer C demands nothing. The market demand at a price of $5 is therefore 50 units. At a price of $2 per unit, A's quantity demanded is 60 units, B's is 50 units, and C's is 15 units, for a total quantity demanded of 125 units. The market demand curve shows the total quantity demanded by all consumers at various prices.

With certain qualifications that we need not go into here, the idea of consumer surplus can be used to examine market demand as well as individual demand. We can sum each consumer's surplus to arrive at the market consumer surplus. As with individual demand curves, consumer surplus for the market demand curve is measured by the difference between the value of the total utility received from consumption and the total amount paid for that consumption. When the price is $2, each person consumes additional units of the good until the marginal valuation of the last unit purchased equals $2. But each consumer gets to buy all the other units for $2 as well. In

EXHIBIT 6   SUMMING INDIVIDUAL DEMANDS TO DERIVE THE MARKET DEMAND

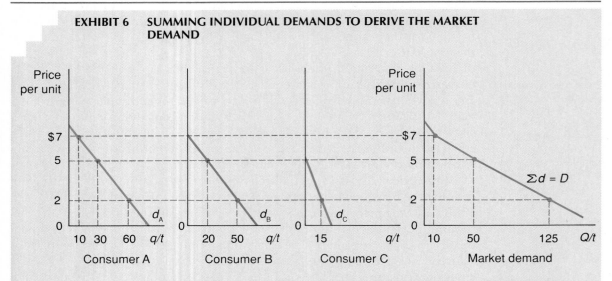

At a price of $2, consumer A demands 60 units, consumer B demands 50 units, and consumer C demands 15 units. Total market demand at a price of $2 is $60 + 50 + 15 = 125$ units. At the higher price of $5, A demands 30 units, B demands 20 units, and C demands nothing. Market demand at $5 is 50 units. At the still higher price of $7, A demands 10 units, and B and C demand nothing. The market demand curve, D, is the horizontal sum of individual demand curves, d_A, d_B, and d_C.

Exhibit 7, the dark shading, bounded below by the price of $2 and above by the demand curve, depicts the market consumer surplus when the price is $2. The light shading represents the increase in consumer surplus if the price drops to $1 per unit.

THE ROLE OF TIME IN DEMAND

Demand measures the desired rate of consumption at alternative prices during a given time period. An important consideration in constructing a demand curve is the time period involved, for it influences the rate of consumption. The longer the time period, the greater the demand, other things constant. The demand for pizza is greater per month than per week or per day.

Because consumption does not occur instantaneously, time also plays another important role in demand analysis. Consumption takes time and, as they say, time is money — time has a positive value for most people. Consequently, the cost of consumption has two components: the *money price* of the good and the *time price* of the good. Goods are demanded because of the services they offer. Your demand for a lawn mower is based on its ability to cut grass; your interest is not in the mower itself but in the service it

EXHIBIT 7   MARKET DEMAND AND CONSUMER SURPLUS

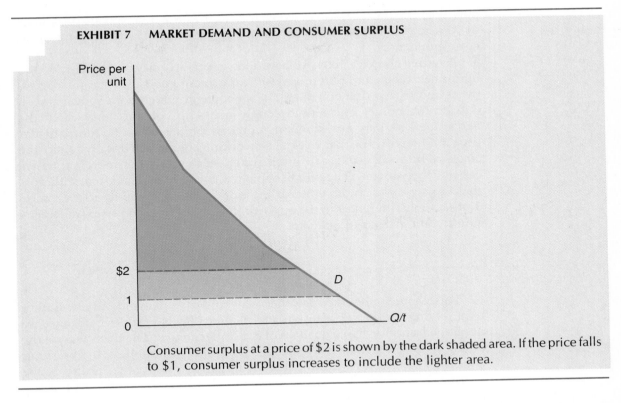

Consumer surplus at a price of $2 is shown by the dark shaded area. If the price falls to $1, consumer surplus increases to include the lighter area.

provides. Thus, you may be willing to pay more for a mower that does the job faster. Similarly, it is not the toaster, automatic dishwasher, or airline ticket to Washington that you demand, but the services these goods provide. Other things held constant, the good that provides the same service in less time is preferred.

The money price of a good is usually the same for all consumers, but the time price of consuming that good differs among individuals, since their opportunity costs of time differ. Your willingness to pay a premium for timesaving goods and services depends on the opportunity cost of your time. This difference in the value of time to different consumers explains many of the consumption patterns observed in the economy.

Consider the alternative ways to get to Europe. You can take the Concorde, a regular airline, or a tramp steamer. Your mode of travel will depend in part on your opportunity cost of time because goods with lower time costs tend to have higher money costs. The Concorde takes less than half the time of other flights, but because the Concorde is much more expensive, only travelers with an extremely high opportunity cost of time will pay such a premium for faster service. Students on their summer vacations may be more inclined to opt for some discount excursion fare or even standby status; for them the lower money cost more than compensates for the higher time cost. Busy executives, however, shepherd their scarce time much more carefully; they pay attention not only to the time spent traveling but also to how they use the travel time. Look around the next time you are on a plane or train and notice who is working on reports or dealing with correspondence.

A retired couple is likely to have a lower opportunity cost of time and so might be expected to purchase fewer timesaving goods, such as microwave ovens and frozen dinners, than, say, a couple in which both spouses work outside the home. The retired couple may clip coupons and search the newspapers for bargains, sometimes going from store to store for particular grocery items on sale that week. The working couple will usually ignore the coupons and sales and will often purchase items at the more expensive convenience stores. The retired couple will be more inclined to drive across the country on vacation, whereas the working couple will fly to a vacation destination. Differences in the opportunity cost of time add an extra dimension to our analysis of demand.

CONCLUSION

This chapter presented another way to derive demand curves. Rather than relying on the substitution and income effects of a price change, we developed a utility-based analysis of consumer choice. The focus was on the utility, or benefits, that consumers receive from consumption. In observing consumer behavior, we assume that for a particular individual, utility can be measured in some systematic way even though different consumers' utility levels cannot be compared. Our ultimate objective is to predict how consumer choice is affected by such variables as a change in price. *We judge a theory not by the realism of its assumptions but by the accuracy of its predictions. Based on this criterion, the theory of consumer choice presented in this chapter has proven to be quite useful.*

Again, we stress that consumers do not have to understand the material presented in this chapter in order to maximize utility. We assume that rational consumers attempt to maximize utility naturally and instinctively. In this chapter we simply tried to analyze that process using a model of consumer choice based on utility analysis. Another way to approach consumer choice, a model based on indifference curve analysis, is developed in the appendix to this chapter.

Summary

1. Utility is a term used to describe the want-satisfying power of goods and services. The utility you receive from consuming a particular good depends primarily on your tastes and preferences. We distinguish between the total utility derived from consuming a good and the marginal utility derived from consuming one more unit of the good. The law of diminishing marginal utility says that the greater the amount of a particular good consumed per

time period, the smaller the increase in total utility received from each additional unit consumed.

2. Utility is a subjective notion because the assessment of the want-satisfying power of consumption must be made by each individual consumer. In this chapter, however, we assumed we could translate an individual's subjective measure of satisfaction into a set of numbers called utils. We were thereby able to predict a consumer's budget allocation decisions as well as the effect of a change in price on quantity demanded. We cannot make utility comparisons across individuals, although we can observe that one consumer has a greater demand for a particular good than does another consumer.

3. The consumer's objective is to maximize utility within the limits imposed by income. In a world without scarcity, utility would be maximized by consuming goods until the marginal utility of the last unit of each good consumed was 0. In a world dominated by scarcity, utility is maximized when the final unit of each good consumed yields the same utility per dollar spent. Put another way, utility is maximized when the marginal utility divided by the price is identical for each good consumed.

4. Utility analysis can be used to construct an individual consumer's demand curve. By changing the price and observing the utility-maximizing levels of consumption, we can generate points along the demand curve. When the price of a good drops, other things constant, the consumer is able to buy all units of the good at the lower price. Thus, we say that consumers typically receive a surplus, or bonus, from consumption, and this surplus increases as the price falls.

5. The market demand curve is simply the horizontal sum of the individual demand curves for all consumers in the market. With some qualifications, consumer surplus for the market demand curve can be measured by the difference between the value of the total utility received from consumption and the total amount paid for that consumption.

6. There are two components to the cost of consumption: the money price of the good and the time price of the good. People with a higher opportunity cost of time are willing to pay a higher money price for goods and services that involve a lower time price.

Questions and Problems

1. (Diminishing Marginal Utility) Some restaurants offer "all you can eat" meals. How is this practice related to diminishing marginal utility? What restrictions must the restaurant impose on the customer in order to make a profit?

2. (Marginal Utility) Consider Exhibit 3 of this chapter; suppose that each number in columns (1) and (5) were multiplied by 2. How would this affect the marginal utility in columns (3) and (7)? Would columns (4) and (8) also be affected?

3. (Marginal Utility) Is it possible for marginal utility to be negative and yet total utility to be positive? Why or why not?

4. (Consumer Equilibrium) Suppose that a consumer has a choice between two goods, X and Y. If the price of X is $2 per unit and the price of Y is $3 per unit, how much of X and Y will the consumer purchase, given an income of $17? Use the following information on marginal utility:

Units	MU_X	MU_Y
1	10	5
2	8	4
3	2	3
4	2	2
5	1	2

5. (Consumer Allocation) Consider two goods, X and Y. Suppose that $MU_X = MU_Y$ and the price of X is less than the price of Y. The rational consumer will increase purchases of X and reduce purchases of Y. Why?

6. (Consumer Allocation) Suppose that MU_X = 100 and that the price of X is $10 and the price of Y is $5. Assuming that the consumer is in equilibrium, what must the marginal utility of Y be?

7. (Time Price and Money Price) In many amusement parks, you pay an admission fee to the park and then you need not pay for each ride. How are rides allocated in such parks? Is there an incentive for some people to sell their places in line? Why or why not?

8. (Utility Maximization) Suppose that the price of X is twice as high as the price of Y. You are a utility maximizer who consumes some of each good.
   a. What must be true about the relationship between the marginal utility levels of the last unit consumed of each good?
   b. What must be true about the relationship between the marginal utility levels of the last dollar spent on each good?

9. (Marginal Utility and Demand) Suppose that you buy five shirts a year when the price of shirts is $30 and ten shirts a year when the price of shirts is $25.
   a. What can you say about the value you place on the third shirt, the seventh shirt, and the twelfth shirt you buy per year?
   b. With diminishing marginal utility, are you deriving any consumer surplus? Explain.

10. (Relative Utility Values) Although utils are purely subjective, you and I consume goods in combinations such that the ratios of the marginal utilities of the last unit consumed of each good are the same for both of us. Why is this true?

APPENDIX
Indifference Curves

The approach used in this chapter requires that we establish some numerical measure of utility in order to determine the optimal bundle of goods and services. Economists have developed another, more sophisticated approach to examining utility and consumer behavior, one that does not require that numbers be attached to specific levels of utility. All this approach requires is that consumers be able to rank their preferences for various combinations of goods. We begin with an examination of consumer preferences.

Consumer Preferences

Indifference curve analysis is an approach to the study of consumer behavior that requires no specific measure of utility. **Indifference curves** show all combinations of two goods that provide the consumer with the same total satisfaction, or total utility. Since each of the alternative bundles of goods yields the same utility, the consumer will be *indifferent* about which combination is actually consumed.

We can best explain the use of indifference curves through an example. In Exhibit 8, the horizontal axis measures the quantity of food a person consumes per period. The vertical axis measures the quantity of clothing the person consumes per period. At point *a*, the person consumes 8 units of clothing and 1 unit of food. In moving from point *a* to point *b*, the consumer is willing to give up 4 units of clothing to get 1 more unit of food. The marginal utility of that additional unit of food is just sufficient to compensate the consumer for the reduction in total utility that results from decreasing clothing consumption by 4 units. Thus, at point *b*, the person is consuming 4 units of clothing and 2 units of food and is indifferent between this combination and the combination reflected by point *a*. In moving from point *b* to point *c*, the consumer is

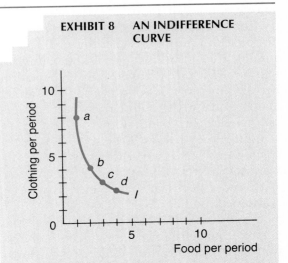

EXHIBIT 8   AN INDIFFERENCE CURVE

An indifference curve shows all combinations of two goods that provide a consumer with the same total utility. Points a through d depict four such combinations. Indifference curves have negative slopes and are convex to the origin.

now willing to give up only 1 unit of clothing to get another unit of food. At point *c*, the consumption bundle consists of 3 units of clothing and 3 units of food. Once at point *c*, the individual is willing to give up only 0.5 unit of clothing to get another unit of food. Combination *d* therefore consists of 2.5 units of clothing and 4 units of food.

We can connect points *a*, *b*, *c*, and *d* to form an indifference curve *I*, which represents all possible combinations of food and clothing that would keep the consumer at the same level of total utility. Since all points on the curve offer the same amount of utility, or satisfaction, the consumer is indifferent among them—hence the name *indifference curve*. Combinations of goods along the indifference curve reflect some constant, though unspecified, level of total utility.

Because both goods yield utility, the consumer prefers more of each rather than less. For the consumer to remain indifferent among bundles of goods, the decrease in utility from consuming less of one good must be just offset by the increase in utility from consuming more of another good. Thus, along an indifference curve there is an inverse relation between the quantity of one good consumed and the quantity of another consumed. The indifference curve slopes downward.

Indifference curves are also *convex to the origin*, which means that they are bowed inward toward the origin: the slope gets flatter as we move down the curve. Here is why. A consumer's willingness to substitute food for clothing depends on how much of each the person is currently consuming. At combination *a*, for example, the individual is consuming 8 units of clothing and only 1 unit of food, so there is much clothing relative to food. Because food is relatively scarce in the consumption bundle, another unit of food has a high marginal value and the consumer would be willing to give up 4 units of clothing to get it. Once the consumer reaches point *b*, the amount of food consumed has doubled and its marginal value has fallen, so the consumer is not quite so willing to surrender clothing to get another unit of food. In fact, the consumer will forgo only 1 unit of clothing to get 1 more unit of food. This moves the consumer from point *b* to point *c*. At point *c*, the consumer is even less anxious to get more food, so is willing to give up only 0.5 unit of clothing to get a fourth unit of food.

The **marginal rate of substitution**, or **MRS**, indicates the amount of one good that a consumer would be willing to give up to get one more unit of another good, as it would leave the consumer equally satisfied. In moving from combination *a* to *b*, the consumer is willing to give up 4 units of clothing to get one more unit of food, so the MRS is 4. In the move from combination *b* to *c*, the MRS drops to 1, and from *b* to *c* it falls to 0.5. Suppose that "food per period" measures meals per day. The consumer is willing to give up 4 units of clothing to get a second meal per day and 1 unit of clothing to get a third meal per

day but only 0.5 unit of clothing to get a fourth meal per day.

As we move down the indifference curve, the amount of food increases and the marginal utility of additional units of food decreases. Conversely, the amount of clothing decreases and its marginal utility increases. Thus, in moving down the indifference curve, the consumer is willing to give up smaller and smaller amounts of clothing to get additional units of food. More generally, consider pairs of goods X and Y. The **law of diminishing marginal rate of substitution** says that as the consumption of good X increases, the amount of good Y that the consumer is willing to give up to get each additional unit of X declines. Because the marginal rate of substitution of X for Y declines with an increase in consumption of X, the indifference curve has a diminishing slope, meaning that it is convex when viewed from the origin.

We have focused on a single indifference curve that indicates some constant but unspecified level of utility. We can use the same approach to generate a series of indifference curves, called an **indifference map**, for a particular consumer's consumption of the two goods in question. Each curve in the indifference map reflects a different level of utility. Such a map is shown in Exhibit 9, where indifference curves for a particular consumer are labeled I_1, I_2, I_3, and I_4. Each consumer will have a different indifference map based on individual preferences.

Curves farther from the origin represent greater consumption levels of both goods and therefore higher levels of total utility. The utility level along I_2 is greater than that along I_1, I_3 is greater than I_2, and so on. Perhaps you can see this best by drawing a ray from the origin and following it to higher indifference curves. As you move out along that line, the combination on each successive indifference curve reflects greater amounts of *both* goods. Since more is preferred to less, each successive indifference curve represents a higher level of utility.

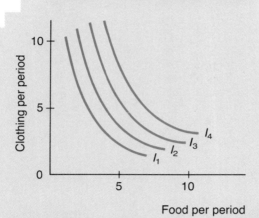

Indifference curves I_1 through I_4 are four examples from a consumer's indifference map. Indifference curves farther from the origin depict higher levels of utility.

Because we confine our analysis to cases in which goods yield positive marginal utility, our indifference curves slope downward.

Let's summarize the properties of indifference curves.

1. *An indifference curve reflects a constant though unspecified level of utility, so the consumer is indifferent among consumption combinations along a given curve.*

2. *Because an increase in the consumption of one good must be offset by a decrease in the consumption of the other good if total utility is to remain constant, indifference curves slope downward.*

3. *Because of the law of diminishing marginal rate of substitution, indifference curves are bowed in toward the origin.*

4. *Indifference curves do not intersect.*

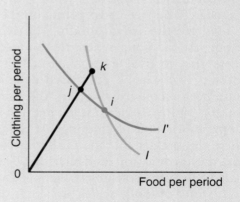

If indifference curves crossed, as at point i, then every point on indifference curve I and every point on curve I' would have to reflect the same level of utility as at point i. But point k is a combination with more food and more clothing than point j and so must represent a higher level of utility. This contradiction means that indifference curves cannot intersect.

One other feature of indifference curves is that they do not intersect. Exhibit 10 shows why. If indifference curves I and I' intersect at point i, then that combination of goods must lie on both indifference curves. Since the consumption of the bundle at point i reflects some specific level of utility and since point i lies on both curves, both curves must reflect this same level of utility.

A ray from the origin intersects the curves at points j and k. Combination k has more of both goods than does combination j. Since more is preferred to less, k must provide greater utility than j. But we already said that if the two indifference curves intersect at i, they must have equal utility. *Because the curves cannot reflect both identical utility and different utility, we conclude that the curves cannot intersect.*

We have not considered consumption combinations in which one good provides negative marginal utility. Such possibilities exist, but they do not interest us because consumers ignore them. No consumer would knowingly increase the consumption of one good to the point where marginal utility was negative.

Given a consumer's indifference map, how much of each good will be consumed? To determine how much will be consumed, we must consider the prices of the goods and the consumer's income. In the next section we will focus on the consumer's budget.

The Budget Line

Suppose the price of food is $4 per unit, the price of clothing is $2 per unit, and the consumer's budget is $20 per period. If the entire $20 is spent on clothing, the consumer can afford to buy 10 units. Alternatively, if the entire $20 is spent on food, the consumer can purchase 5 units. The **budget line** reflects all possible combinations of clothing and food that could be purchased given the consumer's budget and the product prices. In Exhibit 11, the consumer's budget line meets the vertical axis at 10 units of clothing and meets the horizontal axis at 5 units of food. You might think of the budget line as the individual's *consumption possibilities frontier.*

Recall that the slope of any line is the vertical change between two points on the line divided by the corresponding horizontal change. At the point where the budget line meets the vertical axis, the quantity of clothing that can be purchased equals the consumer's income divided by the price of clothing, or I/P_C, where I is income and P_C is the price of a unit of clothing. At the point where the budget line meets the horizontal axis, the quantity of food that can be purchased equals the consumer's income divided by the price of food, or I/P_F, where P_F is the price of a unit of food. The slope of the budget line in Exhibit 11 can be calculated by considering a movement from the vertical intercept to the horizontal intercept. That is, we divide the vertical change ($-I/P_C$) by the horizontal change (I/P_F) as follows:

$$\textbf{Slope} = -\frac{I/P_C}{I/P_F} = -\frac{P_F}{P_C}$$

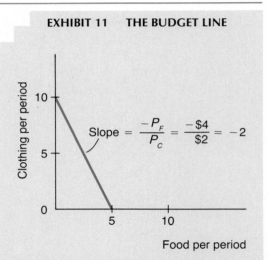

EXHIBIT 11   THE BUDGET LINE

$$\text{Slope} = \frac{-P_F}{P_C} = \frac{-\$4}{\$2} = -2$$

The budget line shows all combinations of food and clothing that can be purchased at fixed prices with a given amount of income. If all income is spent on clothing, 10 units can be purchased. If all income is spent on food, 5 units can be purchased. Points between the vertical intercept and the horizontal intercept represent combinations of some food and some clothing. The slope of the budget line is −2, illustrating that the cost of 1 unit of food is 2 units of clothing.

Along the budget line, the vertical value falls as the horizontal value increases, so the slope is negative. The slope of the budget line equals minus the food price divided by the clothing price; in our example it is −$4/$2, which equals −2. The slope of the budget line indicates what it costs the consumer in terms of forgone clothing to get another unit of food. The consumer must give up 2 units of clothing for each additional unit of food.

As you know, the demand curve shows the quantity that the consumer is willing and able to buy at alternative prices. The indifference curve indicates what the consumer is *willing* to buy. The budget line shows what the consumer is *able* to buy. We must therefore bring together the indifference curve and the budget line to find out what quantity the consumer is both willing and able to buy.

Consumer Equilibrium at the Tangency

We assume that the consumer's objective is to attain the highest level of utility possible, given prices and the consumer's income. We know that indifference curves farther from the origin represent higher levels of utility. The utility-maximizing consumer therefore will select that combination along the budget line in Exhibit 12 that lies on the highest attainable indifference curve. Combination *a* consists of 8 units of clothing costing a total of $16 and 1 unit of food at $4, for a total outlay of $20. Point *a* is on the budget line and thus is a combination the consumer is *able* to consume, but *a* is not on the highest attainable indifference curve. Given prices and income, the consumer maximizes utility at the combination of food and clothing depicted by point *e* in Exhibit 12, where indifference curve I_2 just touches, or is tangent to, the budget line. This utility-maximizing consumption

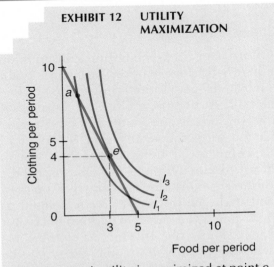

EXHIBIT 12   UTILITY MAXIMIZATION

The consumer's utility is maximized at point *e*, where indifference curve I_2 is just tangent to the budget line.

bundle consists of 4 units of clothing totaling $8 and 3 units of food totaling $12; this combination exhausts the $20 budget.

Since the consumer is maximizing utility at point *e*, this is an equilibrium outcome. There will be no tendency for the consumer to change this consumption pattern as long as prices and the consumer's income and tastes remain unchanged. Note that the indifference curve is tangent to the budget line at the equilibrium point. At that point, therefore, the slope of the indifference curve equals the slope of the budget line. Recall that the slope of the indifference curve is the consumer's marginal rate of substitution, and the slope of the budget line equals minus the price ratio. In equilibrium, therefore, the marginal rate of substitution of clothing for food must equal minus the ratio of the price of food to the price of clothing, or

$$\textbf{Marginal rate of substitution} = -\frac{P_F}{P_C}$$

What is the relation between indifference curve analysis and the marginal utility theory introduced in the chapter? The marginal rate of substitution of clothing for food can also be revealed by the marginal utilities of clothing and food, presented in the chapter. Exhibit 3 indicated that the marginal utility provided by the third unit of food was 12 utils, and the marginal utility provided by the fourth unit of clothing was 6 utils. Since the marginal utility of food (MU_F) is 12 utils and the marginal utility of clothing (MU_C) is 6 utils, the consumer requires 2 units of clothing to give up 1 unit of food. Thus, the marginal rate of substitution of clothing for food equals minus the ratio of food's marginal utility (MU_F) to clothing's marginal utility (MU_C), or

$$\textbf{Marginal rate of substitution} = -\frac{MU_F}{MU_C}$$

We can now generalize the results to say that the slope of the indifference curve equals

− MU_F/MU_C. Since the slope of the budget line equals − P_F/P_C, the equilibrium condition for the indifference curve approach can be written as

$$-\frac{MU_F}{MU_C} = -\frac{P_F}{P_C}$$

which can be easily rearranged to show that

$$\frac{MU_F}{P_F} = \frac{MU_C}{P_C}$$

This equation is the same equilibrium condition for utility maximization that was derived in the chapter using marginal utility theory. The equality says that in equilibrium the last dollar spent on each good yields the same utility. If this equality does not hold, the consumer can increase total utility by adjusting consumption until the equality does hold.

Effects of a Change in Income

We have established the equilibrium consumption bundle for a particular consumer, given that consumer's income and product prices. What happens if the consumer's income changes? Suppose, for example, that the consumer's income is cut in half, from $20 to $10 per period, yet prices remain as before. Exhibit 13 shows the effects of this reduction in income on the equilibrium bundle consumed. Since income falls but prices remain the same, the new budget line is parallel to but below the old budget line. Because of the decrease in income, the budget now buys less of each good. If the entire budget is devoted to clothing, only 5 units can be purchased; if it is devoted to food, only 2.5 units can be purchased. The consumer once again maximizes utility by consuming that combination of goods that is on the highest attainable indifference curve—in this case point e' on indifference curve I'. The drop in income reduces the consumer's ability to purchase goods, resulting in a lower level of utility. (Note that

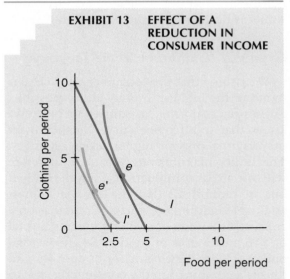

EXHIBIT 13   EFFECT OF A REDUCTION IN CONSUMER INCOME

A reduction in income causes a parallel inward shift of the budget line. The consumer is back in equilibrium at point e', where indifference curve I' is tangent to the new, lower budget line.

food and clothing are both normal goods, since a drop in income results in reduced consumption of both.)

Effects of a Change in Price

What happens to equilibrium consumption if there is a change in price? We begin at point e, our initial equilibrium, in panel (a) of Exhibit 14. At point e, the person consumes 4 units of clothing and 3 units of food. Suppose that the price of food falls from $4 per unit to $3 per unit, other things constant. A drop in the price of food from $4 to $3 means that the consumer could purchase nearly 7 units of food if the entire budget were devoted to food. Since the price of clothing has not changed, however, 10 units of clothing remains the maximum amount that could be purchased. Thus, the budget line's vertical intercept remains fixed at 10 units, but the lower end of the budget line rotates out.

After the price change, the new equilibrium position occurs at *e″*, where the quantity of clothing consumed remains at 4 units, but the quantity of food increases from 3 units to 4 units. Thus, price and quantity demanded are inversely related, other things constant, and we have again derived the law of demand.

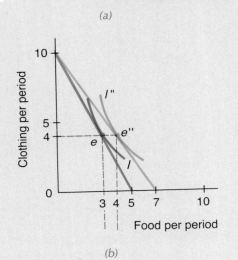

EXHIBIT 14   EFFECT OF A DROP IN THE PRICE OF FOOD

(a)

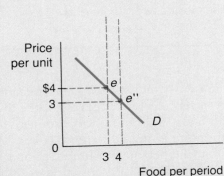

(b)

A reduction in the price of food rotates the budget line outward in panel (a). The consumer is back in equilibrium at point *e″* along the new budget line. Panel (b) shows that a drop in the price of food from $4 per unit to $3 leads to an increase in quantity demanded from 3 units to 4. Price and quantity demanded are inversely related.

The demand curve in panel (b) of Exhibit 14 shows how price and quantity demanded are related. Specifically, when the price of food falls from $4 per unit to $3 per unit, other things constant, the quantity of food demanded increases from 3 units to 4 units. Since the consumer is on a higher indifference curve at *e″*, the consumer is clearly better off after the price reduction.

Income and Substitution Effects

We originally explained the law of demand in terms of an income effect and a substitution effect. We have now developed the analytical tools to examine these two effects more precisely. Suppose the price of food falls from $4 to $2, other things constant. The maximum amount of food that can be purchased with a budget of $20 per period is 10 units, as shown in Exhibit 15, so the budget line rotates out from 5 to 10 units of food. As you can see, after the price change, the quantity of food demanded increases from 3 units to 5 units. The increase in utility shows that the consumer benefits from the price drop.

Through careful analysis, the increase in the quantity of food demanded can be broken down into the substitution effect and the income effect of a price change. When the price of food falls, the change in the ratio of the price of food to the price of clothing is reflected by the change in the slope of the budget line. Suppose, for the sake of exposition, that the consumer tries to maintain the same level of utility after the price change as before. The consumer will increase the quantity of food demanded to the point on indifference curve *I* where the indifference curve is just tangent to *CF*, the dashed budget line. That budget line keeps utility at the old level but reflects the new relative price of food. Thus, we adjust the consumer's budget line to correspond to the new relative prices, but at an income level that keeps the consumer on the same indifference curve.

The consumer moves down along indif-

EXHIBIT 15   SUBSTITUTION AND INCOME EFFECTS OF A DROP IN THE PRICE OF FOOD FROM $4 TO $2 PER UNIT

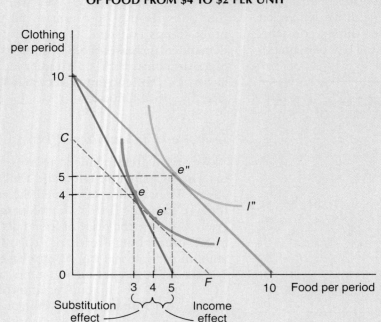

A reduction in the price of food moves the consumer from point e to point e″. This movement can be decomposed into a substitution effect and an income effect. The substitution effect (from e to e′) reflects a reaction to a change in relative prices along the original indifference curve. The income effect (from e′ to e″) moves the consumer to a higher indifference curve at the new relative price ratio.

ference curve *I* to point *e′*, purchasing less clothing and more food. This change in quantity demanded reflects the *substitution effect* of the lower price of food. The substitution effect always increases the quantity demanded of the good whose price has dropped. Since consumption bundle *e′* represents the same level of utility as consumption bundle *e*, the consumer is neither better off nor worse off at point *e′*.

But at point *e′* the consumer is not spending all the income available. The drop in the price of food has increased the amount of food that can be purchased, as shown by the expanded budget line that runs from 10 units of

clothing to 10 units of food. The consumer's *real income* has increased because of the lower price of food. As a result, the consumer is able to attain point *e″* on indifference curve *I″*. At this point, the person consumes 5 units each of food and clothing. Because prices are held constant during the move from *e′* to *e″*, the change in consumption is due solely to a change in real income. Thus, the change in the quantity of food demanded reflects an *income effect.*

We can now distinguish between the substitution effect and the income effect of a drop in the price of food. The substitution effect is shown by the move from point *e* to point *e′* in response to a change in the relative price of food, with the consumer's utility held constant along *I*. The income effect is shown by the move from *e′* to *e″* in response to an increase in real income, with relative prices held constant.

The overall effect of a change in the price of food is the sum of the substitution effect and the income effect. In our example the substitution effect accounts for a 1-unit increase in the quantity of food demanded, as does the income effect. Thus, the income and substitution effects combine to increase quantity demanded by 2 units when the price falls from \$4 to \$2. (Incidentally, notice that as a result of the increase in real income, clothing consumption increases as well—from 4 units to 5 units in our example.) The income effect is not always positive. For inferior goods, the income effect is negative, so as the price falls,

the income effect can offset part or all of the substitution effect.

Conclusion

Indifference curve analysis does not require us to attach numerical values to particular levels of utility, as marginal utility theory does. The results of indifference curve analysis confirm the conclusions drawn from our simpler models. Perhaps the most important conclusion is that demand curves slope downward. Indifference curves provide a logical way of viewing consumer choice, but consumers need not be aware of this approach to make rational choices. As we have said all along, the purpose of the analysis in this chapter is to predict consumer behavior—not to pinpoint what consumers ought to purchase.

Appendix Questions

1. (Slope of Indifference Curve) The slope of an indifference curve equals the marginal rate of substitution. If two goods were *perfectly* substitutable, what would the indifference curves look like? Explain.

2. (Effects of Change in Income) Suppose that a good was income elastic. What would happen to the tangency solutions on a consumer's indifference map as you varied the consumer's level of income?

Cost and Production in the Firm

Each year hundreds of thousands of firms enter the marketplace, and nearly as many leave. Millions of firms make choices about what goods and services to produce and what resources to employ. These firms must make plans while confronting uncertainty about consumer demand, resource availability, and the intentions of other firms. The lure of profit is so strong, however, that eager entrepreneurs are always ready to pursue their dreams.

The previous chapter explored the consumer behavior underlying the demand curve. This chapter examines the producer behavior underlying the supply curve. More specifically, we examine a firm's production and cost of operation as a prelude to an analysis of supply. In the previous chapter we asked you to think like a consumer. In this chapter we want you to think like a producer. Being the consumer may feel more natural (after all, you make purchases every day). But you know more about firms than you may realize because you have been around them all your life — bookstores, video stores, department stores, gas stations, and a variety of fast-food restaurants. Although you probably have not yet managed a firm, you already have some idea how they operate. Topics discussed in this chapter include

- Explicit and implicit costs
- Economic and normal profit
- Increasing and diminishing returns

- Short-run costs
- Long-run costs
- Economies and diseconomies of scale

COST AND PROFIT

As noted in Chapter 4, the firm brings together resources to produce whatever can be sold for a profit. Profit is the difference between the firm's total revenue and its total cost—that is, the difference between the total revenue received from the sale of output and what must be paid to attract resources from their best alternative use.

Explicit and Implicit Costs

To hire resources, the firm must pay their *opportunity cost*—what they could earn from their best alternative use. For resources purchased in resource markets, the corresponding cash payments are good approximations of the opportunity cost. Some resources, however, are owned by the firm (or, more precisely, are owned by the firm's owners), so there are no direct cash payments for their use. For example, the firm does not pay rent to operate in a company-owned building. Similarly, Mom and Pop, the owners and operators of the corner grocery, usually do not pay themselves an hourly wage. *Whether resources are owned by the firm or hired in resource markets, however, resource use involves an opportunity cost to the firm.*

Explicit costs are opportunity costs of a firm's resources that take the form of actual cash payments.

Implicit costs are the firm's opportunity costs of using its own resources or those provided by its owners.

The firm's **explicit costs** are the actual cash payments for resources purchased in resource markets: wages, rent, interest, insurance, and the like. In addition to these direct cash outlays, or explicit costs, the firm also faces **implicit costs**, which are the opportunity costs to the firm of using resources owned by the firm or provided by the firm's owners. Examples include the use of a company-owned building or the time and capital of the firm's owners. Like explicit costs, implicit costs involve an opportunity cost to the firm, but unlike explicit costs, they usually require no cash payment and no entry in the firm's *accounting statement*, which records the firm's revenues, explicit costs, and accounting profit.

Alternative Measures of Profit

A particular example will help to clarify the distinction between implicit and explicit costs. Wanda Wheeler is an aeronautical engineer who earns $30,000 a year working for the Skyhigh Aircraft Company. On her way home from work one day, she gets an idea for a rounder, more friction-resistant airplane wheel. She quits her job to start a business she calls The Wheeler Dealer. To buy the necessary equipment, she withdraws $20,000 in savings that was earning 5 percent interest. She hires an assistant and starts producing the wheel in her garage, which she had been renting to a neighbor for $100 per month.

Sales are slow at first—people keep telling her she is just trying to reinvent the wheel—but her wheel eventually gets rolling. When Wanda and her accountant examine the firm's performance for the year, they are quite pleased. As you can see in Exhibit 1, after paying the assistant's salary and

EXHIBIT 1
ACCOUNTS OF WHEELER DEALER, 1990

Total revenue	$75,000
Less explicit costs:	
Assistant's salary	15,000
Material and and equipment	20,000
Equals accounting profit	$40,000
Less implicit costs:	
Wanda's forgone salary	$30,000
Forgone interest on savings	1000
Forgone garage rental	1200
Equals economic profit	$ 7800

Accounting profit is total revenue minus explicit costs.

covering the costs of raw materials, the firm shows an accounting profit in 1990 of $40,000. **Accounting profit** equals total revenue minus explicit costs—those cash outlays that take the form of payments to nonowners of the firm.

But this accounting profit ignores the opportunity cost of Wanda's own resources used in the firm. First is the opportunity cost of Wanda's time. Remember that she quit a $30,000-a-year job to devote herself full-time to her business, thereby forgoing that salary. She also invested her own savings of $20,000 in the firm, thereby forgoing the 5 percent interest those savings earned—interest amounting to $1000 per year. And recall that she had been renting her garage to a neighbor for $100 per month, so by using her garage for the business, she had to forgo $1200 per year in rental income.

Economic profit is total revenue minus all costs, explicit and implicit.

The forgone salary, interest, and rental income are implicit costs because, although Wanda makes no explicit payment for the resources, she gives up income generated from their best alternative use. **Economic profit** equals total revenue minus all costs, both implicit and explicit, because *economic profit focuses on the opportunity cost of resources.* In Exhibit 1, economic profit equals accounting profit less implicit costs, or $7800.

What would happen to the accounting statement if Wanda decided to pay herself a salary of, say, $20,000 per year? Explicit costs would increase by $20,000, implicit costs would decrease by $20,000, and accounting profits would decrease by $20,000. The economic profit, however, would not change because it already takes into account both implicit and explicit costs.

Normal profit is the profit earned when all resources used by the firm are earning their opportunity cost.

There is one other important type of profit: the profit required to induce the firm's owners to employ their resources in the firm. When all resources used by the firm are earning their opportunity cost, the firm is said to be earning a **normal profit**. Wanda's firm is earning a normal profit when the accounting profit equals the sum of the salary she gave up at her regular job ($30,000), the interest she gave up on her savings ($1000), and the rent she gave up on her garage ($1200). Thus if Wheeler Dealer earns an accounting profit of $32,200 per year—the opportunity cost of the capital, labor, and entrepreneurial ability Wanda supplies to the firm—the company earns a normal profit.

Accounting profit therefore can be divided into normal profit and economic profit. The $40,000 in accounting profit earned by Wanda's firm consists of (1) a normal profit of $32,200, which is sufficient to cover the opportunity cost of all Wanda's resources employed by the firm, and (2) an economic profit of $7800, which is over and above what these resources could earn from their best alternative use. As long as economic profit is positive, Wanda is better off running her own firm than working for the Skyhigh Aircraft Company.

PRODUCTION IN THE SHORT RUN

Keep in mind that the ultimate aim of this chapter is to examine the forces underlying the supply curve. The supply curve describes the relation between the price of a product and the quantity producers are willing and able to offer for sale. The relation between the price and the quantity supplied is determined by the link between cost and quantity produced. But to understand the costs of production, we must first analyze the link between resource use and production.

Production Under the Golden Arches

Suppose a new McDonald's has just opened in your neighborhood, and its business is booming far beyond expectations. The manager responds to the unexpected demand by quickly hiring more workers, but the restaurant still cannot seem to satisfy the demand. The parking lot is always packed, cars are backed up into the street waiting for a space, and there is always a long line at the drive-through window.

Variable resources can be quickly varied to increase or decrease the level of output; fixed resources cannot be varied in the short run.

Fixed and Variable Inputs McDonald's, like other producers, must adjust the quantity of resources used in order to change its output level. Some resources, such as the number of workers, are called **variable resources** because they can be quickly varied to increase or decrease the output level. Adjustments in other resources, however, take more time; the size of the building, for example, cannot be easily altered. Such resources are therefore called **fixed resources**.

*In the **short run**, at least one resource cannot be varied; in the **long run**, all resources are variable.*

Short Run and Long Run When considering the time required to alter the quantity of resources employed, economists distinguish between the short run and the long run. The **short run** is a period so short that at least one resource is fixed. Output can be changed by adjusting the variable resources, but the size, or scale, of the firm is fixed in the short run. In the **long run**, however, all resources can be varied. The amount of time required for a long-run adjustment differs from industry to industry because the nature of the production process differs. For example, the number of franchises McDonald's has in a state can be adjusted more quickly than can the number of electric power plants a utility company has.

The Law of Diminishing Returns

Let's focus on the short-run link between resources and outputs by considering a hypothetical firm called the Smoother Movers moving company. Suppose the company's fixed capital is already in place, and it consists of a warehouse, a large moving van, a pickup truck, and moving equipment. Labor is the only variable resource of significance.

Exhibit 2 presents data showing the relation between the amount of labor employed and output. Labor is measured in workers per day, and output is measured in tons of furniture moved per day. The left column shows the units of labor employed, from 0 to 8. The tons of furniture moved, or the **total physical product**, at each level of employment is in the center column. The right column shows the **marginal physical product (MPP)** of each worker — that is, the amount by which the total physical product, or output, changes with each additional unit of labor, assuming all other resources remain unchanged.

Increasing Marginal Returns Consider now what happens as we add units of labor to the fixed amount of capital. Nothing is produced without labor, so when the quantity of labor is 0, no furniture gets moved and the total physical product is 0. If only one worker is employed, that worker alone must do all the driving, packing, crating, and moving. Some of the larger pieces of furniture such as couches and beds cannot easily be moved by one person. Still, one worker can move 2 tons of furniture per day.

When two workers are employed, total production more than doubles, reaching 5 tons per day, because some division of labor occurs in packing

Total physical product is the total output of goods or services produced by the firm.

Marginal physical product is the change in total physical product that occurs when the usage of a particular resource changes by 1 unit, all other resources constant.

EXHIBIT 2
THE SHORT-RUN RELATION BETWEEN UNITS OF LABOR AND TONS OF FURNITURE MOVED

Units of the Variable Resource (labor/day)	Total Physical Product (tons moved/day)	Marginal Physical Product (tons moved/day)
0	0	—
1	2	2
2	5	3
3	9	4
4	12	3
5	14	2
6	15	1
7	15	0
8	14	−1

and two workers can handle the larger household items much more easily. The marginal physical product resulting from addition of a second worker is 3 tons per day. Addition of a third worker allows greater specialization, which contributes to increased output: two workers can work at one house while the third worker goes to the next job to begin the packing and crating. Thus, each worker is more efficient. The total physical product of three workers is 9 tons per day, which is 4 tons more than is produced by two workers. Because the marginal physical product increases with each additional worker, the firm experiences **increasing marginal returns** as each of the first three workers is added. Marginal returns increase because additional workers can specialize and can therefore make more efficient use of the fixed resources.

A firm experiences ***increasing marginal returns*** *when marginal physical product increases with each additional unit of the variable resource.*

Diminishing Marginal Returns The addition of a fourth worker adds something to the total product, but not as much as was added by the third worker. As more workers are added, the total product increases by successively smaller amounts, so the marginal physical product in Exhibit 2 declines. With each additional worker, the advantages of greater specialization decrease. Indeed, with eight workers, the working area becomes so crowded that workers get in each other's way. Transporting workers to and from moving sites cuts into production because workers take up valuable space on the moving van. As a result, the total product actually declines when an eighth worker is added, so the marginal physical product is negative.

According to the ***law of diminishing marginal returns****, changes in output will eventually diminish as more and more of a variable resource is added to a given amount of fixed resources.*

Beginning with the fourth worker, the **law of diminishing marginal returns** takes hold. This law states that as additional quantities of the variable resource are combined with a given amount of fixed resources, a point is eventually reached where each additional increment of the variable resource yields a smaller and smaller marginal physical product. *The law of diminishing marginal returns is the most important feature of firm production in the short run.* Evidence of diminishing returns is abundant. In your own studies, the productivity of your first hour of studying is likely to be greater than that of your fifth hour at one sitting. In restaurants, "too many cooks spoil the broth." In agriculture, if marginal product continued to increase indefinitely, the world's supply of vegetables could be grown in a backyard simply by adding more and more labor and fertilizer to the fixed plot of land. In construction, as additional floors are added to a skyscraper, the steel must be made stronger, the concrete reinforced more, the water pipes made thicker to withstand the added pressure, and the building's footings driven deeper into the ground; after a certain point these added expenses add less and less value to the building. In medicine, doctors tend to view themselves as a fixed resource, for they can increase total product by hiring nurses and renting offices with more treatment rooms. But the marginal product of these variable inputs evidently shows diminishing returns, because a doctor seldom hires more than two nurses or rents more than a few treatment rooms.

The Total and Marginal Physical Product Curves

Panels (a) and (b) of Exhibit 3 illustrate the total physical product and the marginal physical product, using the data from Exhibit 2. Note that as long as the marginal physical product curve is rising—that is, as long as marginal returns are increasing—the total physical product curve increases by in-

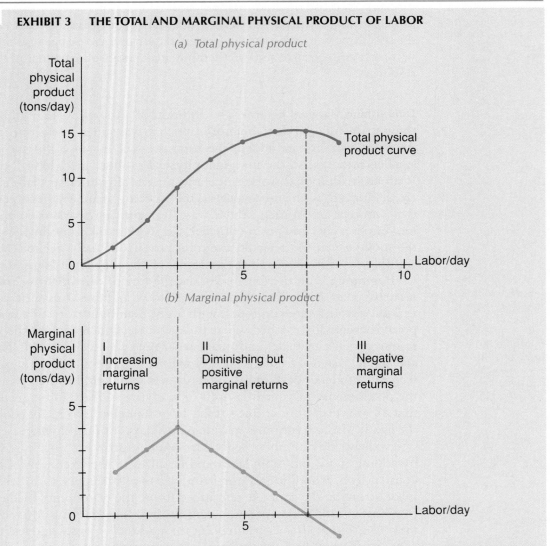

EXHIBIT 3   THE TOTAL AND MARGINAL PHYSICAL PRODUCT OF LABOR

(a) Total physical product

(b) Marginal physical product

In stage I of panel (b), marginal physical product is rising. In panel (a), total physical product is increasing by increasing amounts. In stage II, marginal physical product is decreasing but is still positive. Total product is increasing by decreasing amounts. When marginal product equals 0, total product is at a maximum. Finally, in stage III, marginal product is negative, and total physical product is falling.

creasing amounts. But as the marginal product begins to decline—that is, when marginal returns diminish—total product still increases but at a decreasing rate. At the output level where marginal product becomes negative, the total product curve begins to turn down.

For purposes of exposition, we divide production in the short run into three stages. Increasing marginal returns are experienced by the firm during stage I; diminishing but positive marginal returns are experienced during stage II; and negative marginal returns are experienced during stage III.

COSTS IN THE SHORT RUN

Fixed cost is independent of the firm's rate of output; variable cost increases as output increases.

Now that we have examined the relation between the amount of resources used and the level of output, we can consider how the firm's costs vary with changes in the level of output. Short-run costs are divided into two categories: fixed costs and variable costs. A firm must pay **fixed costs** even if no output is produced. Even if the Smoother Movers do nothing, the firm must pay property taxes, insurance premiums, maintenance costs, plus principal and interest on any loans for its warehouse, trucks, and equipment. By definition, fixed costs do not vary even if output increases. Let's assume that the Smoother Movers face fixed costs of $200 per day.

On the other hand, **variable costs**, as the name implies, vary with output. Whenever output is 0, variable costs are $0; when output increases, variable costs increase. The amount by which variable costs increase depends on the prices of the variable resources employed and the productivity of these resources. In our example, variable costs consist of labor costs. Suppose labor costs are $100 per worker per day. Total variable costs can be found by multiplying $100 times the amount of labor employed.

Total Cost and Marginal Cost in the Short Run

Exhibit 4 presents cost data for the Smoother Movers. The table lists the costs of production associated with alternative levels of output. Column (1) shows the firm's possible levels of output in the short run, measured in tons of furniture per day.

Total Cost Column (2) indicates the total fixed cost (*TFC*) for each level of output. Note that total fixed cost remains constant at $200 per day regardless of the level of output. Column (3) shows the amount of labor required to produce each level of output and is based on the productivity information in the previous two exhibits. For example, moving 2 tons requires one worker, 5 tons requires two workers, and so on. Column (4) lists the total variable cost (*TVC*), which equals the cost of $100 per unit of labor times the quantity of labor employed. For example, the total variable cost of moving 9 tons of furniture per day is $300. Column (5) lists the total cost (*TC*) of each level of output, which is the sum of total fixed cost and

EXHIBIT 4
SHORT-RUN COST DATA FOR THE SMOOTHER MOVERS

Tons Moved per Day (Q) (1)	Total Fixed Cost (TFC) (2)	Workers per Day (3)	Total Variable Cost (TVC) (4)	Total Cost (TC = TFC + TVC) (5)	Marginal Cost $\left(MC = \dfrac{\Delta TC}{\Delta Q}\right)$ (6)
0	$200	0	$ 0	$200	—
2	200	1	100	300	$ 50.00
5	200	2	200	400	33.33
9	200	3	300	500	25.00
12	200	4	400	600	33.33
14	200	5	500	700	50.00
15	200	6	600	800	100.00
15	200	7	700	900	—

total variable cost: $TC = TFC + TVC$. Note that at 0 units of output, variable cost is $0, so total cost equals total fixed cost.

Marginal Cost Of major interest to the firm is how total cost changes as output changes. More specifically, what is the marginal cost of producing another unit? The **marginal cost** of production listed in column (6) is simply the change in total cost divided by the change in output. For example, increasing output from 0 to 2 tons changes total cost by $100 ($300 − $200). The marginal cost of each of the first 2 tons is the change in total cost, $100, divided by the change in output, 2, or $50. The marginal cost of each of the next three units equals $100/3, or $33.33.

> *Marginal cost is the change in total cost divided by the change in ouput.*

Notice in column (6) that marginal cost first decreases, then increases. Changes in marginal cost reflect changes in the marginal productivity of the variable resource employed. Recall from Exhibit 2 that the first three workers showed increasing marginal returns, with each worker producing more output than the last. This greater productivity of labor results in a falling marginal cost for the output produced by the first three workers. Eventually, however, the marginal physical product of the variable resource declines as the firm experiences diminishing marginal returns. *When the firm experiences increasing marginal returns, the marginal cost of output decreases; when the firm experiences diminishing marginal returns, the marginal cost of output increases.*

Thus the marginal cost in Exhibit 4 first falls, then rises because the variable resource contributes first increasing marginal returns, then diminishing marginal returns. Specifically, the variable resource employed by the Smoother Movers shows increasing marginal returns for the first 9 tons of furniture moved and decreasing marginal returns thereafter. Recall that marginal cost equals the increase in total cost divided by the change in Q. Once output reaches 15 units, additional labor adds nothing to output, so the change in Q equals 0 and marginal cost is undefined after output reaches 15 units.

Total and Marginal Cost Curves Exhibit 5 shows the total cost curves and the marginal cost curve for the data in the previous exhibit. Since total fixed cost does not vary with output, it appears as a horizontal line at the $200 level in panel (a). Total variable cost is $0 when output is 0, so the total variable cost curve starts from the origin. Total variable cost increases slowly at first as

EXHIBIT 5   TOTAL AND MARGINAL COST CURVES

(a) *Total cost curves*

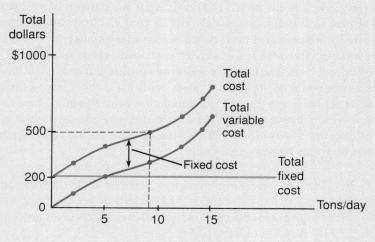

(b) *Marginal cost*

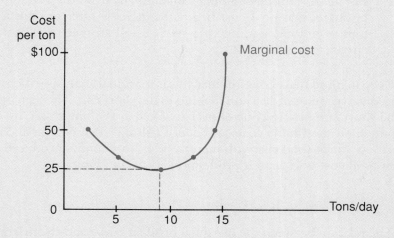

In panel (a), total fixed cost is constant at all levels of output. Total variable cost starts from the origin and increases slowly at first as output increases. When the variable resources generate diminishing marginal returns, total variable cost begins to increase more rapidly. Total cost is the vertical sum of total fixed cost and total variable cost. In panel (b), marginal cost first declines, reflecting increasing marginal returns, and then increases, reflecting diminishing marginal returns.

output increases because of increasing marginal returns generated as more units of the variable resource are employed. As soon as the variable resource reaches the point of diminishing marginal returns, however, total variable cost begins to climb more rapidly as output expands. Overall, the total variable cost curve has a backward S shape.

To derive the total cost curve, we *vertically* sum total variable cost and total fixed cost. Because a constant amount of fixed cost is added to total variable cost, the total cost curve is the total variable cost curve shifted vertically by the amount of fixed cost.

We have already discussed the reasons for the pattern of marginal cost. In panel (b) of Exhibit 5, marginal cost at first declines and then increases, reflecting increasing and then diminishing marginal returns from the variable resource, labor. There is a clear geometric relation between panels (a) and (b) because the change in total cost resulting from a 1-unit change in production equals the marginal cost. With each successive unit of output, the total cost increases by the marginal cost of that unit. Thus, the slope of the total cost curve at each level of output equals the marginal cost at that level of output. The total cost curve can be divided into two sections based on what happens to marginal cost:

1. Because of increasing marginal returns from the variable resource, marginal cost at first declines, so the total cost curve at the outset increases by successively smaller amounts and its slope gets flatter.

2. Because of diminishing marginal returns from the variable resource, marginal cost begins to increase after the ninth unit of output, leading to a steeper and steeper total cost curve.

Keep in mind that economic analysis is marginal analysis. Marginal cost is the key to economic decision making in the short run. The firm operating in the short run has no control over its fixed costs, but it can, by varying output, alter its variable costs and hence its total cost. Marginal cost indicates how much total cost will increase if 1 more unit is produced or how much total cost will drop if production is cut by 1 unit.

Marginal Product and Marginal Cost Curves

The relation between the marginal product curve and the marginal cost curve is expressed by the two panels of Exhibit 6. The upper panel presents the marginal physical product curve from Exhibit 3, and the lower panel presents the marginal cost curve from Exhibit 5. The two panels are lined up to convey the relation between marginal productivity and marginal cost. When the marginal physical product of labor increases, the marginal cost of production decreases. Note that because the marginal physical product increases for the first 3 units of labor, the marginal cost falls for the first 9

EXHIBIT 6   COMPARISON OF THE MARGINAL PHYSICAL PRODUCT CURVE AND THE MARGINAL COST CURVE

(a) Marginal physical product

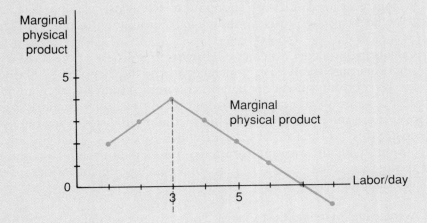

(b) Marginal cost

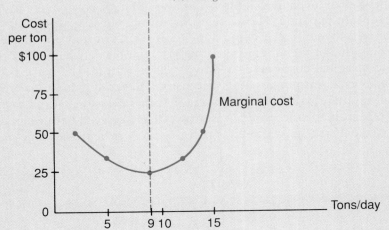

Panel (b) has been placed under panel (a) to convey the relation between the marginal physical product of the variable resource and the marginal cost of output. Because of increasing marginal returns, the marginal physical product increases with the first 3 units of labor employed, so the marginal cost of output falls. Once employment exceeds 3 workers, marginal returns diminish and marginal cost increases.

units of output—the amount produced when three workers are employed. When the marginal physical product of labor declines, as it does beginning with the fourth unit of labor, marginal cost rises.

Average Costs in the Short Run

Although total cost and marginal cost are of most analytical interest, the average cost per unit of output is also important. A producer who knows the average cost of output knows what price will cover costs. There are three average cost measures corresponding to fixed cost, variable cost, and total cost. These average costs are shown in columns (5), (6), and (7) of Exhibit 7.

Calculating Average Cost Let's begin with the easiest of the three cost measures, **average fixed cost**, which equals the fixed cost of $200 divided by the level of output. As the data in column (5) indicate, average fixed cost declines steadily as output increases because $200 in fixed cost is averaged over more and more units of output. Column (6) lists the **average variable cost**, which is total variable cost divided by output. Total cost divided by output yields the **average total cost**, presented in the final column. Both average variable cost and average total cost first decline as output expands and then increase.

Average fixed cost is total fixed cost divided by output; average variable cost is total variable cost divided by output; average total cost is total cost divided by output.

Average and Marginal Cost Curves The average cost data from Exhibit 7 are graphed as average cost curves in Exhibit 8, along with the marginal cost curve introduced in Exhibit 4. The average fixed cost curve falls continually as output expands. The average variable and average total cost curves first fall and then, after reaching a low point, rise; overall, they have a U shape. The shape of the average variable cost curve is determined by the shape of the marginal cost curve. At low levels of output, the marginal cost curve declines as output expands because of increasing marginal returns. This falling marginal cost lowers average variable cost as output expands.

Marginal cost eventually starts to rise, however, because of diminishing marginal returns. As long as marginal cost is below average variable cost,

EXHIBIT 7
SHORT-RUN COST DATA FOR A HYPOTHETICAL FIRM

Total Output (Q) (1)	Total Variable Cost (TVC) (2)	Total Cost (TC = TFC + TVC) (3)	Marginal Cost $\left(MC=\dfrac{\Delta TC}{\Delta Q}\right)$ (4)	Average Fixed Cost $\left(AFC=\dfrac{TFC}{Q}\right)$ (5)	Average Variable Cost $\left(AVC=\dfrac{TVC}{Q}\right)$ (6)	Average Total Cost $\left(ATC=\dfrac{TC}{Q}\right)$ (7)
0	$ 0	$200	$ 0	∞	—	∞
2	100	300	50.00	$100.00	$50.00	$150.00
5	200	400	33.33	40.00	40.00	80.00
9	300	500	25.00	22.22	33.33	55.55
12	400	600	33.33	16.67	33.33	50.00
14	500	700	50.00	14.29	35.71	50.00
15	600	800	100.00	13.33	40.00	53.33

average variable cost declines because the marginal cost pulls down the average. The two curves intersect where marginal cost equals average variable cost. In Exhibit 8, this intersection occurs at 12 units of output. Once marginal cost exceeds average variable cost, the average variable cost curve starts to rise as output expands—higher marginal cost begins to pull up the average. Thus, the marginal cost curve explains why the average variable cost curve has a U shape.

The average total cost curve is the vertical sum of the average fixed cost and the average variable cost curves. Therefore, the shape of the average total cost curve reflects the shapes of the underlying average cost curves. Note that as output increases, the average variable cost and the average total cost

EXHIBIT 8   AVERAGE AND MARGINAL COST CURVES

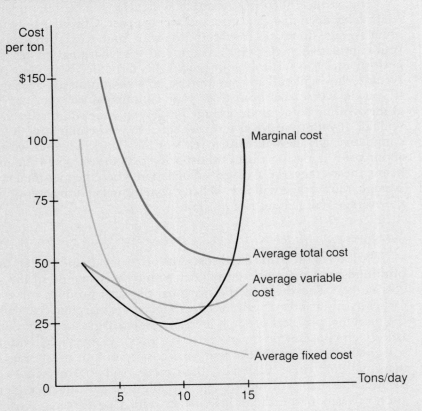

Average fixed cost drops as output expands. Average variable cost and average total cost drop, reach low points, and then rise; overall, they take on U shapes. When marginal cost is below average variable cost, average variable cost is falling. When marginal cost equals average variable cost, average variable cost is at its minimum value. When marginal cost is above average variable cost, average variable cost is increasing. The same relationship holds between marginal cost and average total cost.

curves grow closer and closer together because average fixed cost, which is the vertical difference between the two, becomes smaller.

The marginal cost curve has the same relation to the average total cost curve as to the average variable cost curve, and for the same reasons. When marginal cost is below average total cost, average total cost declines as output expands. The two curves intersect at 14 units of output. At higher levels of output, marginal cost is above average total cost, so average total cost increases as output expands. *Because of these relations, the marginal cost curve intersects both the average variable cost curve and the average total cost curve from below at the lowest point on each of these average cost curves.* Note that the minimum point on the average total cost curve occurs at a greater level of output than does the minimum point on the average variable cost curve because a falling average fixed cost continues to pull the average total cost curve down even after the average variable cost has begun rising.

Perhaps the following example will help you better understand the relation between marginal cost and average cost. Consider how your grade point average fluctuates from term to term. Your average grades determine your cumulative grade point average, and your marginal grades reflect your performance this term. If your grades this term are above your cumulative average, they will pull up your average, so your cumulative average will rise. If you do worse this term than your cumulative average, your marginal grades will be below your average grades, so your cumulative grade point will fall. If your grades this term are equal to your cumulative average, your cumulative average will neither rise nor fall. Thus, whether we are talking about your grades or a firm's short-run cost curves, when the marginal is below the average, the average will fall, and when the marginal is above the average, the average will rise. When the marginal and the average are equal, the average will neither rise nor fall.

Summary of Short-Run Cost Curves

The level of the firm's fixed costs, the price of variable inputs, and the law of diminishing marginal returns determine the shape of all the short-run cost curves. The shape of the marginal physical product curve discussed earlier in the chapter determines the shape of the marginal cost curve. When the marginal physical product increases, the marginal cost of output must fall (given constant prices of variable inputs). Conversely, as diminishing marginal returns set in, the marginal cost of output must rise. Thus, the marginal cost curve first falls, then rises. And the marginal cost curve dictates the shapes of the average variable cost and the average total cost curves. When marginal cost is less than average cost, average cost is falling; when marginal cost is above average cost, average cost is rising. *In short, the shape of short-run cost curves is determined by the increasing and diminishing marginal returns from the variable resource.*

COSTS IN THE LONG RUN

Thus far the analysis has focused on how costs vary as the rate of output expands in the short run for a plant of a given size. In the long run, however, all inputs that are under the firm's control can be varied, so there are no fixed costs. In the long run, the firm is free to select any input combination that appears appropriate, given the resource prices and the level of technology. The long run is best thought of as a planning horizon that is valid only for the firm that has not yet acted on its plans. Once the size of the plant has been selected and resources have been committed, the firm has some fixed costs and is once again back in the short run. Thus, there is a different short-run average total cost curve for each possible plant size. We turn now to the long-run cost curves.

Long-Run Average Cost Curves

Suppose that, because of the special nature of the technology, a company's plant can be one of only three possible sizes: small, medium, or large. Exhibit 9 presents this simple case. The short-run average total cost curves for the three plant sizes are SS', MM', and LL'. Which size plant should the firm build to minimize the average cost of production? The appropriate scale for the plant depends on how much the firm wants to produce. For example, if q is the desired production rate in the long run, the average cost per unit

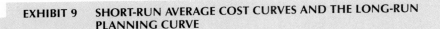

EXHIBIT 9   SHORT-RUN AVERAGE COST CURVES AND THE LONG-RUN PLANNING CURVE

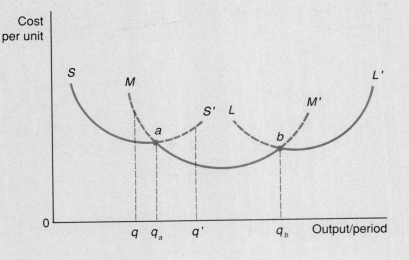

Curves SS', MM', and LL' show short-run average total costs for small, medium, and large plants, respectively. For output less than q_a, average cost is lowest when the plant is small. Between q_a and q_b, cost is lowest with a medium-size plant. If output exceeds q_b, the large plant is best. The long-run average cost curve is $SabL'$.

will be lowest with a small plant. If the desired output level is q', the medium plant size ensures the lowest average cost.

More generally, for any output less than q_a, the average cost of output is lowest when the plant is small. For output levels between q_a and q_b, the average cost is lowest when the plant is of medium size. And for output levels that exceed q_b, the average cost is lowest when the plant is large. Thus, the **long-run average cost curve** connects whichever of the points on the three short-run average cost curves is lowest for each output level. In Exhibit 9, the curve consists of the solid line segments connecting S, a, b, and L'.

Now assume that the number of possible plant sizes is large. Exhibit 10 presents a sample of possible short-run average total cost curves. The long-run average cost curve consists of the portions of the various short-run average cost curves that represent the lowest per-unit cost for each level of output. Each of the short-run cost curves is tangent to the long-run *planning curve*, or *envelope curve*. If we could draw enough cost curves, we would have a different plant size for each level of output. These points of tangency represent the least-cost way of producing each particular level of output, given the technology and resource prices. For example, the short-run average cost curve ATC_1 is tangent to the planning curve at point a, indicating that the least-cost way of producing output level q is with the plant size associated with ATC_1.

*A firm's **long-run average cost curve** indicates the lowest cost of production for each level of output when the firm's plant size is allowed to vary.*

EXHIBIT 10   FAMILY OF MANY SHORT-RUN COST CURVES FORMING A FIRM'S LONG-RUN PLANNING CURVE

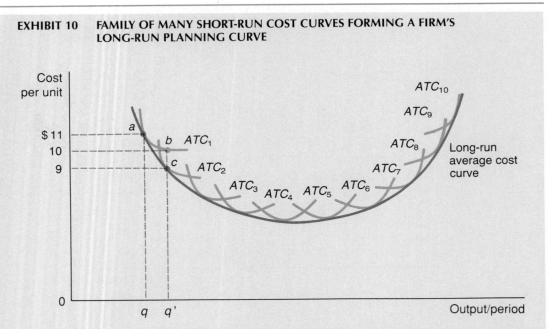

With many possible plant sizes, the long-run average cost curve is the envelope of portions of the short-run average cost curves. Each short-run curve is tangent to the long-run planning curve. Each point of tangency represents the least-cost way of producing a particular level of output.

No other size plant would produce output level q at as low a cost per unit. Note, however, that other output levels along ATC_1 have a lower average cost of production. In fact, for output level q' at point b, the average cost per unit is only $10 per unit, compared to an average cost per unit of $11 for producing q at point a. Point b depicts the lowest average cost along ATC_1. So although the point of tangency represents the least-cost way of producing a particular level of output, it does not represent a least-cost output level for a particular plant size.

If the firm decides to produce output level q', which size plant should it choose to build to minimize the average cost of production? Output level q' could be produced at point b, which represents the minimum average cost along ATC_1. However, the firm could achieve a lower average cost with a larger plant. Specifically, if the firm built a plant of the size associated with ATC_2, the average cost of producing q' would be minimized at point c. *Each point of tangency between a short-run average cost curve and the long-run planning curve represents the least-cost way of producing that particular level of output.*

Economies of Scale

Like short-run average total cost curves, the long-run average cost curve appears to be U-shaped. Recall that the shape of the short-run average total cost curve is determined primarily by the law of diminishing marginal returns. A different principle shapes the long-run cost curve. A firm experiences **economies of scale** when the long-run average cost falls as the firm expands plant size. Consider some sources of economies of scale. *A larger plant size often allows for larger, more specialized machines and greater specialization of labor.* For example, compare the household-size kitchen of a small restaurant with a McDonald's kitchen. At low levels of output, say fifteen meals a day, the smaller kitchen produces meals at a lower average cost than does McDonald's. But if the restaurant became popular and production increased beyond, say, one hundred meals per day, a kitchen on the scale of McDonald's would have the lower average cost. Thus, the long-run average cost curve for the restaurant would fall as plant size increased, reflecting economies of scale.

A firm experiences economies of scale when its long-run average cost falls as it expands plant size.

Diseconomies of Scale

Diseconomies of scale occur when the long-run average cost increases as the scale of operations increases.

Often another force, called **diseconomies of scale**, is eventually set in motion as the firm expands. As the amount and variety of resources employed increase, so does the management task of keeping track of all these inputs. As the work force grows, additional layers of management are needed to monitor production. In the thicket of bureaucracy that develops, communication may become garbled. The top executives have more difficulty keeping in touch with what is happening on the shop floor because information is distorted as it passes through the chain of command. Indeed, in very large organizations rumors become a primary source of information, thereby reducing the efficiency of the organization and increasing average cost.

Let's consider economies and diseconomies of scale in commercial shipping. One rule of naval architecture is that larger ships can go faster. Larger ships can also carry much more cargo. The increase in the cargo-carrying capacity of a ship is more than proportional to the increase in the cost of building and operating the ship. The economies of scale observed in ocean vessels are also found in trucks. For example, hiring a driver costs little more for a 50-foot truck than for a 25-foot truck. Beyond a certain size of ship or truck, however, diseconomies of scale dominate. Ocean-going vessels may become so large that few ports can handle them. Trucks may become so large that they cannot negotiate some roads. (Some trucking companies are able to take advantage of economies of scale by operating tandem trucks on highways and smaller trucks on urban streets.)

We assumed at the outset that in the long run the firm could vary all the inputs under its control. Some inputs, however, are not under the firm's control, and the inability to vary these inputs may be a source of diseconomies of scale, as you will see in the following case study, which describes both economies and diseconomies of scale.

CASE STUDY

At the Movies

Consider economies of scale at the movies. A movie theater with one screen needs someone to sell tickets, someone to operate the concession stand, someone to operate the projector, and someone to take tickets at the door. If the owners add another screen, they do not need to double the work force. The same staff can perform most of these tasks for both screens. Thus, the ticket seller becomes more productive because tickets are sold to both movies. Furthermore, construction costs per screen are reduced because only one lobby and one set of restrooms are required. This is why we see theater owners adding more and more screens at the same location; they are taking advantage of economies of scale.

Economies of scale clearly result from clustering screens together. But why stop at, say, twelve screens? Why not twenty or thirty, particularly in densely populated urban areas, where sufficient demand would warrant such a high level of output? One problem with expanding the number of screens is that scheduling becomes more difficult because the manager must schedule movies' starting and ending times so as to avoid having too many customers arrive and depart at once. Therefore, the average cost of production increases when the number of screens increases.

Another problem theater managers face is that the public roads leading to the theaters are a resource that they cannot control. The congestion around the theater grows with the number of screens at that location. Also, the supply of popular films may not be great enough at any one time to fill so many screens. Finally, time itself is a resource that the firm cannot easily control. Only certain hours are popular with moviegoers. Theater owners can cluster showings during these hours, but they cannot create additional "prime time." Thus theater owners' lack of control over such inputs as the size of public roads, the supply of films, and the hours in the day may contribute to diseconomies of scale.

It is possible for average cost to neither increase nor decrease with changes in firm size. If neither economies of scale nor diseconomies of scale are apparent in the production process, the firm experiences *constant average costs*. It could be that some economies and diseconomies of scale exist simultaneously but have offsetting effects.

Exhibit 11 presents a firm's long-run average cost curve, which is divided into segments reflecting economies of scale, constant average cost, and diseconomies of scale. The rate of production would have to reach point *A* for the firm to achieve the **minimum efficient scale**, which is the lowest rate of output at which the firm takes full advantage of economies of scale. From output level *A* to level *B*, average cost is constant. Beyond point *B*, diseconomies of scale increase average cost.

> The **minimum efficient scale** is the lowest rate of output at which the firm can take full advantage of economies of scale.

Economies and Diseconomies of Scale at the Firm Level

The discussion thus far has referred primarily to a particular plant—the local McDonald's or a nearby cinema—as opposed to the firm more gener-

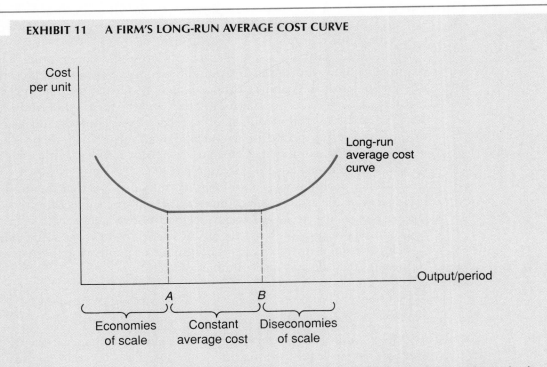

EXHIBIT 11   A FIRM'S LONG-RUN AVERAGE COST CURVE

Up to output level *A*, the long-run average cost curve has a negative slope; the firm is experiencing economies of scale. Point *A* is the minimum efficient scale—the lowest rate of output at which the firm takes full advantage of economies of scale. Between *A* and *B*, the average cost is constant. Beyond output level *B*, the long-run average cost curve slopes upward, reflecting diseconomies of scale.

ally. It is useful, however, to distinguish between economies and diseconomies of scale at the *plant level*—that is, at a particular location—and at the *firm level*. We examine economies and diseconomies of scale at the firm level in the following case study.

CASE STUDY

Burgers by the Billions

McDonald's experiences economies of scale at the plant level because of its specialization of labor and machines, but the company also benefits from economies of scale at the firm level. Operating many separate locations allows the company to standardize menus and operating procedures, to centralize its management training program at Hamburger University, and to spread the cost of its advertising over thousands of individual "plants."

The menu at a local fast-food outlet is the result of intense planning. Every stage of food-preparation is timed and evaluated. Each of the major chains calculates how long it takes employees to do everything from flipping burgers to putting pickles on buns. Before any new product is introduced, labor requirements are monitored closely. For example, before Burger King decided to switch from one cola to another, the company spent more than two years on market research. Reportedly, undercover researchers were sent to competitors' sites to track the time required to inform customers who had asked for Coke that only Pepsi was available.

Some diseconomies also arise in such large-scale operations. The fact that the menu must be uniform around the country means that if customers in some parts of the country do not like a product, it does not get on the menu regardless of its popularity in other areas. McDonald's McRib sandwich never quite caught on in some parts of the country and had to be dropped. Wendy's plans for a gourmet hamburger had to be scrapped because most customers in two states were not familiar with such ingredients as alfalfa sprouts and guacamole.

Another problem with a uniform national menu is that the ingredients must be available around the country and cannot be subject to droughts or sharp swings in price. One chain decided not to add bacon strips as an option on its burgers because the price of pork bellies was so unstable.

Thus, when a firm expands the number of plants, it experiences both economies of scale and diseconomies of scale.

Source: John Koten, "Fast-Food Firms' New Items Undergo Exhaustive Testing," *Wall Street Journal*, 5 January 1984.

Many studies have attempted to determine the shape of the long-run average cost curve for firms in different industries by examining the relation between cost and inputs over time. One finding occurs with enough consistency to deserve mention here. *The long-run average cost curve in many industries appears to be L-shaped, not U-shaped.* There is little evidence of diseconomies of scale. We should note, however, that this finding may be due to the limited range of the data observed. Perhaps researchers found few firms operating in the diseconomies-of-scale range because most firms had determined that they would be less competitive if their costs on average were higher than those of smaller firms. Put another way, it may be that the long-run average cost curve in fact turns upward for firms in most industries, but because firms choose not to become that large, we do not observe empirical evidence of diseconomies of scale.

CONCLUSION

Despite what may appear to be a tangle of short-run and long-run cost curves, *only two relations between resources and outputs underlie all the curves. In the short run, it is increasing and diminishing returns from the variable resource. In the long run, it is economies and diseconomies of scale.* If you understand the sources of these two phenomena, you have mastered the central ideas of this chapter.

In previous chapters we developed a theory of consumer behavior based on utility maximization. We then showed how the downward-sloping demand curve was derived from our theory of consumer choice. In this chapter, by considering the relation between production and cost, we have developed the foundations of the theory of firm behavior. In the appendix we present an alternative way of determining a firm's most efficient combination of resources. Our examination of the relation between resource use and the quantity of output produced in both the short run and the long run forms the basis for deriving an upward-sloping supply curve in the next chapter.

Summary

1. Explicit costs are costs that take the form of payments for resources not owned by the firm. Implicit costs are the opportunity costs of using resources owned by the firm or provided by the firm's owners. Economic profit equals revenue minus both explicit and implicit costs. A firm is said to be earning a normal profit if revenue just covers all implicit and explicit costs.

2. Resources such as labor are called variable resources because they can be easily varied to increase or decrease the output level. Other resources, such as capital, are called fixed resources because more time is required to change the amount used. In the short run, at least one resource is fixed. In the long run, all resources are variable.

3. Short-run increases in the variable resource usually produce increasing marginal returns initially because the additional variable inputs can use the fixed resources more efficiently, taking advantage of increased specialization of the variable resource. The law of diminishing marginal returns indicates that a point is eventually reached where additional units of the variable resource, combined with the fixed resources, yield a smaller and smaller marginal product.

4. The law of diminishing marginal returns is the most important feature of firm production in the short run and is the reason why the marginal cost curve eventually slopes upward as output expands. The law of diminishing marginal returns also explains the shape of the total

variable and total cost curves, as well as the U shapes of the average variable and average total cost curves.

5. In the long run, all inputs under the firm's control are variable, so there are no fixed costs. The firm's long-run average cost curve is an envelope formed by a series of short-run average total cost curves. The long run is best thought of as a planning horizon. The firm selects the most efficient size for the desired level of output. Once the size of the firm has been selected and resources have been committed, some resources become fixed, so the firm is back in the short run. Thus the firm plans based on a long-run perspective but produces in the short run.

6. The long-run average cost curve, like the short-run average total cost curve, is U-shaped. As output expands, average costs at first decline because of economies of scale—a larger plant size allows for more specialized machinery and a more extensive division of labor. Eventually, average costs stop falling. Average costs may be constant over some range. As output expands still further, the plant may encounter diseconomies of scale as the cost of coordinating resources grows. But evidence of diseconomies of scale has been hard to find in empirical research.

Questions and Problems

1. (Explicit Versus Implicit Costs) Old MacDonald is currently raising corn on his 100-acre farm. He can make an accounting profit of $100 per acre. However, if he raised soybeans, he could make $200 per acre. Is the farmer currently earning an economic profit? Why or why not?

2. (Opportunity Costs) Corporate executives often take jobs with the government for much smaller salaries. What are their opportunity costs? Does your answer depend on whether you take a long-run or a short-run view?

3. (Normal Profits) Why is it reasonable to think of normal profits as a type of cost to the firm?

4. (Diminishing Returns) All commercial jets have a pilot and a copilot. How would you interpret the marginal product of the copilot? Why not have a third or fourth pilot for the same flight?

5. (Diminishing Returns) Suppose that you have some farmland. You must decide how many times during the year you will grow your crops. Also, you must decide how to space each plant (or seedling). Will diminishing returns be a factor in your decision making? Relate your answer to Exhibit 3 in this chapter.

6. (Marginal Cost) Explain why the marginal cost curve must intersect the average total cost and the average variable cost curves at their minimum points.

7. (Average Total Cost and Average Variable Cost) Why must average total cost and average variable cost approach each other as output increases? Will this be true for all cost curves?

8. (Short-Run Costs) Which of the following would shift in the short-run marginal cost curve? In which direction might marginal cost shift?
   a. An increase in wage rates
   b. A decrease in property taxes
   c. A rise in the purchase price of new capital
   d. A rise in oil prices (or energy prices)
   e. A sudden change in technology

9. (Long-Run Average Costs) What factors would shift the long-run average cost curve? Would these changes also affect the short-run average cost curves? Why or why not?

10. (Long Run Versus Short Run) What determines the length of the short run? Will this period of time be different for different types of industries?

11. (Marginal Product and Costs) Let L equal units of labor, Q equal units of output, and MPP equal the marginal physical product of labor.
    a. Fill in the table.

L	Q	MPP	TVC	TC	MC	ATC
0	0	—	$ 0	$12	—	
1	6		3	15		
2	15		6			
3	21		9			
4	24		12			
5	26		15			
6	27		18			

    b. At what level of labor do the marginal returns of labor diminish?
    c. What is the implication for marginal cost of the answer to the preceding question?
    d. What is the average variable cost when $Q = 24$?
    e. What is the level of fixed cost?
    f. What is the price of a unit of labor?

12. (Production and Cost) Use the following table to answer the questions below. C is units of capital, L is units of labor, and Q is units of output.

C	L	Q	
5	0	0	Price of labor = $3
5	2	10	$TFC = $20
5	4	16	
5	6	18	
5	8	19	

    a. What is the price of capital?
    b. What is the total cost of producing 10 units of Q?
    c. What is the average cost of producing 16 units of Q?
    d. What is the marginal cost of producing the nineteenth unit of Q?

13. (Short- and Long-Run Costs) Suppose that a firm has only three possible scales of production, with the middle scale of production achieving the lowest average cost of any of the three scales. Let the three short-run average total cost curves be U-shaped and intersect each other as shown below.

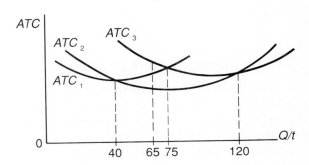

    a. Which scale of production is best when $Q = 65$?
    b. Which scale of production is best when $Q = 75$?
    c. Indicate on the diagram the long-run average cost curve.

APPENDIX
A Closer Look at Production and Costs

In this appendix we develop a model for determining how a profit-maximizing firm will combine resources to produce particular amounts of output. The amount of goods and services that can be produced with a given amount of resources depends on the existing *state of technology*, which is the prevailing knowledge of how resources can be combined. We will therefore begin by considering the technological possibilities available to the firm.

The Production Function and Efficiency

The ways resources can be combined to produce output are summarized by a firm's production function. The **production function** identifies the maximum quantities of a particular good or service that can be produced per time period with various combinations of resources, for a given level of technology. The production function can be presented as an equation, as a graph, or as a table.

The production function summarized in **Exhibit 12** reflects, for a hypothetical firm,

the output resulting from particular combinations of capital and labor. This firm uses only two resources: capital and labor. The amount of capital used is listed in the left-hand column of the table, and the amount of labor employed is listed across the top. For example, if 1 unit of capital is combined with 7 units of labor, the firm can produce 350 units of output per period.

We assume that the firm is aware of the production function, that the firm produces the maximum possible output given the combination of resources employed, and that the same output could not be produced with fewer resources. Since we assume that the production function combines resources efficiently, 350 units is the most that can be produced with that combination of resources. Thus, we say that production is **technologically efficient**.

The assumption that firms are efficient is linked to our earlier assumption that firms maximize profit. If a firm failed to produce efficiently, the same amount of output could be produced using fewer resources. If fewer resources were used, total cost would be lower. Since a firm's profit equals total revenue minus total cost, its profit would be lower if it failed to produce efficiently. *So the assumption of profit maximization implies that firms produce efficiently.*

EXHIBIT 12
A FIRM'S PRODUCTION FUNCTION USING LABOR AND CAPITAL: PRODUCTION PER PERIOD

Units of Capital Employed per Period	Units of Labor Employed per Period						
	1	2	3	4	5	6	7
1	100	150	210	260	300	330	350
2	150	200	260	310	350	375	395
3	210	255	320	370	405	430	450
4	260	310	370	410	445	475	500
5	300	350	405	445	480	510	535
6	330	380	435	475	510	535	555
7	350	390	450	495	530	555	570

Let's return now to the tabular presentation of the production function. We can examine the effects of adding additional labor to an existing amount of capital by starting with some level of capital use and reading across the table. For example, when 1 unit of capital and 1 unit of labor are employed, the firm produces 100 units of output per year. If the amount of labor is increased by 1 unit, with the amount of capital employed held constant, output increases to 150 units, so the marginal physical product of labor is 50 units. If the amount of labor employed increases from 2 to 3 units, other things constant, output goes to 210 units, yielding a marginal physical product of 60 units. By reading across the table at a specific level of capital use, you will discover that the marginal physical product of labor first rises, showing increasing marginal returns from the variable resource (labor), and then decreases, showing diminishing marginal returns. Similarly, by holding the amount of labor employed constant and following a column down, you will find that the marginal physical product of capital also reflects first increasing marginal returns, then diminishing marginal returns.

Isoquants

The information provided in Exhibit 12 can be presented more clearly in graphical form. In Exhibit 13, the quantity of labor employed is measured along the horizontal axis, and the quantity of capital is measured along the vertical axis. Notice from the tabular presentation of the production function in Exhibit 12 that different combinations of resources may yield the same level of output. For example, several combinations of labor and capital yield 350 units of output. The combinations that yield 350 units of output are presented in Exhibit 13 as points *a*, *b*, *c*, and *d*. These points can be connected to form an isoquant, Q_1, which shows all the possible combinations of the two resources that produce 350 units of output. Likewise, Q_2 shows

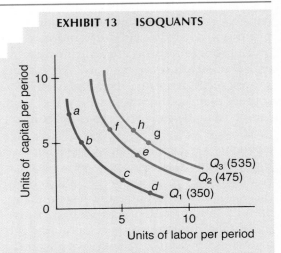

EXHIBIT 13   ISOQUANTS

Isoquant Q_1 shows all technically efficient combinations of labor and capital that can be used to produce 350 units of output. Isoquant Q_2 is drawn for 475 units, and Q_3 for 535 units. Each isoquant has a negative slope and is convex to the origin.

combinations of inputs that yield 475 units of output, and Q_3 shows combinations that yield 535 units of output. (The colors of the isoquants match those of the corresponding entries in the production function table in Exhibit 12.)

An **isoquant** is a curve that shows all the technologically efficient combinations of two resources, such as labor and capital, that produce a certain amount of output. Along a particular isoquant, the amount of output produced remains the same, but the combinations of resources vary.

To produce a particular level of output, the firm can use resource combinations ranging from much capital and little labor to much labor and little capital. For example, a paving contractor can put in a new driveway with ten workers using shovels and hand rollers; the same job can also be done with only two workers, a road grader, and a paving machine. A Saturday afternoon charity car wash to raise money to send the school band to Disney World is labor-intensive, involving perhaps a dozen workers per car. In contrast, a professional car wash is fully automated, requiring only one worker to turn on the machine and collect the money. An isoquant shows such alternative combinations of resources that produce the same level of output. Let's consider some properties of isoquants.

Isoquants Farther from the Origin Represent Higher Output Levels Although we have included only three isoquants in Exhibit 13, there is a different isoquant for every quantity of output depicted in Exhibit 12. Indeed, there is an isoquant for every output level the firm could possibly produce, with isoquants farther from the origin indicating higher levels of output.

Isoquants Slope Down to the Right Isoquants slope down to the right as long as both resources have a positive marginal physical product—that is, as long as both resources contribute to production. If we increase the quantity of labor employed while holding the amount of capital constant, output increases. Therefore, if labor is increased, output can be held constant only if the amount of capital employed is reduced. Hence, along a given isoquant, the quantity of labor employed is inversely related to the quantity of capital employed, so isoquants have negative slopes.

Isoquants Do Not Intersect Since each isoquant refers to a specific level of output, no two isoquants intersect, for such an intersection would indicate that the same combination of resources could with equal efficiency produce two different amounts of output.

Isoquants Are Usually Convex to the Origin Finally, isoquants are usually convex to the origin, meaning that the slope of the isoquant gets flatter down along the curve. To understand why, keep in mind that the slope of the isoquant measures the ability of additional units of one resource—in this case, labor—to

substitute in production for another—in this case, capital.

The slope of the isoquant between any two points is the **marginal rate of technical substitution, MRTS**, between two resources. The $MRTS_{lc}$ indicates the rate at which labor can be substituted for capital without affecting output. When much capital and little labor are used, the marginal productivity of labor is relatively great and the marginal productivity of capital is relatively small, so one unit of labor will substitute for a relatively large amount of capital. For example, in moving from point a to b along isoquant Q_1 in Exhibit 13, we substitute 1 unit of labor for 2 units of capital, so the $MRTS_{lc}$ between points a and b equals 2. But as more units of labor and fewer units of capital are employed, the marginal product of labor declines and the marginal product of capital increases, so it takes more labor to make up for a reduction in capital. For example, in moving from point c to d in Exhibit 13, we substitute 2 units of labor for 1 unit of capital; hence, the $MRTS_{lc}$ between points c and d equals 1/2.

The extent to which one input can be substituted for another, as measured by the marginal rate of technical substitution, is directly linked to the marginal productivity of each input. For example, between points a and b, 1 unit of labor replaces 2 units of capital, yet output remains constant. So labor's marginal physical product, MPP_l—that is, the additional output resulting from an additional unit of labor—must be twice as large as capital's marginal physical product, MPP_c. In fact, all along the isoquant, the marginal rate of technical substitution of labor for capital equals the marginal physical product of labor divided by the marginal physical product of capital, which also equals the absolute value of the slope of the isoquant. Thus we can say that

$$\textbf{Slope of isoquant} = MRTS_{lc} = -\frac{MPP_l}{MPP_c}$$

For example, between points *a* and *b* the slope equals – 2, as does the marginal rate of substitution of labor for capital and the ratio of marginal productivities.

If labor and capital were perfect substitutes in production, the rate at which labor substituted for capital would remain fixed along the isoquant, so the isoquant would be a downward-sloping straight line. Since most resources are *not* perfect substitutes, however, the rate at which one substitutes for another changes along an isoquant. As we move down along an isoquant, more labor is required to offset a decline in capital, so the slope of the isoquant gets flatter, yielding an isoquant that is convex to the origin.

Let's summarize the properties of isoquants.

1. Isoquants farther from the origin represent greater levels of output.

2. Isoquants slope downward.

3. Isoquants never intersect.

4. Isoquants tend to be bowed toward the origin.

Isocost Lines

Isoquants graphically illustrate a firm's production function for all quantities of output the firm could possibly produce. Given these isoquants, how much should the firm produce? More specifically, what is the firm's profit-maximizing level of output? The answer depends on the cost of resources and the amount of money the firm plans to spend.

Suppose a unit of labor costs the firm $15,000 per year, and the rental price for each unit of capital is $25,000 per year. The total cost (*TC*) of production is

$$TC = (W \times L) + (R \times C)$$
$$= \$15,000L + \$25,000C$$

where *W* is the wage rate, *L* is the quantity of labor employed, *R* is the rental price of cap-

ital, and *C* is the quantity of capital employed. An **isocost line** identifies all combinations of capital and labor the firm can purchase for a given total cost. In Exhibit 14, for example, the line *TC* = $150,000 identifies all combinations of labor and capital that cost a firm a total of $150,000. If the firm spends the entire $150,000 on capital, it can rent 6 units per year; if the firm spends the money on labor, it can hire 10 workers per year; or the firm can employ any combination on the isocost line.

The slope of the isocost line equals minus the price of labor divided by the price of capital, or – *W/R*, which indicates the relative prices of the inputs. In our example,

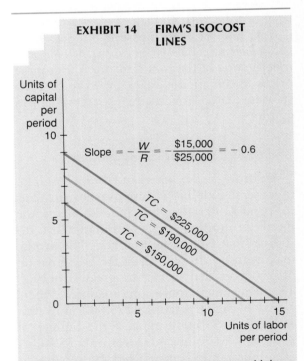

EXHIBIT 14   FIRM'S ISOCOST LINES

Each isocost line shows combinations of labor and capital that can be purchased for a fixed amount of total cost. The slope of each is equal to minus the wage rate divided by the rental rate of capital. Higher levels of cost are represented by isocost lines farther from the origin.

Slope of isocost line $= -\dfrac{W}{R}$

$$= -\dfrac{\$15{,}000}{\$25{,}000}$$

$$= -0.6$$

The wage rate of labor is 0.6 of the rental rate of capital, so hiring 1 more unit of labor, without incurring any additional cost, implies that the firm must rent 0.6 of a unit less of capital.

A firm is not confined to a particular isocost line. A firm can expand production, financing additional resources through the sale of the additional output. Thus, a firm's total cost is not constant but varies with the amount it chooses to produce. This is why in Exhibit 14 we include three isocost lines, not just one, each corresponding to a different level of total cost. In fact, there is a different isocost line for every possible budget. *These isocost lines are parallel because they reflect the same relative prices of resources to the firm.* Resource prices in this model are assumed to be constant no matter how many resources the firm employs.

The Choice of Input Combinations

We bring the isoquants and the isocost lines together in Exhibit 15. Suppose the firm plans to spend $190,000 to purchase resources; the firm can employ any combination of resources that falls along that line. The profit-maximizing firm will select the combination of resources that yields the greatest output. The firm could choose combination *a*, where 7 units of capital totaling $175,000 and 1 unit of labor at $15,000 exhaust the budget of $190,000. At point *a*, however, only 350 units of output would be produced. By moving to point *e*, the firm produces 475 units of output for the same total cost as at point *a*. At point *e*, the firm employs 4 units of capital, for a total of $100,000, and 6 units of labor, for a total of $90,000, so the total budget of $190,000 is exhausted.

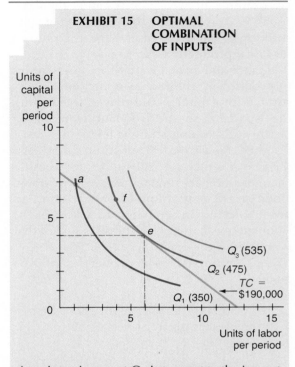

EXHIBIT 15   OPTIMAL COMBINATION OF INPUTS

At point *e*, isoquant Q_2 is tangent to the isocost line. The optimal combination of inputs is 6 units of labor and 4 units of capital. The maximum output that can be produced for $190,000 is 475 units. Alternatively, point *e* determines the minimum-cost way of producing 475 units of output.

This 475 units is the maximum output that can be produced for a total cost of $190,000. Other isoquants, such as Q_3, lie completely above the isocost line and are thus unattainable at the given total cost. *The firm maximizes output (and profit) for a given total cost by choosing that combination of resources where the isocost line is tangent to the highest attainable isoquant.*

We have shown that the combination at *e* yields the maximum output that can be produced for $190,000. We could approach the problem differently. Suppose the firm has decided to produce 475 units of output and wants to minimize its total cost. The firm could select point *f*, where 6 units of capital are combined with 4 units of labor. This combination, however, would cost $210,000 at prevailing prices. Since the profit-maximizing firm wants to produce its chosen output at the minimum cost, it tries to find the isocost line closest to the origin that still touches the isoquant. Only at a point of tangency does a movement in either direction along an isoquant shift the firm away from the origin and to a higher cost level. *So the point of tangency between the isocost line and the isoquant shows both the maximum output attainable for a given cost and the minimum cost required to produce that output.*

Consider what is going on at the point of tangency. At point *e* in Exhibit 15, the isoquant and the isocost line have the same slope. As mentioned already, the slope of an isoquant equals the marginal rate of technical substitution between labor and capital, $MRTS_{lc}$, and the slope of the isocost line equals the ratio of the input prices. So when a firm produces output in the least costly way, the marginal rate of technical substitution must equal the ratio of the resource prices, or

$$MRTS_{lc} = -\frac{W}{R} = -\frac{\$15,000}{\$25,000} = -0.6$$

This equality suggests that the firm will adjust its resource use so that the rate at which one input can be substituted for another in production — that is, the marginal rate of technical substitution — will equal the rate at which one resource can be traded for another in resource markets, which is W/R. If this equality does not hold, it means that the firm, by adjusting its input mix, could produce the same output for a lower cost or produce more output for the same cost.

Recall that the marginal rate of technical substitution equals the ratio of the marginal physical products of the resources. Therefore, we can rewrite the equilibrium condition as

$$-\frac{MPP_l}{MPP_c} = -\frac{W}{R}$$

This equality can be rearranged to yield

$$\frac{MPP_l}{W} = \frac{MPP_c}{R}$$

This last expression says that the firm should employ resources so that the marginal physical product per dollar's worth of each resource is equal. This condition holds when the isoquant is tangent to the isocost line. The least-cost combination requires that the last dollar spent on labor yield the same marginal product as the last dollar spent on capital.

The Expansion Path

Imagine an isoquant representing each possible level of output. Given the cost of resources, we could then draw isocost lines to determine the optimal combination of resources for producing each level of output. The points of tangency in Exhibit 16 show the least costly input combinations for producing several output levels. For example, output level Q_2 can be produced most cheaply using C units of capital and L units of labor. The line formed by connecting these tangency points is the firm's **expansion path**. If the resources are capital and labor, we often refer to this path as the long-run expansion path. The expansion path need not be a straight line, though it will generally slope upward, implying that firms will expand the use of both resources in the long run as output increases. Note that we have assumed that the prices of inputs remain constant as the firm varies output along the expansion path, so the isocost lines are parallel — that is, they have the same slope.

The expansion path is closely linked to the firm's long-run average cost curve. The expansion path indicates the lowest long-run total cost for each level of output. For example, the firm can produce output level Q_2 for TC_2, output level Q_3 for TC_3, and so on. Similarly, the firm's long-run average cost

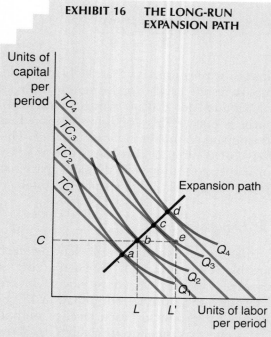

EXHIBIT 16   THE LONG-RUN EXPANSION PATH

The points of tangency between isoquants and isocost lines each show the least expensive way of producing a particular level of output. Connecting these tangency points gives the firm's expansion path.

produce Q_3 would shift from point *e* to point *c*, thereby minimizing the total cost of producing Q_3.

You should note one final point. If the relative prices of resources change, the least-cost combination of those resources will also change, so the firm's expansion path will change. For example, if the price of labor doubles, capital becomes cheaper relative to labor. The efficient production of any given level of output will therefore call for less labor and more capital. With the cost of labor higher, the firm's total cost for each level of output rises; this increase is reflected by an upward shift in the average total cost curve.

Summary

A firm's production function specifies the relation between resource use and output, given prevailing technology. An isoquant is a curve that illustrates the possible combinations of resources that will produce a particular level of output. An isocost line presents the combinations of resources the firm can employ, given resource prices and the amount of money the firm plans to spend.

For a given budget— that is, for a given isocost line—the firm maximizes output by finding the isoquant that just touches, or is tangent to, the isocost line. Alternatively, for a given level of output—that is, for a given isoquant—the firm minimizes its total cost by choosing the isocost line that just touches, or is tangent to, the isoquant. The least-cost combination of resources will depend on the relative cost of resources. So whether the firm's goal is to minimize cost for a given level of output or to maximize output for a given level of cost, the profit-maximizing equilibrium is found where an isocost line is tangent to an isoquant—either the lowest attainable isocost line or the highest attainable isoquant. In equilibrium, the last dollar spent on each resource yields the same marginal physical product.

curve conveys, at each level of output, the total cost divided by the level of output. The firm's expansion path and the firm's long-run average cost curve represent alternative ways of portraying costs in the long run, given resource prices and technology.

We can use Exhibit 16 to distinguish between short-run adjustments in output and long-run adjustments. Let's begin with the firm producing Q_2 at point *b*, which requires *C* units of capital and *L* units of labor. Now suppose that in the short run the firm wants to expand output to Q_3. Since capital is fixed in the short run, the only way to expand output to Q_3 is by expanding the quantity of labor employed to L', which requires moving to point *e* in Exhibit 16. In the long run, capital usage is variable, and the firm that wished to

1. (Choice of Input Combinations) Suppose that a firm's cost of labor is $10 per unit and its cost of capital is $40 per unit.
   a. Construct an isocost line such that total cost is constant at $200.
   b. If this firm is producing efficiently, what is the marginal rate of technical substitution between labor and capital?
   c. Prove your answer to part b using isocost and isoquant curves.
   d. Explain how the output level associated with each isoquant can be used to determine whether the firm is facing economies of scale, diseconomies of scale, or constant average costs. (Assume a straight line expansion path.)

PART FIVE

Market Structure, Pricing, and Government Regulation

C H A P T E R   2 1

Perfect Competition

In the previous chapter we examined the cost curves of individual firms in both the short run and the long run. We discussed how a firm can minimize the total cost of producing a given level of output. In this chapter we will analyze the relation between a firm's cost curves and its supply curve. As we will see, this relation depends on the firm's economic environment.

We have not yet confronted two questions. First, how much will a firm produce? Second, what price will the firm charge? A firm will produce the amount that maximizes profit, but how much is that? In this chapter we find that, given a firm's cost curves, the amount it produces and the price it charges will depend on the demand for the product. We bring together supply and demand to determine the profit-maximizing level of price and output. In the next few chapters we will examine how firms respond to their economic environments in deciding what to produce, in what quantities, and at what price. Topics discussed in this chapter include

- Market structure

- Price takers

- Marginal revenue

- Golden rule of profit maximization

- Loss minimization

- The firm's short-run supply curve

- Industry's long-run supply curve

- Competition and efficiency

- Producer surplus

AN INTRODUCTION TO PERFECT COMPETITION

Market structure describes the important features of a market, such as the number of firms, type of product, ease of entry, and forms of competition.

The decisions a firm makes depend on the structure of the market in which the firm operates. **Market structure** describes the important features of the market, such as the number of firms (are there many or few?), the type of product (do all firms in the market produce identical products or are there differences?), the ease or difficulty of entering the market (is it easy to break into the industry or is market entry blocked by patents or high capital costs?), and the forms of competition among firms (do firms compete only through prices or through advertising and product differentiation as well?). The various features will become clearer as we examine each type of market structure in the next few chapters.

A word about terminology: an industry consists of all firms that supply output to a particular market. The terms "industry" and "market" are used interchangeably throughout the chapter.

Perfectly Competitive Market Structure

Perfect competition is the market structure involving large numbers of fully informed buyers and sellers of a homogeneous product. There are no obstacles to entry or exit of firms.

We begin with **perfect competition**, in some ways the most basic of market structures. *Perfectly competitive* markets are characterized by the following features: (1) there are a large number of buyers and sellers, each of whom buys or sells only a tiny fraction of the total amount exchanged in the market; (2) firms produce a standardized, or *homogeneous*, good (that is, the product of one firm is identical to those of others in the market); (3) all participants in the market are fully informed about the price and availability of all resources, outputs, and production processes; and (4) firms and resources are freely mobile, with no obstacles, such as patents or licenses, to prevent new firms from entering or existing firms from leaving the industry. Given these market characteristics, we can also say that no individual firm will devote resources to product improvement because, with full and perfect information, competitors could immediately copy any improvement. Nor will an individual firm advertise its product because, in the eyes of consumers, one firm's product is identical to those offered by other firms in the market.

A price taker is any firm whose actions have no effect on the market price.

If all these conditions are present in a market, firms in that market are said to be **price takers**. That is, individual firms have no control over the price. Price is determined by market supply and demand. A perfectly competitive firm's capacity is so small relative to the size of the market that the firm's rate of production has no effect on the market supply or the market price. Recall that market supply is determined by summing the individual firms' supply curves. Once the market price has been determined, individual firms can supply all they want at that price. Thus *firms in perfectly competitive markets, as price takers, must offer their product for sale at whatever price is established by the market.*

Some markets, such as the securities markets and world commodity markets, closely approximate perfect competition, but perfect competition is an abstraction that is not usually observed in the real world. It is, however, an important benchmark for evaluating the efficiency of markets.

Demand Under Perfect Competition

Exhibit 1 presents the relation between the market supply and demand curves in panel (b) and the demand curve for the output of a perfectly competitive firm in panel (a). The market price of $5 per unit is determined in panel (b) by the intersection of the market demand curve, D, and the market supply curve, S. Once the price has been established in the market, any firm can sell all it wants at that market price. The demand curve confronted by an individual firm is therefore a horizontal line drawn at the market price. In our example, a firm's demand curve, identified as d in panel (a), is drawn at the market price of $5 per unit. This perfectly elastic demand curve indicates that the firm can sell all it wants at the market price.

As we have said, each firm is a price taker because its output is so small

---

EXHIBIT 1   THE FIRM'S DEMAND CURVE AND MARKET EQUILIBRIUM IN PERFECT COMPETITION

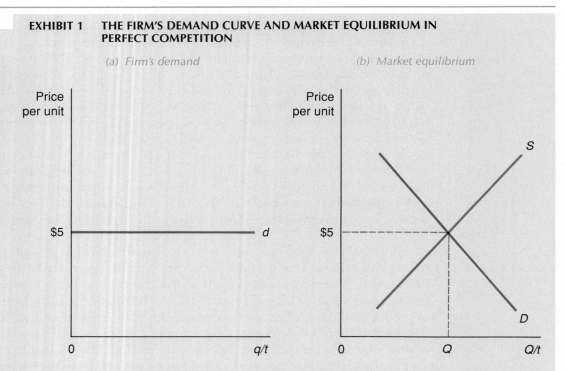

In panel (b), the market price of $5 is determined by the intersection of the market demand and supply curves. The individual perfectly competitive firm can sell any amount at that price. The demand curve facing the competitive firm is horizontal at the market price, as shown by demand curve d in panel (a).

relative to market supply that it has no impact on the market price. Also, because all firms are producing identical goods, no firm can charge more than the market price. If a firm charged $5.50 per unit, customers in this market would simply turn to other suppliers. Any firm is free to charge less than the market price, but why lower the price when any firm can already sell all it wants at the market price?

It has been said, "In perfect competition there is no competition." Ironically, two neighboring corn farmers in perfect competition are not really competing in the sense of being rivals. The amount that one farmer grows will have no effect on the price the other receives per bushel. They both are free to sell as much corn as they choose at the price determined in that market.

SHORT-RUN PROFIT MAXIMIZATION

The assumption here and throughout most of this text is that the firm's objective is to maximize economic profit. The firm's economic profit is equal to its total revenue minus its total cost, where total cost includes both explicit and implicit costs. Implicit cost, you will recall, is the opportunity cost of resources owned and used by the firm and includes a normal profit; economic profit is any profit above normal profit.

The question is, how do firms maximize profit? As we have shown, the perfectly competitive firm has no control over price. What does it control? The firm controls its rate of output. The question then becomes, what rate of output will maximize profit?

Total Revenue Minus Total Cost

The firm maximizes profit by producing the rate of output that maximizes total revenue minus total cost. Columns (3) and (4) in Exhibit 2 list the firm's total revenue and total cost for each rate of output. Remember that total cost already includes a normal profit.

Although Exhibit 2 does not distinguish between total fixed cost and total variable cost, total fixed cost must equal $15, since this is the total cost when output is zero. The fact that the firm incurs a fixed cost indicates that at least one resource must be fixed, so the firm is operating in the short run.

The firm's total revenue per period equals its rate of output multiplied by the market price. The total revenue column for a perfectly competitive firm is simply the price per unit, which is $5 in this example, times the rate of output. Total revenue in column (3) minus total cost in column (4) yields the economic profit per period, which is presented in column (7). As you can see, at very low and very high rates of output, total cost exceeds total revenue, so economic profit is negative. Between 7 units and 14 units of output, total revenue exceeds total cost, so economic profit is positive. Economic profit is maximized (at $12) when output is 12 units per period.

These results are presented graphically in panel (a) of Exhibit 3, which

EXHIBIT 2

SHORT-RUN COSTS AND REVENUES FOR A PERFECTLY COMPETITIVE FIRM

Quantity of Output (Q) (1)	Marginal Revenue (Price) (P) (2)	Total Revenue (TR) (3) = (1) × (2)	Total Cost (TC) (4)	Marginal Cost (MC) (5)	Average Total Cost (ATC) (6) = (4) ÷ (1)	Economic Profit or Loss (7) = (3) – (4)
0	—	$ 0	$15.00	—	∞	– $15.00
1	$5	5	19.75	$ 4.75	$19.75	– 14.75
2	5	10	23.50	3.75	11.75	– 13.50
3	5	15	26.50	3.00	8.83	– 11.50
4	5	20	29.00	2.50	7.25	– 9.00
5	5	25	31.00	2.00	6.20	– 6.00
6	5	30	32.50	1.50	5.42	– 2.50
7	5	35	33.75	1.25	4.82	1.25
8	5	40	35.25	1.50	4.41	4.75
9	5	45	37.25	2.00	4.14	7.75
10	5	50	40.00	2.75	4.00	10.00
11	5	55	43.25	3.25	3.93	11.75
12	**5**	**60**	**48.00**	**4.75**	**4.00**	**12.00**
13	5	65	54.50	6.50	4.19	10.50
14	5	70	64.00	9.50	4.57	6.00
15	5	75	77.50	13.50	5.17	– 2.50
16	5	80	96.00	18.50	6.00	– 16.00

shows the total cost and total revenue curves. As output per period increases by 1 unit, total revenue increases by $5. Therefore the total revenue curve is a straight line emanating from the origin, with a slope of 5. The short-run total cost curve was discussed in the previous chapter. Its backward S shape reflects first increasing marginal returns, then diminishing marginal returns from changes in the variable resource. Total cost therefore increases, first at a decreasing rate and then at an increasing rate.

At rates of output less than 7 units or greater than 14 units, total cost exceeds total revenue, resulting in an economic loss measured by the vertical distance between the two curves. Total revenue exceeds total cost between output rates of 7 units and 14 units; at these outputs the firm makes a profit. *Profit is maximized at the level of output where total revenue exceeds total cost by the greatest amount.* We already know that this distance is greatest when 12 units are produced.

Marginal Cost Equals Marginal Revenue in Equilibrium

Marginal revenue is the change in total revenue resulting from a one-unit change in sales.

Comparing total cost and total revenue is one way to find the profit-maximizing rate of output. A second and more revealing way is to use marginal revenue and marginal cost. Column (2) of Exhibit 2 presents the firm's marginal revenue. **Marginal revenue** is the change in total revenue

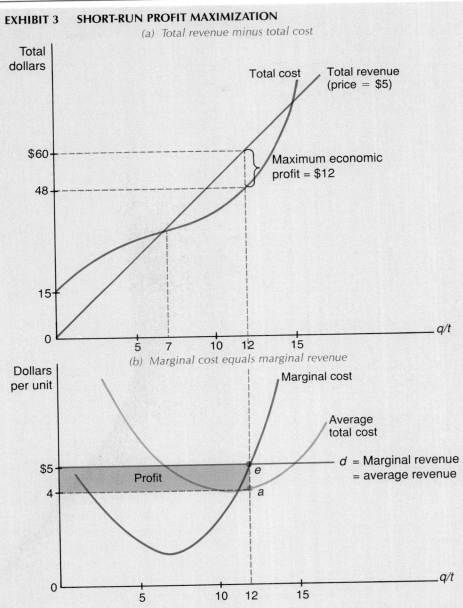

EXHIBIT 3   SHORT-RUN PROFIT MAXIMIZATION

(a) *Total revenue minus total cost*

Total dollars

Total cost

Total revenue (price = $5)

$60

Maximum economic profit = $12

48

15

0   5   7   10   12   15   q/t

(b) *Marginal cost equals marginal revenue*

Dollars per unit

Marginal cost

Average total cost

$5   *e*   *d* = Marginal revenue = average revenue

Profit

4   *a*

0   5   10   12   15   q/t

In panel (a), the total revenue curve for a competitive firm is a straight line with a slope equal to the market price of $5. Total cost increases with output, first at a decreasing rate and then at an increasing rate. Profit is maximized at 12 units of output, where total revenue exceeds total cost by the greatest amount. In panel (b), marginal revenue is a horizontal line at the market price of $5. Profit is maximized at 12 units of output, where marginal cost equals marginal revenue (point *e*). Profit is output (12 units) multiplied by the difference between price ($5) and average total cost ($4), as shown by the shaded rectangle.

divided by the change in output. In perfect competition the firm is a *price taker*; if 1 more unit is sold, total revenue increases by an amount equal to the market price. Thus *in perfect competition the marginal revenue equals the market price*; in this example, the marginal revenue is $5.

Column (5) presents the firm's marginal cost at each level of output. In the last chapter you learned that *marginal cost* is the change in total cost divided by the change in output. Marginal cost first declines, reflecting increasing marginal returns in the short run as more of the variable resource is employed. Marginal cost then increases, reflecting diminishing marginal returns. Average cost also initially declines with increased output, then eventually increases as output expands.

The firm will expand output as long as each additional unit sold adds more to total revenue than to total cost—that is, as long as marginal revenue exceeds marginal cost. Comparing columns (2) and (5) in Exhibit 2, we see that marginal revenue exceeds marginal cost for each of the first 12 units of output. The marginal cost of unit 13, however, is $6.50, compared to a marginal revenue of $5. Producing the thirteenth unit would reduce total profit by $1.50. The change in total profit can be observed in the right-hand column. Since we assume that the firm will maximize profit, the firm will limit its output rate to 12 units per period.

In general, we can say that a firm will expand output as long as marginal revenue exceeds marginal cost, and it will stop expanding before marginal cost rises above marginal revenue. This rule is sometimes called the **golden rule of profit maximization**. In Exhibit 3, the marginal cost curve is below the marginal revenue curve up to 12 units of output, but it rises above the marginal revenue curve for output rates greater than 12.

*According to the **golden rule of profit maximization**, a firm should expand output as long as marginal revenue exceeds marginal cost and should stop expanding output before marginal cost exceeds marginal revenue.*

Measuring Profit in the Short Run

Per-unit cost and revenue data are graphed in panel (b) of Exhibit 3. Marginal revenue is a horizontal line at the market price of $5, which also represents the competitive firm's demand curve. At any point along the demand curve, marginal revenue equals the price. Marginal revenue for the competitive firm also equals the **average revenue**, which is the total revenue divided by the output. Regardless of the output, therefore, the following equality holds at all points on the competitive firm's demand curve:

Average revenue is total revenue divided by output.

Marginal revenue = market price = average revenue

The marginal cost curve intersects the marginal revenue (and demand) curve at point *e*, where 12 units of output are produced. At rates of output to the left of point *e*, marginal revenue exceeds marginal cost, so the firm could increase profit by expanding output. At rates of output to the right of point *e*, marginal cost exceeds marginal revenue, so the firm could increase profit by reducing output.

Profit is identified by the blue rectangle. The height of that rectangle, *ea*, equals the price (or average revenue), $5, minus the average total cost, $4, at that level of output. Thus price minus average total cost yields an average profit of $1 per unit. Total profit per period equals the average profit per unit, denoted by *ea*, times the number of units produced, or $12.

Note that with total cost and total revenue curves, we measure profit by the vertical *distance* between the two curves. But with per-unit curves, we measure profit by an *area* — that is, by the two dimensions that result from multiplying the average profit per unit times the number of units sold.

MINIMIZING SHORT-RUN LOSSES

So far the firm has faced the pleasant problem of choosing the rate of output that maximizes short-run economic profit. But, alas, firms are not always so fortunate. Firms in perfect competition have no control over their price, and sometimes the price is so low that no level of output will yield a profit. Faced with losses at all levels of output, the firm has two options: it can continue to produce at a loss or it can temporarily shut down. Note that even if the firm shuts down, it cannot go out of business in the short run. The short run is a period too short to allow existing firms to leave the industry.

Fixed Costs and Minimizing Losses

Your instincts probably tell you that the firm should temporarily shut down rather than produce at a loss. It's not that simple, however. Keep in mind that the firm has two kinds of cost in the short run: fixed cost, which must be paid even if the firm temporarily shuts down, and variable cost, which depends on the level of output. If the firm shuts down, it must still pay property taxes, fire insurance, and other overhead expenses incurred even when output is zero.

At certain rates of output, the short-run loss the firm incurs by operating may be less than the short-run loss suffered by shutting down. There may be some level of output greater than zero where the firm's revenue will not only cover its variable cost but also cover some portion of its fixed cost. Since the firm's short-run objective is to find the level of output that minimizes its loss, it will continue to produce if the revenues thus generated exceed the variable cost of production.

Consider the same cost data presented earlier in Exhibit 2, but now suppose the market price has fallen from $5 to $3. This new situation is analyzed in Exhibit 4. Because of the lower price, total revenue and total profit have declined at all rates of output. Column (8) indicates that the firm does not earn a profit regardless of the output rate. If the firm produces nothing, its loss is the fixed cost of $15. All output rates result in a loss, but if the firm produces between 6 and 12 units per period, it loses less than it would by shutting down. From column (8) you can see that the loss is minimized at $10 when 10 units are produced. The firm's total cost increases from $15 at zero output to $40 when the output rate is 10. Thus the total cost increases by $25, the variable cost of producing 10 units. Total revenue,

EXHIBIT 4
MINIMIZING LOSSES IN THE SHORT RUN

Quantity of Output (1)	Marginal Revenue (Price) (2)	Total Revenue (3) = (1) × (2)	Total Cost (4)	Marginal Cost (5)	Average Total Cost (6) = (4) ÷ (1)	Average Variable Cost (7)	Total Profit or Loss (8) = (3) − (4)
0	—	$ 0	$15.00	—	∞	—	− $15.00
1	$3	3	19.75	$ 4.75	$19.75	$4.75	− 16.75
2	3	6	23.50	3.75	11.75	4.25	− 17.50
3	3	9	26.50	3.00	8.83	3.83	− 17.50
4	3	12	29.00	2.50	7.25	3.50	− 17.00
5	3	15	31.00	2.00	6.20	3.20	− 16.00
6	3	18	32.50	1.50	5.42	2.92	− 14.50
7	3	21	33.75	1.25	4.82	2.68	− 12.75
8	3	24	35.25	1.50	4.41	2.53	− 11.25
9	3	27	37.25	2.00	4.14	2.47	− 10.25
10	**3**	**30**	**40.00**	**2.75**	**4.00**	**2.50**	**− 10.00**
11	3	33	43.25	3.25	3.93	2.57	− 10.25
12	3	36	48.00	4.75	4.00	2.75	− 12.00
13	3	39	54.50	6.50	4.19	3.04	− 15.50
14	3	42	64.00	9.50	4.57	3.50	− 22.00
15	3	45	77.50	13.50	5.17	4.17	− 32.50
16	3	48	96.00	18.50	6.00	5.06	− 48.00

however, increases from $0 to $30, so with this revenue the firm is able to pay its variable cost of $25 plus $5 of its fixed cost.

Producing Where Total Cost Minus Total Revenue Is Minimized

In panel (a) of Exhibit 5, the firm's strategy of minimizing the short-run loss is presented in terms of the total cost and total revenue curves. The drop in price from $5 to $3 per unit changes the slope of the total revenue curve from 5 to 3, so the total revenue curve is now flatter than in Exhibit 3. Since only the price has changed, the total cost curve is the same as in Exhibit 3. Notice that the total cost curve now lies above the total revenue curve at all output rates. The vertical distance between the two curves measures the firm's loss at each level of output. If the firm produces nothing, the loss is its fixed cost of $15. The distance between the two curves is minimized at an output level of 10 units, where the loss is $10.

Producing Where Marginal Cost Equals Marginal Revenue

Another way to derive the same result is to rely on marginal analysis. The per-unit data from Exhibit 4 are presented in panel (b) of Exhibit 5. The loss-minimizing level of output is found by expanding output as long as

EXHIBIT 5   MINIMIZING SHORT-RUN LOSSES

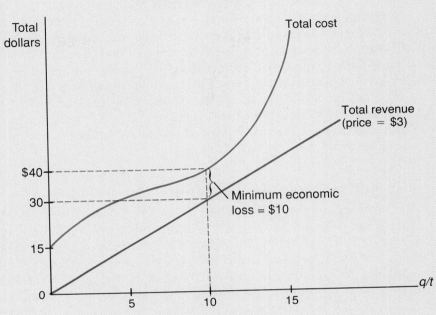

(a) *Total cost and total revenue*

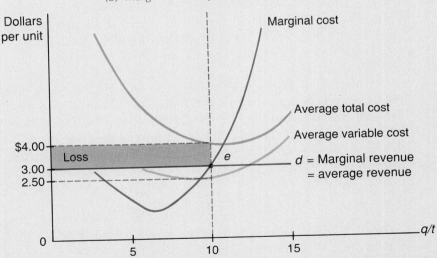

(b) *Marginal cost equals marginal revenue*

Since total cost always exceeds total revenue in panel (a), the firm suffers a loss at every level of output. The loss is minimized at 10 units of output. Panel (b) shows that marginal cost equals marginal revenue at point e. The loss is equal to output (10) multiplied by the difference between average total cost ($4) and price ($3). Since price exceeds average variable cost, the firm is better off continuing to produce in the short run.

marginal revenue exceeds marginal cost, provided that price exceeds average variable cost. The marginal cost and marginal revenue curves intersect at point *e*, where the price is $3 and the output level is 10 units per period.

The average total cost at this level of output is $4, and the average variable cost is $2.50. The difference of $1.50 is the average fixed cost. Since the price of $3 exceeds the average variable cost, the firm is able to cover all its variable cost and a portion of its fixed cost. Specifically, $2.50 of the price pays the average variable cost, and $0.50 covers a portion of the average fixed cost. This leaves a loss of $1 per unit, which, when multiplied by 10 units, yields a total loss of $10 per period. This loss is identified in panel (b) by the red rectangle. If the firm shut down, the loss would be $15 per period. Thus 10 units is the firm's short-run equilibrium rate of output when the market price is $3 per unit.

Shutting Down in the Short Run

In the short run, as long as the firm is able to cover all its variable cost and a portion of its fixed cost, it will produce rather than shut down. If, however, the variable cost of operating exceeds the revenue generated at all levels of output, the firm, by operating, would suffer a loss equal to its fixed cost plus the uncovered portion of its variable cost. Thus, if the price falls below the lowest point on the firm's average variable cost curve, no rate of output will allow the firm to cover even a portion of its fixed cost, so the firm will shut down. After all, why should the firm produce if doing so only increases its loss? As you can see from column (7) of Exhibit 4, if the price falls to $2 per unit, at no output level does the average variable cost drop far enough to be covered by a price of $2. By shutting down, the firm suffers a loss equal only to its fixed cost — a loss that is clearly less than its fixed cost plus a portion of its variable cost.

From column (7) of Exhibit 4 you can see that the lowest price at which the firm would cover its average variable cost is $2.47, which is the average variable cost when output is 9 units. At this price the firm will be indifferent between producing and shutting down, since either way its total loss will be the fixed cost of $15. Any price above $2.47 will allow the firm to cover a portion of its fixed cost and reduce its loss by producing.

The Firm and Industry Short-Run Supply Curves

A firm will vary its output as the price changes. If the price allows the firm to cover its average variable cost, the firm will expand output as long as marginal revenue exceeds marginal cost or reduce output as long as marginal cost exceeds marginal revenue. If the price falls below the average variable cost, the firm will reduce output to zero. The effects of various prices on the firm's output are summarized in Exhibit 6. Points *a*, *b*, *c*, *d*, and *e* are all intersections of the firm's marginal cost curve with different marginal revenue curves. (Recall that for perfectly competitive firms, the marginal revenue curve also represents the firm's demand curve and its average revenue curve.)

EXHIBIT 6   SUMMARY OF SHORT-RUN OUTPUT DECISIONS

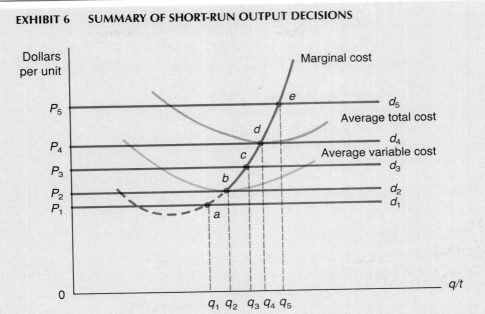

At price P_1, the firm produces nothing because P_1 is less than the firm's average variable cost. At price P_2, the firm is indifferent between shutting down and producing q_2 units of output, because in either case the firm would suffer a loss equal to its fixed cost. At P_3, it produces q_3 units and suffers a loss that is less than its fixed cost. At P_4, the firm produces q_4 and just breaks even, since P_4 equals average total cost. Finally, at P_5, the firm produces q_5 and earns an economic profit. The firm's short-run supply curve is that portion of its marginal cost curve at or rising above the minimum point of average variable cost (point b).

At a price as low as P_1, the firm will shut down rather than produce because no output level generates revenue sufficient to cover average variable cost. At a price of P_2, the firm will be indifferent between producing q_2 and shutting down because either way the loss will equal its fixed cost. If the price is P_3, the firm will produce q_3. Although the firm will incur a loss at a price of P_3, that loss is less than what it would face by shutting down. At P_4, the firm will produce q_4 and will just break even since its average total cost equals the price. When it breaks even, the firm earns a normal profit. If the price rises to P_5, the firm will earn an economic profit.

The Firm's Supply Curve *As long as the price is high enough to cover the firm's average variable cost, the firm will supply the quantity determined by the intersection of its marginal cost and marginal revenue curves.* Thus that portion of the firm's marginal cost curve that rises above the low point on its average variable cost curve becomes the firm's *short-run supply curve*. In Exhibit 6, it is the upward-sloping portion of the marginal cost curve, beginning at point b. The **short-**

*The **short-run supply curve** for a perfectly competitive firm indicates the quantity the firm is willing and able to supply in the short run at each alternative price.*

run supply curve indicates the quantity the firm is willing and able to supply in the short run at each alternative price. If the price is below P_2, the quantity supplied will be zero. The quantity supplied when the price is P_2 or higher is determined by the intersection of the firm's demand curve and its marginal cost curve.

The Industry Supply Curve Exhibit 7 presents an example of how supply curves for just three firms with identical marginal cost curves can be summed horizontally to form the industry, or market, supply curve. (In perfectly competitive industries, there will obviously be many more firms.) At a price below P, no output will be supplied. At a price of P, 10 units will be supplied by each of the three firms, for a market supply of 30 units. At a price above P, say P', each firm will supply 20 units, so the quantity supplied to the market will be 60 units.

Firm Supply and Industry Equilibrium Exhibit 8 shows the relation between the short-run profit-maximizing output of the individual firm and the market equilibrium price and quantity. We assume that there are 1000 firms in this industry. The cost conditions of each firm are assumed to be identical and to reflect the hypothetical average and marginal costs used throughout this chapter. Their individual supply curves (represented by the portion of the marginal cost curve at or rising above the average variable cost) are summed horizontally to yield the market, or industry, supply curve. At a price of $5 per unit, each firm will supply 12 units, for a market supply of 12,000 units. In the short run, each firm is making a profit, represented by the shaded rectangle.

In summary, firms can maximize profits or minimize losses in the short run by adjusting their variable resources. When confronted with a loss, a

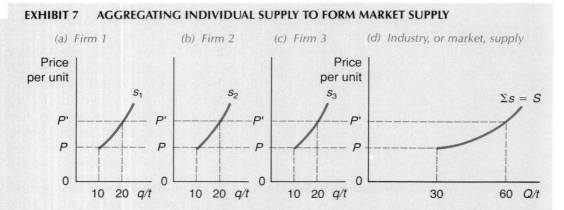

EXHIBIT 7   AGGREGATING INDIVIDUAL SUPPLY TO FORM MARKET SUPPLY

At price P, firms 1, 2, and 3 each supply 10 units of output. Total market supply is 30 units. In general, the market supply curve, panel (d), is the horizontal summation of the individual firm supply curves s_1, s_2, and s_3.

EXHIBIT 8   RELATION BETWEEN SHORT-RUN PROFIT MAXIMIZATION AND MARKET EQUILIBRIUM

(a) Firm

(b) Industry, or market

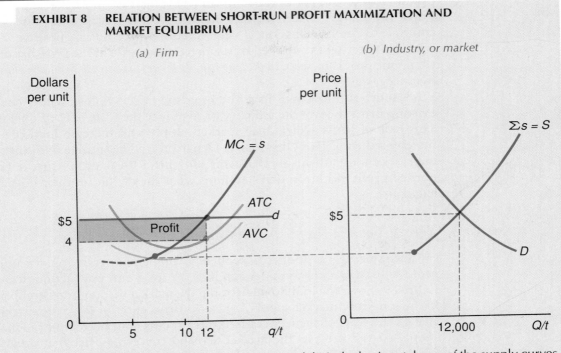

The market supply curve, *S*, in panel (b) is the horizontal sum of the supply curves of all firms in the industry. The intersection of *S* with the market demand curve, *D*, determines the market price, $5. That price, in turn, determines the height of the perfectly elastic demand curve facing the individual firm in panel (a). That firm produces 12 units (where marginal cost equals marginal revenue of $5) and earns an economic profit of $1 per unit, or $12 in total.

---

firm will either produce an output that minimizes its loss or shut down temporarily. So far, so good. Next let's see what happens in the long run.

PERFECT COMPETITION IN THE LONG RUN

In the short run, certain resources can be varied, but others, which determine firm size, are fixed. In the long run, however, firms are free to come and go and to adjust their size—that is, to adjust their scale of operation. There is no distinction between fixed and variable costs in the long run because all resources under the firm's control are variable.

Economic profit will, in the long run, attract new entrants and may encourage existing firms to expand the scale of their operation. Sharp entrepreneurs will be attracted to profit opportunities like bears to honey. Economic profit attracts resources from industries where firms are earning only a normal profit or perhaps are losing money. An increase in the number (or size) of firms in an industry earning short-run economic profits will expand market supply in the long run. This increase in market supply will lower the market price, thereby reducing economic profits. Firms will continue to enter the market as long as economic profits are positive. Firms will stop entering the market only when the decrease in the price has driven economic profits to zero. *In the long run, therefore, the entry of firms will eliminate economic profits.*

A short-run loss will have the opposite effect. A loss will encourage existing firms to leave the industry or to reduce the scale of their operation. This exit of firms will reduce market supply and increase market price, thereby reducing economic losses. Departures will continue until the price increases enough to ensure that remaining firms break even—that is, earn a normal profit, with resources earning what they could in their best alternative use.

Zero Economic Profits in the Long Run

Recognizing the long-run tendency for firms to earn only a normal profit is fundamental to understanding the long-run production decision. Exhibit 9 shows the individual firm and the market in long-run equilibrium. In the long run, market supply adjusts as firms enter or leave the market or change the scale of their operation; this process continues until the market supply curve intersects the market demand curve at a price that equals the

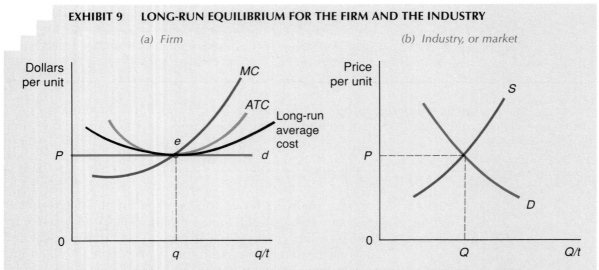

EXHIBIT 9   LONG-RUN EQUILIBRIUM FOR THE FIRM AND THE INDUSTRY

(a) Firm   (b) Industry, or market

In long-run equilibrium, the firm produces *q* units of output and earns a normal profit. At point *e*, price, marginal cost, short-run average total cost, and long-run average cost are all equal. There is no reason for new firms to enter or for existing firms to leave the market. Thus, the market supply curve, *S*, in panel (b) does not shift. As long as market demand, *D*, is stable, the industry will continue to produce a total of *Q* units of output at price *P*.

lowest point on each firm's long-run average cost curve. Any other price would cause further adjustments in the market supply curve, as firms attempted to increase profits or reduce losses. A higher price would generate economic profits and would therefore attract new entrants. A lower price would result in losses, causing some firms to leave the industry.

Competition in the long run cuts economic profit to zero. Because the long run is a time period during which all resources under the firm's control are variable and because firms are driven to maximize profit, *firms in the long run will adjust their scale of operation until their average cost of production is minimized*. Firms that fail to minimize costs will not survive in the long run. At point *e* in Exhibit 9, the firm is in equilibrium, producing *q* units and earning only a normal profit. At point *e*, price, marginal cost, short-run average total cost, and long-run average cost are all equal. No firm in the market has any reason to alter its output and no outside firm has any incentive to enter this industry, since each existing firm is earning a normal, but not economic, profit.

One way to understand the process of competition in the long run is to consider the evolution of a newly emerging industry. Video recorders are fast becoming standard equipment in the typical home. These recorders fueled household demand for videotaped movies. The first videotape rental outlets required customer deposits, rented tapes for as much as $5 per day, and made customers pay a membership fee. Those first entrants were often the only rental stores in the area, and they probably earned an economic profit in the short run. But in the long run this profit attracted many more competitors. The resulting increase in market supply reduced market prices. Competition from the proliferation of rental outlets eliminated membership fees and deposits and forced the rental price down to as low as $1 a day. Stores that could not compete dropped out of the industry. Over the long run, rental stores that remain in business tend to earn just a normal profit.

The Long-Run Adjustment Mechanism

To explore the long-run adjustment mechanism, let's consider how a firm and an industry respond to an increase in demand. Assume that the costs facing each individual firm do not depend on the number of firms in the industry (this assumption will be explained soon).

Effects of an Increase in Demand Exhibit 10 depicts a market in long-run equilibrium, with the market supply curve intersecting the market demand curve at point *a* in panel (b); the price is *P* and the quantity is Q_a. The individual firm supplies *q* at that market price, earning a normal profit. (Remember, a normal profit is built into the firm's average cost curves.) Now suppose the market demand for this product increases from *D* to *D'*, causing the market price to increase in the short run to *P'*. Each firm responds to the increased demand by expanding output along its short-run supply curve to *q'*, the rate at which its marginal cost equals the higher price (which is the firm's marginal revenue). Because all firms expand output, industry output

EXHIBIT 10   LONG-RUN ADJUSTMENT TO AN INCREASE IN DEMAND

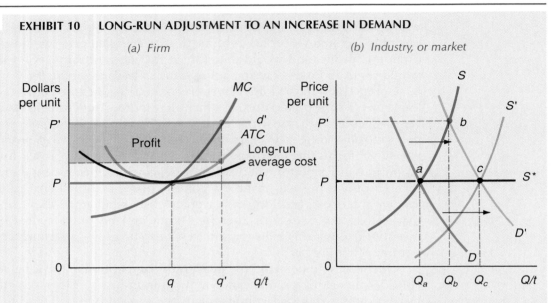

An increase in market demand from D to D' in panel (b) moves the short-run equilibrium point from a to b. Output rises to Q_b, and price increases to P'. The rise in market price causes the demand curve facing the firm to rise from d to d' in panel (a). The firm responds by increasing output to q' and earns an economic profit, identified by the blue rectangle. With existing firms earning economic profits, new firms enter the industry in the long run. Market supply shifts out to S' in panel (b). Output rises further, to Q_c, and price falls back to P. In panel (a), the demand curve shifts back to d, eliminating economic profits. The short-run adjustment is from point a to point b in panel (b), but the long-run adjustment is from point a to point c.

increases to Q_b. Note that in the short run each firm is now earning an economic profit, shown by the blue rectangle in panel (a).

In the long run, resources are attracted to this industry from markets where profits are just normal or where losses are being incurred. The entry of new firms increases supply, causing the market supply curve to shift out and the market price to fall. As long as economic profit is being made in this industry, firms continue to enter it. Thus, the market supply curve shifts out to S', where supply intersects D' at point c, returning the price to its initial equilibrium level, P. Although the market price is back to where it was before the increase in demand, the entry of new firms has increased market quantity to Q_c.

Because of the fall in the market price, the demand curve facing the individual firm shifts from d' back down to d. As a result, each firm reduces output from q' back to q and once again earns just a normal profit. Thus the price of the good in the long run is determined by the minimum point on the firm's long-run average cost curve. Although industry output increases from Q_a to Q_c, each firm's output returns to q. The additional output is provided by the new firms in the industry.

New firms are attracted to the industry by the short-run economic profits arising from the increase in demand. The resulting increase in market supply, however, drives the profits of new and existing firms down to the normal level. In Exhibit 10(b), the short-run adjustment in response to increased demand is from point *a* to point *b*; in the long run, the market equilibrium moves to point *c*.

Effects of a Decrease in Demand Next consider the effect on the long-run market adjustment process of a drop in demand. The initial equilibrium situation in Exhibit 11 is the same as in Exhibit 10. Market demand and supply intersect at point *a* to yield an equilibrium price of *P* and an equilibrium quantity of Q_a. This is a long-run equilibrium, so each firm is earning a normal profit by producing at a point where price, marginal cost, short-run average total cost, and long-run average cost are all equal, as at output rate *q* in panel (a).

Now suppose that the demand for this product declines, as reflected in panel (b) by the shift to the left in the market demand curve, from *D* to *D''*. This decline in demand reduces the market price to *P''*. As a result, the demand curve confronting each individual firm drops from *d* to *d''*. Each firm responds in the short run by cutting its short-run output to *q''*, where

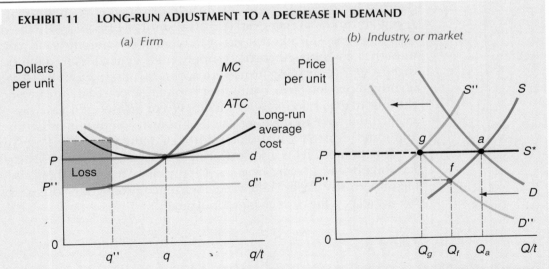

EXHIBIT 11   LONG-RUN ADJUSTMENT TO A DECREASE IN DEMAND

(a) *Firm*

(b) *Industry, or market*

A decrease in demand to *D''* in panel (b) disturbs the long-run equilibrium at point *a*. Prices are driven down to *P''* in the short run; output falls to Q_f. In panel (a), the firm's demand curve shifts down to *d''*. The firm reduces its output to *q''* and suffers a loss. As firms leave the industry in the long run, the market supply curve shifts left to *S''*. Market prices rise to *P* as output falls further to Q_q. At price *P*, the remaining firms once again earn zero economic profit. Thus the short-run adjustment is from point *a* to point *f* in panel (b); the long-run adjustment is from point *a* to point *g*.

the marginal cost equals the lower price. Because each firm cuts output, market output falls to Q_f.

At the lower price, firms suffer losses because the price is below their short-run average total cost (the price must still be above their average variable cost, however, since the firms continue to produce). This loss is indicated by the red rectangle in panel (a). In the long run, losses drive some firms out of the industry. As firms leave, market supply shifts to the left, so the market price increases. Firms continue to leave until the market supply curve shifts to S'', where supply intersects D'' at point g. Output has fallen to Q_g, and price has returned to P. With the price back up to P, the firms still in the industry once again earn a normal profit. Thus, at the conclusion of the industry adjustment process, each firm still in the industry is producing the same rate of output, q, as it did in the initial equilibrium, but market output has fallen from Q_a to Q_g because some firms have left the industry.

THE LONG-RUN SUPPLY CURVE

Thus far we have looked at the industry and firm responses to changes in demand, distinguishing between a short-run adjustment and a long-run adjustment. In the short run, firms adjust output in response to a shift in demand by moving up or down their marginal cost curve (that portion rising above the average variable cost) until the price equals the marginal cost. The long-run adjustment, however, involves the entry and exit of firms until the new short-run market supply curve generates an equilibrium price that provides remaining firms with normal profit. In Exhibits 10 and 11, we identified two long-run equilibrium points generated by the intersection of shifting demand and short-run supply curves. In each case the price remained the same in the long run, but industry output increased in Exhibit 10(b) and decreased in Exhibit 11(b). Connecting these long-run equilibrium points yields the long-run market supply curve labeled S^* in Exhibits 10 and 11. The long-run supply curve in these exhibits is horizontal, or perfectly elastic, reflecting unchanged production costs as the size of the industry adjusts to changes in demand.

Constant-Cost Industries

A **constant-cost industry** can expand or contract without affecting the prices of the resources it employs.

The industry we have depicted thus far is called a **constant-cost industry** because the cost curves do not shift as industry output changes. Resource prices and other production costs remain constant in the long run as industry output increases or decreases. Recall that at the outset of the discussion of the long run we assumed that each firm's costs do not depend on the number of firms in the market. Because each firm's production costs are assumed to be independent of the number of firms in the industry, per-unit production costs in the long run can remain constant as firms enter or leave the industry. *The long-run supply curve for a constant-cost industry is horizontal*, like those depicted in Exhibits 10 and 11.

A constant-cost industry is most often characterized as one that hires only a small portion of the resources available in the resource market. Firms need not increase the price paid for resources to draw them away from competing uses because firms in this industry hire only a small share of the resources available. For example, producers of pencils can expand industry production without bidding up the prices of wood, graphite, and synthetic rubber since the pencil industry uses such a small share of these resources.

Increasing-Cost Industries

*As an **increasing-cost industry** expands, it faces higher average production costs.*

Many industries encounter higher production costs as industry output expands in the long run. These **increasing-cost industries** find that expanding output bids up the prices of some resources, and these higher resource costs cause each firm's cost curves to shift upward. For example, an expansion of the oil industry will bid up the wages of petroleum engineers and geologists, raising average and marginal costs for each oil exploration firm.

To illustrate the equilibrium adjustment process for an increasing-cost industry, we again begin in long-run equilibrium in Exhibit 12(b), where the industry demand curve, D, intersects the short-run industry supply curve, S, at equilibrium point a to yield the price P_a and the quantity Q_a. When the price is P_a, the demand (and marginal revenue) curve facing the firm is d_a in panel (a). The firm produces the rate of output for which marginal cost equals marginal revenue, represented by point a in panel (a). At the equilibrium rate of output, q, the firm is at the low point of its average total cost curve, so the average total cost equals the price and the firm earns no economic profit.

Suppose there is an increase in the demand for this product, reflected by a shift to the right in the demand curve from D to D' in panel (b). The new demand curve intersects the short-run market supply curve at point b, yielding the short-run equilibrium price P_b and quantity Q_b. With an increase in the equilibrium price, each firm's demand curve shifts from d_a up to d_b in panel (a). Each firm expands output as long as its new marginal revenue exceeds its marginal cost. The new short-run equilibrium occurs at point b in panel (a), where each firm produces output q_b. In the short run, each firm earns an economic profit equal to q_b times the difference between the price and the average total cost at that rate of output. So far the sequence of events is identical to that for the constant-cost industry.

The economic profit earned by firms in the industry attracts new entrants in the long run. Because this is an increasing-cost industry, an expansion in the number of firms drives up the prices of some of the industry's resources. These higher resource costs raise each firm's marginal and average cost curves, which shift from MC and ATC up to MC' and ATC', as shown in panel (a) of Exhibit 12. Note that for simplicity we are

EXHIBIT 12   AN INCREASING-COST INDUSTRY

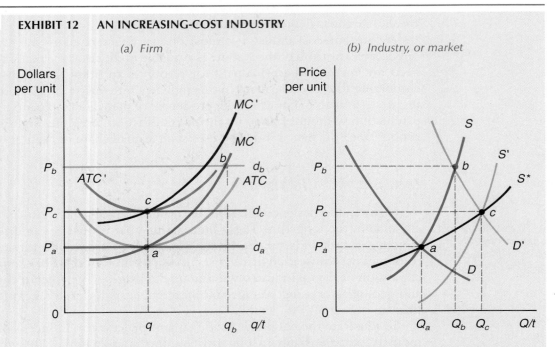

An increase in demand to D' in panel (b) disturbs the initial equilibrium at point a. A short-run equilibrium is established at point b, where D' intersects the short-run market supply curve, S. At the higher price, P_b, the firm's demand curve shifts up to d_b, and its output increases to q_b in panel (a). At point b, the firm is earning an economic profit. New firms enter to try to capture some of the profits. As they do so, input prices are bid up, so each firm's marginal and average cost curves rise. The intersection of the new market supply curve, S', with D' determines the market price, P_c. At P_c, individual firms are earning zero economic profit. Point c is a point of long-run equilibrium. By connecting long-run equilibrium points a and c in panel (b), we obtain the upward-sloping long-run market supply curve, S^*, for this increasing-cost industry.

assuming that the new cost curves are parallel to the old curves, so the minimum efficient plant size remains the same.

The entry of new firms also increases industry supply, thus reducing the price of the industry's output. *New firms enter the industry until the combination of a lower output price and higher production costs drives economic profits to zero.* This occurs when enough new firms have entered the market to shift the short-run industry supply curve out to S', which lowers the price until it equals the minimum on the firm's new average total cost curve. The market price does not fall as far as the initial equilibrium level because each firm now has a higher average total cost.

The intersection of the new short-run market supply curve, S', and the increased market demand, D', determines the new long-run market equilibrium point, identified as point c in panel (b). Point c and point a, the initial long-run equilibrium, are two points on the *upward-sloping* long-run supply curve, denoted as S^*, for this increasing-cost industry.

The firm's costs no longer depend simply on the scale of its plant and its choice of output level, as was the case for firms in constant-cost industries. The costs for firms in increasing-cost industries depend on the number of firms in the market. In increasing-cost industries, short-run economic profits are eliminated by long-run industry expansion for two reasons. First, by increasing market supply, long-run expansion reduces the market price. Second, by bidding up the price of certain resources, long-run expansion increases each firm's production costs. The long-run supply curve for an increasing-cost industry slopes upward, like S^* in Exhibit 12(b), because the firms earn normal profits when production costs rise only if the price also rises.

Decreasing-Cost Industries

*As a **decreasing-cost industry** expands, it faces lower average production costs.*

Firms in some industries may experience lower production costs as output expands in the long run, though this is considered extremely rare. Firms in **decreasing-cost industries** find that as industry output expands, the cost of production falls, causing a downward shift in each firm's cost curves. For example, in the coal mining industry, a major cost is pumping water out of the mine shafts. As more mines in the same area begin operating pumps, the water table in the area falls, so each mine's pumping costs go down.

An increase in market demand results in a higher price in the short run, so firms earn economic profit. This profit attracts new entrants, reducing production costs for all firms in the industry. Decreasing-cost industries have long-run supply curves like the one depicted in Exhibit 13, where point *a* is the initial equilibrium and point *c* is the long-run equilibrium response to the increase in demand. In the long run, the market clearing price, P_c, falls below the initial equilibrium price, P_a. Entry eliminates economic profit in the long run.

In summary, firms in perfect competition can earn an economic profit in the short run, but the entry or exit of firms drives long-run economic profit to zero. This is true whether the industry in question exhibits constant costs, increasing costs, or decreasing costs. Notice that the industry supply curve is less elastic in the short run than in the long run. In the long run, firms can adjust all their resources, so they are better able to respond to changes in price.

We mentioned at the outset that perfect competition serves as a useful benchmark for evaluating the efficiency of markets. Next we will examine the qualities of perfect competition that make it so special.

PERFECT COMPETITION AND EFFICIENCY

There are two concepts of efficiency. The first, called *productive efficiency*, refers to the notion of efficiency developed in the production possibilities

EXHIBIT 13   A DECREASING-COST INDUSTRY

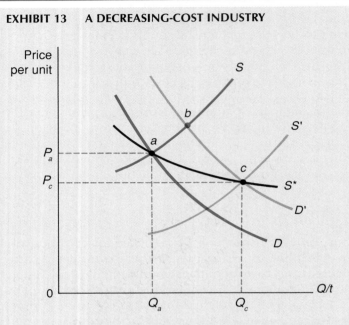

An increase in market demand moves the industry from starting point *a* to short-run equilibrium at point *b*. With each firm earning an economic profit, new firms begin to enter. If entry drives down the cost of production, long-run equilibrium will be reestablished at point *c*, with a lower price than at point *a*. Connecting long-run equilibrium points *a* and *c* yields the downward-sloping long-run market supply curve, *S**, for this decreasing-cost industry.

curve introduced in Chapter 2. The second, called *allocative efficiency*, emphasizes the choice of goods to be produced and the distribution of these goods among consumers.

Productive Efficiency

Productive efficiency is achieved when output is produced with the least costly combination of inputs given the available technology.

    Productive efficiency occurs when whatever level of output the firm decides to produce is produced using the least-cost combination of inputs given the available technology. If firms could produce the same output using fewer resources or could produce more output using the same resources, they are not using resources efficiently. In the long run in perfect competition, the entry and exit of firms ensure that each firm produces at the minimum point on its long-run average cost curve. Firms that are producing less than the minimum efficient level of output must either adjust their size or leave the industry to avoid continued losses. Thus the long-run industry output in perfect competition is produced at the least possible cost per unit. In the perfectly competitive industry, goods are homogeneous and price competition is the only factor of interest to the consumer. Therefore resources are not used up in advertising or in other forms of *nonprice* competition.

Allocative Efficiency

Allocative efficiency is achieved when firms produce the output that is most preferred by consumers.

The fact that goods are produced at the least possible cost does not mean that the allocation of resources is the most efficient one possible. It may be that the goods being produced are not the ones consumers most prefer. This situation is akin to that of the airline pilot who informs the passengers that there is some good news and some bad news: "The bad news is that we are lost; the good news is that we are making record time!" Firms may be producing goods efficiently yet producing the wrong goods. **Allocative efficiency** occurs when firms produce the output that is most preferred by consumers.

How do we know that perfect competition guarantees that the goods produced are those most preferred by consumers? The answer lies with the demand and supply curves. You'll recall that the demand curve reflects the marginal value that consumers attach to each unit they consume, so the price is the amount of money that people are willing to pay for the final unit they consume. We know that, both in the short run and in the long run, the equilibrium price in perfect competition equals the marginal cost of supplying the last unit sold. Marginal cost measures the opportunity cost of using those resources in their best alternative use. Thus supply and demand intersect at the combination of price and quantity where the opportunity cost of the resources employed to produce the last unit of output just equals the marginal value, or the marginal benefit, that consumers attach to that unit of output.

As long as marginal cost equals marginal benefit, the last unit produced is valued as much as or more than any other good that could have been produced using those same resources. There is no way to reallocate resources to increase the value of output. Thus there is no way to reallocate resources to increase the total utility or total benefit consumers enjoy from output. When the marginal cost of each good equals the marginal benefit that consumers derive from that good, the economy is said to pass the test of allocative efficiency.

The Gains from Voluntary Exchange or Trade

If the marginal cost to firms of supplying the good just equals the marginal benefit to consumers, does this mean that market exchange confers no net benefits on participants? The answer is no. Market exchange usually benefits both consumers and producers. Recall that consumers garner a surplus from market exchange because the maximum amount that consumers would be willing to pay for the good exceeds the amount they in fact pay. Exhibit 14 depicts a hypothetical market in short-run equilibrium. The consumer surplus in this exhibit is represented by the blue area below the demand curve but above the market-clearing price of $10.

**EXHIBIT 14   CONSUMER SURPLUS AND PRODUCER SURPLUS FOR A
COMPETITIVE MARKET IN THE SHORT RUN**

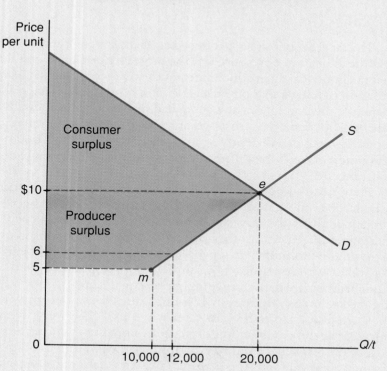

Consumer surplus is represented by the area above the market-clearing price of $10 per unit and below the demand curve; it is shown as a blue triangle. Producer surplus is represented by the area above the short-run market supply curve and below the market-clearing price of $10 per unit; it is shown by the green shading. At a price of $5 per unit, there is no producer surplus. At a price of $6 per unit, producer surplus is the shaded area between $5 and $6.

Producers in the short run also usually derive a net benefit, or a surplus, from market exchange because the amount they receive for their output exceeds the minimum amount they would require to supply the good. Recall that the short–run market supply curve is the sum of that portion of each firm's marginal cost curve that is at or rising above the minimum point on its average variable cost curve. Point *m* in Exhibit 14 is the minimum point on the market supply curve; it indicates that at a price of $5, firms are willing to supply 10,000 units. At prices below $5, the quantity supplied is zero. At point *m*, firms in this industry gain no net benefit from production in the short run because the total industry revenue derived from selling 10,000 units at $5 each just covers the total variable cost incurred by producing that amount of output.

If the price increases to $6, firms supply 12,000 units because the marginal cost of supplying the 12,000th unit is $6. Total revenue increases from $50,000 to $72,000. Part of the increased revenue covers the higher marginal cost of production. But the balance of the increased revenue is a bonus to producers, who would have been willing to supply nearly 12,000 units for less than $6 each. For example, firms would have been willing to supply 10,000 units for only $5 each. In Exhibit 14, at a price of $6 the producer surplus is the green area above the supply curve but below that price. At higher prices, the producer surplus is greater because firms get to sell all their output for the higher price even though they would have been willing to offer most of it for a lower price.

*In the short run, **producer surplus** is the total revenue producers are paid for a commodity minus their total variable cost of producing the commodity.*

In the short run, **producer surplus** is the total revenue producers are paid for a commodity minus their total variable cost of producing the commodity. In Exhibit 14, the market-clearing price is $10 per unit and the producer surplus is depicted by the green area under the price but above the market supply curve. That area represents the market price minus the marginal cost of each unit produced. Allocative efficiency occurs at point *e*, which is the combination of price and quantity that maximizes the sum of consumer and producer surplus.

Note that producer surplus is not the same as profit. Any price that exceeds the average variable cost will result in a producer surplus, even though that price might result in a short-run economic loss. The idea of producer surplus ignores fixed cost because fixed costs are irrelevant to the firm's short-run production decision. Firms cannot avoid paying fixed costs in the short run, no matter what they do. Only marginal cost matters, and marginal cost depends on how variable cost changes as output changes.

Producer surplus is more easily observed in the short run than in the long run. If producer surplus is defined narrowly as total revenue minus total variable cost, producer surplus in the long run for perfectly competitive industries is zero. In long-run equilibrium, all costs are variable and total cost equals total revenue, so there is no producer surplus. But for increasing-cost industries, the definition of producer surplus is often broadened to include the higher incomes to those resource owners whose pay rate increases when industry demand increases. For example, as the number of television broadcasts of professional sports events increases, salaries of professional athletes go up because of the greater demand for their special talents. The rising long-run supply curve in professional sports reflects the rising cost of resources, particularly professional pay. The teams' owners may be earning only a normal profit as demand increases in the long run, but athletes, as suppliers of a specialized resource particular to this industry, earn a producer surplus.

CONCLUSION

Let's reconsider the features that characterize the perfectly competitive market and see how they relate to conclusions developed in this chapter. *First*, there must be a large number of buyers and sellers. This is necessary so that no individual buyer or seller is large enough to influence price. *Second*, firms must produce a homogeneous product. If consumers could distinguish among the output of different producers, they might prefer the output of one firm even at a higher price, so different producers could sell at different prices. In that case not every firm would be a price taker—that is, the firms' demand curves would no longer be horizontal. *Third*, all market participants must have full information about all prices and all production processes. Otherwise, some producers could charge more than the market price, and some uninformed consumers would pay that higher price. Also, through ignorance firms might select outdated technology or fail to recognize the opportunity for short-run economic profits. *Fourth*, all resources must be mobile in the long run, and there must be no obstacles preventing new firms from moving into profitable markets. Otherwise, some firms could earn economic profits in the long run.

Perfect competition is not the form of market most commonly observed in the real world. The markets for agricultural products, stocks, commodities such as gold and silver, and international currencies come close to being perfect. But even if no single example of perfect competition could be found, the model would be a useful tool for analyzing market behavior. As you will see in the next few chapters, perfect competition provides a valuable benchmark for evaluating the efficiency of other kinds of market structures.

Summary

1. Market structure describes important features of the economic environment in which firms operate. These features include the number of competing firms, the ease or difficulty of entering the market, the similarities or differences in the output produced by each firm, and the forms of competition among firms. There are several types of market structures. This chapter examined perfect competition.

2. Perfectly competitive markets are characterized by (1) a large number of buyers and sellers, (2) production of a homogeneous product, (3) full information about the availability and price of all resources and goods, and (4) free and complete mobility of resources. Firms in such markets are said to be price takers because no individual firm can influence the price. Individual firms can vary only the amount they choose to sell at the market price.

3. The market price in perfect competition is determined by the intersection of the market supply and market demand curves. Each firm then faces a demand curve that is a horizontal line drawn at the market price. Because this demand curve is horizontal, it represents the average revenue and the marginal revenue the firm receives at each level of output.

4. In the short run, the price-taking firm maximizes profits or minimizes losses by producing the level of output determined by the intersection of the demand, or marginal revenue, curve with that portion of the marginal cost curve at or rising above the minimum point on the average variable cost curve. For short, we say that the firm chooses that level of output for which marginal cost equals marginal revenue.

5. That portion of the firm's marginal cost curve at or rising above the average variable cost

curve becomes the firm's short-run supply curve. The horizontal addition of all firms' supply curves forms the market supply curve.

6. Because new firms are not free to enter the market in the short run, economic profit is possible. In the long run, however, firms will enter or leave the market until economic profit is driven to zero. In the long run, each firm will produce at the low point on its long-run average cost curve. At this level of output, the price, marginal cost, and average cost will all be equal. Firms that fail to produce at this least-cost combination will not survive in the long run.

7. In the short run, firms will alter their rate of output in response to a change in demand by moving up or down their marginal cost curve. The long-run adjustment to a change in demand involves firms' entering or leaving the market until the remaining firms in the industry earn just a normal profit. As the industry expands in the long run, the industry supply curve reflects either (1) increasing costs, meaning that each firm's production costs rise as the number of firms in the industry expands; (2) constant costs, meaning that firm costs do not change; or (3) decreasing costs, meaning that firm costs fall as the industry expands.

8. Perfectly competitive markets are said to reflect both productive efficiency, because output is produced using the most efficient combination of resources available, and allocative efficiency, because the goods produced are those most valued by consumers. In equilibrium, perfectly competitive markets allocate goods so that the marginal cost of the last unit produced equals the marginal value that consumers attach to that last unit purchased. Voluntary exchange in competitive markets maximizes consumer surplus and producer surplus.

Questions and Problems

1. (Perfect Competition) Some economists have argued that the U.S. stock market is competitive. Discuss the merits and flaws in this view. Consider each assumption involved in perfect competition.

2. (Perfect Competition) Do patents and copyrights hinder competition? Should patents be allowed if they do hinder competition? Why or why not?

3. (Perfect Competition) Some people have claimed that there is strong competition in the U.S. auto market. Give some reasons why this market could not be considered perfectly competitive.

4. (Normal Versus Economic Profits) Company A is making millions of dollars in accounting profits. Yet the same company has decided to quit producing its current product. How is this possible?

5. (Competition) Consider Exhibit 3 in this chapter. Explain why the total revenue curve is a straight line from the origin, whereas the slope of the total cost curve changes.

6. (Profit Maximization) Consider Exhibit 3 in this chapter. Why doesn't the firm choose the output that maximizes average profits (i.e., the output for which average cost is the lowest)?

7. (Price and Marginal Revenue) Explain why price and marginal revenue are identical in the perfectly competitive model.

8. (Minimizing Losses) Consider Exhibit 5 in this chapter. The company portrayed is not able to cover its fixed cost by selling its product. However, it is able to cover its variable cost. How might the firm avoid default on its fixed obligations in the short run?

9. (Entry and Exit of Firms) Why is it reasonable that the short-run competitive model does not allow for the entry and exit of firms? Is entry into an industry intrinsically more difficult than exit from an industry?

10. (Long-Run Industry Supply) Why does the long-run industry supply curve for an increasing-cost industry slope upward? What causes the increasing costs in an increasing-cost industry?

11. (Competitive Industry) Draw the short- and long-run cost curves of a competitive firm in long-run equilibrium.
    a. Show the firm's short-run response to a reduction in the price of a variable resource.
    b. Assuming that the industry is an increasing-cost industry, describe the process by which the industry returns to long-run equilibrium.

12. (Short-Run Competitive Supply) An individual competitive firm's short-run supply curve is the portion of its marginal cost curve that equals or rises above the average variable cost. Explain why this is true.

13. (Short-Run Competitive Supply) Use the following data to answer the questions below.

Q	TVC	Q	TVC
1	$10	5	$31
2	16	6	38
3	20	7	46
4	25	8	55
		9	65

    a. Calculate the marginal cost for each level of production.
    b. Calculate the average variable cost for each level of production.
    c. How much would the firm produce if it could sell its product for $5? for $7? for $10? Explain your answers.

d. Assuming that its fixed cost is $3, calculate the firm's profit at each of the production levels determined in part c.

14. (Long-Run Competitive Behavior) Suppose that a constant-cost industry consists entirely of firms with U-shaped long-run average cost curves. Explain why variation in industry output in response to changes in demand must, in the long run, come from variation in the number of firms rather than from variation in the scale of production by firms in the industry.

15. (Efficiency and Perfect Competition) Use the data below to answer the following questions.

Quantity	Marginal Cost	Marginal Benefit
0	—	—
1	$ 2	$10
2	3	9
3	4	8
4	5	7
5	6	6
6	8	5
7	10	4
8	12	3
9	15	2
10	18	1

    a. Construct the supply-demand diagram for this product and calculate the equilibrium price and quantity.
    b. What is the total (short-run) variable cost to producers of producing this equilibrium amount?
    c. What is the total benefit to consumers of consuming this equilibrium amount?
    d. Compare your answers in parts b and c to the amount that consumers pay (and therefore the revenues producers receive) for this quantity and calculate the amount of consumer and producer surplus associated with this equilibrium quantity.

C H A P T E R   2 2

Monopoly

Monopoly is a Greek word meaning "one seller." Monopolists sell products, such as electricity, postage stamps, and local phone service, that have no close substitutes. You have heard much about the evils of monopoly. You've probably played the Parker Brothers game Monopoly on a rainy day. Now we will sort out fact from fiction. Pure monopoly, like perfect competition, is not as common as other market structures. Yet a study of the sources of monopoly power and the effects of monopoly on the allocation of resources will convey an understanding not only of this market structure but also of the market structures that lie between pure monopoly and perfect competition. Topics discussed in this chapter include

- Barriers to entry
- Price elasticity and marginal revenue
- Long-run profit maximization
- Welfare cost of monopoly
- Price discrimination

BARRIERS TO ENTRY

*A **barrier to entry** is an impediment that prevents new firms from competing on an equal basis with existing firms in an industry.*

Perhaps the single most important feature of a monopolized market is that new firms cannot profitably enter the market in the long run. What factors prevent competitors from entering the monopolist's market? We will examine three kinds of **barriers to entry**: legal restrictions, economies of scale, and the monopolist's control of an essential resource.

Legal Restrictions

One way to prevent new firms from entering a market is to make entry illegal. Patents, licenses, and other legal restrictions provide some producers with legal protection against market entry.

Patents are legal barriers to entry that convey to their holders the exclusive right to supply a product for seventeen years.

Innovation is the process of turning an invention into a marketable product.

Patents and Invention Incentives In the United States, a **patent** awards to the developer of a new product the exclusive right to production for seventeen years. During that time no other firm can produce the good unless authorized by the holder of the patent, so inventors are given a temporary monopoly over the use of their inventions. Originally enacted in 1790, the patent laws encourage inventors to invest the time and money required to make new discoveries. Moreover, these laws give firms the stimulus to turn an invention into a marketable product, a process called **innovation**. If other firms could simply copy successful products, any one firm would be less inclined to incur the up-front costs of developing new products and bringing them to the market.

Licenses and Other Entry Restrictions Governments often promote monopoly by awarding a single firm the exclusive right to provide particular goods and services. Federal licenses give certain firms the right to broadcast radio and TV signals. State licenses are required to provide services such as medical care, haircuts, and legal assistance. Governments confer monopoly rights to sell hot dogs at civic auditoriums, to collect garbage, to provide bus and cab service in and out of town, and to supply services ranging from electricity to cable TV. The government itself may claim the right to provide certain products by outlawing competitors. For example, the U.S. Postal Service has the exclusive right to deliver a broad class of mail, and many states are monopoly sellers of liquor and lottery tickets.

Economies of Scale

A monopoly sometimes emerges when a firm experiences *economies of scale* and thus declining average costs over the full range of market demand, as shown in Exhibit 1. When this is the case, a single firm can satisfy the market demand at a lower cost per unit than could two or more firms operating at smaller levels of output. Thus a single firm will emerge from the competitive process as the sole seller in the market. Cable TV is an industry that exhibits economies of scale. Once the cable has been strung throughout the community—that is, once the fixed cost has been incurred—the marginal cost of hooking up an additional household is relatively small. Consequently, as shown in Exhibit 1, the average cost per household declines as more and more households are tied into the system. The average cost per household would be greater if two or more competing companies each ran their own wires throughout the community.

Because such a monopoly emerges from the natural forces of competition, it is called a *natural monopoly*, to distinguish it from the artificial

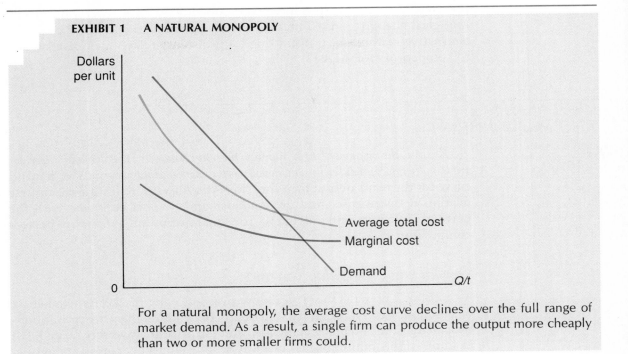

EXHIBIT 1   A NATURAL MONOPOLY

Dollars per unit

Average total cost

Marginal cost

Demand

Q/t

0

For a natural monopoly, the average cost curve declines over the full range of market demand. As a result, a single firm can produce the output more cheaply than two or more smaller firms could.

monopolies created by government patents, licenses, and other official decrees. A new entrant cannot sell enough output to enjoy the economies of scale experienced by an established natural monopolist, so entry into the market is blocked. We will have more to say about the regulation of natural monopolies in a later chapter, when we examine the government regulation of markets.

Control of Essential Resources

Sometimes the source of monopoly power is a firm's control over some nonreproducible resource that is critical to production. For example, the world's diamond trade is operated primarily by the DeBeers Company, which controls the world's diamond mines. Professional sports leagues try to block the formation of competing leagues by signing the best players to long-term contracts and by seeking exclusive use of sports stadiums and arenas. Celebrities have a monopoly over the essential input to their success—themselves. Consequently, the most successful stars carefully control their public appearances to avoid overexposure (this is one reason why the biggest stars seldom appear on TV).

Despite the various barriers to entry, monopolies are rare. Local monopolies are more common than national or international monopolies. The economic profit usually earned by a monopolist provides other firms with a powerful incentive to produce close substitutes. Also, over time, technological change tends to break down the barriers to entry. For example, alternative methods of transmitting long-distance telephone calls gave rise to competitors for AT&T.

REVENUE FOR THE MONOPOLIST

Because the monopoly firm supplies the entire market, the demand curve for goods and services produced by a monopolist is the market demand curve. The demand curve for the firm's output therefore slopes downward, reflecting the inverse relation between price and quantity demanded. This contrasts with the perfectly elastic demand curve for the output of a firm in perfect competition.

Demand and Marginal Revenue

Exhibit 2 presents the typical downward-sloping market demand curve of a monopolist. The quantity sold clearly depends on the price the monopolist charges; the quantity demanded and the price are inversely related. For example, if the monopolist is currently selling 4 units per period and wishes to increase sales to 5 units, the price must drop from $6.75 to $6.50.

When the monopolist sells 4 units at a price of $6.75 per unit, total revenue is $27. The total revenue divided by the quantity, or the average revenue per unit, is $6.75. When the price is $6.50, the monopolist can sell 5 units, for a total revenue of $32.50 or an average revenue of $6.50. Thus, for the monopolist, the average revenue equals the price for any level of sales, and both can be obtained from the demand curve. Therefore *the demand curve is also the monopolist's average revenue curve*, just as the perfectly competitive firm's demand curve is also that firm's average revenue curve.

The relation between price and marginal revenue is more complex. Recall that for the perfectly competitive firm, marginal revenue is always equal to the market price because each firm can sell as much as it chooses at that price. Now consider the marginal revenue the monopolist receives from selling a fifth unit of the good. When the price drops from $6.75 to $6.50, total revenue goes from $27 to $32.50. Thus marginal revenue, which is the change in total revenue resulting from selling one more unit, is only $5.50. *The marginal revenue is less than the price.*

A closer look at Exhibit 2 reveals why the marginal revenue will always be less than the price (except for the first unit sold). The monopolist earns $6.50 on the extra unit sold, as shown by the vertical blue rectangle marked *Gain*. But to sell five units, the monopolist must offer *all* five units for $6.50 each. Thus, by selling the fifth unit, the firm sacrifices $0.25 on each of the first four units, which it could have sold at a price of $6.75. This reduction in revenue from the first four units totals $1 ($0.25 × 4) and is identified in Exhibit 2 by the red rectangle marked *Loss*. The net change in total revenue

EXHIBIT 2 MONOPOLY DEMAND: LOSS AND GAIN IN TOTAL REVENUE FROM SELLING ONE MORE UNIT

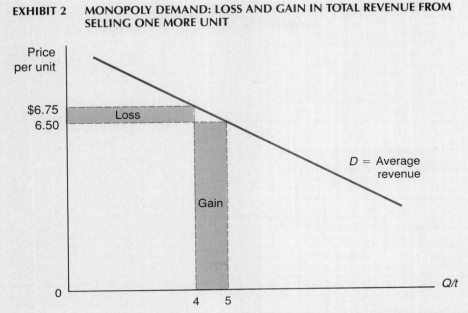

If a monopolist increases production from 4 units to 5, the revenue for the fifth unit sold is $6.50. However, the monopolist loses $1 on the first 4 units, since each unit must now be priced at $6.50 rather than $6.75. Marginal revenue equals the gain minus the loss, or $6.50 − 1.00 = $5.50. Hence, marginal revenue is less than the price ($6.50).

from selling the fifth unit; that is, the marginal revenue from the fifth unit — equals the *Gain* minus the *Loss*, which equals $5.50 ($6.50 − $1). This analysis assumes that all units of the good are sold for the same price; that is, when the price is $6.50, all 5 units must be sold for $6.50 each. Although most markets appear to operate this way, later in this chapter we will consider some cases in which monopolists may be able to charge different prices for different units of the same good.

To calculate the marginal revenue from selling one more unit of output, we must subtract from the amount received for that additional unit the loss resulting from having to sell all units — not just the marginal unit — for the lower price. As we move down the demand curve, marginal revenue is affected by two factors: (1) the amount received from selling another unit declines (since the price drops), and (2) the revenue forgone by selling all units at this lower price increases (since a larger number of units could have been sold for the higher price). Both factors reduce the marginal revenue as the price falls along a given demand curve.

The numbers behind the demand curve in Exhibit 2 are presented in the first two columns of Exhibit 3. The first column lists alternative quantities of the good, and the second column lists the price, or average revenue, corresponding to each quantity demanded. The two columns together represent

EXHIBIT 3
SHORT-RUN REVENUE FOR A MONOPOLIST

Quantity (1)	Price (average revenue) (2)	Total Revenue (3) = (1) × (2)	Marginal Revenue (4)
0	$7.75	$ 0.00	—
1	7.50	7.50	$ 7.50
2	7.25	14.50	7.00
3	7.00	21.00	6.50
4	6.75	27.00	6.00
5	6.50	32.50	5.50
6	6.25	37.50	5.00
7	6.00	42.00	4.50
8	5.75	46.00	4.00
9	5.50	49.50	3.50
10	5.25	52.50	3.00
11	5.00	55.00	2.50
12	4.75	57.00	2.00
13	4.50	58.50	1.50
14	4.25	59.50	1.00
15	4.00	60.00	0.50
16	3.75	60.00	0.00
17	3.50	59.50	− 0.50

the market demand schedule for the good. The monopolist's *total revenue*, which equals price times quantity, is presented in column (3). *Marginal revenue*, the net change in total revenue as a result of selling one more unit, is listed in column (4).

Note that for the first unit sold, marginal revenue and the price are equal. For additional units of output, however, marginal revenue is below the price, and the difference between the two grows larger as the price declines. Marginal revenue is negative for prices below $3.75. This means that the revenue gained from selling one more unit is less than the revenue lost by selling all previous units at the lower price.

Revenue Curves

The data in Exhibit 3 are graphed in Exhibit 4, which shows the demand and marginal revenue curves in panel (a) and the total revenue curve in panel (b). Note that the marginal revenue curve is below the demand curve, and that the total revenue curve is at a maximum when marginal revenue is zero. Take a minute to study these relations—they are important.

Earlier you learned that the price elasticity for a straight-line demand curve decreases as you move down the curve. Where demand is elastic—that is, where the price elasticity of demand is greater than 1—a decrease in the price will increase total revenue. This relation holds because the percentage

EXHIBIT 4   MONOPOLY DEMAND AND MARGINAL AND TOTAL REVENUE

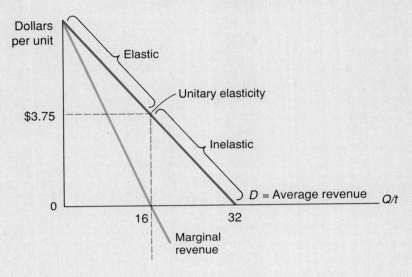

(a) Demand and marginal revenue

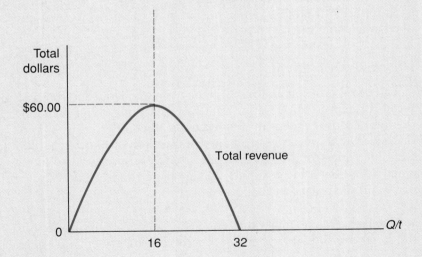

(b) Total revenue

Because a monopolist must lower the price of all units sold in order to sell one more unit, marginal revenue is below demand. Where demand is price elastic, marginal revenue is positive, so total revenue increases as the price falls. Where demand is price inelastic, marginal revenue is negative, so total revenue decreases as the price falls. Where demand is of unitary elasticity, marginal revenue is zero, so total revenue is at a maximum, neither increasing nor decreasing. Note that the marginal revenue curve crosses the horizontal axis where demand is of unitary elasticity and total revenue is at a maximum.

increase in quantity demanded is greater than the percentage decrease in price. On the other hand, where demand is inelastic, total revenue will decline if the price falls because the percentage increase in quantity demanded is less than the percentage decrease in price.

Therefore, *when the demand curve is elastic, marginal revenue is positive and total revenue increases*. From Exhibit 3 you can see that marginal revenue becomes negative if the price drops below $3.75, indicating an inelastic demand at price levels below $3.75. Demand is of unitary elasticity at the price of $3.75. At that price, marginal revenue is zero and total revenue is at a maximum. Finally, *when the demand curve is inelastic, marginal revenue is negative and total revenue decreases*. An understanding of elasticity will be of help later in determining the price and output combination that maximizes the monopolist's profit.

FIRM COSTS AND PROFIT MAXIMIZATION

Given the demand curve, the important question is, how will the monopolist choose among the price-quantity alternatives? We assume that the objective of the monopolist, like that of the perfect competitor, is to *maximize economic profit*. In the case of perfect competition, the firm has to choose the profit-maximizing quantity because the price is given to the firm. The monopolist can choose either the price *or* the quantity, but choosing one determines the other.

Profit Maximization

What are the profit-maximizing price and output for a monopolist? Exhibit 5 repeats the revenue data from Exhibits 3 and 4 and also includes the hypothetical short-run cost data developed in the last chapter. In terms of the cost of production, a monopolist looks like any other firm. For example, since total cost equals $15 when output is zero, fixed cost must equal $15. Given the cost and revenue data, there are two ways to find the price and quantity that maximize profit.

Total Revenue Minus Total Cost The profit-maximizing monopolist employs the same decision rule as the competitive firm. If demand and cost conditions are such that economic profit is possible, the monopolist produces additional output as long as it adds more to total revenue than to total cost. *The monopolist must find the level of output where total revenue exceeds total cost by the greatest amount*. Economic profit is presented in the right-hand column of Exhibit 5. As you can see, the maximum profit is $12.50, which occurs at an output of 10 units and a price of $5.25. At that level of output, total revenue is $52.50 and total cost is $40.00.

Marginal Cost Equals Marginal Revenue *The monopolist maximizes profit by expanding output as long as marginal revenue exceeds marginal cost but must stop before*

EXHIBIT 5
SHORT-RUN COSTS AND REVENUE FOR A MONOPOLIST

Quantity (1)	Price (average revenue) (2)	Total Revenue (3)=(1)×(2)	Marginal Revenue (4)	Total Cost (5)	Marginal Cost (6)	Average Total Cost (7)	Total Profit or Loss (8)
0	$7.75	$ 0.00	—	$ 15.00	—	—	− $15.00
1	7.50	7.50	$ 7.50	19.75	$ 4.75	$19.75	− 12.25
2	7.25	14.50	7.00	23.50	3.75	11.75	− 9.00
3	7.00	21.00	6.50	26.50	3.00	8.83	− 5.50
4	6.75	27.00	6.00	29.00	2.50	7.75	− 2.00
5	6.50	32.50	5.50	31.00	2.00	6.20	1.50
6	6.25	37.50	5.00	32.50	1.50	5.42	5.00
7	6.00	42.00	4.50	33.75	1.25	4.82	8.25
8	5.75	46.00	4.00	35.25	1.50	4.41	10.75
9	5.50	49.50	3.50	37.25	2.00	4.14	12.25
10	**5.25**	**52.50**	**3.00**	**40.00**	**2.75**	**4.00**	**12.50**
11	5.00	55.00	2.50	43.25	3.25	3.93	11.75
12	4.75	57.00	2.00	48.00	4.75	4.00	9.00
13	4.50	58.50	1.50	54.50	6.50	4.19	4.00
14	4.25	59.50	1.00	64.00	9.50	4.57	− 4.50
15	4.00	60.00	0.50	77.50	13.50	5.17	− 17.50
16	3.75	60.00	0.00	96.00	18.50	6.00	− 36.00
17	3.50	59.50	− 0.50	121.00	25.00	7.12	− 61.50

marginal cost exceeds marginal revenue. Again, profit is maximized at $12.50 when output is 10 units. The marginal revenue for unit 10 is $3.00, and the marginal cost is $2.75. Expanding output beyond 10 units would lower profits because additional units add more to cost than they do to revenue. Unit 11, for example, adds $3.25 to cost but only $2.50 to revenue. If the monopolist produced 11 units, profit would fall from $12.50 to $11.75.

Graphical Solution The cost and revenue data in Exhibit 5 are plotted in Exhibit 6, with per-unit cost and revenue curves in panel (a) and total cost and revenue curves in panel (b). The intersection of the two marginal curves at point *e* in panel (a) indicates that profit is maximized when 10 units are sold. At that level of output, we move up to the demand curve to find the profit-maximizing price. When output equals 10 units, the profit-maximizing price is $5.25, as identified by point *a*, and the average total cost is $4.00, as identified by point *b*. The average profit per unit sold equals the price, or average revenue, minus the average total cost: $5.25 − $4.00, or $1.25. The total economic profit is the average profit per unit ($1.25) multiplied by the 10 units sold, for a total of $12.50, as identified by the blue rectangle.

Because the marginal cost curve will never be less than zero, marginal cost will

EXHIBIT 6   MONOPOLY COSTS AND REVENUE

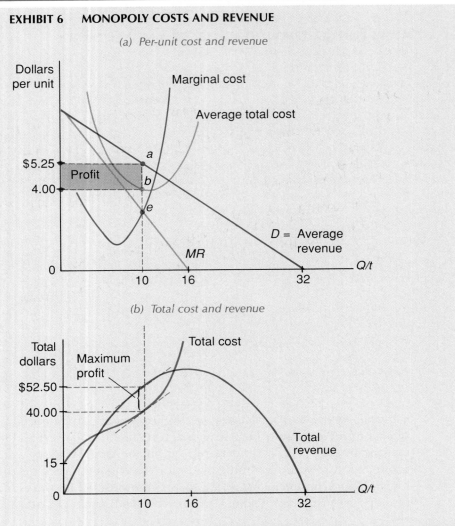

(a) Per-unit cost and revenue

(b) Total cost and revenue

Like other firms, the monopolist maximizes profit where marginal cost crosses marginal revenue—point e in panel (a). The monopolist produces 10 units of output and charges a price of $5.25. Average profit per unit is price minus average total cost, or $5.25 – 4.00 = $1.25 per unit. Total profit, shown by the blue rectangle, is $12.50, the profit per unit multiplied by the number of units sold. In panel (b), profit is maximized where marginal revenue (the slope of the total revenue curve) equals marginal cost (the slope of the total cost curve), at 10 units of output. Profit is total revenue ($52.50) minus total cost ($40.00), or $12.50.

never intersect marginal revenue where marginal revenue is negative. Thus the monopolist will produce only where the demand curve is elastic.

    The firm's profit or loss is measured by the vertical distance between the total revenue and total cost curves in panel (b). The profit-maximizing firm will produce at the level of output where total revenue exceeds total cost by the greatest amount. Thus the firm should expand output as long as the increase in total revenue that results from selling one more unit exceeds the increase in total cost that results from producing that unit. The change in total revenue as a result of a one-unit change in output equals the marginal revenue, or the slope of the total revenue curve. Likewise, the change in total cost resulting from a one-unit change in output equals the marginal cost, or the slope of the total cost curve. The profit-maximizing quantity can be found by determining where the slopes of the total revenue and total cost curves are equal, which is the same as finding the level of output at which marginal cost equals marginal revenue. In panel (b), you can see that the slopes are equal where output is 10 units.

Short-Run Losses and the Shutdown Decision

Monopolists have no guarantee of economic profit. A monopolist is the sole producer of a particular good, but the demand for that good may not be strong enough to generate profits in either the short run or the long run. After all, many new products are protected from direct competition by patents, yet they do not attract enough buyers to survive. And even a monopolist that is initially profitable may eventually suffer losses because of rising costs or falling demand. Coleco, the maker of Cabbage Patch dolls, went bankrupt after that craze died down. In the short run, the loss-minimizing monopolist, like the loss-minimizing perfect competitor, must decide whether to produce or to shut down. If total revenue covers total variable cost, the firm will operate. If total revenue fails to cover total variable cost, the firm will temporarily shut down.

Loss minimization is illustrated graphically in Exhibit 7, where the marginal cost curve intersects the marginal revenue curve at point *e*. At the equilibrium level of output, *Q*, the price, *P*, is above the average variable cost, at point *c*, but below average total cost, at point *a*. Since the firm is able to cover its variable cost and make some contribution to fixed cost, it loses less by producing *Q* than by shutting down. The firm's loss per unit is *ab*, which is the average total cost minus the average revenue, or price. The total loss, identified by the red rectangle, is the average loss per unit, *ab*, times the number of units sold, *Q*. The firm will shut down if the average variable cost curve is above the demand, or average revenue, curve at all output levels.

There Is No Monopolist Supply Curve

For the perfectly competitive firm, the portion of the marginal cost curve that rises above the average variable cost curve is the supply curve because it reflects the quantity the firm is willing and able to supply at each price. If it is able to at least cover its variable cost, the monopolist, like the perfectly competitive firm, maximizes profit (or minimizes losses) by producing where marginal cost equals marginal revenue. For the monopolist, however, unlike the perfectly competitive firm, marginal revenue does not equal the

EXHIBIT 7   THE MONOPOLIST MINIMIZES LOSSES IN THE SHORT RUN

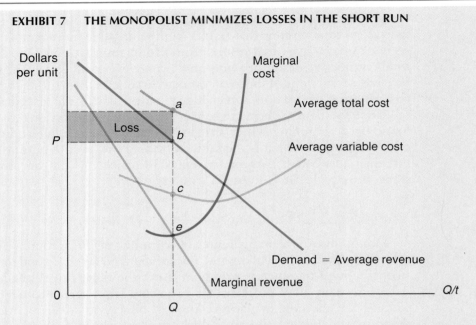

Marginal cost equals marginal revenue at point e. At quantity Q, price P (at point b) is less than average total cost (at point a), so the monopolist is suffering a loss. The monopolist will continue to produce in the short run because price is greater than average variable cost (at point c).

price. The price at the profit-maximizing (or loss-minimizing) level of output is found on the demand curve, which is *above* the marginal revenue and marginal cost curves at that quantity.

So the monopolist's marginal cost curve does not show a unique relation between price and quantity supplied, as was the case for the perfectly competitive firm. For a monopolist, the profit-maximizing quantity supplied, as determined by the intersection of marginal cost and marginal revenue, can result in different prices for different demand curves. For example, in Exhibit 8, *MC* depicts that portion of the monopolist's marginal cost curve that rises above the average variable cost curve. Consider first the demand curve D and the marginal revenue curve *MR*. The marginal cost curve intersects the marginal revenue curve at point e, resulting in an output of Q and a price of P. Suppose that demand increases to D' in such a way that the new marginal revenue curve, MR', also intersects the marginal cost curve at point e. The equilibrium quantity remains unchanged, but the equilibrium price increases to P'. Thus Exhibit 8 indicates that the same equilibrium quantity can be consistent with two different prices. *Since there is no unique relation between price and output, there is no supply curve for the monopolist—no single curve that reflects the amount the monopolist will supply at alternative prices.*

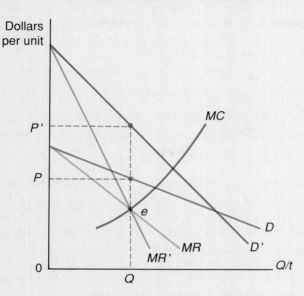

EXHIBIT 8   INCREASED DEMAND MAY NOT AFFECT OUTPUT

When the demand curve is *D*, the monopolist maximizes profit by producing *Q*, the output level for which marginal cost equals marginal revenue. If demand were to increase to *D'*, the marginal revenue curve, *MR'*, would still intersect the marginal cost curve at an output rate of *Q*. The same equilibrium level of output, *Q*, could be associated with two different price levels, *P* or *P'*, depending on demand. The exhibit shows that for the monopolist there is no unique relation between the price level and the quantity supplied. Thus there is no monopolist supply curve.

Long-Run Profit Maximization

With perfectly competitive firms, the distinction between the short run and the long run is important. In the short run, the number and size of firms in a competitive industry are fixed, and these firms may earn economic profits or losses, depending on the demand for the product. In the long run, all resources can vary, so firms will enter or leave the industry until each one is earning just a normal profit, which means zero economic profit. In the case of the monopolist, the distinction between the short run and the long run has less significance because by definition new firms are prevented from entering the market. Hence, there is no tendency for economic profit to be eliminated in the long run by the entry of new firms; economic profit can persist in the long run.

The monopolist's objective in the long run, like that of the perfectly competitive firm, is to find the scale of production that maximizes profit. Even a monopolist that earns economic profit in the short run may find that profits can be increased in the long run by adjusting the size of the firm.

In perfect competition, short-run losses are eliminated in the long run as firms leave the market. But with monopoly, economic loss does not disappear over time through the exit of other firms. If the monopolist cannot eliminate a loss in the long run by changing the scale of the firm to a more efficient size or by increasing the demand, then the firm will put its capital to more profitable use in another industry.

Myths About Monopolies

Although the objective of the monopolist is no different from that of the perfect competitor (both attempt to maximize profit), the following myths keep cropping up in discussions of monopoly.

Gouges Prices One common myth is that the monopolist will charge as high a price as possible. The monopolist, however, is interested in maximizing profit, not price. The amount the monopolist can charge is limited by consumer demand. Given the demand curve used in this chapter, the monopolist could have charged a price of $7.50, but only 1 unit would have been sold at that price. Indeed, the monopolist could have charged $8 per unit, but no product would have been sold. So charging the highest possible price is not consistent with maximizing profit.

Always Earns A Profit Another common myth is that the monopolist always earns a profit. But if the average total cost curve is above the demand curve at all output levels, no combination of price and output will yield a profit. The fact that a firm is the only producer does not guarantee that demand will be great enough to allow the firm to earn even a normal profit. After all, only a fraction of the millions of products that have received U.S. patents have ever earned their inventors a profit.

MONOPOLY AND THE ALLOCATION OF RESOURCES

If monopolists are no more greedy than competitive firms, if monopolists do not charge the highest possible price, and if monopolists are not guaranteed a profit, then what, if any, are the problems that arise from monopoly? The clearest way to answer that question is to compare a monopoly to that benchmark established in the previous chapter: the perfectly competitive industry.

Price and Output Under Perfect Competition

Let's consider first the long-run equilibrium price and output for the perfectly competitive firm and industry. Assume that we are looking at a constant-cost industry, so the long-run supply curve is the horizontal line in Exhibit 9. Because this is a constant-cost industry, the horizontal long-run

EXHIBIT 9   PERFECT COMPETITION AND MONOPOLY

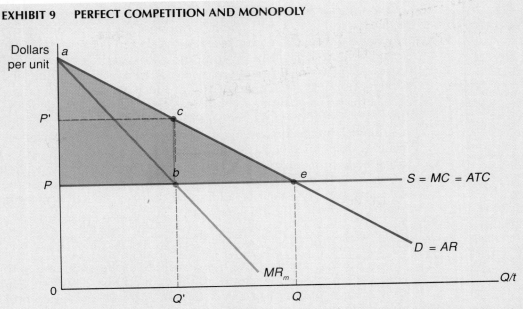

A perfectly competitive industry would produce output Q, determined at the intersection of market demand curve D and supply curve S. The price would be P.

A monopoly that could produce output at the same minimum average cost would produce output Q', determined at point b, where marginal cost and marginal revenue intersect. It would charge price P'. Hence, output is lower and price is higher under monopoly than under perfect competition.

supply curve also equals the marginal cost and the average total cost at each level of output. The competitive industry is in long-run equilibrium where market demand and market supply intersect at point e, yielding price P and quantity Q.

The demand curve indicates consumers' marginal benefit from each level of output. At the equilibrium combination of price and output in perfect competition, the marginal cost to society of producing the final unit of output (as reflected by the horizontal supply curve) just equals the marginal benefit consumers attach to that unit of the good (as reflected by the market demand curve). Because consumers are able to purchase Q units at price P, they enjoy a consumer surplus that is measured by the entire shaded triangle, aeP. You will recall that consumer surplus represents the dollar value of the net benefits consumers enjoy from purchasing Q units of the good at the market price of P.

Price and Output Under Monopoly

If there is only one firm in the industry, the industry demand curve becomes the monopolist's demand curve, and the price the monopolist can charge depends on how much is sold. Because the monopolist's demand curve slopes downward, its marginal revenue curve also slopes downward, as indicated by MR_m in Exhibit 9. Suppose the monopolist can produce at the same constant long-run average cost as can the competitive industry. A firm maximizes profit in the long run by expanding output until marginal cost equals marginal revenue, a condition that holds at point *b* in Exhibit 9. The monopolist will consequently produce output Q' at a price of P'.

At the price-quantity combination associated with point *b*, the marginal cost of the resources used to produce the final unit of output is less than the marginal benefit consumers attach to that unit. The price, or marginal benefit, at point *c* exceeds the marginal cost at point *b*. Thus the value consumers place on an extra unit exceeds the cost of producing it. Society would be better off if output were expanded beyond Q' because the marginal value consumers attach to additional units exceeds the marginal cost of producing those additional units.

Allocative and Distributive Effects

Consider the allocative and distributive effects of monopoly versus perfect competition. As long as the monopolist does not benefit from substantial economies of scale, output is lower and price higher under monopoly than under perfect competition. The monopolist's reduced output and higher price generate economic profit equal to the green rectangle in Exhibit 9. Consumer surplus under perfect competition was the large triangle *aeP*; under monopoly it's reduced to the much smaller blue triangle. By contrasting the situation under monopoly with that under perfect competition, you can see that monopoly profit comes entirely out of what was consumer surplus under competition.

Notice, however, that consumer surplus has been reduced by more than the gain in monopoly profit. Consumers have lost more than the green rectangle; they have also lost the red triangle, which was part of the consumer surplus under perfect competition. Whereas monopoly profit represents benefits transferred from consumers to the monopolist, the red triangle is called the **deadweight loss**, or *welfare loss*, of monopoly because it is a loss to consumers that is not transferred to anyone else. Thus, *if the monopolist can produce output at the same minimum average cost as the competitive firm, the red triangle measures the welfare loss arising from the higher price and reduced output of the monopolist.* The red triangle is a deadweight loss because it represents consumer surplus forgone on units of output that are no longer produced. Empirical estimates of the annual welfare cost of monopoly have ranged from less than 1 percent to about 6 percent of national income. Applied to 1989 income data, these estimates imply a welfare cost as high as $250 billion.

*The **deadweight loss** of monopoly is the forgone consumer surplus (transferred to no one) that arises from the monopolization of an industry.*

PROBLEMS WITH ESTIMATING THE WELFARE COST OF MONOPOLY

Forces at work in the economy could make the actual cost of monopoly different from the welfare loss described in the previous section. We will first consider reasons why monopoly might create a smaller welfare loss than that measured in Exhibit 9 and then reasons why the welfare loss might be greater.

Why the Welfare Loss of Monopoly Might Be Lower Than Estimated

If an industry experiences substantial economies of scale, a monopolist may be able to produce output at a lower cost per unit than can perfectly competitive firms. Therefore the price may be less under monopoly than under competition. Even where there are no significant economies of scale, a monopolist may try to keep the price down to discourage new entry and to protect the firm's long-run potential for profits.

Fear of Potential Rivals The monopolist may keep the price below the short-run profit-maximizing level because high profits are a powerful economic signal to potential rivals. If the monopolist does not have ironclad protection against new firms' entering the industry, it may try to reduce the chances of attracting new competitors. For example, before World War II Alcoa was the only manufacturer of aluminum in the United States. Some observers claim the company kept prices low to discourage potential rivals.

Fear of Public Intervention The welfare loss estimated in Exhibit 9 may overstate the true cost of monopoly because monopolists may, in response to public scrutiny and political pressure, keep prices below what the market could bear. We speak here not about government-regulated monopolies, but about monopolies that curb their profit to avoid public attention and criticism.

Although monopolists would like to earn as great a profit as possible, they realize that if the public outcry over high profit grows loud enough, some sort of government intervention could reduce profits. For example, because of the increase in oil prices during the middle and late 1970s, Congress increased the taxes on oil companies. Firms may try to avoid such a "windfall" profits tax by keeping prices somewhat below the level that would maximize short-run profit.

Why the Welfare Loss of Monopoly Might Be Higher Than Estimated

Another line of thinking, however, suggests that the welfare loss of monopoly may, in fact, be greater than estimated in our simple diagram.

Monopolists Become Inefficient The monopolist, insulated from the rigors of competition in the marketplace, may grow fat and lazy — and become inefficient. Consequently, the firm may not use the least-cost combination of resources. Since some monopolies still earn an economic profit even if output is not produced at the least possible cost, corporate executives may employ resources so as to create a more comfortable life for themselves. Long lunches, afternoon golf, Oriental carpets, and expensive employee benefits may make company life more enjoyable. But these additional expenses also raise the cost of production above what it would be if the firm used the least-cost combination of resources.

Monopolists have also been criticized for being slow to adopt the latest production techniques, being reluctant to develop new products, and generally lacking in innovation. Because monopolists escape the rigors of competition, they may be content to rest on their oars. As the British economist J. R. Hicks remarked, "The best of all monopoly profits is a quiet life."

Not all economists, however, believe that monopolists manage their resources with any less vigilance than people running perfectly competitive firms. Joseph Schumpeter argued that because monopolists are protected from rivals, they are in a position to capture the fruits of any innovation and therefore be more innovative than competitive firms.

Furthermore, if a firm is eroding its monopoly profits through bloated payrolls, company perks, and the failure to innovate, profits will be below their potential. With reduced profits, the value of the firm's stock will be lower than it would be if the firm were more efficient. Lower stock prices provide a strong incentive for outsiders to buy a controlling share of the firm's stock, shape up the operation, and watch profits—as well as the value of the firm's stock—grow. Some economists argue that this *market for corporate control* ensures that even monopolists will not stray too far from the path of efficient production.

Monopolists Expend Resources Trying to Secure and Maintain Monopoly Power If resources must be devoted to securing and maintaining a monopoly position, monopolies may involve more of a welfare loss than simple models suggest. For example, consider radio and TV broadcasting rights, which confer on the recipient the exclusive privilege to use a particular band of the scarce broadcast spectrum. These rights are given away by government agencies to the applicants who are deemed most deserving. Because these rights are so valuable, typically numerous applicants each allocate abundant resources to lawyers' fees, lobbying expenses, and other costs associated with making themselves appear the most deserving. The efforts devoted to securing and maintaining a monopoly position are largely a social waste because they use up scarce resources but add not one unit to output. Activities undertaken by individuals or firms to influence public policy in a way that will directly or indirectly redistribute income to themselves are called **rent seeking**.

Rent seeking is any effort by individuals or firms to shape public policies so as to redistribute income to themselves.

MODELS OF PRICE DISCRIMINATION

The model of monopoly examined thus far is based on the implicit assumption that the monopolist charges all consumers the same price.

Price discrimination
is selling at different prices to different consumers or charging the same consumer different prices for different units of a good, for reasons unrelated to costs.

Under certain conditions, however, the monopolist can increase profits through **price discrimination**, which is the practice of selling output at different prices to different groups of consumers or charging the same consumer different prices for different units of the good, for reasons unrelated to cost. The aim is to charge a higher price to those consumers whose demand is less elastic than to those whose demand is more elastic.

Preconditions for Price Discrimination

In order for a firm to practice price discrimination, certain conditions must exist. First, the demand curve for the product must slope downward, indicating that the producer has some control over the price. This condition holds for the monopolist and, as we will see in the next chapter, for firms in some other market structures as well. Only for perfectly competitive firms does this condition not hold. Second, there must be at least two classes of consumers with different price elasticities of demand. Third, the producer must be able, at little cost, to distinguish between the different classes of consumers. Finally, the monopolist must be able to prevent those buyers who face a lower price from reselling the product to buyers who face a higher price.

Examples of Price Discrimination

Let's consider some examples of price discrimination. Because the costs are paid by their companies and are tax deductible, businesspeople tend to be less sensitive to differences in the price of travel and communication than do households. Businesses therefore have a less elastic demand for travel and communication than do households, so airlines and telephone utilities try to maximize profits by charging the two classes of customers different rates. But how do firms distinguish between households and businesses?

Telephone companies have been able to sort out their customers by charging different rates based on the time of day. Long-distance charges are higher during normal *business* hours than during evenings and weekends, when households, which presumably have a higher price elasticity of demand, make social calls. The airlines try to distinguish between business customers and household customers based on the terms under which tickets are purchased. Households plan their vacations well in advance and often stay for a week or more. They have more flexibility about when they travel and are more sensitive to price than are business travelers. Business travel, on the other hand, is more unpredictable and more urgent and seldom involves a weekend stay. The airlines separate business travelers from vacationers by requiring purchasers of "super-saver" fares to buy tickets well in advance and to spend a weekend at their destination.

Admission to many activities, such as movies and sporting events, is offered at reduced prices to children, students, and senior citizens because these groups presumably are more sensitive to price—that is, they have a more elastic demand. Some firms distinguish among consumers based on the amount of the purchase. For example, industrial users of electricity usually pay lower rates than do households.

A Model of Price Discrimination

Exhibit 10 shows the effects of price discrimination. Consumers are divided into two groups with distinctly different demands. The exhibit shows their demand and marginal revenue curves, along with the producer's marginal cost curve. For simplicity, we assume that the monopolist produces at a constant long-run marginal cost and that this cost is the same for supplying both groups. The consumers in panel (a) generally attach a higher marginal value to each unit of the good than do those in panel (b). In each market the price is determined by finding the level of output that equates marginal cost and marginal revenue. The price elasticity of consumers in panel (b) is greater than that of consumers in panel (a), so consumers in panel (a) are charged a higher price.

Perfect Price Discrimination: The Monopolist's Dream

The demand curve conveys the marginal value consumers attach to each unit consumed. We know that consumers receive a consumer surplus when they are able to purchase all units of the good for a price equal to the marginal value of the last unit consumed. If the monopolist could charge a separate price for each unit consumed—a price equal to the consumers' marginal value of each unit consumed—then the demand curve would

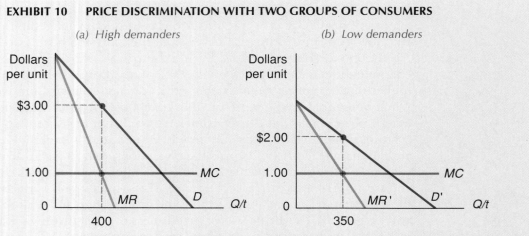

EXHIBIT 10   PRICE DISCRIMINATION WITH TWO GROUPS OF CONSUMERS

A monopolist that faces two groups of consumers with different demand elasticities may be able to practice price discrimination. With marginal cost the same in both markets, the firm sells 400 units to the high-marginal-value consumers in panel (a) and charges them a price of $3 per unit. It sells 350 units to the low-marginal-value consumers in panel (b) and charges them a price of $2.

become the firm's marginal revenue curve. The firm's marginal revenue from selling one more unit would equal the price of that unit. Suppose the monopolist produced at a constant average cost in the long run, as described in the previous two exhibits. The *perfectly discriminating monopolist* would determine the profit-maximizing level of output by setting marginal cost equal to marginal revenue, as at point *e* in Exhibit 11. The firm's economic profit would be defined by the area of the shaded triangle.

By charging a different price for each unit of output, the perfectly discriminating monopolist could convert every dollar of consumer surplus into economic profit. Although this might not be the most equitable way to distribute goods, it would get high marks for allocative efficiency. As in the perfectly competitive outcome, the marginal cost of producing the last unit of output would just equal the marginal benefit consumers attached to that unit. No adjustment in the level of output could make someone better off without reducing monopoly profit. And although consumers would reap no consumer surplus, the total benefits they received from consuming the good would just equal the total price they paid for the good. Note also that because the monopolist would not restrict output, there would be no deadweight loss of monopoly—no welfare triangle.

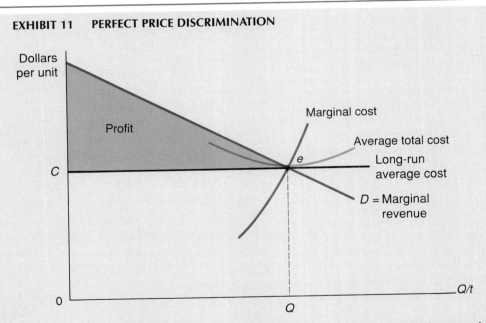

EXHIBIT 11   PERFECT PRICE DISCRIMINATION

If a monopolist can charge a different price for each unit sold, it may be able to practice perfect price discrimination. By setting the price of each unit equal to the maximum amount consumers are willing to pay for that unit (shown by the height of the demand curve), the monopolist can achieve a profit equal to the area of the shaded triangle. Consumer surplus is zero.

CONCLUSION

Pure monopoly, like perfect competition, is seldom observed in the real world. Few firms sell a product for which there are no close substitutes. Economic profit motivates potential rivals to hurdle any barriers to entry. Our examination of pure monopoly and perfect competition, however, has produced a framework that will be helpful for viewing market structures that lie between the two extremes. Monopoly may be rare, but many firms have some degree of monopoly power—that is, they face downward-sloping demand curves. In the next chapter we will consider two market structures in which firms have some monopoly power.

Summary

1. A monopolist sells a product with no close substitutes. A monopoly can persist in the long run only if the entry of new firms into the market is blocked. Three barriers to entry are (1) legal restrictions, such as patents and operating licenses; (2) economies of scale, which make it inefficient for more than one firm to produce the good; and (3) control over an essential resource used in production.

2. Because a monopolist is the sole supplier in a market, the market demand curve is also the monopolist's demand curve. The individual firm can sell more units only if the price is reduced. Because the price must fall for more output to be sold, the monopolist's marginal revenue is less than the price.

3. There is a clear relation among the monopolist's price elasticity of demand, marginal revenue curve, and total revenue curve. When demand is elastic, marginal revenue is positive, and total revenue increases as the price falls. When demand is inelastic, marginal revenue is negative, and total revenue decreases as the price falls.

4. If the monopolist can at least cover its variable cost at some level of output, it can maximize profits or minimize losses by searching for the price-output combination that equates marginal cost with marginal revenue. Because marginal cost is never less than zero, the monopolist never willingly produces where marginal revenue is negative. To put it another way,

the monopolist never produces where demand is inelastic, or where total revenue is declining.

5. In the short run, the monopolist, like the perfect competitor, will shut down unless the price is at or above the average variable cost. But in the long run, the monopolist, unlike the perfect competitor, can earn economic profits as long as the entry of new firms is somehow blocked. There is no supply curve for the monopolist, as there is for the perfectly competitive firm.

6. Resources are usually not allocated as efficiently under unregulated monopoly as under perfect competition. Unlike perfect competition, monopoly usually results in a net welfare loss because the loss in consumer surplus exceeds the gain in monopoly profits.

7. Where conditions permit, a monopolist can increase profits by charging different types of consumers different prices for the same good or charging the same consumer different prices for different units of the good. To increase profits through price discrimination, the monopolist (1) must have at least two identifiable types of consumers with different elasticities of demand, (2) must be able to distinguish between the different types of consumers, and (3) must be able to prevent those consumers who pay the lower price from reselling to those who pay the higher price. A perfect price discriminator charges a different price for each unit of the good, thereby capturing all consumer surplus as economic profit.

1. (Barriers to Entry) What are some barriers to entry into the professional sports industry? For example, why aren't there more professional baseball teams?

2. (Barriers to Entry) In South Korea ginseng and tobacco distribution are state-owned monopolies. What might motivate a government to impose such a barrier to entry?

3. (Monopoly) Are such wonders of the world as the Grand Canyon and the Great Wall of China monopolies because they are one of a kind? Are there substitutes for such places?

4. (Revenue Maximization) Suppose a UFO crashes in your backyard. Ignoring any costs that may be involved, what price would you charge people to come and view the site? Would you allow photographs? Why or why not?

5. (Monopoly) Only one airline has flights to and from some of the South Seas islands. Would this airline qualify as a monopoly? How would such a company price its flights to the islands to maximize profits? Would it price cargo and mail at the same rate per pound? Why or why not?

6. (Demand and Marginal Revenue) Suppose that at a price of $3 per unit, the quantity demanded is 10 units. Explain why, when marginal revenue is equal to $3, quantity demanded must be (roughly) equal to 5 units.

7. (Monopoly) Why is it impossible for a profit-maximizing monopolist to choose any price *and* any quantity it wishes?

8. (Monopoly and Welfare) Why is society worse off under monopoly than under perfect competition? When might monopoly be more efficient?

9. (Price Discrimination) Explain how it may be profitable for Koreans to sell newly produced autos at a cheaper price in the United States than in Korea, even with transportation costs.

10. (Perfect Price Discrimination) Why is the demand curve above marginal cost equal to the marginal revenue curve for the perfectly discriminating monopolist?

11. (Monopoly) Suppose that a certain manufacturer has a monopoly on the sorority and fraternity ring business—a constant-cost industry—because he has persuaded the "Greeks" to give him exclusive rights to their insignia.
    a. Using demand and cost curves, draw a diagram representing the company's profit-maximizing pricing/output decision.
    b. Why is marginal revenue less than price for this company?
    c. On your diagram, show the welfare loss that occurs because the output level is determined by the monopoly situation rather than by a competitive market.
    d. What would happen if the Greeks decided to charge the manufacturer a royalty fee of $3 per ring?
    e. What would happen if the Greeks charged the manufacturer a franchise fee (unrelated to ring production) instead of the royalty fee?

12. (Discriminating Monopoly) Suppose that do-dads are sold to two types of people and that the long-run production costs are constant at $1 per do-dad. Use the following data to answer the questions below. Q_1 represents sales to type 1 people; Q_2 is sales to type 2 people.

P	Q_1	Q_2	$Q_1 + Q_2$	Short-run MC of total Q
$10	4	12	16	$ 1.50
9	6	14	20	2.00
8	8	16	24	3.00
7	10	18	28	7.00
6	12	20	32	12.00
5	14	22	36	20.00
3	18	26	44	40.00
1	22	30	52	80.00

a. Determine the short-run equilibrium price and quantity for this industry, assuming it is competitive.
b. Determine the long-run equilibrium price and quantity for this industry, assuming it is competitive.
c. If do-dads were produced by a non-discriminating monopolist, what price and quantity would maximize short-run profits? long-run profits?
d. If this monopolist could practice price discrimination, what would be the long-run profit-maximizing price and quantity for each group of buyers?

13. (Demand and Marginal Revenue) What is marginal revenue when the value of price elasticity of demand is 1? Explain.

14. (Monopoly and Welfare Loss) Suppose that a firm has a monopoly on a good with the following demand schedule.

P	Q	P	Q
$10	0	$4	6
9	1	3	7
8	2	2	8
7	3	1	9
6	4	0	10
5	5		

a. Calculate the marginal revenue for each output level.
b. What is the profit-maximizing output level if the firm faces constant marginal costs of $3 per unit?
c. Calculate the dollar value of the welfare loss attributable to the fact that this industry is monopolistic rather than competitive.

Between Perfect Competition and Monopoly

Perfect competition and pure monopoly represent the two extreme market structures. Perfect competition is characterized by a homogeneous commodity produced by a large number of sellers who in the long run can enter and leave the industry with ease. Monopoly involves only one seller of a product with no close substitutes; competitors are blocked from entering this market by natural or artificial barriers to entry. These polar market structures are logically appealing and are useful in describing the workings of some markets observed in the economy.

Many markets, however, are not well described by either model. Some markets involve many sellers producing goods that vary slightly, such as the many radio stations that vie for your attention or the convenience stores that blanket metropolitan areas. Other markets consist of a small number of sellers who in some cases produce homogeneous goods, such as oil or steel, and in other cases produce differentiated goods, such as automobiles or breakfast cereal. In this chapter two additional models will be introduced to explain these types of market structures. Topics discussed in this chapter include

- Monopolistic competition
- Product differentiation
- Excess capacity
- Oligopoly
- Competing models of oligopoly
- Mergers

MONOPOLISTIC COMPETITION

During the 1920s and 1930s, economists began formulating models to fit between perfect competition and pure monopoly. Two models of *monopolistic competition* were developed separately. In 1933 at Harvard University, Edward Chamberlin published *The Theory of Monopolistic Competition*. Across the Atlantic that same year, Cambridge University's Joan Robinson published *The Economics of Imperfect Competition*. Although the theories differed, their underlying principles were similar. In this section we will discuss Chamberlin's approach.

Characteristics of Monopolistic Competition

Monopolistic competition is the market structure characterized by a large number of firms selling products that are close substitutes.

The expression **monopolistic competition** is meant to suggest that the market contains elements of both monopoly and competition. Chamberlin used the expression to describe the structure of a market characterized by a large number of producers offering products that are close substitutes but are not viewed as identical by consumers. Because the burgers sold by McDonald's, Burger King, Wendy's, Roy Rogers, and Hardee's can be distinguished from one another, the demand curve each firm faces is not horizontal but downward sloping: each firm has some power over the price it charges. Thus these firms are not *price takers*, as they would be under perfect competition.

Firms in monopolistic competition can enter or leave the market with relative ease. Under monopolistic competition there are enough sellers that they behave competitively. There are also enough sellers that each firm gets lost in the crowd—that is, each firm is so insignificant relative to the market that its price and output policies will be largely ignored by other firms. Hence an individual firm acts *independently*; it is not concerned about how competitors react to any change in its price or output. You will understand the significance of this independent behavior later in the chapter.

Product Differentiation

Product differentiation distinguishes monopolistic competition from perfect competition, where the product is viewed as homogeneous. Sellers can differentiate their products in four basic ways.

Physical Differences The most obvious way products are differentiated is by their physical qualities. The ways that products can differ are seemingly endless: size, weight, taste, texture, and so on. Shampoos, for example, differ in color, scent, thickness, and lathering ability.

Location The number and variety of locations where a product is available represents another dimension of its character. Some products seem to be available everywhere; locating others requires some search and travel. If you live in a metropolitan area, you are accustomed to seeing a large number of convenience stores. Each wants to be closest to you when you need that half gallon of milk—hence a proliferation of stores. These mini grocery stores are selling convenience. Their prices are higher and their selection more limited than those of regular grocery stores, but they are often nearer to customers and they stay open later.

Services Products are also differentiated based on the accompanying services. For example, some pizza sellers deliver; others do not. Some retail stores offer helpful product demonstrations by a well-trained sales staff; other stores are essentially self-service.

Product Image A final way products differ is in the image the producer tries to foster in the mind of the consumer. Whether or not the customer's perception is based on real differences among products does not matter. For example, a clothing manufacturer may try to persuade you that its jeans are special because some celebrity's name is on the back pocket. Some brands of beauty cream sell for $35 a jar, but they contain virtually the same ingredients as other brands selling for less than one-tenth that price. Particular brand names may suggest high quality by the way they are promoted, the form of packaging, or the kind of stores in which they are sold. Producers try to find a particular niche in the consumer's mind through product promotion and advertising.

Price and Output Under Monopolistic Competition

Because the monopolistic competitor offers a product that is differentiated from other products in the industry, each firm has some power to control the price it charges. This "market power" is reflected by a demand curve for the firm's product that slopes downward but is relatively flat. Since many firms are producing goods that are close substitutes, any firm that raises its price can expect to lose some customers to rivals. In contrast, a firm in perfect competition can expect to lose *all* its customers if it raises its price, since it is producing a product that is identical to those of its competitors. Therefore the demand for the monopolistically competitive firm's output is less elastic than the demand for the perfectly competitive firm's output, which is perfectly elastic. At the other extreme, the pure monopolist's demand curve is less elastic than a monopolistic competitor's because, by definition, the monopolist faces no competition for its output.

Recall that the number and similarity of available substitutes for a given product are important determinants of the price elasticity of demand. Therefore the elasticity of the monopolistically competitive firm's demand curve depends on the number of rival firms that produce a similar product and the firm's ability to differentiate its product from those of its rivals. *The firm's demand curve will be more elastic the greater the number of competing firms and the less differentiated the firm's product.*

Marginal Cost Equals Marginal Revenue From our analysis of monopoly, we know that the downward-sloping demand curve faced by the firm in monopolistic competition means that the firm's marginal revenue curve also slopes downward and that it lies below the demand curve. Exhibit 1 depicts demand and marginal revenue curves for a hypothetical firm in monopolistic competition. The exhibit also presents hypothetical cost curves. Note that the shapes of the cost curves do not depend on the nature of the market structure; the forces that determine the cost of production are largely independent of the forces that shape demand.

If a firm can at least cover its variable cost, it will expand production as long as marginal revenue exceeds marginal cost. For short, we can say that *the profit-maximizing level of output is determined by the intersection of the marginal cost and marginal revenue curves, and the profit-maximizing price is found on the demand curve at that level of output.* Panels (a) and (b) in Exhibit 1 identify the price and output combinations that, respectively, maximize short-run profits and minimize short-run losses. The intersection of marginal cost and marginal revenue is identified as point e, the level of output is q, the price is P, and the average total cost is measured on the vertical axis as C.

Maximizing Profits or Minimizing Losses in the Short Run Recall that the short run is a period too short to allow firms to enter or leave the market. Thus firms in monopolistically competitive markets can earn economic profits in the short run. The demand and cost conditions depicted in Exhibit 1(a) indicate that this firm will earn a profit in the short run. At the firm's profit-maximizing level of output, the firm's average total cost is below the price. As noted earlier, the difference between the two is the firm's profit per unit,

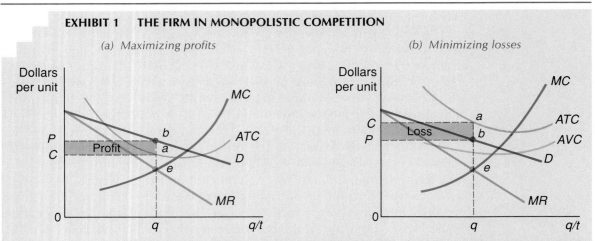

EXHIBIT 1   THE FIRM IN MONOPOLISTIC COMPETITION

The monopolistically competitive firm produces the level of output at which marginal cost equals marginal revenue (point e) and charges the price indicated by point b on the downward-sloping demand curve. In panel (a), the firm produces q units, sells them at price P, and earns a short-run profit equal to (P – C) multiplied by q. In panel (b), the average total cost exceeds the price at the optimal level of output. Thus the firm suffers a short-run loss equal to (C – P) multiplied by q.

and the profit per unit multiplied by the number of units sold yields the total profit, shown by the blue rectangle in panel (a). Note that a monopolistically competitive firm, like a monopolist, has no supply curve. Quantity supplied depends on the intersection of the marginal cost and marginal revenue curves, and the price is found on the demand curve at that quantity.

The monopolistically competitive firm, like other firms, has no guarantee of profit in the short run. The firm's demand and cost curves could be as depicted in panel (b), where the firm's average total cost curve lies above the demand curve, so no level of output would allow the firm to break even. In such a situation the firm must decide whether to produce or to shut down temporarily. The decision rule here is the same as with perfect competition and monopoly: as long as the price is above the average variable cost (as shown in Exhibit 1), the firm should produce and thereby cover at least a portion of its fixed cost. If the price fails to cover the average variable cost, the firm should shut down. Recall that the halt in production may be only temporary; shutting down is not necessarily the same as going out of business. Firms that expect losses to persist will leave the industry but will still incur short-run losses.

Zero Economic Profit in the Long Run

In the long run, the monopolistically competitive firm is in the same profit situation as the perfectly competitive firm. Since there are no barriers to entry, economic profit will attract new entrants into the industry. Because new entrants offer a product that is very similar to those offered by existing firms, new entrants draw many of their customers from existing firms, thereby reducing the demand facing each firm. Eventually, all firms reach the point where they are earning no economic profit; there is then no incentive for additional firms to enter the market. Thus monopolistically competitive firms will in the long run earn no economic profit.

If they incur short-run losses, some firms will leave the industry in the long run, redirecting their resources to activities that are expected to earn at least a normal profit. As firms leave the industry, their customers will switch to the remaining firms, increasing the demand for each firm's product. Firms will continue to leave in the long run until the remaining firms have enough customers to earn a normal profit, but no economic profit.

Exhibit 2 shows the long-run equilibrium for a typical monopolistically competitive firm. In the long run, entry and exit will alter each firm's demand curve until it is just tangent to the total cost curve. In Exhibit 2, this equilibrium is at price P and output level q. Since the average total cost equals the price, the firm earns no economic profit. At all other levels of output, the firm's average total cost is above its demand curve, so the firm would lose money if it reduced or expanded its output level. This same equilibrium point can also be determined by finding the output level where marginal cost equals marginal revenue.

Thus, if entry is easy and if all firms are selling goods that are close but not perfect substitutes, economic profit will, in the long run, draw new

EXHIBIT 2   LONG-RUN EQUILIBRIUM IN MONOPOLISTIC COMPETITION

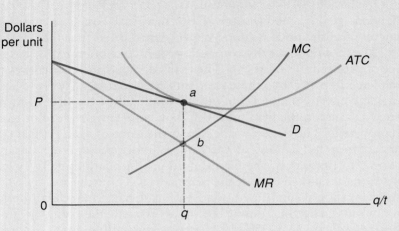

If existing firms are earning economic profits, new firms will enter the industry. The entry of such firms reduces the demand facing each firm. In the long run, demand is reduced far enough that at output q the demand curve is tangent to the average total cost curve (point a) and marginal revenue equals marginal cost (point b). Profit is zero at output q. With zero economic profit, no new firms enter, so the industry is in long-run equilibrium.

entrants into the industry until that profit disappears. Economic losses will force some firms to leave the industry over the long run until remaining firms earn just a normal profit. In summary, *monopolistic competition is like pure monopoly in the sense that firms in each industry face demand curves that slope downward. Monopolistic competition is like perfect competition in the sense that easy entry and exit result in a normal profit in the long run.*

A Comparison of Perfect Competition and Monopolistic Competition

How does monopolistic competition compare with perfect competition in terms of efficiency? In the long run, firms are unable to earn an economic profit in either situation, so what is the difference? The difference lies in the shape of the demand curves facing firms in each of the two market structures.

Exhibit 3 presents the long-run equilibrium price and quantity for firms in each of the two market structures. In each case the average cost curve is tangent to the demand curve faced by the firm. Since the good produced by a perfectly competitive firm is exactly like those produced by other firms in the industry, no firm can charge more than the market price without losing all its customers. So the demand curve for each firm in perfect competition is a horizontal line drawn at the market price, as shown in panel (a), indicating

EXHIBIT 3   MONOPOLISTIC COMPETITION VERSUS PERFECT COMPETITION

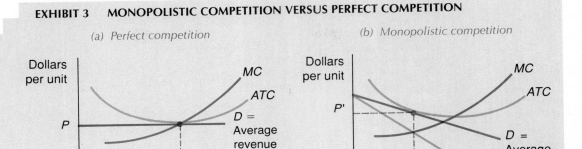

(a) Perfect competition   *(b) Monopolistic competition*

The perfectly competitive firm of panel (a) faces a demand curve that is horizontal at market price *P*. Long-run equilibrium occurs at output *q*, where the demand (average revenue) curve is tangent to the average total cost curve at its lowest point. The monopolistically competitive firm of panel (b) is in long-run equilibrium at output *q'*, where demand is tangent to average total cost. However, since the demand curve slopes downward, the tangency does not occur at the minimum point of average total cost. Hence the monopolistically competitive firm produces less output at a higher price than does a perfectly competitive firm facing the same cost conditions.

that each firm can sell all it wants at the market price but nothing at a higher price. In the long run, entry and exit ensure that economic profit equals zero. Each firm's average cost curve is tangent to its demand curve at the low point of the average total cost curve. Thus output is produced at the lowest possible average cost.

In panel (b), the firm in monopolistic competition faces a downward-sloping demand curve because its product is somewhat differentiated from those produced by other firms. As a result of the entry and exit of other firms in the long run, the downward-sloping demand curve is tangent to the firm's average total cost curve at a point that is not on the lowest portion of the average cost curve. The monopolistic competitor produces at an equilibrium rate of output that lies to the left of the minimum point on its average cost curve. Thus, *if firms have the same cost curves, the firm under monopolistic competition tends to produce less and to charge more than a firm under perfect competition.*

Under perfect competition firms produce where price equals marginal cost, but under monopolistic competition firms produce where price exceeds marginal cost. When the price exceeds the marginal cost, the result is allocative inefficiency. Efficiency could be increased by expanding output because the marginal benefit of additional output exceeds the marginal cost of that output.

Joan Robinson
(1903–1983)

In economics, as in other sciences, occasionally there is a "multiple discovery": two or more people, working independently, publish a new and important idea at nearly the same time. What makes these episodes especially intriguing is that, when we look more closely at the discoveries and the discoverers, we usually find as much difference as similarity.

A good case in point is the concept of "monopolistic competition," which was formulated in the early 1930s by Edward H. Chamberlin and Joan Robinson. Both writers outlined the characteristics of a market in which there were many firms (each too small to affect the behavior of other firms) each of which nonetheless retained some of the characteristics of a monopolist. There the similarity between the theories ends. Chamberlin began with the idea of product differentiation and deduced

from this that firms must produce at higher-than-minimum average cost. Robinson started with the idea that firms produce where costs are still declining and then tacked on the idea that such firms must also face downward-sloping demand curves. Chamberlin viewed a "monopolistically competitive" market as a good thing, arguing that the diversity offered by such a market more than made up for any higher-than-minimum costs. Robinson saw the same market structure as unequivocally bad, arguing that the proliferation of monopolistic competitors amounted to social waste.

Most modern-day economists consider Chamberlin's version of the theory to be the more interesting and well developed of the two. But from a larger perspective, it is clear that Joan Robinson was the more interesting and important economist. Her work on

the theory of monopolistic competition is but a small part of her lifelong contribution. She made many equally important contributions to the theory of economic growth and distribution. Robinson was an early and enthusiastic supporter of Keynesian ideas. She saw in Keynes's model a clear message that the economic system cannot be trusted to work properly without government intervention, and she went on to develop a school of thought that is now called "post-Keynesian" economics.

Joan Robinson was born in Camberley, Surrey, England. She spent her entire academic career at Cambridge University, progressing from student to Lecturer to Reader to Professor. Although her "heretical" views (as she herself called them) may have prevented her from receiving the Nobel Prize, she is widely seen as one of the foremost economists of her age.

Portrait by Peter Lofts Photography

Richard Langlois

Some economists argue that monopolistic competition also results in a wasteful allocation of resources because each firm fails to produce where average cost is at a minimum. For example, consider a crossroads with a gas station on each corner—more than enough stations to service the demands of passing motorists. Although each station earns a normal profit in the long run, the gas pumps are often idle. Or consider the excess capacity in the funeral home business. Industry analysts argue that the nation's 22,000 funeral homes could easily handle 4 million funerals a year, but only half that number of people die. Thus the industry on average operates at only 50 percent of capacity, resulting in higher costs per funeral.

The cost curves in Exhibit 3 are assumed to be identical, but firms in monopolistic competition often try to differentiate their products. Firms in such industries spend more on advertising and other selling expenses than do firms in perfect competition, so cost curves tend to be higher under monopolistic competition. Whether consumers benefit from the greater diversity offered remains a debated question. Some economists, including Joan Robinson, have argued that monopolistic competition results in too many brands, too much promotional effort, and product differentiation that is often artificial. Edward Chamberlin, on the other hand, in outlining his theory of monopolistic competition, argued that the higher cost per unit resulting from excess capacity is the price consumers willingly pay for having a greater selection. According to this view, resources are not wasted because consumers are given a wider choice among gas stations, funeral homes, fast-food outlets, convenience stores, clothing stores, drugstores, computer software, economics textbooks, and many other goods and services. We close our discussion of monopolistic competition by considering a familiar example, computer software and computer magazines.

Personal Computer Products

There are now over 150 relatively well known makers of personal computers, plus hundreds more tiny producers who assemble computers in their basements. The introduction of the personal computer has given rise to many complementary activities, such as the production of software and the publication of personal computer magazines. In 1989 over 3000 software companies were producing over 20,000 different programs. The computer software industry closely approximates monopolistic competition. There are numerous participants. The products are heterogeneous, yet are close substitutes. That is, a given computer program is viewed as somewhat different from the others but not so different that the producer can increase its price without losing some customers to competing software producers. Entry is relatively easy; there are few legal restrictions and no heavy initial start-up costs. A computer whiz can develop a new program using little more than imagination.

In the early days of the industry, producers relied on word of mouth to spread the good news to software buyers. As the use of personal computers grew and the number of software producers increased, advertising to differentiate products also increased. Computer software producers began hiring Madison Avenue advertising firms, which spent multi–million-dollar budgets to reach a growing market. This growth in advertising supported the mushrooming growth of computer magazines. Depending on the definition, there are now between 150 and 400 computer magazines on the market. Each tries to find its niche. For example, a dozen magazines are devoted to IBM personal computers; others specialize in the Apple Macintosh. Thus these magazines are slightly differentiated but so numerous as to comprise a monopolistically competitive industry.

Sources: Theresa Engstrom, "Personal Computers Inspire a Rash of Magazines, but Shakeout Is Seen," *Wall Street Journal*, 9 April 1984; "The Shakeout in Software: It's Already Here," *BusinessWeek* (20 August 1984): 102–104; and William Bulkeley, "Clone-Computer Business Is Booming," *Wall Street Journal*, 7 October 1988.

AN INTRODUCTION TO OLIGOPOLY

Oligopoly is the market structure characterized by a small number of firms whose behavior is interdependent.

Another important market structure is **oligopoly**, which is a market dominated by a few sellers. When we think of "big business," we are thinking of oligopoly. Many industries, including steel, automobiles, oil, breakfast cereals, and tobacco, are oligopolistic. Perfectly competitive firms and monopolistically competitive firms are so numerous that the actions of each have little effect on the behavior of other firms in the industry. Because there are few firms in an oligopolistic market, however, each firm must weigh the effect of its own policies on rivals' behavior. Consequently, oligopoly involves a few sellers who are *interdependent*.

Varieties of Oligopoly

In some oligopolistic industries, such as steel and oil, the product sold is homogeneous; in other industries, such as automobiles and tobacco, the product sold is differentiated. Where the goods being sold are homogeneous, there is greater interdependence among the few dominant firms in the industry. For example, the producers of steel ingots are more sensitive to one another's pricing policies than are the producers of autos, because steel ingots are essentially identical whereas autos differ across producers. A small rise in the price of an ingot will send customers to a rival supplier. Make no mistake, however: auto producers are still sensitive to one another's pricing policies. They just are not as sensitive as steel producers.

Because of this interdependence among firms in the industry, the behavior of a particular firm is difficult to analyze. Each firm will react to other firms' changes in price, output, product quality, and advertising. *Each firm knows that any changes in its own policies will produce a reaction from its rivals.* Whereas perfect competition can be likened to a professional golf tournament, where each player is striving for a personal best, oligopoly is more like a tennis match, where one player's actions depend very much on how and where the opponent hits the ball.

Why have some industries evolved into an oligopolistic market structure, dominated by only a few firms, whereas other industries have not? Although the reasons are not always clear, *an oligopolistic market structure can often be traced to some form of barrier to entry, such as economies of scale, legal restrictions, brand names built up by years of extensive advertising, or control over an essential resource.* The number of firms is small because new firms find it difficult to break into the industry. In the previous chapter we examined barriers to entry as they applied to monopoly. The same principles apply to oligopoly. Perhaps the most significant barrier to entry is economies of scale.

Economies of Scale

If the production process requires a relatively large output before low production costs can be achieved, only a few firms are necessary to produce the total output demanded in the market. Perhaps the best example is the auto industry. Recall that the minimum efficient scale is the lowest rate of output at which the firm takes full advantage of economies of scale. Research shows that an automobile plant of minimum efficient scale can produce enough cars to supply nearly 10 percent of the U.S. market demand. If there were one hundred auto plants, each would supply such a tiny portion of the market that the average cost per car would be higher than if only ten plants manufactured autos.

In the automobile industry, economies of scale are a barrier to entry. Any potential entrant into this industry would have to sell enough cars to reach a scale of operation that would reduce the average cost per car to the low level enjoyed by those firms already in the industry. This situation is illustrated in Exhibit 4, which presents the long-run average cost curve for a typical firm in the industry. Assuming a new entrant can sell only S cars, the average cost per unit for this new entrant, C_a, is much higher than it is for firms that have reached the minimum efficient size, reflected here by output level M. If autos sell for less than C_a, potential entrants can expect to lose money, and this prospect will likely discourage entry.

High Cost of Entry

There is another aspect to the problem faced by potential entrants into oligopolistic industries. The total cost of reaching the minimum efficient size is often great. For example, the cost of building a plant of minimum efficient size may be extremely high. Or promoting a product enough to compete with established brands may require an enormous initial outlay. High start-up costs and the existence of established name brands can be substantial barriers to entry because the future is uncertain. An unsuccessful attempt at securing a place in the market could result in huge losses; the prospect of such losses turns away many potential entrants. Consider, for

EXHIBIT 4   ECONOMIES OF SCALE AS A BARRIER TO ENTRY

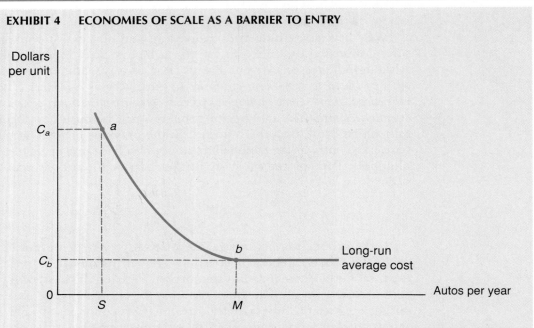

At point b, an existing firm can produce M automobiles at an average cost of C_b. A new entrant that can hope to sell only S automobiles will incur a much higher average cost of C_a at point a. If cars sell for less than C_a, the new entrant will suffer a loss. In this case economies of scale serve as a barrier to entry, protecting the existing firms.

example, the cost required to challenge Coke and Pepsi in the soft drink market.

Under perfect competition all firms sell identical products. There is no incentive to advertise or to promote a particular product, since consumers know that all products are alike. Moreover, producers already can sell all they want at the prevailing market price. Under oligopoly, however, firms often pour resources into differentiating their products. Some of these expenditures have the beneficial effects of providing valuable information to consumers and offering then a wider array of products. But some forms of product differentiation may be of little value. Little information is conveyed when consumers are told that Coke is "it" or that Pepsi is the drink of "a new generation," yet these companies spend millions on such messages. Much of the effort may be aimed at creating an artificial distinction in the consumer's mind between various brands of essentially identical products. Promotional efforts can thus result in a higher average cost curve under oligopoly than under perfect competition. The following case study explores the costs associated with product differentiation in the auto industry.

The Cost of Variety

In the early days of auto manufacturing, cars were very similar. Henry Ford's Model Ts were all the same—same style, same color. He used to say that people could choose any color car they wanted, as long as it was black. Since those days, however, car manufacturers have made an effort to follow Alfred Sloan's motto. Sloan, the head of General Motors from 1937 to 1956, wanted to build a car "for every purse and purpose." In recent years the number of choices has proliferated. Considering the possible combinations of engines, transmissions, colors, and other options, there are more than 69,000 versions of the Ford Thunderbird.

Engineers note that allowing for such variety adds tremendously to the cost of the car. For example, additional costs are necessary to support the sophisticated ordering system and the more complicated factories needed to produce a different car each minute. One study concludes that if the Ford Mustang were introduced today, the price would have to be 25 percent higher just to cover the added costs associated with providing a wider variety of that model.

Because Japanese producers must ship some cars halfway around the world, they have difficulty responding to custom orders. Instead, they concentrate on providing only those features consumers appear to desire most. The Honda Accord, for example, was offered in only thirty-two varieties, including all the combinations of engine, transmission, and color. Some industry analysts argue that this policy has given Japanese manufacturers a significant cost advantage and has allowed them to focus more on quality than on variety. Now that Japanese companies have established plants in the United States, it remains to be seen whether they will continue to limit the number of options offered or will follow a U.S. tradition.

The point is that although consumers like to select cars that most nearly match their own tastes and preferences, this wider selection increases the average cost of cars. Many items cost more when they are customized to particular tastes. A tailor-made suit, for example, is more expensive than one off the rack. A home built to the buyer's specifications costs more than a house built like others in a development. So the wider variety offered by oligopolists is both good and bad. It is good if consumers value the wider choice and are willing to pay the extra cost of variety; it is bad if efforts at product differentiation generate no difference in value to consumers.

Source: John Koten, "Giving Buyers Wide Choices May Be Hurting Auto Makers," *Wall Street Journal*, 15 December 1983.

MODELS OF OLIGOPOLY

Because oligopolists are interdependent, analyzing the behavior of individual producers under oligopoly is more complicated than analyzing that of producers under market structures that assume independent behavior. Since the selling ability of each firm depends on the actions of rival firms, the demand curve facing the individual firm cannot be specified until the behavior of competing firms has been determined. At one extreme, the firms in the industry can behave like monopolists if they are able to coordinate their behavior. At the other extreme, oligopolists may try to act independently and compete so fiercely that price wars erupt.

Although dozens of theories have been developed to explain oligopoly pricing behavior, we will examine only five of the better-known models: (1) the kinked demand curve, (2) cartels, (3) price leadership, (4) game theory, and (5) cost-plus pricing. Each was developed to explain a different type of behavior observed in oligopolistic markets. As we will see, each model has some relevance, though none is entirely satisfactory as a general theory of oligopoly behavior.

The Kinked Demand Curve

Prices in some oligopolistic industries appear to be stable even during periods when altered cost conditions suggest that a price change is appropriate. An often-cited case of price stability occurred in the sulfur industry, where the price remained at $18 per ton for a dozen consecutive years despite major shifts in the cost of production. One oligopoly model sheds light on this apparent price stability. That model is based on the simple idea that if a firm cuts its price, other firms will cut theirs as well, to avoid losing customers to the price cutter. If a firm raises its price, however, other firms will stand pat, hoping to attract customers away from the price raiser. Such expected behavior by competitors leads to the **kinked demand curve**.

*The **kinked demand curve** predicts price stickiness by assuming that one firm's price increases will be ignored by its rivals whereas its price decreases will be imitated.*

To develop the kinked demand curve model, we start at point *e* in Exhibit 5, with the firm producing *q* units at price *P*. If the firm changes its price, its rivals may choose to imitate the price change or to ignore it. Therefore there are two possible demand curves facing the firm in Exhibit 5. The firm's demand curve *DD* is based on the assumption that rivals will not follow any change in price. The firm's demand curve *D'D'* is based on the assumption that rivals will match any change in price. As you can see, *DD* is flatter, or more elastic, than *D'D'*. To see why, suppose that General Motors (GM) raises its prices, but Ford and Toyota do not. In this situation GM will lose far more sales than if other producers also raised their prices. Likewise, if GM cuts prices but Ford and Toyota do not, GM will pick up more sales than if all producers cut prices. Thus, if rivals do not follow price changes, any price increase will drive away more customers and any price decrease attract more customers than if rivals matched price changes. Therefore, each oligopolist's demand curve is more elastic when rivals do not follow price changes than when they do.

If rivals follow a firm's price decreases but do not match its price increases, the oligopolist's demand curve is *DeD'*. That portion of the demand curve reflecting a price increase, *De*, is flatter than that portion of the demand curve reflecting a price decrease, *eD'*. Because the behavior of rivals is different in the case of a price increase and a price decrease, this oligopolist's demand curve has a *kink* at the firm's current price-quantity combination, point *e*.

EXHIBIT 5   THE KINKED DEMAND MODEL OF OLIGOPOLY

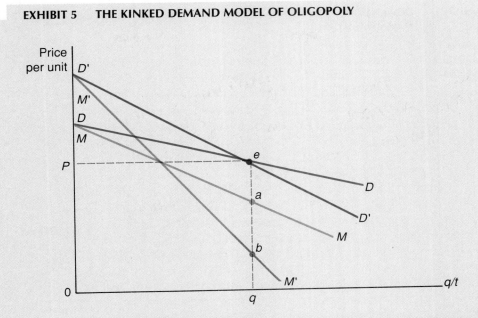

In the initial situation, an oligopolist is at point *e*, selling *q* units at price *P*. The firm's demand curve is *DD* if its competitors do not match its price changes; its demand curve is *D'D'* if competitors do match price changes. Assuming that the firm's rivals match price cuts but not price increases, the relevant demand curve is *DeD'*, with a kink at quantity *q*. *MabM'* is the associated marginal revenue curve, with a gap at quantity *q*.

Marginal Revenue To find the marginal revenue curve for the kinked demand curve, we simply piece together the relevant portions of the underlying marginal revenue curves. Segment *Ma* is the marginal revenue curve applicable to portion *De* of the kinked demand curve. And segment *bM'* is the marginal revenue curve associated with the portion *eD'* of the kinked demand curve. The marginal revenue curve is thus *MabM'*. Because there is a kink in the demand curve, the marginal revenue curve is not a single line; it has a gap at the currently produced quantity. The kinked demand curve and the corresponding marginal revenue curve are depicted in Exhibit 6.

Price Rigidity Within the gap in the marginal revenue curve, *ab*, the firm will not respond to small shifts in the marginal cost curve. Suppose that curve *MC* in Exhibit 6 is the initial marginal cost curve. The point where *MC* crosses the gap in the marginal revenue curve identifies equilibrium quantity *q* and price *P*. If output is reduced below *q*, marginal revenue exceeds marginal cost, so the output reduction decreases profit (or increases losses). If output is expanded beyond *q*, marginal cost exceeds marginal revenue, so the output expansion decreases profit (or increases losses). Thus the

EXHIBIT 6   DEMAND AND MARGINAL REVENUE CURVES FOR THE KINKED DEMAND MODEL

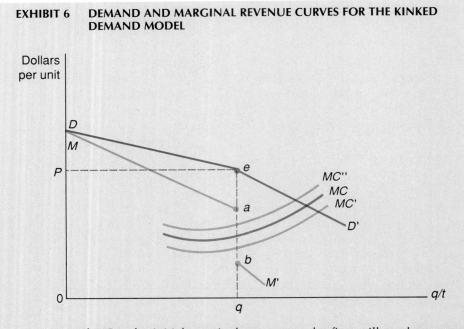

If *MC* is the initial marginal cost curve, the firm will produce quantity *q* (where marginal cost equals marginal revenue) at price *P*. Marginal cost could fall to *MC'* or increase to *MC"* without affecting the quantity produced. Likewise, price *P* will be rigid if marginal cost for output *q* varies between *a* and *b*.

oligopolist maximizes profit or minimizes losses by remaining at output level *q*.

What happens to equilibrium price and quantity if the marginal cost curve drops to *MC'*? Nothing happens, because profit is still maximized at output level *q*. The oligopolist can do no better than to offer quantity *q* at price *P*. The same holds if marginal cost increases to *MC"*—again, there is no change in the equilibrium conditions. It takes a greater shift in the marginal cost curve to produce a change in equilibrium price and quantity. Specifically, the intersection of the new marginal cost curve with the marginal revenue curve must occur above point *a* or below point *b* to change the equilibrium price and quantity. *Because the marginal cost curve can fluctuate within the gap in the marginal revenue curve without affecting the equilibrium price, prices tend to be rigid in oligopolistic industries if firms behave in the manner described by the kinked demand curve.*

Although the kinked demand theory provides an interesting explanation of those price rigidities that have been observed over the years, two basic criticisms have been leveled at it. First, the theory does not explain how the equilibrium price and quantity are initially determined. The theory simply explains why price, once established, is less likely to change in oligopolistic industries. Second, though there is some evidence supporting price rigidity, other evidence suggests that prices are not as rigid as the theory implies, particularly when it comes to price increases. During the inflationary periods of the 1970s and early 1980s, industries characterized as oligopolistic increased prices frequently. Other evidence comparing the frequency of price changes in oligopolies and monopolies suggests that oligopolies changed prices more often than monopolies did, even though the kinked demand theory would imply just the opposite.

Collusion and Cartels

A **cartel** is a collection of firms that agree to coordinate their production and pricing decisions.

Because there are few firms in an oligopolistic market, firms can often *collude*, or agree on price and output levels, in order to decrease competition and increase profit. A **cartel** is a group of firms that agree to coordinate their production and pricing decisions so that each member of the cartel will earn monopoly profits. Cartels can result in many benefits to firms: greater certainty about the behavior of "competitors," an organized effort to block new entry, and, as a result, increased profits.

Colluding firms usually reduce output, increase prices, and block the entry of new firms. Thus consumers suffer because prices are higher, and potential entrants suffer because free enterprise is restricted. Formal collusion and cartels are illegal in this country. The rewards from collusion can be so tempting, however, that firms sometimes break the law. For example, during the 1950s there was evidence of extensive collusion among electrical equipment producers, and some executives went to jail for their participation in the scheme.

In many European countries, formal collusion among firms through cartels not only is legal but is sometimes promoted by government. Some cartels are worldwide in scope, such as the now-familiar Organization of Petroleum Exporting Countries (OPEC). Cartels can operate worldwide (even though they are outlawed in some countries) because there are no international laws to stop them.

Suppose that the firms in an industry establish a cartel. The industry demand curve is presented as D in Exhibit 7. What price will be charged to maximize the industry's profits and how will industry output be divided among participating firms? The first task of the cartel is to determine the marginal cost of production for the cartel as a whole. Since the cartel acts as if it were a monopoly operating many plants, the marginal cost curve in Exhibit 7 represents the horizontal sum of the individual marginal cost curves for the firms in the cartel. The price and total output are determined by the intersection of the aggregate marginal cost curve and the marginal revenue curve. This intersection yields price P and industry output Q.

The cartel has thus determined the price and total quantity that maximizes its profit. So far, so good. Now output must be allocated among members of the cartel. The profit-maximizing solution for the cartel requires that output be allocated so that each firm incurs the same marginal cost on the last unit produced. Problems with maintaining a successful cartel are discussed below.

EXHIBIT 7   CARTEL MODEL WHERE FIRMS ACT AS A MONOPOLIST

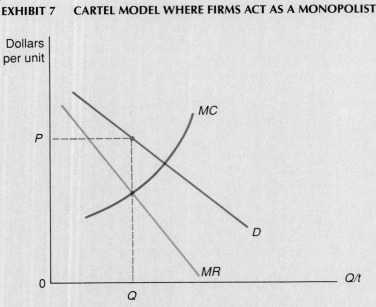

A cartel acts like a monopolist. Here D is the market demand curve, MR the associated marginal revenue curve, and MC the horizontal sum of the marginal cost curves of cartel members. Cartel profits are maximized by producing quantity Q and charging price P.

Differences in Cost If all firms have identical costs, output and profit are easily allocated across firms (each firm produces the same output), but if costs differ, problems arise. The greater the differences in average cost across firms, the greater will be the differences across firms in shares of the cartel's profit. For example, a high-cost firm would need to sell more than a low-cost firm to earn the same total profit, but this allocation scheme would not be consistent with the goal of maximizing cartel profit. Thus there is a conflict between maximizing the total profits of the cartel and equalizing profits among the participants. If firms that experience higher costs are allocated too little output, they could drop out of the cartel, thereby undermining it.

In reality, the allocation of output is typically the result of haggling among cartel members. Firms that are more influential or more adept at bargaining will get a larger share of output. Allocation schemes are sometimes based simply on the historical division of output among firms, or cartel members may divide up the market along geographical lines.

Number of Firms in the Cartel The greater the number of firms in the industry, the more difficult it is to negotiate an acceptable allocation of output. Consensus is harder to achieve as the cartel grows because the chances increase that at least one member will be dissatisfied.

New Entry into the Industry If a cartel cannot block the entry of new firms into the industry, over time new entry will force the price back down to where all firms earn only a normal profit. The profits of the cartel attract entry, entry increases market supply, and increased supply forces the price down. A cartel must therefore be able to block the entry of new firms in order to achieve continued success.

Cheating Perhaps a more fundamental problem in keeping the cartel running is that each oligopolist faces a strong temptation to cheat on the agreement. By lowering its price slightly below the established price, a firm can usually increase its sales and profit. The urge to cheat is strong, especially during economic slumps. Cartel agreements collapse if cheating becomes widespread.

The problems of establishing and maintaining a cartel are reflected in the spotty history of the Organization of Petroleum Exporting Countries. In 1985 the average price of oil reached $34 a barrel. By the end of the decade, the price stood at about $18 a barrel. The price fell partly because of competition among the world's oil producers. Many of the OPEC countries are poor and rely on oil as a major source of revenue, so they fight over the price and their market share. Like other cartels, OPEC also has had difficulty with new entrants. The high prices resulting from OPEC's early success attracted new oil suppliers from the North Sea, Mexico, and elsewhere. Most cartel observers doubt that once-powerful OPEC will ever regain its former control.

More generally, if output is differentiated across firms, if demand or cost conditions are highly variable, or if technology is changing rapidly, it will be difficult to establish and maintain an effective cartel. A successful cartel requires a stable business setting.

Price Leadership

*A **price leader** is a firm whose prices are followed by the rest of the industry.*

An informal, or *tacit,* type of collusion occurs in industries that contain **price leaders**, which set the price for the rest of the industry. A single dominant firm or a few firms establish the market price, and other firms in the industry follow that lead. Any changes in the price are initiated by the price-leading firm. By implicitly settling on a single price, firms in an industry hope to avoid price competition and thereby increase profits.

Historically, the steel industry has been a good example of the price-leadership form of oligopoly. Typically USX (formerly U.S. Steel), the largest firm in the industry, would set the price for various products, and other firms would follow. Congressional investigations of the pricing policy in this industry indicated that smaller steel producers relied on the price schedules of USX. Public pressure on USX to avoid price increases forced the price leadership role onto smaller steel producers, resulting in a rotation of the leadership function among firms. Although the rotating price leadership did reduce conformity among firms in the industry, particularly during the 1970s, close observers of this industry argue that price levels prevailing in the industry were higher than they would have been with no price leadership. As F. M. Scherer has noted, "It seems undeniable that in the absence of what leadership there was, steel prices in the United States, instead of rising, would have fallen sharply between 1974 and 1978, as they did elsewhere in depressed steel markets."[1]

Like other forms of collusion, price leadership is subject to a variety of obstacles. First, the practice often violates antitrust laws. Second, there is no guarantee that other firms will follow the leader, which can be a real problem with price increases. If other firms in the industry do not follow a price increase, the leading firm must either roll back prices or suffer a loss in sales to lower-priced competitors (recall the results from the kinked demand curve model). Third, because oligopolists tend to operate with excess capacity, even if all firms officially follow the price leader, some may cheat on the official price by offering extra services, rebates, or some other deal that lowers the actual price. The incentives to cut prices in order to gain more sales will be particularly strong when the industry is depressed and firms are operating well below capacity. When production is low, so is the marginal cost of producing more output. Finally, the greater the product differentiation across producers, the less effective price leadership will be as a means of organizing oligopolists.

Game Theory

How will firms act when they recognize their interdependence but either cannot or do not collude? Because oligopoly involves interdependence among a few firms, an analogy has been drawn between interacting firms and the players of games such as cards. This approach to analyzing oligopoly was developed by John von Neumann and Oskar Morgenstern in their classic book, *Theory of Games and Economic Behavior*, published in 1944. **Game theory** examines oligopolistic behavior as a series of strategic moves and countermoves among rival firms. Game theory analyzes the behavior of decision makers, or players, whose decisions affect one another, focusing on the players' incentives to cooperate or compete.

Game theory analyzes oligopolistic behavior as a series of strategic moves and countermoves among rival firms.

As an example, consider the market for gasoline in a rural community with only two gas stations. Suppose customers are indifferent between the two brands and consider only the price when choosing between them. Each gas station wants to charge the price that will maximize profits. To keep the analysis manageable, suppose only two prices are possible: a high price or a low price. If both gas stations charge the high price, they split the total quantity demanded and each gas station earns a profit of $1000 per day. If they both charge the low price, they also split the market, but profits are only $700 per day. If one gas station charges the high price but the other

---

[1] F. M. Scherer, *Industrial Market Structure and Economic Performance*, 2d ed. (Chicago: Rand McNally College Publishing Co., 1980), 180.

charges the low price, the low-price station really cleans up, earning $1200 per day. But the high-price station has few customers and earns only $300 per day.

Which pricing strategy will be chosen? The answer depends on the assumptions about firm behavior. One common game-theory assumption is that each firm will try to avoid the worst outcome. The worst outcome is to earn only $300 per day by being the only station charging the high price. The way to avoid this outcome is to charge the low price. So both gas stations will charge the low price and each will earn $700 per day. Note that this payoff is lower than the $1000 each could earn if both charged the high price. If both were charging the high price, however, either one could increase profits to $1200 per day by dropping the price.

Avoiding the worst outcome is only one of several behavioral assumptions that could be used to analyze oligopoly markets in terms of game theory. The specific outcome of such an analysis will depend on the rules of the game and on the assumptions that underlie the analysis. Outcomes can be as volatile as the personalities involved. Some players are more conservative than others, and some are more willing to take risks.

Cost-Plus Pricing

Under **cost-plus pricing**, the price is determined by adding a percentage markup to the average variable cost so as to cover costs that cannot be allocated to any specific product and to provide a profit on the firm's investment.

A final model of oligopoly behavior is based on the observation that many oligopolists employ **cost-plus pricing** strategies. The firms establish a price by calculating the average variable cost per unit and then adding a percentage, called a *markup*. This markup is designed to cover costs that cannot be allocated to specific units of output and to provide the firm with a profit on its investment. This approach seems to ignore the demand curve, since price is determined as a function of cost, not demand.

Cost-plus pricing appears attractive to producers for several reasons. First, it provides a way of coping with uncertainty about the exact shape and elasticity of the demand curve. Second, the very effort of calculating appropriate prices based on marginal analysis is costly, particularly if the firm produces a variety of products. Adopting a simple markup rule greatly simplifies the pricing process. Third, if firms in the industry have similar costs, their use of the same markup percentage will yield uniform prices across the industry, generating an implicit form of price collusion.

Choosing the Target Level of Output and the Markup Because the average variable cost per unit varies with the level of output, the firm must assume some target level of output. For example, the firm may assume that its level of output will be 75 percent of its capacity. A 50 percent markup on an item with an average variable cost of $80 results in a retail price of $120. This markup is designed to cover those elements of cost that do not vary with output, including fixed costs and other costs, such as those for research and development, that cannot be charged against a particular product.

Some producers also build into the price a target rate of profit. For example, General Motors has employed a markup policy aimed at earning a

15 percent after-tax rate of return on its investment. GM estimates that its output will be 80 percent of its capacity. The price is then calculated by adding to the average cost per unit enough of a markup to yield the firm a 15 percent after-tax rate of profit.

An Assessment of Cost-Plus Pricing   Cost-plus pricing has an appealing simplicity, and it grows more attractive as the variety of products sold by the firm increases. A firm such as General Electric produces hundreds of different products, and GE is hard-pressed to attribute such costs as basic research and overhead to particular products. Or consider the problems faced by your favorite grocery store in trying to assign its various costs of doing business to each of the thousands of products it sells. The store finds it easier to use a percentage markup to determine the price of each product. There is abundant evidence that markup pricing is used extensively, particularly in retailing. Firms do not have to be oligopolistic to adopt a cost-plus pricing policy — competitive firms and monopolistically competitive firms may employ the policy as well.

Although cost-plus pricing appears at first to be inconsistent with the use of marginal analysis, some observers argue that the cost-plus approach is, in fact, a profit-maximizing response to complicated and uncertain market conditions. When a number of executives were interviewed about their companies' use of cost-plus pricing, most said that they did not believe profits could be increased by any change in pricing procedures.[2] Apparently these executives believed they were charging the prices that maximized profits. Moreover, close scrutiny of actual policies indicates that *firms do not apply the same markup to all their products but vary the markup inversely with the price elasticity of demand for the product.* The greater the elasticity of demand, the lower the markup. This finding suggests that firms do take demand into account and do employ the markup rule in a way that is consistent with profit maximization.

Comparison of Oligopoly and Perfect Competition

Each of the oligopoly models we have considered was developed to explain certain phenomena observed in oligopolistic markets. Each model, however, has limitations, and at this point none is thought to be a valid depiction of all oligopoly behavior. Consequently, the oligopoly model cannot be compared with the competitive model. We might, however, imagine an experiment in which we took the hundreds of firms that populate a competitive industry and, through a series of giant mergers, combined them to form a half dozen firms. We would thereby transform the industry from perfect competition to oligopoly. How would the behavior of firms in this industry before and after the massive mergers differ?

---

[2] See, for example, Fritz Machlup, *The Economics of Seller Competition* (Baltimore, MD: Johns Hopkins University Press, 1952), 65.

Price Is Usually Higher Under Oligopoly With fewer competitors, these firms would become more interdependent. Oligopoly models presented in this chapter suggest that the firms could conceivably act in concert in their pricing policies. Even cost-plus pricing could be a tool for tacit price collusion if firms faced similar costs and adopted similar markup rules. *If the oligopolists engaged in some sort of implicit or explicit collusion, industry output would be smaller and price would be higher under oligopoly than under perfect competition.*

Higher Profits Under Oligopoly In the long run, easy entry prevents firms in a perfectly competitive industry from earning more than a normal profit. With oligopoly, however, there are presumably barriers to entry that allow firms in the industry to earn long-run economic profits. The barrier to entry might be economies of scale in production or brand name identification built up through years of advertising. Such barriers could be insurmountable for a new entrant. Therefore *we should expect profit rates in the long run to be higher with oligopoly than with perfect competition.*

Profit rates do appear to be positively correlated with the proportion of industry sales made by the largest firms. Some economists view these higher profit rates as a matter of concern, but not all economists share this view. Harold Demsetz, for example, argues that since it is the largest firms in oligopolistic industries that tend to earn the highest rates of return, higher profit rates in oligopolistic industries stem from the greater efficiency arising from economies of scale in these large firms.[3] Many of these issues will be examined in the next chapter, as we explore government's role in regulating the marketplace.

Mergers and Oligopoly

Because large firms are potentially more profitable than small ones, some firms have pursued rapid growth by merging with other firms. In some industries the merging, or joining together, of two firms has contributed to the movement toward oligopoly. Over the last century, there have been three major merger waves in this country. The first occurred between 1887 and 1904. Some of today's largest firms, including USX and Standard Oil, were formed during this first merger movement. These tended to be **horizontal mergers**, meaning that the merging firms produced the same products. For example, the firm that is today USX was formed in 1901 through a billion-dollar merger that involved many individual steel producers and two-thirds of the industry's productive capacity.

The second merger wave took place between 1916 and 1929, when vertical mergers were more common. A **vertical merger** is the merging of one firm with either a firm from which it purchases inputs or a firm to which it sells output. Thus it is the merging of firms at different stages of the

In a *horizontal merger*, one firm combines with another firm that produces the same product.

In a *vertical merger*, one firm combines with a firm from which it purchases inputs or to which it sells output.

---

[3] Harold Demsetz, "Industry Structure, Market Rivalry, and Public Policy," *Journal of Law and Economics* 16 (April 1973): 1–10.

*A **conglomerate merger** involves the combination of firms producing in different industries.*

production process. For example, a steel firm might merge with a firm that mines iron ore. **Conglomerate mergers**, which join firms producing in different industries, were also common during the second merger wave.

The third merger wave occurred during the 25 years following World War II. In that period many large firms were absorbed by other, usually larger, firms. More than 200 of the 1000 largest firms in 1950 had disappeared by 1963 as a result of mergers. In recent years corporate takeovers have become more common, and some of the resulting mergers have been huge. Some of the corporate takeovers eventually lead to smaller conglomerate firms, as the new owners sell off part of the corporation to pay for the purchase. We cannot yet say whether the recent takeover activity forms the basis of a fourth merger wave.

CONCLUSION

This chapter moves us from the extremes of perfect competition and pure monopoly to the gray area inhabited by most firms. Firms in monopolistic competition and firms in oligopoly both face a downward-sloping demand for their products. In choosing the profit-maximizing price-output combination, the firm in monopolistic competition is unconcerned about the effects of this choice on the behavior of competitors. But oligopolistic firms are interdependent and therefore must consider the effects their pricing and output decisions will have on those of other firms. This interdependence complicates the analysis of oligopoly, leaving open a wide array of possible models.

The analytical results derived in this chapter are not as neat as those derived for the polar cases, but we can reach some general conclusions, using perfect competition as our benchmark. Given identical cost curves, monopolistic competitors and oligopolists tend to charge higher prices than perfect competitors. In the long run, monopolistic competitors, like perfect competitors, earn only a normal profit because entry barriers are low. Oligopolists can earn economic profits in the long run if new entry is somehow restricted. In the next chapter we will examine how government policy is often aimed at making firms more competitive.

Summary

1. Whereas the pure monopolist produces output that has no close substitutes, the firm in monopolistic competition must contend with many competitors that offer close substitutes.

Because there are some differences among the products offered by different firms, each monopolistically competitive firm faces a downward-sloping demand curve.

2. Sellers in monopolistic competition differentiate their products through (1) physical qualities, (2) the locations where the product is available, (3) the services provided with the product, and (4) the subjective image of the product in the consumer's mind.

3. In the short run, monopolistically competitive firms that can at least cover their average variable costs will maximize profits or minimize losses by producing where marginal cost equals marginal revenue. In the long run, free entry and exit of firms ensures that monopolistically competitive firms earn only normal profits. In long-run equilibrium, each firm produces where marginal cost equals marginal revenue and where the average total cost curve is tangent to the firm's downward-sloping demand curve.

4. An oligopoly is a market dominated by a few sellers, some of which are large enough relative to the entire market to influence price. In some oligopolistic industries, such as steel, the product is homogeneous; in other oligopolistic industries, such as automobiles and tobacco, the product is differentiated.

5. Because an oligopolistic market consists of few firms, each firm will react to other firms' changes in price, output, product quality, and advertising. Because of this interdependence among oligopolists, the behavior of producers is difficult to analyze. No single model of behavior characterizes oligopolistic markets.

6. In this chapter we observed five possible models of oligopoly behavior: (1) the kinked demand curve, where a firm's rivals follow price decreases but do not follow price increases; (2) the cartel, where firms collude to behave like a monopolist; (3) price leadership, where one firm sets the price for the industry and other firms follow the leader; (4) game theory, which focuses on each firm's strategy, based on the responses of rivals; and (5) cost-plus pricing, where firms determine prices by estimating their average variable cost and adding a percentage markup to cover nonallocated costs and the target rate of profit.

Questions and Problems

1. (Monopolistic Competition) Why would the production of Hollywood movies be an example of a monopolistically competitive industry? What are some of the major firms and how do they differentiate their products?

2. (Monopolistically Competitive Demands) Why does the monopolistically competitive firm's demand slope downward in the long run, even after the entry of new firms?

3. (Oligopoly and Technology) How might changes in technology affect whether an industry remains oligopolistic? That is, might some barriers to entry be affected by technological change?

4. (Kinked Demand) How might a kinked demand curve change if the degree of product differentiation within the oligopoly increased? What can you say about the degree of price rigidity before and after an increase in product differentiation?

5. (Oligopoly) Given a kinked demand curve, will oligopolists always experience economic profits, or could they have short-run losses?

6. (Oligopoly) "If the United Auto Workers union bargains for higher wages at Ford, Ford will simply pass on the additional costs to consumers in the form of higher prices." Must this statement be true? Why or why not?

7. (Cartels) Why would each of the following induce some members of OPEC to cheat on their cartel agreement?

a. Some cartel members are undeveloped countries.
b. Some members are small countries.
c. International debts of some members grow.
d. Expectations grow that some members will cheat.

8. (Price Leadership) Is it reasonable to assume that a price leader will always be the largest producer (that is, the firm with the largest scale)?

9. (Cost-Plus Pricing) How might a firm decide whether its markup was too high or too low? Is this determination governed by market conditions? What is the difference, if any, between sequential markups and profit maximization?

10. (Horizontal Mergers) Why do horizontal mergers seem most likely to occur in those industries that have the potential for substantial economies of scale but have not yet achieved such economies?

11. (Game Theory) Suppose there are only two automobile companies, Ford and Chevy, and Ford believes that Chevy will match any price it sets. Use the following price and profit data to answer the questions below.

If Ford sells for	and Chevy sells for	Ford's profits	Chevy's profits
$ 4,000	$ 4,000	$ 8 mil.	$ 8 mil.
4,000	8,000	12 mil.	6 mil.
4,000	12,000	14 mil.	2 mil.
8,000	4,000	6 mil.	12 mil.
8,000	8,000	10 mil.	10 mil.
8,000	12,000	12 mil.	6 mil.
12,000	4,000	2 mil.	14 mil.
12,000	8,000	6 mil.	12 mil.
12,000	12,000	7 mil.	7 mil.

a. What price will Ford set for its cars?
b. What price will Chevy set, given Ford's price?
c. What is Ford's profit after Chevy's response?

d. If they collaborated to maximize joint profits, what prices would the two companies set?
e. Given your answer to part d, how could undetected cheating on price increase each car maker's profits?

12. (Price Leadership) Consider an oligopolistic industry in which one dominant firm acts as a price leader. Assume that the dominant firm believes that all other firms will respond to its pricing strategy by maintaining their aggregate market share at 50 percent of the total output demanded at the price set by the price leader. Show what this firm's profit-maximizing strategy should be, using demand and "typical" cost curves.

13. (Monopolistic Competition) In the long run, the monopolistically competitive firm earns zero economic profit, which is exactly what would occur if the industry were perfectly competitive. Assuming that the cost curve for each firm is the same whether the industry is perfectly or monopolistically competitive, answer the following questions.

a. Why don't perfectly and monopolistically competitive firms produce the same industry output in the long run?
b. Why is the monopolistically competitive industry said to be economically inefficient?
c. What benefits might cause us to prefer the monopolistically competitive result over the perfectly competitive result?

14. (Cartel) Suppose that a cartel, knowing the industry demand and cost curves, sets industry output so as to maximize industry profits. Using the cost curves of a "typical" cartel member, show why each member is likely to attempt to increase its allocated share once the profit-maximizing price has been determined, if it is certain its efforts will be undetected by the other firms in the cartel.

C H A P T E R   2 4

Regulation, Deregulation, and Antitrust Activity

It has been said that businesspeople praise competition but love monopoly. They praise competition because it harnesses the diverse and often conflicting objectives of various market participants and channels them into the efficient production of goods and services. And it does this as if by an invisible hand. They love monopoly because it provides the surest path to economic profit in the long run—and after all, profit is the firm's objective. The fruits of monopoly are so great they can tempt firms to try to eliminate, or to collude with, competitors. As Adam Smith remarked more than two hundred years ago, "People of the same trade seldom meet together, even for merriment or diversion, but the conversation ends in a conspiracy against the public, or in some contrivance to raise prices."

The tendency of firms to seek monopolistic advantage is understandable, but the pursuit of market power should not be allowed if it prevents an economy from achieving the most efficient use of its scarce resources. Public policy plays a role by attempting to promote competition in those markets where competition seems desirable and to reduce the harmful consequences of monopolistic behavior in those markets where the output can be most efficiently produced by one or a few firms. This chapter discusses the ways in which government regulates business activity. As you will see, there is some disagreement about what government is doing and what it should be doing. Topics discussed in this chapter include

- Market power
- Economic regulation and deregulation
- Social regulation
- Antitrust laws
- Competitive trends of the economy

BUSINESS BEHAVIOR AND PUBLIC POLICY

You'll recall that a monopolist supplies a product with no close substitutes and so can charge a higher price than would prevail if the market were competitive. When a few firms account for most of the sales in a market, those firms are sometimes able to coordinate their actions, either explicitly or implicitly, to approximate the behavior of a monopolist. This ability of one or more firms to maintain a price above the competitive level is termed **market power**. The presumption is that a monopoly or firms acting together as a monopoly will restrict output and charge a higher price than competitive firms. Market power thereby creates a misallocation of resources and shifts wealth from consumers to producers. Other distortions have also been associated with monopolies. Because monopolies are insulated from competition, many critics argue that they are not as innovative as an aggressive competitor would be. Moreover, because of their size, monopolies have been said to exert a disproportionate influence in the political system.

Market power is the ability of one or more firms to maintain a price above the competitive level.

Market Structure, Conduct, and Performance

Economists have developed a branch of economic analysis called **industrial organization** to trace the relationship between the structure of a market and the performance of firms in that market. The *structure* of a particular market, such as the market for steel or personal computers, can be measured by observable characteristics such as the number and size of firms, the extent of product differentiation, and the effectiveness of barriers to entry. Market structure affects the *conduct* of firms in the market — that is, market structure affects how firms behave in such areas as pricing, research and development activity, advertising strategy, and investment policy. And the conduct of firms, in turn, affects their *performance* in the market, as measured by the level of profit, the efficiency of production, and the extent of innovative activity in the industry. Therefore market structure and market conduct are critical factors in determining market performance.

Industrial organization examines the relations among the structure of a market, the conduct of firms in this market, and the performance of firms in this market.

When used to analyze public policies, industrial organization focuses on how to foster the market structure and market conduct that will lead to the most desirable market performance. More specifically, it focuses on *how public policy can enhance social welfare by promoting competition where competition is appropriate and by harnessing the benefits of economies of scale where production by only one or a few firms seems most efficient.*

Government Control of Business

There are three kinds of government policy designed to alter or control the market structure and market conduct of firms: social regulation, economic regulation, and antitrust activity. **Social regulation** consists of government measures that address unsafe working conditions, dangerous products, damage to the environment, and other undesirable side effects, or

Social regulation in-
cludes government
measures designed to
improve health and
safety. *Economic reg-
ulation* is aimed at
controlling price, out-
put, entry, and qual-
ity in markets where
monopoly is inevita-
ble or desirable.

externalities, of production and consumption. Growing concern about the health and safety of workers and consumers has led to the formation of various regulatory agencies to control everything from the permissible level of auto emissions to health warnings on packages of cigarettes.

Economic regulation is concerned with controlling the price, the output, the entry of new firms, and the quality of service in industries where monopoly appears inevitable or even desirable. The regulation of natural monopolies, such as electrical utilities, is an example of this type of regulation. Several other industries, such as communication and land and air transportation, have also been regulated, for reasons that will be discussed later in this chapter. Economic regulation is carried out by various regulatory bodies at the federal, state, and local levels. **Antitrust activity**

Antitrust activity is
aimed at preventing
monopoly and foster-
ing competition.

attempts to prohibit firm behavior aimed at monopolizing or cartelizing a market. Antitrust activity is pursued in court by federal government attor- neys and by individual firms that charge other firms with violations of antitrust laws. Both economic regulation and antitrust activity will be examined in this chapter.

NATURAL MONOPOLIES

As we've seen, because of economies of scale, natural monopolies have a downward-sloping long-run average cost curve over the entire range of market demand. This means that the lowest average total cost is achieved if one firm serves the entire market. As mentioned earlier, cable television is an example of a natural monopoly. The cost per household is lowest when a single company "wires" the community for signal reception. If four cable companies all strung their own wires throughout the community, the average cost per household would be higher.

Exhibit 1 shows the demand and cost conditions for a natural monopoly. A natural monopoly usually faces large capital costs, such as those associ- ated with stringing the wires to transmit electricity, telephone, or cable TV signals, laying the tracks for a railroad, putting a satellite in orbit, building a nuclear power plant, or installing a natural gas transmission line. Because of the heavy capital outlays, the average cost curve slopes downward where it intersects the demand curve. In this situation the cost of production is minimized by having only one producer.

We know that a monopolist, if unregulated, will set price and quantity so as to maximize profit. In Exhibit 1, the monopolist maximizes profit by producing output Q, at which marginal cost equals marginal revenue, and charging price P. However, the monopolist's choice of price and output is inefficient from society's point of view: consumers pay a price that is higher than the marginal cost of producing the good. Because the price, which is consumers' marginal valuation of output, exceeds the marginal cost, there is an underallocation of resources to the production of this good.

EXHIBIT 1   PROFIT MAXIMIZATION FOR THE NATURAL MONOPOLY

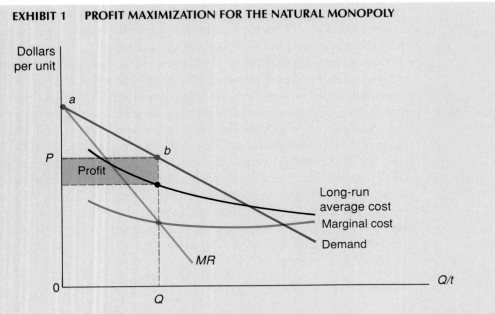

In a natural monopoly, the long-run average cost curve slopes downward at its point of intersection with the market demand curve. The firm produces output Q (where marginal cost equals marginal revenue) and charges price P. This situation is inefficient because price exceeds marginal cost.

Regulation of Natural Monopolies

The government has three options for dealing with natural monopolies. First, the government can do nothing. If left alone, monopolists will maximize profits, as in Exhibit 1. Second, the government can own and operate monopolies, as it does the Tennessee Valley Authority and many urban transit systems. Third, the government can regulate privately operated monopolies, as it does most electrical utilities and local phone services. Regulated industries have come to be known as *public utilities*.

The focus here will be on government regulation rather than government ownership. Many facets of natural monopolies have been regulated, but the object of regulation that captures the most attention is the rates, or prices, these utilities can charge.

Setting Price Equal to Marginal Cost Let's assume that the government regulators decide to make the monopolist act like a perfect competitor — that is, produce at the level of output dictated by allocative efficiency, where price equals marginal cost. The outcome is depicted in Exhibit 2: the price is set at point e, where the demand curve intersects the marginal cost curve, yielding price P' and quantity Q'. Consumers will clearly prefer this outcome over the profit-maximizing solution in Exhibit 1 because the price is lower and

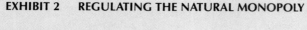

EXHIBIT 2   REGULATING THE NATURAL MONOPOLY

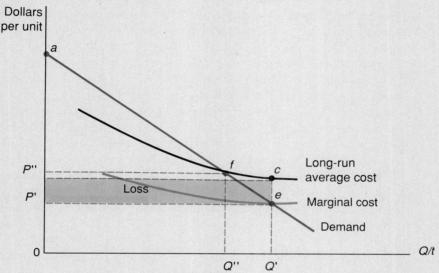

To obtain the efficient level of output, government could regulate the monopolist's price. At price P', the monopoly would produce output Q' — an efficient solution. However, at that price and quantity, the firm would suffer a loss and require a subsidy. As an alternative, the government could set a price of P''. The monopoly would produce output Q'' — an inefficient level. Since P'' equals the average cost, the firm would earn a normal profit and no subsidy would be required.

the quantity supplied is greater. The consumer surplus, a measure of the consumers' net gain, increases from triangle abP in Exhibit 1 to triangle aeP' in Exhibit 2.

Notice, however, that the monopolist now has a problem. At output level Q', the regulated price, P', is below the firm's average total cost, identified as point c. Rather than earning a profit, the monopolist now suffers a loss identified by the shaded rectangle. Forcing the natural monopolist to produce where marginal cost equals price results in an economic loss. Clearly, in the long run the monopolist would go out of business rather than suffer such losses.

Subsidizing the Natural Monopolist How could the regulators encourage the monopolist to stay in business, continuing to produce where marginal cost equals price? One way is for the government to cover the monopolist's losses — to subsidize the firm so that it earns a normal profit. Bus and subway fares are typically below the average cost of providing the service; the difference is made up through a subsidy. For example, the Washington, D.C., subway system receives over $200 million per year in government subsidies; Amtrak also receives substantial subsidies. One problem with the subsidy solution is that, to provide the subsidy, the government must raise taxes, borrow more, or forgo spending in some other area.

Setting Price Equal to Average Cost Although some public utilities are subsidized, most are not. The regulators attempt to establish a price that will provide the monopolist with a "fair return." Recall that the average total cost curve includes a normal profit. Thus setting *price equal to average cost* provides a normal, or "fair," profit for the monopolist. In Exhibit 2, the demand curve and the average cost curve intersect at point *f*, yielding a price of P'' and a quantity of Q''. The regulated monopolist would rather earn an economic profit, as in Exhibit 1; if given no choice, however, the monopolist will continue to operate with a normal profit, since that is what could be earned if the resources were redirected to their best alternative use. But the marginal value that consumers attach to output level Q'' exceeds the marginal cost of that output level. Therefore, social welfare could be enhanced by expanding output until consumers' marginal value equaled the marginal cost of production.

The Regulatory Dilemma Setting price equal to marginal cost yields the *socially optimal* allocation of resources *because the marginal cost of producing the last unit sold equals the consumers' marginal value of that last unit*. Under this pricing rule, however, the monopolist will face recurring losses unless a subsidy is provided. These losses disappear when price is set equal to average cost, thereby ensuring the monopolist a normal profit. But this solution only partially corrects the monopolist's tendency to restrict output; output is still less than would be socially optimal.

Thus the dilemma facing regulators is whether to subsidize the firm and have the monopolist charge the socially optimal price or to allow for a normal profit by setting a price that is higher than is socially optimal. There is no right answer. Compared to the profit-maximizing solution, either approach reduces price, increases output, increases consumer surplus, and eliminates economic profit. Unfortunately, either way, guaranteeing the firm a normal profit may reduce the firm's incentive to produce efficiently.

THEORIES OF ECONOMIC REGULATION

Why does government regulate certain markets? Why not allow market forces to allocate resources? There are two views of government regulation. The first view has been implicit in the discussion thus far—namely, that economic regulation is in the public interest. Regulation is designed to promote social welfare by controlling natural monopolies and by promoting competition where it is economically desirable, thus protecting consumers from harmful business practices.

A second view of regulation is that it is not in the public, or consumer, interest but rather in the special interest of producers. According to this view, *well-organized producer groups expect to profit from regulation and are able to persuade public officials to impose the desired restrictions, such as limiting entry into the industry or preventing competition among existing firms.* Producers have more to gain or lose from regulation than do individual consumers; producers typically are also better organized than consumers and therefore better able to bring about regulations that are favorable to them.

To understand how producer interests could influence public regulation, consider the last time you had your hair cut. Whoever cut your hair probably cuts hair as a profession. Most states regulate the training and licensing of hair professionals. If any new regulations affecting the profession are proposed, such as entry restrictions or license requirements, who has more interest in the outcome of that legislation, you or the person who cuts hair for a living? Producers have a strong interest in matters that affect their specialized source of income, so they play a disproportionately large role in trying to influence such legislation.

As a consumer, you do not specialize in getting haircuts. You purchase haircuts, socks, soft drinks, notebooks, and thousands of other goods and services. You have no *special interest* in legislation affecting hair cutting. Some critics argue that because of this asymmetry in the interests of producers and consumers, business regulations often favor producer interests rather than consumer interests. Well-organized producer groups, as squeaky wheels in the legislative system, receive the most grease in the form of favorable regulations.

Legislation favoring producer groups is usually introduced under the guise of the advancement of consumer interests. Producer groups may argue that unbridled competition in their industry would lead to results that were undesirable for consumers. For example, the alleged problem of "cutthroat" competition among taxi drivers has led to regulations fixing rates and limiting the number of taxis in most large metropolitan areas. Or, regulation may appear under the guise of quality control, as in the case of state control of professional groups such as barbers, doctors, and lawyers, where regulations are viewed as necessary to keep unlicensed "quacks" out of the professions.

The special interest theory may be valid even when the initial intent of the legislation is clearly in the consumer interest. Over time, the regulatory machinery may begin to act more in accord with the special interests of producers, because regulators' political power and strong stake in the regulatory outcome lead them, in effect, to "capture" the regulating agency and prevail upon it to serve producers. This capture theory of regulation was best explained by George Stigler, a Nobel prize winner from the University of Chicago, who argued that "as a general rule, regulation is acquired by the industry and is designed and operated for its benefit."[1]

A more complex variant of the capture theory emphasizes the idea that industry members may not all be of one mind regarding the most favorable

---

[1] George Stigler, "The Theory of Economic Regulation," *The Bell Journal of Economics and Management Science* (Spring 1971): 3.

kind of regulation. For example, small retail stores might support measures that would be opposed by large retail stores; major trucking companies might choose different regulations than independent truckers would. Competing interest groups jockey with one another for the most favorable regulations. Thus it is not simply a question of consumer interests versus producer interests but rather of one producer's interest versus another producer's interest.[2]

Perhaps it would be useful at this point to discuss in some detail the direction that regulation and, more recently, deregulation have taken in particular industries. First we will examine the role of the Interstate Commerce Commission as a regulator of the railroads and trucking.

Rail and Truck Regulation and Deregulation

The *Interstate Commerce Commission* (ICC), established in 1887 to regulate the railroads, was the first federal regulatory agency in this country. The major railroads supported formation of the ICC as a way to stabilize rates and reduce "cutthroat" competition by allocating business among the railroads. The ICC was also supposed to ensure that even small towns would receive railroad service. Thus, at the outset, railroad regulations had several objectives, and it was unclear whether they were primarily in the consumer interest or in the producer interest.

In the 1930s the railroads began to face vigorous competition from the emerging trucking industry. The railroads wanted to avoid competition with trucks, and in 1935 Congress extended the ICC's mandate to cover trucking. The intent of the regulation was to equalize the prices of the two kinds of transportation, so that the two would not compete directly on the basis of price.

The ICC was able to control the structure of the so-called ground transportation industry through regulations about new entry, price competition, and shipping conditions. To control entry, the ICC decreed that no carrier could operate without a license, and it would not issue a new license unless the applicant could show that such entry was "necessary for the public convenience." Existing shippers had a strong interest in presenting evidence to the contrary, so few new licenses were granted. Recall that *the ability to exclude new entrants from a market is a prerequisite for, though not a guarantee of, long-run economic profit.*

Ability to Fix Prices The ICC had control over shipping rates, but much of this power was relegated to rate-setting committees drawn from the rail and trucking industries, an arrangement that allowed the industry members to

---

[2] But just as producer groups may not represent a single interest, consumer groups may not either. For example, major users of electricity prefer rates that decline as usage increases, whereas smaller users do not because they fear that their rates might be higher on average with a declining rate structure. Residents of small rural communities view train service differently from residents in major metropolitan areas.

fix prices legally. Any competitor that wished to charge a lower price had to receive ICC permission. Because such rulings required hearings and often took up to a year to settle, the system discouraged price competition.

Regulating Operating Conditions The ICC also regulated the conditions of service, including the kinds of products that could be hauled, the routes that could be taken, and even the number of cities that could be served along the way. The idea was to limit the versatility of trucks by treating them as if they ran on tracks, thereby reducing any advantage trucks had over the railroads.

Truck routes operated on the "gateway" system, similar to railroad junction points. For example, a trucking firm with a license to ship between points A and B and between points B and C could haul from A to C only if it passed through point B first. Other rules allowed trucks to haul from A to B but not from B to A. So a truck could haul a load from St. Louis to Chicago but could not carry a return load. Such restrictions often required trucks to go hundreds of miles out of their way or to travel empty part of the time. Of course, all this added to the cost of transportation.

Despite the higher cost of shipping created by regulation, *the ability of truckers to fix their prices and restrict entry generally ensured their profitability, because transportation services were much in demand and there were no close substitutes.* In fact, "shipping rights," or the authority to haul particular goods between cities, became valuable and were bought and sold.

Scholars who examined the issue concluded that regulation kept trucking rates higher than the competitive level. As we have seen, the higher rates resulted in part from the production inefficiency caused by the regulations. Regulation also cultivated higher wages in the industry, particularly for the members of the truckers' union, the International Brotherhood of Teamsters. Because regulation strictly limited the entry of new firms and prohibited price competition between particular locations, trucking firms could comply with union demands for higher wages without fear of losing business to rivals with lower prices. Unionized truck drivers captured some of the producer surplus that resulted from regulation.

Deregulation During the 1970s support grew for deregulation in a variety of industries. The Motor Carriers Act of 1980 began the deregulation of trucking. Not only was new entry allowed, but the restrictions on routes, commodities, and the like were reduced. The elimination of "gateways," one-way shipping, and other vestiges of a system aimed at treating trucks as if they were trains reduced duplication and waste. During the first three years of the deregulated environment, an estimated 10,000 small new trucking firms entered the industry. During the same interval, trucking rates dropped substantially in many categories. For example, the average rate per mile for a full truckload of machinery dropped from $1.55 to $1.11, a 28 percent decline. And these drops were all the more dramatic because they came at a time when the cost of fuel was rising.

Winners and Losers Although consumers benefited from falling prices, deregulation also created some losers. More than three hundred trucking firms, some of them very large, went bankrupt, and nearly one-third of the nation's three hundred thousand unionized truck drivers lost unionized jobs. In the wake of deregulation, Teamsters union members were often forced to accept labor contracts that called for wage cuts. Another predictable effect of deregulation was a decline in the value of shipping rights. When shipping certificates were closely regulated, these rights had an estimated aggregate value of $750 million. When entry restrictions were eliminated, however, their value disappeared almost overnight.

Despite the clear efficiency gains from deregulation, the concentrated allocation of the losses to well-identified groups has ensured that the path to full deregulation would not be smooth. The losers (existing shippers, unionized truck drivers) are concentrated groups who know they are losers; the winners (consumers) are widely dispersed and often do not even know that they are winners. As a result, the ICC has been slow to deregulate the railroads, and pressure has been building to "reregulate" trucking. The ICC chairman, supported by the Teamsters union, was slow to push deregulation. In fact, there was so much internal strife on the ICC that the commission met infrequently during the 1980s. Despite foot-dragging by the ICC bureaucracy, the efficiency gains resulting from deregulation have been impressive.

The Railroads and Cross-Subsidization Deregulation may have promoted thriving competition in trucking, but the railroads seemed beyond help, despite the setting of minimum rates, control of competition along rail routes, subsidies, the promotion of mergers among railroads, and other measures designed to prop up this ailing industry. Regulations required railroads to provide service to remote and rural locations that might not receive service based on market demand. The railroads were not allowed to drop unprofitable routes or services, so revenue from profitable routes was used to subsidize operations on unprofitable routes, a policy called **cross-subsidization**. This cross-subsidy from profitable to unprofitable routes contributed to the bankruptcy of some lines. After several railroads in the Northeast went bankrupt, deregulatory measures were introduced to promote efficiency and stability in the industry. One effect of deregulation was that railroads were allowed to abandon unprofitable routes.

*Under **cross-subsidization**, revenue from profitable activities is used to subsidize unprofitable activities.*

Much of the experience with ground transportation regulation and deregulation is also reflected in the case of the airlines, as you will see in the next section.

Airline Regulation

The airline business was closely regulated by the *Civil Aeronautics Board* (CAB), established in 1938. Any potential entrant interested in serving an interstate route had to persuade the CAB that the route needed another airline, a task that proved impossible. During the 40 years prior to deregulation, more than 150 applications for long-distance routes were submitted by potential entrants, *but no new entry was allowed*. The CAB also forced strict compliance with regulated prices. A request to lower prices on any route would result in a rate hearing, where the request was scrutinized by both the CAB and competitors.

Although the CAB, in effect, prohibited price competition in the industry, *nonprice competition was abundant*. Airlines competed on the basis of the frequency of flights, the quality of meals, the width of the seats, even the friendliness of the staff. Such competition, particularly in the area of the frequency of flights, increased operating costs. Frequent flights meant more empty seats; before deregulation, planes on average were nearly half empty. In addition, firms in the industry spent more on promotion, which also raised the average cost of providing airline service. Costs rose until the firms in the industry earned only a normal rate of return. Thus *air fares set above competitive levels plus entry restrictions are no guarantee of economic profit as long as there are no restrictions on nonprice competition or on the number of flights each airline can offer.*

Airline Deregulation

In 1978 Congress passed the Airline Deregulation Act, which reduced restrictions on price competition and on new entry. During the first year of deregulation, the average fare fell by 20 percent. By the end of the 1980s, air fares were lower than they had been at the beginning of the decade. The biggest change was in the number of new entrants: between 1978 and 1983, fourteen new airlines entered the industry. Some major airlines, such as Braniff and Eastern, went bankrupt.

The insulation from price competition had allowed firms to pay higher wages than they would have in a more competitive industry. The Air Line Pilots Association, the union that represented pilots for all the major airlines prior to deregulation, had been able to negotiate extremely attractive wages for its members over the years. A senior pilot, who typically worked less than two weeks a month, earned as much as $150,000 a year in 1983.[3] Just how attractive the pilot's position was became apparent after deregulation. America West Airlines, a nonunion employer that sprouted from deregulation, paid its pilots only $32,000 a year and required them to work forty hours a week, performing dispatch and marketing tasks when they were not flying. Yet America West received some four thousand applications for its twenty-nine pilot vacancies.

Arguments Against Deregulation

Several concerns have been raised about the deregulation of the trucking and airline industries. One of the original rationales for regulation was to

---

[3] For an interesting account of life as a top pilot, see Victor F. Zohana, "End of Glamorous Life Looms for U.S. Pilots As Competition Grows," *Wall Street Journal*, 2 November 1983.

provide service to small towns, and it has been argued that deregulation would strip these smaller communities of their services. Another concern has been that the government would lose the control it had, under regulation, over the quality and safety of airline service. Although it is too early for definitive answers, there is little evidence to indicate that these fears have materialized. For example, despite the demise of the CAB, the Federal Aviation Administration (FAA) still regulates the safety and quality of air service. A study released by the FAA in 1988 indicated that the rate of passenger fatalities in airplane accidents dropped steadily between 1977 and 1987.

Yet competitive trends in the airline industry in recent years raise some troubling questions. Though airline traffic nearly doubled during the 1980s, no new airports were opened and the air traffic control system did not expand. Thus the government did not follow up deregulation with an expansion of airport capacity. Consequently, departure gates and landing rights became the scarce resource in the industry. Those airlines unable to secure such facilities went out of business. Some argue that the major airlines have not pushed for an expansion of airport facilities because this additional capacity could encourage new entry and greater competition. Before deregulation the five largest airlines controlled 63 percent of the passenger business. Deregulation initially promoted a wave of new entry by such upstarts as People Express and New York Air. By the end of the 1980s, however, most of the new entrants had disappeared or had been absorbed by larger airlines. By 1989 the market share of the five largest airlines had climbed to 70 percent.

The course of regulation and deregulation raises some interesting questions about the true objective of regulation. Recall the competing views of regulation: one view holds that regulation is in the public, or consumer, interest; the second view holds that regulation is in the special, or producer, interest. In the ground transportation and airline industries, regulation appeared more in accord with producer interests; the movement toward deregulation apparently sprang from a government policy to promote consumer interests.

ANTITRUST LAWS

Although competition typically ensures the most efficient use of the nation's resources, an individual firm would prefer to operate in a business climate that is more akin to monopoly. If left alone, some firms would attempt to create a monopolistic environment by driving competitors out of business, merging with other firms, or colluding with competitors. In the United States, *antitrust laws* represent an attempt to curb these anticompetitive tendencies. Antitrust policy works in two ways. First, it is aimed at promoting the sort of market structure that will lead to greater competition. Second, it is aimed at controlling market conduct so as to directly reduce or eliminate anticompetitive behavior. Thus *antitrust laws represent an attempt to shape market structure and control market conduct in ways that will promote socially desirable market performance.*

Origins of Antitrust Policy

A variety of economic events that occurred in the last half of the nineteenth century created a political climate supportive of antitrust legislation. Perhaps the two most important factors were (1) technological breakthroughs, which led to more extensive use of capital and a larger optimal plant size in many manufacturing industries, and (2) the rapid growth of the railroads, which lowered the cost of transporting manufactured goods. Economies of scale in production and cheaper transportation extended the geographical boundaries of markets. So firms grew larger and reached wider markets.

Depressions in 1873 and 1883, however, caused a panic among these large manufacturers, which were now committed to the heavy fixed costs associated with large-scale production. Their defensive reaction was to lower prices in an attempt to stimulate sales. Price wars erupted, creating economic chaos. Firms desperately sought ways to stabilize their markets. One solution was for competing firms to form a **trust**, either by merging to form a single enterprise or by simply agreeing on a uniform pricing policy. Early trusts were formed in the sugar, tobacco, and oil industries. Although the activity of these early trusts is still a matter of debate today, they allegedly pursued anticompetitive practices to develop and maintain a dominant market position.

*A **trust** is a merger or collusive agreement among competing firms.*

These practices provoked widespread criticism and earned promoters of trusts the derisive title of "robber barons." Public sentiment lay on the side of the smaller competitors. Farmers, especially, resented the higher prices of manufactured goods, which resulted from the trusts' activity, particularly since the prices farmers were receiving for their own products were declining through the latter part of the nineteenth century. Public dissatisfaction with trusts led eighteen states in the 1880s to enact antitrust laws, which prohibited the formation of trusts. State laws, however, were largely ineffective because the trusts could move across state lines to avoid them.

Sherman Antitrust Act of 1890 In 1888 the major political parties put antitrust planks in their platforms. This consensus culminated in the passage of the Sherman Antitrust Act of 1890. The law contains two main sections:

> Section 1: Every contract, combination in the form of trust or otherwise, or conspiracy, in restraint of trade or commerce among the several states or with foreign nations, is hereby declared illegal.

> Section 2: Every person who shall monopolize, or attempt to monopolize, or conspire with any other person or persons to

monopolize any part of the trade or commerce among the several states, or with foreign nations, shall be guilty of a misdemeanor.

Current penalties for violations include fines of up to $1 million plus possible jail terms.

During the first ten years after its passage, enforcement of the law was hampered by a lack of funds and the absence of a forceful attorney general. Not until President Theodore Roosevelt took office in 1901 was a special Antitrust Division established in the Department of Justice to prosecute offenders. The laws on the books were stiffened in 1914 by additional legislation.

The Clayton Act of 1914 The ambiguous language of the Sherman Act let much anticompetitive activity slip by. Therefore the Clayton Act of 1914 was passed to outlaw certain practices not prohibited by the Sherman Act. Section 2 of the Clayton Act prohibits price discrimination where this practice tends to create a monopoly. You'll recall that price discrimination is charging different customers different prices for the same good or charging the same customer different prices for different quantities of the good. Price discrimination is permitted where the firm can show that it does not reduce competition or where differences in selling costs justify the different prices.

Section 3 of the Clayton Act prohibits tying contracts and exclusive dealing if they substantially lessen competition. **Tying contracts** require the buyer of one good to purchase another good as well. For example, a seller of a patented machine might require customers to purchase unpatented supplies. **Exclusive dealing** occurs when a producer will sell a product only if the buyer agrees not to purchase from other manufacturers. For example, a computer chip maker might sell chips to a computer maker only if the computer maker agreed not to purchase chips elsewhere. The law also prohibits **interlocking directorates**, where the same individual serves on the boards of directors of competing firms. Finally, *mergers* through the acquisition of the stock of a competing firm are outlawed in cases where the merger would substantially lessen competition.

*Under a **tying contract**, a seller of one good requires buyers to purchase other goods as well.*

***Exclusive dealing** occurs when a producer prohibits customers from purchasing from other sellers.*

*In an **interlocking directorate**, the same individual serves on the boards of directors of competing firms.*

Federal Trade Commission Act of 1914 To facilitate antitrust enforcement, the *Federal Trade Commission* (FTC) was established in 1914 to investigate and prosecute what the Federal Trade Commission Act termed "unfair methods of competition." The commission consists of five full-time commissioners appointed by the president for seven-year terms and assisted by a professional staff. A 1919 Supreme Court decision ruled that only the courts could interpret the laws to determine what practices were "unfair," thus limiting the role of the FTC. In 1938 the *Wheeler-Lea Act* gave the FTC the responsibility for prohibiting "deceptive acts or practices in commerce," so the FTC took on the role of policing untrue and deceptive advertising.

The Sherman, Clayton, and FTC acts provided the antitrust framework, a framework that has been clarified and embellished by subsequent amendments. Specifically, the 1936 *Robinson-Patman Act* prohibits firms from selling "at unreasonably low prices" when the intent is to reduce competition. This act was aimed at keeping small merchants in business by preventing manufacturers from giving a price break to large department stores.

A loophole in the Clayton Act was closed in 1950 with the passage of the *Celler-Kefauver Anti-Merger Act*, which prevents one firm from buying the *assets* of another firm if the effect is to reduce competition. This law prohibits both horizontal mergers and vertical mergers where these mergers would tend to reduce competition in a particular industry. For example, a merger of Coke and Pepsi would likely be prohibited.

Antitrust Law Enforcement

Any law's effectiveness depends on the vigor and vigilance of enforcement. The pattern of antitrust enforcement goes something like this. Either the Antitrust Division of the Justice Department or the Federal Trade Commission charges a firm or group of firms with breaking the law. These government agencies are often acting on a complaint by a customer or a competitor. At that point, those charged with the wrongdoing may be able, without any admission of guilt, to sign a *consent decree*, whereby they agree not to continue doing whatever they had been charged with. If the charges are contested, evidence from both sides is presented in a court trial, and a decision is rendered by a judge. Certain decisions may be appealed all the way to the Supreme Court, and in such cases the high court may render new interpretations of existing law.

Those parties who can show injury by firms that have violated antitrust laws can sue the offending company and recover three times the amount of the damages sustained. These so-called *treble damage* suits increased after World War II; more than 1000 cases are initiated each year. Courts have been relatively generous to those claiming to have been wronged. The potential liability for treble damages makes firms more wary of violating antitrust laws.

Since these cases often start with the Justice Department, antitrust law enforcement is affected by the attorney general's inclination to file charges. The vigor of this enforcement varies with the political party in power and with the judicial climate. Antitrust laws were not enforced aggressively until after World War II. Most other industrial countries take a more tolerant view of market power. United States antitrust laws seem to have prevented U.S. firms from adopting many restrictive and predatory practices tolerated elsewhere.

Per Se Illegality and the Rule of Reason

Per se illegality refers to business practices that are declared illegal regardless of their economic rationale or their consequences.

The courts have interpreted the antitrust laws in essentially two ways. One set of practices has been declared illegal **per se** — that is, without regard to economic rationale or consequences. For example, under the Sherman Act, all formal agreements among competing firms to fix prices, restrict output, or otherwise restrain the forces of competition are viewed as illegal *per se*. Under a *per se* rule, in order for the defendant to be found guilty, the government need only show that the offending practice took place; thus the government need only examine the firm's *conduct*.

Another set of practices falls under the **rule of reason**. Here the courts engage in a broader inquiry into the facts surrounding the particular offense—namely, the reasons why the offending practices were adopted and the effect of these practices on competition. The rule of reason was first set forth in 1911, when the Supreme Court held that the Standard Oil Company had illegally monopolized the petroleum refining industry. Standard Oil allegedly had come to dominate 90 percent of the market by acquiring more than 120 former rivals and by implementing predatory pricing tactics to drive remaining rivals out of business. In finding Standard Oil guilty, the Court focused on both its market conduct and the market structure that resulted from Standard Oil's activity, and the Court found that Standard Oil had behaved unreasonably.

Using the rule of reason, the Court in 1920 found U.S. Steel not guilty of monopolization. In this case the Court ruled that not every contract or combination in restraint of trade was illegal—only those that "unreasonably" restrain trade violate antitrust laws. The Court said that mere size was not an offense. Although U.S. Steel clearly possessed market power, the company was not in violation of antitrust laws because it had not unreasonably used that power. The Court changed that view twenty-five years later in reviewing the charges against the Aluminum Company of America (Alcoa). In a 1945 decision, the Supreme Court held that although a firm's conduct might be reasonable and legal, the mere possession of market power—Alcoa controlled 90 percent of the aluminum ingot market—violated the antitrust laws. Here the Court was using market structure rather than market conduct as the test of legality.

Problems with Enforcement of Antitrust Legislation

There is growing doubt about the economic value of some of the lengthy antitrust cases pursued in the past. For example, a government case against IBM began in 1969, when the Antitrust Division sued IBM under Section 2 of the Sherman Act, charging that the company, with nearly 70 percent of domestic sales of electronic data processing equipment, had a monopoly. IBM was also charged with introducing the 360 line of computers so as to eliminate competition. IBM responded that its large market share was based on its innovative products and on its economies of scale. The trial began in 1975, and the government took nearly three years to present its case. Litigation persisted for years. In the meantime many other computer manufacturers emerged both in this country and abroad to challenge IBM's dominance. In 1982 the Reagan administration dropped the case, noting that the threat of monopoly had diminished enough that the case was "without merit."

Too Much Emphasis on the Competitive Model Joseph Schumpeter argued half a century ago that competition should be viewed as a dynamic process. Firms are continually in flux—introducing new products, phasing out old products, trying to compete for the consumer's dollar in a variety of ways. In light of this, antitrust policy should not necessarily be aimed at increasing the number of firms in each industry. In some cases firms will grow large because they are more efficient than rivals at offering what consumers want. Accordingly, firm size should not be the primary concern. Moreover, Vernon Smith has shown through experiments that many of the desirable properties of perfect competition can be achieved with a small number of firms.[4]

Growing Importance of International Markets One yardstick for measuring the market power of a firm is its share of the market. With the growth of international trade, however, the local or even the national market share becomes less relevant. General Motors may dominate U.S. auto manufacturing, accounting for over half of domestic sales by U.S. firms in 1989. But when sales by Japanese and European producers are included, GM's share of the U.S. auto market falls to about one-third. GM's share of world production has declined steadily since the mid-1950s. *Where markets are open to foreign competition, domestic antitrust enforcement makes less economic sense.*

Mergers and Public Policy

The Justice Department has been sensitive to some of its critics, and in 1982 it issued long-awaited guidelines on mergers. Perhaps the most significant feature of the new guidelines is the redefinition of market share. In determining the possible detrimental effects a merger might have on competition, one important factor to consider is the effect of the merger on the level of concentration in that market. The measure of concentration employed until 1982 by the Justice Department was the four-firm **concentration ratio**, which is the sum of the percentage market shares of the top four firms in the market. Suppose that forty-four firms supply a market. Also suppose that the top four firms account for 23 percent, 18 percent, 13 percent, and 6 percent, respectively, of the total market sales, and the remaining forty firms account for 1 percent each. The four-firm concentration ratio is the sum of the shares of the top four firms, which in this case is 60 percent.

*A **concentration ratio** measures the total market share of the largest firms in an industry.*

One problem with the concentration ratio is that it says nothing about the distribution of market share among the four firms. For example, the four-firm concentration ratio is 60 percent if the top four firms each have 15 percent of the market share or if one firm has 57 percent of the market and

---

[4] Vernon Smith, "Markets as Economizers of Information: Experimental Examination of the 'Hayek Hypothesis'," *Economic Inquiry* 20 (1982).

the next three have 1 percent each. Yet clearly an industry in which one firm captures over half the market is less competitive than an industry with four firms of identical size.

To remedy this lack of precision, the Justice Department's new merger guidelines call for the use of the **Herfindahl index**, which is calculated by squaring the percentage market share of each firm in the market and then adding those squares. For example, if the industry consists of one hundred firms of equal size, the Herfindahl index is 100. If the industry is a pure monopoly, the index is 10,000. The index is smaller the more firms there are in the industry or the more equal in size the firms are.

The Herfindahl index provides more information than the four-firm concentration ratio because it gives greater weight to firms with a larger market share. The Herfindahl index for each of the three previous examples is calculated in Exhibit 3. Although each example has the same four-firm concentration ratio, each yields a different Herfindahl index. Note that the index for Industry III is nearly triple that for the two other industries.

The Justice Department's new guidelines also sort all mergers into two bins: horizontal mergers, which involve firms in the same market, and nonhorizontal mergers, which include all others. Of most interest for antitrust purposes are horizontal mergers, such as a merger between competing oil companies. The Justice Department generally challenges any merger in an industry that would have a post-merger Herfindahl index greater than 1800, if the merger would increase the index by more than 100

*The **Herfindahl index** is the sum of the squared percentage market shares of all firms in an industry.*

EXHIBIT 3
COMPUTATION OF THE HERFINDAHL INDEX BASED ON MARKET SHARE IN THREE HYPOTHETICAL INDUSTRIES

Firm	Industry I Market Share (percent)	Market Share Squared	Industry II Market Share (percent)	Market Share Squared	Industry III Market Share (percent)	Market Share Squared
A	23	529	15	225	57	3249
B	18	324	15	225	1	1
C	13	169	15	225	1	1
D	6	36	15	225	1	1
Remaining forty firms (at 1 percent each)	1 each	40	1 each	40	1 each	40
Four-firm concentration ratio	60		60		60	
Herfindahl index		1098		940		3292

points. Mergers in an industry that would have a post-merger index of less than 1000 are seldom challenged. Other factors, such as the ease of entry into the market, are considered for intermediate cases.

COMPETITIVE TRENDS IN THE ECONOMY

For years there has been concern about the sheer size of some firms because of the real or potential power these firms might exercise in both the economic and the political arena. One way to measure the power of the largest corporations is to calculate the share of corporate assets controlled by the one hundred largest firms. What percentage of the nation's assets do the top one hundred manufacturing companies own, and how has this share changed over time?

The largest one hundred firms control about half of all manufacturing assets in the United States, up from a 40 percent share after World War II. Thus the largest firms have increased their share of the country's manufacturing assets. We should recognize, however, that size alone is not synonymous with market power. A very big firm, such as a large oil company, may face stiff competition from other very big oil companies; the only movie theater in an isolated community may be able to raise its price with less concern about competition.

Market Competition over Time

More important than the size of the largest firms in the nation is the market structure in each industry. Various studies have examined the level of competition and change in industry structure over the years. All have used some variation of the concentration ratio as a point of departure, sometimes supplementing this measure with data from the specific industry about barriers to entry and other evidence suggesting whether the largest firms can control prices. Among the most comprehensive of these studies is the research of William Shepherd, who relied on many sources to determine the competitiveness of each industry in the U.S. economy.[5]

Shepherd sorted industries into four groups: (1) pure monopoly, in which a single firm controlled the entire market and was able to block entry; (2) dominant firm, in which a single firm had over half the market share and had no close rival; (3) tight oligopoly, in which the top four firms supplied more than 60 percent of the market, with stable market shares and evidence of cooperation; and (4) effective competition, in which firms in the industry exhibited low concentration, low entry barriers, and little or no collusion.

Exhibit 4 presents Shepherd's breakdown of all U.S. industries into the

---

[5] William G. Shepherd, "Causes of Increased Competition in the U.S. Economy, 1939–1980," *Review of Economics and Statistics* 64 (November 1982).

EXHIBIT 4
TRENDS OF COMPETITION IN THE U.S. ECONOMY, 1939–1980

Competitive Group	Percentage Income Share of Each Category		
	1939	**1958**	**1980**
Pure monopoly	6.2	3.1	2.5
Dominant firm	5.0	5.0	2.8
Tight oligopoly	36.4	35.6	18.0
Effectively competitive industries	52.4	56.3	76.7
	100.0	100.0	100.0

Source: William G. Shepherd, "Causes of Increased Competition in the U.S. Economy, 1939–1980," *Review of Economics and Statistics* 64 (November 1982): 618, Table 2. The income share is the percentage of national income generated by industries in each competitive group.

four categories for the years 1939, 1958, and 1980. The table shows a modest trend toward increased competition between 1939 and 1958, with the percentage of those industries rated as "effectively competitive" growing from 52.4 percent to 56.3 percent of all industries. Between 1958 and 1980, however, there was a clear increase in competitiveness in the economy, with the percentage of effectively competitive industries jumping from 56.3 percent to 76.7 percent.

Exhibit 5 presents Shepherd's findings in greater detail, with the economy broken down into eight broad industrial sectors. The left column lists the sectors. To provide some idea of the relative importance of each sector, the second column lists the income generated by that sector in 1978. The remaining columns list the percentage of industries in each sector that were rated "effectively competitive." The table shows a modest but widespread increase in competition between 1939 and 1958, with increases in seven of the eight industrial sectors. Between 1958 and 1980, according to Shepherd, there were solid gains in the economy's competitiveness, with all sectors showing greater competition.[6]

According to Shepherd, the growth in competition from 1958 to 1980 can be traced to three primary causes: *imports, deregulation, and antitrust activity*. Foreign imports between 1958 and 1980 resulted in increased competition in thirteen major industries, including autos, tires, and steel. According to Shepherd, the growth in imports accounted for one-sixth of the increase in competition. Imports were attractive to consumers because of their superior quality and lower price. Because they were competing with U.S. producers that often had been tightly knit domestic oligopolies, foreign competitors found these U.S. markets relatively easy to penetrate. Finding themselves at a cost and technological disadvantage, domestic

---

[6] He notes, however, that though competition blossomed, market power remained high in many manufacturing industries, such as computers, drugs, and soups, as well as among utilities.

EXHIBIT 5
COMPETITIVE TRENDS IN THE U.S. ECONOMY,
1939–1980, BY INDUSTRY SECTOR

Sectors of Economy	National Income Arising from Each Sector in 1978 (billions of dollars)	Percentage of Each Sector Rated as Effectively Competitive		
		1939	1958	1980
Agriculture, forestry, and fishing	54.7	91.6	85.0	86.4
Mining	24.5	87.1	92.2	95.8
Construction	87.6	27.9	55.9	80.2
Manufacturing	459.5	51.5	55.9	69.0
Transportation and public utilities	162.3	8.7	26.1	39.1
Wholesale and retail	261.8	57.8	60.5	93.4
Finance, insurance, and real estate	210.7	61.5	63.8	94.1
Services	245.3	53.9	54.3	77.9
Totals	1506.4	52.4	56.3	76.7

Source: William G. Shepherd, "Causes of Increased Competition," 618, Table 2.

producers initially responded by seeking trade barriers, such as quotas and tariffs, to reduce foreign competition.

Trucking, the airlines, and telecommunications were among the industries deregulated between 1958 and 1980. We have already discussed some of the effects of this deregulation, particularly in reducing barriers to entry and in eliminating uniform pricing schedules. According to Shepherd's study, the deregulation movement accounted for one-fifth of the increase in competition.

Although it is difficult to attribute an increase in competition to specific antitrust activity, Shepherd concludes that about two-fifths of the increase in competition between 1958 and 1980 can be credited to the effects of antitrust activity. He argues that although imports and deregulation were also important, their benefits could be quickly reversed by a shift toward protectionism and a return to regulation. In contrast, the effects of antitrust legislation are more permanent, and a reversal would require a much greater movement in both legislation and judicial opinion.

CONCLUSION

If we look at all large corporations, we see evidence that the share of corporate assets controlled by the largest firms has been increasing over time, but if we focus on particular industries, the overall degree of competition in the U.S. economy appears to be increasing. How can this paradox be resolved? Many mergers in the years since World War II have been conglomerate mergers, which join firms operating in unrelated markets. If two giant firms from different industries merge, the assets held by the top one hundred firms increase, yet there is no effect on the competitiveness of particular industries.

Shepherd's data go through 1980. What has been the trend in competition since then? On the antitrust front, the trial against American Telephone and Telegraph Company, which began in 1974, was settled in 1982 with AT&T divesting itself of twenty-two companies that provide most of the country's local phone service. As a result, long distance rates are now more competitive. More generally, however, antitrust policy during the decade was not forceful, particularly with regard to the big story during the 1980s: corporate takeovers. Even after adjusting for inflation, the dollar value of corporate acquisitions during the 1980s was more than double that during the post–World War II merger wave. These corporate takeovers could benefit the economy to the extent that more efficient managers replace less efficient managers, but the merging of large firms in the same industry could have negative effects on competition. The effect of these takeovers will be examined more closely later.

The 1980s were a period of more intense international competition. Growing world trade increased competition in the U.S. economy, and at the end of the decade U.S. industries continued to pressure the government for trade protection to reduce competition. For example, despite record industry profits in 1988, U.S. automakers in 1989 were pushing for higher tariffs on imported automobiles.

Deregulation also ran into snags during the 1980s. Airlines are now more concentrated than they were before deregulation. And the bankruptcy of many savings and loan institutions was blamed in part on banking deregulation. The enthusiasm for deregulation appears to have waned. In short, the competitive record of the 1980s can be viewed as two steps forward and one back.

Summary

1. Government regulation of business takes three forms: (1) social regulation, which is aimed at fostering a healthful environment, safety in the workplace, and consumer protection; (2) economic regulation, such as the regulation of natural monopolies; and (3) antitrust activity, which promotes competition and prohibits efforts to cartelize or monopolize an industry. This chapter examined economic regulation and antitrust activity.

2. Natural monopolies are regulated by govern-

ment so that output is greater and prices are lower than they would be if the monopolist were allowed to maximize profits. One problem with regulation is that the price that maximizes social welfare requires the government to subsidize the firm, whereas the price that allows the firm to earn a normal profit does not maximize social welfare.

3. There are two views of economic regulation. The first is that economic regulation is in the public interest because it controls natural monopolies where monopoly is most efficient and promotes competition where competition is most efficient. A second view is that regulation is not in the public, or consumer, interest, but in the special interest of producers.

4. Both the ground transportation and the airline industry were regulated for much of this cen-

tury. Regulation had the effect of restricting entry and fixing prices. Both industries underwent deregulation in the early 1980s. Deregulation increased the number of firms in each industry, but some existing firms could not compete and went bankrupt.

5. The Sherman, Clayton, and FTC acts provided the basic framework for antitrust enforcement, a framework that has been clarified and embellished by subsequent amendments. Antitrust laws are aimed at promoting competition and prohibiting efforts to cartelize or monopolize an industry.

6. Research indicates that competition in U.S. industries has been increasing since World War II. Three reasons for the growth in competition are foreign trade, deregulation, and antitrust activity.

Questions and Problems

1. (Government Control of Business) Which of the three types of regulation of business—social, economic, or antitrust regulation—is the motivation for each of the following?
   a. Marginal cost pricing
   b. Liquor licensing
   c. Building codes
   d. Clayton Act of 1914
   e. The establishment of the Small Business Administration

2. (Regulation) Why do most states require a doctor's prescription to obtain antibiotics? Such regulations do not exist in countries such as Mexico and Taiwan. Should all countries have such laws?

3. (Social Regulation) Recently AIDS has brought the role of the drug regulatory agency known as the FDA into sharp focus. Why might AIDS patients feel resentment toward this agency? How might they circumvent FDA regulations?

4. (Trucking Regulations) "The trucking industry has an unfair advantage over other transportation industries such as the railroads, since it uses the public highways, which were not built exclusively by the trucking companies. Therefore the trucking industry should be regulated." Comment on this assertion.

5. (Regulation) Why might some industries prefer to be regulated rather than face an unregulated environment?

6. (Utility Regulation) It has often been noted that utility stocks tend to go up more slowly than the stock market and to fall more slowly than the market. Is the stability of utility stocks a result of the regulation of the industry? Why or why not?

7. (Antitrust)) Why might a company plead guilty to charges of anticompetitive behavior even though it knew such charges were un-

justified? Would this plea depend on how large the company was?

8. (Antitrust) "The existence of only three or four big auto manufacturers in the United States is prima facie evidence that the market structure is anticompetitive and that antitrust laws are being broken." Evaluate this assertion.

9. (Antitrust) Why might the Herfindahl index be an indication of the relative success of certain firms in an industry rather than a measure of the anticompetitive structure of the industry?

10. (Monopoly Regulation) Compare the impacts of the following policies on the profit and economic inefficiency level of a natural monopoly.
   a. Enacting an excise (sales) tax
   b. Enacting a franchise (lump sum) tax
   c. Setting a price ceiling where marginal cost intersects the demand curve

   d. Setting a price ceiling where average cost intersects the demand curve
   e. Allowing price discrimination in the form of "peak load" pricing

11. (Natural Monopoly) For a natural monpoly, a price equal to marginal cost is economically efficient in the sense that it produces the greatest net benefits to consumers, even though at such a price, the costs of production are not being covered. Explain why this isn't a contradiction.

12. (Discriminating Monopoly) Using demand and cost curves, show why regulation that forces a perfectly discriminating monopolist to charge everyone the same price could lead to a decrease in economic efficiency.

13. (Patents and Deregulation) Discuss whether patents, by restricting access to information and product design, have the effect of decreasing competition.

PART SIX

Resource Markets

C H A P T E R   2 5

Resource Markets

Why does Larry Bird earn more than Big Bird? Supply and demand. Why does prime Iowa corn acreage cost more than scrubland in the Texas panhandle? Supply and demand. Why are the buildings in downtown Chicago taller than those in the farmland of southern Illinois? Supply and demand. Why do M.D.s earn more than Ph.D.s? Supply and demand. You say you've been through supply and demand already? True. But the earlier discussion focused on the product market — that is, the market for final goods and services. Goods and services, however, are produced by resources: land, labor, capital, and entrepreneurial ability. Supply and demand in the resource market determine resource prices and resource uses. The distribution of resource ownership then determines the distribution of income throughout the economy.

Your income depends on the value of your resources in the market, so the discussion of resource markets should be of particular interest to you. Certainly one key element in your career decision is the expected earnings associated with alternative careers. For example, after college should you become a regional sales representative or go on to law school? This chapter and the following few chapters will show how resource supply and demand interact to establish market prices for various resources. Topics discussed in this chapter include

- Resource markets
- Resource demand
- Resource supply
- Earnings differentials

- Economic rent
- Marginal revenue product
- Marginal resource cost
- Elasticity of resource demand

THE DEMAND AND SUPPLY
OF RESOURCES

See if you can answer the following questions about the demand for resources. Consider first the use of land. Old MacDonald has a farm. A neighbor offers him the opportunity to lease an additional plot of farmland. MacDonald figures that farming the extra land would increase total revenue by $600 per year, but it would increase total production costs by $900 per year. Should Old MacDonald lease the extra land? Since the additional cost of farming that land exceeds the additional revenue, the answer is no.

Next, consider labor. A firm's manager knows that hiring one more worker would increase the firm's total cost by $400 per week, but it would increase the firm's total revenue by $500 per week. Should the profit-maximizing firm hire that additional worker? Sure. The firm can increase its profit (or reduce its loss) by $100 per week by hiring the additional worker. As long as the additional revenue resulting from employing another worker exceeds the additional cost, the firm should hire that worker.

What about capital? Suppose that you cut lawns during the summer, earning an average of $10 per lawn. With your push mower you cut about 15 lawns a week, for total earnings of $150. You are content until you read about a larger, faster mower — the Lawn Monster — that would cut your time per lawn in half, allowing you to double the number of lawns you mow per week with the same effort. If you mow 30 lawns per week, with the Lawn Monster, your total revenue will double to $300 per week, but you will have to pay an extra $100 per week for the mower. Should you switch to the Lawn Monster? Since your total cost increases by $100 per week but your total revenue increases by $150 per week, your net revenue increases by $50 per week, so you should move up to the Monster.

The above examples show that *additional units of a resource will be demanded as long as the extra revenue generated by the additional unit exceeds the extra cost*. You should also understand the economic logic behind resource supply. Suppose you are contemplating two jobs that are identical except that one pays more than the other. Is there any question about which job you will take? When other things are held constant, you choose the higher-paying job.

Now turn the example around to consider the case where you must choose between two jobs that are identical in pay. The only difference between them is that one requires you to report for work at 5 A.M., a time of day when your body tends to reject conscious activity, and the other has normal hours. Which job will you choose? Most of us will choose the job that is more in accord with our natural body rhythms. In fact, you may be willing to accept less pay for the job with normal hours rather than start at 5 A.M.

Resource owners will supply additional resources as long as doing so increases their utility. Therefore they will supply their resources to the highest-paying alternative, other things constant. Since other things are not always held constant, however, resource owners must often be paid more to supply their resources to certain uses. In the case of labor, the worker's utility includes both pay and other nonmonetary aspects of the job. Jobs that are dirty, dangerous, exhausting, and of low status are usually less attractive than jobs that are clean, safe, stimulating, and of high status.

The easiest way to understand resource markets is to draw upon what you already know about the market for final goods and services. In the market for goods and services — that is, the product market — households are demanders and firms are suppliers. In the resource market, however, the supply and demand roles are reversed: firms are demanders and households are suppliers. In the product market, households demand the bundle of goods and services that maximizes utility; in the resource market, firms demand the combination of resources that maximizes profit. The assumption of profit maximization ensures that firms will choose the most efficient production process and the least costly combination of resources available.

Exhibit 1 presents the market for a particular resource, in this case the labor market for economists. This market is characterized by an upward-sloping supply curve and a downward-sloping demand curve. This market will converge to the equilibrium wage rate, or the market price, for this type of labor. *Like the supply and demand for final goods and services, the supply and demand for resources depend on the willingness and the ability of buyers and sellers to participate in the market.*

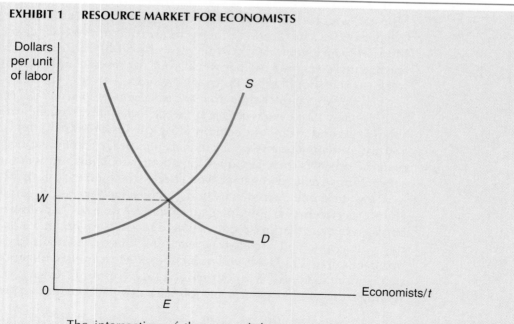

EXHIBIT 1   RESOURCE MARKET FOR ECONOMISTS

The intersection of the upward-sloping supply curve of economists with the downward-sloping demand curve determines the equilibrium wage rate, W, and the level of employment, E.

The Market Demand Curve

Why does a firm employ resources? Resources are used to produce goods and services, which a firm tries to sell for a profit. The firm does not value the resource itself; what the firm values is the resource's ability to produce goods and services. Because the value of any resource depends on the value of what it produces, the demand for a resource is a **derived demand**—derived from the value of the final product. For example, a movie star's earnings per movie are based on that star's appeal at the box office.

The market demand for a resource is the sum of the demands for that resource in all its various uses. For example, the market demand for economists is made up of all the various demands for this type of labor in higher education, industry, finance, and government. Similarly, the market demand for timber consists of its demand in the production of housing, paper products, railway ties, furniture, toothpicks, and so on. The demand curve for a resource, like the demand curve for the goods produced by that resource, slopes downward, as depicted in Exhibit 1. As the price of a resource falls, producers are more willing and more able to employ that resource.

Consider first the producer's greater *willingness* to hire resources as the price falls. In constructing the demand curve for a particular resource, we hold constant the prices of other resources. Consequently, if the price of this particular resource falls, it becomes relatively cheaper compared to other resources the firm could use to produce the same output. Hence, as the price of a resource declines, firms are more willing to hire this resource rather than other, now relatively more costly resources. Thus we observe *substitution in production*—economists for business administrators, coal for oil, or plastic tubing for copper tubing.

A lower price for a resource also increases a producer's *ability* to hire that resource. At a lower price, firms can purchase more resources for the same total cost. If the price of a resource drops by half, a producer can buy twice the amount for the same total cost. This does not mean that the firm *will* buy twice the amount, only that, because price has fallen, the firm *could* buy twice the amount. The amount the firm buys will depend on what happens to the market price of the final good.

*The demand for a resource is a **derived demand**; it is determined by the demand for the product the resource helps to produce.*

The Market Supply Curve

The market supply of a resource is the sum of the individual supplies of all resource owners, such as all economists, to that market. The first reason the supply curve for a resource tends to slope upward is that the resource owners are *willing* to supply more of the good as the price goes up. The higher the price offered for a particular resource, other things constant, the more goods and services the resource owner can buy with the payment obtained for supplying the resource. Hence higher resource prices are more attractive to resource owners than are lower prices.

In constructing the supply curve for a particular resource, we hold constant the prices offered for resources in other markets. As the price offered for a resource rises, suppliers have an incentive to shift out of other resource markets, where prices are now relatively lower, into the market where the price is higher. Resource prices are signals about the rewards for supplying resources to alternative activities, and higher resource prices will draw resources from lower-valued uses. For example, if the wage offered to economists is very low, some economists will supply their labor to other markets, perhaps becoming stock brokers or computer analysts, even though they use few of their economic skills in these other jobs. As the wage offered to economists increases, the quantity of economists supplied will increase, as economists are drawn out of secondary activities.

The second reason for an upward-sloping supply curve is that the resource owners are *able* to supply more of the resource at a higher price. For example, as the price of oil increased in the 1970s, oil exploration became economically feasible in less accessible locations, such as the remote jungles of the Amazon and the stormy waters of the North Sea. It is the higher price offered for the resource that enables resource suppliers to incur the higher cost of supplying the additional output.

Equilibrium and Resource Price Differences

Because of the way resource markets operate, the prices paid for identical resources should, over time, tend toward equality. This should be true even if these resources are supplied to different uses. For instance, consider the wages earned by a group of identical workers supplying their labor to different uses. Assume that the nonmonetary benefits of these jobs, such as their social status, are identical, so we need be concerned only with pay. Under these conditions, if wages differed across uses, workers would move from lower-wage uses to higher-wage uses. This movement would reduce the supply and increase the wage in the lower-wage occupations while increasing the supply and reducing the wage in the higher-wage occupations. Such shifts would continue until wages equalized and nobody had an incentive to move.

In practice, however, we often observe earnings differentials. On average, corporate economists earn more than academic economists, land in the city rents for more than rural land, brain surgeons earn more than tree surgeons, and good pickers of corporate stocks earn more than good pickers of navel oranges. As you will see, these differences can be traced to the workings of supply and demand and can be described as either disequilibrium differentials or equilibrium differentials.

Disequilibrium Differentials Resource markets are often in a transitory state as they move toward equilibrium. So there are sometimes wage differentials among workers who appear equally qualified. Often these differentials reflect market transitions, in which certain industries emerge and others decline. As we have noted, however, the mere presence of differences in the prices of similar resources will encourage resource owners and firms to adjust supply and demand until the prices of identical resources are equal.

For example, the dramatic increase in the use of computers has increased the demand for programmers. As a result, college graduates majoring in computer science expect to earn more than equally talented graduates with other majors. Over time, however, the higher earnings in the computer field will draw more and more students into that field, increasing supply and lowering relative earnings. Meanwhile, the supply of graduates to other fields requiring similar aptitude will fall, increasing the relative earnings in those fields. Over time the increased supply of computer programmers and the decreased supply of graduates in fields such as mathematics and engineering will tend to equalize earnings in these different fields. The process could take years, but when resource markets are free to adjust, **disequilibrium differentials** trigger the reallocation of resources, which equalizes payments for similar resources.

Disequilibrium differentials are differences in resource payments that trigger resource reallocation and pay adjustments.

Equilibrium Differentials Not all resource price differences cause a reallocation of resources. For example, land along New York's Fifth Avenue sells for as much as $36,000 a square yard; for that amount you could buy many acres of farmland in upstate New York. Yet such a differential does not prompt land owners in upstate New York to supply their land to New York City— obviously that's impossible. Resource price differentials that do not precipitate the shift of resources among uses are called **equilibrium differentials**.

Equilibrium differentials are differences in resource payments that do not precipitate resource reallocation.

The price per acre of farmland varies widely, typically reflecting differences in the land's fertility. Such differences do not trigger forces that generate equality. Similarly, certain wage differentials stem from the different costs of acquiring the education and training required to perform particular tasks. This difference explains why brain surgeons earn more than tree surgeons. Other earnings differentials reflect differences in the nonmonetary aspects of similar jobs. For example, most people must be paid more to work in a grimy factory than in a pleasant office. Similarly, corporate economists earn more than academic economists in part because corporate economists typically have less freedom in their daily schedule and in their choice of research topics.

Whereas disequilibrium differentials spur the movement of resources away from lower-paid uses toward higher-paid uses, equilibrium differentials cause no such reallocations. Equilibrium differentials are explained by a lack of resource mobility (urban land versus rural land), differences in the inherent quality of the resource (fertile land versus scrubland), differences in the time and money involved in developing the necessary skills (file clerk versus certified public accountant), and differences in the nonmonetary aspects of the job (lifeguard at Malibu Beach versus prison guard at San Quentin).

Transfer Earnings and Economic Rents

Michael Jordan makes more than $1 million a year playing professional basketball. But he would likely be willing to play for less. The question is, how much less? How much must Mr. Jordan be paid to play basketball rather than do something else? What is his best alternative? Suppose his best alternative is earning $75,000 a year as a college basketball coach. And assume that, if it weren't for the pay difference, he would be indifferent between playing professional basketball and college coaching. Thus he must earn at least $75,000 playing basketball to stay in the profession. This amount represents his **transfer earnings**—the amount he must be paid to prevent him from "transferring," or supplying his talents, to college coaching. His transfer earnings are what he could earn in the best alternative use of his resources. *Transfer earnings can be thought of as the resource's opportunity cost.*

Transfer earnings are what a resource could earn in its best alternative use.

The amount Michael Jordan earns in excess of his transfer earnings is called **economic rent**. Economic rent is that portion of a resource's total earnings that is not necessary to keep the resource in its present use; it is, as they say, pure gravy. Economic rent is a form of producer surplus earned by resource suppliers. The *division* of resource earnings between economic rent and transfer earnings depends on the resource owner's elasticity of supply. In general, *the less elastic the resource supply, the greater the economic rent as a proportion of total earnings.* To develop a feel for the difference between economic rent and transfer earnings, consider the following three cases.

Economic rent is the portion of a resource's total earnings that is not ascribed to transfer earnings.

Case 1: All Earnings Are Economic Rent When a resource has no alternative use, the supply of that resource to a particular market is perfectly inelastic. Hence there are no transfer earnings, and all returns are in the form of economic rent. For example, consider forest land so remote that it has no economic use other than as a source of timber. The supply of this land available to the timber industry is depicted by the vertical curve in panel (a) of Exhibit 2, which indicates that the 10,000 acres have no alternative use. Because the value of this land in its best alternative use is $0, the price of the resource is determined exclusively by its demand. Since the supply is fixed, the price has no effect on the quantity supplied. The economic rent when the equilibrium price of the resource is $10 per acre is shown by the shaded blue area—an amount totaling $100,000. In this case the resource owner earns no transfer earnings; all earnings are economic rent.

Case 2: All Earnings Are Transfer Earnings At the other extreme is the case in which a resource can earn as much in its best alternative use as in its present use. This situation is illustrated by the perfectly elastic supply curve in panel (b) of Exhibit 2. Suppose Exhibit 2(b) depicts the market for janitors in the local school system. At a wage of $10 per hour, the school system can employ as many janitors as it chooses. At a wage of $10 an hour, the school system demands 100 units of labor. If the wage offered falls below $10, however, these workers will find employment elsewhere, perhaps in nearby factories. In this case all earnings are transfer earnings because any reduction in the wage will reduce the quantity of labor supplied to this particular use to 0. The best alternative for these resources also pays a wage of $10 per hour. *Here the demand curve determines the equilibrium quantity hired but not the equilibrium wage; the equilibrium wage is determined exclusively by the supply curve.*

EXHIBIT 2   TRANSFER EARNINGS AND ECONOMIC RENT

(a) *All resource returns
are economic rent*

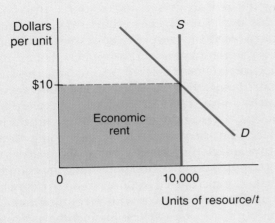

(b) *All resource returns
are transfer earnings*

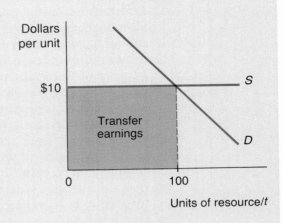

(c) *Resource returns are divided between
economic rent and transfer earnings*

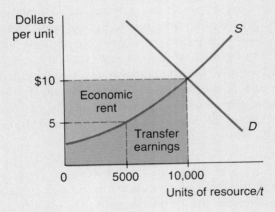

In panel (a), the resource supply curve is vertical, indicating that the resource has no alternative use. The price is demand-determined, and all earnings are in the form of economic rent. In panel (b), the supply curve is horizontal, indicating that the resource can earn as much in its best alternative use. Employment is demand-determined, and all earnings are transfer earnings. Panel (c) shows an upward-sloping supply curve. At the equilibrium price of $10, resource earnings are partly transfer earnings and partly economic rent. Both supply and demand determine the equilibrium price and quantity.

Case 3: Earnings Include Both Economic Rent and Transfer Earnings   Whenever a higher price is needed to increase the quantity of a resource supplied — that is, whenever the supply curve slopes upward — resource owners will collect both transfer earnings and economic rent. This situation is presented in panel (c) of Exhibit 2, where economic rent is represented by the blue area and transfer earnings by the red area. A rising resource price attracts additional resources to this use. Since some resource owners had been willing to supply their resources at a lower price, however, the rising price creates additional economic rent for these resource suppliers. For example, if the price of the resource in panel (c) increases from $5 to $10, the quantity supplied will increase by 5000 units. For those resource suppliers who had been offering their services at a price of $5, the difference between $5 and $10 is additional economic rent. These individuals did not require the higher price to supply their services, but they certainly are not going to turn it down. In the case of an upward-sloping supply curve and a downward-sloping demand curve, both supply and demand determine the equilibrium price and quantity. Note that very specialized resources tend to earn a higher proportion of economic rent than do resources with many alternative uses. Thus Michael Jordan earns a greater *proportion* of his income as economic rent than does a janitor.

To review: When a resource supply curve is vertical (perfectly inelastic), all resource earnings are in the form of economic rent. When resource supply is horizontal (perfectly elastic), all resource earnings are transfer earnings. And when supply slopes upward (an elasticity greater than zero but less than infinity), earnings are divided between transfer earnings and economic rent. *When the supply curve of a resource is vertical, supply determines the equilibrium quantity, but demand determines the equilibrium price.* That is, if a resource is in fixed supply, the demand for the resource will dictate the price and the amount of economic rent. *When the supply curve of a resource is horizontal, demand determines the equilibrium quantity, but supply determines the equilibrium price. When the supply curve slopes upward, both supply and demand determine the equilibrium price and quantity.*

This completes our introduction to resource supply. In the balance of this chapter we take a closer look at the demand side of resource markets. The determinants of the demand for a resource are largely the same whether we are talking about land, labor, or capital. Thus the demand for resources can be examined more generally. The supply of different resources, however, has certain peculiarities depending on the resource, so the supply of specific resources will be taken up in the next three chapters.

A CLOSER LOOK AT RESOURCE DEMAND

In Chapter 2 you learned that the art of economic reasoning involves marginal analysis — that is, focusing on adjustments to the status quo.

Although production usually involves the cooperation of many inputs, we will cut the analysis down to size by focusing on the use of a single resource and assuming that the quantities of all other resources are constant. We will then show the relevance of this approach to all resources. As in the past, we will assume that the firm's objective is to maximize profit.

The Firm's Demand for One Resource

You may recall that when we introduced the firm's cost, we considered the example of a moving company, where labor was the only variable resource in the short run. By varying the amount of labor employed, we examined the relation between the quantity of labor employed and the amount of output produced per day. The same idea is used in Exhibit 3, where all but one of the firm's inputs are held constant. The first column in the table lists units of the variable resource, in this case labor. The second column presents the total output, or total physical product, and the third column presents the marginal physical product. The marginal physical product of labor shows how much additional output is produced by each additional unit of labor. The first unit of labor has a marginal physical product of 10 units, the second unit has a marginal physical product of 9 units, and so on.

The marginal physical product declines as more labor is used, reflecting the law of diminishing marginal returns. Recall that the law of diminishing marginal returns states that as additional units of the variable resource are

EXHIBIT 3
THE MARGINAL REVENUE PRODUCT WHEN A FIRM SELLS IN A COMPETITIVE MARKET

Units of Variable Resource (1)	Total Physical Product (TPP) (2)	Marginal Physical Product (MPP) (3)	Product Price (4)	Total Revenue (5) = (2) × (4)	Marginal Revenue Product (MRP) (6)
0	0	—	$2	$ 0	—
1	10	10	2	20	$20
2	19	9	2	38	18
3	27	8	2	54	16
4	34	7	2	68	14
5	40	6	2	80	12
6	45	5	2	90	10
7	49	4	2	98	8
8	52	3	2	104	6
9	54	2	2	108	4
10	55	1	2	110	2
11	55	0	2	110	0
12	53	−2	2	106	−4

combined with a given amount of other resources, a point is eventually reached where each additional unit yields a smaller marginal physical product. In Exhibit 3 diminishing marginal returns set in immediately — that is, right after the first unit of output.

Although labor is used here as the variable resource, we could examine the marginal physical product of any resource. For example, we could consider how many lawns you could cut per week if you varied the quantity of capital. You might start off with very little capital — imagine cutting grass with a pair of scissors — and eventually move up to the Lawn Monster and beyond. By holding labor constant and varying the quantity of capital, we could compute the marginal physical product of capital. Likewise, we could compute the marginal physical product of land by examining crop production for varying amounts of land, holding other inputs, such as the amount of farm labor and capital, constant.

Marginal Revenue Product

Marginal revenue product is the change in total revenue when an additional unit of a resource is hired while the quantities of other resources are held constant.

The first three columns of Exhibit 3 show what happens to the firm's output as the quantity of labor is varied. For the profit-maximizing firm, however, the important question is, what happens to the firm's *revenue* as a result of hiring additional labor? The firm wants to determine the **marginal revenue product** of labor, which is how total revenue changes when an additional unit of labor is employed, given that the quantities of other resources are held constant. You could think of the marginal revenue product as the firm's "marginal benefit" from hiring one more unit of the resource. A resource's marginal revenue product will depend on two factors: (1) the amount of additional output produced and (2) the price of that output.

Selling as a Price Taker The calculation of the marginal revenue product (MRP) is simplest when the firm sells its output in a perfectly competitive market, which is the assumption underlying Exhibit 3. Since the individual firm in perfect competition cannot affect the market price of its product regardless of how much it sells, the firm's selling price does not vary with output. The firm is said to be a *price taker* because it must accept, or "take," whatever price is determined in the market. The marginal revenue product, listed in column (6), is the change in total revenue that results from changing input usage by one unit. For the competitive firm, the marginal revenue product is simply the price, in this case \$2, multiplied by the marginal physical product, or $MRP = P \times MPP$. (For this reason the marginal revenue product in perfect competition is sometimes called the *value of the marginal product*, but we will not use that expression.) Because of diminishing returns, the marginal revenue product falls steadily as additional units of the input are employed.

Selling as a Price Searcher If the firm has some market power in the product market, the demand curve that firm faces slopes downward. To sell more output, the firm must lower its price. The firm, consequently, must search for the price that will maximize profit. Hence firms with market power — that is, firms that face a downward-sloping demand curve for their product — are often called *price searchers*. Exhibit 4 repeats the first two columns of Exhibit 3; the remaining columns reflect the revenue of a firm selling as a price searcher. Column (2) lists total output for each level of labor employed. Column (3) presents the price at which consumers will demand that quantity of total output. Together, columns (2) and (3) represent the demand schedule for the good because they list the price at which consumers will demand each level of output. Total output multiplied by the price at which that output can be sold yields the firm's total revenue, which is presented in column (4). Note that the marginal physical product column has been omitted because it is not directly used in the calculations.

The marginal revenue product of labor, which is the change in total revenue resulting from a one-unit change in the quantity of labor employed, is listed in column (5). For example, the 10 units produced by the first unit of labor can be sold for $4 each, yielding total revenue of $40. The second unit of labor adds 9 units to the total product, but in order to sell these additional units, the firm must lower the price from $4 to $3.52. Since we assume that this price searcher cannot price discriminate, all units must be sold for $3.52. Total revenue increases by $26.88, which is the marginal revenue product for the second unit of labor. *The marginal revenue product for a firm with market power is most easily determined by computing the change in total revenue resulting from a one-unit change in the input.*

Recall that for firms selling in competitive markets, the marginal revenue

EXHIBIT 4
THE MARGINAL REVENUE PRODUCT WHEN A FIRM SELLS AS A PRICE SEARCHER

Units of Variable Resource (1)	Total Physical Product (TPP) (2)	Product Price (3)	Total Revenue (4) = (2) × (3)	Marginal Revenue Product (MRP) (5)
0	0	—	—	—
1	10	$4.00	$ 40.00	$ 40.00
2	19	3.52	66.88	26.88
3	27	3.14	84.78	17.90
4	34	2.78	94.52	9.74
5	40	2.50	100.00	5.48
6	45	2.25	101.25	1.25
7	49	2.05	100.45	− 0.80
8	52	1.90	98.80	− 1.65
9	54	1.80	97.20	− 1.60
10	55	1.75	96.25	− 0.95
11	55	1.75	96.25	0.00

product equals the marginal physical product times the price. For firms with some market power, however, this relationship does not apply because the price must fall before the firm can sell the additional output. The marginal revenue product for competitive firms declines only because of diminishing marginal returns. For firms with market power, however, it declines both because of diminishing returns and because the selling price of the good must be reduced in order to sell increased output.

Marginal Resource Cost

Marginal resource cost *is the change in total cost when an additional unit of a resource is hired.*

A **resource price taker** *faces a given market price for the resource; its demand for the resource does not affect the price of the resource.*

Given the firm's marginal revenue product curve, can we determine how much labor the firm should employ to maximize profits? Not yet, because we know only one side of the equation. We also need to know how much this resource costs the firm. Specifically, what is the **marginal resource cost**— that is, what is the additional cost to the firm of employing one more unit of the resource? Marginal resource cost is simplest to calculate when the firm is a price taker in the resource market. A **resource price taker** hires such a tiny fraction of the available resource that its actions have no effect on the price of the resource. Thus the price taker faces a given market price for the resource and decides only on the quantity to be hired at that price.

For example, if the market wage for factory workers is $10 per hour, a firm that is a price taker in this labor market can hire as much labor as it wants at that wage. Therefore the marginal resource cost of labor is $10 per hour regardless of how much is employed. The marginal resource cost of $10 is represented by the flat line drawn at the $10 level in Exhibit 5. The marginal resource cost curve is the horizontal supply curve faced by the price taker. Exhibit 5 also shows the marginal revenue product curve based on the schedule presented in Exhibit 3. The marginal revenue product curve indicates the additional revenue the firm receives as a result of employing each additional unit of labor.

Given a marginal resource cost of $10 per hour, how much labor will the profit-maximizing firm purchase? The firm will continue to hire labor as long as doing so adds more to revenue than to cost—that is, as long as the marginal revenue product exceeds the marginal resource cost. The firm will stop hiring labor only when the two are equal. If the marginal resource cost equals $10, the firm will hire 6 units of labor. The golden rule of equating marginal cost with marginal revenue applies to all the firm's input decisions, just as it did to the firm's output decisions. Stated more formally, the golden rule of resource utilization is that the firm should hire additional inputs up to the level where

Marginal resource cost = marginal revenue product

This rule holds for all resources employed. In a competitive labor market, we can say that profit-maximizing resource use occurs when the market wage equals the marginal revenue product. Based on data presented thus far, we cannot say exactly what the firm's profit will be because we have not

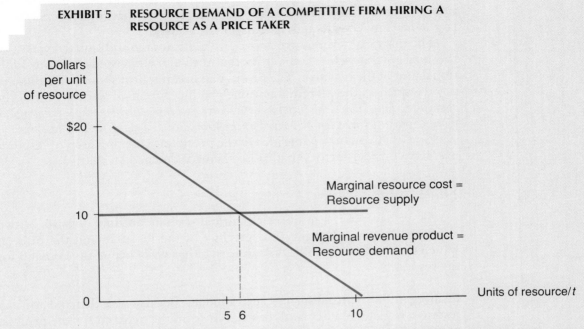

**EXHIBIT 5   RESOURCE DEMAND OF A COMPETITIVE FIRM HIRING A
RESOURCE AS A PRICE TAKER**

For a competitive firm, the downward-sloping marginal revenue product curve is its demand curve for the resource. If the firm is a price taker in the resource market, it faces a horizontal resource supply curve. It can hire as much of the resource as it desires at a constant marginal resource cost. The firm will hire up to the point where the marginal revenue product equals the marginal resource cost.

included information about the cost of the firm's other inputs. We do know, however, that a seventh worker would add $10 to cost but only $8 to revenue, reducing the firm's profit by $2.

Whether the firm sells its output as a price taker or as a price searcher, the profit-maximizing level of employment occurs where the marginal revenue product of labor equals its marginal resource cost. Similarly, the profit-maximizing levels of other resources, such as land and capital, will occur where their respective marginal revenue products equal their marginal resource costs. Regardless of what it is, the firm will hire a resource only if it "pulls its own weight" — only if the resource yields a marginal revenue at least equal to its marginal cost.

Several chapters back we developed a rule for determining the profit-maximizing level of output. Profit is maximized when the marginal cost of output equals its marginal revenue. Likewise, profit is maximized when the marginal resource cost equals the resource's marginal revenue product. Though the first rule focuses on the quantity of output and the second rule focuses on the quantity of the resource, the two approaches are equivalent ways of deriving the same principle. For example, the firm selling output in a competitive market maximizes profit by hiring 6 units of labor when the wage is $10 per unit. The sixth unit of labor produces 5 units of output, which sell for $2 per unit, for a marginal revenue product of $10. The marginal cost of that output is $10/5, or $2, and the marginal revenue is $2, so the marginal cost equals the marginal revenue.

The marginal revenue product curve indicates the additional revenue, or the "marginal benefit" to the firm, that results from employing each additional unit of the resource. The profit-maximizing firm should be willing to pay as much as the marginal revenue product for an additional unit of the resource. *Thus, when the firm buys a resource in a competitive market, the marginal revenue product curve can be viewed as the firm's demand curve for that resource.*

Now that you have some idea of the profit-maximizing level of resource use, let's consider factors that cause resource demand to shift.

Shifts in the Demand for Resources

As we have said, a resource's marginal revenue product consists of two elements: the marginal physical product of the resource and the price at which that product is sold. A change in either will change the demand for the resource.

Changes in the Demand for the Final Product Because the demand for any resource is a derived demand, based as it is on the demand for the product produced by the resource, any change in the demand for that product will change the firm's resource demand. For example, an increase in the demand for automobiles will increase their market price and thereby increase the marginal revenue product of labor employed to produce automobiles. More specifically, if the price in a competitive product market doubles from $2 to $4, the marginal revenue product will also double. You may want to recalculate total revenue and marginal revenue product in Exhibit 3 to verify this.

Other Inputs Employed Although the analysis thus far has focused on a single input, in practice resources are used in conjunction with one another. The marginal physical product of any resource depends on the quantity and quality of other resources used in the production process. Sometimes the resources are *complements*, such as a truck driver and a truck. If the relationship is complementary, a reduction in the price of one resource will increase the demand for the other. If the price of bigger and better trucks falls, bigger and better trucks will be purchased. This increase in capital will increase the marginal productivity of labor because labor will have more to work with. A driver of a big rig will be able to haul more goods than a driver of a pickup truck. An increase in the quantity and quality of trucks will increase the marginal revenue product of truck drivers, so the demand for truck drivers will shift to the right.

One reason why a truck driver in the United States usually earns over $15 an hour and a rickshaw driver in the Far East earns more like $0.15 an hour is the *truck*. The rickshaw driver pulls a cart that may be valued at less than $100 and that can move only as fast and as far as the driver's legs will take it; the truck driver is behind the wheel of a machine that may have cost more than $100,000 and that can haul heavy weights great distances at high speed. The truck makes the driver more productive. *More generally, the greater the quantity and quality of complementary resources used in production, the greater the marginal productivity of the resource in question and the greater the demand for it.*

Sometimes resources are *substitutes.* If resources are substitutes, an increase in the price of one will increase the demand for the other. For example, an increase in the price of oil will increase the demand for coal.

Changes in Technology and Training Technological improvements can enhance the productivity of any resource. The development of fuel-efficient cars has increased the number of miles that can be squeezed out of a gallon of gasoline, so the productivity of gasoline has increased. An improved word processing program will increase the productivity of an author or typist. A training program that teaches workers how to operate machinery will obviously increase their productivity. (Imagine someone who has driven only the family car trying to operate a road grader.) Thus *any technological improvement or training program that enhances the quality of a resource will increase its marginal productivity and will consequently increase the demand for that resource.*

Price Elasticity of Resource Demand

We can examine the elasticity of demand for a resource, just as we examined the elasticity of demand for final products. The price elasticity of demand for a resource equals the percentage change in the quantity of the resource demanded divided by the percentage change in its price. A variety of forces influence the price elasticity of demand for a resource. Some of these relate to the fact that the demand for a resource is a derived demand; others relate to the productivity of the resource itself.

Price Elasticity of Demand for the Final Product By causing the product price to rise, an increase in the resource price reduces the quantity demanded of the final product and therefore reduces employment of the resource. And a larger drop in the quantity demanded of the product triggers a larger drop in the quantity demanded of the resource. Hence, *the more elastic the demand for the final product, the more elastic the demand for the resources used to produce it.*

Ease of Substitution In the previous section we mentioned that some resources are substitutes. *The more abundant and the more similar the substitutes are in production, the more easily one resource can be substituted for another and the more elastic the demand for both resources.* For example, to the baker white eggs and brown eggs are virtually identical, so an increase in the relative price of white eggs will increase the use of brown eggs. The demand for white eggs is price elastic, as is the demand for brown eggs. On the other hand, there are no close substitutes for jet fuel, so an increase in its price will not cause airlines to switch to other forms of energy, at least not in the short run. Thus the demand for jet fuel is relatively inelastic in the short run.

The Resource's Share of Production Cost *The greater the resource's cost as a fraction of the total product cost, the more elastic the demand for that resource, other things constant.* For example, because the cost of lumber represents a relatively large share of housing costs, an increase in the price of lumber substantially raises the cost of a new house, thereby reducing the quantity of housing demanded and, in turn, reducing the quantity of lumber demanded. On the other hand, the cost of electrical wire makes up only a tiny fraction of the cost of new housing. Therefore a rise in the price of electrical wire will have little impact on the quantity of housing demanded and will consequently have little effect on the quantity of wire demanded for housing construction.

Time Finally, as with consumer demand, *the longer the time period under consideration, the greater the elasticity of demand for the resource.* For example, if the price of steel increases, auto manufacturers cannot quickly switch to substitutes. Over time, however, they can change production processes and perhaps redesign cars so that the quantity of steel required for auto production declines. Or consider the nation's experience with oil. The price increases in the 1970s had relatively little effect on the quantity of oil demanded in the short run. In the long run, however, higher oil prices precipitated substitution away from oil. More fuel-efficient cars and airplanes were developed, coal was substituted for oil in electricity production, and the "reinvented" coal-fired locomotive replaced the diesel locomotive.

Hiring Resources as a Price Searcher

Determining optimal resource use for a price taker in the resource market is quite straightforward. But what if a firm hires such a large fraction of the available resource that the quantity of the resource supplied to the firm depends on the price the firm pays for the resource? If the quantity of the resource supplied to the firm depends on the price the firm pays, the firm is a **resource price searcher**. Resource price searchers are also called *monopsonists*. A resource price searcher typically faces an upward-sloping resource supply curve—that is, the quantity of the resource supplied to the firm increases only if the price per unit of the resource increases.

*A **resource price searcher** faces an upward-sloping supply curve for the resource.*

Suppose the firm is an aircraft designer that employs such a large proportion of the total supply of aeronautical engineers that the amount of this kind of labor supplied to the firm depends on the wage the firm offers. The first column in Exhibit 6(a) lists the quantity of labor hired, and the second column shows the wage the firm must pay to attract that quantity of labor to the firm. Together, the first two columns represent the supply of labor schedule faced by a firm that is a price searcher in the resource market. This schedule is presented in the form of a supply curve in Exhibit 6(b). A hypothetical marginal revenue product schedule is listed in the final column in Exhibit 6(a) and is plotted as the marginal revenue product curve in Exhibit 6(b).

If the firm cannot practice wage discrimination, it must raise the wage paid to all its engineers in order to hire more. Consequently, the marginal

**EXHIBIT 6   RESOURCE DEMAND FOR A FIRM HIRING A RESOURCE
AS A PRICE SEARCHER**

(a) MRC and MRP schedules

Units of Variable Resource (1)	Wage (2)	Total Resource Cost (TRC) (3)	Marginal Resource Cost (MRC) (4)	Marginal Revenue Product (MRP) (5)
0	—	$ 0	—	—
1	$ 8	8	$ 8	$20
2	9	18	10	18
3	10	30	12	16
4	11	44	14	14
5	12	60	16	12
6	13	78	18	10
7	14	98	20	8
8	15	120	22	6

(b) MRC and MRP curves

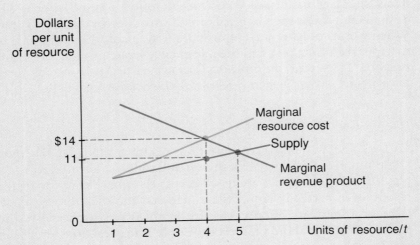

A resource price searcher faces an upward-sloping resource supply curve. The marginal resource cost lies above that supply curve. The firm will hire the resource up to the point where the marginal revenue product equals the marginal resource cost (4 units) and will pay a wage read off the resource supply curve ($11).

resource cost exceeds the wage required to attract the marginal unit of labor. For example, according to the supply schedule, the firm must pay $9 to attract a second unit of labor. But if the firm pays $9 for a second unit, it must also pay $9 for the first unit. If the firm hires 2 units of labor, it cannot pay the second unit more than the first. Hence the total cost increases by $10 when 2 units rather than 1 unit of labor are hired ($9 for the second unit plus

$1 more for the first unit). The $10 marginal resource cost for the second unit exceeds the wage of $9 required to attract that second unit.

Likewise, if the firm decides it needs 3 units of labor, it must pay $10 per unit to attract 3 units to the firm, for a total labor cost of $30. The labor cost for hiring 3 units is $12 more than the $18 cost of hiring 2 units, so the marginal resource cost of the third unit is $12. Compare columns (2) and (4) in Exhibit 6(a) and you will see that after the first unit of labor is hired, the marginal resource cost exceeds the wage, and the difference grows as more labor is employed. This growing difference is reflected most clearly by the distance between the labor supply curve and the marginal resource cost curve in Exhibit 6(b).

The firm maximizes profit by hiring additional units of the resource as long as these marginal units add more to revenue than to cost. Specifically, the firm hires additional resources until *the marginal resource cost equals the marginal revenue product*. In Exhibit 6, the marginal resource cost curve and the marginal revenue product curve intersect where 4 units of labor are employed. As the supply curve indicates, the firm must offer a wage rate of $11 to attract 4 units of labor, for a total resource cost of $44. The wage rate required to attract 3 units of labor is $10, for a total resource cost of $30. Thus the marginal resource cost of the fourth unit of labor is $14 ($44 − $30), which is also the marginal revenue product for the fourth unit of labor. When 4 units of labor are employed, the wage of $11 per hour is below the marginal resource cost and the marginal revenue product of the fourth unit of labor. Thus, *when the firm hires labor as a resource price searcher, in equilibrium the marginal revenue product of labor exceeds the wage rate*.

Summarizing Four Market Possibilities

Let's review the market conditions examined thus far. The possibilities are summarized in the matrix shown in Exhibit 7. The two roles a firm may play in hiring resources are listed across the top. Either the firm may hire resources in perfectly competitive markets, and therefore be a *resource price taker*, or it may hire resources as a resource price searcher. A resource price searcher can hire more of a resource only if the resource price is increased.

Possible situations confronting a resource price taker are depicted in parts (a) and (c) of Exhibit 7, where the marginal resource cost is a horizontal line drawn at the market-determined resource price. Possible situations confronting a resource price searcher are illustrated in parts (b) and (d), where the marginal resource cost curve is an upward-sloping line drawn above the resource supply curve. Recall that the resource price-searcher's marginal resource cost curve exceeds the resource supply curve because the firm, in order to attract more resources, must pay *all* units of the resource the higher supply price.

The two roles a firm may play in product markets are listed along the left-hand side of Exhibit 7. The firm may sell its output in a perfectly competitive product market, in which case the firm is a price taker in the product market, as shown in parts (a) and (b). If the firm is a price taker in the

EXHIBIT 7   RESOURCE MARKET EQUILIBRIUM UNDER ALTERNATIVE MARKET CONDITIONS

(a) *Firm is a price taker in both the resource and the product markets*

(b) *Firm is a price taker in the product market and a price searcher in the resource market*

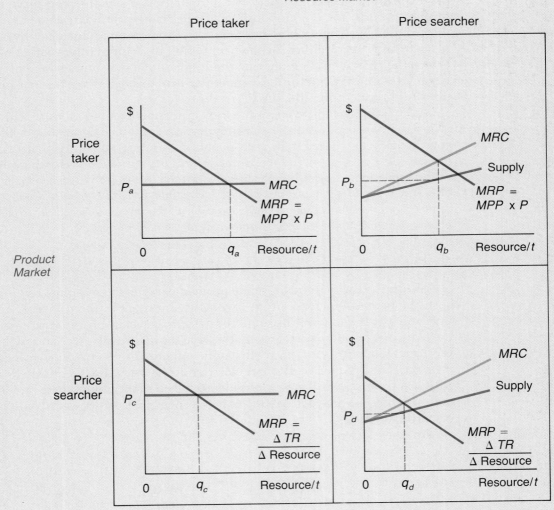

Resource Market

Price taker   Price searcher

Product Market

(c) *Firm is a price taker in the resource market and a price searcher in the product market*

(d) *Firm is a price searcher in both the product and the resource markets*

product market, its resource demand is simply the resource's marginal physical product multiplied by the market-determined product price.

Rather than being a price taker in the product market, the firm may have some market power in the product market, as shown in parts (c) and (d). If the firm is a price searcher in the product market, the marginal revenue product curve slopes downward both because the marginal physical product falls as more of the resource is employed and because the price of the product must fall if more output is to be sold. The marginal revenue product curve reflects the combined effects of both a declining marginal physical product and a declining price. For simplicity, we say that the marginal revenue product for a monopolist equals the change in total revenue resulting from employing each additional unit of the resource. Incidentally, the marginal revenue product for the firm selling in a competitive market also equals the change in total revenue resulting from a one-unit change in the resource employed, but for the competitive firm this reduces to the marginal physical product times the price.

As we said, Exhibit 7 presents the four possible combinations that arise when the two product market structures are combined with the two resource market structures. In each panel, the resource quantity that maximizes the firm's profit is determined by the point where the marginal revenue product equals the marginal resource cost. Note that *when the firm hires a resource in a competitive market, the marginal revenue product equals the equilibrium price of the resource, but when the firm is a price searcher in the resource market, the marginal revenue product exceeds the equilibrium price of the resource.*

Optimal Use: More than One Resource

As long as the marginal revenue product exceeds the marginal resource cost, the firm can increase profit by employing more of the resource. The firm will increase resource use until the marginal revenue product just equals the marginal resource cost. Stating this rule more formally, we can say that the firm will hire labor up to the point where labor's marginal revenue product, MRP_L, equals its marginal resource cost, MRC_L, or $MRP_L = MRC_L$. Likewise, the firm will employ capital up to the point where capital's marginal revenue product, MRP_K, equals its marginal resource cost, MRC_K, or $MRP_K = MRC_K$.

Another way of writing each expression is

$$\frac{MRP_L}{MRC_L} = 1 \quad \text{and} \quad \frac{MRP_K}{MRC_K} = 1$$

so

$$\frac{MRP_L}{MRC_L} = \frac{MRP_K}{MRC_K} = 1$$

Thus, *to maximize profit the firm should employ resources so that the last dollar spent on each resource yields one dollar's worth of marginal revenue product.* In other words, the last dollar spent on each resource should yield the same marginal revenue product. To see the logic of this equality, suppose the marginal revenue product from the last dollar's worth of labor employed exceeds the marginal revenue product from the last dollar's worth of capital employed. Since the marginal productivity of labor exceeds the marginal productivity of capital, the firm's profits can be increased by spending more on labor and less on capital. Spending can be shifted from capital to labor until the last dollar spent on each resource yields a dollar's worth of marginal revenue product.

At the beginning of the chapter, we asked why the buildings at the center of Chicago are taller than those farther out. One rule of optimal resource use is that firms combine resources in a way that conserves the use of the scarcest resource. Land is more expensive at the center of a large city because of the convenience of the location. Land and capital are to a large extent substitutes in the production of building space. When land is more expensive, builders substitute additional capital for land, building *up* instead of *out*. Hence buildings are taller when they are closer to the center of the city and are tallest in cities where the land is relatively more expensive. Buildings in Chicago and New York are taller than buildings in Bismarck and Tucson, for example.

The high price of land in metropolitan areas has other implications for the efficient employment of resources. For example, in New York City, as in many large cities, vending carts on street corners specialize in everything from hot dogs to doughnuts. Why are there so many carts? Consider the resources used to supply hot dogs: land, labor, capital, entrepreneurial ability, plus hot dogs, buns, and other ingredients. Which of these do you suppose is most expensive in New York City? As we have noted, space there is very costly. Retail space along Fifth Avenue rents for as much as $400 a year per square *foot*. Since a hot dog cart requires about three square yards to operate, it could cost more than $10,000 a year to rent the required space. Aside from the necessary public permits, however, space on the public sidewalk is free. Profit-maximizing street vendors substitute free public sidewalk space for costly commercial rental space.

CONCLUSION

The framework we have developed focuses on marginal analysis of resource use to determine the equilibrium resource price. Resources cooperate to produce output, much as the musicians in an orchestra combine to produce music. The firm uses each resource up to the point where the marginal revenue product of that resource equals its marginal resource cost. The objective of profit maximization ensures that firms will employ the least-cost combination of resources. Using the least-cost combination of resources implies that the last dollar spent on each resource yields a marginal revenue product of one dollar. If this were not so, firms could lower their cost by adjusting their resource mix.

Summary

1. Firms demand resources to maximize profits. Households supply resources to maximize utility. Any differences between the profit-maximizing goals of firms and the utility-maximizing goals of households are reconciled through voluntary exchange in resource markets.

2. Because the value of any resource depends on the value of what it produces, the demand for a resource is a derived demand—derived from the value of the final product. A resource demand curve slopes downward because firms are more willing and able to increase the quantity demanded as the price of a resource declines. A resource supply curve tends to slope upward because resource owners are more willing and able to increase the quantity supplied as their reward for supplying the resource increases.

3. Differentials in the market prices of similar resources stem from a variety of sources, but we can classify them into two broad categories. Price differentials that do not precipitate a shift in resources among uses are called equilibrium differentials. Price differentials that trigger the reallocation of resources to equalize prices for similar resources are called disequilibrium differentials.

4. Resource earnings can be divided into (1) transfer earnings, the amount that must be paid to a resource owner to supply resources for a particular use, and (2) economic rent, the portion of a resource's total earnings that is not necessary to keep the resource in its present use. If a resource has no alternative use, earnings consist only of economic rent; if a resource has many alternative uses, transfer earnings predominate.

5. In a competitive resource market, a firm's resource demand curve equals the marginal revenue product of that resource. If a firm sells its output in a perfectly competitive market, the marginal revenue product equals the marginal physical product of the resource times the price of the product. If a firm has some market power in the product market, it must take into account both changes in the marginal physical product of resources and reductions in the price necessary to sell additional output.

6. The demand for a resource will increase if there is an increase in either its marginal physical product or the price of the product produced with the resource. An increase in the use of a complementary resource will increase a resource's marginal productivity.

7. The marginal resource cost is the marginal cost to the firm of employing one more unit of the resource. If a firm hires resources in competitive markets, the firm is a resource price taker and has no control over resource prices. If the price a firm pays for a resource depends on the quantity of the resource it employs, the firm is a price searcher in the resource market. Both the price taker and the price searcher in the resource market maximize profits by employing each resource to the point where the marginal revenue product equals the marginal resource cost.

Questions and Problems

1. (Resource Demand) How might the elasticity of demand for a resource depend on the substitutability among resources in the production process?

2. (Supply of Resources) Suppose that worker A speaks only German and worker B speaks only English; otherwise they are identical in their skills. Consider the relative elasticities of supply for their labor in
   a. the Federal Republic of Germany.
   b. the United States.
   c. all other places.

3. (Resource Demand) Suppose that good A has a perfectly inelastic demand. Would the resources used to produce good A have to have a perfectly inelastic demand? Why or why not?

4. (Transfer Earnings Versus Economic Rent) "If the supply of a resource has unitary elasticity, transfer earnings will be equal to economic rent—at every resource price." Evaluate this assertion.

5. (Diminishing Returns) To have diminishing returns, one must add a variable resource to a set of fixed resources. Why must we assume that some fixed resources are present?

6. (Price Taker's Marginal Revenue Product) If a competitive firm hires another full-time worker, total output will increase from 100 units to 110 units per month. Suppose the wage is $200 per week. What market price will allow the additional worker to be hired?

7. (Competitive Resource Market) Explain why a competitive resource market requires that the resource price (that is, the wage rate) be equal to the marginal resource cost to the firm.

8. (Resource Price Searcher) Explain why a price searcher in the product market need not be a price searcher in the resource market. Are all resource price searchers necessarily also product price searchers? Why or why not?

9. (Resource Price Searcher) Why must a resource price searcher pay a higher wage to all of its workers in order to hire an additional worker?

10. (Complements in Production) Many countries are predominantly agrarian. How would the amount of fertilizer available affect the marginal product, and thus the income, of the farmers in such societies?

11. (Resource Demand) Use the following data to answer the questions below.

Units of Labor	Units of Output
0	0
1	7
2	13
3	18
4	22
5	25

   a. Calculate the marginal revenue product (MRP) for each unit of labor if output sells for $3 per unit.
   b. If labor costs $15 per hour, how much labor will get hired?
   c. Construct the demand curve for labor based on the above data and the $3 per unit output price.
   d. Using your answer to part (b), compare total revenue to the total amount paid to labor. Who gets the difference?
   e. What would happen to your answers to parts (b) and (c) if the price of output increased to $5 per unit?

12. (Economic Rents) Top athletes in baseball, football, basketball, and hockey earn considerably more than a million dollars per year. Yet in many cases their transfer earnings are far lower. Explain the magnitude of their economic rents in terms of the demand for and supply of their services.

13. (Exploitation of Labor) Labor can be said to be exploited if it is not paid what it is worth.
   a. How should "worth" be measured?
   b. Does exploitation occur when labor is hired by a price searcher in the product market? by a resource price searcher? Explain using diagrams of the labor market.

14. (Efficient Resource Use) Earlier you learned that a firm combines resources efficiently by choosing the combination for which the marginal rate of technical substitution between resources equals the price ratio of the resources. Show that this principle is formally equivalent to the efficiency rule presented in this chapter—namely, that each resource should be hired until its marginal revenue product equals its price.

C H A P T E R   2 6

Labor Markets and Wage Determination

In 1988 the median earnings of full-time workers in the United States were about $20,000. File clerks averaged about $11,000, and the heads of the country's eight hundred largest companies averaged about $1 million. High school principals averaged $53,000, some $2000 more than the earnings of full professors at the college level. Heart surgeons averaged about $300,000 per year—triple the average earnings of general practitioners. Professional baseball players averaged $485,000—more than twice the average for professional hockey players and more than five times what members of Congress earned. Michael Jackson earned $60 million. The money leader in 1988 was Michael Milken, who earned $200 million as a junk bond banker—an impressive sum, but less than the $550 million he earned the year before.

What determines the wage structure in the economy? You don't need a course in economics to figure out why corporate presidents earn more than file clerks, or why heart surgeons earn more than general practitioners. But why do baseball players earn more than hockey players? And why do high school principals earn more than college professors? Will we see a similar pattern in the year 2000? You can be sure of one thing: supply and demand play a central role in the development of a wage structure. We have already examined what determines the demand for labor or any other resource. Demand depends on the resource's marginal revenue product. In this chapter we focus on the market supply of labor, then bring supply and demand together to arrive at the market wage. Topics discused in this chapter include

- Theory of time allocation
- The backward-bending supply curve for labor
- Nonwage factors and labor supply
- Why wages differ
- Information problems in labor markets
- The functional distribution of income

INDIVIDUAL LABOR SUPPLY

You, as a resource supplier, have a labor supply curve for each of the many possible uses of your labor. To some markets your quantity supplied is zero over the realistic range of wages. (We say "over the realistic range" because if the wage were high enough, say $1 million per hour, there might be no activity to which you would not supply labor.) In those cases where your quantity supplied is zero over the realistic range of wages, it may be because you are *willing* but *unable* to perform the job (for example, airline pilot, professional golfer, novelist), or it may be because you are *able* but *unwilling* to do so (for example, soldier of fortune, gym teacher, economist).

Therefore you have as many supply curves as there are labor markets, just as you have demand curves for the markets in goods and services. Your labor supply to each market depends on the opportunity cost of your time—how much you could earn from other activities. Each supply curve is developed under the assumption that the wages offered in other markets do not change, just as each demand curve is developed under the assumption that prices of related goods are constant over the time period under consideration.

Labor Supply and Utility Maximization

Recall the definition of economics: it is the study of how individuals choose to use their scarce resources to produce, exchange, and consume products in an attempt to satisfy their unlimited wants. Individuals attempt to use their limited resources so as to maximize their utility. Two sources of utility are of special interest to us in this chapter: the consumption of goods and services and the enjoyment of leisure. The utility derived from consuming goods and services is obvious and serves as the foundation of consumer demand. Leisure time spent relaxing, sleeping, eating, and in recreational activities also represents a valuable source of utility. Leisure can usually be viewed as a normal good that, like other goods, is subject to the law of diminishing marginal utility. Thus, the more leisure time you have, the less you value each additional unit. Sometimes you may have so much leisure that you are "just killing time." As that well-known economist/cat Garfield once lamented, "Spare time would be more fun if I had less to spare."

Three Uses of Time You can use your time in three ways. First, you can undertake **market work**, selling your time in the labor market in return for

Market work is time sold as labor in return for a money wage.

Nonmarket work is time spent producing goods and services in the home or acquiring an education.

Leisure is time devoted to nonwork activities.

money. When you offer yourself for employment, you surrender control over the use of your time to the employer in return for a wage. Second, you can undertake what we will call **nonmarket work**, using time to produce your own goods and services. Nonmarket work includes the time you spend doing your laundry, preparing your meals, or typing a term paper. Nonmarket work also includes the time spent in acquiring skills and education to enhance the value of your time in the future. Although the time you spend attending class, reading, and studying course material provides no instant payoff, you are betting that the skills and perspective you gain will be rewarded later. Third, you can convert time directly into **leisure**—nonwork uses of your time. (Some of you may specialize in leisure.)

Work and Utility Unless you are one of the fortunate few, work is not a pure source of utility, as it often generates some boredom, discomfort, or aggravation. In short, time spent working can be a source of *disutility*—the opposite of utility. You work nonetheless because work allows you to afford goods and services. You expect that the utility generated by the goods and services made possible through work will exceed the disutility of that work. Thus the net utility of work—the utility of the consumption made possible through work minus the disutility of the work itself—makes work an attractive use of your time. In the case of market work, you earn wages, which are used to buy goods and services. In the case of nonmarket work, you either produce goods and services directly, as in making yourself an egg salad sandwich, or you expect to increase your future earnings through education.

Utility Maximization Within the limits of a 24-hour day, 7 days a week, you balance your time among market work, nonmarket work, and leisure so as to maximize utility. As a rational consumer, you attempt to maximize utility by allocating your time so that the expected marginal utility of the last unit of time spent in each activity is identical. Thus, in the course of a week, the marginal utility of the last hour of leisure equals the net marginal utility of the last hour of market work, which equals the net marginal utility of the last hour of nonmarket work. In the case of time devoted to acquiring skills, you must consider the marginal utility expected from the future increase in earnings that will result from your enhanced productivity.[1]

Perhaps at this point you are saying, "Wait a minute. I don't allocate my time with that sort of precision or logic. I just sort of bump along, doing what feels good." We do not claim that you are even aware of making such marginal calculations. But as a rational decision maker, you allocate your scarce time to satisfy your wants, or to maximize utility. And utility maximization, or "doing what feels good," implies that you act "as if" you used

---

[1] We will develop a way of analyzing choices involving future production and consumption in a later chapter, when we consider human capital more explicitly.

time to derive the same expected net marginal utility from the last unit of time spent in each alternative use.

You probably have settled into a rough plan (for meals, work, entertainment, study, sleep, and so on) that accords with your overall objectives and appears reasonably rational. This plan is probably in constant flux as you make expected and unexpected adjustments in the use of your time. For example, this morning you may have slept later than you planned; last weekend you may have failed to crack a book, despite good intentions. Over a week or a month, however, your use of time is roughly in line with an allocation that maximizes utility as you perceive it. Put another way, given the various constraints on your time, money, energy, and other resources, if you could change your use of time to increase utility, you would do so. You may emphasize current utility over future utility, but that's your choice.

Thus this time-allocation process ensures that at the margin the expected utility from the last unit of time spent in each activity is equal. Because information is costly and because the future is uncertain, you sometimes make mistakes in allocating time; you do not always get what you expect. Some mistakes are minor, such as going to see a movie that proves to be a waste of time. But other mistakes can be costly. For example, you may now be preparing for a field of study that will be too crowded by the time you graduate, or you may now be acquiring skills that will become obsolete because of changing technology in the form of a computer chip no bigger than a housefly.

Implications The model of time allocation that has been described thus far has several implications for individual choice. First, consider the choice between market and nonmarket work. The higher your market wage, other things constant, the greater the opportunity cost of nonmarket work. Hence individuals with a high market wage will produce less for themselves, other things constant. Surgeons are less likely to mow their own lawns than are butchers. By the same logic, the higher the expected earnings right out of high school, other things constant, the higher the opportunity cost of college.

Alternatively, the more productive people are in nonmarket work, other things constant, the less labor they will supply to the market. Those proficient at preparing meals or handy around the house will do more for themselves and hire fewer of these services in the market. And those who find education useful and productive will be more inclined to spend time in school. Conversely, those who find boiling water difficult will eat out more frequently, and those who are all thumbs around the house will hire various services; both will be more inclined to supply their labor to market work rather than to nonmarket work. In summary, utility maximization implies that individuals will use nonmarket work to produce those goods they can provide more cheaply than the market can.

How Will You Spend Your Summer?

To breathe life into the time-allocation problem, consider your choices for the summer. You can take the summer off, spending it entirely on leisure, as perhaps a fitting reward for a rough academic year. You can supply your time to market work. Or you can undertake nonmarket work, such as cleaning the basement or attending summer school. As a rational decision maker, you will select that combination of leisure, market work, and non-market work that you expect will maximize your utility. And the optimal combination is likely to involve allocating some time to each activity. For example, even if you work during the summer, you might still consider taking one or two classes at the local university. After all, many students hold down part-time jobs during the academic year.

Suppose that the only summer job available is some form of unskilled labor, such as working at a car wash or in a nearby fast food restaurant. For simplicity, let's assume that you view all available jobs to be equally attractive (or unattractive) in terms of their nonmonetary aspects. (These nonmonetary aspects will be discussed in the next section.) Since in your view there is no difference among these unskilled jobs, the most important question for you in deciding how much market labor to supply is, what is the market wage for unskilled labor?

Suppose the wage is $3 per hour—not even the minimum wage. At a wage that low, you may decide to work around the house, attend summer school full-time, hitchhike across the country to find yourself, take a really long nap, or perhaps do some combination of these. In any event, you will supply no market labor at such a low wage. The market wage must rise to $4 per hour before you will supply any market labor. Suppose that at a wage of $4 per hour you will supply 20 hours per week, perhaps taking fewer summer courses and shorter naps.

What if the wage increases to $5 per hour, everything else held constant? The higher wage raises the opportunity cost of the time you spend in other activities, so you substitute market work for other uses of your time. You decide to work 30 hours per week, earning a total of $150 a week. At $6 per hour you are willing to cut more into studying or surfing, increasing your quantity of market labor supplied to 40 hours per week, for weekly earnings of $240. At $7 per hour you provide 48 hours of market labor per week, earning $336 per week, and at $8 per hour you increase your quantity supplied to 55 hours, for $440 per week. At a wage of $9 you go to 60 hours per week; you are starting to earn serious money: $540 per week.

Finally, what if the wage offered is $10 per hour, a wage you consider to be very attractive indeed? You cut back to 55 hours per week, and you earn $550 per week—more than you did when the wage was $9 per hour. To explain why you may eventually reduce your quantity of market labor supplied as the wage rate rises, we must analyze in more detail the impact of wage increases on the utility-maximizing allocation of time among leisure, nonmarket work, and market work.

Substitution and Income Effects An increase in the wage rate affects your choice between market work and other uses of your time in two ways. First, at a higher wage, each hour of work buys more goods and services, so a higher wage provides you with an incentive to work more—to substitute work for other activities that now have a higher opportunity cost. This effect is referred to as the *substitution effect* of a wage increase; it encourages you to allocate more time to market work. Something else also happens as the wage rate increases, however. A higher wage means a higher income, and a higher income means that you demand more of all normal goods. Since leisure is a normal good, a higher income increases your demand for leisure, thereby reducing your allocation of time to market work. The higher wage rate therefore has an *income effect*, which tends to reduce the quantity of market labor supplied.

Consequently, as the wage goes up, the substitution effect causes you to supply more time to market work and the income effect causes you to supply less time to market work and to demand more leisure time. In the case of your summer job possibilities, the substitution effect dominates the income effect for wage rates of up to $9 per hour, resulting in a greater quantity of market labor supplied as the wage rises to $9. When the wage hits $10 per hour, however, the income effect exceeds the substitution effect, causing a net reduction in the quantity of labor supplied to market work.

Backward-Bending Labor Supply Curve The hypothetical market labor supply curve that we have described is presented in Exhibit 1. As you can see, this

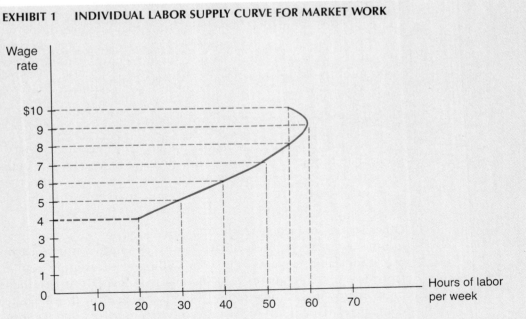

EXHIBIT 1   INDIVIDUAL LABOR SUPPLY CURVE FOR MARKET WORK

When the substitution effect of a wage increase outweighs the income effect, the quantity of labor supplied increases with the wage rate. At some wage (here, above $9), the income effect dominates. Above that wage, the supply curve bends backward; further increases in the wage rate reduce the quantity of labor supplied.

supply curve slopes upward until a wage of $9 per hour is reached, and then it begins to bend backward. The *backward-bending supply curve* gets its shape from the fact that the income effect of a higher wage eventually outweighs the substitution effect, so the quantity of market labor supplied at some point declines with an increase in the wage. We often see evidence of a backward-bending supply curve, particularly among high-wage individuals, who reduce their work and consume more leisure. For example, doctors often play golf on a weekday afternoon. Entertainers typically perform less as they become more successful. Unknown bands play hours for peanuts; name bands play less for more. In fact, the income effect of rising wages during this century has been used to explain the decline in the average work week in the United States from 53 hours in 1900 to less than 40 hours per week in 1990.

Flexibility of Hours Worked The model we have been describing assumes that workers have some control over the number of they hours work per week. At first blush this assumption appears to conflict with the standard work week of, say, 40 hours. The assumption that workers are able to vary the hours worked seems reasonable, however, in view of the opportunity to work overtime or to work part-time in different jobs. In this way workers can bundle together their most preferred quantity of hours (for instance, 40 hours in a restaurant and 15 hours at a car wash). Workers also have some control over the timing and length of their vacations. More generally, individuals can control the length of time they stay in school, when and to what extent they enter the work force, and when they choose to retire. Thus the worker actually has more control over the number of hours worked than you might think if you focused on the standard work week.

Nonwage Determinants of Labor Supply

The quantity of market labor supplied depends on a variety of factors other than the wage rate, just as the quantity of a good demanded depends on factors other than the price. What are the nonwage factors that go into a decision about your supply of labor to the market during the summer?

Other Sources of Income Although some jobs are rewarding in a variety of nonmonetary ways, the primary reason people work is to earn money to buy goods and services. Thus your willingness to supply your time to the labor market depends on your income from other sources, including savings, borrowing, family support, and scholarships. If your household income is relatively high or if you received a generous scholarship, you may feel less need to earn additional income during the summer. "In-kind" support is also important. For example, you may live at home, where your parents provide your room and board, or you may drive one of the family cars. The greater these other sources of income, the less inclined you will be to supply your time to market work, other things constant.

Nonmonetary Factors in General Labor is a special kind of resource. Unlike capital and land, which can be provided regardless of the whereabouts of the resource owners, time supplied to market work requires the seller of that time to be on the job. Because the individual must be present to deliver labor, such *nonmonetary factors* as the difficulty of the job and the quality of the work environment have important effects on the labor supply. The labor supply curve shows the relation between the wage rate and the quantity of market labor you are willing and able to supply, other things constant. Among the other things held constant are these nonmonetary factors. Thus far we have been able to ignore the role of nonmonetary factors by assuming no difference in them among the unskilled jobs from which you could choose. Now we will look more realistically at these nonmonetary factors.

Job Amenities Consider the different job amenities you might encounter. For a full-time student, a library job that allows you to study much of the time is more attractive than a job that affords no study time. A job in the college cafeteria may allow you to eat all you want at no extra charge; you may find this feature attractive. Some jobs allow you to work flexible hours; others impose a rigid work schedule. Is the workplace air-conditioned or do you have to sweat it out? The more attractive these on-the-job amenities are to you, the more labor you will supply to that particular market, other things constant.

One job quality that is generally valued is latitude in the use of time on the job. As we said earlier, when you sell your labor in the resource market, you surrender the use of your time to the control of a manager or entrepreneur. The amount and the intensity of this control depend on the kind of job. If you are like most people, the more closely you are monitored and directed, other things constant, the less willing you are to supply labor to that market. Thus closely monitored workers must be paid more than those whose jobs allow more personal discretion. College professors typically earn less than people in private industry with a similar education. This is partly because professors are subject to less direction in the classroom and in their research interests. Thus professors pay for their "academic freedom" by earning a lower salary than they could in positions where someone was always looking over their shoulder.

The Value of Job Experience You are more inclined to take a job that provides what potential future employers will view as valuable experience; serving as the assistant treasurer for a nearby business looks better on a resume than serving hash at the college cafeteria. Some people are willing to accept relatively low wages now because of the promise of higher wages later. For example, new lawyers are eager to fill clerkships for judges, though the pay is low and the hours long, because these positions provide experience that will be valued by potential future employers. Some individuals accept relatively low pay to work for certain government agencies because the experience and the personal contacts developed will be valuable later in the private sector, especially to private sector employers who deal with that particular government agency. Thus, the greater the investment value of a position in terms of enhancing your future earning possibilities, the more labor you will supply to that market, other things constant.

Taste for Work Just as consumers' tastes for goods and services differ, tastes in work also differ among labor suppliers. Some people like physical labor and avoid any job that would keep them desk-bound. Some can't stand the sight of blood; others choose to be surgeons. Some fear flying; others want to be pilots. Often writers and artists stick with their professions even if the pay is low and employment is not always available; apparently the satisfaction gained from the creative process offsets the low expected pay. In fact, some people evidently have such a strong preference for certain kinds of work that they are willing to perform those duties free, such as people who serve as auxiliary police officers or as volunteer fire fighters.

As with the taste for goods and services, we do not attempt to explain the taste for work. We simply argue that your supply of labor will be greater to those jobs that are more in accord with your tastes. Voluntary sorting based on tastes allocates workers among different jobs in a way that tends to minimize the disutility associated with work. This is not to say that everyone will be perfectly matched to his or her most preferred occupation. The cost of acquiring information about jobs and the cost of changing jobs may prevent some matchups that might otherwise seem desirable, but people will tend to find jobs that suit them. We are not likely, for example, to find airline pilots who are afraid of heights or zoo keepers who are allergic to animals.

Market Supply

In the previous section we considered those factors, both monetary and nonmonetary, that influence individual supply. *The market supply of labor to a particular market is the horizontal sum of all the individual supply curves.* If an individual supply curve of labor bends backward, does this mean that the market supply curve of labor also bends backward? Not necessarily. Since different individuals have different opportunity costs and different tastes for work, the bend in the supply curve occurs at different wages for different individuals. Exhibit 2 shows how just three individual labor supply curves can be summed to yield a market supply curve that slopes upward over the realistic range of wages.

WHY WAGES DIFFER

The market supply curve combines with the market demand curve for labor to yield the equilibrium wage and the equilibrium level of employment in the market. Just as both blades of a pair of scissors contribute equally to cutting cloth, both the supply of and the demand for labor determine the market wage rate. Therefore differences in wages across markets can be traced to differences in either labor supply or labor demand.

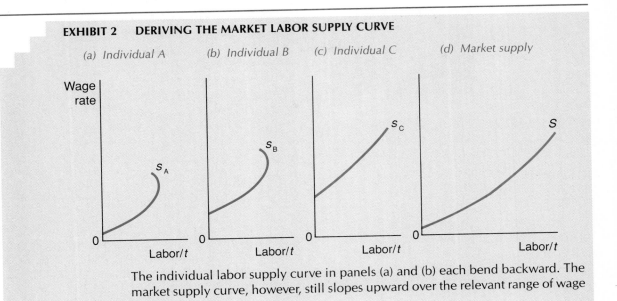

EXHIBIT 2   DERIVING THE MARKET LABOR SUPPLY CURVE

(a) *Individual A*   (b) *Individual B*   (c) *Individual C*   (d) *Market supply*

The individual labor supply curve in panels (a) and (b) each bend backward. The market supply curve, however, still slopes upward over the relevant range of wage rates.

In the previous chapter we discussed the elements that influence the demand for resources, and we examined labor in particular. In brief, a firm is willing to hire labor up to the point where labor's marginal revenue product equals its marginal resource cost—that is, where the last unit employed earns the firm just enough to cover its cost. Since we have already discussed the factors that affect the demand for labor, we consider in this section primarily those forces that affect market supply.

Differences in Training and Education Requirements

Some jobs pay more than others because they require a long and costly training period. Costly training reduces market supply because fewer individuals are willing to incur such an expense. But the training increases the productivity of each additional unit of labor, thereby increasing the demand for these skills. Reduced supply and increased demand both have a positive effect on the equilibrium wage. Dentists are paid more than dental hygienists primarily because of the great difference in the time and expense required to train for the two jobs.

Differences in Ability

Because they are more able and talented, some individuals are paid more than others with identical training and education levels. Two lawyers may have had identical educations, but one earns twice as much as the other because of differences in underlying ability. Most executives have extensive training and business experience, but only a few become chief executives of

Gary S. Becker
(b. 1930)

What is economics? In the nineteenth century the classical writers saw their subject as restricted to purely "economic" activities: business, finance, material well-being. By the 1930s, however, economists had begun to see their task quite differently. Today economics deals not with a particular sphere of human activity but with a particular aspect of *all* human activity: the aspect that involves allocating scarce resources, whatever those resources might be.

There is no better example of this transformation in economics than the work of Gary Becker. From racial discrimination to education to crime to the intimate decisions within the family, Becker has pioneered the application of economic perspectives to areas of human life previously

considered "noneconomic." Largely thanks to him, economic ideas have now spread so widely into subjects once the domain of other disciplines that angry cries of "economic imperialism!" routinely reverberate from the walls of sociology, philosophy, history, and other university departments.

To see his approach more clearly, consider another area he has written about: the economics of crime and punishment. Crime, Becker argues, is from the economist's point of view an occupation like any other. The decision to engage in criminal activity — as in any activity — will hinge on the costs and benefits involved. The higher the punishment if the criminal is caught and the higher the probability of getting caught, the less criminal activity there will be, other

things constant. Conversely, the more lucrative the criminal opportunities relative to other opportunities (the lower the opportunity cost of engaging in crime), the more crime there will be, other things constant. Also, since crime is an extremely risky business, it is likely to attract people with a taste for taking chances, just as low-risk occupations (like being an economist?) are likely to attract people who are averse to risk.

Gary Becker was born in Pottstown, Pennsylvania. He received his undergraduate degree from Princeton University and his Ph.D. from the University of Chicago. He taught at Columbia University, where he became a full professor at age 30, only five years after leaving school. Since 1970 he has been a professor at the University of Chicago.

Portrait by The University of Chicago

Richard Langlois

large corporations. From actors to professional athletes, pay differences reflect differing abilities.

Differences in Risk

Jobs vary in the degree of risk of work-related injury or death. Research indicates that jobs with a higher probability of injury or death, such as coal mining, pay a higher wage. Workers are also paid more, other things constant, in fields where the chances of being unemployed are greater, such as construction.

Problems of Labor Mobility

Identical workers may earn different wages because each sells labor in a different market. Wages are often lower in rural areas than in metropolitan areas in part because there are fewer employers in rural areas and therefore less demand for labor. This difference in wages creates an incentive to migrate to high-wage areas. But some workers do not migrate, perhaps because they are unaware of the higher-paying alternatives or they are reluctant to leave their home towns. Generally, however, individuals have a strong incentive to sell their resources in the market where these resources are valued most.

Did you ever notice that place kickers in professional football have names that are difficult to pronounce? These kickers are drawn to the United States by the attractive salaries available in the National Football League. Likewise, physicians are paid more in the United States than in any other country in the world. Consequently, foreign-trained physicians have a strong incentive to practice medicine in the United States. Indeed, every year more than 10,000 physicians migrate to the United States. Some Americans seek their fortune abroad, such as basketball players drawn by the high pay in European professional leagues.

Differences in Job Status

Other things constant, employers must pay workers more to perform jobs that are dirty, smelly, noisy, dangerous, boring, irregular, or of low social status. This does not mean that jobs of low social status must pay more than all other jobs. After all, a janitor earns less than a computer programmer. What it means is that, *other things constant*, jobs of lower status must pay more than jobs of higher social status that require the same skills.

Job Discrimination

Sometimes individuals are paid different wages because of racial or sexual discrimination in the job market. Although such discrimination is illegal, history shows that certain groups have systematically earned less than others of apparently equal ability. The reasons underlying the differences in average earnings between males and females are discussed in the following case study.

CASE STUDY

Comparable Worth

Comparable worth calls for pay to be determined by job characteristics rather than by supply and demand.

Despite laws in this country requiring affirmative action and equal pay for equal work, women on average still earn only about 65 percent as much as men earn. After adjusting for several factors, such as the tendency of women to interrupt their careers for child rearing, we find that the differential between the sexes shrinks but does not disappear. One explanation for this pay gap is that women have crowded into certain occupations, such as secretarial work and nursing, because other job opportunities have been blocked by discrimination and restrictive sex roles. The increased supply of (female) labor to these crowded professions has lowered the prevailing wage.

Some advocates of women's rights are promoting a notion called **comparable worth** as a way of addressing pay differences. The comparable worth approach calls for each job to be evaluated based on that job's requirements — the training necessary, previous experience needed, and so on. Pay is then based on this evaluation. Proponents of comparable worth believe that such a system would eliminate situations in which men working in jobs requiring few skills are paid more than women working in occupations requiring greater skills.

Pay differences were dramatized in a 1984 strike of clerical and technical workers against Yale University. The predominantly female labor union noted that administrative assistants, who were mostly female and whose pay averaged $13,424 per year, performed work that required, in the union's view, at least as much training and experience as the work performed by the university's truck drivers, who were mostly men and whose pay averaged $18,470.

Comparable pay laws have been adopted in more than a dozen states as well as in Australia and Great Britain. Female workers in Washington state won a discrimination suit that could cost the state government nearly $1 billion. Legislation has been proposed that would require the federal government to reevaluate all of its jobs, with the idea of raising the pay for jobs held mainly by women. Some major employers, such as BankAmerica and AT&T, have begun to integrate comparable worth into their compensation schemes.

Would basing pay on some standard of comparable worth reduce pay differentials between males and females? And what other effects would it have on the economy? Put aside for the present any consideration of the administrative cost of setting up the bureaucracy needed to establish and police such a system, and assume that such a bureaucracy could accurately calculate and assess the skills associated with each position. Experts conclude that implementation of comparable worth standards would increase women's wages in the affected professions by at least 10 percent, with the biggest increases coming in nursing and teaching. As a result, the average cost of labor would also increase, but not by as much.

Basing pay on comparable worth reduces the allocative role of the job market. As a result of comparable worth laws, there could be a modest decrease in job opportunities for women. If wages in some professions are low because of crowding and if comparable worth laws raise the pay in these crowded occupations, then more women (and men) will attempt to crowd into these fields as the wage becomes relatively more attractive. To the extent that employers base their hiring on the marginal productivity of labor, they will cut back on the quantity demanded in these fields. Thus fewer will be employed in these historically female professions, but those who find jobs will earn more than before.

Sources: Barbara Bergman, "The Economic Case for Comparable Worth," in Heidi Hartmann, ed., *Comparable Worth: New Directions for Research* (Washington: National Academy Press, 1985), 78–85; Mark Aldrich and Robert Buchele, *The Economics of Comparable Worth* (Cambridge, Mass.: Ballinger, 1986); Ronald Ehrenberg and Robert Smith, "Comparable Worth Wage Adjustments and Female Employment in the State and Local Sector," *Journal of Labor Economics* 5 (January 1987): 43–62.

INFORMATION PROBLEMS IN LABOR MARKETS

In our market analysis of the supply and demand for particular kinds of labor, we typically assume that workers are identical. In equilibrium, each worker in the market is assumed to be paid the same wage, which is equal to the marginal revenue product of the last unit of labor hired. Problems arising from differences in the quality of workers have been downplayed in our formal analysis.

Differences in the quality of workers present no particular problem as long as the effect of these differences on the workers' productivity can be readily observed. If the productivity of each particular worker is easily quantified through a measure such as the quantity of oranges picked, the number of shoes stitched, or the number of papers typed, that measure itself can and does serve as the basis for pay. But because production often takes place through the coordinated efforts of several workers, it is usually easier to pay workers by the hour rather than attempt to keep a detailed account of each worker's contribution to total output.

Often the pay is some combination of an hourly rate and an additional incentive linked to a measure of productivity. A sales representative typically receives a base salary plus a commission tied to the quantity sold. At times the task of evaluating marginal product is left to the consumer rather than the firm. Workers who provide personal services, such as waiters and waitresses, have a pay structure based heavily on tips. Since this service is by definition "personal," customers are considered to be in the best position to judge the quality of service and to tip accordingly.

Adverse Selection Problem

Adverse selection occurs when unobservable labor skills are misvalued in the market.

An **adverse selection** problem arises in the labor market when labor suppliers have much better information about their productivities than employers do, because the abilities of workers are not observable before employment. A given wage tends to attract the least productive workers available in the labor pool; the most productive workers view the given wage as below the value of their marginal productivity.

Let's assume that an employer wants to hire a program coordinator for a new project, a job that calls for imagination, organizational skills, and the ability to work independently. The employer would like to attract the most qualified person, but because the qualities demanded are not directly observable, the employer must rely on proxy information, such as education and previous employment history. The pay level advertised for the position is not the marginal revenue product of the best person in the market; it is more likely the average marginal revenue product of all those in the market. Individual workers have a good idea of their own intelligence and creativity and are able to evaluate this wage in view of their own abilities and opportunity cost. The really talented people will find that the salary offered by the employer is below the true value of their abilities and will be less inclined to apply for the job. Less talented individuals, however, particularly those who meet all the proxy qualifications (that is, "look good on paper"), will find that the offered wage exceeds the true value of their marginal productivity and thus will be more likely to pursue the job. This adverse selection will make the recruiting task more difficult because the pool of applicants will be of below-average ability.

Signaling

Adverse selection gives rise to signaling. Because the true requirements for many positions are qualities that are unobservable in an interview, the employer must rely on proxy measures, such as educational attainment, in evaluating potential employees. A proxy measure is called a **signal**. A signal serves as a useful way of screening applicants as long as it is a true indicator of the unobservable quality of interest.

*A **signal** is a proxy measure for unobservable employee characteristics.*

In order to identify the best workers, employers must find signals that less productive individuals will have significantly more difficulty acquiring. A signal that can be acquired with equal ease or difficulty by all workers, regardless of their productivity, does not provide a useful way of screening applicants. If, for example, more productive workers find it easier to succeed in college than do less productive individuals, a good college record is a signal worth using to distinguish more productive workers from less productive workers. In this case education may be significant not so much because it enhances worker productivity as because it enables employers to distinguish among workers.

Principal-Agent Problems

A second problem that arises when people on one side of the market have better information than those on the other side is explained by the principal-agent model. This expression is used to describe a relation in whch one party, known as the **principal**, makes a contractual agreement with another

In a ***principal-agent relationship***, the principal makes an agreement with an agent in the expectation that the agent will act in the principal's behalf.

party, known as the **agent**, in the expectation that the agent will act on behalf of the principal. You could confront a principal-agent problem when you deal with an insurance agent, a stock broker, a lawyer, or a garage mechanic, to name a few. In each case you, the principal, hire an agent who has more expertise than you in providing the service. More generally, any employer-employee relationship is a principal-agent relation.

In this age of specialization, there are many tasks we do not do for ourselves because someone else either does them better or has a lower opportunity cost of time. Suppose your objective is to get your car repaired, but you have little knowledge of cars. The mechanic you hire may have other objectives, such as maximizing on-the-job leisure or maximizing the garage's revenue. Suppose that your car has only a loose wire, but the mechanic inflates the bill by charging you for service you do not really need. You, as principal, are poorly served by the mechanic, your agent. Principal-agent problems arise when the goals of the agent differ from those of the principal.

There are ways of reducing the consequences of the principal-agent problem. An incentive structure or an information-revealing system can be developed to reduce the problems associated with the lopsided availability of information. For example, some garages provide written estimates before a job is done and return the defective parts to the customer after the job is done as evidence of the necessity of the repair.

These are just a few of the information problems that arise in the market for labor. Hiring and paying workers based on their marginal product is often more easily said than done. But the marginal productivity theory of resource use is a good first approximation of how resource markets work.

FUNCTIONAL DISTRIBUTION OF INCOME

One way to develop an overview of resource markets and labor's role in particular is to consider how income is distributed among resource owners: what share of the income goes to suppliers of labor and what share goes to suppliers of each of the other resources? In this final section we will examine how the income of the United States as a whole is divided among resource owners.

Exhibit 3 shows the proportion of national income that goes to (1) wages and salaries, (2) proprietors' income, (3) corporate profits, (4) interest, and (5) rent. Over time, wages and salaries have claimed by far the largest share of national income, most recently about three-fourths of the total. This statistic understates the proportion going to labor, however, because a portion of proprietors' income consists of wages as well: the proprietor of a corner store typically works long hours, and much of what is counted as the proprietor's income is in fact compensation for the proprietor's labor.

Exhibit 3 also shows the sharp decline over time in the share of national income received by proprietors. A generation ago the income received by

EXHIBIT 3
FUNCTIONAL DISTRIBUTION OF INCOME:
PERCENTAGE SHARE OF EACH SOURCE OF INCOME

Time Period	Wages and Salaries (1)	Proprietors' Income (2)	Corporate Profits (3)	Interest (4)	Rent (5)
1900–1909	55.0	23.7	6.8	5.5	9.0
1910–1919	53.6	23.8	9.1	5.4	8.1
1920–1929	60.0	17.5	7.8	6.2	7.7
1930–1939	67.5	14.8	4.0	8.7	5.0
1940–1948	64.6	17.2	11.9	3.1	3.3
1949–1958	67.3	13.9	12.5	2.9	3.4
1959–1963	69.9	11.9	11.2	4.0	3.0
1964–1970	71.6	9.6	12.1	3.5	3.2
1971–1979	74.6	7.4	9.8	6.3	1.9
1980–1989	73.0	7.9	7.9	10.2	1.0

Sources: Irving Kravis, "Income Distribution: Functional Shares," *International Encyclopedia of Social Sciences*, vol. 7 (New York: Macmillan Co. and Free Press, 1968), 134; *The Annual Report of the Council of Economic Advisors*, 1990, Table C-24. Figures after 1963 are not fully consistent with prior figures, but they convey a reasonably accurate picture of income trends.

Mom and Pop from their corner store was counted as proprietors' income; the people who ring up your Pepsi today are more typically earning salaries and wages as employees of a corporate chain of convenience stores, such as 7–Eleven.

The major problem with Exhibit 3 is that the categories and definitions do not really match the tidy definitions we have used. We already noted that proprietors' income includes labor income. Additionally, the column heads Corporate Profits, Interest, and Rent do not correspond closely to the terms *economic profit*, *interest*, and *economic rent* as they are used in this book. Yet the definitions in Exhibit 3 bear enough similarity to the way economists view the world to make the table of interest to us. *The most important conclusion is that labor's share of total income is relatively large and has grown during this century.* This conclusion still holds even if the definitions of each income category are changed somewhat.

CONCLUSION

This chapter has employed the tools of supply and demand to examine how labor markets work and why wages differ across professions and across individuals within professions. The interaction of the supply of and demand for labor determines wage rates, the level of employment, and the distribution of income across households. Our emphasis has been on market forces. To a large extent, we have ignored the influence of institutional forces, such as labor unions, large corporations, and government. The effect of unions on the labor market is the topic of the next chapter.

1. The supply of labor shows the relationship between the wage rate and the quantity of market labor people are willing and able to supply. The demand for labor shows the relation between the wage rate and the quantity of market labor firms are willing and able to demand. The intersection of supply and demand determines the equilibrium wage rate.

2. People allocate their time so as to maximize utility. There are three uses of time: market work, nonmarket work, and leisure. A higher market wage means that each hour of market work yields more in terms of the goods and services that can be purchased, so a higher wage provides an incentive to substitute market work for other uses of time. But the higher the wage, the higher the income, and as income increases, people consume more of all normal goods including leisure. The net effect of a higher wage on an individual's quantity of market labor supplied depends on both the substitution effect and the income effect.

3. The quantity of market labor supplied also depends on a variety of factors other than the wage, including (1) other sources of income, (2) job amenities, (3) the future value of job experience, (4) the amount of discretion allowed in the use of time while working, and (5) taste for the work.

4. Market wages differ because of (1) differences in training and education requirements, (2) differences in the skill and ability of workers, (3) differences in the riskiness of the work, both in terms of the workers' safety and the chances of getting laid off, (4) problems of labor mobility, and (5) racial and sexual discrimination.

5. Wages are determined on the basis of the marginal productivity of workers. Problems arise if differences in worker productivity cannot be readily determined by employers. Adverse selection occurs because workers are more familiar with their own productivity than employers are. When the productivity of workers is not directly observable, employers sometimes hire workers based on some signal that appears to be related to productivity, such as education. This system of screening applicants is effective as long as more productive workers find it easier to send the correct signal than less productive workers do.

6. The principal-agent model describes a relation in which one party, known as the principal, makes a contractual agreement with another party, known as the agent, in the expectation that the agent will act on behalf of the principal. Principal-agent problems arise when the goals of the agent differ from those of the principal.

7. During this century wages and salaries have grown as a percentage of total resource income, and they now account for about three-quarters of the total. Proprietors' income and rent have fallen as a percentage of the total.

Questions and Problems

1. (Utility Maximization) Explain how the consumption of goods, the supplying of labor, and the consumption of leisure affect utility and one another.

2. (Labor Supply) Suppose that the substitution effect of an increase in the wage rate exactly offsets the income effect for all wage levels. What would the market supply of labor look like in this case? Why?

3. (Labor Supply) Many U.S. companies have a problem with worker absenteeism. How is this problem related to market labor supply and, in particular, to the level of wages? What other considerations are there?

4. (Equilibrium Differentials) Suppose that two jobs are exactly the same except that one is performed in an air-conditioned workplace. How might an economist measure the value workers place on such a job amenity?

5. (Labor Supply) What type of education and general skills are needed to improve the productivity of the labor force? Do you believe that high schools and colleges provide such an education? Why or why not?

6. (Risk and Labor Supply) Suppose that you have a choice between a job that results in the loss of one life in a hundred and another job that includes no such risk. If the no-risk job pays $20,000 per year, what income would be necessary to induce you to take the risky job?

7. (Adverse Selection and Signaling) Suppose that you were charged with the responsibility of recruiting for a major corporation. What signals would you use to reduce the problem of adverse selection? How might these signals be faulty indicators of productivity?

8. (Principal-Agent) Export management companies help firms market their products in foreign countries. Are such export management companies principals or agents? What skills must employees of such companies possess to be successful?

9. (Distribution of Income) How might technological advances affect the functional distribution of income in an economy?

10. (Distribution of Income) Why is land reform essential to bring about a more equitable functional distribution of income in some countries? What dangers exist for countries with very unbalanced distributions?

11. (Equilibrium Wage) Use a labor supply-demand diagram to predict the impact on the equilibrium wage and quantity of market labor of each of the following:
    a. An increase in the income tax
    b. A reduction in labor productivity
    c. An increase in the level of unemployment compensation

12. (Labor Supply and Indifference Curves) Using indifference curves relating leisure to all other goods, show how a backward-bending labor supply curve could be consistent with utility maximization.

13. (Comparable Worth) Suppose legislation is passed mandating equal pay for all jobs that require the same skills and training.
    a. What kinds of problems will this create if such jobs have different nonpay attributes?
    b. How might employers respond to such legislation?

14. (Labor Supply) Determine the hourly wage rate necessary to induce you to work this summer. What factors did you take into account in determining this wage rate?

C H A P T E R   2 7

Unions and Collective Bargaining

Few aspects of the labor market are more in the news than the activities of labor unions. Labor contract negotiations, strikes, picket lines, confrontations between workers and employers—all these fit neatly into TV's "action news" format. Each September, for example, along with another football season we get pictures of striking teachers walking picket lines somewhere in the country. This drama may cause you to miss the real economic significance of unions. Also, you may have developed the mistaken impression that the majority of workers belong to unions and that strikes occur frequently. In this chapter we will step back from the charged rhetoric typically used to discuss union-employer relationships to review the history of the union movement in the United States, examine more carefully the economic effects of unions, and discuss recent trends in union membership. Topics discussed in this chapter include

- Craft unions
- Industrial unions
- Collective bargaining
- Tradeoff between wages and employment
- Union objectives
- Recent trends in union membership

A BRIEF HISTORY OF THE LABOR MOVEMENT IN THE UNITED STATES

In 1860, before labor unions achieved national prominence, the workday for nonfarm employees averaged about 11 hours, and people normally worked a 6-day week. Those employed in steel mills, paper mills, and breweries typically worked 12 hours a day, 7 days a week. Working conditions were often frightful: insurance company estimates indicate that about 1 out of 15 workers was seriously injured each year. Mining and metal processing were particularly dangerous. To be compensated for injuries, a worker had to sue the employer and prove the employer's negligence. Most workers did not know how to sue their employers. Child labor was also common. In 1880 a million children between the ages of 10 and 15 were in the work force; this number had doubled to 2 million by 1910, when one-fifth of those between 10 and 15 held full-time jobs.

Immigration during the period sent millions of new workers streaming into the work force, competing for jobs and keeping wages relatively low. Employers were therefore assured of a ready pool of workers despite poor working conditions.

Early Labor Organizations

The first unions in the United States date back to the early days of national independence, when employees in various crafts, such as carpenters, shoemakers, and printers, formed local groups to seek higher wages and shorter hours. Such **craft unions** confined membership to workers with a particular skill or craft. In the 1850s, because improved transportation systems extended markets beyond the local level, unions in the same trade began widening their membership to regional and even national levels. The National Typographical Union, formed in 1852, was soon followed by several other national craft unions.

A **craft union** confines membership to workers with a particular skill or craft.

Knights of Labor The first major national labor organization in the United States was the *Knights of Labor*, formed in 1869. Its objectives were generally more political than economic, but the Knights sought an 8-hour workday and the abolition of child labor. Within 20 years the union had over 750,000 members. But the union lacked focus and tried to include as members both skilled and unskilled labor, a combination that proved difficult to organize.

American Federation of Labor The various craft unions that had developed during the nineteenth century did not find the Knights of Labor appealing. Consequently, these craft unions formed their own national organization, called the *American Federation of Labor (AFL)*. The AFL was founded in 1886 under the direction of Samuel Gompers, a cigar maker. It was not a union but rather an organization of national unions, with each member union retaining its autonomy.

By the beginning of World War I, the AFL, still under the direction of Gompers, was viewed as the voice of labor. The Clayton Act of 1914 exempted trade union negotiations from antitrust law, meaning that *unions in competing companies could join forces in an attempt to raise wages.* Union membership jumped during World War I, but dropped after the war as the government retreated from its support of union efforts. Membership dropped by half between 1920 and 1933.

A New Deal for Labor

The Great Depression set the stage for a new era in the labor movement. The unemployment rate reached 25 percent, prices dropped, and output fell by more than 33 percent between 1929 and 1933. President Franklin D. Roosevelt believed that higher prices and wages were necessary to pull the economy out of its disastrous slump. Government support for organized labor was, he thought, a way to boost wages. The *Norris-La Guardia Act* of 1932 provided this support by sharply limiting the courts' ability to stop strikes. Furthermore, *yellow-dog contracts*, under which workers had to agree not to join a union as a condition of employment, were declared unenforceable by the courts.

Wagner Act Another important law passed during this period was the *Wagner Act* of 1935, which required employers to bargain with unions that represented the majority of the workers. The act also made it illegal for employers to interfere with their employees' right to unionize. To investigate unfair labor practices and to oversee union elections, the law established the *National Labor Relations Board*. The act has come to be known as the Magna Carta of the U.S. labor movement.

The Congress of Industrial Organizations Such favorable legislation nourished the growth of a new kind of union, organized along industry lines. The *Congress of Industrial Organizations (CIO)* was established in 1935 to serve as a national organization of unions in mass-production industries, such as autos and steel. Whereas the AFL had organized workers in particular crafts, such as plumbers and carpenters, the CIO was made up of unions whose membership embraced all workers in a particular industry, including unskilled and semiskilled workers. This **industrial union** approach proved successful, and in 1937 the steel workers' union joined the CIO, bringing into the organization more than 200,000 members. In 1938 the charismatic leader of the United Mine Workers, John L. Lewis, became president of the CIO. Workers in the auto and rubber industries were able to organize through the use of *sit-down strikes*, in which workers occupied the plants but did not work, thereby paralyzing operations.

*An **industrial union** includes all workers in a particular industry, both skilled and unskilled.*

The Labor Movement After World War II

After World War II, economic conditions and public sentiment appeared to turn against unions. Postwar inflation seemed to be aggravated by a series of strikes, and in November 1946 the United Mine Workers defied a court order to return to work after a long and bitter strike. In response, Congress in 1947 passed the *Taft-Hartley Act*, which attempted to limit strikes that would affect the public's safety and welfare. The president, by obtaining a court order, could stop a strike for 80 days, during which time the parties could continue to negotiate.

The Taft-Hartley Act also prohibited the **closed shop**, which requires workers to join a union before they can be hired. Moreover, the act permitted individual states to pass **right-to-work** laws outlawing the **union shop**, which requires workers to join the union once they are hired. Twenty-one states eventually outlawed union shops in favor of **open shops**, which allow employers to hire both union and nonunion workers. With an open shop, the nonunion employees, once hired, do not have to join the union.

All this shop talk can become confusing, so let's summarize. There are three types of shops: (1) *closed shops*, which require workers to join the union before they can be hired and which were outlawed by the Taft-Hartley Act; (2) *union shops*, which require workers to join the union once employed and which are legal in the majority of states, and (3) *open shops*, which do not require union membership and which are the only kind of union shops allowed in the twenty-one "right-to-work" states. Not surprisingly, union membership as a percentage of the work force is about one-third lower in right-to-work states than in other states.

Despite the Taft-Hartley Act, the union movement flourished, with membership growing from less than 4 million, or about 12 percent of nonfarm wage and salary workers, in 1930 to more than 17 million, or about 34 percent, in 1955. The AFL and the CIO merged in 1955.

During the 1950s organized labor suffered from allegations of corruption and misconduct on the part of union leaders. Congressional investigations led to the passage in 1959 of the *Landrum-Griffin Act* to protect the rights of rank-and-file union members against abuses by union leaders. The act regulated union elections, required union officials to file financial reports, and made theft of union funds a federal offense. This act has been called the Bill of Rights for union members because it is aimed at guaranteeing each member's right to open elections and honest union leadership.

COLLECTIVE BARGAINING AND OTHER TOOLS OF UNIONISM

Now that you have some idea of the labor movement's history, let's consider the tools used by unions to exert some control over wages and working conditions. We begin with a discussion of collective bargaining.

Collective Bargaining

Collective bargaining is the process by which representatives from union and management negotiate a mutually agreeable contract specifying wages, employee benefits, and working conditions. The actual contract can run to many pages of fine print written in language only a lawyer could understand. Once an agreement has been reached, union representatives must carry it back to the membership for a vote. If it is rejected, the union can vote to strike or to continue negotiations.

Mediation and Arbitration

If negotiations over a contract reach an impasse and if the public interest is involved, government officials may ask an independent mediator to step in. A **mediator** is an impartial observer who listens to both sides separately and makes suggestions about how each side could adjust its position to resolve differences. If a resolution appears possible, the mediator will bring the parties together to iron out a contract. The mediator has no power to impose a settlement on the parties.

In certain critical sectors, such as police and fire protection, where a strike would seriously harm the public interest, an impasse in negotiations is sometimes settled through **binding arbitration**, whereby a neutral third party evaluates both sides of the dispute and issues a decision that the parties are committed to accept. Some disputes skip the mediation and arbitration steps, going directly from impasse to strike.

*In **mediation** an impartial observer attempts to resolve differences between union and management. Under **binding arbitration** both parties must accept an impartial observer's resolution of the dispute.*

The Strike

A major source of union power in the bargaining relationship is the threat of a **strike**, which is the union's attempt to withhold labor from the firm. The purpose of a strike is to stop production, thereby forcing the firm to accept the union's position. But a strike imposes significant costs on union members, who forgo pay and benefits for the duration of the strike and risk losing their jobs. Union funds and other sources may provide some support during a strike, but the typical striker's income falls substantially.

*A **strike** is a union's attempt to withhold labor from a firm.*

Thus strikes can be very costly for both sides. In 1989, for example, a strike at Eastern Airlines forced the company into bankruptcy and cost many union members their jobs as the company attempted to operate with nonunion workers. The threat of a strike hangs over labor negotiations and can serve as a real spur to reach an accord. *Although usually neither party wants a strike, both sides must act as if they would endure a strike rather than concede on key points.*

Since the strike's success depends on blocking the supply of labor to the firm, unions usually picket the targeted employer to prevent or discourage so-called strike-breakers, or "scabs," from working. Not surprisingly, violence occasionally erupts during confrontations between striking and non-striking workers. Although reports of strikes are often in the news, most bargaining agreements — well over 95 percent — are reached without a strike. Strike activity declined during the 1980s, and by the end of the decade only 2 of every 10,000 workdays were lost because of strikes.

THE ECONOMIC EFFECTS OF UNIONS

Union members, like everyone else, have unlimited wants, but no union can regularly get everything it desires. Because resources are scarce, choices must be made. One could prepare a menu of union desires: higher wages, more employee benefits, greater job security, better working conditions, and so on. To keep the analysis manageable, we will focus initially on a single objective: higher wages. We will examine three possible ways of increasing wages: (1) inclusive, or industrial, unionism; (2) exclusive, or craft, union-ism; and (3) increasing the demand for union labor.

Inclusive, or Industrial, Unions

The first model we will consider characterizes strong industrial unions, such as the auto and steel unions, which attempt to set the industry-wide wage for each class of labor. In Exhibit 1(b), the market supply and demand for a particular class of labor are presented as S and D. In the absence of a union, the equilibrium wage is W and the equilibrium employment level is E. At the market wage, each individual employer faces a horizontal, or perfectly elastic, supply of labor, as reflected by s in Exhibit 1(a). Thus each firm, as a price taker, can hire as much labor as it wants at the market wage of W. The firm hires labor up to the point where the marginal revenue product, or the firm's demand for labor, equals the marginal resource cost, or the firm's supply of labor; this amount is represented by quantity e in Exhibit 1(a). In equilibrium each worker hired is paid a wage just equal to what the marginal worker earns for the firm.

Now suppose that the union is able to negotiate a minimum wage in this industry of W', meaning that no labor will be supplied at a lower wage, but any amount desired by the firms, up to the quantity identified at point a in Exhibit 1(b), will be supplied at the floor wage. In effect, the supply of union labor is perfectly elastic at the union wage up to point a. If more than a is demanded, however, the floor wage no longer applies; the upward-sloping portion, aS, becomes the relevant part of the labor supply curve. For an industry facing a floor wage of W', the entire labor supply curve is $W'aS$, which has a kink where the floor wage joins the upward-sloping supply curve.

Once this floor wage has been established, each individual firm faces a horizontal supply curve for labor at the collectively bargained wage, W'. As the price of labor goes up, each employer demands less labor, as reflected by the firm's drop in employment from e to e' in Exhibit 1(a). Consequently, higher wages lead to a reduction in total employment; the quantity de-manded by the industry drops from E to E' in Exhibit 1(b). At wage W' the amount of labor supplied, E'', exceeds the amount demanded, E'.

In the absence of a union, this excess supply of labor would cause unemployed workers to lower their asking wage. But union members agree *collectively* to a wage, so workers cannot individually offer to work for less, nor can employers hire them at a lower wage. Because the number of union members willing and able to work exceeds the number of jobs available, the union must develop some mechanism for rationing the available jobs, such as awarding jobs based on seniority. *With the inclusive, or industrial, union,*

EXHIBIT 1   EFFECT OF A UNION'S WAGE FLOOR

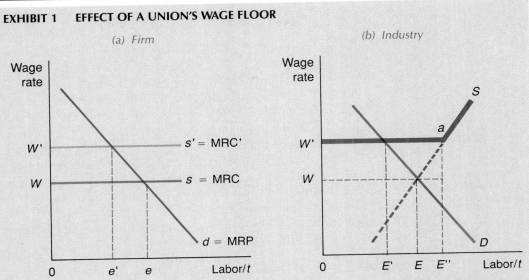

(a) *Firm*   (b) *Industry*

In panel (b), the equilibrium wage rate is *W*. At that wage the individual firm of panel (a) hires labor up to the point where the marginal revenue product equals *W*. Each firm hires quantity *e*; total employment is *E*.

If a union can negotiate a wage *W'* above the equilibrium level, the supply curve facing the firm shifts up to *s'*. The firm hires fewer workers, *e'*, and total employment falls to *E'*. At wage *W'* there is an excess supply of labor equal to *E'' − E'*.

wages are higher and total employment lower than they would be in the absence of a union.

Those who cannot find union employment will look for jobs in the nonunion sector. The increased supply of labor in the nonunion sector drives down the nonunion wage. So wages are relatively higher in the union sector, first because unions bargain for a wage that exceeds the market clearing wage and second because those unable to find employment in the union sector supply their labor to the nonunion sector. This increased supply of labor to the nonunion sector reduces the nonunion wage. *Evidence suggests that union wages in the United States are on average about 15 to 20 percent higher than nonunion wages.*[1]

Exclusive, or Craft, Unions

One way to increase wages while avoiding the excess labor supply created by the industrial-union approach is for the union to somehow shift

---

[1] The most comprehensive discussion of the economic impact of unions is provided by Richard B. Freedman and James L. Medoff in *What Do Unions Do?* (New York: Basic Books, 1984), especially Table 3-1.

the supply curve to the left, as shown in panel (a) of Exhibit 2. Successful supply restrictions of this type require that two conditions be met. First, the union must be able to restrict its membership, and second, the union must be able to force all employers in the industry to hire only union members. The union can restrict its membership with high initiation fees, long apprenticeship periods, difficult qualification exams, and other devices designed to slow down or discourage new membership. But, as we will see later, unions have difficulty requiring all firms in the industry to hire only union workers.

Whereas wage setting is more typical of the industrial unions, restricting supply (and employment) is more characteristic of the craft unions, such as unions of carpenters, plumbers, and bricklayers. Groups of professionals such as doctors, lawyers, and accountants also impose entry restrictions through education and examination standards. Such restrictions, though usually proposed on the grounds that they protect the public, are often no more than self-serving attempts to increase earnings by reducing supply.

Increasing Demand for Union Labor

A third way to increase the wage is to increase the demand for union labor, by shifting the labor demand curve outward from D to D'' in panel (b)

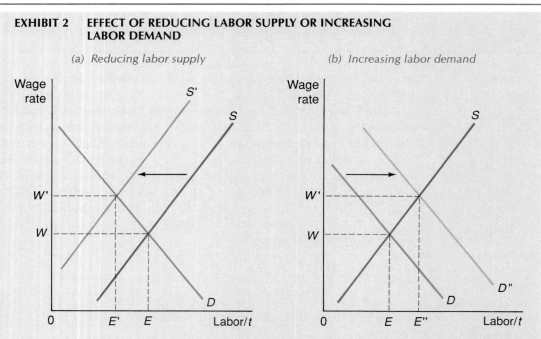

EXHIBIT 2   EFFECT OF REDUCING LABOR SUPPLY OR INCREASING LABOR DEMAND

(a) Reducing labor supply

(b) Increasing labor demand

If a union can restrict labor supply to an industry, the supply curve shifts to the left from S to S', as in panel (a). The wage rate rises from W to W' but at the cost of a reduction in employment from E to E'. In panel (b), an increase in labor demand from D to D'' raises both the wage and the level of employment.

of Exhibit 2. This approach is an attractive alternative *because it increases both wages and employment*, so there is no need to ration jobs or to restrict union membership.

Increase Demand for Union-Made Goods The demand for union labor may be increased through a direct appeal to consumers to buy only union-made products (as in the familiar refrain "Look for the union label"). Because the demand for labor is a derived demand, an increase in the demand for union-made products will increase the demand for union labor.

Restrict Sales of Nonunion-Made Goods Another way to increase the demand for union labor is to restrict the supply of products that compete with union-made products. Again, this approach relies on the derived nature of labor demand. The United Auto Workers have over the years supported restrictions on imported cars. Fewer imported cars means a greater demand for cars produced by U.S. workers, who are mostly union members.

Increase Productivity Some observers claim that the efficiency with which unions organize and monitor the labor-management relationship increases the demand for union labor. According to this theory, unions increase worker productivity by minimizing conflicts, resolving differences, and at times even straightening out workers who are goofing off. In the absence of a union, for example, an individual worker may be reluctant to complain to the employer about some unsatisfactory element of the job. Instead, the really dissatisfied worker may simply look for another job, thereby causing job turnover, which is costly to the firm. With a union, however, workers have union channels through which they can more comfortably complain, and the negotiated responses they receive may reduce their urge to leave the firm. Quit rates are in fact significantly lower among union workers. If unions increase the productivity of workers in this way, the demand for union labor will increase.

Featherbedding is an attempt to increase the number of union workers required to perform a particular task.

Featherbedding Still another way unions attempt to increase the demand for union labor is by **featherbedding**, which is an attempt to ensure that more union labor is hired than producers would prefer. Featherbedding is often a response to the introduction of labor-saving technology. For example, when the diesel engine replaced the coal-fired engine, locomotives no longer needed someone to shovel coal. For years after the adoption of the diesel engine, however, the railroad unions required such a crew member. Similarly, unions often fight technological developments in electronic composing and typesetting, which have reduced the labor requirements of newspapers; some require that ready-to-use advertising layouts be reset by hand. For the same reason, court transcribers refuse to permit tape recordings of legal proceedings; painters' unions often prohibit the use of spray guns, limiting members to paintbrushes; and musicians object to the use of taped music.

Featherbedding does not create a true increase in demand, in the sense of shifting the demand curve to the right; instead, it forces firms to hire a quantity to the right of their demand curve. The union tries to limit a firm to either hiring a certain number of workers or hiring none. Thus the union attempts to dictate not only the wage but also the quantity that must be hired at that wage, thereby moving the employers to the right of their demand for labor curve. An example of featherbedding is considered in the following case study.

CASE STUDY

Feather-bedding on Broadway

Broadway producers have long claimed that the restrictive work rules of the theatrical unions are a primary source of the increases in the cost of Broadway tickets. Union contracts specify not only the pay level but also the number of workers required for each position. For example, union rules require a backstage crew of at least four, regardless of the show, and the box office must be staffed by three people. At some theaters union rules require a certain number of musicians, whether or not they are needed in a particular show. (Victor Borge, at the end of his solo piano performance on Broadway, asked musicians required by union rules to be present for the evening to line up for the curtain call, even though none had played a single note.)

To the extent that these union work rules raise ticket prices, the continued employment of union members depends on the elasticity of demand for theater tickets. With the top price per ticket over $50, there is evidence that the demand has been elastic enough to put many theater employees out of work. Less than half of the theaters on Broadway are operating, and many union members are unemployed. Featherbedding rules require each theater to hire a specified number of employees, but these rules cannot dictate that theaters stay in business.

Because union staffing requirements are based on the number of seats in the theater, new shows have moved to smaller theaters off Broadway, shifting to the larger Broadway theaters only after their success seems assured. Producers have also reduced staffing requirements by simply reducing the number of seats that can be sold — in some cases by simply blocking off the balcony.

Sources: "Unions Are Losing Their Star Billing On Broadway," *Business Week*, 26 November 1984; Robert Lenzner, "Economics Is Dimming the Lights of Broadway," *Boston Globe*, 1 February 1987.

We have examined three ways in which unions can attempt to raise members' wages: (1) by negotiating a floor wage above the equilibrium wage for the industry and somehow rationing the limited jobs among union members, (2) by restricting the supply of labor, and (3) by increasing the demand for union labor. Unions can attempt to increase the demand for union labor in several ways: (1) through a direct public appeal to buy only union-made products, (2) by restricting the supply of products made by nonunion labor, (3) by making union labor more productive through lower turnover costs, and (4) through featherbedding, which forces employers to employ more workers than they would prefer.

UNION OBJECTIVES

Thus far we have assumed that unions attempt to maximize wages. Although this appears to be a reasonable assumption, union behavior at times seems to suggest other possible objectives, which we will explore in this section. Keep in mind during this discussion, however, that unions may adopt a variety of goals, depending on the circumstances, so no single model can capture all the variation.

Maximize Employment

Let's turn to the market for a particular type of labor. In Exhibit 3, the demand curve is labeled D and the supply curve is labeled S. Without a union, the competitive market wage is W and the equilibrium quantity of labor is E. Firms in this industry are price takers in the resource market. Now suppose workers in the industry form a union. Consider the alternative wage and employment policies the union could adopt.

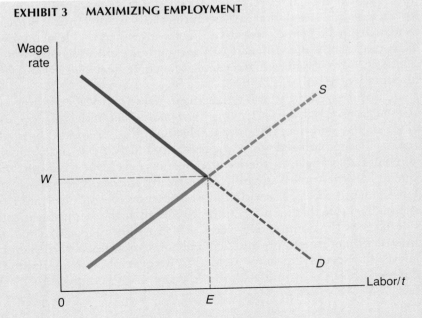

EXHIBIT 3   MAXIMIZING EMPLOYMENT

W is the equilibrium wage. At any other wage, employment is either the quantity demanded or the quantity supplied, whichever is less. Employment is maximized at E when the wage rate is at equilibrium.

The union could attempt to *maximize the number of workers employed in the industry*. In Exhibit 3, employment is maximized at E when the competitive wage, W, is selected. Any wage higher than W lowers employment, since the quantity demanded is reduced, and any wage below W lowers employment, since the quantity supplied is reduced. The relevant portions of the supply and demand curves are drawn as solid lines (in contrast to the broken lines for the rest of the curves) to underscore the dominance of what is called the "short side" of the market. Note that at a wage above W, the demand curve determines employment, and at a wage below W, the supply curve determines employment. *So the competitive wage rate maximizes employment, but the workers do not need a union to achieve this objective.*

Maximize the Wage Bill

*Employment multiplied by the wage rate is the **total wage bill**.*

Another possible objective for the union is to maximize the **total wage bill**, which is employment multiplied by the wage rate. Consider the union as a monopoly seller of labor to firms that are price takers. To induce firms to hire additional labor, the union must lower the wage. But as the union lowers the wage, the wage earned by those workers who were already employed in the industry must also fall. As a result, the union's *marginal revenue* will always be less than the wage.

The union's marginal revenue (MR) curve in Exhibit 4 shows how much the total wage bill changes for each one-unit change in employment. As long as the marginal revenue curve is positive, lower wages will increase the total wage bill. Recall that as long as the elasticity of demand is greater than one, marginal revenue is positive. Therefore, when the demand for labor is elastic, a lower wage will increase the total wage bill. When labor demand is inelastic, however, marginal revenue is negative, so a lower wage will reduce the total wage bill.

Consider again the wage that maximizes total wages in this example. *The total wage bill is maximized where marginal revenue is equal to zero*, so a wage floor of W^* will maximize the total wage bill. Put another way, the total wage bill is maximized where the elasticity of labor demand is equal to one, which is at point b on the labor demand curve. But the floor wage that maximizes the total wage bill in this example creates an excess supply of labor, identified as bc, so jobs must somehow be rationed among union members. Note that in this example the wage that maximizes the total wage bill exceeds the competitive wage, which is the wage associated with the intersection of the supply and demand curves at point a. If the labor supply curve intersected the labor demand curve at point b in Exhibit 4, the competitive wage would also be the wage that maximized the total wage bill.

Maximize Economic Rent

Some observers have suggested that *union leaders attempt to maximize the difference between the market wage and the opportunity cost of workers' time in its best*

EXHIBIT 4   MAXIMIZING THE TOTAL WAGE BILL

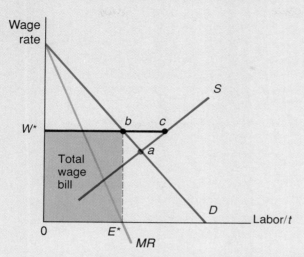

A union that is interested in maximizing the total wage bill paid to its members should negotiate wage W^*. With employment at E^*, the union's marginal revenue is zero. Further increases in employment will cause the wage bill to decrease. Wage W^* is read off the labor demand curve at point *b*. There is excess labor supply at that wage.

alternative use — that is, to maximize the *economic rent* earned by union workers. This approach explicitly takes each member's opportunity cost into account. (Recall that the total earnings of any resource can be divided between the amount necessary to attract the resource to a particular use, called transfer earnings, and any payment over and above transfer earnings, called economic rent.) The labor supply curve represents the minimum amount workers must be paid to "transfer," or to supply, each additional unit of labor. The height of the supply curve at each level of employment represents workers' opportunity cost of providing that marginal unit of employment.

For example, the labor supply curve in Exhibit 5 shows that only 10,000 hours of labor are supplied at a wage of $5 per hour because at that wage most workers have higher-paying alternatives. If the wage increases to $7.50 per hour, however, an additional 10,000 hours are supplied by workers whose opportunity cost is greater than $5 but less than $7.50. All workers who would have supplied their labor at a wage of $5 earn an economic rent of at least $2.50 when the wage is $7.50.

In order to maximize economic rent, the union should expand employment until the marginal revenue from supplying additional units of labor equals the opportunity cost of supplying those additional units of labor. In Exhibit 5 the union's marginal revenue curve and the labor supply curve intersect at point *a*, where the opportunity cost of time, or transfer earnings,

EXHIBIT 5   MAXIMIZING ECONOMIC RENT

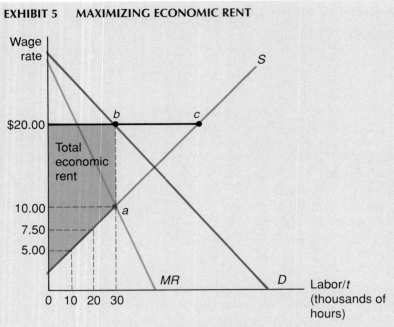

At point a the union's marginal revenue curve intersects the labor supply curve. The corresponding employment level (here, 30,000 hours) maximizes economic rent to employed workers. However, there is excess supply at the corresponding wage rate (here, $20 per hour).

is $10 per hour, and the quantity supplied is 30,000 hours. The rent-maximizing wage rate of $20 is found at point *b* on the labor demand curve. If the union leaders can negotiate a wage floor of $20 per hour, the economic rent earned on the last unit of labor employed is the wage rate of $20 minus the opportunity cost of the last unit hired, $10. So at a floor wage of $20 per hour, each employed worker earns at least $10 per hour in economic rent.

The total economic rent is reflected by the blue shaded area above the supply curve but below the floor wage of $20. This economic rent represents pure gravy to the workers because it reflects a payment over and above their opportunity cost—it is a payment over and above their transfer earnings, the amount required to attract each additional unit of labor to this market.

There are problems with the rent-maximizing solution, however. Unions are made up of a variety of workers with different backgrounds and different opportunity costs, so it probably would be difficult for a union to pursue such a well-defined objective as rent maximization. And even if rent maximization were achieved, there would be a large excess supply of labor at the floor wage (*bc* in Exhibit 5), which would create much frustration among union members. Nonetheless, it is still useful to assume that one union goal is rent maximization, because this assumption allows us to compare unions to profit-maximizing monopolists.

This section explored several possible union goals other than simply maximizing the wage, including maximizing (1) employment, (2) the total wage bill, and (3) economic rent. A competitive market accomplishes the first goal naturally — without unions. The second goal is achieved by finding the wage floor that equates the union's marginal revenue to zero. As we've just seen, achieving the third goal — maximizing the economic rent received by union members — requires union leaders to negotiate the wage floor that equates the union's marginal revenue to the opportunity cost of the last unit hired. But achieving either the second or third goal is likely to create excess supply, requiring the union to ration jobs. Thus unions may adopt a variety of goals, depending on the circumstances.

Some analysts believe union officials pursue wage-employment strategies that ensure the survival and growth of the union, keep most union members happy, and keep the leadership in office. Recent empirical work on union goals suggests that whatever their goals, unions appear to be sensitive to the tradeoff between the wage level and the employment level.

RECENT TRENDS IN UNION MEMBERSHIP AND BARGAINING POWER

Picture, if you will, a typical union member at work. You probably imagine a blue-collar worker with a hard hat, tending a steel furnace or perhaps working on an assembly line. This conception may have been accurate at one time, but such a worker is no longer typical. Only one in three union workers is in the goods-producing sector, and even fewer union members are in the heavy industries, such as autos and steel. A more typical union member these days is a schoolteacher.

In 1955 about one-third of nonfarm wage and salary workers belonged to unions. Union membership as a percentage of the work force declined during the 1960s, 1970s, and 1980s, so by 1988 only one-sixth of nonfarm wage and salary workers belonged to unions. Union membership rates are highest among government employees, over one-third of whom are unionized, and lowest among service workers in the private sector, less than 10 percent of whom belong to unions.

The decline in union membership in recent decades is due in part to structural changes in the economy. Unions have long been more important in the industrial sector than in the service sector. But employment in the industrial sector, including manufacturing and mining, declined from one-third of the work force in 1960 to one-quarter in 1988. During the same interval, service employment increased from 58 percent to over 70 percent of the work force.

The bar graph in Exhibit 6 indicates recent union membership rates by age and sex. The rates for men, indicated by the blue shaded bars, are higher than the rates for women, in part because men tend to be employed more in manufacturing and women more in the service sector. The highest membership rates are for middle-aged males. Though the exhibit does not show

EXHIBIT 6   UNION MEMBERSHIP AS A PERCENT OF TOTAL WAGE AND SALARY EMPLOYMENT BY AGE AND GENDER FOR 1988

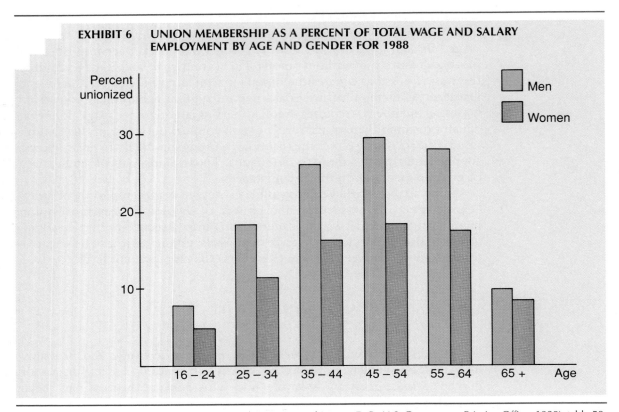

Source: U.S. Department of Labor, *Employment and Earnings* (Washington, D.C.: U.S. Government Printing Office, 1989), table 59.

it, blacks have a higher union membership rate than whites, in part because blacks are more often employed by government and heavy industries such as autos and steel, where the membership rate tends to be higher.

Compared with those of other industrialized countries, the United States' union participation rate of about 17 percent is relatively low. In Sweden over 95 percent of the nonfarm wage and salary workers are unionized. In Australia 56 percent are unionized. About half the work forces in both Britain and Italy are unionized. The rate in West Germany is 43 percent, and in the Netherlands and Canada, 35 percent. Japan and France have a rate of 28 percent.

Let's examine recent developments that have contributed to current trends in unionization in the United States.

Public Employee Unions

Union membership among public employees climbed sharply during the 1970s but leveled off during the 1980s. With increased membership in public employee unions has come the ticklish problem of strikes by such groups. Whereas some consumers suffer modest inconveniences if, say, auto workers go on strike, a strike by police personnel or fire fighters could jeopardize public safety. Most states have passed laws restricting strikes by public employees. The issue of public employee strikes was dramatized in 1981, when the Professional Air Traffic Controllers Organization (PATCO) called a strike. As federal employees, they were prohibited by law from striking, and they were fired by President Reagan. The firings sent a strong signal to other public employee unions. We examine the event more closely in the following case study.

CASE STUDY

PATCO's Billion-Dollar Gamble

On August 3, 1981, PATCO struck for higher wages and better working conditions. PATCO's strike was a big gamble because, by undertaking an illegal strike, union members put at risk secure jobs that at the time paid an average of $35,000 per year (which amounts to about $50,000 in 1990 dollars). PATCO made three major demands: a $10,000 across-the-board raise for all controllers, a 32-hour work week, and retirement after 20 years of service at 75 percent of the retiree's highest pay. President Reagan warned the controllers that unless they returned to work by August 5, they would be fired. True to his word, the President fired the 11,345 controllers who ignored the back-to-work ultimatum.

The graph in Exhibit 7 crudely approximates the market for air traffic controllers. In the absence of a union, the equilibrium wage and employment level would have been W and E, respectively. PATCO, however, had been able to force the wage floor up to an average of $35,000 per year for the 15,000 controllers, an attractive salary for a job that requires no college education. As you can see, there was excess supply at the prevailing wage. The overwhelming number of applications from people wishing to replace the striking controllers (over 200,000 people applied for the 11,345 openings) was evidence of the excess supply.

The supply curve represents the opportunity cost of offering labor services as an air traffic controller. The opportunity cost for the last worker hired, identified as C in Exhibit 7, was below the actual wage paid. Given the narrow nature of their job experience and the fact that most controllers had no college degree, their alternatives probably paid much less than a controller's salary. The shaded area is a rough approximation of the economic rent earned by air traffic controllers. Those who were fired lost this economic rent.

Fired workers paid a very high price for their strike. What was their best alternative wage? A survey of 900 former controllers showed that about 60 percent had annual *household* incomes, which include the earnings of spouses, of less than $25,000 three years after the strike. Thus we can conservatively estimate that in 1981 the average alternative wage was about $20,000, implying an average economic rent of $15,000 per ex-controller, for a total annual economic rent of $170 million; this stream of economic rent has a present value of about $2 billion.

There is more to the job than money, however. If the best alternative was an easier, more pleasant job, the dollar difference in pay would have over-

EXHIBIT 7   LABOR MARKET FOR AIR TRAFFIC CONTROLLERS

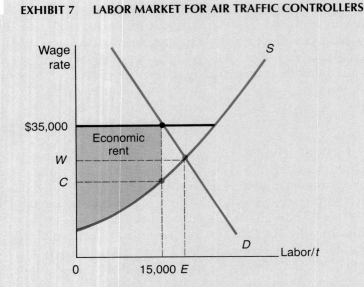

In the absence of a union, the equilibrium wage and employment level would have been *W* and *E*. At the negotiated wage of $35,000 per year, 15,000 PATCO controllers were employed. The corresponding economic rent was about $170 million.

stated the true economic rent of the job. But most air traffic controllers apparently enjoyed the tension and the prestige associated with the job. As one former controller lamented, "It's hard to get out of your blood. It's the most exciting thing that most of us will ever do." Many said that guiding traffic produced a deep sense of satisfaction. According to one researcher who has tracked many controllers since 1981, most have since found other work, "but they have suffered a substantial drop in income and prestige in occupation."

Source: Roger Lowenstein, "For Fired Air-Traffic Controllers, Life's OK, but Not Like Old Times," *Wall Street Journal*, 1 August 1986.

Competition from Nonunion Suppliers

Since the Middle Ages, craft unions have attempted to increase their wages by restricting output. Weavers from the city would sometimes make forays into the countryside to destroy looms and other weaving devices, thereby shutting off this competing source of labor. Competition from nonunion suppliers is still a major problem facing many unions today. Although unions usually can prevent existing employers from hiring nonunion workers, they cannot block the entry of new nonunion firms, nor can they always restrict imports. Since 1955, for example, U.S. imports have increased from 5 percent to 12 percent of GNP. The United Auto Workers has lost one-third of its membership since 1979 to foreign competition.

Even more troublesome to the UAW, three Japanese auto producers have established nonunion production facilities in the United States.

In competitive markets high-cost producers will not survive. Union membership among construction workers fell sharply over the last decade because many union members were unable to find union jobs. In the face of nonunion competition, these unions have been forced to make concessions over wages and work rules to compete. In some parts of the country, unions are permitting construction contractors to hire a larger proportion of apprentices, who are typically paid only half the union scale, and unions are allowing their members to work on the same jobs as nonunion members, which was unheard of a few years ago.

Industry Deregulation

For the last twenty years, the Teamsters Union has negotiated union wages for truckers through a national contract. Trucking regulations that blocked new entry into the industry and prevented existing firms from competing on the basis of price provided an environment conducive to union demands. But the deregulation of several major industries, including trucking, airlines, intercity bus lines, and telecommunications, has reduced the union's negotiating power in these industries.

Although the Teamsters Union can prevent unionized firms from hiring nonunion drivers, it cannot prevent other firms from entering the industry. The Motor Carrier Act of 1980 allows any existing or new trucking firm to operate on any route and to change rates on short notice. Deregulation of the trucking industry dropped the floor that had propped up the rates of all companies, both union and nonunion. The demise of regulation set off rate competition, leading to business failures and eliminating nearly one-third of the jobs controlled by the Teamsters. Since deregulation, more than 10,000 low-cost, nonunion operators have entered the industry, nearly doubling the number of nonunion carriers. The union was obliged to give up its automatic cost-of-living adjustment and to agree to a lower wage for new employees, creating a *two-tiered wage structure*.

Unionization and Technological Change

Some blue-collar workers, such as members of the United Mine Workers, have lost jobs as a result of automation. With employment stagnant in the so-called smokestack industries, the union movement looked to emerging high-technology areas as a source of new membership. Unions made a special effort in the 1970s and 1980s to organize high-tech workers but were largely unsuccessful. Aside from some defense contractors, the electronics industry remains mostly nonunion. Union organizers could not deal with the high job turnover created by the rapid entry and exit of firms in the high-technology industries. Moreover, progressive managers in many high-tech firms encouraged worker participation and often provided lavish bonuses and perks. Thus the workers in such firms were not good prospects for unionization.

Government's Safety Net

In the last thirty years, the federal government has broadened worker protection against unfair dismissal, plant closings, worker injuries, and unemployment. Social Security, medicare, and other government transfer programs buffer workers from the ravages of poor health and old age. *As government provides a broader menu of social insurance, workers feel less compelled to rely on unions for protection.*

The Urge to Merge

With their membership shrinking, unions have adopted new tactics in an attempt to ensure their survival. One alternative has been to merge with other unions. Mergers can reduce costs per member by spreading out expenses for staff and headquarters, and the larger membership can enhance the union's political clout. Some unions have even resorted to unfriendly takeovers of rival unions. Since 1980 there have been more than thirty union mergers. One problem with the merger solution is that the interests of the resulting organization may be seriously divided. An unlikely marriage between the Pottery Workers Union and the Seafarers International Union lasted only eighteen months before different interests caused the parties to part.

CONCLUSION

When unions first appeared in our nation's history, working conditions were dreadful. Hours were long, pay was low, and workplaces were hazardous. The last century brought revolutionary improvements in the conditions of the average worker. The real income of workers increased many times over, the workplace grew safer, and the workweek became much shorter. We cannot credit all these improvements to the development of organized labor. The growth in labor productivity supported higher wages and better benefits. But the labor movement clearly focused attention on the problems and helped develop the political consensus to introduce employee-oriented legislation. Although union members were always a minority of the work force, never exceeding one-third of the total, just the threat of unionization encouraged some nonunion employers to match benefits available in unionized firms. So the effects of unions spilled over to nonunion firms.

At one time, because of government regulations, foreign trade restrictions, and the lack of competition from nonunion firms, unions dominated some industries. But deregulation, technological change, and growing competition from nonunion firms both here and abroad have seriously challenged union positions in industries such as steel, autos, trucking, airlines, and construction. As markets grow more competitive, employers have a harder time passing higher union labor costs along to consumers. Unions to some extent have become victims of their own success.

Summary

1. The formation of labor unions in the United States was in part a response to long hours and poor working conditions in the nineteenth and the early twentieth century. Unions received a boost from government during the Great Depression, when several laws were passed to improve unions' legal standing.

2. Unions and employers attempt to negotiate a mutually agreeable labor contract through collective bargaining. A major source of the unions' power is the threat of a strike, which is an attempt to withhold labor from the firm.

3. Inclusive, or industrial, unions attempt to establish a floor wage that exceeds the free market wage. But a wage above the market-clearing wage creates an excess supply of labor, so the union must somehow ration jobs among its members. Exclusive, or craft, unions try to raise the wage by restricting the supply of

labor. Another way to raise union wages is to increase the demand for union labor.

4. Unions may pursue goals other than maximizing the wage. The maximization of employment occurs as a result of natural market forces and requires no union. Unions can attempt to maximize the total wage bill paid to union members or to maximize total economic rent, but these policies usually create an excess supply of labor, requiring job rationing. No single goal accounts for all union behavior.

5. Union membership as a percentage of the labor force has been decreasing for several decades. In 1988 only about one-sixth of the nonfarm labor force was unionized, compared to one-third in 1955. Unions' problems have included competition from nonunion workers, competition from imports, industry deregulation, a greater public safety net, and technological change.

Questions and Problems

1. (Labor History) What historical reasons can be given for the development of labor organizations?

2. (Unions and the Law) Why was the passage of federal laws rather than state or local laws important to the large labor organizations, such as the AFL-CIO?

3. (Strikes) How might a large company protect itself against a protracted strike? Use coal mining as an example in your answer.

4. (Strikes) Why would strikes be most effective in industries where there were very high fixed costs?

5. (Unions and Employee Benefits) Why have past tax laws encouraged unions to ask for higher employee benefits rather than just higher wages?

6. (Union Behavior) Will economic rents for union workers increase if unions are successful in raising the demand for the products the workers produce? Will transfer earnings also increase? Why or why not?

7. (Union Behavior) Show that maximizing the wage bill always leads to greater employment than maximizing economic rent.

8. (Unions and Business) Why might unions and business lobby together in Washington, D.C., to protect the industry from foreign competition? Who would oppose such lobbying?

9. (Wage Bill Maximization) Use the data below to answer the following questions.

Quantity of Labor	Marginal Revenue Product
0	—
1	$50
2	45
3	40
4	33
5	20
6	5
7	0

a. If the firm's supply of labor is perfectly elastic at $20, how much labor will get hired?

b. What labor price would maximize the total wage bill?

c. Who gains and who loses if a union succeeds in changing the labor price to the level you calculated in part b?

10. (Wage Differentials) Using supply-demand diagrams, show what happens to wage differentials between unionized and non-unionized sectors of the labor force when the union negotiates a wage rate for the unionized sector that is above the labor-market equilibrium.

11. (Union Behavior) Using a supply-demand diagram for labor, compare the effects on wages and employment in a unionized industry of each of the following:
   a. Conducting a "Buy American" plan
   b. Featherbedding
   c. Negotiating a minimum wage above the market-clearing wage

APPENDIX
Bilateral Monopoly

Throughout the chapter we assumed that wages are determined through negotiations between the labor union and the entire industry. Since each firm hires labor as a price taker in the labor market, each firm can hire as much labor as it chooses at the negotiated wage. The model of a union bargaining with the entire industry describes much of what is observed in labor markets.

On occasion, however, negotiations are between a union and an employer that is the only demander of the union's labor, or a **monopsonist**. The employer in this case is a price searcher in the labor market. *A monopsonist faces a labor supply curve that slopes upward.* For simplicity, we begin by examining the situation of this resource price searcher in the absence of a union, as depicted in Exhibit 8. The labor supply curve, S, determines the wage the firm must pay at each level of employment; the marginal resource cost curve for labor is above the labor supply curve. In the absence of a union, the profit-maximizing firm will hire labor up to the point where labor's marginal resource cost equals its marginal revenue product. In Exhibit 8, the profit-maximizing level of employment is E, and the profit-maximizing wage as found on the supply curve is W.

Thus *a profit-maximizing monopsonist pays nonunionized labor a wage below labor's marginal revenue product.* In the absence of a union, workers have little power in dealing with the employer. A worker can only decide whether or not to work for the firm at the wage offered by the employer. Workers whose opportunity cost is at or below W will work for the firm; those with a higher opportunity cost will not.

In contrast, the union, as a monopoly supplier of labor to the firm, has some power to negotiate the wage. The union's power rests in its willingness and ability to withhold all labor—to strike—if the employer does not comply. Thus both sides have some economic power: the firm as the only employer of this

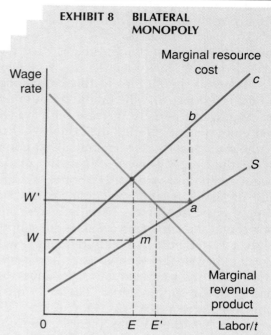

EXHIBIT 8   BILATERAL MONOPOLY

If a monopsonist faces a nonunionized workforce, the profit-maximizing employment level occurs where the marginal resource cost curve intersects the marginal revenue product curve. At that level of employment, E, the equilibrium wage, W, is found at point m, which lies on the red labor supply curve, S. If the monopsonist faces a unionized workforce and the union can establish a wage floor, such as W', the labor supply curve consists of the green horizontal line $W'a$ plus the upward-sloping segment aS on the red supply curve. The monopsonist's marginal resource cost curve consists of the line segments $W'a$, ab, and bc. The monopsonist maximizes profits by operating where the marginal resource cost of labor is equal to its marginal revenue product, which yields an employment level E' at the floor wage W'.

type of labor, and the union as the only supplier of this type of labor. The union will try to push wages up, and the profit-maximizing firm will try to pay no more than it has to for a given amount of labor. **Bilateral monopoly** describes the situation in which a single seller, in this case a union, bargains with a single buyer, or monopsonist. Since both sides have some power, the wage will depend on the relative bargaining skills of each side. Economic theory alone cannot predict what the agreed-upon wage will be.

Of special significance in this bargaining model is the fact that the union, by pushing up wages, can initially increase both wages *and* employment. Notice in Exhibit 8 that without unions, workers are initially at point *m* on their supply curve. When the union negotiates a floor wage of W', both the wage and the level of employment increase. The supply curve for union labor now remains horizontal at the bargained wage until supply level *a* is reached. For employment levels greater than *a*, the supply curve is the upward-sloping line segment *aS*. Thus the union's labor supply curve is $W'aS$, with a kink at point *a*.

Given this kinked supply curve, the monopsonist's marginal resource cost curve for labor consists of two separate segments. For quantities of labor less than *a*, the marginal resource cost curve is given by the horizontal segment, $W'a$, which is the floor wage. Within this range of employment, the firm can hire more labor at the floor wage, so the marginal resource cost is constant and equal

to that wage. For employment levels greater than *a*, the labor supply curve slopes upward, so hiring another unit of labor means paying a higher wage to all workers. Thus, for labor quantities greater than *a*, that portion of the marginal resource cost above the supply curve becomes the relevant segment.

The *marginal resource cost curve* is therefore indicated by the line segments $W'a$, *ab*, and *bc*. The kink in the labor supply curve creates a gap in the firm's marginal resource cost curve as reflected by the dashed line segment, *ab*. In Exhibit 8, the intersection of the firm's marginal resource cost curve for labor and its marginal revenue product curve for labor yields a wage of W' and employment of E'. In this example, both the wage and the level of employment are greater with a union than without.

In summary, when a labor union negotiates with the main employer of that type of labor, a bilateral monopoly exists. The resulting wage will depend on the relative bargaining strength and skills of each side. When a labor union negotiates with a monopsonist, both the wage rate and the employment level can be increased over the levels achieved in the absence of a union.

Appendix Questions

1. (Bilateral Monopoly) What is the marginal resource cost curve for a monopsonist that faces collective bargaining with a union?

2. (Bilateral Monopoly) Refer to Exhibit 8 to answer the following questions.

   a. Show the gains and losses to the employee and the employer if workers receive the union-negotiated wage W' rather than the nonunion wage W.
   b. What wage rate is the economically efficient wage? Why?

C H A P T E R   2 8

Capital and Entrepreneurial Ability

So far the discussion of resources has focused primarily on labor. This emphasis is appropriate since labor income represents more than three-quarters of all resource income. The returns to labor, however, depend largely on the amount and quality of the other resources employed. A farmer driving a huge tractor is more productive than one who scrapes the soil with a stick. In this chapter we discuss the returns to nonlabor resources, particularly capital and entrepreneurial ability. As we will see, entrepreneurial ability is in many ways the most important resource for determining the wealth of nations, but it is also the most elusive.

One problem that crops up in discussions of resources is that economists sometimes use the same term in slightly different ways or to define different things. For example, the term *interest* is used to mean both the amount earned for lending money and the return earned by capital as a resource. Another term that can be a source of confusion is *rent*. Earlier we distinguished between transfer earnings, the payment necessary to attract a resource to a particular use, and economic rent, the surplus over transfer earnings. Economic rent is not strictly required to keep a resource in a particular use. Often we refer to the return on land as rent, because land is typically thought to be in fixed supply and the return on a resource in fixed supply consists entirely of economic rent. Describing the return on land as rent is quite appropriate, but that particular meaning of rent will not receive special treatment in this chapter. Topics discussed in this chapter include

- Time, consumption, and production • Market for loans

- Roundabout production   • Present value and discounting

- Optimal investment   • Theories of profit

- Investing in human capital

THE ROLE OF TIME IN CONSUMPTION
AND PRODUCTION

Time plays an important role in both production and consumption. In this section we will first consider the effect of time on the production decision and show why firms are willing to pay for the use of household savings. Next we will consider time in the consumption decision and show why households must be rewarded for deferring consumption, or saving. Then, bringing together the desires of borrowers and the desires of savers, we will look at the equilibrium rate of interest.

Production, Saving, and Time

Suppose Old MacDonald is a primitive farmer. Isolated from any neighbors or markets, he literally scratches out a living on a plot of land, using only crude sticks as farm implements. While a crop is growing, none of it is available for present consumption. Since production takes time, MacDonald must rely on food saved from prior production to support himself during the time required to grow the crop. The longer the growing season lasts, the more savings required. Thus, even in this simple example, it is clear that *production cannot occur without savings.*

Suppose that with his current inputs, consisting of land, labor, and some crude sticks, Old MacDonald grows about 100 bushels of corn per year. He soon realizes that if he had a plow — a type of investment good, or capital — his productivity would increase. Making a plow is a major undertaking in such a crude setting, however. That task would keep Old MacDonald away from the fields for a year. Thus the plow has an opportunity cost of 100 bushels of corn. Old MacDonald will be unable to institute this temporary drop in production unless he has saved enough food from previous harvests to allow him to forgo the annual crop.

During the time required to produce capital, Old MacDonald must rely on his savings from prior production. Should Old MacDonald invest his time in the task of making the plow? The answer depends on the costs and benefits of the plow. We already know that the cost is 100 bushels — the forgone output. The benefit depends on how long the plow will last and how much it will increase crop production. Suppose Old MacDonald figures that the plow will last his lifetime and will increase production by 20 bushels per year. He must decide whether the benefit of increasing corn production by 20 bushels per year exceeds the opportunity cost of 100 bushels sacrificed to make the plow. The answer will depend on how strongly the farmer prefers present consumption over future consumption.

Roundabout production is the production of capital goods that can then be used to produce consumer goods.

If Old MacDonald makes the plow, he will be engaging in **roundabout production**. Roundabout production involves producing capital goods rather than consumer goods. These capital goods are then used to increase the production of consumer goods. An increased amount of roundabout production in an economy means that more capital accumulates, so more consumer (and capital) goods can be produced in the future. Advanced industrial economies are characterized by much roundabout production and abundant capital accumulation.

We have yet to discuss production in an economy with money or even with barter. Nonetheless, we have demonstrated why production cannot occur without savings. *Production requires savings because both direct and roundabout production require time—time during which goods and services are not available from current production.* Now let's modernize the example by introducing the ability to borrow. Many farmers visit the bank each spring to borrow enough "seed money" to support their families until their crops are produced and sold. Businesses often borrow at least a portion of the start-up funds needed to get going. Thus in a modern economy, production need not rely on each producer's prior savings. Banks and other financial institutions, by accepting deposits and then lending the accumulated funds, transfer money between savers and producers. Financial markets for trading stocks and bonds also help to channel savings to producers.

Consumption, Saving, and Time

Did you ever burn the roof of your mouth biting into a slice of pizza before it had cooled sufficiently? Have you done this more than once? Why does such self-mutilation persist? It persists because that bite of pizza is worth more to you now than the same bite five minutes from now. In fact, you are even willing to risk burning your mouth rather than wait until the pizza has lost its destructive properties. In a small way this phenomenon reflects the fact that you and other consumers value *present* consumption more than *future* consumption: you and other consumers have a **positive rate of time preference**.

A positive rate of time preference means that present consumption is valued more than future consumption.

Because present consumption is valued more than future consumption, you are willing to pay a higher price to consume something now rather than later. And prices often reflect this greater willingness to pay. Consider the movies. You pay more if you go to see a movie at a first-run theater than if you wait until it shows up at other theaters. (If you are very patient, you can wait to see it on TV.) The same is true for books. If you are willing to wait until a new book is available in paperback, you can usually buy it for less than one-third of the hardback price. Photo developers, dry cleaners, and fast food restaurants tout the speed of their services, knowing that consumers are willing to pay more for this earlier availability, other things constant.

Because present consumption is valued more than future consumption, households must be rewarded if they are to postpone consumption; in other words, saving must be rewarded. By saving their money in financial institutions such as banks, households refrain from spending a portion of their income on present consumption in return for the promise of a greater ability to consume in the future. Interest is the reward offered to households to forgo present consumption. Specifically, the **interest rate** is the amount of money earned by savers for giving up the use of $1 for a year. If the interest rate is 10 percent, a saver earns $0.10 per year for each dollar saved in a financial institution.

The greater the interest rate, other things constant, the more consumers are rewarded for saving, so the greater the opportunity cost of present consumption in terms of future consumption. For example, at an interest rate of 5 percent, a household can place $100 in an account and end up with $105 a year from now. So $100 worth of consumption today has an opportunity cost of $105 in consumption a year from now. At an interest rate of 10 percent, $100 worth of consumption today has an opportunity cost of $110 in consumption a year from now.

Consequently, the greater the interest rate offered for saving, other things constant, the greater the quantity of money households are willing to save. Banks pay interest on consumer savings because the banks can, in turn, lend these savings to those who need money, such as farmers, at the higher interest rate. The banks play the role of *financial intermediaries* in what is known as the market for loanable funds. The **loanable funds market** brings together savers, or suppliers of loanable funds, and borrowers, or demanders of loanable funds, to determine the market rate of interest. The **supply of loanable funds** reflects the positive relation between the market rate of interest and the quantity of savings, as shown by the upward-sloping supply curve in Exhibit 1.

*The **interest rate** is the amount paid for the use of a dollar for one year.*

*The **loanable funds market** brings together savers, or suppliers of loanable funds, and borrowers, or demanders of loanable funds, to determine the market rate of interest.*

*The **supply of loanable funds** reflects the positive relation between the market rate of interest and the quantity of savings supplied to the economy.*

Optimal Investment

In a market economy characterized by specialization and exchange, Old MacDonald no longer has to produce his own capital, nor does he have to rely on his own savings. He can invest in capital using borrowed funds. Also, current production can be financed with current, rather than past, savings when the borrowers and savers are different entities.

Suppose Old MacDonald is interested in buying a tractor. There are many sizes of tractors on the market, from the small garden variety to giants. Column (1) of Exhibit 2(a) lists the available sizes in 40-horsepower increments, from the smallest to the largest. The total and marginal physical products of each tractor are listed in columns (2) and (3). Note that other resources are constant (in this case, the farmer's labor, land, seeds, and fertilizer).

Without capital, Old MacDonald can grow 100 bushels of corn per year. The smallest tractor will allow him to double production to 200 bushels per year; thus the smallest size tractor has a marginal physical product of 100 bushels. With the next largest size, total output increases from 200 to 280 bushels, so the marginal physical product of that size tractor is 80 bushels. Note that in this example diminishing marginal returns set in almost imme-

EXHIBIT 1   SUPPLY OF LOANABLE FUNDS

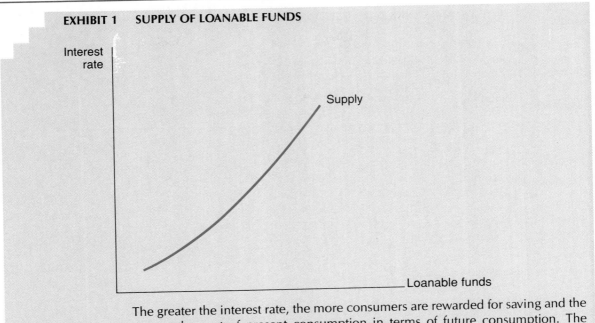

The greater the interest rate, the more consumers are rewarded for saving and the greater the cost of present consumption in terms of future consumption. The greater the interest rate, the greater consumers' willingness to save; the supply of loanable funds slopes upward.

diately. The marginal physical product continues to decrease as the tractors get larger, dropping to zero for the 240-horsepower tractor. Though the exhibit does not show it, the marginal physical product would be negative for tractors larger than 240 horsepower. (You might imagine a tractor so large that Old MacDonald would have trouble maneuvering it on his relatively small plot.)

Suppose Old MacDonald sells corn in a perfectly competitive market, so he is a price taker in the market for corn. He can sell all he wants at the market price of $4 per bushel. This price is multiplied by the marginal physical product from column (3) to yield each tractor's *marginal revenue product* in column (4).[1] The marginal revenue product in this example is the change in total revenue resulting from increasing the tractor size by 40 horsepower.

The purchase price of each tractor is listed in column (5). The smallest tractor sells for $1000, the next largest for $2000, and so on, the price increasing by $1000 with each 40-horsepower increase in size. Thus the marginal cost of buying a larger tractor is $1000, as listed in column (6).

---

[1] If the product is sold in a market where the firm has some market power, proper calculation of the marginal revenue product requires that the firm consider the impact of increased output on the product's price.

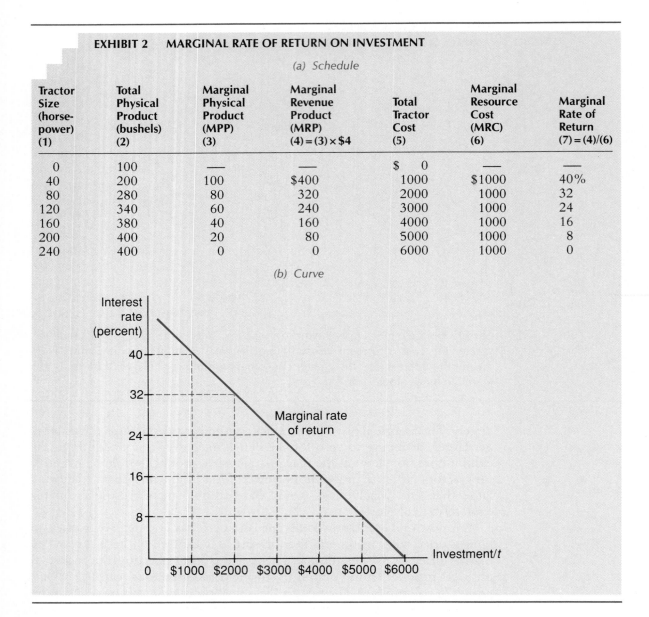

EXHIBIT 2   MARGINAL RATE OF RETURN ON INVESTMENT

(a) Schedule

Tractor Size (horse-power) (1)	Total Physical Product (bushels) (2)	Marginal Physical Product (MPP) (3)	Marginal Revenue Product (MRP) (4) = (3) × $4	Total Tractor Cost (5)	Marginal Resource Cost (MRC) (6)	Marginal Rate of Return (7) = (4)/(6)
0	100	—	—	$ 0	—	—
40	200	100	$400	1000	$1000	40%
80	280	80	320	2000	1000	32
120	340	60	240	3000	1000	24
160	380	40	160	4000	1000	16
200	400	20	80	5000	1000	8
240	400	0	0	6000	1000	0

(b) Curve

The ***marginal rate of return on investment*** *is equal to capital's marginal productivity (its marginal revenue product) as a percentage of the marginal expenditures on capital (its marginal resource cost).*

Suppose the tractors are so durable that they last indefinitely, that operating expenses are negligible, and that the price of corn is expected to remain at $4 per bushel in the future.

Old MacDonald must decide how much to invest in a tractor. The first task in determining the optimal investment is to compute the marginal rate of return that could be earned by investing in tractors of different sizes. Given the circumstances described thus far, the **marginal rate of return on investment** is equal to the capital's marginal productivity (its marginal revenue product) as a percentage of the marginal expenditure on capital (its marginal resource cost). The smallest tractor yields a marginal revenue product of $400 per year and has a marginal resource cost of $1000. Thus the smallest tractor has a marginal rate of return of $400/$1000, or 40 percent per year, as shown in column (7) of Exhibit 2(a). The next largest tractor has a marginal revenue product of $320 per year and a marginal cost of $1000, so the marginal rate of return equals $320/$1000, or 32 percent per year. By dividing the marginal revenue product of capital in column (4) by the marginal resource cost of that capital in column (6), we get the marginal rate of return on investment in column (7). The data in column (7) are depicted in Exhibit 2(b) as a downward-sloping curve which reflects the marginal rate of return on investment.

Given the marginal rate of return, how much should Old MacDonald invest? Suppose he must borrow the money to invest. The amount he must pay to borrow depends on the *market rate of interest*, which is the rate of interest determined by the supply and demand for loanable funds. Old MacDonald will make the largest investment for which the marginal rate of return equals or exceeds the market rate of interest. For example, if the market rate of interest is 20 percent, Old MacDonald will invest $3000 in the 120-horsepower tractor. That size tractor yields a marginal return of 24 percent, a rate exceeding the 20 percent rate of interest on the borrowed funds. Investing another $1000 in the next largest tractor would yield a marginal return of only 16 percent, a rate below the cost of borrowing. If the market rate of interest dropped to 10 percent, the 160-horsepower tractor would become the most profitable investment. And if the interest rate dropped to 8 percent, Old MacDonald would buy the 200-horsepower tractor for $5000.

As long as the marginal rate of return on investment exceeds the market rate of interest, which is the marginal cost of borrowing, the farmer should increase the size of the tractor purchased. *Old MacDonald should increase his investment to the point where the marginal rate of return on that investment just equals the market rate of interest.* The marginal rate of return curve therefore shows how much will be invested at each interest rate. In other words, the marginal rate of return curve represents Old MacDonald's *demand curve for investment*.

Would the example change if Old MacDonald already had the money saved and did not need to borrow? Not as long as he can save at the market rate of interest. For example, if the market rate of interest were 8 percent, Old MacDonald would invest his savings in a tractor as long as the marginal rate of return on the investment equaled or exceeded the 8 percent rate earned on savings. Rather than invest in a tractor with a marginal return of less than 8 percent, Old MacDonald would leave his money in savings, where it could earn the market rate of 8 percent. Thus as long as he can borrow and save at the same interest rate, Old MacDonald ends up with the same size tractor whether he uses borrowed funds or his own savings.

The simplified principles developed here can be generalized to other firms. The major demanders of loans are firms that borrow to invest in capital goods, such as machines, trucks, and buildings. At any time each firm has a variety of possible investment opportunities. These opportunities can be ranked by each firm from best to worst based on their expected marginal rates of return. Firms will finance all investments whose expected rates of return exceed the market rate of interest; they will increase their investment until their expected marginal rate of return just equals the market rate of interest. When other inputs are held constant, as they were on Old Mac-Donald's farm, the demand for investment slopes downward.

Let's review the procedure used to determine the optimal amount of investment. First, compute the marginal revenue product of the investment. Next, determine the marginal rate of return on the investment; this can be done for our simple example by dividing its marginal revenue product by its marginal resource cost. The firm will increase investment as long as the marginal rate of return on investment exceeds the market rate of interest. The market rate of interest represents the opportunity cost of investing either borrowed funds or savings. Finally, the marginal rate of return curve is the firm's demand for investment — that is, it shows the amount invested at each alternative interest rate.

Investing in Human Capital

The tractor has a substantial impact on the farmer's ability to produce. Similarly, education and training that improve the farmer's knowledge of farming also enhance productivity. Rather than invest in a larger tractor, Old MacDonald could invest in his own education — he could invest in human capital. For example, by taking agricultural courses at a nearby college, Old MacDonald could increase his knowledge of plant science, fertilizers, soil drainage, agricultural economics, and other subjects that would make him a more productive farmer.

Old MacDonald might read through the course descriptions and decide how valuable each course would be. Although the costs of investing in human capital are incurred when the courses are taken, the benefits come in the future as the new knowledge is applied. Old MacDonald might estimate the expected marginal rate of return for each course, then order the courses from most desirable to least desirable, based on their expected returns.

How many courses should Old MacDonald take? The answer depends on the expected marginal rate of return on each course and the market rate of interest. If Old MacDonald has enough savings to pay the cost of education, his opportunity cost will be the interest he could have earned on his savings, which will depend on the market rate of interest. If he borrows the funds, the annual cost, again, will depend on the market rate of interest. Old MacDonald should increase his course load as long as the marginal rate of return on human capital investment exceeds the market rate of interest. Investing in human capital can be analyzed the same way we analyzed investing in physical capital.

Note that in our simple model Old MacDonald must predict marginal rates of return for tractors and college courses. To do that, he must predict not only the marginal physical product of these investments but also the price of corn in the future. Because of technological change and other possible changes in market supply and demand, producers face an uncertain future, so the investment decision is often risky. In addition, our simple model assumes that Old MacDonald can borrow and save at the same interest rate. But financial intermediaries, such as banks, typically charge a higher interest rate to borrowers than they pay to lenders. Thus Old MacDonald would likely be charged more interest to borrow than he could earn on savings; consequently, investing with borrowed funds involves a higher opportunity cost. The point is that investment decisions are generally more complicated than the one presented here.

The Market Demand for Loans

We have now examined why firms are willing to pay interest to borrow money: money gives firms a command over resources that makes roundabout production possible. For the economy as a whole, if the supply of other resources and the level of technology are fixed, diminishing marginal productivity causes the marginal rate of return on investment — the demand for investment — to slope downward. The **demand for loanable funds** is based on the marginal rate of return these borrowed funds yield when invested in capital. Each firm has a downward-sloping demand for loanable funds, reflecting a declining marginal rate of return on investment. With some qualifications, firms' demands for loanable funds can be summed horizontally to yield the demand for loanable funds by all firms.

The **demand for loanable funds** reflects the negative relation between the market rate of interest and the quantity of loanable funds demanded.

But firms are not the only demanders of loanable funds. As we have seen, households value present consumption more than future consumption; they are often willing to pay extra to consume now rather than later. One way to ensure that goods and services are available now is to borrow money for present consumption. Mortgages, car loans, and credit card purchases are examples of household borrowing. The household's demand for loanable funds, like the firm's demand, slopes downward, reflecting consumers' greater ability and greater willingness to borrow at lower interest rates, other things constant. The government sector and the rest of the world may also be demanders of loanable funds. Thus the market demand curve for loanable funds, presented in Exhibit 3, is the total demand by firms, households, governments, and the rest of the world.

By bringing the supply and demand for loanable funds together, as in Exhibit 3, we can determine the market rate of interest. The equilibrium interest rate, i, is the only rate that will exactly match up the wishes of both borrowers and savers. Any change in the supply or demand for loanable funds will change the equilibrium rate of interest. For example, some technological breakthrough might increase the productivity of investment, thereby increasing its marginal rate of return and increasing the demand for loanable funds. The demand for loanable funds will shift out to the right, as shown in the movement from D to D' in Exhibit 3; an increase in the demand for loans raises the equilibrium rate of interest from i to i'.

EXHIBIT 3   MARKET FOR LOANABLE FUNDS

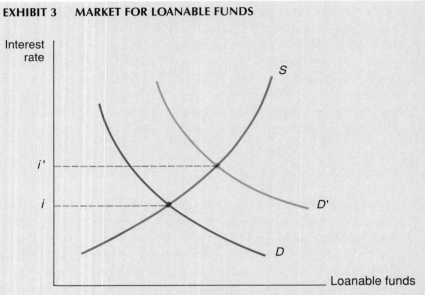

Because of the declining marginal rate of return on capital, the demand for loans is inversely related to the rate of interest. The equilibrium rate of interest, *i*, is determined at the intersection of the demand and supply curves for loans. An increase in the demand for loans from *D* to *D'* leads to an increase in the equilibrium rate of interest from *i* to *i'*.

Real Versus Nominal Interest Rates

Thus far we have discussed interest rates under the assumption that "other things are constant." One of the factors implicitly held constant has been the expected rate of inflation in the economy. Let's consider how a change in expected inflation affects the market for loanable funds. If the rate of inflation is expected to increase, savers will be less willing to save because each dollar they save will buy less in the future. Conversely, borrowers will be more willing to borrow because each dollar they repay will be worth less than the dollar they borrowed. Therefore an increase in the anticipated rate of inflation decreases the supply of loanable funds and increases the demand, thereby increasing the equilibrium **nominal rate of interest**. The nominal rate of interest — the rate of interest that appears on the loan agreement — is the interest rate discussed in the media. It measures the interest rate in terms of the actual dollars paid, even if the value of these dollars has been eroded by inflation.

*The **nominal rate of interest** is the interest rate expressed in current dollars — that is, dollars not adjusted for inflation.*

*The **expected real rate of interest** is the expected interest rate expressed in dollars of constant value — that is, dollars adjusted for expected inflation.*

If inflation is expected to be 6 percent, lenders must earn 6 percent interest just to maintain the same real purchasing power when the loan is repaid. The **expected real rate of interest** is the nominal rate of interest less the expected inflation rate; it measures the expected increase in the future purchasing power of savers when they forgo present consumption. For example, if the nominal rate is 10 percent and the expected inflation rate is 6 percent, the expected real rate of interest is 4 percent. If inflation is expected to be zero, the nominal rate of interest and the expected real rate are identical.

The realized real rate of interest is the nominal rate of interest minus the actual inflation rate.

Finally, the **realized real rate of interest** is the nominal rate of interest minus the actual inflation rate. The realized real rate of interest is not known until the loan is repaid. Given the nominal rate of interest, the higher the actual inflation rate, the lower the realized real rate of interest. *Economic decisions are based on the expected real rate of interest, not the realized real rate of interest.* If the rate of inflation is predicted accurately, the expected real rate of interest will equal the realized real rate of interest.

Why Interest Rates Differ

So far we have been talking about the market rate of interest, implying that only one interest rate prevails in the loanable funds market. At any particular time, however, a range of interest rates can be found in the market. Why? Let's consider some reasons.

The pure rate of interest is the interest rate on a risk-free loan.

Risk Some borrowers are more likely to repay their loans than others. Differences in the risk associated with various borrowers are reflected in differences in the interest rate negotiated. As a point of reference, the **pure rate of interest** is the rate charged on a risk-free loan. In the United States, the federal government is thought to be the most reliable borrower around, so the closest thing to a risk-free rate is the rate on funds borrowed by the federal government. As loans become more risky, the interest rate on these loans rises, reflecting the higher risk. For example, a bank would charge more interest on a loan to a new video rental store than on a loan to IBM.

The term structure of interest rates is the relation between the duration of a loan and the interest rate charged.

Duration of the Loan The future is uncertain, and the further into the future we try to predict, the more uncertain our predictions are. One source of uncertainty about a loan based on a fixed nominal rate of interest is the course of inflation. If the actual inflation rate exceeds the expected rate over the period of the loan, the purchasing power of repaid dollars will be lower than expected. The longer the period of repayment, the greater the risk of higher-than-expected inflation. Thus loans extended for longer periods usually carry a higher interest rate to compensate the lender for the greater risk of higher-than-expected inflation. The **term structure of interest rates** refers to the relationship between the duration of a loan and the interest rate charged. The term structure depends on expectations about inflation and on the supply and demand for loans with different maturity dates.

Cost of Administration The costs of executing the loan agreement, monitoring the conditions of the loan, and collecting the payments on the loan are called the *administration costs* of the loan. These costs as a proportion of the total cost of the loan decrease as the size of the loan increases. For example, the administration costs on a $100,000 loan will be less than ten times greater than the costs on a $10,000 loan. Consequently, that portion of the interest charge reflecting the cost of administering the loan will be smaller when the loan is larger. So the larger the loan, other things constant, the lower the interest rate.

Tax Treatment Differences in the tax treatment of different types of loans will also affect the market rate of interest. For example, the interest earned on funds loaned to state and local governments is not subject to federal income taxes. Since lenders are interested in their after-tax rate of interest, state and local governments can pay lower pre-tax interest rates than other borrowers.

PRESENT VALUE
AND DISCOUNTING

Because present consumption is valued more than future consumption, present and future consumption cannot be directly compared. A way of standardizing the discussion is to measure all consumption in terms of its present value. **Present value** is the current value of a payment or payments that will be received in the future. For example, how much would you pay now to acquire the right to receive $100 one year from now? Put another way, what is the present value of receiving $100 one year from now?

Present value is the value today of a payment to be received in the future.

Present Value of Payment One Year Hence

Suppose that the market interest rate is 10 percent, so you can either lend or borrow money at that rate. One way to determine how much you would pay for the right to receive $100 one year from now is to ask how much you would have to save, at the market rate of interest, to end up with $100 one year from now.

Here is the problem we are trying to solve: what amount of money, if saved at a rate of 10 percent, will accumulate to $100 one year from now? We can calculate the answer with a simple formula. Let PV stand for the unknown present value. We can say

$$\text{PV} \times 1.10 = \$100$$

or

$$\text{PV} = \frac{\$100}{1.10} = \$90.91$$

Thus $90.91 is the present value of receiving $100 one year from now; it is the most you would be willing to pay today to receive $100 one year from now. Rather than pay more than $90.91, you would simply deposit your $90.91 at the market rate of interest and end up with $100 a year from now.

Discounting *is the procedure of converting a sum of money to be received in the future into its present value. The interest rate used for this conversion is the* **discount rate**.

The procedure of dividing the future payment by 1 plus the prevailing interest rate in order to express it in today's dollars is called **discounting**. The interest rate that is used to discount future payments is called the **discount rate**.

The present value of $100 to be received one year from now depends on the interest rate used to discount that payment. *The higher the interest rate, or discount rate, the more the future payment is discounted and the lower its present value.* In other words, the higher the interest rate, the less you need to save now to yield a given amount in the future. For example, if the interest rate is 15 percent, the present value of receiving $100 one year from now is $100/1.15, which equals $86.96. Conversely, the lower the interest rate, or discount rate, the less the future income is discounted and the greater its present value. A lower interest rate means that you must save more now to yield a given amount in the future. As a general rule, the present value (PV) of receiving M dollars one year from now when the interest rate is i is

$$PV = \frac{M}{1+i}$$

For example, when the interest rate is 5 percent, the present value of receiving $100 one year from now is

$$PV = \frac{\$100}{1+0.05} = \frac{\$100}{1.05} = \$95.24$$

Present Value for Payments in Later Years

Now consider the present value of receiving $100 two years from now. What amount of money, if deposited at the market rate of interest of 5 percent, would yield $100 two years from now? Again, let PV represent the unknown amount of money. At the end of the first year, its value would be $PV \times 1.05$, which would then earn the market rate of interest during the second year. At the end of the second year, the deposit would have accumulated to $PV \times 1.05 \times 1.05$. Thus we have the equation

$$PV \times 1.05 \times 1.05 = PV \times (1.05)^2 = \$100$$

Solving for PV yields

$$PV = \frac{\$100}{(1.05)^2} = \frac{\$100}{1.1025} = \$90.70$$

If the $100 were to be received three years from now, we would discount the payment over three years:

$$PV = \frac{\$100}{(1.05)^3} = \$86.38$$

More generally, the present value formula for receiving M dollars in year t at interest rate i may be written as

$$PV = \frac{M}{(1 + i)^t}$$

Because $1 + i$ is greater than 1, the more times it is multiplied by itself, the greater the denominator will be. Thus *the present value of a given payment will diminish the further in the future that payment is to be received.*

Present Value of an Income Stream

The previous method is used to compute the present value of a single sum to be paid at some time in the future. Most investments, however, yield a stream of payments over time. In cases where the payments are to be made over a period of years, the present value of each payment can be computed individually, and then the results can be summed to yield the present value of the entire payment stream. For example, the present value of receiving $100 next year and $150 the year after is simply the present value of the first year's payment plus the present value of the second year's payment. If the interest rate is 5 percent, the present value equals

$$PV = \frac{\$100}{1.05} + \frac{\$150}{(1.05)^2} = \$231.29$$

Present Value of an Annuity

An **annuity** is a given sum of money received each year for a specified number of years.

A given sum of money received each year for a specified number of years is called an **annuity**. Such a payment is called a *perpetuity* if it continues indefinitely into the future, as it would in the earlier example of the productivity gain stemming from Old MacDonald's purchase of a tractor. The present value of receiving a certain amount forever seems like a very large sum indeed. But because payments are valued less the further in the future they are to be received, it turns out that the present value of receiving a particular amount forever is not much more than that of receiving it for, say, 20 years.

To determine the present value of receiving $100 each year forever, we need only ask how much money must be deposited in a savings account to yield $100 in interest per year. When the interest rate is 10 percent, a deposit of $1000 will earn $100 per year. Thus the present value of receiving $100 a year indefinitely when the interest rate is 10 percent is $1000. More generally, we can use the formula $PV = A/i$, where A is the amount received each year.

Old MacDonald, by increasing his tractor size from 160 to 200 horse-power, expected to earn $80 more per year from a marginal investment of $1000. Thus his marginal rate of return was 8 percent. At a market rate of interest of 8 percent, the present value of a cash flow of $80 discounted at 8 percent would be $80/0.08, which equals $1000. Thus, at the margin, Old MacDonald was willing to invest in capital an amount that would yield a cash stream with a present value just equal to the amount invested. To develop a better feel for present value and discounting, consider the following case study.

<table>
<tr><td>

CASE STUDY

The Million-Dollar Lottery?

</td><td>

Since New Hampshire introduced the first state-run lottery in 1964, many states have followed suit, and payoffs of millions of dollars are now common. As a winner of a million-dollar lottery, you might expect to be handed a check for a million dollars. Instead, you would typically be paid in installments, such as $50,000 per year for twenty years. Though this adds up to a total of a million dollars, you now know that such a stream has a present value of less than the advertised million. To put this payment schedule in perspective, keep in mind that at a discount rate of 10 percent, the $50,000 received in the twentieth year has a present value of only $7450. If today you deposited $7450 in an account earning 10 percent interest, you would wind up with $50,000 in twenty years.

At 10 percent the present value of a $50,000 annuity for the next twenty years is $425,700. Thus the present value of the actual payment stream is less than half of the promised million, which is the reason lottery officials pay it out in installments. Incidentally, we might consider the present value of receiving $50,000 per year forever. Using the formula $PV = A/i$, where A equals $50,000 and i equals 10 percent, we have $PV = \$50,000/0.10 = \$500,000$. Since the present value of receiving $50,000 for twenty years is $425,700, continuing the $50,000 annual payment indefinitely adds only $74,300 to the present value. This shows the dramatic effect of discounting on the present value of payments after year 20.

</td></tr>
</table>

This discussion of present value and discounting concludes our treatment of capital and interest. There remains only one more resource to discuss, a resource that in some respects is more important than any other: entrepreneurial ability. Entrepreneurial ability is the wellspring of economic vitality and the source of a rising standard of living.

ENTREPRENEURIAL ABILITY AND PROFIT

Though it is difficult to teach, some four hundred colleges now offer courses in it. Though it is difficult to measure, business publications look for it in all the rising stars whose success they track. And though it is difficult to analyze, new books on the topic appear almost daily. What is it? *Entrepreneurial ability.* Perhaps no other economic resource is more widely discussed yet so poorly understood. There is no market for entrepreneurial ability in the sense in which we usually think of markets. In fact, the reason firms are formed is because entrepreneurs believe they will be better off running their own firms than working for other firms. They are their own bosses—that is, they hire themselves—because there is no formal market for their special kind of ability.

An **entrepreneur** is a profit-seeking decision maker who organizes an enterprise and assumes the risk of the enterprise. *An entrepreneur establishes a firm, acquires the right to direct resources in that firm, assumes responsibility for paying these resources, and claims any profit or loss that is left over after all other resources have been paid.* The right to control resources does not necessarily mean that the entrepreneur must manage the firm. But the entrepreneur must have the power to hire and fire the manager; the entrepreneur must have the power to control the controller.

*An **entrepreneur** is a profit-seeking decision maker who organizes an enterprise and assumes the risk of the enterprise.*

The Entrepreneur Can Supply Other Resources

Recall that a firm's total revenue minus all the payments to resource owners other than the entrepreneur can be considered accounting profit. To arrive at economic profit, we must carefully subtract from accounting profit that portion of the entrepreneur's income that is a return for supplying resources other than entrepreneurial ability. To the extent that the entrepreneur provides any resources other than entrepreneurial ability, an implicit return should be assigned to those inputs based on what those resources could earn in resource markets.

For example, economic profit should exclude any salary to the entrepreneur for managing the firm. Managers can be viewed as another form of labor, albeit a rather special kind, and the manager's salary should not be confused with profit. The services of managers, like those of teachers and steelworkers, are bought and sold in the labor market. Similarly, any money invested by the entrepreneur in the firm should be assigned imputed interest equal to the market rate of interest paid on investments involving a comparable degree of risk—what we have referred to as a normal profit. Economic profit is then the amount over and above all of these imputed payments for resources supplied by the entrepreneur other than entrepreneurial ability. The net result can be an economic loss rather than an economic profit.

Imagine that a posh new restaurant called the Blue Beagle is opening in your community. Suppose that the founder of the Blue Beagle borrows money from a bank to start the restaurant and selects a manager to hire all other employees and to lease or buy a building, furniture, and everything else the operation requires. The entrepreneur promises to pay all these resource owners at least the market return for putting their resources under the manager's direction. Otherwise, these resources would go elsewhere. In the operation of the Blue Beagle, the entrepreneur, by hiring the manager and agreeing to pay all resource suppliers, supplies no resources other than entrepreneurial ability. The entrepreneur nonetheless controls the restaurant and is liable for its success or failure.

Since all the resources except entrepreneurial ability are either rented or hired, who is the Blue Beagle's owner and what does the owner own? The restaurant's owner is the entrepreneur. *The "firm" owned by the entrepreneur consists of a bundle of contracts or agreements between the entrepreneur and resource suppliers.* The entrepreneur has acquired the right to direct and control these resources in return for a promise to pay their owners a specified amount. At the end of the year, the entrepreneur can consider as economic profit whatever is left after all other resource suppliers have been paid. The entrepreneur is what we referred to earlier as the *residual claimant* — someone who claims the residual left over after all costs, both explicit and implicit, have been subtracted from revenues. If revenues fail to cover outlays, however, the entrepreneur is obliged to make up the shortfall. The entrepreneur is last in line to be paid and is the chief bag-holder should anyone be left holding the bag.

It is not the management of resources that distinguishes the entrepreneur; it is the control over the decision as to who manages resources. Even if the entrepreneur decided to serve as the restaurant's manager, the entrepreneur as manager would likely still delegate to the chef many decisions about resource use — which assistant chefs to hire, what ingredients to purchase, how to combine these ingredients. In fact, the entrepreneur could serve as the chef, maitre d', cashier, dishwasher or in whatever capacity was most needed at the time. Therefore, do not think entrepreneurs have to manage (though they often do); *entrepreneurs simply must have the power to appoint the manager and to claim the profit or loss that arises from the manager's decisions.*

Why Entrepreneurs Often Invest in the Firm

The entrepreneur rarely has the limited role described in the restaurant example. Entrepreneurs usually provide at least a portion of the funds required to start and maintain a business. Since it is not strictly necessary for the entrepreneur to provide resources in addition to entrepreneurial ability, why do entrepreneurs generally provide funds to the firm?

In our example the entrepreneur borrowed from the bank the funds necessary to finance the restaurant's operations. In reality a bank would be most reluctant to lend all of the funds required to start a firm, especially one as risky as a new restaurant. Although the entrepreneur would promise to repay the bank, the restaurant could go bankrupt. And, as noted in Chapter 4, under the corporate business structure, an entrepreneur's liability is limited to his or her own investment in the firm. Even if the firm were not incorporated, the entrepreneur, in the face of huge losses, could file for personal bankruptcy.

Because of the possibility of bankruptcy and default, lenders typically want entrepreneurs to supply additional resources to the firm. The entrepreneur's supply of funds to the firm reassures wary creditors in at least two ways. First, when the entrepreneur's own assets are tied up in the firm, the individual is likely to exercise greater care and vigilance in shepherding all the firm's resources, including the bank's funds. Second, the entrepreneur's investment in the firm — called owner's equity — serves as a buffer, providing creditors and other resource suppliers with some insulation against a default in the event that the firm's costs exceed its revenues in a particular year. Losses can be covered out of owner's equity rather than out of payments due to some other resource owner, such as the bank.

ENTREPRENEURSHIP AND THEORIES OF PROFIT

Profit plays an important role in a market economy because profit incentives direct the allocation of resources. Profit, therefore, deserves much attention. There is no single theory explaining the source of economic profit in the capitalist system. Rather, there are several theories of profit, each of which focuses on a different role played by the entrepreneur. Here we examine three entrepreneurial roles that represent potential sources of economic profit.

The Entrepreneur as Broker

Perhaps the simplest view of the entrepreneur is that of a broker whose aim is to "buy low and sell high." Entrepreneurs bid against one another for the available resources, and this bidding establishes market prices for the various resources. Entrepreneurs contract with resource suppliers and combine the resources to produce goods and services. The difference between what the entrepreneur pays for resources (including the opportunity cost of any other resources supplied by the entrepreneur) and the revenue received from sales equals the entrepreneur's economic profit. Thus entrepreneurs earn an economic profit by selling output for more than it costs to produce the output.

At the first sign of economic profit, however, other entrepreneurs will enter this industry. If markets are perfectly competitive, economic profit will be driven to zero in the long run, and entrepreneurs will earn just a normal rate of return on resources they supply to the firm, including their entrepreneurial ability.

The Entrepreneur as Risk Bearer

Some economists think of the profit earned by entrepreneurs as arising from the risk associated with venturing into a world filled with uncertainty. According to this theory of profit, a portion of the return received by entrepreneurs is a payment for their willingness to bear that risk. But the consideration of risk bearing as a source of economic profit gives rise to a more general treatment of risk and return for various resource owners. We can speak of two sources of risk for resource owners: (1) the risk of not getting paid after the resource is provided and (2) the risk of a drop in the market value of the resource.

Risk of Not Getting Paid Despite the entrepreneur's guarantees, resource suppliers, particularly suppliers of loans, often face the possibility of not being paid. If resource owners take a risk by turning the use of their resources over to the entrepreneur, they will require greater compensation than they would if their payment were assured. In this sense, resource suppliers are risk bearers, and they are typically compensated for bearing risk. Consequently, if we define profit as a return for risk bearing, the greater resource payment required for bearing risk can be considered profit. Resource suppliers who do not get paid obviously suffer an economic loss.

Think of the resource owners as standing in line waiting to receive the payment guaranteed them by the entrepreneur, not knowing when or if the cashier's window will close. Some owners try to put themselves first in line by requiring payment before their resource is supplied, by requiring payment before other resources are paid, or by requiring the entrepreneur to post *collateral*—valued assets that can be claimed by the resource supplier should payment not be forthcoming. Labor suppliers typically are paid weekly or biweekly, so little labor is extended without compensation. Lenders, however, usually extend the entire amount up front and are repaid in installments or at the end; lenders thus often require collateral. If resource suppliers have doubts about getting paid, they will demand a higher return for their services. This additional payment can be considered a return for risk bearing.

Risk of a Decline in the Value of the Resource The capitalist system is based on the private ownership of resources and the right of resource owners to contract freely for the lease or sale of their resources. An important feature of capitalism is the right of a resource owner to the gain or the loss in the value of that resource. Thus resource owners bear the risk associated with acquiring or developing resources. Although we typically associate risk bearing with the acquisition of physical capital, investment in human capital is often no more certain.

Right now you are acquiring human capital that you hope will serve you for a lifetime. Your decision to specialize in a particular area, such as economics, accounting, chemistry, or engineering, involves some risk because you cannot know what return this investment will yield in the future. You can only guess how changes in tastes, technology, taxes, and the supply of resources will shape the future supply and demand for your particular resource.

Many college students are understandably tempted to train for that first job; the tendency is to acquire very specific skills. *The more specific your human capital is, however, the more risk you assume in an uncertain and changing world.* Thus there is a risk involved in investing in human capital just as there is in investing in physical capital, and a portion of the return on human capital could be identified as an economic profit or an economic loss.

The Entrepreneur as Innovator

A variation of the idea of the entrepreneur as broker is the view that entrepreneurs are resource suppliers earning profits arising from successful innovations. If entrepreneurs can make an existing product more cheaply than competitors do or can introduce a new product demanded by consumers, they will be able to earn at least short-run economic profits. The possibility of economic profits serves as a powerful motive for innovations. Whether these profits continue in the long run will depend on the ability of other firms to imitate the cost-saving activity or the new product. If the entrepreneur is somehow able to acquire monopoly power, economic profit can be earned in the long run as well. For more about the entrepreneur as innovator, see the profile of Joseph Schumpeter in this chapter.

The idea of the entrepreneur as innovator harks back to our earlier discussion linking economic profit to monopoly. The entrepreneur may have patented an innovation that provides the firm with market power. We will briefly mention some other sources of market power here as well. The entrepreneur may be the sole owner of a key resource used in production. The entrepreneur may have secured a monopoly position through government regulation of the industry. Or economies of scale in production may provide the entrepreneur with the market power needed to earn an economic profit in the long run.

Profit and the Supply of Entrepreneurs

The ranks of entrepreneurs are in constant flux, as some emerge from the labor market to form their own enterprises and others return to the labor market after failing with their own firms or selling successful firms. The total supply of entrepreneurial ability is influenced by a variety of forces, such as the pace of technological change, the tax laws, and the market return on the other resources entrepreneurs could supply.

Evidence suggests that most new firms fail within two years. What encourages someone to take on such a risk rather than settle for the predictable salary, vacation time, health benefits, and other amenities that typically come with serving as an employee rather than as an employer? Why do seventeen million people in this country call themselves boss?

One strong economic incentive for founding a firm is that any entrepreneur who can develop a profit-making operation can typically sell the firm for a price equal to the present value of the expected profit stream. For example, suppose you put together a company that yields a profit of $25,000 per year. At a 5 percent discount rate, the present value of such a stream, if it is expected to continue indefinitely, is $25,000/0.05, or $500,000. The present value will be even higher if profits are expected to grow. A growing stream of future profits is what becomes capitalized into

Joseph A. Schumpeter
(1883–1950)

Businesspeople are not troubled by the concept of profit: they know it when they see it. But for economists, profit has long been a somewhat elusive—or at least controversial—concept. Some have seen profit as merely the wages of management; others have viewed it as a reward for bearing risk; and Marxist economists have always maintained that profit is extracted from laborers through exploitation. But one of the most brilliant and challenging formulations of the theory of profit arose from a somewhat unlikely source: an urbane, aristocratic Viennese named Joseph Schumpeter.

Profit, said Schumpeter, is neither a wage nor the fruits of exploitation; it is not even a reward for bearing risk. Profit, he argued, is a residual: it's what's left over after all the factors of production have been paid. In the ordinary course of things, there is no such profit. But an enterprising individual who creates a new technology or opens a new market generates profit—at least for a while, until imitators swarm in to copy the innovation and drive profit back to zero. These path-breaking entrepreneurs, as Schumpeter called them, are not only the source of profit. They are also the source of the momentum and drive of the entire economic system. Innovations are the wellspring of economic growth, and entrepreneurs are the fountainhead of innovation. Capitalism, Schumpeter said in a famous phrase, is a "perennial gale of creative destruction."

In the United States of the 1990s, Schumpeter's theory conjures up images of "cowboy capitalism" and the dynamism of Silicon Valley. But the author of the theory himself calls to mind a different picture. Joseph Schumpeter was a flamboyant and cultured European of the old school. He was born in Triesch in the Austro-Hungarian Empire and moved to Vienna as a lad when his widowed mother married an aristocrat. A star student at the University of Vienna, he published his first book at the age of 25. After a multifarious career (including positions as Austrian finance minister and as president of a failed bank), he settled into academia, ending up at Harvard University in the 1930s.

Schumpeter was one of the widest-ranging thinkers of his time. In a massive 1939 tome, he traced depressions and recessions to cycles in entrepreneurship and to the "clustering" of innovations. His most famous work was published in 1942. *Capitalism, Socialism, and Democracy* presented a dark and ironic argument that capitalism must eventually fail—not because of its weaknesses but because its very *success* will undermine the attitudes and values that support it.

Richard Langlois

the value of a firm. Some entrepreneurs are motivated by the ability to *capitalize* on a successful firm.

To close our look at entrepreneurs, we offer the following case study of the entrepreneur who developed Lotus 1-2-3.

CASE STUDY

Feasting in the Land of Lotus

Milton Kapor's job background hardly seemed to qualify him to become a successful producer of computer software. He had held various jobs, ranging from disk jockey to instructor of transcendental meditation. One day he traded his stereo for an Apple computer, and therein lies the tale. He was enraptured by the Apple and soon developed his programming skills to the point where he reportedly took only two months to write two business applications programs that he sold for more than a million dollars!

With these funds and with additional support, both financial and entrepreneurial, from a *venture capital firm*, he founded the Lotus Development Corporation in 1982. In less than a year, Lotus 1-2-3 became the industry's best-selling business program, with sales of $50 million the first year. In October 1983 the company made its first public offering of stock, making Kapor's stock in the company worth $70 million. In a few short years, Lotus grew out of his basement to become a firm with over 2200 employees and annual sales exceeding $500 million.

The other side of this success story is the venture capital firm that invested $2.1 million in Kapor's company in 1982. Venture capitalists shop around, investing in promising new firms. Such investors could be considered entrepreneurs in that, by becoming part owners, they share the responsibility of guaranteeing the payments of the other resources, they share in the control of these resources, and they are residual claimants of any profit or loss. When Lotus made its public offering in 1983, the stock held by the venture capitalists became worth $70 million, or about thirty-three times their investment only a year earlier.

In July 1986 Kapor resigned as chairman of Lotus. Evidently, he did not find the job of managing people as attractive as founding an empire. Since Kapor was viewed as the imaginative force behind Lotus, the day after he resigned the price of a share of company stock dropped by $2.25, an amount that at the time represented about 10 percent of the stock's value. Investors apparently believed that Kapor's special skills could not be easily replaced.

Source: "A Software Whiz Logs Off," *Newsweek*, 21 July 1986, 32.

CONCLUSION

Capital and entrepreneurial ability are more complicated resources than this chapter has conveyed. For example, the investment demand curve looks more like a moving target than like the stable relation drawn in Exhibit 2(b). An accurate depiction of the investment demand curve calls for knowledge of the marginal physical product of capital and the price of output both now and in the future. But the marginal physical product changes from period to period with changes in technology and in the employment of other resources. And the future price of the product can vary widely. Consider, for example, the dilemma of someone who invested in an oil well at the beginning of the 1980s. The price of a barrel of oil during the decade varied between $10 and $36.

Likewise, the chapter implied that entrepreneurial ability can be dissected and analyzed. But if the skills of the entrepreneur could be learned step by step like the skills of a plumber or an accountant, anyone could take a course and start a new firm. Entrepreneurship is a much more elusive skill, which is why successful entrepreneurs earn economic profits.

Despite the limitations of the discussion, you now have some knowledge of the economic roles of capital and entrepreneurial ability. This chapter brings to a close our treatment of resource markets. In the next chapter we will examine the results of the operation of resource markets by focusing on the distribution of income in the United States.

Summary

1. Production cannot occur without savings because both direct production and roundabout production require time—time during which the resources required for production must be paid. Because present consumption is valued more than future consumption, consumers must be rewarded if they are to defer consumption. Interest is the reward paid to savers for forgoing present consumption and the cost paid by borrowers to increase present consumption.

2. The marginal rate of return on investment equals the marginal revenue product of capital as a percentage of the marginal resource cost of capital. The profit-maximizing firm invests up to the point where its marginal rate of return equals the market rate of interest, which is the opportunity cost of investing borrowed funds or savings.

3. The nominal rate of interest measures the interest rate in terms of the actual dollars paid, even if dollars have lost purchasing power because of inflation. The nominal rate of interest equals the targeted real rate of interest plus the expected inflation rate. At any given time, market rates of interest may differ because of differences in risk, maturity, administrative costs, and tax treatment.

4. An entrepreneur is a profit-seeking decision maker who guarantees payment for the other resources in return for the right to direct these resources in the firm. The entrepreneur is also the residual claimant of any profits or losses of the firm. The entrepreneur need not supply any resource other than entrepreneurial ability, though entrepreneurs usually also supply capital and resource management.

5. There is no single theory explaining the profit earned by entrepreneurs. Entrepreneurs have been viewed as brokers who earn a profit by buying resources for less than they charge for the product of those resources. They have been viewed as risk bearers who earn a profit by taking chances. And they have been viewed as innovators who earn a profit by developing new products and by producing existing products for less.

Questions and Problems

1. (Capital in Production) Why would seed also be considered part of Old MacDonald's savings? Should seed be considered part of the capital stock? Why or why not?

2. (Marginal Efficiency of Capital) Consider Exhibit 2 in this chapter. If the marginal resource cost rose to $2400, what would be the optimum stock of capital? If the interest rate then rose to 16.6 percent, what would be the optimum stock of capital?

3. (Human Capital) Why are banks more willing to lend to medical students than to graduate students in education? What other variables besides interest rates affect the ability to accumulate human capital?

4. (Real Interest Rates) Is it possible for the realized real rate of interest to be negative? If so, what would cause this?

5. (Taxes and Investment) How does the tax deductibility of mortgage interest payments affect the demand for housing and building construction?

6. (Present Value) How would the present value of an investment project change if interest rates rose?

7. (Bond Prices) Why is $10,000 a reasonably close approximation of the price of a bond paying $1000 each year for thirty years at 10 percent interest?

8. (Entrepreneurs) The success and value of entrepreneurship are easiest to identify in small businesses. How would you identify the effect or value of entrepreneurship in large corporations? Give some examples of entrepreneurs in such settings.

9. (Valuing Entrepreneurship) *The Concise Oxford Dictionary* defines the business term *goodwill* as a "privilege granted by the seller of an established business, of trading as the seller's recognized successor; the amount paid for this." How might a company's goodwill be a measure of previous entrepreneurship?

10. (Profits) Some people claim that profits are bad or can be excessive. Support or refute this claim in light of the discussion in this chapter.

11. (Present Value) Suppose you are hired by your state government to determine the profitability of a lottery offering a grand prize of $10 million paid out in equal installments over twenty years. Show *how* you calculate the cost to the state of paying out such a prize.

12. (Loanable Funds Market) Using a supply-demand diagram for loanable funds, show the effect of each of the following on (nominal) interest rates:
    a. An increase in the expected rate of inflation
    b. An increase in the productivity of capital
    c. A decrease in the tax rate on savings

13. (Human Capital) Suppose you are considering enrolling in a graduate school program costing a total of $40,000. You expect that the graduate degree will increase your annual income by $5000. Calculate the interest rate that would make such an investment in human capital a good one.

14. (Entrepreneurship) Suppose you currently hold a $30,000-per-year job with an expected rate of salary increase of 5 percent per year. You are considering quitting and starting your own business with expected first-year costs of $50,000 and first-year revenues of $60,000. You anticipate that costs will increase annually by 3 percent and revenues will increase annually by 10 percent. If your discount rate is 5 percent and you expect to work for twenty years, show how you would decide whether or not to start your own business. (Ignore all other factors, such as risk.)

C H A P T E R   2   9

Income Distribution and Poverty

Income in a market economy depends primarily on the productivity of the household's resources. The problem with allocating income according to productivity is that some people have difficulty earning income. Those born with mental or physical disabilities may be unable to earn a living. Others may face limited job choices and reduced wages because of age, a poor education, or discrimination in the marketplace. Still others may be unable to work because they must care for small children.

In this chapter we will first examine the distribution of income in the United States, with special attention to poverty in recent years. We will then discuss and evaluate the "social safety net": public policies aimed at helping the poor. We will also consider the impact of the changing family structure on the incidence of poverty, focusing in particular on the age, race, and gender of the head of the household. We will explore the effects of discrimination on the distribution of income and close the chapter by examining recent welfare reforms. Topics discussed in this chapter include

- Personal distribution of income
- Lorenz curve
- Official poverty level
- Public policy and poverty

- The feminization of poverty
- Poverty and discrimination
- Negative income tax
- Recent welfare reforms

THE DISTRIBUTION OF HOUSEHOLD INCOME

The best way to consider the distribution of income is to focus on the family as an economic unit. After dividing the total number of families into five groups of equal size, ranked according to income, we can examine what percentage of income is received by each group. Such a division is presented in Exhibit 1. Notice that in 1929 families in the lowest, or poorest, fifth of the population received only 3.5 percent of the income, whereas families in the highest, or richest, fifth received 54.4 percent of the income. Thus the richest 20 percent of the families received over half the income.

Notice also that the richest group's share of income dropped from 54.4 percent in 1929 to 43.0 percent in 1947. What caused this drop in the amount going to the top group? The Great Depression erased many personal fortunes, and World War II brought more people into the labor force and increased the average wage. Beginning with 1947 the data display a remarkable stability, with the share going to the lowest fifth hovering around 5 percent and the share to the highest fifth ranging between 40.4 and 43.7 percent. To give you some idea of the levels of income involved, the upper limit for families in the poorest 20 percent was $14,450 in 1987. The lower limit for families in the top 20 percent was $52,920. So the middle 60 percent had family incomes between those two amounts.

The distribution of income in the United States is quite similar to that in other developed countries throughout the world, including Canada, France, West Germany, Great Britain, Japan, Italy, and the Soviet Union. Income in many developing countries, such as India, Brazil, Kenya, and Mexico, tends to be more unevenly distributed, with half or more of all income going to the richest 20 percent of the population.

EXHIBIT 1
**THE DISTRIBUTION OF MONEY INCOME AMONG FAMILIES
FOR SELECTED YEARS SINCE 1929**

Percentage Share

Year	Lowest Fifth	Second-Lowest Fifth	Middle Fifth	Second-Highest Fifth	Highest Fifth
1929	3.5%	9.0%	13.8%	19.3%	54.4%
1947	5.0	11.9	17.0	23.1	43.0
1957	5.1	12.7	18.1	23.8	40.4
1967	5.5	12.4	17.9	23.9	40.4
1977	5.2	11.6	17.5	24.2	41.5
1987	4.6	10.8	16.9	24.1	43.7

Source: U.S. Bureau of the Census, *Current Population Reports*, series P-60, no. 162 (Washington, D.C.: U.S. Government Printing Office, 1989).

The Lorenz Curve

The Lorenz curve is another way of picturing the distribution of income in an economy. As shown in Exhibit 2, the cumulative percentage of families is measured along the horizontal axis, and the cumulative percentage of income is measured along the vertical axis. The **Lorenz curve** shows the percentage of total income received by any given percentage of recipients when incomes are arrayed from smallest to largest.

Any given distribution of income can be compared to an equal distribution of income among families. If income were evenly distributed, the poorest 20 percent of the population would receive 20 percent of the total income, the poorest 40 percent of the population would receive 40 percent of the income, and so on. The Lorenz curve in this case would be a straight line with a slope equal to 1.0, as shown in Exhibit 2.

As the distribution becomes more uneven, the Lorenz curve is pulled down and to the right, away from the line of equal distribution. The Lorenz curves in Exhibit 2 were calculated for 1929 and 1987, based on the data in Exhibit 1. As a point of reference, point *a* on the 1929 Lorenz curve indicates that in that year the bottom 80 percent of families had 45.6 percent of the income and the top 20 percent had 54.4 percent of the income. Point *b* on the 1987 Lorenz curve shows that in that year the bottom 80 percent had about 56.3 percent of the income; the income share of the top 20 percent was down to 43.7 percent. The Lorenz curve for 1987 is closer to the center than the

*The **Lorenz curve** shows the percentage of total income received by a given percentage of recipients when incomes are arranged from smallest to largest.*

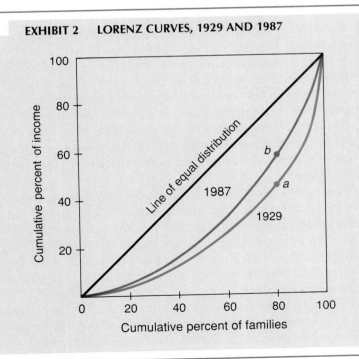

EXHIBIT 2   LORENZ CURVES, 1929 AND 1987

one for 1929; the shift indicates that the distribution of income among families has become more even.

Families receive income from two primary sources: resource earnings and transfer payments from the government. Exhibits 1 and 2 measure money income after cash transfers but before taxes. Thus the distributions shown in Exhibits 1 and 2 omit the effects of taxes and of in-kind transfers, such as food stamps and free medical care for poor families. The tax system as a whole tends to be mildly progressive, so families with higher incomes pay a larger fraction of their income in taxes. In-kind transfers benefit the lowest-income groups the most. Consequently, if the representations of the distribution of income in Exhibits 1 and 2 incorporated the effects of taxes and in-kind transfers, the share of income going to the lower groups would increase, the share going to the higher groups would decrease, and income would appear more evenly distributed.

The income distribution figures include only reported sources of income. If people receive payment "under the table" to evade taxes, or if they earn money through illegal activities, their actual income will exceed their reported income. The omission of unreported income will distort the data in the first two exhibits only if such income as a percentage of total income differs across income levels. For example, if people who appear to be poor based on official reports actually earn significant amounts of unreported income, then the distribution of income will be more even than the official data indicate.

Why Do Family Incomes Differ?

*The median is the middle number in a series of numbers arranged from smallest to largest; the **median income** is the middle income in a series of incomes so ranked.*

In 1988 the median income of all families in the United States was $32,191. The **median income** is the middle income when incomes are ranked from lowest to highest. In any given year, half the families are above the median income and half are below it. Since most income comes from selling labor, variations in family income often stem from differences in the number of workers in each family. Thus *one reason incomes differ across households is that the number of family members who are working differs.* For example, median income in 1988 for families with two earners was 60 percent higher than for families with only one earner and nearly three times higher than for families with no earners.

Family incomes also differ for all the reasons labor income differs, such as differences in education, ability, job experience, and so on. Exhibit 3 relates the average earnings of males to two important factors affecting earnings: education and age. Age is measured on the horizontal axis and average earnings on the vertical axis. The bottom, middle, and top lines reflect the average earnings for those with elementary, high school, and college educations, respectively.

The relation between income and education is clear. At every age, those with more education earn more, on average. Age also has an important effect on income. Those just entering the work force tend to be at the bottom of

EXHIBIT 3   AVERAGE EARNINGS OF MALES BASED ON AGE AND EDUCATION: 1986

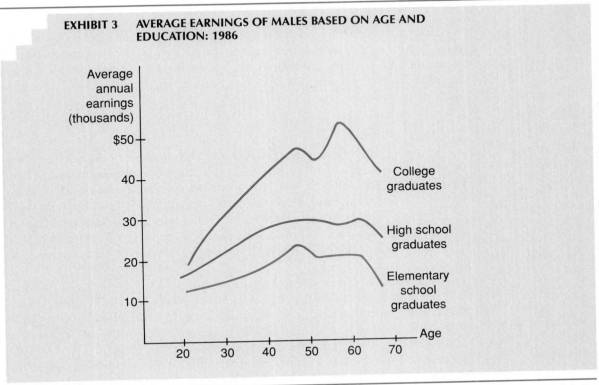

Source: U.S. Bureau of the Census, *Current Population Reports*, series P-60, no. 159 (Washington, D.C.: U.S. Government Printing Office, 1989).

the scale, but as workers mature, they acquire valuable job experience, get promoted, and earn more. As workers continue to grow older, however, their incomes level off and eventually fall with the onset of retirement. Thus average income initially increases with age, reaches a peak, then drops off. Note in Exhibit 3 that income peaks at a younger age for those with only an elementary education. Less educated workers tend to rely more on physical work, whereas more educated workers rely more on mental work. Advancing age takes more of a toll on physical productivity than on mental productivity.

Differences in earnings based on age and education reflect the normal *life-cycle* pattern of income and are not matters of public concern. In fact, most income differences across households reflect the normal workings of resource markets, where workers are rewarded according to their productivity. High-income households tend to be headed by well-educated, middle-aged individuals and to have two people from the household working. Low-income households tend to be headed by single parents who are young, female, poorly educated, and not working. When incomes are very low, however, they become a matter of public concern, as we will see in the next section.

POVERTY AND THE POOR

Since poverty is such a relative concept, how do we measure it objectively and how do we ensure that our measure can be applied with equal relevance over time? The federal government has developed a method for calculating an official poverty level; this level has become the benchmark for poverty analysis in this country.

Official Poverty Level

To derive the official poverty level, the Department of Agriculture first estimates the cost of minimum food consumption requirements. Then, based on the assumption that the poor spend about one-third of their income on food, the official poverty level is calculated by multiplying these food costs by three. Adjustments are made for family size and for inflation. The official poverty level of money income for a family of four was $12,100 in 1989; families of four at or below that income level were regarded as living in poverty.

Each year the Census Bureau conducts a survey comparing individual families' annual cash incomes to the annual poverty threshold applicable to that family. The percentage of the population below the official poverty level since 1959 is shown in Exhibit 4. The biggest decline in the rate of poverty came prior to 1970; the rate dropped from 22.4 percent in 1959 to 12.1 percent in 1969 (between points *a* and *b* in Exhibit 4). During that period the number of poor people as measured by the official government definition dropped from about 40 million to 24 million. The poverty rate bottomed out at 11.1 percent in 1973, fluctuated between 1973 and 1979, then rose between 1979 and 1983. Despite a decline since 1983, the rate most recently was still higher than in 1973.

But poverty is a relative term. If we examined the distribution of income across the countries of the world, we would find huge gaps between rich and poor nations. For example, the official U.S. poverty level of income exceeds by many times the average income for three-fourths of the world's population.[1] Also, an income at the U.S. poverty level today provides a standard of living that would have been considered attractive by most people who lived in the United States at the turn of the century, when only 15 percent of families had flush toilets, only 3 percent had electricity, and only 1 percent had central heating.

Public Policy and Poverty

What should the government response to poverty be? Families in which the head of the household has a job are much more likely to escape poverty than are families without employment. Thus the government's first line of

---

[1] See the World Bank, *World Development Report 1989* (New York: Oxford University Press, 1989), table 1.

EXHIBIT 4   PERCENTAGE OF POPULATION BELOW THE OFFICIAL POVERTY LEVEL SINCE 1959

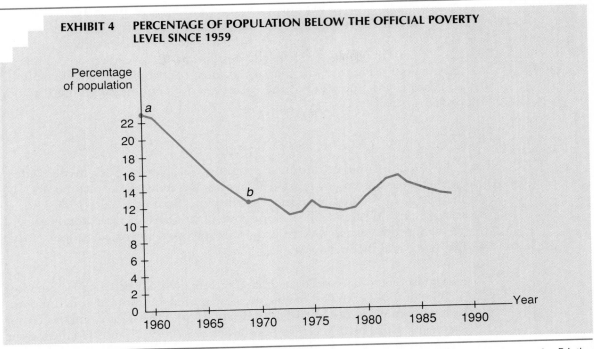

Source: U.S. Bureau of the Census, *Current Population Reports*, series P-60, no. 163 (Washington, D.C.: U.S. Government Printing Office, 1989).

defense in fighting poverty is to promote a healthy economy and to provide the education and training that enhance job opportunities.

Yet even when the unemployment rate is relatively low, some people may remain poor because they lack marketable skills, must care for small children, or face discrimination in the labor market. The government has several alternatives when confronted with the problems of poverty: (1) it can do nothing, relying on private charity and support from relatives to help the poor; (2) it can intervene in private markets with measures designed to help the poor, such as laws prohibiting discrimination based on gender or race; or (3) it can wait until private markets have cleared and then tax the income of those with higher incomes to provide transfers to the poor.

Let's consider the first alternative: leaving the care of the poor to private charity. Private charity is in some ways an ideal form of redistribution. Since charitable contributions are voluntary, they probably provide utility to both the donor and the recipient. Those who make donations benefit from knowing that the poor receive money, and the poor benefit from receiving those donations. But most people are inclined to let others support the poor, so voluntary charity is insufficient. How much of your income or time did you contribute to charity this past year? On average those aged 18 to 24 contribute less than 1 percent of their income to charity.[2]

To overcome the problem of insufficient voluntary contributions, voters agree to tax themselves to help the poor. Many people are more willing to aid the poor if they are sure that others must contribute as well. Such public choices provide more aid to the poor than does voluntary giving through private charity.

Programs to Help the Poor

Although some government programs to help the poor involve direct market intervention, the most visible programs redistribute income after the market has provided an initial distribution. Since the mid–1960s, social welfare expenditures at all levels of government have increased dramatically. We can divide social welfare programs into two major categories: social insurance and income assistance.

Social Insurance   The social insurance system is designed to replace the lost income of those who worked but are now retired, temporarily unemployed, or unable to work because of total disability or work-related injury. By far the major social insurance program is *Social Security*, established during the Great Depression to provide retirement income to those with a work history and a record of contributing to the program. Medicare provides health insurance for short-term medical care for those aged 65 and older, regardless of income. Other social insurance programs include unemployment insurance and worker's compensation, both of which require beneficiaries to have a prior record of employment.

The social insurance system deducts what may be thought of as insurance premiums from worker payrolls and provides higher benefits to those with higher earnings before retirement, disability, or unemployment. These programs protect some families from poverty, particularly the elderly receiving Social Security, but they are aimed more at those with a work history.

Income Assistance   Income assistance programs—what we usually call "welfare"—provide money and in-kind assistance to the poor. Unlike social insurance programs, income assistance programs do not require the recipient to have worked or to have contributed to the program. Income assistance programs are means tested. In a **means-tested** program, a household's income and/or assets must be below a certain level in order for the members of the household to qualify for benefits. People who qualify for assistance are *entitled* to the program; hence these programs are sometimes

*A **means-tested** program requires that a household's income and/or assets be below specified levels in order for household members to qualify for benefits.*

[2] This statistic is from Virginia Hodgkinson, Murray Weitzman, and the Gallup Organization, Inc., *Giving and Volunteering in the United States: 1988 Edition* (Washington, D.C.: Independent Sector, 1988).

called *entitlement programs*. The major cash transfer and in-kind transfer programs are listed in Exhibit 5. As you can see, the federal government is the primary source of funding for most welfare programs; most of the money supports in-kind transfer programs.

The two primary *cash transfer* programs are *Aid to Families with Dependent Children (AFDC)*, which provides cash to poor households with children, and *Supplemental Security Income (SSI)*, which provides cash to the indigent elderly and the totally disabled. Cash transfers vary inversely with household income from other sources. AFDC began with the Social Security legislation and was originally aimed at providing support for widows with young children. The cost is divided between the state and federal governments, though the federal government pays a higher proportion of the total in poorer states. In 1988, 3.8 million families received an average AFDC transfer of $355 per month. Because benefit levels are set by each state, they vary widely. For example, benefit levels in California average nearly five times those in Mississippi.

The Supplemental Security Income program provides support for elderly and disabled poor. The federal portion of this program is uniform across states, but states can supplement federal aid. Benefits averaged $253 per month to 4.4 million recipients in 1987. Benefit levels in California

EXHIBIT 5
ANTIPOVERTY EXPENDITURES BY PROGRAM AND BY LEVEL OF GOVERNMENT: 1987 (billions of dollars)

Program	Source of Revenue			Percent of Expenditures
	Federal	State and Local	Total	
Cash Transfers	$22.8	$13.8	$36.6	28.9%
AFDC	10.0	8.4	18.4	14.5
SSI	10.8	2.9	13.7	10.8
Earned Income Tax Credit	2.0	—	2.0	1.6
General Assistance	—	2.5	2.5	2.0
Medical Care	28.0	25.4	53.4	42.2
Medicaid	28.0	22.0	50.0	39.5
General Assistance	—	3.4	3.4	2.7
Food Assistance	19.8	1.2	21.0	16.8
Food stamps	12.5	—	12.5	9.9
School lunch program	3.3	—	3.3	2.6
Other food programs	4.0	1.2	5.2	4.3
Housing Assistance	13.2	—	13.2	10.4
Energy Assistance	1.9	0.2	2.1	1.7
Total Expenditures	85.7	40.6	126.3	100.0
Percent of spending by government level	67.9%	32.9%	100.0%	

Source: Developed from data found in U.S. Bureau of the Census, *Statistical Abstracts of the United States: 1989*, table 570, 349.

average twice those in Mississippi. The federal government also funds the *Earned Income Tax Credit*, which allows the working poor to receive as an income tax refund more than they paid in taxes. Most states offer modest *General Assistance* aid to those who are poor but do not qualify for AFDC or SSI.

In addition to cash transfer programs, a variety of *in-kind transfer* programs provide health care (through Medicaid), food stamps, and housing assistance to the poor. *Medicaid* is by far the largest welfare program, costing more than all cash transfer programs combined. It was the only major poverty program to show any real growth during the 1980s. Medicaid pays for medical care for all those with incomes below a certain level who are aged, blind, disabled, or in families with dependent children. The qualifying level of income is set by each state, and some states are very stringent. Therefore the proportion of poor covered by Medicaid varies greatly across states. Some states also offer General Assistance to provide health care coverage to those who are poor but not eligible for Medicaid.

Food stamps are vouchers that can be redeemed for food. The program is aimed at reducing hunger and providing for proper nutrition in poor households. The cost is paid by the federal government, and benefits are uniform across states. The number of beneficiaries of the program rose from fewer than a half-million people in 1965 to 22 million by 1981. A tightening of eligibility requirments in the early 1980s reduced coverage to only 19 million people by 1987. In 1989 the monthly allowance was raised 10 percent and the eligibility requirements were liberalized. As of October of 1989, a family of four was eligible for up to $331 per month.

Housing assistance programs include direct assistance for rental payments and subsidized low-income housing. Spending for housing assistance has more than doubled since 1980. About 4 million households received various low-income housing subsidies in 1987. Other in-kind programs listed in Exhibit 5 include *school lunch programs* for poor children and *energy assistance* to help pay the heating costs of poor households.

Expenditures and the Rate of Poverty

Payments for social insurance programs and income assistance programs at all levels of government totaled about $615 billion in 1989, or about 12 percent of GNP. Most of the funding went to social insurance programs rather than to programs aimed more specifically at the poor. Income assistance programs—what we typically think of as welfare programs—amounted to only about 3 percent of GNP.

Exhibit 6 indicates what happened since 1960 to federal expenditures aimed specifically at assisting poor people—the cash and in-kind transfer programs listed in Exhibit 5. Expenditures are measured in constant dollars, so outlays are in real terms, or inflation-adjusted dollars. The most rapid growth occurred between 1970 and 1981 (points *a* and *b*), when real expenditures nearly tripled, growing by an average of 9.6 percent per year.

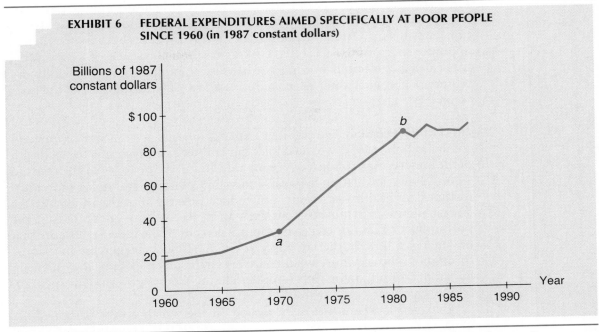

EXHIBIT 6   FEDERAL EXPENDITURES AIMED SPECIFICALLY AT POOR PEOPLE SINCE 1960 (in 1987 constant dollars)

Source: *Budget of the United States Government* (Washington, D.C.: U.S. Government Printing Office, various years).

Since 1981 real spending has fluctuated, and has shown a modest trend upward.

If you compare Exhibit 6 with Exhibit 4, which presented the poverty rate since 1959, you will notice that the decline in the poverty level ceased just when federal outlays for the poor showed their greatest increase. Were efforts to eradicate poverty facing diminishing returns?

Exclusion of In-Kind Transfers One reason official poverty statistics seem unaffected by the greater welfare spending during 1970–1981 is that the Census Bureau includes only *money transfers* in the definition of income. It ignores the value of in-kind transfer programs, such as Medicaid, food stamps, and housing assistance. When official poverty statistics were first collected in the 1960s, in-kind transfers were minimal, so neglecting these transfers did not bias the results. But in-kind programs expanded during the 1970s and most recently accounted for over 70 percent of all welfare spending. Ignoring in-kind transfers in the definition of income biases the poverty statistics, making the official figures higher than the actual values. When poverty data are reestimated to include the value of in-kind transfers, the revised poverty rate is one-third lower than the official estimate. For example, the percentage of the population defined as poor in 1988 drops from 13.1 to 8.3.

Despite the growth in in-kind benefit programs, many of the poor still do not receive them, though some households above the poverty line do.

Only about two of five poor households receive Medicaid; a similar proportion receives food stamps. Only one of six poor households receives a housing subsidy. Often the poor do not receive benefits because they fail to apply for them, but just as often coverage is limited because of long waiting lists (such as for public housing) or because some states establish eligibility requirements (such as for Medicaid) that allow only the poorest of the poor to qualify.

Effect of the Economy For another explanation of why the war on poverty has stalled since 1973 we must look beyond welfare programs to the health of the underlying economy. "A rising tide lifts all the boats" — so goes the old axiom about the relation between a thriving economy and rising individual fortunes. A healthy economy can reduce poverty more than all but the largest increases in government assistance. As we saw at the outset, the bottom fifth of families receives about 5 percent of the income, a figure that has changed little in the last forty years. A 10 percent increase in income throughout the economy would have raised the income of this lowest group by about $15 billion in 1988 — more than the federal government spent on AFDC that year.

Between 1959 and 1969, the period during which poverty dropped the most, the economy showed the strongest growth; real family income grew on average by more than one-third. Between 1969 and 1979, however, the economic growth slowed. Twice as many people were unemployed in 1979 as in 1969. The effect of the growth in transfer spending during the 1970s may have been to compensate in part for a flat economy, with the result that poverty rates remained relatively unchanged. Poverty rates climbed in the early 1980s because the economy was weakening, then began to fall after 1983 as the economy improved.

To develop a fuller understanding of the extent and composition of poverty over time and to examine the trend in poverty, we must look behind the totals. We next examine the composition of the poor.

WHO ARE THE POOR?

Who are the poor, and how has the composition of this group changed over time? We will slice the poverty statistics in several ways to examine the makeup of the group. Keep in mind that we are relying on official poverty statistics, which ignore the value of in-kind transfers and so to some extent overstate the problem.

Poverty Among Young Families

Earlier we looked at the poverty rate of the entire population. Now we will focus on poverty in families. The poverty rate since 1959, based on the age of the head of the family, is presented in Exhibit 7. The first row lists the poverty rate for all families regardless of age. The largest reduction in the

EXHIBIT 7

OFFICIAL POVERTY RATE OF FAMILIES BY AGE OF HOUSEHOLD HEAD FOR SELECTED YEARS SINCE 1959

Age of Household Head	1959	1968	1970	1975	1980	1987
All families	18.5%	10.0%	10.1%	9.7%	10.3%	10.8%
Under 25	26.9	13.2	15.5	21.0	21.8	29.5
25–44	16.5	9.3	9.5	10.3	11.8	12.6
45–54	15.0	7.0	6.6	6.6	7.6	7.0
65 and over	30.0	17.0	16.5	8.9	9.1	7.2

Source: U.S. Bureau of the Census, *Current Population Reports*, series P-60, no. 163 (Washington, D.C.: U.S. Government Printing Office, 1990).

overall rate was between 1959 and 1968, when the poverty rate declined from 18.5 percent to 10.0 percent. There was, however, no general improvement during the last two decades.

Poverty is highest in families where the head of household is under 25 years old. Older heads of households have a lower poverty rate, especially in more recent years. Although earnings tend to be lowest for those just entering the labor market, the data show more than a simple age–wage effect, as *the poverty rate among young families has grown since 1968*. In 1968 the poverty rate for families headed by someone under 25 was only one-third greater than the rate for all families, but by 1987 these younger families had a poverty rate nearly *triple* the average.

The most dramatic reversal of poverty has occurred among families where the head of household is 65 or over. In 1959 the elderly group was the poorest, with a poverty rate of 30 percent. By 1987 the poverty rate for the elderly group had dropped to 7.2 percent, among the lowest rates of any age group. In fact, *families with a head aged 65 or over were the only ones to have a lower rate most recently than in any previous year*. Particularly in light of the fact that the poverty rate among young families more than doubled between 1968 and 1987, the rate reduction among the elderly has been remarkable.

This reduction in poverty among the elderly can be attributed to a tremendous growth in Social Security and Medicare spending, which grew from $42 billion in 1959 to over $298 billion in 1988, measured in 1988 dollars. In 1988 Social Security and Medicare spending matched the country's expenditures for national defense and was more than double what the federal government spent on income assistance programs. Social Security has been credited with lifting 15 million Americans above the poverty line. Though not welfare programs in a strict sense, Social Security and Medicare have been extremely successful in reducing poverty among the elderly.

Poverty and Public Choice

In a democratic country such as ours, public policies depend very much on the political power of the interest groups represented. In recent years the elderly have become a strong political force. Unlike most interest groups, the elderly are a group we all expect to join one day. The elderly actually are represented by four constituencies: (1) the elderly themselves, (2) those under 65 who are concerned about the benefits to their parents or other elderly relatives, (3) those under 65 who are concerned about their own benefits in the future, and (4) those such as doctors and nursing home operators who earn their living by caring for the elderly.

Moreover, the voter participation rate of those 65 and over tends to be higher than that of other age groups. Specifically, those between 65 and 74 vote at more than twice the rate of those under 34. The political muscle of the elderly has been flexed whenever a question of Social Security benefits has come up. In 1985, for example, at a time when Congress was seeking ways to address a $200 billion federal deficit, a proposal to delay for several months a cost-of-living increase in Social Security benefits was defeated amid much posturing among members of Congress about how the country could not solve the deficit at the expense of the elderly. Yet as we have seen, the poverty rate among the elderly is now lower than that of nearly all other groups. Congress had less difficulty trimming programs specifically targeted at low-income people.

We close this section by considering a group with perhaps the most urgent needs of any group yet with little political power: the homeless.

CASE STUDY

The Street People

A recent study by the National Academy of Sciences concludes that on any given night, 735,000 people in the United States have no home and must sleep on streets, in shelters, or in some other makeshift quarters. Most of these people are alone, but about one-fourth of them are in families. Children in families make up about 100,000 of the homeless. Research suggests that homeless families consist mainly of young, single women with two or three children who were receiving AFDC and had received it longer than other welfare families.

Homelessness appears to be more prevalent in cities with strong rent controls and other housing restrictions. These government restrictions result in very low vacancy rates in rental units and high housing prices. Rent controls discourage the construction of new rental housing. Because the supply of housing is restricted, people who might otherwise move into better housing instead stay put. There is thus little turnover of housing, and no "filtering down" of housing to the low end of the housing market. Affordable housing is therefore more scarce in cities with greater housing restrictions, such as New York, Boston, and Berkeley, than in cities with fewer housing restrictions, such as Kansas City and Pittsburgh.

Some homeless individuals have serious mental problems. Most studies report that between one-fifth and one-third of the homeless are deinstitutionalized mental patients. In the mid-1950s the nation's mental hospitals began releasing patients on a large scale. Newly developed miracle drugs effective in treating mental illness were supposed to follow these patients into society, helping them lead productive lives. Some former patients made a successful transition, but many ended up homeless and on the street. Fewer than one-fourth of those discharged are in any kind of mental health program. And most of the young homeless who are mentally ill have never received any in-patient treatment.

Since most street people have no permanent address, they have problems registering for the few welfare programs for which they qualify. It is difficult for someone who calls a Dumpster home to receive mental health treatment or public assistance. There is episodic support, most of it in-kind, from shelters, soup kitchens, and emergency rooms, but coverage varies widely across regions. Many homeless feel safer on the streets even when shelters are available. The problem of the homeless suggests that there is a major hole in the social service safety net.

Sources: Ellen L. Bassuk, "Mental Health Needs of Homeless Persons," *The Harvard Medical School Mental Health Letter* 3, no. 7 (January 1987): 4–6; Associated Press, "100,000 U.S. Children Under 18 Found Homeless on Any Given Night," *Hartford Courant*, 20 September 1988; Gregory Fossedal, "Homelessness and the U.S. Housing Mess," *Wall Street Journal*, 12 March 1990.

Poverty, Gender, and Race

One way of classifying the incidence of poverty is by the age of the household head; the race and gender of the household head is another. Exhibit 8 illustrates family poverty rates since 1959 based on race and gender of the head of household.[3] Poverty rates for all four groups declined sharply during the 1960s, showed modest declines during the 1970s, and flattened out during the 1980s. The decline was most dramatic among families headed by black males. Overall, the 1987 poverty rates were higher for female-headed households than for male-headed households. Also, poverty rates among black families were about twice those among white families. *The highest poverty rate was among black families headed by females; the lowest rate was among white families headed by males.*

Children born outside marriage are likely to have available less resources than other children, since the father in such cases typically assumes little responsibility for child support. The percentage of births to unmarried mothers is about four times higher today than it was in 1960. Also, between 1965 and 1975 the divorce rate doubled, and it has since remained at the higher level. Because of the rising divorce rate, even children born to married couples now face a higher likelihood of living in a one-parent household before they grow up. Divorce usually reduces the resources available for the children.

Even though the poverty *rates* for female-headed households have shown some improvement since 1959, increases in the number of unwed mothers and in the divorce rate have made female-headed households the fastest

[3] The experience of other ethnic and racial groups would be of interest as well, but census data over the full period are available only for whites and blacks. Only in recent years have figures for persons of Hispanic origin been collected.

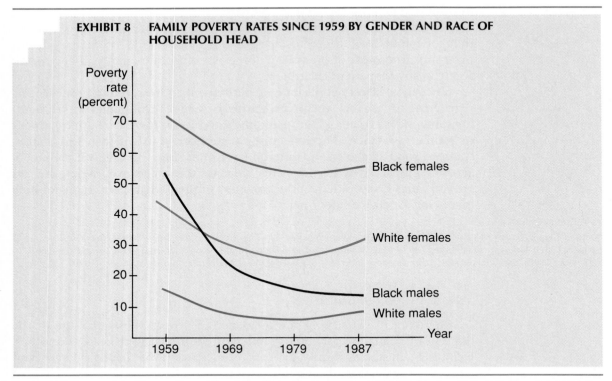

EXHIBIT 8   FAMILY POVERTY RATES SINCE 1959 BY GENDER AND RACE OF
            HOUSEHOLD HEAD

Source: U.S. Bureau of the Census, *Current Population Reports*, series P-60, no. 163 (Washington, D.C.: U.S. Government Printing Office, 1990).

growing group of poor people. In 1960 only one household in fourteen was headed by a woman. By 1987 one family in five was headed by a woman. With the increase in female-headed households, the *number* of poor from these households climbed, even though the poverty *rate* among such families improved somewhat. In 1959 only 6.6 million poor people lived in female-headed households. By 1987 this number had nearly doubled to 11.7 million. In contrast, the number of poor living in male-headed households dropped during the same period from 26.9 million to 11.9 million. The sharp decline in poverty in male-headed families suggests the strong role played by the economy during the period. Since 1960 the economy has generated over 50 million new jobs. Male-headed households were in the best position to gain from this economic growth because they typically had one more potential wage earner than did female-headed households.

The percentage of all the poor in female-headed families increased from 20 percent in 1959 to 49 percent in 1987. *Poverty has therefore become increasingly feminized, in part because female-headed households have become much more common in the population as a whole.* Because female-headed households have grown more rapidly among blacks, the feminization of poverty has been more dramatic in black households. Female-headed households are often concentrated in the poorest areas of central cities, where crime and drug abuse compound the problem of poverty, creating a group of poor termed the *underclass*. Underclass families must cope not only with poverty but also with the daily effects of crime and drug addiction in the neighborhood. Some children are born to drug-addicted mothers. In 1989, for example, an estimated 10,000 babies were born in New York City to substance-abusing mothers.[4] Perhaps the expression "no-parent households" should be introduced to reflect the sad circumstances of such children.

In 1987, 71 percent of poor blacks were in families headed by women; in contrast, only 35 percent of poor whites were in families headed by women. The high poverty rate among female-headed households and among black households raises the question of whether discrimination exists either in the job market or in the availability of transfers. In an earlier chapter we considered discrimination against women and examined the issue of comparable worth. In the next section we consider discrimination against blacks.

POVERTY AND DISCRIMINATION

Family income comes from two primary sources: resource earnings—typically labor—and transfer income. The question we ask is this: are the lower family income and greater incidence of poverty among blacks the result of discrimination in job markets or discrimination in the availability of transfer programs, or are there other explanations? We should note that discrimination can occur in many ways: in school admissions, in school funding, in housing, in employment, in career advancement. Also, discrimination in one area can affect opportunities in another. For example, housing discrimination may reduce job opportunities because the black family cannot move within commuting distance of the best employers.

The legacy of discrimination can affect career choices long after discrimination has ceased. A black man whose father and grandfather found job avenues blocked may be less inclined to pursue an education or to accept a job that requires a long training program. Thus discrimination is a complex topic, and we cannot do it justice in this brief section.

Discrimination in the Job Market

Job market discrimination can take many forms. An employer may fail to hire a black job applicant because the applicant lacks training, but this lack of training may arise from discrimination in the schools, in union apprenticeship programs, or in training programs run by employers. For example, evidence suggests that black workers receive less on-the-job training than otherwise similar white workers.

We will first consider the difference between the earnings of nonwhite and white full-time workers. In 1939 nonwhite workers earned less than half of what white workers earned. The earnings gap based on race has been

4 "Crack Mothers, Crack Babies and Hope," *New York Times*, 31 December 1989.

reduced, especially since 1965. By 1980, among full-time workers, non-white males earned 71 percent of what white males earned, and nonwhite females earned 95 percent of what white females earned. Such data are very crude, of course, since they fail to account for differences in education, job experience, or other characteristics that can affect productivity and pay.

What happens when we adjust for education? Exhibit 9 compares median family incomes of blacks and whites. For each group, median family income increases with education, as expected, but at each level of education, white family income is higher than black family income. The gap between white and black families is greatest when the head of household has attended high school. Median incomes of blacks as a percentage of those of whites are highest among the least educated and among the most educated.

But Exhibit 9 does not take into account other factors that affect family income, such as the number of earners in the household or their job experience. The lower family income among blacks, for example, may reflect the fact that a larger proportion of black households are headed by women and thus tend to have one fewer wage earner. And many blacks with college degrees tend to be recent graduates with less job experience than the typical white with a college degree.

We attempt to adjust for more variables in Exhibit 10, which presents ratios of the standardized hourly wage rate of black males to that of white males. These data not only account for education and age but also adjust for marital status, geographic location, veteran status, and the probability of employment in the public sector. The idea was to adjust for those factors that could contribute to the worker's productivity. The data indicate that, among workers who completed high school, blacks earned less than otherwise similar whites at all age levels. Among recent college graduates,

EXHIBIT 9
MEDIAN MONEY INCOME OF FAMILIES BY EDUCATION AND RACE: 1988

Education	Race		Black/White Income Percentage
	Black	White	
Elementary school			
Less than 8 years	$12,149	$15,264	79.6%
8 years	13,210	18,718	70.6
High school			
1–3 years	12,166	22,653	53.4
4 years	20,263	30,958	65.4
College			
1–3 years	25,115	37,324	67.3
4 years or more	36,568	50,908	71.9

Source: U.S. Bureau of the Census, *Current Population Reports*, series P-60, no. 162 (Washington, D.C.: U.S. Government Printing Office, 1989).

EXHIBIT 10
THE RATIO OF BLACK TO WHITE WAGE RATES FOR MALES AS OF 1980

	Years of Schooling	
Age	12	16
22	0.90	1.18
27	0.83	1.10
32	0.84	0.99
37	0.94	0.98
42	0.90	0.94
47	0.86	0.89
52	0.82	0.86

Source: Computed based on data reported in Daniel S. Hamermesh and Albert Rees, *The Economics of Work and Pay*, 3d ed. (New York: Harper & Row, 1984), table 13.3, 319.

however, blacks earned more than whites. Only among workers 42 and older did blacks earn markedly less than whites. Thus there may be job discrimination against older and less educated blacks, but there was no evidence of discrimination against blacks who graduated from college within the previous ten years.

Could other explanations besides job discrimination account for the differentials found in Exhibit 10? Though the data adjust for the *years* of schooling, some research suggests that black workers, particularly older black workers, received a lower *quality* of schooling than white workers.[5] This quality difference could account for at least a portion of the remaining difference in standardized wages, particularly among those with only a high school education. Although any differences attributable to a poorer quality education would not reflect job discrimination, they might well reflect discrimination in the funding of schools.

Finally, even though Exhibit 10 accounts for the age of workers, there is evidence that black and white workers of the same age have not acquired the same amount of job experience. Black males who worked full-time in 1980 were less likely than white workers to have worked full-time their entire working lives. This implies that for any given age group, black workers are likely to have less job experience than white workers, and, again, this difference in experience could account for some of the difference in wages between the two groups. Differences in job experience may reflect past discrimination in hiring or a greater reluctance among employers to provide training programs for black workers.

Affirmative Action

The Equal Employment Opportunity Commission, established by the Civil Rights Act of 1964, monitors cases involving unequal pay for equal work and unequal access to promotion. Executive Order 11246, signed by President Lyndon Johnson, requires all companies doing business with the federal government to set numerical hiring, promotion, and training goals. The objective was to ensure that these firms did not discriminate in hiring on the basis of race, sex, religion, or national origin. Today that executive order governs employment practices in 73,000 firms employing nearly 35 million workers. Attention has been focused on hiring practices and equality of opportunity at the state level as well.

The federal focus on employment practices appears to have improved employment opportunities for blacks. Black employment increased sharply in those firms required to file affirmative action plans.[6] The percentage of the black labor force employed in white-collar jobs increased from 16.5 percent

---

[5] See Finis Welch, "Black-White Differences in Returns to Schooling," *American Economic Review* 63 (September 1973): 893–907.

[6] See the evidence provided in James Smith and Finis Welch, "Black Economic Progress After Myrdal," *Journal of Economic Literature* 27 (June 1989): 519–563.

in 1960 to 40.5 percent in 1981. Recent Supreme Court decisions, however, have questioned the constitutionality of some affirmative action plans, and many employers are scrutinizing their plans in light of these decisions. So whether employment gains from affirmative action will continue remains unclear.

Discrimination in Transfer Programs?

Market-related earnings represent the primary source of income for most households, but many households rely on government transfers. Are the lower family income and higher incidence of poverty among blacks linked to unequal treatment of blacks in the welfare system? Are blacks more likely than whites to fall through the safety net provided by social service programs? For example, blacks living in rural areas of the South must often travel to the county seat to apply for welfare; does this affect their participation rate?

Exhibit 11 presents the percentage, by race, of families and unrelated individuals who received federal cash transfers. There is also a separate breakdown for those below the poverty line. No matter which group we examine, there is no evidence that blacks participate any less than whites in the transfer system.

In summary, evidence presented in this section suggests that older black men and less-educated black men earn less for comparable jobs than do whites. Part of this difference may reflect differences in the quality of education and in job experience, differences that could themselves be the product of discrimination. There is no evidence that blacks have less access to government transfer programs.

We should note that black families are not a homogeneous group. In fact, the distribution of income is more uneven among black families than it is among the population as a whole. More black families have moved into the middle class. The percentage of black families earning more than $35,000, adjusted for inflation, increased from 13 percent in 1967 to 22 percent in 1988. The average black person today has a high school education; in 1960

EXHIBIT 11
PERCENTAGE OF FAMILIES AND UNRELATED INDIVIDUALS WHO RECEIVED CASH TRANSFERS

	Families		Unrelated Individuals	
	Black	**White**	**Black**	**White**
All income levels	56.0%	42.5%	45.5%	43.9%
Below the poverty level	75.3%	57.5%	63.5%	53.5%

Source: U.S. Bureau of the Census, *Statistical Abstract of the United States* (Washington, D.C.: U.S. Government Printing Office, 1984), table 766, 459. Data are for 1982.

the average black person had only a junior high school education. But among the poorest of blacks, matters have worsened. Between 1967 and 1988, the percentage of black families with real incomes under $10,000 increased from 28 to 30 percent. Thus the good news has been the emergence of a flourishing black middle class; the bad news has been the emergence of a black underclass living in female-headed households, often in the poorest sections of central cities.

SOME UNINTENDED CONSEQUENCES OF INCOME ASSISTANCE

On the plus side, antipoverty programs increase the consumption possibilities of poor families, and this is critical, especially since children are the largest poverty group. But programs to assist the poor may have secondary effects that limit their ability to reduce poverty. Here we consider some secondary effects.

Work Disincentives

Society tries to provide families with an adequate standard of living but also wants to ensure that only the most needy receive benefits. This results in a system in which benefits are reduced sharply as earned income increases. Efforts to reduce benefits as earned income increases in effect impose a high marginal tax rate on that earned income. This high marginal tax rate could discourage employment and self-sufficiency.

As we have seen, income assistance consists of a bundle of cash and in-kind programs. Because these programs are designed to help the poor and only the poor, the level of benefits is inversely related to income from other sources. For example, a family of four receiving food stamp benefits would find those benefits reduced by $30 per month for each $100 of outside income. Thus the *marginal tax rate* on earned income (as reflected by the reductions in food stamp benefits) is 30 percent under this program. Any increase in earnings would also cause a decline in benefits received from AFDC, Medicaid, housing assistance, energy assistance, and other programs.

If a bite is taken from each program as earned income increases, working may result in little or no increase in total income. In fact, over certain income ranges the welfare recipient may lose well over $1 in benefits for each $1 in earnings. Thus the marginal tax rate can exceed 100 percent! When you consider that holding even a part-time job involves additional expenses, such as transportation and child care costs, not to mention the loss of free time, such a system of incentives can frustrate those who would like to work their way off welfare. Just how much the higher marginal tax rates reduce the incentive to work remains unclear. We do know that only about one of every twenty persons receiving AFDC is employed. Twice as many welfare recipients worked in the mid-1970s. These high marginal tax rates also encourage welfare recipients not to report earned income; some may work "off the books" for cash or may become involved in illegal activities.

What if the high marginal tax rates discourage recipients from working? The longer people are out of the labor force, the more their job skills deteriorate, so when they do seek employment, their marginal product and their pay are lower than when they were last employed. This lowers their expected wage and makes work less attractive. Some economists argue that in this way welfare benefits can lead to long-term dependency.

Does the system of incentives created by high marginal tax rates create a dependency among welfare recipients? How could we examine such a question? High turnover among welfare recipients would be evidence of little dependency. If, however, the same families were found to be poor year after year, this would be a matter of concern.

To explore the possibility of welfare dependency in the United States, a University of Michigan study tracked five thousand families over a number of years, paying particular attention to economic mobility both from year to year and from one generation to the next.[7] The study first examined poverty from year to year, or dependency within a generation. It found that for most recipients welfare lasted less than a year, but there were some long-term recipients who were on welfare for at least eight years. The second and more serious concern was, do the children of the poor end up in poverty as well? Is there a cycle of poverty? To answer this question, the Michigan study examined the relation between the income of one generation and that of the next generation. The results indicate that only a minority of those who grow up in welfare homes become dependent on welfare. For white women there was a modest link between the welfare dependence of parent and child. For black women there was no link.

One way to look at the cycle-of-poverty question more generally is to examine how much mobility there is in the income distribution from one generation to the next. In the Michigan study, parents were divided into five equal groups based on income; their grown children were also placed in five groups according to income. The point was to see if the children of poor parents also tended to be poor. Exhibit 12 presents the mobility between generations for the sample tracked by the University of Michigan study. The five groups of parents, from poorest to richest, are listed in the left-hand column; the five groups of children, also ranked from poorest to richest, are listed across the top.

The first row of the table indicates how the children of the poorest parents fared with respect to income. A total of 44 percent of the children of the poorest parents were themselves among the poorest fifth of their genera-

[7] Greg J. Duncan, Richard D. Coe, and others, *Years of Poverty, Years of Plenty* (Ann Arbor: University of Michigan Press, 1984).

EXHIBIT 12
INTERGENERATIONAL MOBILITY

Parents	Young Adults Forming Households				
	Poorest Fifth	Second-Lowest Fifth	Middle Fifth	Second-Highest Fifth	Highest Fifth
Poorest fifth	44%	27%	18%	9%	2%
Second-lowest fifth	23	24	19	19	15
Middle fifth	11	23	23	26	17
Second-highest fifth	10	17	22	26	25
Highest fifth	9	13	19	23	36

Source: Computed based on Greg J. Duncan, Richard D. Coe, and others, *Years of Poverty, Years of Plenty* (Ann Arbor, Mich.: University of Michigan Press, 1984).

tion; 27 percent moved up to the next highest fifth, 18 percent jumped to the middle fifth, and so on. In contrast, among children of the wealthiest parents, only 9 percent found themselves among the poorest fifth, 13 percent in the next poorest, and so on. Although having poor parents does not doom one to be poor, those with parents in the poorest group were five times more likely to be in the bottom group than those with parents in the wealthiest group. Conversely, the chances of ending up in the wealthiest group were eighteen times greater if one's parents were in that group than if they came from the poorest group. If the children of all income groups had an equal opportunity of joining the highest group, the children of the poor would be just as likely to end up rich as poor.

WELFARE REFORM

There is much dissatisfaction with the welfare system, both among those who pay for the programs and among those who receive the benefits. A variety of welfare reforms have been suggested in recent years, ranging from dismantling many federal programs to increasing federal control so as to ensure more uniform support levels across states. One possible reform, introduction of the so-called negative income tax, has been the subject of a massive social experiment.

Negative Income Tax

*The **negative income tax** is a cash transfer program in which benefits are reduced as earnings rise.*

A **negative income tax** (NIT) gives cash transfers to poor families, providing them with a guaranteed minimum income and allowing them to keep a portion of any earnings. The program is called a negative income tax because the cash transfer is reduced as the family's earnings rise. Let's see how a NIT works.

Suppose that the program guarantees a family of four at least $8000 per year regardless of the family's earnings. If the family has no earnings, it will receive $8000 in transfers. The cash transfer decreases as the family's earned income increases; the amount by which transfers are reduced depends on the negative income tax rate. For example, if the negative income tax rate is 40 percent, transfers will be cut by $0.40 for each $1 earned. If the family earns $6000, its $8000 cash transfer will be reduced by $6000 x 0.40, or $2400. Thus the family's total income will be $6000 in earnings plus $5600 in transfers, for a total of $11,600.

As the family's earned income increases, the tax rate (or benefit-reduction rate) on these earnings reduces the family's net cash transfer. If the family earns $20,000, its negative income tax is $8000 (that is, $20,000 × 0.40), which reduces the transfer to zero. Such a family is at the *break-even point*, which is where the tax and the subsidy cancel out. Thus we can specify three components to the negative income tax: the guaranteed minimum, G; the negative tax rate, r; and the break-even point, B. They are related as follows: $B = G/r$. If you know the value of any two variables, you can solve for the third.

Critics of the NIT argued that providing people with a guaranteed income would reduce their incentive to work. The federal government set up an extensive series of economic experiments to observe the effects of providing a guaranteed minimum income on work incentive and on family stability. The experiments began in 1968 and lasted ten years, eventually involving 8700 people. The tests ran for different intervals in different parts of the country. The most extensive experiments ran from 1971 to 1978 in Seattle and Denver.

The important question for the researchers was whether the guaranteed minimum reduced work effort. The results suggest that it did. In the Seattle and Denver experiments, the number of hours worked fell on average by 9 percent for husbands and by 20 percent for wives. The greatest effect appeared to be among young males not yet heading households, who reduced their work effort by 43 percent. This latter outcome is troubling, because young males are considered to be most in need of developing the work skills and job discipline required to establish themselves in the work force.

Another concern of experimenters was the effect of the NIT on the stability of the family. There is some indication that a guaranteed income had a destablilizing effect on the family, as divorce rates were above average among participants in the experiment, particularly among households with no children. The results concerning work effort and family stability have been interpreted differently by different researchers, but the net effect of the experiments has been to deflate enthusiasm for a negative income tax as a solution to the problem of poverty.

Recent Reforms

Few women on welfare hold jobs. Some analysts believe that one way to reduce poverty is to provide welfare recipients with job skills and to find jobs for those who are able to work. Some sort of "workfare" component for welfare recipients has been introduced in over thirty-five states. In such states, as a condition of receiving AFDC, the head of the household has to agree to search for work, participate in education and training programs, or take some form of paid or unpaid position. The idea was to acquaint those on welfare with the job market so that they need not depend on welfare. Evidence from various states indicates that programs involving mandatory job searches, short-term unpaid work, and training can be operated at low cost and do affect employment.

Reforms at the state level set the stage for federal reform. When Congress began deliberating on welfare reforms in early 1987, Senator Daniel Patrick Moynihan outlined three guidelines for developing a new system. First, the primary responsibility for child support should rest with the child's parents. Second, the able-bodied mother of a child should have a responsibility to support her child by working, at least part-time. And third, the government should provide time-limited child support to the extent that parental support is inadequate.[8] In Moynihan's view, therefore, public assistance should be viewed as a short-term supplement to family income.

Federal welfare reform was debated for nearly two years before a bill was finally passed. The Family Support Act of 1988, the first substantial welfare reform since 1935, appears consistent with Senator Moynihan's guidelines. To increase the incentive to work, welfare recipients are assured one year of day care assistance and Medicaid after they work their way out of the AFDC program. The reform is aimed at smoothing the transition from welfare dependency for some of the 3.5 million single mothers on welfare. By providing day care and Medicaid for a year, the measure reduces the marginal tax rate associated with employment.

To encourage spouses to stay together, the Family Support Act requires all states to provide benefits for families with a father who is present but unemployed (half the states already provided such coverage). Another provision requires that in two-parent welfare families where neither parent is employed, one parent should work at least sixteen hours a week in unpaid community service. The objective is to help people develop job skills and make a social contribution.

The measure also calls for deducting from the paycheck of the absent parent child support payments that are legally due. But half of the children receiving AFDC were born outside marriage, and in many cases the whereabouts of the father is unknown. Also, since AFDC aid is reduced by child support payments, the mother has little economic incentive to identify the father for support.

Whether the measure will have any real impact on poverty remains to be seen. Though state governments endorse the reforms, the act has attracted little public support.

---

[8] Maureen Dowd, "Moynihan Opens Major Drive to Replace Welfare Program," *New York Times*, 24 January 1987.

CONCLUSION

Government redistribution programs have been most successful at reducing poverty among the elderly, whose poverty rates have been cut in half since 1970. But poverty rates among children have increased by one-third. Most of the income transfers in the economy are not from the government but rather within the family, from parents to children. Thus any change in a family's capacity to earn income has serious consequences for dependent children. Family structure appears to be a primary determinant of family income. The poorest income group, the underclass, consists primarily of minority, female-headed households concentrated in the poorest sections of our central cities. The problem of poverty in the central cities is compounded by the crime and drug addiction that can make daily life there terrifying. Those who suffer most are the children. One fifth of the children in the United States live in poverty — over 12 million in all. Children are the innocent victims of the changing family structure.

Summary

1. Money income in the United States became more evenly distributed across households between 1929 and 1947, but this distribution has changed little since 1947.

2. During the 1960s the economy boomed and the poverty rate fell, reaching a low of 11.1 percent in 1973. Between 1973 and 1979, the level of poverty fluctuated but showed no substantial decline. Since 1983 the poverty rate has fallen somewhat, but it is still higher than it was in 1973.

3. Since 1959 poverty rates have dropped the most among the elderly and among families headed by black males. Families with a head of household under 25 were the only group to experience an increase in the poverty rate since 1959. A major contributor to poverty has been the increase in female-headed households.

4. Black men who are older and who have a high school rather than a college education appear

to earn less for comparable jobs than do white men. Affirmative action provisions seem to have increased employment opportunities among blacks. There is no evidence that blacks have less access to cash transfer programs.

5. Among the unintended effects of income assistance is a high marginal tax rate on earned income, which may discourage employment and create welfare dependency. Although some families depend on welfare for long periods, there is little evidence of a cycle of poverty from one generation to the next.

6. The results of experiments with a negative income tax suggest that providing families a guaranteed income through cash transfers may reduce the incentive to work. Welfare reforms introduced by the states set the stage for federal welfare reforms, which tried to promote the transition from welfare to work.

1. (Depressions and the Rich) "The only people who benefit from a depression are the rich, who can adequately protect themselves." Evaluate this statement in light of Exhibit 1 in the chapter.

2. (Lorenz Curve) Construct a Lorenz curve using the following hypothetical income data for a country with only five households: H1, $10,000; H2, $4000; H3, $3000; H4, $2000; H5, $1000.

3. (Poverty in the United States) How would you explain the drop in Exhibit 4 in the percentage of the population below the official poverty level during the 1960s? Why did the percentage rise during the early 1980s? Are these statistics deceptive?

4. (Poverty in the United States) Should the U.S. government attempt to completely eliminate poverty? Why or why not?

5. (Economic Growth and Poverty) "Economic growth is more effective than welfare programs in reducing poverty in the United States." Evaluate this statement.

6. (Poverty and Age) Why has poverty been rising dramatically among younger households and falling dramatically among elderly households?

7. (Poverty and Gender) Why are female-headed households more vulnerable to poverty than male-headed households are?

8. (Discrimination and Earnings) What types of discrimination can drive a wedge between what whites earn and what nonwhites earn? Consider discrimination in schooling, for example. How could you detect such discrimination?

9. (Welfare and the Underground Economy) How might the implicit tax on earned income (in the form of the loss of benefits from government assistance programs) affect the underground economy? How might some people avoid the implicit tax?

10. (Negative Income Tax) Give some reasons why the experiment with a negative income tax, as discussed in the chapter, might have led to a reduction in work effort. How could adjustments be made to reduce this loss of incentives?

11. (Indifference Curve Analysis) Using an indifference curve diagram that relates food to "all other goods," show the impact on utility of an in-kind transfer of food. (Hint: Such a transfer would allow the consumer to increase his or her consumption by the amount of the transfer, but not change the prices of the goods.) Compare the result to that of a pure cash transfer of equal dollar value.

12. (Impact of Transfer Programs) Suppose that cash transfers tend to decrease work effort. How would this affect your interpretation of before- and after-transfer income distributions as a measure of the impact of the cash transfer program?

13. (Charitable Contributions) Suggest a reason why people who voluntarily give money to charities tend to give less than they give through government.

14. (Income Distribution) Suppose the data in Exhibit 3 yield the following income-age relationships:

Age	Income (average)
22–32	$25,000
32–42	35,000
42–52	43,000
52–62	48,000
62–72	35,000

Calculate a Lorenz curve for each of the following age distributions:

	22–32	32–42	42–52	52–62	62–72
a.	20%	20%	20%	20%	20%
b.	15%	25%	25%	20%	15%
c.	15%	20%	30%	25%	10%

A Closer Look at Firms, Governments, and Externalities

A Closer Look at the Firm

The firm has been viewed thus far as a "black box" that hires resources on the basis of their marginal products, combines these resources efficiently to produce the profit-maximizing level of output, and sells this output for the profit-maximizing price. We have assumed that the firm knows what resources to employ and in what quantities. We have also assumed that the firm is aware of the latest technology, the price, quality, and availability of all resources, and the demand for its product.

We have said little about the internal structure of the firm or its finances, because our objective has been to understand how the price system coordinates the use of resources, not to understand the internal workings of the firm; in this chapter we will step inside the factory gate to consider some assumptions about the firm and its behavior. In some cases we will point out limitations of the idealized model of the firm; in other cases we will show that the model's usefulness does not necessarily rely on a particular assumption. In still other instances we will extend the model of the firm to make it more realistic. Overall, this chapter should help you develop a deeper understanding of the firm's role in the economy. Topics discussed in this chapter include

- Transaction costs
- Shirking and monitoring
- Vertical integration
- Economies of scope
- Contestable markets

- Corporate finance
- The separation of ownership from control
- The market for corporate control

THE RATIONALE FOR THE FIRM AND THE SCOPE OF ITS OPERATION

The model of perfect competition assumes that all participants in the market are fully informed about the price and availability of all inputs, outputs, and production processes. Such an assumption slights the role of the entrepreneur. If everyone had easy access to all the information required to make decisions, there would be little need for entrepreneurs. So far we have assumed that the firm is headed by a brilliant decision maker with a computerlike ability to calculate all the marginal productivities. This individual knows everything necessary to solve complex production and pricing problems.

The irony is that if the black box characterization of the firm were accurate—that is, if the marginal products of all inputs could be easily measured and if prices for all inputs could be determined without cost—then there would be little reason for production to take place in firms. In a world characterized by perfect competition, perfect information, and frictionless exchange, the consumer could bypass the firm, purchasing inputs in the appropriate amounts and paying each resource owner accordingly. Someone who wanted a table could buy timber, have it milled, contract with a carpenter, contract with a painter, and end up with a finished product. The consumer could carry out transactions directly with each resource supplier.

In this section we will explore two theories of why production is carried out within the firm. The first theory argues that the development of the firm is a response to the transaction costs of using the market directly. The second focuses on the role of the entrepreneur as a monitor of the "shirking" that arises when output is produced by a team of resource suppliers. As you will see, these are not so much competing theories of the firm as rationales that emphasize different functions of the firm.

The Firm Reduces Transaction Costs

Over fifty years ago, in a classic article titled "The Nature of the Firm," Ronald Coase asked the fundamental question "Why do firms exist?"[1] Why do people organize in the hierarchical structure of the firm and coordinate their decisions through a central authority rather than simply rely on market exchange? Coase's answer would not surprise today's students of economics: *organizing activities through the hierarchy of the firm is often more efficient than market exchange because production requires the coordination of many transactions among many resource owners.* The costs of transacting business through market relations are, according to Coase, often higher than those of undertaking the same activities within the firm.

---

[1] *Economica* 4 (November 1937): 386–405.

Coase's major insight was that economic activity is best understood in terms of the transaction costs involved in any system of exchange between individuals. The exchange relation between individuals is contractual in nature. When you buy any product, you agree to pay a certain amount—a contract is implicit. With major purchases, such as homes or cars, you actually sign contracts. Many resource owners sign contracts specifying the terms of supply. Thus contractual relations abound.

The firm itself is most easily understood in terms of a particular kind of contractual relation, called the *authority relation*. The entrepreneur agrees to pay the resource owner a specified amount in return for the authority to direct the use of that resource in the firm. The owner therefore sells the right to control the resource to the entrepreneur, who may do the managing or may hire a manager. In the market, resources are allocated based on prices, but in the firm, resources are guided by the decisions of managers. Coase argues that firms emerge when the transaction costs involved in using the price system exceed the costs of organizing those same activities through direct managerial controls in a firm.

Consider again the example of the consumer purchasing a table by contracting directly with all the different resource suppliers, from the grower of timber to the individual who paints the table. Using resource markets directly involves (1) the cost of determining what inputs are needed and (2) the cost of negotiating a separate agreement with each resource owner for each specific contribution to production. Where inputs are easily identified, measured, priced, and hired, production can be carried out through markets rather than within the firm. For example, getting your house painted is a relatively simple production task; you can buy the paint and brushes and hire painters by the hour. In this case you, the consumer, become your own painting contractor, hiring inputs in the market and combining these inputs to do the job.

Where the costs of determining inputs and negotiating a contract for each specific contribution are high, the consumer minimizes transaction costs by purchasing the product from a firm rather than hiring all the inputs directly through markets. For example, attempting to buy a car by contracting with the hundreds of resource suppliers required to put one together would be time-consuming and costly. What type of skilled labor should be hired and at what wages? How much steel, aluminum, and other materials should be purchased? How should the resources be combined and in what proportions? The task is impossible for someone who lacks special knowledge of car production. Consequently, it is more efficient for a consumer to buy a car produced by the firm than to contract separately with each resource supplier.

At the margin there will be some activities that could go either way, with some consumers using firms and some hiring resources directly in the markets. The choice will depend on the skill and opportunity cost of time of each consumer. For example, some people may not want to be troubled with hiring all the inputs to get their houses painted; instead, they will simply contract with a firm to do the entire job for an agreed-upon price — they will hire a contractor.

Shirking and the Entrepreneur

Like Coase, Armen Alchian and Harold Demsetz contend that the contractual arrangements typically associated with the capitalist firm are often more efficient than those contractual arrangements found exclusively in markets.[2] The very existence of firms, they argue, can be inferred from an analysis of rational behavior. Teams of resource suppliers working on a complex product can produce more in cooperation with one another than they can separately. Hence they have an incentive to coordinate their actions. But a special problem arises with team production: the tendency of team members to shirk. **Shirking** is the tendency to goof off or otherwise take it easy on the job.

Shirking is the tendency not to work as hard as required.

Because of the complex interdependence of inputs and because the contribution of each input typically cannot be observed directly in the final product, there is no way of keeping track of each worker's contribution. Hence there is no way of dividing revenues among the team members based on their respective contributions. Consequently, some other kind of allocation scheme is needed to divide the revenue arising from team production, such as an equal sharing of revenues. Since each worker's earnings are unrelated to his or her actual contribution, these sharing schemes give rise to the problem of shirking.

Although individual workers bear the full cost of their effort, each receives only a portion of what that effort produces. If a particular worker takes it easy, this reduction in effort is enjoyed exclusively by that "shirker" whereas the resulting diminished productivity is divided among all members of the group and is thus largely borne by others. Equal sharing of the fruits of production involves a fundamental asymmetry in incentives: the product of any individual's effort must be shared with all other members of the group, whereas the benefits of shirking, such as on-the-job leisure, are enjoyed exclusively by the shirker. Since each member will find it attractive to shirk, the group's total product will fall. As a result, each member may be worse off than if no shirking had occurred.

Even if some group members identify the problem, it is not easily solved. Alchian and Demsetz contend that the usual market mechanism, whereby outsiders can offer to replace shirkers, will not work because an outsider cannot identify the shirkers. Moreover, how can new members be prevented from shirking once they join the team? If the marginal products of team members could be monitored somehow so that shirking could be identified, this would resolve the problem.

---

[2] "Production, Information Costs, and Economic Organization," *American Economic Review* 62 (December 1972): 777–795.

The question that Alchian and Demsetz address is, how can this monitoring be carried out most efficiently? One possibility is to rotate jobs so that members of the team take turns serving as monitor. This approach, however, surrenders the benefits arising from specialization of the monitoring task. Moreover, the monitor has the incentive to shirk at that task, since monitoring costs are borne solely by the monitor whereas the benefits are shared by all. Thus who will monitor the monitor?

Because of the critical role of the monitor, the incentives must be structured so as to elicit the efficient amount of monitoring. Alchian and Demsetz argue that the best way to do this is to establish the monitor as the central contracting authority with each of the team's members and to give the monitor the right to all the revenue in excess of contractual payments to other team members. Each member is paid based on the estimated marginal revenue product, according to a contract between the monitor and each team member. The monitor then gets to keep any difference between total revenues and contractual costs. Under these circumstances there are clear incentives for the monitor to police shirking up to the point where the monitor's marginal cost of policing just equals the monitor's marginal gains from reducing that shirking.

This structure gives the monitor the incentive and the authority to adjust the contract in accordance with the observed marginal productivity of each resource. Rational team members should support such a move because these contracts are entered into voluntarily and team members are paid their marginal revenue products. Moreover, team members need not be concerned about shirking by other team members. *The result is a hierarchical relation based on voluntary contracting. Workers surrender control over their resources to the monitor in return for a contractual guarantee of payment.*

What we end up with is a description of the firm, where the monitor is the entrepreneur who guarantees payment in return for control. The firm emerges as the dominant form of organization whenever the net value of team production exceeds the net value of carrying out production through market arrangements—that is, whenever production is more efficiently organized within a firm than through market exchange.

The Scope of the Firm

We have explained why firms exist: firms minimize both the transaction and the production costs of economic activity. Next we ask, what is the efficient scope of the firm? The theory of the firm described in earlier chapters has been largely silent on questions concerning the boundaries of the firm—that is, on the appropriate degree of vertical integration. **Vertical integration** is the expansion of a firm into stages of production earlier or later than those in which the firm has specialized. For example, a steel company may decide to mine its own ore or to form its steel into various components. A large manufacturer employs an amazing variety of production processes, but on average about half of the cost of production goes to purchasing inputs from other firms.

Vertical integration is the expansion of a firm into stages of production earlier or later than those in which the firm has specialized.

What determines which activities the firm will undertake and which it will purchase from other firms? Should IBM manufacture its own computer chips or buy them from another firm? The answer depends on a comparison of the costs and benefits of internal production versus market purchases. The point bears repeating: internal production and markets are alternative ways of organizing transactions. The choice will depend on which form of organization is the more efficient way to carry out the transaction in question. Keep in mind that market prices coordinate transactions *between* firms, whereas managers coordinate activities *within* firms. The market coordinates resources by integrating the independent plans of separate decision makers, but a firm coordinates resources through the conscious direction of the manager. Coordination through a market is often more efficient than coordination within a firm because the market requires less conscious activity.

Thus the usual assumption is that transactions will be organized by markets unless market exchange presents problems. Sometimes, for example, it is difficult to use markets because the item in question is not standardized or the exact performance requirements are hard to specify. Consider, for example, trying to contract with another firm to supply research and development services. The amount of uncertainty involved in the purchase of such a nonspecific service makes it difficult to write, execute, and enforce contracts covering all possible circumstances that could arise. Many contingencies cannot be addressed adequately during contract negotiations, so events not covered in the contract inevitably occur. Since market participants do not like surprises, such incomplete contracts create a potentially troublesome situation. Thus, conducting research and development within the firm often involves a lower transaction cost than purchasing it in the market. Coase's analysis of transaction costs helps explain why production often can be carried out more efficiently in the firm than through market transactions. His analysis also suggests the appropriate amount of vertical integration in the firm.

At this point it will be useful to discuss specific criteria the firm considers in deciding whether to purchase a particular input in the market or produce it internally.

Bounded Rationality of Managers To direct and coordinate activity in a conscious way in the firm, the manager must comprehend how all the pieces of the puzzle fit together. As the firm takes on more and more activities, the manager starts losing track of things and the quality of managerial decisions suffers. The larger the firm, the longer the lines of communication between the manager and the production worker who must implement the decision. One limit to the extent of vertical integration is the manager's **bounded rationality**, which limits the amount of information the manager can comprehend about the firm's operation. When the firm takes on additional functions, it can experience diseconomies similar to those it experiences when it expands output beyond the efficient scale of production.

Bounded rationality limits the amount of information a manager can comprehend.

Minimum Efficient Scale In the long run, the average cost of production is minimized when the firm achieves its minimum efficient scale. For example, suppose that economies of scale in the production of dishwashers are exhausted when the production rate reaches 100,000 units per year, as shown by the average cost curve in panel (a) of Exhibit 1. Steel is an important component of household appliances. The question is, should the dishwasher manufacturer integrate backward into steel production? Sup-

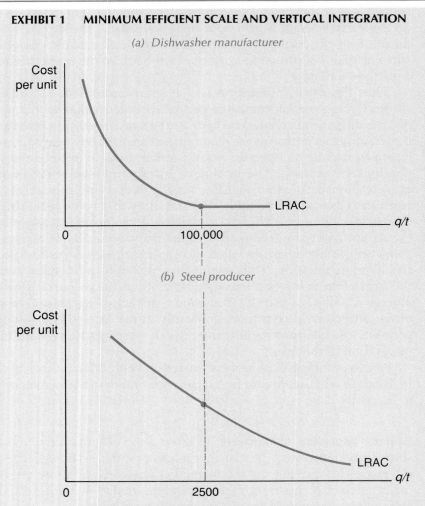

EXHIBIT 1   MINIMUM EFFICIENT SCALE AND VERTICAL INTEGRATION

(a) Dishwasher manufacturer

(b) Steel producer

The dishwasher manufacturer of panel (a) is producing at the minimum efficient scale of 100,000 units per period. That level of production requires 2500 tons of steel. If the manufacturer produced its own steel, the cost would be much higher than if it purchased steel from a steel producer operating on a much larger scale. As panel (b) shows, at 2500 tons, economies of scale in steel production are far from exhausted.

pose that economies of scale in steel production are not exhausted until production reaches a rate of 1 million tons per year. If each dishwasher requires 50 pounds of steel, the dishwasher manufacturer needs only 2500 tons of steel per year—a tiny fraction of the amount produced at the minimum efficient scale for steel plants. As you can see in panel (b) of Exhibit 1, if only 2500 tons of steel were produced per year, the cost per ton would be very high relative to the cost that could be achieved at minimum efficient size. The dishwasher manufacturer therefore minimizes production costs by buying steel from a steel firm of optimal size rather than trying to produce its own steel. More generally, *other things equal, firms should buy an input in the resource market when the cost is lower than it would be if the input were internally produced.*

Easily Observable Quality If an input is well defined and its quality is easily determined at the time of purchase, it is more apt to be purchased in the market than produced internally, other things constant. For example, a flour mill will typically buy its wheat in the market rather than grow its own, as the quality of the wheat can be easily assessed upon inspection. In contrast, the quality of other inputs can be determined only during the production process. Firms whose reputations depend on the operation of a key component are likely to produce that component, especially if the quality of that component cannot be easily observed by inspection. For example, suppose that the manufacturer of a sensitive measuring instrument requires a crucial gauge, the quality of which can be observed only as the gauge is assembled. If the firm produces the gauge itself, it can closely monitor quality.

Number of Suppliers A firm wants an uninterrupted source of component parts. When there are many interchangeable suppliers of a particular input, a firm is more likely to purchase that input in the market than produce it internally, other things constant. Not only does the existence of many suppliers ensure a dependable source of components, but competition among the many suppliers keeps the component price down. If the resource market is so unstable that the firm cannot rely on a consistent supply of the component, the firm may produce the item to insulate itself from the vagaries of that market.

Economies of Scope Thus far we have considered issues affecting the optimal degree of vertical integration. Sometimes firms branch out into product lines that do not have a vertical relation. **Economies of scope** exist when it is cheaper to combine two or more product lines in one firm than to produce them separately. Outlays for buildings, research and development, advertising, and product distribution can be minimized when spread over different products. For example, car dealers sell not only new cars but also used cars; they sell car service and repairs too. Farmers often grow a variety of crops and raise different kinds of farm animals. A major food company may produce breakfast cereals, baked goods, and a variety of other food products. With economies of scale, the cost per unit of output falls as the scale of

Economies of scope exist when it is cheaper to combine two or more product lines in one firm than to produce them separately.

Oliver E. Williamson
(b. 1932)

Individuals and businesses sometimes find it profitable to invest in specialized assets of various kinds—unique machines, for example, which are not easily sold or transferred to other uses, or employees with special skills. Most often, specialized assets of this sort create problems for the smooth functioning of markets. Someone who plays a unique part in a specialized and complex production process can threaten to pull out unless the other parties involved agree to transfer most of the gains of production to that person. (Think of the star professional athlete walking out of camp until management agrees to a higher salary.) This possibility creates friction in the marketplace. And, as we saw, a market works best when it is contestable—that is, when there are no irreversible commitments or specialized assets to prevent competitors from quickly entering the market.

But the market also has ways of making good use of irreversible commitments and specialized assets. Sometimes, in fact, an irreversible commitment can help make contracts go through more smoothly. In order to persuade you to combine your specialized assets productively with my assets, I can agree to make an irreversible commitment of my own. My commitment becomes a kind of insurance that I won't pull out of the contract, because doing so would hurt me as much as you.

More generally, the market has a nifty device for reducing the difficulties posed by specialized assets. It's called a business firm. If one party—the firm—owns all the unique machines and other specialized assets used in production, there is no longer a threat of a holdout. One reason for the existence of firms, then, is that common ownership is sometimes less costly than

contractual arrangements when there are specialized assets involved.

The author of many of these ideas is a professor at Berkeley named Oliver Williamson. Born in Superior, Wisconsin, and educated at MIT, Stanford, and Carnegie-Mellon, Williamson has made a career of opening up the "black box" of the firm and looking inside. In the 1960s he did pioneering work on the behavior of managers within corporations. Since then he has developed an approach to theory called transaction-cost economics. This approach attempts to explain market behavior and organizational structure by recognizing that firms face not only normal costs of production but also various other, less visible costs of transacting and exchanging. The difficulties caused by the use of specialized assets, for example, are one source of such transaction costs.

Portrait by University of California, Berkeley

Richard Langlois

the firm increases; with economies of scope, per unit production costs fall when the firm produces more than one kind of product.

CONTESTABILITY

A market is **contesta-ble** as long as firms can enter or leave at will—as long as no irreversible invest-ments are required to enter.

Another assumption of our analysis of firm behavior thus far is that perfect competition requires a large number of firms. Research suggests, however, that as long as firms can enter and leave the market with ease, existing firms will be unable to earn an economic profit in the long run regardless of how many firms are in the market. Such markets are said to be **contestable**. Even though only one firm may now be serving the market, as long as there are no entry or exit barriers, other firms will enter and "contest" this market if the existing firm charges a price that provides economic profits. A contestable market is one in which the potential entrant can serve the same market and has access to the same technology as the existing firm.

Suppose that you cut grass in your neighborhood during the summer. All you need is the family lawn mower, some gasoline, and some time. If you are the only one in your neighborhood who offers these services, are you a monopolist? Well, you are a monopolist in the sense that you are the only seller of services in this particular market, but you are not necessarily a monopolist in the sense that you have market power. Because no special skills are required and because most homes already have a lawn mower, entry into this business is easy. No irreversible investments need to be made.

An investment is said to be *irreversible* if, once the investment is made, the asset is dedicated to the production of a particular good and cannot easily be redirected toward producing another good. For example, auto manufacturers and cosmetic surgeons make irreversible investments in capital. Entrepreneurs are less willing to risk entering a market if entry requires irreversible investments, because irreversible investments result in sunk costs. *Sunk costs* are those fixed costs that cannot be recovered even in the long run. The larger the sunk costs involved, the larger the economic profit necessary to attract a new firm into the industry, other things constant. Therefore, whenever irreversible investments in human or physical capital must be made in order to produce in a particular market, that market is not likely to be contestable.

How high would the price you charge for cutting lawns have to rise to attract rivals? Since the mower in most households is underutilized, its opportunity cost is near zero. The gasoline is also a relatively minor expense. Hence only the opportunity cost of time is important. Suppose the opportunity cost of your time is the same as that of potential competitors. If you charge a price that yields an economic profit—that is, that pays you more than the opportunity cost of your time—you will be undercut (or mowed down?) by new entrants. This market is contestable because entry barriers are relatively low.

Let's consider an example of contestability on a larger scale. Suppose only one airline offers passenger service between two cities. If other airlines can easily send planes into that market when profits rise and assign the planes to different routes if profits fall, the market is contestable. *In summary, a large number of firms are not necessary to ensure the competitive outcome as long as firms will be challenged by new entry whenever they earn more than a normal profit.*[3]

CORPORATE FINANCE

During the Industrial Revolution, labor-saving machinery made large-scale production more profitable, so manufacturers began to require large capital investments. The corporate structure served these capital needs and by 1920 accounted for most employment and output in the economy. In Chapter 4 we examined the pros and cons of the corporate form of business organization, but thus far we have said little about corporate finance.

As was noted in Chapter 4, a corporation is a legal entity, distinct from its shareholders, created by the state. To incorporate a business, the owners must draw up a *certificate of incorporation* and send it to the secretary of state where the business seeks incorporation. The corporation may own property, earn profits, sue or be sued, and incur debt. Stockholders are liable only to the extent of their investment in the firm. Use of the abbreviation "Inc." or "Corp." in the company name serves as a warning to potential creditors that shareholders will not accept unlimited personal liability. *Corporations acquire funds for investment in three ways: by selling stock, by retaining part of their profit, and by borrowing.*

Stocks

Corporations *float new stock issues* to raise money for working capital and for new plant and equipment. Suppose, for example, you have incorporated the Chocolate Chip Cookie Corporation (4C) and want to raise $1 million by issuing stock in the company. First you must provide details of the firm's operation in a lengthy *registration statement* filed with the *Securities and Exchange Commission*, or SEC, the federal body that regulates securities markets. You must also prepare a *prospectus*, which conveys the most important of these facts to any potential purchasers of the new issue.

The new stock issue is purchased by an *investment banker* for a negotiated price, say $100 per share for the 10,000 shares issued. The investment banker then sells the issue to the public. Investment bankers *underwrite* the issuance of new securities by guaranteeing the corporation a certain price before the securities are sold to the public. As an underwriter, the investment banker incurs the risk of price fluctuations while a new issue is being sold.

---

[3] For an extensive discussion of contestability, see Elizabeth E. Bailey and William J. Baumol, "Deregulation and the Theory of Contestable Markets," *Yale Journal on Regulation* 1, no. 2 (1984): 111–137.

A *share* of stock represents a claim to a *share* of the company's assets and earnings, as well as the right to vote on corporate directors and on other matters. A person who bought 10 percent of the shares issued would own 10 percent of the company, be entitled to 10 percent of any profit, and have 10 percent of the votes.

Corporations must pay corporate income tax on any profits. After-tax profits are either paid as dividends to shareholders or reinvested in the corporation. Reinvested profits, or *retained earnings*, allow the firm to grow. Stockholders expect dividends, but the corporation is not bound by contract to pay dividends. Once shares are issued, their price tends to fluctuate directly with the firm's prospects for earning profits.

Bonds

> A **bond** is a piece of paper reflecting the corporation's promise to pay the holder a fixed sum of money on the designated maturity date plus an annual interest payment, or coupon, until the date of maturity.

Another way the corporation can raise money is by borrowing. The corporation can go directly to a bank for a loan or can issue bonds through an investment banker. A **bond** is a piece of paper reflecting the corporation's promise to pay the holder a fixed sum of money on the designated *maturity date* plus an annual interest payment, or *coupon*, until the date of maturity. For example, a corporation might issue 10,000 bonds, each with the promise to pay the holder $1000 at the end of twenty years plus an annual interest payment, or coupon, of $100.

The payment stream for bonds is much more predictable than that for stocks. Unless the corporation goes bankrupt, it is obliged to pay bondholders $100 every year for twenty years and to return the $1000 at the end of that time. Furthermore, stockholders are last in line when resource holders get paid, so bondholders get paid before stockholders. Thus investors consider bonds less risky than stocks.

But bond prices may still fluctuate for two reasons. First, if a firm's poor performance raises the possibility that bondholders might not get their money, bond prices will fall. Second, *whenever the interest rates go up, the market value of previously issued bonds goes down*. In our example, the interest on a $1000 bond was $100 per year. What if, after those bonds were sold, the interest offered on comparable new bonds rose to $120 per year? Nobody would pay $1000 for a bond paying a coupon of only $100 when newer bonds selling for $1000 were paying a coupon of $120. Consequently, the only way a bond offering an interest payment of $100 would sell is if its price were reduced. *Because bond prices fluctuate inversely with the firm's economic strength and with movements in the interest rate, bond ownership involves some risk.*

Securities Exchanges

Once stocks and bonds have been issued and sold, holders of these securities are free to sell them on *security exchanges*. In the United States there are ten security exchanges registered with the SEC. The New York Stock Exchange is by far the largest, trading the securities of over two thousand major companies and handling over 80 percent of the trades that occur. Next largest is the American Stock Exchange, which is also in New York City. A few smaller regional exchanges are located in major cities around the country. The wishes of buyers and sellers are expressed on the exchange floor through open auction among stock brokers or traders. The over-the-counter (OTC) market trades securities that are not listed on organized stock exchanges. On the OTC market, buyers and sellers are matched electronically by the computerized National Association of Securities Dealers Automated Quotation (NASDAQ) system.

Nearly all the securities traded each day are *secondhand securities* in the sense that they have already been sold by the issuing company. So the bulk of the transactions do not provide funds to firms in need of investment capital. Most money goes from a securities seller to a securities buyer. *Institutional investors*, such as banks, insurance companies, and mutual funds, account for over half the trading volume on the New York Stock Exchange. By providing a *secondary market* for securities, exchanges raise the *liquidity* of these securities—that is, the exchanges make the securities more readily exchangeable for cash.

The secondary markets for stocks also determine the current market value of the corporation. The market value of a firm at any given time can be found by multiplying the share price times the number of shares. For example, if 4C stock is selling at $200 per share, the market value of the firm equals $200 times the 10,000 outstanding shares, or $2 million. Securities prices give the firm's management some indication of the wisdom of raising new capital through new stock issues or new bond issues. The more profitable the company, other things constant, the higher the value of shares on the stock market and the lower the interest rate that would have to be paid on new bond issues.

More successful firms will receive more for selling new issues and therefore will not have to dilute ownership much to issue new shares. For example, suppose 4C has done so well that a share of stock, which initially sold for $100, has doubled in price to $200. Suppose also that managers at 4C would like to raise an additional $1 million by issuing new stock. If the new shares sell for $200 each, only 5000 new shares need be sold to raise $1 million. Owners of the original issue will still own 10,000, or two-thirds, of the 15,000 shares outstanding after the new issue is sold. If, however, 4C has foundered from the start and its stock has dropped to $50 per share, 20,000 shares will have to be sold at that price to raise $1 million in new funds. Buyers of the new issue will control two-thirds of the company. A struggling firm will also have to pay a higher interest rate on new bonds than will a more profitable firm. *Thus capital markets allocate funds more readily to successful firms than to firms in financial difficulty.* Some firms may be in such sad financial shape that they cannot issue new securities. Capital markets promote the survival of the fittest.

The third function performed by securities markets is in the market for corporate control, which we will discuss next.

CORPORATE OWNERSHIP AND CONTROL

Up to this point we have assumed that firms attempt to maximize profits. Earlier we described the entrepreneur as the individual responsible for guaranteeing payment to owners of the other resources in return for the opportunity to direct the use of these resources in the firm and the right to any profit or loss. We said that the entrepreneur need not actually manage the firm's resources as long as the entrepreneur has the power to hire and fire the manager — that is, as long as the entrepreneur controls the manager.

Managerial Behavior in Large Corporations

In a small firm there is usually little danger of the hired manager's not following the wishes of the owner. A manager who does not respond to the owner's desires will be replaced by one who does. As the modern corporation has evolved, however, its ownership has become widely distributed among many stockholders, leaving no single stockholder with either the incentive or the ability to control the manager. Economists since the days of Adam Smith have been concerned with what is known as the **separation of ownership from control** in the large corporation.

Separation of ownership from control occurs when no single stockholder has the incentive or ability to control the management of a corporation.

Various economists have formulated theoretical models suggesting that, when freed from the control of a dominant stockholding influence, managers will attempt to pursue their own selfish goals rather than those of the firm's owners. The alternatives vary from model to model, but emphasis has focused on such goals as maximizing the firm's rate of growth or increasing the perquisites and discretionary resources available to the managers, such as attractive surroundings, corporate jets, and other amenities. Managers may pursue firm growth because they want to enjoy the power, security, and status associated with a growing firm. As goals other than profit are pursued, so the argument goes, the firm's resources are used less efficiently, resulting in a lower level of profit. Thus the stockholders — the owners of the firm — suffer because managers are not furthering owners' best interests.

Constraints on Managerial Discretion

Analysts have identified a variety of constraints that can serve as checks on wayward management. The nature and effectiveness of each constraint will be examined next.

Economics of Natural Selection Some economists argue that even if managers are freed from the control of a dominant stockholder, the rigors of competition in the product market will force them to maximize profits. The "economics of natural selection" ensures that only the most efficient firms will be able to survive. Other firms simply will not earn enough profit to attract and retain resources and so will eventually go out of business.

The problem with this argument is that although pressure to pursue profits may arise when firms sell their product in competitive markets, many large corporations are at least partially insulated from intense product competition. Either because government regulations protect their firms from competition or because the firms enjoy some degree of market power, many managers have a certain amount of discretion in how they use their firms' resources. Such managers could divert corporate resources into activities reflecting their own interests yet still earn enough profit to ensure their firms' survival.

Managerial Incentives Other economists have examined the manager's incentive structure. If executive pay is linked closely to the firm's profit, the compensation scheme may encourage the manager to pursue profit even in the absence of a dominant stockholder or competition in the product market. Evidence suggests that at least a portion of the typical manager's compensation is tied to the firm's profitability through some type of bonus pay scheme or stock option plan.

Even if the manager's income is tied to profit, the manager will not necessarily attempt to maximize profit. The manager in a large corporation who diverts profit to other ends will simply forgo some income. This profit diversion may be "cheap" in view of the small fraction of the firm's shares typically owned by management. For example, if the manager owns 1 percent of the firm's shares and can divert $10,000 of potential profits to buy an expensive desk, this diversion will cost the manager only $100 in forgone pretax profits. After corporate taxes and personal income taxes, the cost is less than half that amount. Thus the existence of a link between executive pay and firm profit is not necessarily evidence that managers will attempt to maximize profit; it is only evidence that profit diversion will involve some personal cost, which may be quite small.

Stockholder Voting Each year stockholders have an opportunity to attend the company meeting and elect the board of directors. Couldn't stockholders join forces to oust an inefficient manager? What about that "corporate democracy" so often heralded on Wall Street? In fact, chances of an effective stockholder revolt are slim. The average stockholder does not have the information, the resources, or the incentive to challenge management. Most shareholders either ignore the voting altogether or dutifully pass their votes to the managers.

The dissatisfied stockholder, however, does have one very important alternative. The stockholder can "fire" the manager and the firm simply by selling shares in the corporation. Some economists contend that the possibility of a widespread vote of no confidence provides a check on managerial discretion that may ultimately lead to corporate reform. According to this argument, as dissatisfied stockholders sell their holdings, the share price drops and the firm becomes more attractive as a target for a reform-minded capitalist. A so-called *corporate raider* can buy a controlling interest in the firm at a relatively low price, reform or replace the management, and then benefit when the firm's improved prospects for profit lead to an appreciation in the value of shares. The effects of this market discipline will be examined next.

The Market for Corporate Control

The market for corporate control has been championed by many economists as an efficient mechanism for allocating and reallocating corporate assets to those who value them most highly. If the firm's assets are undervalued in the stock market, some entrepreneur has an incentive to "buy low and sell high"—that is, to buy firms that own undervalued resources and take measures to increase the value of these resources.

The effectiveness of this market in checking managerial abuses depends on the existence of someone with (1) the ability to identify firms that are performing below potential, (2) access to the resources necessary to carry off a successful takeover, and (3) the savvy to turn the situation around. There are a variety of reasons why this market may not operate perfectly.

A major problem with the market for corporate control is that outsiders have difficulty determining whether a firm is being run efficiently. Often when a firm performs poorly, it is unclear whether the management is poor or the assets of the firm are not what they seem. Management is likely to be better informed than a potential corporate raider. Some types of information are more public than others, however. For example, the value of oil reserves tends to be widely known in that industry. Thus, when an oil firm's market value falls significantly below the underlying value of the firm's assets, we expect a takeover to be attempted, as happened frequently during the 1980s.

Other problems arise during a takeover attempt. Although the corporate raider would prefer to quietly buy up a controlling interest in the firm, such a major purchase would not go unnoticed in the stock market. Moreover, once a single person or entity acquires 5 percent ownership in a firm, that position in the market must be registered with the SEC, thereby becoming public information.

*A **tender offer** is an attempt to attain a controlling interest in a firm by purchasing shares at a premium over the market price.*

A corporate raider usually attempts to acquire a controlling interest through a public **tender offer** for the firm's shares, in which stockholders are offered more than the prevailing share price. For example, a raider may offer to pay $30 per share for stock that had been trading at $20 per share prior to the takeover attempt. If a controlling number of shares are tendered by shareholders, the raider will purchase them and the takeover will be successful. If too few shareholders agree to sell, however, the deal will fall through and the tender offer will be withdrawn or amended.

The evidence indicates that successful takeovers increase the wealth of stockholders in the company that is taken over. Estimates of the amount by which shares appreciate vary from study to study, ranging between 16 and 34 percent. There is evidence that the value of the acquiring company's shares increases as well, though by a smaller amount. Thus stockholders appear to benefit from takeover activity.

The incumbent managers have access to all the firm's resources in defending themselves against an unwanted suitor. They are in a position to adopt strategies designed either to make the firm less attractive as a takeover target or to make a takeover more difficult. Defensive strategies range from costly legal actions to newspaper advertisements urging stockholders to reject the tender offer. The recent wave of takeover activity has created a colorful vocabulary for describing the offensive and defensive strategies of each side in a takeover. What follows is a brief glossary of these expressions.

Golden parachutes are provisions that guarantee lavish payments to incumbent managers if they are fired as a consequence of a takeover. About half of the five hundred largest corporations have golden parachutes.[4] These lucrative severance agreements have been criticized because they seem to protect managers' interests at the stockholders' expense. Defenders argue that the practice gives management the security necessary to be unbiased in negotiating with possible merger partners.

A *white knight* is someone or some firm that comes to the rescue of a firm facing an unwanted takeover. The target firm, when confronted with the possibility of being swallowed up by an unsolicited takeover, often seeks out a "white knight" as a merger partner. Incumbent managers presumably expect to receive kinder treatment from a white knight than from a hostile suitor.

Greenmail is a premium paid by a target company to buy back its own shares from a potential raider. The expression alludes to the fact that management is forced to pay an inflated share price to avoid the takeover — blackmail paid in green money. As a defensive strategy, paying greenmail to one raider can be counterproductive in that it often attracts another. Supporters of greenmail say that to the extent that these share repurchases make attempts at takeovers less risky for would-be corporate raiders, they stimulate the market for corporate control by increasing the number of attempted takeovers. Critics claim that the management is using the company's resources to prevent a takeover that may, in fact, be in the stockholders' best interests.

Junk bonds are bonds issued by a corporate raider to help finance a takeover. Junk bonds either are not rated by the bond-rating companies or are rated among the poorest of risks. In a typical takeover involving junk bonds, the corporate raider first visits major financial institutions, asking them to agree to purchase bonds in the event that the raider's tender offer elicits a sufficient number of shares. As collateral for these junk bonds, the raider pledges the assets and expected profits of the target company. Because these bonds offer a high interest rate, financial institutions often find them attractive. When the necessary commitments have been lined up, a tender offer is made to the public. If enough shares are tendered, the raider sells the

---

[4] According to a recent Securities and Exchange Commission ruling, stockholders may also get to vote on such provisions. See Kevin Salwin, "Ruling by SEC May Threaten Parachute Plans," *Wall Street Journal*, 18 January 1990.

bonds to raise enough money to buy the shares. If too few shares are tendered, the deal falls through and no bonds are sold.

Poison pills are actions taken by the management of a target firm to make that firm less attractive (that is, poison) to potential raiders. These actions may include selling valuable assets, merging with another firm to create antitrust problems for potential raiders, buying back the firm's shares and thereby loading the firm up with debt, or imposing heavy costs for replacing the existing management (that is, creating golden parachutes). Some oil companies, for example, sold their much-sought-after oil reserves so that they would not be taken over.

A leveraged buyout is a corporate takeover that is financed mostly by debt. A firm's financial leverage is measured by the ratio of its debt to its equity. The higher this ratio, the more the firm is said to be *leveraged*, or dependent on debt. Corporate acquisitions that are financed primarily by debt result in firms that are highly leveraged, so debt-driven acquisitions are called leveraged buyouts. The debt resulting from a leveraged buyout is often repaid by selling off parts of the acquired company. Leveraged buyouts allow a corporate raider with little personal wealth to acquire a large corporation by using debt secured with the assets and potential profits of the acquired firm. The gamble, if successful, can yield a huge payoff to the raider. Not all leveraged buyouts succeed, however, as the following case study shows.

CASE STUDY

Too Much Leverage

In April 1988, Robert Campeau, a Canadian real estate developer, paid $6.6 billion to acquire Federated Department Stores. A year earlier, Campeau had purchased Allied Stores for $3.7 billion. Both acquisitions were financed by borrowed funds, acquired mostly through junk bonds, and thus the deals were leveraged buyouts. As security, Campeau pledged the assets and earnings of the newly acquired companies.

To manage the huge debt, Campeau planned to cut operating costs and sell off parts of the vast retailing empire the two companies comprised. Over 10,000 employees were laid off, and retail chains, such as Bonwit Teller, Brooks Brothers, and I. Magnin, were sold. But proceeds from these sales were less than expected, and the remaining stores faced substantial debt service requirements, which drained the cash needed to pay other bills. By the summer of 1989, store suppliers were reluctant to provide goods on credit since they were unsure of payment.

To reduce the debt, Campeau attempted to sell the crown jewel of his acquisitions, Bloomingdale's. But nobody was willing to pay what Campeau thought the chain was worth. Federated and Allied were left in an impossible position since their debt service requirements far outstripped their expected cash flows. On January 15, 1990, after failing to make scheduled interest payments on $2.3 billion in debt, Federated and Allied filed for bankruptcy. The filing affected more than 100,000 employees at 258 stores, about 300,000 suppliers, plus bondholders and other creditors.

Whether these stores can work their way back to solvency remains to be seen.

The stores were well managed and highly regarded, but they could not support the crushing debt that resulted from the leveraged buyout. Financial analysts argue that Campeau paid too much for the firms and lenders were too willing to finance such a costly acquisition, particularly since Campeau had no experience in retailing. This was not the only leveraged buyout to sour. Corporate bond defaults in the United States more than doubled from about $5 billion in 1988 to about $12 billion in 1989. They were projected to more than double again to $25 billion in 1990. These defaults cooled the market for new issues of junk bonds and slowed the trend in leveraged buyouts these bonds finance.

Sources: "An Extra $500 Million Paid for Federated Got Campeau in Trouble," *Wall Street Journal*, 11 January 1990; "Bankruptcy Petition Brings Fresh Risks for Allied, Federated," *Wall Street Journal*, 16 January 1990; "Campeau Bankers Are Posing Some $2.3 Billion Questions," *New York Times*, 14 January 1990.

CONCLUSION

The firm has evolved through a natural selection process as the form of organization that minimizes both transaction and production costs. According to this theory of natural selection, those forms of organization that are most efficient will be selected by the economic system for survival. Attributes that result in profits will be rewarded, and those that do not will fall by the wayside. The form of organization selected may not be optimal in the sense that it cannot be improved upon, but it will be the most efficient form among those that have been tried. If there is a way to organize production that is more efficient than the firm, some entrepreneur will stumble upon it one day and be rewarded with greater profits. Thus the improvement may not be the result of any conscious design. Once a more efficient way of organizing production is uncovered, others will imitate the successful innovation.

Summary

1. According to Ronald Coase, firms exist because production often can be accomplished more efficiently through the hierarchy of the firm than through transactions carried out in markets. Because production requires the extensive coordination of transactions among many resource owners, all this activity can be carried out better under the direction of a manager in a firm than by consumers' specifying detailed performance contracts with many separate suppliers.

2. Alchian and Demsetz argue that in team production it is often difficult to observe each team

member's marginal contribution to the finished product. Team members may therefore have an incentive to goof off, or "shirk." This shirking can be reduced by appointing a monitor to police shirking in the firm. The monitor can contract with each resource supplier, then keep any difference between total revenues and contractual costs. The monitor, as residual claimant, therefore has a clear incentive to see that other resource suppliers do not shirk.

3. The extent to which a firm vertically integrates will depend on both the transaction and the production costs of economic activity. Other things equal, the firm is more likely to buy a component part than produce it if (1) the item can be purchased for less than the firm would have to pay to produce it, (2) the item is well defined and its quality is easily observable, or (3) there are a large number of interchangeable suppliers. Economies of scope exist when it is cheaper to combine two or more product lines in one firm than to produce them separately.

4. A large number of firms is not necessary to ensure the competitive outcome as long as firms are challenged by new entry whenever they earn more than a normal profit. A contestable market is one in which a potential entrant can serve the same market and has access to the same technology as an existing firm. Whenever irreversible investments in human or physical capital must be made in order to produce in a particular market, that market is not likely to be contestable.

5. Corporations secure investment capital from three sources: stock issues, retained earnings, and borrowing. Once new stocks and bonds are issued, these securities are bought and sold on securities exchanges. Stock prices tend to vary directly with the firm's profitability. Bond prices are also sensitive to the firm's profitability. Bondholders receive more predictable returns on their investments than do stockholders, but they must take into consideration the risk of default. Bond prices tend to vary inversely with prevailing interest rates.

6. The ownership of the modern corporation is typically fragmented among many stockholders, with no stockholder owning a dominant share. The fact that a poorly performing firm can be bought at a bargain price, shaped up, and sold for a profit is said to keep management behavior in accord with stockholders' interests.

Questions and Problems

1. (Internal Production Versus the Market) What economic factors determine whether a firm has its own legal staff or retains an outside law firm to handle its litigation?

2. (Shirking) What is the difference between the shirkers in a group and the less-skilled employees? Can this difference always be observed and monitored?

3. (Monitoring) What problems might arise in the practical application of Alchian and Demsetz's "monitor system"?

4. (Internal Production Versus the Market) Ashland Oil, Inc. is an oil refiner that buys its crude oil in the marketplace. Larger oil companies, such as Texaco, have their own crude oil production facilities. How would you explain this situation?

5. (Contracting) Department stores, among other enterprises, often contract with janitorial services to clean the store every night. Why doesn't the store simply hire its own janitors?

6. (Contracting) When you deposit money in a bank, you are really lending the money to

firms and home purchasers who borrow from the bank. The bank typically makes a profit on this transaction. What is it doing for you — that is, what keeps you from lending your money directly to the borrowers without paying the "middleman"?

7. (Production and Information) How does the technology of information processing influence both economies of scale and economies of scope?

8. (Contestable Markets) What are the differences and similarities between contestable and competitive markets?

9. (Contestable Markets) The concentration ratio (the percentage of market activity conducted by a few of the largest firms in the industry) is often used as a measure of competitiveness within a given industry.

   a. Are there problems with using this measure, given the contestable markets hypothesis?
   b. What factors should be taken into account

in determining the validity of this hypothesis?

10. (Corporate Finance) When a firm needs to raise capital, it can do so by issuing stocks or bonds. What are some of the factors management must take into account in determining which method to use?

11. (Managerial Behavior) Why might separation of ownership from control possibly lead to lower profitability for the firm?

12. (Managerial Behavior) How might the objectives of stockholders and the objectives of a growth-oriented management conflict?

13. (Corporate Takeovers) Who stands to gain and who stands to lose in a corporate takeover? Is the economy helped by such takeovers?

14. (Corporate Indebtedness) Why do corporate takeovers frequently lead to a rise in corporate indebtedness? Does corporate indebtedness benefit the economy? Why or why not?

C H A P T E R 3 1

Public Choice

The effects of government are all around us. The clothes you put on this morning were manufactured according to government regulations about everything from the working conditions of textile employees to the label providing washing instructions. Your breakfast cereal was made from grain grown on subsidized farms; the milk and sugar you put on your cereal were also subject to government price supports. The condition of the vehicle in which you rode to school was regulated by government, as was the driver's speed and sobriety. Your education has been subsidized in a variety of ways by government. Government has a pervasive influence on all aspects of your life and on the economy.

Yes, government is big business. The federal government spends well over $1 *trillion* per year, including more than $1 million just on paper clips. In Chapter 4 we introduced the roles government plays in the economy, and we have considered the effects government has on market competition, natural monopolies, labor unions, and income redistribution, among other things.

Until now we have assumed that government makes optimal decisions in response to the shortcomings of the private market—that when confronted with a failure in the private market, government adopts and implements the appropriate program to address the problem. But this is easier said than done. There are limits to the effectiveness of government activity, just as there are limits to the effectiveness of private sector activity. Sometimes a government "solution" may be worse than the market failure. Indeed, implementing a government program for every instance of private market failure would be like awarding the prize in a talent contest to the only other contestant after hearing the first.

In this chapter we will trace the government decision-making process and explore problems that arise with public choice. Beginning with the problem of majority rule in direct democracy, we proceed to complications that arise when public choices are delegated to elected representatives, who, in turn, delegate the implementation of these choices to government bureaus. Topics discussed in this chapter include

- Negative-sum games
- Median voter model
- Cyclical majority
- Representative democracy
- Rational ignorance

- Special interest legislation
- Rent seeking
- Underground economy
- Bureaucratic behavior

THE ECONOMY AS A GAME

One useful way of understanding the role of government is to think of the economy as a kind of game, which initially involves two major groups of players: consumers and producers. The players pursue their own self-interests: consumers attempt to maximize utility, and producers attempt to maximize profit. Economic coordination in a market economy hinges on players' ability to secure the rights and obligations of property as well as to enforce contracts. From time to time disagreements arise about property rights or the interpretations of contracts.

Players can either police themselves, as they do in card games, or hire an umpire or referee, as they do in most sports. A market economy often requires some third party (government) to resolve disputes, protect the rights to resources, and enforce contracts. Also, government may provide public goods and services and control activities that involve externalities in production or consumption—a topic addressed in the next chapter.

Fairness of the Game

Participants in a game often attach a value to the fairness, or equity, of the game. Fairness can be viewed from two perspectives. First, are the rules of the game fair to all participants—that is, is the *process* fair? A game may not be fair because the cards are marked, one player can see another's hand, or a group of players conspires against another player.

Fairness can also be viewed in terms of the results of the game. Is the *outcome* of the game fair? Suppose a few skilled or lucky players win all the chips. Some argue that if the rules are fair, then the outcome must by definition be fair, even if there are big winners and losers. Others argue that even fair rules will not result in a fair outcome if the players are not on equal footing at the outset. For example, what if certain players begin the game with fewer chips than the others? Or what if some players lack the skill to play well? Do these differences among players make the game less fair? If by fairness we mean that every player has an equal opportunity to win, differences in the initial endowment of chips or in the ability to play the game need to be taken into account. If players believe it is important that the *result* be fair, the rules can be changed to bring about what is viewed as a fairer outcome.

Kinds of Games

*A game is a **positive-sum game** if total winnings exceed total losses; if winnings just offset losses, it is a **zero-sum game**; if losses exceed winnings, it is a **negative-sum game**.*

By comparing the total amount of winnings and losses, we can classify games into three categories. If the winnings exceed the losses, the game is a **positive-sum game**; if the winnings are just offset by the losses, the game is a **zero-sum game**; and if the losses exceed the winnings, the game is a **negative-sum game**. Poker is a zero-sum game because the total amount of the winnings just equals the total amount of the losses. Most gambling activities, such as horse racing and state lotteries, are negative-sum games because the "house" and the government take a cut of the amount wagered.

Many people mistakenly think of market activity as a zero-sum game. Intuition suggests that the gains from one side of the market must come at the expense of the other side. But a key feature of market activity ensures that most exchanges will yield positive gains. Because market exchange is *voluntary*, participants expect to be at least as well off after engaging in market exchange as before. Product demanders expect consumer surplus, and resource suppliers typically expect producer surplus. Thus market exchange is usually a positive-sum game.

Rules and Behavior

Rules and rule changes can affect either the way the game is played or the distribution of winnings when the game is over. Laws such as those governing minimum wages, pollution controls, import restrictions, affirmative action, and farm price supports affect the conditions of market production and exchange. They influence what resources are used, in what quantities, and often at what price. These rules thereby have a direct effect on how the game is played.

Another set of rules redistributes the winnings when the game is over. Taxes and transfers redistribute earnings after production and exchange have taken place. The problem is that the way the winnings are reallocated can also influence the way the game is played. For example, what if all the winnings were divided equally among the players when the game was over? What effect do you suppose this would have on the intensity and quality of play? It's possible that players would not accord the same attention to the game as they would if it were "for keeps." Likewise, each individual's incentives to work, to invest, and to take risks will be affected by the redistribution of earnings.

Allowing changes in the rules can introduce other distortions that affect the efficiency and equity of the game. A player can either devote resources toward winning under the existing rules (sharpening game skills or playing with greater intensity) or spend time trying to change the rules to his or her advantage. Some rule changes can be of the positive-sum variety, actually helping players by making the game more efficient. Rule changes are known as **Pareto optimal** if at least one player is made better off and none is made worse off. Changes in the rules that help one player or class of players, however, often harm other players. In fact, rule changes may in the aggregate result in more harm to the losers than gain to the winners; such changes thus have a negative sum.

As you can see, the introduction of rules and rule changes can affect the economy in a variety of ways. Choices about the rules of the game are typically public choices. We turn now to a closer examination of the public choice process.

*Any change to the status quo is **Pareto optimal** if it makes at least one person better off while making no one worse off.*

PUBLIC CHOICE IN DIRECT DEMOCRACY

Government decisions about the supply of public goods and services and the collection of revenues are public choices. In a democracy public choices usually require approval by a majority of the voters. In some cases we can explain the choice of the electorate by focusing on the preferences of the median voter.

Median Voter Model

*The **median voter model** predicts that under certain conditions the preference of the median, or typical, voter will dominate other choices.*

The **median voter model** predicts that under certain conditions the preference of the median, or typical, voter will dominate other choices. Consider the logic behind the median voter model. Suppose you and two roommates have just moved into an apartment, and the three of you must decide on furnishings. You all agree that the common costs will be divided equally among the three of you and that majority rule will prevail, with one vote per person. The issue at hand is whether to rent a TV and, if so, of what size. The problem is that you each have different preferences. The more studious of your roommates considers a TV to be an annoying distraction. Your other roommate, a real TV fan, prefers the 36-inch screens often seen in bars and other cultural centers. Although by no means a TV addict, you enjoy watching TV as a relief from the rigors of academe; you think a 19-inch screen would be just fine. What to do, what to do?

Exhibit 1 illustrates your preferences and those of your roommates. The horizontal axis specifies the size of the TV screen, and the vertical axis indicates the order of preferences for the different sizes. Your studious roommate's preference is shown by the blue line, the TV fan's preference is shown by the green line, and your preference is shown by the red line. We focus on three possibilities: no TV, a 19-inch TV, and a 36-inch TV. Your

EXHIBIT 1   PREFERENCES FOR SIZE OF TV SCREEN

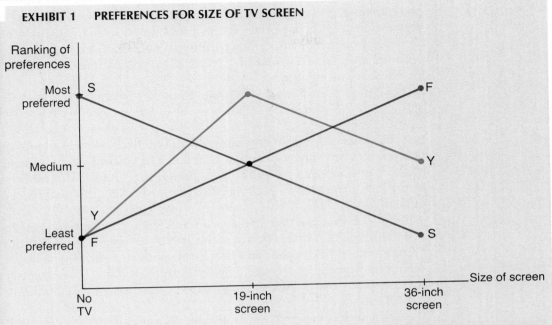

S prefers no TV most and a 36-inch screen least. F prefers just the opposite. The median voter, Y, prefers a 19-inch screen most and no TV least. In this case the 19-inch screen will be selected because there are more votes for it than for either of the other two options. The median voter's preference prevails.

studious roommate, S, most prefers the option of no TV, has medium preference for the 19-inch TV, and least prefers the 36-inch set. The order of preferences of the TV fan, F, are just the opposite. You, Y, most prefer the 19-inch screen but would rather have the 36-inch TV than no TV at all. Spend a moment becoming familiar with the figure.

You all agree to make the decision by voting on two alternatives at a time, then pairing the winning alternative against the remaining alternative until one choice dominates the others. When a motion for no TV is paired with a motion to rent the 19-inch set, the 19-inch set gains majority support because this option gets both your vote and the TV fan's vote. When a motion for the 36-inch screen is then paired with the motion for the 19-inch screen, the 19-inch screen wins a majority again, this time because your studious roommate sides with you rather than voting for the super screen.

Majority voting in effect delegates the public choice to the person whose preference is the median for the group. You, as the median voter in this case, can have your way; if you had wanted a 12-inch screen, you could have received majority support for that size. Similarly, *the median voter in an electorate often determines public choices. Political candidates try to get elected by appealing to the median voter.* This is one reason why there often appears to be little difference among candidates.

Note that under majority rule, only the median voter receives his or her preference. All other voters are required to go along with what the median voter wants. Thus the other voters usually end up paying for what they consider to be either too much or too little of the good. In contrast, under voluntary exchange in private markets, each consumer can purchase the desired amount of a good.

Logrolling

Logrolling *is the trading of support between voters.*

The outcome preferred by the median voter is less likely to prevail when many issues are subject to public choice. **Logrolling** occurs when voters pledge support for one issue in exchange for support on another issue. Logrolling can result in outcomes that do not reflect the preferences of the median voter.

Suppose that another choice you and your roommates need to make collectively is that of a stereo system. In this case your studious roommate prefers a powerful, expensive system, one with teeth-rattling speakers. You again prefer a more moderately priced system, and the TV fan would rather have no stereo at all. Thus you happen to be the median voter in this decision as well.

As the median voter, you would have your way under majority rule. If we introduce the possibility of logrolling, however, your choice may no longer dominate. Your two roommates realize that they are not getting their first choices in either decision. Suppose that the studious roommate agrees to vote for the super TV screen in return for the TV fan's vote for the powerful stereo system. By trading votes, or logrolling, they each get a first choice in one of the two decisions. You, as the median voter, no longer cast the deciding vote. This exchange of support usually results in greater outlays for the two items than would have been the case without such logrolling.

Cyclical Majority

Even without logrolling, a clear majority choice may not emerge. Suppose, for example, that the TV fan, as a purist, prefers no TV to any TV smaller than the super size. F's preference is shown by the green line in Exhibit 2; preferences of S and Y are the same as before. If under these circumstances the 19-inch screen is up for a vote against the giant screen, the 19-inch screen will win a majority, as before. If a motion for the 19-inch screen is then paired with the option of no TV, however, the no-TV alternative will gain a majority, winning both the studious roommate's vote and the TV fan's vote. If the no-TV option is then paired with the motion for a 36-inch screen, the large screen will win your vote and the TV fan's vote, thereby gaining a majority.

There is no dominant choice in this case. Although the 19-inch option defeats the 36-inch option, the no-TV option defeats the 19-inch option, and then the 36-inch option defeats the no-TV option. No matter which alternative wins in a particular pairing, there is always another option that

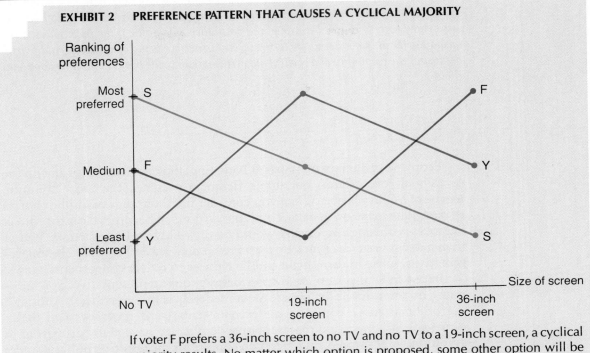

EXHIBIT 2   PREFERENCE PATTERN THAT CAUSES A CYCLICAL MAJORITY

If voter F prefers a 36-inch screen to no TV and no TV to a 19-inch screen, a cyclical majority results. No matter which option is proposed, some other option will be preferred by a majority of voters.

With a cyclical majority, no choice dominates all others. The outcome of a vote depends on the order in which the issues are considered.

can beat that winner. Instead of a clear majority, there is a **cyclical majority**, with the outcome depending on the order of voting. What causes this cycle is that the TV fan prefers no TV to any TV smaller than the giant one. Thus the TV fan's ordering does not rank TV size from highest to lowest in a direct way.

Perhaps an application to public finance will clarify the notion of a cyclical majority. Consider the preferences for education in your home town. Suppose that high-income families prefer that the public schools be first-rate. Families of middle income and below are not able to afford the taxes needed to pay for a top-quality school system and so prefer a moderate budget. High-income voters believe that if the schools are not going to be first-rate, then private schools are the appropriate choice for their children. If high-income families feel obliged to send their children to private schools, they will no longer support public school spending and will prefer a low budget to a moderate budget. Thus the most affluent families prefer the highest school budget, but if they can't have it, they prefer a low school budget to a moderate budget. This set of preferences will lead to a cyclical majority in public choices regarding the school budget.

You should remember several points from this discussion of majority rule. *First, when a single issue is under consideration, majority rule often reflects the views of the typical, or median, voter. Second, under majority rule all but the median voter will usually be required to purchase either more or less of the public good than he or she would have preferred. Thus majority rule means that there are likely to be many dissatisfied voters. Third, because of the possibility of logrolling, the preferences of the median voter may not dominate when several issues are being considered. And fourth, because of the possibility of a cyclical majority, majority rule may result in no dominant choice.*

REPRESENTATIVE DEMOCRACY

People vote directly on issues at New England town meetings and on the occasional referendum, but direct democracy is not the most common means of public choice. When you consider the thousands of public choices that must be made on behalf of individual voters, it becomes clear that direct democracy through referenda would be unwieldy and impractical. Rather than make myriad decisions by direct referenda, voters typically elect representatives, who, in turn, make public choices to reflect constituents' views.

In our federal system each voter helps choose representatives at a minimum of three levels of government: federal, state, and local. Although logrolling is more common under representative democracy than under direct voting, direct and representative democracy have many properties in common. For example, under certain conditions the resulting public choices reflect the preferences of the median voter. The question of representation, however, raises a special set of issues that we will explore in this section.

Goals of the Participants

We assume that consumers maximize utility and firms maximize profit, but what about governments? As noted in Chapter 4, there is no common agreement about what governments maximize or, more precisely, what elected officials maximize. One theory that appears to parallel the rational self-interest employed in private choices is that elected officials attempt to *maximize their political support.* Political support can take the form not only of votes but also of campaign contributions and in-kind support, such as the efforts of campaign workers.

When representative democracy replaces direct democracy, there is a greater possibility that elected representatives will cater to special interests rather than serve the interests of the majority. The problem arises because of the asymmetry between special interests and the common interest. Let's consider only one of the thousands of decisions that are made each year by elected representatives: funding of an obscure federal program that subsidizes wool production in the United States. Under the wool subsidy program, the federal government establishes and guarantees a floor price to be paid to sheep farmers for each pound of wool they produce. The guaranteed price was $1.53 per pound at a time when the world market price was $0.61 per pound, thereby providing wool producers with a subsidy of $0.92 per pound.[1] During deliberations to renew the subsidy program, the only person to testify before Congress was a representative of the National Wool Growers Association, who noted how vital the subsidy was to the nation's economic welfare. The federal subsidy costs taxpayers over $75 million per year. Why didn't a single representative of taxpayer interests testify against the subsidy? Why were sheep farmers able to pull the wool over the taxpayers' eyes?

Rational Ignorance

Households consume so many different public and private goods and services that they have neither the time nor the incentive to understand the effects of public choices on every one of these products. Voters realize that they each have but a tiny possibility of influencing the outcome of public choices. Moreover, even if an individual voter is somehow able to affect the outcome, the impact of the chosen policy on that voter is likely to be small. For example, even if a taxpayer could successfully stage a grass-roots campaign to eliminate the wool subsidy, that individual would probably save less than $1 per year in federal income taxes. Therefore, unless voters have concentrated interests, they adopt a policy of **rational ignorance**, which means that they remain largely oblivious to the costs and benefits of the thousands of proposals considered by elected officials. The costs of acquiring and acting on such information are typically greater than any expected benefits.

Voters often exhibit ***rational ignorance*** *because the costs of understanding and voting on a particular policy exceed the expected benefits of doing so.*

In contrast, consumers have a greater incentive to gather and act upon information about decisions they make in private markets because they benefit directly from the knowledge acquired. *In a world where information and the time required to acquire and digest it are scarce, consumers concentrate on private choices rather than public choices because the payoff in making wise private choices is usually more immediate and more direct.* The consumer in the market for a new car has an incentive to examine the performance records of different models rather than get stuck with a lemon. That consumer can then choose between Ford and Toyota. But the same individual has less incentive to examine the performance records of candidates for public office because that single voter has virtually no chance of deciding the election. Moreover, if political candidates try to please the median voter, their positions will be quite similar anyway, in which case it matters little who gets elected.

Distributions of Costs and Benefits

In a representative democracy there is always the possibility that an influential minority may be able to use the public sector to transfer wealth from the majority to itself. The costs imposed by a particular legislative

---

[1] The prices quoted are for 1983, as noted by James Bovard in "A Subsidy Both Wooly-Headed and Mammoth," *Wall Street Journal*, 17 April 1985.

measure may be either narrowly or widely distributed over the population, depending on the issue. Likewise, the benefits may be conferred on only a small band of voters or they may affect much of the population.

The more widespread the costs or benefits of a legislative measure, the less they will affect any individual. Alternatively, the more concentrated the costs or benefits, the more important they become to those affected. The possible combinations of costs and benefits yield four alternative types of distributions: (1) widespread costs and widespread benefits, (2) widespread costs and concentrated benefits, (3) concentrated costs and concentrated benefits, and (4) concentrated costs and widespread benefits.

Special interest legislation involves concentrated benefits but widespread costs.

The distribution of traditional public goods, such as national defense and a system of justice, tends to be a positive-sum game. Such goods typically have widespread costs and benefits. In other words, nearly everyone pays and nearly everyone benefits from this category of distribution. With **special interest legislation**, benefits are concentrated but costs are widespread. For example, if some special interest group, such as the wool producers, can get Congress to adopt legislation that fleeces just $1 from each taxpayer and transfers it to the wool producers, this yields that special interest over $85 million. Accommodating special interests is often a negative-sum game. **Competing interest legislation** involves both concentrated costs and concentrated benefits; consider the impact of a tariff on importers of shoes versus domestic manufacturers of shoes, or the effect of airline deregulation on the Airline Pilots Association versus the airline stockholders. Though resolving a competing interest issue may appear to be a zero-sum game because the gains and losses of the competing interests seem to offset each other, it will be a negative-sum game if the resolution generates economic inefficiencies.

Competing interest legislation involves concentrated costs and concentrated benefits.

When legislators propose imposing costs in a concentrated way to confer benefits widely, the special interest group whose ox is being gored will cry foul and discourage the passage of such legislation. Meanwhile, the potential beneficiaries will remain rationally ignorant of the proposed legislation, so they will provide little political support for such a measure. For example, whenever Congress considers imposing a tax on a particular industry, that industry floods Washington with lobbyists and mail, usually noting how the tax will lead to economic ruin, not to mention the decline of Western civilization as we know it today. Thus legislation that imposes costs on a small group but confers benefits widely has less chance of being passed than do measures that confer benefits narrowly but spread costs widely.

In the following case study, we consider the redistributive and efficiency effects of a specific example of special interest legislation: farm subsidy programs.

*Farm
Subsidies: The
Negative-Sum
Game*

The Agricultural Marketing Agreement Act was enacted in 1937 to prevent what had been viewed as "ruinous competition" among farmers. In the years since, the government has introduced a variety of policies to set floor prices for a wide range of farm products. For example, the federal government pays millions of dollars to subsidize the production of honey in this country. A much more extensive and expensive program involves the price supports in the dairy industry.

Exhibit 3 depicts the market for milk. Suppose that in the absence of government intervention, the market price of milk is $2 per gallon and the equilibrium quantity is 100 million gallons per week. By producing at the long-run equilibrium, dairy farmers earn a normal rate of return. Con-

EXHIBIT 3   EFFECTS OF MILK PRICE SUPPORTS

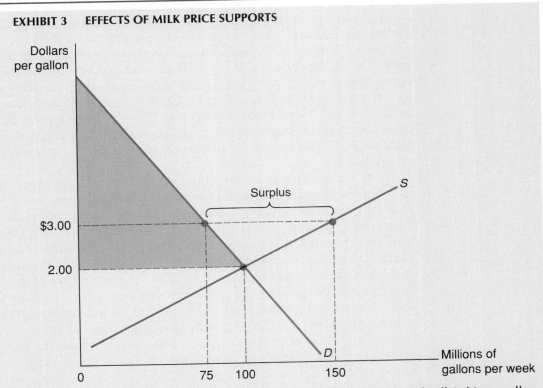

In the absence of government intervention, the market price of milk is $2 per gallon and 100 million gallons are sold per week. If Congress establishes a floor price of $3 per gallon, then the quantity supplied will increase and the quantity demanded will decrease. To maintain the higher price, the government must buy up the surplus milk at $3 per gallon.

Consumers are worse off as a result of this policy. In addition to paying an extra $1 per gallon, they must pay for government purchases of surplus milk as well as for storing that milk. In the long run, farmers are no better off, since the policy drives up the prices of resources specialized to dairy farming.

sumers as a group capture the consumer surplus shown by the blue-shaded area. Recall that consumer surplus is the difference between the most that consumers would have been willing to pay for each unit of the good and the price actually paid.

But suppose that dairy farmers persuade Congress that such a price is too low, so legislation establishes a floor price for milk of, say, $3 per gallon. The higher floor price provides farmers with an incentive to increase the quantity supplied to 150 million gallons per month. In response to the higher price, however, consumers reduce their quantity demanded to 75 million gallons per month. To make the higher price stick, the government must buy the 75 million gallons of "surplus" milk generated by the floor price.

Consumers end up paying dearly to subsidize the farmers. First, the price per gallon increases by $1. Second, taxpayers must pay for government purchases of surplus milk. And third, taxpayers must then pay for storing all that surplus milk as butter, cheese, and powdered milk products. Consider the price the typical consumer-taxpayer now pays for a gallon of milk. The consumer pays $3 per gallon for milk purchased on the market; the consumer as an average taxpayer pays another $3 for the gallon the government buys, plus, say, an extra $0.50 per gallon to store that government purchase. Instead of paying just $2 — the price in the absence of government price supports — the typical consumer-taxpayer is milked for a total of $6.50 per gallon, or an extra outlay of $4.50 per gallon of milk consumed.

How do the farmers make out? Each farmer receives an extra $1 per gallon over the price that would have prevailed in a free market. As farmers increase their output, however, the marginal cost of production increases; at the margin, the higher price the farmer receives is just offset by higher production costs. Still, farmers gain some producer surplus, identified in Exhibit 3 by the area above the supply curve that is between the market price of $2 and the supported price of $3. The long-run effect of the subsidy, however, will be to bid up the cost of resources specialized to dairy farming, such as cows and grazing land. Farmers who own these resources will be able to capitalize, but farmers who purchase them after the subsidy is introduced will end up earning just a normal rate of return. So with free entry into the dairy industry, most farmers in the long run earn just a normal rate of return despite the billions of dollars spent on the program.

If the extra $1 per gallon were pure profit, farm profit would increase by $150 million. But consumer-taxpayer costs increase by $337.5 million: $75 million for the extra cost of each of the 75 million gallons consumers purchase, plus $225 million in higher taxes for the 75 million surplus gallons purchased by the government, plus $37.5 million to store the 75 million surplus gallons. Thus consumer-taxpayer costs are more than double the farmers' maximum possible gain of $150 million.

The government subsidy program is therefore a negative-sum game, as the sum of all the gains and losses is less than zero. This does not mean that nobody gains — all farmers gain in the short run, and farmers who owned specialized resources at the time the subsidy was granted probably gain in the long run. But a negative-sum game implies that the whole process is inefficient. That is, everyone would be better off if the government made a direct payment to farmers.

Between 1986 and 1989, farm subsidies averaged over $15 billion per year, with dairy subsidies averaging $2 billion per year. In 1988 the federal government bought the equivalent of nearly 9 billion pounds of milk. The federal government spends more on farm subsidies than on Aid to Families with Dependent Children. Some state subsidies support even higher prices.

The dairy industry is protected in other ways. Since 1980 U.S. milk prices have been double or triple the average price on world markets, yet imports are restricted. Other laws promote the consumption of dairy products. For example, laws in many states prohibit restaurants from serving margarine unless customers specifically request it instead of butter.

Although a direct income transfer between taxpayers and dairy farmers that was not tied to milk production would be more efficient, such a transparent special interest proposal could attract the public's attention and be doomed. Special interest legislation is often promoted under the cover of some greater good. The purported goal of farm subsidies, for example, is to save the family farm, even though in actuality an overwhelming share of the subsidies goes to giant agribusiness, not to family farmers.

Sources: James Bovard, "The Sacred Cows That Keep Milk Prices Higher," *Wall Steet Journal*, 5 May 1989; "The Bitter Butter Battle," *Wall Street Journal*, 31 March 89.

RENT SEEKING

An important feature of representative democracy is the incentive and political power it offers participants to employ legislation to increase their wealth, either through direct transfers or through favorable public expenditures and regulations. Special interest groups, such as farmers, try to persuade elected officials to approve measures that provide the special interest with some market advantage or some outright transfer or subsidy. Such benefits are sometimes called *rents*—in yet another use of that term. The term in this context implies that the government transfer or subsidy constitutes a payment to the resource owner that is over and above the earnings necessary to call forth that resource. The activity that interest groups undertake to elicit these special favors from government is called **rent seeking**.

Rent seeking is the expenditure of resources in an attempt to obtain favorable treatment from government.

Competition among groups to obtain rents has been of growing concern among public choice scholars. As a firm's profitability becomes more and more dependent on decisions made in Washington, resources are diverted from productive activity to rent seeking, or lobbying. One firm may thrive because it secured some special advantage at a critical time; another firm may fail because its managers were more concerned with productive efficiency than with rent seeking.

Let's consider, for example, the market depicted in Exhibit 4. Suppose

EXHIBIT 4   MONOPOLY PROFIT, RENT SEEKING, AND WELFARE LOSS

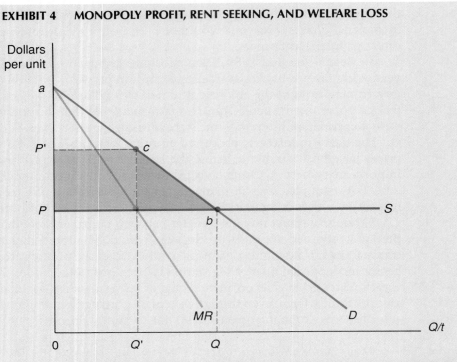

A competitive industry will produce at point b, with output Q and price P. All firms will earn a normal profit, and consumers will enjoy a consumer surplus equal to the area abP. If government decides to allow the industry to become monopolized, output will fall to Q' and price will rise to P'. The monopolist will earn a profit shown by the blue-shaded area.

The welfare loss to society includes the loss of consumer surplus, identified by the red-shaded welfare triangle. In addition, potential monopolists will devote resources to rent seeking—an additional welfare loss.

that the good under consideration is produced in a constant-cost industry, so its long-run supply curve, S, is horizontal at a level equal to the minimum point of the firm's long-run average cost. With no barriers to entry, firms will enter this industry until the market supply intersects the market demand at point b, where output equals Q, price equals P, and all firms earn a normal profit. Consumers enjoy the consumer surplus of abP.

Now suppose that the government for some reason decides that this good should be supplied by an unregulated monopolist and invites applications for the designation of monopoly supplier. Once entry by other suppliers is restricted, the designated unregulated monopolist will be able to reduce market output to Q', raise the price to P', and earn an economic profit identified by the blue rectangular area. Consumer surplus declines from abP to acP'. The entry barrier could be import quotas, a tariff on foreign goods, operating licenses, or some other device that effectively blocks entry.

Many would–be monopolists will be understandably interested in securing this monopoly profit and will expend resources on campaign contributions, lobbyists, public relations, and other efforts to win the right to produce as a monopolist. We pointed out in an earlier chapter that the welfare loss associated with monopoly includes the portion of lost consumer surplus that is not transferred to the monopolist, identified by the red triangle in Exhibit 4. But with many potential monopolists competing for the profits, the total cost of monopoly is now larger than this simple welfare triangle. *The welfare cost includes the cost of resources devoted to rent seeking, since this use results in no output that is of social value.* Firms competing for rents may be expected to spend in the aggregate an amount equal to the present value of the flow of economic profits identified by the blue rectangle. The government frequently bestows some special advantage on a producer or group of producers, and abundant resources are expended to secure these rights. For example, *political action committees*, known more popularly as PACs, contributed $170 million to congressional campaigns in 1988, a 70 percent increase from four years earlier.

Rent Seeking and Efficiency

To the extent that government transfers reduce the net return individuals expect from working and investing, less work and less investment may occur. If this happens, not only will income be transferred but also potential income will go unearned. Moreover, to the extent that special interest groups engage in rent-seeking activities, they shift resources from productive endeavors that create income to activities that focus simply on transferring income. *Resources that are employed in an attempt to get government to redistribute income or wealth are largely unproductive because they do nothing to increase output and often end up making it smaller.* And often many firms compete for the same government advantage, thereby wasting still more resources.

As economist Mancur Olson of the University of Maryland notes, special interest groups typically have little incentive to make the economy more efficient.[2] In fact, special interest groups will usually support legislation transferring wealth to them even if the measure reduces the economy's overall efficiency. Thus special interest groups have an incentive to support negative-sum transfers. For example, suppose that lawyers are able to push through a measure that has the effect of increasing their incomes by a total of $1 billion per year, or about $1400 per lawyer. Suppose that, as a result of this measure, litigation increases and insurance premiums go up, raising the total cost of production by $5 billion. Lawyers themselves will have to bear part of this higher cost, but since they account for only about 1 percent of the spending in the economy, they will bear only about 1 percent of the higher cost—a total of $50 million, or about $70 per lawyer. Thus the

---

[2] Mancur Olson, *The Rise and Decline of Nations* (New Haven, CT: Yale University Press, 1982).

legislation is a bargain for lawyers because it increases each lawyer's income by $1400 but increases each lawyer's costs by only $70.

There are hundreds of special interest groups representing farmers, physicians, lawyers, teachers, manufacturers, barbers, and so forth. With many competing groups, the situation becomes, in Olson's words, "like a china shop filled with wrestlers battling over the china, and breaking far more than they carry away."[3] Olson argues that most redistribution is not from the upper- and middle-income groups to the lower-income groups but from one middle-income group to another middle-income group, and from all income groups to certain high-income groups.

Olson is far less concerned about incentive problems associated with redistribution to the poor than about the major distortions that arise when special interest groups get into the act. Since the poor are by definition contributing less to the economy's output, the incentive problems created by redistributing the wealth to them are relatively modest compared to the loss that arises when the country's best minds are occupied with devising schemes to avoid taxes, developing and enforcing restrictive work rules, and engaging in other practices that transfer income to favored groups at the expense of market efficiency. For example, the pursuit of tax loopholes encourages some of the best and the brightest to become tax lawyers and accountants.

Think of the economy's output in a particular period as depicted by a pie. The pie is the total value of goods and services produced. In deciding on answers to the "what," "how," and "for whom" questions introduced in Chapter 2, rule makers have three alternatives: (1) they can introduce changes that will yield a bigger pie (that is, positive-sum changes), (2) they can decide simply to carve up the existing pie differently (zero-sum changes), or (3) they can start fighting over the pie, causing some of it to end up on the floor (negative-sum changes).

THE UNDERGROUND ECONOMY

*The **underground economy** is a term used for all market activity that goes unreported to the government.*

A government subsidy promotes production, as we saw in the case study on milk price supports. Conversely, a tax discourages production. Perhaps it would be more accurate to say that when government taxes production, less production is *reported*. If you worked as a waiter or waitress, did you faithfully report all your tips to the Internal Revenue Service? To the extent that you did not, your income became part of the underground economy. The **underground economy** is a term used for all market activity that goes unreported to the government. Although tax evasion is the primary reason why certain market exchanges go unreported, some types of economic activity are not reported because they are illegal. Thus income arising in the

---

[3] Mancur Olson, "What We Lose When the Rich Go on the Dole," *The Washington Monthly* (January 1984): 49.

underground economy ranges from the earnings of drug dealers to those of moonlighting carpenters.

The introduction of a tax has two effects. First, owners will supply less of the taxed resource because the tax reduces the net return expected from supplying the resource. Second, in an attempt to evade taxes, some market participants will divert their economic activity from the formal, reported economy to an underground, off-the-books economy. Thus, when the government taxes market exchange or the income arising from that exchange, less formal market activity occurs. For example, a plumber and an accountant may barter services to evade taxes, rather than paying each other in money that would have to be reported as income.

We should take care to distinguish between tax *avoidance* and tax *evasion*. Tax avoidance is a legal attempt to arrange one's economic affairs so as to pay the least tax possible. Tax evasion is illegal; it takes the form of either failing to file a tax return or filing a fraudulent return by understating income or overstating deductions.

Although there are no official figures on the size of the underground economy, federal agencies have developed estimates. The Census Bureau estimates that its official figures capture only 90 percent of U.S. income. An Internal Revenue Service survey estimated that in 1981 about 13 percent of taxes due were not paid. This figure was higher than the IRS estimate from a decade earlier, suggesting that the underground economy was growing faster than the economy as a whole. These studies suggest a value of between $450 billion and $700 billion for the underground economy in 1990.

One motive for lowering the rates on personal income taxes in the 1986 tax reform was to encourage those in the underground economy to join the mainstream of recorded economic activity. A lower marginal tax rate reduces the benefit of tax evasion. With a top marginal tax rate of 50 percent, the person who has gone underground evades a maximum of $0.50 in taxes for each $1 earned. But the tax reform of 1986 dropped the highest marginal rate to 33 percent, so the tax evader now saves at most only $0.33 in federal income taxes.

Those who pursue rent-seeking activity and those involved in the underground economy view government from opposite perspectives. Rent seekers want government to become actively involved in transferring wealth to them, whereas those in the underground economy want to evade any government contact. Subsidies and other advantages bestowed by government draw some groups closer to government; taxes encourage others to go underground.

BUREAUCRACY AND REPRESENTATIVE DEMOCRACY

Elected representatives approve legislation, but the task of implementing that legislation is typically left to various government departments and agencies. The organizations charged with implementing legislation are usually referred to as **bureaus**; bureaus are government agencies whose activities are financed by appropriations from legislative bodies.

Ownership and Funding of Bureaus

We can get a better feel for government bureaus by comparing them to corporations. Ownership of a corporation is based on the proportion of shares owned by each stockholder. Stockholders are the residual claimants of any profits or losses arising from the firm's operations. Ownership in the firm is *transferable*; the shares can be sold in the stock market. In contrast, taxpayers, by dint of their citizenship, are in a sense the "owners" of government bureaus in the jurisdiction in which they live. If the bureau earns a "profit," taxes will be reduced; if the bureau operates at a "loss," as most do, this loss must be covered by taxes. Each taxpayer has just one vote, regardless of the taxes paid. Ownership in the bureau is surrendered only if the taxpayer dies or moves out of the relevant jurisdiction; it is not transferable—it cannot be bought and sold.

Whereas firms derive their revenue when customers voluntarily purchase their products, bureaus are typically financed by a budget appropriation from the legislature. Most of this budget comes from taxpayers. On occasion bureaus will earn revenue through the sale of output at specified user charges, but even then they often receive supplementary assistance through budget appropriations. Because of these differences in the forms of ownership and the sources of revenue, bureaus have different incentives than do profit-making firms, so we are likely to observe different behavior in the two organizations.

Ownership and Organizational Behavior

A central assumption of economics is that people behave rationally and respond to economic incentives. The more compensation is linked to individual incentives, the more people will behave in accord with those incentives. If a letter carrier's pay is based on the customers' satisfaction, the letter carrier will make a greater effort to deliver mail promptly and intact.

The firm has a steady stream of consumer feedback when its product is sold in free markets. If the price is too high or too low to clear the market, the firm will know as surpluses or shortages develop. Not only is consumer feedback abundant, but the firm's owners have an incentive to act on that information in an attempt to satisfy consumer wants. The promise of profits also creates incentives to produce the output at minimum cost. Thus the firm's owners stand to gain from any improvement in customer satisfaction or in production efficiency.

Since public goods and services are not sold in free markets, government bureaus receive little consumer feedback. There are no prices and no obvious shortages or surpluses. For example, how would you know whether there was a shortage or a surplus of police protection in your community? (Would gangs of police hanging around the doughnut shop indicate a surplus?)

Not only do bureaus receive less consumer feedback than do firms; they also have less incentive to act on the information available. Because any "profits" or "losses" arising in the bureau are spread among all taxpayers and because there is no transferability of ownership, bureaus have less incentive to satisfy customers or to produce their output using the least–cost combination of resources. (Laws prevent bureaucrats from taking home any "profit" in brown paper bags.)

Some pressure for customer satisfaction and cost minimization may be communicated by voters to their elected representatives and thereby to the bureaus. This discipline, however, is likely to be less precise than that operating in the firm, particularly since any gains or losses in efficiency are diffused among all taxpayers. For example, suppose that you are a citizen in a state with a million taxpayers and you become aware of some inefficiency that is costing taxpayers a million dollars a year. If you undertake measures that succeed in correcting the shortcoming, you save yourself about a dollar per year in taxes.

Because of differences between public and private organizations—both in the owners' ability to transfer ownership and to appropriate profits—we expect bureaus to be less concerned with satisfying consumer demand and minimizing costs than private firms are. A variety of empirical studies have attempted to compare costs for products that are provided by both public bureaus and private firms. Though the results are not conclusive, several studies indicate that private firms appear to be more efficient than public bureaus in providing such services as fire protection and garbage collection.

Bureaucratic Objectives

Assuming that bureaus are not simply at the beck and call of the legislature—that is, assuming that bureaucrats have some autonomy—what sort of objectives will they pursue? One widely discussed theory of bureaucratic behavior has been put forth by William Niskanen. Niskanen argues that bureaus attempt to *maximize their budgets*, for along with a big budget comes size, prestige, amenities, and staff, which are valued by bureaucrats.[4]

How do bureaucrats maximize the bureau's budget? According to Niskanen, bureaus supply their output to the legislature as monopolists. Rather than charge a price per unit, bureaus offer the legislature the entire amount as a package deal in return for the requested appropriation. According to this theory, the legislature has little ability to dig into the budget and cut particular items. If the legislature proposes cuts in the bureau's budget, the bureau will threaten to make those cuts as painful to the legislature and its constituents as possible. For example, if town officials attempt to reduce

---

[4] William A. Niskanen, Jr., *Bureaucracy and Representative Government* (Chicago, IL: Aldine-Atherton, 1971).

the school budget, school bureaucrats, rather than increase teaching loads, may threaten to eliminate kindergarten, dissolve the high school football team, or do away with the school band. Similarly, any attempts by Congress to cut the defense budget may elicit threats by the Pentagon to close military installations located in the districts of key members of Congress. If such threats are effective in forcing the legislature to back off from any cuts, the government budget turns out to be larger than taxpayers would prefer. *Budget maximization results in a budget higher than that desired by the median voter.*

Private Versus Public Production

Simply because public goods and services are financed by the government does not mean that they must be produced by the government. Profit-making firms have government contracts to provide everything from fire protection to the operation of prisons. The mix of firms and bureaus varies over time and across jurisdictions. Elected officials may contract directly with private firms to produce public output. For example, a city council may contract with a firm to handle garbage-collection services for the city. Elected officials may also use some combination of bureaus and firms to produce desired output. For example, the Pentagon, a giant bureau, hires and trains military personnel, yet contracts with private firms to develop and produce various weapon systems. State governments typically hire contractors to build roads but use bureaus to maintain them.

When governments produce public goods and services, they are using *the internal organization of the government*—the bureaucracy—to supply the product. When governments contract with private firms to produce public goods and services, they are using *the market* to supply the product. Legislatures might prefer to deal with bureaus rather than with firms for two reasons. First, in situations where it is difficult to specify a contract that clearly spells out all the possible contingencies, the internal organization of the bureau may be more responsive to the legislature's concerns than the management of a firm would be. Second, to the extent that legislators view bureaus as a source of political patronage and discretion, they may prefer bureaus because bureaus provide more opportunities to reward friends and supporters with jobs than firms would.

Using market competition to supply services that are not well defined, such as the guidance provided by a social worker, may lead to poor service. A private firm that wins the contract might be tempted to shade on quality, particularly if the quality of the service can be determined only by direct observation when the service is provided. For example, suppose that government put social work out for bid, selected the lowest bidder, then attempted to monitor the quality of the service through direct observation. The government would find direct monitoring too costly. These services thus might best be provided by a government bureau. Because the bureau is less concerned with minimizing costs, it has less reason to lower quality to reduce cost.

James M. Buchanan
(b. 1919)

Thomas Jefferson wrote the Declaration of Independence in 1776, the same year that Adam Smith published *The Wealth of Nations*. This is a coincidence, but a particularly symbolic one. The system of political thought developed by Jefferson and the other Founding Fathers has much in common with the economics developed by Smith. The Founding Fathers tried to design political institutions that would limit abuses of political power. In much the same way, Smith saw the economic institutions of the market as limiting economic power and channeling self-interest in beneficial directions. The separation of powers among the three branches of government is just one of the "checks and balances" that preoccupied political thought in the early republic.

The connection between economic and political thought grew weaker over the years. Economists concentrated on market phenomena; to the extent that they men-

tioned the political process at all, they tended to assume that governments acted in an uncomplicated and disinterested manner to correct imperfections in the market. Recently, however, the gap between economics and politics has begun to close, and economists are returning to the insights of two hundred years ago.

The most influential figure in this reunion of economics and politics is James Buchanan. A founder of the Public Choice School, Buchanan has spent his career examining political decision making through the same lens economists use to look at market decision making. In part, this has involved recognizing that governments—like markets—are composed of many individuals who respond to incentives in a rational way. In markets, competition for profits both guides and disciplines economic agents; in the political world, the quest for votes and other forms of political support plays a similar role. Thinking in these terms pro-

vides a way of analyzing what goes on inside a legislature or a government bureau.

But not only has Buchanan's work brought economic ideas to bear on politics; it has also brought political concerns back into economics. Buchanan's writings have often centered on questions of constitutional design and political philosophy. Like the country's early political writers, he is concerned with setting up institutions that constrain abuses of political power and channel the interests of political agents in the same directions as those of the citizens they serve.

James Buchanan was born in Murfreesboro, Tennessee. He attended Middle Tennessee State, the University of Tennessee, and the University of Chicago, where he earned a Ph.D. in 1948. Most of his career has been spent in Virginia, first at the University of Virginia, later at Virginia Polytechnic Institute, and now at George Mason University. Buchanan won the Nobel Prize in economics in 1986.

Portrait by Carl Zitzmann/George Mason University

Richard Langlois

CONCLUSION

This chapter examined how individual preferences are reflected in public choices. We began with direct voting based on majority rule, moved on to problems arising from representative democracy, and finally examined bureaus, the organizations that usually implement public choices. An earlier chapter on income redistribution focused on direct transfers to poor people. Here we considered indirect transfers, which arise because of changes in the rules governing economic activity in the private sector. Price supports, import restrictions, and other indirect transfers do not show up in the budget but often have a profound effect on the economy. Whenever governments become involved in the workings of the economy to favor one group over another, some resources are shifted from productive activity to rent-seeking activity—that is, efforts to persuade the government to confer benefits on certain groups. Individual incentives may also be distorted in a way that reduces total output.

Governments attempt to address failures in the private economy. But simply turning problems of perceived market failure over to government may not always be the best solution, because government has failings of its own. Perhaps we should be more sensitive to government failure. Participation in markets is based on voluntary exchange. Governments, however, have the legal power to enforce public choices. We should employ at least as high a standard in judging the performance of government as we do in judging the private market, where decisions are based on voluntary exchange.

Summary

1. Under certain conditions public choice under majority rule reflects the preferences of the median voter, requiring other taxpayers to buy either more or less of the public good than they would prefer. Logrolling, or vote trading, produces public choices that may represent the preferences of a minority of voters rather than those of the median voter. When a cyclical majority arises, no clear public choice emerges.

2. Producers have an abiding interest in any legislation that affects their livelihood. Consumers, however, purchase thousands of different products and have no special interest in legislation affecting any particular product. Con-

sumers are said to adopt a posture of rational ignorance about producer-oriented legislation because the costs of keeping up with special interest issues outweigh the expected benefits.

3. The intense interest that producer groups express in relevant legislation, coupled with rational ignorance on the part of the mass of voters on most issues, leaves government vulnerable to rent seeking by special interests. Elected officials interested in maximizing their political support may have a tendency to serve producer interests rather than consumer interests—that is, to serve special interests rather than the public interest.

4. Much of the redistribution of wealth that occurs through the process of public choice is not from rich to poor but from all taxpayers to some special interest groups. The harm special interest groups inflict on the economy often outweighs the benefits they reap, so this type of redistribution is a negative-sum game.

5. Bureaus differ from firms in the amount of consumer feedback they receive, in their incentive to minimize costs, and in the transferability of their ownership. Because of these differences, bureaus may not be as efficient or as sensitive to consumer preferences as firms are.

Questions and Problems

1. (Median Voter) In a single-issue vote, such as the television example in the chapter, will the median voter necessarily always get his or her most preferred outcome? If not, how would you alter the preferences in Exhibit 1 to show this?

2. (Majority Vote) We often hear that in the United States we are governed by the principle of majority rule. Is it true that there must always be a majority?

3. (Representative Government) What would guide a senator in deciding how to vote on an issue that did not directly affect his or her constituency? Is logrolling an important consideration here? Why or why not?

4. (Party Affiliation) Why might it be important to a person running for office to have a party affiliation? Does the existence of political parties reduce the transaction costs involved in voting?

5. (Consumer Interest Lobbies) Why might consumer interest groups in Washington be less effective than producer lobbies?

6. (Voting) Why does 50 percent of the U.S. voting population consistently fail to vote?

7. (Logrolling) Is it possible for lobbies to engage in a type of logrolling? How?

8. (Political Action Committees) How might the emergence of political action committees have contributed to the soaring costs of running a political campaign? Why are seats in the government, which pay relatively poorly, becoming so expensive to obtain?

9. (Subsidies) "To subsidize the price of milk or other agricultural products is not very expensive considering how many consumers there are in the United States. Therefore, there is little harmful effect from such subsidies." Evaluate this point of view.

10. (Underground Economy) Why is it important to reduce the size of the underground economy? How might the government do so?

11. (Efficiency and Price Supports) Suppose that the government decides to guarantee an above-market price for a good by buying up any surplus at that above-market price. Using a conventional supply-demand diagram, illustrate the following gains and losses of a price support:
    a. The loss of consumer surplus
    b. The gain of producer surplus
    c. The tax cost of running the government program (assuming no storage costs)
    d. The net efficiency loss, assuming that the government-purchased products are distributed to consumers (Hint: this loss is caused purely by overproduction of the good.)

12. (Median Voter) The text describes circumstances under which the outcome of a vote will be the one desired by the median voter. Using a single-issue example with three

voters, answer the following questions:

a. Why did the vote result in the outcome it did?

b. Would the outcome have been different if non-median voters' feelings about the preferred choice had been stronger or less strong?

c. Is the outcome likely to be the economically efficient one? Why or why not?

13. (Representative Government) Political parties typically produce "middle of the road" platforms rather than taking extreme positions. Is this consistent with the concepts of the median voter and rational ignorance discussed in the text?

14. (Cyclical Majority) Compare the preferences shown in Exhibits 1 and 2. What is the key difference between them that leads to a cyclical majority in Exhibit 2? Does such a pattern of preferences necessarily lead to a cyclical majority?

C H A P T E R   3 2

Externalities and the Environment

Toilets in Athens, Greece, flush directly into the Aegean Sea. The river at the port of Bilbao, Spain, is fouled from raw sewage and from 110 waste dumps. The air in Paris has more lead and carbon monoxide than that of any other major city in the world. In the United States, beaches have been choked with sewage and medical trash, the air in some cities is dangerous, and the ground has been poisoned with toxic waste. What does all this have to do with economics? Plenty.

Market prices can efficiently direct the allocation of resources only as long as property rights are well defined and can be easily enforced. Property rights to clean water and air, peace and quiet, and scenic vistas are hard to establish and enforce. This chapter will examine how the lack of property rights to some key resources results in inefficient use of these resources. The focus will be on how externalities affect resource allocation and on public policies to promote greater efficiency. Externalities may be either negative—for example, air pollution—or positive—for example, the general improvement in the civic climate that results from education. This chapter will concentrate primarily on negative externalities. Topics and terms discussed in this chapter include

- Negative and positive externalities

- Private property rights

- Renewable resources

- The common pool problem

- Marginal social cost and marginal social benefit

- The greenhouse effect

- The market for pollution rights

- The Coase theorem

EXTERNALITIES AND THE COMMON POOL PROBLEM

Private property rights allow individuals to control the use of certain resources now and in the future and to charge others for their use.

In an economic system that allows for private property rights, specific individuals own the rights to a resource and have an abiding interest in using that resource efficiently. For example, you own your clothes, your compact disc player, and your time. **Private property rights** allow individuals to control the use of certain resources now and in the future and to charge others for their use. Property rights are defined and enforced by government, by informal social actions, and by ethical norms. But not all resources are owned as private property, because specifying and enforcing some property rights would be too costly. For example, how could specific individuals claim and enforce a right to the air or to fish in the ocean?

Renewable Resources

A resource may be defined as renewable if periodic use of it can be continued indefinitely.

A resource may be defined as **renewable** if periodic use of it can be continued indefinitely. Thus fish are a renewable resource if the amount taken does not jeopardize each species's ability to sustain itself. Timber is a renewable resource if trees are felled and replanted at rates that provide a steady supply. The atmosphere and rivers are renewable resources to the extent that they can absorb or recycle emissions. More generally, biological resources such as fish, game, forests, rivers, grasslands, and agricultural soil are renewable if they are shepherded appropriately.

The common pool problem is that resources to which there is unrestricted access will tend to be overused or overharvested until the net marginal value of additional use drops to zero.

When renewable resources are commonly owned and their use is unrestricted, these resources often are subject to the **common pool problem**: commonly held resources tend to be overused or overharvested. The atmosphere is a commonly owned resource. Since nobody in particular owns the right to the atmosphere, producers tend to use the air as a dump for gases that are unwanted byproducts of their production processes. Air pollution is a negative externality imposed by polluters on society. As noted in Chapter 4, *negative externalities* are unpriced byproducts of production or consumption that impose costs on other consumers or other firms. For example, sulfur dioxide emitted from coal-fired power plants mostly in the Midwest is often cited as the cause of the acid rain that is killing lakes and trees in the Northeast. Some spray cans release fluorocarbons into the atmosphere; these gases are said to cause thinning of the ozone layer that protects us from the sun's ultraviolet rays. Carbon dioxide emissions and other gases are said to form a blanket that is trapping the sun's heat and causing global warming.

Pollution and other negative externalities arise because there are no enforceable property rights to commonly owned resources, such as the air. Market prices usually fail to reflect the costs that negative externalities impose on society. For example, electric rates in the Midwest do not reflect the negative externalities, or *external costs*, that sulfur dioxide emissions impose on those downwind of power plants. The cost of a can of hairspray powered by fluorocarbons does not reflect the effect of gas emissions on the ozone layer.

The price you pay for gasoline does not reflect the costs imposed by the dirtier air your driving creates.

External Costs with Fixed Technology

Suppose the demand for electricity in the Midwest is depicted by *D* in Exhibit 1. Recall that demand reflects consumers' marginal benefit for each level of consumption. The horizontal supply curve reflects the *marginal private cost* of production incurred by the electricity producers. If producers base their pricing and output decisions on their private marginal costs, the equilibrium quantity of electricity used per month is 50 million kilowatt hours and the equilibrium price is $0.10 per kilowatt hour. At that price and

EXHIBIT 1   **NEGATIVE EXTERNALITIES: THE MARKET FOR ELECTRICITY IN THE MIDWEST**

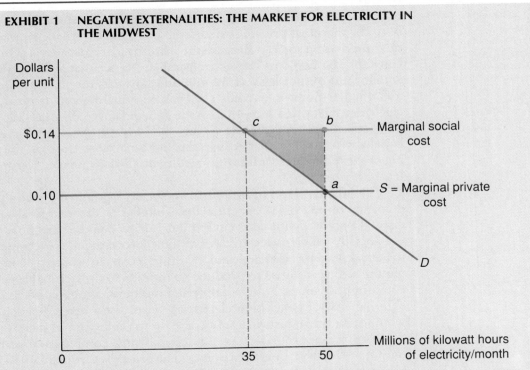

If producers base their output decisions on marginal private cost, 50 million kilowatt hours of electricity are produced per month. The marginal external cost of electricity production reflects the cost of pollution imposed on society. The marginal social cost curve includes both the marginal private cost and the marginal external cost. If producers base their output decisions on marginal social cost, only 35 million kilowatt hours are produced, which is the optimal level of output. The total social gain from basing production on marginal social cost is reflected by the blue triangle.

output level, the marginal private cost of production just equals the marginal benefit enjoyed by consumers of electricity.

But research suggests that the sulfur emitted by coal-fired power plants during the production of electricity is carried by the prevailing winds and gives rise to acid rain, which kills lakes and forests and corrodes buildings, bridges, and other capital. Electricity production, therefore, involves not only the private marginal cost of the resources employed but also the external cost of using the atmosphere as a gas dump. Suppose that the marginal external cost imposed on the environment by the generation of electricity is $0.04 cents per kilowatt hour. If the only way of reducing the emission of sulfur is by reducing the output of electricity, then the relation between the production of electricity and the production of pollution is a fixed one. Thus we say that pollution occurs *with fixed production technology.*

The marginal external cost of $0.04 cents per kilowatt hour is reflected by the vertical distance between the marginal private cost curve and the marginal social cost curve in Exhibit 1. The **marginal social cost** includes both the marginal private cost and the marginal external cost that production imposes on society. Because the marginal external cost is assumed to be constant, the two cost curves are parallel. Notice that at the private sector equilibrium output level of 50 million kilowatts, the marginal social cost, identified at point *b*, exceeds society's marginal benefit from that unit of electricity, identified at point *a* on the demand curve. The last kilowatt hour of electricity produced costs society $0.14 to produce but has a marginal benefit of only $0.10. Because the marginal cost exceeds the marginal benefit, the private equilibrium results in a *market failure.* Too much electricity is produced.

The efficient level of output from society's point of view is where the demand, or marginal benefit, curve intersects the marginal social cost curve — a point identified as *c* in Exhibit 1. How could output be restricted to the socially efficient level of 35 million kilowatts? If government policy makers knew the demand and marginal cost curves, they could simply require electric utilities to produce no more than the optimal level. Or they could impose on each unit of output a pollution tax equal to the marginal external cost of generating electricity. If correctly determined, such a tax would raise the industry supply curve up to the marginal social cost curve.

With the appropriate tax, the equilibrium combination of price and output moves from point *a* to point *c*. The price rises from $0.10 to $0.14 per kilowatt hour, and output falls to 35 million kilowatts. Setting the tax equal to the marginal external cost results in a level of output that is socially efficient; at point *c*, the marginal social cost of production equals the marginal benefit.

Notice that pollution is not eliminated at point *c*, but the utilities no longer generate electricity whose marginal social cost exceeds its marginal benefit. The total social gain from reducing production to the socially optimal level of output is shown by the blue triangle in Exhibit 1. This triangle also measures the total social cost of ignoring the negative externalities in the production decision; it reflects the total amount by which the

The **marginal social cost** curve includes both the marginal private cost and the marginal external cost of production or consumption.

marginal social cost exceeds the marginal benefit of the good if 50 million kilowatts are produced.

Though Exhibit 1 offers a tidy solution, the external costs of pollution often cannot be easily calculated or taxed. At times government intervention may result in more or less production than the optimal solution calls for.

External Costs with Variable Technology

The above example assumes that the only way to reduce the total amount of pollution is to reduce output. But power companies can usually change their resource mixes to reduce emissions, particularly in the long run. To examine the optimal amount of pollution under variable technology, consider Exhibit 2. The horizontal axis measures the percentage by which pollution is reduced, or abated. If all firms made their production decisions based simply on their marginal private cost, then little or no pollution abatement would occur, so the percentage of abatement would be close to zero. Alternatively, if somehow all pollution could be eliminated, the economy would be at 100 percent pollution abatement.

EXHIBIT 2   THE OPTIMAL LEVEL OF POLLUTION ABATEMENT

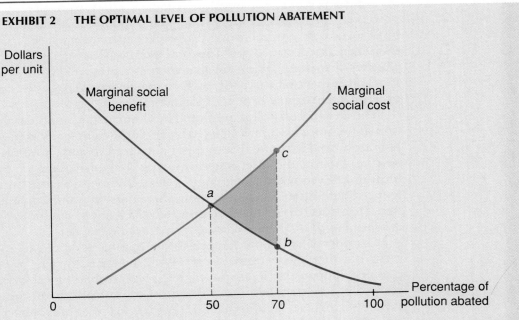

The optimal level of pollution abatement is found at point *a*, where the marginal social cost of abatement equals its marginal social benefit. If some higher level of abatement were dictated by the government, the marginal social cost would exceed the marginal social benefit, and social waste would result. The total social waste resulting from a higher-than-optimal abatement level is indicated by the red triangle.

On the cost side, pollution can be abated by adopting cleaner production technology. For example, coal-burning plants can be fitted with smoke scrubbers to reduce toxic emissions. But the production of cleaner air, like the production of other goods, is subject to diminishing marginal returns. For example, cutting emissions of the largest particles may involve simply putting a screen over the smokestack, but eliminating successively finer particles requires more sophisticated and more expensive processes. Thus the marginal social cost of pollution abatement slopes upward, as shown in Exhibit 2.

The marginal social benefit curve includes both the marginal private benefit and the marginal external benefit from production or consumption.

The **marginal social benefit** curve reflects all the benefits society derives from marginal improvements in pollution abatement. When pollution is at unhealthy levels, improvements in the level of air quality can save lives and will be valued by society more than improvements in air quality when the air is already relatively clean. Thus cleaner air, like other goods, has a declining marginal benefit to society. The marginal social benefit curve from additional abatement therefore slopes downward, as shown in Exhibit 2. The optimal level of pollution abatement is found at point *a*, where the marginal social cost of further abatement equals the marginal social benefit of that abatement. In this example the optimal abatement level is 50 percent.

What if the government decreed that the level of abatement should exceed 50 percent? For example, suppose a law were passed setting 70 percent as the minimum acceptable level of pollution abatement. The marginal social cost, *c*, of achieving that level of abatement exceeds the marginal social benefit, identified as *b*. The total social waste associated with dictating a higher-than-optimal level of abatement is represented by the red triangle, *abc*. This is the total amount by which the marginal cost of cleaning the air exceeds the marginal benefit of cleaner air.

The idea that all pollution should be eliminated is a popular misconception. If pollution occurs with fixed technology, completely eliminating that pollution would require that output be reduced to zero. Completely eliminating carbon dioxide emissions would require that everyone stop breathing. Even when technology is flexible enough that pollution can be reduced with little change in output, there must be some amount of pollution if firms are to operate efficiently. *Pollution should be abated only as long as the marginal benefit of further abatement exceeds its marginal cost.*

Consider what would happen to the optimal level of pollution abatement if either the marginal cost or the marginal benefit of abatement changed. Suppose, for example, that some technological breakthrough allowed producers to remove harmful emissions from the air more cheaply. As shown in panel (a) of Exhibit 3, the marginal cost of reducing pollution would fall, thereby increasing the optimal level of pollution abatement from 50 percent to 65 percent. The simple logic is that *the lower the marginal cost of reducing pollution, other things constant, the greater the optimal level of pollution abatement.*

An increase in the marginal benefit of pollution abatement would have a similar effect. For example, what if we discovered that cleaner air reduced the incidence of certain types of cancer more than was previously believed?

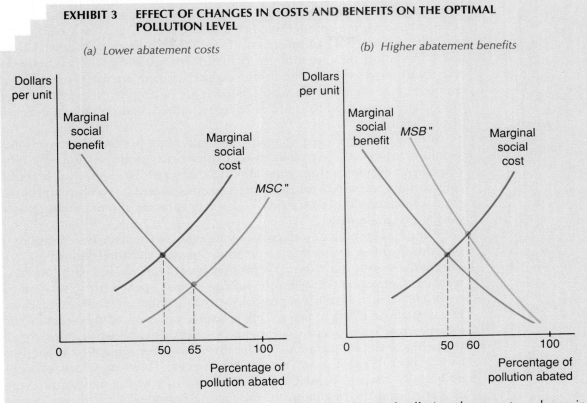

EXHIBIT 3   EFFECT OF CHANGES IN COSTS AND BENEFITS ON THE OPTIMAL POLLUTION LEVEL

(a) Lower abatement costs

(b) Higher abatement benefits

Either a reduction in the marginal social cost of pollution abatement, as shown in panel (a), or an increase in the marginal social benefit, as shown in panel (b), will increase the optimal level of pollution abatement.

The marginal benefit of cleaner air would increase, as reflected in panel (b) of Exhibit 3 by a shift up in the marginal benefit curve. As a result, the optimal level of pollution abatement would increase from 50 percent to 60 percent. *The greater the marginal benefit of reducing pollution, other things constant, the greater the optimal level of pollution abatement.*

Resolving the Common Pool Problem

Because property rights do not attach to commonly owned resources, individual exploiters of fresh air, clean water, wildlife, timber, grasslands, and other renewable resources tend to ignore the effects of their activities on the resources' ability to renew themselves. As stocks diminish from overuse or overharvesting, a resource grows more scarce. For example, unregulated fishing has resulted in years of massive harvesting of the ocean's bounty, which has depleted the stock of fish.

The common pool problem of resource exploitation can be reduced if some central authority imposes restrictions on resource use. By imposing an appropriate removal or depletion tax or by restricting output, a regulatory authority can force competitive firms to use the resource at a rate that is socially optimal. For example, in the face of the tendency to overfish and to catch fish before they are sufficiently mature, the government has imposed a variety of restrictions on the fishing industry. There are limits on the total amount of the catch , on the size of fish that can be caught, on the duration of the fishing season, on the kind of equipment used, and on other aspects of the business.

More generally, when imposing and enforcing private property rights would be too costly, government regulations may improve allocative efficiency. For example, stop signs allocate the scarce road space at a traffic intersection, size limits restrict lobster fishing, hunting seasons control the stock of game, and official study hours may calm the din in the dormitory during certain hours.

But not all production restrictions are equally efficient. For example, at one time fishing authorities set a limit only on the total industry catch during the season, allowing all firms to fish until the *total* industry limit was reached. Consequently, when the fishing season opened, there was a mad scramble to catch as much as possible before the industry limit was reached. Firms made no effort to fish selectively, since time was of the essence. And the catch reached processors all at once, creating a peak-load problem for all segments of the industry. Also, each firm had an incentive to expand its fishing fleet to catch more in those few weeks. Thus large fleets of technologically efficient fishing vessels would sit in port for most of the year, except during the beginning of the fishing season. Each firm was acting rationally, but the collective effect of the regulation was grossly inefficient in terms of social welfare. Allocating a certain amount of output to each company would have proven much more efficient.

The Greenhouse Effect

As we have said, the absence of well-defined property rights encourages polluters to use the air, water, and land as waste dumps. For example, the carbon dioxide content of the atmosphere is on the rise, primarily as the result of burning fossil fuels in power plants, homes, and automobiles. Worldwide, carbon dioxide emissions from burning fossil fuels average about one metric ton per person per year. In the United States, the figure is about five metric tons per person per year.

*The **greenhouse effect** occurs because carbon dioxide and other gases form a blanket around the globe, preventing some of the sun's heat from escaping and thus causing heat buildup.*

Carbon dioxide and other gases form a blanket around the globe, preventing solar heat from escaping and thus causing heat to build up. The gases act like the glass in a greenhouse—hence the expression **greenhouse effect**. The greenhouse effect is said to be causing the earth's atmospheric temperature to rise. Although the issue is still subject to debate, some experts believe that the earth's overall temperature will rise by from 3 to 8 degrees Fahrenheit by the middle of the next century. Because of the resulting glacial melting, sea levels will rise to flood coastlines. Ocean currents that dictate weather patterns will grow stronger. Thus, such a temperature rise could have a significant impact on weather systems and plant life.

The atmosphere has the ability to cleanse itself of a certain level of emissions, but other global events have reduced this ability, as we see in the following case study.

CASE STUDY

Destruction of the Tropical Rain Forests

The tropical rain forests have been called "the lungs of the world" because they naturally recycle carbon dioxide by transforming it into oxygen and wood, thus helping to maintain the world's atmospheric balance. But the world's demand for timber products has caused loggers to cut down much of the tropical forest. Worse yet, farmers burn down these forests to create pastures and farmland. Burning the world's forests has a double-barreled effect. The burning itself adds yet more harmful gases to the atmosphere, and eliminating these natural recycling regions reduces the atmosphere's ability to cleanse itself. So both the loss of trees and the burning of forests contribute to the greenhouse effect.

Forest acreage throughout the world has declined by 15 percent over the last decade, and the rate of decline is now accelerating. The amount of Amazon jungle that has been cleared in the last decade is equal to an area the size of France. In Central America the forests have been cleared for cattle ranches. Haiti is now a treeless wasteland, and once-lush El Salvador is a semi-desert. At current rates of destruction, no forests will be left in Central America by 1995. Commercial logging has been so extensive in the African countries of Ghana and the Ivory Coast that the business is already winding down, leaving behind poverty and devastation. According to the World Bank, two-thirds of the countries that export tropical forest products will be out of trees in a decade.

The loss of the tropical forests causes other negative externalities as well. As long as the tropical forest has its canopy of trees, it remains a rich, genetically diverse ecosystem. Tropical forests cover only 7 percent of the earth's land (down from 10 percent originally) but contain *half* of the world's species of plants and animals, thus representing an abundant source of fruits, crops, and medicines. One-fourth of the prescription drugs used in the United States are derived from tropical plants. Scientists recently discovered that the seeds of a certain tropical plant may help cure some types of cancer. Biologists estimate that ten thousand species are lost forever each year because of deforestation. Yet most tropical plants have not yet been tested for their medicinal properties.

Small-time farmers and wood gatherers and big-time lumber companies are stripping the tropical forests. Once the forests are cut down, the tropical soil is eroded by rains and baked by the sun and soon runs out of nutrients. Once the nutrients are lost, the system is not very resilient. It takes a century for a clearcut forest to return to its original state. The policy of cutting down everything in sight is of benefit only to loggers, who usually do not own the land and thus have little interest in its future.

The world's rain forests are located in countries that tend to be relatively poor: Brazil, Zaire, Peru, Indonesia, and the Philippines. Colonization schemes in the Amazon are heavily subsidized by the Brazilian government to draw people from the crowded cities and reduce poverty. In the state of Rondonia, for example, a native population that numbered 10,000 in 1960 had swelled to more than 1 million by 1985. The smoke of burning forests at times grows so thick that the capital of Rondonia must close its airport for days. Brazil is destroying its forests to provide jobs. Though eliminating the rain forests is not in the planet's long-run interest, the decision has a short-run economic appeal to Brazil and other developing countries desperate for jobs. Since the soil quickly loses its nutrients to erosion and the sun, however, few Brazilian settlers have become successful farmers.

Sources: "Exotic Herb May Speed Colon Cancer Detection," *Wall Street Journal*, 27 July 1989; "Playing with Fire," *Time*, 18 September 1989, pp. 76–85.

The ongoing destruction of tropical rain forests illustrates the common pool problem. Since nobody in particular owns the trees and land on the Brazilian frontier, or the atmosphere that is cleansed by the trees, the only way to capture the value of the forest is to cut down the trees. When the taking of lumber is "first come, first served," forests will be cut down prematurely and the resource will not be carefully shepherded. The positive effects that the trees have on the atmosphere and on the land's value — for example, in preventing erosion and shading the soil from the tropical sun — are ignored in the logging decision. *It is the lack of well-defined, transferable property rights to the trees, the land, and the atmosphere, not the greed of peasants and timber companies, that leads to inefficient, or wasteful, uses of resources.* Selective cutting and replanting would allow the forest to be harvested more efficiently over the long run and would provide a renewable source of forest products.

The Coase Analysis of Externalities

In the traditional analysis of externalities, it is assumed that market failures arise because people ignore the external effects of their actions. Suppose a laboratory that tests delicate equipment is located next to a manufacturer of heavy machinery, and the vibrations caused by the manufacturing process throw off the delicate machinery in the lab next door. Professor Ronald Coase of the University of Chicago would point out that the external cost in this case is not imposed by the machinery producer on the testing lab — rather, it *arises from the incompatible activities of the two parties.* The externality is the result both of vibrations created by the factory *and* of the location of the testing lab next door. One efficient solution to this externality problem might be to modify the machines in the factory; others might be to make the equipment in the testing lab more shock resistant or to move the lab elsewhere.

According to Coase, the most efficient solution to an externality problem depends on which party can avoid the problem at the lower cost. Suppose the factory has determined that it would cost $2 million to reduce vibrations enough to allow the lab to function normally. For its part, the testing lab has concluded that it cannot alter its equipment to reduce the effects of the vibrations, so its only recourse would be to move the lab elsewhere at a cost of $1 million. Based on these costs, the efficient resolution to the externality problem is for the testing lab to relocate.

Coase argued that if the government assigns property rights to one party or another, the two parties will agree on the efficient solution to an externality problem as long as transaction costs are low. This efficient solution will be achieved regardless of which party is assigned the property right. Suppose the government awarded the testing lab the right to operate free of vibrations from next door, so the testing lab had the right to ask the factory to reduce its vibration. Rather than cut vibrations at a cost of $2 million, the factory could offer to pay the lab to relocate. Any payment by the factory that was greater than $1 million but less than $2 million would make both firms better off, since the lab would receive more than its moving cost and the factory would pay less than its cost of reducing vibrations. Thus the lab would move, which is the efficient outcome.

Alternatively, suppose the factory was awarded the right to generate vibrations in its production process. For the factory, this would mean business as usual. The lab might consider paying the factory to alter its production method, but since the minimum payment the factory would accept would be $2 million, the lab would rather move at a cost of $1 million. Thus, whether property rights were awarded to the lab or to the factory, the lab would move, which is the efficient outcome. The **Coase theorem** argues that as long as bargaining costs are small, the assignment of property rights will generate an efficient solution to an externality problem regardless of which party is assigned the property rights. A particular assignment of property rights determines only who incurs the externality costs, not the efficient outcome.

Inefficient outcomes do occur, however, when the transaction costs of arriving at a solution are high. For example, an airport located in a populated area may have difficulty negotiating with all the surrounding residents about noise levels. Or a power plant emitting sulfur dioxide would have trouble negotiating with the millions of people scattered across the downwind states.

*The **Coase theorem** contends that as long as bargaining costs are small, an efficient solution to the problem of externalities will be achieved by the assignment of property rights, regardless of which party is assigned the rights.*

A Market for Pollution Rights

According to Coase, the assignment of property rights is often sufficient to resolve the market failure typically associated with externalities; further government intervention is not necessary. If pollution can be easily monitored and polluters easily identified, the government may be able to achieve an efficient solution to the problem of pollution simply by selling the right to pollute. For example, firms that dump *effluents* into a river evidently value the ability to discharge their waste matter in this way; for them the river provides an inexpensive outlet for effluents that otherwise would have to be disposed of at greater cost. In fact, the river provides services just like other resources, and the demand for this effluent transportation system slopes downward.

The demand for the river as a discharge system is presented as D in Exhibit 4. The horizontal axis measures the amount of effluent dumped into the river per day, and the vertical axis measures firms' marginal benefits of disposing of their effluent in this way. With no restrictions on pollution—that is, if all are free to discharge their wastes into the river—the daily discharge rate can be found where the the marginal benefit of discharging effluents goes to zero—that is, where the demand curve hits the horizontal axis, which is at output level Q in Exhibit 4. Dumping will continue as long as it yields some private marginal benefit. Thus, if dumping remains unreg-

EXHIBIT 4   OPTIMAL ALLOCATION OF POLLUTION RIGHTS

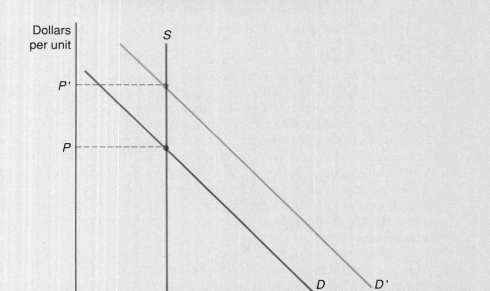

Suppose the demand for a river as an outlet for pollution is D. In the absence of any environmental controls, pollution will occur up to point Q, where the marginal benefit of further pollution equals zero. If regulatory authorities establish Q^* as the maximum allowable level of pollution and then sell the rights to pollution, the market for these pollution rights will clear at price P. If the demand for pollution rights increases to D', the market-clearing price will rise to P'.

ulated, the river will become choked with whatever polluters choose to dump there.

The river, like the atmosphere and the soil, can absorb and recycle a certain amount of pollution each day without deteriorating in quality. Suppose voters in the jurisdiction that encompasses the river make the public choice that the river should be clean enough for swimming and fishing. The maximum level of effluent discharge that is consistent with this river quality is Q^* in Exhibit 4. Hence, if the river is to be preserved at the specified level of quality, the "supply" of the river as a discharge resource is fixed at S.

If polluters can be easily identified and monitored, government regulators can somehow allocate an amount of pollution rights equal to Q^*. If polluters are simply given these rights, there will be excess demand for them, since the quantity supplied is Q^* but the quantity demanded at a price of zero is Q. An alternative that has been receiving increasing attention recently is to *sell* the specified quantity of pollution rights at the market-clearing price. The intersection of the supply curve, S, and the demand curve, D, yields the market-clearing price, P, at which pollution rights could be sold; this price per unit of discharge is often called an *effluent fee*.

With the sale of pollution rights for price P, the marginal private cost that polluters must incur increases from zero to P. This higher cost creates an economic incentive for polluters to reduce their daily discharge rate to Q^*. So the government could sell Q^* discharge rights for price P and be assured that the river quality would be maintained. The beauty of this system is that only those producers that value the discharge rights the most will buy them. Producers that attach a lower marginal value to river dumping obviously have cheaper ways of resolving their effluent problems, including changing their production functions to reduce their pollution. If conservation groups wished to maintain a higher river quality than was implied by the government's standard, they could purchase pollution rights but not exercise them.

What if new firms located along the river and wanted to discharge effluents? This additional demand for discharge rights is reflected in Exhibit 4 by the higher level of demand, D'. This greater demand would bid up the price of discharge rights to P'. Regardless of the comings and goings of would-be dischargers, the total quantity of discharge rights is restricted to Q^*, so the river's quality will be maintained. Thus the value of discharge rights, but not the total quantity discharged, may fluctuate over time.

If the right to pollute could be sold, monitored, and enforced, then what had been a negative externality problem could be solved through market allocation, once rights to the river as an effluent transportation system had been established. Historically, the U.S. government has relied on setting discharge standards and fining offenders and has used pollution rights only in some metropolitan areas. But in 1989 a pollution rights market for fluorocarbon emissions was established, and in 1990 a pollution rights market for sulfur dioxide was proposed.[1]

---

[1] See Dick Thompson, "Giving Greed a Chance," *Time*, 12 February 1990, 67.

Unfortunately, legislation dealing with pollution is affected by the same problems of representative democracy that affect other public policy questions. Polluters have a special interest in government proposals relating to pollution, and they will fight measures to limit pollution. But members of the public remain rationally ignorant about pollution legislation. So pollution regulations may be less in accord with the public interest than with the special interests of polluters.

Positive Externalities

Until now we have considered only negative externalities. Externalities can sometimes be positive, or beneficial. *Positive externalities* are created when the unpriced byproduct of consumption or production benefits other consumers or other firms. For example, people who get innoculated against a disease reduce their own likelihood of contracting the disease, but they also reduce the chance of transmitting the disease to others. Innoculations thus provide *external benefits* to others. Education also confers external benefits on society as a whole because those who acquire more education become better citizens, are better able to support themselves and their families, pay more taxes, are more able to read road signs, and are less likely to resort to violent crime to earn a living.

The effect of external benefits on the optimal level of consumption is illustrated in Exhibit 5, which presents the supply and demand for education. The demand curve, *D*, represents the private demand for education, which reflects the *marginal private benefit* obtained by those who acquire the education. More education is demanded at a lower price than at a higher price.

The benefits of education, however, spill over to others in society. If we add these positive externalities, or the *marginal external benefit*, to the marginal private benefit of education, we get the marginal social benefit of education. Thus the marginal social benefit includes all the benefit society derives from education. The marginal social benefit curve appears above the private demand curve in Exhibit 5. At each level of education, the marginal social benefit exceeds the marginal private benefit by the marginal external benefit generated by that particular unit of education.

If determining how much education to acquire were a strictly private decision, the amount purchased would be determined by the intersection of the private demand curve, *D*, with the supply curve, *S*. The supply curve reflects the marginal cost of producing each unit of the good. This intersection, identified as point *e* in Exhibit 5, yields output level *Q*. At that level of education, the marginal cost of education equals the marginal private benefit.

But is *Q* the optimal level of education from the society's point of view? What if one more unit of education were produced? The marginal social benefit of producing an additional unit of education exceeds the marginal cost, so net social welfare increases when output is expanded beyond *Q*. *As long as the marginal social benefit of education exceeds its marginal cost, social welfare*

EXHIBIT 5   **EDUCATION AND POSITIVE EXTERNALITIES**

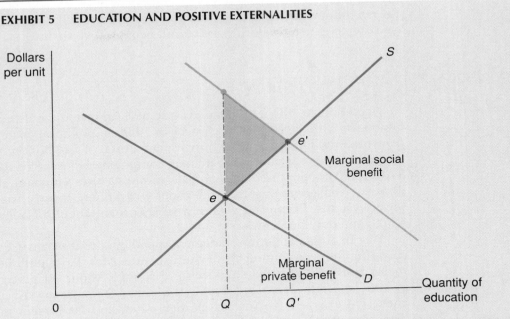

In the absence of government intervention, the quantity of education demanded is Q, at which the marginal cost equals the marginal private benefit of education. However, education also conveys a positive externality on the rest of society, so the marginal social benefit exceeds the private benefit. At quantity Q, the marginal social benefit exceeds the marginal cost, so more education is in society's best interest. In such a situation, government will try to encourage an increase in the quantity of education to Q', at which the marginal cost equals the marginal social benefit.

is increased by expanding output. Social welfare is maximized at point *e'* in Exhibit 5, where Q' units of education are provided—that is, where the marginal social benefit equals the marginal cost, as reflected by the supply curve. The blue triangle identifies the net increase in social welfare that results when the quantity of education increases from Q to Q'.

Thus society is better off if the amount of education provided exceeds the level that would prevail if determining how much education to acquire were a strictly private choice. *When positive externalities are present, private markets provide less than the socially optimal quantity of the good.* Hence, like negative externalities, positive externalities typically point to *market failure*, which is why government often gets into the act. For example, government attempts to encourage people to acquire more education by requiring students to stay in school until they are 16 years old, by providing free primary and secondary education, and by subsidizing public higher education. Given the presence of external benefits, public policy attempts to increase the level of output beyond the private optimum.

Note that an external effect can be simultaneously positive and negative.

For example, suppose your stereo system can be heard by your neighbors. If one neighbor enjoys the music you play but another neighbor can't stand it, your stereo generates both positive and negative externalities.

POLLUTION IN THE UNITED STATES

According to the U.S. Department of Commerce, an estimated $71 billion, or $300 per capita, was spent in 1987 on pollution abatement and control in the United States.[2] Firms spent a total of $44 billion, mostly to install and operate pollution abatement equipment. Households spent about $10 billion to purchase and operate motor vehicle emission abatement devices. And governments spent about $15 billion, mostly to construct sewer systems. Firms and government also spent about $2 billion on research and development.

We can divide pollution abatement spending into three main categories: spending for air pollution abatement, spending for water pollution abatement, and spending for solid waste disposal. About 40 percent of the pollution abatement expenditures in the United States go toward cleaner air, another 40 percent go toward cleaner water, and 20 percent go toward disposing of solid waste.

Federal efforts to clean up the environment are coordinated by the *Environmental Protection Agency (EPA)*. Four federal laws underpin federal efforts to protect the environment: the Clean Air Act of 1970, the Clean Water Act of 1972, the Resource Conservation and Recovery Act of 1976, which governs solid waste disposal, and the *Superfund* law, a 1980 law focusing on toxic waste dumps. In this section we will consider, in turn, air pollution, water pollution, disposing of solid waste, and Superfund activities.

Air Pollution

In the Clean Air Act of 1970, Congress set national standards for the amount of pollution that could be emitted into the atmosphere. Congress thereby recognized air as an economic resource, which, like other resources, has alternative uses. The air can be used, for example, as a source of life-giving oxygen, as a prism for viewing breathtaking vistas, or as a garbage dump for carrying away unwanted soot and gases. The 1970 act gave Americans the right to breathe air of a certain quality and at the same time gave producers the right to emit certain specified pollutants into the air.

Smog is the most visible form of air pollution. Automobile emissions account for 40 percent of smog. Another 40 percent comes from consumer products, such as paint thinner and fluorocarbon sprays, dry cleaning

---

[2] Kit Farber and Gary Rutledge, "Pollution Abatement and Control Expenditures, 1984–87," *Survey of Current Business*, June 1989: 19–26.

solvents, and baker's yeast byproducts. Only 15 percent comes from manufacturing. The Clean Air Act mandated a reduction of 90 percent in auto emissions, leaving it to the industry to achieve this target. At the time, auto maufacturers complained that the objective was impossible, but by 1989 average emissions for new vehicles were only 4 percent of their 1970 level. Although air pollution is still a problem, U.S. pollution levels are down on average since the 1970s.

Water Pollution

Two major sources of water pollution are sewage and chemicals. For many decades cities had an economic incentive to dump their sewage directly into waterways rather than incur the expense of cleaning it up first. Frequently, the current or tides would carry the effluent away to become someone else's problem. Although each community found it rational (based on a narrow view of the situation) to dump into the river or sea, the combined effect of these individual choices was pollution-choked waterways. Thus sewage is a negative externality imposed by a community on other communities.

Most of the EPA's money over the years has gone to build sewage treatment plants. Real progress has been made in lessening sewage-related water pollution. Hundreds of once-polluted waterways have been cleaned up enough to permit swimming and fishing. The majority of U.S. cities now have modern sewage control (notable exceptions include Boston, which dumps sewage directly into Boston Harbor, and New York City, which teams up with New Jersey to dump raw sewage into the Atlantic Ocean, using a discharge point 106 miles off Cape May, New Jersey).

Chemicals are another source of water pollution. Chemical pollution may conjure up an image of a chemical company dumping in the river, but only about 10 percent of water pollution comes from *point* pollution, which means pollution from factories and other fixed industrial sites. About two-thirds of the chemical pollutants in water come from what is called *nonpoint* pollution, derived mostly from runoff of pesticides and fertilizer from agriculture. Congress has been reluctant to limit the use of pesticides, though pesticides pollute water and contaminate food. Industrial America seems an easier target than Old MacDonald's farm.

In 1970 Congress shifted control of pesticides from the U.S. Department of Agriculture to the newly formed EPA. But the EPA already had its hands full administering the Clean Water Act, so it turned pesticide regulation over to the states. Most states turned the job over to their departments of agriculture. But these state agencies tend to promote the interests of farmers, not to restrict what farmers can do. The EPA now reports that in most states pesticides have fouled the ground water. The EPA also argues that pesticide residues on food pose more health problems than do toxic waste dumps or air pollution. According to EPA estimates, some six thousand cancer deaths a year are caused by just one-third of the *approved* pesticides that have been tested. Over fifty thousand pesticides on the market today have never been tested for their long-term health effects.

Toxic Waste and the Superfund

The U.S. synthetic chemical industry has flourished in the last forty years, and about fifty-five thousand chemicals are in common use. Some have harmful effects on humans and other living creatures. These chemicals can pose risks at every stage of their production, use, and disposal. New Jersey manufactures more toxic chemicals than any other state and, not surprisingly, has the worst toxic waste burden. Prior to 1980 the disposal of toxic waste created get-rich-quick opportunities for anyone who could rent or buy a few acres of land to open a toxic waste dump. One site in New Jersey took in 71 million gallons of hazardous chemicals between 1973 and 1976, chemicals that damaged nearby trees and houses.[3]

Prior to 1980, once a company paid someone to haul away its wastes, it was no longer responsible for them. The Comprehensive Environmental Response, Compensation and Liability Act of 1980, known more popularly as the *Superfund* law, requires any company that generates, stores, *or* transports hazardous wastes to pay to clean up any wastes that improperly disposed of. A producer or hauler that is the source of even one barrel of pollution dumped at a site can be held responsible for cleaning up the entire site.

The Superfund law gives the federal government authority over sites contaminated with toxins. But to get an offending company to comply with its edicts, the EPA frequently must sue the company. So the process is slow, and over 80 percent of the Superfund budget, which is financed by a tax on manufacturers, has been spent on court costs and consultants' fees rather than on site cleanups. As of 1989, only 48 of the 1175 sites designated for cleanup under the Superfund law had actually been cleaned up. Often the contaminated sludge has simply been moved from one dump to another, eventually requiring another cleanup. In some cases the costs of cleanup far exceed the value of the land in question.

Congress never established criteria for allocating the Superfund, so the attention of the program's administrators has been drawn from one hot spot to another, more in response to the squeaky political wheel and to media hype than on the basis of any economically rational plan. A recent EPA study claims that the health hazards of Superfund sites have been vastly exaggerated. Chemicals in the ground often move very slowly, sometimes taking years to move a few feet, so the threat they pose is only to those living nearby. In contrast, air pollution represents a more widespread threat because the air is so mobile. Those who are neighbors of toxic waste sites know it and can exert political pressure to get something done. But those who may in the future develop some disease from air or water pollution do

---

[3] See Jason Zweig, "Real-Life Horror Story," *Forbes*, 12 December 1988.

not know it now; thus many of them see no reason to press their elected officials for legislation that mandates clean air and clean water. Because of their greater media appeal and political urgency, toxic waste dumps tend to receive more attention than air or water pollution.

Solid Waste

In 1987, Islip, Long Island, with little space left in its municipal landfill, piled 3186 tons of garbage on a barge, hoping to dump it elsewhere. The barge wandered from port to port, but nowhere did people want the garbage in their backyard. After traveling 6000 miles, the barge returned to New York, where the garbage was burned and buried. The "barge to nowhere" illustrates another major environmental problem in the United States: the nation is running out of places to dump the 160 million tons of garbage generated yearly. We generate about 3.6 pounds of garbage per resident per day in this country — double the quantity produced in 1960 and the largest amount per capita in the world. The throwaway tendency of advanced economies leads them to generate three times the garbage of less developed countries. A toaster that goes on the fritz, for example, is more likely to be sent to the dump than to the repair shop. It's cheaper to buy a new toaster for $30 than to pay up to $40 per hour to have it repaired, assuming you can find a repair shop. (Look up "Small Appliance Repair" in the Yellow Pages and see if you can find even one such repair shop in your area.)

Eighty percent of the nation's garbage is bulldozed and covered with soil in landfills. Not only are landfills an unsightly mess, but toxic materials deposited in landfills may leach into the soil, contaminating wells and aquifers. Therefore the prevailing attitude is NIMBY (Not In My Back Yard): everybody wants the garbage picked up but nobody wants it put down anywhere near his or her backyard.

As a result, the country is running out of places to dump garbage. According to the EPA, 70 percent of the nation's landfills were closed between 1978 and 1988, although the annual production of solid waste increased by 16 percent. Only 5500 landfills remain, and half of those are expected to close by 1993. New Jersey, for example, exports 55 percent of its solid waste to such places as Ohio, Pennsylvania, and Kentucky. The cost of dumping in some parts of the country exceeds $100 per ton.

Only about 20 million of the 160 million tons of garbage generated annually in the United States are recycled. What gets recycled is dictated largely by economics: scrap iron and steel, aluminum, paper, and glass. Aluminum can manufacturers now recycle half the cans produced. About one-third of the newspapers and half of the cardboard boxes produced are recycled. Much of the paper is shipped to Korea and Taiwan, where it becomes packaging material for U.S. imports such as VCRs and compact disc players. As the cost of solid waste disposal accelerates, state and local governments are instituting economizing measures, such as requiring households to sort their trash, charging households by the pound for trash pickups, and requiring deposits on bottles.

About 15 million tons of garbage are burned each year, most in trash-to-energy plants, where the heat from incineration generates electricity. Until recently such plants looked like the wave of the future, but a decline in energy prices, less favorable tax treatment in the 1986 tax reform act, and environmental concerns over the siting of incinerators have taken the steam out of the trash-to-energy movement.

So about 80 percent of our garbage goes to landfills, and only 20 percent is incinerated or recycled. In contrast, the Japanese recycle 40 percent of their waste and incinerate 33 percent, leaving only 27 percent to be deposited in landfills. Japanese households sort their trash into as many as twenty-one categories. Land costs much more in Japan than it does in the United States, and so the Japanese use that scarce resource more efficiently than we do.

CONCLUSION

Market prices can direct the allocation of resources only as long as property rights are well defined and can be easily enforced. The lack of well-defined property rights can give rise to the overuse of commonly owned resources. Pollution of air, land, and water arises not so much from the greed of producers and consumers as from the fact that these commonly owned resources are subject to the common pool problem.

Over 5 billion people inhabit the globe, and the population increases by about 80 million each year. In the next fifty years, the population is projected to exceed 10 billion; 90 percent of this growth will occur in less developed countries, where most people eke out a living. Growing population pressure, coupled with a lack of incentives to shepherd commonly owned resources, results in denuded forests, polluted air and water, overgrazed grasslands, and overplanted soil.

Ironically, because of tighter pollution controls, more developed economies tend to be less polluted than developing countries, where there is less industry but much more pollution from what industry there is. The air in places such as Mexico City and Lagos, Nigeria, is dangerous. Winter smog in Mexico City sends thousands to the city hospital each year with respiratory problems. Visitors to China's cities report rarely seeing the sun through the smoke and smog. People there cover their mouths with masks when the smog is especially thick. Farmers in Central America douse their crops with pesticides long banned in the United States. Most developing countries have such profound economic problems that pollution control is not high on their list of priorities.

1. Private choices will result in too little output when positive externalities exist and too much output when negative externalities exist. Public policy should subsidize or otherwise promote the production of goods generating positive externalities and should tax or otherwise discourage the production of goods generating negative externalities.

2. The optimal amount of pollution abatement occurs where the marginal social cost of pollution abatement equals the marginal social benefit of that abatement. A decrease in the marginal cost of pollution abatement or an increase in the marginal benefit of pollution abatement increases the optimal level of abatement.

3. The thermal blanket of carbon dioxide and other gases building up in the atmosphere causes the greenhouse effect. The world's tropical rain forests have served to recycle noxious gases and convert them into oxygen and wood; the destruction of these forests has reduced the environment's ability to cleanse itself.

4. The Coase theorem argues that as long as bargaining costs are small, assigning property rights to one party leads to an efficient solution to the problem of externalities. An example of the Coase theorem in action is the sale of pollution rights.

5. In the last two decades, progress has been made in cleaning up the nation's air and waterways. The air is cleaner because of stricter emissions standards for motor vehicles; the water is cleaner because of billions spent on sewage treatment facilities. Though much of the federal attention and federal budget goes toward cleaning up toxic waste dumps, this pollution does not pose as great a threat to the population as a whole as other forms of pollution such as smog and pesticides.

Questions and Problems

1. (Positive Externalities) Consider the situation illustrated in Exhibit 5, in which external benefits exist. Show on the diagram the welfare (deadweight) loss associated with producing at the point where marginal private benefit equals supply instead of where marginal social benefit equals supply.

2. (Negative Externalities) Consider the situation illustrated in Exhibit 1, in which a negative externality exists. If the government simply sets the price of electricity at the optimal level (that is, where the marginal social cost equals the demand), why is the net gain equal to triangle *abc* even though consumers now pay a higher price for electricity?

3. (Externalities) When students rent local housing, they often drive up rents in the neighborhood, causing a loss of utility to existing residents. Is this an externality? Explain.

4. (Coase Theorem) Suppose a firm pollutes a stream that has recreational value only when it is unpolluted. Why does the assignment of property rights to the stream lead to the same (efficient) level of pollution whether the firm or the recreational users own the stream?

5. (Efficiency Costs of Externalities) Use the data below to answer the following questions.

Quantity	Marginal Private Benefit (Demand)	Marginal Private Cost (Supply)	Marginal Social Cost
0	—	$ 0	$ 0
1	$10	2	4
2	9	3	5
3	8	4	6
4	7	5	7
5	6	6	8
6	5	7	9
7	4	8	10
8	3	9	11
9	2	10	12
10	1	11	13

a. What is the external cost per unit of production?

b. At what level will the economy produce if there is no regulation of the externality?

c. At what level should the economy produce to achieve economic efficiency?

d. Calculate the dollar value of the net gain to society from correcting the externality.

6. (Externalities and Economic Efficiency) Describe the specific externality, if any, of each of the following, and discuss the implications of each for economic efficiency:

a. Crabbing in the Chesapeake Bay
b. Airport runway noise
c. Cloud seeding
d. Smoking on airplanes

7. (Education and Positive Externalities) Discuss the following proposition: "Education should be subsidized because society is better off when education consumption increases."

8. (Negative Externalities) Show why, in general, the optimal amount of a negative externality is not zero.

9. (Reduction of Negative Externalities) Suppose you wish to reduce a negative externality by imposing a tax on the activity that creates the externality. If the amount of the externality produced per unit of output increases as output increases, show how to determine the correct tax by using a supply-demand diagram.

10. (Public Goods) In a sense, a public good (one that, once produced, is available for all whether or not they pay) is an example of an externality. Explain.

PART EIGHT

The International Setting

C H A P T E R   3 3

International Trade

This morning you put on your Jordache jeans from Taiwan, laced up your Reebok shoes from Korea, and pulled on your Benetton sweater from Italy. After a breakfast that included ham from Poland and coffee from Brazil, you climbed into your Japanese Toyota fueled by Saudi Arabian oil and headed for a lecture by a visiting professor from Yugoslavia. Americans buy Japanese cars, French wine, Swiss clocks, and thousands of other goods from around the globe. Foreigners buy wheat, personal computers, aircraft, and thousands of other products from the United States. The world is a giant shopping mall, and Americans are big spenders.

International trade is trade not between countries but between individuals in different countries. In this chapter we will examine the gains from international trade and the effects of trade restrictions on the allocation of resources. At times the chapter gets a bit technical, but we will base the discussion primarily on the familiar concepts of supply and demand. Topics discussed in this chapter include

- Gains from international trade
- Absolute and comparative advantage
- Tariffs
- Import quotas
- Welfare loss from trade restrictions
- Arguments for trade restrictions

THE GAINS FROM TRADE

A family from Georgia that sits down to a meal of Kansas prime rib and Idaho potatoes has been involved in interstate trade. No doubt you have little difficulty understanding why the the residents of one state trade with those of another. Back in Chapter 2 we looked at the gains arising from specialization and exchange. You may recall the discussion of how you and your roommate could maximize output by specializing. Just as individuals benefit from specialization and exchange, so do states and, indeed, nations. To enjoy the gains that arise from specialized production, countries engage in international trade. *With trade, each country can concentrate on producing those goods and services that it produces most efficiently.*

A Profile of Imports and Exports

Some nations are more involved in international trade than others, just as some states are more involved in interstate trade than others. For example, exports account for about half the GNP in the Netherlands; about one-third of the GNP in West Germany, Sweden, and Switzerland; and about a quarter of the GNP in Canada, Yugoslavia, and the United Kingdom. Despite the perception that Japan has a giant export sector, only about 13 percent of Japanese production is involved in international trade.

In the United States, foreign trade amounts to about 10 percent of GNP. Though small relative to GNP, foreign trade plays a vital role in the economy. The two main types of U.S. exports are (1) high-technology manufactured products, such as computers, aircraft, and telecommunication equipment, and (2) agricultural products, such as corn, wheat, and soybeans. Half of U.S. imports are manufactured goods, such as automobiles from Japan and color TVs from Taiwan. Approximately 20 percent of our imports are petroleum and related products, and about 10 percent are agricultural products, such as cocoa, coffee, sugar, and bananas. The United States depends on imports for some key inputs. Nearly all the bauxite used to produce aluminum is imported; most of the platinum and chromium and all of the manganese, mica, diamonds, and nickel are imported.

The primary change in U.S. exports over the last two decades has been a growth in the dollar value of machinery exports; the primary change in imports has been the fourfold increase in the percentage of our import expenditures devoted to petroleum imports. Canada is the United States's largest trading partner; Japan is the next largest. Other important trading partners include Mexico, West Germany, Great Britain, South Korea, France, Hong Kong, Italy, and Brazil.

Absolute and Comparative Advantage

The rationale behind some international trade is obvious. The United States cannot mine bauxite because the mineral is unavailable here; likewise, a country without coal deposits cannot mine that mineral. It is more revealing, however, to examine the gains from trade where the cost advantage is not quite so clear. Suppose that just two goods — food and clothing — are produced and consumed and that there are only two countries in the world — the United States, with a labor force of 100 million workers, and the mythical country of Izodia, with 200 million workers. The conclusions we derive from our simple model will have general relevance to the pattern of international trade.

Exhibit 1 presents each country's production possibilities schedule *in the absence of trade*, based on the size of the labor force and the productivity of workers in each country. We assume that labor is fully and efficiently employed. Since no trade occurs between countries, Exhibit 1 presents each country's *consumption possibilities schedule* as well.

Suppose that each worker in the United States can produce either 6 units of food or 3 units of clothing per day. If all 100 million U.S. workers produce food, 600 million units can be produced per day, as reflected by combination C_1 in part (a) of Exhibit 1. If all workers produce clothing, the United States can produce 300 million units per day, as reflected by combination C_6. Combinations in between represent possible mixes of output if some workers produce food and some produce clothing. Because a U.S. worker can produce either 6 units of food or 3 units of clothing, the opportunity cost of producing 1 more unit of clothing is 2 units of food. Increasing clothing production by 60 million units requires shifting 20

EXHIBIT 1
PRODUCTION POSSIBILITIES SCHEDULES
FOR THE UNITED STATES AND IZODIA

(a) *United States*

Units Produced (per worker per day)	Production Possibilities at Full Employment of 100 Million Workers (millions of units per day)					
	C_1	C_2	C_3	C_4	C_5	C_6
Food 6	600	480	360	240	120	0
Clothing 3	0	60	120	180	240	300

(b) *Izodia*

Units Produced (per worker per day)	Production Possibilities at Full Employment of 200 Million Workers (millions of units per day)					
	I_1	I_2	I_3	I_4	I_5	I_6
Food 1	200	160	120	80	40	0
Clothing 2	0	80	160	240	320	400

million workers away from food production. Therefore food production falls by 120 million units.

In Izodia workers are less educated, less capital is available per worker, and land is less fertile than in the United States. So each Izodian worker is less productive than each U.S. worker and can produce only 1 unit of food or 2 units of clothing per day. If all 200 million Izodian workers specialize in food production, the country can produce 200 million units of food per day, as reflected by combination I_1 in part (b) of Exhibit 1. If all Izodian workers are involved in clothing production, 400 million units of clothing can be produced per day, as reflected by combination I_6. Some intermediate production possibilities are also listed in the exhibit. Since each worker can produce either 1 unit of food or 2 units of clothing per day, the opportunity cost in Izodia of producing 1 more unit of clothing is 0.5 unit of food. Note from the combinations in part (b) of the table that producing an additional 80 million units of clothing reduces food production by 40 million units, as 40 million workers shift from food production to clothing production.

Thus a U.S. worker can produce 6 units of food per day compared to only 1 unit for an Izodian worker. Also, a U.S. worker can produce 3 units of clothing per day, compared to only 2 units for an Izodian worker. Because they have access to more physical capital, better education, and more training, workers in the United States can produce both more food and more clothing per day than can workers in Izodia. U.S. workers have an *absolute advantage* in the production of both goods because each good can be produced in less time.

Since it has an absolute advantage in the production of both commodities, should the United States be self-sufficient, producing both food and clothing, or can the United States gain from trade? We learned the answer in Chapter 2, when we observed the gains from trade between you and your roommate. In that example, even though you were better at both typing and ironing than your roommate, you each benefited from specialization based on *comparative advantage*.

As long as the *relative* production costs of the two goods differ in the United States and Izodia, there are gains to be made from specialization and trade. In the United States the opportunity cost of producing 1 more unit of clothing is 2 units of food, compared to only 0.5 unit of food in Izodia. *Since the opportunity cost of producing clothing is higher in the United States than in Izodia, both countries will gain if Izodia concentrates on producing clothing and exports some to the United States and the United States concentrates on producing food and exports some to Izodia.*

Production Possibilities Frontiers

We can illustrate the gains from trade by converting the data in Exhibit 1 to a production possibilities frontier for each country, as shown in Exhibit 2. In each diagram the amount of clothing produced is measured on the horizontal axis and the amount of food on the vertical axis. Production

EXHIBIT 2   PRODUCTION POSSIBILITIES FRONTIERS FOR THE UNITED STATES AND IZODIA WITHOUT TRADE

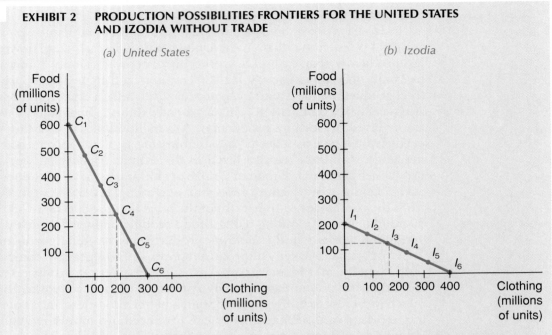

Panel (a) shows the U.S. production possibilities curve; its slope indicates that the opportunity cost of an additional unit of clothing is 2 units of food. Panel (b) shows production possibilities in Izodia; an additional unit of clothing costs 0.5 unit of food. Clothing is relatively cheaper to produce in Izodia.

combinations for the United States are designated in panel (a) by C_1, C_2, and so on; production combinations in Izodia are designated in panel (b) by I_1, I_2, and so on. Because we assume that each country's resources are perfectly adaptable to the production of each commodity, each production possibilities curve is a straight line.

Exhibit 2 illustrates the possible combinations of food and clothing that residents of each country can produce and consume if all resources are fully and efficiently employed and there is no trade between the two countries. Suppose that U.S. producers maximize profit and U.S. consumers maximize utility with the combination of 240 million units of food and 180 million units of clothing—combination C_4. This combination will be called the *no-trade equilibrium*. Suppose also that Izodians have a no-trade equilibrium, identified as combination I_3, of 120 million units of food and 160 million units of clothing.

The Gains from Specialization and Exchange

Since the opportunity cost of producing goods is different in the two countries, mutual gains from trade are possible. *According to the law of* comparative advantage, *each producer should specialize in the good for which its opportunity cost is lower than that of other producers.* As we have already determined, the opportunity cost of producing clothing is 2 units of food in the United States, but only 0.5 unit of food in Izodia. Thus both countries can gain if Izodia specializes in clothing and the United States specializes in food.

Terms of trade *indicate how much of one good will be exchanged for a unit of another good.*

Before countries can trade, the **terms of trade** must be established; that is, the two countries must know how much of one good will be exchanged for each unit of another good. If market forces establish terms of trade whereby the United States can buy clothing for less than 2 units of food and Izodia can sell clothing for more than 0.5 unit of food, both countries will be better off with trade.

Suppose that the two countries have an *exchange ratio* whereby 1 unit of clothing trades for 1 unit of food. At this ratio the United States sacrifices less food by trading with Izodia for clothing than by producing clothing, so U.S. workers specialize in the production of food. Similarly, Izodians sacrifice less clothing by trading with the United States for food than by producing food, so Izodians specialize in the production of clothing. Exhibit 3 shows that with terms of trade that set 1 unit of food equal to 1 unit of clothing, Americans and Izodians can consume anywhere along or below their blue consumption possibilities frontiers. The amount each country actually consumes will depend on its relative preferences for food and clothing. Suppose Americans select point *C* in panel (a) and Izodians select point *I* in panel (b).

Without trade, the United States produced and consumed 240 million units of food and 180 million units of clothing. With trade, the country produces where the production possibilities frontier hits the vertical axis and then trades down along the new consumption possibilities frontier. Thus Americans produce 600 million units of food, consume 400 million units, and exchange the other 200 million units they produce for 200 million units of clothing, as reflected by point *C* in panel (a). Through exchange Americans are able to increase their consumption of both food and clothing.

Without trade, Izodians produced and consumed 120 million units of food and 160 million units of clothing. With trade, Izodia produces where the production possibilities frontier hits the horizontal axis and then trades up along its new consumption possibilities frontier. Thus Izodians consume 200 million of the 400 million units of clothing they produce and exchange the remaining 200 million units of clothing for 200 million units of food, as reflected by point *I* in panel (b). Izodians, like Americans, are able to increase their consumption of both food and clothing through trade. How is this possible?

Just as a country must allocate its resources efficiently in order to operate on its production possibilities frontier, the world must allocate its resources efficiently in order to maximize world production. Since Izodia is relatively more efficient in the production of clothing and the United States is relatively more efficient in the production of food, total world production of both products increases if Izodia specializes in clothing and the United States specializes in food.

**EXHIBIT 3   PRODUCTION (AND CONSUMPTION) POSSIBILITIES FRONTIERS
WITH TRADE**

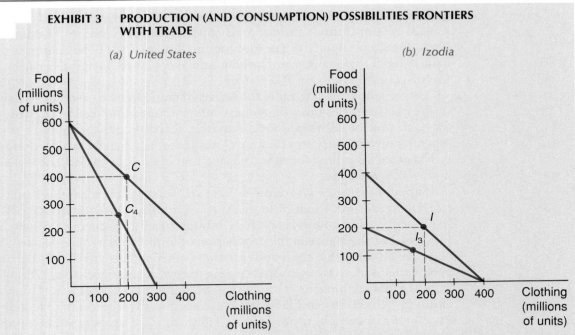

(a) United States   *(b) Izodia*

If Izodia and the United States can trade at the rate of 1 unit of clothing for 1 unit of food, both can benefit. Consumption possibilities at those terms of trade are shown by the blue lines. The United States was previously producing and consuming combination C_4. By trading with Izodia, it can produce only food and still consume combination C—a combination that contains more food and more clothing than combination C_4 does. Likewise, Izodia can attain the preferred combination I by trading its clothing for U.S. food. Both countries are better off as a result of international trade.

Specifically, without specialization, total food production was 360 million units (240 million units in the Unites States plus 120 million units in Izodia) and total clothing production was 340 million units (180 million units in the United States plus 160 million units in Izodia). With specialization, food production increases to 600 million units and clothing production increases to 400 million units, enabling consumption of both goods to rise in each country. The only constraint on trade is that, for each good, total world production must equal total world consumption. This means that the amount of food the United States exports must equal the amount of food Izodia imports. The same goes for clothing.

Thus both countries are better off after trade because the consumption in each country increases. *Despite the absolute advantage held by the United States in the production of both goods, differences in the opportunity cost of production between nations ensure that specialization and exchange can result in mutual gains.* Remember that comparative advantage, not absolute advantage, is the source of gains from trade.

We simplified trade relations in our example to highlight the gains from specialization and exchange. We assumed that each country would completely specialize in producing a particular good, that resources were equally adaptable to the production of either good, that the costs of transporting the goods from one country to another were inconsequential, and that there were no problems in arriving at the terms of trade.

Reasons for International Specialization

Countries trade with one another—or, more precisely, people in one country trade with those in another—because each side expects to gain from the exchange. How do we know what each country should produce and what goods should be traded?

Differences in Resource Endowments Trade is often prompted by differences in resource endowments. Two key resources are labor and capital; countries differ not simply in the amount of labor and capital with which they are endowed but in the quality of each. A well-trained labor force will be much more productive than an uneducated and unskilled labor force. Sophisticated capital reflecting the most recent technological developments will be more productive than out-of-date capital. Some countries, such as the United States and Japan, have an educated labor force and have accumulated an abundant stock of modern capital. Both resources result in greater productivity per worker, making each nation very competitive in producing goods that require skilled labor and sophisticated capital.

Some countries have fertile land in abundance and a favorable growing season. The United States, for example, has been called the breadbasket of the world because of its rich farmland. Honduras has the ideal climate for growing bananas. Coffee is grown best in the climate and elevation of Colombia, Brazil, or Jamaica. Thus the United States exports wheat and imports coffee and bananas. Differences in the seasons across countries also serve as a basis for trade. For example, during winter months Americans import fruit from Chile and Canadian tourists travel to Florida for sun and fun. During summer months Americans export fruit and American tourists travel to Canada for fishing and camping.

Mineral resources are often concentrated in particular countries: oil in Saudi Arabia, bauxite in Jamaica, diamonds in South Africa, coal in the United States. The United States has abundant coal but not enough oil to satisfy domestic demand. Thus the United States exports coal and imports oil. More generally, countries export those products that they can produce more cheaply in return for those that are unavailable domestically or are more costly to produce than to buy from other countries.

Differences in Tastes Even if all countries had identical resource endowments and combined those resources with equal efficiency, each country would still gain from trade as long as tastes and preferences differed among countries. And consumption patterns do appear to differ, often because of custom or religion. For example, the per capita consumption of beer in Germany is triple that in Norway and Spain. The English like tea; Americans, coffee. Algeria has an ideal climate for growing grapes, but it also has a large Moslem population that abstains from alcohol. Thus Algeria exports wine.

Economies of Scale If production is subject to *economies of scale* — that is, if the cost per unit of production falls as productive capacity expands — countries can gain from trade by having each nation specialize in one product. Such specialization allows each nation to produce at a higher output level, which reduces average production costs. The primary reason for establishing the Single Integrated Market by 1992 in Western Europe is to offer European producers a very large open market of over 320 million consumers so that producers can increase production, experience economies of scale, and become more competitive in international markets.

TRADING ON THE WORLD MARKET

So far we have analyzed the case in which each country fully specializes in the production of a particular good. How does international trade affect prices and output in domestic markets when two countries both produce a certain good? In this section we will rely on supply and demand analysis to develop an understanding of international markets.

*The **world price** is the price determined by the world supply and world demand for a product.*

The **world price** is the price determined by the world supply and demand for a product. It is the price at which any supplier can sell output on the world market and at which any demander can purchase output on the world market. If there are enough buyers and sellers throughout the world, no single country's supply or demand for the good can affect the world price. Thus the world price faced by each country is similar to the market price faced by each firm in perfect competition. Let's consider the market for a particular product: steel.

World Price Is Above the Domestic Equilibrium Price

Exhibit 4(a) shows hypothetical curves reflecting the long-run supply and demand for steel in the United States. The world price per ton of steel is measured on the vertical axis. The U.S. demand curve for steel intersects the U.S. producers' supply curve at a price of $150 per ton. Therefore a price of $150 per ton is the market-clearing price that would prevail in the United States without international trade. U.S. demanders are willing to buy all of the 100 million tons per month offered by U.S. producers at that price, so the United States does not export steel. U.S. suppliers are willing to sell all of the 100 million tons per month that U.S. demanders wish to purchase at that price, so the United States does not import steel.

What if the world price of steel is $200 per ton — a price *above* the $150 per ton price that would prevail in the United States in the absence of trade?

EXHIBIT 4   THE DOMESTIC MARKET AND WORLD MARKET FOR STEEL

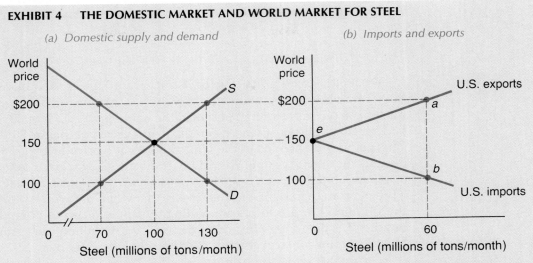

(a) *Domestic supply and demand*

(b) *Imports and exports*

Panel (a) shows the domestic supply and demand for steel in the United States. At a world price of $150 per ton, U.S. consumers demand all that U.S. producers supply. Panel (b) shows that no U.S. steel is exported or imported at that price.

At world prices above $150 per ton, U.S. producers supply more than enough to satisfy domestic quantity demanded. The excess is exported. The U.S. export line in panel (b) shows the volume of exports at prices above $150. If the world price is below $150, domestic quantity demanded exceeds domestic quantity supplied. The difference is made up by imports.

If international trade is prohibited, the world price is irrelevant, and only the price determined in the United States matters. But if U.S. producers can easily export steel to the rest of the world, they will increase the quantity supplied when the world price rises above $150 per ton. You can see from the supply curve in panel (a) that when the world price rises, U.S. suppliers increase the quantity supplied from 100 to 130 million tons per month. Because of the higher price, U.S. demanders reduce the quantity they demand to 70 million tons per month.

The amount by which the quantity supplied by U.S. producers exceeds the quantity demanded in the United States equals the amount of steel exported by U.S. producers. Thus, when the world price equals $200, 60 million tons of steel are exported from the United States. U.S. exports and imports as a function of the world price are illustrated in panel (b) of Exhibit 4. In that panel the vertical axis again presents the world price of steel, but the horizontal axis measures the amount of steel that is imported or exported based on the world price. At point *e* on the horizontal axis of panel (b), the world price is $150 per ton and imports and exports equal zero. When the world price is $200, the United States exports 60 million tons of steel, a combination identified as point *a* in panel (b). By connecting points *e* and *a*, we can form an upward-sloping *export line*. At each point on this export line, the quantity exported by the United States is equal to the difference in panel (a) between the U.S. quantity supplied and the U.S. quantity demanded at that price.

World Price Is Below the Domestic Equilibrium Price

What if the world price is below $150 per ton? If U.S. steel buyers cannot buy from abroad, the world price of steel is irrelevant. If, however, U.S. buyers can purchase foreign output at the world price, the United States will become an importer of steel when the world price falls below $150 per ton. The quantity demanded in the United States at a price below $150 per ton exceeds the quantity supplied by U.S. producers, so *the excess demand in U.S. markets is satisfied by purchases from foreign producers*. Suppose the world price is $100 per ton. In Exhibit 4(a) you can see that when the price is $100 per ton, the amount U.S. producers are willing to supply drops to 70 million tons, but the U.S. quantity demanded increases to 130 million tons. At that price 60 million tons of steel are purchased on the world market.

The quantity of steel imported by the United States when the price is $100 per ton is shown by point *b* in panel (b). At any prices below $150 per ton, the quantity of imports is equal to the excess quantity demanded, shown in panel (a); with these quantities we can construct the *import line* in panel (b), which starts at a price of $150 (point *e*) and slopes down to the right.

To summarize: When the world price of steel is $150 per ton, the quantity of steel demanded in the United States equals the quantity supplied by U.S. producers, so steel is neither imported nor exported. When the world price is above $150, the quantity of steel supplied by U.S. producers exceeds the quantity demanded by U.S. buyers, so steel is exported. And when the world price is below $150, the quantity demanded by U.S. buyers exceeds the quantity supplied by U.S. producers, so steel is imported. The world price therefore determines whether the United States is an importer, an exporter, or neither.

The Rest of the World

To simplify our analysis, let's suppose that there is just one other country in the "rest of the world": Japan, a major producer and user of steel. To keep the accounting simple, we'll convert all Japanese prices into U.S. dollars. Japan's domestic supply and demand for steel, along with its supply of exports and demand for imports, are presented in Exhibit 5. As you can see from panel (a), when the world price of steel is $100 per ton, the quantity supplied by Japanese producers just equals the quantity demanded in Japan. In panel (b), therefore, there are no imports or exports when the world price is $100 per ton. But at a world price above $100 per ton, Japanese producers supply more steel than is demanded in Japan, so the difference is exported to the world market, as shown in panel (b). The reverse is true for prices below $100; in that case the quantity demanded in Japan exceeds the quantity

EXHIBIT 5   THE DOMESTIC JAPANESE MARKET AND THE WORLD MARKET FOR STEEL

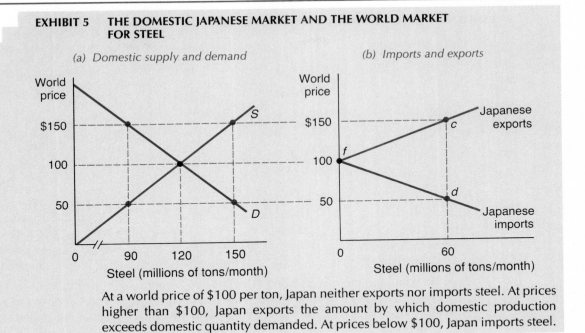

(a) Domestic supply and demand

(b) Imports and exports

At a world price of $100 per ton, Japan neither exports nor imports steel. At prices higher than $100, Japan exports the amount by which domestic production exceeds domestic quantity demanded. At prices below $100, Japan imports steel.

Japanese producers supply, and the difference becomes Japan's imports, as shown in panel (b).

Determining the World Price

The world price of steel is determined by international supply and demand. In our simplified model, *the world price is found where the exports of one country equal the imports of the other country.* To determine the world price of steel, we combine elements of Exhibit 4 and 5. Panel (a) of Exhibit 6 again presents the supply and demand for steel in the United States, and panel (c) presents the same information for Japan.

The U.S. *import* line and the Japanese *export* line are shown in panel (b). The U.S. export line and the Japanese import line are not shown because, given the supply and demand conditions, the United States will not export steel and Japan will not import it. From Exhibits 4 and 5 you can see that U.S. producers would like to export steel if the world price rises above $150, but Japanese buyers are willing to import steel only at prices below $100. Since the lowest price at which U.S. producers would like to export exceeds the highest price at which Japanese buyers would like to import, U.S. exporters and Japanese importers will do no business.

But at a price above $100 per ton, Japanese producers are willing to export, and at a price below $150 per ton, U.S. buyers are willing to import. International trade will occur at a world price between $100 and $150 per ton. Specifically, the intersection of the Japanese export line with the U.S.

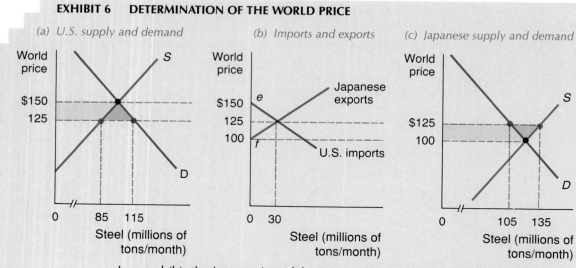

EXHIBIT 6   DETERMINATION OF THE WORLD PRICE

(a) *U.S. supply and demand*   (b) *Imports and exports*   (c) *Japanese supply and demand*

In panel (b), the intersection of the Japanese export and U.S. import lines determines the nature of trade between the two countries. At a world price of $125 per ton, Japan exports 30 million tons of steel to the United States. In the United States prices are lower and the quantity consumed is greater as a result of trade. The blue areas reflect the gain in consumer surplus. In Japan prices are higher and the quantity produced is greater. The green areas indicate the gain in producer surplus. The net gains in the two countries are shown by the darkly shaded triangles in panels (a) and (c).

import line yields the world equilibrium price of steel. (Again, we are assuming that the world market consists only of these two countries.) Given the supply and demand for steel in the two countries, the equilibrium world price will be $125 per ton. At that price Japan will export 30 million tons of steel per month to the United States.

The Net Effect of Trade on Social Welfare

Let's consider the gains from trade in each country. *The net change in social welfare is determined by summing the net changes in consumer and producer surpluses.* In panel (a) of Exhibit 6, you can see that at a price of $125 per ton, 115 million tons per month are demanded in the United States. At that price 85 million tons are supplied by U.S. producers and 30 million tons are imported from Japan. In the United States the price is lower and the quantity consumed is greater than would be the case without trade. The two blue shaded areas in panel (a) reflect the gain in U.S. consumer surplus resulting from the lower world price. But the lower price also means that U.S. producers supply less steel and thus forgo some producer surplus, as indicated by the light blue area in panel (a). Hence the light blue area represents the surplus transferred from domestic steel producers to domestic consumers of steel. But the gain in consumer surplus exceeds the loss in producer surplus by the area of the dark blue triangle. Thus the lower price of steel generates a net gain in welfare in the United States.

The situation is reversed in Japan, as shown in panel (c). At a world price of $125 per ton, Japan produces 105 million tons per month for its domestic market and exports the other 30 million tons to the United States. Japanese producers are better off with international trade because they get to sell more output for a higher price than they could if they were limited to their domestic market. The two green shaded areas in panel (c) represent the gain in producer surplus for Japanese steelmakers, who can sell steel at a world price of $125 per ton instead of the $100 price prevailing in Japan without international trade. The light green area represents the consumer surplus lost as a result of the higher price and lower domestic consumption. Therefore that portion of the gain in producer surplus in panel (c) comes at the expense of forgone consumer surplus. But since the gain in producer surplus exceeds the loss in consumer surplus (indicated by the dark green triangle), net social welfare increases in Japan.

TRADE RESTRICTIONS

Despite the benefits of international trade, nearly all countries at one time or another erect barriers to impede or block free trade among nations. In this section we will consider the effects of restrictions and the reasons they are imposed.

Tariffs

*A **tariff** is a tax on imports (or exports).*

A **tariff** is a tax on imports. (Tariffs can also be applied to exports, but we will focus on import tariffs.) A tariff can be either *specific*, such as a lump–sum tariff of $5 per barrel of oil, or *ad valorem*, a percentage of the cost of imports at the port of entry. Let's consider the effects of a specific tariff on a particular good. In Exhibit 7, *D* is the domestic demand for sugar and *S* is the amount supplied by domestic producers. Suppose that the world price of sugar is $0.10 per pound. With free trade, domestic consumers can buy any amount desired at the world price, so the quantity demanded is 70 million pounds per month, of which 20 million pounds are supplied by domestic producers and 50 million pounds are imported. Domestic producers cannot charge more than the world price, since domestic buyers can purchase as much sugar as they want at $0.10 per pound in the world market.

Now suppose that a specific tariff of $0.05 is imposed on each pound of sugar imported, raising the price of imported sugar from $0.10 to $0.15 per pound. Domestic producers can therefore raise their price to $0.15 per pound as well without losing sales to imports. With the higher price, the quantity supplied by domestic producers increases to 30 million pounds per month, but the quantity demanded by domestic consumers declines to 60 million pounds per month. Because the quantity demanded has declined and

EXHIBIT 7   EFFECT OF A TARIFF

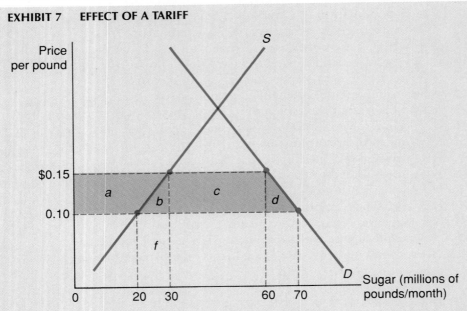

At a world price of $0.10 per pound, domestic consumers demand 70 million pounds per month and domestic producers supply 20 million pounds per month; the difference is imported. With the imposition of a $0.05 per pound tariff, the domestic price rises to $0.15 per pound, domestic producers increase production to 30 million pounds, and domestic consumers cut back to 60 million pounds. Imports fall to 30 million pounds. At the higher domestic price, consumers are worse off; their loss of consumer surplus is the sum of areas *a*, *b*, *c*, and *d*. Area *a* represents an increase in producer surplus: a transfer from consumers to producers. Areas *b* and *f* reflect the portion of additional revenues to producers that is just offset by the higher production costs of expanding domestic output by 10 million pounds. Area *c* shows government revenue from the tariff. The net welfare loss to society is the sum of area *d*, which reflects the loss of consumer surplus resulting from the drop in consumption, and area *b*, which reflects the higher marginal cost of producing domestically output that could have been produced more cheaply abroad.

the quantity supplied by domestic producers has increased, imports decline from 50 million to 30 million pounds per month.

Since the price is higher after the tariff, consumers are worse off. The loss in consumer surplus is identified in Exhibit 7 by the blue and red shaded areas. Because both the domestic price and the quantity of sugar supplied by domestic producers have increased, the total revenue received by domestic producers increases by the area *a* plus *b* plus *f*. But only the light blue area, *a*, represents an increase in net income to domestic producers — an increase in producer surplus. The increase in revenue represented by the area *b* plus *f* just offsets the higher cost of production that results from expanding domestic output from 20 million to 30 million pounds. The red triangle, *b*, represents a net welfare loss to the domestic economy, reflecting the higher marginal cost of expanding domestic production by 10 million pounds rather than purchasing that output from foreign producers at $0.10 per pound.

Government revenue from the tariff is identified by the light blue area, *c*, which equals the tariff of $0.05 per pound multiplied by the 30 million pounds that are imported. Tariff revenue represents a loss to consumers, but since the tariff is revenue to the government, this loss can potentially be offset by a reduction in taxes or an increase in public services.

The red triangle, *d*, represents the loss in consumer surplus that results from the 10 million pound drop in quantity demanded. This loss is not redistributed as a gain to anyone else, so area *d* reflects a net welfare loss of the tariff. The two red triangles, *b* and *d*, therefore measure the domestic economy's net welfare loss, or the deadweight loss; the triangles measure a net loss in consumer surplus that is not offset by a net gain to anyone else.

Of the total loss in consumer surplus resulting from the tariff, area *a* is redistributed to domestic producers (and suppliers of resources specific to the industry), area *c* becomes tariff revenue for the government, and the two red areas, *b* and *d*, are deadweight losses. All of these amounts—the amount redistributed, the tariff revenue, and the deadweight losses—depend on the slopes of the domestic supply and demand curves. The steeper the supply curve, the smaller the increase in domestic production resulting from a given tariff and the smaller the deadweight loss resulting from a higher marginal cost of domestic production. The steeper the demand curve, the smaller the decrease in quantity demanded for a given tariff and the smaller the dead-weight loss resulting from a reduction in quantity demanded.

Recognizing the losses associated with tariff restrictions, the United States, after World War II, invited its trading partners to negotiate less stringent trade restrictions. The result was the **General Agreement on Tariffs and Trade (GATT)**, which was an international trade treaty adopted in 1947 by twenty-three countries, including the United States. Each member of GATT agreed to reduce tariff rates and to treat all member nations equally with respect to trade. The agreement resulted in thousands of tariff reductions; the number of signers has since grown to ninety-two. International trade increased in the 1950s and 1960s, partly in response to a lowering of tariffs. GATT has become a permanent international organization. Members of GATT agree to honor the *most-favored nation clause*, which means that tariff reductions granted to one country are extended to other trading members of GATT. Multilateral negotiations since 1947 have focused primarily on reducing tariffs. As a result, nontariff barriers such as quotas have become increasingly important.

The ***General Agreement on Tariffs and Trade (GATT)*** *is an international tariff-reduction treaty adopted in 1947 by the United States and twenty-two other nations.*

Import Quotas

An **import quota** is a legal limit on the quantity of a particular commodity that can be imported per year. Quotas are often targeted at exports

An **import quota** is a
legal limit on the
quantity of a particu-
lar commodity that
can be imported per
year.

from certain countries. For example, a quota may limit the number of autos
that can be imported from Japan or the amount of ham that can be imported
from Poland. To have an impact on the market, a quota must limit imports to
less than would be imported under free trade; such a quota is referred to as an
effective quota.

Let's consider the effect of a quota on the domestic market for sugar. In
panel (a) of Exhibit 8, the domestic supply of sugar is *S* and the domestic
demand is *D*. Suppose that the world price of sugar is $0.10 per pound. With
free trade, that price would prevail in the domestic market, and 70 million
pounds per month would be demanded. Domestic suppliers would provide
20 million pounds and importers 50 million pounds. With a quota of 50
million pounds or more per month, the domestic price would be the same as
the world price of $0.10 per pound, and domestic sales would be 70 million
pounds per month. Any more stringent quota, however, would reduce the
supply of imports, which, as we will see, would raise the domestic price.

Suppose that a quota of 30 million pounds per month is established. As
long as the price in the U.S. market is at or above the world price of $0.10
per pound, foreign producers supply 30 million pounds to the U.S. market.
So at price levels at or above $0.10 per pound, the total supply of sugar to the
domestic market is found by adding 30 million pounds of sugar to the
amount supplied by domestic producers. At the world price of $0.10,
domestic producers supply 20 million pounds, and importers supply the
limit of 30 million pounds, for a total quantity supplied of 50 million
pounds. At prices above $0.10, domestic producers can and do expand their
quantity supplied in the U.S. market, but imports are restricted by the quota
to 30 million pounds.

Domestic and foreign producers will never sell their output for less than
$0.10 per pound in the U.S. market because they can always sell it for $0.10
per pound on the world market. Thus the supply curve from both domestic
production and imports becomes horizontal at the world price of $0.10 per
pound and remains horizontal until the supply reaches 50 million pounds.
For prices above $0.10 per pound, the supply curve equals the horizontal
sum of the supply curve of domestic producers, *S*, and the quota of 30
million pounds. The domestic price is found where the new supply curve
intersects the domestic demand curve, which in panel (a) of Exhibit 8 occurs
at point *e*. An effective quota, by limiting imports, raises the domestic price
of sugar above the world price and makes the quantity demanded lower than
it would be under free trade. Note that the quota in the example yields the
same equilibrium price and quantity as does the tariff we examined earlier.

Panel (b) of Exhibit 8 focuses on the redistributional and efficiency
effects of the quota. The decline in consumer surplus after the quota is
imposed is depicted by the blue and red shaded areas. The loss in consumer
surplus represented by the blue area *a* is converted into the gain in producer
surplus resulting from the higher price. Because the value of area *a* is simply
transferred from domestic consumers to domestic producers, there is no
loss in domestic welfare. The blue rectangle *c* shows the gain to those
permitted by the quota to sell 30 million pounds per month at the domestic

EXHIBIT 8   EFFECT OF A QUOTA

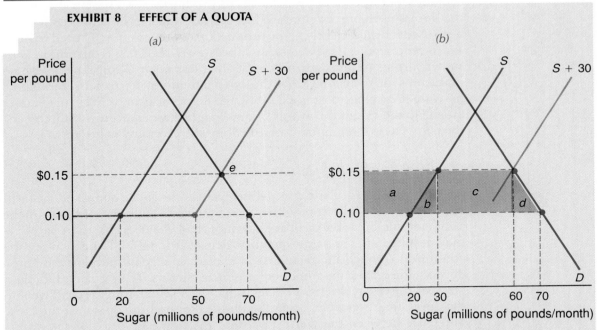

In panel (a), *D* is the domestic demand curve and *S* is the domestic supply curve. When the government establishes a sugar quota of 30 million pounds per year, the supply curve from both domestic production and imports becomes horizontal at the world price of $0.10 per pound and remains horizontal until the supply reaches 50 million pounds. For higher prices, the supply curve equals the horizontal sum of the domestic supply curve, *S*, and the quota. The new domestic price, $0.15 per pound, is determined by the intersection of the new supply curve, *S* + 30, with the domestic demand curve, *D*. Panel (b) shows the welfare effect of the quota. As a result of the higher domestic price, consumer surplus is reduced by the amount of the shaded area. Area *a* represents a transfer from domestic consumers to domestic producers. Rectangular area *c* shows the gain to those who can import sugar at the world price and sell it at the higher domestic price. Triangular area *b* reflects a net loss; it represents the amount by which the cost of producing an extra 10 million pounds of sugar in the United States exceeds the cost of producing it abroad. Area *d* also reflects a net loss—a reduction in consumer surplus as consumption falls. Thus the blue shaded areas illustrate the loss in consumer surplus that is captured by domestic producers and those who are permitted to fulfill the quota, and the red triangles illustrate the minimum net welfare cost.

price of $0.15 per pound. To the extent that the gains from the quota go to foreign exporters rather than to domestic importers, area *c* reflects a net loss in domestic welfare.

The red triangle *b* shows the amount by which the domestic marginal cost of producing another 10 million pounds exceeds the world price of the good. This triangular area represents a deadweight loss to the domestic economy, because sugar could have been produced more cheaply abroad and the domestic resources employed to increase sugar production could have been used more efficiently in the production of other goods. The red triangle *d* also represents a deadweight loss, because it reflects a reduction in consumer surplus (resulting from the fact that less sugar is consumed) with no offsetting gain to anyone. Thus the two red triangles in panel (b) of Exhibit 8 measure the welfare cost imposed on the domestic economy by an effective quota. To the extent the profits of quota rights (area *c*) accrue to foreigners, the net welfare loss imposed on the domestic economy is greater.

Comparison of Tariffs and Quotas

Consider the similarities and differences between the quota and the tariff we have discussed, both of which raised the domestic price of sugar by the same amount. Since the tariff and the quota had identical effects on the price, they resulted in the same quantity demanded. In both cases domestic consumers suffered the same loss in consumer surplus and domestic producers gained the same amount of producer surplus. The primary difference between the two restrictive policies is that the revenue from the tariff went to the domestic government, whereas those allocated the quota captured the difference between the world price and the domestic price. If the profits from quotas accrue to foreigners, then the domestic economy is better off with a tariff than with a quota.

Currently the United States grants quotas to specific countries. These countries, in turn, award these rights to their exporters through a variety of means. The value of these export rights has been estimated recently to exceed $7 billion, with more than half of this amount due to quotas on textiles and apparel.[1] By rewarding domestic producers with higher prices and foreign producers with the right to sell goods to the United States, the quota system creates two groups of rent seekers intent on securing and perpetuating these quotas. Lobbyists for foreign producers work the halls of Congress seeking the right to export to the United States. This strong support from producers, coupled with little opposition from consumers (who remain rationally ignorant), led to quotas that have lasted for decades. Steel quotas have been in effect for over twenty years, apparel quotas for over thirty years, and sugar quotas for over fifty years.

Quotas are so attractive to foreign producers that, in the absence of quotas, producers sometimes restrict their exports to the United States under *voluntary export restraints*, or *VERs*. For example, between 1981 and 1985 Japan restricted its sales of automobiles to the United States. By limiting the supply of Toyotas, Nissans, and Hondas, such restrictions resulted in higher U.S. prices for these automobiles and higher prices for domestically produced autos.

Some economists have argued that if quotas are to be used, the United

---

[1] See C. Fred Bergsten, "Reform Trade Policy with Auction Quotas," *Challenge* (May/June 1987): 5.

States should auction off quota allocations to foreign producers, thereby capturing the difference between the world price and the U.S. price. Auctioning off quotas would not only increase federal revenue but also reduce foreign pressure for quotas.

Other Trade Restrictions

Besides tariffs and quotas, there are a variety of other restrictions on free trade. A country may provide *export subsidies* to encourage firms to export or *low interest loans* to foreign buyers to promote exports of large capital goods. Some countries impose *domestic content requirements* specifying that a certain percentage of a final good's value must be produced domestically. Other requirements concerning health, safety, or technical standards often discriminate against foreign goods. For example, European countries prohibit imports of beef from hormone-fed cattle, a measure aimed at U.S. beef producers. Purity laws in West Germany bar the importation of many non-German beers. Differing technical standards force manufacturers to make seven different models of the same TV for the European Community.

ARGUMENTS FOR TRADE RESTRICTIONS

In view of their distributional effects and the welfare loss they can cause, trade restrictions often appear to be little more than welfare programs for the protected domestic industries. Given the welfare loss that results from these restrictions, it would be more efficient simply to transfer money from domestic consumers to domestic producers. But such a blatant transfer would probably be politically unpopular. Arguments for trade restrictions avoid mention of transfers to domestic producers and instead cite loftier concerns. As we shall now see, some of these arguments have more validity than others.

National Defense Argument

Certain industries are said to be in need of protection from import competition because they produce output that becomes vital in time of war. Because of their strategic importance, industries such as weapons manufacturing are sometimes insulated from foreign competition by trade restrictions. Thus national defense considerations outweigh concerns about efficiency and equity.

How valid is this argument? Trade restrictions may shelter the defense industry, but other methods of sheltering it, such as government subsidies to U.S. producers, might be more efficient. Or the government could stockpile basic military hardware so that maintaining productive capacity would become less essential. Since nearly all industries can make some claim on national defense grounds, instituting trade restrictions on this basis can get out of hand. For example, one reason domestic wool producers benefit from protective policies is that wool is said to be critical to the production of military uniforms.

Infant Industry Argument

The infant industry argument was formulated as a rationale for protecting emerging domestic industry from foreign competition. When production is subject to economies of scale, new domestic firms may need to be insulated from mature foreign competitors until the domestic firms reach sufficient size to be competitive. Trade restrictions are thus viewed as *temporary* devices for allowing domestic firms to achieve sufficient economies of scale to compete with established foreign producers.

The first problem with this argument is that it is more relevant to developing economies than to mature ones. Another problem is how to identify which industries merit protection. Finally, when do domestic firms become old enough to look after themselves? The very existence of protection may foster production inefficiencies that firms may not be able to outgrow. The short-run cost of such restrictions is the deadweight loss from higher domestic prices. Long-run costs may be incurred as well if the industry never realizes the expected economies of scale and thus never becomes competitive. As with the national defense argument, policy makers should be careful in adopting trade restrictions based on the infant industry argument. Here again, production subsidies are more efficient than import restrictions.

Antidumping Argument

Dumping *is the sale of a commodity abroad for less than its price in the domestic market.*

Dumping is the sale of a commodity abroad for less than its price in the domestic market. Exporters may be able to sell the good for less overseas because of subsidies that the exporting country provides in an effort to foster exports. Or firms may simply find it profitable to practice price discrimination by charging lower prices in foreign markets than they charge at home, where demand is less elastic. Critics of dumping argue that the domestic government should impose a tariff to nullify the impact of the lower dumping price on domestic producers.

What's wrong with foreign producers' selling goods for less in the United States than in their own countries? Why should U.S. consumers be prevented from buying products for as little as possible even if these low prices are the result of a foreign subsidy? If the dumping is *persistent*, the lower price may increase consumer surplus by an amount that will more than offset losses to domestic producers. Thus there is no good reason why consumers should not be allowed to buy imports for a persistently lower price.

An alternative form of dumping, termed *predatory dumping*, is the *temporary* sale of a product at a lower price abroad in order to drive out competing producers. Once the competition has been eliminated, so the theory goes, the exporting firm can raise the price. Predatory dumping may also be a way to discourage the development of domestic production of a good. Domestic firms would not find entry into this industry attractive because they could not sell at the low price that results from dumping. By driving out established firms or by discouraging domestic entry, the dumpers may place themselves in a position to monopolize the market. The trouble with this theory is that, once importers monopolize the industry and raise their prices, the resulting monopoly profits might still attract entry. Also, it would be difficult to block entry from around the world. There are very few documented cases of predatory dumping.

Sometimes dumping may be *sporadic*, as firms occasionally try to unload excess inventories. Sporadic dumping can be unsettling for domestic industry, but the economic impact is not a matter of great public concern. Regardless, all dumping is prohibited in the United States by the Trade Agreement Act of 1979, which calls for the imposition of tariffs when a good is sold for less in the United States than in its home market. In addition, GATT allows for the imposition of offsetting tariffs when products are sold for "less than fair value" and when there is "material injury" to domestic producers.

Jobs and Income Argument

One rationale for trade restrictions that is commonly heard in the United States today is that they protect U.S. jobs and wage levels. Using trade restrictions to protect domestic jobs is a strategy that dates back to the days of the mercantilists, who considered a favorable balance of trade to be the path to domestic prosperity. One problem with such a policy is that other countries will likely retaliate by restricting *their* imports to save *their* jobs, so international trade is reduced, jobs are lost in export industries, and potential gains from trade are not realized.

Wages in other countries, especially developing countries, are often a small fraction of wages in the United States. Looking simply at differences in the wage rate narrows the focus too much, however. Wages represent just one component of the total production cost and may not necessarily be the most important. Employers are interested in the labor cost per unit of output, which depends on both the wage rate and labor productivity.

The high wage rate in the United States exists in part because of the high marginal productivity of U.S. workers. U.S. labor productivity remains the highest in the world. This high productivity can be traced to education and training and to the abundant machines and other physical capital that make workers more productive. Workers in the United States also benefit from a business climate that is relatively stable and provides appropriate incentives to produce. How about the lower wages in many competing countries? These low wages can often be linked to workers' lack of education and training, the meager amount of physical capital that accompanies each worker, and a business climate that is less stable and that offers fewer productive incentives. In areas where higher U.S. wages are supported by higher U.S. output per worker, the labor cost per unit of output may be as low, if not lower, in the United States than in many countries with low wages and low productivity.

But once multinational firms build plants and provide technological know-how in developing countries, U.S. workers lose some of their competitive edge, and their relatively high wages could price some U.S. products out of the world market. This has already happened in the stereo industry and consumer electronics industries. Over time, as labor productivity in developing countries increases, wage differentials among countries will narrow, much as wage differentials between Northern states and Southern states have narrowed. As technology and capital spread, U.S. workers cannot expect to maintain wage levels that are far above those in other countries.

Domestic producers do not like to compete with foreign producers whose costs are lower, so they often push for trade restrictions. But if restrictions negate any cost advantage a foreign producer might have, the law of comparative advantage becomes inoperative and domestic consumers are denied access to the lower-priced goods.

Declining Industries Argument

Where an established domestic industry is in jeopardy of being displaced by lower-priced imports, there could be a rationale for *temporary* import restrictions to allow the orderly adjustment of the domestic industry. After all, domestic producers employ many industry-specific resources—both specialized machines and specialized labor. This physical and human capital is worth less in its next best alternative use. If the extinction of the domestic industry is forestalled through trade restrictions, specialized machines can be allowed to wear out naturally and specialized workers can retire voluntarily or gradually pursue more promising careers.

Thus, in the case of declining domestic industries, trade protection is viewed as a temporary measure to help lessen shocks to the economy and allow for a slower transition to a new industrial mix. But the protection offered should not be so generous as to encourage continued investment in the industry. Protection should be of specific duration and should be phased out over that period.

The clothing industry is an example of a declining U.S. industry. A 1989 study by the Federal Trade Commission estimated that U.S. consumers pay 58 percent more for textiles and apparel because of high tariffs and restrictive quotas. The 22,390 U.S. jobs saved as a result of trade restrictions paid an average of $16,000 per year, but each job cost U.S. consumers an average of $551,000 per year in higher prices! What's more, because tariffs and quotas are relatively higher on low-priced products, the poor pay proportionately more for these trade restrictions.

Although particular workers suffer in the short run as imports displace workers, many more jobs have been created by private enterprise than have been destroyed by imports. And even where foreign competition appears to have displaced U.S. workers, foreign companies have built plants in the United States and employed U.S. workers. For example, a dozen foreign television manufacturers and all major Japanese automobile manufacturers have plants in the United States. In fact, a U.S. consumer who buys a Honda is more likely to own a car produced in the United States than is a U.S. consumer who buys a Pontiac Le Mans.

Since 1960 the number of jobs in the United States has nearly doubled. To acknowledge this job growth is not to deny the problems facing those workers who are displaced by imports. Some displaced workers, particularly those in blue-collar jobs in steel and other unionized industries, are not apt to find jobs that pay as well as the jobs they lost. As with infant industries, however, the problems posed by declining industries need not be solved by trade restrictions. To support the affected industry, the government could offer wage subsidies or special tax breaks that decline over time.

Problems with Protection

Trade restrictions raise a number of problems in addition to the ones already mentioned. First, protecting one stage of production often requires protecting downstream stages of production. Protecting the U.S. textile industry from foreign competition, for example, raises the cost of cloth to U.S. clothing manufacturers, reducing their competitiveness. Thus, if the government protects domestic textile manufacturers, it must also protect the domestic garment industry. Otherwise, foreign garment manufacturers will fashion lower-priced foreign textiles into garments for export to the United States, where they will sell for less than U.S.-made garments made from higher-priced U.S. textiles.

Second, the cost of protection includes not only the deadweight loss arising from the higher domestic price but also the cost of the resources used by domestic producers and groups to secure the favored protection. The cost of rent seeking—lobbying fees, propaganda, legal actions—can amount to as much as or more than the direct deadweight loss of restrictions.

A final problem with restrictions is policing and enforcing the myriad quotas, tariffs, and other restrictions. Consider the following case study.

CASE STUDY

Enforcing Trade Restrictions

The United States is the richest, most attractive market in the world. Trade restrictions often make U.S. markets even more appealing to foreign producers because U.S. prices exceed world prices. Thus we should not be surprised when some U.S. importers try to skirt trade restrictions, either avoiding tariffs or illegally importing goods that are controlled by quotas. A diverse array of goods is imported in violation of quotas, including clothing, sugar, coffee, gems, and steel pipes. It has been estimated that more than 10 percent of all imports are illegal.

Restrictions affect not only the quantity of imports but also the quality. Nearly all schemes to import clothing illegally involve fraudulent documents intended to misrepresent the clothing so that it fits into some quota or qualifies for a lower tariff. Sometimes the garments are altered to evade detection. For example, because imports of men's running shorts are controlled by a quota, the shorts in one shipment reportedly had a flimsy inner lining basted in so that they would pass for swimming trunks, which face no quotas.

Because the United States allows some countries more generous quotas than others, exporters in a country under tight control sometimes ship their goods through a country with a liberal ceiling. For example, Japan typically makes so little clothing for export that the United States imposes no clothing quota for imports from Japan. As a result, clothing made in Korea is often shipped through Japan to evade U.S. quotas on Korean goods. Similarly, because Nepal is not subject to a clothing quota but India is, India ships clothing to the United States through Nepal.

Higher tariffs are often imposed on lower-priced products. Foreign steel companies have been accused of falsely inflating the price of steel to avoid import duties on low-priced steel. Allegedly part of the higher price paid by importers was secretly rebated by steel producers through a variety of schemes. Producers of other steel products have mislabeled and falsely weighed them to avoid certain restrictions.

Some foreign producers and U.S. importers are said to engage in "port shopping," or testing various ports to see where inspections are most lax. Documents are often forged. U.S. Customs inspectors are responsible for policing all this activity. These inspectors have their work cut out for them in view of the thousands of tariffs, quotas, and other trade restrictions in effect and the myriad ways to get around them.

Source: Anthony De Stefano, "Customs Agents Fight Often Losing Battle Against Illegal Imports," *Wall Street Journal*, 26 January 1986.

CONCLUSION

Comparative advantage, specialization, and trade allow people to use their scarce resources most efficiently to satisfy their unlimited wants. International trade arises from voluntary exchange among buyers and sellers pursuing their self-interest. Despite the clear gains from free trade, restrictions on international trade date back hundreds of years.

Those who benefit from trade restrictions are the domestic producers (and their resource suppliers) who are able to sell their output for a higher price because of the restrictions. But these producers may not be winners in the long run. If the domestic industry is competitive, the profit from protection will attract new entrants until the profits in this industry are just normal. Protection insulates the industry from the rigors of global competition, in the process stifling innovation and leaving the industry vulnerable to technological change. For example, although the U.S. steel industry is one of the most protected, the industry has a declining workforce and dwindling profits. Under a system of quotas, the winners' circle also includes those who have secured the right to import the good at the world price and sell it at the domestic price.

Consumers who must pay higher prices for protected goods suffer from trade restrictions, as do the domestic producers who use imported intermediate goods. Other losers are U.S. exporters, who face higher trade barriers if foreigners retaliate. Even if other countries do not retaliate, U.S. trade restrictions reduce the gains from comparative advantage and thereby reduce world income. With world income lower, U.S. exporters find that their foreign markets have shrunk. Some of these losers may go out of business; other firms may never start producing. To the extent that protected industries expand and thereby drive up resource prices, other producers using these same resources are losers.

Trade restrictions are often imposed gradually over a period of years. Because the domestic adjustments to them are slow and because the losers are scattered throughout the economy, the losers often fail to attribute their losses to the offending restriction. Often they do not know that they are losers, or they fail to connect their troubles with trade policy. On the other hand, those who benefit from trade restrictions are usually a well-defined group who can clearly identify the source of their gains. *One reason trade restrictions exist is that most losers do not know they are losers, whereas winners know what is at stake.* Producers have an abiding interest in trade legislation, but consumers remain rationally ignorant. Congress tends to support the group that makes the most noise, so trade restrictions persist, despite the clear gains that could be had from free trade.

Summary

1. Even if a country has an absolute advantage in producing all goods, that country should specialize in producing the good for which it has a comparative advantage—that is, the good for which its opportunity cost of production is lower than that of other countries. If each country specializes and trades according to the law of comparative advantage, all countries will be better off.

2. Tariffs and effective import quotas raise prices in domestic markets. The primary difference between a tariff and a quota is in the distribution of the gains resulting from higher domestic prices.

3. Tariff revenues go to the government and could be used to lower taxes; quotas confer benefits on those with the right to buy the good at the world price and sell it at the higher domestic price. Both restrictions harm domestic consumers more than they help domestic producers, though tariffs at least yield government revenue.

4. Despite the gains from free trade and the net welfare losses arising from tariffs and quotas, trade restrictions have been a part of trade policy since the days of the mercantilists. Some of the reasons given for instituting trade restrictions include fostering national defense, giving infant industries time to grow, preventing foreign producers from dumping goods in domestic markets, protecting domestic jobs, and allowing declining industries time to phase out.

Questions and Problems

1. (Resources and Trade) Malaysia exports tin and rubber. Why have these resources become progressively less important to the world economy? Explain why the decline in the importance of these resources could hinder the growth of the Malaysian economy.

2. (U.S. Trade) What reasons would you give for the rise in importance of international trade to the U.S. economy? Will these reasons continue to have an influence in the future?

3. (Differences in Tastes and Trade) What products might the U.S. Virgin Islands trade with the Bahamas, which were formerly British, and Martinique, which is French? Is trade possible among islands that are so much alike?

4. (Absolute and Comparative Advantage) Suppose that each worker in the United States can produce 8 units of food or 2 units of clothing. In Izodia, which has the same number of workers, each worker can produce 7 units of food or 1 unit of clothing. Why does the United States have an absolute advantage in both goods? Which country enjoys a comparative advantage in food? Why?

5. (Specialization and Consumer Welfare) Why do economists believe that consumers are better off when countries specialize in the goods for which they have a comparative advantage and then trade with each other?

6. (World Equilibrium Price) Diagram the domestic supply and demand for steel, assuming that the world equilibrium price is the same as the domestic equilibrium price. If there is an increase in foreign supply, what will happen in the domestic market for steel?

7. (Tariffs) Very high tariffs usually cause black markets and smuggling. How is government revenue reduced by such activity? Relate your answer to the graph in Exhibit 7 in this chapter. Does smuggling have any social benefits?

8. (Voluntary Quotas or Restraints) The United States tried to limit Japanese exports to the United States by way of voluntary restraints. Why did the U.S. government lose revenues by adopting this approach rather than using tariffs?

9. (Quotas) The Immigration Service in the United States allows only a certain number of individuals to apply each year for U.S. citizenship. Quotas are set for each country. How might the Immigration Service allocate such privileges among so many applicants?

10. (Efficiency and Production Possibilities) The data from the production possibilities tables in Exhibit 1 can be used to construct a world production possibilities frontier.
    a. Draw a graph illustrating this joint production possibilities curve. (Hint: Start with all resources producing food and then gradually switch resources into clothing as efficiently as possible.)
    b. Why does this curve have a kink in it?
    c. Explain why it is necessary for one or both countries to specialize in production in order to be on the joint production possibilities curve.
    d. Why does the trading rate between the countries have to fall between 0.5 and 2 units of food per unit of clothing?
    e. How do the relative gains from trade between the two countries depend on what terms of trade are established?

11. (Absolute Versus Comparative Advantage) Explain why the potential gains from trade depend on relative rather than absolute resource costs for the goods produced.

12. (Restricting Trade) Suppose that the world price for steel is below the U.S. domestic price, but the government requires that all steel used in the United States be domestically produced.

a. Use a diagram like the one in Exhibit 8 to show who gains and who loses from such a policy.

b. How could you estimate the net welfare loss (deadweight loss) from such a diagram?

c. What kind of response to such a policy would you expect from industries (like au-tomobile producers) that use U.S. steel?

13. (Restricting Trade) Industries hurt by cheap imports typically argue that restricting trade will save U.S. jobs. What's wrong with this argument? Are there ever any reasons to support such an argument?

C H A P T E R   3 4

International Finance

A U.S. firm that plans to buy a machine from a British manufacturer will be quoted a price in British pounds. Suppose that machine costs 10,000 pounds. How many dollars will it cost? The cost in dollars will depend on the current exchange rate. When buyers and sellers from two countries trade, two national currencies are almost always involved. Supporting the flows of goods and services are flows of currencies that connect all international transactions. The exchange rate between two currencies—the price of one in terms of the other—is the means by which the price of a good in one country is translated into the price to the buyer in another country. The willingness of buyers and sellers to strike deals therefore depends on the rate of exchange between currencies. In this chapter we will examine the international transactions that determine the relative value of the dollar. Topics discussed in this chapter include

- Balance of payments

- Deficits and surpluses

- Foreign exchange markets

- Floating exchange rates

- Purchasing power parity

- Fixed exchange rates

- Development of the international monetary system

- Managed float

BALANCE OF PAYMENTS

A country's gross national product conveys an idea of the flow of economic activity that occurs within that country during a given period. To account for their dealings with other countries, countries keep track of their international transactions. A country's **balance of payments** is a summary statement reflecting all economic transactions that occur during a given time period between residents of that country and residents of other countries. *Residents* include individuals, firms, and governments.

International Economic Transactions

Balance of payments statements measure economic transactions that occur between countries, whether they involve goods and services, real or financial assets, or transfers. Because the balance of payments reflects the volume of transactions that occur during a particular time period, usually a year, the balance of payments measures a *flow*.

Some transactions included in the balance of payments do not involve payments of money. For example, if *Time* magazine ships a new printing press to its Australian subsidiary, no money payment occurs, yet an economic transaction involving another country has taken place and must be included in the balance of payments. Similarly, if you send money to friends or relatives abroad, if CARE sends food to Africa, or if the Pentagon sends military assistance to Central America, these transactions must be captured in the balance of payments. So remember that although we speak of the *balance of payments*, a more descriptive phrase would be the *balance of economic transactions*.

Balance of payments accounts are maintained according to the principles of double-entry bookkeeping, in which one side of the ledger reflects liabilities, or debits, and the other side reflects assets, or credits. The total debits must be in balance with, or equal to, the total credits—hence the name balance of payments. The balance of payments involves a comparison between the outflow of payments to the rest of the world, which are entered as debits, and the inflow of receipts from the rest of the world, which are entered as credits.

International trade statistics were the first commercial data compiled on a regular basis. Until the nineteenth century, tariffs—or taxes—on imports were an important source of government revenue, so governments kept records about the amount and kind of imports. Furthermore, mercantilism was based on the idea that countries should export more than they import, so records were kept on exports as well. In fact, *for many countries data on international trade were often more reliable than data on domestic trade*. The next sections describe the major accounts in the balance of payments.

Merchandise Trade Balance

*The **merchandise trade balance** equals the value of merchandise exported minus the value of merchandise imported.*

The **merchandise trade balance** equals the value of merchandise exported minus the value of merchandise imported. The merchandise account reflects trade in tangible products, such as French wine and U.S. computers, and is often referred to simply as the *trade balance*. The value of U.S. merchandise exports is listed as a credit in the U.S. balance of payments account because U.S. residents must *be paid* for the exported goods. The value of U.S. merchandise imports is listed as a debit in the balance of payments account because U.S. residents must *pay* for the imported goods. If the value of merchandise exports exceeds the value of merchandise imports, there is a *surplus* in the merchandise trade balance, or, more simply, a *trade surplus*. If the value of merchandise imports exceeds the value of merchandise exports, there is a *deficit* in the merchandise trade balance, or a *trade deficit*. The merchandise trade balance is reported on a monthly basis and influences the stock market and other financial markets. The trade balance depends on a variety of factors, including the relative strength of the domestic economy compared to other economies and the relative value of the domestic currency compared to other currencies.

The U.S. merchandise trade balance since 1979 is presented in Exhibit 1. Because imports have exceeded exports nearly every year, the balance has been in deficit, as reflected by the bottom line. Note that during recessions, which are indicated by shading, imports were relatively flat, as was the

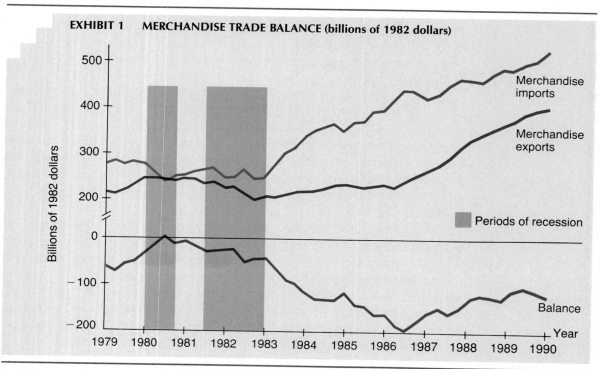

EXHIBIT 1   MERCHANDISE TRADE BALANCE (billions of 1982 dollars)

Source: Department of Commerce, Bureau of Economic Analysis, National Income and Product Accounts.

overall trade deficit. Since 1983 the U.S. economy has expanded. *When aggregate demand increases, the demand for all goods, including imports, increases.* So the U.S. demand for imports has grown. Between 1983 and 1987, the U.S. trade deficit grew each year, as imports have climbed faster than exports. Since 1987 exports have climbed faster than imports, so the trade deficit has declined.

Balance on Goods and Services

The merchandise trade balance focuses on the flow of goods, but services are also traded internationally. *Services* are intangibles, such as transportation, insurance and banking services, military transactions, and tourist expenditures. Services also include the income earned from foreign investments less the income earned by foreigners from their investment in the domestic economy. Services are often called the "invisibles." The value of U.S. service exports is listed as a credit in the U.S. balance of payments account because U.S. residents receive payments for these services. The value of U.S. service imports is listed as a debit in the balance of payments account because U.S. residents must pay for the imported services.

*The **balance on goods and services** is the difference between the value of exports of goods and services and the value of imports of goods and services.*

The **balance on goods and services** is the difference between the value of exports of goods and services and the value of imports of goods and services. Currently produced goods and services that are sold or otherwise provided to foreigners form part of the nation's output. The production of these goods and services generates income during the current period. Conversely, imports of goods and services form part of the nation's expenditures—part of consumption, investment, and government expenditures. Allocating imports to each of the major expenditure components is an accounting nightmare, so we usually just subtract imports from exports to yield *net exports*. Thus the gross national product equals total expenditures for consumption, investment, and government, plus net exports.

Unilateral Transfers

Unilateral transfers consist of government transfers to foreign residents, foreign aid, personal gifts to friends and relatives abroad, personal and institutional charitable donations, and the like. For example, money sent abroad by a U.S. resident to friends or relatives would be included in U.S. unilateral transfers. U.S. net unilateral transfers equal the unilateral transfers received by U.S. residents minus the unilateral transfers sent to foreign residents. U.S. net unilateral transfers have been negative each year since World War II, and since 1984 they have exceeded $12 billion per year. The United States places no restrictions on money sent out of the country.[1]

---

[1] Federal authorities do, however, require reporting of the source of cash exports of $10,000 or more. This measure is aimed at reducing money laundering overseas.

Other countries, particularly developing countries, strictly limit the amount of money that may be sent abroad.

The **balance on current account** is the sum of net unilateral transfers and the balance on goods and services.

When we add net unilateral transfers to the exports of goods and services minus the imports of goods and services, we get the **balance on current account**. Thus *the current account includes all transactions in currently produced goods and services plus net unilateral transfers.* It can be negative, reflecting a current account deficit; positive, reflecting a current account surplus; or zero.

Capital Account

The **capital account** records international transactions involving purchases or sales of assets.

The current account records international transactions involving goods, services, and transfers. The **capital account** records international transactions involving purchases or sales of assets. When economists talk about capital, they usually mean those physical and human resources employed to produce goods and services. But sometimes *capital* is used as another word for *money*—money used to acquire financial assets, such as stocks, bonds, and bank balances. U.S. capital outflows result when Americans purchase foreign assets. U.S. capital inflows result from foreign purchases of U.S. assets.

Investors purchase foreign assets in order to earn a higher rate of return or to diversify portfolios. High real interest rates in the United States (relative to those in the rest of the world), such as occurred during the 1980s, usually result in a net inflow of capital. Also, in recent years many developing countries have experienced debt problems. These debt problems have had two effects on the U.S. capital account. First, U.S. banks have become more cautious in lending to developing countries; second, the United States has become more attractive as a safe place to invest. Thus capital outflow declined during the 1980s and capital inflow increased.

Between 1917 and 1982, the United States was a net capital exporter, and the net return of all this foreign investment over the years improved our balance on current account. In 1983, for the first time in sixty-five years, the United States became a net importer of capital. Each year since then, U.S. imports of capital have exceeded exports of capital, meaning that Americans owe foreigners more and more. *The United States is now the world's largest debtor nation.* This is not as bad as it sounds, since foreign investment in the United States adds to America's productive capacity and promotes employment. But the return on foreign investment in the United States flows to foreigners, not to Americans. This means that the United States will no longer earn more from foreign investments than it pays out to foreigners. Since 1981, net investment income has been falling. In fact, net investment income dropped from $22.3 billion in 1987 to $2.2 billion in 1988 and only $1.0 billion in 1989. The smaller the net investment income, the more difficult it becomes to offset a deficit in the merchandise trade balance.

In the double-entry system, payments must always balance over a given

The *official reserve transactions account* reflects the flow of gold, currencies, and Special Drawing Rights among central banks.

period—debits must equal credits. The **official reserve transactions account** indicates the net amount of international reserves that shift among central banks to settle international transactions. (Many government publications show this not as a separate account but as part of the capital account.) International reserves consist of gold, dollars, other major currencies, and a special-purpose reserve currency called Special Drawing Rights, or SDRs.

Statistical Discrepancy

As we have said, the U.S. balance of payments is a record of all transactions between U.S. residents and foreign residents over a specified period. It is easier to describe this record than to compile it. Despite efforts to capture all international transactions, some go unreported. Yet, as the name *balance of payments* clearly states, debits must equal credits—the entire balance of payments account must be in balance. To ensure that the accounts balance, a residual account called the *statistical discrepancy* was created. An excess of credits in all other accounts is offset by an equivalent debit in the statistical discrepancy account, or an excess of debits in all other accounts is offset by an equivalent credit in the discrepancy account.

The statistical discrepancy provides analysts with both a measure of the net error in the balance of payments data and a means of satisfying the double-entry bookkeeping requirement that total debits must equal total credits. Some analysts believe that the United States's positive statistical discrepancy in recent years reflects large, secret money flows into the country. Wealthy people from countries with unstable governments or with high taxes may be purchasing U.S. financial assets to shelter their wealth. For example, as of 1990, wealthy Venezuelans had invested an estimated $60 billion of capital abroad, much of it in the United States.

Deficits and Surpluses

Nations, like households, operate under a cash-flow constraint. Expenditures cannot exceed income plus cash on hand and borrowed funds. We have distinguished between *current* transactions, which are the income and expenditures from exports and imports, and capital transactions, which are international investments and borrowing. Any surplus or deficit in the current account must be balanced by other changes in the balance of payments accounts. The current account has been in deficit since 1982, meaning that the amount we spent on imports and sent as unilateral transfers to foreigners has exceeded the amount foreigners spent on our exports and sent as unilateral transfers to us.

Exhibit 2 presents the most recent U.S. balance of payments statement. All payments from foreigners to U.S. residents are entered in the credits column using a plus sign (+), because they result in a flow of funds to U.S. residents. All payments to foreigners from U.S. residents are entered in the debits column using a minus sign (−), because they result in a flow of funds to foreign residents. Deficits in the current account and in the official reserve transactions account were offset by surpluses in the capital account and in the statistical discrepancy.

To see how the table works, suppose a U.S. car dealer buys a Porsche from the West German manufacturer for $50,000. This purchase is entered as a debit in the U.S. current account. If the Porsche company deposits the funds in its account with a U.S. bank, the deposit is entered as a credit in the U.S. capital account. Or Porsche may deposit the funds in its German bank, which in turn lends them to a German importer to pay for U.S. exports— thereby creating an offsetting credit entry in the U.S. current account. Or the German bank may lend the funds to a German resident to purchase some

EXHIBIT 2
U.S. BALANCE OF PAYMENTS: 1989
(billions of dollars)

Item	Debits	Credits	Balance
Current Account			
1. Merchandise exports		+ 361.9	
2. Merchandise imports	− 475.1		
3. Trade balance (1 + 2)			− 113.2
4. Service exports		+ 238.5	
5. Service imports	− 216.9		
6. Goods and services balance (3 + 4 + 5)			− 91.6
7. Net unilateral transfers	− 14.3		
8. Current account balance (6 + 7)			− 105.9
Capital Account			
9. Outflow of U.S. capital	− 100.4		
10. Inflow of foreign capital		+ 189.3	
11. Capital account balance (9 + 10)			+ 88.9
Official Reserve Transactions Account			
12. Increase in U.S. official assets abroad	− 25.3		
13. Increase in foreign official assets in U.S.		+ 7.4	
14. Official reserve balance (12 + 13)			− 17.9
15. Statistical discrepancy		+ 34.9	
TOTAL (8 + 11 + 14 + 15)			0.0

Source: *Survey of Current Business*, U.S. Dept. of Commerce, March 1990.

U.S. bonds — also a credit entry in the U.S. capital account. Or the German bank may exchange the dollars for marks at the German central bank. The central bank's international reserves rise by $50,000 — a credit entry in West Germany's official reserve transactions account. Or the West German central bank may use the $50,000 to purchase a U.S. Treasury security — again, generating a credit entry in the country's official reserve transaction account. The initial debit entry in the U.S. current account for the purchase of the Porsche will generate some sort of offsetting credit entry, either in the current account as an export, in the capital account, or in the official reserve transactions account.

If a country runs a deficit in its current account, it is because the amount of foreign currency the country earns by selling its exports falls short of the amount of foreign currency needed to pay for its imports. The additional foreign currency must be provided by a net capital inflow (international loans, foreign purchases of domestic stocks and bonds, and so forth) or through official government transactions in foreign currency. If the value of exports exceeds the value of imports, the domestic economy earns the excess foreign exchange. This excess could be held in a bank account or used to purchase foreign stocks and bonds.

When all transactions are considered, the balance of payments always balances, though specific accounts may not be in balance. A deficit in a particular account should not necessarily be viewed as a source of concern, nor should a surplus be viewed as a reason for elation. The deficit in the U.S. current account in recent years has been offset by a net inflow of capital from abroad. As a result of the net inflow of capital, foreigners are acquiring larger claims on U.S. assets. If this growing foreign claim on U.S. assets becomes a matter of public concern, government officials may consider policies aimed at increasing net exports of goods and services and reducing net imports of capital.

Some developing countries have had particular problems repaying their loans to the industrialized countries. We close this section with a case study of Brazil's foreign debt problems.

CASE STUDY

Brazil and the Banks

On the morning of Friday, February 20, 1987, Brazil's finance minister notified seven hundred banks around the world that Brazil was suspending interest payments on $67 billion in bank loans. Later that day Brazilian President Jose Sarney appeared on television to announce that his country "won't pay debt with hunger." Brazil was beset with staggering economic problems, including a 600 percent inflation rate. In 1989 inflation jumped to over 1700 percent per year.

Brazil is one of the world's largest debtor nations, with a total debt at the time of the moratorium of $108 billion, the largest of any developing country. Interest alone was about $10 billion per year, or 4 percent of the country's GNP. Some say that Brazil's move was aimed at forcing lenders to renegotiate the terms of their loans to Brazil's advantage. Brazil had already stopped paying the principal on its foreign debt in 1982. Rather than forgo interest altogether, lenders might be willing to settle for some smaller amount.

The largest holder of Brazilian debt is Citibank, with $4.6 billion at the time the moratorium on interest payments was declared. Chase Manhattan and Bank of America each held an estimated $2.7 billion. After Brazil's declaration, the stock prices of the big banks fell. In 1988 Brazil negotiated a complicated financial agreement with lenders, but inflation exceeding 1700 percent in 1989 killed the deal, sending the market value of Brazilian debt into a dive. In July of 1985, Brazilian debt was selling for about 80 percent of its redemption value; by 1989 that figure had dropped to about 33 percent of redemption value. Investors evidently had little confidence that the debt would ever be paid. The United States Export–Import Bank placed Brazil in its riskiest loan category.

Brazil's troubles point up just how interrelated the world economy has become. For better or worse, the United States is now very much a part of the world economy. We used to say that if the United States sneezed, the rest of the world would catch cold. Today economic viruses are spread with equal ease in both directions.

Sources: Peter Truell and Roger Cohen, "Brazil Debt Action Poses Challenge for Major Banks," *Wall Street Journal*, 23 February 1987; William Rhodes, "An Insider's Reflection on the Brazilian Debt Package," *Wall Street Journal*, 14 October 1988; "How Latin America's Economies Look After a Decade's Decline," *New York Times*, 11 February 1990.

FOREIGN EXCHANGE RATES AND MARKETS

Now that you have some idea about the international flow of products and capital, we can take a closer look at the forces that determine the underlying value of the currencies involved in these transactions. We begin by looking at exchange rates and the market for foreign exchange.

Foreign Exchange

The margin note: *The **exchange rate** is the price of one country's currency measured in terms of another country's currency.*

***Foreign exchange** is the currency of another country that is needed to carry out international transactions.*

The **exchange rate** is the price of one country's currency measured in terms of another country's currency. Exchange rates are determined by the interaction of the households, firms, private financial institutions, and central banks that buy and sell foreign currencies. The exchange rate fluctuates to equate the quantity of foreign currency demanded with the quantity of foreign currency supplied. The market in which the currencies are traded is called the foreign exchange market. **Foreign exchange** is the currency of another country that is needed to carry out international transactions. Typically, foreign exchange is made up of bank deposits denominated in the foreign currency. When foreign travel is involved, foreign exchange may consist of foreign paper money.

The foreign exchange market incorporates all the arrangements used to buy and sell foreign exchange. The foreign exchange market is not a physical place but a network of telephones and telex systems connecting large banks all over the world. Perhaps you have seen pictures of foreign exchange traders in New York, London, or Tokyo amid a tangle of telephones. The foreign exchange market is like an all-night diner—it never closes. Some trading center is always open somewhere in the world.

Since the exchange rate is a price, we can explain its determination using the conventional tools of supply and demand: the equilibrium price of foreign exchange is the one that equates quantity demanded with quantity supplied. To simplify the analysis, let's suppose that the United States and Great Britain are the only two countries in the world, so the supply and demand for pounds in the United States is the supply and demand for foreign exchange from the U.S. perspective.

Consider the market for pounds in terms of dollars. The price, or exchange rate, is specified in terms of the number of dollars required to purchase one British pound. An increase in the number of dollars needed to purchase a pound indicates a weakening, or a **depreciation**, of the dollar. A decrease in the number of dollars needed to purchase a pound indicates a strengthening, or an **appreciation**, of the dollar.

Depreciation of a currency is an increase in the amount of the currency needed to purchase one unit of another currency.

Appreciation of a currency is a decrease in the amount of the currency needed to purchase one unit of another currency.

Demand for Foreign Exchange

U.S. residents need pounds to pay British residents for goods and services, to purchase British assets, to make loans in Great Britain, or simply to send cash gifts to Britain. Whenever U.S. residents need pounds, they must buy pounds in the foreign exchange market, paying for them with dollars.

A drop in the dollar price of foreign exchange, in this case the pound, means that fewer dollars are needed to purchase each pound, so the dollar prices of British goods, which have price tags listed in pounds, become cheaper. The cheaper it is to buy pounds, the lower the dollar price of British goods, the larger the quantity of British goods demanded by U.S. residents, and the greater the quantity of pounds demanded by U.S. residents, other things constant.

Exhibit 3 illustrates the quantity of foreign exchange demanded at each exchange rate. The horizontal axis measures the quantity of foreign exchange, or pounds, and the vertical axis measures the number of dollars required to purchase each pound. The demand curve for foreign exchange, identified as *D*, indicates that the fewer dollars needed to acquire a pound, other things constant, the greater the quantity of foreign exchange that will be demanded. Some of the factors held constant along the demand curve are the incomes of U.S. consumers, the expected inflation rates in the United States and Britain, the pound prices of British goods, the preferences of U.S. consumers, and the interest rates in the United States and Britain. People

EXHIBIT 3   THE FOREIGN EXCHANGE MARKET

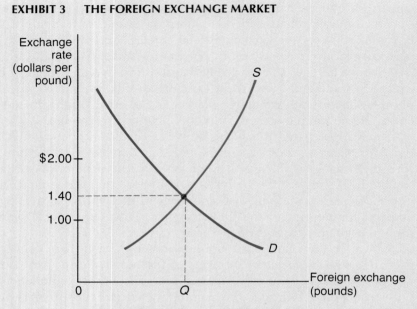

The fewer dollars needed to purchase one unit of foreign exchange, the lower the price of foreign goods and the greater the quantity of foreign goods demanded. The greater the demand for foreign goods, the greater the amount of foreign exchange demanded. The demand curve for foreign exchange slopes downward. An increase in the exchange rate makes U.S. products cheaper for foreigners. The increased demand for U.S. goods implies an increase in the quantity of foreign exchange supplied. The supply curve of foreign exchange slopes upward.

have many different reasons for demanding foreign exchange, but in the aggregate the quantity demanded is inversely related to the price.

Supply of Foreign Exchange

The supply of foreign exchange is generated by the desire of foreign residents to acquire dollars — that is, to exchange pounds for dollars. Foreign residents want dollars to buy U.S. goods and services, to buy U.S. assets, to make loans in dollars, or simply to make cash gifts in dollars to their U.S. friends and relatives. Furthermore, people from countries suffering from economic and political turmoil may want to hold dollars as a hedge against the inflation of their own currencies. The dollar has long been accepted as an international medium of exchange.

The British offer pounds in the foreign exchange market to acquire the dollars they need. An increase in the dollar-per-pound exchange rate, other things constant, makes U.S. products cheaper for foreigners, since foreign residents need fewer pounds to get the same number of dollars. Suppose a week's vacation at Disney World costs $3000. When the exchange rate is

$1.50 per pound, that vacation costs a British tourist 2000 pounds; when the exchange rate is $2 per pound, the vacation costs only 1500 pounds. The number of trips to Disney World demanded by British residents increases as the dollar-per-pound exchange rate increases, so more pounds will be supplied on the foreign exchange market to buy dollars.[2]

More generally, the higher the dollar-per-pound exchange rate, other things constant, the greater the quantity of pounds supplied to the foreign exchange market. The positive relation between the dollar-per-pound exchange rate and the quantity of pounds supplied on the foreign exchange market is expressed in Exhibit 3 by the upward-sloping supply curve for foreign exchange (again, pounds in our example). The supply curve is drawn holding other things constant, including British incomes and preferences, expectations about the rates of inflation in Britain and the United States, and interest rates in Britain and the United States.

The supply of pounds also reflects the British demand for dollars. When the dollar-per-pound exchange rate is low, dollars are expensive in terms of pounds so British residents demand fewer dollars (supply fewer pounds). When the dollar-per-pound exchange rate is high, dollars are cheap in terms of pounds so British residents demand more dollars (supply more pounds). Thus if we were to draw the British demand curve for dollars, we would measure the pound price per dollar on the vertical axis and the quantity of dollars demanded on the horizontal axis. The British demand curve for dollars would slope downward, with more demanded as the pound price of the dollar fell.

Determining the Exchange Rate

Exhibit 3 brings together the supply and demand for foreign exchange to determine the exchange rate. At an exchange rate of $1.40 per pound, the quantity of pounds demanded equals the quantity of pounds supplied. Once it is achieved, the equilibrium rate of exchange remains constant until a change occurs in one of the factors that affect supply or demand. When the exchange rate is allowed to adjust freely, or to *float*, in response to market forces, market rate will clear continually, as the quantities of foreign exchange demanded and supplied are equated.

What if the initial equilibrium is upset by a change in one of the underlying forces that affect supply or demand? Suppose an increase in U.S. income causes Americans to increase their demand for all normal goods, including products imported from Britain. An increase in income will shift

---

[2] As the exchange rate rises, the British have a greater incentive to buy more U.S. goods and services since their prices in terms of pounds have decreased. As more is bought at lower prices, however, the total expenditure of British pounds rises only if the percentage increase in quantities of U.S. products demanded by the British exceeds the percentage decrease in their prices in terms of pounds. If the percentage increase in quantities demanded is *less* than the percentage decrease in the price in terms of pounds, the supply curve of British pounds will slope downward.

the demand curve for foreign exchange to the right, as Americans seek more pounds to buy more cashmere sweaters, Jaguars, and trips to London.

This increased demand for pounds is shown in Exhibit 4 by a shift to the right in the demand curve for foreign exchange. The supply curve does not change. The shift in the demand curve from D to D' leads to an increase in the exchange rate from $1.40 per pound to $1.60 per pound. Thus the pound rises in value, or appreciates, while the dollar falls in value, or depreciates. The higher exchange value of the pound prompts British residents to increase the quantity of pounds supplied on the foreign exchange market to purchase more American products, which are now cheaper in terms of the pound. The amount of the increase in the quantity supplied is the difference between Q' and Q.

Any increase in the demand for foreign exchange or any decrease in its supply, other things constant, causes an increase in the number of dollars required to purchase one unit of foreign exchange, which is a depreciation of the dollar. On the other hand, any decrease in the demand for foreign exchange or any increase in its supply, other things constant, causes a reduction in the number of dollars required to purchase one unit of foreign exchange, which is an appreciation of the dollar.

EXHIBIT 4   EFFECT ON THE FOREIGN EXCHANGE MARKET OF AN INCREASE IN DEMAND

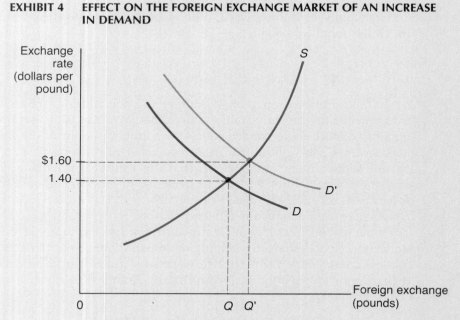

The intersection of supply curve S and demand curve D determines the exchange rate. At an exchange rate of $1.40 per pound, the quantity of pounds demanded equals the quantity supplied. An increase in the demand for pounds from D to D' leads to an increase in the exchange rate from $1.40 to $1.60 per pound.

Arbitrageurs and Speculators

Arbitrageurs simultaneously buy currency at one price and sell it at a higher price to take advantage of temporary differences in exchange rates.

Exchange rates between specific currencies are nearly identical at any given time in the different markets around the world. For example, the price of a dollar in terms of the pound is the same in New York, Tokyo, London, Zurich, Istanbul, and other financial centers. This equality is ensured by **arbitrageurs**—individuals who take advantage of any temporary difference in exchange rates across markets by buying low and selling high. Their actions tend to equalize exchange rates across markets. For example, if one pound cost $1.59 in New York and $1.60 in London, an arbitrageur could buy, say, $1,000,000 worth of pounds in New York and at the same time sell these pounds in London for $1,006,289, thereby earning $6289 minus the transaction costs of executing the trades.

Because the arbitrageur buys and sells simultaneously, no risk is involved. The arbitrageur increases the demand for pounds in New York and increases the supply of pounds in London. Therefore the dollar price of pounds rises in New York and falls in London. Even a tiny difference in exchange rates across markets will prompt arbitrageurs to act, and this action will quickly eliminate discrepancies in exchange rates across markets. Exchange rates may still change because of market forces, but they tend to change in all markets simultaneously.

Speculators buy or sell foreign exchange in hopes of profiting by trading the currency at a different exchange rate later.

The demand and supply of foreign exchange arises from many sources: from importers and exporters, investors in foreign assets, tourists, arbitrageurs, and speculators. **Speculators** buy and sell foreign exchange in hopes of profiting by trading the currency at a different exchange rate later. By taking risks, speculators aim to profit from market fluctuations. In contrast, arbitrageurs take no risks, since they *simultaneously* buy and sell a currency.

Purchasing Power Parity

*The **purchasing power parity theory** predicts that exchange rates between two national currencies will adjust in the long run to reflect the price level differences between the two countries.*

As long as trade across borders is unrestricted and as long as exchange rates are allowed to adjust freely, the **purchasing power parity theory** predicts that exchange rates between two national currencies will adjust in the long run to reflect the price level differences in the two countries. A given basket of internationally traded goods should therefore sell for similar amounts in different countries (except for differences reflecting transportation costs and the like). Suppose a given basket of traded commodities that costs $1500 in the United States costs 750 pounds in Great Britain. According to the purchasing power parity theory, the equilibrium exchange rate between the United States and Great Britain should be $2 per pound. If this were not the case—if the exchange rate were, say, $1.50 per pound—then the basket of goods could be purchased in Great Britain for 750 pounds and sold in the United States for $1500. The $1500 could then be exchanged for 1000 pounds, yielding a profit of 250 pounds (minus any transaction costs). Selling dollars and buying pounds drives up the dollar price of pounds.

The purchasing power parity theory is more a predictor of the long-run tendency than of the day-to-day relationship between changes in the price level and the exchange rate. For example, a country's currency generally appreciates when its inflation rate is lower than the rest of the world's and depreciates when its inflation rate is higher. Because of trade barriers, central bank intervention in exchange markets, and the fact that some products are not traded or are not comparable across countries, the purchasing power parity theory may not explain exchange rates at a particular point in time. For example, the theory did not accurately predict events during the first half of the 1980s, when the dollar appreciated against key currencies despite a U.S. inflation rate that exceeded key foreign inflation rates. But the theory is helpful in explaining long-run trends.

*Under a system of **flexible exchange rates**, the exchange rate is determined by the forces of supply and demand.*

What we have been describing thus far is a system of **flexible exchange rates**, in which the exchange rate is determined by the forces of supply and demand. Flexible, or *floating*, exchange rates adjust continually to the myriad forces that buffet the foreign exchange market. Consider how the exchange rate is linked to the balance of payments. Debit entries in the current and capital accounts increase the demand for foreign exchange, and credit entries in these accounts increase the supply of foreign exchange. In the absence of government intervention in the foreign exchange market, the current account and the capital account, on average, sum to zero. If planned debit transactions exceed planned credit transactions, the domestic currency depreciates; if planned credit transactions exceed planned debit transactions, it appreciates.

The wild swings in exchange rates that sometimes occur with flexible exchange rates have forced policy makers to consider alternatives, such as some combinations of flexible and fixed exchange rates. Let's look now at how fixed rates work.

Fixed Exchange Rates

*Under a system of **fixed exchange rates**, central banks buy and sell currency to keep the exchange rate within a narrow band of values.*

When exchange rates are flexible, government officials have little direct role in the foreign exchange market. If government officials try to set exchange rates, however, active central bank intervention is necessary to establish and maintain these **fixed exchange rates**. Suppose that monetary officials select what they perceive to be an appropriate rate of exchange between the dollar and the pound. They undertake to *fix*, or to "peg," the exchange rate within a narrow band around the particular value selected. Let's assume that the exchange rate is set at $2 per British pound, with a permitted margin of fluctuation of 1 percent on either side of the pegged rate. Therefore dollars per pound can vary from $1.98 to $2.02, but monetary authorities will not permit the rate to stray outside this narrow band.

To explore the mechanics of fixed exchange rates, let's begin with a situation in which the equilibrium exchange rate is exactly $2 per pound, as indicated in Exhibit 5 by point *e*, the intersection of *D* and *S*. Since the equilibrium rate equals the fixed rate, monetary authorities need not intervene in the foreign exchange market.

**EXHIBIT 5   CENTRAL BANK INTERVENTION TO MAINTAIN AN EXCHANGE
RATE CEILING**

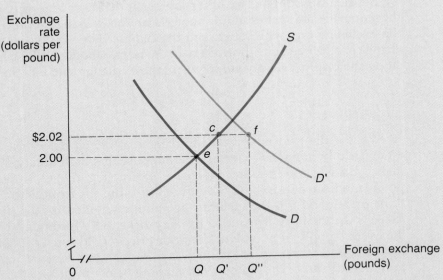

Point e, the intersection of demand curve D and supply curve S, determines an
exchange rate within a band of 1 percent on either side of $2 per pound. An
increase in the demand for foreign exchange from D to D' would drive the
exchange rate above the permitted margin of fluctuation. To maintain the exchange
rate within the band, monetary authorities must sell pounds for dollars at an
exchange rate of $2.02 per pound. That is, the Bank of England must sell (Q" − Q')
pounds to maintain a fixed exchange rate.

Enforcing a Rate Ceiling

Suppose that consumer income in the United States increases, causing
the demand curve for foreign exchange to shift to the right as the U.S.
demand for imports rises. If the resulting increase in the equilibrium exchange rate is within the limits set by the government, the increase in
demand will prompt no action by monetary authorities. But if the increase
in demand is large enough to increase the equilibrium price above $2.02 per
pound, monetary authorities will intervene.

The shift to the right from D to D' in Exhibit 5 will result in an
equilibrium exchange rate above $2.02. At the ceiling exchange rate of
$2.02, the quantity of pounds demanded (point f) exceeds the quantity
supplied (point c). To keep the dollar-per-pound rate from rising above
$2.02, monetary authorities must sell pounds for $2.02 in the foreign
exchange market. As long as the foreign exchange market has a ready supply
of pounds at this ceiling rate, traders will be willing to exchange pounds for
dollars at that rate. *By providing pounds at $2.02, monetary authorities, such as the
Bank of England, can prevent the exchange rate from rising above the designated rate.*

In Exhibit 5, we can identify the amount of foreign exchange (pounds) sold by the Bank of England in a given period of time as the difference between Q'', the quantity demanded when the exchange rate is \$2.02, and Q', the quantity supplied by other sources at that exchange rate. As long as the monetary authorities supply enough foreign exchange at the ceiling rate, the exchange rate will not exceed the ceiling. The supply of foreign exchange in effect becomes horizontal to the right of point c, which is the point along the original supply curve where the exchange rate hits the ceiling.

Enforcing a Rate Floor

What if the exchange rate is in danger of falling below the floor rate established by monetary authorities? Suppose that high inflation in Britain makes British goods more expensive, decreasing the U.S. demand for pounds, reflected in Exhibit 6 by the shift to the left from D to D''. At the floor price of \$1.98, the quantity of pounds supplied by the market, Q', exceeds the quantity demanded by the market, Q''. Without intervention, the excess supply of pounds at the floor price would force the equilibrium exchange rate lower, to the point where supply and demand intersect. To prevent the value of the pound from slipping below the floor rate, monetary authorities must be willing to buy pounds at the floor rate, thus taking the excess supply of pounds off the market. As long as there is a ready demand for pounds at the floor rate, other traders will be unwilling to exchange dollars for pounds at less than that rate. Since the central bank buys any excess pounds at the floor rate (up to point g on the supply curve), to the right of point h the demand curve becomes horizontal at the floor price.

Through such intervention in the foreign exchange market, monetary authorities can stabilize the exchange rate, keeping it within the specified band. In sum, the situation under fixed exchange rates around a narrow band is as follows: at the exchange rate floor, the demand curve is horizontal; within the permitted margin of exchange rate fluctuations, the supply curve slopes upward and the demand curve slopes downward; and at the exchange rate ceiling, the supply curve is horizontal. Government transactions to enforce the fixed exchange rate enter into the official reserve transactions account of the balance of payments. Excess demand for foreign exchange at the ceiling rate implies that total debits exceed total credits in the current and capital accounts. This deficit is offset by central banks' official transactions.[3]

If the equilibrium exchange rate is sometimes above and other times below the floor, the central bank will be alternately buying and selling foreign exchange. Its reserves may therefore fluctuate around a constant

---

[3] Currency transactions by the central bank will also affect a country's money supply unless the bank tries to offset, or "sterilize," the transactions by buying or selling other central bank assets. An official reserve transactions surplus increases the money supply; a deficit decreases the money supply.

EXHIBIT 6   CENTRAL BANK INTERVENTION TO MAINTAIN AN EXCHANGE RATE FLOOR

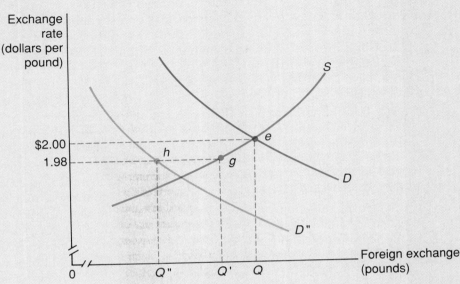

Point *e*, the intersection of demand curve *D* and supply curve *S*, determines an exchange rate within a band of 1 percent on either side of $2 per pound. A decrease in the demand for foreign exchange from *D* to *D″* would drive the exchange rate below the permitted margin of fluctuation. To maintain the exchange rate within the band, monetary authorities must sell dollars for pounds at an exchange rate of $1.98 per pound. That is, the Bank of England must buy ($Q'-Q''$) pounds to maintain a fixed exchange rate.

*A **devaluation** of the domestic currency is an increase in the official pegged value of foreign currency. A **revaluation** is a reduction in the official pegged value of foreign currency.*

average level. The possibility of reserve depletion arises when a permanent change in demand or supply causes the equilibrium exchange rate to remain continually above or below the pegged rate on a long-term basis. When this occurs, the government has several options for eliminating the exchange rate disequilibrium. Suppose there is excess demand at the ceiling rate, as in Exhibit 5. First, the pegged exchange rate can be increased: a **devaluation** of the domestic currency. (A decrease in the pegged exchange rate is called a **revaluation**.) Second, the government can impose restrictions on imports or on capital outflows to directly reduce the demand for foreign exchange. Third, the government can adopt contractionary fiscal or monetary policies that reduce the country's income level, increase interest rates, or reduce inflation relative to that of the country's trading partners, thereby indirectly decreasing the demand for foreign exchange. Finally, the government can allow the disequilibrium to persist and ration the available foreign currency through some form of foreign exchange controls.

HISTORY AND DEVELOPMENT
OF THE INTERNATIONAL MONETARY SYSTEM

*Under the **gold stan-dard**, the currencies of most countries were convertible into gold at a fixed rate.*

From 1879 to 1914, the international financial system operated under a **gold standard**, whereby the currencies of most countries were convertible into gold at a fixed rate. The U.S. dollar could be redeemed at the U.S. Treasury for one-twentieth of an ounce of gold. The British Treasury would exchange one-fourth of an ounce of gold for one pound sterling. Since each pound sterling could buy five times as much gold as each dollar, one pound sterling exchanged for $5.

The gold standard provided a predictable exchange rate, one that did not vary as long as currency could be redeemed for gold at the announced rate. But the money supply in each country was determined largely by the flow of gold between countries, so each country had little control over its own monetary policy. A balance of payments deficit theoretically caused a country's money supply to drop; a surplus caused a country's money supply to rise. Also, the supply of money throughout the world depended on the vagaries of gold discoveries. When gold production was slow and the money supply did not keep pace with the growth in economic activity, the result was a drop in the price level, or *deflation*. When gold production was up and the growth of the money supply exceeded the growth in economic activity, the result was a rise in the price level, or *inflation*. For example, gold discoveries in Alaska and South Africa in the late 1890s expanded the U.S. money supply, leading to inflation.

The Bretton Woods Agreement

During World War I, many countries could no longer convert their currencies to gold, and the gold standard eventually collapsed, disrupting international trade during the 1920s and 1930s. Once an Allied victory in World War II appeared certain, the Allies met in Bretton Woods, New Hampshire, in July of 1944 to formulate a new international monetary system. Because the United States was not ravaged by World War II and had a strong economy, the dollar was selected as the key reserve currency in the new international monetary system. All exchange rates were fixed in terms of the dollar, and the United States, which held most of the world's gold reserves, stood ready to convert foreign holdings of dollars into gold at a fixed rate of $35 per ounce. Even though exchange rates were fixed by the Bretton Woods accord, *other* countries could adjust their exchange rates if there was a fundamental disequilibrium in their balance of payments—that is, a large and persistent deficit or surplus.

Special Drawing Rights (SDRs) are a form of international reserve currency created by the International Monetary Fund.

The Bretton Woods agreement also created the International Monetary Fund (IMF) to set rules for maintaining the fixed exchange rates and to make loans to countries with temporary balance of payments problems. The IMF, which has more than 140 member countries, also standardized financial reporting for international trade and finance. The IMF now issues a paper substitute for gold called **Special Drawing Rights**, or **SDRs**, which function as international reserves. Whereas the supply of gold depends on discoveries and the cost of production, SDRs can be created by the IMF to satisfy the world's demand for international reserves. Within limits, each central bank can exchange its own currency for SDRs. Note that SDRs are used exclusively to make settlements between central banks.

Demise of the Bretton Woods System

During the latter part of the 1960s, inflation began heating up in the United States, and the dollar became overvalued at the official exchange rate, meaning that the gold value of the dollar exceeded the exchange value of the dollar. With the dollar overvalued, foreigners redeemed more dollars for gold. To stop this outflow of gold, some adjustments in the international monetary system had to be made. On August 15, 1971, President Richard Nixon closed the "gold window," refusing to exchange gold for dollars. In December 1971 the ten richest countries of the world met in Washington and devalued the dollar by 8 percent. The hope at the time was that this devaluation would put the dollar on firmer footing and would save the "dollar standard." With inflation rising at different rates around the world, however, an international monetary system based on fixed exchange rates was doomed.

In 1971 U.S. merchandise imports exceeded merchandise exports for the first time since World War II. When the trade deficit tripled in 1972, it became clear that the dollar remained overvalued. In early 1973 the dollar was devalued another 10 percent, but this did not quiet foreign exchange markets. The dollar, for twenty-five years the anchor of the international monetary system, suddenly became a hot potato, and speculators began betting the dollar would fall more. Dollars were exchanged for West German marks because the mark appeared to be the most stable currency. Monetary officials at the Bundesbank, West Germany's central bank, exchanged marks for dollars to defend the official exchange rate and to prevent an appreciation of the mark. After selling $10 billion worth of marks, the Germans threw in the towel and stopped defending the dollar. As soon as the value of the dollar was allowed to float against the mark, the Bretton Woods system, already on shaky ground, collapsed.

Why didn't West Germany want the mark to appreciate? Appreciation of the mark makes West German goods more expensive abroad and foreign goods cheaper in West Germany. By increasing the supply of marks while increasing the demand for dollars, central bankers hoped to keep the value of their own currency from rising.

The Current System: Managed Float

*The **managed float system** combines features of freely floating exchange rates with intervention by central banks.*

The Bretton Woods system has been replaced by a **managed float system**, which combines features of a freely floating exchange rate with occasional intervention by central banks as a way of moderating exchange rate fluctuations among the world's major currencies. A group of European countries have formed the European Monetary System, through which they attempt to align the values of their respective currencies. Members of the European Monetary System have even developed a new monetary unit called the European Currency Unit, or ECU, which they hope will one day become one of the world's key currencies, perhaps replacing the dollar in international transactions. Most smaller countries peg their currencies to one of the major currencies (such as the U.S. dollar or the French franc), to Special Drawing Rights, or to a "basket" of major currencies.

Exchange rates between the West German mark, the Japanese yen, and the U.S. dollar remain highly unstable, particularly because of international speculation about official efforts to stabilize exchange rates. Major criticisms of flexible exchange rates are that (1) they are inflationary, since they free monetary authorities to follow expansionary policies, and (2) they have very often been volatile, especially since the late 1970s. This volatility creates much uncertainty and risk for importers and exporters, increasing the cost of international trade and thus reducing its volume. Furthermore, exchange rate volatility can lead to wrenching changes in the competitiveness of a country's export sector and of those domestic producers who must compete with imports. These changes in competitiveness cause swings in employment, resulting in calls for protectionism.

Policy makers are always on the lookout for an international monetary system that will perform better than the current managed float system with its fluctuating currency values. *Their ideal is a system that will foster international trade, lower inflation, and promote a more stable world economy.* International finance ministers have acknowledged that the world must find an international standard and establish a more stable exchange rate.

Return to the Gold Standard?

Some critics of the current international monetary system recommend a return to the gold standard based on fixed exchange rates, with all currencies convertible into gold. They argue that if currency could be redeemed for gold by foreign central bankers at fixed rates, then the threat of a loss of gold reserves would discipline monetary authorities. If monetary authorities chose a policy that generated an inflation rate that exceeded the rate in other countries, the country's currency would become overvalued. This would result in a balance of payments deficit and a subsequent loss of gold reserves. The threat of the loss of gold reserves would thus moderate domestic monetary policy. Fixed rates would also provide more predictability in trade policy.

Why not return to the gold standard? Supporters of flexible exchange rates argue that different countries have different tolerances for unemployment versus inflation. Flexible exchange rates allow these countries to follow unique stabilization policies leading to different tradeoffs between unemployment and inflation. Also, the disinflationary policies of the major central banks in the 1980s show that monetary authorities are capable of stabilizing inflation without resorting to fixed exchange rates. Finally, supporters of flexible exchange rates argue that the extreme volatility of exchange rates in the 1970s and 1980s was a response to, not the cause of, such turbulent economic developments as two oil-price shocks, high and uneven rates of inflation throughout the world economy in the 1970s followed by a major contraction of the world economy in the early 1980s, the crash of the U.S. stock market in 1987, and the sharp drop in the Japanese stock market in 1990. A fixed exchange rate regime would have been unable to withstand this turbulence unless the major industrial nations imposed restrictions on international flows of trade and capital.

Critics of the gold standard note that in recent years the price of gold has been determined by a free market, and its price per ounce has varied greatly — from $300 to $900. They fear that pegging the value of currency to a commodity whose value has varied so much would cause price levels to undergo similar swings. Also, a return to the gold standard would most benefit the world's largest gold producers, South Africa and the Soviet Union. These countries could thereby play a more critical role in international finance. Neither country is a close ally of the United States. There does not appear to be overwhelming support for a gold standard, but there is interest in some sort of stabilizing reform. *But no exchange rate system functions well without coordinated action among countries on common macroeconomic policies.*

CONCLUSION

At one time the United States was largely self-sufficient. A technological lead over the rest of the world, an abundance of natural resources, a well-trained work force, a modern and extensive capital stock, and the ability to convert its currency into gold made the United States the envy of the world. The dollar was the world's premier international currency — readily accepted and prized.

The situation has changed. The United States is now very much a part of the world economy, not only as a major exporter but also as the largest importer in the world. U.S. multinational corporations are an international presence and have spread advanced technology around the world. As a result of the spread of technology and capital, U.S. workers now face stiff competition from abroad. U.S. banks have loaned billions to developing countries throughout the world, and Americans have borrowed billions from abroad; we are now the world's largest debtor.

As a result of chronic balance of payments deficits, enormous numbers of dollars circulate in the world markets. Many of the loans made by U.S. banks to developing countries have soured, and the banks must now rely on the vagaries of the world economy to see if and when these loans will be repaid. Although the dollar remains the unit of transaction in many international settlements — OPEC, for example, still states oil prices in dollars — the wild gyrations of exchange rates have made those involved in international finance wary of putting all their eggs in one basket. Traders therefore hedge against a decline in the dollar. The international monetary system is now going through a difficult adjustment period as it gropes for a new source of stability after the collapse of the Bretton Woods agreement.

Summary

1. The balance of payments reflects all economic transactions across national borders. The current account measures the flow of (1) merchandise, (2) services, including investment income, military transactions, and tourism, and (3) unilateral transfers, or public and private transfers to foreign residents. The capital account reflects international flows involving purchases or sales of assets.

2. Currencies support the flow of goods and services across international borders. The intersection of the supply and demand for currency on the foreign exchange market determines the equilibrium exchange rate.

3. Under our current system of fluctuating, or floating, exchange rates, the value of the dollar relative to other currencies varies over time. An increase in the demand for dollars or a reduction in their supply in the foreign exchange market, other things constant, will cause an increase in the value of the dollar relative to other currencies, or appreciation. Conversely, a reduction in the demand for dollars or an increase in their supply will cause a decrease in the value of the dollar, or depreciation.

4. For much of this century the international monetary system was based on fixed exchange rates. A managed float has been in effect for the major currencies since the demise of the Bretton Woods system in the early 1970s. Although central banks have often tried to stabilize exchange rates, recent swings in exchange rates have troubled policy makers.

Questions and Problems

1. (The Versatility of the Dollar) In general, an American cannot use U.S. currency to buy products in Rome or London. However, some places, especially border towns such as Windsor, Ontario, and Nuevo Laredo, Mexico, do accept U.S. dollars. Why does this practice exist in border towns? Why would we expect the practice in countries that have exchange controls, which give rise to black markets?

2. (The Demand for Money and Dollars) What is the difference between the demand for the U.S. dollar and the U.S. domestic demand for money?

3. (Current and Capital Accounts) An important debate in international finance is whether, under flexible exchange rates, changes in the current account are caused by movements in the capital account or vice versa. Choose one side and argue your point.

4. (Balance of Payments Accounting) Explain which entry in the U.S. balance of payments is relevant to each of the following:
   a. A Hong Kong financier buys some U.S. corporate stock.
   b. A U.S. tourist in Paris buys some perfume.

c. IBM-Japan sells computers to a pineapple company in Hawaii.

d. U.S. farmers make a gift of food to starving children in Ethiopia.

e. The U.S. Treasury sells a thirty-year bond to a Saudi Arabian prince.

f. A West German student buys a U.S. textbook in France.

g. A U.S. company deposits dollars in a Eurodollar account in Hong Kong.

5. (Recessions and the Trade Balance) Explain why recessions in the United States (which are not currently world recessions) tend to reduce the U.S. trade deficit.

6. (Flexible Exchange Rates) Why must the balance on capital account and the balance on current account sum to zero (on average) when exchange rates are flexible?

7. (Flexible Exchange Rates) Explain why, under flexible exchange rates, if the price of the dollar is above its equilibrium level, the balance of payments will be in deficit.

8. (Trade Balances) Why is it unreasonable to expect all countries, regardless of their level of development, to have balanced trade (that is, exports equal to imports)?

9. (The European Currency Unit) Of what value would it be to the members of the European Monetary System to have their own currency?

10. (Developing Countries' Debt) John Maynard Keynes is credited with saying that if you borrow $1000 from a bank and can't pay it back, then it's your problem, but if you borrow $1000 million from a bank and can't pay it back, it's the bank's problem. How does Keynes's humorous remark relate to the problem of the debt of developing countries?

11. (Trade Deficits) Suppose the United States ran a balance on goods and services surplus by exporting goods and services while importing nothing.

a. How would such a surplus be offset elsewhere in the balance of payments accounts?

b. If the level of U.S. production does not depend on the balance on goods and services, how does running this surplus affect our *current* standard of living?

c. How will such a surplus probably affect our *future* standard of living?

12. (Exchange Rate Determination) Using a supply-demand diagram for foreign exchange (for example, the pound or yen) against dollars, determine the likely impact of each of the following on the strength of the dollar against foreign exchange, other things constant.

a. An increase in U.S. interest rates

b. An increase in the U.S. money supply

c. An increase in U.S. productivity

d. An increase in U.S. citizens' preferences for imported goods

13. (Exchange Rate Determination) Use the data below to answer the following questions:

Price of pounds (in $)	Q_D (of pounds)	Q_S (of pounds)
$4.00	50	100
3.00	75	75
2.00	100	50

a. Construct the supply and demand curves for pounds, and determine the equilibrium exchange rate (dollars per pound).

b. Construct the supply and demand curves for dollars, and determine the equilibrium exchange rate (pounds per dollar).

14. (Purchasing Power Parity) According to the theory of purchasing power parity, what will happen to the value of the dollar (against foreign currencies) if the U.S. price level doubles and price levels in other countries stay constant? Why is the theory more suitable to analyzing events in the long run?

15. (Fixed Versus Floating Exchange Rates) Compare the adjustment processes necessary to eliminate trade imbalances under the fixed and the floating exchange rate models.

a. By what means do central banks and governments maintain fixed exchange rates?

b. What are the benefits and costs of each model?

C H A P T E R   3 5

Problems of Developing Countries

The sun rises on all of us around the world, but we face the day under very different circumstances. Some of us arise from a comfortable bed in a nice home, select the day's clothing from a diverse wardrobe, choose from a variety of foods for breakfast, and drive to school or to work in one of the family's personal automobiles. Most other people are less fortunate. Three-fourths of the 5 billion people on earth do not have spacious homes, closets full of clothes, or pantries full of food. They own no automobile, and many have no job. Their health is poor, as is their education. More than likely they cannot read or write.

So far this book has focused on the United States, one of the richest countries on earth. In this chapter we turn to problems confronting developing countries. We should acknowledge at the outset that no single theory of economic development has gained general acceptance, so this chapter will focus less on a theory of economic development than on the differences between developed and developing countries. Thus the chapter will be more descriptive than theoretical. Topics discussed in this chapter include

- Third World economies
- Developing countries
- Absolute poverty level
- Productivity and development

- Obstacles to development
- Foreign aid
- Third World debt problems

WORLDS APART

Countries are classified in a variety of ways based on their level of economic development. The *First World* is the name given to the economically advanced capitalist countries of Western Europe, North America, Australia, New Zealand, and Japan. First World countries were the first to experience long-term economic growth during the nineteenth century. These countries are more commonly called *industrial market countries*. The *Second World* is the name given to economically advanced socialist countries in Eastern Europe, including the Soviet Union and other Soviet-type countries, such as Poland. (Keep in mind that even though countries of Eastern Europe are socialist countries, as time goes on they are relying more on markets.) The *Third World* consists of about 140 developing countries in Asia, Africa, and Latin America. Third World economies may be capitalist, socialist, or a mix. These countries tend to have a low level of per capita income, a low standard of living, and a high rate of population growth, and they rely on First and Second World countries for technology. Third World countries are also called **developing countries** and less-developed countries, or LDCs. In this chapter we will refer to them as developing countries.

Developing countries are typified by high rates of illiteracy, high unemployment, rapid population growth, and exports of primary products.

Developing Countries

The term *developing countries* is an expression adopted by the United Nations to describe countries with high rates of illiteracy, high unemployment, extensive underemployment, rapid population growth, and exports consisting of agricultural products and raw materials. Typically, more than half the labor force in developing countries is in agriculture. Farming methods are relatively primitive, and farm productivity is low. Thus most people in these countries are living from hand to mouth, so to speak.

The differences in economic activity across countries are profound. For example, the United States, with its 250 million people, has a gross national product that exceeds the combined gross national products of *all* developing countries. Thus, the United States, with only 5 percent of the world's population, produces more than the combined output of three-quarters of the world's 5 billion plus population.

To get a general feel for the differences between developed and developing countries, consider the following comparison. Income for a typical family of four in the United States was a little more than $35,000 in 1989. That family, though by no means rich, has a comfortable standard of living. Each of the children has a bedroom. The children will finish high school and will probably go to college. Compare this family with a typical extended family in rural Asia. The Asian household is likely to be much larger, including grandparents, aunts, and uncles. The combined annual income of this family, including both money income and in-kind income (such as the value of food they grow), is about $300. The family lives in a one-room shack without electricity, running water, or sanitation. Family members work the land as tenant farmers. Of the four school-age children, only one attends school regularly, and that child can expect to get through only three or four grades. The family eats only one meal a day — a meal that does not change and is never enough to ward off hunger. Family members are frequently ill, but health care often is not available, as most of the doctors are located in urban areas, where higher-income families reside.

Classification of Economies

The developing nations vary greatly, ranging from the tragically poor economies of Sub-Saharan Africa to the booming economies of the Far East. It is helpful therefore to draw finer distinctions among developing countries.

The economic criterion used most often to compare living standards across nations is per capita gross national product. We caution that making intercountry comparisons of GNP is tricky, because countries employ different national income accounting procedures and all measures must be translated into comparable accounting formats and a common currency. One problem with international comparisons is determining the appropriate exchange rate for translating different countries' GNP statistics into a common currency. The exchange rate problem is compounded when some countries produce a significant amount of output that is not traded across international boundaries. Furthermore, although official international comparisons based on per capita GNP usually include an estimate of the value of food produced and consumed by the farm households, other nonmarket activities are not captured by GNP. Thus international comparisons that compare only GNP per capita tend to underestimate the quantity of goods and services available per person in developing countries, which have more nonmarket production than do industrial nations.

The World Bank attempts to estimate comparable GNP figures for all reporting countries and then uses these figures to classify economies. The World Bank divides reporting countries into three major groups based on their per capita GNP. In 1987 there were (1) fifty-two low-income economies with a per capita income of $480 or less, (2) eighty-two middle-income economies with a per capita income exceeding $480 per year but less than $6000, and (3) forty-one high-income economies with a per capita GNP of $6000 or more. The low- and middle-income countries are often referred to as *developing* countries, and the high-income countries are often referred to as *industrial market* countries (though some of the high-income countries have economies that are still developing). Another group of ten countries, primarily socialist countries such as the U.S.S.R. and Cuba, do not report data on their economic status and consequently are classified by the World Bank as *nonreporting nonmember economies.*

Data on total population, average real GNP per capita, and average growth in income are summarized in Exhibit 1 for all reporting countries with a population of 1 million or more. Despite the problems associated with estimating comparable income figures, Exhibit 1 presents a reasonable

EXHIBIT 1

POPULATION, GNP PER CAPITA, AND ANNUAL GROWTH RATE
(for countries with a population of 1 million or more)

Classification	Population, mid-1987 (millions)	Real GNP per Capita	
		1987 Dollars	Annual Growth Rate, 1965–1987 (percent)
1. Low-income economies	2,822.9	290	3.1
China and India	1,866.0	300	3.9
Other	956.9	280	1.5
2. Middle-income economies	1,038.5	1,810	2.5
3. High-income economies	777.2	14,430	2.3
4. Nonreporting economies	371.5	Not reported	

Source: Based on data presented by the World Bank in *World Development Report 1989* (New York: Oxford University Press, 1989), Table 1.

picture of economies throughout the world. Low-income economies, which had an average per capita income of $290 in 1987, account for over half of the world's population. Developing countries (those in the first two groups plus six of the high-income countries) account for 78 percent of the world's population.

The giants among the poorest countries are China and India, which together account for more than a third of the world's population. China and India had a higher level of real GNP per capita as well as a higher level of growth in GNP per capita than did the other low-income economies. Among low-income countries other than China and India, the average growth rate in GNP per capita was only 1.5 percent per year from 1965 to 1987. On average, per capita income in the high-income economies was about fifty times that in the low-income economies—quite an incredible difference.

Exhibit 2 presents GNP per capita for selected countries, arranged from left to right in descending order. Switzerland, the richest country in the world in 1987, had a GNP per capita that was about thirteen times that of Costa Rica. But per capita GNP in Costa Rica was, in turn, about thirteen times that of Ethiopia, the poorest country in the world. Costa Rica no doubt feels poor relative to industrialized nations, but it appears well off compared to the poorest developing countries. Thus there is a tremendous range of productive performance around the world.

Can the degree of poverty throughout the world be measured in some objective way? The **absolute poverty level** defines the level of income needed to satisfy the basic physical requirement for food, clothing, and

The **absolute poverty level** defines the income needed to satisfy basic physical needs.

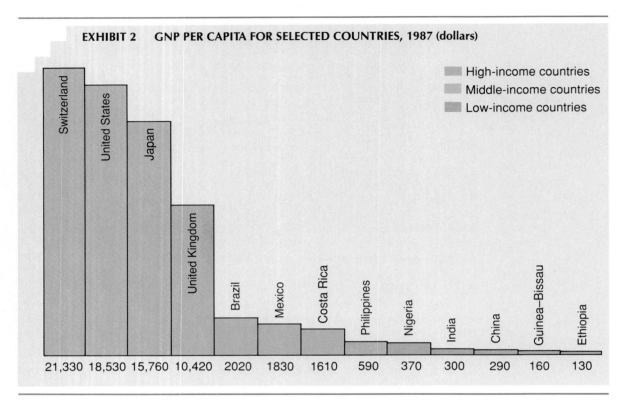

EXHIBIT 2   GNP PER CAPITA FOR SELECTED COUNTRIES, 1987 (dollars)

High-income countries
Middle-income countries
Low-income countries

Switzerland	United States	Japan	United Kingdom	Brazil	Mexico	Costa Rica	Philippines	Nigeria	India	China	Guinea-Bissau	Ethiopia
21,330	18,530	15,760	10,420	2020	1830	1610	590	370	300	290	160	130

Source: Based on data presented by the World Bank in *World Development Report 1989* (New York: Oxford University Press, 1989), Table 1.

shelter to ensure survival. Based on this criterion, about 40 percent of the population in developing countries lives in absolute poverty.[1]

Health and Nutrition

Differences in stages of development among countries are reflected in a number of ways besides per capita income levels. For example, many people of the Third World suffer from poor health as a result of malnutrition and disease. Life expectancy in the least-developed African countries averaged 51 years in 1987, compared with 64 years in other developing economies and 76 years in industrial economies. The average life expectancy worldwide ranged from 39 years in Guinea-Bissau to 78 years in Japan.

Infant Mortality Rates Health differences among countries are dramatized by infant mortality rates. In 1987, among the least-developed African countries, an average of 115 of every 1000 infants died during their first year,

---

[1] See M. S. Ahluwalia, N. Carter, and H. Chenery, "Growth and Poverty in Developing Countries," *Journal of Development Economics* 6 (September 1979).

compared with 71 for all low- and middle-income countries and 10 for high-income countries. Thus babies born in the poorest countries were eleven times more likely to die than babies born in high-income countries. Mortality rates for selected countries are presented in Exhibit 3. Note that Japan, the country with the highest life expectancy in the world, also has the lowest infant mortality rate. Similarly, the country with the shortest life expectancy — Guinea-Bissau — has one of the highest infant mortality rates.

Malnutrition People living in much of Africa, West Asia, and South Asia don't have enough food to maintain good health. Those in the very poorest countries consume only half the calories of those in high-income countries. Even if an infant survives the first year, malnutrition can turn normal childhood diseases, such as measles, into life-threatening events. Malnutrition is a primary or contributing factor in more than half of all deaths among children under 5 in low-income countries. Diseases that are well controlled in the industrial countries — malaria, whooping cough, polio, dysentery, typhoid, and cholera — become epidemics in poor countries. Many of these diseases are water borne, and residents of urban areas in less-developed countries are often unable to obtain safe drinking water.

EXHIBIT 3   MORTALITY RATE PER 1000 INFANTS FOR SELECTED COUNTRIES: 1987

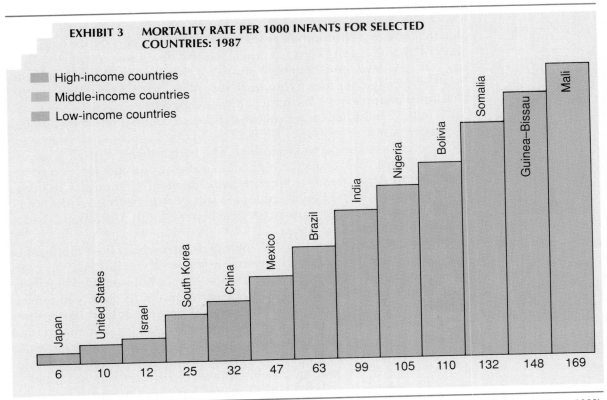

High-income countries
Middle-income countries
Low-income countries

Japan	United States	Israel	South Korea	China	Mexico	Brazil	India	Nigeria	Bolivia	Somalia	Guinea-Bissau	Mali
6	10	12	25	32	47	63	99	105	110	132	148	169

Source: Based on data presented by the World Bank in *World Development Report 1989* (New York: Oxford University Press, 1989), Table 32.

Availability of Physicians Life expectancy and infant mortality rates are a reflection, in part, of how well the health care system operates. The number of physicians in a country is one measure of the availability of health care. The population per physician in 1984 was about twelve times larger in low-income economies than in high-income economies. The poorest countries of Africa had the fewest physicians and the Soviet Union the most physicians. The pattern for nurses is similar to that for physicians. High-income economies had sixteen times more nurses per capita than low-income economies.

Not only do developing countries have fewer physicians, but these physicians tend to locate in urban areas, where only about one-fourth of the population lives. Physicians locate near the people who can most afford their services, and higher-income people tend to live in urban areas. For example, in 1987 only 27 percent of India's population resided in urban areas, but 80 percent of the physicians practiced there.

High Rates Of Population Growth

This year about 80 million people will be added to the world's population of 5 billion people. More than 70 million of these people will be born in developing countries. Developing countries are identified not only by their low incomes and high mortality rates but also by their high birth rates. In fact, the birth rate—the number of births per 1000 people—is one of the best ways of distinguishing between developed and developing countries. Birth rates in less-developed countries are twice those in developed countries. Few developing countries have a birth rate of less than 20 per 1000, but no developed country has a birth rate above that level.

Families tend to be larger in less-developed countries because children are viewed as a source of labor for the farm and as a source of economic and social security as the parents get older. The higher infant mortality rates in poorer countries also engender higher birth rates, as parents strive to ensure a sufficiently large family. Evidence from developing countries indicates that when women have better employment opportunities outside the home, fertility rates decline. As women become better educated, they tend to earn more and have fewer children.

Much international aid to developing countries has taken the form of medical care and programs to improve hygiene. These advances have allowed people in developing countries to live longer, but increased longevity has placed a greater strain on the limited resources in those economies. Therefore improved health does little to avert poverty, at least in the short run. For example, in Sri Lanka modern medicine has eliminated malaria and has doubled the population growth rate. Other major diseases have also been wiped out. With 40 percent of the population in developing countries already living at the level of absolute poverty, a greater survival rate is a mixed blessing in the short run. Over the long run, however, improved health leads to increased labor productivity and thus to higher income levels.

Despite improvements in medical care, death rates are still higher in developing countries than in developed countries. But these higher death rates are not great enough to offset the higher birth rates. Thus since 1980 the population in developing countries has grown by an annual average of 2.0 percent or more, compared with only 0.6 percent in industrial countries. The annual population growth rates since 1965 for major groupings of countries are presented in Exhibit 4, along with projections to the year 2000. For most groupings annual growth has been slower since 1980 than it was between 1965 and 1980. The countries of Sub-Saharan Africa, the poorest countries in the world, grew the fastest.

Because of the high birth rates in developing countries, children under 15 make up almost half the total population there. In developed countries children are only about a quarter of the population. In some developing countries the growth rate in population has exceeded the growth rate in real GNP, so the standard of living as measured by per capita GNP has been falling.

EXHIBIT 4
AVERAGE ANNUAL POPULATION GROWTH RATE (percent)

Classification	1965–1980	1980–1987	1987–2000 (projected)
1. Low-income economies	2.3	2.0	1.9
China and India	2.2	1.6	1.5
Other	2.6	2.8	2.6
Sub-Saharan Africa	2.7	3.2	3.1
2. Middle-income economies	2.4	2.2	1.9
3. High-income economies	0.9	0.7	0.5
4. Nonreporting economies	1.0	1.0	NA

Source: Based on data presented by the World Bank in *World Development Report 1989* (New York: Oxford University Press, 1989), Table 26.

Women in Developing Countries

Throughout the world, poverty is greater among women, particularly women who head households. Because women often must work in the home as well as in the labor market, poverty can impose a special hardship on them. In many cultures women's responsibilities include gathering firewood and carrying water, tasks that are especially burdensome if firewood is scarce and water is far from home. The percentage of households headed by women varies from country to country, but exceeds 40 percent in some areas of the Caribbean and Africa.

Women in developing countries tend to be less educated than men. In the countries of Sub-Saharan Africa and South Asia, for example, only half as many women as men complete high school. Women have fewer employment opportunities and earn lower wages than men do. Women are often on the fringes of the labor market, working long hours in agriculture. They also have less access to other resources, such as land, capital, and technology.

Intracountry Income Distribution

Per capita income differs not only across countries but also across households within countries. A standard procedure for measuring the distribution of household income is to group households from poorest to richest. After dividing the total number of households into five groups of equal size, we can examine what percentage of income is received by each group. Income distribution studies have been conducted for various countries around the world, and some of the results are presented in Exhibit 5. Countries are divided simply into developing and industrial; within each division countries are listed from lowest to highest based on their average per capita income. Bangladesh, the poorest country, is listed first; in Bangladesh the poorest fifth of the households received 6.6 percent of the income, and the richest fifth received 45.3 percent.

All countries show some degree of income inequality, but income in developing countries tends to be less evenly distributed than income in

EXHIBIT 5
PERCENTAGE SHARE OF HOUSEHOLD INCOME BY GROUPS OF HOUSEHOLDS FOR SELECTED COUNTRIES

Country	Year	Lowest Fifth	Second-lowest Fifth	Middle Fifth	Second-highest Fifth	Highest Fifth
Developing Countries						
Bangladesh	1980–1981	6.6	10.7	15.3	22.1	45.3
India	1975–1976	7.0	9.2	13.9	20.5	49.4
Kenya	1976	2.6	6.3	11.5	19.2	60.4
Sri Lanka	1980–1981	5.8	10.1	14.1	20.3	49.8
Indonesia	1976	6.6	7.8	12.6	23.6	49.4
Brazil	1972	2.0	5.0	9.4	17.0	66.6
Hungary	1982	6.9	13.6	19.2	24.5	35.8
Israel	1979–1980	6.0	12.0	17.7	24.4	39.9
Industrial Countries						
West Germany	1978	7.9	12.5	17.0	23.1	39.5
Sweden	1981	7.4	13.1	16.8	21.0	41.7
Japan	1979	8.7	13.2	17.5	23.1	37.5
United States	1980	5.3	11.9	17.9	25.0	39.9

Source: Based on data presented by the World Bank in *World Development Report 1989* (New York: Oxford University Press, 1989), Table 30.

industrial market countries. One reason is that industrial market countries have more income redistribution programs—for example, a progressive income tax and social welfare programs. In developing countries about two-thirds of the very poor scratch out a living as subsistence farmers or as farm workers. Although poverty is primarily a rural phenomenon, most government spending in developing countries occurs in urban areas, perhaps because urban poverty is more visible and because government officials who make budget decisions live in urban areas.

Economist Simon Kuznets, who won the Nobel Prize for economics in 1971, has suggested that during the early stages of economic development, income tends to be unevenly distributed, but as an economy develops, the distribution of income tends to become more equal. The data in Exhibit 5 lend some support to Kuznets's hypothesis.

One final note: Though developing countries have many similarities, they also have differences. For example, some developing countries, such as Cuba and South Korea, have literacy rates that rival those in industrial countries.

PRODUCTIVITY AND DEVELOPMENT

We have examined some of the symptoms of poverty in developing countries, but not why poor countries are poor. At the risk of appearing too simplistic, we might say that poor countries are poor because they do not produce many goods and services. In this section we will examine why some developing countries experience such low productivity.

Low Labor Productivity

Labor productivity, measured in terms of output per worker, is very low in low-income countries. Why is this so? Labor productivity depends on the amount of capital, land, and other resources that are combined with labor. The greater the availability of other resources, the greater the productivity of labor. A worker digging a ditch with a backhoe is much more productive than one using only a shovel.

One way to raise productivity is to invest more in human and physical capital. This investment must be financed by either domestic savings or foreign funds. Income per capita is typically too low in developing countries to permit extensive investments to be financed with internal funds. In poor countries with unstable governments, the wealthy minority may invest in more stable foreign economies. There are thus few domestic funds available for investment in either human or physical capital, and without sufficient capital workers are less productive.

Technology and Education

What exactly is the contribution of education to the process of economic development? Richard Easterlin of the University of Southern California argues that the spread of technology underlying modern economic growth depended largely on the acquisition of skills and motivation through formal schooling.[2] Education makes people more receptive to new ideas and methods. Thus the nations with the most advanced educational systems were also the first to develop. In this century the leader in schooling and in economic development has been the United States. In Latin America, Argentina was the most advanced nation educationally a hundred years ago and is one of the most developed Latin American nations today. The growth of education in Japan during the nineteenth century contributed to its people's ready acceptance of technology and thus to its remarkable economic growth in the twentieth century.

In most developing countries, education claims a large share of the public budget, yet literacy levels remain low. For example, in the least-developed countries only 37 percent of the adult population is literate. Among developed countries 97 percent of the population is literate. The percentage of the population enrolled in school at various levels differs sharply across countries. In high-income economies an average of 39 percent of those aged 20 to 24 are enrolled in post-secondary education, compared with 18 percent in middle-income economies and only 3 percent in low-income economies. Post-secondary enrollment data for selected countries are presented in Exhibit 6. The United States is by far the leader in post-secondary education. Among the poorest countries, less than 1 percent of the relevant population pursues higher education.

Poor Use of Labor

Another feature of developing countries is that they use labor less efficiently than developed nations. Poor use of labor results from both unemployment and underemployment. *Underemployment* occurs when people are working less than they would like to—a worker seeking full-time employment may find only a part-time job, or a highly skilled worker may be employed in a low-skill job. *Unemployment* occurs when those who are willing and able to work cannot find jobs. Unemployment is measured primarily in urban areas, because in rural areas farm work is usually an outlet for labor even if most workers are underemployed.

The unemployment rate in developing nations on average is about 10 to 15 percent of the urban labor force. Unemployment among young workers—those 15 to 24—is typically twice that of older workers. In developing nations about 30 percent of the combined urban and rural workforces is either unemployed or underemployed.

Although two-thirds of the labor force in developing countries works in agriculture, only one-third of GNP in these countries arises from agriculture. Agricultural productivity is low because of the large number of farmers relative to the amount of land farmed. In some developing countries

---

[2] Richard Easterlin, "Why Isn't the Whole World Developed?" *Journal of Economic History* 61 (March 1981): 1–17.

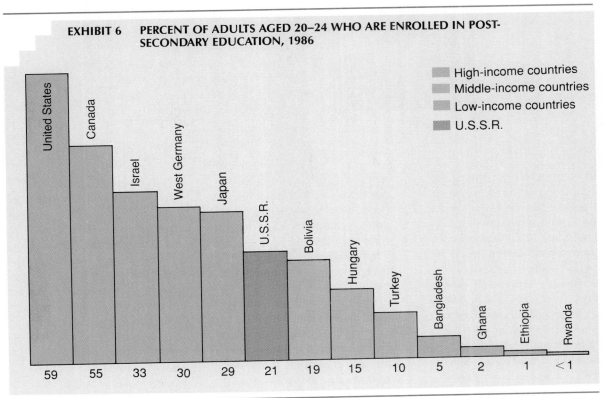

EXHIBIT 6   PERCENT OF ADULTS AGED 20–24 WHO ARE ENROLLED IN POST-SECONDARY EDUCATION, 1986

High-income countries
Middle-income countries
Low-income countries
U.S.S.R.

United States — 59
Canada — 55
Israel — 33
West Germany — 30
Japan — 29
U.S.S.R. — 21
Bolivia — 19
Hungary — 15
Turkey — 10
Bangladesh — 5
Ghana — 2
Ethiopia — 1
Rwanda — < 1

Source: Based on data presented by the World Bank in *World Development Report 1989* (New York: Oxford University Press, 1989), Table 29.

the average farm is as small as two acres. Productivity is low also because few other inputs, such as capital and fertilizer, are employed. Even where more land is available, the absence of capital limits the amount of land that can be farmed. In the United States a farmer and modern tractor can farm hundreds of acres, but in developing countries a farmer with a hand plow or an ox-drawn plow can farm maybe 10 to 20 acres. As you would expect, U.S. farmers are much more productive than farmers in developing countries.

Low productivity obviously results in low income, but low income can, in turn, affect worker productivity. Poor nutrition during the formative years of life can retard mental and physical development. These difficult beginnings may be aggravated by poor diet and health in later life, making the worker poorly suited for formal employment. Low productivity may result from an inability to work in a competitive setting. Thus *low income and low productivity may reinforce each other*. Poverty results in an inadequate diet and insufficient attention to health care. In turn, poor diet and lack of appropriate medical care can reduce the worker's productive ability.

Obstacles to Development

We have already considered several obstacles to economic development: (1) the strain on the poor nations' resources caused by the explosive popula-

W. Arthur Lewis
(b. 1915)

In the nineteenth century, the countries that today make up the industrialized First World were themselves developing countries. And the economic theory dominant during that period—what we now call "classical economics"—was very much concerned with problems of economic development. To writers such as David Ricardo (1772–1823) and John Stuart Mill (1806–1873), the key to economic growth lay primarily in the manufacturing sector. These writers believed that manufacturers, unlike the other sectors of society (laborers and the owners of agricultural land), would accumulate capital by plowing back most of their profits into new investments. Because of population growth, workers would be in almost limitless supply at the "subsistence wage," the wage rate at which a worker family could just barely survive.

As the Western world became increasingly developed by the late nineteenth century, economists turned away from this kind of analysis and be-

gan addressing other questions. Most of this book has been about those newer concerns. But many countries—nations of the so-called Third World—still face urgent problems of economic development that are not entirely unlike those Western Europe once faced. So perhaps it is not surprising that when economists began addressing the difficulties of Third World development after World War II, they first looked back to the classical economists.

The person who opened up this approach—and who helped create the modern field of economic development—is W. Arthur Lewis. Born in a developing country, he was well aware of the problems of the Third World; trained in England, he was well schooled in the legacy of British economics. Lewis put these influences together in a famous 1954 paper that set forth what is called the "dual-economy" model of economic development.

Like Ricardo and Mill, Lewis envisioned an economy

in which growth comes from capital accumulation in a "capitalist" sector, which represents mostly, but not exclusively, urban manufacturing. This "growth sector" contrasts with a stagnant "traditional" sector, which is predominantly rural and agricultural. Because of population pressure and low productivity in the traditional sector, the capitalist sector can draw on an almost limitless supply of labor at a subsistence wage.

This dual-economy model has been the subject of much scrutiny, but it remains an important way of thinking about economic development. The author of the model was born in St. Lucia, in the West Indies. He attended the London School of Economics and the University of Manchester before beginning a stellar career of academic achievement combined with administration and public service. In 1963 Lewis was knighted by Queen Elizabeth, and in 1979 he won the Nobel Prize.

Richard Langlois

tion growth, (2) poor nutrition and health, (3) lack of capital, (4) lack of education, and (5) poor use of labor. Here we consider other factors that affect a developing country's productivity and growth.

International Trade The economies in most developing countries are geared to producing primary products, such as farm goods and raw materials, rather than manufactured products. Primary products also make up the bulk of exports from developing countries, just as manufactured goods make up the bulk of exports from developed countries. Developing countries need to trade with developed countries in order to acquire the capital and technology that will increase labor productivity both on the farm and in the factory. To import capital and technology, developing countries must first acquire foreign exchange. Foreign aid and private investment are sources of foreign exchange in developing countries, but exports usually generate more than half of the annual flow of foreign exchange.

One problem with exporting primary products rather than finished goods is that the prices of primary products, such as coffee, cocoa, sugar, and rubber, fluctuate more widely than the prices of finished goods. Developing countries must also confront industrial countries' protectionist measures, which discriminate against primary products. Exports from developing countries must contend not only with tariffs but also with nontariff barriers such as sugar quotas. Developing countries' share of world trade has been falling since 1950. But some of the obstacles to international trade are imposed from within, as reflected in the following case study.

CASE STUDY	The conditions seemed right in Egypt for Mohammed Marzouk to develop a business that made cotton underwear for export. After all, Egypt grows the best cotton in the world. Quality cotton combined with low labor costs seemed like a sure winner. So why is Egyptian underwear too costly to compete on the world market? As developing countries grow desperate for exports, why can't Egypt compete?
A Hard Sell in Egypt	

The thin cotton yarn used to weave the cloth is produced by government-owned spinning companies. These companies have a monopoly in the production of yarn from raw cotton, and the price of this yarn has tripled since 1978. But the government-produced yarn tends to be inferior and breaks easily. To protect the state monopoly, a duty of 65 percent is imposed on imported yarn. So although Egyptian cotton is of fine quality, the production chain is only as strong as its weakest link, and yarn spinning is the weak link.

Although wages are low, total labor costs are high because labor productivity is low as well. Since the yarn breaks so easily, workers must rewind and wax it before knitting can begin. The objective is to detect irregularities in the yarn that could damage machinery or produce holes in fabric. Because there is little modern machinery, much other work must be done by hand as well. For example, each finished article is pressed with a hand iron. When steam is needed, the presser sips water and spits.

Egypt, like many Third World countries, is plagued by bureaucratic snarls and petty corruption that gum up the wheels of commerce. Mr. Marzouk employs workers whose primary job is to run interference with the government bureaucracy. As many as thirty-four government signatures are needed to ship an order for export. At each step along the way, someone's palm must be greased with *baksheesh*, or bribes, to move the paperwork along.

One of Mr. Marzouk's biggest problems is the apparently arbitrary treatment he receives from the government. His factory was started in 1976 under an investment law that conferred a five-year income tax break. But because of this tax break, another government agency decided that he should pay more for electricity, so he pays triple the rate charged most other customers. Because of the uncertainty created by the arbitrary nature of government regulations, Marzouk is reluctant to expand, even though he has $1 million worth of crated machinery plus 14 acres of land on which to build.

Source: Barbara Rosewicz, "Factory Owner Joins Egypt's Exports Push but Runs into Hurdles," *Wall Street Journal*, 11 November 1985.

Migration and the Brain Drain Migration plays an important role in the economies of developing countries. A major source of foreign exchange in some countries is the money sent home by migrants who find jobs in developed countries. Thus migration provides a valuable safety valve for poor countries, but there is a negative aspect as well. Often the best and the brightest professionals, such as doctors, nurses, and engineers, migrate to developed countries after they have been trained at great expense to the developing country. Since human capital is such a key resource, this "brain drain" can have devastating effects on the developing country.

Natural Resources Some countries are richer than others because they are blessed with natural resources. The difference is most striking when we compare countries with oil reserves and those without. Some developing countries of the Middle East are classified as high-income economies because they are lucky enough to be sitting atop major oil reserves. But oil-rich countries are the exception. Many developing countries, such as Chad and Ethiopia, have little in the way of natural resources. Developing countries without oil reserves were in trouble during the 1970s, when oil prices rose. Oil had to be imported, and these imports drained the oil-poor countries of precious foreign exchange. A few countries, however, such as Japan and South Korea, have managed to do very well despite their lack of natural resources.

Technological Know-How Knowledge is a resource, and the lack of knowledge can diminish the productivity of other resources. If knowledge is insufficient, other resources may not be used efficiently. For example, a country may be endowed with fertile land, but the land may subdivided into such small parcels that farmers cannot take advantage of economies of scale.

Or a poor country may have adequate land but may lack knowledge of irrigation and fertilization techniques. Or farmers may lack the know-how to rotate crops so as to avoid soil depletion.

Financial Institutions Another requirement for development is an adequate and trusted system of financial institutions. Investment is critical to growth. An important source of funds for investment is the savings of households and firms. If financial institutions fail to serve as intermediaries between borrowers and lenders, the lack of funds for investment becomes an obstacle to growth. Developing countries have special problems because banks are not held in high regard. At the first sign of economic problems, many depositors withdraw their funds. Since banks cannot rely on a continuous supply of deposits, they cannot make loans for extended periods. Government-imposed ceilings on the interest rates that banks can offer savers and can charge lenders also restrict the market for loans in developing countries.

Attitudes Customs and conventions can also be obstacles to development. In developed market economies resource owners tend to supply their resources where they are valued most highly, but in developing countries links to the family or clan may be the most important consideration. For example, in some cultures children are expected to remain in the father's occupation even if they are better suited to some other line of work. Family businesses may resist growth because such growth would involve hiring people from outside the family.

Infrastructure Some development economists believe that the single most important ingredient in economic development is the political organization and the administrative competence of the government. Production and exchange often rely on an infrastructure of communication and transportation networks provided by the public sector. Roads, bridges, airports, harbors, and other transportation facilities are vital to commercial activity. Reliable mail service, telephone communication, and a steady supply of water and electricity are also essential for advanced production techniques. Imagine how difficult it would be to run even a personal computer if the supply of electricity were continually interrupted. Many developing countries tend to have serious deficiencies in their infrastructures.

Entrepreneurial Ability A country can have abundant supplies of land, labor, and capital, but without entrepreneurial ability the other resources will not be combined efficiently to produce goods and services. Unless a country has a class of entrepreneurs who are able to bring together resources and take the risk of profit or loss, development may never begin. Many developing countries were until recently under colonial rule, a system of government that offered the local population little opportunity to develop entrepreneurial skills.

Government Monopolies Government officials often decide that local, private sector entrepreneurs are unable to generate the kind of economic growth the country needs. State enterprises are therefore created to do what government believes the free market cannot do. State-owned enterprises, however, have multiple objectives other than producing goods efficiently — objectives that include maximizing employment and providing jobs for friends and relatives of government officials. Economies may be less productive if people respond not to the normal market incentives but to rent-seeking opportunities arising from government advantage. Consider the following case study.

Indonesia is a country of 180 million people spread across an archipelago in the Indian Ocean. The country is rich in natural resources, including oil, yet economic development has been hampered by bureaucratic red tape and corruption. At the center is President Suharto, who has conferred monopoly privileges on his family and friends. For example, friends and relatives hold the exclusive rights to import steel, plastic, tin, cotton, industrial machinery, and other key resources.

Based on the strength of government-granted monopolies, President Suharto's children have been able to build an economic empire. One of the president's sons has an interest in more than fifty companies that make products ranging from baby food to petroleum. Another son is the sole distributor of several key petrochemicals produced by the state oil company. Most of these businesses started with lucrative government contracts, government decrees, or government licenses conferring the right to import or to produce the goods and services in question. Forms of government intervention have included (1) awarding import licenses, often to a single company; (2) imposing quotas to control imports; (3) designating "approved traders" to restrict the number of firms that may distribute a product; and (4) licensing investment to block the new entry of firms.

Because of government-imposed monopolies, the prices of products in Indonesia are higher than those prevailing on the world market. All imported plastic must flow through a company controlled by Suharto's children, an arrangement that is said to add 15 to 20 percent to the domestic price of plastics. A family monopoly on the importing of cold-rolled sheet steel — a key input in products ranging from appliances to cars — has raised the price of steel 25 to 45 percent above the world price. All tin must be purchased from a tin monopoly, an arrangement that is said to raise the domestic price of tin by 60 to 70 percent. The domestic cement industry is protected from imports, and thus domestic cement costs twice as much as cement sold on the world market.

The higher domestic prices for resources impose a burden on Indonesian consumers and also raise the prices of goods produced with these resources, making Indonesian products less competitive on world markets. The consequent reduction in exports limits the foreign exchange available for purchasing modern machinery from abroad and for making other investments that could advance the Indonesian economy.

Thus these monopolies stifle competition, increase costs for consumers, and hinder the development of an export sector that can compete on the world market. In this environment, political connections become more important than ability or expertise; free enterprise is thereby discouraged. Businesses are better off trying to develop contacts in high places than trying to produce goods and services more efficiently. In his autobiography President Suharto speaks approvingly of the industry shown by his children. That book was published by a company owned by his daughter.

Although Indonesia may be run like a family business, the political environment has at least been relatively stable since Suharto was first elected president in 1965. And political stability is an important prerequisite for economic growth in developing countries. Indonesia's per capita GNP has grown by 4.5 percent per year since 1965, more than most other countries, though the country is still classified as a low-income economy.

Sources: Steven Jones and Raphael Pura, "Indonesian Decrees Help Suharto's Friends and Relatives Prosper," *Wall Street Journal*, 24 November 1986; Barry Wain, "An Indonesian of Few Words Spills the Beans," *Wall Street Journal*, 25 March 1989.

Governments in some developing countries have difficulty pursuing policies conducive to development. Often the gains from economic development are widespread, but the beneficiaries, such as consumers, do not recognize the source of their gains. On the other hand, the losers tend to be concentrated, such as producers in a particular industry, and they know quite well the source of their losses. So the government has difficulty removing the impediments to development, because the potential losers fight reforms that might affect their livelihood while the potential winners remain largely silent.

Though most people would benefit from freer markets, some would be significantly worse off in the short run. In Egypt, for example, large food subsidies drain the government's budget, leaving little funding for development projects. Yet attempts to remove these subsidies resulted in widespread urban riots that forced the government to reverse its decision. In Peru, devaluations of the currency designed to encourage exports and discourage imports (thereby generating more foreign exchange for development) caused the overthrow of the government.

INTERNATIONAL ISSUES OF DEVELOPMENT

We have already seen that because poor countries do not generate enough savings to fund an adequate level of investment, these countries often rely on foreign capital. In this section we will look more specifically at the relationship between developing nations and the rest of the world, beginning with foreign aid.

Foreign Aid

Foreign aid is any international transfer made on concessional (that is, especially favorable) terms for the purposes of promoting economic development. Foreign aid includes both grants that need not be repaid and loans that have more favorable repayment terms than the recipient could secure in normal markets. Concessional loans have lower interest rates, longer repayment periods, or grace periods during which payments are reduced or waived. Foreign aid need not be money; it may come in the form of capital goods, technical assistance, food, and so forth.

Some foreign aid is from a specific country, such as the United States, to a specific country, such as the Philippines. Country-to-country aid is called *bilateral* assistance. Other aid is through international bodies such as the International Bank for Reconstruction and Development (IBRD), also known as the World Bank. Assistance provided by organizations that use funds from a number of countries is called *multilateral*. The World Bank was organized at the Bretton Woods Conference and established as an affiliate of the United Nations in 1946. It provides loans and grants to support activities that are viewed as prerequisites for development, such as health and education programs or basic development projects like dams, roads, and communications networks. The World Bank gets its money through contributions from member nations and through bond issues in private capital markets. Loans must be used for specifically approved projects.

The World Bank Group consists of two other lenders in addition to the International Bank for Reconstruction and Development: the International Development Association and the International Finance Corporation. Because IBRD loans are not made unless there is reasonable assurance that the borrower can service and repay the loan, some countries do not qualify for these loans. The International Development Association (IDA) was formed to provide financing to poor credit risks. IDA loans usually include terms considered more favorable to the developing countries—that is, lower interest rates and longer repayment periods. The International Finance Corporation makes loans directly to private enterprises in developing countries.

During the last four decades, the United States has provided the developing world with over $400 billion in aid. Since 1961 most foreign aid by the United States has been coordinated by the U.S. Agency for International Development (AID). This agency concentrates primarily on health, education, and agriculture, providing both technical assistance and loans. AID emphasizes long-range plans to meet the basic needs of the poor and to promote self-sufficiency. Foreign aid is a controversial, though relatively small, part of the federal budget. In 1988 official U.S. aid amounted to only 0.25 percent of U.S. GNP—a lower percentage than in many other industrial countries. The U.S. government spends much more to subsidize U.S.

farmers than it spends on aid to the billions of people in developing countries.

Does Foreign Aid Work?

There are two sources of controversy over foreign aid. First, it is unclear whether foreign aid *supplements* domestic saving, thus increasing growth, or simply *substitutes for* domestic saving, increasing consumption rather than investment. In general, foreign aid provides additional purchasing power and thus the possibility of increasing investment, capital imports, or consumption.

A second major controversy concerns the motivation of the donor. Geopolitical and commercial motives often appear more influential than humanitarian motives. Much bilateral funding, for example, is tied to purchases of goods and services from the donor nation. Assistance programs can sometimes be counterproductive. For example, in the 1950s the United States began the "Food for Peace" program, but some governments sold the food to finance poorly conceived projects. Moreover, the availability of low-priced food drove down food prices, hurting farmers in the countries that received the aid. Per capita food production in Africa has fallen since 1960.

Development aid often becomes a source of discretionary funds that benefit not the poor but their leaders. More than 90 percent of the funds distributed by AID go to governments, whose leaders assume responsibility for their distribution.

Third World Debt Problems

As we have said, economic development requires that developing countries receive capital, or investment funds, from abroad because they do not generate enough domestic saving to meet their investment needs. The oil price increases of 1973 were a major shock to the development process. Most developing countries were oil importers, so they soon experienced deficits in their trade balances. To offset these trade deficits, many countries borrowed in international capital markets. At the time their economies seemed vigorous, so foreign banks were willing to lend them money to get through the period of high oil prices.

Some developing countries, such as South Korea, immediately began adjusting to the new economics of higher oil prices, and by the late 1970s these countries were growing again at a healthy rate. But some other developing countries borrowed and borrowed as long as anyone would lend them money. Rising interest rates during the 1970s increased the cost of borrowing. Countries continued to import more than they exported and did little to address the fundamental imbalances in their economies, in part because any belt-tightening would have been politically unpopular. Their debts mounted.

The worldwide recession in the early 1980s was a crippling blow to many developing nations. The recession was followed by high real interest rates, declining commodity prices, dramatic shifts in exchange rates, and a cutoff of private lending to most developing countries. These shocks hit middle-income indebted countries hard. The value of their commodity exports was falling, making debt service more difficult and further credit unavailable. Net investment in these countries consequently fell during the 1980s, as did per capita incomes.

One major problem of developing countries has been their deteriorating trade position. They export raw materials, whose prices fluctuate wildly. In recent years the prices of raw materials have fallen as demand has softened and as substitutes have been developed for some products, such as rubber. Since the prices of manufactured imported goods did not fluctuate as much, developing countries received less money from exports than they spent on imports. To close the trade gap, developing countries tried to restrict imports. Because imported food often is critical to survival, developing countries were more likely to cut back on imports of capital goods—the very items needed to promote growth and productivity.

The key to development is how foreign borrowing is used in the domestic economy and how the developing economy adjusts to a changing world. South Korea has one of the highest levels of external debt per capita in the world, but this borrowed money has been invested and managed wisely, so South Korea has had little difficulty servicing its debt.

What if the debt were simply forgiven, as has been proposed by politicians in both developed and developing countries? Debtor nations would experience short-term benefits, but in the long run they would have difficulty attracting further capital. Once lenders realized that future loans could be canceled as well, they would be unwilling to lend or would lend only at interest rates that reflected the greater risk of default. Therefore, to avoid default, debts are usually rescheduled, and a set of conditions is placed on the debtor nation so that it will institute economic reforms. The debt repayments and government belt-tightening called for by the World Bank and the International Monetary Fund often reduce the growth of the economy and leave countries more vulnerable to economic, social, and political upheavals. Recently, however, the United States dropped its longstanding opposition to debt forgiveness and announced plans to write off about 20 percent of its loans to sixteen of the poorest African nations.

CONCLUSION

As we said at the outset, because no single theory of economic development has become widely accepted, the emphasis in this chapter has been more descriptive than theoretical. We can readily define the features that distinguish developing and industrial economies, but we are less sure how to foster growth and development. In conclusion, we point out what are perhaps some important prerequisites to development.

A stable political environment with well-defined property rights seems important. Little private sector investment will occur if the investors believe their capital might be appropriated by government or destroyed by civil unrest. Education is also key to development, maybe not so much because of its direct effect on productivity as because those who are more educated tend to be more receptive to new ideas. One might argue that one reason developing countries have not yet fully developed is the lack of sufficient entrepreneurship. Until a country "grows its own" entrepreneurs, one source of entrepreneurship is the capital and expertise that flow into the country from abroad.

Much hope has been held out for foreign aid as a spur to development. Foreign aid may have raised the standard of living in some developing countries, but it has not increased their ability to be self-supporting at that higher standard of living. Many countries are doing less of what they had done well. Their agricultural sectors have suffered. No country receiving U.S. aid in the past twenty years has moved up in status from less developed to developed. Outside aid has often insulated government officials from the troubles of their own economies.

Summary

1. Developing countries are distinguished by low levels of real GNP per capita, poor health and nutrition, high birth rates, low levels of education, and saving rates that are too low to finance sufficient investment.

2. Worker productivity is low in developing countries because the stock of physical and human capital is low, technological advances are not widely diffused throughout the economy, financial markets are not well developed, individual incentives are not appropriately structured, and government may serve the cause of the group in power rather than the public interest.

3. The secret to growth and a rising standard of living is increased productivity. Developing nations therefore try to stimulate investment, to foster education and training programs, and to provide the infrastructure necessary to support economic development. Economic development often involves government planning, foreign technical assistance, and foreign aid.

4. Increases in productivity do not occur without prior saving, but most people in developing countries live from hand to mouth and have little opportunity to save. Also, even if people had the money to save, financial institutions in developing countries are not well developed, and capital seeks a more stable investment climate elsewhere.

Questions and Problems

1. (Developing Countries) How would you explain why agricultural production in developing countries is usually low? Is the law of diminishing returns important to your answer? Why?

2. (Per Capita Real Income) What arguments are there for using real per capita GNP to compare living standards between countries? What weakness does this measure have?

3. (Developing Countries) Why is a higher survival rate a mixed blessing for developing countries? That is, what problems does a developing country face when life expectancy increases?

4. (Developing Countries and Trade) How might a country that is predominantly agricultural grow into an industrial economy? Is saving an important feature of growth? What about import substitution, whereby imported products are replaced by domestically produced goods?

5. (Growth and Foreign Exchange) How does a country that wants to import more productive capital and technology get the foreign exchange to do so?

6. (Political Stability and Development) Why is political stability a key element in a country's ability to grow? Consider the effect of political instability on capital.

7. (Growth and Fixed Exchange) In an effort to spur growth, governments in developing countries often fix the price of their currency at low levels. How might fixing the rate in this way help stimulate growth? What problems might it cause?

8. (Low Wages and Growth) Sometimes it is argued that low wages for labor are essential for growth. How is this argument dependent on exchange rates?

9. (Domestic Aggregate Demand) Why is it important to develop a strong domestic economy if the economy as a whole is to continue to grow?

10. (Heavy Industry and Growth) Many developing countries believe they must produce steel and autos in order to experience fast economic growth. Why is this policy usually misguided? Consider the issue of comparative advantage.

11. (Per Capita Real Income) How do differences in each of the following affect the usefulness of per capita real income as a means of comparing living standards across countries?
   a. Income distribution
   b. The level of nonmarket activity using resources
   c. The level of externalities generated by income production
   d. The amount of leisure consumption

12. (Developing Versus Industrial Market Economies) Compare developing and industrial market economies on the basis of each of the following general economic characteristics, and relate the differences to the process of development:
   a. Diversity of the industrial base
   b. Distribution of resource ownership
   c. Educational level of the labor force

13. (Economic Growth) Countries that need new capital and technology often institute "austerity programs" centered around increasing exports. What is the purpose of such programs and why do they often create political instability?

14. (Foreign Aid) Foreign aid, if it is to be successful in enhancing economic development, must lead to a more productive resource base. Describe some of the problems in achieving such an objective through foreign aid.

C H A P T E R   3 6

The Soviet Economy

In Chapter 2 we considered the three questions that every economic system must answer: what to produce, how to produce it, and for whom to produce it. Laws regarding resource ownership and the role of government in resource allocation determine the "rules of the game"—the incentives and constraints that guide the behavior of individual decision makers. Under pure capitalism the rules of the game include private ownership of resources and the coordination of economic activity by price signals generated by competitive markets; market coordination answers the three questions. Under a command economy the rules of the game include government ownership of resources and the allocation of resources through central planning rather than through market forces. No country exhibits either capitalism or a command economy in its pure form.

This book has focused on how market forces operate in a mainly capitalist economy such as that of the United States. Although government has an important role in the U.S. economy, other economies rely on government more extensively. Some countries carefully limit the private ownership of resources such as land and capital. Each country employs a slightly different system of resource ownership, resource allocation, and individual incentives to answer the three economic questions.

In this chapter we will examine the economic system in the Soviet Union, one of the largest economies in the world. On one Sunday in February of 1990, in more than thirty cities from Siberia to the southern republic of Georgia, hundreds of thousands of Soviets rallied for democracy, in the first nationwide protest since the Revolution of 1917. That same month the Communist party agreed to surrender its monopoly on government control. Thus the Soviet Union is currently undergoing dramatic reforms in its economic and political system and may be poised for another revolution. We will consider how the economy has operated in the past, and we will evaluate its performance. Topics discussed in this chapter include

- Planned socialism
- Market socialism
- Bureaucratic coordination
- Material balance system

- Performance of the Soviet economy
- The Soviet elite
- *Perestroika*

INTRODUCTION TO ALTERNATIVE ECONOMIC SYSTEMS

An *economic system* is the set of mechanisms and institutions that resolve the what, how, and for whom questions. Several criteria are used to distinguish among economic systems: who owns the resources, what decision-making process is used to allocate resources, and what type of incentives guide activities.

Planned and Market Socialism

Capitalism means private ownership of all resources; *communism* means state ownership of all resources, including labor. Thus under communism a worker has no claim to labor earnings. Workers provide their labor in service to the state. No countries practice communism in its pure form. The countries that are typically referred to as communist are, in fact, socialist.

Socialism means state ownership of all resources other than labor. Under **planned socialism** the state directs these resources by means of economic plans and central decision making. The state attempts to motivate labor through both philosophical and economic incentives. Under **market socialism** incentives are largely economic, planning is decentralized, and market forces are used to allocate economic resources.

Just as pure capitalism and communism represent polar cases not found in the real world, planned socialism and market socialism are not found in their pure form. The Soviet Union can best be described as a planned socialist economy, as resources other than labor are publicly owned, resource allocation is by plan, and decision making is centralized. Yugoslavia's economy is the best example of market socialism, but other countries, including China and the Soviet Union, are experimenting with combinations of socialism and capitalism. With McDonald's golden arches appearing in Moscow in 1990, can other signs of capitalism be far behind? Several once-socialist countries of Eastern Europe, including Poland, Hungary, Czechoslovakia, and Romania, have become more market oriented, and as of 1990 East Germany is negotiating a reunification with West Germany, an

Under **planned socialism** the state owns all resources other than labor and directs them by means of economic plans and central decision making.

Under **market socialism** the state owns all resources other than labor, but market forces are used to allocate most resources.

industrialized market economy. The extensive changes taking place in Eastern Europe have blurred the distinction between planned economies and market economies.

Kinds of Coordination

An economic system coordinates the activities and interaction of individuals and organizations. We distinguish between two types of coordination: market coordination and bureaucratic coordination. In *market coordination* the relation between buyers and sellers is horizontal; that is, from a legal perspective, buyers and sellers are on equal footing. Both are motivated by self-interest. Their self-interests are coordinated by means of agreed-upon prices. Transactions occur because each party hopes to benefit, not because one side has the power to coerce the other. Exchange is voluntary.

In *bureaucratic coordination* control is exercised through an administrative hierarchy. The coordinating relation is vertical, from the higher level of the organization to the lower level. Administrative pressure and legal restraints force individuals and organizations to accept orders and restrictions from above. The transactions among levels in the bureau need not involve money, but when they do, the lower level of the organization depends on the higher level for its finances. The decision makers in the bureaucracy control the allocation of resources as well as the distribution of income.

Governments in planned economies rely primarily on *central plans* rather than on market signals to answer the three economic questions. Bureaucratic coordination rather than market coordination determines the method of producing goods and services. Decisions about how to produce goods and services are based on historical experience and technological know-how. To ensure that the directions of the central planners are followed, the government relies on persuasion, coercion, and a mix of economic incentives.

Why would a country want a planned economy? The leaders can establish whatever priorities they believe are best for the economy and can pursue these objectives using the full authority of the state. The state can ensure that savings are sufficient to promote the capital formation required for growth and development. The problem of unemployment can be solved by creating enough enterprises to hire all those seeking employment.

Communism, Socialism, and the Soviet Union

Adam Smith provided the theoretical underpinnings and intellectual justification for capitalism, and Karl Marx provided the same support for socialism, which he considered a stage in economic development on the way to communism. Under communism the means of production are owned by the state, and the income that results from production is shared by all citizens according to their needs.

According to communists, capitalism is doomed because of an alleged long-run tendency toward declining profits, increased unemployment, subsistence wages, and successively more severe economic crises. Communists believe that modern industrial economies will eventually achieve communism, but only after a long period of socialism. During the socialist stage of evolution, the state will own and operate the means of production, distribution, and exchange, but workers will have a right to their labor and each person will be paid based on the work performed. After the economy's productive capacity is built up enough to provide for everyone, the state will wither away and pure communism will arise. *People will work according to their ability and receive according to their needs.* Thus socialism is a transitory economic system, a step on the road to communism.

The writings of Marx inspired the Russian Revolution of 1917, which overthrew the czarist form of government. The Soviet Union was formed in 1922, and since 1928 it has been guided by a series of one-year and five-year plans. The economy is based on "socialist ownership of the means of production." With limited exception, the central government owns all the land, natural resources, and capital goods, as well as nearly all businesses and most urban housing. Virtually all the industrial sector is owned by the state.

The Soviet Union is a country of about 280 million people. Its land area is almost two and a half times that of the United States and sixty times that of Japan. When a family in Moscow sits down to dinner, fellow citizens of the Soviet Far East are greeting the next day's sunrise. The Soviet Union has the world's longest frontier, bordering a dozen countries and a dozen seas of three oceans. Ethnically the Soviet Union is very diverse; there are Russians, Ukranians, Uzbeks, Byelorussians, and many more groups. Since the current borders were established as recently as the end of World War II, ethnic feelings are still very powerful among the fifteen republics, and some of the republics are seeking independence. Given the economic and political reforms now under way in the Soviet Union, who knows what that country will look like in the future.

Under a constitution adopted in 1977, the political foundation of the country is the *Soviets*, or Councils, of People's Deputies. The Communist party is, according to the Soviet constitution, "the leading and guiding force of the Soviet society and the nucleus of its political system." In 1990 the Communist party agreed to surrender its historic monopoly on power and proposed constitutional changes that would create a Western-style presidency and cabinet system of government.

Central Planning

Until quite recently leaders of the Soviet Communist party believed that central planning could direct resources better than could market coordination. Party leaders establish priorities and present them to the State Planning Agency, called *Gosplan*, which develops long-term economic and social plans and generally supervises their execution. Regional Gosplans take the plans and provide directives to regional ministries, which formulate orders to individual plant directors. Included in these orders governing the production of intermediate and final goods are the kinds and amounts of commodities that the industrial plant should produce, the wages to be paid,

Karl Marx
(1818–1883)

On the whole, economics is not a profession from which one expects larger-than-life political figures to emerge. But there is one famous political economist whose name is synonymous with a political movement that governs more than half the world's population. His name, of course, is Karl Marx.

Marx was a political economist in the classical British tradition of David Ricardo (1772–1823), from whom he borrowed a number of key ideas. But Marx was also a German philosopher, influenced especially by the writings of G. W. F. Hegel (1770–1831). In Hegel's scheme of things, history moved according to predictable stages through a clash of contradictory opposites, what he called the process of *dialectic*. Marx adapted this philosophy to economics and sought to map out the stages of economic history and to analyze the "internal contradictions" of capitalism.

Capitalism emerged from the contradictions of an earlier stage of history—the feudalism of the Middle Ages. In contrast to feudalism, capitalism is a dynamic system that unleashed productive forces never before seen in history. But for Marx, the system also contained the seeds of its own destruction. Whereas Adam Smith looked at the economy of market prices and saw an invisible hand, Marx looked at the price system and saw chaos. Because capitalists mainly produce goods to be sold to others (rather than producing for their own immediate uses), there was, according to Marx, no effective way of coordinating production and use. This problem would lead, he believed, to ever-deepening crises (depressions) followed by consolidation of capital ownership into fewer and fewer hands. Eventually, he predicted, exploited workers would rise up against the capitalists and take over the system the capitalists had created. The result would be communism, the final stage of history. About the details of this stage Marx was almost completely silent, preserving the mystery which appears to be the soul of prophecy.

Karl Marx was a dark, intense, brooding figure. Born into an upper-class family in Trier, Germany, the young Marx studied philosophy at the University of Bonn. Unable to find an academic job, he edited a number of radical journals, fleeing from country to country as the authorities tried to suppress him. Eventually he settled in London with his wife, Jennie, the daughter of a German nobleman. There he lived in dire poverty, often dependent on handouts from his friend and coauthor Friedrich Engels (1820–1895). Marx toiled every day from 10 in the morning until 7 in the evening, always in the same seat in the library of the British Museum, to produce his prodigious four-volume tome *Capital*, one of the most famous and important books in the history of ideas.

Richard Langlois

the prices to be charged, and the profit to be earned. Thus Gosplan personnel and others involved in the planning process translate the priorities established by the Communist party into specific directives for each enterprise.

Individual plants are operated by directors, or plant managers, who are appointed by the government with the approval of the local Communist party. Although they are far from entrepreneurs, plant directors have some discretion over how to combine resources to meet the output objectives established by the planning hierarchy. As we will see later, often plant directors must be creative to meet their production goals.

Household income in the Soviet Union consists almost exclusively of labor earnings: wages and salaries paid to employees of government enterprises and bureaus. Since the state owns nearly all resources except labor, any return on resources other than labor is income from state-owned enterprises. This nonlabor income is either turned over to the state to finance government activities or kept by the enterprise to support expansion. The state, not the enterprise, determines the share of profits the enterprise retains.

Supply and Demand

*The **material balance system** was designed by central planners to ensure a balance of supply and demand for important types of industrial output.*

How can central planning coordinate hundreds of different resources in thousands of different enterprises? The system of central planning developed in the Soviet Union during the 1930s is called the **material balance system**. Under this system central authorities control only the most important industrial output, leaving decisions about less important output to the lower levels of the planning hierarchy. For example, Gosplan in Moscow plans the production of steel, energy, motor vehicles, and machine tools. Lower-level planners guide the production of shoes, clothing, and household services. Items of still lower priority are not planned for at all and may be left to market coordination.

The planning machinery must achieve a material balance of supply and demand. For example, Gosplan sets a target for steel production based on past experience and technological know-how. Suppose the economy's productive capacity is 100 million tons of steel per year. The Soviet Union has already agreed to export 20 million tons, leaving a possible domestic supply of 80 million tons. Based on past experience, Gosplan knows how much steel will be demanded to meet output targets for motor vehicles, machine tools, construction, and other uses. Gosplan selects a target for steel production that will equate the quantity of steel supplied with the anticipated quantity demanded, thereby achieving a *material balance* through bureaucratic coordination rather than through market coordination. Gosplan follows the same approach for each other critical commodity, as well as for labor, machinery, and finance.

The five-year plan for the economy is actually the result of bargaining among planning elements: Gosplan, Communist party officials, the various ministries, and the plant managers. After much haggling up and down the hierarchy, a final plan is prepared and submitted to the central government for approval. Once approved, the economic plan becomes law, determining how many employees each enterprise can hire, what resources it can expect through supply channels, and how much bank credit will be available. The plan is broken down by week, month, quarter, and year.

Capitalist economies equate quantity supplied with quantity demanded through the invisible hand of market coordination; centrally planned economies use the visible hand of bureaucratic coordination. If supply and demand are not in balance, something has to give. In capitalist systems what gives is the price. In centrally planned economies what usually gives is the plan itself. A common problem in centrally planned economies is that actual production often falls short of planned production. If the quantity supplied falls below the planned amount, Gosplan reduces the quantity each sector receives. These are not across-the-board cuts. Critical sectors such as heavy industry and the military are cut the least, and lower-priority sectors such as consumer products are cut the most. When supplies are low, Soviet consumers often pay a higher "price" in terms of the time spent waiting in line.

The Soviet approach to central planning is not the only alternative to capitalism but rather one of many. The Chinese, for example, have used sample surveys to gauge public sentiment on policy questions. A study of economic planning in different countries and in different periods would uncover much diversity.

Labor Markets

Under socialism the state owns all resources other than labor. Except during times of war, most Soviet workers have some discretion in their choice of occupation and place of work. Most workers are hired in an independent labor market. The manager of an enterprise also has some discretion over whom to hire.

Central planners set relative wages to reflect market realities, the plans of the state, and the nature of the work performed—its complexity, the responsibility involved, and other relevant features. Other things constant, those involved in more arduous or unhealthy work—coal miners and metalworkers, for example—earn more than other industrial workers do. Thus there is a Soviet labor market, and wage differentials are not very different from those observed in capitalist markets. As a way of providing production incentives, the state requires that many industrial workers be paid by the amount produced rather than by the hour. The 1989 strike by Siberian coal miners points up the labor discontent even in a system theoretically controlled by the workers.

Having a choice of occupations allows workers to select jobs that more nearly suit their preferences, and this greater discretion enhances worker productivity. The government, however, has been concerned about the high job turnover that has resulted from worker discretion in employment and has attempted to restrict mobility in various ways. Wages, bonuses, housing availability, and other amenities have been tied explicitly to length of employment in a particular job. University graduates and others with specialized training receive administrative assignments to particular jobs and are expected to hold these jobs for several years. More generally, movement into large cities is restricted through a system of internal passports. Housing availability is also a limiting factor.

PERFORMANCE OF THE SOVIET ECONOMY

In 1986 Mikhail Gorbachev addressed the Communist Party Congress in a six-hour speech in which he called the economy "a mess." He identified three reasons for the stagnation of the Soviet economy: (1) the bureaucracy had become so overburdened that it could no longer administer the economy, (2) technical progress was too slow, and (3) so many public officials were using their office for personal gain that corruption was a national scandal. In this section we will take a closer look at how the Soviet economy has performed, and in the process you should come to understand better the strengths and weaknesses of central planning.

Economic Growth

How has the Soviet system performed based on the standards typically used to evaluate an economic system? The Communist party began with a relatively undeveloped agrarian economy and created one of the world's largest economies. Central planning mobilized resources by forcing a high rate of capital formation and by shifting labor from agriculture to industry.

After adjusting official Soviet figures, experts said the Soviet economy grew at a rate of about 5 percent per year between 1930 and 1980, a faster rate than that of any industrial economy except Japan. The growth rate in the United States was only 3 percent. This impressive Soviet growth rate appeared to lend credibility to the economy and its leadership. Any inefficiencies arising from central planning were not evident during these decades, in part because of the economy's access to cheap and plentiful resources, particularly labor. The Soviet Union, like other developing countries, showed dramatic growth because millions of workers were moving from the rural agricultural sector, where productivity was low, into the urban industrial sector, where productivity was high. The government speeded up the transition and forced the necessary capital formation. Once all available workers had shifted out of agriculture, however, the era of abundant labor ended.

During the 1981–1985 planning period, production increased at an annual rate of only 2 percent—only half the amount called for in the Eleventh Five-Year Plan. According to official estimates, economic growth exceeded 2 percent in 1986 but fell below that figure during the next three years. In 1990, Soviet economists acknowledged privately that Soviet output actually fell by 2 to 4 percent in each of the preceding four years.[1] The drop in the growth rate of the Soviet economy has been attributed to a shortage of labor, poor labor morale, little government credibility, and some loss of ideological fervor at the top. Also, the allocation of an estimated 14 to 16 percent of the Soviet national income to military expenditures (compared to about 5 percent in the United States) drew resources away from capital formation. Except for military and space applications, the Soviet Union lagged behind other industrial countries in the development of technology, especially computers and software, and this lag contributed to the relative slowdown.

Prices, Shortages, and Consumer Satisfaction

As we've said, most prices in the Soviet system are determined not by market forces but by central planners. As a result, consumers have little to say about what gets produced. Once set, prices tend to be inflexible (for example, the price of a cabbage slicer is stamped on the metal). In the spirit of equity, Soviet planners price many consumer goods below the market-clearing level, so shortages (or "interruptions" in supply, as the Soviets call them) are common. Rents have not changed since 1928. Until the recently instituted price increases, the price of bread had not changed since 1954 and, by 1990, amounted to only 7 percent of its production cost. Meat prices had not changed since 1962.

The planning process may call for a certain amount of soap to be produced per period and sold for a particular price. In Exhibit 1, the amount produced is identified as Q. The quantity supplied depends not on how much consumers would be willing to pay but on the priority that soap holds in the larger scheme of the economy. Thus the supply of soap is fixed. Note that a price of P would equate quantity demanded and quantity supplied. In fact, the price of soap and many other consumer goods is established by bureaucrats, not by markets. Because prices, once set, tend to be inflexible, they are often below the market-clearing level. In Exhibit 1, a price of P' results in a shortage of soap.

Necessities such as housing, electricity, and basic food are cheap, but because their prices are set below the market-clearing level, they are also in short supply. Food is rationed in most of the fifteen Soviet republics. Evidence of shortages includes long waiting lines at retail stores, empty store shelves, and the "tips" shop operators expect for supplying scarce consumer goods. Some scarce goods are diverted to the black market, where they sell at a premium over set prices. Shortages of medicine, soap, tooth-brushes, toothpaste, needles, thread, and diapers are especially common. Probably the scarcest good in the Soviet Union over the years has been

---

[1] Gerald F. Seib and Peter Gumbel, "Despite Arms Progress, New Tensions Mark U.S.-Soviet Relations," *Wall Street Journal*, 29 May 1990.

EXHIBIT 1   SUPPLY AND DEMAND FOR SOAP

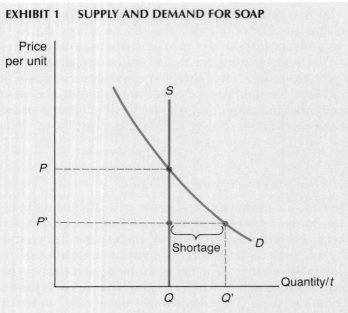

Under central planning, the amount of soap produced is *Q*. A price of *P* would equate quantities supplied and demanded. However, the price is usually held below the market-clearing level. A price of *P'* results in a shortage.

housing. Couples may wait years for a cooperative apartment. Quality is also a problem because producers try to meet production quotas rather than satisfy consumers. Plant managers do not score extra bureaucratic points by producing a garment that is in style and in a popular size. Tales of shoddy products abound. Thus *necessities are scarce because the price is set below the market-clearing level.*

Soviet officials try to discourage the consumption of luxuries such as automobiles by allocating few of the economy's resources to their production. For example, Soviet automobiles are of poor quality by our standards. But because so few automobiles are produced, the prices are relatively high, and waiting lists are long. For the typical Soviet worker, the purchase of a new Lada — the Soviet version of a 1965 Fiat — requires seven years' wages and a five-year wait. Even used cars are scarce. A four-year-old Lada cost about $15,000 in 1990 — one and a half times the typical yearly household income. In the United States this would be comparable to a four-year-old Ford Escort's selling for $50,000.

A pair of Soviet-made pantyhose costs about $10; a 21-inch color television costs about $1000. On the black market, Japanese VCRs were reportedly selling for up to $2500, and blank videotapes for $67. With such strong demand, the Soviets began producing their own brand of VCR, the Electronika VM, which sells for $875 but which has no recording function (evidently because of the security problems posed by such a function). There are few tape rental stores, and the pickings of titles are slim — mostly reruns from Soviet TV. Despite the poor choice of movies and limited capability of the VCR, buyers face a ten-year waiting list for the Electronika VM, according to press reports.[2] Many consumer products taken for granted in the West are not produced at all in the Soviet Union. For example, Soviet industry makes no dishwashers or toasters, and although hair dryers are supposedly produced, none can be found for sale.

Compared to what they sell for in the United States, necessities are relatively cheap and luxuries relatively expensive in the Soviet Union. But shortages of both types of goods often occur because prices are set below the market-clearing level. The market system is not an expression of the "anarchy of production," as Soviets have claimed, but a sophisticated feedback mechanism that offers producers a detailed picture of consumer demand. Central planning without feedback results in allocative inefficiency. And selling products for less than the cost of production requires huge government subsidies. The Soviet government ran up deficits during the 1980s that increased from 2.5 percent of GNP in 1985 to 13.1 percent in 1989; the latter deficit was larger than the U.S. federal deficit both in absolute amount and as a percentage of GNP. Because there is no well-developed market for government bonds, the deficits have been financed with a monetary expansion, which has led to greater inflationary pressure.

What would happen if prices were allowed to seek the market-clearing level? Such an experiment was performed by Poland in early 1990; it is discussed in the following case study.

CASE STUDY

Prices Get Real in Poland

For over four decades, most prices in Poland reflected the decisions of central planners rather than the forces of market competition. Food production was heavily subsidized by the state. Because prices were artificially low, lines were long and store shelves were bare. On January 1, 1990, the newly elected Solidarity government began dismantling central planning and made a leap of faith into a market economy. Food subsidies ended.

During the first month of the new program, shopkeepers responded to their new freedom to set prices. The good news was that, for the first time in decades, prized goods appeared in abundance on store shelves and there were no lines. Meats crowded the butchers' shelves; cheesecakes adorned display cases; bananas bunched in abundance. The bad news was that inflation jumped to 67 percent during the first month, and the high prices scared off consumers. With the average Polish family spending over half its income on food, few could afford the higher prices. Since goods weren't selling, meat went bad, cheesecakes aged, and bananas turned brown.

With store prices so high, a black market of sorts developed. Farmers did their own butchering, selling crude cuts of uninspected meats from the

---

2 "VCRs Are in a Sorry State in the U.S.S.R.," *Hartford Courant*, 6 August 1986.

backs of their trucks. And with stores doing little business, Polish consumers witnessed an event seldom seen in four decades of central planning: a sale. The country's leading department store had a 30-percent-off sale.

Storekeepers had believed that the market system meant they could charge whatever prices they wanted. They soon discovered that they could charge only what consumers were willing to pay. Thus, after decades of price suppression, prices in Poland, in fits and starts, were seeking their equilibrium level.

Sources: Marilyn Greene, "Family Hopes Results Worth the Sacrifice," USA Today, 20 February 1990; Barry Newman, "Poles Find the Freeing of the Economy Lifts Supplies—and Prices," Wall Street Journal, 21 February 1990.

Problems with Agriculture

Most agricultural output in the Soviet Union is produced on state-owned farms or on cooperatives that are closely controlled by the state. The remainder is produced on privately owned farms or by cooperative members who are permitted to farm private plots in their spare time. Those who work on cooperative farms do not receive wages but share in the income of the farm. State policy, however, has been aimed at keeping farm prices low, which has kept farm incomes low as well.

In the 1930s Joseph Stalin pursued a policy of rapid industrialization and the collectivization of farms. Collective farms have been a problem ever since peasants were forced to join them. Soviet planners tried to organize farming like other industries, but collectivization initially contributed to a famine, killing millions of peasants. A farm is not a factory that can be shut down for the holidays. The care and feeding of plants and animals is no less urgent on weekends. Perhaps it is no coincidence that farms in most economic systems tend to be owner-operated. Even the Chinese recognize that farming is not like other industries; they have a system of incentives that rewards farmers who are especially productive.

Bureaucracies abound in the Soviet Union, and the agricultural sector has its share. For example, the details of how teams of farmers are to be rewarded are worked out by the Union-Republic Council of Ministers, the Ministry of Agriculture, the Ministry of Fruit and Vegetables, the State Committee for the Supply of Production Equipment to Agriculture, the Ministry of Procurement, the State Committee on Labor and Social Questions, and the All-Union Central Council of Trade Unions. Get the idea? In the Ministry of Agriculture alone there are three million bureaucrats—more than in the entire U.S. government.

As in the United States, agriculture in the Soviet Union has become increasingly mechanized over the last few decades and has therefore come to rely on inputs from the industrial sector. But the marriage of industry and agriculture has not been a happy one. For example, industry produces huge tractors, but without the support equipment (threshers, reapers, and the like) required to take advantage of their size. Tractors are left to rust in the freezing winters because there are no sheds to store them in. Farm machinery is scrapped at a much higher rate in the Soviet Union than elsewhere because spare parts and trained mechanics are both scarce. Between 1976 and 1980, industry provided 1.8 million tractors to the agricultural sector, but the stock of tractors rose by only about 250,000. During that same period, farmers received 539,000 grain combines, but the stock of combines rose by only 33,000.[3]

Enough mechanics are trained, but Soviet planners have difficulty keeping them down on the farm because they are paid much more in urban areas. Despite the infusion of new equipment, about one-fourth of some Soviet crops rot in the field because of equipment shortages. Ironically, farm products are more widely available in major cities, such as Moscow, than in rural areas where the food is grown. Two million rural residents travel to Moscow each day to shop. Pravda recently reported that one rural region supplies Moscow with 38,000 tons of meat per year—and then residents of that same rural area travel to Moscow to buy half of it back.

In summary, poor morale, low farm prices, unreliable equipment, and interrupted supplies of key inputs combine to dampen work incentives on the farm and reduce farm productivity. The Soviet Union has undergone a complete change: once the world's largest grain exporter, it is now the world's largest grain importer. Industrial production also suffers from the limitations of central planning, as you will see in the following case study.

CASE STUDY

The Informal Economy

There are really three economies in the Soviet Union: (1) the official economy, where things are done by the book, according to orders from on high; (2) the so-called second economy, the Soviet version of the underground economy, where individuals buy and sell to promote their self-interest; and (3) the "informal economy," where Soviet managers pursue official objectives by skirting the official rules. In this case study we will examine the informal economy.

The resource distribution system in the Soviet economy is not the well-oiled operation envisioned by the central planners. For example, enterprises often fail to receive critical resources and are sent resources they can't use. Because of the chronic problem of inadequate and late resources, factory workers often have little to do. The pace of the work is therefore uneven, with workers idle for days, then frantically trying to meet the month's production quota once the required supplies or replacement parts arrive.

To alleviate these problems, managers frequently barter with other enterprises for critical resources or buy resources on the black market. More importantly, rather than depend on a sporadic supply system, the enterprise frequently manufactures its own key replacement parts. For example, in the Soviet Union only about 4 percent of standard metalworking products are

---

[3] These examples are found in Gale Johnson and K. M. Brooks, *Prospects for Soviet Agriculture in the 1980s* (Bloomington, IN: Indiana University Press, 1984).

produced in specialized plants. The rest are produced by the enterprises that use the products. In contrast, in the United States 70 percent of these products are produced by specialized firms.

Thus Soviet enterprises try to reduce the risk of interrupted supplies by bringing activities inside the firm. Plants of all sizes often design and produce equipment for their own use. An automobile plant may make its own robots, a shoe plant may make its own machines and glue, and a computer center may develop its own computer programs. If an enterprise wants to expand, it may use its own workers to put up a new building. Some enterprises have even built their own power generators in areas where electricity is frequently interrupted.

Self-reliance is not confined to obtaining resources. Because many consumer goods are so scarce, enterprises also produce goods and services for employee consumption. That is, many industrial firms raise crops and livestock on the side, much as a U.S. firm might provide day care facilities for its employees with small children. The resources needed to produce these other products are siphoned from official channels, acquired through barter, or purchased on the black market.

Thus self-service is the implicit motto of Soviet enterprise. Because the transaction costs of relying on the bureaucratic hierarchy as a source of supply are high, more and more activities are brought inside the enterprise. The informal economy reflects abundant entrepreneurial spirit on the part of plant directors. Rather than serving as perfunctory underlings who carry out orders in the chain of command, they try to satisfy their production quotas while providing employees with goods and services that are hard to get on the market.

But this intramural activity violates one of the basic axioms of efficiency: the division of labor. As an individual enterprise expands into more and more activities, workers are spread thinner, so they perform all jobs less efficiently. Each worker becomes a jack-of-all-trades but a master of none. The plant director's attention span is strained, and the coordination of resources becomes a problem. Many studies in the Soviet Union show that in-house production costs more than production in specialized plants. Soviet planning officials are understandably concerned about the loss of production as enterprises seek self-sufficiency.

Source: V. Kontorovich and V. Shlapentokh, "Soviet Industry Grows Its Own Potatoes," *Wall Street Journal*, 11 January 1985.

Secondary Effects of Socialist Ownership of Property

Because in a socialist economy everyone owns state property, nobody in particular owns it. Since those who allocate and use resources do not immediately benefit from that use, resources are sometimes wasted. For example, an estimated 10 percent of all fertilizer is lost on its way from factory to fields because it is shipped in unsuitable freight cars or is improperly stored. At six hundred railroad stations, fertilizer is just dumped on the open ground. Also, about one-third of the harvest reportedly deteriorates before it reaches consumers, and some food is allowed to spoil in stores.[4]

Soviet workers are said to have little regard for equipment that belongs to the state. New trucks or tractors may be dismantled for parts, or working equipment may be sent to a scrap plant. Pilfering of state-owned property is a high art and a favorite sport. The 1986 Program of the Communist Party called for "the adoption of all measures for the defense of socialist property." The political elite has been trying to persuade Soviet citizens to regard themselves as the "masters of their enterprise."

In contrast, the Soviet people take better care of their personal property than do people in capitalist countries. For example, personal cars run for twenty years or more on average—twice the official projected automobile life. The incentives of private ownership are also evident on the farm. Each farmer on the collective is allowed a small plot of land on which to cultivate crops for personal consumption or for sale at prices determined in unregulated markets. Income earned by farmers from their private plots is taxed at rates that vary inversely with what the farmer produces on the collective. The tax rate is low, but it increases sharply if the farmer fails to achieve the established workday quota on the collective. This tax system is an attempt to ensure that farmers do not neglect their collective work in favor of their private plots. Despite the small size of the plots and the taxes on earnings from these plots, farmers produce a disproportionate share of output on private plots. Privately farmed plots constitute only 3 percent of the Soviet Union's farmland, but they supply 30 percent of all meat, milk, and vegetables and 60 percent of all potatoes.

The Soviet Union lacks an adequate refrigeration and transportation system for distributing fruits and vegetables throughout the country. This vacuum creates an opportunity for enterprising farmers in the warmer regions to fill suitcases with fresh produce and fly north on Aeroflot to Moscow or Kiev, where this produce is sold at public markets. Heavily subsidized airline passenger service makes this possible. In urban areas many mechanics, carpenters, plumbers, and tailors moonlight in the second economy, accounting for a substantial share of the service sector. Everyday life would grind to a halt without these free spirits.

Innovation

Despite the emphasis on technical progress in Soviet planning, the technological gap between the Soviet Union and major capitalist countries is great and has not diminished in the last two decades. To supplement their own technological developments, Soviet officials buy, borrow, or steal technology from capitalist countries. Yet *the problem in the Soviet Union is not so much that the latest technology is not available as that it is not diffused throughout*

---

[4] These examples are provided in Vladimir Shlapentokh, "Soviet Ideas on Private Property Invite Abuse of Capital Stock," *Wall Street Journal*, 20 March 1986.

the economy. The reluctance of plant managers to develop or employ new technologies is described in the following case study.

No major U.S. corporation could compete without computers to facilitate the coordination of resources in the firm by providing data about payroll, inventories, production, sales, and other details. Computers are especially important for an economy in which resources are coordinated through a hierarchy rather than through markets. Thus computers were considered to be a natural tool of the Soviet Union's centrally planned economy. The Ninth Five-Year Plan, introduced in 1971, established the goal of connecting all levels of the Soviet economy through a computer network. The various ministers could then serve as field marshals, redeploying resources as needed. This objective has received continued support in subsequent five-year plans. But scientific breakthroughs are not usually achieved on schedules established in five-year plans.

Although the Soviet Union has acquired Western computer technology, the Soviets have had difficulty producing modern computers and have not exploited the computer's tremendous capabilities. Their most sophisticated memory chip can hold only 256,000 bits of data, whereas U.S. and Japanese chips can hold over a million bits. The number of personal computers produced in the Soviet Union in 1987 was estimated to be only 40,000, compared to a U.S. output of nearly 5 million that year. Recently, only about one-third of plants with at least five hundred employees had mainframe computers, compared with 100 percent coverage in the United States. Fewer than 10 percent of smaller firms use computers. The computers now commonly in use are copies of mainframes that IBM stopped making more than a decade ago.

Another problem is getting plant directors to accept and use computers. This problem springs from the role that information plays in the Soviet system. Central planners often present enterprises with unrealistic production targets, creating chronic shortages of resources. When plant directors fall short of their targets, they tend to exaggerate the results they did get. If by some chance they exceed targets, they tend to downplay the results so that their future targets will not be raised.

Plant directors also hoard key resources to avoid production delays. These excess inventories must be concealed from the higher-ups; otherwise the supply of resources would be reduced. Because Soviet managers frequently acquire resources through barter or on the black market, they need slush funds to support these transactions. Supervisors may therefore pad the payroll to provide the necessary funds.

Information is a source of power. Plant directors are understandably wary of computers because an accurate accounting system would put this power in the hands of superiors who survey plant directors' performance. The director with anything to hide would be tripped up by a computer disseminating accurate reports to the higher authorities. Information that fell into the wrong hands could prove incriminating. Because plant directors have an incentive to distort information, they view computers as tools of the hierarchy rather than as management tools.

The plant manager who does want to develop a computer system faces many obstacles. Any enterprise fortunate enough to acquire a computer must confront a bureaucratic maze to get the computer into operation. The training and abilities of the state employees who service and repair computers leave much to be desired. Once installed, computers break down more frequently than would be accepted in the West. Moreover, Soviet telecommunications is of such poor quality that electronic data transmission is slow, and computer links are often interrupted, creating severe problems for computer operations.

Central planners have provided plant directors with incentives to use computers, but these incentives can have perverse effects. Some computer executives, for example, receive bonuses for the number of tasks performed by the computer system and the number of subsystems operating. Consequently, rather than developing a unified accounting system, managers introduce many subsystems, and the result is cumulative inefficiency.

Reaching the goal of a computerized Soviet economy seems impossible in the near future. Plant managers appear reluctant to accept the rope they think could be used to hang them. Furthermore, growth in the use of computers, particularly personal computers, has been hampered by the state control of information. In a country where typewriters and duplicating machines are considered potential tools of sedition, a word processor and printer pose a threat to the leadership. Nearly all computers in the Soviet Union are in state-run institutions and are closely guarded.

Sources: Daniel Seligman, "The Great Soviet Computer Screw-Up," *Fortune* (8 July 1985): 32–36; "Soviet Technology," *Business Week* (7 November 1988): 68–86.

THE DISTRIBUTION OF INCOME AND CONSUMPTION

Another way of evaluating the performance of an economic system is in terms of equity. How evenly are the fruits of production distributed among Soviet households?

Income Distribution

The average household income in the Soviet Union in 1990 was the equivalent of about $10,000. Wage and salary inequality across households in the Soviet Union is roughly comparable to the inequality found in other industrial countries. Income is more evenly distributed in the U.S.S.R. than in the United States, although the difference is not substantial. Most Soviet income consists of wages and salaries, and tax rates on this income tend to be only mildly progressive, rising to a maximum of 13 percent. But money income has less significance in the Soviet Union because many goods are in short supply and cannot be purchased without waiting in line or having an inside connection. The Soviet Union has a well-defined class structure, and not all people are created equal, as we will see next.

Soviet Elite

The *intelligentsia* forms the artistic, social, technical, and political vanguard of the Soviet elite. Socialist dogma called for a "withering away" of the state as a classless communism emerged, but Stalin held that in the meantime special rewards were required to call forth productive capabilities. Thus Stalin fostered social stratification, and the Soviet elite has flourished.

Although there are no exact definitions or reliable statistics, the Soviet ruling class, or *nomenklatura*, has about 250,000 members. Counting family members, this ruling class makes up less than 1 percent of the population. Exhibit 2 gives an idea of how the elite are distributed across occupations. Note that 7.5 percent of the elite are enterprise directors (but only a fraction of directors qualify for elite status). Salaries of the elite in academic and research positions average about four times that of the average worker. As we will see, rank has its privilege not only in pay but in virtually every aspect of Soviet life.

Consumption Ordinary citizens of Moscow might spend hours in line trying to buy meat, but members of the Soviet elite can shop at the famous Kremlin canteen. This shop, which stocks the best food available at the lowest prices anywhere, accepts payment only in *kemliovka* coupons. Members of the *nomenklatura* receive part of their pay in *kemliovka*. The Central Committee building in Moscow has three dining rooms on different floors, each serving a different category of official. The food is said to be as good as in the best restaurants, but the prices are considerably lower. The most select restaurant has a military guard at the door.

EXHIBIT 2
ELITE PERSONNEL BY OCCUPATION DURING THE 1970s

Occupation	Percentage
Enterprise directors	7.5
Intelligentsia (academicians, artists, editors)	17.6
Government and trade union officials	26.5
Military, police, and diplomats	13.2
Communist party officials	35.2

Source: Based on data presented in Abram Bergson, "Income Inequality Under Soviet Socialism," *Journal of Economic Literature* 22 (September 1984), Table 10.

Housing Housing is heavily subsidized and in short supply, and it is allocated by bureaus rather than by markets. The best housing goes to top Communist party officials, who until recently were entitled to second homes—plush country retreats called *dachas*. Housing distinctions by rank can be observed in a research complex, where a Soviet academy member—the cream of academe—merits a separate cottage. In that same complex, a family of four headed by a professor rates only 604 square feet of living space—about the area of an efficiency apartment. A service worker's family has to make do with only half that space.[5]

Social Mobility

In the United States wealth and power are passed from one generation to another through genes, education, and inheritance. The same is true in the Soviet Union. Since most resources are owned by the state, private wealth is limited primarily to savings deposits, government bonds, and other personal possessions. Interest rates in the Soviet Union are fixed at a low level, but there is little or no inheritance tax, so large sums can be passed along to the next generation.

How does one join the elite? The surest way is to be born into it. Children of the elite have a much better chance of being accepted into the right schools. Young men from elite families are routinely appointed to *nomenklatura* positions, and their sisters marry those who hold such positions. (Soviet women from elite families usually do not seek employment.) For an outsider, the best route in the past has been to join the Communist party and capture someone's attention. *Perestroika*, or Soviet economic reform, may change this, but the jury is still out.

Tales of bribery and abuse of official positions are so pervasive that Gorbachev felt obliged to express concern about the problem in his 1986 speech to the Communist Party Congress. Interviews with thousands of emigrants from the Soviet Union suggest the widespread use of bribery to obtain first jobs and university positions. When bureaucratic coordination replaces market coordination, some nonmarket system of rationing must be used to deal with excess demand. Bribes replace long lines and may actually be more efficient, though not necessarily more equitable.

SOVIET REFORMS

The word *reform* means different things in different countries. In the United States reform often implies greater bureaucratic intervention because of a perceived market failure, such as reform of the way hazardous waste is handled or reform of corporate takeover activity. In the Soviet Union,

---

[5] This example is found in Abram Bergson, "Income Inequality Under Soviet Socialism," *Journal of Economic Literature*, 22 (September 1984): 1059.

however, reform is more a reaction to bureaucratic failure, and the solution is to introduce more market mechanisms into the resource allocation system.

Economic reform in the Soviet Union has had a checkered past. Most economic reforms have been aimed at changing policies adopted during the Stalin era. First introduced by Nikita Khrushchev in 1957, economic reform was halted by Leonid Brezhnev in 1965, revived by Yuri Andropov in 1983, and slowed by Konstantin Chernenko in 1984. Gorbachev introduced major reforms in 1986 with *glasnost* and *perestroika*. **Glasnost** refers to the new openness in Soviet affairs: a greater willingness to let the Soviet people and the rest of the world know what's going on in the Soviet Union. Because of *glasnost*, Soviet intellectuals have more freedom to think, to speak, and to write.

Perestroika is a restructuring of the economy to promote more decentralization, less bureaucracy, and greater individual incentives. *Perestroika* has been resisted by many bureaucrats who could lose their jobs. Thus far *perestroika* has not resulted in greater availability, better quality, or more variety in consumer goods. *Perestroika* has only heightened the expectations of Soviet consumers. Ironically, *glasnost*, the greater openness, has made people more aware of nationwide shortages of consumer goods. Because of *glasnost*, consumer shortages are now publicly admitted, and public grievances are being aired for the first time since the Russian Revolution.

Industrial Reforms

Decentralization is a Soviet code word for introducing private incentives into the economy. Gorbachev's economic experiment is to allow enterprises to retain a majority of their profits. Plant managers are now given a freer hand in solving problems, regulating the size of their workforce, and negotiating wages and prices, so central planners have less direct control. For example, the number of targets a plant manager must meet has been reduced from forty to eight. Factories are encouraged to compete with each other.

Among Gorbachev's reforms has been the creation of incentive funds. A material incentive fund provides bonuses to the enterprises that perform well relative to their sales and profit targets. A production and development fund is designed to allow more internal financing for those enterprises that meet their profit targets and are efficiently managed. The idea is to promote efficient use of capital resources by allowing only the most efficient firms to expand. To deal with the question of quality, central planners have changed their pricing system to pay producers less for lower-quality goods and more — up to 30 percent more — for higher-quality goods.

According to the official Soviet news agency, Tass, under the Gorbachev reforms workers in collectives will become "full-fledged masters of their enterprises and will independently decide practically all matters related to the production and social development of a mill or factory."[6] Under *per-*

Glasnost is the new openness in Soviet affairs: a greater willingness to let the Soviet people and the rest of the world know what's going on in the Soviet Union.

Perestroika is a restructuring of the economy to promote more decentralization, less bureaucracy, and greater individual incentives.

---

[6] "Soviets Seek to Relax Controls on Economy," *Hartford Courant*, 8 February 1987.

estroika new regulations affecting thousands of factories and mills allow managers to "combine elements of centralized guidance and socialist self-management by the work collective." The new laws are quite significant. Work collectives will pay salaries and research and development costs out of their revenues. Another change in the law allows Soviet enterprises to develop ties with companies from capitalist countries in order to create joint enterprises and encourage technology transfer.

Gorbachev's reforms call for sharp staff reductions at central ministries by 1991 and further dismantling of the centralized pricing system. These efforts to provide more incentives to meet targets, to produce high-quality goods, and to earn profits will move Soviet industry away from planned socialism and toward market socialism.

Allowing for Private Enterprise

The first day of May, 1987 — May Day — marked a declaration of independence of sorts for private enterprise in the Soviet Union. On that day for the first time self-employed individuals could tailor a suit, change a spark plug, drive a taxi, or sand a floor. In all, private individuals became eligible to offer twenty-nine categories of services. Two to three million people were affected. Those offering services need a license and become liable for income tax; they also must hold a full-time public sector job. In preparation for the new law, penalties for receiving "unearned income" were increased. Self-employed workers can allow family members to assist in the business but cannot hire outsiders. The change in the law simply ratified what had been happening in the second economy. This way the state can keep better track of these activities and can tax them.

Earlier we discussed the greater agricultural productivity on private plots. Although the country clearly benefits from the greater output, this example of capitalism has long irritated Communist officials. In 1961 the Party Congress called for the elimination of private plots by 1980, but the Soviets now seem to recognize the benefits of private incentives. Gorbachev proposed that a fixed amount of the harvest from cooperatives be turned over to the state. The balance could then be sold at market prices for whatever the cooperatives and state farms could get. Soviets are looking for ways to reintroduce the incentives associated with private property as a spur to production. For example, in 1989 the Soviet government announced that it would begin paying farmers in foreign currency for wheat and other crop production in excess of their average production in the early 1980s.

In early 1990, Soviet legislators moved further in the direction of allowing private property. The Supreme Soviet approved legislation that permits Soviet citizens to lease land (at prices set by the government) and bequeath leases to their children. The legislation represents a major modification of the policy of state control of land, which has been in effect since Stalin, but it stops short of legalizing full private ownership of property by strictly forbidding the sale of land. Additional legislation was passed in March, 1990, allowing Soviet citizens to own factories and other production assets.

Citizens will be able to hire workers and retain any profit from the production and sale of their products. The new law also allows Soviet citizens to own houses, apartments, and other buildings (although they are still unable to own land).

Centralized planning is a comfortable habit for the Soviet elite. Private production represents competition for the state monopoly. The success of Gorbachev's reforms depends on the support of the Soviet elite. This group is powerful and has a clear interest in the status quo. A Communist party official's wife was quoted in *Pravda* as challenging Gorbachev: "We are the elite, and you will not pull us down. You don't have the strength. We'll rip the flimsy sails of your restructuring."[7]

But the exalted position of the Soviet elite is showing signs of erosion. In 1990 the government announced that members of the Politburo, the Communist party's ruling body, will no longer be provided country dachas. Also, retired Politburo members will have to do without the three household workers and the cars provided by the government.[8]

The economic reforms have been accompanied by political reforms. In 1989 the Supreme Soviet, for the first time in seventy years, rejected nominees backed by the Communist party. More generally, President Gorbachev proposes to reduce government's role in the economy by removing 15 million bureaucrats from government payrolls over the next ten years. As a first step, the number of ministries is to be cut from fifty-two to thirty-two. And as noted earlier, the dominance of the Communist party in affairs of state seems to be coming to an end.

CONCLUSION

Central planning and control make it difficult to address the complexities of developing and operating a modern economy. Capitalism has outshone socialism in terms of technical progress and matching production to market needs. The consumer reigns supreme under capitalism. Capitalism is more efficient than socialism as a way to satisfy a variety of consumer wants, for products from compact disc players to microwave popcorn. Capitalism thrives where it is permitted and even where it's prohibited.

Few observers are optimistic that *perestroika* will put more consumer goods on store shelves soon. Seventy years of bureaucratic inflexibility cannot be cleared away overnight. There is much underemployment in agriculture, which employs 20 percent of the Soviet labor force—far more than the 3 percent figure for the United States. Efforts to streamline bloated factory payrolls have increased unemployment to 15 percent or more in six southern Soviet republics. The Soviet system has no unemployment insur-

---

[7] As reported in "Gorbachev's Opposition," *Newsweek* (18 May 1987): 48.

[8] "No More Dachas," *Wall Street Journal*, 21 February 1990.

ance or retraining programs, so the high unemployment has created unrest and even some rioting.

Because prices have been kept so low for so long, policy makers fear a drastic increase in inflation should prices be allowed to seek their own level. Moreover, since little in the way of consumer goods has been available, Soviet consumers have been forced to save their money, and the huge hoards of cash could fuel inflation if prices were allowed to adjust when and if more appealing consumer goods became available.

In May 1990, Soviet officials proposed a five-year reform aimed at shifting from a centrally planned economy to a "regulated market economy." The plan would raise consumer prices sharply, close inefficient factories, establish a modern banking system, and allow for private ownership of what had been state enterprises. Because these reforms had the potential to seriously destabilize the economy during the transition period, Soviet officials sought a clear indication of public support for the plan. Therefore, they announced that the proposals would be voted on in the first-ever national referendum in Soviet history. Despite the planned referendum, the announcement of the proposed reforms caused panic buying of consumer staples throughout the Soviet Union. As a result, the sale of consumer goods to other than local residents was prohibited in some areas, such as Moscow. Although President Gorbachev tried to calm consumer fears, early evidence suggests that the road to reform will not be a smooth one.

Intellectuals received greater freedom from *glasnost*, but *perestroika* has yet to deliver the goods to consumers. *Glasnost* has allowed consumers to learn how bad conditions are throughout the fifteen Soviet republics. The success or failure of *perestroika* depends on whether the restructured system can deliver the goods, such as soap, sausage, and sugar.

Summary

1. Economic systems can be classified based on the ownership of resources, the way these resources are allocated to produce goods and services, and the incentives used to motivate people.

2. In capitalist systems resources are owned by individuals and are allocated through market coordination. People are motivated by self-interest. In socialist economies resources are owned by the state, and people are motivated by a combination of self-interest and patriotic interest in social welfare. Under planned socialism resources are directed by bureaucratic coordination. Under market socialism resources are directed by market coordination.

3. Gosplan is the Soviet Union's state agency that develops the central plan for production targets in major industrial sectors. Production decisions for less important commodities are relegated to a lower level of the planning bureaucracy or in some cases are left to the market. Usually the quantity of resources demanded exceeds the quantity supplied, and the amount obtained by the consumer sector is therefore restricted.

4. There are three economies in the Soviet Union: (1) the official economy as established by the central plan; (2) the "second economy," the Soviet version of the underground economy; and (3) the "informal economy," where Soviet managers pursue official objectives by skirting the official rules. The second economy and the informal economy evolved in response to shortcomings of the official economy.

5. Several reforms have been introduced in recent years to decentralize decision making, to provide greater production incentives to the workers, and to allow more room for private markets, particularly in the service sector.

Questions and Problems

1. (Socialism) Is there any reason why socialist economies couldn't have as much diversity in the production of goods as capitalist economies do? How does your answer depend on how much central planning is undertaken by the government?

2. (Capitalism) Many socialists stress the fact that in market economies there is much waste due to the production of useless luxuries for the rich. Also, they claim that consumers are often fooled into buying products they do not really want through advertising ploys. How would you respond to such claims?

3. (Ownership of Resources) Socialists argue that no person was responsible for creating the natural resources found in a country. Therefore these resources should be publicly owned. What problems do you see with this line of reasoning? Consider also the efficiency of private ownership.

4. (Material Balance System) Would the Soviet method of material balance planning necessarily lead to a burdensome expansion of the bureaucracy? How might lags in decision making cause problems?

5. (Internal Passports) Why might the authorities in centrally planned economies attempt to prevent migration through the use of internal passports?

6. (Soviet Reform) What has been Gorbachev's criticism of Soviet economic performance?

7. (China and Socialism) One of the periods of greatest economic growth in China was shortly after the communist revolution of 1949. How might you explain this short-term economic success of central planning?

8. (Specialization) Explain why central planning in the Soviet Union has led many companies to abandon specialization of production in favor of self-reliance and independence of production.

9. (Private Agriculture) Of what value to the Soviet economy is the private production of agricultural goods? How does the government tax such production? Should privatization be extended to other facets of the Soviet economy?

10. (Soviet Computerization) Why are managers in the Soviet Union wary of widespread computerization of companies and enterprises? Could such computerization reduce the amount of fraud and waste in the Soviet system?

11. (Rationing Without Prices) In Exhibit 1, the price is set in such a way that there is a shortage of soap.
    a. Do any consumers lose out relative to the situation in which the price clears the market?
    b. Is a "black market" likely to develop for soap? Why?

12. (Rationing Without Prices) In China there are

"friendship stores," which typically carry imported goods that can be purchased only with foreign exchange certificates, not with domestic currency. Can you suggest any reasons for having such stores?

13. (Centrally Owned Resources) In an economy in which the state owns resources like land and capital, such resources are often wasted. Can you explain such waste in terms of the "common pool problem" discussed in the chapter on externalities and the environment?

14. (*Perestroika*) Mikhail Gorbachev has pushed hard for the restructuring of the Soviet economy. What kinds of problems are generated by *perestroika* in the short run, and who would you expect to fight against such a restructuring?

Glossary

A

Absolute advantage   The ability to produce something with fewer resources than other producers use

Absolute poverty level   The level of income at which people can satisfy their basic physical needs, but no more

Accounting profit   A firm's total revenue minus its explicit costs

Activists   Those who consider the private sector to be relatively unstable and able to absorb economic shocks only with the aid of discretionary fiscal policy

Actual investment   The amount of investment actually undertaken during a year, equal to planned investment plus unplanned changes in inventories

Adverse selection   The problem that arises when a buyer or seller engages in an unfavorable transaction because information about the other party is incomplete or inaccurate; for example, unobservable labor skills may be misvalued in the market because of a lack of information

Agent   A person who performs work or a service on behalf of another person, the principal

Aggregate demand curve   A curve representing the relation between the general price level and the amount of aggregate output demanded per period of time

Aggregate expenditure   Total planned spending on final goods and services at a given price level; the total of $C + I + G + (X - M)$

Aggregate expenditure function   A relationship showing, for a given price level, the total amount of planned spending for each level of income; the total of $C + I + G + (X - M)$

Aggregate income   The sum of all income earned by resource suppliers in an economy during a given time period

Aggregate output   The total quantity of final goods and services produced in an economy during a given time period

Aggregate supply curve   A curve representing the relation between the general price level and the amount of aggregate output supplied per period of time

Allocative efficiency   The condition that exists when firms produce the output that is most preferred by consumers so that the marginal cost of each good just equals the marginal value that consumers derive from that good

Annuity   A given sum of money received each year for a specified number of years

Antitrust activity   Government activity aimed at preventing monopoly and fostering competition

Applied research   Research aimed at answering specific questions or applying scientific discoveries to the development of specific products

Appreciation (of currency)   A decrease in the number of units of a particular currency needed to purchase one unit of another currency

Arbitrageur   A person who engages in arbitrage, which is the practice of simultaneously buying a currency at one price and selling it at a higher price to take advantage of temporary differences in exchange rates across markets

Asset   Anything of value that is owned

Association-causation fallacy   The incorrect idea that if two variables are associated in time, one must necessarily cause the other

Automatic stabilizers   Structural features of government spending and taxation that smooth fluctuations in disposable income over the business cycle

Autonomous investment   Investment that is independent of the level of income

Average fixed cost   Total fixed cost divided by output

Average revenue   Total revenue divided by output

Average total cost   Total cost divided by output; the sum of average fixed cost plus average variable cost

Average variable cost   Total variable cost divided by output

B

Balanced budget multiplier   A factor that shows the effect on equilibrium output demanded of equal-sized changes in government purchases and taxes; the multiplier is 1, indicating that the change in equilibrium output demanded is the same size as the change in government purchases and taxes

Balance of payments   A record of all economic transactions between residents of one country and residents of the rest of the world during a given time period

Balance on current account   A section of a country's balance of payments that measures the sum of the country's net unilateral transfers and its balance on goods and services

Balance on goods and services A section of a country's balance of payments that measures the difference in value between a country's exports of goods and services and its imports of goods and services

Balance sheet A financial statement that shows assets, liabilities, and net worth at a given point in time

Bank holding company A corporation that owns banks

Bank notes Papers promising a specific amount of money in gold to bearers who presented them to issuing banks for redemption; an early type of money

Barrier to entry Any impediment that prevents new firms from competing on an equal basis with existing firms in an industry

Barter The direct exchange of one good for another without the use of money.

Basic research Research aimed at acquiring knowledge without regard for how the knowledge will be used

Behavioral assumption An assumption that describes the expected behavior of economic actors

Bilateral monopoly A situation in which a single seller bargains with a single buyer, or monopsonist

Binding arbitration Negotiation in which both parties in a union-management dispute agree to accept an impartial observer's resolution of the dispute

Bond A paper representing a firm's promise to pay the holder an annual interest payment until the date of maturity and a fixed sum of money on the designated maturity date

Bounded rationality The feature of human consciousness that places a limit on the amount of information an eco-

nomic agent, such as a manager, can comprehend

Budget line A line showing all combinations of two goods that can be purchased at given prices with a fixed amount of income

Bureau A government agency charged with implementing legislation and funded by appropriations from a legislative body

Business cycle The rise and fall of economic activity relative to the long-term growth trend of the economy

C

Capital All buildings, equipment, and human skill used to produce goods and services

Capital account The record of a country's international transactions involving purchases or sales of assets

Cartel A collection of firms that agree to coordinate their production and pricing decisions

Change in demand A shift in a given demand curve caused by a change in one of the determinants of demand for a particular good

Change in quantity demanded Movement along the demand curve for a good in response to a change in the price of the good

Change in quantity supplied Movement along the supply curve for a good in response to a change in the price of the good

Change in supply A shift in a given supply curve caused by a change in one of the variables that influence supply

Checkable deposits Deposits in financial institutions against which checks can be written

Circular flow model A model describing the flow of resources, products, and income among economic actors

Closed shop A workplace

where workers are required to join a union before they can be hired

Coase theorem As long as bargaining costs are small, an efficient solution to the problem of externalities will be achieved by assigning property rights.

Collective bargaining The process by which union and management negotiate a mutually agreeable contract

Collusion The joint determination of price and output by two or more firms in order to eliminate price competition

Command economy An economic system characterized by centralized economic planning and public ownership of resources

Commercial banks Depository institutions that make short-term loans primarily to businesses

Commodity money Anything that serves both as money and as a commodity

Common pool problem The problem that unrestricted access to resources results in their being overused until the net marginal value of additional use drops to zero

Comparable worth The principle that pay should be determined by job characteristics rather than by supply and demand

Comparative advantage The ability to produce something at a lower opportunity cost than other producers face

Competing interest legislation Legislation that imposes costs on one group and provides benefits to another group

Complements Goods that are related in such a way that an increase in the price of one leads to a decrease in the demand for the other

Concentration ratio A measure of the market share of the largest firms in an industry

Conglomerate merger A merger involving the combination of firms producing in different industries

Constant-cost industry An industry that can expand or contract without affecting the prices of the resources it employs

Constant elasticity of demand The type of demand that exists when price elasticity of demand takes on the same value at every point along the demand curve

Consumer equilibrium The condition in which an individual consumer's budget is completely exhausted and the last dollar spent on each good yields the same utility

Consumer price index (CPI) A measure over time of the cost of a fixed "market basket" of consumer goods and services

Consumer surplus The difference between the maximum amount that a consumer is willing to pay for a given quantity of a good and what is actually paid

Consumption All household purchases of final goods and services

Consumption function The relation between the level of income in an economy and the amount households spend on consumption

Contestable market A market that firms can enter or leave at will and that requires no irreversible investments

Contractionary gap The amount by which actual output in the short run falls below the economy's potential output

Corporate profits A component of the government measure of national income; the net revenues received by incorporated business before corporate income taxes are subtracted

Corporation A legal entity owned by stockholders whose liability is limited to the value of their stock

Cost-plus pricing A method of determining the price of a good by adding a percentage markup to the average cost

Cost-push inflation A continuous rise in the price level caused by reductions in aggregate supply

Craft union A union whose members have a particular skill or work at a particular craft

Cross-price elasticity of demand The percentage change in the quantity demanded of one good divided by the percentage change in the price of another good

Cross-subsidization The use of revenues from profitable activities to subsidize unprofitable activities

Crowding out The displacement of interest-sensitive private spending that occurs when increased government spending drives up interest rates

Cyclical majority A situation in which no choice dominates all others, and the outcome of a vote depends on the order in which issues are considered

Cyclical unemployment Unemployment that occurs because of declines in the economy's aggregate output

D

Deadweight loss A loss of consumer surplus that is not transferred to anyone else; it arises, for example, from monopolization of an industry or imposition of restrictions on international trade

Decision-making lag The time needed to decide what changes to make in government policy after a macroeconomic problem is identified

Decreasing-cost industry An industry that faces lower resource prices as it expands

Deflation A sustained and continuous decrease in the price level

Demand A relation showing how much of a good consumers are willing and able to buy at each possible price during a given period of time, other things constant

Demand curve A curve showing the quantity of a commodity demanded at various possible prices, other things constant

Demand deposits Accounts at financial institutions that pay no interest and on which depositors can write checks to obtain their deposits at any time

Demand for loanable funds The relation between the market rate of interest and the quantity of loanable funds demanded, other things constant

Demand-pull inflation A continuous rise in the price level caused by increases in aggregate demand

Demand-side economics The use of government policies to regulate aggregate demand so as to promote full employment and price stability

Dependent variable A variable whose value is affected by the value(s) of some other variable(s)

Depository institutions Commercial banks and other financial institutions that accept deposits from the public

Depreciation (of capital) The value of capital stock used up during a year in producing GNP

Depreciation (of currency) An increase in the number of units of a particular currency needed to purchase one unit of another currency

Depression A severe reduction in an economy's total production accompanied by high unemployment lasting several years

Derived demand Demand for a resource that is derived from demand for the product the resource helps to produce

Devaluation (of a domestic currency) An increase in the official pegged price of foreign currency in terms of the domestic currency

Developing countries Nations typified by high rates of illiteracy, high unemployment, rapid population growth, and exports of primary products

Direct (positive) relation See positive relation

Discounting Determining the present value of a sum of money to be received in the future

Discount rate The interest rate charged by the Federal Reserve to financial institutions that borrow reserves; also, the interest rate used in discounting

Discouraged worker A person who has dropped out of the labor force because of lack of success in finding a job

Discretionary fiscal policy The deliberate manipulation of government spending or taxation in order to promote full employment and price stability

Diseconomies of scale Forces that cause a firm's average cost to increase as the scale of operations increases in the long run

Disequilibrium differentials Differences in resource prices that trigger resource reallocation and price adjustments

Disinflation A reduction in the rate of inflation

Disposable income The income households have available to spend or save after paying personal taxes

Division of labor The organization of production of a single good into separate tasks in which people specialize

Double coincidence of wants A situation in which two traders are willing to exchange their products directly

Dumping The sale of a commodity abroad for less than its price in the domestic market

E

Economic profit A firm's total revenue minus all its explicit and implicit costs

Economic regulation Government measures aimed at controlling prices, output, market entry and exit, and product quality in situations where monopoly is inevitable or desirable

Economic rent The portion of a resource's total earnings above transfer earnings; earnings above the amount necessary to keep the resource in its present use

Economics The study of how people choose to use their scarce resources in an attempt to satisfy unlimited wants

Economies of scale Forces that cause reductions in a firm's average cost when the scale of operations is increased in the long run

Economies of scope Forces that make it cheaper to combine two or more product lines in one firm than to produce them separately

Effectiveness lag The time necessary for changes in monetary or fiscal policy to have an effect on the economy

Efficiency The condition that exists when there is no way resources can be reallocated to increase the production of one good without decreasing the production of another

Efficiency wage theory The idea that keeping wages high (above the level required to attract a sufficient pool of workers) makes workers compete to keep their jobs and results in greater productivity

Elastic demand The type of demand that exists when a percentage change in price causes a greater percentage change in quantity demanded

Employee compensation A component of the government measure of national income made up of wages and salaries plus payments by employers to cover Social Security taxes, medical insurance, and other fringe benefits

Entrepreneur A profit-seeking decision maker who organizes an enterprise and assumes the risks involved

Entrepreneurial ability Managerial and organization skills combined with the willingness to take risks

Equation of exchange The quantity of money, M, multiplied by its velocity, V, equals nominal income, which is the product of the price level, P, and real GNP, Y.

Equilibrium The condition that exists in a market when the plans of buyers match the plans of sellers

Equilibrium differentials Differences in resource prices that do not precipitate resource reallocation or price adjustments

Excess reserves Reserves held by depository institutions in excess of required reserves

Exchange rate The price of one country's currency measured in terms of another country's currency

Exclusive dealing The situation that occurs when a producer prohibits customers from purchasing from other sellers

Expansion path A curve showing the firm's optimal combination of resources for each rate of output

Expansionary gap The amount by which actual output in the short run exceeds the economy's potential output

Expected real rate of interest The expected interest rate expressed in dollars of constant value

Expenditure approach A method of calculating GNP that involves adding up expenditures on all final goods and services produced during a year

Explicit costs Opportunity costs of a firm's resources that take the form of actual cash payments

Externality An unpriced by-product of consumption or production that harms or benefits individuals not involved in the transaction

F

Fallacy of composition The incorrect belief that what is true for the individual or part must necessarily be true for the group or whole

Featherbedding An attempt to increase the number of union workers required by contract to perform a particular task

Federal budget deficit The excess of the federal government's annual expenditures over its annual revenues

Federal funds market A market for day-to-day lending and borrowing of reserves among financial institutions

Federal funds rate The interest rate prevailing in the federal funds market

Federal Reserve System The central bank and monetary authority of the United States, known as "the Fed"

Fiat money Money not redeemable for any commodity; its status as money is conferred by the government

Fiduciary money Paper money redeemable for gold or another valuable commodity

Final goods and services Goods and services sold to final or ultimate users

Financial intermediaries Institutions that serve as go-betweens, accepting funds from savers and lending those funds to borrowers

Financial markets Markets in which financial claims are traded, made up of banks and other institutions that facilitate the flow of funds from savers to borrowers

Firms Economic units that hire resources to produce goods and services for sale

Fiscal policy The use of government purchases, taxes, and borrowing to influence aggregate economic activity

Fixed cost Any production cost that is independent of the firm's rate of output

Fixed exchange rates Rates determined by a system in which central banks buy and sell currency to peg the rate within a narrow band of values

Fixed resource Any resource that cannot be varied in the short run to increase or decrease the level of output

Flexible exchange rates Rates determined by the forces of supply and demand without government intervention

Flow A variable that measures the amount of something over an interval of time

Foreign aid An international transfer made on especially favorable terms for the purpose of promoting economic development

Foreign exchange The currency of another country needed to carry out international transactions

Fractional reserve banking system A banking system in which only a portion of deposits in the depository institutions are backed up by reserves

Frictional unemployment Unemployment that arises because of the time needed to match qualified job seekers with available job openings

Functional relation A relation between two variables in which the value of one variable depends on the value of the other variable

G

Game theory A model that analyzes oligopolistic behavior as a series of strategic moves and countermoves by rival firms

General Agreement on Tariffs and Trade (GATT) An international tariff-reduction treaty adopted in 1947 by the United States and twenty-two other countries

Glasnost A Russian word that refers to the new openness in Soviet affairs

Gold standard An arrangement in which the currencies of most countries are convertible into gold at a fixed rate

Golden rule of profit maximization A firm will continue to expand the level of output as long as marginal revenue exceeds marginal cost.

Good A tangible item that is used to satisfy wants

Government budget A plan for government expenditures and revenues for a specified period, usually a year

Government purchases Spending for goods and services by all levels of government

Greenhouse effect The formation of a blanket of carbon dioxide and other gases around the earth, causing heat buildup

Gresham's Law People tend to trade away inferior money and hoard the best.

Gross investment The value of all investment during a period, including investment required to replace capital used up during the production process

Gross national product (GNP) The total value of all final goods and services produced in an economy during a given year

H

Herfindahl index The sum of the squared percentage market shares of all firms in an industry; a measure of the level of concentration in that industry

Horizontal merger A merger in which one firm combines with another firm that produces the same product

Hyperinflation A very high rate of inflation

Hypothesis A statement about relationships among key variables

I

Implementation lag The time needed to introduce a change in monetary or fiscal policy

Implicit costs A firm's opportunity costs of using its own resources or those provided by its owners without a corresponding cash payment

Implicit price deflator A price index for the economy's aggregate output, measured as the ratio of nominal GNP to real GNP multiplied by 100

Import quota A legal limit on the quantity of a particular commodity that can be imported per year.

Income approach A method of calculating GNP that involves adding up all payments to owners of resources used to produce output during a year

Income effect The effect on quantity demanded of a change in consumers' purchasing power caused by a change in the price of a good

Income elasticity of demand The percentage change in quantity demanded divided by the percentage change in income

Increasing-cost industry An industry that faces higher resource prices as it expands

Increasing marginal returns The result when marginal physical product increases with each additional unit of a resource that is used, other resources held constant

Independent variable A variable whose value affects, but is not affected by, the value(s) of some other variable(s)

Indifference curve A curve showing all combinations of two goods that provide a consumer the same level of total utility

Indifference map A set of indifference curves representing each possible level of total utility to be derived by a particular consumer from the consumption of two goods

Industrial organization A branch of economics that examines the relation between the structure of a market and the

conduct and performance of firms in that market

Industrial union A union of both skilled and unskilled workers from a particular industry

Inelastic demand The type of demand that exists when a change in price has relatively little effect on quantity demanded; the percentage change in price exceeds the percentage change in quantity demanded

Inferior good A good for which demand decreases as consumer income rises

Inflation A sustained and continuous increase in the price level

Inflation rate The annual percentage change in the price level

Injection Any payment of income other than by firms or spending other than by domestic households, including investment, government purchases, transfer payments, and exports

Innovation The process of turning an invention into a marketable product

Intercept The point where a line or curve in a graph crosses the horizontal or vertical axis

Interest The return resource owners receive for the use of their capital; the reward offered to households to forgo present consumption

Interest rate The amount of money paid for the use of a dollar for one year

Interlocking directorate An arrangement whereby one individual serves on the boards of directors of competing firms

Intermediate goods and services Goods and services purchased for further reprocessing and resale

Inventories Stocks of finished or in-process goods maintained by producers

Inverse (negative) relation See **negative relation**

Investment All output pro-

duced during a year but not used for present consumption

Isocost line A line showing all combinations of two resources that a firm can purchase for a given total cost

Isoquant A curve showing all technologically efficient combinations of two resources that can produce a given amount of output

K

Kinked demand curve A curve that illustrates price stickiness—if one firm cuts its prices, other firms in the industry will cut theirs as well, but if the firm raises its prices, other firms will not change theirs

L

Labor The physical and mental effort of humans

Labor force All noninstitutionalized individuals sixteen years of age and older who are either working or actively looking for work

Labor force participation rate The ratio of the number in the labor force to the working-age noninstitutionalized population

Land Plots of ground and other natural resources used in the production of goods and services

Law of comparative advantage The individual or country with the lowest opportunity cost of producing a particular good should specialize in producing that good.

Law of demand The quantity of a good demanded is inversely related to its price, other things constant.

Law of diminishing marginal rate of substitution The amount of good A a consumer is willing to give up to get one additional unit of good B declines as the consumption of B increases.

Law of diminishing marginal returns When more and more of a variable resource is added to a given amount of a fixed resource, the resulting changes in output will eventually diminish.

Law of diminishing marginal utility The more of a good consumed per period, the smaller the increase in total utility from consuming one more unit, other things constant.

Law of increasing opportunity cost As more of a particular good is produced, larger and larger quantities of an alternative good must be sacrificed if the economy's resources are already being used fully and efficiently.

Leading economic indicators Economic statistics that foreshadow future changes in business activity

Leakage Any diversion of aggregate income from the domestic spending stream, including saving, taxes, and imports

Legal tender Anything that creditors are required to accept as payment for debts

Leisure Time devoted to nonwork activities

Liability Anything that is owed to another individual or institution

Liquidity A measure of the ease with which an asset can be converted into money without significant loss in its value

Loanable funds market The market in which savers (suppliers of funds) and borrowers (demanders of funds) come together to determine the market rate of interest

Logrolling The trading of support for one issue for support for another issue between voters

Long run In microeconomics, a period during which all the firm's resources are variable; in macroeconomics, a period during which previous wage contracts and resource price agreements can be renegotiated

Long-run average cost curve A curve that indicates the lowest cost of production at each level of output when the firm's plant size is allowed to vary

Lorenz curve A curve showing the percentage of total income received by a given percentage of recipients whose incomes are arranged from smallest to largest

Lump-sum tax A tax that collects a fixed amount of revenue regardless of the level of income

M

M1 A measure of the money supply consisting of currency and coin held by the nonbank public, checkable deposits, and traveler's checks

M2 A monetary aggregate consisting of M1 plus savings deposits, small time deposits, and money market mutual funds

M3 A monetary aggregate consisting of M2 plus negotiable certificates of deposit

Macroeconomics The study of the behavior of entire economies

Managed float system An exchange rate system that combines features of freely floating rates and intervention by central banks

Marginal A term meaning "incremental" or "decremental," used to describe a change in an economic variable

Marginal cost The change in total cost divided by the output

Marginal physical product The change in total physical product, or output, that occurs when the usage of a particular resource changes by 1 unit, all other resources constant

Marginal propensity to consume The fraction of a change in income that is spent on consumption; the change in consumption spending divided by the change in income that caused it

Marginal propensity to import The fraction of a change in income that is spent on imported goods and services; the change in total spending on imports divided by the change in income that caused it

Marginal propensity to save The fraction of a change in income that is saved; a change in saving divided by the change in income that caused it

Marginal rate of return on investment The marginal revenue product of capital expressed as a percentage of its marginal cost

Marginal rate of substitution (MRS) A measure of how much of one good a consumer could give up to get one more unit of another good while remaining equally satisfied

Marginal rate of technical substitution (MRTS) The rate at which a firm can substitute one resource for another without affecting the level of output

Marginal resource cost The change in total cost when an additional unit of a particular resource is hired

Marginal revenue The change in total revenue resulting from a 1-unit change in sales

Marginal revenue product The change in total revenue when an additional unit of a resource is hired, other things constant

Marginal social benefit The total of the marginal private benefit and the marginal external benefit of production or consumption

Marginal social cost The total of the marginal private cost and the marginal external cost of production or consumption

Marginal utility The change in total utility derived from a 1-unit change in consumption of a good

Marginal valuation The dollar

value of the marginal utility derived from consuming each additional unit of a good

Market   A set of arrangements through which buyers and sellers carry out exchange at mutually agreeable terms

Market demand curve   A curve showing the quantity of a good demanded by all consumers at various possible prices, other things constant; also, a curve showing the sum of the demands for a resource in all its various uses

Market failure   A condition that arises when unrestrained operation of markets yields socially undesirable results

Market power   The ability of one or more firms to maintain a price above the competitive level

Market socialism   An economic system in which the state owns all resources other than labor, but uses market forces to allocate the resources

Market structure   The important features of a market, such as the number of firms, type of product, ease of entry, and forms of competition

Market supply curve   A curve showing the quantity of a good supplied by all producers at various possible prices, other things constant; also, a curve showing the sum of all individual supplies of a particular resource to a market

Market work   Time sold as labor in return for a money wage

Material balance system   A system of central planning designed to ensure a balance of supply and demand for important types of industrial output

Means-tested program   A benefit program that requires that recipients' incomes and/or assets be below specified levels

Median   The middle number in a series of numbers arranged from smallest to largest

Median income   The middle income in a series of incomes ranked from smallest to largest

Median voter model   Under certain conditions the preference of the median, or typical, voter will dominate other public choices.

Mediation   The efforts of an impartial observer who helps resolve differences between union and management

Medium of exchange   Anything that facilitates trade by being generally accepted by all parties in payment for goods or services

Merchandise trade balance   The value of a country's merchandise exports minus the value of its merchandise imports

Microeconomics   The study of the economic behavior of individual decision makers

Minimum efficient scale   The lowest rate of output at which a firm takes full advantage of economies of scale

Model   See **theory**

Monetarism   A school of thought that emphasizes the effects of changes in the supply of money on economic activity

Monetary aggregates   Measures of the economy's money supply

Monetary policy   Regulation of the money supply by the Fed in order to influence aggregate economic activity; the Fed's role in supplying money to the economy

Monetary theory   The study of the effect of money on the economy

Money   Anything that is generally acceptable in exchange for goods and services

Money market mutual fund   A collection of short-term interest-earning assets purchased with funds collected from many shareholders

Money multiplier   The multiple by which the money supply increases as a result of an increase in excess reserves in the banking system

Monopolistic competition   A market structure characterized by a large number of firms selling products that are close substitutes

Monopoly   The single producer of a product for which there are no good substitutes

Monopsonist   The sole purchaser of a particular resource or good

Multiplier   The ratio of a change in equilibrium income to the initial change in expenditure that brought it about

N

National income   The amount of aggregate income earned by suppliers of resources employed to produce GNP; net national product plus government subsidies minus indirect business taxes

Natural monopoly   A situation in which one firm can serve a market more cheaply than two or more firms can

Natural rate hypothesis   The natural rate of unemployment is largely independent of the stimulus provided by monetary or fiscal policy.

Natural rate of unemployment   The unemployment rate that occurs when the economy is producing its potential level of GNP

Near moneys   Financial assets that are like money but that do not serve as mediums of exchange

Negative income tax   A cash transfer program in which benefits are reduced as earnings rise

Negative (inverse) relation   A relation between two variables such that an increase in the value of one causes a decrease in the value of the other

Negative-sum game   A game in which total losses exceed total winnings

Net exports   The value of a country's products purchased by foreigners minus the value of foreign products purchased by its residents

Net interest A component of the government measure of national income, made up of the interest received by individuals, excluding interest paid by consumers to businesses and interest paid by government

Net investment Gross investment minus depreciation

Net national product GNP minus depreciation; a measure of the value of aggregate output available for use

Net wealth The difference between the values of a household's assets and liabilities

Net worth The difference between the values of an institution's assets and liabilities

Nominal rate of interest The interest rate expressed in current dollars

Nominal value A value measured in current dollars

Nominal wage The wage measured in terms of current dollars

Nonactivists Those who consider the private sector to be relatively stable and able to absorb economic shocks without discretionary government policy

Nonmarket work Time spent producing goods and services in the home or acquiring an education

Normal good A good for which demand increases as consumer income rises

Normal profit The profit required to induce a firm's owners to employ their resources in the firm; the profit earned when all resources used by the firm are earning their opportunity costs

Normative economic statement A statement that represents an opinion, which cannot be proved or disproved

O

Official reserve transactions account A section of a country's balance of payments that reflects the flow of gold, Special Drawing Rights, and currencies among central banks; the sum of the current account and the capital account

Oligopoly A market structure characterized by a small number of firms whose behavior is interdependent

Open market operations Purchases and sales of government securities by the Federal Reserve in an effort to change the money supply

Open shop A workplace that hires both union and nonunion workers

Opportunity cost The benefit expected from the best alternative forgone when an item or activity is chosen

Other-things-constant assumption The assumption that variables other than the variable of interest remain unchanged over time; it simplifies analysis by permitting economists to focus on one variable at a time

P

Paradox of thrift If all households try to save more, they may be unable to do so because the reduced consumption ultimately lowers income.

Pareto optimal A change in the status quo that makes at least one person better off while making no one worse off

Partnership A firm with multiple owners who share the firm's profits and bear unlimited liability for the firm's debts

Patents Legal barriers to entry that convey to their holders the exclusive right to supply a product for a certain period of time

Perestroika A Russian word that refers to the restructuring of the Soviet economy to promote decentralization, less bureaucracy, and greater individual incentives

Perfect competition A market structure in which there are large numbers of fully informed buyers and sellers of a homogeneous product and there are no obstacles to entry or exit of firms

Perfectly elastic demand curve A horizontal line reflecting the fact that any price increase reduces quantity demanded to zero

Perfectly elastic supply curve A horizontal line reflecting the fact that any price decrease reduces the quantity supplied to zero

Perfectly inelastic demand curve A vertical line reflecting the fact that a price change has no effect on the quantity demanded

Perfectly inelastic supply curve A vertical line reflecting the fact that a price change has no effect on the quantity supplied

Permanent income Income that individuals expect to receive on average over the long term

Per se illegality A category of illegality in antitrust law, applied to business practices that are deemed illegal regardless of their economic rationale or their consequences

Personal income The amount of before-tax income received by households; national income less income earned but not received plus income received but not earned

Phillips curve A curve showing possible combinations of the inflation rate and the unemployment rate, given the expected price level

Physical capital Manufactured items used to produce goods and services

Planned investment The amount of investment firms plan to undertake during a year

Planned socialism An economic system in which the state owns all resources other than labor and directs them by means of economic plans and central decision making

Positive (direct) relation A relation between two variables such that an increase in the value of one causes an increase in the value of the other

Positive economic statement A statement that can be proven or disproven by reference to facts

Positive rate of time preference A characteristic of consumers who value present consumption more highly than future consumption

Positive-sum game A game in which total winnings exceed total losses

Potential output The economy's maximum sustainable level of output, given the supply of resources and state of technology; the level of real GNP produced when the actual price level equals the expected level

Present value The value today of a payment to be received in the future

Price discrimination Selling the same good at different prices to different consumers or charging the same consumer different prices for different units of a good

Price elasticity of demand A measure of the responsiveness of quantity demanded to a price change; the percentage change in quantity demanded divided by the percentage change in price

Price elasticity of supply A measure of the responsiveness of quantity supplied to a price change; the percentage change in quantity supplied divided by the percentage change in price

Price leader A firm whose prices are followed by the rest of the industry

Price taker Any firm that faces a given market price for its output and whose actions have no effect on the market price

Principal A person who enters into a contractual agreement with an agent in the expecta-tion that the agent will act on behalf of the principal

Producer surplus The total revenue producers receive for a commodity less their total vari-able cost of producing it

Product market A market in which goods and services are exchanged

Production function An equation, graph, or table that shows the maximum output that can be produced per pe-riod with particular combina-tions of resources, given the available technology

Production possibilities fron-tier A curve showing all combinations of goods that can be produced when available re-sources are used fully and efficiently

Productive efficiency The condition that exists when out-put is produced with the least-cost combination of inputs, given the level of technology

Productivity A measure of output per unit of a particular input

Profit The return resource owners receive for their entre-preneurial ability

Proportional income tax A tax that collects the same per-centage of every level of income

Proprietors' income A com-ponent of the government mea-sure of national income, made up of the earnings of farmers and other unincorporated businesses

Public good A good that, once produced, is available for all to consume, regardless of who pays and who does not

Purchasing power parity the-ory Exchange rates between two countries will adjust in the long run to reflect price level differences between the countries.

Pure capitalism An economic system characterized by private ownership of resources and the use of prices to coordinate eco-nomic activity in free, com-petitive markets

Pure rate of interest The in-terest rate on a risk-free loan

Q

Quantity theory of money The velocity of money is stable and predictable, so changes in the money supply have predict-able effects on nominal income.

Quota A legal limit on the quantity of a particular com-modity that can be imported or exported

R

Rational expectations A school of thought that claims people form expectations based on all available information, in-cluding the probable future ac-tions of government policy makers

Rational ignorance A stance adopted by voters when they find that the costs of under-standing and voting on a par-ticular issue exceed the expected benefits of doing so

Real income Income mea-sured in terms of the goods and services it can buy

Realized real rate of interest The nominal rate of interest minus the inflation rate

Real value A value measured in terms of dollars of fixed purchasing power

Real wage The wage measured in terms of the quantity of goods and services it will purchase

Recession A decline in an economy's total production lasting six months or longer

Recognition lag The time needed to identify a macro-economic problem and assess its seriousness

Renewable resource A re-source that can be used peri-odically for an indefinite length of time

Rent The return resource owners receive for the use of their land

Rental income of persons A component of the government measure of national income, consisting mainly of the imputed rental value of owner-occupied housing

Rent seeking Any effort by individuals or firms to obtain favorable treatment from government

Required reserve ratio The proportion of deposits a financial institution is legally required to hold in the form of reserves

Required reserves The dollar amount of reserves a financial institution is legally required to hold

Resource market A market in which resources are exchanged

Resource price searcher A firm that faces an upward-sloping supply curve for a resource

Resource price taker A firm that faces a given market price for a resource and whose actions do not affect the price of the resource

Revaluation(of a domestic currency) A reduction in the official pegged price of foreign currency in terms of the domestic currency

Right-to-work laws Laws that outlaw closed shops and union shops

Roundabout production The production of capital goods that can then be used to produce consumer goods

Rule of reason A principle used by a court to examine the reasons for certain business practices and their effects on competition before ruling on their legality

S

Saving function The relationship between saving and level of income

Say's Law The production of a given amount of aggregate output creates an equivalent demand for that output.

Scarce A term used to describe a resource when there is not enough of it to satisfy all of the people's wants, or desires, for it

Seasonal unemployment Unemployment caused by seasonal shifts in labor supply and demand

Secondary effects Effects of economic actions that develop slowly over time as people react to events

Seigniorage The difference between the face value of money and the cost of coining it, which is received as revenue by the issuer of the coins

Separation of ownership from control The situation that exists when no single stockholder has the incentive or ability to control the management of a corporation

Service An intangible activity that is used to satisfy a want

Shirking The tendency not to work as hard as required

Shortage An excess of quantity demanded over quantity supplied at a given price

Short run In microeconomics, a period during which some of a firm's resources cannot be varied; in macroeconomics, a period during which some resource prices, especially those for labor, are fixed by agreement

Short run supply curve A curve that indicates the quantity a firm is willing and able to supply at each price in the short run

Signal A proxy measure of unobservable characteristics

Simple money multiplier The reciprocal of the required reserve ratio, or $1/r$

Slope A measure of the steepness of a line, expressed as the ratio of the change in the value measured along the vertical axis to the change in the value

measured along the horizontal axis

Social regulation Government measures designed to improve health and safety

Sole proprietorship A firm with a single owner who has the right to all profits and who bears unlimited liability for the firm's debts

Special Drawing Right (SDR) A form of international reserve currency created by the International Monetary Fund; its value is a weighted average of the values of the major national currencies

Special interest legislation Legislation that generates concentrated benefits but imposes widespread costs

Specialization The focusing of individuals' efforts on the production of a single good or service

Speculators Those who buy and sell foreign exchange in hopes of profiting from fluctuations in exchange rates over time

Stagflation A contraction of a nation's output accompanied by inflation

Standard of value A common unit for measuring the value of every good or service

Sterilization The Fed's use of open-market operations to offset the effects of its foreign currency transactions on the domestic money supply

Stock A variable that measures the amount of something at a particular point in time

Store of wealth Anything that retains its purchasing power over time

Strike A union's attempt to withhold labor from a firm

Structural deficit A measure of what the federal budget deficit would be if the economy were producing its potential level of output

Structural unemployment Unemployment that arises because the skills demanded by employers do not match the skills of the unemployed or because the unemployed do not live where the jobs are located

Substitutes   Goods that are related in such a way that an increase in the price of one leads to an increase in demand for the other

Substitution effect   A change in the pattern of consumption caused by a change in the price of a good; when the price of a good falls, consumers will substitute it for other relatively expensive goods

Sunk cost   A cost that cannot be recovered and that is therefore irrelevant when an economic choice is being made

Supply   A relation showing how much of a good producers are willing and able to sell at various prices during a given time period, other things constant

Supply curve   A curve showing the quantity of a good supplied at various prices, other things constant

Supply of loanable funds   The relation between the market rate of interest and the quantity of savings supplied to the economy

Supply shocks   Unexpected events that (often temporarily) affect aggregate supply

Supply-side economics   The use of tax reductions to stimulate production so as to increase aggregate supply

Surplus   An excess of quantity supplied over quantity demanded at a given price

T

Tangent   A straight line that just touches, but does not cross, a curve at a particular point

Tariff   A tax on imports or exports

Tax incidence   The ultimate burden of paying for a tax

Technologically efficient production   Production that yields the maximum possible output given the combination of resources employed; production accomplished with the least amount of resources

Tender offer   An attempt to attain a controlling interest in a firm by purchasing shares at a premium over the market price

Terms of trade   An indication of how much of one good will be exchanged for a unit of another good

Term structure of interest rates   The relationship between the duration of a loan and the interest rate charged

Theory or **model**   A simplification of reality designed to capture the important elements of the relationship under consideration

Thrift institutions   Depository institutions that make long-term loans primarily to households

Time-series graph   A graph showing the behavior of one or more variables over time

Token money   Coins whose face values exceed their metallic values

Total physical product   The total output of goods and services produced by a firm

Total revenue   Price multiplied by the quantity sold at that price

Total utility   The total satisfaction a consumer derives from consuming a certain quantity of a good

Total wage bill   Employment multiplied by the wage rate

Transaction costs   The costs of time and information required to carry out an exchange

Transactions demand for money   The demand for money to support the exchange of goods and services

Transfer earnings   What a resource could earn in its best alternative use; the earnings required to keep the resource in its present use

Transfer payments   Cash or in-kind benefits given to individuals as outright grants from the government

Trust   A merger of or collusive agreement among competing firms

Tying contract   An arrangement in which a seller of one good requires buyers to purchase other goods as well

U

Underemployment   A situation in which workers are overqualified for their jobs or work fewer hours than they prefer

Underground economy   All economic activity not reported to the government

Unemployment rate   The number of unemployed individuals expressed as a percentage of the labor force

Union shop   A workplace where workers must join the union after being hired

Unitary elastic demand   The type of demand that exists when a percentage change in price causes an equal percentage change in quantity demanded

Util   A unit of utility—a subjective measure that is unique to an individual

Utility   The satisfaction received from consuming a good or service

V

Value added   The difference at each stage of production between the value of a product and the cost of materials needed to make it

Variable   Any quantity that can take on different values

Variable cost   Any production cost that increases as output increases

Variable resource   Any resource that can be quickly varied in the short run to increase or decrease the level of output

Velocity of money   The average number of times per year a dollar is used to purchase final goods and services

Vertical integration The expansion of a firm into stages of production earlier or later than those in which it has specialized

Vertical merger A merger in which one firm combines with another from which it pur-

chases inputs or to which it sells output

W

Wages The return resource owners receive for their labor

Wealth The total value of a household's or an economy's assets

World price The price at which a good or service is traded internationally; it is determined by the world supply and demand for a product

Z

Zero-sum game A game in which total winnings just equal total losses

Index